CAMBRIDGE LIBRARY COLLECTION

Books of enduring scholarly value

History

The books reissued in this series include accounts of historical events and movements by eye-witnesses and contemporaries, as well as landmark studies that assembled significant source materials or developed new historiographical methods. The series includes work in social, political and military history on a wide range of periods and regions, giving modern scholars ready access to influential publications of the past.

The Dispatches of Field Marshal the Duke of Wellington

Arthur Wellesley (1769–1852), the first Duke of Wellington, was one of the most successful military figures of the early nineteenth century. After fighting in the fourth Anglo-Mysore war in India, his successes during the Peninsular War (1809–14) and his victory at the Battle of Waterloo (1815) established his reputation as a brilliant military tactician. These volumes, first published between 1834 and 1839, contain the letters, dispatches, instructions and general military orders Wellington wrote throughout his military career. Edited by his private secretary, Colonel John Gurwood (1790–1845), they offer a wealth of fascinating details concerning Wellington's campaigns in India and Europe, from mundane administrative tasks to discussions of tactics, personnel and intelligence-gathering. These volumes are reissued from the 1844 revised edition, and provide invaluable information for the study of warfare during this period. Volume 3 covers his Peninsular campaigns between 1808 and 1810.

Cambridge University Press has long been a pioneer in the reissuing of out-of-print titles from its own backlist, producing digital reprints of books that are still sought after by scholars and students but could not be reprinted economically using traditional technology. The Cambridge Library Collection extends this activity to a wider range of books which are still of importance to researchers and professionals, either for the source material they contain, or as landmarks in the history of their academic discipline.

Drawing from the world-renowned collections in the Cambridge University Library, and guided by the advice of experts in each subject area, Cambridge University Press is using state-of-the-art scanning machines in its own Printing House to capture the content of each book selected for inclusion. The files are processed to give a consistently clear, crisp image, and the books finished to the high quality standard for which the Press is recognised around the world. The latest print-on-demand technology ensures that the books will remain available indefinitely, and that orders for single or multiple copies can quickly be supplied.

The Cambridge Library Collection will bring back to life books of enduring scholarly value (including out-of-copyright works originally issued by other publishers) across a wide range of disciplines in the humanities and social sciences and in science and technology.

The Dispatches
of Field Marshal
the Duke of Wellington

*During his Various Campaigns
in India, Denmark, Portugal, Spain,
the Low Countries, and France*

VOLUME 3

EDITED BY JOHN GURWOOD

CAMBRIDGE
UNIVERSITY PRESS

CAMBRIDGE UNIVERSITY PRESS

Cambridge, New York, Melbourne, Madrid, Cape Town, Singapore,
São Paolo, Delhi, Dubai, Tokyo, Mexico City

Published in the United States of America by Cambridge University Press, New York

www.cambridge.org
Information on this title: www.cambridge.org/9781108025171

© in this compilation Cambridge University Press 2010

This edition first published 1844
This digitally printed version 2010

ISBN 978-1-108-02517-1 Paperback

THE

DISPATCHES

OF

FIELD MARSHAL THE DUKE OF WELLINGTON,

DURING

HIS VARIOUS CAMPAIGNS.

MONUMENTUM ÆRE PERENNIUS.

AN ENLARGED EDITION, IN EIGHT VOLUMES.

THE

DISPATCHES

OF

FIELD MARSHAL

THE DUKE OF WELLINGTON,

DURING

HIS VARIOUS CAMPAIGNS

IN

INDIA, DENMARK, PORTUGAL, SPAIN, THE LOW COUNTRIES, AND FRANCE.

COMPILED FROM OFFICIAL AND OTHER AUTHENTIC
DOCUMENTS,

BY COLONEL GURWOOD, C.B., K.C.T.S.

*ESQUIRE TO HIS GRACE AS KNIGHT OF THE BATH, AND DEPUTY LIEUTENANT
OF THE TOWER OF LONDON.*

VOLUME THE THIRD.

LONDON:

PARKER, FURNIVALL, AND PARKER,
MILITARY LIBRARY, WHITEHALL.

M.DCCC.XLIV.

CONTENTS OF THE THIRD VOLUME.

INTRODUCTION.

THE SERVICES OF

FIELD MARSHAL THE DUKE OF WELLINGTON,

IN EUROPE.

Major General the Hon. Sir Arthur Wellesley, soon after his return to England from India, in September 1805, was appointed to the command of a brigade in an expedition fitted out in the autumn of that year to proceed to Hanover, under the command of Lord Cathcart: but the consequences of the battle of Austerlitz induced the government to recall this force; and the troops composing it were placed on the coast for future operations, or for the defence of the country against threatened invasion.

In the mean time, Marquis Cornwallis had died at Ghazypoor, near Benares, on the 5th Oct. 1805, shortly after his arrival in India as the new Governor General; and, on the 30th Jan. 1806, Major Gen. Sir A. Wellesley succeeded his Lordship as Colonel of the 33rd regt., of which he had been Lieutenant Colonel above 12 years.

On the return of the expedition from Hanover, in the beginning of 1806, Sir A. Wellesley was appointed to the command of a brigade of infantry, stationed at Hastings, in the Sussex district; to the discipline, manœuvre, and minute details of which he paid the most scrupulous attention.* He had been elected to serve in the new Parliament for the borough of Rye; and in his place in the House of Commons, by a simple statement of facts, he repelled the unworthy attacks made upon Lord Wellesley's brilliant administration of the extensive Empire of India.†

---

* There is no situation, and there are no circumstances, that will not, in some manner or other, be stamped with the superior principles of the thorough soldier. An intimate friend having in familiar terms inquired of Sir A. Wellesley, when at Hastings, how he, having commanded armies of 40,000 men in the field; having received the thanks of Parliament for his victories; and having been made Knight of the Bath, could submit to be reduced to the command of a brigade of infantry? 'For this plain reason,' was the characteristic answer, 'I am *nimmukwallah*, as we say in the East; that is, I have eat the King's salt, and, therefore, I conceive it to be my duty to serve with unhesitating zeal and cheerfulness, when and wherever the King or his government may think proper to employ me.' This maxim has the more force from there being officers in the army, who, unfortunately, having declined subordinate employment from flattering themselves with superior pretensions, have repented their decision during the remainder of their lives; and it is for this reason that the Compiler has presumed to draw the attention of those who may hereafter be placed in similar circumstances to this great military principle, as well as to the example of the Duke of Wellington.

† See 'Hansard's Debates.' Mr. Paul's motions for the impeachment of Marquis Wellesley, 1805 and 1806.

In the month of April, 1807, a new administration was formed. The Duke of Richmond was appointed Lord Lieutenant of Ireland; and Sir A. Wellesley, Chief Secretary, and consequently he was sworn of the King's Privv council.

In the month of August, in the same year, war was declarea against Denmark; and on the 8th Sept. Adm. Gambier and Lord Cathcart, commanding a combined expedition, took possession of the city and citadel of Copenhagen. Major Gen. Sir A. Wellesley commanded the division of reserve; and at Kioge, on the 29th Aug., had an affair with the enemy, described in his dispatch to Lord Cathcart, the Commander of the land forces.

On the 7th Sept., in conjunction with Sir Home Popham, Captain of the fleet, and Lieut. Col. Murray,* D. Q. M. G. of the British forces under Lord Cathcart, Sir A. Wellesley drew up and signed the articles of capitulation of the town and citadel of Copenhagen, in conjunction with the Danish officers deputed by Gen. Peymaun, the Commander in Chief of His Danish Majesty's forces in Zealand.

In Feb. 1808, Major Gen. Sir A. Wellesley being in his place in the House of Commons, the Speaker, having returned the thanks to other General officers, members of the House, for their conduct at Copenhagen, thus particularized Sir A. Wellesley on that occasion :

' But I should indeed be wanting to the full expression of those sentiments which animate this House, and the whole country, if I forbore to notice that we are on this day crowning with our thanks one gallant officer, long since known to the gratitude of this House, who has long trodden the paths of glory, whose genius and valor have already extended our fame and empire, whose sword has been the terror of our distant enemies, and will not now be drawn in vain to defend the seat of Empire itself, and the throne of his King. I am charged, Sir Arthur Wellesley, to deliver the thanks of this House to you, and I do accordingly thank you, in the name of the Commons of the United Kingdom, for your zeal, intrepidity, and exertion displayed in the various operations which were necessary for conducting the siege, and effecting the surrender of the navy and arsenal of Copenhagen.'

Major Gen. the Hon. Sir A. Wellesley replied as follows :

' Mr. Speaker; I consider myself fortunate that I was employed by His Majesty on a service which this House has considered of such importance as to have marked with its approbation the conduct of those officers and troops who have performed it. The honor which this House has conferred upon my honorable friends and myself is justly considered by the officers of the navy and army as the highest which this country can confer : it is the object of the ambition of all who are employed in His Majesty's service, and to obtain it has doubtless been the motive of many of those acts of valor and good conduct which have tended so eminently to the glory, and have advanced the prosperity and advantage of this country. I can assure the House that I am most sensible of the great honor which they have

* Gen. Sir G. Murray, G.C.B., &c.

done me, and I beg leave to take this opportunity of returning you, Sir, my thanks, for the handsome terms, respecting myself, in which your kindness to me has induced you to convey the resolution of the House.'

On the return of the expedition from Zealand, Sir A. Wellesley resumed his duties as Secretary for Ireland.*

In the spring of 1808 a force was assembled at Cork, with a view, as it was supposed, to some expedition against the Spanish colonies of South America; but extraordinary changes took place towards the latter end of 1807 and the beginning of 1808, in the affairs of Spain and Portugal, by French intervention, or rather invasion, and by the consequent national appeals from the inhabitants of those countries to Great Britain for aid to rescue them from the flagrant usurpation of Napoleon Buonaparte. The corps assembled at Cork was accordingly placed under the command of Sir A. Wellesley, and directed to proceed to the aid of the patriotic movement in the Peninsula. It sailed for Coruña on the 12th July, and finally landed, on the 1st Aug., at Lavos, at the mouth of the river Mondego, in Portugal.

The battles of Rolica and Vimeiro, fought on the 17th and 21st Aug. 1808, were followed by an armistice, and subsequently by the Convention of Cintra,† according to the stipulations of which the French army, commanded by Gen. Junot, was afterwards embarked at Lisbon, in British vessels, and landed at La Rochelle, in October.

An Inquiry was ordered by the King to be made into the Armistice and the Convention, and into all the circumstances connected with them; and a board of General officers was assembled for that purpose, at the great hall in Chelsea College, in the months of November and December, 1808.

In the mean time the British army at Lisbon being left disposable for other services, the greater part of it was marched into Castille, under the command of Lieut. Gen. Sir J. Moore, and was joined on the Duero, in December, by an additional force, under Sir D. Baird, which had landed at Coruña.

In the month of November, the French armies having been greatly reinforced, and the Spaniards having been successively defeated at Tudela and in other battles, the city of Madrid fell again into the hands of the enemy. Buonaparte, who had arrived to superintend in person the operations in Spain, directed, in the month of December, a combined movement of several corps, under the command of Marshal Soult, against the army under Sir J. Moore, which consequently retreated into Galicia; and a battle took place on the 16th Jan. 1809, at Coruña, where Sir J. Moore was killed in the hour of victory.

Sir A. Wellesley, on his return from Portugal after the battle of Vimeiro, again resumed the duties of his office as Chief Secretary for Ireland; and the Court of Inquiry held at the Royal College at Chelsea having concluded, in December he proceeded to Dublin.

---

* See ' Hansard's Debates.' The official and other dispatches, although full of local interest with regard to Ireland, are not inserted in this work.

† Erroneously called the ' Convention of Cintra,' that document having been framed and signed at Lisbon. This misnomer arose from the copy of the Convention having been forwarded by Lieut. Gen. Sir H. Dalrymple to the Sec. of State in a dispatch, dated Cintra, 3rd Sept. 1808. The error, however, having become fixed and habitual, the usual name has been retained.

Parliament having reassembled in January, 1809, he returned to London to attend the House of Commons; and on the 27th Jan., when in his place, he received the Thanks of the House for his conduct at the battle of Vimeiro in the following terms:

'LIEUT. GEN. SIR ARTHUR WELLESLEY; After the events of last year, it was impossible that Parliament should reassemble without directing its earliest attention to the services of the British army in Portugal; and amidst the contending opinions which have prevailed upon other questions, the public voice has been loud and general in admiration of your splendid achievements.

'It is your praise to have inspired your troops with unshaken confidence and unbounded ardor; to have commanded, not the obedience alone, but the hearts and affections of your companions in arms; and having planned your operations with the skill and promptitude which have so eminently characterised all your former exertions, you have again led the armies of your country to battle, with the same deliberate valor and triumphant success which have long since rendered your name illustrious in the remotest parts of this Empire.

'Military glory has ever been dear to this nation, and great military exploits in the field and upon the ocean have their sure reward in Royal favor and the gratitude of Parliament. It is, therefore, with the highest satisfaction, that, in this fresh instance, I now proceed to deliver to you the Thanks of this House; and I do now accordingly, by the command and in the name of the Commons of the United Kingdom of Great Britain and Ireland, thank you for the distinguished valor, ability, and conduct displayed by you on the 17th and 21st Aug. last in Portugal; on the latter of which days you obtained at Vimeiro, over the army of the enemy, a signal victory, honorable and glorious to the British arms.'

Sir A. Wellesley rose and made the following answer:

'MR. SPEAKER; I beg leave to express my acknowledgments to the House for the high honor which they have conferred upon me, by the notice which they have taken, and the approbation they have conveyed, of my conduct during the time I commanded His Majesty's troops in Portugal.

'No man can value more highly than I do the honorable distinction which has been conferred upon me, a distinction which it is in the power of the representatives of a free people alone to bestow, and which it is the peculiar advantage of the officers and soldiers in the service of His Majesty to have held out to them as the object of their ambition, and to receive as the reward of their services.

'I beg leave to return to you, Sir, my thanks for the handsome terms in wreturn to you, Sir, my thanks for the handsome lity, for me, has induced you to convey the approbation of the House.'

The House of Lords passed the following resolutions, which were communicated to Sir A. Wellesley:

'House of Lords, 23rd Jan. 1809.

'Resolved, *Nem. dissent.*, That the Thanks of this House be given to Lieut. Gen. the Rt. Hon. Sir A. Wellesley, K.B., for the distinguished valor, ability, and conduct displayed by him on the 17th and 21st of Aug. last in Portugal; on the latter of which days he obtained at Vimeiro, over the army of the enemy, a signal victory, honorable and glorious to the British arms.

'Resolved, *Nem. dissent.*, That the Thanks of this House be given to Major Gen. Spencer, Major Gen. Hill, Major Gen. Ferguson, Brig. Gen. Acland, Brig. Gen. Nightingall, Brig. Gen. Bowes, Brig. Gen. Fane, Brig. Gen. Anstruther, and the several officers of the army, for their skill and gallant exertions against the enemy in the battles of Roliça and Vimeiro, by which they reflected so much lustre on His Majesty's arms.

'Resolved, *Nem. dissent.*, That the House doth highly approve of, and acknowledge, the steady and disciplined valor displayed by the non-commissioned officers and private soldiers of the army on the above occasion, and that the same be signified by the commanders of the several corps, who are desired to thank them for their distinguished and exemplary conduct.'

To these resolutions, conveyed to him by the Lord Chancellor, Lieut. Gen. Sir A. Wellesley wrote the following answer:

To the Rt. Hon. the Lord Chancellor, &c. London, 28th Jan. 1809.

' I have had the honor of receiving your Lordship's letter of the 24th inst., containing copies of the unanimous resolutions of the House of Lords, conveying the approbation of their Lordships of my conduct and that of the General and other officers, non-commissioned officers, and soldiers comprising the army which I commanded in Portugal, and their Lordships' desire that I should communicate their Lordships' vote to the respective General officers and to the officers commanding the corps employed in the service in that country.

' I have received the mark of distinction which the House of Lords have conferred upon me with sentiments of gratitude and respect proportionate to the high sense I entertain of the greatness of the honor which it carries with it; and I shall have great pleasure in communicating to the officers and the troops the distinguished reward of their exemplary conduct which their Lordships have conferred upon them.

' I beg leave, at the same time, to express to your Lordship my thanks for the expressions of personal civility with which your Lordship has conveyed to me the commands of the House.'

Early in the year 1809, after the battle at Coruña, Portugal again became the seat of active military operations, Marshal Soult having invaded its northern provinces from Galicia, and taken possession of Oporto on the 29th March. Lisbon was thrown into alarm, and the Regency urgently implored the further aid and protection of the British nation. Reinforcements were embarked, and Lieut. Gen. Sir A. Wellesley, having resigned the office of Chief Secretary in Ireland and his seat in Parliament, was sent again to command the British army in Portugal. He sailed on the 15th April in the *Surveillante* frigate, which was nearly lost close to St. Katherine's, at the back of the Isle of Wight, in the night after quitting Spithead. On his arrival at Lisbon, on the 22nd April, he assumed the command of that army, with which, in the following years, he liberated the Peninsula from its French invaders, and ultimately placed the British standard at Bordeaux and Toulouse. He returned to England on the 23rd June, 1814, a Field Marshal, and took his seat in the House of Lords at once as Baron, Viscount, Earl, Marquis, and Duke!

After the capitulation of Paris, and the consequent peace in 1814, during the adjustment of the state of Europe at the Congress of Vienna, Napoleon Buonaparte suddenly re-appeared in France in March, 1815. He again rallied under his eagles a complete and organised army of Frenchmen, animated by enthusiasm for their Emperor, and excited by the recollections of their former victories. He attacked the allied Prussian and British armies, then in the Low Countries, under Prince Blücher and the Duke of Wellington, at Ligny and at Waterloo.

The battles of the 16th and 18th of June, 1815, undoubtedly the most important military events of modern times, were attended by results and advantages sufficient for the glory of many such armies as those of the allies thus engaged. The French army, defeated and dispersed at Waterloo, never rallied; Buonaparte fled from the field of battle, and lost his Empire for ever; Paris again capitulated; and the peace of Europe and of the World was settled on the basis on which it rests at this moment.

OFFICIAL AND OTHER DISPATCHES

OF

FIELD MARSHAL THE DUKE OF WELLINGTON.

DENMARK AND THE PENINSULA.

To Lieut. Col. Malcolm.   London, 25th Feb. 1806.

I RETURNED from the Continent only a few days ago, and have not yet had leisure to read the Indian papers which have come into my hands, in order to enable me to form an opinion of the state of affairs up to the latest period. I think it possible, however, that you will have peace; and that may be permanent, or otherwise, in proportion to our own firmness, and the means of the enemy of disturbing our tranquillity. So many principles, however, have been abandoned or overturned, that we must look for peace from a course of accidental circumstances, and not from the steady adherence to any settled system of policy.

I will try to get a living for your brother, but you see that a revolution (commonly called a change) has taken place in the government of this country. *We* are not actually in opposition, but we have no power; and if I get any thing for your brother, it must be by the influence of private friendship.

I don't think that this government can last very long. You can have no idea of the disgust created by the harshness of their measures, by the avidity with which they have sought for office, and by the indecency with which they have dismissed every man supposed to have been connected with Pitt. His friends will, I think, remain connected, and will act together as a body, and a most formidable one they will be to any government on account of their numbers.

I am tolerably well in health, and I shall be quite well if I can continue to spend a few weeks at Cheltenham in this summer. The regiment which they have given me, and the staff, have made me rich.

As soon as I shall have read all the Indian papers, which I have got, I will sit down and write to you a long dispatch upon them.

There is a report about London, which I cannot bring myself to give credit to, that you had been kicked by a horse, and that your leg had, in consequence, been amputated. I was employed for two days ascertaining this report, and at last I found that you had been bit by a horse in the arm : I only hope not by *Sultan*.

To Lieut. Col. Malcolm.   Hastings, 31st July, 1806.

I have received your letters up to the 14th Jan., for which I return you many thanks. The subjects to which they relate are too large to be discussed in a letter which must go to the post this afternoon, in order to be dispatched by the ships which will sail in a few days. I shall therefore satisfy myself by telling you that I consider that you have acted a part entirely consistent with your own character, and in strict conformity with my sentiments, in every thing that you have done. The arrangement with Scindiah is precisely that which you and I recommended long before, and which I urged, and, I believe, was ordered when I was in Bengal in 1804. I thought also at that time, and so did you, that the Rajpoots ought to have been subjugated to the control of Scindiah's government, as the only mode of re-establishing it; the state in which it must exist, if it is to exist at all. This object might with care and justice have been effected at that time, if the state of Scindiah's government had permitted it; and I am not sufficiently acquainted with all that has passed between the Rajpoots and our government since the period of Monson's defeat, to be able to decide that we ought not to deliver them over to Scindiah, notwithstanding the favorable change which has taken place in the state and dispositions of his councils.

I regret that it has been necessary to allow Holkar to exist, and to be at large. I should be induced to suspect that he will never allow us to be at peace; and without peace we cannot reduce the debt, which must be the great object at present. However, if it was necessary to allow him to exist, I see but one amendment which could have been made to the treaty with him; that is, to have kept permanently Umber and Chandore in the Deccan, and some place of similar consequence in Hindustan, either in our own hands or those of our allies, as a perpetual memorial to the whole world that we had defeated him. The powers of India will not now believe that our moderation alone has occasioned the treaty which has been concluded; and I shall not be surprised if it give ground for a belief, the most erroneous, that Holkar's power and his mode of warfare had been more destructive to us than the resources and the efficiency and discipline of the armies of the other Marhattas.

In respect to the necessity of peace with Holkar, no man can be a judge of it who has not been in this country, who has not sat in the House of Commons, and had means of ascertaining the public opinion at its fountain head. I really believe, that in the opinion of the majority of people in this country, it would have been better to cede the whole of Oude to Holkar than to continue the war with him.

As for myself, I am here in the command of a few troops stationed in this part of the coast, the old landing place of William the Conqueror. You will have seen that I am in Parliament, and a most difficult and unpleasant game I have had to play in the present extraordinary state of parties. I have desired Sydenham to send you a copy of a speech which I made upon the budget.

I have seen your brothers, Pulteney and Charles, both well. The former is in the *Donegal*, off Brest; the other unemployed in London. But Sir Thomas, whom I saw likewise, expects to be able to get a ship for Charles soon. I have tried a job for a relation of yours,   *   *   *   *   *   but without success; but I will not lose sight of him. God bless you, my dear Malcolm; don't stay too long in India.

P.S. Pray remember me most kindly to Wilks and all friends in Seringapatam.

To Lieut. Col. Malcolm.   Deal, 10th Dec. 1806.

I hear that the ships will soon sail from Portsmouth, and I will not allow them to go without a few lines, although I have but little to tell you. I know no more of public news than what you will see in the newspapers, which, indeed, in these days contain every thing. You will read with horror the accounts of the French successes against the King of Prussia; but will learn with pleasure that, considering the line of policy which that government had adopted for some years, those successes are not likely to do us any material mischief immediately, whatever may be the eventual consequence in relation to our ally the Emperor of Russia. Of the truth of this opinion I am thoroughly convinced, from a personal knowledge of facts, as well as because I know it is entertained by some for whose judgment I entertain the greatest respect.

As for India, I know but little respecting it. If I had been employed in North America, I might be informed and consulted on the measures to be adopted in India; but as it is, that is out of the question. Lord Minto will sail soon, I believe early in next month; and Gen. Hewitt, who is appointed Commander in Chief, will go with him, or shortly after him. You will find this to be a sensible and goodnatured gentleman, and well disposed to carry on his business in the manner which experience has proved to be most suitable to the country. I doubt whether his health or his age will permit him to remain long or to be very active in the field.

The last letter which I received from you was dated from Cawnpore, in May, I believe; but I sent it to Lord W., who has kept it. You are already acquainted with my opinion, generally, about your peace with Holkar and your treaty with Scindiah. I only wish that you had kept any thing from the former which might have been held out as a perpetual signal and memorandum to all India that he had been defeated by us; for I am apprehensive that the opinion, to which I know all were inclined, that Holkar's system of warfare was the same with the old Marhatta system, that it was the best against us, and that Scindiah was ruined by his adoption of a more regular system, than which nothing can be more erroneous, may occasion another war with a confederacy. I know that we have no danger to apprehend from this war if we keep up, not so much the strength of our armies as an equipment, and if our troops are commanded by officers who know how to make use of them. But I dread the expense and the effect which the renewal of these wars will have in this country; and I know full well that there are many delicate questions to be settled in the Marhatta Empire, the arrangement of which, in peace, will require all the impression from former victories, all the vigor, all the prudence, and all the temper which have brought us through our former difficulties. The fault which I find with the peace with Holkar therefore is, that it has strengthened an erroneous opinion which deprives us of the greatest advantage of our victories, viz., their impression, and that in this manner it will increase the chance of war upon the occasion of the arrangement of every question which remains to be settled in the Marhatta Empire. The want of this impression renders the exercise of a vigorous administration nearly impracticable, excepting in a state of constant preparation for war, which, after all, is nearly as expensive as war itself; and yet I don't see how the government in India is to be carried on excepting with vigor.

I see no material objection to the treaty with Scindiah, and I believe that I recommended that the treaty of peace should be arranged upon the principles of that treaty; and that a treaty to a similar purport should be concluded with Scindiah when the treaty of peace was arranged differently.

You will have heard with astonishment of ——'s attack upon Lord Wellesley. The impudence of this gent. in setting himself up for Westminster has afforded an opportunity of unveiling him to the public, and his character is now well known. Only think of that fellow standing for Westminster, and having been not far from carrying his election ! ! ! He is not now in Parliament, and I doubt whether he will ever come in ; and if he should not be in the House of Commons, it is not quite clear that any body will undertake the cause which he will have left. But whether there should be such a person or not, I have some reason to believe that the House will not allow the business to be brought forward again, although from the state of parties I am afraid that it will not be got rid of in the manner which would be most agreeable and honorable to Lord W. and his friends. You, who know him well, will be aware of the impression which all that has passed upon this subject, and the state of the public mind on Indian subjects generally, have made upon him. I shall not pretend to describe it to you in a letter; and I cannot venture to enter into particulars on many subjects on which I should write for your information, considering the danger to which letters are exposed on their passage, and the bad consequences which have resulted, and must always result, from the publication of intercepted correspondence.

Your brother is well, and off Brest in the *Donegal.* Charles has got a ship, and is, I believe, still at Plymouth. I have been endeavoring to do something for ——'s brother, who is to be married to your sister, but hitherto without success. Remember me most kindly to Wilks, Barclay, Symonds, and Piele, and all friends at Seringapatam; also to Col. Close when you write to him.

To Lieut. Col. Malcolm.   London, 23rd Feb. 1807.

I had intended to write to you by Lord Minto, but he left town very suddenly while I was hunting at Hatfield, and he had sailed before I heard of his departure from London. But I hear that the Indiamen are to sail immediately, and I shall not suffer them to go without a letter.

I shall not pretend to give you an account of the state of public affairs, of which you will be enabled to form a better judgment by a perusal of the newspapers than by any thing I could write to you. The minority are certainly very strong in Parliament, and, I think, are getting on a little in the country. But they will never be so popular as Pitt was; and I think that there are symptoms in this country and in Ireland which require the serious attention of every man who wishes for the continuance of the Empire and the prosperity of Great Britain. They are coming to their senses greatly about India, and I know that Tierney has some good principles in relation to that country, and that he would govern it well if he had the power. A revolution is also in progress, slowly but very certainly, in the public mind, respecting the former system of government there, and that according to which affairs ought to be administered there in future. The Court of Directors are certainly less hostile than they were towards Lord Wellesley; and, as for me, I have the most certain proofs that they are desirous that I should serve them again. All this looks well, and I am sanguine in my expectations that all difficulties upon these subjects will soon have been overcome.

You will have been astonished at the career of —— ——, —— ——, your quondam friend and *protege*. He certainly was nearly being the representative of Westminster, owing partly to the unpopularity of Sheridan; partly to his own impudence; and partly to the power which Horne Tooke and Cobbett have acquired over the public mind. I was the first person who discovered that the characteristics of —— were perseverance, effrontery, and impudence; and when you conceive such a character, you will not be astonished at all at what he has done, notwithstanding the kicks, cuffs, and buffeting which we gave him last year in Parliament, and all that he still threatens. He is not now in Parliament, and —— ——, who was one of his supporters last year, has announced his intention of moving a resolution on the transactions in Oude. He brings no charge, however, and he does not mean to criminate Lord Wellesley; and he has particularly stated that he does not think there is the smallest ground for attributing to Lord Wellesley the waste of the public money. We shall beat him, whatever may be the nature of his resolution. Another gentleman, —— ——, has given notice of a day for moving again for the printing the Carnatic papers, with a view to the consideration of the transactions in the revolution in that country. We shall beat him likewise. You will readily believe that Lord Wellesley is much annoyed by all this; but his mind is more composed, and he is more reconciled to his situation than he was last year.

Alas! my dear Malcolm, what has come over the army of Fort St. George? What are we to believe? Is it possible that the Princes at Vellore can have corrupted the detachment at Hyderabad, at the distance of 500 miles? Surely these Princes in confinement, and possessing but limited pecuniary means, could never have had the power of creating a general interest in their favor throughout the whole of the Native army of Fort St. George, dispersed as it is over thousands of miles!!! I am all

anxiety upon this subject, and yet I have not received a line from a soul.
Nobody believes the accounts which are received from India upon this
subject, notwithstanding the credit and character of those who have transmitted them; and the mind of every man is filled with suspicion and
alarm. Surely those followers who went through the difficulties and
dangers of the Marhatta campaigns cannot have broken their allegiance!
I can never believe it, till I shall see it proved in the clearest manner.

I wish that you were *now* in England; but I doubt whether it will be
of any use to you to come hereafter. Government have some thoughts of
sending an embassy to Persia; ——— —— as the ambassador. I put
a spoke in his wheel the other day, I think, in a conversation with ———,
and urged him to get Lord Howick to appoint you. God knows whether
I have succeeded in the last object, although I made it clear that ———
was an improper man, and that you were the only one fit for the station.
I do not recommend it to you to be in a hurry to come to England.
Expenses here are very heavy, and fortunes very large. Notwithstanding
all the taxes and the rise in price of every article in life, there is more
luxury than ever, more appearance of riches in the country, and more
persons with large fortunes, and fewer with fortunes of a moderate extent, than there were formerly. You could not exist in the way you would
like under a much larger fortune than you possess; and take my word
for it, you will lose nothing by staying away from England a little longer.
Pray don't forget to remember me to all my friends, particularly to Wilks,
Close, Barclay, Symonds, Piele, Cole, if he should be with you, Buchan,
&c., &c. Tell ——— that I have endeavored to serve him in his difficulties. The Court of Directors are outrageous against him, for no
reason whatever; and I am not sure that I have prevailed with ——— to
prevent them from venting their rage in paragraphs in a general letter.
God bless you.

To the Duke of Richmond.   London, 24th July, 1807.
You will have heard of the intended expedition from this country, the
object of which is to attack the Danish island of Zealand, and to endeavor
to obtain possession of the Danish fleet. The success, in my opinion,
depends in a great measure upon the possibility of bringing the Danish
army over from Holstein. If that should be possible, I think the success
very problematical, as it may be depended upon that the Danes will be
joined and assisted by the French, and, if the first can pass unmolested
by our ships, the last will find no difficulty in passing.

However, whatever may be the chance of success of the expedition, it
would not answer for me to allow it to go on without expressing a desire
to be employed upon it; I accepted my office in Ireland solely on the
condition that it should not preclude me from such service when an opportunity should offer; and I am convinced that, although you may feel
some inconvenience from my temporary absence, supposing that it is
intended that I should return to you, or from the loss of the assistance
of an old friend, supposing that it is not, you would be the last man to
desire or to wish that I should do any thing with which I should not be
satisfied myself: and I acknowledge that I should not be satisfied if I

allowed any opportunity of service to pass by without offering myself. Under these circumstances, I have desired to be employed, and I understand that, if the expedition should go on, I am to go with it.

I do not know, and I have not asked, whether I am to return to my office when this *coup de main* shall have been struck, or shall have failed. All that I am to tell you is, that nothing will give me greater satisfaction than to assist you so long as I can be useful to you; and that I have been desired by Lord Hawkesbury and Lord Castlereagh to settle with Long to take charge of my business in Parliament whilst I shall be absent.

I shall write to you the particulars of every thing I shall hear or learn upon this subject. In the mean time I tell you that I heard a piece of news this morning, which looks very like a stop to the expedition, viz., that the Danes had already begun to move their troops out of Holstein. If that is the case, we shall probably not go. In this state of uncertainty, I have not written to Lady Wellesley upon this subject, and it is as well not to say any thing to her about it, till it shall be positively settled that we are to go.

To Lieut. Gen. Lord Cathcart, K.T.   Kioge, 19th Aug. 1807.

According to the intention which I announced to your Lordship on the evening of the 27th, I moved to Roeskild Kroe, and placed Col. Reden at Vallensbrek; and Gen. Linsengen marched yesterday morning to Roeskild: by these different movements his force became the right instead of the left.

Having had reason to believe that the enemy still remained at Kioge, I determined to attack him this day. I settled with Gen. Linsengen, that he should cross the Kioge rivulet at Little Salbye, and turn the enemy's left flank, while I should move along the sea road towards Kioge, and attack him in front.

Both divisions broke up this morning, and marched according to the plan concerted. Upon my approach to Kioge, I found the enemy in force on the north side of the town and rivulet, and they commenced a cannonade upon the patroles of hussars in my front; they had 3 or 4 regular battalions formed in one line, with cavalry on both flanks, and apparently a large body beyond the town and rivulet. At the time agreed upon with Gen. Linsengen, I formed my infantry in one line, with the left to the sea, having the 2 squadrons of hussars upon the right. There had been some appearance of a movement by the enemy to their left; and I had not had any communication with Gen. Linsengen, and was not certain that he had passed the rivulet: I therefore thought it proper to make the attack in an *echelon* of battalions from the left; the whole covered by the 1st batt. 95th regt.,* and by the fire of our artillery. It fell to the lot of the 92nd regt. to lead this attack, and they performed their part in the most exemplary manner, and were equally well supported by the 52nd and 43rd.

The enemy soon retired to an intrenchment which they had formed in front of a camp on the north side of Kioge, and they made a disposition

---

* Afterwards the Rifle Brigade, but at this time, and until the end of the war, known as the 95th

of their cavalry upon the sands to charge the 92nd in flank, while they should attack this intrenchment. This disposition obliged me to move Col. Reden's hussars from the right to the left flank, and to throw the 43rd into a second line; and then the 92nd carried the intrenchment, and forced the enemy to retreat into the town in disorder. They were followed immediately in the most gallant style by Col. Reden and his hussars, and by the 1st batt. 95th regt., and afterwards by the whole of the infantry of my corps. Upon crossing the rivulet, we found Gen. Linsengen's corps upon our right flank, and the whole joined in the pursuit of the enemy.

Major Gen. Oxholm, the second in command, who had joined the army with 4 battalions last night from the southern island, attempted to stand in the village of Hersolge, but he was attacked briskly by the hussars, with detachments of which were Capt. Blaquiere and Capt. Cotton of the Staff, and by a small detachment of the 1st of the 95th; and he was compelled to surrender, with Count Wedel Jarlsburg, several other officers, and 400 men.

The loss of the enemy has been very great, many have fallen, and there are nearly 60 officers and 1100 men prisoners. In their flight they have thrown away their arms and clothing, and many stands of the former have fallen into our hands. I believe that we have taken 10 pieces of cannon; but I have not yet received all the reports from the detachments employed in the pursuit of the enemy. I have not seen Gen. Linsengen, as he is still out with his hussars; but I understand that the enemy had destroyed the bridges at Little Salbye, which was the cause of the delay of his operations upon their flank.

I cannot close this letter without expressing to your Lordship my sense of the good conduct of the troops; all conducted themselves with the utmost steadiness; but I cannot avoid mentioning particularly the 92nd regt., under the command of Lieut. Col. Napier; the 1st batt. 95th regt., under the command of Lieut. Col. Beckwith; the British artillery, under the command of Capt. Newhouse; the Hanoverian hussars, under Col. Reden, and the Hanoverian light artillery, under Capt. Sympher, as a corps that had particular opportunities of distinguishing themselves: I am also much obliged to Gen. Linsengen and to Brig. Gen. R. Stewart, for the assistance I received from them in the formation and execution of the plan by which the enemy have been defeated. The officers of the Staff have also rendered me much assistance; and I must particularly mention Capt. Blaquiere and Capt. Colin Campbell.

P.S. We have taken a large store of powder and other military stores in this town, which I propose to destroy, if I should not be able to prevail upon the Captain of one of His Majesty's ships to take charge of them.

To Lord Hawkesbury.   Roeskild Kroe, 28th Aug. 1807.

Lord Rosslyn landed at Kioge, and joined the army before Copenhagen, on the 22nd and 23rd, and on that day we found that the battery which had been constructed on the extremity of our left had not been so effectual a protection against the fire of the gun boats as had been expected. In fact, in an engagement between our gun craft and battery on our left on one side, and the Crown battery and the enemy's gun boats on the other, on the 23rd, the enemy had the best of it, and our boats were obliged to draw off. Lord Cathcart therefore determined to move on his centre and right; and on the morning of the 24th the whole line, with the exception of the extremity of the left, moved forward and established themselves without opposition in a line, at the distance of about 1700 yards from the town; and my riflemen in the centre of the guards on the right were pushed considerably more forward into the suburbs. On the 25th, Lord Rosslyn took up my position on the lines, as I was destined to destroy the collection of Danish troops and peasants which had been making in the neighbourhood of Roeskild; and on the 25th, in the afternoon, there was some appearance of an intention in the enemy to make a sortie to drive in the riflemen and light infantry of the guards, which occupied the faubourgs in front of our line. I went down and assisted Lord Rosslyn, and we soon drove in the enemy entirely, and have established ourselves within 700 yards of the town, on the bank of the reservoirs of water for the supply of Copenhagen. The left made a forward movement at the same time, with the exception of its flank; so that on the morning of the 26th, when I marched, the army was securely established in a position within 700 yards of the works of the town. Lord Cathcart intended to establish mortar batteries at that distance, and then to summon the town. Since my departure I hear that he has given them 24 hours to consider of his propositions; and I learn that our battery upon the left has been more successful against the enemy's craft; that one vessel has blown up, and two have been sunk; and that on the right, where the enemy had brought gun craft, between Amag and the island of Zealand, a battery which has been constructed for the protection of the right flank has been equally successful. Unless the enemy should consent to our terms, I conclude that Lord Cathcart will commence the bombardment to-morrow morning. I acknowledge that I should prefer an establishment upon Amag, as a more certain mode of forcing a capitulation than a bombardment. In fact, the Danes are fighting only for their credit; it would be disgraceful not to bear a bombardment; but no city with a population of 70,000 or 80,000 inhabitants can be expected to hold out when cut off from all supplies of provisions. Besides, I think that it behoves us to do as little mischief to the town as possible, and to adopt any mode of reducing it, rather than bombardment. However, I am aware that no man can judge of the propriety of any particular plan of operations so well as the person who conducts them, and knows every thing; and therefore I conclude that there are some strong reasons against the occupation of Amag, of which I am not aware: one of these is certainly the necessity of sending a detachment to disperse the collection of troops making near Roeskild, upon which service I am now employed with my own corps, and a part of the cavalry under Gen. Linsengen. I made a good forced march upon them yesterday, but they avoided me, and are gone down to Kioge, and I propose to try again to-morrow. But the country is so much against us, that I can get no information excepting from our own patroles, and this deficiency of intelligence may protract the defeat or dispersion of the corps. The troops continue very healthy, and behave tolerably well;

they have done very well in the little affair which we have had before Copenhagen. Pray communicate this letter to Lord Castlereagh.

To Lord Hawkesbury.   Bræsenborg, 3rd Sept. 1807.

I marched on the morning after I wrote to you last, and defeated the Danish army at Kioge ; I don't believe they have now a man in Zealand, excepting the cavalry and a few infantry at Vordinborg, endeavoring to escape to the island of Falster, and my cavalry are gone after them. Not a man would have made his retreat if —— —— had carried into execution his part of the plan ; but, as it is, they have been sufficiently beat to prevent their assembling again. I cannot tell you how the siege is going on ; from what I have heard, however, I believe that the mortar batteries were prepared only yesterday.   *   *   *   *
We had possession of the ground for them on the 25th at night, and their mortar batteries were not prepared to open till the 2nd Sept. in the morning! Although the success at Kioge must have some effect upon the garrison of Copenhagen, I conceive that it will still be necessary to occupy Amag, and I have proposed a plan to Lord Cathcart for that purpose, which I am willing to carry into execution myself now that I have nothing more to do in this part of the country, or to aid any other officer to carry it into execution, if he should think it necessary to employ another.

To Lord Hawkesbury.   Head quarters near Copenhagen, 8th Sept. 1807.

Lord Cathcart sent for me the day before yesterday from my detachment in the country,* and in the course of that night I settled with the Danish commissioners the capitulation of the town and citadel of Copenhagen, which, of course, will be sent to England by this opportunity. I have only to observe upon this instrument that it contains the absolute and unconditional cession of the fleet and naval stores, and gives us the possession of those military points which are necessary in order to enable us to equip and carry away the vessels. This was all that we wanted ; and in every thing else I did all in my power to conciliate the Danes.

They certainly are much irritated against us, so much so that the

---

* Lieut. Gen. Lord Cathcart, K.T., to Visct. Castlereagh. Copenhagen, 8th Sept. 1807.

On the evening of the 5th Sept. a letter was sent by the Danish General, to propose an armistice of 24 hours, for preparing an agreement on which articles of capitulation might be founded. The armistice was declined, as tending to unnecessary delay, and the works were continued ; but the firing was countermanded, and Lieut. Col. Murray was sent to explain that no proposal of capitulation could be listened to, unless accompanied by the surrender of the fleet.

This basis having been admitted by a subsequent letter, on the 6th, Major Gen. Sir A. Wellesley, whom I had sent for, for this purpose, from his command in the country, where he had distinguished himself in a manner so honorable to himself and so advantageous to the public, was appointed, with Sir H. Popham and Lieut. Col. Murray, to prepare and sign articles of capitulation ; and those officers having insisted on proceeding immediately to business, the capitulation was drawn up in the night between the 6th and 7th.†

† See Marten's Treaties, &c.

Danish officers who settled the capitulation apprehended a riot among the sailors and the Burgher militia on account of the cession of the fleet; and the officers of the navy, in particular, were likely to be much irritated. On this account, and because we command it completely from the citadel and dockyard, I did not ask for the Crown battery; and indeed I must add that we have no claim to this work, not having, I believe, fired one shot into it from the moment we approached the place.

I might have carried our terms higher; and in contemplation of a notion hinted in a letter from Lord Castlereagh to Lord Cathcart, of keeping possession of Zealand, I might have gone so far as to demand the cession of the town entirely. But I have to observe that we are not aware what was the inducement to agree to any capitulation; I suspect it was want of powder, and, if it was so, they must have agreed to any terms; but if their only inducement was, as they said, the damage which they had received, and the greater damage they might receive, from the bombardment, terms which went to place us in their town, or to disgrace their burghers or their marine, particularly their officers, might have been rejected. Then I was to consider the state of the siege, their means of defence, and your call from England for the troops; none of which afforded inducements to press heavier terms upon them.

As to Lord Castlereagh's hint to Lord Cathcart, more as a point for deliberation than any thing else, it is quite out of the question. In the first year it would be necessary to have in Copenhagen a garrison of 10,000 men, and twice that number in the country. Those numbers might be diminished afterwards in proportion as we should conciliate the Danes to us and our government, and as we should bring the native population forward in our defence. But it could not be much diminished, and the naval blockade would be to be kept up necessarily until the Crown Prince and the powers of Europe should have consented to our possessing the island.

I have gone thus far into the consideration of the terms of the capitulation, which I must add are highly satisfactory to the army, not in order to justify them, for I am convinced that you and your friends will approve of them, but in order to show you that I took the whole subject into consideration; and I have only now to add that the Admiral and Lord Cathcart authorised us to take the fleet on the terms on which we first offered to hold it.

I am going this morning to join my corps in the country in order to draw it in gradually. I shall ask Lord Cathcart's leave to go to England immediately, and I hope to see you soon after you will receive this letter.

To Col. Malcolm.   Dublin Castle, 15th Oct. 1807.

I received your letters, written in March, a few days ago upon my return from Zealand; and I took care to communicate to Mr. Dundas your sentiments on the state of the army and on the causes which have led to the unpleasant temper which appears to exist in it. I agree with you entirely in some of your opinions on the causes which have produced this temper, particularly among the officers; and I also agree in your opinions on the remedies which ought to be adopted. Firmness of temper and uniformity and good sense in conduct by the government would soon bring all about; and I have no doubt whatever that if it should please the government here to send me to India again, I should have it in my power to re-establish the temper and spirit of the army in the manner in which it existed in our better times. I acknowledge, however, that I have not much fear for the safety of India, even if things should remain some time longer as they are. No country was ever lost by the mutiny, much less by the discontent, of its troops; and I am not quite certain that in order to produce radical good, it is not requisite to show the necessity of a complete change in respect to Indian manners and opinions, and to let matters continue for some time longer in the unpleasant state in which they are. But I have no inclination to refuse my services in that country, if they should be called for at present, or to do any thing here to serve those for whom I must ever retain the strongest sentiments of gratitude and affection.

I don't think it probable that I shall be called upon to go to India. The fact is that men in power in England think very little of that country, and those who do think of it feel very little inclination that I should go there. Besides that, I have got pretty high upon the tree since I came home, and those in power think that I cannot well be spared from objects nearer home. At the same time the Indians in London are crying out for my return.

I shall not pretend to give you any news. You will see the accounts of our Zealand expedition, which has had great effect in London, and has added to the popularity and strength of the ministry. The Danes did not defend themselves very well, and I think we might have taken the capital with greater ease than we forced them to the capitulation which I settled with them. I am now come here in consequence of the disturbed state of this country, and I shall stay here until the meeting of Parliament. I strongly recommend you not to return home as long as your health will permit you to remain in India, and as you can retain office. Take my word for it, you are not yet sufficiently rich; you will have to return there, and you may possibly find it difficult to get employment in the line to which you are so well suited, and to which you have always been accustomed.

Remember me most kindly to Wilks, Close, Barclay, and all friends.

To Lieut. Col. Malcolm.   London, 25th Feb. 1808.

I beg leave to congratulate you on your marriage, and to assure you that I rejoice most sincerely in an event which is so likely to contribute to your happiness. I beg that you will present my best respects to Mrs. Malcolm, to whom I hope you will introduce me at the first convenient moment.

My time has been so much occupied by my official and other duties, that I have really not had a moment which I could devote to my friends in India. I assure you, however, that I have not forgotten them or their kindness to me, the continued mark of which is the most pleasing circumstance of my life. I am employed in this country much in the same way that I was in India; that is to say, in everything: but there are circumstances in this country which render all employment unpleasant, and make it difficult to perform those services to the public in which every good man must be desirous to have a share.

Lord Wellesley has got the better of the impressions that the base attacks upon him had made upon his mind. He has lately made a most distinguished speech in the House of Lords, and I have no doubt will come forward frequently in the same way. I hope that we shall be able to bring the House of Commons to a vote on the Oude case, in the course of next week; not that I think that it signifies essentially whether we do or not, as time has had its usual effect upon the sense or folly of the public, and has convinced them that the man they have been in the habit of abusing was the best Governor for India. It is desirable, however, to come to a vote on this question, as several of Lord Wellesley's Indian friends are anxious about it, as well as others who have more respect than I have for what passes in Parliament. —— —— is arrived, and appeared inclined to bring himself before the House of Commons; a plan from which I advised him to desist, and rather to pocket all his grievances and affronts than to expose himself to an attack for years, to defend himself from which would occupy his whole time, and expose him to frequent mortifications. I shall recommend the same line of conduct to my friend ———, who, I find from a letter received from him, is likewise disposed to bring himself before the House of Commons.

I think the state of India is uncomfortable. I don't like the continued want of confidence between the officers and soldiers of the army of Fort St. George; still less so do I like the proceedings of ———— in Persia. I am convinced they would have been of no avail if the government had sent you to Persia, as I recommended long ago. However, it cannot now be helped. The state of affairs in Persia creates great anxiety here, but it is of that nature that you have occasionally witnessed in timid and undecided men, who fear something they know not what, and are more afraid of the remedy than they are of the danger to which they are exposed. Pray remember me most kindly to Wilks, Close, Barclay, Symonds, Freere and Mrs. Freere, and Purneah, and all friends at Seringapatam.

To the Rt. Hon. H. Dundas.   Dublin Castle, 20th April, 1808.

I have perused with great attention the paper which you enclosed with your letter of the 15th. My opinion is, that you ought to make an effort to meet the enemy, if possible, upon the Indus; although that opinion is much qualified by a variety of considerations which I shall now suggest to you.

1st. The art of crossing rivers is now so well understood, and has been so frequently practised, and so invariably, I believe, with success, in the late wars in Europe, that we cannot hope to defend the Indus, as a barrier. It is true that the enemy will not be in possession of the resources and means which they could apply to such an operation on a river in Italy or in Germany; but they will experience no want of such resources as that country will afford; and I have made as good a bridge with the basket boats

(which are described in Cæsar, and are in use all over India, the materials
for which are to be found every where) as I could have made of the best
pontoons. I acknowledge, therefore, that although, in this impending
war, I should seize Attock at an early period, I should endeavor to make
the Indus the seat of its operations; I have no great reliance upon that
river as the barrier to India.

2ndly. If it be true that we cannot rely upon the defence of the Indus,
although it is desirable to try it, and to carry the war into the countries
on its banks, the question is, what preparatory steps ought to be ordered
from hence? We must look to the state of the finances, to the fears and
jealousies which will be excited throughout India by a very large early
preparation, to a corresponding preparation by those in whom those fears
and jealousies will be excited, to the state of inefficiency and apathy in
which an army becomes in that country when long assembled in preparation and does not act.

The measures which I should recommend would be founded, 1st, upon
the conviction that the Indus cannot be completely defended, do what you
will; and, 2ndly, upon the considerations above referred to, of the inconvenience and evils resulting from a large early preparation to meet the
enemy on that river.

I shall not now enter into a detailed consideration of all the points to
which I have above referred. I shall only tell you that experience has
convinced me, and, I believe, the late Lord Lake, that active operations
are not to be carried on in those countries without the assistance of large
bodies of the *country light troops*. In this supposed war they would be
absolutely necessary, to enable us to cope at all with the same description
of troops which will be brought from the northern parts of Asia by our
enemies; and I leave you to judge of the extent of abuse and expense
which will attend the employment of troops of this description before the
period of their active operations will arrive.

The measure which I should recommend to you would be to assemble
your British army in the cantonments upon the Ganges and the Jumna,
and in the neighbourhood of Delhi; to form your magazines for its support;
to adopt all the preparatory measures for its taking the field at the shortest
notice which do not create large expense, and even those which do create
a large expense, the completion of which would require much time; to
form arrangements with the chiefs and leaders of the country light troops
for their junction with the British army, when their services should be
called for.

Then I should assemble in the field in front of Delhi a large corps consisting of from 6000 to 10,000 men, including a good proportion of the
British cavalry and a body of from 2000 to 3000 of country light troops,
and provided with a small battering train, the object of which should be to
cover the cantonments of the army, and to be in readiness to move with
rapidity and seize ——, as soon as intelligence should be received of the
intended advance of the enemy. The main body of your army would follow
and support this corps, and either the defence of the Indus might be undertaken, or any other measure might be adopted which would appear most
advisable at the time.

If the battle is to be fought upon the Indus, it will be absolutely necessary to station reserves upon the Bundelcund frontier, on the Jumna, and one in the country of the Seiks. But I do not now propose to enter so much into detail upon this subject as to point out the situation of these reserves. The station for the Bombay troops in Guzerat ought to depend upon the temper and inclinations of Scindiah and Holkar. If all is right in these quarters, the Bombay troops might be assembled at Ahmedabad, from whence they would threaten the enemy's right flank; if not, I am afraid it would be necessary to move them towards Dohud. It is certain, however, that the enemy cannot spread in the direction of Guzerat; and indeed the Bombay troops would not find it an easy matter to move northward, excepting in the winter, from Ahmedabad, on account of the difficulty of the Desert, and of the Ajmeer and Oudepoor countries.

Before I left India I gave in a plan for the positions of the subsidiary forces serving with the Peshwah and the Nizam, which, however, I am afraid that they have never been able to carry into execution. It went to the establishment of these corps upon the river Godavery, in communication with each other. If this plan had been adopted, no foreigners could enter the Deccan. Even as it is, not a shot has been fired in the Deccan since the year 1803. But if this great attack should be made upon Hindustan, the subsidiary forces must be moved up to the northern frontier, towards the Taptee. If Scindiah should misbehave, one of them should move across the Taptee and Nerbudda, and co-operate with the Bombay troops against him; and this corps ought to be replaced in the Peshwah's territories by the advance of a corps of the same strength from Mysore. Then you ought to have on the frontier of Mysore a reserve in the field.

In respect to the flotilla, the expense of it will be enormous, and the utility very doubtful. The enemy cannot spread to the Lower Indus; if they could, they would then fall in with the pirates, who would stop them, or they must subdue the pirates. If we send a flotilla to the Lower Indus, we must begin by subduing the pirates, and, when we shall have effected that object, as we cannot afford a sufficient army to protect ourselves there, we shall have deprived ourselves of our best barrier in that quarter, for the enemy would not be able to do more than drive the pirates from their establishments on the continent, considering the naval means which the latter have.

My opinion therefore is, that, instead of forming a large flotilla, we should encourage the pirates in the mouths of the Indus and in the gulf to defend themselves; and that we should aid them to that end as far as may be in our power. However, 1 may be mistaken upon this point, for I do not exactly recollect all that bears upon it, and I am writing to you without either paper or a map to refer to.

P.S. I sail to-night, and hope to be in London on Monday.

To the Duke of Richmond.   London, 4th June, 1808.

      *   *   *   *   *   *

The government has lately been talking to me about taking the command of the corps which is to be assembled at Cork, which is destined for Spain, but nothing is yet settled about it. I am convinced that I need make no apology to you for taking it, for if you were in my situation you would do the same; nor need I say much to produce a conviction upon your mind, that if this service should separate me from you, it will be a source of the greatest regret to me. Till this is certain it is useless to say more upon the subject; but I cannot inform you even of the chance that it may happen without expressing to you how sensible I am of all your

---

H. R. H. the Commander in Chief to Lieut. Gen.* the Hon. Sir A. Wellesley, K.B.

Horse Guards, 14th June, 1808.

His Majesty having been graciously pleased to appoint you to the command of a detachment of his army, to be employed upon a particular service, I have to desire that you will be pleased to take the earliest opportunity to assume the command of this force, and carry into effect such instructions as you may receive from His Majesty's ministers.

The force which His Majesty has been pleased to place under your command consists of the following corps:

Royal artillery		
Royal Staff corps, detachment		
29th foot		With Major Gen. Spencer.
*32nd .. 1st batt.		
*50th		
*82nd		
*5th		
*9th		
*38th		
*40th		To proceed from Cork.
60th .. 5th ..		
*71st .. 1st ..		
*91st		
95th, 4 companies		
4th Royal Vet. batt.		

And the Staff† appointed to this force is composed as follows:

Major Gens. Spencer, Hill, Ferguson.
Brig. Gens. Nightingall, Fane, Catlin Craufurd.

On all subjects relating to your command you will be pleased to correspond with me, and you will regularly communicate to me all military transactions in which you may be engaged, reporting to me all vacancies that may occur in the troops under your command; and as the power of appointing to commissions is not vested in you, you will be pleased to recommend to me such officers as may appear to you most deserving of promotion, stating the special reasons, where such recommendations are not in the usual channel of seniority.

As the regiments marked thus (*), under your command, have 2nd battalions attached to them, and which remain in this country, it is necessary that I should acquaint you that the first battalions under your orders being composed exclusively of the senior officers of their respective ranks, such vacancies as may occur therein, by promotion or casualty, must unavoidably be supplied by officers from the 2nd battalions, who will be ordered immediately to join, on such vacancies being made known to me.

Should you have occasion to recommend any gentleman for an ensigncy, you will be pleased to make known his address, in order that, if His Majesty should be pleased to confirm the recommendation, he may be directed to join the corps immediately on his appointment.

You will transmit, monthly, returns of the troops under your command to the Sec at War, and to the Adj. General, for my information; and you will strictly adhere to His Majesty's regulations, in regard to the pay, clothing, and appointments of the troops; and your special attention must necessarily be directed to their discipline, and to the interior economy of the different corps, which is so

essential,

---

* Sir A. Wellesley had been promoted to the rank of Lieut. General on the 25th April, 1808.

† The names of the other military and civil Staff officers are too numerous for insertion.

kindness and confidence in me, and how happy I should have been to have continued to assist you in the performance of the arduous duties which you have undertaken.   The ministers are not yet quite agreed about sending me, and I think that they are rather inclined to keep me.

Don't mention this subject, as I don't write it to Lady W. till it shall be positively determined.

P.S. I enclose Mr. Rennie's report on the Howth harbour.

---

essential, not only to the comfort of the soldier, but to the preservation of his health under every change of climate to which he may be exposed.

Under the head of pay, I have to direct your attention to the instructions of the Paymasters General to their deputy, respecting the usual stoppages being deducted from the pay of the several Staff officers, and to which you are requested to give the most punctual attention.

You will be vested with the usual powers of convening General Courts Martial, upon which subject I have to observe that, as great inconvenience has arisen to the service from officers commanding on foreign stations having permitted prisoners to return to England prior to the proceedings and opinion of the Court Martial having been submitted to the King, I have to request that, in all cases where any person whatever may be tried by a General Court Martial, and where your powers are not sufficient to enable you to decide finally upon the proceedings, opinion, and sentence of the Court, you do not permit the prisoner to return to England until His Majesty's commands shall have been duly communicated to you through the proper channel for that purpose.

I have likewise to acquaint you, that as many General officers, from the best motives, have taken upon themselves to commute sentences of capital punishment to transportation for a term of years, or for life, when it is found that no such power is delegated by His Majesty, and, consequently, that the whole of the proceedings may be thereby rendered nugatory, it will be necessary that your particular attention should be given to the powers granted to you by His Majesty's warrant on this subject, in order to prevent you from inadvertently falling into a similar irregularity.

It is particularly desirable that the officer, and the head of the Q. M. Gen.'s staff, should be directed to keep a journal, or other memorandum, descriptive of the movements of the troops, and occurrences in which they are engaged ; as also, that he should take and collect plans of the harbours, positions, or fortified places, in which the troops may be, for the purpose of being transmitted to me and lodged in the military depot.

In all points where any question or doubt may arise, and in which you may be desirous of receiving further and more specific instructions, you will always find me ready to pay the earliest attention to your representations.

Visct. Castlereagh * to Lieut. Gen. the Hon. Sir A. Wellesley, K.B.

Downing Street, 21st June, 1808.

Our accounts from Cadiz are bad ; no disposition there or in the neighbourhood of Gibraltar to move ; Gen. Spencer returning to Gibraltar : the proceedings, however, in the northern provinces were not then known.   It is material to know the effect produced by that effort which may be hourly expected.

The cabinet are desirous of postponing, till they hear again, their final decision on your instructions, being unwilling you should get too far to the southward, whilst the spirit of exertion appears to reside more to the northward.

Hitherto, no time, in fact, has been lost, as your equipment cannot be assembled at Cork for some days.   The arms and cavalry transports are not yet got to Portsmouth, and it is better to bring the whole together than to trust to junctions on the coast of Spain.

You will have the goodness to order the transports to be kept fully victualled whilst in port, that you may carry with you a full supply.

* Secretary of State for the Department of War and Colonies until Nov. 1809, when he was succeeded by the Earl of Liverpool.

To Major Gen. Hill.*   Dublin Castle, 23rd June, 1808.

I rejoice extremely at the prospect I have before me of serving again with you, and I hope that we shall have more to do than we had on the last occasion on which we were together.

I propose to leave town for Cork as soon as I shall receive my instructions from London. I understand that every thing has sailed from England which is to go with us; and the horses belonging to the Irish Commissariat will be at Cork, I hope, before the transports shall have arrived in which they are to be embarked. Let me hear from you if you learn any thing respecting them. The dragoons are to come direct from England to the rendezvous, and will not detain us at Cork.

I enclose a list of the names of the officers appointed to be D. A. A. G. and D. A. Q. M. G. Major Arbuthnot † will probably be in Dublin this day, and I shall send him to Cork immediately, and you will put him in charge of the A. G.'s department. You will put the senior of the list of A. D. Q. M. G. in charge of that department, and give him the enclosed return of camp equipage and stores embarked in the *Grinfield* transport. I had understood that I was to have had stores of this description for 8000 men; and I shall be obliged to you if you will desire the head of the Q. M. G.'s department to inquire whether there are in the transport any more camp equipage stores besides those contained in the enclosed return.

I beg you to arrange for the embarkation of the D. A. A. G., and the D. A. Q. M. G.: probably they and the Commissaries had best go in the horse ships.

I understand there is a vessel at Cork to carry 36 horses for the officers, besides those intended for the Commissariat horses; and I shall be obliged to you if you will desire that spare room may be kept for my horses, and those of my aides de camp, which will arrive at Cork in a day or two.

There remains nothing now but to brigade the troops, which may be a convenience for the present, and give us the assistance of the General officers in the different arrangements which may be necessary on board the transports. But what we shall do now can only be temporary, as the whole corps must necessarily be new modelled when we join Gen. Spencer. The Veteran battalion must be put out of the question, as that corps must go into the garrison of Gibraltar.

The corps might be brigaded as follows: the 95th and the 5th batt. of the 60th; the 5th, 9th, and 38th; the 40th, 71st, and 91st. You will alter this arrangement, if the corps belonging to your brigade are not put together, and you will put such (if all the corps of your brigade are not embarked for this service) corps as you please with the 9th. Let Gen. Fane then command the light brigade; Gen. Craufurd the Highlanders; and Gen. Ferguson, who belongs to Spencer's corps, that brigade which has been, and will hereafter be yours. The Veteran battalion to report to Gen. Fane, until it shall be otherwise disposed of.

Pray let me hear from you, and acquaint me with all your wants, and

* The late Gen. Lord Hill, G.C.B.
† Lieut. Gen. Sir T. Arbuthnot, K.C.B.

whether I can do any thing for you here. You will readily believe that I have plenty to do, in closing a government in such a manner as that I may give it up, and taking the command of a corps for service; but I shall not fail to attend to whatever you may write to me.

To Major Gen. Hill. Dublin Castle, 25th June, 1808.

I desired Torrens to write to you yesterday, to tell you it was probable that we should be detained till the cavalry should come round from Portsmouth; and I have now to request that you will make arrangements with

---

Visct. Castlereagh to Lieut. Gen. the Hon. Sir A. Wellesley, K.B.

Downing Street, 30th June, 1808.

The occupation of Spain and Portugal by the troops of France, and the entire usurpation of their respective governments by that power, has determined His Majesty to direct a corps of his troops, as stated in the margin, to be prepared for service, to be employed, under your orders, in counteracting the designs of the enemy, and in affording to the Spanish and Portuguese nations every possible aid in throwing off the yoke of France.

You will receive, enclosed, the communications which have been made by the deputies of the principality of Asturias, and the kingdom of Galicia, to His Majesty's government, together with the reply which His Majesty has directed to be made to their demand of assistance.

I also enclose a statement of the supplies which have been already dispatched to the port of Gijon, for the use of the people of Asturias.

As the deputies from the above provinces do not desire the employment of any corps of His Majesty's troops in the quarter of Spain from whence they are immediately delegated; but have rather pressed, as calculated to operate a powerful diversion in their favor, the importance of directing the efforts of the British troops to the expulsion of the enemy from Portugal, that the insurrection against the French may thereby become general throughout that kingdom as well as Spain, it is therefore deemed expedient that your attention should be immediately directed to that object.

The difficulty of returning to the northward with a fleet of transports, at this season of the year, renders it expedient that you should, in the first instance, proceed with the armament under your orders off Cape Finisterre. You will, yourself, precede them in a fast sailing frigate to Coruna, where you will have the best means of learning the actual state of things, both in Spain and Portugal; and of judging how far the corps under your immediate orders, either separately or reinforced by Major Gen. Spencer's corps, can be considered as of sufficient strength to undertake an operation against the Tagus.

If you should be of opinion, from the information you may receive, that the enterprise in question cannot be undertaken without waiting for reinforcements from home, you will communicate, confidentially, to the provisional government of Galicia, that it is material to the interests of the common cause that your armament should be enabled to take an anchorage to the northward of the Tagus, till it can be supported by a further force from home; and you will make arrangements with them, for having permission to proceed with it to Vigo, where it is conceived it can remain with not less security than in the harbour of Ferrol, and from which it can proceed to the southward with more facility than from the latter port.

In case you should go into Vigo, you will send orders to Major Gen. Spencer to join you at that place, should he have arrived off the Tagus, in consequence of the enclosed orders; and you will also transmit home such information as may enable His Majesty's ministers to take measures for supporting your corps from hence.

With a view to the contingency of your force being deemed unequal to the operation, an additional corps of 10,000 men has been ordered to be prepared for

service,

the agent of transports, that the soldiers embarked may have fresh provisions and vegetables every day ; and that the stock of provisions in the transports may be kept up to the original quantity which each is capable of containing. I also think it very desirable that the soldiers should have permission to go ashore as they may wish, under such regulations as you may think proper; and that the regiments should be sent ashore and exercised in their turns.

I request you to arrange these matters with the agents of the transports, which can easily be done by a good management of the ships' boats. I shall let you know as soon as I hear any thing certain of the cavalry.

---

service, and which, it is hoped, may be ready to proceed in about 3 weeks from the present time. I enclose such information as we are in possession of with respect to the enemy's force in Portugal; a considerable proportion of which is said to have been lately moved to Almeida, on the north-eastern frontier. You will, no doubt, be enabled to obtain more recent information at Coruna, in aid of which Lieut. Col. Brown has been ordered to proceed to Oporto, and to meet you, with such intelligence as he can procure, off Cape Finisterre.

An officer of engineers, acquainted with the defences of the Tagus, has also been sent off the Tagus to make observations, and to prepare information for your consideration with respect to the execution of the proposed attack on the Tagus. The result of his inquiries he will be directed to transmit also to the rendezvous off Cape Finisterre, remaining himself off the Tagus till your arrival.

You are authorised to give the most distinct assurances to the Spanish and Portuguese people, that His Majesty, in sending a force to their assistance, has no other object in view than to afford them the most unqualified and disinterested support; and in any arrangements that you may be called upon to make with either nation, in the prosecution of the common cause, you will act with the utmost liberality and confidence, and upon the principle that his Majesty's endeavors are to be directed to aid the people of Spain and Portugal in restoring and maintaining against France the independence and integrity of their respective monarchies.

In the rapid succession in which events must be expected to follow each other, situated as Spain and Portugal now are, much must be left to your judgment and decision on the spot.

His Majesty is graciously pleased to confide to you the fullest discretion to act according to circumstances for the benefit of his service; and you may rely on your measures being favorably interpreted, and receiving the most cordial support.

You will facilitate, as much as possible, communications between the respective provinces and colonies of Spain, and reconcile, by your good offices, any differences that may arise between them in the execution of the common purpose.

Should any serious division of sentiment occur, with respect to the nature of the provisional government which is to act during the present *interregnum*, or with respect to the Prince in whose name the legal authority is considered as vested by the captivity or abdication of certain branches of the Royal family, you will avoid, as far as possible, taking any part in such discussions, without the express authority of your government.

You will, however, impress upon the minds of persons in authority, that, consistently with the effectual assertion of their independence, they cannot possibly acknowledge the King or Prince of Asturias as, at present, possessing any authority whatever, or consider any act done by them as valid until they return within the country, and become absolutely free agents. That they never can be considered free so long as they shall be prevailed on to acquiesce in the continuance of French troops either in Spain or Portugal.

The entire and absolute evacuation of the Peninsula, by the troops of France, being, after what has lately passed, the only security for Spanish independence, and the only basis upon which the Spanish nation should be prevailed upon to treat or to lay down their arms.

To Brig. Gen. the Hon. C. Stewart.*   Dublin Castle, 25th June, 1808.

I enclose some papers which I have received respecting the state of the transports at Cork. The troops are certainly too much crowded; and I recommend that those which can be quartered within one day's march of Cork may be landed, unless it be certain that we shall go immediately. The troops would be on board before I should get to Cork, if they should be landed and marched only one day's march into the country; and they would certainly benefit by this arrangement.

To Major Gen. Hill.   Dublin Castle, 29th June, 1808.

I received your letter of the 27th this morning, and I am glad to find that you can make arrangements for landing the corps so frequently. It will tend much to the health of the men, and will make them feel less unpleasantly the heat and confinement of the transports.

* Gen. the Marquis of Londonderry, G.C.B., brother to the late Marquis of Londonderry, K.G., then Lord Castlereagh.

Visct. Castlereagh to Lieut. Gen. the Hon. Sir A. Wellesley, K.B.
                                           Downing Street, 30th June, 1808.

Since my instructions to you, No. 1, were closed, advices have been received from Sir C. Cotton, off the Tagus. The intelligence therein conveyed does not require that I should vary any part of those instructions, except in so far as to direct that, instead of going yourself to Coruna, you should send a confidential officer to that port, to execute that part of your instructions, and to meet you off Cape Finisterre, or to follow you to the Tagus. You will, of course, feel it of the most pressing importance that your armament should proceed off the Tagus, not separating yourself from it, with the least possible delay. The artillery preparation, which was ordered to be in readiness for 1st July, with a view to another service, has been embarked with 6 additional 10 inch mortars, and will sail from the river to-morrow. It will be directed to proceed immediately off the Tagus. 2 additional battalions, at present cantoned in the neighbourhood of Cork, the 36th and 45th, consisting of about 1200 men, have been ordered to embark, and join your force; for the reception of which, and to prevent the troops already embarked from being too much crowded, 3000 tons of transports sailed this day from the Downs, with a fair wind; as did also the 20th light dragoons from

I consider, therefore, that every part of your equipment has been forwarded from hence; and, I trust, you will find the whole ready to proceed upon your arrival at Cork. But if the 2 last regiments should not have been actually embarked, you will not delay your departure, but will order them to follow you off the Tagus. 30,000 stand of arms, and an equal number of pikes, have been sent, which you will make such use of as the public service may appear to you to require. A supply of money has also been sent, for the use of your troops. Any demands for military stores, which you may receive from the provinces which have declared against France, you will send home, and it will be the earnest wish of His Majesty's government to comply with them as far as circumstances will permit.

With respect to the money, 200,000l. has been ordered to be sent to Ferrol, for the immediate use of the Spanish patriots, till further arrangements can be made. It would much facilitate their financial operations, if they could give circulation in Spain to a paper currency, secured upon their South American finances; this, together with a moderate duty upon imposts, would furnish them with immediate resources, and, in proportion as a currency of the nature alluded to could be thrown into circulation, it would have the effect of attaching the soldiers to the national cause.

I mention this subject that, in any communication you may have with the persons in authority, you may press it on their attention.

There is camp equipage complete, including havresacks and canteens for 4000 men, on board the *Grinfield*, which sailed from Portsmouth on the 21st June; and for the same number on board the *Tuscan*, which sailed from Portsmouth on the 23rd. As soon as these vessels shall arrive, you will direct the regiments to make returns for the number of canteens and havresacks that they may require, which are to be issued upon these returns from the Q. M. G.'s stores. But they are to be kept in their packages in the regimental store of each regiment, and are not to be issued to the soldiers until further orders shall be given.

To Major Gen. Hill.   Dublin Castle, 3rd July, 1808.

I have received my instructions, and I understand that the cavalry, and some ships to receive the 36th and 45th regts., sailed from the Downs and Portsmouth on the 30th. I shall be at Cork on Wednesday; and I hope that we shall sail immediately afterwards.

The horses of the Commissariat will be at Cork on Tuesday and Wednesday; and I shall be obliged to you if you will arrange with Gen. Floyd respecting their early embarkation. I should have taken horses of the artillery if I could have got them; but, alas! I could not, and have, therefore, taken those which will probably only do our work till we shall get others.

I have written to Malcolm a long letter, respecting the arrangements of the transports into divisions, a code of signals for the army, and return of transports and flat bottomed boats; so that we may make all our arrangements for landing whilst we shall be on the passage. He will probably speak to you on these subjects, and I shall be obliged to you if you will give him all the assistance and information in your power. Tell Arbuthnot that I shall be obliged to him to have my horses embarked in the transport allotted for the staff horses. He had better send up to Cork to one of the officers of Gen. Floyd's staff to desire that the horses may be forwarded to Cove.

To Brig. Gen. Lee.   Cork, 7th July, 1808.

According to the desire which you expressed in the conversation which I had with you at Lord Harrington's on Wednesday, I proceed to give you my opinion on the nature and circumstances of the command which you are about to exercise in the county of Limerick. In the first place, I must point out to you that the situation of a General officer commanding in a district in Ireland is very much of the nature of a Dep. Governor of a county or a province: he becomes necessarily charged with the preservation of the peace of the district placed under his command; and the government must confide in his reports and opinions for the adoption of many measures relating solely to the civil administration of the country. From these circumstances it is obvious that it is the duty of every General officer to make himself acquainted with the local circumstances of his district, and with the characters of the different individuals residing within it, in order that he may decide for himself according to the best of his judgment and information, and that he may not be misled by others.

This duty will be still more obvious by a consideration of certain circumstances which exist in nearly all parts of Ireland. It frequently happens that disturbances exist only in a very small degree, and probably only partially, and that the civil power is fully adequate to get the better of them : at the same time, the desire to let a building to government for a barrack; the desire to have troops in the county, either on account of the increased consumption which they occasion of the necessaries of life, or because the increased security which they would give to that particular part of the country would occasion a general rise in the value and the rent of land, which probably at that moment might be out of lease; or, in some instances, the desire to have the Yeomanry called out on permanent duty; occasions a representation that the disturbances are much more serious than the facts would warrant. Upon these occasions, letter after letter is written to the Commanding officer and to government; the same fact is repeated through many different channels; and the result of an inquiry generally is, that the outrage complained of is by no means of the serious nature or of the extent which has been stated.

The obvious remedy for this evil, and that which is generally resorted to, is to call for informations on oath of the transactions which are complained of: but this remedy is not certain; for it frequently happens that the informations on oath are equally false with the original representations. The General officer, then, has no remedy excepting, by his acquaintance and communication with the magistrates and gentlemen of the county, to acquire a knowledge of characters, and to become acquainted with all the circumstances which occur.

It frequently happens that the people who do commit outrages and disturbances have some reason to complain; but, in my opinion, that is not a subject for the consideration of the General officer. He must aid in the preservation of the peace of the county, and in the support of the law; and he who breaks the law must be considered in the wrong, whatever may have been the nature of the provocation which he has received.

It is possible that grievances may exist in the county of Limerick; provisions may be too dear, or too high a rent may be demanded for land; and there may be no poor laws; and the magistrates may not do their duty as they ought by the poor; but these circumstances afford no reason why the General officer should not give the military aid which he may have at his command to preserve the peace, to repress disturbance, and to bring those to justice who may have been guilty of a violation of the law.

In respect to the gentlemen of the county in which you are posted, I recommend to you to attend particularly to the Lord Chief Baron O'Grady. You will find him well informed of the transactions in the county of Limerick, and well acquainted with characters, and disposed to assist your judgment. I also recommend to your attention Mr. Dixon, the late high sheriff of the county; and Col. Vereker, the member for the city of Limerick. There may be, and certainly are, other gentlemen in the county of Limerick on whose information you can depend; but I have requested Mr. Trail, to whom I send this letter, to apprise you confidentially of the names of those whom you ought to consult.

I arrived here last night, and I find that the 20th light dragoons and the 3000 tons of shipping for the infantry are not arrived. The Irish Commissariat horses, for the draught of the artillery, are not yet all arrived, and will not be on board until Saturday. I propose to wait till that day for the dragoons and the additional tonnage, and, if they should not have arrived, I shall sail with what is ready, and let the rest follow.

By some accident, which, from not having seen the agent of transports, I cannot yet account for, we have four transports, as stated underneath, which have not been returned to me in any statement from the Transport Board or from your brother. These vessels have enabled Gen. Floyd to embark the 95th, and to make some provision for the embarkation of the 36th. But it appears to me that the whole are too much crowded, and if the additional tonnage does not arrive to-morrow, I shall settle to leave behind the Veteran battalion, or the 36th, to follow with the additional tonnage and the 20th dragoons, to give more space to all the troops in the transports. If the additional tonnage should arrive, and I should find that I do not want these four ships, I shall leave them behind.

Upon a review of your instructions, and a consideration of the state of affairs in Spain, according to the last accounts, I rather think that, as soon as I have got every thing away from Cork, I shall best serve the cause by going myself to Coruña, and joining the fleet off Cape Finisterre or the Tagus. I propose accordingly to go on board one of the craft, and I expect to be at the rendezvous before the troops.

Since I wrote to you yesterday, the ships having on board the 20th light dragoons, excepting the *Rebecca*, *Albion*, and *Jackall*, the *Minerva* laden with hay, the *Britannia* and *Harford* with arms, and the *Britannia* with intrenching tools, have arrived. The empty transports have not, however, yet appeared; and I propose in the morning to land part of the Veteran battalion, to make room for the whole of the 36th, and I shall then sail with the first fair wind. All the horses of the Commissariat will be on board early to-morrow.

Upon consulting with Malcolm, I find that no inconvenience can result from my going to Coruna, and that he should make Cape Finisterre in his passage to the Tagus at all events. As I must derive the greatest advantage from going there, I shall therefore embark in one of the smaller vessels, and join the fleet again when it comes off the Cape.

I have the honor to acquaint you that camp equipage for 8000 men only has been provided for the army about to sail under my command, and I have it not in my power to make the necessary issue to the 36th and 45th regts. I therefore request that you will be pleased to give the necessary orders that camp equipage for 1500 men may be issued from the stores of this place, and delivered over to the Dep. Assistant at the head of the Q M. G.'s department at Cove.

I likewise beg leave to acquaint you that the camp kettles provided for the use of my force are of the Flanders pattern, the size of which would cause considerable inconvenience in the service in which it is probable I shall be engaged: and having been given to understand that small tin kettles are in store here, I request you will be pleased to cause an issue to be made of them for the use of the troops under my command. The D. A. Q. M. G. at Cove will give to the Assist. Commissary Gen. at Cork the necessary receipt for the same, as well as for the camp equipage for the 36th and 45th regts.

Visct. Castlereagh to Lieut. Gen. the Hon. Sir A. Wellesley, K.B.

Downing Street, 15th July, 1808.

Since my dispatches to you of the 30th ult., marked ' Secret,' Nos. 1 and 2, the enclosed intelligence has been received from Major Gen. Spencer with respect to the state of the enemy's force in Portugal.

The number of French troops immediately in the vicinity of Lisbon (so far as this information can be relied on) appearing much more considerable than it was before reported to be by Sir C. Cotton, His Majesty has been pleased to direct a corps of 5000 men, consisting of the regiments mentioned in the margin,* to be embarked, and to proceed, without loss of time, to join you off the Tagus.

His Majesty has been further pleased to direct, that the troops under Lieut. Gen. Sir John Moore, which are arrived from the Baltic, as soon as they shall be refreshed, and their transports can be re-victualled, should also proceed, without delay, off the Tagus.

The motives which have induced the sending so large a force to that quarter are, 1st, to provide effectually for an attack upon the Tagus; and, 2ndly, to have such an additional force disposable, beyond what may be indispensably requisite for that operation, as may admit of a detachment being made to the southward, either with a view to secure Cadiz, if it should be threatened by the French force under Gen. Dupont, or to co-operate with the Spanish troops in reducing that corps, if circumstances should favor such an operation, or any other that may be concerted.

His Majesty is pleased to direct that the attack upon the Tagus should be considered as the first object to be attended to. As the whole force (of which a statement is enclosed), when assembled, will amount to not less than 30,000 men, it is conceived that both services may be amply provided for; the precise distribution as between Portugal and Andalusia, both as to time and proportion of force, must depend on circumstances, to be judged of on the spot; and should it be deemed advisable to fulfil the assurance which Lieut. Gen. Sir H. Dalrymple appears to have given to the Supreme Junta of Seville, under the authority of my dispatch of the 6th inst., that it was His Majesty's intention to employ a corps of his troops, to the amount of 10,000 men, to co-operate with the Spaniards in that quarter, a corps of this magnitude may, I should hope, be detached without prejudice to the main operation against the Tagus, and may be reinforced, according to circumstances, after the Tagus has been secured: but if, previous to the arrival of

* RAMSGATE.

Under Brig. Gen. Anstruther:					
9th foot, 2nd batt.	.	.	.	.	675
43rd	..	.	.	.	861
52nd	..	.	.	.	858
97th		.	.	.	769

HARWICH.

Under Brig. Gen. Acland:					
2nd or Queen's foot	.	.	.	.	813
20th	.	.	.	.	689
95th, 2 companies	.	.	.	.	180
					4845
2 companies of artillery	.	.	.		200
					5045

To the Duke of Richmond.   Cove, 9th July, 1808.

     *   *   *   *   *   *   *

I have got all the troops on board, and we shall sail as soon as the wind shall be fair. It is now blowing strong from the S. W., and I am afraid will last. If you should have occasion to write to me, direct to Cork. As I find from Malcolm that he must make Cape Finisterre on his way to the Tagus, I propose to go in the *Crocodile* to Coruna, in the first instance, as soon as I shall get every thing out of this harbour, and shall join the convoy again off Cape Finisterre. I shall derive much information and advantage from this step.

---

of the whole force under orders from England, Cadiz should be seriously threatened, it must rest with the senior officer off the Tagus, at his discretion, to detach, upon receiving a requisition to that effect, such an amount of force as may place this important place out of the reach of immediate danger, even though it should, for the time, suspend operations against the Tagus. As the force which may be called for on the side of Cadiz can only require a field equipment, the ordnance preparation which has been sent with a view to the reduction of the Tagus will remain at that station.

With the exception of the ordnance preparation sent for the attack of the forts on that river, it has not been deemed necessary to encumber the army with any larger detail of artillery than what belongs to a field equipment, with a proportion of horses.

Exclusive of the period for which the transports are provided, a due proportion of victuallers will accompany the armament, which, with the supplies which may be expected to be derived from the disposition and resources of the country, it is conceived, will remove all difficulty on this head, so long as the army shall continue to act near the coast.

The great delay and expense that would attend embarking and sending from hence all those means which would be requisite to render the army completely moveable immediately on its landing, has determined His Majesty's government to trust, in a great measure, to the resources of the country for their supplies.

There is every reason to believe, from the ardor of the inhabitants, both of Spain and Portugal, that so soon as a British army can establish itself on any part of the coast, not only numbers will be anxious to be armed and arrayed in support of the common cause, but that every species of supply which the country produces for subsisting and equipping an army will be procurable; it therefore becomes the first object of consideration (if a direct and immediate attack upon the defences of the Tagus cannot in prudence be attempted), on what part of the coast between Peniche, on the north, and St. Ubes, on the south of that river, a position can be taken by the British army, in which its intercourse with the interior may be securely opened, and from whence it may afterwards move against the enemy, endeavoring, if possible, not only to expel him from Lisbon, but to cut off his retreat towards Spain.

A proportion of cavalry, as far as the means of transport exist, will accompany the troops, which can be hereafter increased, according as circumstances shall point out.

Visct. Castlereagh to Lieut. Gen. the Hon. Sir A. Wellesley, K.B.

                                    Downing Street, 15th July, 1808.

I am to acquaint you that His Majesty has been pleased to intrust the command of his troops serving on the coasts of Spain and Portugal to Lieut. Gen. Sir H. Dalrymple, with Lieut. Gen. Sir H. Burrard, second in command.

The Lieut. General has been furnished with copies of your instructions up to the present date exclusive. These instructions you will be pleased to carry into execution with every expedition that circumstances will permit, without awaiting the arrival of the Lieut. General, reporting to him your proceedings. And, should you be previously joined by a senior officer, you will, in that case, communicate to him your orders, and afford him every assistance in carrying them into execution.

To Lieut. Cheeseman, R.N., Agent of Transports.   Cork, 10th July, 1808.

In consequence of no hospital ship having yet arrived for the use of the army under my command, I have to request that you will forthwith appropriate an empty transport, for the reception of such medical staff and sick as the Dep. Inspector of Hospitals may send on board the same.

Return of the effective force embarked, and under the command of the Rt. Hon. Lieut. Gen. Sir A. Wellesley, K.B.   Cork, 13th July, 1808.

Regiments.	Field officers.	Captains.	Subalterns.	Staff.	Staff serjeants.	Serjeants.	Drummers.	Rank and file.	Horses.
Royal engineers	..	2	4	..	..	1	..	11	..
Royal artillery	2	4	5	2	1	8	5	345	..
Royal artillery drivers	..	..	1	..	1	1	1	46	..
20th light dragoons	2	2	6	3	..	19	3	346	215
5th foot	3	10	27	6	..	53	21	987	..
9th	3	9	22	5	..	51	21	950	..
36th	2	9	28	4	..	49	22	589	..
38th	3	10	28	6	..	54	22	956	..
40th	3	9	29	6	..	54	19	920	..
45th	3	8	17	6	..	38	22	500	..
60th .. 5th batt.	2	7	18	6	..	54	22	930	..
71st	2	8	23	5	..	50	21	875	..
91st	3	8	24	5	..	51	20	907	..
95th .. 2nd batt.	1	4	13	1	..	20	8	399	..
4th R. Vet. batt.	1	6	14	4	..	47	20	744	..
Total	30	96	259	59	2	550	227	9505	215

ROWLAND HILL, Major General.

Visct. Castlereagh to Lieut. Gen. Sir H. Dalrymple.   Downing Street, 15th July, 1808.

Permit me to offer you my congratulations on the flattering commands I have been charged to convey to you from His Majesty, and to request you will, at the same time, accept my personal thanks for the zeal and ability with which you have discharged your public duties during the late important period.

I trust the force which has been provided will enable you to give a new and decisive turn to affairs both in Portugal and Spain.

Permit me to recommend to your particular confidence Lieut. Gen. Sir A. Wellesley. His high reputation in the service as an officer would in itself dispose you, I am persuaded, to select him for any service that required great prudence and temper, combined with much military experience.

The degree, however, to which he has been for a length of time past in the closest habits of communication with His Majesty's ministers, with respect to the affairs of Spain, having been destined to command any operation that circumstances might render necessary for counteracting the views of France against the Spanish dominions in South America, will, I am sure, point him out to you as an officer of whom it is desirable for you, on all accounts, to make the most prominent use which the rules of the service will permit.

G.O.   10th July, 1808.

Regulating the number of commissioned and non-commissioned officers to be sent on board the hospital ship in charge of sick men. [Not in the General Orders from whence this copy was made, although mentioned in the Index of them.]

To Visct. Castlereagh.   Cove, 10th July, 1808.

The wind is still contrary, but we hope it will change so as to sail this evening. We are unmoored, and shall not wait one moment after the wind may be fair.

I see that people in England complain of the delay which has taken place in the sailing of the expedition; but, in fact, none has taken place; and even if all had been on board we could not have sailed before this day. With all the expedition which we could use, we could not get the horses of the artillery to Cork till yesterday, and they were immediately embarked; and it was only yesterday that the 20th dragoons arrived, and the ships to contain the 36th regt. and a detachment of the 45th, which arrived yesterday evening and embarked. Your instructions to me left London on the Friday evening, and I was at Cork on the following Wednesday, which is as much expedition as if the instructions had come by the post.

I leave here, at the disposal of government, 1668 tons of shipping. The resident agent will report the names of the ships to the Transport board.

To Visct. Castlereagh.   H.M.S. *Crocodile*,* off Coruña, 21st July, 1808.

I have the honor to inform you, that having adverted to the tenor of

* The *Crocodile* was commanded by the Hon. G. Cadogan, now Earl Cadogan.

H. R. H. the Commander in Chief
     to Lieut. Gen. Sir H. Dalrymple.   Horse Guards, 21st July, 1808.

His Majesty having been graciously pleased to appoint you to the command of a large division of his army, to be employed on a particular service, I have to notify to you the several corps, General and Staff officers, which compose this army, and to desire that you will use your best endeavors to carry into effect such instructions as you may receive from His Majesty's ministers.

In transmitting to you a list of your force, I have felt it my duty, with the view of giving you every information and assistance in my power, to annex to it an outline of the manner in which it appears to me that it would be most advisable to brigade the army: but, although I have given this plan every possible consideration, yet I mean you should fully understand it is intended solely for your guidance, in the event of the circumstances of your situation rendering it practicable and easy; and by no means to curb you in any other arrangements you may think it advisable to adopt, under the pressure of local or other difficulty.

The 4th Royal Veteran battalion is not included in this dislocation, as that corps is at present intended for the garrison of Gibraltar; but it may, possibly, be in your power to take a more serviceable corps from thence in lieu of it, bearing in mind that this battalion is not to be permanently stationed at Gibraltar, but to be sent eventually to Madeira.

[*The remainder of this letter is the same as that addressed to Lieut. Gen. Sir A. Wellesley at p. 16, beginning with the words* ' On all subjects,' *and is therefore not repeated.*]

Visct. Castlereagh
     to Lieut. Gen. the Hon. Sir A. Wellesley, K.B.   Downing Street, 21st July, 1808.

In the event of your deeming it may be advantageous that the troops now proceeding from England should be disembarked at any point on the coast of Portugal north of the Tagus, I am to suggest to you the propriety of your requesting Sir C. Cotton to station one of his cruisers to the northward of the Berlings,† with such information as you may deem material to communicate to the senior officer in command of the troops; and I shall intimate to the officers in charge of the troops proceeding from hence, that they should be prepared, at that point, to receive an intimation from you of the actual state of things in the Tagus.

† Rocks on the coast of Portugal, opposite Peniche.

your Lordship's instructions of the 30th ultimo (Nos. 1 and 2), I deemed it expedient to quit the fleet containing the troops under my command,

---

Horse Guards, 20th July, 1808.

List of the several Corps, General and Staff officers, composing a large division of His Majesty's army, to be employed upon a particular service.

His Majesty has been pleased to direct that the undermentioned corps should be formed into one army, viz. :

SIR JOHN MOORE'S CORPS.

3rd light dragoons, King's German Legion .	562	
British artillery	374	
German ditto	320	
* 4th Foot, 1st batt.	971	
* 28th	020	
52nd	951	
* 79th	995	
* 92nd	934	
95th, 3 companies	300	
Royal Staff corps	50	
1st Light batt., K.G.L.	907	
2nd Light batt., K.G.L.	903	
1st Line batt.	725	
2nd	761	
5th	753	
7th	679	
Garrison company	48	
		11,253

MAJOR GEN. SPENCER'S CORPS.

Royal artillery	245	
Royal Staff corps	45	
* 6th foot, 1st batt.	946	
29th	806	
* 32nd	874	
* 50th	948	
* 82nd	929	
		4,793

SIR A. WELLESLEY'S CORPS.

20th light dragoons	394	
Royal artillery	226	
* 5th foot, 1st batt.	990	
9th	833	
* 36th	591	
* 38th	957	
* 40th	926	
* 45th	670	
60th .. 5th batt.	936	
* 71st .. 1st	903	
* 91st	917	
95th, 4 companies	400	
4th Royal Veteran batt.	537	
		9,280

FORCE NOW EMBARKING.

British artillery, one company } Number not known.		
German .. .. }		
2nd foot, or Queen's	731	
9th, 2nd batt.	633	
20th	530	
43rd, 2nd batt.	721	
52nd	654	
95th, 2 companies	200	
97th	694	
18th light dragoons	640	
		4,803

His

as soon as it was clear of the coast of Ireland, on the 13th inst.; and I arrived here in this ship yesterday.

I have had several conferences with the Junta of Galicia since my arrival, the general result of which has been, that the whole of Spain, with the exception of the kingdoms of Navarre and Biscay, are in arms against the French; and that in many places detachments of the French troops had been defeated by the Spanish people. The information, however, which has been received by the Junta of Galicia is not of an official nature;

His Majesty has further been pleased to direct, that Lieut. Gen. Sir H. Dalrymple shall have the chief command thereof, and that Lieut. Gen. Sir H. Burrard be second in command, when the staff of this army will consist as follows, viz.:

Lieut. Gen. Sir H. Dalrymple, Commander of the forces.
Lieut. Gen. Sir H. Burrard, second in command.
Lieut. Gens. Sir J. Moore, the Hon. J. Hope, Mackenzie Fraser, Lord Paget, the Hon. Sir A. Wellesley.
Major Gens. J. Murray, Lord W. Bentinck, Hon. E. Paget, Spencer, Hill, Ferguson.
Brig. Gens. Acland, Nightingall, R. Stewart, the Hon. C. Stewart, H. Fane, R. Anstruther, Catlin Craufurd.
Brig. Gen. H. Clinton, 1st Foot Guards, *Acting* Adj. Gen.
Lieut. Col. Murray, 3rd Foot Guards, *Acting* Q. M. Gen.
Bt. Lieut. Col. Torrens, 89th Foot, Military Secretary.

His Majesty has further been pleased to command that the following should be the outline of the dislocation of the troops, subject to the discretion of the General commanding.

The reserve, under the command of Lieut. Gen. Sir J. Moore and Major Gen. the Hon. E. Paget.

Regiments	Brig. Gen.	Lieut. Gen.
18th light dragoons		
20th	Brig. Gen. the Hon. C. Stewart.	
3rd light dragoons, K.G.L.		
52nd foot, 1st batt.		
52nd .. 2nd ..	Brig. Gen. R. Anstruther.	
95th, 9 companies		
43rd foot, 2nd batt.		
60th .. 5th ..	Brig. Gen. R. Stewart.	
1st light batt., K.G.L.		
2nd		
2nd, or Queen's foot		
4th, 1st batt.	Brig. Gen. Acland.	Lieut. Gen. the Hon. J. Hope.
28th		
79th		
91st	Major Gen. Ferguson.	
92nd		
6th		
29th	Major Gen. Spencer.	Lieut. Gen. Lord Paget.
32nd		
5th		
50th	Brig. Gen. Nightingall.	
82nd		
9th		
9th, 2nd batt. ..	Major Gen. Hill.	Lieut. Gen. Mackenzie Fraser.
40th, 1st . ..		
36th		
45th	Brig. Gen. Fane.	
97th		
20th		
38th	Brig. Gen. Catlin Craufurd.	Lieut. Gen. the Hon. Sir A. Wellesley.
71st		
4 batts. of Infantry of the King's German Legion.	Major Gen. J. Murray.	

and I am not enabled to state positively where these occurrences have taken place, or to what extent, although I imagine that there is no doubt that these French corps have been defeated in the manner reported in the private letters received by individuals.

The Galician army, joined by that of Castille, (the whole consisting of 50,000 men, of which 20,000 are stated to have been regular troops,) was posted at Rio Seco, in the province of Valladolid, and was attacked on the 14th inst. by a French corps, under the command of Marshal Bessieres, consisting of 20,000 men (of which 4000 were cavalry), which had been at Burgos : in the commencement of the action the Spanish troops had the advantage ; but towards the close of the day the French cavalry charged the left of the Spanish line, which consisted of the Castillian peasantry, and which was broken and defeated, with the loss of 7000 men, some officers of distinction, and 2 pieces of cannon. The loss of the French troops in the action is stated to have been 7000 men and 6 pieces of cannon. On the following day the Spanish army retired to Benavente, on the Esla ; from which measure the French have acquired the command of the course of the Rio Douro, and are in a situation to impede the communication between this province and those to the southward, and to the eastward, likewise in arms against the French. The Junta of Galicia have given their consent to my using the port of Vigo, if I should find it necessary, to afford shelter to the fleet, or even to land the troops there.

It appears, from the intelligence which I have received here, that the total number of the French troops still in Portugal is about 15,000 men, of which number 12,000 are at Lisbon and in the neighbourhood ; and Almeida is occupied by a small corps. The 3 provinces north of the Rio Douro are in arms against the French ; and there is a corps of Portuguese troops in Oporto, the number of which is stated to be 10,000 men ; besides these, a Spanish corps, consisting of 2000 men, commenced their march on the 15th inst., from a port in the southern part of Galicia, towards Oporto, where I expect they will arrive about the 24th or 25th inst.

I have not received any account of Gen. Spencer, from which I can form a judgment whether that officer will have it in his power to proceed to Lisbon, according to the tenor of your Lordship's instructions of the 30th June and 2nd July. I propose to sail from hence this night, and to go to Oporto in this ship ; and I shall be directed in the future operations of the army, for the execution of your Lordship's instructions, by the intelligence which I shall receive there. I shall request Capt. Malcolm to follow me with the convoy to Oporto.

To Visct. Castlereagh.   Coruna, 21st July, 1808.

I arrived here yesterday, and I propose to go to sea again this day, to meet the fleet, which however has not yet appeared off the coast.

Since my arrival I have had frequent conversations with the Junta ; and Mr. Stuart,* who arrived also yesterday, will send by this conveyance to Mr. Canning an account of all the intelligence which we have received

* Lord Stuart de Rothesay, G.C.B. ; afterwards minister at Lisbon, and ambassador at the Hague, at Paris, and Petersburgh. He was at this period employed in establishing communications with Spain.

from them respecting the present situation of affairs in Spain. The general result, however, appears to me to be, that the whole of the Spanish nation, with the exception of the provinces of Biscay and Navarre, and those in the neighbourhood of Madrid, are in a state of insurrection against the French; that several French detachments in different parts of the country had been destroyed, viz., a corps under Lefebre, which had been attacked four times, near Zaragoza, in Aragon, particularly on the 16th and 24th June, a corps which I believe to have been under the command of Dupont; and it is said that Dupont was taken prisoner in an action fought between Andujar and La Carolina, before the 23rd June; and two corps defeated in Catalonia before the 19th June, one on its march to Montserrat, and the other to Zaragoza. The Catalonians have also got possession of the fort of Figueras, in the neighbourhood of Rosas, and have blockaded the French troops in Barcelona. As, however, the communication, which was never very perfect between one province and the others, has been impeded by the march and position of the French armies, and particularly by their late success at Rio Seco, to which I shall presently refer, the Junta have no official accounts of any of these actions; but they give credit to those they have received, copies of which will be transmitted to Mr. Canning by Mr. Stuart. He will also send the account which the Junta have received of the action at Rio Seco. The army of Castille and Galicia united was posted at that place, which is in the province of Valladolid; and their intention, as is stated, was either to have attacked the French corps under Marshal Bessieres at Burgos, or to have marched upon Madrid. But I suspect that they would have confined their operations to the arrangement of the insurrection towards Madrid, and to cutting off the communication between the French troops stationed there and in Biscay and Navarre. It is said that they intended to attack Marshal Bessieres on the 16th, but he attacked them on the 14th: his infantry was at first defeated by the Spaniards, with the loss of 7000 men; but afterwards his cavalry fell upon the left wing of the Spanish army, which consisted of the peasants of Castille, and defeated it.

I understand that the Spanish army, which consisted of 50,000 men, lost about 7000 men and 2 pieces of cannon; and that they had taken and still retain 6 pieces belonging to the French. The Spaniards retired either on that night or on the next day to Benavente on the Esla. The worst of this action is, that it has given the French possession of the whole course of the Douro, and by obliging the Galician troops to retire from Rio Seco, it has interrupted the communication between this province and those to the southward and eastward.

I understood that the Junta were much alarmed when they received the account of this defeat; but the arrival of the money yesterday has entirely renewed their spirits; and I did not see either in them or in the inhabitants of this town any symptom either of alarm or doubt of their final success. The capture of Santander by the French is not considered an event of any importance; and it is said here that a corps was actually on its march from the Asturias to retake that place.

It is impossible to convey to you an idea of the sentiment which prevails here in favor of the Spanish cause. The difference between any two men is whether the one is a better or a worse Spaniard, and the better Spaniard is the one who detests the French most heartily. I understand that there is actually no French party in the country; and at all events I am convinced that no man now dares to show that he is a friend to the French. The final success must depend upon the means of attack and defence of the different parties, of the amount of which it is impossible for me at present to form an opinion. If it be true that the several French corps which I have above enumerated have been cut off, it is obvious that Buonaparte cannot carry on his operations in Spain, excepting by the means of large armies; and I doubt much whether the country will afford subsistence for a large army, or whether he will be able to supply his magazines from France, the roads being so bad and the communications so difficult. If this be true, his object must be to gain possession of the northern provinces, and this can be done only by the invasion and possession of the Asturias. I think, therefore, that our government ought to direct its attention particularly to that important point, and to endeavor to prevail upon the Asturians to receive a body of our troops. I consider this point so important, that I should not be surprised if Buonaparte, finding that he cannot penetrate by land, should make an effort to reach the Asturias by sea; and I should therefore recommend to you to reinforce the squadron which is here, and let it cruise between Cape Ortegal and Santander. It might come here in case of a gale from the northward.

I suggested to the Junta to fit out the ships at Ferrol for this service; but they said it would divert their attention and their means from other more important objects; and that, although they were aware of its importance, they would prefer relying, for the naval defence which they might require, on the assistance to be received from Great Britain.

It will be necessary that you should assist all the Spanish provinces with money, arms, and ammunition. Notwithstanding the recent defeat of the Galician army, the Junta have not expressed any anxiety to receive the assistance of British troops; and they again repeated this morning that they could put any number of men into the field, if they were provided with money and arms; and I think that this disinclination to receive the assistance of British troops is founded in a great degree on the objection to give the command of their troops to British officers.

The Junta here have expressed a great wish to unite in a general Cortes with the other provinces; but, in addition to the difficulties which must attend the adoption of this measure, from the position of the French armies, I understand that there are others referable to the desire which each of the kingdoms of which Spain is composed has, that the Cortes should be established within itself.

If the French should be obliged to quit Madrid, it is probable that this difficulty would be overcome; and till that period, or until the strength of the French army shall have been driven from the centre of Spain, I am not quite certain that it is not as well that each of the kingdoms should be governed by its own Junta. I am convinced that the general zeal and exertion of each are greater, at present, than would be manifested if the whole Kingdom were under the direction of one body.

In respect to my own operations, I find that Junot has collected, it is supposed, 12,000 men at Lisbon; and the French still hold Almeida, and other points in Portugal, with 3000 more. The 3 northern provinces of Portugal are in a state of insurrection, and there is a Portuguese army at Oporto, to join which 2000 Spanish troops have marched from Galicia, and they will arrive there about the 24th or 25th.

From the intelligence which I have received here, I can form no opinion whether I shall be joined by Gen. Spencer or not. Mr. Stuart heard from the *Brilliant*, on his passage, that Gen. Spencer had left Cadiz, after the Spaniards had got possession of the French fleet, and had gone to Ayamonte, at the mouth of the Guadiana, to stop the progress of a French corps which was coming by that route from Portugal into Andalusia. They had heard nothing here of this movement; but they had heard a report that 5000 British troops had been in Gen. Castanos' army, and had behaved remarkably well, but on what occasion, and what troops, they did not know.

I understand that there is a Spanish corps of 20,000 men in Estremadura, at Almaraz, on the Tagus, which corps will impede the communication between Junot and the army at Madrid; and it may be reasonably expected that the number of French now in Portugal will be the number which we shall have to contend with. The Junta express great anxiety respecting my operations in Portugal, and have strongly recommended me not to attempt to land at Lisbon, or in the neighbourhood of the French army. They urge, as an objection to this measure, that I shall thereby entirely lose the advantage of the co-operation of the Spanish and Portuguese forces at Oporto, who will not be able to approach Lisbon till they have heard that I have disembarked; and they recommend that I should disembark at Vigo or Oporto, and bring the allies with me to Lisbon. It is impossible for me to decide upon this or any other measure till I shall know more of the situation of affairs. I should have no doubt of success, even without Gen. Spencer's assistance, or that of the allies, if I were once ashore; but to effect a landing in front of an enemy is always difficult, and I shall be inclined to land at a distance from Lisbon.

I now intend to look for the fleet this night, and if we should not find it, I shall leave one of Capt. Hotham's squadron upon the rendezvous, with directions for Malcolm to follow me, and go in the *Crocodile* to Oporto, where I shall be able to decide upon the measures which I shall adopt.

To the Duke of Richmond.   Coruna, 21st July, 1808.

I arrived here yesterday, and propose to sail again this evening to join the fleet off Cape Finisterre. I have not yet determined in what manner I shall attack the French in Portugal; whether by disembarking in the neighbourhood of Lisbon, or at a distance, so as to insure a junction without the co-operation of the Portuguese and Spanish troops at Oporto.

Affairs here appear to be in a prosperous state. The Spaniards have defeated and destroyed several French detachments; viz. one under Dupont to the southward, one under Lefebre in Aragon, and two in Catalonia. They have taken the fort of Figueras, near Rosas, in the Pyrenees, and have blockaded the French troops in Barcelona. But the great army of Galicia, consisting of 50,000 men, received a check on the 14th of this month from the French corps under Marshal Bessieres. The French had not more than half the number, and lost about 7000 men, which is about the number the Spaniards lost; but the French cavalry, the Spaniards having none, charged the peasants of Castille, who were in the left wing, and gained the victory. The Spaniards lost 2 pieces of cannon, the French 6; and the Spanish army has retreated about 20 miles from the field of battle towards this province.

This check does not appear to have affected the spirits, or to have diminished the hopes, of people here. They say that they do not require men, and have not asked me to give them assistance. It is impossible to describe to you the state of enthusiasm in which they all are. They manifested the greatest satisfaction upon our arrival, received us with the utmost civility and cordiality, illuminated the town at night, and the whole of the inhabitants attended us to our boat when we returned on board the frigate at night.

There is no such thing as a French party in the country, and I believe there is no man who dares to avow that he wishes well to the French cause.

From all this it is very obvious to me that the French will make no progress in Spain, excepting by the aid of very large armies; and I doubt whether they will find it practicable to subsist by the means which the country can afford, or to supply their magazines from France, owing to the difficulty and badness of the communication.

*   *   *   *   *   *   *   *

To C. Stuart, Esq.   H.M.S. *Crocodile*, off Cape Finisterre, 23rd July, 1808.

I find that the 2 ships which I imagined contained the stores for the Asturias are not in the fleet, notwithstanding that they were reported to me at Cork by the Commanding officer of my artillery. I conclude, therefore, that they have really arrived at Gijon, and that the officer is not so correct as the editor of the Oviedo gazette.

I hear that the actions at Zaragoza were an attack upon the place by the French, who have been frequently repulsed. I hear also that the French have concentrated their force at Lisbon, and that the insurrection has extended itself to that city. The French troops cannot show themselves outside of it. We hear from San Sebastian, that King Joseph has entered Spain, and had passed that fortress. He was received by the constituted authorities, but not by the people.

To Gen. Sir J. Pulteney, Bart., Sec. at War.   H.M.S. *Donegal*, at Sea, 25th July, 1808.

I have the honor to acknowledge the receipt of your letter of the 5th inst., communicating to me His Majesty's appointment to serve as a Lieut. General on the Staff, with 2 aides de camp, upon a particular service, from the 23rd inst.; and I beg leave to acquaint you that His Majesty's commission, to serve as Commander of the forces upon the service in which I am at present engaged, is dated the 14th June 1808, from which period the Staff of the army have been appointed and doing duty. I therefore request that you will transmit to me, at your earliest convenience. an authority to issue pay to the Staff of the army from that date; or to inform me in what manner those are to be paid who were not before upon the Staff in Ireland.

To Visct. Castlereagh.   H.M.S. *Crocodile*, off Oporto. 25th July. 1808.

I avail myself of the opportunity of the return of the *Peacock* to propose to send the fleet to the Mondego to make all the arrangements for landing; to go down to communicate with the Admiral; and by the time I shall have returned, all will be ready to go on shore, either at the Mondego or Peniche, or farther to the southward if the Admiral thinks it advisable.

I have heard nothing positive of Gen. Spencer, excepting that he was fortunately, there are none in the country; indeed, I may say. none to arm the troops which the Bishop of Oporto and the Junta of this place have assembled. They have at present a corps of about 5000 men, regular troops and militia, including 300 cavalry at Coimbra, armed with 1000 muskets got from the fleet, fowling pieces, &c., and 12,000 peasantry, mostly unarmed, I believe. The regular troops are composed of detachments of different corps, and cannot in any respect be deemed an efficient force. Besides these, there are 300 Spanish infantry, about 1500 regular Portuguese infantry, and some militia volunteers and peasantry, here.

The corps of Spanish infantry, which had commenced its march from Galicia, as I informed you in my last letter, is not yet arrived. It was stopped on the frontier, because there were no orders at Braganza to allow it to enter the country; and, although the Bishop expects it, the Portuguese officers appear to think that the success of the French against the Spanish army on the 14th has diverted this corps from the cause in this country. Under all the circumstances, I have determined to take forward the Portuguese corps now at Coimbra, and to collect every thing else upon this place. The Bishop is much alarmed respecting the success of the French in the province of Valladolid. It is reported here that there has been a second action; and I saw a letter last night from the Bishop of Santiago, stating that Gen. Cuesta, the Castillian Commander in Chief, had informed him that he had gained a victory in this action, and had actually in his camp 1500 horses taken from the French cavalry; and it is, at the same time, reported that the French are actually in Benavente. It is impossible to learn the truth.

I have received a letter from Sir C. Cotton, of the 9th inst., in which he advises me to leave the fleet to windward, and to go down to the Tagus to confer with him. He has occupied a post with 400 marines at Figueira on the Mondego, in front of Coimbra, at which place, or at Peniche, he thinks it will be most advisable for me to land. I therefore propose to send the fleet to the Mondego to make all the arrangements for landing; to go down to communicate with the Admiral; and by the time I shall have returned, all will be ready to go on shore, either at the Mondego or Peniche, or farther to the southward if the Admiral thinks it advisable.

I have heard nothing positive of Gen. Spencer, excepting that he was with Sir C. Cotton in the beginning of this month, his corps having been landed, merely to preserve the health of the men, near Cape St. Mary's. I conclude, therefore, that I shall find him with the fleet off the Tagus. The French corps is concentrated at or about Lisbon, and is said to consist of from 13,000 to 14,000 men. Sir C. Cotton says they are adding to the fortifications of the town, of a citadel within the town, and of Fort St. Julian.

The measures to be adopted for this country are to supply it with arms and money. I saw a statement last night, from which it appears that they could get together 38,000 men with ease, if they had arms or money to pay them. If I should find the troops at Coimbra to be worth it, I propose to arm them.

To Major Gen. Spencer.　　　　H.M.S. *Crocodile,* off the Tagus, 26th July, 1808.

I have the honor of receiving your letters of the 15th and 16th inst.

As the instructions which I have received from His Majesty's ministers positively direct me to make an attack upon the French troops in the Tagus, if I should find the force under my command sufficient to enable me to make it; as these instructions were framed at the instance of the Juntas of Galicia and Asturias; and as the Junta of Galicia, with which I have communicated lately at Coruna, have again pressed me to carry into execution the object of those instructions; and, above all, as I am convinced that the most effectual mode in which Great Britain can serve the Spanish cause is by driving the French out of Portugal, and thus to make that Kingdom the point of communication between the northern and southern parts of Spain itself, I cannot avoid urging you to embark the troops under your command, as soon as you shall receive this letter, and to proceed to the Tagus, when you shall receive further orders from me.

If, when you receive this letter, you should be engaged in any active operations, the relinquishment of which would, in your judgment, be detrimental to the Spanish cause, you will not obey this order, but still continue such operations; but if you should not be so actually engaged, and should embark as ordered, you will take care to apprise the Junta of Seville of the motives which have induced His Majesty s ministers to make an effort to wrest the Kingdom of Portugal from the power of the French; and of the reasons for which I think that I shall most effectually forward the interests and objects of the Spanish nation, by persevering in carrying into execution the orders I have received, as detailed in the first part of this letter.

To Major Gen. Spencer.　　　　　　　　　　　　　　26th July, 1808.

In case you should quit Cadiz according to the instructions contained in my dispatch of this date, it occurs to me, from the representation you have made of the wants of the Junta of Seville, that the Spanish nation

G.O.　　　　　　　　　　　　　　　　　　　　　26th July, 1808.
Regulations to be observed in the event of a landing being determined on in Mondego bay. [Not in the General Orders from whence this copy was made, although mentioned in the Index of them.]

would be most effectually served, and the minds of the principal persons among them would be reconciled to your departure, if their pecuniary distresses could be relieved by an immediate advance of money.

I therefore beg you to inform them, if they can procure money for a bill on the Lords Commissioners of the Treasury of England, that you are authorised to draw upon them for £100,000; and I authorise and beg you to give bills on the Lords of the Treasury for that sum of money, which you will pay to the persons who may be appointed to receive it by the Junta of Seville and you will take their receipt for the same.

I think it probable that His Majesty may have directed a sum of money to be sent to the Junta of Seville, as he has to that of Galicia, which has been received; and if you should be able to procure the money for the bills which I have above requested you to give, I beg of you to leave a letter for the gentleman who may come up with the money which may be sent by His Majesty's directions, in which you will inform him that you have made this advance; and you will request him to send to the Tagus, for the use of the army, an equal sum out of the money which it is supposed he will have brought out from England.

To Major Gen. Spencer.   26th July, 1808.

As Lieut. Col. Bathurst is appointed D. Q. M. G. to the troops under my command, and Mr. Hunter Dep. Paymaster General, I feel great inconvenience from the want of the assistance of those officers; and as I believe Major Rainey is present with your corps, who can take charge of the Q. M. G.'s department, I request you to send Lieut. Col. Bathurst and Mr. Hunter to join me immediately, in the schooner which will take you this dispatch.

As I understand that some of the transports you have with you are heavy sailers, and as it is most desirable to the King's service that your corps should arrive here at an early period, I recommend you to apply to Lord Collingwood, to allow some of the troops to come here in men of war, as being the most expeditious mode of sending them.

To Visct. Castlereagh.   26th July, 1808.

I have the honor to inform you that I joined the fleet off Cape Finisterre on the 22nd inst., and continued my voyage in this ship to Oporto (leaving them to follow me), where I arrived on the 24th, and the fleet on the following morning.

I saw the Bishop of Oporto, who is at the head of the Junta, and the General officers commanding the Portuguese troops, on that night; and I learned from them, and from Lieut. Col. Brown, that the Portuguese troops, militia, and regulars which had been collected, amounted to about 5000 men, and were posted at Coimbra, in the province of Beira, about 80 miles from Oporto, towards Lisbon. That, besides these troops, there were in advance about 1200 peasants armed in different modes, and a corps of about 1500 Portuguese infantry, and 300 Spanish infantry, at Oporto, besides volunteers and peasants. The whole of these troops, however, are badly armed and equipped. The peasantry have, I believe, no arms but pikes, and those called regular infantry are composed of individuals belonging to different corps of the Portuguese army. The corps of Spanish infantry, consisting of 2000 men, which I informed your Lordship in my letter of the 21st inst. was ordered to march from Galicia into Portugal, had not left the former kingdom by the last accounts, and was not expected at Oporto.

A post at Figueira upon the river Mondego, which falls into the sea at Mondego bay, is occupied by 300 marines belonging to the fleet under the command of Capt. Bligh, of H.M.S. *Alfred*, which was likewise detained there.

On my arrival at Oporto, I received from Sir C. Cotton a letter of the 9th inst., a copy of which I enclose, in which the Admiral recommends that I should leave the fleet at anchor to the northward, and go to the mouth of the Tagus to communicate with him, as he thought it probable that it would be deemed advisable that the troops should land at Mondego bay, or at Peniche. I have accordingly requested Capt. Malcolm to anchor at Mondego, and I am now on my passage to the mouth of the Tagus.

While I was at Oporto I requested the Bishop to supply me with 150 horses for the remount of the 20th light dragoons, of which corps there are nearly that number of men dismounted. I also requested him to supply the troops with 500 mules, of a description which could be applied either to draft or carriage, which I propose to apply to the carriage of the musket ammunition and intrenching tools, (there being with the army no ammunition, tumbril, or intrenching tool carts,) of a certain quantity of provisions, and if I should find it necessary, of the camp equipage of the army. The Bishop promised that I should have the horses and mules at Coimbra by the time that the army would be disembarked, if I should determine to disembark at Mondego bay. I also made arrangements with him for the supply of fresh meat for the troops, and of forage and grain for the horses of the cavalry and artillery, and for the mules with the army.

Having made all these arrangements, in the course of the night of the 24th inst. I embarked from Oporto, on the morning of the 25th joined the fleet, and am now on my passage to the Tagus.

To Major Gen. Spencer.   26th July, 1808.

The public letters, which Capt. Cooke * will deliver to you with this, will apprise you of my wishes that you should come here as soon as possible, and of the reasons for which I wish that you should do so.

In addition to those stated in my public letter, I have to mention to you, that, from all that I have heard, I think there is reason to believe that Buonaparte is not now very strong in Spain; and that he has not at his command the means of reinforcing his troops sufficiently to strike any blow which can have a permanent effect. It is obvious that Dupont to the southward does not think himself sufficiently strong for Castanos, otherwise he would not halt and take up a defensive position. Even supposing that we should deem it expedient eventually to return and carry on operations in the south of Spain, it is not probable, from the general state of

---

* The late Major Gen. Sir H. F. Cooke, K.C.H.

the French, that any great misfortune can happen before we return. In the mean time the Spaniards will acquire strength and experience; and I must observe that nothing we can do can be so useful to them as to get possession of and organise a good army in Portugal. On the other hand, if the efforts of the Spanish nation should fail, and if the French are now able to obtain possession of Cadiz, I do not think the presence of your corps would be of much avail to prevent the occurrence of this misfortune; while its presence here is of the utmost importance, to enable me to perform the operations intrusted to me, the success of which would be a great benefit to Great Britain: even if all should unfortunately fail. Therefore, in either and all the views of the case, whether Spain is to continue or to fail, Portugal is an object, and your presence here is most necessary. You will find, on your arrival with Adm. Cotton, instructions for your operations.

Do not delay on account of the bill which you are to draw for 100,000*l.*, but leave Tucker or somebody to settle it with the Junta with the bills in his hands.

Memorandum for disembarkation.   29th July, 1808.

In the event of a landing being determined upon in Mondego bay, a signal will be made to Capt. Malcolm, when it will be settled at what period it may be proper to move the horse ships, and the ships having the ordnance on board, into the river.

The infantry will be directed to be landed from the transports in the roads, and to be rowed in the boats up the river, and landed on the south bank of it: Gen. Fane's brigade first, excepting the Veteran battalion, which is to remain on board: then Gen. Ferguson's; then Gen. Craufurd's.

In the mean time the following arrangements are to be made:

1st. The havresacks and canteens now in the regimental stores are to be given out to the men.

2nd. Tin camp kettles are to be issued from the Q. M. G.'s stores to the regiments.

3rd. The Commissary must issue to each of the Paymasters of regiments, on account of the Paymaster Gen., the sum of £1000 for each of the regiments, and in that proportion for the artillery, dragoons, and 95th companies, which he will receive from the *Donegal*. A month's pay may also be issued on the same account to the officers of the Staff.

4th. Gen. Hill will inform the officer commanding the 20th light dragoons that he is to receive a sufficient number of horses to mount all his men; that he will therefore be prepared to land the horse appointments of the men who have at present no horses.

5th. The following arrangement to be made respecting baggage. The men to land, each with one shirt and one pair of shoes, besides those on them, combs, razor, and a brush, which are to be packed up in their great coats. The knapsacks to be left in the transports, and the baggage of the officers, excepting such light articles as are necessary for them. A careful serjeant to be left in the head quarter ship of each regiment, and a careful private man in each of the other ships, in charge of the baggage;

and each officer who shall leave any baggage in a transport must take care to have his name marked on each package, and each numbered, and give a list of what he leaves to the soldier in charge of the baggage, in order that he may get what he may require.

6th. The men will land with 3 days' bread and 2 days' meat, cooked.

7th. The Commanding officer of artillery is to land the 3 brigades of artillery, each with half the usual proportion of ammunition, the forge cart, &c. He will also land 500,000 rounds of musket ammunition for the use of the troops, for which carriage will be provided.

8th. Each soldier will have with him 3 good flints.

9th. Besides the bread above directed to be landed with the soldiers, 3 days' bread to be packed up in bags, containing 100 lbs. each, on board each of the transports, for the number of soldiers who shall be disembarked from it.

10th. Mr. Commissary Pipon to be directed to attach a Commissary, and the necessary number of clerks, &c., to each brigade, to the cavalry and to the artillery. He will hereafter receive directions to take charge of the bread above directed to be prepared, and to make his arrangements for victualling the troops.

11th. Three days' oats to be landed with each of the horses.

12th. The horses of the Irish Commissariat to be handed over, when landed, to the Commanding officer of the artillery, who will allot the drivers to take charge of them; and then the officers and drivers belonging to the Irish Commissariat to place themselves under the orders of Mr. Pipon.

13th. The officers commanding companies will make an arrangement for purchasing mules for the carriage of camp equipage, for which they have received an allowance in the embarkation money

To Adm Sir Ch. Cotton, Bart.   H.M.S. *Donegal*, off Figueira, 30th July, 1808.

I arrived here this day, and have received dispatches from England, dated the 15th inst., from which I learn that a reinforcement to the amount of 5000 men is likely to arrive here immediately.

I propose to disembark here the day after to-morrow, but I shall not move forward till I shall hear of my reinforcement from England, or of the arrival of Gen. Spencer. I think it probable that he will now come here, for I understand that Gen. Castanos defeated Dupont in an action fought on the 20th inst., and that Dupont surrendered on condition that he should be sent to France by sea. If this should be true, there can be nothing to detain Gen. Spencer in that quarter.

I propose to look at Peniche as I shall march towards Lisbon, and if there should be any prospect of early success, I shall attack the place. But in order to be able to effect this object I must have 24 pounders; and the necessity there may be to have this ordnance at Peniche, and the desire which I have to profit as long as possible by the assistance of Capt. Bligh, induce me to ask you to allow the *Alfred* to remain with us as long as may be possible. I shall not ask to detain either that ship or the *Donegal*, as soon as the moment shall arrive at which you may have it in your power to attack the fleet. If either the fleet having on board the ordnance stores. or Gen. Spencer's corps, or the reinforcements from England, should go to the mouth of the Tagus, I shall be obliged to you if you will order them here, directing that they may keep in shore, in case we should have occasion to communicate with them.

Capt. Malcolm will write to you about the marines, who shall be sent in the *Blossom* and *Lively*.

To Visct. Castlereagh.   H.M.S. *Donegal,* off Figueira, 1st Aug. 1808.

I have the honor to inform you, that when on my passage from the fleet to the mouth of the Tagus, I fell in with H. M. S. *Plantagenet,* on the 26th July, in which was embarked Capt. Cooke, of the Coldstream Guards, who delivered to me the dispatches from Gen. Spencer, of which I enclose copies, by which I was informed that that officer had landed at Puerto de Sta Maria, and had determined to remain in the province of Andalusia. After consulting with Sir C. Cotton upon the situation of affairs in Portugal and Spain, I thought it proper to send Gen. Spencer orders to re-embark his whole corps and to join me, unless he should be engaged in any active operation, the relinquishment of which he should deem detrimental to the cause of the Spaniards. As Gen. Spencer, in his letter, and more particularly in a verbal message by Capt. Cooke, represented the great distress for money which was felt by the Junta of Seville, I desired him to draw upon England for £100,000, and to pay that sum to the person they should appoint to receive it.

I have the honor to enclose copies of the letters which I have written to Gen. Spencer upon this occasion, in which the reasons which induced me to give these orders are sufficiently detailed; and they will, I hope, justify me for having given them, without being under the necessity of troubling your Lordship with my reasons for thinking that it was probable that Dupont was not sufficiently strong for Gen. Castanos; that Gen. Spencer's corps was useless at Cadiz, while the operations of mine in Portugal were cramped for want of its assistance; that a junction of the two corps was necessary to enable either to perform any effectual service; and that, in the general situation of affairs in Spain, as well as in Portugal, it was most important to drive the French out of Portugal.

The orders which I gave appeared to me to be entirely in conformity with the intentions and object of His Majesty's government, and to be consistent with those which your Lordship gave to the General in your letter of the 30th June; and although it appears by your Lordship's dispatch of the 15th July, which I received here from Lord Burghersh on the 30th, that it was His Majesty's intention to assist the Spanish nation with a body of his troops in Andalusia, I did not think it proper to recall those which I had sent to Gen. Spencer on the 26th. The second orders would not have reached him till the 3d or 4th of Aug., when he would have carried the first into execution, and would probably be far advanced on his passage; and I received accounts on my arrival here, on the same day, to which I gave credit, that Gen. Castaños had defeated Gen. Dupont on the 20th inst., and there was no longer any immediate necessity for the assistance of the British corps in that quarter of Spain. These accounts have been still further confirmed by others arrived this day, from which it appears that Gen. Dupont, and all the French troops to the southward of the Sierra Morena, had surrendered, on condition, that they should be sent to France by sea.

The information of the state of the enemy's force in Portugal, communicated to me by Gen. Spencer, (which, however exaggerated the accounts he had received may be, deserve attention,) and the expectation held out by your Lordship, that a reinforcement would arrive here at an early period, have necessarily induced me to delay the commencement of the operations of the troops under my command till the arrival of the corps from England, or of Gen. Spencer. The General will have received

---

G. O.   Mondego bay, 31st July, 1808.

The troops are to understand that Portugal is a country friendly to His Majesty, that it is essentially necessary to their own success that the most strict obedience should be preserved, that properties and persons should be respected, and that no injury should be done which it is possible to avoid. The Lieut. General declares his determination to punish in the most exemplary manner all who may be convicted of acts of outrage and of plunder against the persons or property of any of the people of the country.

It is almost essential to the success of the army that the religious prejudices and opinions of the people of the country should be respected, and with this view the Lieut. General desires the following rules may be observed:

1st. No officer or soldier belonging to the army is to go to any place of religious worship, during the performance of Divine service in such places, excepting with the permission of the officer commanding his regiment, and the General officer commanding the brigade to which he belongs.

2nd. When an officer or soldier shall visit a church, or any other place of religious worship, from motives of curiosity, at periods when Divine service is not performed, he is to remain uncovered while in the church.

3rd. When the Host passes in the streets, officers and soldiers, not on duty, are to halt and front it; the officers to pull off their hats, and the soldiers to put their hands to their caps. When it shall pass a guard, the guard will turn out and present arms; when a sentry the sentry must present arms.

Until further orders the troops will receive rations from the Commissary. The rations will consist for each day of 1 lb. of bread or biscuit, and 1 lb. of meat, salt or fresh. If the soldiers should have fresh meat, they are not entitled to spirits or wine; if they should have salt meat, and upon all occasions when it can be got for them, they shall have each one quarter of a pint of spirits, or a pint of wine. The troops are also entitled in camp to 3 lbs. of wood each man.

The women, that is to say, 6 for each company of 100 men, will receive half a ration *per diem*, and the children a quarter; but no spirits or wine will be issued to women or children.

Horses will receive a ration of 10 lbs. of hay and 10 lbs. of oats, if hay and oats should be delivered. If there should be none in store, the ration will be 14 lbs. of Indian corn or barley, and 10 lbs. of straw.

The number of days for which an issue is to be made will be stated in G. O. the day previous to the issue, and the returns and receipts are to be given to the Commissary according to the following regulations, viz.:

A return of the effectives of each regiment of infantry and cavalry present entitled to draw provisions agreeably to the following forms, signed by the paymaster and commanding officer of each corps, is to be sent the day previous to the issue to the Assist. Commissary, from whom the supplies are to be drawn. On the day of delivery a receipt, in *triplicate*, is to be produced to the Assist. Commissary, agreeably to the form herewith, signed as above, and by the quarter master, the commanding officer being held responsible for the accuracy, as well of the return as of the receipt.

When detachments are stationed at a distance from the head quarters of their regiments, the commanding officers thereof are to conform to the regulations above laid down for the commanding officers of regiments. On the 24th of each month inclusively, a general receipt in *triplicate* is to be furnished to the Assist. Commissary for the whole period from the 25th of the preceding month to the 24th of the present one, both inclusive, which receipt, in *triplicate*, is to be signed by the commanding officer and quarter master, and in which are to be recapitulated the different periods of delivery from that particular magazine, by which means the receipts before given, as temporary vouchers, are to be cancelled.

Assist

my letter of the 26th, I hope, on the 28th and I expect that he will be ready to sail by the 31st. The length of his passage to the Tagus, and to this place, must then depend upon the winds, which have blown from the southward since the 28th.

The enemy's position in the neighbourhood of the Tagus appears so strong, that it is considered impracticable to make a landing in that quarter, without diverting the attention by an attack to the northward. The plans of attack on Cascaes Bay would fail, because it is stated to be impossible to approach the coast sufficiently with the large ships to silence

---

Assist. Commissaries are to be allotted to each brigade and corps of the army, as will be stated in General Orders; but in case any regiment or detachment should cease to receive its provisions from one assistant in the course of the month, the general receipts in *triplicate*, as above stated, must be given to each Assist. Commissary for the number of days which each regiment may have received its provisions from each Commissary.

The staff of the army will be guided in drawing their supplies by the foregoing regulations.

The aides de camp of Generals will sign receipts in like manner for the staff they belong to, which are likewise to be cancelled by a general one in *triplicate*, on the 24th of each month, or after the deliveries made from that particular depôt. Each department to give receipts in the manner as before directed for the whole of that department at the station.

If any detachment of the troops should at any time receive provisions and firewood from the inhabitants, the officer commanding the regiment or detachment will give a receipt in writing in the following form :

i. Received from ——, magistrate of the town of ——,
Wood . . . — lbs.
Meat . . . — lbs.
Bread . . . — lbs.
Wine . . . — qts.
for the —— soldiers of the —— regt. under my command, for —— days, from the —— to the —— of —— inclusive.   (Signed)   ———, officer commg.

If detachments should consist of soldiers of more than one regiment, a separate receipt is to be given for those of each regiment. If forage is received, the receipt must run in the following form :

ii. Received from ——, magistrate of the town of ——, —— rations of forage, consisting of 10 lbs. of straw, and 14 lbs. of barley or Indian corn each, for —— horses belonging to the —— regt. (or if a General or field officer on the staff, the name of each officer), from the —— to the ——, both days inclusive.   (Signed)   ———, officer commg.

The receipts for carriages must be drawn in the following manner :

iii. Received from ——, magistrate for the town of ——, a cart with 2 bullocks, for the use of —— regt., of —— or detachment under my command, which went —— miles.
(Signed)   ———, officer commg.

The receipts must be given every 3 days for provisions and forage ; and for carriages when they shall be discharged, by commanding officers of corps and detachments.

Aides de camp of General officers, and others who sign these receipts, will take care that they are drawn out in the regular form.

The officers and soldiers are to understand that they are to pay for every thing they require from the country, excepting provisions, forage, wood, and carriages allowed by the public. For these articles when required, and not issued by the Commissary, they will make requisitions in the country, and give receipts; but they are to make these requisitions only by order of a General or other officer commanding a brigade or detachment : and in case any officer should pass his receipt for any article for which he ought to pay, or should sign a receipt for which he may not be authorized by the officer commanding the brigade or detachment to which he belongs, the Commissary will receive directions to charge such articles to the officer who shall have given the receipt, and such officer will also be liable to the penalties of disobedience of orders.

Officers to land with as little baggage as possible. [Not in the General Orders from whence this copy was made, although mentioned in the Index of them.]

the Fort of Cascaes, and the other works erected for the defence of the bay; and although the ships of war might be able to pass Fort St. Julian, the Fort Bugio, and the other works by which the entrance of the Tagus is defended, it is not imagined that these forts could be silenced by their fire, so as to enable the troops to land at Paco d'Arcos, as was proposed. Between Cascaes and the Cape Roca, and to the northward of Cape Roca, there are small bays, in which small bodies of men could be disembarked in moderate weather. But the surf on the whole of the coast of Portugal is great, and the disembarkation in these bays of the last divisions of the troops, and of their necessary stores and provisions, would be precarious, even if a favorable moment should have been found for the disembarkation of the first. The vicinity of the enemy, and the want of resources in the country in the neighbourhood of the Rock of Lisbon, for the movement of the necessary stores and provisions for the army, would increase the embarrassment of a disembarkation in that quarter. All these considerations, combined with a due sense of the advantages which I shall derive from the co-operation of the Portuguese troops, have induced me to decide in favor of a landing to the northward.

There is no place to the northward of Lisbon which would at all answer for a place of disembarkation nearer than Mondego, excepting possibly Peniche. But the fort upon that peninsula is strong, and is occupied by the enemy with a sufficient garrison, and could not be taken without heavy ordnance; and the ordnance and ammunition, which your Lordship informed me in your dispatch of the 30th June was to sail from the river on that day, has not yet arrived.

I shall consider the possession of the harbour and city of Lisbon as the immediate object of our operations, which must be attained by that of the forts by which the entrance of the Tagus is guarded. It is probable that it will be necessary to attack two of these forts, Cascaes and St. Julian, with heavy ordnance; and it is obvious that the enemy will not allow us to undertake those operations till he shall have been driven from the field.

The positions which he would take for the defence of these posts must be all turned from the heights to the northward of Lisbon, and, indeed, unless prevented by our possession of these heights, the enemy would have it in his power to renew the contest in different positions, until he should be driven into Lisbon or retire. The last will be rendered difficult, if not impossible, excepting in boats across the Tagus, by the adoption of the line of attack by the heights to the northward, which I also prefer, as being more likely to bring the contest to the issue of a battle in the field.

I have this day commenced my disembarkation in the river of Mondego, because I was apprehensive that any further delay might tend to discourage the country, and because I shall experience greater facilities in making the arrangements for the movement and supply of the army when it shall be on shore than while it shall continue afloat. The landing is attended with some difficulties even here, and would be quite impossible if we had not the cordial assistance of the country, notwithstanding the zeal and abilities of the officers of the navy; and in all probability Gen. Spencer and the reinforcements from England will arrive before the troops at present here shall be on shore: if either should arrive, I propose to commence my march.

I have the honor to inform your Lordship that I have issued 5000 stands of arms for the purpose of arming the Portuguese regular troops, who, it is intended, should co-operate with the British army in the attack on the French in this country.

To the Duke of Richmond.   H.M.S. *Donegal,* off the Mondego, 1st Aug. 1808.

Nothing has occurred since my last letter excepting that I have been to the Tagus to communicate with Sir C. Cotton, and the result is a determination to make our landing to the northward of the Mondego river.

Spencer has sent me a paper of information stating that the French force in Portugal amounts to 20,000 men; and although he knows I have only 10,000, and that he was not employed on any service to the south, he had determined to remain on shore at Xerez near Cadiz: but I have ordered him to join me, and I expect him in a day or two; and as I don't believe the French have so many as 20,000 men, I shall commence my operations as soon as he with his 5000, or a reinforcement expected from England of 5000 men, shall join me. He sent this same account to England, where they took the alarm, and ordered out 5000 men and Moore's corps of 10,000 men, with several general officers, senior to me, and Sir Hew Dalrymple to command the whole army. I hope that I shall have beat Junot before any of them shall arrive, and then they will do as they please with me. I think it possible, however, that the ministry may wish me to return to you.

I have commenced my landing, which will not be completed, on account of the difficulties of this iron coast, till either Spencer or the English reinforcement shall arrive.

What becomes of Lord Chatham in all this?

P.S. General Castaños has certainly beat Dupont in an action fought in Andalusia on the 20th July. Dupont surrendered, with his whole army, on condition of being sent to France by sea.

To Visct. Castlereagh.   H.M.S. *Donegal,* 1st Aug. 1808.

I have nothing to add to my public letter of this date, excepting to tell you I have reason to believe Gen. Spencer's account of the French force in Portugal is exaggerated. I intended to make the attack with my own corps, aided by the Portuguese, if it should have turned out that he could not join me, according to my orders of the 26th July, until I received your letter of the 15th, in which you announce the reinforcements; and I shall now march on, of course, as soon as one of the corps shall arrive.

Pole and Burghersh have apprised me of the arrangements for the future command of this army; and the former has informed me of your kindness towards me, of which I have experienced so many instances, that I can never doubt it in any case. All that I can say upon that subject is, that whether I am to command the army or not, or am to quit it, I shall do my best to insure its success; and you may depend upon it that I shall not hurry the operations, or commence them one moment sooner than they ought to be commenced, in order that I may acquire the credit of the success.

The government will determine for me in what way they will employ me hereafter, whether here or elsewhere. My opinion is, that Great

Britain ought to raise, organize, and pay an army in Portugal, consisting of 30,000 Portuguese troops, which might be easily raised at an early period; and 20,000 British, including 4000 or 5000 cavalry. This army might operate on the frontiers of Portugal in Spanish Estremadura, and it would serve as the link between the kingdoms of Galicia and Andalusia: it would give Great Britain the preponderance in the conduct of the war in the Peninsula; and whatever might be the result of the Spanish exertions, Portugal would be saved from the French grasp. You know best whether you could bear the expense, or what part of it the Portuguese government would or could defray. But if you should adopt this plan, you must send everything from England; arms, ammunition, clothing, and accoutrements, ordnance, flour, oats, &c. These articles must find their way to the frontier, partly by the navigation of the Douro and Tagus, and partly by other means.

P.S. The ground I have for believing that Castaños has beaten Dupont is, that I have read a copy of his dispatch to the Junta of Seville, published in the Coimbra gazette. Its purport is nearly what I have stated in my dispatch, excepting only that Dupont may have surrendered with his army, and that the French force in the Sierra Morena, not engaged in the action of the 20th, may have capitulated, on condition of being sent to France by sea. I do not understand Portuguese well enough to say whether this is not the case, and somebody has taken away the gazette.

2d P.S. You will observe that I have exceeded my authority in ordering Spencer to draw for £100,000 upon England, and to advance that sum to the Junta at Seville; of which act I hope you will see the propriety, and that you will send me an approbation of it. I must mention, however, that since I did it, I have heard that Sir H. Dalrymple had refused to advance them any money, although he had an authority.

To Lieut. Col. Trant. H.M.S. *Donegal,* 1st Aug. 1808.

I have just received your letter of this day; and I shall write to the Bishop in order to have it ascertained whether or not the Portuguese troops under Gen. Freire are to co-operate with me. If they should do so, I shall send you a project for the march combined with that of the British troops.

You are mistaken in supposing that I shall march on Wednesday, or that any day is fixed for my march; but I shall take care to give you due notice of it, and will beg you to communicate it to Gen. Freire, and to press him not to move forward until I shall be ready. The arms were sent on shore this day, and you shall have the 10,000 flints. I prefer the mares to the stallions for our cavalry.

To the Juiz de Fora* at Figueira. H.M.S. *Donegal,* 1st Aug. 1808.

As a part of the troops under my command have landed, and their horses, and the mules and cattle belonging to the people of the country, which are with the camp, situated near the village of Lavos, are in want of grain and forage, I shall be much obliged to you if you will give

---

* The magistrate in a Portuguese town.

directions that forage and grain may be collected at Lavos for the use of the cattle, and mules, and horses, for which the Commissary will pay.

1st. The troops will land with 4 days' bread and 2 days' meat; and it will be necessary to keep up that supply at the village of Lavos, so that, when the army shall march, the troops may carry, each man, 4 days' bread.

2d. Besides this quantity of bread to be carried by the men themselves, a quantity, equal to 3 days' consumption for 10,000 men, must be carried, if possible, on the backs of mules; viz., 2 bags, or 224 lbs., on each mule; this will require 130 mules.

3d. Besides these 7 days' bread to move with the troops, the Lieut. General desires that 10 days' bread, 5 days' meat, and 10 days' spirits, for 10,000 men, should move from Lavos about the same time, by the carts of the country, to be formed into a depôt about 70 miles in advance. This will require

					Carts.
Bread	.	.	.	.	170
Meat	.	.	.	.	100
Spirits	.	.	.	.	37
			Total	. .	307

These carts must be levied, and will be relieved at Leiria.

4th. The Medical department will require 2 carts to march with the army, carrying 24 bearers for wounded men, a case of utensils, and a medicine chest.

5th. The artillery will require, to move with the army, 250 mules, each to carry 2000 rounds of musket ammunition.

6th. The Q. M. Gen.'s department will require 30 mules to carry intrenching tools.

7th. The Commissary Gen. will make arrangements for supplying the troops at Lavos with bread, meat, spirits, and wood.

8th. The Commissary Gen. will see in the G. O. to what day the troops, as they disembark, will have bread and meat, and he will provide accord-singly for their subsistence.

9th. The horses will land, each with 3 days' forage and oats: provision must be made for them after the 3d inst.; but as the demand must be small, it is concluded that the country will experience no difficulty in supplying their wants, and therefore no provision is made for carrying forward forage or oats.

10th. The muleteers and carmen are to be provisioned from this date, and their cattle foraged.

11th. Bread, &c. to be landed from the ships accordingly.

Proclamation by the Commanders in Chief of His Britannic Majesty's Land and Sea Forces, employed to assist the loyal Inhabitants of the Kingdom of Portugal.

People of Portugal! The time is arrived to rescue your country, and restore the government of your lawful Prince.

His Britannic Majesty, our most gracious King and master, has, in compliance with the wishes and ardent supplications for succour from all parts of Portugal, sent to your aid a British army, directed to co-operate with his fleet, already on your coast.

The English soldiers, who land upon your shore, do so with every sentiment of friendship, faith, and honor.

The glorious struggle in which you are engaged is for all that is dear to man, the protection of your wives and children; the restoration of your lawful Prince; the independence, nay, the very existence of your kingdom; and for the preservation of your holy religion. Objects like these can only be obtained by distinguished examples of fortitude and constancy.

The noble struggle against the tyranny and usurpation of France will be jointly maintained by Portugal, Spain, and England; and in contributing to the success of a cause so just and glorious, the views of His Britannic Majesty are the same as those by which you are yourselves animated.

Memorandum for the Commissary General.   Lavos, 3d Aug. 1808.

1st. The 130 mules allotted to carry three days' bread for the army should be divided into three divisions, each consisting of 35 mules, and to be handed over to the Assist. Commissary attached to each of the brigades, the remaining 25 being handed over to the Commissary attached to head quarters.

2d. The Assist. Commissaries are to be directed to give the muleteers each a ration of bread and meat daily, and to forage the mules.

3d. The 250 mules for the artillery must be mustered and set apart, and an Assist. Commissary must be appointed to take charge of them and forage them, and give rations to the drivers.

4th. 12 of the best mules, now with the army, to be selected for draft, and these will answer for the intrenching tools, instead of the 30 before ordered. These must be handed over to the chief Engineer, and the Commissary General must provide rations for the mules and muleteers.

5th. A head muleteer, or *capataz*, to be appointed to superintend each division attached to the Assist. Commissaries of brigades, and to every 50 of the mules attached to the artillery, for the carriage of musket ammunition, and to the 100 mules ordered to be retained in the next article. These head muleteers, if not otherwise paid in the service, to receive one shilling *per diem*, besides rations.

6th. 100 mules, with drivers, to be retained in case of the arrival of reinforcements, and 150 carts, in addition to those ordered to be retained for particular service on the 1st inst.

7th. The mules and carts for the service being ascertained, the Commissary Gen. should select them from the numbers now attending camp: he must put all the carts ordered on the 1st inst., and those and the mules ordered this day, in charge of an Assist. Commissary Gen., who will muster them, forage the mules and cattle, and give rations of bread and meat to the drivers.

8th. All the carts and mules above this number to be discharged.

9th. A head driver must be appointed for every 50 carts, ordered by the Memorandum of the 1st inst., and by the 5th article of that of this day; and if not already in the service, this man to be paid one shilling a day besides his ration.

10th. The carts and mules must do all the duty of the army till they shall be required to perform the particular services allotted to them in the Memorandum of the 1st and of this day.

To Col. Trant.   Lavos, 3d Aug. 1808.

I received your letter of the 2d this morning. I shall be perfectly satisfied if I can get 5000 regular troops and 2000 irregulars; upon which subject I have begged Col. Brown to communicate with the Bishop; and I am decidedly of opinion that it is necessary to watch the enemy's movements from the northward, and upon the Douro, with the remainder of the Portuguese troops that can be collected; for I acknowledge that I give no credit to the truth of the reported second or third Spanish victories at Benavente.

It is very evident from your account that the Portuguese are not accu-

---

[The G. O. in Italics not in the General Orders from whence this copy was made, although mentioned in the Index of them.]

G. O.   Lavos, 3d Aug. 1808.
Relative to the turning out of the line, mounting of guards, piquets, &c.
The order of battle of the army is to be 2 deep, and as follows, beginning with the right:

> Major Gen. Ferguson's brigade.
> Brig. Gen. Catlin Craufurd's ditto.
> Brig. Gen. Fane's ditto, on the left.

There is to be a howitzer and 3 pieces of cannon attached to each of the brigades of infantry. The 9 pounder brigade with that under Major Gen. Ferguson, and the remainder of the artillery not allotted, will be in reserve.

On marching days the piquets coming off duty will either be fixed previous to the march, and their place in the order of march will be stated in orders, or they will not be fixed till the army shall have reached its ground. In the same manner the piquets coming off duty will either join their regiments, or follow the army as a rear guard, as will be directed in the orders for the march.

When the army shall move from its left, the 95th and 5th batt. 60th will lead the column in the ordinary course. When the army shall move from its right, the 95th and 5th batt. 60th must form the advanced guard, and lead the column from the right of the two corps with the howitzer and 6 pounders attached to Gen. Fane's brigade.

The Lieut. General requests the General officers commanding brigades will, on all occasions of march and formation of the line of their respective brigades, place the light infantry companies belonging to the several regiments under their command in a separate corps under the command of a field officer. In the ordinary formation on parade, and in route marches, these corps of light infantry will be on the left of the brigade. In formation in front of the enemy they will be in front or in rear, according to circumstances; and in the marches of columns to take up a position, they will be on the reverse flank of the column. The light infantry companies will, however, encamp, and do all duties with the regiments.

The cavalry is to be in reserve; and its position, as well in the line as in the column of march, will be pointed out in the orders of the day. One subaltern and 20 men must, however, be a piquet every day with a view of furnishing the necessary patroles, and keeping up the communication.

Sentries to be relieved every hour during the day.
Order respecting fires in camp.
The ration of a muleteer, or bullock driver, is to be 1 lb. of bread and $\frac{1}{2}$ lb. of meat *per diem*; that of a mule 10 lbs. of straw and $\frac{1}{4}$ of an alquier of barley or Indian corn; that of a bullock 10 lbs. of straw of Indian corn.

rately informed even of the first action which was fought, not on the 12th, but the 14th July; and not at Benavente, to which town the Spanish troops retreated, but at Rio Seco.

I think that it would be attended with good consequences if I could see Gen. Freire; and if you will settle a meeting with him, I will go over to Monte Mor o Velho on any day, at any hour, he will fix.

I understood that you did not want any ammunition for the Portuguese troops.

Are the 75,000 rounds to be fixed at Leiria for them?

To Lord Burghersh. Lavos, 3d Aug. 1808.

I received this morning your letter of yesterday, and your report is very satisfactory. I have heard this day that the infantry and artillery have nearly completed their embarkation, and I hope we shall have everything on shore to-morrow.

I should like much to have a report of the state of things at Viseu; and I have nothing else for you to do here at present. If I should move before your return, which is not very probable, you can easily overtake me.

I think that, if I can get 5000 good Portuguese troops and 2000 regulars, it is as much of that description as I should want; more would only embarrass us; and I think it very desirable that we should have an eye to the cause of Douro. I suspect the truth of these second and third Spanish victories in the neighbourhood of Benavente, and I see clearly, that at all events, the intelligence respecting them, given to Col. Trant, is not correct; for he is mistaken respecting the date even of the first action, which took place on the 14th, and not on the 12th; and he says that a reinforcement came from Andalusia, which is the western kingdom of the Peninsula.

The same reasons therefore which induced me to confine my requisition of Portuguese troops to 5000, and to recommend a collection of troops to watch the enemy's movements from the northward, still exists.

To Adm. Sir Charles Cotton, Bart. Lavos, 4th Aug. 1808.

I have just had the honor of receiving your dispatches of the 29th and 31st ult., by the *Scout*.

In the letter which I had the honor of addressing to you on the 31st July, I requested that in case the fleet having on board the equipment for the heavy ordnance, or that having Gen. Spencer, or that having a reinforcement from England, should arrive at the Tagus, you would order them to Figueira; and I conclude that you will have ordered the fleet of transports, having on board Gen. Spencer's corps, to come here immediately.

Upon a full consideration of all that passed between you and me upon the subject of disembarkations to be made in the bay of Lisbon, or to the northward, and in the neighbourhood of the Rock, I was convinced that it was a very hazardous undertaking for those who should attempt it, as well as for those who should depend upon the assistance and co-operation of the troops intended to be disembarked in that quarter.

In respect to a disembarkation in the country south of the Tagus, it appeared to me to be a division of our force, likely to be attended with bad consequences to one, if not to both of our divisions; and therefore, upon the whole, I thought it better to concentrate our force at the earliest possible period, and to land the whole here, as being in every respect the most convenient landing place, and the most eligible spot from which to proceed to the attack of the enemy's force in Portugal. On this ground, I requested you to send Gen. Spencer here, and in expectation of his arrival, I have disembarked my own corps, and wait only for his junction to commence my operations. I am fully aware of the advantage to be derived by diverting the enemy's attention to the Bay of Lisbon, during my advance towards that city; and, accordingly, I propose to send a battalion to the fleet, which is not very capable of making an active march, but may enable you, with the assistance of the marines of the fleet, to make a very seasonable diversion in my favor.

I had heard a report that a detachment of the French army had crossed the Tagus, and I entertained some apprehensions for the fate of the Spanish detachment at Alentejo; and I am now happy to find, from such good authority, that it has returned northward.

To Lieut. Col. Brown.   Lavos, 4th Aug. 1808.

I have just received your letter of the 3d, and am much obliged to you for the exertions you have made to procure the mules for us : if you can get us 100, that number will, I imagine, be sufficient.

I shall be very glad to see you and Mr. Walsh here as soon as you can come over. I expect Gen. Spencer with his corps every moment, and I propose to march as soon as he shall arrive.

We shall be much distressed for the want of about 150 draft mules, to complete the draft of Gen. Spencer's artillery, which I was in hopes I should have had from the 500 which I expected Mr. Walsh would have purchased for me. Can he, or you, or the Portuguese Commander in Chief do any thing to assist us in this way? Are there no draft mules left in the country?

I am obliged to you for my chaise and cart, which I request you to send over as soon as you can. The Bishop *must*, however, receive payment for them. Tell Col. Trant that I do not write to him, as I have nothing particular to say. I have received from Sir C. Cotton, and from Seville, the official accounts of Castaños' victory. The French, who had crossed the Tagus on the 26th, had retired again to this side of the river before the 31st. You may tell the gentlemen at Coimbra, and the Bishop, that this is certain.

To Lord Burghersh.   Lavos, 5th Aug. 1808.

I am very much obliged to you for your letter of the 4th inst.

The difficulties and inconveniences attending the state of the arms of the Portuguese troops will, I hope, be removed entirely as soon as they will receive the English arms which I have sent to them, and some ammunition. I am obliged to you for your routes: one of them, that of the left column, is the best road of the three; but I am afraid that we shall not be able to use it, as in one very important part of it there is no communication between that road and the others on its right.

Loison has returned across the Tagus: the situation of my friends, the Spaniards, gave me some uneasiness when I heard that he had passed.

Spencer has arrived, and his corps will probably be here to-morrow. You had better return, therefore, as I shall march as soon as they will be on shore.

To Lieut. Col. Trant. Lavos, 6th Aug. 1808.

I received your letter of the 5th at 3 this morning. I shall meet Gen. Freire at Monte Mor, at 12 to-morrow.

I was apprehensive that the Spaniards in Alentejo would suffer, when I heard that the French detachment had crossed the Tagus; but I was in hopes that they had not time to effect any thing of importance, when I heard they had returned before the 31st. I hope now that the Spaniards retreated in good time, and that they have lost only their rear guard.

There is nothing so foolish as to push these half disciplined troops forward; for the certain consequence must be, either their early and precipitate retreat, if the enemy should advance, or their certain destruction. I am determined not to move a man of my army till I am fully prepared to support any detachment I may send forward; and for this reason I object to send any troops to Leiria, in answer to various applications which

---

[The G. O. in Italics not in the General Orders from whence this copy was made, although mentioned in the Index of them.]

G. O. Lavos, 5th Aug. 1808.

Soldiers not to go beyond the limits of the camp, without a pass signed by the commanding officer of the regiment.

Outlying piquets and outposts not to turn out, by way of compliment, unless ordered.

Capt. Jarvis, D. A. A. G., will take charge of all deserters who have or may hereafter come in from the enemy. The Dep. Commissary Gen. will issue pay and rations to the people according to a weekly return, which Capt. Jarvis will present to him for that purpose; and one of the Commissary Gen.'s department will muster the men under his command on the 24th of each month, agreeably to the form established for the British service.

G. O. *Parole. Battle.* Lavos, 6th Aug. 1808.

His Majesty has been graciously pleased to appoint the undermentioned officers to serve on the staff of the forces under the command of the Rt. Hon. Lieut. Gen. Sir A. Wellesley from the 14th June last inclusive:

Major Gens. Spencer, Hill, and Ferguson.
Brig. Gens. Nightingall, Fane, and Catlin Craufurd

(The names of the officers of the general staff here follow.)

Officers commanding corps and detachments will immediately send in all carts, now in their possession, belonging to the Commissary General's department, to his depot at Lavos, where they are to remain.

Three days' bread and 3 days' forage will be issued to-morrow at daylight; the former from the Assist. Commissaries of brigades, and the latter from the Commissariat depot at Lavos from the 9th inst. inclusive. Half a pint of wine will be issued this evening at 5 o'clock by the Assist. Commissaries of brigades.

Weekly states of brigades, and corps not brigaded, will be sent in future to the D. A. G.'s office every Monday morning at 8 o'clock.

The following orderlies to be furnished, till further orders, by the 20th light dragoons:

Lieut. Gen. commanding	2
Major Gen. Spencer	2
General officers, each	1
D. A. Gen.	1
D. Q. M. Gen.	1

have been made to me by a Portuguese Commissary, who has applied for protection, being, as he says, employed to collect supplies for the British troops, and which will probably fall into the hands of the enemy, if he should not be supported.

I have uniformly objected to sending any detachment or any person forward till I should be enabled effectually to protect them; and I should have sent on in ample time to secure everything for the army that it could require, or that Leiria could afford. It is unfortunate, therefore, that this gentleman has been sent forward, particularly if the consequence should be the loss of the supplies which Leiria might otherwise have afforded.

To Adm. Sir C. Cotton, Bart.   Lavos, 6th Aug. 1808.

I have had the pleasure of receiving your letter of the 2d, by the *Nautilus*, which brought Gen. Spencer, and arrived here the day before yesterday. His troops are now coming in. They will land to-morrow, I hope, and I shall begin my march immediately.

I am very much obliged to you for leaving the *Alfred* with us. I shall give Capt. Bligh the plan of our marches, and shall arrange with him for our communication, from which I hope not only to derive some advantage in the way of subsistence, but to communicate to you intelligence of our movements. I propose besides to have daily communication by messengers with Capt. Malcolm, at Figueira, until he shall move from hence.

I sent my letters to England by the *Blossom*, which will have reached you. The *Crocodile* is still here; and I thought it best to refrain from asking Capt. Malcolm to send her till I should find it absolutely necessary, which has not been the case yet, as vessels have been going down every day.

I am much obliged to you for ordering the ordnance vessels to join us. Your friends from ———— are still here. The arms which I propose giving them are those which the Portuguese troops will give up when they shall have received their new arms, and they are not yet arrived from Coimbra. They are perfectly satisfied with their arms, which, I understand, are serviceable. But if, when they shall arrive, I should find they are not so, I propose giving them 500 stands of new arms. They were a little alarmed when they heard that the French had crossed the Tagus, and I have not seen them since I heard from you that they had returned again.

P.S. I have written to you officially respecting the proclamation, in

---

A. G. O.   Lavos, 6th Aug. 1808.

Major Gen. Spencer's corps being expected, the following regiments will, in the morning, move out of their tents, and keep themselves in the position which will be pointed out to them by an officer of the Q. M. G.'s department : the 71st, 36th, 40th, 91st, and 45th regts.

The 29th and 82nd regts. will occupy the tents of the 45th and 36th ; the 50th the tents of the 71st ; and the 6th and 32nd those of the 40th and 91st regts.

Till the arrival of the regiments ordered to occupy the tents, small guards of those which will leave them must remain in charge of them.

The corps which are to hut, will apply at 5 o'clock this evening to the D. Q. M. G., near head quarters, for bill hooks, and 60 will be issued to each regiment. Commanding officers are requested to give particular directions that these bill hooks may not be lost or damaged, as the troops will require them in their future operations.

which I have made only a verbal alteration, and I have had a better translation made of it.

To Adm. Sir C. Cotton, Bart.   Lavos, 6th Aug. 1808.

I have had the honor of receiving your letter, in which you have enclosed the draft of a proclamation which, in your opinion, ought to be published to the Portuguese nation upon the commencement of the military operations. As I concur entirely in opinion with you, I have affixed your name and my own to a copy of this proclamation, and have directed that it may be published at Coimbra. I shall circulate it in the country, and send a certain number of copies to you.

To Brig. Gen. Acland, &c., commanding corps arriving on the coast of Portugal.
                                                          Lavos, 7th Aug. 1808.
Having been informed by a dispatch from the Sec. of State, dated 15th

---

G. O.   Lavos, 7th Aug. 1808.
Major Gen. Spencer's corps having joined the army, the regiments will be brigaded as follows, from the right:

1st brigade	5th regt. 9th .. 38th ..	Major Gen. Hill. Brigade Major Fordyce. Assist. Commissary Capt. Hamilton.
2d brigade	29th regt. 82d ..	Brig. Gen. Nightingall. Brig. Major Stewart. Assist. Commissary Lieut. Nelson.
5th brigade	45th regt. 50th .. 91st ..	Brig. Gen. Catlin Craufurd. Brigade Major Blair. Assist. Commissary Aylmer.
4th brigade	6th regt. 32d ..	Brig. Gen. Bowes. Brigade Major Butler. Assist. Commissary Turton.
2d brigade	36th regt. 40th .. 71st ..	Major Gen. Ferguson. Brigade Major Talbot. Assist. Commissary Dillon.
6th, or light brigade	2d batt. 95th. 5th batt. 60th.	Brig. Gen. Fane. Brig. Major M'Neil. Assist. Commissary Lamont.

The foregoing will be the general formation of the brigades in one line, excepting that the light brigade will be ordered to take post in front or in rear, or on either flank, according to circumstances. The cavalry will be in reserve, and posted as may be necessary. A half brigade of artillery will be attached to each brigade of infantry. Howitzers will be attached to the 1st, 2d, 5th, and 6th brigades, and the 9 pounder brigade will be in reserve.

Major Gen. Spencer being second in command, is not to be put on duty as a General officer. The Lieut. General requests that he will give such orders to the troops, from time to time, as he may judge necessary, reporting them to the Lieut. General when he finds it convenient; and the Major General's orders are at all times to be obeyed, although they may be contradictory to those previously issued by the Lieut. General. Capt. Bradford, D. A. A. G., is attached to Major Gen. Spencer.

Brig. Gen. Bowes, on the staff of the troops at Gibraltar, being present with the army, will command the 4th brigade till further orders.

Capt. Hamilton of the 5th regt., Lieut. Nelson of the 40th, and Cornet Turton of the 6th dragoons, are appointed to act as assistants in the Commissary General's department until further orders, and they will report themselves to D. C. Gen. Pipon.

Serj. Major Scates, of the 6th regt., is appointed Dep. Provost Marshal of the army.

Estimates of subsistence, to the 24th inst. inclusive, will be made out immediately by the different corps not yet paid up to that period, and they are to be sent in to the Dep. Paymaster General as soon as he arrives.

Half a pint of wine to be issued to the troops this evening at 5 o'clock.

The light brigade and artillery attached to it to receive one day's salt provisions at an
                                                                            early

July, that you were ordered to proceed from England to join the army under my command, I beg that, upon the receipt of this letter, you will proceed along the coast of Portugal till you shall join the *Alfred,* Capt. Bligh, with a convoy, which ship will attend the movements of the army; and you will receive from Capt. Bligh instructions to guide your future operations.

To Visc. Castlereagh.   Lavos, 8th Aug. 1808.

I have the honor to inform you that Major Gen. Spencer arrived in Mondego bay on the night of the 5th inst., and was followed by a part of the corps under his command on the 6th, and the remainder on the 7th, and the whole have been disembarked in the course of yesterday and this day. The General had determined to embark, in obedience to your Lordship's instructions of the 30th June, on the 21st July, when he received intelligence of the defeat of Dupont, and he consequently had not seen my instructions to him of the 26th July, copies of which I transmitted to your Lordship in my last letter.

I have received your Lordship's letter of the 21st July; and I had already requested the Captains commanding H. M. ships off Cape Finisterre to communicate to all vessels and convoys coming from England that the army under my command was landing in Mondego bay.

I propose to commence my march on the day after to-morrow, and I have the honor to enclose the copy of a letter, which I have left here to be delivered to Sir H. Burrard, in which I have communicated to him the state of affairs in Spain and Portugal, as far as I have been able to obtain a knowledge of them. I have sent a copy of this letter to Sir H. Dalrymple.

To the Duke of Richmond.   Camp at Lavos, 8th Aug. 1808.

Since I wrote to you last Gen. Spencer has joined me, on the 6th and 7th, and his corps have landed yesterday and this day. My advanced guard will move to-morrow, and the army on the 10th. The enemy is nearly in the situation in which he was. He has a corps of about 2000 men in my front; and he has sent a corps of 4000 or 5000 men across the Tagus into Alentejo, apparently with an intention to open his communication

---

early hour to-day, and to cook it this evening, and to keep it; and all the troops to receive one day's salt provisions to-morrow from the Assist. Commissaries of brigades.

A General Court Martial to assemble at 8 o'clock to morrow morning at Major Arbuthnot's quarters, near head quarters, for the trial of such prisoners as shall be ordered before it.

Major Gen. Hill, President.

Six field officers, and 6 captains, to be furnished by the 1st, 2d, and 6th brigades.

Capt. Jarvis, D. A. A. G., to officiate as Dep. Judge Advocate, to whom the names and ranks of the members of the Court, with a list of the evidences, must be sent in the course of this afternoon to Major Arbuthnot's quarters.

A. G. O.   Lavos, 7th Aug. 1808.

All carts and mules belonging to the Commissariat. in possession of any of the corps, to be returned *forthwith* to the Commissary's depôt, at Lavos, in compliance with the orders of the 5th inst.

with Spain, and to suppress the commotion in the Portuguese province of Alentejo, and to drive out 2000 or 3000 Spanish troops which had advanced from Spanish Estremadura. He will not succeed in opening a communication with Spain; and if he does not look sharp, I shall be at Lisbon before that detachment can return.

To Lieut. Gen. Sir H. Burrard, Bart.   Lavos, 8th Aug. 1808.

Having received instructions from the Sec. of State, that you were likely to arrive on the coast of Portugal with a corps of 10,000 men, lately employed in the north of Europe under the orders of Sir J. Moore, I now submit to you such information as I have received regarding the general state of the war in Portugal and Spain, and the plan of operations which I am about to carry into execution, in obedience to the orders of the Sec. of State.

The enemy's force at present in Portugal consists, as far as I am able to form an opinion, of from 16,000 to 18,000 men, of which number there are about 500 in the Fort of Almeida, about the same number in Elvas, about 600 or 800 at Peniche, and 1600 or 1800 in the province of Alentejo, at Setuval, &c.; the remainder are disposable for the defence of Lisbon, and are in the forts of St. Julian and Cascaes, in the batteries along the coast as far as the Rock of Lisbon, and in the old citadel of Lisbon, to which the enemy have lately added some works.

Of the force disposable for the defence of Lisbon, the enemy have lately detached a corps of about 2000 men under Gen. Thomière, principally, I believe, to watch my movements, which corps is now at Alco-

---

G. O.   Lavos, 8th Aug. 1808.

Brig. Gen. Fane's brigade, with the artillery attached to it, and a captain's detachment of 50 men of the 20th light dragoons, to march in the morning, carrying 4 days' bread, and one day's meat cooked. They will this day receive 3 days' bread, and forage to the 12th inst. inclusive.

Whenever the troops are ordered to march, they are to receive one day's meat as soon as possible after the order is issued, which is to be cooked immediately, and carried by the men on the following day.

The Lieut. General requests the commanding officers of regiments to pay the most strict attention in carrying into execution, at the earliest possible period, all orders that are issued, particularly those respecting provisions. The consequences of inattention to this point must be, as no other arrangement can afterwards be made, that the men will be without provisions, as was the case yesterday with the 82nd regt. The provisions for this corps, which according to the orders ought to have been carried by the men in their havresacks, were sent in a separate boat with a guard, which could not arrive at Lavos till 4 this morning.

The Lieut. General is also under the necessity of drawing the attention of the officers of the army to an order twice issued to send to the Commissary's depôt all carts and mules detained in camp. He now requests the General officers commanding brigades will send round the lines, and cause all carts, not absolutely hired by individuals, to be sent to the Commissary's depôt in charge of a guard. As there are also several of the public mules detained in camp by officers, the Lieut. General hopes those who have them will send them back *forthwith*.

The practice of pressing carts and mules is positively forbid. If carts are wanted for any service, application must be made for them to the Commissary General; and if the public service will admit of it, the individuals applying will be accommodated as far as may be possible.

The captains of companies of the corps lately joined with Major Gen. Spencer, will immediately provide mules for the conveyance of the camp kettles of their respective companies.

Half a pint of wine per man to be issued at 5 o'clock this evening by the respective Commissaries of brigades.

baca; and another corps, of 4000 men, under Gen. Loison, was sent across the Tagus into Alentejo, on the 26th of last month: the object of which detachment was to disperse the Portuguese insurgents in that quarter; to force the Spanish corps, consisting of about 2000 men, which had advanced into Portugal as far as Evora from Estremadura, to retire; and thus to be enabled to add, to the force destined for the defence of Lisbon, the corps of French troops which had been stationed at Setuval and in the province of Alentejo. At all events, Loison's corps will return to Lisbon, and the French corps disposable for the defence of that place will probably be about 14,000 men, of which at least 3000 must be left in the garrison and forts on the coast and in the river.

The French army under Dupont in Andalusia surrendered, on the 20th of last month, to the Spanish army under the command of Gen. Castaños; so that there are now no French troops in the south of Spain.

The Spanish army of Galicia and Castille, to the northward, received a check at Rio Seco, in the province of Valladolid, on the 14th July, from a French corps supposed to be under the command of Gen. Bessieres, which had advanced from Burgos.

The Spanish troops retired on the 15th to Benavente, and I understand there has since been an affair between the advanced posts in that neighbourhood; but I am not certain of it, nor am I acquainted with the position of the Spanish army, or of that of the French, since the 14th July. When you shall have been a short time in this country, and shall have observed the degree to which the deficiency of real information is supplied

---

A. G. O.　　　　　　　　　　　　　　　　　　　　　　Lavos, 8th Aug. 1808.

Each staff surgeon must provide himself, without delay, with a sufficient horse or mule to be employed solely for carrying the surgical field equipment, for which a sum, not exceeding £18, will be allowed to every surgeon actually in possession of a mule or horse for the above purpose, and also 1s. 6d. *per diem* will be allowed each staff surgeon for the hire of a native, as a batman, so long as he may be actually employed. Hospital mates will be allowed 1s. *per diem* for the hire of a native, as a servant, to be paid quarterly by the Commissary General, on a return certified by the head of the medical department, according to the following form:

Return of servants, not soldiers, employed by the undermentioned Staff surgeons and Hospital mates, from 25th June to 24th Sept. 1808, inclusive.

Name.	Country.	Period, from	to	With whom serving.	Number of days.	Amount at per diem. £. s. d.

Commanding officers of regiments and detachments are requested to report in the course of this day, to the D. A. G., the number of men incapable of marching on account of sickness.

A mule will be sent to the quarter master of each regiment by the Commissary General for the purpose of carrying the bill hooks delivered to the corps. This mule will march with the regiment, and is not to be employed for any other purpose. The quarter master will receive directions from the Commissary General respecting the payment of the muleteer, and forage for the mule.

Capt. Taggart will land as soon as possible with the detachment of the Irish Commissariat waggons under his command, and march forthwith to the village of Lavos. where he will report himself to the D. C. G. This detachment will bring on shore 4 days' bread and 2 days' meat, cooked, and adhere strictly to the General Orders issued to the troops already landed respecting the men's necessaries, &c.

by the circulation of unfounded reports, you will not be surprised at my want of accurate knowledge upon these subjects.

It is, however, certain that nothing of importance has occurred in that quarter since the 14th July, and from this circumstance I conclude that the corps of Marshal Bessières attacked the Spanish army at Rio Seco, solely with a view to cover the march of King Joseph Bonaparte to Madrid, where he arrived on the 21st July.

Besides the defeat in Andalusia, the enemy, as you may probably have heard, have been beaten off in an attack upon Zaragoza, in·Aragon; in another upon the city of Valencia (in both of which actions it is said that they have lost many men); and it is reported, that in Catalonia two of their detachments have been cut off, and that they have lost the Fort of Figueras in the Pyrenees, and that Barcelona is blockaded: of these last mentioned actions and operations I have seen no official accounts, but the report of them is generally circulated and believed. At all events, whether these reports are founded or otherwise, it is obvious that the in-surrection against the French is general throughout Spain; that large bodies of Spaniards are in arms (among others, in particular, an army of 20,000 men, including 4000 cavalry, at Almaraz, on the Tagus, in Estre-madura); that the French cannot carry on their operations by means of small corps. I should imagine from their inactivity, and from the mis-fortunes they have suffered, that they have not the means of collecting a force sufficiently large to oppose the progress of the insurrection and the efforts of the insurgents, and to afford support to their different detached corps; or that they find they cannot carry on their operations, with armies so numerous as they must find it necessary to employ, without magazines.

In respect to Portugal, the whole Kingdom, with the exception of the neighbourhood of Lisbon, is in a state of insurrection against the French; their means of resistance are, however, less powerful than those of the Spaniards. Their troops have been completely dispersed, their officers had gone off to Brazil, and their arsenals pillaged, or in the power of the enemy. Their revolt, under the circumstances in which it has taken place, is still more extraordinary than that of the Spanish nation. The Portuguese may have, in the northern parts of the Kingdom, about 10,000 men in arms, of which number 5000 are to march with me towards Lisbon; the remainder, with a Spanish detachment of about 1500 men, which came from Galicia, are employed in a distant blockade of Almeida, and in the protection of Oporto, which is at present the seat of government. The insurrection is general throughout Alentejo, and Al-garve to the southward, and Entre Minho e Douro, and Tras os Montes, and Beira, to the northward; but for want of arms the people can do nothing against the enemy.

Having consulted Sir C. Cotton, it appeared to him and to me, that the attack proposed upon Cascaes Bay was impracticable, because the bay is well defended by the Fort of Cascaes, and the other works constructed for its defence, and the ships of war could not approach sufficiently near to silence them. The landing in the Paço d'Arcos in the Tagus could not be effected without silencing Fort St. Julian, which appeared to be impracticable to those who were to carry that operation into execution.

There are small bays within, and others to the northward of the Rock of Lisbon, which might admit of landing troops; but they are all defended by works which must first have been silenced: they are of small extent, and but few men could have landed at the same time: there is always a surf on them, which affects the facility of landing at different times so materially, as to render it very doubtful whether the troops first landed could be supported in sufficient time by the others; and whether the horses for the artillery and cavalry, and the necessary stores and provisions, could be landed at all. These inconveniences attending a landing in any of the bays near the Rock of Lisbon would have been aggravated by the neighbourhood of the enemy to the landing place, and by the exhausted state of the country in which the troops would have been landed.

It was obviously the best plan, therefore, to land in the northern parts of Portugal, and I fixed upon Mondego bay, as the nearest place which afforded any facility for landing excepting Peniche; the landing place of which peninsula is defended by a fort occupied by the enemy, which it would be necessary to attack regularly, in order to place the ships in safety. A landing to the northward was further recommended, as it would insure the co-operation of the Portuguese troops on the expedition to Lisbon. The whole of the corps placed under my command, including those under the command of Gen. Spencer, having landed, I propose to march on Wednesday. I shall take the road by Alcobaça and Obidos, with a view to keep up my communication by the sea coast, and to examine the situation of Peniche; and I shall proceed towards Lisbon by the route of Mafra, and by the hills to the northward of that city.

As I understood from the Sec. of State that a body of troops under the command of Brig. Gen. Acland may be expected on the coast of Portugal before you will arrive, I have written to desire that he will proceed from hence along the coast of Portugal to the southward; and I propose to communicate with him by the means of Capt. Bligh, of the *Alfred*, who will attend the movements of the army, with a few transports, having on board provisions and military stores. I intend to order Brig. Gen. Acland to attack Peniche, if I should find it necessary to obtain possession of that place; and if not, I propose to order him to join the fleet stationed off the Tagus, with a view to disembark in one of the bays near the Rock of Lisbon, as soon as I shall approach sufficiently near to enable him to perform that operation

If I imagined that Gen. Acland's corps was equipped in such a manner as to be enabled to move from the coast, I should have directed him to land at Mondego, and to march upon Santarem, from which situation he would have been at hand either to assist my operations or to cut off the retreat of the enemy, if he should endeavor to make it either by the north of the Tagus and Almeida, or by the south of the Tagus and Elvas. But as I am convinced that Gen. Acland's corps is intended to form part of some other corps, which is provided with a commissariat; that he will have none with him; and, consequently, that his corps must depend upon the country; and as no reliance can be placed upon the resources of this country, I have considered it best to direct the General's attention to the sea coast. If, however, the command of the army remained in my hands, I should certainly land the corps which has been lately under the command of Sir J. Moore at Mondego, and should move it upon Santarem.

I have the honor to enclose a return of the troops under my command, and the copy of a letter which I have written to Capt. Malcolm, of the *Donegal*, in which the mode of disposing the transports is stated.

To Lieut. Col. Robe, R.A.   Lavos, 8th Aug. 1808.

I have the honor to acknowledge the receipt of your letter of this date, representing the inadequacy of the assistance in the Civil department of the Ordnance with which you have been provided for this service; the same being only one clerk of stores, who is also Paymaster, and 5 conductors of stores, 2 of whom have never yet joined.

I have to acquaint you, in reply thereto, that although I fully concur with you in considering the establishment insufficient for the performance of all the duties required of it, yet I do not consider myself warranted in giving my authority for the increase of the same, or of granting any allowance to persons holding the temporary appointments in the Ordnance department, until the sanction of the Board be obtained. It is, therefore, not in my power to make the appointment *pro tempore*, specified in the scale annexed to your letter.

I have likewise to acquaint you, in reply to your letter of this date, respecting the appointment of a Brigade Major, in consequence of the junction of the two detachments, by the arrival of Major Gen. Spencer's corps, that however the extension of your duties may render the assistance of such a Staff officer necessary, I have it not in my power to make the appointment, nor to issue allowance to any officer acting in that capacity, without the concurrence of the Board of Ordnance.

To Capt. Malcolm, H.M.S. *Donegal.*   Lavos, 8th Aug. 1808.

The following appears to be the result of the conference which I had with you this morning, respecting the future disposition of the fleet of transports for the convenience and benefit of the service.

That the ships stated in the margin shall sail under convoy of H. M. S. *Alfred*, on the day that the army shall march from this place. I shall communicate to Capt. Bligh the project of the march of the army, and shall request of him to bring to an anchor off the places in the neighbourhood of which we may be on the different days, in order that (if we should require it) we may communicate with him.

That such of the transports as may be, in your opinion, capable of keeping the sea should remain with you at anchor, or otherwise off the Mondego; and that all the remainder should be ordered into Oporto or the Mondego. I beg of you to let me know the names and numbers of each, and their contents. It would be desirable that an officer should be left with each division, to facilitate getting the ships out of these harbours in case an enemy should approach.

That measures should be adopted for giving the Veteran battalion more space; and that in addition to the ships in which that corps is now embarked, 3 of the ships allotted to the 6th regt. should be given to them, and I beg that you will let me know their names. This regiment is then to be sent to the fleet off the Tagus, and it is desirable that the officer who shall take them under his convoy should keep as near to the coast as may be possible.

I shall establish a daily communication with you, and shall let you know regularly my progress; from which you will be enabled to judge, according to circumstances, when it may be necessary for you to move from Mondego bay.

To Visct. Castlereagh.   Lavos, 8th Aug. 1808.

My dispatch contains the fullest information upon every subject, and I have nothing to add to it. I have had the greatest difficulty in organising my commissariat for the march, and that department is very incompetent, notwithstanding the arrangements which I made with Huskisson upon the subject. This department deserves your serious attention. The existence of the army depends upon it, and yet the people who manage it are incapable of managing anything out of a counting house.

I shall be obliged to leave Spencer's guns behind for want of means of moving them; and I should have been obliged to leave my own, if it were not for the horses of the Irish Commissariat. Let nobody ever prevail upon you to send a corps to any part of Europe without horses to draw their guns. It is not true that horses lose their condition at sea.

I have just heard that Joseph Buonaparte left Madrid for France, accompanied by all the French, on the 29th of last month.

I have received your private letter of the 21st July, for which I am much obliged to you. I shall be the junior of the Lieut. Generals; however, I am ready to serve the government wherever and as they please.

To Lieut. Gen. Sir H. Dalrymple.   Lavos, 8th Aug. 1808.

I have been apprised by the Sec. of State that His Majesty has been pleased to appoint you to command his troops employed in this part of Europe, and it becomes my duty to make you acquainted with the situation of affairs in Portugal.

In order to perform this duty in the best manner in my power, I have the honor to enclose the copy of a letter and of its enclosures, which I have written to Lieut. Gen. Sir H. Burrard, who is expected to arrive on the coast of Portugal to command a corps of troops.

To Lieut. Gen. Sir H. Dalrymple.   Lavos, 8th Aug. 1808.

I have the honor to inform you that when I commanded His Majesty's troops employed in this part of the world, I deemed it proper to authorise and direct Major Gen. Spencer, who was at that time, as I imagined, at or near Cadiz, to draw upon the Lords Commissioners of His Majesty's Treasury for the sum of £100,000, and to advance that sum to such persons as the Junta of Seville shall appoint to receive it.

I gave these directions in consequence of the impression I received from Major Gen. Spencer by letter, and verbally by Capt. Cooke, A. A. Gen., of the great distress to which the Junta of Seville were reduced; and from a knowledge which I had, that His Majesty would be disposed to relieve that distress by an advance of money, from what he had been graciously pleased to do in respect of the Junta of Galicia. I desired Gen. Spencer to apprise, by letter, the person who I thought it likely would be sent from England with money for the use of the Junta of Seville, that he had made this advance, and to request him to send £100,000 of the money with which he might be charged to Portugal for the use of the army. Major Gen. Spencer left the coast of Spain before he received these instructions, and, consequently, the Junta of Seville did not receive the aid which I had intended to afford them; and I now apprise you of these circumstances, in order that you may adopt such measures in respect to them as you may think proper.

I apprised the Sec. of State, in a letter which I addressed to him on the 1st Aug., that I had given Gen. Spencer the directions to which I have above referred.

To Lieut. Gen. Sir H. Dalrymple.   Lavos, 8th Aug. 1808.

I have the honor to acknowledge the receipt of your letters of the 16th and 24th July, for which I am much obliged to you. Major Gen. Spencer arrived in Mondego bay on Friday the 5th, and a part of his corps followed him on the 6th. They were disembarked yesterday and this day; but I am sorry to say, that we have not been joined by the detachment of artillery and ordnance which you stated, in your letter of the 24th, that you had directed to join us.

Memorandum for the march of the brigade commanded by Brig. Gen. Fane.
Lavos, 8th Aug. 1808.

Major Gen. Fane will be pleased to march to-morrow morning at 3 o'clock with the brigade under his command (60th regt., 95th regt., 50 dragoons, and detachment of Royal artillery), and take his post in front of St. Giao. Capt. Douglas, A. Q. M. G., will point out the ground. Capt. Gower will attend the column from the camp to show the road. In the evening he will be pleased to push forward some dragoons, with a detachment of 200 infantry, as far as may be judged expedient; and should intelligence be received that the enemy are not at Leiria or in the neighbourhood, Gen. Fane will cause the town of Leiria to be occupied by this detachment either to-morrow evening or on Wednesday morning. Should he find that the enemy are in any force at or in the neighbourhood of Leiria, he will withdraw the detachment and remain in front of St. Giao until he receives orders from Sir A. Wellesley, to whom he will transmit the earliest intelligence he may obtain.

Brig. Gen. Fane will be pleased to cause a detachment to remain in camp to deliver over the camp equipage of the 60th and 95th regts. to the storekeeper, who will be on the ground at 3 o'clock, A.M. to receive it. The tents are to be packed up in bales ready for embarkation, with the number on each bale marked on the outside, and they are to be packed on the waggons by the detachments of the regiments.

An Assist. Commissary will attend the brigade to supply provisions.

He will also make every inquiry respecting the resources which the army may be likely to find at and near Leiria; and Brig. Gen. Fane will be pleased to give him any assistance he may require to execute this duty.

Memorandum for Col. Trant.

5000 stands of English arms will be landed to-morrow morning at Figueira, to be at the disposal of Col. Trant. The intention in landing these arms is, that they should be given to the regular Portuguese troops under the command of Gen. Freire. Of the 5000 stands which they will give up, 500 must be delivered to Col. Trant, in order that they may be given to the deputies of Sines, for whom the Admiral has requested to have 500 stands of arms. These deputies will have a note for Col. Trant, to request him to deliver those arms to them.

Col. Trant will inform me if musket ammunition should be wanted for the 5000 arms. Col. Trant will inquire from Gen. Freire, if a small advance of money would be likely to stimulate the exertions of his troops; and will let me know what amount will be required.

To Major Gen. Hill.   Lavos, 9th Aug. 1808.

I enclose the copy of the orders which I gave Gen. Fane, since which,

G. O.   Lavos, 9th Aug. 1808.

The army will march to-morrow by the right; the mounted dragoons to lead, followed by the 3rd, 5th, and 4th brigades of infantry. The staff corps to precede the column of infantry, and the dismounted dragoons to go to Lavos as a guard to the Commissariat. In addition to the dismounted dragoons, a captain's guard of 50 men, from the 4th brigade, will remain as an escort to the military chest and the Commissariat stores.

All other guards, piquets, and other duties, to be called in at an early hour in the morning; and the tents to be struck and packed in the cases, and the number of tents in each case to be marked upon them, in sufficient time to enable the whole line to move off at 4 o'clock. A small guard to be left by each regiment in charge of the tents, for the purpose of loading them on the carts, and delivering them over to the Commissariat, after which the guards will proceed and join their regiments.

The artillery, dragoons, 45th and 91st regts., will receive 4 days' bread; the staff corps, the 3rd and 4th brigades, 3 days' bread, to complete them all to the 13th inst. inclusive; and the whole will receive one day's meat, to be cooked this afternoon for to-morrow. The issue of these provisions to be made by the Commissary at 3 o'clock this afternoon.

Dr. Deane, physician to the forces, will remain behind to superintend the management of the sick of the brigades left embarked. The assist. surgeons are to act under his directions; and all such arrangements and removals of sick, as he may deem beneficial, are to be complied with.

A stoppage of 4d. per diem, being the difference between the hospital stoppage and that for rations for each sick man requiring extra allowances of wine, vegetables, &c., is to be paid to the medical officer in charge, to provide those necessaries. The purveyor will advance money for this purpose, on account of the paymasters of regiments which have left sick in the ships.

Such sick as are considered incapable of marching, to be at 3 o'clock this afternoon at the Commissary's store in the village of Lavos, where Dr. Deane, physician to the forces, will be ready to take charge of them, and embark them on board the *Enterprise* hospital ship, No. 196. A subaltern officer of Gen. Craufurd's brigade will collect them according to a return which will be furnished him by the D. A. G., and march them down and deliver them over to Dr. Deane.

Such corps as may have had any of their ammunition damaged, will send requisitions, without delay, to the commanding officer of artillery for the number of rounds wanting to complete.

The General Court Martial, of which Major Gen. Hill is the President, is adjourned, and the members will return to their duty.

Three days' grain, and one day's straw for to-morrow, to be issued to-day by the Commissary to the artillery, cavalry, and other horses entitled.

Officers may receive money on account of their bât and forage allowance about to be issued, on application to the Dep. Commissary General.

having received intelligence that rendered it possible that the enemy might be in strength at Leiria, I have directed him to halt, till further orders, at a wood about a mile in front of the advanced post on the high road to Leiria. You will march with your own brigade, and Gen. Ferguson's will join Gen. Fane where he is directed to halt; and you will proceed with the whole to St. Giāo, where you will halt and put up for this day. There is a position with water in front of St. Giao, towards Leiria, which may answer for you. If you should hear that the enemy are already in possession of Leiria, it is not worth while to drive them out this afternoon; but if you should have reason to believe that they are not in possession of Leiria, I recommend that you should allow 200 of the riflemen and a few dragoons to feel their way into Leiria, as it is very important, if the enemy be not already there, that they should not be allowed to get in there this night.

If you should obtain possession with your 200 men, support them with your whole corps, at as early an hour as possible in the morning, and take up your position in front of Leiria, and halt there to-morrow; but if you should find the enemy in possession of Leiria when you arrive at St. Giao, and you should not send on the detachment of the rifle corps, you will halt at St. Giāo in the morning, till I shall join you, which will probably be at 5 or 6 o'clock, and you will be prepared to march at that hour.

P.S. I have desired Ferguson to move with his brigade as soon as he shall have got his bread, and join Gen. Fane, and then proceed on the

---

A. G. O. Lavos, 9th Aug. 1808.

Capt. Taggart's troop of the Irish Commissariat drivers will remain under the orders of the Dep. Commissary General. The other troop will be attached to the Royal Artillery, and will immediately receive their orders from Lieut. Col. Robe.

Brig. Gen. Bowes will be pleased to direct the supernumerary camp kettles of the 8th regt. to be sent to-morrow to Lavos, with the camp equipage.

The Dep. Commissary General will hereafter arrange the payment of the muleteers attached to the artillery, and Lieut. Col. Robe will draw rations for them for the present.

Memorandum.

The formation of the column of march to-morrow morning:

The dragoons to march off from their ground, and form half a mile in front of the artillery park by 4 o'clock A. M.

The 29th and 82nd to follow, and form with the head of their column upon the hill near the artillery park.

The staff corps, and the artillery of the 3rd brigade, will form in the rear of the cavalry.

The 5th and 4th brigades will form with the head of their column upon the cross road leading from their ground just on the right of the artillery, and will take their place in the column of march as it passes them.

The artillery will take care to be in front of the brigades to which they are attached.

The reserve artillery and depot mules, &c., will follow the infantry; then the baggage of head quarters and General officers, the baggage of brigades in succession, the medical stores, the Commissariat mules, &c., depots.

A captain to be left with the equipage, until carts take it off the ground, with a subaltern's guard from Brig. Gen. Nightingall's brigade, a subaltern's guard from Brig. Gen. Bowes' brigade, and a serjeant and 12 privates from the 50th regt. Men for this duty to be selected who are the least capable of marching.

If the camp equipage is got off the ground to-morrow, these guards will proceed forward and join their respective corps; if not, they will remain with the camp equipage until it is removed, and afterwards repair to Figueira, and apply to Capt. Malcolm, R.N., for a transport to embark in.

high road to St. Giao. You will do well to order your brigade to proceed on its march when it shall be ready with bread, &c., and join Gen. Fane yourself immediately, and proceed on to St. Giao with the first brigade that will join you.

To Capt. Bligh, H.M.S. *Alfred*.   Lavos, 9th Aug. 1808.

You will probably receive instructions from Capt. Malcolm to take under your charge certain victualling and ordnance store ships, the names of which are in the margin, with a view to take them down the coast of Portugal, and to endeavor to keep up a communication with the army under my command on its advance towards Lisbon. With this view it is necessary that I should apprise you of the project of my marches, and I have accordingly the honor to inform you that the army will be at Leiria on Thursday the 11th, and at Alcobaça on Friday the 12th, or Saturday the 13th. I mention the last day, as it is possible that I may have to halt one day at Leiria for the Portuguese troops.

I think it desirable that you should not appear off the coast of Nazareth till Friday evening, as otherwise you would acquaint the enemy with my intended route   If I should wish you to be there earlier I shall write to you from Leiria.

At Nazareth you shall hear from me respecting my future plans.

To Lieut. Gen. Sir H. Burrard, Bart.   Camp, 8 miles N. of Leiria, 10th Aug. 1808.

Since I wrote to you on the 8th inst., I have received letters from Mr. Stuart and Col. Doyle from Coruna, of which I enclose copies : from these you will learn the state of the war in that part of Spain; and you will observe that Mr. Stuart and Col. Doyle are of opinion that Marshal Bessieres will take advantage of the inefficiency of the Galician army under Gen. Blake, to detach a corps to Portugal to the assistance of Gen. Junot.

We have not yet heard of this detachment, and I am convinced it will not be made until King Joseph Buonaparte shall either be reinforced to such a degree as to be in safety at Madrid, or till he shall have effected his escape to France; with which view, it is reported, he left Madrid on the 29th of last month : I have therefore, I conceive, time for the operations which I propose to carry on, before a reinforcement can arrive from Leon, even supposing that no obstacles could be opposed to its march in Spain or in Portugal; but it is not probable that it can arrive before the different reinforcements will arrive from England; and as Marshal Bessieres had not more than 20,000 in the action at Rio Seco on the 16th of July, I conceive that the British troops that will be in Portugal will be equal to contend with any part of that corps which he may detach.

The possibility that in the present state of affairs the French corps at present in Portugal may be reinforced, affords an additional reason for taking the position at Santarem, which I apprised you in my letter of the 8th I should occupy, if the command of the army were to remain in my hands after the reinforcements should arrive : if you should occupy it, you will not only be in the best situation to support my operations, and to cut off the retreat of the enemy; but if any reinforcements of French troops should enter Portugal, you will be in the best situation to collect your whole force to oppose them.

To C. Stuart, Esq.   Camp, 8 miles N. of Leiria, 10th Aug. 1808.

I had the pleasure of receiving, this morning, your letter of the 2d, for which I am very much obliged to you.

I do not think that Bessieres will venture to make a detachment towards this country till King Joseph Buonaparte shall be in safety in Madrid, or shall have made good his retreat into France, upon which it is said that he had already set out on the 29th of last month.

In either of these cases, I think it probable that an effort will be made to reinforce Junot, which however will be opposed by many natural obstacles in this country, as well as by the forces in Spanish Estremadura, through which province I conclude the reinforcement will pass rather than through the Portuguese provinces of Tras os Montes and Entre Minho e Douro. At all events, I hope to bring to a conclusion the operations, with the conduct of which I am entrusted, before this reinforcement can enter Portugal; and if I should not, I have reason to expect that 15,000 men will soon arrive here under the command of Sir Harry Burrard, who will be more than a match for Junot and Bessieres together.

I was joined by Gen. Spencer on the 6th and 7th. This corps landed in Mondego bay on the 7th and 8th. The advanced guard marched yesterday, and I have marched this day. I shall have with me about 5000 Portuguese troops, of which there are about 10,000 in all. The other 5000 are employed partly in taking care of Oporto, and partly in a distant blockade of Almeida; but these last have marched to Castello Branco, I believe, to join the Spanish detachment which is watching Loison's motions. This General left Lisbon on the 26th July, with 4000 or 5000 men (I believe before he knew that we were arrived on the coast), crossed the Tagus, and attacked at Evora a Spanish detachment of about 1000 men from the province of Estremadura, which had entered Alentejo, and some Portuguese peasants and troops, whom he entirely defeated. The object of this march appears to have been to relieve the garrison of Elvas, which has been effected, and to give a check to the insurrection in that part of Portugal. Loison was at Elvas on the 3d Aug., and he is now expected, and his arrival apprehended in all parts of Portugal. But I imagine that he will hasten back to oppose me. Be so good as to communicate this letter to Col. Doyle.

I am concerned that our friends of the Junta do not get on well. If we are lucky in this country, and can beat Junot well, and take Elvas

---

G. O.   Lugar, 10th Aug. 1808.

The 3rd brigade will throw out a piquet to its right, the 4th to its left, and the 5th to its front, near the village of Lugar.

The meat brought for to-day to be cooked; and if the Assist. Commissaries of brigades come up in time, they will issue one day's meat for to-morrow, to be cooked this evening.

The artillery, dragoons, the 3rd, 4th, and 5th brigades, will march at 4 o'clock tomorrow morning, and in the same order as to-day.

and Almeida, we might soon have a general Cortes. I have heard nothing from the south of Spain since the capitulation of Dupont.

To the Dep. Commissary Gen.   Leiria, 11th Aug. 1808.

I beg that you will make a requisition upon the Portuguese Commissary or magistrates here for 80 waggons with bullocks, to be in this town to morrow, in order to release a similar number arrived from Lavos with the army, which are to be discharged.

To Lieut. Col. Gordon*, Mil. Sec. to H.R.H. Com. in Chief.   Leiria, 11th Aug. 1808.

I have the honor to acquaint you, for the information of H. R. H. the Commander in Chief, that I found, before the landing of the army under my command in this country, that the exigencies of the service required that I should make an issue of bat and forage money to the officers of the different regiments, and forage money to the officers of the Staff. In my orders for the payment of the same, I have been entirely guided by the schedule of rates enclosed in H. R. H.'s letter of the 14th June, with the exception of the Deputy Commissary General, to whom I was induced to authorise an issue of 20 rations, in consequence of that allowance being specified in his instructions from the Lords of the Treasury. As many officers of the army have, however, made strong representations to me upon the subject of their allowances, I feel it my duty to refer them to the consideration of his Royal Highness, who will, of course, be better able to judge how far it may be proper to make them known to the Lords of the Treasury.

I have been informed that the A. A. G.'s have been in the habit of receiving, for many years back, 10 rations of forage money; but at present they only receive 6 rations, which is 4 less than what is allowed to Aides

* Gen. Sir Willoughby Gordon, G.C.B., Quarter Master General.

G. O.   Leiria, 11th Aug. 1808.

The duties of field officer and adjutant to the piquets of the line are discontinued, and will be performed by brigades, commencing to-day. Each brigade to furnish both an outlying and inlying piquet of a captain and 50 men, with a proportion of officers and noncommissioned officers from each regiment, under the orders of a field officer of the brigade. Care to be taken that the sentries of the outlying piquets of each brigade are double, and communicate with those of the brigades or corps to their right and left whenever circumstances will admit of it. The General officer of the day will visit such of the piquets as he may think necessary, and they will receive their orders from him. All the field officers of piquets will report to him whenever any thing particular occurs.

In column of march the light infantry companies of brigades will move at the head of their respective brigades, and be thrown out to either flank as circumstances may require.

The pioneers of brigades will also march in future at the head of their brigades in front of the light infantry companies, and the mules or horses conveying the camp kettles of companies, and the surgeons' field chest, and the bill hooks, will march in the intervals between the divisions, and be made to keep up with their respective corps.

The line of parade or defence of the brigades and corps will always be established when they take up their ground after a march; and if the troops are required to halt, they will make their huts as near to that line as possible.

Commanding officers of corps are referred to His Majesty's regulations respecting the number of bâtmen allowed to officers, and will take care that it is on no account exceeded.

A pint of wine per man to be issued this evening, at 5 o clock, by the respective Assist. Commissaries of brigades; and such corps as did not receive meat yesterday for to-day, will be supplied with it immediately. Meat for to-morrow to be issued to the army as soon after daylight in the morning as possible.

de Camp and Brigade Majors, although the latter are Staff situationsof an inferior rank. The Surgeons of regiments have likewise represented to me that the present regulation deprives them of the means of carrying their medicine chest, which has of late years been provided for by their being on a footing with Captains *with* companies. By the present issue, and in conformity with the schedule above referred to, they are paid as Captains *without* companies, and have no allowance for the carriage of the medicine chest but the 10*l.* allowed as preparation money on embarkation in England.

These are the principal and best founded objections to the schedule of rates of bat and forage money transmitted to me by his Royal Highness, which, it appears, had been approved of by the Lords of the Treasury, notwithstanding that their Lordships have departed from it in the instructions which they have given to the Dep. Commissary Gen. I shall not, however, deviate from the orders of his Royal Highness.

To Lieut. Col. Gordon.   Leiria, 11th Aug. 1808.

I have the honor to inform you that the corps of His Majesty's troops placed under my command, which sailed from Cork on the 10th July, arrived off the coast of Portugal on the 23d of that month, and on the 26th the fleet of transports anchored in Mondego bay, at the recommendation of Adm. Sir C. Cotton, and I went to the fleet at the mouth of the Tagus, to communicate personally with the Admiral on the service, the performance of which had been entrusted to us. After a full consideration of the subject, it appeared to us both that a landing in the bay, or in the neighbourhood of the Rock of Lisbon, was a very difficult and precarious operation, whether viewed in relation to the strength of the works erected for their defence, to the impossibility of approaching them with the ships of war, or to the state of the surf and its increase with different winds. To these circumstances were to be added the neighbourhood of the enemy to the probable place of landing, with the whole of his forces, and the impossibility of procuring in the country so near Lisbon, and exhausted as it was, all the means which were requisite to move the provisions and stores which were necessary for the troops.

We considered also, that by making a landing further to the northward we should have the advantage of the co-operation of the Portuguese troops, and of the means of the countries in insurrection against the French government for the supply of His Majesty's troops. We therefore determined to land in Mondego bay, on the northern bank of which, at the entrance of the river, the Admiral had already occupied a small Portuguese redoubt, with 300 marines.

I returned to the fleet on the 30th July, and on the 1st Aug. I commenced the disembarkation of the troops, which, on account of the surf which prevails along the coast of Portugal, was not completed till the 5th. On the 6th Gen. Spencer's corps, which had remained on shore in Andalusia till the 21st, when the General heard of the surrender of the French army under Gen. Dupont to the Spanish troops under Gen. Castanos, arrived in Mondego bay, and was landed on the 7th and 8th. In the mean time all the arrangements had been made for the march of the army, and for the supply of the troops on their way to Lisbon; and the advanced guard moved on the 9th, and the main body yesterday, when the former arrived here, and the latter this day. The Portuguese troops have also broken up from the positions they had for some time occupied in the neighbourhood of Coimbra and they will arrive here to-morrow.

The French army in Portugal is said to consist of about 16,000 men in the whole, of which number about 5000 or 6000 occupy Lisbon, Forts St. Julian and Cascaes, and the other works erected for the defence of the Tagus and of the Bay of Lisbon; 800 in Peniche, 600 in Almeida, 600 in Elvas, and, it is said, 1600 in Setuval: of the disposable force about 4000 are at Alcobaca, about 16 miles from hence, under Gens. Laborde and Thomiere; and the remainder, under Gens. Junot and Loison, are in the neighbourhood of Santarem, on the high road to Lisbon. There are many strong positions on both roads, which I imagine the enemy intend to contest. I shall march by the first, as, although circuitous, I shall be enabled to communicate with a small fleet of victualling and store ships, under charge of Capt. Bligh, of H. M. S. *Alfred,* who will attend the march of the army.

I have the satisfaction to inform you that the people of the country have done everything in their power to assist His Majesty's troops, and have received them in every respect as friends. I have the pleasure to add, that the troops, on the other hand, have conducted themselves remarkably well, and I have not heard one complaint of them since the army landed.

To Lieut. Col. Gordon.   Leiria, 11th Aug. 1808.

I have but little to add to my public letter of this day, which, of course, you will lay before his Royal Highness.

Some letters which I have received from Col. Doyle and Mr. Stuart, dated the 2d, at Coruna, mention the inefficiency of the Galician army, and the probability that it will be employed only to cover the frontiers of Galicia. They therefore suspect that Bessieres, whose corps is at or in the neighbourhood of Leon, will detach to the aid of Junot.

I do not imagine that Bessières will venture to make any detachment until King Joseph Buonaparte shall have made his retreat into France, with which view he left Madrid on the 29th July. If I am right in this conjecture, Bessieres' detachment will not be in Portugal, even if its march should not be delayed by the difficulties of the country and by the efforts of the inhabitants of Spain and Portugal, until after I shall be in Lisbon, or, at all events, until our reinforcements shall have arrived.

To Lieut. Gen. Sir H. Burrard, Bart.   Leiria, 11th Aug. 1808.

In my official letters of the 8th and 10th I have apprised you of the state of the war in this country and in Spain, and I shall adopt this mode of communicating to you what I know of the resources of this country, and those matters of which it will be convenient to you to be apprised in the operations which you will have to conduct.

In the first place, in the present season of the year, you cannot depend upon the country for bread. Portugal never fed itself during more than 7 months out of 12. The common consumption of the country is Indian corn; and the little which there is in the country cannot be ground at this season of the year, as the mills are generally turned by water, and there is now no water in the mill streams; you must therefore depend upon your transports for bread. Wine and beef you will get in the country; and in a short time, straw and Indian corn, or barley, for your horses; but the supply of these articles will not last long: this, however, is a consideration for a future period.

I conclude that you will have come equipped with horses to draw your artillery; you will want, therefore, mules to draw the carriages of your reserve musket ammunition, and some to carry a few days' provisions to march with the troops. I have ordered 150 draught mules at Oporto, with which, if they had come in time, I should have drawn Gen. Spencer's brigade of artillery, and you will of course take them. If you will write to the Bishop of Oporto about them, he will send them to you. As for mules for carriage, I am afraid you will get none; for I believe my corps has swept the country, very handsomely, of this animal. You must therefore depend for the carriage of your bread upon the carts of the country, drawn by bullocks; each of these will carry about 600 lbs., and will travel in a day about 12 miles; but I do not believe that any power that you could exert over them, particularly when they shall have already made an exertion against the enemy, by the assistance which they have given to me, would induce the owners of the carts to go from their homes a greater distance than to the nearest place where you could get carts to relieve them. I think, therefore, that, if you should determine to march upon Santarem, you should, in the first instance, form a magazine of bread upon Leiria. Santarem is about 30 miles distant from hence; and this place is about 27 miles from the landing place in the Mondego. A magazine here would be safe, until the enemy should quit the Tagus to join a corps, which should enter Portugal by the Douro for his relief. You might be here as soon as he, and, at all events, your magazine would not be in danger unless he should quit the Tagus, which would give you possession of that river, and all the facilities of forming your magazine wherever you might please, as high up as Abrantes. With a view, therefore, to your first operation in Portugal, which I will suppose to be to march to Santarem, I would recommend to you to form a magazine of 10 days' bread and 5 days' meat, in case of accidents, at Leiria; and then to keep that quantity up or to increase it as you may find it convenient for your purposes at Santarem. You will probably find it convenient to increase it, in which you will experience no difficulty. You will find the people of this country well disposed to assist you with every thing in their power, but they have very little in their power, and they have been terribly plundered by the French.

I shall desire the Commissary to let your Commissary know the price of the hire of carts and mules, and of other articles purchased by him The Q. M. G. shall be directed to make your Q. M. G. acquainted with every thing relative to the roads, &c.

To Gen. Freire, Portuguese Army.   Calvario, 13th Aug. 1808.

Lieut. Col. Trant informed me this morning of the distress which your troops were likely to suffer from want of bread, and he earnestly urged me, on the part of your Excellency, to issue bread to the Portuguese troops from the British Commissariat.

I must beg leave to call to your Excellency's recollection what I have repeatedly told you, that it was not in my power to supply the Portuguese troops with bread; and, in fact, when your Excellency shall reflect upon my situation in this country, the distant prospect that Portugal will, in

---

M. G. O   Leiria, 12th Aug. 1808.

The General Court Martial, of which Major Gen. Hill is the President. will reassemble at 9 o'clock this morning, at the D. A. G.'s office, near head quarters, for the trial of two deserters from the —— regt., and such other prisoners as may be ordered before it. All evidences to be immediately warned to attend.

The army will march to-morrow morning. The hour and order of march will be hereafter specified.

The three light companies of Major Gen. Hill's brigade, under the command of a field officer, to assemble on the bridge leading to the great Lisbon road, to wait there till further orders.

G. O.   Leiria, 12th Aug. 1808.

Representations having been made that Assist. Commissaries —— and —— have in some instances disobeyed the orders of the Dep. Commissary General, the Lieut. General contents himself at present with thus noticing the circumstance; but should a similar complaint be again made to him, his disapprobation will be marked in a much stronger manner.

The Assist. Commissaries of brigades are distinctly to understand that the issues of provisions and forage they may be required to make by the General Orders, must always be punctually delivered at the particular hour specified.

The army to be completed by the Assist. Commissaries of brigades, at 3 o'clock, to 4 days' bread up to the 16th inst. inclusive, and an issue of one day's forage to be likewise made from the commissariat stores in the principal square of the town.

Head quarters, the general staff of the army departments, and the artillery not attached to brigades, and other unattached corps, will, in future, draw their provisions and forage from Assist. Commissary Aylmer.

Regimental surgeons will send returns to the D. A. G.'s office, addressed to the Inspector of Hospitals, of the medicines and surgical field equipments with them for immediate use, specifying the manner in which they are conveyed.

The brigade majors are henceforward always to encamp or quarter themselves close to their respective brigades; and whenever they have occasion to be absent, must appoint an adjutant to do their duty. They are also to report, in writing, to the D. A. G., the quarters of their respective brigadiers whenever they change them.

A. G. O.   Leiria, 12th Aug. 1808.

The sick inspected this morning by the staff surgeons, and found incapable of marching, are to be sent, as soon as possible, under the charge of an assistant surgeon from each brigade, to the Portuguese hospital in town, where a medical staff officer will attend to receive them, under the charge of Dr. Hume, and the usual stoppages for men in hospital are to be charged against them.

The 2d, 3d, and 4th brigades will each send, in the course of this afternoon, to head quarters, a serjeant as permanent orderly to the Lieut. General.

The army will march to-morrow morning at 4 o'clock, in 2 columns, by their right; the right column composed of the 20th light dragoons, the staff corps, the 6th, 1st, 3d, and 5th brigades of infantry, the artillery park, and the commissariat depôt. This column will be conducted by Major Rainey, A. Q. M. G. Capt. Gomm will conduct the 3d and 5th brigades in the second line through the town.

The left column, composed of 50 dragoons of the 20th, and 50 of the Portuguese cavalry, the 2d and 4th brigades of infantry and Portuguese troops, will proceed by Batalha. This column will be conducted by Capt. Langton. Ensign Laing, of the staff corps, will lead the 4th brigade from their present ground through the town.

All waggons will be kept with the right column. One gun, without a car, will proceed with the left column; the remainder of the half brigade of artillery, attached to the 2d brigade, will join and accompany the park.

All guards, excepting that over the commissariat stores, and the Provost Marshal's, to be withdrawn in the morning, and to join their corps before the army marches.

The parole and countersign are in future to be given out at sunset, until further orders.

The General Court Martial, of which Major Gen. Hill is the President, is dissolved.

any reasonable time, be able to supply the wants of bread by the British troops; the distance at which we are placed from Great Britain, from whence we must draw our supplies of bread, under these circumstances; and, above all, that I have not made any previous arrangements to answer so extraordinary a demand on the part of your Excellency, you will, I am convinced, do me the justice to believe, that in declining to comply with your wishes, upon this occasion, I have been actuated solely by an attention to those circumstances attending our situation at the present moment, which are most likely to have a fatal influence on the success of the service in which we are both employed.

I beg leave to recal to your Excellency's recollection what I told you at Oporto, that I could only supply bread to the British troops; that I repeated this to you at Monte Mor o Velho; and I apprised you in both these conferences that I should require wine and meat for my soldiers, and straw and corn for the horses and cattle attached to the army. I moved forward in great haste, and at great inconvenience to the army, in order to save the depôt formed at Leiria, as I understand, for the use of the British troops. But when I arrived there, having learned from the Portuguese Commissary, that if he delivered the bread to my troops, there would be none for those under the command of your Excellency, I declined to ask for it, and actually received nothing at Leiria excepting wine for one day.

I am really much concerned that your Excellency's troops should suffer

---

G. O.   Calvario, 13th Aug. 1808.

The army will march at 4 o'clock to-morrow morning.

It is the Lieut. General's desire that, in route marching, a regular steady pace should be preserved by the leading divisions of corps, without reference to those immediately preceding them. It is even desirable that each company or division should be led at an uniformly regular pace by its officer, without attention to the exact preservation of intervals, which is of less importance.

As it is found inconvenient for the mules carrying the camp kettles to march in the intervals of divisions according to the orders of the 11th inst., they will in future follow in rear of their respective brigades; but the mule or horse carrying the surgeon's field chest will proceed in rear of its particular regiment.

No baggage whatever is to precede the light and 1st brigades when the army marches by the right; nor the light and 2d when marching by the left. The mules of both, with the led horses of officers and of the cavalry, will march in the rear of the latter of the two front brigades, and all the wheel carriages will follow the artillery park.

The Dep. Commissary General will issue rations for the prisoners in the Provost guard, on the requisition of the Dep. Provost Marshal.

A. G. O.   Calvario, 13th Aug. 1808.

Brig. Gen. Fane will be pleased to inspect the 20th light dragoons, at 6 o'clock this evening, upon their own ground, and report as soon as possible to the Lieut. General the number of men, horses, and saddles, effective and serviceable, belonging to that corps.

The army will march at half-past 4 o'clock to-morrow, in 2 columns, from their right. The right column will consist of 50 dragoons and the 1st brigade, with the half brigade of artillery attached to it. The commissariat will follow in rear of this column. Capt. Gomm, D. A. Q. M. G., will conduct it, and Capt. Mawe will lead the head of the commissariat depôt. The left column will be composed of the British and Portuguese cavalry, the 6th brigade, the staff corps, the 3d, 5th, 4th, and 2d brigades, with their artillery. They will form on their own parades. The cavalry will move off at half-past 4 o'clock along the road on its right, guided by Major Rainey, A. Q. M. G.; the 6th brigade will follow the cavalry; the 3d the 6th, and the 5th the 3d. Capt. Langton, D. A. Q. M. G., will guide the 4th and 2d brigades to the road. The park of artillery and spare ammunition will follow the left column. The 50th regt. will remain on its present ground until half-past 7 o'clock, when it will move off, and follow in rear of the baggage of the left column.

any distress; but you must be aware that the arrangements for providing for them have not fallen upon me; and that I have not required a greater proportion of the resources of the country (particularly not bread) than is necessary for those of His Majesty; and I trust that your Excellency will see the propriety of adopting some arrangement which will provide effectually for the subsistence of the army which you will march to Lisbon; at the same time, that you will allow His Majesty's troops to enjoy such of the resources of the country as I have above mentioned, which they require.

As it is now certain that Gen. Loison has marched from Thomar towards Torres Novas, I do not see any inconvenience that can result to your Excellency from halting at Leiria this day, or perhaps to-morrow, at which time I hope you will have it in your power to make the arrangements for your supply which I have recommended.

To Lieut. Col. Trant.   Calvario, 13th Aug. 1808. ½ past 4, P.M.

I have just received your letter of this date, and I am concerned to find that the arrangements to enable the Portuguese army to take the field, in co-operation with the British troops, have been so much neglected as to render that measure impracticable. I have written to Gen. Freire this day upon the subject of his supplies, upon which I have nothing further to say. As to his plan of operations, I do not see what purpose it is to answer, in view to the result of the campaign; and I certainly can never give my sanction to any thing which appears so useless, and so crudely digested, so far as even to promise to communicate with or aid the person who is carrying it into execution.

I have one proposition to make to Gen. Freire, that is, that he should send me his cavalry and his light infantry, and a corps of 1000 regular infantry, to be employed as I choose, and I engage to give these men their bread; and for meat, wine, and forage, they shall fare as well as our troops. If he will accept of this proposition, let the troops join me to-morrow at Alcobaça. If he does not, I beg that he will carry on such operations as he may think proper.

I shall execute the orders which I have received from my government without the assistance of the Portuguese government; and Gen. Freire will have to justify himself with the existing government of Portugal, with his Prince, and with the world, for having omitted to stand forward upon this interesting occasion, and for having refused to send me the assistance which it is in his power to give. I propose sending the correspondence which has passed on this subject to the Bishop of Oporto.

In respect to yourself, as it appears to me that no object is answered by your remaining with Gen. Freire, with whom I do not see how I can have any communication, you may as well come away, if he should persist in his intention not to send me the cavalry or the infantry; otherwise, or if he should intend to co-operate more nearly in our plan of operations, I shall beg of you to stay with him.

P.S. Upon again reading over the plan of operations, it appears to me to be decided upon, as the army is to march this night; if so, I see no reason whatever why you should stay with Gen. Freire.

To Lieut. Col. Trant.   Alcobaca, 14th Aug. 1808.

The army arrived here at 10 this morning, the enemy having retreated from their position in the night, of which circumstance I beg you to acquaint Gen. Freire.

I now beg leave to communicate to you, for his information, the few observations which I intended to make upon the plan of operations which he intended to adopt with his own corps. I have to observe, in the first place, that it is entirely foreign to any co-operation with me; and it must be considered as distinct in itself, and unconnected with my troops.

It is obvious, that whether I am too weak to contend with Gen. Junot, or sufficiently strong for him, there is nothing in common between the Portuguese troops and me. My object is to obtain possession of Lisbon, and to that I must adhere, whatever may be the consequence, till I shall have attained it, as being the first and greatest step towards dispossessing the French of Portugal. They may fight an action with me and retire, or they may retire without fighting, or, what I hope is least probable, they may defeat me. In the last hypothesis, I have no assistance from Gen. Freire; and in the first two, which I hope are the most probable, I must give my attention to obtaining possession of Lisbon and the Tagus, and leave Gen. Junot to retreat where he pleases and to do what he pleases.

I should like to know what it is most probable he will do, in case he should be either defeated by me, or retire and leave me to march unmolested to Lisbon? He will fall upon that which is most justly called the *noyau* of the Portuguese army; the new foundation and hopes of the monarchy; which will as certainly be destroyed as it exists, if Gen. Freire persists in adopting this plan of operations.

Let him contemplate the relative strength of the two armies; and let him reflect upon the consequences of an action between Gen. Junot and me. With his superiority of cavalry is it possible that, supposing I am successful in the action, they will not remain sufficiently unbroken to be able still to destroy that which Gen. Freire commands; and will Junot thus have any other object? But Gen. Freire reckons upon my pursuing Junot, and not allowing this misfortune to befal the Portuguese troops: so I will, when I shall be certain of the possession of Lisbon and the Tagus; but positively not till that moment.

Let us now examine why this plan is adopted? The General says it is necessary in order to subsist his troops: I say it is not! He could find

---

G. O.   Alcobaca, 14th Aug. 1808.

The army will march at half-past 4 to-morrow morning; the order of march will be given out in the evening.
(*The detail of the issue of provisions and forage.*)

A. G. O.   Alcobaca, 14th Aug. 1808.

The army will march to-morrow, in two columns, by the right.
(*The detail as before, with little variation.*)

A body of Portuguese cavalry and infantry, which has joined the army, will march in rear of the right column; but from the lateness of the hour at which it arrived this night, it will not move to-morrow until 8 o'clock. Lieut. Col. Trant, A. Q. M. G., will do duty with this corps, and all communications with it are to be made through the medium of that officer.

some subsistence everywhere, and good arrangements would bring plenty. In this very town I got this day as much bread as would have subsisted the whole Portuguese army; and I am convinced, from what I see of the country next the sea coast, through which I shall march, that it is the richest in Portugal. I declare that I think the plan of operations proposed is so defective and dangerous, that I would recommend to the General, if he will not accompany me, rather to remain at Leiria, or march here; and he can be supplied at either place; and to wait in security the event of a contest which must take place in a few days.

The enemy are said to be at Obidos, where I shall march to-morrow.

P.S. The Portuguese detachment allotted to me are not yet arrived, but I conclude they will be here this evening.

To Capt. Bligh, H.M.S. *Alfred.*   Alcobaca, 14th Aug. 1808.

The head of 120 carts are just about to leave this place, to bring away the bread and oats, for which I wrote this morning; and I hope they will return here, loaded, to-morrow. The dragoons and their horses will go in the morning, at daylight, for their saddles, &c., and I shall order them to return in the evening.

The enemy have retired to Obidos, about 20 miles from hence; and I propose to follow them in the morning, leaving the articles which you will land for me to follow. If they should quit Obidos, I shall occupy that place to-morrow; and on the next day I shall reconnaitre Peniche. If the enemy should stay at Obidos, I shall either attack them or turn them on the next day; that is, Tuesday. I should think that they will stay, as I imagine that Loison has joined the detachment which was here with about 5000 men. They had 3000 or 4000 here.

It might be very useful to me if you would appear off Peniche with your little fleet on Tuesday morning, the 16th inst. It is possible that I may not reconnaitre that place till Wednesday, or possibly not at all; as I may find another line of operation more convenient to me in a view to my ultimate destination. But if I should not go to Obidos, or if I should give up all thoughts of communicating with you at Peniche, I shall take care to send you a letter by this place, which will be forwarded to you from Nazareth.

I have not yet finally determined upon our next point of communication after Peniche, for the reasons which I have above stated. I rather believe it will be Ericeira, near Mafra; but upon this point I shall write to you again this night, after I shall have more perfectly ascertained roads, distances, position of the enemy, &c. Everything is going on well; but the Portuguese troops have not joined us.

I propose to send you this night three French Commissaries, who were taken 2 days ago at Thomar. I shall write you a line with them.

P.S. If you should have an opportunity, let the Admiral and Malcolm know that you have heard from me.

To Visc. Castlereagh.   Caldas, 16th Aug. 1808.

I have the honor to enclose copies of letters which I have received some days ago from Mr. Stuart and Col. Doyle, from Coruna, and copies of letters which I have in consequence written to Sir H. Burrard, to be delivered to him upon his arrival on the coast of Portugal.

To Visc. Castlereagh.   Caldas, 16th Aug. 1808.

I marched from Lavos on the 10th, and was joined at Leiria on the 12th by the Portuguese troops under Gen. B. Freire, consisting of between 5000 and 6000 men. But I am concerned to inform your lordship that they have not accompanied me any farther. Since my arrival in this country, Gen. B. Freire, and the other Portuguese officers, had expressed a wish that the British Commissariat should support the Portuguese troops from the British stores during the campaign; particularly in a meeting which I had with them at Oporto on the night of the 24th July, and in another at Monte Mór o Velho on the 7th inst.; and upon both these occasions I told them explicitly that it was impossible to supply their wants from the British stores; that those stores were formed with a view to the consumption of the British only, and that but during a short time; and that it was a proposition of a novel nature to require an army landing from its ships not only to supply its own consumption of bread, but likewise that of the army of the state to whose assistance it had been sent. I told the Portuguese officers, however, that I believed I should not have occasion to call upon the country to supply bread during my march towards Lisbon; but that I should require beef, wine, and forage, all of which the Bishop of Oporto engaged should be supplied to me.

Before I marched to Leiria, the Portuguese officers earnestly urged

---

G. O.   Caldas, 15th Aug. 1808.

(*The detail of the issue of provisions and forage, and the order of the march.*)

Three days' bread to be issued to the troops to-morrow, to complete them to the 19th inst. inclusive.

G. O.   Caldas, 16th Aug. 1808.

The army will march to-morrow: the hour and order of march will be made known in the evening.

(*Detail of the issue of provisions and forage.*)

The Lieut. General being informed that many irregularities are committed, and risk incurred by the soldiers strolling to a distance from their lines, the General officers, and officers commanding corps, will be pleased to put a stop to this practice, and prevent the soldiers from going beyond their lines without a written pass, signed by a commissioned officer; and they are not to enter any town or village without their side arms, and being dressed in the uniform of their corps. Such soldiers as may be taken up for a disobedience of this order, are not to receive the allowance of wine given from time to time to the troops as an indulgence only.

Regimental surgeons will report the state of their sick, personally, to the Inspector of Hospitals, without delay, and the same is to be done on every halting day.

The Portuguese troops, acting with the army, are to be provisioned by the Dep. Commissary General in the same manner as the British.

General officer for the day, to-morrow, Brig. Gen. Bowes.

A. G. O.

The army will move off from their present ground at half-past 4 o'clock to-morrow morning, and assemble in contiguous columns of brigades, right in front, in the plain on this side the castle of Obidos.

(*Detail of the order of march.*)

One captain, 2 subalterns, 2 serjeants, 1 drummer, and 50 R. and F., from the 2d brigade, to be added to the guard already over the commissariat depôt and military chest, at 4 o'clock to-morrow morning; and the officers and non-commissioned officers of these guards are held responsible that their men keep sober, and abstain from taking any of the public stores placed under their charge.

my early advance, to secure a magazine which had been formed at that
place, as I understood, for the use of the British troops, and my advance
certainly saved it from the enemy. But I received no supply from the
magazine, which was left entire for the use of the Portuguese army. On
the evening, however, of the arrival of the Portuguese army at Leiria,
some very extraordinary messages were sent to me respecting their supplies; and in a conversation which I had with him that night, Gen. Freire
expressed his anxiety upon the subject. The plan of the march for the
next morning was communicated to him, and the hour for the departure
of the Portuguese troops was fixed. Instead of making the march, however,
as had been agreed upon, I received from Gen. Freire a proposition for a
new plan of operations, which was to take the Portuguese troops to a distance from the British army, by Thomar, towards Santarem, unless I
should consent to feed the whole of them; and the pretext for the adoption
of this plan was the probable want of supplies on the road which I had
proposed to take, and their great plenty in the proposed quarter; and that
the Portuguese troops would be in a situation to cut off the retreat of the
French from Lisbon.

In my reply, I pointed out the inefficiency and danger of this plan,
and requested the General to send me 1000 infantry, all his cavalry, and
his light troops, which I engaged to feed; and I recommended to him
either to join me himself with the remainder, or at all events to remain at
Leiria. or at Alcobaca, or somewhere in my rear, where at least his own
troops would be in safety. He has sent me the troops which I have required, to the amount of 1400 infantry, and 260 cavalry; but he has
announced to me that he intends to persevere in his proposed plan of
operations for the remainder of his army, notwithstanding that I have
informed him that I have found resources in the country fully adequate
to the subsistence of his troops.

I have been thus particular in detailing to your Lordship the circumstances which have attended, for I am certain they have not occasioned,
the separation of the Portuguese army from that of His Majesty. There
must have been in the magazine at Leiria bread for the Portuguese
troops for 2 days. I found at Alcobaca a sufficiency to last them one day,
and more might have been procured; and this town would have afforded
ample supplies.

Gen. Freire has been apprised of this state of the resources, and yet he
perseveres in his plan; and I acknowledge that I can attribute it only to
his apprehensions, which, however, he has never hinted to me, that we are
not sufficiently strong for the enemy. I am convinced that he can have
no personal motive for his conduct, as I have been always on the most
cordial good terms with him; I have supplied him with arms, ammunition,
and flints, and have done every thing in my power for his army; and only
on the day before he communicated to me the alteration of his plan for
the march of his army, he voluntarily placed himself and his troops under
my command.

Having found the resources of the country more ample than I expected,
I should certainly have undertaken to feed his army according to his
desire; as I consider it of importance, on political rather than on military

grounds, that the Portuguese troops should accompany our march; only that I have found the British Commissariat to be so ill composed as to be incapable of distributing even to the British troops the ample supplies which have been procured for them; and I did not wish to burden them with the additional charge of providing and distributing supplies to the Portuguese army. Besides, as I have above explained to your Lordship I do not believe the motive stated is that which has caused the determination to which I have adverted.

I marched from Leiria on the 13th, and arrived at Alcobaca on the 14th, which place the enemy had abandoned in the preceding night; and I arrived here yesterday. The enemy, about 4000 in number, were posted about 10 miles from hence at Rolica; and they occupied Obidos, about 3 miles from hence, with their advanced posts. As the possession of this last village was important to our future operations, I determined to occupy it; and as soon as the British infantry arrived upon the ground, I directed that it might be occupied by a detachment consisting of 4 companies of riflemen of the 60th and 95th regts.

The enemy, consisting of a small piquet of infantry and a few cavalry, made a trifling resistance and retired; but they were followed by a detachment of our riflemen to the distance of 3 miles from Obidos. The riflemen were there attacked by a superior body of the enemy, who attempted to cut them off from the main body of the detachment to which they belonged, which had now advanced to their support; larger bodies of the enemy appeared on both the flanks of the detachments; and it was with difficulty that Major Gen. Spencer, who had gone out to Obidos when he heard that the riflemen had advanced in pursuit of the enemy, was enabled to effect their retreat to that village. They have since remained in possession of it, and the enemy have retired entirely from the neighbourhood.

In this little affair of the advanced post, which was occasioned solely by the eagerness of the troops in pursuit of the enemy, I am concerned to add that Lieut. Bunbury, of the 2d batt., 95th regt., was killed, and the Hon. Capt. Pakenham* wounded, but slightly; and we have lost some men, of whose numbers I have not received the returns.

Besides the corps of about 4000 men, commanded by Gens. Laborde and Thomiere, which is retiring in front of the army by the sea road towards Lisbon, there is another corps, consisting of about 5000 men, assembled at Rio Maior, under Gen. Loison, which I conclude will retire by the great Lisbon road, and they will probably join near Lisbon with whatever troops can be spared from the defence of the fortifications.

Loison's corps has lately been employed in Alentejo against a Spanish detachment of about 1000 men, and the Portuguese insurgents in that quarter, and with a view to the relief of Elvas. I understand that it has suffered much in the expedition, as well by the fatigue of the marches which it has made as by the opposition it has met with.

When I was at Alcobaca I communicated with Capt. Bligh, of the *Alfred*, who was detained off Nazareth with a convoy of victuallers and ordnance store ships, and he landed a supply, which I hope to receive this evening;

* Major Gen. the Hon. Sir Hercules Pakenham, K.C.B.

and he is now off Peniche, where I intend, if possible, to communicate with him to-morrow morning.

To Visct. Castlereagh.   Caldas, 16th Aug. 1808.

I have but little to add to my letters of this day. We are going on as well as possible; the army in high order, and in great spirits. We make long marches, to which they are becoming accustomed; and I make no doubt they will be equal to anything when we shall reach Lisbon. I have every hope of success. The affair of the advanced posts of yesterday evening was unpleasant, because it was quite useless; and was occasioned, contrary to orders, solely by the imprudence of the officer, and the dash and eagerness of the men: they behaved remarkably well, and did some execution with their rifles.

I send you the history of our separation from the Portuguese army, that you may communicate upon it with De Sousa.* If you should determine to form a Portuguese army, you must, if possible, have nothing to do with Gen. Freire. The fact is, they are afraid of the French; they are incapable of making any arrangement to feed their troops; and they are not a little afraid of them.

Our artillery horses are not what we ought to have. They have great merit in their way as cast horses of dragoons, and Irish cart horses, bought for £12 each! but not fit for an army that, to be successful and carry things with a high hand, ought to be able to move.

To the Duke of Richmond.   Caldas, 16th Aug. 1808.

We are getting on as well as possible. The army is in high spirits, and beginning to march tolerably well, and I have every prospect of success. The enemy are retiring before us in two divisions, one of 4000, the other of 5000 men; and I would try to cut off one of them, only they out-march us.

The Commissariat horses do as well as they can; but they are not exactly what we ought to have.

We had yesterday evening a little affair of advanced posts, foolishly brought on by the over-eagerness of the riflemen in the pursuit of an enemy's piquet, in which we lost Lieut. Bunbury of the 95th, killed, and Pakenham, slightly wounded, and some men of the 95th and 60th. The troops behaved remarkably well, but not with great prudence.

I am perfectly well. The troops very healthy, notwithstanding that they are in the sun all day, and in the dew all night, for they have no tents.

P.S. I have written to Longford, to desire him to apprise his mother and his family of his brother's wound; but if he should be out of the way, and you should have reason to believe that Lady Wellesley will hear of it before she will see Longford, give her the enclosed letter.

To Visct. Castlereagh.   Villa Verde, 17th Aug. 1808.

The French Gen. Laborde having continued in his position at Rolica, since my arrival at Caldas on the 15th inst., I determined to attack him

---

* Ambassador at the Court of London. Afterwards Conde de Funchal.

in it this morning. Roliça is situated on an eminence, having a plain in its front, at the end of a valley, which commences at Caldas, and is closed to the southward by mountains, which join the hills forming the valley on the left. Looking from Caldas, in the centre of the valley, and about 8 miles from Roliça, is the town and old Moorish fort of Obidos, from whence the enemy's piquets had been driven on the 15th; and from that time he had posts in the hills on both sides of the valley, as well as in the plain in front of his army, which was posted on the heights in front of Rolica, its right resting upon the hills, its left upon an eminence on which was a windmill, and the whole covering 4 or 5 passes into the mountains on his rear.

I have reason to believe that his force consisted of at least 6000 men, of which about 500 were cavalry, with 5 pieces of cannon; and there was some reason to believe that Gen. Loison, who was at Rio Maior yesterday, would join Gen. Laborde by his right in the course of the night.

The plan of attack was formed accordingly; and the army, having broken up from Caldas this morning, was formed into 3 columns. The right, consisting of 1200 Portuguese infantry, 50 Portuguese cavalry, destined to turn the enemy's left, and penetrate into the mountains in his rear. The left, consisting of Major Gen. Ferguson's and Brig. Gen. Bowes' brigade of infantry, 3 companies of riflemen, a brigade of light artillery, and 20 British and 20 Portuguese cavalry, was destined, under the command of Major Gen. Ferguson, to ascend the hills at Obidos, to turn all the enemy's posts on the left of the valley, as well as the right of his post at Roliça. This corps was also destined to watch the motions of Gen. Loison on the enemy's right, who, I had heard, had moved from Rio Maior towards Alcoentre last night. The centre column, consisting of Major Gen. Hill's, Brig. Gen. Nightingall's, Brig. Gen. C. Craufurd's, and Brig. Gen. Fane's brigades (with the exception of the riflemen detached with Major Gen. Ferguson), and 400 Portuguese light infantry, the British and Portuguese cavalry, a brigade of 9 pounders, and a brigade of 6 pounders, was destined to attack Gen. Laborde's position in the front.

The columns being formed, the troops moved from Obidos about 7 o'clock in the morning. Brig. Gen. Fane's riflemen were immediately detached into the hills on the left of the valley, to keep up the communication between the centre and left columns, and to protect the march of the former along the valley, and the enemy's posts were successively driven in. Major Gen. Hill's brigade, formed in three columns of battalions, moved on the right of the valley, supported by the cavalry, in order to attack the enemy's left; and Brig. Gens. Nightingall and Craufurd moved with the artillery along the high road, until at length the former formed in the plain immediately in the enemy's front, supported by the light infantry companies, and the 45th regt. of Brig. Gen. Crau-

---

G. O. Casas de Suano, 17th Aug. 1808.

The army will be under arms at the usual hour in the morning, before daylight, and in readiness to march at 5 o'clock; the disposition of the march will be made known in the morning.

General officer for the day, to-morrow, Brig. Gen. Fane.

furd's brigade; while the 2 other regiments of this brigade(the 50th and 91st), and half of the 9 pounder brigade, were kept up as a reserve in the rear.

Major Gen. Hill and Brig. Gen. Nightingall advanced upon the enemy's position, and at the same moment Brig. Gen. Fane's riflemen were in the hills on his right, the Portuguese in a village upon his left, and Major Gen. Ferguson's column was descending from the heights into the plain. From this situation the enemy retired by the passes into the mountains with the utmost regularity and the greatest celerity; and notwithstanding the rapid advance of the British infantry, the want of a sufficient body of cavalry was the cause of his suffering but little loss on the plain. It was then necessary to make a disposition to attack the formidable position which he had taken up.

Brig. Gen. Fane's riflemen were already in the mountains on his right; and no time was lost in attacking the different passes, as well to support the riflemen as to defeat the enemy completely.

The Portuguese infantry were ordered to move up a pass on the right of the whole. The light companies of Major Gen. Hill's brigade, and the 5th regt., moved up a pass next on the right; and the 29th regt., supported by the 9th regt., under Brig. Gen. Nightingall, a third pass; and the 45th and 82d regts., passes on the left. These passes were all difficult of access, and some of them were well defended by the enemy, particularly that which was attacked by the 29th and 9th regts. These regiments attacked with the utmost impetuosity, and reached the enemy before those whose attacks were to be made on their flanks.

The defence of the enemy was desperate; and it was in this attack principally that we sustained the loss which we have to lament, particularly of that gallant officer, the Hon. Lieut. Col. Lake, who distinguished himself upon this occasion. The enemy was, however, driven from all the positions he had taken in the passes of the mountains, and our troops were advanced in the plains on their tops. For a considerable length of time the 29th and 9th regts. alone were advanced to this point, with Brig. Gen. Fane's riflemen at a distance on the left, and they were afterwards supported by the 5th regt., and by the light companies of Major Gen. Hill's brigade, which had come upon their right, and by the other troops ordered to ascend the mountains, who came up by degrees.

The enemy here made 3 most gallant attacks upon the 29th and 9th regts., supported as I have above stated, with a view to cover the retreat of his defeated army, in all of which he was, however, repulsed; but he succeeded in effecting his retreat in good order, owing principally to my want of cavalry; and, secondly, to the difficulty of bringing up the passes of the mountains, with celerity, a sufficient number of troops and of cannon to support those which had first ascended. The loss of the enemy has, however, been very great, and he left 3 pieces of cannon in our hands.

I cannot sufficiently applaud the conduct of the troops throughout this action. The enemy's positions were formidable, and he took them up with his usual ability and celerity, and defended them most gallantly. But I must observe, that although we had such a superiority of numbers employed in the operations of this day, the troops actually engaged in the heat of the action were, from unavoidable circumstances, only the 5th, 9th, 29th, the riflemen of the 95th and 60th, and the flank companies of Major Gen. Hill's brigade; being a number by no means equal to that of the enemy. Their conduct therefore deserves the highest commendation.

I cannot avoid taking this opportunity of expressing my acknowledgments for the aid and support I received from all the General and other officers of this army: I am particularly indebted to Major Gen. Spencer for the advice and assistance I received from him; to Major Gen. Ferguson, for the manner in which he led the left column; and to Major Gen. Hill, and Brig. Gens. Nightingall and Fane, for the manner in which they conducted the different attacks which they led.

I derived most material assistance also from Lieut. Col. Tucker and Lieut. Col. Bathurst, in the offices of D. A. and D. Q. M. Gen., and from the officers of the Staff employed under them. I must also mention that I have every reason to be satisfied with the artillery under Lieut. Col. Robe. I have the honor to enclose herewith a return of killed, wounded, and missing.

To Visc. Castlereagh. Lourinha, 18th Aug. 1808.

I have the honor to enclose a return of the killed and wounded in the affair between the outposts of the 15th inst., reported in my letter to your Lordship of the 16th.

Return of the killed, wounded, and missing of the Army under the command of Lieut. Gen. the Hon. Sir A. Wellesley; K.B., on the 17th of Aug. 1808.

	Officers.	Non-commis. officers and drummers.	Rank & File.	Horses.	Total loss of officers, non-commissioned officers, and rank and file.
Killed	4	3	63	1	70
Wounded	20	20	295	2	335
Missing	4	2	68	..	74

To Lieut. Gen. Sir H. Dalrymple. Lourinha, 18th Aug. 1808.

I have the honor to enclose the copy of a letter which I have addressed to the Sec. of State, in which I have reported the circumstances of an action which I had with one of the enemy's corps yesterday.

To Visc. Castlereagh. Lourinha, 18th Aug. 1808.

Since I wrote to you last night I have heard from Brig. Gen. Anstruther that he is on the coast, off Peniche, with the fleet of victuallers and store ships, in charge of Capt. Bligh, of the *Alfred*, with a part of the force detached from England under Brig. Gen. Acland, in consequence of the receipt of orders which I had left at Mondego bay for Gen. Acland, which he had opened.

I have ordered Brig. Gen. Anstruther to land immediately, and I have moved to this place in order to protect his landing and facilitate his junction.

Gen. Loison joined Gen. Laborde in the course of last night at Torres Vedras, and I understand that both begin their march towards Lisbon this morning; I also hear that Gen. Junot has arrived this day at Torres Vedras, with a small corps from Lisbon; and I conclude that the whole of the French army will be assembled between Torres Vedras and the capital in the course of a few days.

To Lieut. Col. Gordon.   Lourinha, 18th Aug. 1808.

The army marched from Leiria on the 13th to Calvario, and on the 14th to Alcobaça, which place the enemy had abandoned in the night of the 13th. I was joined at Alcobaça by 1650 Portuguese troops, viz., 1000 regular infantry, 400 light troops, and 250 cavalry; and I engaged to feed these troops in the same manner as those of His Majesty are fed. The Portuguese Gen. Freire stated, as his reason for not joining me with the whole corps, that he could not find subsistence for it on the route towards Lisbon, which I intended to take; and as I deemed it desirable on political, rather than on military grounds, to have with the British army a corps of Portuguese troops, I desired him to send the corps which joined me at Alcobaca, which I engaged to feed.

On the 15th I marched to Caldas, in 2 columns. As the possession of the town and Moorish fort of Obidos was important to me, with a view to my future operations, I directed that it might be taken possession of by four companies of riflemen, shortly after the infantry of the army had reached Caldas; and they were detached to Obidos, under Major Travers, of the 95th. The enemy's piquet, which was in the village, retired when Major Travers approached, and fired upon the riflemen, and were pursued

---

M. G. O.   Casas de Suano, 18th Aug. 1808.

The following new distribution of brigades to take place on leaving this ground :

The 6th, or light brigade, to consist of the 50th regt., 4 companies of the 95th, and 5 companies of the 60th.

One company of the 60th to be attached to each of the following brigades : the 1st, 2d, 3d, 4th, and 5th; and to join them as soon as possible.

G. O.   Lourinha, 18th Aug. 1808.

The Lieut. General was perfectly satisfied with the conduct of the troops in the action of yesterday, particularly with the gallantry displayed by the 5th, 9th, 29th, 60th, and 95th, to whose lot it principally fell to engage the enemy.

From the specimen afforded yesterday of their behaviour in action, the Lieut. General feels confident that the troops will distinguish themselves whenever the enemy may give them another occasion ; and it is only necessary for him to recommend to them a steady attention to the preservation of order and regularity, and strict obedience to the commands which the officers may give.

Returns of the killed, wounded, and missing, in the action of yesterday, to be sent as soon as possible, through the major of brigade, to the D. A. G., and lists of all officers of corps, specifying ranks and dates of commissions, to Lieut. Col. Torrens, Military Secretary.

(*Detail of the issue of provisions, &c.*)

The army will march to-morrow : the time and order of march will be hereafter notified. General officer for the day, to-morrow, Brig. Gen. C. Craufurd.

by a small detachment to the distance of nearly 3 miles from Obidos. The riflemen were there attacked by a superior body of the enemy, who attempted to cut them off from the main body of the detachment, which had now advanced from Obidos to their support. Larger bodies of the enemy then appeared on both flanks of the detachment; and it was with difficulty that Major Gen. Spencer, who had gone out to Obidos, when he heard that the riflemen had advanced in pursuit of the enemy, was enabled to effect their retreat to that village. In this affair, which was occasioned solely by the eagerness of the troops in pursuit of the enemy, we sustained a loss, of which I enclose a return. Capt. Pakenham s wound is so slight that he has continued to do his duty with his regiment. The loss of the enemy in this affair was not inconsiderable, and much larger than that sustained by His Majesty's troops.

The enemy having still continued in his position at Roliça, I attacked him on the 17th, and I enclose a copy of the letter which I have written to the Sec. of State, in which the particulars of this action are detailed. I have nothing to add to this letter, excepting to request you to represent to his Royal Highness my admiration of the conduct of the troops throughout the day.

I heard this morning, at 9 o'clock, that Gen. Anstruther had joined the convoy of victuallers and store ships stationed off Peniche, under Capt. Bligh, of the *Alfred*, with 2500 men of the force detached from England, under Brig. Gen. Acland. I have directed that this force may land in this neighbourhood; and I have moved here this morning in order to protect his landing, and favor his junction with me. They will, I hope, land to-morrow.

Gen. Loison joined Gen. Laborde at Torres Vedras last night, and they retreated this morning at daylight; and Gen. Junot, with a small corps from Lisbon, arrived at Torres Vedras at an early hour this day. I imagine that the whole of the French troops will join immediately, with a view to impede my march upon Lisbon.

To Visc. Castlereagh.   Lourinha, 18th Aug. 1808.

My dispatch of yesterday and of this day will inform you of the state of affairs here. I never saw such desperate fighting as in the attack of the pass by Lake, and in the 3 attacks by the French on our troops in the mountains. These attacks were made in their best style, and our troops defended themselves capitally; and if the difficulties of the ground had not prevented me from bringing up a sufficient number of the troops and of cannon, we should have taken the whole army. They say that the French lost 1500 men, which is a large amount; but I think they had more than 6000 men in the action.

As soon as Anstruther shall have landed I shall give you a goodaccount of the remainder of the French army; but I am afraid I shall not gain a complete victory; that is, I shall not entirely destroy them for want of cavalry.

P.S. I enclose a letter for Mr. Borough about Lake's death, and onefor Lord Longford, to tell him that his brother is quite well.

To Adm. Sir C. Cotton, Bart.   Lourinha, 18th Aug. 1808.

I have the pleasure to inform you that I beat Laborde's corps yesterday, in an action of which the circumstances are detailed in the enclosed dispatch to Sir H. Dalrymple, which I request you to peruse, and forward to him by the first opportunity. I hear that the enemy have lost 1500 men. Our loss is about 70 killed, about 350 wounded, and a few missing, officers included.

I expect to have another brush with the whole of his army in a day or two; and at all events to be in your neighbourhood before long. If Junot, who is with the army, should retire, I shall be at Mafra on the day after to-morrow, I hope; but I recommend to you not to land your marines, &c. till you hear further from me. 2500 men, under Gen. Anstruther, are with Capt. Bligh, and I propose to land them to-morrow.

To the Duke of Richmond.   Camp at Lourinha, 18th Aug. 1808.

You will see that we have beaten a French corps yesterday. The action was a most desperate one between the troops engaged. I never saw such fighting as in the pass by the 29th and 9th, or in the three attacks made by the French in the mountains. These were in their best style; at the same time, if I could have got a sufficient number of troops up in time, I should have taken or destroyed their whole corps.

The whole French army is now collected, and I have come here to favor Anstruther's landing and junction. He will join me to-morrow with 2500 men.

To R. Borough, Esq.   Lourinha, 18th Aug. 1808.

I do not recollect the occasion upon which I have written with more pain to myself than I do at present, to communicate to you the death of your gallant brother-in-law.* He fell in the attack of a pass in the mountains, at the head of his regiment, the admiration of the whole army; and there is nothing to be regretted in his death, excepting the untimely moment at which it has afflicted his family,† and has deprived the public of the services of an officer who would have been an ornament to his profession, and an honour to his country.

It may at the moment increase the regret of those who lose a near and dear relation, to learn that he deserved and enjoyed the respect and affection of the world at large, and particularly of the profession to which he belonged; but I am convinced, that however acute may be the sensations which it may at first occasion, it must in the end be satisfactory to the family of such a man as Col. Lake, to know that he was respected and loved by the whole army, and that he fell, alas! with many others, in the achievement of one of the most heroic actions that have been performed by the British army.

I cannot desire to be remembered to Mrs. Borough.

---

* Lieut. Col. the Hon. G. A. F. Lake, 29th regt.
† Gen. Lord Lake, the father, died early in the year.

To Visc. Castlereagh.*   Vimeiro, 20th Aug. 1808.

I have had no opportunity of sending my dispatch of the 17th to your Lordship till this day, and I now transmit it by Capt. Campbell,† my aide de camp, to whom I beg leave to refer your Lordship for any further information you may require; at the same time, I beg leave to recommend Capt. Campbell to your Lordship as an officer of great merit: he has served with me for some years in my family, and I have always had reason to be satisfied with his conduct.

To Visc. Castlereagh.   Vimeiro, 20th Aug. 1808.

Anstruther is on shore, and I expect him in camp every moment. I shall be near Mafra to-morrow. The enemy have their advanced guard in front of Torres Vedras, and the main body of their army collected in the

---

* Visc. Castlereagh to Lieut. Gen. the Hon. Sir A. Wellesley, K.B.
                                        Downing Street, 19th Aug. 1808.
I have received and laid before the King your 2 dispatches of the 26th and 28th July (a), giving a detail of your operations, from the time of your landing at Oporto till the disembarkation of your forces in the Mondego River, in immediate expectation of being reinforced by the division under Major Gen. Spencer. This circumstance, connected with the surrender of Gen. Dupont's army, the retreat of Marshal Bessieres, and the evacuation of Madrid, joined to the assistance you must have received from the Portuguese, will have enabled you to commence your operations without delay; and the fullest reliance is placed not less on your decision than on your prudence.

I am also to express His Majesty's approbation of the authority you thought it incumbent upon you to give Major Gen. Spencer, for making an advance of money to the Spaniards, and of your taking upon yourself the responsibility of that measure, in case Major Gen. Spencer should have felt the necessity of acting in conformity to your instruction.

(a) *Note.* There having been no dispatch of the 28th July, it is supposed that this is a clerical error, and that the passage should run thus: ' your 2 dispatches of the 26th July and 1st Aug.'

† Lieut. Gen. Sir Colin Campbell, K.C.B.

G. O.   Vimeiro, 19th Aug. 1808.
The army will march at 5 o'clock to-morrow morning : the order of march will be made known in the morning.
                    (*Detail of the issue of provisions, &c.*)
General officer for the day, to-morrow, Major Gen. Hill.

Pass Order.
Three days' bread, from the 22d inclusive, to be issued this evening by the Assist. Commissaries of brigades. The Dep. Commissary General will also issue 3 days' bread to the Portuguese troops acting with the army.

A. G. O.   Vimeiro, 19th Aug. 1808.
The army will halt to-morrow; excepting the 6th brigade with their guns, and the 2d brigade with their guns, the British cavalry (excepting 50 to be left in camp), with 50 of the Portuguese cavalry, which will march to-morrow morning at 3 o'clock, without great coats or havresacks, under the command of Major Gen. Spencer.

The rifle and light companies of the 1st, 3d, 4th, and 5th brigades, will occupy, at the same hour, the present position of the light brigade, under the orders of Major Gen. Hill, the General officer of the day.

Brig. Gen. Fane will draw out, on the road leading to Lourinha, precisely at 3 o'clock, left in front, and the 2d brigade and cavalry will immediately follow him.

The 3d brigade will send immediately a captain and 50 men to the north of the village of Vimeiro, on the road by which the army entered it this morning, and the cavalry will patrole constantly from it during the night on the road to Lourinha.

rear of that town. I understand that they have got together everything
that Portugal can afford.

Col. Brown, who has got charge of my letters to you, has not had an
opportunity of going on board ship till this day. I intended to have sent
them by my aide de camp, Capt. Campbell, in order that he might get the
promotion usual upon such occasions ; but I hope that I shall have another
and a better occasion to send him home : if I should not, I trust that he
will not lose his promotion by my having omitted to send him on the
present occasion.

To Capt. Bligh, H.M.S. *Alfred*.   Vimeiro, 20th Aug. 1808. ½ past 11, A.M.

I am much obliged to you for your letter of yesterday. I have just
been down at Maceira, where I hope that you will land the bread, ammunition, &c., and the saddles. It appears a very good landing place, and
there is a good road, and it is no great distance from thence here ; but if
you should think that place inconvenient, I will contrive to communicate
with any other place at which you may land them.

I propose to march to-morrow towards Mafra ; I shall be glad if you
will be off Ericeira to-morrow evening. I shall contrive to communicate
with you either to-morrow or next day, and to fix on the next place of
rendezvous. I apprehend no accidents ; but I should like to keep the
transports for a few days, in case of the occurrence of any. They might
also be useful in turning any position the enemy might take in the neighbourhood of the Rock of Lisbon.

P.S. If Gen. Acland should join you, keep him with you, and desire him
to let me know it immediately.

To Lieut. Col. Gordon.   Vimeiro, 20th Aug. 1808.

I avail myself of the delay which has taken place in the departure of the
ship which will take my dispatches to England, to acquaint you, for the

---

G. O.   Vimeiro, 20th Aug. 1808.
   The army will march at half past 4 o'clock to-morrow morning. Half a pint of wine
per man, and one day's meat for to-morrow, to be issued at 4 o'clock this evening to all the
troops, excepting the 7th, or Brig. Gen. Anstruther's brigade, which will receive one pint of
wine per man.
   Returns of the number of bill hooks in possession of the several corps to be sent immediately to the D. Q. M. G.
                       (*Detail of guards ordered.*)
   The several regiments of infantry will forthwith send in to the Dep. Commissary General
20 camp kettles each, for the purpose of supplying the 7th brigade, who are unprovided with
them ; and the 95th will, for the same object, furnish 8 camp kettles. As soon as the whole
are collected, the Dep. Commissary General will issue an equal proportion of them to the
2d batts. of the 9th, 43d, and 52d regts., and the 97th regt., and will allot to each of
those corps one cart for the conveyance of the kettles.
   No wine being procurable, an issue of spirits will be made to the troops.
   A piquet of 20 Portuguese and 10 British cavalry, with an infantry piquet to be furnished by the 5th brigade, consisting of one captain, 2 subalterns, and 100 men, with non-
commissioned officers in proportion, will be posted, at 7 o'clock this evening, at a large house
on the hill in rear of Brig. Gen. C. Craufurd's brigade, which piquet will patrole the front
of the ravine, as far as the sea, during the night.

Night Pass Order.
   The army will halt to-morrow. The men to sleep accoutred to-night, in readiness to
turn out, and to be under arms at 3 o'clock in the morning.

information of the Commander in Chief, of the death of that gallant officer, Lieut. Col. Stewart, of the 9th regt, in consequence of the severe wounds he received in the action of the 17th; and I request that you will, at the same time, represent to His Royal Highness that the conduct of Major Molle, who was also wounded upon this occasion, was such during the action as to merit my warmest approbation; and I therefore beg leave to submit his name to the favorable consideration of His Royal Highness to succeed to the Lieutenant colonelcy unfortunately vacated by the decease of Lieut. Col. Stewart.

Should Major Molle be promoted upon this occasion, I request you will be pleased to submit to His Royal Highness, that the succession should go in the regiment in favor of Capt. Aylmer, Lieut. Finlay, and Ensign Curzon.*

To Visc. Castlereagh.   Vimeiro, 21st Aug. 1808. 6, A.M.

Sir H. Burrard will probably acquaint your Lordship with the reasons which have induced him to call Sir J. Moore's corps to the assistance of our army, which consists of 20,000 men, including the Portuguese army, which was to join this morning, notwithstanding former determinations to the contrary, and is opposed by, I am convinced, not more than 12,000 or 14,000 Frenchmen, and to halt here till Sir John's corps shall join. You will readily believe, however, that this determination is not in conformity with my opinion, and I only wish that Sir Harry had landed and seen things with his own eyes before he had made it. Gen. Acland's brigade landed last night.

The French are in and about Torres Vedras. Junot's corps, which arrived last, is the advanced guard, and the others are in the rear, nearly on the ground to which Laborde retreated after the battle of the 17th.

* The Hon. Wm. Curzon, afterwards killed at the battle of Waterloo.

G. O.   Vimeiro, 21st Aug. 1808.

Lieut. Gen. Sir A. Wellesley congratulates the army on the signal victory they have this day obtained over the enemy, and returns them his warmest thanks for their resolute and heroic conduct. He experienced the sincerest pleasure in witnessing various instances of the gallantry of the corps, and has, in particular, to notice the distinguished behaviour of the Royal artillery, 20th light dragoons, the 36th, 40th, 43d, 50th, 52d, 60th, 71st, 82d, 95th, and 97th regts.

It will afford the Lieut. General the greatest pleasure to report to the Commander in Chief the bravery displayed by all the troops, and the high sense he entertains of their meritorious and excellent conduct throughout the day.

The brigade under the orders of Brig. Gen. Acland is denominated the 8th brigade. The two companies of the 95th, attached to it, will join those with the 6th brigade; and one rifle company of the 60th will be transferred immediately from the 6th to the 7th brigade, and another from the 6th to the 8th brigade.

Returns of the killed, wounded, and missing, in the action of to-day, to be sent to the D. A. G.'s office before 8 o'clock this evening.

An allowance of spirits, and one day's meat for to-morrow, to be issued to the troops as soon as possible.

General officer for the day, to-morrow, Brig. Gen. Nightingall.

A guard, consisting of 1 serjeant, 1 corporal, and 18 privates from the 4th brigade, to be sent immediately to Lieut. Gen. Sir H. Burrard's quarters, in the village of Maceira on the river side, near the sea shore, and the following guards to be relieved at 5 o'clock this evening, by the 1st brigade.

(*Detail of guards.*)

To Lieut. Gen. Sir H. Burrard, Bart.*   Vimeiro, 21st Aug. 1808.

I have the honor to inform you, that the enemy attacked us in our position at Vimeiro this morning.

The village of Vimeiro stands in a valley, through which runs the river Maceira; at the back, and to the westward and northward of this village, is a mountain, the western point of which touches the sea, and the eastern is separated by a deep ravine from the heights, over which passes the road which leads from Lourinha, and the northward to Vimeiro. The greater part of the infantry, the 1st, 2d, 3d, 4th, 5th, and 8th brigades, were posted on this mountain, with 8 pieces of artillery, Major Gen. Hill's brigade being on the right, and Major Gen. Ferguson's on the left, having one battalion on the heights separated from the mountain. On the eastern and southern side of the town is a hill, which is entirely commanded, particularly on its right, by the mountain to the westward of the town, and commanding all the ground in the neighbourhood to the southward and eastward, on which Brig. Gen. Fane was posted with his riflemen, and the 50th regt, and Brig. Gen. Anstruther with his brigade, with half a brigade of 6 pounders, and half a brigade of 9 pounders, which had been ordered to the position in the course of last night. The ground over which passes the road from Lourinha commanded the left of this height, and it had not been occupied, excepting by a piquet, as the camp had been taken up only for one night, and there was no water in the neighbourhood of this height. The cavalry and the reserve of artillery were in the valley, between the hills on which the infantry stood, both flanking and supporting Brig. Gen. Fane's advanced guard.

The enemy first appeared about 8 o'clock in the morning, in large bodies of cavalry on our left, upon the heights on the road to Lourinha; and it was soon obvious that the attack would be made upon our advanced guard and the left of our position; and Major Gen. Ferguson's brigade was immediately moved across the ravine to the heights on the road to Lourinha, with 3 pieces of cannon; he was followed successively by Brig. Gen. Nightingall, with his brigade and 3 pieces of cannon, Brig. Gen. Acland, and his brigade, and Brig. Gen. Bowes, with his brigade. These troops were formed (Major Gen. Ferguson's brigade in the first line, Brig. Gen. Nightingall's in the second, and Brig. Gen. Bowes' and Acland's in columns in the rear) on those heights, with their right upon

---

* Lieut. Gen. Sir H. Burrard to Visc. Castlereagh.   Maceira, 21st Aug. 1808.

The report, which I have the honor to enclose to your Lordship, made at my request by Lieut. Gen. Sir A. Wellesley, conveys information which cannot but prove highly gratifying to His Majesty.

On my landing this morning, I found that the enemy's attack had already commenced; and I was fortunate enough to reach the field of action in time to witness and approve of every disposition that had been, and was afterwards made, by Sir A. Wellesley; his comprehensive mind furnishing a ready resource in every emergency, and rendering it quite unnecessary to direct any alteration.

I am happy on this occasion to bear testimony to the great spirit and good conduct displayed by all the troops composing this gallant army in this well contested action.

I send this dispatch by Capt. Campbell, aide de camp to Sir A. Wellesley, no person being better qualified to give your Lordship information.

the valley which leads into Vimeiro, and their left upon the other ravine, which separates these heights from the range which terminates at the landing place at Maceira. On the last mentioned heights the Portuguese troops, which had been in the bottom near Vimeiro, were posted in the first instance, and they were supported by Brig. Gen. C. Craufurd's brigade. The troops of the advanced guard, on the heights to the southward and eastward of the town, were deemed sufficient for its defence, and Major Gen. Hill was moved to the centre of the mountain, on which the great body of the infantry had been posted, as a support to these troops, and as a reserve to the whole army; in addition to this support, these troops had that of the cavalry in the rear of their right.

The enemy's attack began in several columns upon the whole of the troops on this height; on the left they advanced, notwithstanding the fire of the riflemen, close to the 50th regt, and they were checked and driven back only by the bayonets of that corps. The 2d batt. 43d regt. was likewise closely engaged with them in the road which leads into Vimeiro; a part of that corps having been ordered into the churchyard, to prevent them from penetrating into the town. On the right of the position they were repulsed by the bayonets of the 97th regt., which corps was successfully supported by the 2d batt. 52d, which, by an advance in column, took the enemy in flank.

Besides this opposition given to the attack of the enemy on the advanced guard by their own exertions, they were attacked in flank by Brig. Gen. Acland's brigade, in its advance to its position on the heights on the left, and a cannonade was kept up on the flank of the enemy's columns by the artillery on those heights. At length, after a most desperate contest, the enemy was driven back in confusion from this attack, with the loss of 7 pieces of cannon, many prisoners, and a great number of officers and soldiers killed and wounded. He was pursued by a detachment of the 20th light dragoons; but the enemy's cavalry were so much superior in numbers, that this detachment has suffered much, and Lieut. Col. Taylor was unfortunately killed.

Nearly at the same time the enemy's attack commenced upon the heights on the road to Lourinha: this attack was supported by a large body of cavalry, and was made with the usual impetuosity of French troops. It was received with steadiness by Major Gen. Ferguson's brigade, consisting of the 36th, 40th, and 71st regts.; and these corps charged as soon as the enemy approached them, who gave way, and they continued to advance upon him, supported by the 82d, one of the corps of Brig. Gen. Nightingall's brigade, which, as the ground extended, afterwards formed a part of the first line by the 29th regt, and by Brig. Gen. Bowes' and Acland's brigades; whilst Brig. Gen. C. Craufurd's brigade and the Portuguese troops, in two lines, advanced along the height on the left. In the advance of Major Gen. Ferguson's brigade, 6 pieces of cannon were taken from the enemy, with many prisoners, and vast numbers were killed and wounded.

The enemy afterwards made an attempt to recover part of his artillery, by attacking the 71st and 82d regts., which were halted in a valley in which it had been taken. These regiments retired from the low grounds in the valley to the heights, where they halted, faced about, and fired, and advanced upon the enemy, who had by that time arrived in the low ground, and they thus obliged him again to retire with great loss.

In this action, in which the whole of the French force in Portugal was employed, under the command of the Duc d'Abrantes in person, in which the enemy was certainly superior in cavalry and artillery, and in which not more than half of the British army was actually engaged, he has sustained a signal defeat, and has lost 13 pieces of cannon, 23 ammunition waggons, with powder, shells, stores of all descriptions, and 20,000 rounds of musket ammunition. One General officer has been wounded (Brenier) and taken prisoner, and a great many officers and soldiers have been killed, wounded, and taken.

The valor and discipline of His Majesty's troops have been conspicuous upon this occasion, as you, who witnessed the greatest part of the action, must have observed; but it is a justice to the following corps to draw your notice to them in a particular manner: viz, the Royal artillery, commanded by Lieut. Col. Robe; the 20th light dragoons, which has been commanded by Lieut. Col. Taylor; the 50th regt., commd. by Col. Walker; the 2d batt. 95th foot, commd. by Major Travers; the 5th batt. 60th regt., commd. by Major Davy; the 2d batt. 43d, commd. by Major Hull; the 2d batt. 52d, commd. by Lieut. Col. Ross; the 97th regt., commd. by Lieut. Col. Lyon; the 36th regt, commd. by Col. Burne; the 40th, commd. by Lieut. Col. Kemmis; the 71st, commd. by Lieut. Col. Pack; and the 82d regt, commd. by Major Eyre. In mentioning Col. Burne and the 36th regt. upon this occasion, I cannot avoid adding that the regular and orderly conduct of this corps throughout the service, and their gallantry and discipline in action, have been conspicuous.

I must take this opportunity of acknowledging my obligations to the General and Staff officers of the army. I was much indebted to Major Gen. Spencer's judgment and experience in the decision which I formed in respect to the number of troops allotted to each point of defence, and for his advice and assistance throughout the action. In the position taken up by Major Gen. Ferguson's brigade, and in its advances upon the enemy, that officer showed equal bravery and judgment; and much praise is due to Brig. Gen. Fane and Brig. Gen. Anstruther for their gallant defence of their position in front of Vimeiro, and to Brig. Gen. Nightingall, for the manner in which he supported the attack upon the enemy made by Major Gen. Ferguson.

Lieut. Col. G. Tucker, and Lieut. Col. Bathurst, and the officers in the departments of the Adj. and Q. M. Gen., and Lieut. Col. Torrens and the officers of my personal staff, rendered me the greatest assistance throughout the action.

I have the honor to enclose herewith a return of the killed, wounded, and missing.

P.S. Since writing the above I have been informed that a French General officer, supposed to be General Thiebault,* the chief of the Staff, has been found dead upon the field of battle.

* It was not General Thiebault.

Return of the killed, wounded, and missing of the Army under the command of Lieut. Gen. the Hon. Sir A. Wellesley, K.B., on the 21st Aug. 1808.

	Officers.	Non-commis. officers and drummers.	Rank & File.	Horses.	Total loss of officers, non-commissioned officers, and rank and file.
Killed	4	3	128	30	135
Wounded	37	31	466	12	534
Missing	2	3	46	1	51

To Lieut. Gen. Sir H. Burrard, Bart.　　　　　　　　Vimeiro, 22d Aug. 1808.

According to the directions which I have received from the Sec. of State, I have the honor to enclose instructions which I have received from him, and a return of the troops which have been hitherto under my command.

To H.R.H. the Duke of York.　　　　　　　　Vimeiro, 22d Aug. 1808.

I have omitted to address your Royal Highness till I should have something to communicate deserving your Royal Highness' attention; and I hope that the action which the troops fought yesterday will be deemed of that description.

I wrote to Col. Gordon on the 18th, from Lourinha, and gave him a detailed account of occurrences here up to that date. On the 19th I moved to Vimeiro, in order to be more certain of protecting the disembarkation of Gen. Anstruther's brigade, which I expected would have been made at Maceira. Brig. Gen. Anstruther landed on that evening, and in the night of the 19th and 20th, about 8 miles north of Maceira, and joined on the morning of the 20th. It was my intention to move, on the

---

Morning Pass Order.　　　　　　　　Vimeiro, 22d Aug. 1808.

Commanding officers of corps will send without delay to the Dep. Adj. Gen. returns of the number of French prisoners in their charge, and particularly the rank and names of the officers.

Letters for England will be received at the D. A. G.'s office in Vimeiro at 11 o'clock this forenoon for the purpose of being forwarded.

G. O.

All regimental medical officers will repair *forthwith*, with all their surgical articles, to the General Hospital in Vimeiro, where Dr. Shapter will give them orders.

The 97th regt. is transferred from the 7th to the 8th brigade, and will join the latter immediately.

(*Detail of the issue of provisions, guards, &c.*)

A. G. O.

The army will hold itself in readiness to march to-morrow morning; the hour and order of march will be notified hereafter.

G.O.　　　　　　　　22d Aug. 1808.

The horses of the country, whether belonging to the Portuguese dragoons or to the army, and all mules, &c., must be provided with forage of the country by their owners giving receipts for the same. [Not in the General Orders from whence this copy was made, although mentioned in the Index of them.]

morning of the 21st, by the route of Mafra, by which I should have turned the left of the enemy's position at, and in the rear of, Torres Vedras; and I intended that Brig. Gen. Acland's brigade, which appeared in the offing in the middle of that day, should be landed at Maceira in the evening, and join the army on that night. Lieut. Gen. Sir H. Burrard, however, arrived off Maceira on the evening of the 20th, and determined that the army should halt at Vimeiro till it should be reinforced by Sir J. Moore's corps, which was to be re-embarked in Mondego bay. The disembarkation of Gen. Acland's brigade was effected in the evening, and during the night of the 20th, and they joined the army about 6 in the morning of the 21st.

During the night of the 20th and 21st my patroles gave me intelligence of movements by the enemy; but as we were so very inferior in cavalry, my patroles could not go to any distance, and of course their reports were very vague, and not founded on very certain grounds. But I thought it probable that if I did not attack the enemy, he would attack me; and I prepared for the conflict at daylight in the morning, by posting the 9 pounders, and strengthening my right, where I expected the attack, from the manner in which the enemy had patrolled towards that point in the line during the 19th and 20th. He appeared, however, about 8 o'clock on the 21st, on the left, and an action commenced, of which a detailed account is given in the enclosed copy of a letter which I have written upon it to Sir H. Burrard. I likewise enclose a plan of the ground, which will more clearly explain the nature of the different movements made by the enemy and by our troops.

I cannot say too much in favor of the troops: their gallantry and their discipline were equally conspicuous; and I must add, that this is the only action that I have ever been in, in which everything passed as it was directed, and no mistake was made by any of the officers charged with its conduct. I think if Gen. Hill's brigade and the advanced guard had moved upon Torres Vedras, as soon as it was certain that the enemy's right had been defeated by our left, and our left had pursued their advantage, the enemy would have been cut off from Torres Vedras, and we should have been at Lisbon before him; if, indeed, any French army had remained in Portugal. But Sir H. Burrard, who was at this time upon the ground, still thought it advisable not to move from Vimeiro; and the enemy made good their retreat to Torres Vedras

Sir H. Dalrymple arrived this morning, and has taken the command of the army.

P.S. I have not yet been able to procure a plan of the ground, and I therefore transmit this letter without it.

To Visc. Castlereagh.   Vimeiro, 22d Aug. 1808.

After I wrote to you yesterday morning, we were attacked by the whole of the French army, Sir H. Burrard being still on board the ship, and I gained a complete victory. It was impossible for troops to behave better than ours did; we only wanted a few hundred more cavalry to annihilate the French army.

I have sent my report upon this action to Sir H. Burrard, who will send it home. You will see in it that I have mentioned Col. Burne, of the 36th regt , in a very particular manner; and I assure you that there is nothing that will give me so much satisfaction as to learn that something has been done for this old and meritorious soldier.* The 36th regt are an example to this army.

Sir Harry did not land till late in the day, in the midst of the attack, and he desired me to continue my own operations ; and as far as I am personally concerned in the action, I was amply rewarded for any disappointment I might have felt in not having had an opportunity of bringing the service to a close, by the satisfaction expressed by the army that the second and more important victory had been gained by their old General. I have also the pleasure to add, that it has had more effect than all the arguments I could use to induce the General to move on, and I believe he will march to-morrow. Indeed, if he does not, we shall be poisoned here by the stench of the dead and wounded ; or we shall starve, everything in the neighbourhood being already eaten up.

From the number of dead Frenchmen about the ground, and the number of prisoners and wounded, I should think their loss could not be far short of 3000 men. The force which attacked us was very respectable, and probably not short of 14,000 men, including 1300 dragoons and artillery, and 300 chasseurs à cheval.

Sir Hew Dalrymple arrived last night, and will land this morning.

To the Duke of Richmond.   Camp at Vimeiro, 22nd Aug. 1808.

Sir H. Burrard came here on the night of the 20th, but did not land, and, as I am the most fortunate of men, Junot attacked us yesterday morning with his whole force, and we completely defeated him. You will see the account of the action. The French have lost not less than 3000 men.

Since I wrote to you last, I came here to facilitate Anstruther's landing and junction, which took place on the 20th, in the morning. In the evening Acland came up from the Tagus, and I landed him immediately, and he joined us before the action yesterday morning ; but Sir Harry did not come up till the action was nearly over.

Although we had, when Acland joined, not less than 17,000 men, and between 6000 and 7000 Portuguese in our neighbourhood, Sir Harry did not think these sufficient to defeat 12,000 or 14,000 Frenchmen, but determined to wait for Moore's corps, notwithstanding all that I could urge upon the subject. The action of yesterday has, however, had more effect than all my eloquence, and I believe he will march on to morrow. If he would have allowed me to move that part of the army yesterday evening, which had not been engaged in the morning, the French would not have stopped till they reached Lisbon.

---

* This officer was shortly afterwards rewarded by the government of Carlisle being conferred on him.

Au Quartier Général de l'Armée Anglaise, le 22 Août, 1808.

Suspension d'Armes arrêté entre Mons. le Chevalier Arthur Wellesley, Lieutenant Général, et Chevalier de l'ordre du Bain, d'une part; et Mons. le Général de Division Kellermann, Grand Officier de la Légion d'Honneur, Commandeur de l'ordre de
la Couronne de Fer, Grande Croix de l'ordre du Lion de Bavière, de l'autre part; tous
deux chargés de pouvoirs des Généraux respectifs des Armées Françaises et Anglaises.

Art. 1. Il y aura à dater de ce jour une suspension d'armes entre les
armées de Sa Majesté Britannique et de Sa Majesté Impériale et Royale,
Napoléon I., à l'effet de traiter d'une Convention pour l'évacuation du
Portugal par l'armée Française.

Art. 2. Les Généraux en Chef des deux armées, et M. le Commandant
en Chef de la flotte Britannique à l'entrée du Tage, prendront jour pour
se réunir dans tel point de la côte qu'ils jugeront convenable pour traiter
et conclure la dite Convention.

Art. 3. La rivière de Sizandre formera la ligne de démarcation établie
entre les deux armées. Torres Vedras ne sera occupé ni par l'une ni par
l'autre.

Art. 4. M. le Général en Chef de l'armée Anglaise s'obligera à com-
prendre les Portugais armés dans cette suspension d'armes, et pour eux la
ligne de démarcation sera établie de Leiria à Thomar.

Art. 5. Il est convenu provisoirement que l'armée Française ne pourra
dans aucun cas être considérée comme prisonnière de guerre; que tous
les individus qui la composent seront transportés en France avec armes et
bagages, et leurs propriétés particulières quelconques dont il ne pourra
leur être rien distrait.

Art. 6. Tout particulier, soit Portugais, soit d'une nation alliée à la
France, soit Français, ne pourra être recherché pour sa conduite politique;
il sera protégé, ses propriétés respectées, et il aura la liberté de se retirer
du Portugal dans un terme fixé avec ce qui lui appartient.

Art. 7. La neutralité du port de Lisbonne sera reconnue pour la flotte
Russe, c'est à dire, que lorsque l'armée ou la flotte Anglaise seront en
possession de la ville et du port, la dite flotte Russe ne pourra être ni in-
quiétée pendant son séjour, ni arrêtée quand elle voudra sortir, ni pour-
suivie lorsqu'elle sera sortie, qu'après les délais fixés par les lois
maritimes.

Art. 8. Toute l'artillerie du calibre Français, ainsi que les chevaux de
la cavalerie, seront transportés en France.

Art. 9. Cette suspension d'armes ne pourra être rompue qu'on ne se
soit prévenu quarante-huit heures d'avance.

Fait et arrêté entre les Généraux désignés ci-dessus au jour et l'année
ci-dessus.

ARTHUR WELLESLEY.   Le Gén. de div. KELLERMANN.

Article Additionnel. Les garnisons des places occupées par l'armée
Française seront comprises dans la présente Convention, si elles n'ont
point capitulé avant le 25 du courant.

ARTHUR WELLESLEY.   Le Gén. de div. KELLERMANN.

To Capt. P. Malcolm, H.M.S. *Donegal.*   Ramalhal, 23d Aug. 1808.

Torrens wrote to you on the night of the 21st to apprise you of the complete victory which we had gained; one of the consequences of which has been a suspension of arms between the French and us, preparatory to the evacuation of the country by them; the conditions of which I signed last night.

Although I signed these conditions, I beg that you will not believe that I entirely approve of the manner in which the instrument is worded.

You will receive a public letter from me upon this subject this day, in which I have requested you to bring the whole of your fleet of transports to the mouth of the Tagus, with the exception of the horse ships, which are to go to England.

P.S. It would be very convenient to us if you would communicate with Capt. Bligh as you pass by. I shall be much obliged to you if you will have another cask of my claret broken up and put in chests such as the last, and leave one of them with Bligh for me.

To Capt. Malcolm, H.M.S. *Donegal.*   Ramalhal, 23d Aug. 1808.

I have the honor to inform you that an agreement for the suspension of hostilities between the British and French armies, preparatory to the arrangement of a Convention for the evacuation of Portugal by the latter, was signed last night by the direction of the Commander in Chief.

The Commander in Chief has desired me to inform you that he has received orders to send to England all the horse transports now in Portugal, with the exception of those which will have brought out the 18th light dragoons; and he concludes that you will receive orders from the Admiral to send them to England without loss of time. He wishes, however, that all the other transports, whether in the Mondego river, at Oporto, or off Maceira, should be brought to the mouth of the Tagus without loss of time; and he has desired me to request that you will give directions that they may be sent to that station.

To Charles Stuart, Esq.   Ramalhal, 25th Aug. 1808.

Since I wrote to you last we have been very actively employed in this quarter, and with some success.

On the 17th inst. I attacked and defeated Laborde's corps, consisting of about 6000 men, in the neighbourhood of Roliça, about 6 or 7 miles to the south of Obidos. On the following day, the French troops under Gen. Junot, Gen. Loison, and Gen. Laborde, joined in the neighbourhood of Torres Vedras, to the amount of from 12,000 to 14,000 men. I marched on the same day towards Lourinha, to protect the landing of a brigade of infantry under Gen. Anstruther, which brigade joined me on the 20th at Vimeiro, near Maceira; and I was joined by another brigade of infantry, under Gen. Acland, early in the morning of the 21st, which brigade had landed in the course of that night. The French army attacked me in my position at Vimeiro, on the 21st, at about 8 in the morning; and it was completely defeated, with the loss of 13 pieces of cannon, and a vast number of killed, wounded, and prisoners. Sir H. Burrard, who had come into the roads of Maceira on the night of the 20th, landed

during the action on the morning of the 21st; and if I had not been prevented, I should have pursued the enemy to Torres Vedras on that evening, and, in all probability, the whole would have been destroyed.

On the 22d, in the morning, Sir H. Dalrymple arrived; and in the
evening Gen. Kellermann came in with a proposition to suspend hostilities, with a view to make a Convention for the evacuation of Portugal by
the French.

In the agreement which Sir Hew entered into upon this occasion there
was an article stipulating that the Russians should be allowed to use the
port of Lisbon as a neutral port, which was referred to the Admiral, who
has refused to consent to it; and the General has this day given notice to
Junot that the suspension of arms will be at an end on the 28th at noon,
unless a Convention for the evacuation of Portugal by the French, by
sea, should be agreed upon before that day.

This is the general outline of the state of affairs here. Sir J. Moore's
corps is in the roads of Maceira, and I believe is to be landed. Besides
this, we have 6000 Portuguese troops at Lourinha; and I believe there is
a detachment of Spanish and Portuguese troops about Santarem and
Abrantes.

The retreat of the French is, however, open through Arentejo towards
Elvas; and I have but little doubt that if we should not get them out of
Portugal by sea, they will secure themselves in Elvas and Almeida, and
we shall have the pleasure of attacking those places regularly, or of
blockading them in the autumn. If we should be able to get them away
by sea, it will be possible to push our troops into Spain at an early period.
I request you to furnish Col. Doyle with such information from this
letter as may be useful to him.

The French troops are now assembled at Cabeca de Montachique, and
extending towards Mafra. We are behind Torres Vedras, which town is
not occupied by either party.

Memorandum handed to Sir H. Dalrymple* by Sir A. Wellesley, for Lieut. Col. Murray,
    charged with the negotiation for a Convention.   Ramalhal, 23d Aug. 1808.

I. It would be very desirable to instruct Col. Murray at an early hour

* Lieut. Gen. Dalrymple to Lieut. Col. Murray, Q.M.G.   Ramalhal, 25th Aug. 1808.

I have the honor to enclose a letter, which you will deliver to the French Commander in Chief, and you will apprise his Excellency, that as Gen. Kellermann
appeared to attach much importance to the article respecting the Russians, and as
it is exceedingly inconvenient and disadvantageous to the British army to be liable
to the agreement for an unlimited suspension of hostilities, you will inform his
Excellency, that I shall consider that to which I have agreed to be at an end at
12 o'clock at noon on the 28th.

In case his Excellency should manifest a desire to continue the negotiations for
a Convention on the basis of the remaining articles of the agreement, I authorise
you to enter upon and conclude it, with such officer as shall be appointed by the
Commander in Chief of the French army, upon the terms specified in the enclosed
memoranda, subject to the ratification of the Admiral and myself; and in case
you should find this disposition to exist in his Excellency's mind, and if you
should enter upon the negotiation under these powers, you are authorised to
apprise the Commander in Chief of the French army, that I shall have no objection to a renewal of the agreement for the suspension of hostilities for a definite
period, to enable the officers employed to bring the negotiations to their result.

this day, to urge the Admiral to have a communication with the Russian Admiral, in which the latter should be informed, that whatever might be the result of the negotiations between Sir Hew and the Duc d'Abrantes, the Russian fleet should not be molested if they conducted themselves as they ought in a neutral port, and took no part in the contest.

II. If the Admiral should consent to this arrangement in favor of the Russians, and the Russians should be satisfied upon this point, the French Commander in Chief should be pressed upon the following points in the negotiation for the Convention.

1st. The fort of Peniche to be evacuated in 2 days; the forts of Elvas and La Lippe in 4 days; the fort of Almeida in 5 days. The French army to cross the Tagus, and evacuate Lisbon and all the forts on the Tagus in 4 days from the signature of the Convention, and to be prepared to embark in 7 days, or as soon afterwards as the British Commander in Chief may appoint.

The British army, in the mean time, to have the use of the port of Lisbon and the navigation of the Tagus.

2dly. The mode of paying for the hire of the transports to be settled.

3dly. The ports to be settled to which they are to go. Rochefort or Lorient would answer best, as being the greatest distance from Spain and the Austrian frontier.

4thly. Security to be required for the transports going to the ports appointed, and for the return of the transports; as 50 of those sent with the army of Egypt were detained in France.

5thly. Some mode to be devised to make the French Generals disgorge the church plate which they have stolen.

6thly. An exchange of prisoners to be settled.

7thly. There are no horse transports; and the French must be permitted to leave Commissaries to sell the horses, or to hire vessels to transport them to France; but certainly not the cavalry itself.

Plan for the operations of the Army.

Ramalhal, 26th Aug. 1808.

1. The whole army to march to-morrow morning, the 27th, to the heights on this side of Torres Vedras. This must depend upon the result of Lieut. Col. Murray's mission. If Junot should declare himself ready to negotiate, the General would probably not be disposed to show his army so near the line of demarkation; if not, the more ready to appear to move the better.

2. On the 28th, the brigades, as follow, to march by their left to Sobral, viz.

Major Gens. Hill, Ferguson.
Brig. Gens. Nightingall, C. Craufurd, Fane, Bowes.
The 20th light dragoons; the Portuguese cavalry; the Portuguese infantry under Col. Trant; one brigade of 9 pounders; 2 brigades of 6 pounders; spare ammunition, &c, being in Col. Robe's park.

3. The infantry of Lieut. Gen. Moore's corps, to the amount of 5000 or 6000 men, to be landed as soon as possible, and to be assembled in this camp. Three brigades of artillery and their horses, and the cavalry

likewise, to be landed and assembled in the same place. It is supposed that this debarkation may be completed by the 28th in the evening.

4. On the 29th, in the morning, the troops which remain in this camp to march upon Enxara dos Cavalleiros, on the road to Cabeca de Montachique. The Portuguese army at Lourinha on the same day to St. Pedro de Codiera, on the road to Mafra, and the corps at Sobral to St. Antonio de Tojal. If it should be found that the French troops still remain in the position at Cabeca de Montachique, these troops will move on the following day, the 30th, by Loures, to attack the enemy at Cabeca de Montachique in the rear, while they will be attacked in front by the troops from Enxara dos Cavalleiros; and the Portuguese troops will on that day, the 30th, move to Mafra. These corps will communicate as follows: on the 28th by Runa to Ramalhal; on the 29th by Runa and Torres Vedras to Enxara dos Cavalleiros; on the 30th by the same route, unless the enemy should retire. If the enemy should retire, then by Cabeca de Montachique and Loures.

5. The remainder of the infantry of Sir J. Moore's corps to be landed as soon as possible after the first disembarkation of infantry, cavalry, and artillery. This corps of infantry to be assembled as a reserve in the camp at Vimeiro, and to march on the 30th by the road towards Mafra and Cintra, keeping up its communication with the sea, and receiving its supplies of provisions from the shipping.

6. All the ships now in the roads at Maceira to be moved to the mouth of the Tagus, with the exception of a victualler, an ordnance store ship, a hay and oat ship, and a medicine ship, to remain with Capt. Bligh, who will communicate daily with the corps to be assembled in the camp at Vimeiro, and to be marched by the route of Mafra.

7. The other corps to be victualled as follows: The troops now in camp to receive 3 days' bread for the 29th, 30th, and 31st, on the 28th in the morning at daylight. The corps to march to Sobral, to be attended by their brigade Commissariat mules, carrying 3 days' bread, and 3 days' meat to be driven with them. The horses of the cavalry and artillery, on the 28th in the morning, to receive 3 days' grain for the 29th, 30th, and 31st.

8. Three days' bread to be sent with this corps in waggons for the Portuguese infantry and cavalry.

9. The waggons in the Commissariat depot carrying above 100,000 lbs. of bread and meat, spirits, &c., to attend the movement of the corps, to march on the 29th from camp to Enxara dos Cavalleiros. Calculating the consumption of these troops at 15,000 rations daily, they will have bread to last till the 4th Sept.

10. In order to make this arrangement complete, it will be necessary to get up 560 bags of bread this day, the 26th, which it is supposed were landed yesterday; to lay the whole of the bread down in this camp tomorrow morning, the 27th; to land 960 bags more on the 27th at Maceira; and to send the empty carts on the 27th to Maceira, so that they may be full on the 28th, and ready to move on the 29th. The corps which will land and come on to the camp at Torres Vedras on the 27th should have 5 days' bread with them, to the 31st inclusive.

To Lord Mulgrave, First Lord of the Admiralty.   Ramalhal, 26th Aug. 1808.

As my command is at an end, I hope I may be permitted to trouble you with a few lines on the co-operation which I have received from the navy. I have long been in the habits of friendship and intimacy with Capt. Malcolm, of the *Donegal;* but it is impossible for me to describe the zeal, the ardor, and the kindness with which he entered into all my views; and the whole army will bear testimony to the exertions which he and all the officers of the navy acting under him made to provide for their convenience on the passage, to land them with celerity, and to provide for all their necessities and comforts when they were on shore. His views in all these respects were fully carried into execution by Capt. Adam, of the *Resistance,* and Capt. Cadogan, of the *Crocodile;* and, after our arrival on the coast of Portugal, by Capt. Bligh, of the *Alfred,* from whom we received some most essential assistance. There were other Captains of the navy with whom we have had at different times occasion to communicate, and I must say that the same desire to render us every assistance in their power has animated them all; which I attribute in a great degree to the disposition which, throughout the service, has been manifested by Capt. Malcolm, who was principally charged with its conduct.

I also beg leave to recommend to your Lordship's favor and protection Lieut. Fleetwood, the agent of transports, who superintended the fleet in which the army under my command was embarked. He is the most active, intelligent, and zealous of all the officers that I have seen in that line of the naval profession, and he really deserves promotion. If his services should be continued in the transport line of the profession, benefit will be derived from his promotion, as his sphere will be enlarged, and the armies to which he may be attached in future will not suffer the inconvenience which that under my command did, of having him superseded by an officer without any of his qualifications, in the midst of the service. I have to add that Capt. Malcolm is equally satisfied with Lieut. Fleetwood.

To the Commissioners of the Transport board.   Ramalhal, 26th Aug. 1808.

As Lieut. Gen. Sir H. Dalrymple has taken the command of the army, which was lately under my orders, I take this opportunity of drawing your attention to the conduct of Lieut. Fleetwood, the agent of transports attached to that army. I cannot say too much in praise of his zeal, intelligence, and activity; and I have great pleasure in adding, that his conduct has given equal satisfaction to Capt. Malcolm, of the *Donegal,* to whom the conduct of the naval part of the service was intrusted. I therefore hope that you will apply to the Lords Commissioners of the Admiralty to promote Lieut. Fleetwood, and otherwise reward him as you may think proper.

To Lieut. Gen. Sir H. Dalrymple.   Ramalhal, 26th Aug. 1808.

I have the honor to enclose herewith a schedule of recommendations for promotion, in consequence of the casualties which took place in the action of the 21st inst., together with some memorials in support of these officers' claims, and also a memorial from Brevet Lieut. Col. Davies, of the 36th regt.; all of which I request you will be pleased to forward to the Commander in Chief, for his Royal Highness' favorable consideration.

You will be pleased to observe, that I have recommended the succession in the 20th light dragoons, according to the seniority of the officers, as they stand in the detachment at present serving with this army; and although it may interfere in some instances with the regimental priority of rank, I have considered the recommendation in favor of the officers named in the schedule as a justice due to the gallantry which that corps displayed in the action of the 21st inst., particularly in the case of Major Blake, who is a most deserving officer.

To the Duke of Richmond.   Ramalhal, 27th Aug. 1808.

I wrote to you after the battle of the 21st. On the 22d, in the morning, Sir H. Dalrymple arrived; and on that evening Gen. Kellermann came in to ask for a suspension of hostilities, to give time for the negotiation of a Convention for the evacuation of Portugal by the French by sea. Sir Hew consented to this, and desired me to sign it, notwithstanding that I neither negotiated nor approved of it.

This agreement contained many improper stipulations; among others, it gave the French 48 hours' notice of an intention to put an end to it. It likewise contained a stipulation in respect to the Russians which ought never to have been admitted; and it was in other respects objectionable on account of its French *verbiage*. I have not got a copy of it. The objections to it have, however, since been considerably removed, by the refusal of the Admiral to consent to the stipulation respecting the Russians, and by the determination of the suspension of hostilities to-morrow at 12 o'clock, unless Murray, who is negotiating the Convention, should be of opinion that an additional period of 24 hours is necessary to enable him to perform his work. I am ready to march in the evening, and Sir J. Moore next day; and, whether there is a Convention or not, I hope to be in Lisbon by the beginning of September.

I approve of allowing the French to evacuate the country, for I am convinced that, if we did not, we should be obliged to attack Elvas, Fort la Lippe, Almeida, and Peniche, regularly, or blockade them, and thus the autumn would pass away; and it is better to have 10,000 or 12,000 additional Frenchmen on the northern frontier of Spain, and the English army in Spain, than the Frenchmen in Portugal, and the English blockading them in strong places. This necessity would have been avoided, if Sir H. Burrard would or could have carried on with Sir J. Moore's corps the operations upon Santarem, which I recommended to him, by which the French would certainly have been cut off from Elvas and Almeida.

The French got a terrible beating on the 21st. They did not lose less, I believe, than 4000 men; and they would have been entirely destroyed, if Sir H. Burrard had not prevented me from pursuing them. Indeed, since the arrival of the great generals, we appear to have been palsied, and every thing has gone on wrong.

I am getting plans done for you of both the battles of the 17th and 21st, and I will write to you if any thing further should occur. I am not very well pleased, between ourselves, with the way in which things in this country are likely to go on, and I shall not be sorry to go home, if I can do so with propriety; in which case I shall soon see you. But I don't like to desire to go, lest it should be imputed to me that I am unwilling to serve where I don't command.

P.S. I have heard nothing of Ireland since I left it. Pray, remember me most kindly to the Duchess, and Louisa, &c., and Lady Edward. Lord FitzRoy has been very useful to me; and I have this day lent him to Sir H. Dalrymple, to go to the French head quarters.

To Lieut. Gen. Sir H. Dalrymple.　　　　　　Torres Vedras, 29th Aug. 1808.

I have the honor to enclose herewith a letter from Brig. Gen. Anstruther, covering a representation from Major Hull, of the 43d regt., respecting the inadequacy of the present establishment of subalterns and non-commissioned officers to carrying on the duties of the 2d battalion of that corps in the field; and also a statement of the services of Major Hull,* whom I am induced to recommend for the lieutenant colonelcy, for the reasons stated in Brig. Gen. Anstruther's letter, should His Majesty be pleased to appoint an additional Lieut. Colonel to the 43d regt.

I request that you will be pleased to forward these papers to the Commander in Chief, for his Royal Highness' favorable consideration.

To Capt. P. Malcolm, H.M.S. *Donegal.*　　Torres Vedras, 29th Aug. 1808, ½ past 5, P. M.

Capt. Dalrymple arrived this morning with the Convention, signed by Gen. Kellermann and Col. Murray; but it was so objectionable in many parts, that a meeting of the General officers was called to deliberate upon and settle the alterations to be made in it, which meeting I attended. The result of the meeting was a proposal to make certain alterations, which I acknowledge I do not think sufficient, although the treaty will answer in its amended form. In the mean time the army remains on its present ground, very much against my opinion.

I am afraid that I am so much connected with the credit of this army, that I cannot remain with it without falling as it will fall. If I could be of any use to men who have served me so well, I would stay with them for ever; but as matters are situated, I am sure that I can be of no use to them; I am convinced they cannot render any service, and I have determined to go home immediately.

At the same time I must say that I approve of allowing the French to evacuate Portugal, because I see clearly that we cannot get them out of Portugal otherwise, under existing circumstances, without such an arrangement; and we should be employed in the blockade or siege of the places which they would occupy during the season in which we ought and might be advantageously employed against the French in Spain. But the Convention, by which they should be allowed to evacuate Portugal, ought to be settled in the most honorable manner to the army by which they have been beaten; and we ought not to be kept for 10 days

* Afterwards killed in command of the 1st batt. 43d regt., at Gen. R. Craufurd's affair on the Coa, the 24th July, 1810.

on our field of battle before the enemy (who sued on the day after the action) is brought to terms. I am quite annoyed on this subject.

Definitive Convention for the evacuation of Portugal by the French Army.

The Generals commanding in chief of the British and French armies in Portugal, having determined to negotiate and conclude a treaty for the evacuation of Portugal by the French troops, on the basis of the agreement entered into on the 22d inst., for a suspension of hostilities, have appointed the undermentioned officers to negotiate the same in their names: viz., on the part of the General in Chief of the British army, Lieut. Col. Murray, Q. M. G.; and on the part of the French army, M. Kellermann, General of Division, to whom they have given authority to negotiate and conclude a Convention to that effect, subject to their ratification respectively, and to that of the Admiral commanding the British fleet at the entrance of the Tagus. These 2 officers, after exchanging their full powers, have agreed upon the articles which follow:

Art. 1. All the places and forts in the kingdom of Portugal, occupied by the French troops, shall be delivered up to the British army, in the state in which they are at the period of the signature of the present Convention.

Art. 2. The French troops shall evacuate Portugal, with their arms and baggage: they shall not be considered as prisoners of war; and, on their arrival in France, they shall be at liberty to serve.

Art. 3. The English government shall furnish the means of conveyance for the French army, which shall be disembarked in any of the ports of France between Rochefort and Lorient inclusively.

Art. 4. The French army shall carry with it all its artillery of French calibre, with the horses belonging to it, and the tumbrils supplied with 60 rounds per gun. All other artillery, arms, and ammunition, as also the military and naval arsenal, shall be given up to the British army and navy, in the state in which they may be at the period of the ratification of the Convention.

Art. 5. The French army shall carry with it all its equipments, and all that is comprehended under the name of property of the army, that is to say, its military chest, and the carriages attached to the field Commissariat and field hospital; or shall be allowed to dispose of such part of the same on its account, as the Commander in Chief may judge it unnecessary to embark. In like manner all individuals of the army shall be at liberty to dispose of all their private property of every description, with full security hereafter for the purchasers.

Art. 6. The cavalry are to embark their horses, as also the Generals and other officers of all ranks: it is, however, fully understood, that the means of conveyance for horses, at the disposal of the British Commander in Chief, are very limited. Some additional conveyance may be procured in the port of Lisbon. The number of horses to be embarked by the troops shall not exceed 600, and the number embarked by the Staff shall not exceed 200. At all events, every facility will be given to the French army to dispose of the horses belonging to it which cannot be embarked.

Art. 7. In order to facilitate the embarkation, it shall take place in 3 divisions, the last of which will be principally composed of the garrisons of the places, of the cavalry, the artillery, the sick, and the equipment of the army. The first division shall embark within 7 days from the date of the ratification, or sooner if possible.

Art. 8. The garrison of Elvas and its forts, and of Peniche and Palmella, will be embarked at Lisbon; that of Almeida at Oporto, or the nearest harbour. They will be accompanied on their march by British Commissaries charged with providing for their subsistence and accommodation.

Art. 9. All the sick and wounded who cannot be embarked with the troops are intrusted to the British army: they are to be taken care of whilst they remain in this country at the expense of the British government, under the condition of the same being reimbursed by France, when the final evacuation is effected. The English government will provide for their return to France, which shall take place by detachments of about 150 or 200 men at a time. A sufficient number of French medical officers shall be left behind to attend them.

Art. 10. As soon as the vessels employed to carry the army to France shall have disembarked it in the harbours specified, or in any other of the ports of France, to which stress of weather may force them, every facility shall be given them to return to England without delay, and security against capture, until their arrival in a friendly port.

Art. 11. The French army shall be concentrated in Lisbon, and within a distance of about 2 leagues from it. The English army will approach within 3 leagues of the capital, and will be so placed as to leave about one league between the 2 armies.

Art. 12. The forts of St. Julian, the Bugio, and Cascaes, shall be occupied by the British troops on the ratification of the Convention. Lisbon and its citadel, together with the forts and batteries as far as the Lazaretto or Traffaria, on one side, and Fort St. Joseph on the other, inclusively, shall be given up on the embarkation of the second division, as shall also the harbour, and all the armed vessels in it of every description, with their rigging, sails, stores, and ammunition. The fortresses of Elvas, Almeida, Peniche, and Palmella, shall be given up as soon as the British troops can arrive to occupy them: in the mean time, the General in Chief of the British army will give notice of the present Convention to the garrisons of those places, as also to the troops before them, in order to put a stop to all further hostilities.

Art. 13. Commissaries shall be named on both sides to regulate and accelerate the execution of the arrangements agreed upon.

Art. 14. Should there arise any doubt as to the meaning of any article, it shall be explained favorably to the French army.

Art. 15. From the date of the ratification of tne present Convention all arrears of contributions, requisitions, or claims, whatever, of the French government against the subjects of Portugal, or any other individuals residing in this country, founded on the occupation of Portugal by the French troops in the month of Dec. 1807, which may not have been paid up, are cancelled; and all sequestrations laid upon their property, moveable or immoveable, are removed, and the free disposal of the same is restored to the proper owners.

Art. 16. All subjects of France, or of powers in friendship or alliance with France, domiciliated in Portugal, or accidentally in this country, shall be protected. Their property of every kind, moveable and immoveable, shall be respected ; and they shall be at liberty either to accompany the French army or to remain in Portugal; in either case their property is guaranteed to them, with the liberty of retaining or of disposing of it, and passing the sale thereof into France, or any other country where they may fix their residence : the space of one year being allowed them for that purpose. It is fully understood that shipping is excepted from this arrangement; only, however, in so far as regards leaving the port; and that none of the stipulations above mentioned can be.made the pretext of any commercial speculation.

Art. 17. No native of Portugal shall be rendered accountable for his political conduct during the period of the occupation of this country by the French army, and all those who have continued in the exercise of their employments, or who have accepted situations under the French government, are placed under the protection of the British Commanders : they shall sustain no injury in their persons or property, it not having been at their option to be obedient or not to the French government. They are also at liberty to avail themselves of the stipulations of the 16th article.

Art. 18. The Spanish troops detained on board of ship in the port of Lisbon shall be given up to the General in Chief of the British army, who engages to obtain of the Spaniards to restore such French subjects, either military or civil, as may have been detained in Spain, without being taken in battle, or in consequence of military operations, but on occasion of the occurrences of the 29th of last May and the days immediately following.

Art. 19. There shall be an immediate exchange established for all ranks of prisoners made in Portugal since the commencement of the present hostilities.

Art. 20. Hostages of the rank of field officers shall be mutually furnished on the part of the British army and navy, and on that of the French army, for the reciprocal guarantee of the present Convention. The officer of the British army shall be restored on the completion of these articles which concern the army, and the officer of the navy on the disembarkation of the French troops in their own country. The like is to take place on the part of the French army.

Art. 21. It shall be allowed to the General in Chief of the French army to send an officer to France with intelligence of the present Convention. A vessel will be furnished by the British Admiral to carry him to Bordeaux or Rochefort.

Art. 22. The British Admiral will be invited to accommodate his Excellency the Commander in Chief and the other principal officers on board of ships of war.

Done and concluded at Lisbon, this thirtieth day of August, one thousand eight hundred and eight.

GEORGE MURRAY, Q. M. G.
KELLERMANN, Général de division.

Additional Articles to the Convention of the 30th Aug. 1808.

Art. 1. The individuals in the civil employments of the army, made prisoners, either by the British troops or by the Portuguese, in any part of Portugal, will be restored, as is customary, without exchange.

Art. 2. The French army shall be subsisted from its own magazines up to the day of embarkation, the garrisons up to the day of the evacuations of the fortresses.   The remainder of the magazines shall be delivered over in the usual form to the British government, which charges itself with the subsistence of the men and horses of the army, from the above mentioned periods until their arrival in France, under the conditions of their being re-imbursed by the French government for the excess of the expense, beyond the estimation to be made by both parties, of the value of the magazines delivered.   The provisions on board the ships of war, in possession of the French army, will be taken on account by the British government, in like manner with the magazines of the fortresses.

Art. 3. The General commanding the British troops will take the necessary measures for re-establishing the free circulation of the means of subsistence between the country and the capital.

Done and concluded, &c. &c., and signed as before.

To Visc. Castlereagh.   Camp, N. of Torres Vedras, 30th Aug. 1808.

A Convention, signed by Gen. Kellermann and Col. Murray, for the evacuation of Portugal by the French troops, was brought here yesterday morning; but it was not ratified by the General, in consequence of his finding some fault with it.   It was altered, but not as I thought as it ought to have been, and was returned to Junot yesterday afternoon.   In the mean time, the army has halted in its position; with the only difference, that we have a corps in Torres Vedras, instead of 3 miles from that town.   In short, in 10 days after the action of the 21st, we are not farther advanced; or, indeed, as I believe, so far advanced as we should and ought to have been on the night of the 21st.

I assure you, my dear Lord, matters are not prospering here; and I feel an earnest desire to quit the army.   I have been too successful with this army ever to serve with it in a subordinate situation, with satisfaction to the person who shall command it, and of course not to myself.   However, I shall do whatever the government may wish.

To Lieut. Gen. Sir H. Dalrymple.   Sobral de Monte Agraço, 1st Sept. 1808.

As it is probable that you will take an early opportunity of communicating with England, I think it proper at this time to submit to you the enclosed state of the horses attached to the artillery, with the corps which has hitherto been under my command.   As it was not deemed expedient that I should take with me horses belonging to the artillery, horses belonging to the Irish Commissariat were embarked for the purpose of drawing the artillery, which horses were of a very inferior description, being either cast horses from the dragoons, or horses purchased in Ireland at a very low price, viz., £12 or £13 each; and they were never intended to be applied to this purpose.   They have, however, performed the service hitherto, but with the aids and losses stated in the enclosed papers; and you will observe that there are at this moment 76 of them with incurable diseases.

As these horses were never intended to perform the service of the artillery, and as I have every reason to believe that mules will not answer to draw our ordnance carriages, and that the country does not afford horses of a proper description, I cannot avoid recommending to you to call the attention of His Majesty's government to this subject at an early period; and to require•an immediate supply of 300 artillery horses to draw the brigades of ordnance which have been hitherto attached to this corps, if you should have reason to expect that you shall require any further active service from those guns.

I had already apprised the Sec. of State of the inadequacy of these horses to the service required of them.

While writing upon this subject, it is proper to remind you, that there is another brigade of 6 pounders belonging to the corps hitherto called mine, three pieces of which are in the ships, and three were left at Leiria, as the horses were unable to draw them on.

To C. Stuart, Esq.   Sobral, 1st Sept. 1808.

In the last letter which I wrote to you I believe I informed you of our actions on the 17th and 21st Aug.; and that the Commander in Chief had agreed to a suspension of hostilities with the French, with a view to the settlement of a Convention for their entire evacuation of Portugal.

Since I wrote that letter I have received yours (I think) of the 19th Aug., which I have given to Sir H. Dalrymple, and he will of course write to you. I trouble you now only because Sir R. Wilson's departure for Oporto affords a favorable opportunity of sending a letter, and I consider it desirable that you should be apprised of the state of affairs here.

The agreement for the suspension of hostilities, concluded on the night of the 22nd Aug., ended in a Convention for the evacuation of Portugal by the French, signed on the 30th of that month. As far as I have learnt, the Convention contains nothing material, excepting that the French are to be taken to a port in France; that they are to embark within 7 days; that till they are embarked they are to remain in possession of Lisbon and a circuit of 2 leagues; and we are to have Fort St. Julian, Cascaes, and all the forts on the coast and in the interior, upon the ratification of the Convention. They are to give up the Spanish prisoners on the General engaging to use his good offices that Frenchmen taken in Spain, not having engaged in hostilities, should likewise be released. There is nothing else in the Convention that I have heard of that is of any importance. The Russians, Danes, &c., are left at our mercy.

As far as I have any knowledge of them, I have many objections both to the agreement for suspending hostilities and to the Convention for the evacuation of Portugal by the French. I approve, however, of the principal point in the latter, viz., to allow them to evacuate: and it is useless to trouble you with my objections to the mode in which that point has been brought about.

My reasons for thinking that we have done right in allowing them to evacuate are as follow :

1st. Sir H. Burrard and Sir H. Dalrymple having determined that they would bring Sir J. Moore's corps down to Lisbon, instead of placing it in a situation in which it would have the means of cutting off the enemy's retreat across the Tagus, he would have been enabled to secure himself in Elvas and Almeida, and the campaign would have been spent in the siege or blockade of those places. Admitting that the army which will evacuate Lisbon will be immediately carried to the frontiers of Spain, I conceive it better to have that army in that situation, and our army acting in Spain, in co-operation with the Spanish troops, than to have the French troops occupying strong places in Portugal, and our army occupied in the siege or blockade of them.

2dly. The Commander in Chief and those who surround him appeared very unwilling to advance towards Lisbon, even after our victory of the 21st Aug., without the assistance of Sir J. Moore's corps ; and as the period of his arrival at Maceira, the place of disembarkation, was very uncertain, and delays at this season of the year were very dangerous, and we had already had on the 22d Aug. some very bad weather, of which a continuance was certainly to be expected early in this month, when the fleet of transports, with which a communication was also lately necessary to us, must have quitted the coast, I considered our only chance of reaching Lisbon at all to be by negotiation.

If we had not negotiated we could not have advanced before the 30th, as Sir J. Moore's corps was not ready till that day. The French would at that time have fortified their positions near Lisbon, which it is probable we should not have been in a situation to attack till the end of the first week in this month. Then, taking the chances of the bad weather depriving us of the communication with the fleet of transports and victuallers, and delaying and rendering more difficult and precarious our land operations, which after all would not have been effectual to cut off the retreat of the French across the Tagus into Alentejo, I was clearly of opinion that the best thing to do was to consent to a Convention and allow them to evacuate Portugal.

The detail of this Convention, and of the agreement for suspending hostilities, is a question of another kind, upon which it is useless that I should trouble you ; and I write what I have above written only that you may be aware of the general grounds on which I acquiesced in the Convention, as far as its principal point goes, some of which, I believe, induced the General himself to consent to it.

I do not know what Sir H. Dalrymple proposes to do, or is instructed to do ; but if I were in his situation I would have 20,000 men at Madrid in less than a month from this time. I propose recommending to him to arm and accoutre the Spanish troops, and to send them into Spain.

We, that is, my corps, are only 24 miles from Lisbon, and I believe the army about the same distance, on the side of Mafra.

To the Duke of Richmond.   Sobral, 1st Sept. 1808.

A Convention was signed on the day before yesterday, for the evacuation of Portugal by the French, and they will be off in the course of 7 days. I have not seen the Convention, and I know it contains some matter of which I disapprove, as much as I did of the agreement for the suspension of hostilities, but it is useless to trouble you with my objections to it. I told you in my last letter that I thought it right to agree to the main point in the Convention, viz. the evacuation; and it is not of much importance in what manner that is carried into execution.

The armies are now situated as follows: my corps is on the left, about 24 miles from Lisbon, and I shall march to-morrow to Bucellas and Tojal, where I shall be about 12 miles from thence; and the army, consisting of Moore's corps, and Anstruther's and Acland's brigades, are this day at Mafra, and will be to-morrow at Cintra. They will occupy St. Julian and Cascaes, and we shall remain in these situations until the French shall evacuate. We got all the forts in the interior and on the coast immediately upon the ratification of the Convention.

I shall wait till I see the French fairly off, by which time I hope that I shall hear from ministers whether they wish me to return to my office. If they do, I shall be with you immediately; and I assure you that, considering the way in which things are likely to be carried on here, I shall not be sorry to go away.

Remember me most kindly to the Duchess and the children.

P.S. Lord FitzRoy is come back from Lisbon, and gives a fine account of Junot, who was very civil to him.

To the General Officers.　　　　　　Zambujal, 12 miles N. of Lisbon, 3d Sept. 1808.

I have had the honor of receiving your letter of this day, and I assure you that it is a source of great gratification to me to find that my conduct in the command, with which I was lately intrusted by His Majesty, has given you satisfaction.

As my efforts were directed to forward the service on which we were employed, I could not fail to receive your support and assistance; and to the cordial support and friendly advice and assistance which I invariably received from you collectively and individually, I attribute the success of our endeavors to bring the army into the state in which it was formed to meet the enemy on the days on which the gallantry of the officers and soldiers was stimulated by your example, and their discipline aided and directed by your experience and ability.

Under these circumstances my task has been comparatively light, and I imagine that its difficulty has been overrated by your partiality; but I have a pride in the reflection that as I should not deserve, so I should not possess, your regard, if I had not done my duty; and with these sentiments, and those of respect and affection for you all, I accept of that testimony of your esteem and confidence which you have been pleased to present to me.

The General officers who landed with the troops at the Mondego to Lieut. Gen. the Hon. Sir A. Wellesley, K.B.　　　　　　Camp at St. Antonio do Tojal, 3d Sept. 1808.

Anxious to manifest the high esteem and respect we bear towards you, and the satisfaction we must ever feel in having had the good fortune to serve under your command, we have this day directed a piece of plate, value 1000 guineas,* to be prepared and presented to you.

The enclosed inscription, which we have ordered to be engraved on it, expresses our feelings on this occasion.

B. Spencer, Major Gen.	B. F. Bowes, Brig. Gen.
R. Hill, Major Gen.	H. Fane, Brig. Gen.
R. Ferguson, Major Gen.	J. Catlin Craufurd, Brig. Gen.
M. Nightingall, Brig. Gen.	

'Inscription.

'From the General officers serving in the British army, originally landed at Figueira, in Portugal, in the year 1808, to Lieut. Gen. the Rt. Hon. Sir A. Wellesley, K.B., &c., their Commander.

'Major Gen. Spencer, second in command, Major Gens. Hill and Ferguson, Brig. Gens. Nightingall, Bowes, Fane, and Craufurd, offer this gift to their leader, in testimony of the high respect and esteem they feel for him as a man, and the unbounded confidence they place in him as an officer.'

Visc. Castlereagh to Lieut. Gen. the Hon. Sir A. Wellesley, K.B.

Downing Street, 4th Sept. 1808.

I received by your aide de camp, Capt. Campbell, your dispatches of the 16th and 17th Aug., the first containing the account of the affair at Alcobaca, which obliged the enemy to retire his advanced posts; the other of the 17th, containing the account of your attack, with the troops under your command, on the advanced corps of the enemy, in their formidable position near Obidos, and of their entire defeat.

These dispatches having been laid before His Majesty, I am to convey to you His Majesty's entire satisfaction in the able, spirited, and decisive conduct you have displayed, by which so much credit has been reflected upon His Majesty's arms, and the progress of the army towards the complete reduction of the enemy was so greatly facilitated.

His Majesty has also signified his royal pleasure, that his most gracious approbation should be signified by you to Major Gen. Spencer, and to the Generals and other officers under your command, for the skill, valor, and perseverance they exhibited, and to the troops in general, for the courage, coolness, and determination which appear to have marked their conduct.

Visc. Castlereagh to Lieut. Gen. Sir H. Burrard, Bart. Downing Street, 4th Sept. 1808.

I received by Capt. Campbell, aide de camp to Lieut. Gen. Sir A. Wellesley, your dispatch of the 21st ult., enclosing the report to you from that General, of the signal victory obtained by His Majesty's forces under his orders, when attacked, at Vimeiro, by the whole of the French force in Portugal, commanded by Gen. Junot in person.

Having laid the same before His Majesty, I am directed by His Majesty to desire that you will signify to Lieut. Gen. Sir A. Wellesley, that the disposition made by him to receive the enemy, and the skill and valor displayed by him in effecting their total defeat, have afforded His Majesty the highest satisfaction.

The conduct of Major Gen. Spencer, and of the other Generals and officers who so ably executed the orders they had received, and displayed so many instances of judgment and valor, is highly honorable to themselves and acceptable to His Majesty.

You will be pleased to communicate the satisfaction His Majesty feels in the deliberate and steady bravery by which his troops distinguished themselves, reflecting at once equal honor upon the character and discipline of his army— qualities by which alone success in war can be permanently looked for.

The delicacy and honorable forbearance which determined you, though present in the action, not to interfere with the arrangements previously made by Lieut. Gen. Sir A. Wellesley, and then in progress of execution, has been observed by His Majesty with approbation.

* This piece of plate was afterwards augmented in value by the additional subscriptions of Gens. Anstruther and Acland, and the field officers of the army who served under the orders of Major Gen. Sir A. Wellesley, at the battle of Vimeiro.

To Capt. P. Malcolm, H.M.S. *Donegal.*   Zambujal, 5th Sept. 1808.

I received your letter of Saturday this morning, having been at Cintra yesterday morning, and not having returned here till late in the evening. I lament the situation of our affairs as much as you do, and I did every thing in my power to prevent it; but my opinion was overruled. I had nothing to do with the Convention as it now stands; and I have never seen it to this moment.

I have not heard from your brother yet, but I suppose his letter is coming to me. I will see you soon if I can. I have stronger reasons, public as well as private, but I shall not decide hastily or in anger upon any subject.

P.S. Give my best love to Cadogan, and tell him that I lament the result of our labors as much as he does, but that it is not my fault. I have only to regret that I put my name to an agreement of which I did not approve, and which I did not negotiate. If I had not done it, I really believe that they would not have dared to make such a Convention as they have made; notwithstanding that that agreement was never ratified, and is now so much waste paper.

To Lieut. Col. Murray, Q. M. G.   Zambujal, 5th Sept. 1808.

I hope you will be able to make a good arrangement for the performance of the duty required from me in the Asturias, for which I deem myself incapable. If it were not so, I believe your experience of the zeal with which I served Lord Cathcart would convince you that I would not decline performing any duty which the government could require from me. I shall not conceal from you, however, that I consider myself in a very different situation in this army from that in which Lord Cathcart placed me; and I acknowledge that I cannot venture to do many things which I did for him, because it is evident that there exists a want of confidence which never existed in respect to me in any former instance. This, however, did not affect my decision in the service required of me yesterday, which I certainly should have undertaken if I had been capable of performing it.

To Lieut. Gen. Sir H. Dalrymple.   Zambujal, 5th Sept. 1808.

When I had the honor of recommending to you to appoint a successor to Capt. Preval of the Foreign Engineers, as Captain of Guides, I apprised you of the bad state of health of that officer, who had then requested me to apply to you for leave to go to England for his recovery, which request he has since repeated. I therefore beg leave to recommend that Capt. Preval may have leave to go to England for the recovery of his health.

I cannot make this request without, at the same time, mentioning my sense of Capt. Preval's services, not only in his capacity of engineer, but in that of Captain of Guides. In Portugal the services of an officer in the latter capacity are most essential, there being no map of the country, and no person capable of giving information of a topographical nature; and of all those whose services have contributed to the success of the late operations, there is none who, in his line, stands higher than Capt. Preval.

Under these circumstances, I recommend this application for leave of absence to your favorable attention. And as his duty has been most laborious, and attended by some responsibility, I beg leave to recommend that he may have the pay and allowances of a D. A. Q. M. G. from the 1st Aug., on which day he commenced to perform it. I have to mention that if the command of the army had remained in my hands, I should have given him that appointment, which I observe that you have given to his successor in the Corps of Guides.

To Visc. Castlereagh.   Zambujal, 12 miles N. of Lisbon, 5th Sept. 1808.

Your brother Charles communicated to me your letter of the 20th Aug. to Sir H. Dalrymple, of which Sir Hew himself communicated to me different parts yesterday; and I proceed to give you my opinion on the points to which it relates. I must apprise you, however, that our information here of the state of affairs in Spain is very defective; that we, or at least I, do not know what is the position, what are the numbers, what are the means, or what ought to be the objects of the French army in Spain; and I am equally ignorant of the state of the force of the Spaniards.

I rather believe, however, that the French army in Spain now consists of about 40,000 men, of which number about 5000 are cavalry, and that they are under the command of Marshal Bessieres, and are stationed somewhere about Vitoria, in Biscay. The probability that they will be reinforced must depend upon the state of affairs in the other parts of Europe, of which I have no knowledge whatever; but if the attention of the French government is not called to other quarters, we must expect that the French army in Spain will be increased at an early period to a very large amount.

The amount of the force with which operations can be carried on in Spain is another and a very material consideration, which bears upon the whole question; and, from all that I have heard of the state of the resources in the country, I should doubt whether it will be practicable to carry on operations in Spain with a larger corps than 40,000 men. There may be other *corps de reserve*, and employed in operations on other lines, or on the same line, in the protection of convoys from France, &c.; but it is not probable that the corps in front will exceed 40,000 men. You must consider this, however, as a mere matter of opinion, founded upon general information of the state of the resources in Spain, in which I may be much mistaken.

The next point for consideration is the force of the Spaniards: I really know of nothing that they have in the shape of an army capable of meeting the French, excepting that under Gen. Castanos. Gen. Cuesta has some cavalry in Castille; Gen. Galluzzo some more in Estremadura; and Blake's army of Galicia may in time become an efficient corps. But those armies of peasantry, which in Murcia, Valencia, and Catalonia, have cut up French corps, must not be reckoned upon (at least at present) as efficient armies to meet the French troops in the field. It is most probable that they will not, and indeed cannot, leave their provinces; and if they could, no officer could calculate a great operation upon such a body.

I doubt not that, if an accurate report could be made upon their state, they want arms, ammunition, money, clothing, and military equipments of every description; and although such a body are very formidable and efficient in their own country, and probably equal to its defence, they must not be reckoned upon out of it; and in any case it is impossible to estimate the effect of their efforts. In some cases equal numbers will oppose with success the French troops; in others, 1000 Frenchmen, with cavalry and artillery, will disperse thousands of them, and no reliance can be placed on them in their present state.

The result, then, of my information of the present state of the Spanish force to be opposed to the French, is, that there are about 25,000 men under Castanos, now ready, and about the same number under Blake in Galicia, upon whom you may reckon as efficient troops. All the rest may become so, and may be useful in different ways even at present, but you must not found the arrangement for a great military operation on their utility or efficiency. I understand that government had promised 10,000 men to Castaños, and I have no doubt whatever that a corps well equipped, consisting of about 15,000 men, including a proportion of British cavalry and artillery, would be highly useful to him. This would make his army 40,000 men, of which the British corps would be the best troops that could be found anywhere; and this army, aided by the insurrection from the other kingdoms of Spain, would be the operating army against what I have supposed to be the French operating army. This British corps should advance from Portugal, to which kingdom it would be in the mean time a defence.

You should leave in Portugal a British corps of 5000 men, to be stationed at and in the neighbourhood of Lisbon, with probably a small garrison in Elvas. The object in stationing this corps in Portugal is to give strength to the government which you will establish here, and to render it independent of the factions and intrigues by which it will be assailed on all sides. You ought to send to Lisbon, in the quality of the King's Ambassador, a discreet person, who could superintend the management of the affairs of this country, particularly the expenditure of the money which you must supply for its wants, and its application to the purposes for which it will be given, viz., to provide a military defence.

The next consideration is the employment of the remainder of the army now in Portugal, amounting by estimate to about 10,000 men, with an additional corps of 10,000 men assembled and ready in England, and some cavalry. I acknowledge that I do not think the affairs in Spain are in so prosperous a state as that you can trust, in operations within that kingdom, the whole disposable force which England possesses, without adopting measures of precaution, which will render its retreat to the sea coast nearly certain. Besides this, I will not conceal from you that our people are so new in the field, that I do not know of persons capable of supplying, or, if supplied, of distributing the supplies, to an army of 40,000 men (British troops) acting together in a body. Even if plenty could be expected to exist, we should starve in the midst of it, for want of due arrangement. But the first objection is conclusive. We may depend upon it that whenever we shall assemble an army the French will consider its defeat and destruction their first object, particularly if Buonaparte should be at the head of the French troops himself; and if the operations of our army should be near the French frontier, he will have the means of multiplying, and will multiply, the numbers upon our army in such a degree as must get the better of them. For the British army, therefore, we must have a retreat open, and that retreat must be the sea.

Our operations carried on from Portugal and the north of Spain would, as you truly observe, involve us in a line of operations much too long. The retreat would be difficult, if not impossible. This objection, you will say, would apply equally to the corps of 15,000 men proposed to be employed with Castaños. 1st, I conceive that there is a great deal of difference between the risk of the loss of such a corps as this, and that of the loss of the whole of the disposable force of Great Britain. 2dly, it does not follow that, because the whole British army could not make its retreat into Portugal, a corps of 15,000 could not. 3dly, it does not follow that this corps of 15,000 men would necessarily retreat upon Portugal; being a part of Castaños' army, it might retire with his troops into Andalusia, leaving the frontiers of Portugal to be defended by the Portuguese and the British corps of 5000 men, till those, or a part of them, would again be brought round to the Tagus, or could enter Portugal by Algarve. I conclude, then, that although this corps might be risked, and its retreat to the sea should be considered in some degree *en l'air*, that of the whole disposable force of Great Britain ought to be, and must be, saved.

The only efficient plan of operations in which the British troops can be employed, consistently with this view, is upon the flank and rear of the enemy's advance towards Madrid, by an issue from the Asturias. If it be true, as is stated by the Asturian deputies in London, that their country is remarkably strong, and that it is secure from French invasion; if it be true that the ports of Santander and Gijon, the former particularly, are secure harbours in the winter; and if the walls can give to both, or either, the means of making an embarkation, even if the enemy should be able to retreat through the mountains; the Asturias is the country we should secure immediately, in which we should assemble our disposable force as soon as possible, and issue forth into the plains, either by Leon or the pass of Reynosa. The army could then have a short, although probably a difficult communication with the sea, which must be carried on by mules, of which there are plenty in the country; it could co-operate with Blake's Galician army, and could press upon the enemy's right flank and rear, and turn his position upon the Ebro, which it is evident he intends to make his first line. To secure the Asturias as soon as possible, you may depend upon it, is your first object in Spain, and afterwards to assemble within that country your whole disposable force, after marching the detachment to Castaños.

There are some points of detail which must be attended to in these arrangements. The army now in this country might either be marched into Leon, or it might be embarked and transported to Gijon or Santander. The latter would be the quickest operation; by the adoption of the former, its artillery, in its present form, might accompany it; but it must be recollected, that if the artillery should be kept in its present form, in case of retreat it must be left behind in the plains; as I understand there is no carriage-road across the mountains of Asturias.

The troops, then, now in this country ought to be embarked in the

Tagus, and sent to the Asturias; and ordnance carriages ought to be sent from England without loss of time, which can be taken to pieces, and carried by hand, or when put together can be drawn by horses.   The reports, which will be made by the officers sent to those countries, will state whether cavalry can pass through them : I should think they might; as I see that wherever a mule can go a horse can likewise.   If so, the cavalry from England should likewise be landed in Asturias; if not, the cavalry should be landed at Coruña or Ferrol, and join the army in the plains, through the passes of Galicia, which we know are practicable for cavalry.

There remains now to be considered only the operations of the Sicilian corps, consisting of 10,000 men.   In the present state of affairs the government will probably not deem it expedient to remove this corps from the Mediterranean.   If the Spaniards should be able to make any head against the French on the left of their line in Catalonia, and on the Lower Ebro, this corps might reinforce that part of the Spanish insurrection, keeping its retreat always open to the sea.   This, however, would be very difficult, the French being in possession of Barcelona; and probably the siege of that place, aided by the insurgents of Catalonia, would be the most this corps would perform.   And whether the operation should be successfully included, or the corps should be forced to re-embark in consequence of the approach of the stronger French force, it would materially aid the operations of the troops in the centre of Spain.

The result of all these operations, which must for the present be distinct, would be to confine the French to their line of the Ebro for the present, and eventually to oblige them to retire upon their own frontier.   Time would be gained for the further organization of the Spanish government and force; by the judicious and effectual employment of which the British government would be enabled to withdraw its troops from Spain, to employ them in other parts of Europe.   As for preventing the retreat of the French from Spain, it is quite out of the question.   They have possession of all the fortresses on this side of the Pyrenees, through which mountains there are not less than 40 passes by which troops could march.   Besides, if it were possible under these circumstances to place an army in their rear, with the object of cutting them off from France, you might depend upon it that all France would rise as one man for their relief, and the result would be the loss of the army which should be so employed.

In respect to your wish, that I should go into the Asturias to examine the country, and form a judgment of its strength, I have to mention to you that I am not a draftsman, and but a bad hand at description.   I should have no difficulty in forming an opinion, and a plan for the defence of that country, provided I was certain that it would be executed.   But it would be an idle waste of my time, and an imposition upon you, if I were to go into that country with the pretence of giving you, or any General officer you should employ there, an idea of the country; and it would be vain and fruitless to form a plan for the defence of the country which would depend upon the execution of another.   Indeed, this last would only bring disgrace upon me, and would disappoint you.   Under these circumstances, I have told Sir H. Dalrymple that I was not able to perform the duty in which you had desired I should be employed; that I was not a topographical engineer, and could not pretend to describe in writing such a country as the Asturias; and he appeared to think that some of the gentlemen of the Q. M. G.'s department might be more usefully employed on this service. I hope you will not believe that I feel any disinclination to performing any service in which you may think I can be of use to you; and that I have discouraged the idea of employing me on that proposed, solely from my incapacity of performing it as it ought to be performed, and from a certainty that you were not aware of the nature of the service which you required from me when you wrote to Sir H. Dalrymple.

To Visc. Castlereagh.   Zambujal, 5th Sept. 1808.

You will receive from me by this opportunity a long letter upon our future operations. This relates solely to my private views. It is quite impossible for me to continue any longer with this army; and I wish, therefore, that you would allow me to return home and resume the duties of my office, if I should still be in office, and it is convenient to the government that I should retain it; or if not, that I should remain upon the Staff in England; or, if that should not be practicable, that I should remain without employment. You will hear from others of the various causes which I must have for being dissatisfied, not only with the military and other public measures of the Commander in Chief, but with his treatment of myself. I am convinced it is better for him, for the army, and for me, that I should go away; and the sooner I go the better.

Since I wrote to you on the 30th, the Convention has been returned, ratified by Junot, but materially altered. I understand that we have not a sufficiency of the Tagus to give us a secure harbour; we have not got the navigation of the river; and as we did not insist upon having Belem castle, which was asked for by the alteration of the 29th, the transports cannot be watered without going into that part of the river occupied by the Russians and the French troops, to which I understand the Admiral will not consent. I have not seen the Convention, and I do not know what it contains.

To Lieut. Gen. Sir H. Dalrymple.   Zambujal, 6th Sept. 1808.

I have the honor to enclose a letter which I have received from Major Gen. Ferguson, in which he excuses himself for having omitted to march from hence with troops yesterday morning, owing to indisposition; and he has desired me to request you would give him leave to go to England for a short time on urgent private affairs. It has come to my knowledge that Major Gen. Ferguson was ordered from England at a very short notice, and he has made me acquainted with the nature of the business which induces him to wish to return there for a short time, which appears to be of great importance to his family, and of a nature to require his presence. I therefore take the liberty of requesting that he may have the leave of absence which he requires.

To the Bishop of Oporto.   Zambujal, 6th Sept. 1808.

I have had the honor of receiving your Lordship's letter of the ——, and I have not failed to lay before the Commander in Chief, Sir H. Dalrymple, the paper containing a memorandum of those points which your Lordship wished him to consider in the negotiation of any Convention with the French army. I conclude that his Excellency will address your Lordship upon those subjects.

I must inform your Lordship, that the battle of the 21st Aug. was the conclusion of my command of the British forces in Portugal. Indeed a senior officer, Sir H. Burrard, was in the field towards the close of the action, and directed the operations which were carried on after that battle was concluded. Sir H. Dalrymple, the present Commander in Chief, landed on the morning of the 22d Aug.; and on that evening he negotiated in person with the French General Kellermann an agreement for the suspension of hostilities. I was present during the negotiation of this agreement; and, by the desire of the Commander in Chief, I signed it. But, as I have above informed your Lordship, I did not negotiate it; nor can I in any manner be considered responsible for its contents.

This agreement was followed by a negotiation with the French Commander in Chief, of a Convention for the evacuation of Portugal by the French army, through the medium of Col. Murray, the Q. M. G. of the army, which Convention has been concluded and ratified by the Commanders in Chief of both armies, and is now in the progress of execution. I have not seen this Convention, and cannot inform your Lordship of its contents; but I doubt not but that it will be laid before your Lordship by the Commander in Chief.

I have thought proper to trouble your Lordship with this detailed account of the share which I have had in these transactions, in order that your Lordship may not attribute to me the omission to apprise you of their nature, which I am convinced was only accidental. But as I consider myself, and the army which I commanded, to be particularly obliged to your Lordship, such an omission would have been unpardonable in me; and I am happy to take this opportunity of relieving myself from the imputation of it by apprising your Lordship of the mode in which they were carried on, and of the share which I had in them.

To Lieut. Col. Murray, Q.M.G. Zambujal, 6th Sept. 1808.

I am sorry to be obliged to trouble you again about our money and Commissariat concerns. We have not now one shilling here: money is due to the officers, to the troops, and to the people of the country. The money belonging to us, and allotted to pay these demands, and landed from the *Donegal* by my order, has been taken by Mr. Kennedy.

The accounts of the officers and soldiers of the army to the 4th Aug. are unsettled, for the reasons which I stated to you in my last letter upon this subject. The corps are separating, 5 battalions having already marched away; and the Dep. Paymaster, who alone can settle accounts, pay balances and outstanding demands, is ordered away, and is now at head quarters, under the pretence that his powers are at an end, there being a senior officer in the pay department present.

I am well aware that his powers are at an end as to all current and future payments; but it is the first time that I have ever heard that a pay officer, either dismissed or superseded in his office, was so far deprived of his powers as to be disabled from settling accounts and making payments, which ought to have been settled and made during the period in which his powers were in full force. Who is to settle these accounts and pay these demands, if Mr. —— is disabled from doing so? Certainly not Mr. Smith, the present Dep. Paymaster Gen.; for his powers, excepting under a special order from the Commander in Chief, cannot have a retrospect. I can assure you that I have no desire to retain these gentlemen who belonged to the army I commanded one moment longer than may be necessary to enable them to bring their concerns to a conclusion.

I hope that you will be able to settle this point with the Dep. Paymaster Gen. and Mr. Kennedy, and to send us Mr. —— and the money immediately; if not, I must trouble his Excellency upon it.

We should know where the Commissariat depôt is, in order that I may send for bread for the troops for the 10th, 11th, and 12th, otherwise I shall not have it in time for the issue on the 10th.

To Lieut. Gen. Sir H. Dalrymple. Zambujal, 9th Sept. 1808.

In reference to the order of the 8th inst., relative to the bât and forage allowance to be issued to the troops, of which, for your convenience, I enclose a copy, I have the honor to enclose a copy of the orders which I received from H.R.H. the Commander in Chief upon the same subject; in conformity with which I regulated the issues lately made to the troops under my command.

As the difference of the issue is considerable, particularly to the officers of the inferior ranks of the army, which I am convinced it cannot be the intention of H. R. Highness should prevail, to the prejudice and disadvantage of those officers who have served during the whole of the campaign in this country, I beg to know whether you have any objection to my ordering fresh returns for bât and forage to be made out by the regiments, charging the sums for each rank according to the general orders of the 8th inst., and to my directing the late Paymaster Gen. of the army, lately under my command, to pay the same, and charge those sums in his accounts to the 24th Aug.?

To Visc. Castlereagh. Zambujal, 9th Sept. 1808.

Your brother Charles is, I imagine, at Lisbon, and will make you acquainted with the state of affairs there. I write to you only in reference to the recommendation I made you some days ago to appoint a proper person to be the King's Ambassador here. Since I wrote that letter I have heard so much of Lord R. Fitzgerald, from various quarters, that I cannot avoid recommending you to turn your thoughts to him. I am but little acquainted with him myself; but I hear an excellent character of him.

I fear that Sir Hew will make a mistake respecting the appointment of a Regency at Lisbon. My intention was to have issued a proclamation, and to have called the Regency appointed by the Prince to re-assume their functions, with the exception of the members (by name) who had been confidentially employed by the French; and in the same proclamation, I should have desired the remaining *true* members of the Regency to fill

up the vacancies by election, according to the powers given to them of
electing successors to vacancies by the very act which appoints them. I
should then have exerted the influence, which I should have undoubtedly
had at this moment over them, to induce them to elect the Bishop of
Oporto and others, who it is important should belong to the government;
and thus the government would have been legally constituted, without
the unnecessary interference of a foreign power. I have discussed the
whole plan more than once with Sir Hew, and I have pointed out the
mode of execution, &c.; but, instead of adopting it, I now hear that he is
going to appoint a Regency, by his own authority; which measure will
only add tenfold to the difficulties with which the new government will
have to contend at its outset. I wrote to your brother, however, on this
subject, to beg him to make one more effort to keep Sir Hew right; and,
if I can, I will see your brother to-morrow.

I send you two letters which I wrote to Sir H. Burrard, besides the first
which I sent you, which are important to show you my view of the campaign in this country.

To the Duke of Richmond.   Zambujal, 9th Sept. 1808.

Nothing particular has occurred since I wrote to you last: the French
are about to evacuate Lisbon, under the Convention, as soon as the transports shall be ready; and the Russians have concluded a convention with
the Admiral from their fleet, under which they are to be taken to a British
port. I have neither seen one nor the other of these conventions, and I
cannot tell you their contents; but I am convinced that neither are what they
ought to be, considering the success of the army. The country has, however, acquired the honour of reconquering the country, and of restoring
the rightful ruler to this government; and with these advantages I hope
they will be satisfied.

I have only to regret that I signed the agreement for the suspension of
hostilities without having negotiated. I have already told you the reasons
why I did so, but I doubt whether good nature, and a deference to the
opinion of an officer appointed Commander in Chief on the day of his
taking the command, and to his orders, and a desire to avoid being considered the head of a party against his authority, will be deemed sufficient
excuses for an act which, on other grounds, I cannot justify. I have had
nothing to do, however, with any subsequent transaction, excepting to
advise stronger measures, and that the Commander in Chief should insist
on better terms.

I am sick of all that is going on here, and I heartily wish I had never
come away from Ireland, and that I was back again with you. Remember
me kindly to the Duchess.

To Lieut. Gen. Sir H. Dalrymple.   Zambujal, 10th Sept. 1808.

I had the honor of receiving, in the night, the letter which you wrote
to me yesterday. My wish is, at all times, to render myself as useful as
may be in my power to the officer under whose command I may be
serving; and this desire is limited only by the doubt which I may entertain of my fitness for the employment held out to my acceptance. The

view which I have taken of the state of affairs in Spain has long ago suggested to me the propriety of placing in that kingdom a person of the description stated by yourself, possessing full powers, the means of exerting them on all parts of Spain, and of communicating and treating with all the local juntas of government.

In order to be able to perform the important part allotted to him, this person should possess the confidence of those who employ him; and, above all, in order that he may recommend, with authority, a plan to the Spaniards, he should be acquainted with those of his employers, the means by which they propose to carry them into execution, and those by which they intend to enable the Spanish nation to execute that which will be proposed to them.

I certainly cannot consider myself as possessing those advantages, personally, which would qualify me for the situation you have proposed for me; and you must be the best judge whether you have made up your own mind, and are enabled to instruct me, and are inclined to confide in me, to the extent which in my opinion will be necessary, in order to derive any general advantage from such a mission. It is true that one might be undertaken with more limited views and objects than those above adverted to, and which are discussed in the letter which I have the honor to receive from you; and it might be confined to the mere arrangement with Gen. Castaños, or the military committee at Madrid, of a plan for the remaining part of the campaign. This mission, however, would require a full and clear explanation of views and means; and the person who undertakes it must have the confidence of his employer, and must be certain that the plan, which he would arrange under these circumstances, would be carried into execution.

I beg that you will consider me ready to be employed in any manner you may think proper; and I have above pointed out the powers and instructions which can alone, in my opinion, render the employment of any person, in the situation which you have held out to me, at all useful to the army or to the country.

To Visc. Castlereagh.   Zambujal, 12th Sept. 1808.

Nothing particular has occurred since I last wrote to you. I have been in Lisbon, and the French appear much dissatisfied with the mode in which the Convention is executed; but I can give no opinion whatever whether their complaints are well or ill founded, as I have not seen the Convention, and am not accurately acquainted with its contents.

I enclose copies of letters which have passed between Sir H. Dalrymple and me, respecting an offer which he made to send me to Madrid, upon which I think it probable that he will write to you, and, in my opinion, you will be a better judge on the subject by reading the letters. The object of my letter was to show Sir Hew that a mission to Madrid was at present no light matter, in whatever view it were taken; and that the officer who was to be sent there, if he were to do anything, must be instructed, and must be trusted. I would not trouble you with this comparatively trifling subject, only that I am convinced that Sir Hew will tell you that I declined the mission to Madrid.

You will observe what he says of Castaños' demand for cavalry, from which I should judge that he does not propose for, or to accept of infantry.

To Lieut. Col. Murray, Q.M.G.   St. Antonio de Tojal, 15th Sept. 1808.

I have received your note respecting Mr. Walsh and Mr. Kennedy. I do not know what influence my opinion respecting the former gentleman can have upon the measures of the latter respecting him, for it appears to me that the question between them is entirely one of justice and law, as far as I have acquired any knowledge of it. But as my opinion in favor of Mr. Walsh may be of use to him on other grounds, it is but fair towards him that I should make you acquainted with it.

When the army under my command landed in Portugal, a contract was made with a Mr. Archer, a merchant of Figueira, for the supply of beef for the troops, and it was soon found that Mr. Archer could not perform the contract at the rate at which he agreed to take it; and, in point of fact, he gave notice of its discontinuance, at the specified time of one fortnight, before the army marched from Lavos.

A contract was then made with Mr. Walsh, at a higher rate and upon different terms; and I understand that Mr. Walsh placed himself, for the remainder of Mr. Archer's period of the contract, in the situation of Mr. Archer. I believe it is notorious throughout the army that they were well supplied with beef from that time forward. The consumption was greater than 15,000 rations; and it is unnecessary that I should detail our marches to point out the difficulty of supplying it.

I believe the army which was under my command afforded a rare instance of a British army on its march, shortly after its landing in a foreign country, which did not experience any want. At the same time I must do Mr. Walsh the justice to add, that the bullocks which were consumed as beef were of the best kind, and were all brought from the north of Portugal, in order that the army might not be disappointed in its demand upon the country for draught cattle.

In this situation things stood, when, on the 20th, 5000 additional troops landed under Gens. Anstruther and Acland, and I believe twice as many more, and many General officers, staff, servants, &c., before the end of the month; and I have no doubt that the consumption of the army, which under my command was estimated at 16,000 rations, now amounts to nearly 40,000. I cannot say at what period the contract was enlarged, but certainly not during the period that I had any thing to say to the operations or means of the army; and at all events, supposing it were made commensurate to the increased demand on the 20th, would it have been unreasonable in Mr. Walsh to have asked for some indulgence in point of time for his supplies, considering that they must come from the countries to the northward, the French being still in possession of Lisbon, Alentejo, and every thing about Lisbon? But, in point of fact, has Mr. Walsh failed? I do not know how he stands with the army; but I know that the troops here have always had fresh beef, excepting a part of them on one day. I know also, that many bullocks were lost in the confusion, amongst the Commissariat, of the battle of the 21st; I believe some on the 17th; and I know that nearly a day's consumption for the whole corps was lost by one Assist. Commissary on the night of the rain and thunder-storm, on the ground at Ramalhal. If all these circumstances are taken into consideration, I think it will be found that Mr. Walsh has great merit in having supplied us as he has done. I know I never saw any British contractor who did his duty so well; and that, at all events, Mr. Kennedy has no right, and no man has a right, to discontinue a contract legally made with him, without giving him the notice required by the terms of the contract itself. If Mr. Walsh has not performed his contract, nor given satisfaction to Mr. Kennedy, let him pay the penalty of non-performance; but do not let Mr. Kennedy do that which is illegal, and certainly unjust.

Having written thus much in favour of Mr. Walsh, I must add, in justice to myself, that I was entirely unacquainted with that gentleman till I arrived in Portugal. I first saw him at Oporto, where he was introduced to me by Col. Brown; and he interested himself in a supply of mules which the Bishop engaged to give for the army. His zeal for the success of our operations brought him to Figueira, where he found Mr. Archer unequal to the performance of the task which he had undertaken; and he undertook it, and has performed it, at all events, to the satisfaction of those persons who conducted the operations at that period.

P. S. In mentioning the difficulties with which Mr. Walsh had to contend, I have omitted to advert to those which occurred on the march and arrival of the bullocks with the army, by duties levied by the Bishop of Oporto, and other impediments incidental to their advance by the Portuguese army, upon which I had a correspondence with Gen. Freire.

To Lieut. Gen. Sir J. Moore, K.B.   Lumiar, 17th Sept. 1808.

I write to you on the subject to which this letter relates with the same freedom with which I hope you would write to me on any point in which you might think the public interests concerned.

It appears to me to be quite impossible that we can go on as we are now constituted; the Commander in Chief must be changed, and the country and the army naturally turn their eyes to you as their commander. I understand, however, that you have lately had some unpleasant discussions with the King's ministers, the effect of which might be to prevent the adoption of an arrangement for the command of this army, which, in my opinion, would be the best, and would enable you to render those services at this moment for which you are peculiarly qualified. I wish you would allow me to talk to you respecting the discussions to which I have adverted, in order that I may endeavor to remove any trace which they may have left on the minds of the King's ministers, having the effect which I have supposed.

Although I hold a high office under government, I am no party man, but have long been connected in friendship with many of those persons who are now at the head of affairs in England; and I think I have sufficient influence over them, that they may listen to me upon a point of this description, more particularly as I am convinced that they must be as desirous as I can be to adopt the arrangement for the command of this army which all are agreed is the best. In these times, my dear General, a man like you should not preclude himself from rendering the services of which he is capable by an idle point of form. Circumstances may have occurred, and might have justified the discussions to which I have referred; but none can justify the continuance of the temper in which they are carried on: and yet, till there is evidence that it is changed, it appears to be impossible for the King's ministers to employ you in the high situation for which you are the most fit, because during the continuance of this temper of mind there can be no cordial or confidential intercourse.

In writing thus much I have perhaps gone too far, and have taken the permission for which it was the intention of this letter to ask; but I shall send it, as it may be convenient for you to be apprised of the view which I have already taken of these discussions, as far as I have any knowledge of them, in deciding whether you will allow me to talk to you any further about them. If you should do so, it would probably be most convenient to us both to meet at Lisbon, or I can go over to you, if that should suit you better.

To Lieut. Gen. Sir H. Burrard, Bart. Lumiar, 17th Sept. 1808.

I received yesterday your letter of the 15th, enclosing that which you had received from the Sec. of State respecting the action of the 21st Aug.

I beg that you will accept my acknowledgments for the handsome terms in which you have expressed yourself upon this occasion; and with your permission I shall communicate that letter to the General officers and troops which were under my command. At the same time I cannot avoid taking this opportunity of expressing how very sensible I was of the mark you gave me of your confidence during the action of the 21st, in allowing me to bring the operations of that battle to a close, and of your kindness to my friend Capt. Campbell in making him the bearer of your dispatches.

To Lieut. Gen. Sir H. Dalrymple. Lumiar, 17th Sept. 1808.

The embarkation of the French troops having brought to a final close the operations of the army in Portugal, and as in the present state of the season some time must elapse before the troops can enter upon any other active operation; and as I understand you have sent Lord W. Bentinck on the service for which you had thought me qualified, and it is not probable that there will be an opportunity for active service, or that you will require my assistance at this particular moment, or for some time to come, I am induced to request your permission to go to England.

The situation of my office of Chief Sec. in Ireland, of which the duties have been done lately by a gentleman who is now dead, renders it desirable, under these circumstances, that I should be in England as soon as possible, to ascertain whether it is His Majesty's pleasure that I should continue to hold it, or that I should relinquish it. I have therefore to request' that you will give me leave to go to England by the first ship that shall sail.

To Lieut. Col. Murray, Q.M.G. Lisbon, 19th Sept. 1808.

I am going to-morrow, and I regret that it was so late when I reached head quarters yesterday that I could not endeavor to find you before I came away.

I do not conceal from you that I am not quite satisfied with our situation; but nothing should have induced me to go away if I had thought there was the smallest prospect of early active employment for the army; and I should not go now if my poor friend Mr. Trail were not dead, and if it were not necessary that I should be in England, if possible, to know whether I am to retain my office or to resign it, and if there were a probability of another early opportunity of going home. I intend to return as soon as I can. I request you to command me if I can do any thing for you. I shall not embark, I believe, before 12 to-morrow, and, at all events, you can write to me to the Irish office, London.

In regard to matters personal to myself, I shall not enter into them; I wish that Sir Hew had given me credit for a sincere desire to forward his views, whatever they might be; and I think I could have been of as much use to him as I believe I have been to other officers under whose orders I have served. He is the only one of whom I have not been the right hand for some years past; and at the same time I must say that I felt the same inclination to serve him that I had to serve the others.

I have heard from Anstruther that the Bishop of Oporto will accept the office of President of the Regency.

To Major Gen. Beresford.   Lisbon, 19th Sept. 1808.

I enclose to you a letter which I have received from Senhor Fernandez Thomas, a gentleman belonging to this country, from whom I have received more real assistance and service than I have from all the others of the subjects of Her Most Faithful Majesty, with the exception only of the Bishop of Oporto.

It is extraordinary that after I have been the instrument of the British government, which has had the principal share in restoring the Portuguese monarchy, I should be obliged to apply to you to exert the influence which I am convinced you will have over the government that may be established in Portugal, to obtain for this gentleman the objects for which he is solicitous. But I am satisfied you will believe me when I assure you that he deserves them, and much more, from his government, for his faithful and efficient services; and that your friendship for me will induce you to intercede for him with the persons who may exercise the powers of government, which I ought to have been in the situation to do for him myself. I shall desire him to wait upon you.

To Senhor Fernandez Thomas.   A Lisbonne, ce 19 Sept. 1808.

Je viens de recevoir la lettre que vous m'avez fait l'honneur de m'écrire, et je puis vous assurer que je prendrai toutes les occasions qui me seront offertes, pour faire savoir, au gouvernement qui sera établi dans ce pays-ci, les grands services que vous avez rendus à l'armée Anglaise.

Il est malheureux que je ne suis pas moi-même dans une situation dans laquelle je pourrai vous être aussi utile que je voudrais; mais je viens de recommander vos services au Général Beresford, qui commande à Lisbonne, dans une lettre dont je vous envoie la copie; et je vous prie de passer chez lui aussitôt que vous le pouvez.

Je vous promets aussi de ne pas oublier de vous recommander à M. de Sousa, l'Ambassadeur Portugais en Angleterre, auquel j'espère que je pourrais demander la grace de vous recommander au gouvernement.

To Lieut. Col. Murray, Q.M.G.   Lisbon, 20th Sept. 1808.

I wish that you would speak to Sir H. Dalrymple upon the temper in which the Spanish officers who have come from the army of Estremadura are, and upon the language of dissatisfaction which I understand they hold in every house in Lisbon. As it is no business of mine, I have not inquired much into the causes of their complaints; but if I were in Sir Hew's situation I would not only arm and equip completely the Spanish soldiers set free in Lisbon, but also the army in Estremadura.

The way, depend upon it, that is most agreeable to, as well as most for the interest of, the people of England, is to conciliate the Spanish nation, and to bring the largest possible number of Spaniards into the field in the shape of an army; and I know from experience that the government will sanction any expense incurred with these views.

I enclose a letter which I received some time ago from Lord Castlereagh, in which he conveys the King's approbation of an order which I had given to Gen. Spencer to make an advance of £100,000 to the Junta of Seville; and I understand that the King likewise approved of an advance of £10,000 made by Gen. Spencer. Under the circumstances I conceive that Sir Hew will act upon sure grounds in incurring any expense for these people; and as they are already formed in regiments, and actually assembled under officers, and want only arms to become efficient soldiers, they are just the people to whom arms ought to be given.

I hope that the opinions which I have above given upon this occasion will be received as they ought to be; and that it will not be believed that I give them from any desire to interfere in what is no particular concern of mine.

To the Duke of Richmond.   Plymouth, 4th Oct. 1808.

As soon as I heard of the death of Mr. Trail, I determined to return home without loss of time; and whether I am to continue to hold my office or to relinquish it, it will be a convenience to you that I should be in the way when his successor in the first case, or mine in the second, shall be appointed. Accordingly I sailed from Lisbon on the 20th Sept., and arrived here this day; and I shall go to Ireland as soon as possible. Pray write to me to London.

The French troops were nearly all embarked, and 2 divisions had sailed when I came away, and our troops were in possession of Lisbon; and as the equinoctial rains were expected at every moment, it is impossible to commence any further operation by land.

I have not heard from England since the end of August, and the only letter I have received from you since I left Ireland is dated the 8th Aug.

To Visc. Castlereagh.   London, 6th Oct. 1808.

I have the honor to inform your Lordship that I arrived in London this day, by leave of the Commander of the Forces in Portugal; and having seen a copy of his Excellency's letter to your Lordship, dated at

Cintra, the 3d Sept., in which it would appear, from an inaccuracy of expression, that I had agreed upon and signed certain articles ' for the suspension of hostilities on the 22d Aug. ;' I beg leave to inform your Lordship that I did not negotiate that agreement; that it was negotiated and settled by his Excellency in person, with Gen. Kellermann, in the presence of Lieut. Gen. Sir H. Burrard and myself, and that I signed it by his Excellency's desire. But I could not consider myself responsible in any degree for the terms in which it was framed, or for any of its provisions.

At the same time, adverting to the situation which I had held in Portugal previously to his Excellency's arrival, I think it but just to inform your Lordship, that I concurred with the Commander of the Forces in thinking it expedient, on the 22d Aug., that the French army in Portugal should be allowed to evacuate that kingdom, with their arms and baggage, and that every facility for this purpose should be afforded to them.

I deemed this to be expedient, in the relative state of the two armies on the evening of the 22d, considering that the French army had then resumed a formidable position between us and Lisbon; that they had the means of retiring from that position to others in front of that city; and, finally, of crossing the Tagus into Alentejo, with a view to the occupation, in strength, of the forts of Elvas, La Lippe, and eventually Almeida.

As Lieut. Gen. Sir J. Moore's corps had been diverted from the occupation of the position at Santarem, which had been proposed for them, there were no means to prevent, and no increase of numbers could have prevented, the French army from effecting these objects.

The British army, after waiting for and receiving its reinforcements, would thus have been precluded from the use of the Tagus for some time longer; and as it depended for its supplies of provisions and ammunition upon its communication with the fleet, which, in the end of August, would have become most precarious by the coast, it would have been involved in difficulties for the want of necessaries, which would have been aggravated by the increase of its numbers.

To these circumstances, which affected the immediate situation of the army and its existence in Portugal, there were other considerations to be added respecting its future operations. I considered it most important that the British army in Portugal should be at liberty at an early period to march into Spain. Not only no arrangements for the march into Spain could be made till the French should have evacuated Elvas and Almeida, and we should have possession of the Tagus and the Douro, but the army must have attacked and taken these places by regular sieges before His Majesty could have restored the government of his ally, or could have moved his troops to the assistance of the Spaniards. I need not point out to your Lordship the difficulties of these operations, their increase in the season in which they would have been undertaken, or the time which they would have lasted.

These circumstances, affecting the situation, the objects, and the future operations of the army, were to be attributed to the fact, that the enemy occupied, in a military point of view, the whole of Portugal, having every stronghold in their hands; that their situation on the evening of the 22d Aug. enabled them still to avail themselves of these possessions, and to strengthen them as they might think proper; and I conceived that an army, whose retreat was open, and which possessed such advantages, had a fair claim to be allowed to have the facility of withdrawing from the country entirely. On these grounds, therefore, I concurred with the Commander of the Forces in the opinion that the French might be allowed to evacuate Portugal.

To the Duke of Richmond. London, 10th Oct. 1808.

You will readily believe that I was much surprised when I arrived in England to hear of the torrents of abuse with which I had been assailed; and that I had been accused of every crime of which a man can be guilty, excepting cowardice. I have not read one word that has been written on either side, and I have refused to publish, and don't mean to authorise the publication of a single line in my defence.

I think, however, that the King and his ministers, and my friends, have a right to an explanation of the cause for which my name appeared to the armistice of the 22d Aug., as I have already told you in a former letter, written from Portugal, in which I entered into the details of what passed on that occasion, and stated generally my motives for signing that instrument.

I think that Sir H. Dalrymple's letter of the 3d Sept. has, by fixing upon me, by a purposed inaccuracy of expression, the odium of negotiating that instrument, enabled me to explain the share I had in it to the King's ministers and to the King.

I enclose a copy of the letter which I have written to the Sec. of State upon this subject, in which you will see that not only I have explained this point, but I have thought it but just and fair to Sir H. Dalrymple to avow that I was of opinion that the French ought to be allowed to evacuate Portugal, and my reasons for entertaining that opinion *on the evening of the 22d Aug.* This is the whole amount of what I shall do in my defence at present; the rest I shall leave to chance, and to the result of the inquiry into Sir H. Dalrymple's conduct.

I propose, however, if I should have time, to write you a narrative of the whole campaign, stating the measures which I had adopted, and the principles on which I had adopted them, how far they were carried into execution, and the consequences which resulted from a departure from them on the arrival of the officers who relieved me.

I shall be obliged to you if you will show the enclosed paper, in confidence, and not on any account to be copied or printed, to the Chancellor, Attorney and Solicitor General, Lord Edward, and any friends of mine in Ireland.

I hope to be able to go to you in a few days.

P.S. Pray remember me most kindly to the Duchess and Lady Mary, and give my love to Louisa and Charlotte.

Visc. Castlereagh to Lieut. Gen. the Hon. Sir A. Wellèsley, K.B.

Downing Street, 13th Oct. 1808.

Your letter.of the 6th inst. has been received, and laid before the King; and having also been. brought under the consideration of His Majesty's confidential servants, I am to acquaint you that a copy thereof will be communicated to Lieut. Gen. Sir H. Dalrymple on his arrival in England.

To Lieut. Col. Gordon.   London, 15th Oct. 1808.

I am about to set out for Ireland, as some time must elapse before the nature of the inquiry to be instituted on Portuguese affairs will be decided on, and I am wanted in that country. If the inquiry should be delayed till the officers shall return, I shall go to Spain immediately; if it should be commenced at an early period, I shall go to Spain as soon as I shall be dismissed; and, in either case, I should think that my stay in Ireland will be short.

I promised my brother in law, Capt. Pakenham, of the 95th, that I would speak to you in his favor. He is anxious to get a majority, and his time is about out. He was with me in Zealand: he was wounded on the 15th Aug., and served in both the actions of the 17th and 21st afterwards; and he is really one of the best officers of riflemen that I have seen. I shall be very much obliged to you if you will keep his promotion in your mind.

Having said so much of his military character, it is scarcely fair to him, or to you, to mention that he is the member for the county of Westmeath, and a steady friend; but the Secretary in Ireland must take care of a claim even on this ground.

To Lieut. Col. Gordon.   Dublin Castle, 21st Oct. 1808.

I am afraid that I did not explain myself sufficiently about Capt. Pakenham's wish to be promoted. His object is to purchase, which will possibly facilitate his advancement.

I agree with you in thinking that I cannot leave these countries till the mode and period of the inquiry into the late transactions in Portugal will have been determined upon. If the inquiry is to be made immediately, I can give my evidence and go: if, as I think it most probable, it cannot be made till other officers, besides myself, are in the way to be examined, I can go, and return, when they will, to attend the inquiry. This is my notion at present; but, of course, the decision must rest with those who are at the head of affairs.

I am obliged to you for your Spanish news. The Spaniards must either accelerate their operations upon the French corps now in Spain, or take up their position to oppose the French reinforcements marching into that country. If the reinforcements should catch those engaged in the operations, they will make a woeful example of them.

To Sir J. Sinclair, Bart.   Dublin Castle, 21st Oct. 1808.

I have had the pleasure of receiving your two letters, and I am much concerned that I was not at home when Lieut. Col. Shrapnell did me the favor to call upon me in London. I shall have great pleasure in testifying at any time the great benefit which the army, lately under my command, derived from the spherical case shot in two actions with the enemy, a benefit which I am convinced will be enjoyed whenever they shall be judiciously and skilfully used.

I consider it, however, to be very desirable that this invention, and the use which the British army have made of it, should not be made public. Our enemies are not aware of the cause of the effect of our artillery, of which they have complained; and we may depend upon it that any public mention, or notice, of the benefit which we have derived from this description of shot, would induce them immediately to adopt it.

At the same time I consider Col. Shrapnell to be entitled to a reward for his ingenuity and the science he has proved he possesses by the perfection to which he has brought this invention, and, more particularly so, because I am of opinion that the public interests require that the advantages which we have derived from the use of the shot should not be made public, and he is thus deprived of the fame and honor which he would have enjoyed.

I am ready to give this opinion whenever it may be wished, and to assist by every means in my power to produce a reward for Lieut. Col. Shrapnell.

I have thought proper to trouble you so far on this subject, as you have expressed a great interest in it.

To Major Gen. Spencer.   Dublin Castle, 22nd Oct. 1808.

I received your very kind letter yesterday upon my arrival here, and I am very much obliged to you for it. I had intended to write to you from London, but I was much hurried while I was there, and I found that there was no ship going to Coruña, where I think a letter is most likely to reach you.

You will have seen in the newspapers the attacks which have been made upon me, as well as upon Sir H. Dalrymple and Sir H. Burrard; and that I have my full share, at least, of the blame with which the public have received the Convention in Portugal. I never approved of but one point in that Convention, viz., the allowing the French to withdraw with their arms and baggage. This I thought expedient, viewing the relative state of the two armies on the evening of the 22d Aug.; that the French had their retreat open, and that we had at that time no means of preventing it; and considering that we should, in all probability, be glad, in the month of December, to give them the same terms which we had given in August: so far I approved; but I disapproved of the whole of the detail of both the Armistice and the Convention.

However, notwithstanding the calumny and abuse of which I am the object, for measures not my own, and against which I gave my opinion, I have neither lost my temper nor my spirits; and I look with pride and satisfaction at the confidence and kindness of yourself and the officers of the army, who, after all, are the best judges of my conduct, and at the affection of my friends. The King, the Prince of Wales, and the Duke of York, received me most graciously; and I think I may defy the mob of London.

The transactions in Portugal must be inquired into; and my intention is to wait with patience for the result of the inquiry, for my justification with the public. I shall adopt no illegitimate means of setting them right, and shall neither publish any thing myself, nor authorise a publication by any body else; nor shall I, in order to raise myself in the public opinion, state circumstances respecting the difference of opinion between Sir H. Burrard and myself, on the 20th and 21st Aug., although those circumstances led to the expediency of allowing the French to evacuate Portugal. As the truth, however, must be told upon the inquiry, it is very possible that those circumstances may come out; but they shall not be brought forward by me, unless I should be questioned upon them.

The worst of this inquiry is, that I fear it may keep me for some time from the army. I must wait, until it is decided in England what course shall be taken in respect to Sir H. Dalrymple. If his conduct is to be inquired into immediately, I shall go over and give my evidence, and then join the army, and shall possibly see you before much time will elapse. If it should not be inquired into, till more officers than me are in the way to be examined, I shall then join the army also immediately. In short, in either case I hope to see you soon; and I have come over here only to arrange the business of my office till Sir Hew shall arrive, and the mode and period of the inquiry shall be settled. I enclose you a letter which I have received from Mrs. ——. I wish that I could have done something more substantial for her.

Pray remember me kindly to Hill, and all friends with the army.

P.S. I conclude that Nightingall is on his way home. Ferguson is better, and is gone to Scotland, but will soon be back, and will join the army. I shall be much obliged to you to desire somebody to buy 2 or 3 mules for me, and leave them for me at Coruña. The American Consul, Dos Santos, will take care of them for me.

To J. W. Croker, Esq. Dublin Castle, 23d Oct. 1808.

I have just received your letter of the 17th inst., and I am very much obliged to you for the kindness towards me which dictated it.

I acknowledge that I have not read even one, much less all, the calumnies which have been circulated against me during my absence in Portugal; but, upon a full consideration of the case, I have determined that I will not publish myself, or authorise others the publication of any thing in my defence. The late transactions in Portugal must be inquired into; and the result of that inquiry will show what share I had in them, and how far I deserve what has been said against me.

I am, however, as much obliged to *you* for your kind offer of assistance as if I had accepted your services.

P.S. I wish that you would call upon me at the Castle about 2 o'clock, as I want to speak to you.

To ———. Dublin Castle, 25th Oct. 1808.

I have had the honor to receive your letter of the 23rd inst. I am highly flattered by your favorable opinion, and much obliged by your intention to enlighten the public mind in respect to the late transactions in Portugal. But, as I have determined that I will neither publish, nor authorise the publication of, any thing upon that subject, I must decline to answer the queries which your letter contains relating to it.

To Major Barclay. Dublin Castle, 28th Oct. 1808.

I have received your letter of the 25th Feb., and my Marhatta prize money, and my bazaar money to the period of my departure, for which I return you my thanks. I rejoice to find that you are employed by Sir G. Barlow, and I have no doubt but that you will make yourself useful to him.

You will have heard that I commanded the army in Portugal for some time, and I was equally, if not more fortunate against the French, than I was against the Marhattas. I never saw such desperate fighting as we had on the 17th Aug., or troops receive such a beating as the French did on the 21st; and it is unfortunate that I was not allowed to carry my own measures into execution after the action of that day. If I had, we should have destroyed them entirely. As usual, I had an unanimous army, who would have undertaken any thing for me; and I took care that the troops should be well provided with every thing they wanted.

You will also have seen that the public are not satisfied with the result of the transactions in Portugal; and I think they have attributed to me more than my share of the blame for them. When the action of the 21st Aug. was not followed up, when the principle of all my measures was altered, and the corps which I had proposed should cut the French off from their strongholds south of the Tagus was diverted from its destination, it was very clear to me that we should never get the French out of Portugal excepting by an agreement; and that we should be very glad to make an agreement with them in December, after we should have lost half our army, if we had refused to make it in August. You will see my reasoning upon this subject detailed more fully in a letter to the Secretary of State, of which I enclose a copy. So far I agreed with the arrangements of that period. As to every thing else, I objected to it not in the form of protest, as is stated by my zealous defenders in the newspapers, but in reasoning with the Commander in Chief; and I signed the armistice, not because he ordered me, for I certainly might have declined it, but because he desired me, and I did not choose, and did not think it proper for me, to set myself up as the head of a party against him on the day of his arrival.

I have no objection to your showing the enclosed to any friend of mine in the East Indies, for I consider that all my friends have a right to an explanation of the reasons which induced me to sign my name to the armistice; but it must not be printed on any account, and no copy must be taken of it, as I am determined that I will not publish, or authorise the publication by others, of a single line upon this subject.

Pray remember me most kindly to all my friends. I don't write by this opportunity to Malcolm, because I think it possible that he may be in Persia, and my letter might fall into hands which ought not to possess it. But I beg you to show him this letter, if he should be in India; and tell him that his brother Pulteney was our Commodore on the expedition to Portugal, that I lived with him in the *Donegal* for some time, and that he is in great style. His ship appears to have been made head-quarters by most of the Generals who came successively from England after I had marched. If Malcolm should be in Persia, and you should think the communication with him secure, write him the purport of this letter and of the enclosed.

I received a letter from Col. Close while I was in Portugal; and I will write to him as soon as I can get a moment's leisure. In the mean time I beg you to communicate to him and to Wilks the enclosed letter, and this if you like it.

Present my best respects to Sir G. Barlow.

Dublin Castle, 9th Jan. 1809.

P.S. I have had no opportunity of sending this letter till now.

You will have seen that I have been in London since I wrote it, to attend the Court of Inquiry, of which you will see the ridiculous report in the newspapers. I enclose a printed copy of the narratives and statements which I put on the minutes of the Court; which you may show as well as this letter to my friends.

Visc. Castlereagh to H.R.H. the Commander in Chief. Downing Street, 29th Oct. 1808.

I am to signify to your Royal Highness, His Majesty's pleasure, that a full investigation by a Court of Inquiry should be made as soon as possible into the late Armistice and Convention concluded in Portugal, and into all the circumstances connected therewith.

It is considered, from the nature of the transaction, that the proceeding by a Court of Inquiry, in the first instance, will best bring before His Majesty a full explanation of all the considerations and causes which may have influenced the conclusion of the said Armistice and Convention, and ultimately lead to a just judgment thereupon.

I am further to state to your Royal Highness the importance of giving to this inquiry every degree of solemnity and publicity which usage and precedent have in like cases admitted of; and that the court be specially instructed, not only to report an opinion upon the matter referred to them, but also to submit to His Majesty what it may be, in their judgment, fit to be done thereupon.

Your Royal Highness will be pleased to receive His Majesty's pleasure, with respect to the proper measures for carrying these His Majesty's commands into execution.

To ————.   Dublin Castle, 3rd Nov. 1808.

I have received your letter of the 28th Oct., and I am very sensible of your kindness towards me; but I have determined that I will not publish, and I will not authorise the publication of a single word on the subject to which you refer. The inquiry which must be made into the late transactions in Portugal must show the public that they have done me great injustice.

I am happy to hear of your hopes of the amendment of the state of the county of Kerry. With every desire on the part of the Lord Lieutenant to appoint you to a situation which you will like better than that which you now fill, I apprehend that it will be found most difficult to appoint you to one, of which the duties will not take up a great part of your time. The office which you now hold allows of your residence in the county of Kerry, which is a great benefit to the public, and I should think must be a convenience to you.

To Capt. P. Malcolm, R.N.   London, 12th Nov. 1808.

I am very much obliged to you for your letter of the 11th, and particularly so for the kindness towards me which has induced you to stay at home to be examined before the Court of Inquiry. It will meet on Monday, but, I imagine, will not proceed to the examination of evidence for a day or two.

When you come to town, I can give you a bed here, and you will be as heartily welcome as I have often been in your ships.

To Visc. Castlereagh.   London, 14th Nov. 1808.

After I saw you on Saturday I spoke to Col. Gordon, and he agreed entirely in opinion with me, that it was expedient to recommend Gen

Spencer to the King, at an early period, for some mark of His Majesty's favor; but he promised to speak to the Duke of York upon the subject.

I have always been of opinion that I should not be able to convince the public of the goodness of my motives for signing the armistice; and the late discussions in Middlesex and elsewhere, and the paragraphs in the newspapers, which, after all, rule every thing in this country, tend to convince me that it is determined that I shall not have the benefit of an acquittal; and that the news-writers and the orators of the day are determined to listen to nothing in my justification. I am therefore quite certain that the government will not be able to recommend me for any mark of the King's favor, to which they might otherwise think me entitled. If this turns out to be true, the ministers will be obliged to recommend that a mark of the King's favor should be conferred on Gen. Spencer, and not on me, although both were employed on the same service, and this after an inquiry will have been held in which my conduct will have been investigated. They will be obliged to adopt this line, notwithstanding that I hope they will be convinced of the propriety of my conduct, and the goodness of my motives in every instance; or they must determine not to confer upon Gen. Spencer those marks of the King's favor which his services undoubtedly merit.

I have no doubt of the alternative which the ministers will be inclined to adopt. I am convinced that Spencer himself will urge them not to think of him, if the King's favor cannot be extended to me, and thus he will lose what he so well deserves. I am convinced that this will be the result of any further delay.

I wish, therefore, that you would immediately recommend Spencer for what you think he ought to have. There can be no doubt of his merit on every ground; and nobody can with reason complain that an injustice is done to me, because even my most sanguine friends cannot think that I am in a situation to receive any mark of His Majesty's favor.

I wish you would turn this subject over in your mind, and you will discover that great difficulties will be avoided by adopting immediately the measure which I most earnestly recommend.

P.S. It is said that Spencer would not like to accept any mark of the King's favor at present; but I am convinced that I shall be able to prevail with him.

To the Duke of Richmond.   London, 18th Nov. 1808.

*   *   *   *   *   *   *

I attended the Court of Inquiry yesterday, and the whole day was employed in reading the dispatches to and from me. Afterwards Sir H. Dalrymple read something from a paper, complaining of the misrepresentations in the newspapers, which he attributed to me and my friends; this gave me an opportunity, which I wished for, of explaining that I acted by his desire, and not by his order, in signing the armistice. The newspapers have, as usual, misrepresented what both of us said; but I have made a note of what I said from the short hand writer's notes, which I propose to put on the minutes to-morrow, of which note I enclose a copy.

I think that the Court of Inquiry will be over in about a week if they stick to their business as they ought.

To the Rt. Hon. —— Dublin Castle, 25th Oct. 1808.

I have received your letter of the 24th inst., and I should be very happy to have an opportunity of forwarding your views for the promotion of your step-son, Mr. * * * *, and I will accordingly make application for his promotion to the Commander in Chief. I must inform you, however, that an officer is rarely, if ever, promoted from an Ensigncy to a Lieutenancy in a regiment to which he does not belong; and this injustice to Ensigns in the regiment to which it may be desired to promote him is never done when such regiment is employed on active service. I must also inform you that the promotion of Mr. * * * * to a Lieutenancy in a regiment now employed in Portugal or Spain would not, of course, place him in either of those countries, as each of these regiments has a 2d battalion, now in England or Ireland, and he would be in the first instance the junior Lieutenant of the 2d batt. Under these circumstances the application which I shall make for Mr. * * * * 's promotion will probably not be successful; and if successful, will not accomplish the object which you have in view in making it; but still I shall make it to H.R.H. the Commander in Chief, in order to show my respect for you, and my desire to gratify you.

To Lieut. Col. Gordon, Military Secretary. Dublin Castle, 29th Oct. 1808.

I enclose a letter to me, and a memorial to H. R. H., which I have received from Major Travers, of the 95th regt.; and I can assure you with great truth that no troops could behave better on all occasions than those of the detachment of the 95th regt.; and there was no officer of his rank with whom I had more reason to be satisfied than Major Travers, during the period that I commanded the army. From the nature of the country, and the description of troops, such as the 95th are, they were probably more exposed and more frequently engaged than the others; and as I have had many opportunities of testifying, they always conducted themselves well.

To Lieut. Gen. ——. Dublin Castle, 30th Oct. 1808.

Your letter of the 26th Aug. was sent to Portugal, and did not arrive there till after I had quitted that country, and I only received it two days ago. I should not have recommended you in any case to serve with the Portuguese troops, because their conduct was not likely to do you credit; and I doubt the expediency of your serving with the Spaniards, for, to tell you the truth, I don't give credit to the histories we see in the papers of their successes. The public opinion and hope must be kept up in Spain, as in other countries, by success; and it is a venial offence to conceal disasters and exaggerate successes, of which I know the Spanish provincial governments are guilty. Our foolish editors of newspapers copy from the Spanish newspapers all they see, and the gulls of England believe all that the English newspapers tell them.

In point of fact the Spaniards have had no great success excepting against Dupont, and in the defence of Zaragoza. From the manner in which the story of the first was told, and supported by evidence, and comparing that with the histories of other successes, I am convinced that, if there is any foundation for them, it is but very small; and that the corps of French troops said to have been cut off in Catalonia, Valencia, Murcia, and Estremadura were at most straggling battalions, or probably even individuals. With regard to the last, I believe that the Spaniards have a good intrenched position at Zaragoza, which the citizens have defended manfully; but on the other hand, the French have never been able to attack it with heavy cannon.

Under these circumstances, and adverting to the temper of the public, I should doubt the expediency of your serving with the Spaniards. They must meet with severe reverses; and with their usual liberality, the good people of England will be disposed to attribute to an English general the reverses of their friends the Spaniards, which they do not at present expect, and will not believe can happen under any other circumstances whatever. I therefore recommend to you not to go to the Spaniards at present; but if you should still wish it, I'll bear your wishes in mind, and try what I can do for you when I shall return to the army, which I hope will be in a short time.

To Adm. Whitshed.   Dublin Castle, 31st Oct. 1808.

I am very much obliged to you for your kind letter of the 29th, which I have just received. I think that if I had been allowed to bring the operations in Portugal to a conclusion, the public would not have been so much displeased with them as they appear to be with the late transactions in that country. However, that is a misfortune to be lamented, and cannot now be avoided; but I hope it will be a lesson to our ministers, in future, not to incur the risk of altering the principle on which an operation is conducted in the middle of it. Pray make my best respects to Mrs. Whitshed.

To the Duke of Portland, K.G.   Dublin Castle, 1st Nov. 1808.

I have the honor to enclose a letter which has been transmitted to me for your Grace from Capt. Baker, of H.M.S. *Kangaroo*. In forwarding this letter to your Grace, I cannot avoid to mention to you that Capt. Baker waited upon the coast of Portugal for some days for my dispatches, with great politeness to me; that I believe it is usual to give promotion to an officer who brings home dispatches upon important events, such as those to which the dispatches in question referred; and that I have recommended Capt. Baker in consequence.

To Mr. ——.   London, 19th Nov. 1808.

I have received your letter, and am much obliged to you. I must always consider it a gross injustice to those who are obliged to appear before the Court of Inquiry to publish any part of the proceedings till the whole will be concluded, and that such publication must tend to mislead the public. The Court of Inquiry has desired that its proceedings should not be published; and, therefore, although I should be happy to assist you in any way, I must decline either to furnish you with materials, or to correct any thing for you, till the whole shall be brought to a conclusion, and it should be understood that there is no objection to publication in any quarter.

THE

COURT OF INQUIRY

INTO THE

CONVENTION.

———————

A SELECTION ONLY IS GIVEN OF THOSE PARTS OF THE PROCEEDINGS IN WHICH
LIEUT. GEN. SIR ARTHUR WELLESLEY APPEARED BEFORE THE COURT.

COURT OF INQUIRY.

GEORGE R.

'WHEREAS We were pleased, in the month of July, 1808, to constitute and appoint Lieut. Gen. Sir H. Dalrymple, Kt., to the command of a body of our forces employed to act on the coasts of Spain and Portugal, or in such other part of the Continent of Europe as he might afterwards be directed to; and the said Lieutenant General did, pursuant to our instructions transmitted to him, proceed to Portugal, and did, on the 22d Aug. 1808, land in that country, and take upon himself the command of the said body of our forces accordingly; and whereas it appears that on the same day (22d Aug.), and subsequently to his having assumed the command, an armistice was concluded,*

'We think it necessary that an inquiry should be made, by the General officers after named, into the conditions of the said Armistice and Convention,† and into all the causes and circumstances (whether arising from the previous operations of the British army, or otherwise) which led to them, and into the conduct, behaviour, and proceedings of the said Lieut. Gen. Sir H. Dalrymple, and of any other officer or officers who may have held the command of our troops in Portugal, and of any other person or persons, as far as the same were connected with the said Armistice and Convention, in order that the said General officers may report to us touching the matters aforesaid, for our better information.

'Our will and pleasure therefore is, and we do hereby nominate and appoint the General officers of our army whose names are respectively mentioned in the list ‡ annexed, to be a Board, of which we do hereby appoint Gen. Sir D. Dundas, K.B., to be President, who are to meet accordingly for the purposes above mentioned. And you are hereby required to give notice to the said General officers, when and where they are to meet for the said examination and inquiry; and you are hereby directed to summon such persons as may be judged necessary by the said General officers (whether the General officers employed in the expedition or others) to give information touching the said matters, or whose examination shall be desired by those employed in the said expedition. And the said General officers are hereby directed to hear such persons as shall offer to give information touching the same; and they are hereby authorised, empowered, and required, strictly to examine into the matters before mentioned, and to report a state thereof as it shall appear to them, together with their opinion thereupon; and also with their opinion whether any and what further proceedings should be had thereupon. All which you are to transmit to our Commander in Chief, to be by him laid before us for

---

* See the Armistice and Convention already printed, pp. 104, 105, 106.

† The Inquiry into the Convention (commonly called the Convention of Cintra, although framed and signed at Lisbon) was held at the Royal College at Chelsea, from the 14th Nov. to the 27th Dec. 1808.

The proceedings are of too great length to insert in detail in this work: the compiler has, therefore, extracted those passages only in which Sir A. Wellesley, in his several addresses, narratives, questions, and answers, appeared before the Court; in addition to which a summary of the proceedings is added. As is usual on Courts of Inquiry and Courts Martial, the questions are put to those who are examined, in the second person, through the Judge Advocate. They are answered sometimes in the second, and at other times in the third person, and are thus inserted in the proceedings. This will account for the want of perspicuity in the answers in this respect; but they are copied *verbatim* from the proceedings published 'by authority.'

‡ Gens. the Earl of Moira, Peter Craig, and Lord Heathfield; and Lieut. Gens. the Earl of Pembroke, Sir G. Nugent, and O. Nicholls.

our consideration. And for so doing this shall be, as well to you as to our said General officers and all others concerned, a sufficient warrant.

'Given at our Court at St. James's, this first day of Nov. 1808, in the 49th year of our reign.

'By His Majesty's command,

'J. Pulteney.

'To Our right trusty and well beloved Councillor, the Hon. R. Ryder, Judge Advocate Gen. of our Forces, or his Deputy.'

At a meeting of the Board of General officers appointed to inquire into the Convention, &c. in Portugal, by His Majesty's Warrant bearing date the 1st Nov. 1808, at the Great Hall in Chelsea College, on Monday the 14th day of the same month :

President : Gen. Sir D. Dundas, K.B. ·

Members : Gen. F. Earl of Moira, Gen. P. Craig, Gen. F. Lord Heathfield, Lieut. Gen. G. Earl of Pembroke, K.G., Lieut. Gen. Sir G. Nugent, Bart., Lieut. Gen. O. Nicholls.

Sir A. Wellesley addressed the Board as follows :

' I hope that in delivering this my narrative to the Court I shall be permitted to make a few observations upon the paper which has been read by Sir H. Dalrymple.

' I have as much reason to complain as he has that the writers in the newspapers should for some weeks past have amused the public with supposed accounts and comments on the late transactions in Portugal, and most particularly that they should have ventured to state some of them from what they call authority from me or my friends.

' I never said, nor ever authorised any body to say, and more I can venture to say, that no person connected with me, as my relations, friends, or aides de camp, or otherwise in the service, ever gave any authority to any publisher of a news-paper, or anybody else, to declare that I was compelled, or even ordered, to sign the paper to which my name appears. It is true that I was present when the Armistice was negotiated by the Commander in Chief, and I did assist in his negotiations, and I signed it by desire of the Commander in Chief : but I never said, and never will say, that the expression of the desire of the Commander in Chief was in the shape of an order which it was not in my power to disobey, much less of compulsion. I thought it my duty to comply with this desire of the Com-mander in Chief from the wish which I have always felt, according to which I have always acted, to carry into effect the orders and objects of those placed in command over me, however I might differ in opinion with them. I certainly did differ in opinion with the Commander in Chief upon more than one point in the detail of what I was thus called upon to sign, as I shall show hereafter ; but as I concurred in and advised the adoption of the principle of the measure, viz., that the French should be allowed to evacuate Portugal, for reasons which I shall state at a future period, I did not think proper to refuse to sign the paper on account of my disagreement on the details.

' I have thought it necessary to say thus much upon this subject ; and I now beg leave to deliver in a narrative of my proceedings from the time I took upon me the command of the army at Cork to the moment at which I delivered over the command to Lieut. Gen. Sir H. Burrard, on the afternoon of the 20th.'

Sir A. Wellesley accordingly delivered in his narrative ; which was laid upon the table, together with the narrative delivered in by Sir H. Dalrymple.

Sir A. Wellesley, on a subsequent day, read the narrative, which he had before delivered in, as follows :

'Gen. Sir D. Dundas,

'My Lords and Gentlemen,

' Having received the directions of the Judge Advocate General to attend you here this day, with as much detailed information in writing as I may think proper to offer, of my proceedings from the time I sailed with the troops from Ireland to the time I gave up the command to Lieut. Gen. Sir H. Burrard, I have now the honor to submit to the Court of Inquiry copies of my dispatches to the Sec. of State, detailing my proceedings.

' As these proceedings are fully detailed in the dispatches which contain an account of my motives for my actions at the moment I carried them into execution, I should be satisfied if the Court were to form an opinion upon a consideration of their contents; but as the Court have expressed a desire, at the same time, to have a narrative of my proceedings, I have drawn one out principally from the dispatches.

' I sailed from Cork in the *Donegal* on the 12th July; I went on board the *Crocodile* on the 13th, and sailed to Coruña, where I arrived on the 20th July. I there found that the French had, on the 14th, defeated the armies of Castille and Galicia, under Gens. Cuesta and Blake; but, having sounded the Junta respecting their wish to have the assistance of the army under my command, in the existing crisis of their affairs, they declared explicitly that they did not want the assistance of troops; but, eventually, arms and ammunition, and money immediately. A sum of £200,000 for their use had arrived on the 20th, and their requisition for arms and ammunition was sent home immediately. The Junta of Galicia at the same time expressed the greatest anxiety that the troops under my command should be employed in driving the French out of Portugal, as they were persuaded that the Spaniards of the north and south of the Peninsula could never have any decided success independently of each other, and could never make any great simultaneous effort to remove the French from Spain till they should be driven from Portugal, and the British troops in that Kingdom should connect the operations of the northern and the southern Spanish armies. The Junta of Galicia, at the same time, strongly recommended to me to land in the north of Portugal, in order that I might bring forward and avail myself of the Portuguese troops which the government of Oporto were collecting in the neighbourhood of that city. I have to observe to the Court, that they will not see, in my dispatches to the Sec. of State from Coruña, the detail of the wishes and sentiments of the Junta on my plan of operations, because they did not come regularly within the scope of a military dispatch; but the subject is mentioned in my dispatch to Gen. Spencer of the 26th July.

' I sailed from Coruña on the 22d, and joined the fleet off Cape Finisterre next day, and quitted it again at night, and went to Oporto, in order to hold a conference with the Bishop and the General officers in the command of the Portuguese troops. On my arrival at Oporto, on the 24th, I received a letter from the Admiral, Sir C. Cotton, in which he recommended to me to leave the troops either at Oporto or at the mouth of the Mondego river, and to proceed to Lisbon in a frigate, to communicate with him before I should determine upon the plan of operations and the landing place. The result of the conference which I had on the night of the 24th with the Bishop and the General officers of the Portuguese army was an agreement, that about 5000 Portuguese troops should be sent forward to co-operate with me against the enemy; that the remainder of the Portuguese troops, amounting to about 1500, and a Spanish corps of about 1500 men, then on its march from Galicia, and another small Spanish corps of about 300 men, and all the Portuguese armed peasantry, should remain in the neighbourhood of Oporto, and in the province of Tras os Montes; a part to be employed in the blockade of Almeida, and a part in the defence of the province of Tras os Montes, which province was supposed to be threatened by an attack from the French corps under Marshal Bessières, since the defeat of the Spanish armies under Blake and Cuesta at Rio Seco, on the 14th July. The Bishop of Oporto likewise promised to supply the army under my command with mules and other means of carriage, and with slaughter cattle.

' I sailed from Oporto on the morning of the 25th, and joined the fleet, and settled with Capt. Malcolm that it should go to Mondego bay; and I left it again that night, and went to the mouth of the Tagus to confer with the Admiral. I joined him on the evening of the 26th; and I there received letters from Gen. Spencer, at Puerto de Sta Maria, in which he informed me that he had landed his corps in Andalusia, at the request of the Junta of Seville, and he did not think it proper to embark it again till he should receive further orders from me; and he appeared to think that my presence in Andalusia, and the assistance of the troops under my command, were necessary to enable Gen. Castaños to defeat Gen. Dupont.

'As I was of opinion that the most essential object for the Spaniards, as well as for us, was to drive the French from Portugal, and that neither his corps nor mine was sufficiently strong, when separate, to be of much service anywhere, and that when joined they might effect the object which had been deemed of most importance in England, and in Galicia, I immediately dispatched orders to Gen. Spencer to embark his troops, unless he should be actually engaged in an operation which he could not relinquish without loss to the Spaniards, and to join me off the coast of Portugal.

'The result of the information which I received from Gen. Spencer, of the strength of the French army in Portugal, was, that they consisted of more than 20,000 men. The accounts of their numbers which I received from the Admiral, and had received from the Portuguese, did not make their force so large; but, upon the whole, I was induced to believe that they had not less than from 16,000 to 18,000 men. Of this number they had from 600 to 800 in the fort of Almeida, 600 or 800 in Elvas, 800 in Peniche, 1600 or 1800 in Setuval, and the remainder were considered about 14,000, disposable for the defence of Lisbon, and the forts on the Tagus. The whole of this disposable force was at this time in the neighbourhood of Lisbon, excepting about 2400 men at Alcobaça, under Gen. Thomière.

' I considered with the Admiral the propriety of carrying into execution any of the proposed plans of attack upon the Tagus, or upon the coast in the neighbourhood of the Rock at Lisbon; and it appeared to us both that all the attacks upon the river, which had been proposed to government, were impracticable; that the attack upon Cascaes bay was likewise so; that a landing in any of the small bays in the neighbourhood of the Rock was a matter of considerable difficulty at any time, and that there was a risk that if a part of the army, or even the whole army were landed, the state of the surf which prevails upon the whole coast of Portugal might prevent the disembarkation of the rear in the one case, and of the stores and provisions which were necessary in the other. At all events, the disembarkation would be made in the neighbourhood of the whole disposable force of the French army; and the British troops would be exposed to their attack on their landing, probably in a crippled state, and certainly not in a very efficient state. By making our disembarkation in one of the bays near the Rock of Lisbon, it was certain that we should not have the advantage which, at that time, we expected to derive from the co-operation of the Portuguese troops. It appeared to us that the fort of Peniche, which was garrisoned by the enemy, would prevent the disembarkation under the shelter of that peninsula; and therefore it appeared to the Admiral and to me, that it would be most advisable to disembark the troops in the Mondego river.

'I quitted the Admiral off the Tagus on the 27th, and joined the fleet of transports off the Mondego on the 30th. I there received information from government, dated the 15th July, that they intended to reinforce the army under my command with 5000 men, under the command of Brig. Gen. Acland, in the first instance, and eventually with the corps, consisting of 10,000 men, which had been under the command of Sir J. Moore in Sweden; and that Sir H. Dalrymple was appointed to command the army. I was likewise directed to carry into execution the instructions which I had received, if I conceived that my force was sufficiently strong.

' Besides these dispatches from government, I received information, on my arrival at the Mondego, of the defeat of the French corps under Dupont by the Spanish army under Castaños, on the 20th July; and I was convinced that Gen. Spencer, if he did not embark immediately upon receiving intelligence of that event, would do so as soon as he should receive my orders of the 26th July: I therefore considered his arrival as certain, and I had reason to expect the arrival of Gen. Acland's corps every moment, as I had been informed that it was to sail from Harwich and the Downs on the 19th July. I also received accounts. at the same time, that Gen. Loison had been detached from Lisbon across the Tagus into Alentejo on the 27th July, in order to subdue the insurrection in that province, and open the communication with Elvas. The insurgents had lately been joined by about 1000 men from the Spanish army of Estremadura, and the insurrection had made considerable progress, and was become formidable in Alentejo.

'I therefore considered that I might commence the disembarkation of the troops, without risk of their being attacked by superior numbers before one or both the reinforcements should arrive; and I was induced to disembark immediately, not only because the troops were likely to be better equipped, and more able to march in proportion as they should have been longer on shore, but because I had reason to believe that the Portuguese had been much discouraged by seeing the troops so long in the ships after the fleet had arrived in Mondego bay; and I was certain they would suspect our inclination or our ability to contend with the French, if they had not been disembarked as soon as I returned from the Tagus. I therefore determined to disembark as soon as the weather and the state of the surf would permit us, and we commenced the disembarkation on the 1st Aug.

'The difficulties of landing, occasioned by the surf, were so great, that the whole of the corps were not disembarked till the 5th, on which day Gen. Spencer arrived, and his corps on the 6th. He had embarked at Puerto de Sta Maria on the 21st July, when he had heard of the defeat of Dupont by Castaños, and had not received the dispatches addressed to him by me on the 26th July. Gen. Spencer disembarked on the 7th and 8th, on which night the whole army was in readiness to march forward.

'From the 1st Aug. to that day the time had been usefully spent in procuring the means for moving with the army the necessary stores, provisions, and baggage, and in arranging those means in the most advantageous manner to the different departments: the cavalry and the artillery received a large remount of horses, means were procured of moving with the army a sufficient supply of ammunition and military stores, and a seasonable supply of hospital stores; but I determined to march towards Lisbon by that road which passes nearest to the sea coast, in order that I might communicate with Capt. Bligh, of the *Alfred*, who attended the movements of the army with a fleet of victuallers and store ships. The communication with this fleet, however, it was obvious, would be very precarious, as well on account of the state of the surf on the coast, in the different points of rendezvous which had been settled, as because it might happen that it would be more advantageous to the army to take another line of march, passing farther inland. I therefore made arrangements for carrying with the army such a supply of the articles of first necessity as should render it independent of the fleet till it should reach the Tagus, if circumstances should prevent the communication with the fleet, or should render it advantageous to relinquish it.

'In the same period of time I also armed the Portuguese troops, and ascertained, as far as lay in my power, the degree of their discipline and efficiency, and recommended and superintended their organisation. I offered such a sum of money as the funds of the army could afford, to defray any expense which it might be deemed necessary to incur in their equipment for the field, which was declined by the Portuguese General officers; and I met these gentlemen at Monte Mór o Velho on the 7th, and arranged with them the plan of our operations and march, which was delayed for the main body of the army till the 10th, at their desire, for the convenience of the Portuguese troops.

'On the 8th I wrote a letter to Sir H. Burrard, which I left with Capt. Malcolm, of the *Donegal*, to be delivered to him upon his arrival at the Mondego, detailing all the circumstances of our situation, and recommending for his consideration a plan of operations for the corps under the command of Sir J. Moore. The Court will find the copy of this letter enclosed in my dispatch to Lord Castlereagh of the 8th Aug.

'The advanced guard marched on the 9th, supported by the brigades under Gen. Hill and Gen. Ferguson, as I had heard that Gen. Laborde had collected his own corps and Gen. Thomière's, consisting of from 5000 to 6000 men, in the neighbourhood of Leiria, which place he threatened, as it contained a magazine formed for the use of the Portuguese army. On the 10th the main body followed, and the advanced guard arrived at Leiria on the 10th, and the main body on the 11th.

'I received a letter from Mr. Stuart and Col. Doyle at Coruña, on the 10th, detailing the inefficient state of the Galician army under Gen. Blake; that that General had separated his troops, which consisted of infantry, from the cavalry under Gen. Cuesta; and that neither were in a condition to act offensively against

Bessières, or even to follow that General if he should march into Portugal, or to attack him if he should make any considerable detachment to that quarter. At the same time I received the intelligence of the retreat of Joseph Buonaparte from Madrid on the 29th July; and I concluded that Bessières, instead of moving out, or detaching towards Portugal, would cover the retreat of Joseph Buonaparte towards the French frontier. Whether he did so or not, it was obvious to me that I should have time for my operations against Junot before Bessières could arrive in Portugal to interrupt them; and it was probable that Gen. Acland's corps, or Sir J. Moore's, would arrive and land in Portugal before Bessières could come from the north of Spain.

'Adverting, therefore, to the advanced state of the season, the necessity of communicating with the sea coast, and the certainty that that communication would be nearly impracticable after the month of August, and to the still dispersed state of the French forces in Portugal, I considered it to be important to endeavor to perform those operations to which the army was equal, and for which it was fully equipped and prepared, without loss of time. I communicated, however, the intelligence which I had received from Mr. Stuart, and my opinion upon it, to Sir H. Burrard, in a letter which I addressed to him on the 10th Aug.; a copy of which, and of a private letter to Sir H. Burrard, the Court will find in my dispatch to the Sec. of State of the 18th Aug.

'The Portuguese army, consisting of about 6000 men, including 500 cavalry, arrived at Leiria on the 12th, where the whole force was then assembled.

'The French General Loison, who, I have informed the Court, had been detached across the Tagus into Alentejo, on the 26th or 27th July, with between 5000 and 6000 men, had withdrawn the greatest part of the garrison of Setuval, consisting of 1600 men, by which he had been joined, and he had immediately marched towards Evora, where he defeated and dispersed a Spanish detachment, consisting of 1000 men, and the force of the insurrection of Alentejo collected in that town; he then marched to Elvas, re-victualled that place, suppressed the insurrection, and re-established the French authority in Alentejo, and made arrangements for the purchase and collection of the grain of that province. He crossed the Tagus again at Abrantes, and marching down that river, he arrived at Thomar, about 16 miles to the south east from Leiria, on the evening of the 11th, on which day the British army arrived at Leiria.

'The corps under Laborde was at the same time at Alcobaca, about 16 miles from Leiria to the south west, and the object of the French officers had evidently been to join at Leiria before the British troops could arrive there. This town is on the high road from Lisbon to the north of Portugal, to the eastward of which, and nearly parallel to the road, there is a chain of high mountains which runs from Leiria nearly to the Tagus, over which chain there is no good passage for carriages. In consequence of the early arrival, therefore, of the British troops at Leiria, Gen. Loison was obliged to return to the southward before he could effect his junction with Gen. Laborde, who was thus exposed to be attacked when alone, and was attacked on the 17th Aug. The Court will find in my dispatch to the Sec. of State of the 16th Aug., from Caldas, an outline of the operations of Loison's corps, of which what I have here stated is a more detailed account.

'All the arrangements for the march having been made, and communicated to the Portuguese officers, the army marched on the 13th, in 2 columns, to Calvario, and on the 14th, in 2 columns, to Alcobaça, from whence Gen. Laborde had retreated in the course of the preceding night. The Portuguese troops had not marched from Leiria, as had been arranged and as I had expected, under the pretence that they had no provisions; and I received on the 13th, in the evening, a letter from Col. Trant, who was employed by me to communicate with the Portuguese General, in which he informed me of the General's intention to halt at Leiria, unless I should consent to supply the Portuguese troops with provisions from the British Commissariat on the march to Lisbon. He also explained a plan of operations, which Gen. Freire proposed to carry into execution, by which he would have been left without any communication with the British army, exposed to be attacked by the French army, if they should choose to abandon the defence of Lisbon and the Tagus, and proceed to the northward and eastward, or even if they should be compelled to retire after an action with the British troops.

' In my reply to this communication I pointed out the impossibility of my complying with the demand for provisions, and the danger which would result from the adoption of the plan of operations proposed for the Portuguese corps. I urged the Portuguese General, in the most earnest terms, to co-operate with me in the deliverance of his country from the French, if he had any regard to his own honor, to the honor of his country, or of his Prince; and I pointed out to him the resources of which he could avail himself to feed the army. I then proposed to him that, if he should not march with his whole corps, he should send to join me 1000 regular infantry, all his light troops and his cavalry, which troops I engaged to feed, as the utmost I could undertake to perform in that way.

' These troops, in number, 1000 regular infantry, 400 light troops, and 250 cavalry, joined me at Alcobaça, on the evening of the 14th, with Col. Trant, and remained with me during the remainder of the operations. The main body of the Portuguese corps, instead of carrying into execution the plan of operations which I had originally proposed, or that which Gen. Freire had substituted, adopted the measure of safety which I had recommended in the event of his determination not to join me, and remained at Leiria, and afterwards at Caldas and Obidos, till the 22d Aug.

' On the arrival of the army at Alcobaça, I immediately opened a communication with Capt. Bligh, of the *Alfred*, who had been for 2 days waiting with the fleet of victuallers and store ships off Nazareth. A supply of bread and oats was immediately landed; and I appointed Peniche, which place I intended to reconnaitre, as our next point of communication.

' The army marched on the 15th, in two columns, to Caldas, where it halted the 16th, to allow the Commissariat to come up, and to receive the supplies which had been landed at Nazareth. On the 15th, in the evening, there was a skirmish between the troops of the advanced guard of Laborde's corps and our riflemen, in which the latter sustained some loss. But we kept possession of the post at Obidos, which commands the valley of Caldas. The details of this affair are published in the Gazette, as are those of the action of the 17th.

' Throughout that day we had reason to believe that Gen. Loison, who had moved from Rio Maior on the evening of the 16th, would be found on Laborde's right, and the disposition for the attack was made accordingly. During the action a French officer, who was dying of his wounds, informed me that they had expected Loison to join them that day at 1 o'clock by their right, which was the reason for which they stood our attack ; that their numbers were 6000 ; and that their loss had been severe. Intelligence to the same purport was received from other prisoners; and as a small patrole of French infantry appeared at no great distance from the left of our position on the 17th at dusk, and I heard that Loison's corps was at that moment arriving at Bombarral, which was about 5 miles from the field of battle, I concluded that the junction had been intended, and was prevented only by our early attack. At all events great caution was necessary in all the movements of that day ; and, indeed, the nature of the ground over which the troops were obliged to move rendered a very rapid attack impossible.

' The two French corps joined on that night, and retired beyond Torres Vedras, which was 10 miles from the field of battle towards Cabeça de Montachique. My intention was to march to Torres Vedras on the morning of the 18th ; and the troops were under arms, and the orders for the march had been issued, when I received from Gen. Anstruther an account of his arrival on the coast, and of his junction with Capt. Bligh. My original intention had been to employ the corps under Gen. Acland and Gen. Anstruther in the siege of Peniche, if I should find it necessary to undertake it; or if I should not, to send them down the coast to effect a landing in some of the bays in the neighbourhood of the Rock of Lisbon, in the rear of the enemy, while I should press upon their front. But the disappointment which I experienced in the hope of co-operation of the Portuguese troops, which were with me in the action of the 17th, and above all, the determined and gallant resistance of the enemy in that action, induced me to be of opinion that I ought to land Gen. Anstruther's brigade, and Gen. Acland's when it should arrive, and to join those troops to the army. I therefore marched on the 18th to Lourinha, from whence I communicated again with Gen. Anstruther, and, on the 19th, to Vimeiro, which appeared on the whole to be the position best calculated to secure the junction of Gen. Anstruther, at the same time that it was a march in advance on our route. On account of the calms, the fleet which was anchored off the Berlings could not stand in till late on the 19th, and Gen. Anstruther did not land till that evening, and he formed a junction with 2 brigades detached from our left on the morning of the 20th, and took his position in the advanced guard.

'Between the 18th and 20th the French corps had assembled at and about Torres Vedras, the troops last arrived under Junot forming the advanced guard, in a strong position in front of the town; and the divisions of Laborde and Loison, the main body, in another strong position behind it. Their cavalry was very active throughout the days of the 19th and 20th; they covered the whole country, patrolled frequently up to our position, and on the 20th one patrole was pushed into the rear of our right, as far as the landing place at Maceira. Under these circumstances we could gain no detailed information of the enemy's position excepting that it was very strong, and occupied by their whole force.

'My intention was to march on the morning of the 21st, and orders were issued accordingly. I should have pushed the advanced guard as far as the heights of Mafra, and should have halted the main body about 4 or 5 miles from that place. By this movement the enemy's position at Torres Vedras would have been turned, and I should have brought the army into a country of which I had an excellent map and topographical accounts, which had been drawn up for the use of the late Sir C. Stuart;* and the battle, which it was evident would be fought in a few days, would have had for its field a country of which we had a knowledge, and not very distant from Lisbon, into which town, if we had been successful, we might have entered with the retreating enemy.

'I was informed in the middle of the day of the 20th, that Gen. Acland's brigade was in the offing, and I made arrangements for their disembarkation as soon as they should arrive; and in the evening of this day Sir H. Burrard arrived in Maceira roads in the *Brazen.* He immediately assumed the command of the army.

'The Court will observe that the last of my dispatches to the Sec. of State is dated the 18th, and the account of my proceedings on the 19th and 20th, the last 2 days of my command, is made from memory, assisted by a reference to private letters written at the time; and if the Court should wish it, it can be substantiated by evidence.'

Sir A. Wellesley delivered in copies of several dispatches, but which were not read, other copies having been already laid before the Board and read.

The Board desiring that Sir A. Wellesley's narrative should be again read, the Judge Advocate General accordingly read the same.

A paper containing questions prepared by the Board having been delivered to Sir A. Wellesley at their last meeting, Sir A. Wellesley now returned the same with his answers in writing. The questions, with the answers, were then read, viz. :

'Q. When did you receive orders to take the command of a considerable body of troops assembled at Cork?

'A. I received the orders of H. R. H. the Commander in Chief on the 15th June. I received the instructions of the Sec. of State, of the 30th June, in Dublin, on the 3d July, and I set out from thence on the 5th, and arrived at Cork on the 6th July.

'Q. When did you sail from Cork, and with what numbers?

'A. I sailed from Cork on the 12th July, with about 9064 men, including the 4th Royal Veteran Battalion, 275 artillery and drivers, and about 300 cavalry, of which 180 were mounted.

'Q. What were the orders and instructions under which you sailed, and the principal objects of your expedition?

'A. The orders and instructions which I received are before the Court; from the Commander in Chief, of the 14th June, and from the Sec. of State, of the

---

* Lieut. Gen. the Hon. Sir C. Stuart, K.B., brother of the first Marquis of Bute, and father of Lord Stuart de Rothesay. He had commanded a British force for some time in Portugal.

30th June. I have not copies of the instructions from the Sec. of State : I gave the originals to Lieut. Gen. Sir H. Burrard, and he returned me copies, which I have, by some accident, mislaid. The general object of the expedition was to aid the Spanish and Portuguese nations ; the principal object was to attack the French in the Tagus. But I considered myself authorised by my instructions to pursue any other object, if I thought it more likely to conduce to the benefit of the Spanish and Portuguese nations.

'Q. What were the particulars of your progress until you arrived in Mondego bay ?

'A. The particulars of my progress are detailed in my dispatches of the 21st and 26th July, and 1st Aug., to the Sec. of State, and in my narrative.

'Q. What reasons determined your arrival in Mondego bay, your subsequent landing on the 1st Aug., your remaining there until the 9th, and your proceeding on that day towards Lisbon ?

'A. The reasons which determined my arrival and subsequent landing in Mondego bay, on the 1st Aug., are detailed in my dispatches to the Sec. of State of that date, in my letter to Sir H. Burrard of the 8th Aug., and in my narrative. The reasons which occasioned my remaining there till the 9th Aug., and my proceeding on that day towards Lisbon, are detailed in my dispatches to the Sec. of State of the 1st and 8th Aug., in my letters to Sir H. Burrard of the 8th and 10th Aug.. and in my narrative.

'Q. On your arrival at Mondego bay, what knowledge had you of expected reinforcements from England, and what orders respecting them : did troops join you at Mondego bay, and in what numbers ?

'A. On my arrival at Mondego bay on the 30th July, from the Tagus, I received a letter from the Sec. of State, dated the 15th July, announcing that Brig. Gen. Acland was ordered to sail with 5000 men to join me; and that Sir H. Burrard was ordered to sail with 10,000 men, which had been in Sweden under Sir J. Moore, for the same purpose; also that transports had been sent to convey to Portugal one regiment (the Buffs) from Madeira ; and I received orders, in a letter dated the 21st July, from the Sec. of State, to give notice, by ships of war stationed off the coast, where I should be found ; and other orders to carry into execution the object of my instructions, if I should think my force sufficient : these are, I think, the heads of my instructions ; but I am not certain, as I have no copy of them. I was joined at the Mondego on the 6th Aug. by Gen. Spencer, with 4314 rank and file, and 71 artillery and drivers.

'Q. On your march of the 9th Aug. what knowledge had you of reinforcements from England, and what orders respecting them ?

'A. The knowledge and orders as above detailed. There were reports by ships arrived from England, but nothing official on which I could rely.

'Q. What was the object of your march forward on the 9th, before the arrival of reinforcements from England ; what were your numbers ; and were any Portuguese corps on your left assisting, and with which you were in communication ?

'A. The objects of my march are stated in my dispatch to Sir H. Burrard, of the 8th Aug., and in my narrative. My numbers were upon the whole (having left the 4th Royal Veteran battalion on board ship) about 12,300 rank and file. There was besides a Portuguese corps in communication with me on my left, consisting of about 6000 men, under Gen. Freire ; exclusive of this Portuguese corps, there was a corps consisting of 1500 Spanish infantry, under the Marques de Valladares, and about the same number of Portuguese troops belonging to the defence of Oporto, and the blockade of Almeida, collected near Guarda, which moved towards Abrantes, in consequence of Loison's march across the Tagus : it was thought he intended to go to Almeida.

'Q. What was your progress until you reached Caldas, in the neighbourhood of the enemy ?

'A. My progress is detailed in my narrative : I was with the army between Lavos and Leiria on the 10th, at Leiria on the 11th and 12th, at Calvario on the 13th, at Alcobaça on the 14th, and at Caldas on the 15th Aug.

'Q. In what manner was your army supplied with provisions during your march, and what resources did you draw from the country ?

'A. The army received biscuit, fresh meat, and wine ; the two latter drawn from the country. I had arranged with the Bishop when I was at Oporto, on the night of the 24th July, that the government should take measures to supply us with slaughter cattle; but in case of failure from this quarter, I had authorised a contract for slaughter cattle for the army with Mr. Archer, of Figueira, which was afterwards renewed with Mr. Walsh, of Oporto.

'Q. On your arrival at Caldas, what was the number and state of your horses, artillery, carriages, of your ammunition, provisions, and of your dependence for future supplies?

'A. On the arrival of the army at Caldas, we had a sufficient number of horses to draw one brigade of 9 pounders, and 2 brigades of 6 pounders, with the carriages attached to them. I must inform the Court, that the expedition which sailed from Cork under my command was originally destined to go to the coast of Spain, to be prepared to act as circumstances might require; and as it was very uncertain that the troops would ever land in Spain, and it was thought that the horses of the artillery would suffer and might be lost to the service by being kept so long in the transports, as it was probable we might be on the coast of Spain unemployed, it was expedient to equip the ordnance sent on the expedition with horses taken from the Irish Commissariat. These are generally horses cast from the cavalry or bought at low prices, such as £12 or £13 each; and although not bad horses, they are not so good and efficient as those belonging to the artillery: about 298 were originally embarked in Ireland, and I believe all arrived safe at the mouth of the Mondego river; we lost 4 or 5 in the disembarkation, and there were 8 or 10 unfit for service; so that we had originally 282 Irish horses: besides this number, I gave 20 mares to the artillery, out of a number sent from Oporto by the Bishop; but of this the Court will see an accurate return in a letter from Sir H. Dalrymple to the Sec. of State, read to the Court on Saturday. These mares answered well to carry the officers and non-commissioned officers attached to the brigades, who are usually mounted, and the Irish horses were in the draught; we put 2 in addition to the usual numbers in each carriage, on account of the heaviness and badness of the roads, the heat of the weather, and their low condition. In this manner we got on very well, and had a sufficient number for all our purposes on our arrival at Caldas, not less, I should think, than 300. The ordnance consisted of 18 pieces of cannon, of which there were one 9 pounder brigade, and 2 6 pounder brigades, all complete in every respect, with the usual proportion of ammunition; besides which there was a quantity of spare ammunition for the 9 pounders carried upon the carts of the country; the exact amount I cannot now tell, but more than sufficient for a battle in the field.

'The soldiers had, each of them, 60 rounds of musket ammunition: besides this quantity there were 90 mules attached to the reserve of the artillery to carry musket ammunition, each mule with 2000 rounds; and there were 500,000 rounds on the carts. The army marched from Lavos on the 10th Aug., with 17 days' bread, viz., 4 days' bread on the men's backs, 3 days' bread on mules, and 10 on carts; there were, besides, 5 days' salt meat, and 10 days' spirits. Of this quantity of course 7 days' bread was consumed on the 16th; but nearly 3 days' bread was received at Nazareth on the 14th, so that on the 16th Aug. the army had 14 days' bread. Besides the salt meat, the contract provided that there should always be 3 days' fresh meat in camp. I do not believe that, upon our arrival at Caldas, the contractor had fulfilled his contract to that extent; but the supply was regular, and it was certain that his bullocks were coming up regularly.*

* Sir D. Dundas: 'The Court will observe in my letter to the Sec. of State, written from Caldas on the 16th Aug., that a complaint is made of the inefficiency of the Commissariat.

'As conclusions may be drawn from this letter which it was never my intention should be drawn from it, I beg leave, in justice to the individuals composing the Commissariat attached to the army lately under my command, to state, that I did not intend to complain of their want of zeal in the service, or of any deficiency of exertion on their part.

'The fact is, that I wished to draw the attention of the government to this important branch of the service, which is but little understood in this country. The evils of which I complained are probably to be attributed to the nature of our political situation, which prevents us from undertaking great military operations, in which the subsistence of armies becomes a subject of serious consideration and difficulty; and these evils consisted in the inexperience of almost every individual belonging to the Commissariat, of the mode of procuring, conveying, and distributing the supplies which were to be got for the use of the troops.

'I hope that the Court will allow this explanation to stand upon their minutes.'

' I do not recollect that at this time we had used either salt meat or spirits. We procured wine in nearly every village in the country; our dependence upon future supplies of bread was upon our communication with the shipping; and I had appointed Capt. Bligh, of the *Alfred*, to communicate with the army off Peniche on the 16th or 17th. Our dependence of meat was upon the contractor (who, I must say, never failed us until the numbers of the army were increased) and upon the shipping; and for ammunition upon the same.

' Q. Why did you direct your march to Lisbon by a road near the coast, in preference to another line near the Tagus?

' A. I directed my march by the road of the coast for the reasons in my letter to Sir H. Burrard, of the 8th Aug., and in my narrative, and in my answer to the last question.

' Q. At Caldas, what information had you of the strength and position of the enemy, and what of your expected reinforcements?

' A. The information I had of the enemy at Caldas was, that Gen. Laborde was in my front at Roliça, with Gen. Thomière's corps, which had been reported to me 2400 men, and his own, which had been reported 2600; in the whole 5000. Besides these troops, they were joined in the battle of the 17th by 400 men of the garrison of Peniche. I judged the strength of the French corps in that action to have been 6000 men, from the view I had of them, and that was the number reported to me during the action, as I have stated in my narrative: Laborde himself, however, says that they had not nearly that number. Gen. Loison's corps was at Rio Maior during the whole of the 16th; this corps was reported to be from 5000 to 7000 men; they took 9000 rations from the country; Loison's corps marched from Rio Maior about 7 o'clock in the evening of the 16th, and I heard of his march at 11 o'clock. Besides these corps of Loison's, I heard at Caldas that Junot was on his march from Lisbon with 3000 or 4000 men; I had no intelligence at Caldas of my expected reinforcements.

' Q. Where did you first meet with considerable opposition from the enemy?

' A. I first met with considerable opposition from the enemy on the 17th Aug. near Roliça.

' Q. What were your proceedings from Caldas to Vimeiro?

'A. My proceedings from my departure from Caldas until my arrival at Vimeiro are detailed in my dispatch of the 17th Aug. to the Sec. of State, and in my narrative.

' Q. What knowledge on the 20th had you of the enemy's strength and position?

' A. I knew on the 20th that all the enemy's disposable force was collected at Torres Vedras; that the advanced guard was on the heights in front of the town, the main body to the southward of it. I had no particular details of their position; but I do not believe that they extended at all to their left towards the road to Mafra.

' Q. What were your intentions and proceedings with respect to moving forward next day?

' A. I had ordered the army to march on the morning of the 21st, and I intended to march, and should have marched, as I have stated in my narrative.

' Q. How was the army circumstanced on the 20th with respect to provisions and ammunition, and what was your prospect as to future supplies and difficulties?

' A. On the 20th the army had consumed 5 days' of 14 days' bread it had on the 16th; but the fleet had arrived at Maceira, and the communication was open with it, and we received a supply of 3 days' bread on that day, making 12 days' bread for the original numbers. 2 days' salt meat and spirits had at this time been consumed, and the supply of fresh meat was complete. It must be observed, however, that the consumption of the army had been increased by above 4000 men, or one third of the original numbers who drew rations. This reinforcement landed with 4 days' bread: therefore it may be calculated that the army, including these reinforcements, had in camp and the means of moving, on the 21st Aug., above 9 days' bread.

' The Portuguese troops (1650 in number), whom I had engaged to supply with bread, were supplied, in the first instance, by some which the French had left behind at Alcobaça, and another quantity found at Caldas.

' The ammunition expended in the action of the 17th was replaced on the 20th Aug; and all the equipments of the army were as complete as when we were at Caldas on the 16th.

'Q. What reinforcements, and at what places and days, joined you on your march from Caldas, and previous to your victory at Vimeiro on the 21st?

'A. Brig. Gen. Anstruther joined with his brigade, consisting of 2400 men, at Vimeiro, on the morning of the 20th, and Brig. Gen. Acland, with his brigade, consisting of about 2750 men, at Vimeiro, on the night of the 20th.

'Q. What orders and instructions relative to your proceeding did you receive from England, from the 9th Aug. to the 21st?

'A. I did not receive any orders or instructions from England relative to my proceeding between the 9th and the 21st Aug.

'Q. When did you give up the command of the army to Lieut. Gen. Sir H. Burrard?

'A. Sir H. Burrard assumed the command of the army on board H. M. S. *Brazen*, when I went on board that vessel on the evening of the 20th Aug. to report to him.

'Q. As you expected Sir H. Burrard to arrive early in August, what steps did you take to give him previous information, and to acquaint him of your proceedings from time to time?

'A. I wrote to Sir H. Burrard on the 8th, 10th, and 12th Aug.; and copies of my letters are before the Court. I sent him a copy of my dispatch of the 17th Aug., addressed to the Sec. of State, to Capt. Malcolm, of the *Donegal*, to be delivered to him; besides this, I wrote to Capt. Malcolm, of the *Donegal*, nearly every day.

'Q. What position do you understand did the enemy take on the evening of the 21st Aug.?

'A. I understand that the enemy spent the evening of the 21st Aug. in endeavoring to form the different corps of their army again, and to regain Torres Vedras; some of their corps arrived at Torres Vedras at about 12 o'clock at night of the 21st; others not until late in the day of the 22d Aug. When the French retired from the field at Vimeiro, they drew off to the northward towards Lourinha; and from thence they got into the road to Torres Vedras.

'Q. What were the numbers of the enemy's cavalry at the battle of Vimeiro?

'A. As far as I could judge and learn, they had from 1200 to 1400 cavalry.

'Q. What were the numbers of British and Portuguese cavalry in the said battle?

'A. We had about 210 mounted men of the 20th dragoons, and 260 of Portuguese cavalry.'

The Board now proceeded further to examine Sir A. Wellesley.

'Q. Had Sir A. Wellesley any communication with Santander, or other means of knowing what was the wish of the inhabitants of Biscay, relative to assistance from the British army?

'A. When I was at Coruña I received a letter from Sir T. Dyer, who was employed by His Majesty's government in communication with the Junta of Asturias, in which Sir Thomas informed me that, as I understood him, he had held out a prospect to the Junta of Oviedo that the troops under my command would land in Asturias; and he informed me that this communication had been received with satisfaction by the Junta at Oviedo, and he rather urged me to disembark at Santander, in order that I might attack the French corps which at that time had got possession of that city. I communicated with the Junta of Galicia upon this subject among others, who I conceived were interested in the position of the French corps at Santander, and I was informed by them that measures had been adopted which they thought likely to be effectual to drive this French corps from Santander, which measures afterwards proved to be successful. I had no communication whatever with any of the people of Biscay, which province was not, as I understood at that time, in insurrection against the French.

'Q. Had you any correspondence with the Spanish Generals, or did you make any suggestion to them on the importance of gaining the passes of the Pyrenees, and thereby preventing the entrance of French reinforcements into Spain?

'A. I had no correspondence with the Spanish Generals.

'Q. Is the inference accurate that you thought the army under your immediate command adequate to the expulsion of Junot's force from the positions at Lisbon, when you, in a letter dated the 10th Aug., advised Sir H. Burrard to march with the expected reinforcements to Santarem to cut off the enemy's retreat?

A. I did consider the force which marched from Lavos under my command, to be sufficient to deprive the French of Lisbon and of the forts upon the Tagus.

' Q. What alteration, if any, took place in that opinion in consequence of the actual arrival of Lieut. Gen. Sir J. Moore with the division under his orders?

' A. No alteration whatever in respect to the actual capacity of the army, from its strength, to obtain possession of Lisbon and of the forts upon the Tagus.

' Q. You have stated that you would have undertaken the supply of the Portuguese troops had it not been for the insufficient construction of the British Commissariat. Is this conclusion from that statement just, that the country afforded considerable supplies of provisions, if due means could be applied to collect them?

' A. The country afforded us no provisions excepting beef and wine, and I believe that from the time I landed in Portugal to the time I quitted the army on the 20th Sept., the troops only received biscuit from the ships. As I have stated in my narrative, a small quantity of bread was left behind by the French at Alcobaça, and a small quantity at Caldas; and besides this, after I had given up the command when the army arrived in the neighbourhood of Torres Vedras, a small quantity of flour was got, which had likewise been left behind by the French. While I commanded the army this bread supplied the consumption of the Portuguese troops, 1650 in number, who were with me, and afterwards I believe that the officers of the army received some baked bread from the Commissariat. But I am of opinion that no exertion would have drawn from Portugal a supply of bread sufficient for that army. My opinion, as stated in my letter, and in my explanation of my letter, went to the arrangement and distribution of supplies as well as to the collection of them.

' Q. The answer to the former question having nearly restricted itself to bread and flour, to what extent could beef or other articles of sustenance have been furnished by the country?

' A. Wine could be procured in the villages occupied by the army, in almost every one of its positions, in sufficient quantities for one day's or probably two days' consumption; but I have seen the wine exhausted, in more than one instance, when the army has halted more than one or two days in the same place, and I believe that latterly the Commissary General was not able to supply the troops with wine. As long as I commanded the army there was no want of fresh beef; and as the carts of the country were drawn by bullocks, the draught cattle might have been killed for food for the troops; but without resorting to this resource, it was very soon found that the supplies of cattle for slaughter were not sufficient in Portugal for a large army. And in point of fact, before I quitted the army, a very large proportion, I believe more than half, was fed upon salt provisions, and I believe the whole army has since received nothing else. The cattle on which the army under my command was fed, supplied under the contracts with Mr. Archer and Mr. Walsh, all came from the north of Portugal, and, excepting 10 or 12 head received at Leyria, and the same number at Caldas, I do not recollect that the country which was the immediate seat of our operations ever supplied us with any.

' Q. The Portuguese General, Freire, in his letter of the 2d Sept. to Sir H. Dalrymple, states that the fort of Peniche had been on the point of surrendering to him. How was the fact?

' A. I never heard of it: it could not have occurred during the time I commanded the army, as neither that General nor his corps were near that fort.

' Q. Did you understand that the Juntas in Spain were in general at first averse to a British force landing in Spain?

' A. I did understand that the Junta of Galicia were not desirous of having the co-operation of a British army with their own troops under the command of Gen. Blake. They were not averse to our landing in Spain, as they consented to my landing in Vigo, if I should find it convenient, and indeed recommended that measure, as Vigo was the only port which could afford protection to our transports on the west coast of the Peninsula, excepting the Tagus. I also understood that the Junta of Seville, and the persons in authority in Andalusia, had no very great desire that Gen. Spencer's corps should co-operate with General Castaños, although they were desirous that Gen. Spencer's corps should land at Puerto de Sta. Maria, and eventually cover Gen. Castaños' retreat, in case he should have been defeated by Dupont. I wish to explain to the Court, that this opinion is formed from my communications with the Junta of Galicia as far as respects them : and in those communications they expressed a most anxious desire that we should carry on our operations in Portugal, and drive the French out of that Kingdom, and that afterwards the British army should be the point of connexion between the northern and southern armies of Spain.

' Q. Did you receive communications of similar wishes from any of the chief Juntas or persons in authority in Spain ?

' A. None.

' Q. Was the expulsion of the French from Portugal, in your opinion, of essential service to the Spaniards ; and had the British force, in the first instance, landed in Spain, might not the French force under Junot have been employed against Spain ?

' A. I consider the expulsion of the French from Portugal as an object of the greatest consequence to the Spanish nation. There is no doubt whatever, that if the apprehension of the employment of the disposable force of Great Britain in Portugal had been removed from the mind of the French General, in Portugal, he might have moved a large proportion of his army into Spain.'

Sir A. Wellesley, on being asked by the Board, said he had no persons whom he wished to call as witnesses.

Capt. P. Malcolm, of H. M. S. *Donegal*, was examined by the Board.

' Q. Were you employed on the coast of Portugal in assisting and forwarding the movements of the army during any and what period of Lieut. Gen. Sir A. Wellesley's command on that coast?

' A. The whole of the time that Sir A. Wellesley commanded.

' Q. State in general the difficulties or facilities that present themselves in landing troops, or horses, or artillery, or provisions, on the coast of Portugal from the Tagus to Oporto, in the months of August and September, and whether you actually experienced any and what difficulties on the above occasion.

' A. There is always a very great difficulty in landing on the coast of Portugal in those months, owing to the swell, which causes a considerable surf upon the beach. At Mondego bay there is a river, but at the mouth of the river there is a bar on which generally there is a very considerable surf. During the time that I was there, there were only 4 or 5 days that we could pass it without danger in common boats; but at the Mondego we got a large supply of boats of the country, schooners, and larger boats, which facilitated the landing very much. I know of no other place between Oporto and the Rock of Lisbon where boats of the country could have been procured, except at Ericeira : I was not there, but I understand that boats could have been procured there. I believe, also, that boats could have been procured, and that the landing is tolerable, at Peniche, but I have not seen it; the latter place was in possession of the enemy. During the whole time we were employed landing the troops, we constantly experienced very great difficulty and danger in landing the troops, both at the Mondego and Maceira.

' Q. Could the boats of the country obtained at the Mondego be carried to the southward ?

' A. They would have been of no use at any other part, because they could not land on the open beach.

' Q. Between the Mondego and the Tagus are there any bays, or protecting promontories, where a fleet of transports can anchor in safety in those months and in boisterous weather ?

' A. No, none. The whole coast is exposed to westerly winds, and the anchorage very bad. The prevalent winds are from the north, but about the end of August they frequently blow from the south-west, as we experienced. I believe that under the Berlings off Peniche there is a shelter for a few ships, but the anchorage is not good. The river Mondego will admit ships not drawing more than 11 feet of water, for about 20 or 25 vessels.

' Q. (By desire of Sir A. Wellesley.) Do you recollect that on one night in August you were obliged to put to sea in the *Donegal* from the roads of Maceira, that you made the signal to the transports to put to sea, that many anchors were lost; and how many, to the best of your recollection ?

' A. On the 20th Aug. the wind came from the south-west. I weighed, and made the signal for the convoy so to do: the convoy then consisted of 230 or 240 vessels. About one half of the convoy succeeded in getting under weign, the others were obliged to remain at anchor. Next day the wind shifted, and on my return to Maceira roads I found about 60 of the convoy had lost their anchors in attempting to weigh, and I have no doubt, had the breeze increased to a common gale, that many of the vessels would have been lost; they were then mostly reduced to their last anchor, and the bottom is very rocky. The transports, on board which Sir J. Moore's troops were, were very badly found, and not calculated to beat off a lee shore.

'Q. Do you recollect that many boats were swamped in the surf at Maceira, and particularly some flat-bottomed boats, and how many were lost entirely?

'A. The boats in landing at Maceira were almost constantly filled in going in by the surf. I suppose we lost about 20 entirely, and several men: 6 or 7 belonging to the artillery and German Legion were drowned. The day before (the 30th Aug.) I left Maceira I could only find 30 or 40 boats from all the fleet that were fit for service, although carpenters had been constantly employed all the night in repairing them.'

Sir A. Wellesley observed, that he wished to make some observations upon Sir H. Dalrymple's narrative, which he would reduce to writing, and, by permission of the Board, read to them at some future period of the inquiry.

Sir A. Wellesley now read the following address:

'Gen. Sir D. Dundas, My Lords and Gentlemen,

The Court will permit me, I hope, to begin the address with which I have to trouble them with some few observations upon that part of Lieut. Gen. Sir H. Dalrymple's narrative which refers to the operations of the army while under my command in Portugal, in which, of course, I feel much interested. It appears that the General had at a very early period conceived an opinion that I had undertaken an operation of extreme difficulty and hazard; and yet he entertained the intention of leaving me to conclude it as I could, and of joining at the Mondego the reinforcements expected from England. Indeed, he states that he acted upon this intention, and that he communicated it to me by his aide de camp; but I can assure the Court that yesterday was the first time I heard of it.

'I do not mean now to extenuate the difficulty and the hazard of the enterprise which I undertook when I commenced my march from the Mondego; I am addressing myself to persons too well acquainted with the operations of war not to appreciate them; but I contend for it, notwithstanding the opinion, as at present stated, of an officer of so much more experience than myself, that the means which I had in my power, those which I expected, and the measures which I adopted and recommended, were more than adequate to overcome the difficulties, and remove the risks of the operations which I conducted, excepting those inseparable from all military operations. The Court have already before them, in my dispatches to the Sec. of State, to Sir H. Burrard, and my narrative, the reasons which induced me to land, and to march without waiting for further reinforcements; upon which I would wish to rely. But what has fallen from Sir H. Dalrymple renders it necessary for me to trouble them with something further upon this part of the subject.

'The questions, as arising out of his statement, are, whether I was in the first instance sufficiently strong to get the better of the enemy in the field; and if I were, whether I adopted the best means of getting the better of him. In respect to my strength, in comparison of the army of the enemy, I do not desire to be judged by the result of the campaign, as far as it was conducted by me, but by the commencement, at which time the measures were adopted, from which, as it was truly stated, it would not have been easy, and I certainly had no inclination to withdraw.

'My strength then consisted of nearly 13,000 British troops, and I had the assistance of 6000 Portuguese troops, from whose co-operation I expected to derive advantages; in which expectation, I admit, I was subsequently disappointed. But I will ask this Court, what would have been said, and deservedly said, and felt of me, throughout the army and the country, and by the government by which I was intrusted, if, with such a force, I had hesitated to advance upon the enemy? I have already told the Court, in my narrative, that I did not believe his force was more than 16,000 to 18,000 men, only 14,000 of which number could be disposable in the field. The largest account we received, which was deemed an exaggerated one, of the strength of the enemy, made them 20,500; and even admitting those numbers to be correct, the troops disposable for the field could not have equalled in numbers those which I had under my command and co-operating with me.

'It appears that I was not mistaken upon this subject, for, in point of fact, the largest number at which I have ever heard the French force estimated in the battle of the 21st Aug. was 16,000 men; and I, who saw them, did not think they had more than 14,000; every man of which, excepting the cavalry, who remained untouched, were actually engaged, and particularly Gen. Kellermann's reserve. Now if all this be true, I may fairly conclude, that if the enterprise was hazardous and difficult, I was not without means of bringing it to a fortunate conclusion.

'The next question is, whether, having adequate means in my power, I adopted proper measures to effect my object. Sir H. Dalrymple says, that, by the line of march I adopted, all the strong positions were in the hands of the enemy; but I can assure him that he will find it very difficult to adopt any line of march in Portugal which will not afford strong positions to an enemy acting on the defensive. But there was one advantage attending the line which I adopted, which was, that it rendered the enemy's superior cavalry useless, in the way in which he ought and would have employed it, if I had adopted any other line.

'If I had adopted the line by the high road from Lisbon to the north, by Santarem, I must have kept up my communication with the Mondego; which would have weakened my force for operations in the field, and after all, the enemy with his cavalry must have broken in upon it. By adopting the line by the sea coast, and depending for my supplies upon the shipping, my communication was so short that it defended itself; I was enabled to keep my force collected in one body; and I had my arsenals and magazines close to me whenever I required to communicate with them. Having taken this line myself, I proposed that by Santarem to Sir H. Burrard, for Sir J. Moore's corps; by which it might have been adopted with safety, as I was upon the sea line.

'The Lieut. General has stated, that by the line I adopted I left all the strong positions in the enemy's hands. I do not know what positions were in the enemy's hands of which I could have deprived him, or he could have been deprived by the adoption of any other line of march. If the march had been made, as I had ordered it on the 21st Aug. in the morning, the position at Torres Vedras would have been turned; and there was no position in the enemy's possession excepting that in our front at Cabeça de Montachique and those in the rear of it; and I must observe to the Court, that if Sir J. Moore's corps had gone to Santarem as proposed, as soon as it disembarked in the Mondego, there would have been no great safety in these positions, if it was, as it turned out to be, in our power to beat the French in the field.

'I will not follow the example of Sir H. Dalrymple in entering into a discussion on the probable effects of the battle of the 21st Aug., if a certain line of action had been adopted, because an officer supposed to be concerned in that question is not present; and I dare say that opportunities will not be wanting of entering into that part of the subject. It has been my misfortune to have been accused of temerity and imprudence, as well as of excess of caution, in the late transactions in Portugal; but without appealing to the result of what happened at the moment I gave over the command of the army, I may safely assert, that whatever might be the difficulty of the operation I had undertaken, means existed to bring it to a fortunate conclusion; that there was no ground for the apprehension for my safety, which Sir H. Dalrymple seems to have entertained; and that under the instructions which I had received, I should have been blamed deservedly if I had not commenced my operations as soon as I thought I had a sufficient force.

'The next point to which I shall take the liberty of drawing the attention of the Court is the share which I am supposed to have had in the negotiation of the Armistice and the Convention. In that part of the question which I have discussed hitherto I am wholly and solely responsible; in that part which follows, I am held responsible for the advice I am supposed to have given in character, at least, if not in person and in my profession. It is important for me, therefore, to show what advice I really did give, in what view I gave it, and what would have been the result if the measures which I recommended had been pursued. I did recommend and concur in the measure of allowing the French to evacuate Portugal with their arms and baggage; and here I must observe, that it was particularly understood in the negotiation of the Armistice, that in the words "property of all descriptions," was to be included only military baggage and equipment; that this understanding was carried into execution by a separate article of the Convention; and that the commissioners for executing the Convention acted upon this principle.

'When the measure of allowing the French to evacuate Portugal was to be taken into consideration, viz., on the evening of the 22d Aug., it was necessary to review the situation, the means, and the resources of the two armies, and our own objects. The enemy had collected their forces after the defeat of the 21st, and were about to resume the position of Cabeça de Montachique, from whence their retreat was open to other positions in front of Lisbon, and from thence across the Tagus into Alentejo. They had all the facilities in their power to make these movements, and when they should have reached Lisbon, the possession of that river by the forts and by the Russian fleet, and the great number of boats of which they would have had the use, would have enabled them to cross in one body, covered by the citadel and the high grounds; and they would scarcely have lost their rear guard. In Alentejo they had provided ample supplies. As I have stated in my narrative of my proceedings from the 12th July to the 20th Aug., Loison had re-established the French authority in that province, during his expedition towards Elvas in the month of July, and the grain which it had produced was purchased for the use of the French army. I know this circumstance, not only from the reports of the country, but from intercepted letters written to Loison by the French agents in Alentejo, which were shown to me. On their arrival in that province, the French would have had to march, unmolested, by the finest road in Portugal, to Elvas, which is a fortress at least of the second order among the fortresses in Europe; where they would have placed a part of their corps in garrison, and they would have sent the remainder across the upper Tagus to Almeida. This place was already provisioned in some degree; and that part of their force, which the French would have detached to Almeida, would have experienced no difficulty in relieving the distant blockade kept up by the Portuguese peasantry, and in throwing in such quantities of provisions as they would have required.

'Sir J. Moore's corps had been ordered, on the evening of the 20th, to join the army; for which corps a disposition had been proposed for the purpose of preventing the French from carrying into execution the plan of operations which I have supposed, and which it is certain they would have adopted after their defeat in the field. Sir J. Moore's corps could have supported itself at Santarem, as proposed, only by keeping up its communication with the Mondego; because the victuallers and transports could lie in safety in that river only; and the country on the banks of the Mondego, and under the authority of the government of Oporto, could alone furnish the means of keeping up that communication to any efficient purpose. When Sir J. Moore's corps, therefore, was called down to join the army, it could operate only as it was intended by Sir H. Burrard that it should operate, in immediate aid and communication with that under my command, depending for its subsistence upon the means which had been provided for the army, and the whole bearing upon the enemy's front. Our operations, when we should have joined, would have been those of a superior army pressing upon an inferior on its retreat; but nothing which we could have done would have cut off this retreat; the enemy must have been in Lisbon before us; the Tagus would have been the enemy's to the last moment of their passage; and, after they should have crossed, the necessity of possessing ourselves of the forts on the river, and the Russian fleet in the first instance, and the want of boats, which the enemy would have carried off, would have given them ample time to make all their arrangements in Alentejo before our troops could reach them. But in carrying on these operations we should have been involved in many difficulties and distresses, which might have again placed in a state of risk all the objects of the campaign.

'The communication with the shipping on the coast of Portugal is at all times precarious; and becomes more so towards the end of August, and is at length quite impracticable. In fact, many boats were swamped in the last week in

August, vessels lost their anchors, and more than once the fleet was obliged to go to sea in danger. On the 22d Aug. there were 11 days' bread in camp for the original force which marched from Lavos on the 9th and 10th Aug.; the troops which had landed on the 20th had brought 4 days' bread for themselves, and the supply for the whole might have been for 8 or 9 days, and no means could be procured of moving a larger quantity : no bread whatever could be procured in the country ; and, in point of fact, I believe that, excepting a few thousand rations of bread left behind by the French at Alcobaça, Caldas, and Torres Vedras, and which were given to the Portuguese troops, the country supplied not a single ration from the time the troops landed till I came away on the 20th Sept.

' It was obvious, then, that when Sir J. Moore's corps should land at Maceira, and should nearly double the consumption of the army, without increasing the means of procuring and conveying its supply, there was a risk of its being in want. Sir J. Moore's corps could not be expected to be on shore and in a situation to commence its operations till the end of August, during which period the enemy would have fortified his position at Cabeça de Montachique, and in the rear towards Lisbon ; and it would have been unreasonable to expect to be able to force or turn them in less than ten days. During the whole of this period, as well as during the time that would be employed in landing Sir J. Moore's corps, the whole army would have subsisted, and would have depended, upon the means which had been collected and provided for the subsistence of half of it; and it would have been certain of a supply only at the time it should reach and be in possession of the river Tagus so as to admit the transports.

' After we should have obliged the enemy to cross the Tagus, and we should have possessed ourselves of the forts on that river, and of the Russian fleet, and we should have crossed that river with the British army, we must have placed ourselves in a situation to invest Elvas for a blockade or a regular siege. In either case, the army would have been exposed to the effects of a bad climate in the worst season of the year ; and in the latter case, they would have had to move the means for the siege from Abrantes, beyond which place the Tagus would not have carried them, to the scene of action, a distance of not less than 60 miles. After having performed this operation, the army would have been obliged to renew it in order to obtain possession of Almeida. I am convinced that we should not have had possession of Elvas till late in December; and I think it more than probable that we should have been glad to allow the French to evacuate Portugal in that month instead of August, if we had persevered, after having sustained the loss of a great part of our army by sickness, and of 3 months of most valuable time with reference to further operations.

' I conceived that the objects of His Majesty and of the Spanish nation were, that the British army should co-operate with the Spanish armies. I believed that the only mode in which the operations of the Spanish corps could be brought to bear upon the same object, was by the influence which the co-operation of a British army would give to the government; and I believed that it was important to the Spanish nation to have the co-operation of 30,000 British soldiers in Spain, to receive the assistance of 4000 Spanish soldiers, who were prisoners to the French, and of about 2000 who were employed in Portugal.

' I considered these objects to be so important as to counterbalance the disadvantage of throwing 20,000 additional French troops, at no very remote period, upon the Pyrenees; that the Spanish nation would gain, even upon a comparison of numbers, not less than 16,000 good troops; but, if I were not mistaken in my political speculations upon this subject, they would likewise acquire strength in their own union, the amount of which could not be estimated; which strength, I well knew, they could acquire from no other source excepting Portugal, if a British army were to give it to them, as I knew that this country could not afford to send out another army of sufficient strength. I may have been mistaken in my speculations upon this subject; but, in point of fact, the Spanish nation do now enjoy the very advantages from the Convention to which I have above referred, and which I had in contemplation at the time the Armistice was negotiated; and besides these advantages they have acquired another, viz., the service of the army of Estremadura, consisting of between 14,000 and 16,000 men, a part of them cavalry, which had been employed on the frontiers of Portugal, and have been equipped from the stores of Elvas, and are on their march towards the frontiers of

France; and not a man of the French army which evacuated Portugal under the Convention has yet been brought, or can be brought for some time, upon the frontiers of Spain.

' In reference to political and military objects, then, at least in my view of them, the measure of allowing the French to evacuate Portugal was an advantage. If I was mistaken in my view of this advantage, it was a mistake into which I fell with the Spaniards themselves; for the army of Dupont, which was really in a situation to be obliged to surrender, was allowed to evacuate Andalusia by sea, and to serve again, under the Convention made by the Spanish General Castaños. If, however, it was an advantage, there is another question attending it, which is, was it disgraceful *per se* ? I am not now discussing the detail of the Convention; but the mere measure of allowing the French to evacuate Portugal.

' Those who argue upon this part of the subject contend, that the French ought to have been forced to lay down their arms. It is certainly a very desirable object, at all times, to oblige the army of an enemy to lay down its arms; but the question here was one of means. I wish that those who think that the French ought to have been obliged to lay down their arms had reviewed the history of all or of any of the armies which have been forced to adopt that extremity, and had compared their situation with that of the French army in Portugal. Those armies have invariably been surrounded by bodies superior in numbers, in equipments, or in efficiency ; and have been distressed, or in the utmost danger of immediate distress, for the want of provisions, and without hope of relief. I need not point out to this Board, that the French army in Portugal were not in that situation, and were not likely to be in such a situation. In fact, they had the military possession of Portugal; they had their magazines in the country, the fortresses, and the harbours; and they incurred no risk of distress from the want of provisions; but we, who were to oblige them to lay down their arms, did incur that risk, till we should obtain possession of the Tagus. But this is not all. Let the measure of allowing the French to evacuate Portugal be compared with other measures of the same description which have been not only approved, but deservedly, in my opinion, extolled in this country. Let the situations of the garrisons of Cairo and Alexandria be compared with the situation of the French army in Portugal; and I believe it will be admitted that the latter possessed advantages which the former did not; at the same time that those who had to decide upon this measure in Portugal knew that there must have been other objects for the British troops in that country, which the situation of Europe, at the time of the Convention in Egypt, did not hold out to the British troops employed there.

' But although I concurred in the general principle of the measure of evacuation, and advised it, I did not agree in all the details either of the Armistice or of the Convention. In the first place I must inform this Board that in the first interview I had with Sir H. Dalrymple, after his arrival in Portugal, on the morning of the 22d Aug., I, who am supposed to have been his adviser, and am here now for no crime excepting my supposed advice, had reason to believe that I did not possess his confidence; nay, more, that he was prejudiced against the opinions which I should give him. I had an opportunity of talking to him upon business that morning, as I can prove ; in consequence of which I formed this belief; of which, if it is desired, I will state the grounds. I may have been mistaken in it; but I certainly entertained it, as I can prove, if the Board wish it, by an examination of those to whom I confided it. But I think the Board will be inclined to admit that I might have had grounds for believing that Sir H. Dalrymple was prejudiced against the opinions which I should give him, when they shall recollect his own account of the opinions he entertained of the operations I had conducted even before he landed.

' Gen. Kellermann arrived at the advanced sentries of the British army between 1 and 2 o'clock of the 22d, and sent in a flag of truce to announce that he wished to speak to me, who, of course, he supposed commanded the army. It is true, as stated by Sir H. Dalrymple, that there was an alarm in the camp when he arrived, which was occasioned by a Portuguese officer who had come from Gen. Freire, at Lourinha, and who represented Gen. Kellermann's escort, which he had seen, as the whole French army. The Commander of the Forces was to do me the honor of dining with me on that day, and as he was then riding into the village of Vimeiro, I asked him whether I should go up to the out-posts and speak to

Gen. Kellermann? His answer was " No ; that the General had desired to speak to him, the Commander of the army, and that he would receive him at my quarters. Gen. Kellermann was brought there, and he arrived at about half past 2.

'Shortly after his arrival, Sir Hew sent for me into the room in which they were, and communicated to me the object of Gen. Kellermann's mission, which was repeated by Kellermann in my presence, and he afterwards read from a paper a memorandum of the wishes of the French Commander in Chief. Sir H. Dalrymple, Sir H. Burrard, and I withdrew into an inner room to deliberate upon Kellermann's propositions ; but we had not the paper, as I had refused to take it, conceiving that the negotiation then going on ought to be confined to a mere suspension of hostilities. When we had gone into the inner room, I told Sir H. Dalrymple that I considered that it was advisable to allow the French to evacuate Portugal, for reasons upon which I am afraid I have already delayed the Court too long ; and I said that I did not conceive that there existed any objections at that moment to granting the French a suspension of hostilities for 48 hours, for the purpose of negotiating a Convention for the evacuation of Portugal. Whether Sir Hew acquiesced in my opinion upon this subject, or I in his, I do not recollect, nor is it material ; but I know that we all agreed that there was no objection to allow the French to evacuate Portugal by sea. I then told Sir Hew that I thought there was an objection, in point of form, to allow the negotiation then going on to extend to other objects than the mere suspension of hostilities ; and that for that reason I had declined to take from Kellermann the paper which he had read to us ; but of which I told him that I accurately remembered all the particulars. He was of opinion, however, that as long as we agreed upon the material point, viz., that the French should be allowed to evacuate Portugal by sea, it was useless " to drive them to the wall upon a point of form ;" and in this manner this objection was overruled.

'After dinner the negotiation with Kellermann was continued. The first point which was discussed was the property which the French were to carry off with them, which was explained by him to mean only the " *military baggage and equipments.*"

'The next point of difficulty was that respecting the Russians, which at first stood in a form different from that in which it stands in the Armistice ; and upon this point I stated to Sir H. Dalrymple my opinion, that the French ought not to be allowed to stipulate for the Russians at all. He would not allow the article in respect to the Russians to stand as at first proposed by Kellermann, under which they would have returned to the Baltic unmolested ; and, in point of fact, the French General at first consented, as I understood, to leave out the stipulation in respect to the Russians, on the ground that it was a point referable to the Admiral. He brought it forward again, however, in the shape in which it now stands, and the Commander of the Forces consented to allow it to remain in the treaty, with the condition, that, if the Admiral did not agree to it, it must be struck out.

'When Gen. Kellermann first proposed the arrangement in respect to the Russians, as it now stands in the Armistice, the Commander of the Forces, Sir H. Burrard, and I, withdrew into the inner room ; and I told his Excellency what had passed between Admiral Sir C. Cotton and me, upon this subject, in a conference which I had with the Admiral, when I was at the mouth of the Tagus, on the 26th and 27th July. The Admiral had then told me, that he had heard that the Russian Admiral intended to remain neutral in the contest between the British and the French troops ; and would claim the neutrality of the port of Lisbon ; and Sir C. Cotton asked me what I thought upon that claim ? I told him that I thought the only way of getting rid of it was, to be so quick in our operations, that there would be no time for the Portuguese to make it before he would attack the Russian fleet ; and that it was a subject upon which it would be necessary to make reference to England. I pointed out to Sir Hew, however, that this was a claim which might be made by the Russians on their own account, or by the Portuguese in favor of the Russians, but not by the French. The Commander of the Forces appeared to be of opinion that as the question was, in fact, understood by Kellermann to be referable to the Admiral, it was not important whether this agreement was in the arrangement or not.

'It is true, as stated by Sir H. Dalrymple, that there was a long, and the longest, discussion, upon the point relating to the Russians ; but it related to a claim made by Gen. Kellermann, that the Russian fleet should be allowed to depart from Lisbon, and that the British fleet should not be allowed to pursue them for a limited time. The Commander of the Forces, however, insisted that they should have no more in the port of Lisbon than the rights of a neutral nation; and this point was yielded by Gen. Kellermann.

'The next point of importance was that relating to the length of time during which the suspension of hostilities should last; and Sir H. Dalrymple admits that I proposed to limit the duration of the suspension of hostilities to 48 hours only, whereas that he preferred the proposal of Gen. Kellermann, that the suspension should be unlimited in the first instance, and followed by a limited suspension of 48 hours when either party should wish to put an end to it.

' I shall consider presently the advantage which I conceived the limited term of suspension had over the unlimited term, in the then situation of the two armies. But I shall now consider this circumstance in another point of view. First, I am called the negotiator of this instrument, and in this important point the plan of the French General is adopted instead of mine, by the Commander of the Forces. But, secondly, I am called the adviser of these measures, and for this crime of advice I am here. Now although I must submit to incur disgrace and punishment, where I shall be found to deserve those misfortunes, I must say that I think it is a new measure of punishment which appears invented for me; that I, a subordinate officer, am to be punished for advising measures which were not conducted according to my advice. I say that this point was most important in a view to the state of our resources, to the state of the season, and to the tone in which the Convention should be negotiated; and above all, it was important in a view to the threats of the French in respect to the Russians. If there was any foundation for those threats, which I acknowledge I imagined there was, and that they would have received assistance from the Russians; if the Admiral refused his consent to the article respecting the Russian fleet, which I was sure he would do; it was most important that if the negotiations should then be broken off, and notice given of the conclusion of the suspension of hostilities, a period of 48 hours should not be allowed to the French to equip and prepare the Russians before we should begin our operations. If we derived any advantage, which I contend we did not, from prolonging the suspension of hostilities, I was sure that we could always prolong it. But whatever may have been the opinion of the Commander of the Forces on the 22d, and whatever may be Sir H. Dalrymple's opinion now, he was of a different opinion on the 25th Aug.; and, in point of fact, when he began to negotiate, he did at my suggestion give notice of the conclusion of the suspension of hostilities in 48 hours from noon of the 26th Aug., as appears by his instructions of the 25th Aug. to Lieut. Col. Murray.

' After the articles were settled, Sir H. Dalrymple says, that Gen. Kellermann asked him who should sign the Armistice, and he said himself, and he was about to sign it, when Gen. Kellermann informed him that my name was in the title, and that it was not usual for an officer of the rank of Commander in Chief to sign an instrument with one of inferior rank. I am afraid that Sir H. Dalrymple's memory has not served him very well upon this occasion: if my name had been at that time inserted in the title of the instrument, as the negotiator of it, Gen. Kellermann could have no reason to ask who was to sign it; and if this question was asked by Gen. Kellermann after the instrument was drawn up, and Sir H. Dalrymple was about to sign it, he was about to sign it without reading the instrument; for if he had read it, he would have seen that my name was used in it. The fact is, that when the terms had been generally settled, Gen. Kellermann was dictating the fair copy of the instrument to the officers who were writing it, and before he wrote or dictated the title, he asked Sir H. Dalrymple who was to sign it? and Sir Hew said himself. Gen. Kellermann then represented that he (Sir Hew), being Commander in Chief, ought not to sign an agreement with an inferior officer, and proposed that I should sign it. Sir H. Dalrymple then came into another room, where I was, and told me that Gen. Kellermann had proposed that I should sign the instrument, and he asked me whether I had any objections to doing so. My answer was, that I would sign any paper he wished me to sign.

' It may not be very important at what period Sir H. Dalrymple had intended to sign the instrument; but this is very obvious, that he had intended to sign it, which he would not have done if I had negotiated it; and, indeed, the very question asked by Gen. Kellermann showed who was the negotiator; for if it had been me, or if it had been Sir H. Burrard, there would have been no doubt, and the question would have been useless ; but as Sir H. Dalrymple was the negotiator himself, and it was not regular for an officer commanding in chief to sign an agreement with an officer of inferior rank, Gen. Kellermann was obliged to inquire who should sign; and in point of fact proposed me. I repeat that I was not in the room at the time this conversation between Gen. Kellermann and Sir H. Dalrymple took place; but as I went into the room more than once while the officers were writing the instrument, which was after I had been asked and had consented to sign it, I know it must have been when the title was making out, and not when the whole was drawn up. When it was drawn up I read it over, and at the table gave it to Sir H. Dalrymple to read, with an observation, that it was an extraordinary paper. He answered that it did not contain anything that had not been settled, and I then signed it. This is the mode in which this agreement was negotiated ; and I repeat that I never considered myself in any manner responsible for its contents, or for the manner in which it was drawn up. It is perfectly true that I advised the principle of the arrangement, that I assisted the Commander in Chief in discussing the different points with Gen. Kellermann, and that I gave him my opinion when he asked it, and when I thought it desirable to give it him. But I was not the negotiator, and could not be, and was not so considered, the Commander of the Forces being present in the room deciding upon all points, and taking part in all discussions. If, indeed, the Commander of the Forces had given me instructions to negotiate this instrument, and I had then negotiated and signed it, I might have been responsible for its contents, or at all events for the manner in which it was drawn up; but as it is, my signature is a mere form. But this instrument, about which so much has been said, and respecting which I have troubled the Court so much at length, is in point of fact a dead letter; it was never ratified by any of the parties in whose name it was concluded, and no one article in it was ever carried into execution, excepting that by which hostilities were suspended. From the beginning, my object had been to keep the Russians clear from the French. I have shown that I endeavored to effect that object in the negotiation of the Armistice ; and I will now show the subsequent measures which I adopted with a view to effect the same object in the subsequent negotiations. ' At 3 o'clock on the morning of the 23d, the army marched under my command to Ramalhal. Lieut. Col. Murray had been sent off from Vimeiro at an early hour, to communicate to the Admiral the contents of the agreement for suspending hostilities ; and upon my arrival at the ground at Ramalhal, I gave to the Commander of the Forces a paper, of which what follows is a copy.' *

' The object of the paper was to get the Russians out of the hands of the French ; and I did think that it was a matter of indifference what arrangement was made with them, or what became of the Russian fleet, provided it was not allowed to return to the Baltic. I was, and am still of opinion, that the best arrangement would have been to leave them in the port of Lisbon, on the ground of its neutrality. Two events might have occurred, either of which would have placed them in our hands; and in the mean time the officers and seamen would not have been sent back to Russia to co-operate in the war against the Swedes. ' One of the events is the declaration of Russia against the Spaniards and Portuguese, the other the re-entry of the French into Portugal. But whatever may have been the nature of the terms to be granted to the Russians, it appeared to me most important that the French should have nothing to do with the negotiations affecting their fleet. I beg to observe to the Court that it always occurred to me, that one of the practical effects of the Convention with the French for the evacuation of Portugal must have been to give to the Russians the benefit of the neutrality of the port of Lisbon. The Convention must have provided for the occupation of the forts of the Tagus by the British troops, and at this time the Portuguese flags would be hoisted. It would be impossible for the British Admiral to go in and attack the Russians while the arrangement under the Convention should be in the course of execution ; and while they would have continued in this state the Russians would have time to claim, and the Portuguese to grant, the

* See p. 98.

neutrality of the port. The question then must have been referred to the British government, and would have been discussed between them and the Portuguese.

' I do not know whether Sir H. Dalrymple sent instructions to Lieut. Col. Murray according to the recommendation contained in the paper which I have just read ; but I rather believe he did not, as he appeared to be convinced that the Admiral would not agree to the terms proposed for them under the 7th article of the agreement for suspending hostilities. Lieut. Col. Murray returned to Ramalhal from the Admiral in the night of the 24th, and having called upon me to inform me that the Admiral would not consent to the terms proposed for the Russians, I desired him to tell the General that, in my opinion, he ought to inform the French Commander in Chief, as soon as possible, that he should consider the suspension of hostilities at an end in 48 hours.

' I waited upon Sir H. Dalrymple at daylight on the morning of the 25th, in company with Capt. Malcolm of the Navy ; and, in his presence, I told him that I thought that he ought immediately to put an end to the suspension of hostilities, on the ground of the Admiral's dissent from the articles, without specifying which of them ; and to leave it to the French Commander in Chief to renew the negotiation for the evacuation of Portugal, if he should think proper, but that we ought to lose no further time in advancing. I then pointed out to Sir H. Dalrymple the practical inconvenience which resulted at that moment from his having allowed the French a suspension of hostilities for an unlimited period of time, followed by a limited period of 48 hours.

' Sir H. Dalrymple told me that as soon as Lieut. Col. Murray should have rested himself he would draw up a report of what had passed between him and the Admiral, on which he should be better able to form his opinion. In the course of that morning he sent for me again, and he showed me the report which Lieut. Col. Murray had made. I again recommended to him to put an end to the suspension of hostilities, on the ground of the Admiral's dissent, without entering into details, and to leave it to the French Commander in Chief to recommence the negotiation for the evacuation, if he should think proper. Sir H. Dalrymple was, however, of a different opinion, and determined to communicate, through Lieut. Col. Murray, to the French Commander in Chief the Admiral's sentiments on the agreement for suspending hostilities ; because Lieut. Col. Murray informed us that, when he was leaving the *Hibernia*, with Junot's aide de camp, the latter had asked him whether anything had passed with the Admiral likely to break off the negotiation, and had urged the propriety of informing Junot if that was the case. The Lieut. Colonel had replied, that he did not think that any thing had occurred which ought to preclude further negotiation.

' The Commander of the Forces having thus determined that he would communicate to the French Commander in Chief, in detail, the Admiral's sentiments on the Armistice, Lieut. Col. Murray's instructions were drawn, by which he was ordered to give notice of the end of the suspension of hostilities in 48 hours ; and he was authorised to negotiate a Convention with the French for the evacuation of Portugal, on the terms contained in the paper which I had delivered to the General on the 23d Aug., and which I have just read to the Court.

' Thus, then, between the 23d and 25th, I took two opportunities of endeavoring to effect the object I had in view, viz., to separate the Russians from the French ; and I really believe that, if the Commander of the Forces had not been influenced by his desire to perform with good faith that to which he thought Lieut. Col. Murray had bound him by his conversation with Junot's aide de camp, and had not stated to Junot the detail of the Admiral's sentiments respecting the Russians, the negotiation would have been continued with the French only, and the Russians would have been left to their fate. But the Court will see that I made another effort to effect this same object on the 27th, and that, in point of fact, it was effected ; and that the General gave orders that the negotiation should be broken off entirely, if it was not so understood.

' Lieut. Col. Murray went to Lisbon on the 25th ; and on the 27th, in the morning, Sir H. Dalrymple sent for me and Sir J. Moore, and not Sir H. Burrard, as stated by Sir H. Dalrymple, to communicate to us a letter received from Lieut. Col. Murray, and another from Junot. Lieut. Col. Murray reported that Junot had agreed to continue the negotiation without reference to the article of the Armistice relative to the Russians ; and that the suspension of hostilities would terminate at a particular hour named, unless the negotiation, in which he was engaged with Gen. Kellermann, should be brought to a conclusion.

'Gen. Junot appeared, by his letter, to think that the suspension of hostilities was still indefinite, and to consider the negotiation of the Military Convention as depending upon the negotiation of the Naval Convention between the British and the Russian Admirals.

'I recommended to the General to instruct, and I drew for him instructions to Lieut. Col. Murray, which are in the collection of papers dated the 27th Aug., which I will now read, by which he was directed to call upon Gen. Kellermann to explain and reconcile the difference between his (Lieut. Col. Murray's) statement and the General's intention, and that contained in Junot's letter to Sir H. Dalrymple; and to break off the negotiation, and to come away within the period limited for the suspension of hostilities, if this explanation should not be satisfactory; but that if the explanation should be satisfactory, he was to continue the negotiations; and if further time was necessary to enable him to bring them to a conclusion, he was permitted to suspend hostilities for a further period of 24 hours. Lieut. Col. Murray was also directed to inform Gen. Kellermann that it was expected that, in future, Junot should confine to the channel of Lieut. Col. Murray any communication he had to make to Sir H. Dalrymple.

'Sir H. Dalrymple says, in his narrative, that there was but little difference between Junot's letter and Lieut. Col. Murray's. I have not got Lieut. Col. Murray's letter, but, as well as I recollect, the difference was very material. At all events, it appears from the letter of the 27th, that Junot's notion was inconsistent with the intention of the Commander of the Forces, which intention was to allow the French to have nothing to say to the Russian negotiation; and that was what Lieut. Col. Murray was ordered to set right in this letter written by me. I never saw the answer to this letter, nor do I know any thing further of the negotiation till the 29th; but I believe the Court will be of opinion, that if the plan detailed in that letter had been carried into execution, there would have been no occasion for treating with the Russians and the French at the same time.

'On the 28th, that part of the army which had been originally under my command marched to the neighbourhood of Torres Vedras, leaving Gen. Anstruther's and Gen. Acland's brigades, and a part of Sir J. Moore's corps, which had been landed, in the camp at Ramalhal. On the 29th, in the morning, Sir H. Dalrymple sent for me to Ramalhal, where I went to take into consideration a Convention which had been agreed upon between Gen. Kellermann and Lieut. Col. Murray, and had been ratified by Gen. Junot, dated the 28th Aug. There were present at head quarters, Sir H. Burrard, Sir J. Moore, Lieut. Gen. Hope, Lieut. Gen. Mackenzie Fraser, and myself; and the Convention was taken into consideration article by article. It was altered in many important particulars.

'1st. The article respecting property was placed on a proper footing; the French were to be allowed to carry off only their military equipments; and were to restore property of all descriptions which had been taken from the churches or the inhabitants of Portugal.

'2dly. The security given to the purchasers of property from the French was not afforded by the alteration made.

'3dly. The French were to find the transports for their own cavalry.

'4thly. The Commander of the Forces engaged to use his good offices, instead of stipulating for indemnity, for the inhabitants of Portugal in the French interest, during the time they should remain in Portugal.

'5thly. The French were required to evacuate all the Forts on the right of the Tagus immediately, as far up as Belem; and Lisbon itself, when the second division should embark.

'I was most anxious, and pressed upon Sir H. Dalrymple that they should be required to evacuate Lisbon, and to cross the Tagus forthwith, according to the plan recommended in the paper which I had given him on the 23d, in order to give us possession of the harbour, and the use of the navigation of the river; because, as I told him, he would not be able to conduct the service, and do all that would be necessary to refit the army, unless he should have a free and easy communication between every corps of the army and the transports; that this would be impossible even with the possession of Belem; if the French were to continue in Lisbon with a circuit of 3 leagues; and that the navigation of the

Tagus, at an early period, was necessary in a view to the future operations of the army. Sir H. Dalrymple overruled this proposition of mine, and directed that the article might stand as I have above stated, viz., giving to the French a circuit of 2 leagues round Lisbon, with a league of distance between their posts and ours ; and to us the possession of all the forts on the right bank of the Tagus, including Belem.

'I beg that the Court will not understand, that this meeting of the Lieutenant Generals of the army, at Sir H. Dalrymple's quarters, or that any of the meetings which I had with him during the course of these negotiations, were at all of the nature of *councils of war.* They were merely meetings of General officers with whom the Commander of the Forces chose to converse on the subjects then under his consideration ; but, whatever might be the opinion of any, or the whole of those officers, he decided for himself; and, in this last meeting of the 29th Aug., he decided for himself upon every proposition. I never knew for what reason the improvements made in the Convention in this meeting of the 29th Aug. were not carried into execution. I returned to Torres Vedras after the meeting was concluded ; head quarters were moved there on the following day, the 30th ; but I did not see the Commander in Chief, and I marched to Sobral with my division on the morning of the 31st. When I was near Sobral, I received a message from the Commander in Chief, acquainting me that the Convention had arrived, signed by Gen. Kellermann and Lieut. Col. Murray, and desiring to see me; but I was so far from Torres Vedras, that I conceived I should not be able to arrive there in time, and I did not go; and the Court will see that my name is not in the list of those officers who were present at this meeting, as read by Sir H. Dalrymple. I understand, however, that the Commander in Chief ratified the Convention on that day, without any of the alterations made by the meeting of General officers on the 29th Aug. ; and, in point of fact, I never saw the Convention till I arrived in England.

'I have now stated to the Court all that I had to do with the treaties, and the opinions I gave to the Commander of the Forces at different periods while they were negotiating; and I really believe that if a Convention for the evacuation of Portugal had been concluded according to the terms which Sir H. Dalrymple admits I recommended to him on the 23d Aug., and with which he actually instructed Lieut. Col. Murray on the 25th Aug., the country would have been satisfied. But there is one article in the Convention particularly disapproved of in this country, of which I approved, notwithstanding that it is not contained in that paper which I gave to the Commander of the Forces on the 23d. It relates to the Spanish prisoners, who were certainly at the time of the Convention completely and entirely in the power of the French. The Court will observe that the principle upon which I thought that any Convention ought to be made with the French was, that they had the military possession of the country; and that their retreat was open to Elvas and Almeida: they had in their power to do as they pleased with their Spanish prisoners; and I conceived that they had a fair claim to be allowed for them in the negotiation. The exchange of the Frenchmen taken in Spain, not in military operations, for these Spaniards, appeared to me to be not an unreasonable arrangement; and it was one to which I had reason to believe the Junta of Galicia, at least, would not object. The only objection which I saw to the article was, that the Commander of the Forces engaged to obtain the release of the Frenchmen, instead of engaging to use his good offices to obtain their release; and he appears to have directed that an alteration might be made in this article, by his letter to Lieut. Col. Murray of the 29th Aug., which I heard read to the Court.

'It will be necessary that I should call evidence to support part of this statement; but I will trouble the Court as little as possible. I have called no evidence yet; and I beg leave now to declare, that the officers at home from the army are here on leave of absence, either on account of their health or their private affairs; and have not been called, and are not detained by me.'

Lieut. Col. Torrens was examined by Sir A. Wellesley's desire.

'Q. Do you recollect my having had a conversation with you on the night of the 22d Aug., or the morning of the 23d, respecting my having signed the Armistice?

'A. At daylight on the morning of the 23d, Sir A. Wellesley mentioned to me the occurrences which had taken place the evening before ; and mentioned that he had signed the Armistice by the desire of Sir H. Dalrymple, although he totally disapproved of many points in it, and of the tone of the language in which it was drawn up.

'Q. Did I state to you what parts of it I disapproved of?

'A. You principally stated that you disapproved of the article that provided for the neutrality of the Russians, and of the 48 hours which had been given to the enemy, from the termination of the Armistice, before hostilities should again commence.

'Q. Do you recollect my having expressed to you great uneasiness on the 22d, upon finding that I did not possess the confidence of the Commander in Chief?

'A. I do recollect that Sir A. Wellesley did express, after he had had a meeting with the Commander of the Forces upon his landing at Maceira, that he had to regret that it was apparent that he had not the confidence of the Commander of the Forces, or words to that effect.

'Q. Did I state to you my reasons?

'A. You did.

'Q. State them.

'A. Sir A. Wellesley told me, that upon the landing of Sir H. Dalrymple, he had gone to him to represent to him the necessity of an advance, and that he stated his reasons for thinking it necessary. Sir H. Dalrymple replied, that he had just arrived, and was consequently unable to form any judgment upon the matter; upon which, an officer of the Staff spoke apart to Sir H. Dalrymple, and then followed Sir A. Wellesley, and told him, it was the desire of the Commander of the Forces that he should make preparations for the march of the army, and give what orders he thought necessary for it.

'Q. Was that officer of the staff, Lieut. Col. Murray?

'A. Yes.

'Q. Do you recollect that I told you that Lieut. Col. Murray had spoken to the Commander of the Forces upon the necessity of marching, in consequence of my having urged that necessity upon him (Lieut. Col. Murray) after the Commander of the Forces had declined to attend to my recommendation?

'A. I certainly did understand from Sir A. Wellesley that Lieut. Col. Murray had urged the necessity of an advance to the Commander of the Forces, in consequence of having had a conference with him, Lieut. Col. Murray, on the subject; but I cannot recall to my recollection whether, or not, Sir A. Wellesley told me that he had had this conference with Lieut. Col. Murray after he had urged the matter himself to the Commander of the Forces.'

Capt. Malcolm was again examined by Sir A. Wellesley's desire.

'Q. Do you recollect to have waited upon the Commander in Chief, Sir H. Dalrymple, in company with me on the morning of the 25th Aug. ?

'A. I do.

'Q. Do you recollect Sir A. Wellesley having recommended to the Commander in Chief, to announce to Gen. Junot the termination of the suspension of hostilities in 48 hours, without reference to the detail which had been received of the sentiments of the Admiral, respecting the article of the Armistice regarding the Russians, and to leave to Gen. Junot to renew the negotiation if he thought proper?

'A. Yes, I do.

'Q. Will you state what passed?

'A. On my going into the room, Sir H. Dalrymple informed Sir Arthur, that the Admiral would not agree to that part of the Armistice that regarded the Russian fleet; Sir Arthur replied that he thought so. Sir Hew asked Sir Arthur for his opinion as to what steps ought to be taken; Sir Arthur said, he thought it most advisable to inform Gen. Junot in general terms that the Admiral disapproved of the Armistice; that he saw no necessity for pointing out the particular article which he disapproved, and proposed that Gen. Junot should be told that the suspension was to be at an end in 48 hours, as had been agreed upon by the Armistice, and to leave it to Gen. Junot to propose terms again if he thought proper.'

Sir A. Wellesley now read an extract of a G. O., which was admitted by Sir H. Dalrymple, viz.

' G. O., Parole, Portugal.   Head Quarters, Ramalhal, 27th Aug. 1808.

' The rapid and skilful march, performed by the army commanded by Lieut. Gen. Sir A. Wellesley, marked in its progress by the talent of the General and the gallantry of the troops, and terminated by a victory greatly glorious to both, seemed to have accomplished the immediate object in view, without further operation in the field.

' Should that expectation be disappointed, the army will again advance, greatly augmented by the arrival of troops much more valuable from their composition than their numbers; and if by this means there will remain less opportunity for the army at large to acquire renown by the encounter of an army so greatly inferior in force, there will be greater occasion to display patience and cheerfulness under such privations as the exhausted state of the country and other circumstances must necessarily produce.

' H. Clinton, Adj. Gen.'

The Board now proceeded to question Major Gen. Spencer, by desire of Sir A. Wellesley :

' Q. Were you aware that it had been arranged with Capt. Malcolm, that the *Alfred* should attend the movements of the army along the coast from the Mondego, in charge of the victuallers and store ships, as that ship was armed with 24 pounders, and the ammunition for sieges expected from England was for 24 pounders ?

' A. The *Alfred*, 74 gun ship, was ordered, by Sir A. Wellesley's wish, for the express purpose of supplying the army with whatever heavy ordnance the Commander in Chief might require.

' Q. Were you aware that, before the army was in a situation to attack Peniche, or any other fortified place, the ordnance store ship, loaded with ammunition for 24 pounders and heavy mortars and stores for them, had joined the fleet, in charge of the *Alfred* ?

' A. It joined the fleet a long time before they could have been required.'

Sir A. Wellesley was questioned by the Board :

' Q. Had you heavy artillery on travelling carriages in the ordnance store ship ?

' A. There were mortars, but no guns in the ordnance store ship.'

Lieut. Col. Torrens was asked, by Sir A. Wellesley's desire,

' Q. Do you recollect, that on the day the army marched from Vimeiro to Ramalhal, I wrote a paper as soon as the army had taken up its ground, for the use of Sir H. Dalrymple, which I gave you to copy, to the following purport :

' " 1st. It would be very desirable, &c. to *Ramalhal, 23d* Aug. 1808 ? " *

' A. When the army took up its ground at Ramalhal on the 23d Aug., Sir A. Wellesley wrote the memoranda which he has just read to the Court, and I copied it.

' Q. Did I then take the original to Sir H. Dalrymple ?

' A. Immediately after 1 copied it, Sir A. Wellesley himself carried the original to Sir H. Dalrymple.'

The Dep. Judge Advocate Gen. to the Rt. Hon. Sir A. Wellesley, K.B.   10th Dec. 1808.

I have the honor to inform you, by the desire of Gen. Sir D. Dundas, that the Board of Inquiry will on Tuesday next request of you to state all your proceedings from the time when you met Sir H. Burrard on board ship, on the 20th Aug., till the morning of the 22d, when Sir H. Dalrymple arrived and took the command; and to specify the several interviews which you had with Sir H. Burrard during that period, the nature of the reports you made to him, the propositions (if any) which you laid before him, and the orders or directions which

* See p. 98.

you received in consequence, with such explanatory reasons as occurred at the time in support of such propositions.

I am desired to add, that the Board may have some other questions to propose to you, but they would be glad to have the amount of the above set forth in the shape of a narrative, in order to save time.

Sir A. Wellesley now read a paper in answer to the above letter, as follows:

'GEN. SIR D. DUNDAS; MY LORDS AND GENTLEMEN,

'Having been out of town at Brighton, I did not receive, till my return yesterday afternoon, the letter of the Judge Advocate General, of the 10th Dec., in which the Court have called upon me for a narrative of all my proceedings from the time I saw Lieut. Gen. Sir H. Burrard, on the 20th Aug., till the morning of the 22d, when Lieut. Gen. Sir H. Dalrymple arrived, and an account of the several interviews I had with, and the reports I made to, Lieut. Gen. Sir H. Burrard in that interval. I beg leave to inform the Court, that even if the time which by accident has been allowed me to draw up this narrative had been longer, I should have asked their permission to decline to make it in the present stage of their proceedings. I am perfectly ready to answer verbally, or in writing, any questions which the Court may put to me, and to give them every information in my power; but Lieut. Gen. Sir H. Burrard was my commanding officer, and it rests with him to give such a narrative as he may think proper of all the circumstances which occurred during the period before referred to; and I have no doubt whatever that it will be perfectly correct.

'I may possibly feel it necessary afterwards to address observations to the Court, and to call certain witnesses before them, for which I shall hope for their indulgence.'

Sir H. Burrard now read a narrative of his proceedings, from which the following is extracted:

'About the close of the action, when it was evident that the enemy must be everywhere repulsed, Sir Arthur came up to me and proposed to advance: I understood he meant the movement to be from our right and towards Torres Vedras, with some circumstances I cannot now relate, as they are imperfect in my memory, it not having struck me at the time, or till very lately, that it would be necessary for me to account for every thing that passed on this subject: I answered that I saw no reason for altering my former resolution of not advancing, and, as far as my recollection goes, I added that the same reasoning which before determined me to wait for the reinforcements had still its full force in my judgment and opinion. I am certain Brig. Gen. Clinton and Lieut. Col. Murray were with me at the time, (with others of my Staff,) for they both immediately afterwards assured me that in their opinion I had well decided.

'Q. (By desire of Sir A. Wellesley to Sir H. Burrard.) Did you ever hear that it was a standing order of the army when under my command, that the troops, when ordered to march, should cook a day's provision?

'A. I think I have.

'Q. The troops having on the 20th had orders to march on the 21st, would they not have in their havresacks, during the action of the 21st, the provision for that day?

'A. Certainly, if they had received orders to march.

'Q. Did I not inform you on the evening of the 20th that I had ordered the army to march on the following morning?

'A. I understood from Sir Arthur that he intended to march, and very probably he told me that he had ordered it.

'Q. Having stated to the Board that I proposed to you on the field of battle to pursue the enemy upon one occasion, do you recollect my having proposed it to you a second time, in consequence of a message which I had received from Gen. Ferguson?

'A. I do remember that Sir Arthur did mention something of the kind to me, and, if I understood him right, it was to pursue on the left where there was open ground, and where the enemy's cavalry might have acted: Gen. Ferguson's brigade was then much in advance.

'Q. Do you recollect that the ground in front of the position of Gen. Fane's and Gen. Anstruther's brigades was bounded by a hill covered with pine, to which the right flank of those brigades would have been exposed, if they had pursued that part of the enemy's army engaged with and defeated by them?

' A. I know there was a hill in their front, and some pine wood on it.

' Q. Do you recollect that in describing to you the disposition I had made of the army, and the orders which I had given to the different corps, I informed you that I had ordered Gen. Fane and Gen. Anstruther not to be induced to quit their position on any account, without receiving orders from me?

' A. I was informed that Gen. Fane's and Gen. Anstruther's brigades were not to advance to follow the enemy; but I did not understand that it was an order that had been given to them before they were engaged. Whether Sir Arthur told me, or somebody else, I do not recollect.

' Q. Do you recollect that the plan, according to which I proposed to you to follow up our advantages, was to move the brigade upon the right wing, Gen. Hill's, Gen. Fane's, and Gen. Anstruther's upon Torres Vedras by the high road, and to follow the beaten enemy with the other 5 brigades and the Portuguese troops?

' A. I did not understand it in that detail: I understood that Sir A. Wellesley intended to march the brigades from his right upon Torres Vedras. The rest I do not recollect as part of the plan mentioned to me.

' Q. Do you recollect the first time I proposed to you to pursue the enemy, I mentioned the plan of the march to Torres Vedras, and the second time the pursuit of the left to what you consider open ground?

' A. I did not consider them as one and the same plan; I thought that Gen. Ferguson's brigade was getting too far, and I wished it to be stopped; but I do not know that Sir A. Wellesley mentioned it as the plan of the pursuit of the enemy by the right to Torres Vedras, and in front, with the other brigades.

' Q. Was the period, at which you state that you saw one of the corps of Gen. Ferguson's brigade in advance, and in a run, before or after you had decided that the enemy should not be pursued, and before or after the last attack made by a corps of French infantry upon the 71st and 82d regts.?

' A. I think the attack made upon the two corps last mentioned was the very last of the action. What I have before said of the 71st must have happened prior to that.

' Q. Were not the 36th and 40th regts. in the same brigade with the 71st, and on the same ground, and this brigade supported by the 29th regt., and in the rear by the brigades of Gen. Bowes and Gen. Acland, in column of brigades, throughout the action; and, at its close, by that of Gen. C. Craufurd and the Portuguese detachment close on the left?

' A. I believe they were. The exact situation of the Portuguese, and the brigade with them, I cannot speak to so well.'

Sir A. Wellesley, by the Board:

' Q. Was the high road which our right must have taken to Torres Vedras nearer to it than that which the enemy, who was engaged on our left, must have taken, to have reached that place?

' A. I should think it was; the enemy must have gone by the road which falls into the high road from Lourinha to Torres Vedras. Our right would have marched by the direct road from Vimeiro to Torres Vedras.'

Sir A. Wellesley was further questioned by the Board:

' Q. Had our troops followed promptly their first success, was there in your opinion a probability of our being able to have intercepted a great part of the French army that had been repulsed by our left wing, and who were retiring and in confusion?

' A. The enemy's left, which was engaged with our right, retired by a road which leads along the heights towards Lourinha, on a different side of the valley from that on which our left stood, and it began to retire at much about the same time that the attack began upon the left, consequently the left could not have been immediately employed in pursuit of those troops which had been engaged on our right. Those troops I believe continued in confusion in the woods which were on that side of the valley during a considerable part of the day, and this confusion

M 2

was considerably increased, and its duration lengthened, by the attack made by our cavalry. I certainly think that if the left wing of the army had followed up its advantages as I proposed, not only many prisoners would have been taken belonging to the left wing of the French army, but likewise belonging to the right, and that the whole of them were in such confusion, that, giving them full credit for great facility and discipline in forming after having been broken, it would have been very difficult, if not impossible, to form again.

' Q. From the suggestion mentioned by you as having come from Major Gen. Ferguson, for following the French on the left, it should appear that some pause, if not a close of the action had then taken place : whence did that cessation occur ?

' A. When the enemy were beaten on the left, I went to Sir H. Burrard, who was on the field of battle, and proposed to him the pursuit of the enemy. I did it in the way of a continuance or a renewal of the discussion I had had with him in the *Brazen* on the preceding evening, and I told him that that was his time to advance; that he ought to move the right wing to Torres Vedras, and pursue the beaten enemy with the left. I also stated to him that we had 12 days' provisions in camp, and plenty of ammunition for another battle. Sir H. Burrard was of opinion that our advantages ought not to be followed up, much for the same reasons as he had stated the night before, and he desired that I would halt the troops on the ground which they then occupied : at this time the 71st and 82d were in a valley, the 40th and 36th immediately in their rear on the side of the valley, and the other troops formed in succession for their support. Nearly about the same time the last attack was made by a body of the enemy's infantry upon the 71st and 82d, and was repulsed, as is stated in my report to Sir H. Burrard; and it was after that, as well as I can recollect, that Gen. Ferguson sent his aide de camp, Capt. Mellish, to inform me that great advantages might be derived from the continuance of our advance; and I took Capt. Mellish to Sir H. Burrard to endeavor again to prevail upon him to allow us to continue in the pursuit of our advantages.

' Q. Then it was not exactly the pursuit of fugitives, but a movement after a repulsed enemy, which you recommended to Sir H. Burrard?

' A. Certainly; the second proposition did not go to the pursuit of the French army in the shape of fugitives, although they were still in great confusion.

' Q. At the close of the action on our left, was any considerable part of the enemy that had engaged our right then in sight?

' A. No.

' Q. [By desire of Sir H. Burrard to Sir A. Wellesley.] If our army had preserved their order in pursuing, must not the French have gained ground of them in retiring in very loose order; and if our infantry broke in their pursuit, would not the enemy have had a good opportunity of acting with their cavalry?

' A. In order to answer that question, I must state to the Court what I conceive would have been the operations of the two armies, if the plan proposed had been adopted. By the march of the right to Torres Vedras, the enemy would have been cut off from Lisbon by the nearest road to that place; if they had retired upon Torres Vedras in the state of confusion supposed by the question, they would have been between two bodies of our troops. If they had chosen to go round by the other road to Lisbon, by Villa Franca and Alemquer, it is perfectly true that infantry not formed would have got faster over the country than infantry which would have been under the necessity of preserving its order; but I conceive that an army in that situation, followed even at a slower rate by a victorious enemy, is absolutely incapable of forming, or of appearing again in the shape of an army. There is no doubt but that our infantry must have kept its order and the connection between one corps and another in this proposed pursuit; but by its order I do not mean at all times a formation in line.

' Q. Do you know what number of guns the enemy retreated with?

' A. According to their order of battle, they had 21 guns in the action; we took 13 and a great number of ammunition waggons; and if the statement of the order of battle is correct, which I believe it is, they had 8 left.

' Q. How do you know that the reserve infantry of the enemy were engaged?

' A. I know it from several circumstances: 1st; I saw them engaged: 2dly; several prisoners belonging to the reserve were taken, and are now in England:

3dly; Gen. Kellermann, who commanded the reserve, told me they were engaged, and Gen. Junot, who commanded the army, told me that he attributed the loss of the battle to the impetuosity of the reserve, whom he could not restrain: and, lastly; I heard from many French officers that every corps in the army, excepting the cavalry, was engaged.

' Q. Having said you saw the reserve engaged, how did you know that it was the reserve engaged at the time?

' A. I knew it from the period at which they were introduced into the action; I knew it also from the circumstances of the line of march by which they approached to the attack of our troops; and by comparing what I saw with the accounts given to me by the French officers, of the line of attack adopted by that corps of the French army.

' Q. Might not there have been a second line of infantry, as well as a reserve, in an attack of that sort?

' A. Such was the nature of the country, that any number of troops might have been concealed in it, and might have been destined to co-operate in the attack, and it would have been difficult, if not impossible, for us to see them; but I had seen nearly the whole, if not the whole, of the French troops on their march in columns in the morning; and, judging from the numbers I saw, and comparing those numbers with those which I conceived to be the numbers of their disposable troops for action in the field, I did not conceive that they had any second line besides the reserve, although it might have been possible to conceal such a body of troops in the hills. I must also mention that I saw the tails of their columns.

' Q. What was the distance of the right of Gen. Hill's brigade from the left of Gen. Ferguson's at the close of the action?

' A. I should think nearly 3 miles. I must however observe that, from the nature of this action, the right and left wings of both armies were disconnected; that there was a valley which ran from the point near where the action finished to Vimeiro, which separated the left wing of the British army from the right wing, and also disconnected the two wings of the French army. At the same time, such was the nature of the ground, and it was so completely occupied by the troops which were on it, which troops were so completely supported by those in their rear, that we could feel no inconvenience from this circumstance.

Major Gen. Spencer was further questioned, by desire of Sir A. Wellesley:

' Q. Whether the line of infantry, which you saw, was seen by you after the attack had been repulsed by our left, or do you mean after the attack had been repulsed by Gen. Fane and Gen. Anstruther's brigades?

' A. After the attack of the whole.

' Q. Was that line of French infantry formed near the road to Torres Vedras, or is that part of the scene of action which was to the northward, and lay towards Lourinha?

' A. It was towards the northward, and near the Torres Vedras road.

' Q. Having mentioned that you heard of the arrival of a body of French infantry of 3000 or 4000 men on the evening of the 21st, did you hear this report from any authority excepting the general report in the country?

' A. I did not hear of it from any authority, but it was the report in the camp.

' Q. Were you present when I recommended to Sir H. Burrard to continue the pursuit of our advantages on the field of battle on the 21st Aug.?

' A. I was not.

' Q. Did you, as second in command to Sir A. Wellesley in that action, consider the defeat of the enemy to be so decided as to warrant his pursuit?

' A. I considered the enemy as beaten in the centre and left, and should have supported Sir A. Wellesley in that opinion.'

Major Gen. Ferguson was further questioned, by desire of Sir A. Wellesley:

' Q. Were you present when I proposed to Sir H. Burrard, on the field of battle, on the 21st Aug., to continue the pursuit of our advantages?

' A. I was not: I was with my brigade.

' Q. Do you recollect, that after you had received an order to halt, you sent Sir A. Wellesley a message by Capt. Mellish, to inform him that, if allowed to continue to advance, you could gain important advantages?

' A. I did send such a message.

'Q. Describe to the Court what those advantages were.

'A. A column of the enemy completely broken, and consisting, in my opinion, of from 1,500 to 2,000 men, had, in their confusion, gone into a hollow, and were thereby placed in a situation to have been cut off from their main body, by a movement in advance by the corps under my command.

'Q. Did you consider that part of the enemy with which the troops under your command were engaged on the 21st Aug. to be so beaten as to render it expedient to continue the pursuit of our advantages?

'A. As they had lost all their artillery, and were retiring in the utmost confusion, it certainly was my opinion that our army should have continued to advance.

'Q. Did you see any troops formed at the end of the action, excepting cavalry?

'A. None regularly formed; some battalions of their infantry occasionally halted, in my opinion, for the purpose of carrying off their wounded.

'Q. (By the Board.) From whom did you receive the order to halt which has been alluded to by Sir A. Wellesley?

'A. I understood from Sir H. Burrard.

'Q. Under what circumstances did that order find you?

'A. With one battalion in front of the village of Pereganza, and another battalion in the rear of it to support the advance. The village of Pereganza was the last hollow where the enemy made a stand, and were driven out of it by the 71st regt., which is the battalion alluded to in the advance of the village : the enemy were then retiring in the greatest confusion.

'Q. (By the Board.) Had you had heavy artillery on travelling carriages, with proper horses, would the nature of the roads have allowed you to carry them forward with the army by Torres Vedras to Lisbon; or could such guns have been transported by the draught oxen of the country?

'A. In my opinion, certainly not.'

Lord Burghersh, Capt., 3d regt. of dragoon guards, was examined by desire of Sir A. Wellesley.

'Q. Was your Lordship present when I recommended to Sir H. Burrard, on the field of battle, on the 21st Aug., to continue the pursuit of our advantages?

'A. I was.

'Q. Was your Lordship also present during the conversation I had with Sir H. Burrard in the *Brazen*, on the evening of the 20th Aug.?

'A. I was.

'Q. Does your Lordship recollect Sir A. Wellesley having on that occasion recommended to Sir H. Burrard to continue our operations, according to the plan on which they had been conducted by Sir A. Wellesley till that moment, and his having pointed out to Sir H. Burrard, particularly, the inconveniences and disadvantages which would result from his bringing Sir J. Moore's corps from the Mondego to join the army?

'A. I remember Sir A. Wellesley having recommended to Sir H. Burrard to allow the army to move forwards on the morning of the 21st, as it had been ordered; as a reason for that, that the army was so near the French army as to make it no longer doubtful that one of the two must attack; and that by advancing, the British army would act on the offensive, and, in Sir A. Wellesley's opinion, reach Mafra before he should be forced to a general engagement; and, by reaching that position, he should have turned the French positions, and come more immediately in front of Lisbon, with which ground he was so acquainted as to make him anxious to meet the enemy upon it. As an objection to waiting for Gen. Sir J. Moore's corps, he thought it must be at least 10 days before they could be landed and become serviceable at Vimeiro.

'Q. Does your Lordship recollect, that, when I urged Sir H. Burrard, on the field of battle, on the 21st Aug., to continue the pursuit of our advantages, I began the conversation by a reference to our discussion of the preceding evening?

'A. I do not perfectly remember the manner in which Sir A. Wellesley pressed it to Sir H. Burrard. I remember his urging him to advance, giving as a reason that his right was some miles nearer to Torres Vedras than the enemy; that he had 4 brigades that had not been engaged; and that Torres Vedras was the pass by which the enemy must retire to Lisbon.

'Q. Does your Lordship recollect that Sir A. Wellesley urged Sir H. Burrard to march the right wing of the army upon Torres Vedras and to continue the pursuit of the enemy with the troops which had been just then engaged with the left wing?

'A. I do; saying at the same time that, in his opinion, by that movement no part of the French army could reach Lisbon.'

Sir A. Wellesley was examined by desire of Sir H. Burrard.

'Q. Did the French cavalry patrole on the night of the 19th Aug., how near the British camp, and where?

'A. I do not recollect that the French cavalry patrolled very near the British camp on the night of the 19th Aug.; they certainly did so very early on the morning of the 20th. A division of the British army had been detached at an early hour on that morning, under Gen. Spencer, towards Lourinha, to facilitate the junction of Gen. Anstruther's brigade, which had landed in a bay to the southward of Peniche. This division was posted upon a height between Lourinha and Vimeiro, and the French cavalry patrolled very close to it.

'Q. Do you think it possible for 16,000 or 17,000 men to commence a march within 9 miles of a French army that has cavalry far out-numbering your own, without its being known to the French in an hour's time?

'A. I think, that under certain circumstances of country and of position, it is possible for an army to march, and that the march should not be known to the enemy at the distance of 3 miles in less than 2, if not 3 hours.

'Q. Was not Torres Vedras 9 miles from Vimeiro; and is it not the general practice of all armies to be under arms before daylight; and was it not the practice in the English army?

'A. Torres Vedras is about 8 or 9 miles from Vimeiro; the British army was always under arms an hour before daylight.

'Q. Are there no cross roads, or other means by which the French could approach your march in your way to Mafra?

'A. Yes.

'Q. Is there not a road from Torres Vedras, that, by coming by Ponte do Rol, would bring the enemy within reach of you, near the creek, by Fort Porto Novo?

'A. There is a road, I believe, from Torres Vedras to Ponte do Rol.

'Q. Are not the creeks formed by mountain torrents, with a bar that is dry in summer?

'A. Yes.

'Q. Do not those mountain torrents generally form difficult passes, with steep hills or mountains on their sides?

'A. Yes.

'Q. Is not Torres Vedras much nearer to Mafra than Vimeiro, and how much?

'A. I should imagine that Torres Vedras must be about 12 miles from Mafra; Vimeiro cannot be less than from 17 to 19 miles.

'Q. If the French had fallen back upon Mafra from Torres Vedras, when you quitted Vimeiro, could they not have been reinforced by all the men that could possibly be spared for a short time from Cascaes and the other forts; and did you know that there was no good position near Cintra and Colares?

'A. I conceive that the enemy could not have been at Mafra before us, if we marched as we always did, before day in the morning. If we could have got to Mafra before them, their line of retreat must have been by Cabeça de Montachique. I always estimated the force which the French had in Lisbon, St. Julian, and Cascaes, and the batteries, to be 3000 men: they were troops in whom much confidence was not placed for operations in the field, being principally Hanoverians, Italians, and people from Dalmatia; and as the Admiral was anchored off Cascaes with the fleet, and had with him the Royal Veteran batt. for the purpose of alarming the enemy upon those points, and it was settled with him that, as we should advance, he should make a disembarkation with the Veteran batt. and the marines of the fleet, in some of the bays in the neighbourhood of the Rock of Lisbon, I conceived that the French would not have ventured to weaken the garrisons of the forts on the Tagus and on the sea coast.

'Q. Did you mean to attack Cascaes or St. Julian, and how did you propose to procure heavy cannon, if necessary?

'A. I did mean to attack both Cascaes and St. Julian; and I always considered that those operations would have followed the battle which, it was evident, we should have in the field with the enemy. It had been settled in England, that I should have the use of the heavy cannon I wanted from the ships of the fleet, and ammunition for 24 pounders, and mortars with ammunition were sent from England in a store ship, and joined the fleet before we were in a situation to undertake any siege. I conceive that when the enemy should have been defeated in the field, and I should have been in possession of the right bank of the Tagus, and of the sea coast, as far as the Rock of Lisbon, I should have been able to land the artillery I should have required for the siege of those places, if not in Cascaes Bay, where the horses of the 18th dragoons landed in the beginning of September, or in Paço d'Arcos, in some of the bays between Cascaes and Cape Roca.

' Q. Are you sure you could have landed heavy cannon from the ships, and in any weather; and had you proper carts, or other conveyance, for moving the cannon to the points where they might be wanted ?

' A. I cannot be certain that I could have landed heavy cannon from the ships, because this must have depended upon the state of the weather, which is very precarious; but I thought it very probable that the weather would have allowed me to land heavy cannon in one of those bays; and it is now certain that it would, as the horses of the 18th dragoons were landed in Cascaes bay.

' Q. How many days did you think it would have taken you to get possession of Cascaes or St. Julian; or would you have attacked them both together; and how long would it have taken you to take both by siege ?

' A. I never made my mind up to that point : they are neither of them very strong, although it would have been necessary to break ground before both ; and I do not conceive that the army would have been sufficiently strong to undertake both sieges at the same time.

' Q. Is not Lisbon nearer Santarem than Santarem is to Lavos, on the Mondego ?

' A. Santarem is about 56 miles from Lisbon, and it is about the same distance from Lavos.

' Q. Could not the French have seized all the mules of Lisbon, and with them the horses and mules of the Royal stables, and would it not have assisted them very much in going to Santarem ?

' A. Certainly; they had great resources of every description, which could have been of use to them in any expedition of that description.

' Q. Could not their cavalry have marched to Santarem in a short time, had they been pressed, and their infantry crossed over to Aldea Galega; and is not that the high road to Elvas ?

' A. Their cavalry could have moved with great celerity to any point; and there were boats in sufficient numbers in the Tagus, and at their command, to pass the French army to Aldea Galega at once.

' Q. Could you not from Caldas or Obidos (after the action of the 17th) have reached Santarem before the force under Sir J. Moore could equip and march from the Mondego for that place; and had not you as good means of equipment as that army could find after you left the Mondego; and could you not have received biscuit from S. Martinho or Nazareth, from the victuallers, had you so wished ?

' A. After the action of the 17th I was nearer Santarem than Sir J. Moore's corps was when it was in the Mondego, and could certainly have arrived there before Sir J. Moore could have arrived in a state of equipment from the Mondego. I conceive that there were two distinct lines of operations in Portugal, and two modes of supporting those operations; one by the sea coast, and depending upon the communication with the coast for supplies of all kinds; the other by Santarem, and depending for its support upon its communication with the Mondego. There was shelter in that river for the small victuallers and transports, which then in fact would have come a depôt, and the country on the banks of the Mondego, which was settle and organised under the government of Oporto, would have afforded means, even after the army under my command was equipped, of keeping up the communication between the Mondego and Leiria, which place would have furnished the means of communicating with the army at Santarem. As there was no shelter for the transports at S. Martinho and Nazareth, and those places had not been settled under the government of Oporto, and Nazareth had been burnt by the French, the depôt could not have been formed at those places; and if it had been possible to have formed it, there would have been no means of communicating; therefore, I conceive that after the action of the 17th Aug., it was not expedient that I should change my line of operations in a view to those reasons only, and that it was best that the corps which should take the line of Santarem should communicate with the Mondego.

' Q. Do you not think that the victuallers that would have provisioned Sir J. Moore's corps at Santarem would also have victualled you had you been there?

' A. If I had been at Santarem, and all the previous arrangements had been made for supporting the corps under my command at that place, as detailed in my letters of the 8th, 10th, and 12th Aug., to Sir H. Burrard, I conceive that the corps under my command might have been victualled.

' Q. Is it not double the distance from Santarem to Lavos, on the Mondego, as it is from Caldas to Santarem; and do you suppose it was impossible to land Gen. Anstruther's brigade anywhere, so as to join you at Caldas?

' A. I should think it about 40 miles, if not more, from Caldas to Santarem. I was not informed of the arrival of Gen. Anstruther's brigade till the morning of the 18th Aug.; they were then off the Berlings, to the southward of Caldas, and I could not have landed them nearer to Caldas than where they did land, without sending them back to the northward against the wind, and either halting in my position, or falling back to Caldas again, after the action of the 17th Aug., to facilitate a junction.

' Q. How far was it from where Gen. Anstruther landed to Obidos?

' A. From 15 to 20 miles.

' Q. How far is it from Santarem to Monte Mor o Novo, on the high road from Aldea Galega to Elvas and Fort La Lippe?

' A. Monte Mór o Novo is about 60 miles.

' Q. Did not the event prove that it was possible for the cavalry of Sir J. Moore's army, with his artillery horses and his light regiments, to land at Maceira and to follow the army?

' A. Yes.

' Q. Might not the rest of the force have landed at Maceira, formed a depot of provisions, and taken a position there, at the same time that the reinforcements most wanted would have joined your division?

' A. I conceive that the formation of a depôt of provisions and stores at any point on the coast was very precarious, and, in the end of August and beginning of September, became daily more so. It might have been effected in a long course of fair weather, but it was an operation which could not be calculated upon.

' Q. Had the artillery horses landed, could not those with your army have been given over to the Commissariat, or a proportion of the worst from each corps?

' A. They might have been disposed of in that or any other manner; but it would have been useless to give them to the Commissariat, as there were no carts with the Commissariat, or in the country, which could be drawn by horses.

' Q. If the horses of the artillery had been landed, could not the waggons have also been landed, and have been made useful for the Commissariat?

' A. I conceive that there were not more waggons with the artillery than were required to carry the stores of the artillery; but those waggons might be employed to carry provisions, if the Commander in Chief of the army should think proper.

' Q. Was there no ground at or near Mafra or Lisbon fit for cavalry to act on?

' A. In my opinion cavalry can be used with advantage in nearly all parts of Portugal, not in large bodies any where, but every where in small; and there was ground between Mafra and Lisbon on which cavalry could have acted with advantage.

' Q. Did you not understand that the 18th light dragoons embarked in the river Thames on the 25th and 26th July, and had you not just cause to expect them off Maceira by the 21st or 22d Aug., or was it intended that they should proceed further, without running down the coast for intelligence?

' A. I do not recollect that I ever heard at what time the 18th light dragoons embarked; as well as I can recollect, I imagined that they were to come from England with Sir J. Moore's corps.'

Sir A. Wellesley was also asked by the Board :

'Q. The possibility of the French army's crossing the Tagus, had the terms proposed by Gen. Junot been rejected, and thereby engaging the British army in a tedious and difficult campaign, has been stated by you: could not Gen. Junot have so transported his forces across the Tagus immediately after the 22d Aug. ?

'A. I do think he might.

'Q. How is this conclusion to be resisted; that Gen. Junot thought the conditions of the Convention more advantageous to the French interest, than the protracting the campaign in the manner which is represented to have been in his power?

'A. When I considered the expediency of allowing the French to evacuate Portugal by sea, I took into consideration the British interests and British objects only, and the objects of their allies, as connected with those of Great Britain. I considered that the French army, from the relative situation of the 2 armies in Portugal, and from its having the military possession of the country, had a fair military right to withdraw by sea with their arms and baggage; and I do not think it necessary for me to account for the motives of Gen. Junot in preferring the evacuation by sea to another line of operation.; which, without wishing to say anything personally disrespectful of him, might have been bad or unworthy motives, as well as views for the interests of his country.'

Lieut. Col. Torrens was again examined by Sir A. Wellesley :

'Q. Were you present in the *Brazen* when I had a conversation with Sir H. Burrard, on the evening of the 20th Aug. last?

'A. I was.

'Q. State what you recollect.

'A. I was present in the *Brazen* when Sir A. Wellesley made his report to Sir H. Burrard, upon the arrival of that officer in Maceira roads. Sir A. Wellesley represented to him the state of the army under his command, and the situation of that of the enemy, and the principle on which he had conducted the operations from the landing at Mondego; and further stated, that he had issued orders for the march of the army the next morning. Sir H. Burrard replied that he did not consider it advisable to advance from that position till the army should be reinforced by the division under the command of Sir J. Moore. Sir A. Wellesley observed, that he thought-it of the utmost importance to push forward by the way of Mafra, with a view of turning the enemy's left flank, and to endeavor to bring the French army to the issue of a battle in the field, as near to Lisbon as possible, that we might avail ourselves of a short distance from the Tagus, by following up the victory, so as to prevent the French crossing that river. And he further stated, that he was desirous of this contest taking place near to Lisbon, having an actual survey of all the country in the vicinity of that town. Sir A. Wellesley further added, that if Sir J. Moore's corps should be brought down to Maceira, Sir H. Burrard must relinquish all the advantage which might have been expected from his marching that body upon Santarem, with the view of cutting off the retreat of the French army by the northward. Sir H. Burrard again repeated, that he thought it advisable to bring down Sir J. Moore's corps, to render certain those operations which appeared to him to be doubtful. Sir Arthur then asked Sir H. Burrard whether he had received his letters of the 8th and 10th Aug., which recommended the march of this reinforcement upon Santarem. Sir Harry replied that he had received those letters; but he did not in my presence make any comment or observation upon that proposed operation. Sir H. Burrard then wrote a letter to Sir J. Moore, which I did not see; but I understood it to be an order for him to come down the coast with his division. I beg leave to state, that to the best of my recollection this is the substance of the conversation that passed, though I cannot pledge myself to the exact words.

'Q. Do you recollect my stating to Sir H. Burrard the probability that if we did not move to attack the French, they would attack us?

'A. I do remember Sir A. Wellesley making that observation to Sir H. Burrard, and adding at the same time, that a great expenditure of provisions would be occasioned by waiting on that ground for Sir J. Moore, who could not be expected for some days.

'Q. Do you recollect my stating to Sir H. Burrard the probable increased difficulties of supplying the army with provisions when its numbers should be in creased, without any proportional increase of means?

'A. I do perfectly recollect your making that observation.

'Q. Do you recollect my stating to Sir H. Burrard the probability that, if the enemy did not attack us, they would fortify their positions between our army and Lisbon, during the delay of our march; and my stating to him the difficulty of turning fortified positions with cannon in that country, on account of the narrowness of the roads?

'A. I do, perfectly; adding at the same time that the badness of the roads, as well as the narrowness of them, would render the turning of the enemy's flank in any position he might take up extremely difficult.

'Q. Do you recollect my sending you with orders to Gen. Fane's and Gen. Anstruther's brigades before or immediately at the commencement of the battle of the 21st Aug.?

'A. I do recollect Sir A. Wellesley sending me with orders, both to Gen. Fane and Gen. Anstruther, at the commencement of the battle of the 21st Aug.

'Q. What were they?

'A. Sir A. Wellesley desired me to ride as fast as I could to Gen. Anstruther and to Gen. Fane, and to convey to them his orders that they should not move from the position which they occupied in front of the village of Vimeiro, without further directions from Sir Arthur. On my arrival at that position, I found that Gen. Fane had advanced a little way in front, and was engaged with some French light troops. I followed him, and delivered those orders, and he consequently retired: this was about half-past nine in the morning; but I cannot speak with any degree of accuracy.

'Q. Did I state to you the reason for giving those orders, and what was it?

'A. Yes, partly: I understood from Sir A. Wellesley that those orders originated from the nature of the ground in front of that position, which would render it ineligible to remove from it, particularly as he observed a large French column forming in the wood in front, and evidently preparing to make a vigorous attack upon the centre.

'Q. Were you present when I recommended to Sir H. Burrard, on the field of battle, on the 21st Aug., to continue the pursuit of our advantages?

'A. I was.

'Q. State what passed.

'A. Immediately after we had defeated the right column of the French army, which had made its attack upon our left, and were then retreating in a precipitate manner, Sir A. Wellesley rode to Sir H. Burrard, and said, "Sir Harry, now is your time to advance: the enemy are completely beaten, and we shall be in Lisbon in 3 days. We have a large body of troops, which have not been in action; let us move them from the right on the road to Torres Vedras, and I will follow them with the left." Sir H. Burrard replied, that he thought a great deal had been done, very much to the credit of the troops; but that he did not think it advisable to move off the ground in pursuit of the enemy. Sir A. Wellesley remarked at the time that the troops were perfectly ready to advance, having provisions ready cooked in their havresacks, according to the orders of the day before.

'Q. Do you recollect my mentioning that the troops had plenty of ammunition; that there was 12 days' bread in camp for the original number of the army, and a sufficiency of every kind of store in the reserve for the artillery?

'A. I recollect Sir A. Wellesley mentioning that there was plenty of ammunition; that the mules with the reserve musket ammunition were in the rear of the brigades; that we had abundance of ordnance stores and plenty of provisions; but I cannot call to my recollection whether he specified at that time the number of days' provisions we had in camp.

'Q. Did I order the army on the 20th to march on the morning of the 21st?

'A. You did.

'Q. Did I countermand those orders when I returned from the *Brazen* on the evening of the 20th?

'A. Sir A. Wellesley countermanded those orders immediately on his arrival in camp, on the evening of the 20th, in consequence of directions he had received from Sir H. Burrard to that effect.

'Q. (By desire of Sir H. Burrard.) How long a time elapsed from the French being defeated in the centre till the end of the action?

'A. The right column of the French arrived at the point of attack on our left in about 10 minutes or a quarter of an hour after his left column was defeated by our centre: I cannot speak with any accuracy as to the length of the action on the left; it might probably be an hour, more or less.

'Q. When Sir A. Wellesley asked me whether I had received his dispatches of the 8th, 10th, and 11th Aug., did I tell him that I had sent them to Sir J. Moore by Col. Donkin from S. Martinho?

'A. I do not recollect that Sir H. Burrard made that communication in my presence.'

Sir A. Wellesley then addressed the Board as follows:

'GEN. SIR D. DUNDAS; MY LORDS AND GENTLEMEN,

'Two or 3 points have been adverted to in the narrative of Sir H. Burrard, and some circumstances have been stated in evidence, upon which I wish to trouble the Court with some observations. The first and principal of these is the reason stated by Lieut. Gen. Sir H. Burrard for not deeming it expedient to place Lieut. Gen. Sir J. Moore's corps at Santarem, as proposed by me in my letters of the 8th, 10th, and 12th Aug., which are before the Court, because, as Lieut. Gen. Sir H. Burrard states, it would not, in his opinion, have been sufficiently strong to oppose the enemy, if he had retreated by that road.

'I beg to refer the Court to my dispatches of that period, which I consider the fairest documents to which I can refer, as when they were written I had certainly no notion that the subjects to which they related would ever have become the topic of discussion here. The Court will see, that in these dispatches I always considered the possession of Lisbon and of the Tagus to be the great object of the campaign both to us and the French; that for this object a battle would be fought in the field, in which I thought I had reason to expect success; and that the enemy would, after this battle, endeavor to retire across the Tagus to Elvas, or along the right bank of the Tagus by Santarem towards Almeida.

'If the Court will refer to the paper drawn by the French engineer, laid before them by Lieut. Gen. Sir H. Dalrymple, they will see that these are the lines of retreat recommended by the officers of the engineers to the French Commander in Chief. Now the occupation of the position at Santarem by Sir J. Moore's corps was calculated to cut off these lines of retreat; in the first supposed case, by the facility and celerity with which the Tagus would have been crossed; in the second, as it was upon the road which the enemy must have taken. But as I set out with the certainty, that the French would not, nay, could not, abandon Lisbon and the Tagus, without fighting a battle for those possessions, I may conclude that, after that battle, they would have been so much weakened as that Sir J. Moore's corps would have been a match for them; and, at all events, it is not to be supposed that, if this battle had been fought, they would not have been followed by a part, if not the whole of the army, which, in this supposition, would have defeated them. Indeed, the Court will have observed, by my correspondence with Sir H. Burrard, that I considered this position at Santarem to be so little dangerous, and, at the same time, so advantageous, that if the brigades of Brig. Gens. Acland and Anstruther had been equipped to act independently of any other body of troops, I should have ordered those brigades to occupy it.

'The next point on which I wish to observe is the mode in which I proposed and intended that this corps should be supplied at Santarem. The Court will see this mode, and all the difficulties which attended it, discussed in my letters to Sir H. Burrard; and I have no doubt whatever that he would have been able to procure carts in the country, on the Mondego, to enable him to form at Leyria the proposed depôt, and at that place the means of moving what should be required to Santarem. I also wish to say a few words upon the strength of the corps under my command, in comparison with that of the enemy.

'I marched from Lavos on the 10th Aug. with 13,000 men, and I was joined by and expected the co-operation of 6000 Portuguese troops: I was disappointed in this expectation on the 13th Aug., when I was engaged in an operation against a detachment of the enemy, which promised the utmost success, from which I could not with propriety withdraw, and which ended in the battle of the 17th Aug. On the 18th I heard of the arrival of Gen. Anstruther's brigade, and on the 20th, in the evening, when Lieut. Gen. Sir H. Burrard decided that he would alter the principle on which we had before carried on our operations, Gen. Acland was arrived in Maceira roads with his brigade, and he was landed on that night. The force then consisted of between 16,000 and 17,000 men, British troops, and 1650 Portuguese troops, actually in camp. We had been successful in the action of the 17th, and the army was in the highest order and the highest spirits ; well equipped, supplied with 12 days' provisions for the original number, and everything it required for its future operations.

' In discussing and considering the propriety of the decision of Lieut. Gen. Sir H. Burrard, or of my previous operations, it would not be fair to estimate the enemy's force at larger numbers than 20,000 men, of which they were reported to consist, by Gen. Spencer, in his report to government from the mouth of the Tagus. From this number the garrisons of Elvas, Almeida, and Peniche were to be deducted, which I always reckoned at 2000 men ; then there were the forts of St. Julian, Cascaes, the citadel of Lisbon, Bugio, Belem, and the batteries on the Tagus and the coast, as far as the Rock of Lisbon, which would have required at least 3000 more. This would have left the enemy with only 15,000 men for operations in the field, while we had above 18,000 men.

' If it is contended that the estimate of the enemy's strength ought to be made according to their embarkation returns, instead of according to Gen. Spencer's return of their force, a deduction ought to be made, from the amount of 24,000, of the real numbers of the garrisons of Almeida, Elvas, and Peniche, and of 3000 men for the garrisons upon the Tagus and upon the coast ; and, if but a small allowance is made for non-combatants, it will still turn out that the force to be met in the field did not exceed 15,000 or 16,000 men. From this statement it will appear that the force of 3000 or 4000 men, which it was reported had arrived at Torres Vedras after the action, could not have existed ; and, in point of fact, it was a report circulated by Gen. Junot, and indeed the fact was published in the newspapers of Lisbon, with other false accounts of the circumstances of the action.

' In respect to other points I shall not observe upon them, as the evidence is before the Court, who will judge of it. I consider it proved and admitted that I recommended on the evening of the 20th Aug. that the army should not halt, and that the proposed disposition for Sir J. Moore's corps should not be altered ; that the enemy were completely defeated in the action of the 21st Aug., on all points of attack, and that I proposed to Sir H. Burrard the pursuit of them.

' The Court have before them my reasons for advancing on the 10th Aug., and for thinking that I was strong enough for the enemy ; and for recommending to Lieut. Gen. Sir H. Burrard a perseverance in the plan of operation which I commenced ; and, in my evidence of yesterday, my reason for thinking that most beneficial consequences would have resulted if the enemy had been pursued. Upon all these points of difference of opinion between Lieut. Gen. Sir H. Burrard and me, the Court will form their judgment upon the evidence. I think it necessary, however, to detain the Court for a short time upon another part of the subject which has been under their consideration.

' Although I am decidedly of opinion that the most decisive consequences would have resulted from the march as proposed, and the pursuit of the enemy on the 21st Aug. after the battle, yet it does not follow that the measure of allowing the French to evacuate Portugal was not right on the evening of the 22d. On the 21st Aug. the enemy were defeated and in confusion ; and I have explained the grounds which I have for thinking that the most advantageous consequences would have resulted from a pursuit. On the 22d, in the evening, when the question of the evacuation was considered and decided, the enemy was no longer in confusion, and they had resumed the position of Cabeça de Montachique, between us and Lisbon. The relative situation of the two armies was then to be taken into consideration, as well as in the other case ; but that of the French army had been materially improved by our omission to pursue our advantages ; and we were then to look to our relative means of annoying each other, and our own objects. I have already detailed to the Court, in a former statement, the relative situation and means of the two armies at that period of time ; and I conceive that the battle of the 21st Aug. could be taken into consideration in the discussion of the question, whether the French should be allowed to evacuate Portugal or not, only in this way, viz., that it was a trial of strength between the two contending armies, and it proved the superiority of that of His Majesty. It was also clear to me that the

French would not risk another action; that their object was to secure a retreat across the Tagus; and that they would use their positions in front of Lisbon to facilitate and secure that object. As I have already explained to the Court, we had no means on the 22d of preventing them from effecting that object, from which I did, and do still think, it was important to us to preclude them, excepting by a Convention for the evacuation of Portugal.'

Sir A. Wellesley was asked by Sir H. Burrard:

'Q. Had not the British army the same means of advancing by Mafra on the morning of the 23d, when Sir H. Dalrymple ordered it to march, as it had on the 20th, when Sir A. Wellesley intended it should march; and does Sir A. Wellesley know that the French would not have risked another battle, nor attempted his flank upon his march, or been at Mafra before him?

'A. I do think the army might have marched to Mafra with as much facility on the 23d as I thought it might on the 21st. There was this difference, however, that on the 23d I believe Mafra was occupied by a French corps, and there was none there on the 21st. I must also state to the Board, that the object of the march to Mafra would on the 23d have been defeated, because, as I have just informed them, there was no chance of bringing the French into another action. They would have acted, according to my opinion, in Portugal as they did in Egypt; they tried their strength once in the field, and, having failed, they would in Portugal have continued to retreat till they could have got into safety. I do not believe that any corps could have fallen on the flank of the march on the 23d, because no Frenchman remained in Torres Vedras, or nearer than Cabeca de Montachique, on the evening of the 22d.

'Q. Did that French corps that was at Mafra retreat from Torres Vedras, and was that the nearest way to Lisbon, or to go up the country?

'A. That French corps must have been in the action, and must have retreated through Torres Vedras. The shortest road from Torres Vedras to Lisbon, and of course up the country, is not through Mafra, but it is, in my opinion, entirely consistent with an intention to cross the Tagus, and retreat up the country, to occupy all the forts which were likely to impede or delay the advance of the British troops.

'Q. (By the Board to Sir A. Wellesley.) Would your occupation of Torres Vedras on the evening of the 21st have prevented the French from gaining the Cabeça de Montachique?

'A. Our occupation of Torres Vedras on the evening of the 21st would have placed us on the shortest road from the position of the two armies to Cabeça de Montachique, as we should have been in a situation, by a subsequent movement, to occupy not only Cabeça de Montachique, but the other positions in front of Lisbon, before the French could have reached them.

'Q. Would not the French, in the course of the retreat from the field of battle, have passed through Torres Vedras previous to the time that the British army could arrive there?

'A. The French, as I explained in my evidence yesterday, retreated from all points of attack to the northward, apparently with an intention of falling in with the road from Torres Vedras to Lourinha, by which they had advanced to the attack. I conceive that, after the action was over, the right of our army in particular was nearer to Torres Vedras than the enemy, and therefore I should think that the right of our army would have been at Torres Vedras before any part of the enemy could have reached that town in their retreat.

'Q. Gen. Spencer yesterday described a line of the enemy at the distance of 3 miles: was that corps further from Torres Vedras than the right of the British army?

'A. I cannot say that I recollect to have seen that corps. According to Gen. Spencer's description, he saw it formed about an hour after the enemy had been defeated upon our left, and, as he said, to the northward and upon the road to Torres Vedras. If that is an accurate description of the position of that corps, it must have been much about the same distance from Torres Vedras as our right was.

'Q. Had the army advanced at the time you recommended it, would not our right have been nearer to Torres Vedras by pushing on than that corps which was said to have been formed an hour after the action had taken place?

'A. I should conceive that that corps must have been on the ground on which

Gen. Spencer states he saw it, or at no great distance from it, about the time that I proposed to Sir H. Burrard to pursue the enemy, although probably not formed.

'Q. Do you think that the French corps which attacked your right retired upon Torres Vedras, or took another route?

'A. The right of the army, properly so called, was not attacked. The attack was made upon the right of the centre, and all the French troops which attacked Gen. Fane's and Gen. Anstruther's brigades retired to the northward, as I have before explained, with the exception possibly of some small detachments, of which, however, I saw none.'

Sir A. Wellesley addressed the Board as follows :

'GEN. SIR D. DUNDAS ; MY LORDS AND GENTLEMEN,

'At a former meeting of the Court, Lieut. Gen. Sir H. Dalrymple expressed a wish that the Court should have before it a copy of the letter which I was supposed to have addressed to the Bishop of Oporto on the 24th Aug.; and I then told the Court that I would lay before them all the letters I had written to the Bishop of Oporto, of which I had copies among my papers.

'I find that I have the copies of only 2 letters, although I have written many, which I now lay before the Court [*these letters were not deemed necessary, and were therefore withdrawn*]; and I should have taken an earlier opportunity of laying those letters before the Court, only that one of them relates to transactions in which Sir H. Burrard was a party; and I was unwilling to make it public during his absence.

'In respect to the letter supposed to have been written by me on the 24th Aug. I repeat that I have no recollection of having written it; and I have no copy of it; and I think it probable, from an inaccuracy of the date, from the address, and some of the expressions, that I did not write it; but I adopt as my own all the sentiments which it contains. It congratulates the Bishop upon the prospect of the evacuation of Portugal by the French, which the Court will have observed I always considered a subject of congratulation; and it states that the agreement for the suspension of hostilities contains nothing else that is remarkable, excepting a stipulation that the port of Lisbon should be considered a neutral port in respect to the Russians.

'It is well known and admitted, that there was another part of that agreement to which I entertained objections; but in respect to the Portuguese, it did contain nothing remarkable, excepting this stipulation; and this remark, if I wrote the letter, rather tends to confirm that which I have always stated were my sentiments in respect to this stipulation.

'This mode of laying a private letter before a Court is not regular, any more than the mode of calling for a letter of this description; but if the Court should be desirous of seeing this, or any other letters of mine to the Bishop of Oporto in an official shape, they may call for them at the office of the Sec. of State for Foreign Affairs, through which channel, I doubt not, they can be procured.'

Sir H. Burrard now addressed the Board as follows :

'I trust the Board of Inquiry will not think it improper to grant me the liberty to offer a few observations upon what happened on the 21st Aug., when it was my opinion (unswayed, I trust, by any unworthy motives) that it was not expedient to follow the enemy towards Torres Vedras. In the first place, I did not believe that the enemy's whole force was engaged in that action; neither do I think that it is proved it was known to have been so in fact, when it was proposed to me to advance from the right.

'I very freely acknowledge that I did not understand that a corps of such considerable numbers as is stated was cut off from the main body of the enemy on the left of our position; but it was impressed upon my mind that they were towards Major Gen. Ferguson's front, inclining towards their own force; and I considered it improper to attack them in that situation. This appeared so much the more necessary to me, as I had determined, from the situation our right appeared to me to be in, not to advance to Torres Vedras, and I still think that I determined properly.

'The extensive line the British army occupied was not in favor of our advancing.

The distance from right to left was, I still think, 4 miles. The centre of the enemy had been necessarily disengaged an hour and a half; time enough for them to have formed a line near 3 miles distant in our front, with 8 pieces of cannon, and a large body of cavalry, of which we had none.

'At the time Sir A. Wellesley came up to me, and publicly proposed to me to advance, I felt the situation it placed me in, and that it was not likely my determination should please a British army, who had so much signalised itself; that will, I believe, be sufficient proof that I acted to the best of my judgment, and those who know me will be convinced, very much against my feelings.

'My sentiments on the uncommon situation in which I then stood were well known to those of my staff about me. The want, at this moment, of every one of those gentlemen who were with me on the 21st Aug., I sincerely feel and regret, and am convinced the Board will also feel for the person who stands in so unusual a predicament; at the same time, if there has been any error in judgment, it is all my own; I decided for myself, from what I saw and heard, and take most decidedly the whole responsibility upon myself. But I trust that the Board, upon a review of the whole case, will have sufficient reason to be convinced that it would have been unwise to have risked much, when so superior a force was at hand to reinforce the British army, which must have rendered vain the future efforts of the enemy, and have decided the contest with less loss to the public service than by what I conceive a precarious operation.'

Sir A. Wellesley again addressed the Board, viz.

'I trust that the Court will permit me to address a few words to them upon this occasion.

'Although I did differ, and do still differ, in opinion with Lieut. Gen. Sir H. Burrard, respecting the measures adopted immediately after the battle of the 21st Aug., I hope it will not be deemed presumptuous in me as an inferior officer to declare to the Court and to the public the opinion which I have always entertained, that Sir H. Burrard decided upon that occasion upon fair military grounds, in the manner which appeared to him to be most conducive to the interests of the country; and that he had no motive for his decision which could be supposed personal to me, or which as an officer he could not avow.'

Sir H. Burrard was further examined by Sir H. Dalrymple.

'Q. Was not Sir H. Burrard present at the conference with Gen. Kellermann at Vimeiro, on the subject of the Armistice on the 22d Aug.?

'A. I was called in by Sir H. Dalrymple.

'Q. Had I not, in your opinion, reason to presume, from what passed on that occasion, that both Sir A. Wellesley and yourself cordially approved the Convention for the evacuation of Portugal by the French troops, as a general measure, and that you both seemed to acquiesce in the several arrangements ultimately settled for the Armistice?

'A. I did, and I thought Sir A. Wellesley did so generally : there were a great many objections stated at times, which upon conversation were given up.

'Q. Did I not send for you and Sir A. Wellesley on the morning of the 25th Aug., after the arrival of Lieut. Col. Murray from on board the British Admiral's ship, to consider upon the measures next to be pursued, and again on the morning of the 27th, for a similar purpose?

'A. I was sent for, I believe, on both those occasions; but I made no memoranda of the dates.

'Q. Was not a treaty signed by Lieut. Col. Murray, but which I refused to ratify, read article by article, in presence of yourself, Sir J. Moore, Lieut. Gens. Hope, Mackenzie Fraser, and Sir A. Wellesley; and were not the observations and proposed alterations on each article written down by Sir A. Wellesley?

'A. The whole of that is true, to the best of my knowledge and recollection.

'Q. Was not the definitive Convention ratified in your quarters at Torres Vedras, in presence of yourself, Sir J. Moore, Lieut. Gen. Hope, and Lieut. Gen. Mackenzie Fraser; and have I not just grounds to believe that none of those Lieut. Generals disapproved of the measures of ratifying that treaty?

'A. They were present at the time, called in by Sir H. Dalrymple, and I saw him sign it; and from the characters of such men, I do not suppose that they would have allowed him to do so, without stating their objections, if they had any. Of their sentiments I know no further.

'Q. (By desire of Sir A. Wellesley.) Do you recollect that, when the Armistice was negotiated, Gen. Kellermann read from a paper a statement of the wishes of the French Commander in Chief?

'A. I do recollect that after some conversation he took a paper out and read it.

'Q. Do you recollect my refusing to take that paper, and telling the Commander of the Forces, when we went into the inner room, that I had done so, because I thought that the agreement then to be negotiated ought to be confined to a suspension of hostilities?

'A. I think I recollect Sir Arthur's refusing a paper, but I do not recollect the precise conversation that passed on that occasion.

'Q. Do you recollect the use of these words by the Commander of the Forces, " that as there was no difference of opinion upon the substance of the negotiation, it was not worth while to push the French to the wall upon the form ?"

'A. I think those sentiments were expressed; but I cannot at this time recollect who it was that said them.

'Q. Do you recollect that the demand of the French in favor of the Russians would, in the first instance, have gone to allow the Russians to return to the Baltic with their fleet?

'A. I must say that I was very often in and out of the room; that I had dispatches to send to England; and I cannot exactly recollect that circumstance.

'Q. Do you recollect my having said to the Commander of the Forces, that you and I having been employed last year to bring one fleet out of the Baltic, could not but advise him not to allow another to return there, and that the Commander of the Forces, in consequence, determined that he would not allow the article to stand as it was at first proposed?

'A. I recollect Sir A. Wellesley having made use of those expressions.'

REPORT.

' May it please your Majesty,

We, the underwritten General officers of the army, in obedience to your Majesty's warrant, which bears date the 1st day Nov. 1808, commanding us strictly to examine and inquire into the conditions of a suspension of arms, concluded on the 22d Aug. 1808, between your Majesty's army in Portugal and the French force in that country; and also into a definitive Convention, concluded with the French General commanding, on the 31st Aug. following, &c., &c.; most humbly report to your Majesty, that it appears that the operations of the army under Sir A. Wellesley, from his landing in Mondego bay, the 1st Aug., until the conclusion of the action at Vimeiro, the 21st Aug., were highly honorable and successful, and such as might be expected from a distinguished General at the head of a British army of 13,000 men, augmented on the 20th and 21st to 17,000, deriving only some small aid from a Portuguese corps (1600 men), and against whom an enemy not exceeding 14,000 men in the field was opposed; and this before the arrival of a very considerable reinforcement from England under Lieut. Gen. Sir J. Moore, which, however, did arrive, and join the army from the 25th to the 30th Aug.

' It appears a point on which no evidence adduced can enable the Board to pronounce with confidence, whether or not a pursuit, after the battle of the 21st, could have been efficacious; nor can the Board feel confident to determine on the expedience of a forward movement to Torres Vedras, when Sir H. Burrard has stated weighty considerations against such a measure. Further it is to be observed, that so many collateral circumstances could not be known in the moment of the enemy's repulse as afterwards became clear to the army, and have been represented to the Board. And considering the extraordinary circumstances under which two new Commanding Generals arrived from the ocean and joined the army, (the one during, and the other immediately after, a battle, and those successively superseding each other, and both the original Commander, within the space of twenty-four hours,) it is not surprising that the army was not carried forward until the second day after the action, from the necessity of the Generals being acquainted with the actual state of things and of their army, and proceeding accordingly.

' It appears that the Convention of Cintra, in its progress and conclusion, or at least all the principal articles of it, were not objected to by the 5 distinguished Lieut. Generals of that army; and other General officers who were on that service, whom we have had an opportunity to examine, have also concurred in the great advantages that were immediately gained to the country of Portugal, to the army and navy, and to the general service, by the conclusion of the Convention at that time.

' On a consideration of all circumstances, as set forth in this Report, we most humbly submit our opinion that no further military proceeding is necessary on the subject; because, howsoever some of us may differ in our sentiments respecting the fitness of the Convention in the relative situation of the two armies, it is our unanimous declaration, that unquestionable zeal and firmness appear throughout to have been exhibited by Lieut. Gens. Sir H. Dalrymple, Sir H. Burrard, and Sir A. Wellesley, as well as that the ardor and gallantry of the rest of the officers and soldiers on every occasion during this expedition have done honor to the troops, and reflected lustre on your Majesty's arms.

' All which is most dutifully submitted.

' DAVID DUNDAS, Gen.	' PEMBROKE, Lieut. Gen.
' MOIRA, Gen.	' G. NUGENT, Lieut. Gen.
' PETER CRAIG, Gen.	' OL. NICOLLS, Lieut. Gen.
' HEATHFIELD, Gen.	

' 22d Dec. 1808.'

H.R.H. the Commander in Chief to Lieut. Gen. Sir H. Dalrymple.

Horse Guards, 20th Jan. 1809.

In obedience to His Majesty's commands to me, received through the Sec. of State, I transmit to you the enclosed copy of a paper containing the decision which His Majesty has taken upon the review of the proceedings of the Board of Inquiry, together with the copy of Lord Castlereagh's dispatch, which accompanied it.

Visc. Castlereagh to H.R.H. the Commander in Chief. Downing Street, 18th Jan. 1809.

The proceedings of the Board of General officers, appointed by His Majesty to inquire into, and to report upon, the Armistice and Convention, lately concluded in Portugal, which were communicated to me by the Judge Advocate Gen., at the desire of your Royal Highness, for the information of His Majesty's ministers, having been fully considered, and their opinion thereupon humbly submitted for His Majesty's consideration: I have received the King's commands to transmit to your Royal Highness the decision His Majesty has taken upon the review of these proceedings, a copy of which your Royal Highness will receive enclosed; and to desire that your Royal Highness will be pleased to cause the necessary communication to be made to Lieut. Gen. Sir H. Dalrymple accordingly.

Visc. Castlereagh to H.R.H. the Commander in Chief. Downing Street, 18th Jan. 1809.

The King has taken into his consideration the report of the Board of Inquiry, together with the documents and opinions thereunto annexed.

While His Majesty adopts the unanimous opinion of the Board, that no further military proceeding is necessary to be had upon the transactions referred to their investigation, His Majesty does not intend, thereby, to convey any expression of His Majesty's satisfaction at the terms and conditions of the Armistice or Convention.

When those instruments were first laid before His Majesty, the King, reserving for investigation those parts of the definitive Convention in which His Majesty's immediate interests were concerned, caused it to be signified to Sir H. Dalrymple, by His Majesty's Sec. of State, that His Majesty, nevertheless, felt himself compelled at once to express his disapprobation of those articles in which stipulations were made directly affecting the interests or feelings of the Spanish and Portuguese nations.

At the close of the inquiry, the King (abstaining from any observations upon other parts of the Convention) repeats his disapprobation of those articles, His Majesty deeming it necessary that his sentiments should be clearly understood, as to the improriety and danger of the unauthorised admission into Military Conventions of articles of such a description, which, especially when incautiously framed, may lead to the most injurious consequences.

His Majesty cannot forbear further to observe, that Lieut. Gen. Sir H. Dalrymple's delaying to transmit, for his information, the Armistice concluded on the 22d Aug., until the 4th Sept., when he, at the same time, transmitted the ratified Convention, was calculated to produce great public inconvenience, and that such public inconvenience did, in fact, result therefrom.

To the Duke of Richmond.   London, 23rd Nov. 1808.

*   *   *   *   *   *   *

The Court of Inquiry is going on as well as I could wish. I made my statement respecting the Armistice and the Convention yesterday; and I was obliged to go further into the subject than I intended, owing to the attacks which Sir H. Dalrymple had made upon me, not only on the opening of the Court, but in his narrative of his proceedings. The consequence is, that he cannot escape censure. If he had done what a gentleman ought to have done, and what he has done before the Court of Inquiry, viz. relieve me from the responsibility of negotiating the Armistice in his answer to the letter of the Sec. of State, by which my letter of 6th Oct. was communicated to him; and if he had not attacked me when he first addressed the Court of Inquiry, and in his narrative, I should have defended for him the measure of allowing the French to evacuate Portugal, and should not have said one word about the details of the Convention. I only hope that Burrard will be a little more fair, or a little more candid, than Sir Hew has been. You see that the papers have already changed their tone about the evacuation; and, excepting personal abuse of me and misrepresentation of what I have said, they do what one would wish.

I will send you copies of my narrative of my own proceedings, and of my statement on the negotiations in reply to Sir H. Dalrymple.

To the Duke of Richmond.   London, 25th Nov. 1808.

*   *   *   *   *   *

I have received your two letters of the 21st. I will do what I can for ———, but, of course, just at present I have but little communication with the Horse Guards, and that little is by letter.

The Court of Inquiry is going on as well as I could wish.

The news from Spain is very bad. Blake is certainly defeated, and his army dispersed. The French are at Valladolid, and the head of Moore's column at Salamanca, and Baird at Lugo, in Galicia. Baird says that his communication with Moore will be cut off. It is obvious that these British corps cannot form a junction in Spain, and Moore must retire into Portugal, and Baird to the sea, and embark, in order to join at all. I don't think the British corps in any danger. Moore is certainly a most unlucky fellow!

To the Duke of Richmond.   London, 30th Nov. 1808.

*   *   *   *   *   *

There is nothing new. I don't believe the stories in the newspapers of Blake's victories; nor do I believe that his defeat has been so complete as Baird has stated it to be : but, from all I have seen and heard of the Spanish armies, I am very well convinced that, if they are not already defeated and dispersed, they will be so before long. It does not appear to me that either Moore or Baird is in any danger.

The Court of Inquiry have adjourned till next Tuesday, to give time to ———— to come over. We expect him every moment; and I imagine that what remains to be investigated will not take more than 2 or 3 days. I hope, therefore, to be able to leave town for Ireland by the end of the week.

To Lord Burghersh.   Dublin Castle, 11th Jan. 1809.

I have received your letter of the 5th, and I have put the memorial of your friend in a train of examination, and that which can be done will be done for him.

The report of the Court of Inquiry is indeed an extraordinary production. Opinions, like colors, are now matters of taste, and may in this view of them be inconsistent with each other. But a Court of this description ought, if it touches facts, to state them correctly; and a principal member, if he observes upon the subject, ought not to pass unnoticed or to contradict the principal fact bearing upon the question on which he observes.

To the Duke of Richmond.   London, 22d Jan. 1809.

I arrived here on Saturday evening, and found that the government had been in much greater strength on the first day of the session than they had expected, and the opposition very weak; and I understand that the spirit of both houses is favorable to us, and that the attendance is likely to be good.

I have seen Lord Liverpool, and he has desired me to tell you that, if you should find any of the counties determined to assemble in the manner pointed out by the Act of Parliament, to petition the Lord Lieutenant to proclaim any districts under the Insurrection Act, it is desirable that you should consult the Chancellor and the Chief Justices, and that you should transmit your own and their opinion, and the grounds upon which it is formed, in a dispatch to him; in order that he may take the opinion of the Cabinet upon the measure of proclaiming any district, before you should adopt it. He says, however, that if you should be of opinion that it would be advisable to proclaim any district as soon as possible after the gentlemen of the county will have petitioned that it should be proclaimed, he begs that you will consider the dispatch written to you last year as containing the King's authority to do so; and that in this case you need not wait to receive the opinion of the Cabinet.

Charles Stewart arrived in town on Saturday morning, bringing dismal accounts of the state of the army which had arrived at Coruña on the 11th, closely followed by Soult's corps, which arrived there on the 13th. The transports were at Vigo, and did not arrive till the 14th. Paget arrived this evening, and brings an account of an action fought on Monday, in which the French were defeated and repulsed with considerable loss; but Moore was killed; and Baird badly wounded, his arm had been carried off by a cannon ball at the socket. The army had embarked in the night, Monday, and on the morning of Tuesday; and it is believed the whole were on board, and the wind was fair to take them out of Coruña. Considering the situation of the army, I think this action a fortunate event, notwithstanding the loss of these two men; for I doubt whether they could have come off at all, and I am convinced they could not have come off with honor, if the French had not attacked them.

I believe the whole are coming home; but this is secret.

To Major Gens. Spencer and Hill, to Brig. Gens. Acland, Nightingall, Bowes, and Craufurd; and also to Major Gen. Ferguson and Brig. Gen. Fane, to whom, being members of the House of Commons, the words in italics are not to be addressed.

London, 28th Jan. 1809.

I have the honor to communicate to you, by order of the House of Lords, the unanimous resolution of their Lordships, *and, by order of the House of Commons, the resolution of the Commons*, declaring the approbation *of those bodies respectively* of your conduct while serving with the army under my command in Portugal.

I beg leave to congratulate you upon receiving this distinguished reward of your distinguished conduct in Portugal.

P.S. I request you to communicate the resolutions of the Houses of Lords and Commons to the staff officers who served under your directions in Portugal.

To the Commanding officers of regiments and corps.   London, 28th Jan. 1809.

I enclose, by order of the House of Lords, the unanimous resolutions of their Lordships, and, by order of the House of Commons, the resolutions of the Commons, declaring the approbation of those bodies respectively of the conduct of the General and other officers, non-commissioned officers, and soldiers composing the army lately under my command in Portugal, while serving in that country.

I beg you will communicate to the officers, non-commissioned officers, and soldiers under your command, these honorable marks of the approbation of the houses of Parliament of their exemplary conduct.

Memorandum on the defence of Portugal.   London, 7th March, 1809.

I have always been of opinion that Portugal might be defended, whatever might be the result of the contest in Spain; and that in the mean time the measures adopted for the defence of Portugal would be highly useful to the Spaniards in their contest with the French.

My notion was, that the Portuguese military establishments, upon the footing of 40,000 militia and 30,000 regular troops, ought to be revived; and that, in addition to these troops, His Majesty ought to employ an army in Portugal amounting to about 20,000 British troops, including about 4000 cavalry. My opinion was, that even if Spain should have been conquered, the French would not have been able to overrun Portugal with a smaller force than 100,000 men; and that, as long as the contest should continue in Spain, this force, if it could be put in a state of activity, would be highly useful to the Spaniards, and might eventually have decided the contest.

It is obvious, however, that the military establishments of Portugal could not be revived without very extensive pecuniary assistance and political support from this country; and the only mode in which it appeared to be safe, or even practicable to give this assistance and support, or to interfere at all in a military way in the concerns of Portugal, was to trust the King's Ambassador at Lisbon to give or withhold such sums as he might think necessary for the support of military establishments only, and to instruct him to see that the revenues of Portugal, whatever they might be, were in the first instance applied to the same objects. By the operation of these powers and instructions, it is probable that he would have had a complete control over the measures of the Portuguese government; and we might have expected by this time to have in the field an efficient Portuguese army.

As it was not possible, however, to adopt these measures at that time, and as the attention of the government has necessarily been drawn to other objects, it is probable that the military establishments of Portugal have made but little progress; and in considering the extent of the British force required for the defence of that country, and the other measures to be adopted, the small extent of the Portuguese force, and the probability of an early attack by the enemy, must be considered on the one hand; and, on the other, the continuance of the contest in Spain, and the probability that a very large French force will not be disposable in a very short period of time for the attack upon Portugal.

I would still recommend the adoption of the political measures above suggested, with a view to the revival of the military establishments in Portugal. It is probable that the expense of these measures will not in this year exceed a million sterling. But if they should succeed, and the contest should continue in Spain and in Portugal, the benefit which will accrue from them will be more than adequate to the expense incurred.

The British force employed in Portugal should, in this view of the question, not be less than 30,000 men, of which number 4000 or 5000 should be cavalry; and there should be a large body of artillery.

The extent of force in cavalry and artillery, above required, is because the Portuguese military establishments must necessarily be deficient in these two branches; and British or German cavalry and artillery must be employed with the Portuguese infantry.

The whole of the army in Portugal, Portuguese as well as British, should be placed under the command of British officers. The Staff of the army, the Commissariat in particular, must be British; and these departments must be extensive in proportion to the strength of the whole army which will act in Portugal, to the number of detached posts which it will be necessary to occupy, and in a view to the difficulties of providing and distributing supplies in that country. In regard to the detail of these measures, I recommend that the British army in Portugal should be reinforced as soon as possible with some companies of British riflemen, with 3000 British or German cavalry; that the complement of ordnance with that army should be made 30 pieces of cannon, of which 2 brigades of 9 pounders; that these pieces of ordnance should be completely horsed; that 20 pieces of brass (12 pounders) ordnance upon travelling carriages should be sent to Portugal, with a view to the occupation of certain positions in the country; that a corps of engineers for an army of 60,000 men should be sent there, and a corps of artillery for 60 pieces of cannon.

I understand that the British army now in Portugal consists of 20,000 men, including cavalry. It should be made up 20,000 infantry at least, as soon as possible, by additions of riflemen and other good infantry, which by this time may have been refitted after the campaign in Spain. The reinforcements may follow, as the troops shall recover from their fatigues.

The first measures to be adopted are to complete the army in Portugal with its cavalry and artillery, and to horse the ordnance as it ought to be. As soon as this shall be done the General and Staff officers should go out; as it may be depended upon that as soon as the newspapers shall have announced the departure of officers for Portugal, the French armies in Spain will receive orders to make their movements towards Portugal, so as to anticipate our measures for its defence. We ought therefore to have every thing on the spot, or nearly so, before any alarm is created at home respecting our intentions.

Besides the articles above enumerated, 30,000 stands of arms, clothing, and shoes, for the Portuguese army, should be sent to Lisbon as soon as possible.

To the Rt. Hon. Robt. Dundas.   London, 17th March, 1809.

I return your paper, which I have perused with great attention. The object of Munro's alteration appears to be nothing more than to appoint a Commissary General, whose particular business shall be to superintend the execution of their duties by the different paymasters of districts, acting in the capacities of garrison storekeepers and commissaries of provisions. This alteration of the system may be desirable, as it is quite impossible for the military board to superintend immediately the execution of the duties. But the alteration of the system should be limited to the appointment of a Commissary General: the arrangements ought to be left as they now are; and it is possible that the improvements which the Commissary General may introduce into the department may occasion savings which may compensate for the expense of the salary and establishments. As an additional saving, I should recommend that the Commissary General might be the garrison storekeeper at the Presidency. But I doubt whether the saving on this head will prove great; there are several causes which lead to the expense and abuse of this department which no regulation can remedy. One of them is the want of good granaries in all the newly conquered countries, and another is the large quantities of vermin in the granaries, which destroy grain; another the climate, which destroys much of the rice when beat out of the husk, and which will not keep in the husk more than one or two seasons in those countries in which heavy rains fall. To these evils, for which there is no remedy, may be added the dishonesty of the Native servants, who cannot even under the best regulations be charged with the care of the stores: and it must be obvious that they have more scope for their roguery in the care of grain than they have in any other article.

This circumstance would afford good reasons for not involving the Company in the ruinous sale and purchase of stores, for it may be certain that the Native servants, and not improbably the European storekeeper, derive a profit from both the sale and repurchase. But this is a point of the department which might be better settled by the Commissary General upon the spot, and, indeed, the use of such an officer would be to superintend the execution of the detail of the duties of the department.

What I have above stated refers to a state of peace. Munro is much mistaken if he supposes that the Commander in Chief at Fort St. George can ever relieve himself in war, from this responsible part of his duty, by the appointment of a Commissary General. A Commissary General may often, upon the expectation of war and in the preparation for military operations, be useful in pointing out to the Commander in Chief the supplies he would require, and where they were to be stored; but the Commander in Chief of an army in India, as well as in every other country, must be his own Commissary General if he means that his army is to be fed.

I enclose to you the copy of a memorandum, which I gave to Lord Wellesley when I was in India, at the moment Lord Lake's army was in such distress for provisions, pointing out the detail of the mode in which I had conducted this branch of the service.* You will observe the extent and variety of the details which it embraces, and how impossible it would be for any man, excepting the Commander in Chief himself, to superintend them and to combine them for the public service.

In discussing these questions I observe that neither Munro nor Gen. Macdonell, nor Mr. Petrie, have adverted to the supplies or the operations of the army under my command. In fact, the business was then carried on chiefly in conformity with the regulations; and I was never stopped for one moment for want of supplies. It is true, however, that we paid more than ordinary attention to this branch of the service.

To the Duke of Richmond. London, 28th March, 1809.

I intended to write to you yesterday, but was prevented, to inform you that Lord Castlereagh had offered me the command of the troops in Portugal, which I have, of course, accepted. This will separate me from you, at which I feel much concern; but I will take care to leave all your business in good order, and to inform the person who will be appointed to succeed me, whoever he may be, of all your plans, and of the mode in which I intended to have carried through the measures of government in this session of Parliament.

Sir E. Littlehales has written to me respecting leave of absence for himself; but I rather think that, as I am to leave you, you will find it more convenient that he should not quit Ireland, at least till my successor shall have taken possession of his office, which I suppose he will not do till after the session of Parliament in June.

* See vol. i., p. 1354.

To Dom Domingos de Souza Coutinho.*   Portsmouth, 13th April, 1809.

I have had the honor of receiving your letter of the 9th inst., and I am much flattered by the regret you express that it was not in my power to wait upon you on Saturday last. I considered it important, however, not to delay my departure for one moment after I had received my instructions from His Majesty's ministers, and I had made all the arrangements to which it was necessary that I should attend previous to my departure from England. If I had suspected that I should have been detained here by contrary winds till this time, I should have had great pleasure in waiting upon you. I am likewise much flattered by your expressions of satisfaction upon my appointment to command in Portugal. I only hope that I may arrive there in time to be of any service, and you may depend upon my making every exertion which zeal for the Portuguese nation and for the honor of His Majesty's arms can induce me to make.

I shall pay attention to the different subjects to which you have referred in your letter; and I shall do every thing in my power to satisfy the government and people of Portugal in respect to them, and to conciliate their good will upon all others.

I recommend to you to mention to Mr. Canning your wishes, that a part of the ammunition and arms intended for the kingdom of Portugal should be sent to Oporto; and that the ammunition should be sent out made up, rather than that the materials should be sent; as he will be more able than I am to effect the alterations which you desire.

I am apprehensive, however, that to send a part of the arms and ammunition intended for Portugal to Oporto may interfere with another arrangement which Mr. Canning had in contemplation, to make Lisbon the depôt of all the stores intended by Great Britain for the service of His Majesty's allies in the Peninsula.

To the Duke of Richmond.   Portsmouth, 14th April, 1809.

I am still detained here by contrary winds, which have blown for these 2 days past with considerable violence. †

In the mean time affairs are in a critical state in Portugal. We have accounts from thence of as late a date as the 3rd April. Soult, who had advanced from Galicia, and had defeated some small Portuguese corps at Chaves and Braga, had advanced to Oporto, which town he took on the 29th March. His corps consisted of about 15,000 men. There was another French corps, of about 10,000 men, advancing from Salamanca, and had arrived at San Felices, on the road to Almeida.

Marshal Victor, at the head of another, consisting of about 35,000, had lately driven the Spanish army, under Cuesta, from the bridge at Almaraz, upon the Tagus; and had since destroyed Cuesta's army, in an action fought upon the Guadiana; and had afterwards arrived about the 1st April at Badajoz.

* Portuguese minister at the Court of London, afterwards Conde de Funchal.
† The *Surveillante* frigate, in which Sir A. Wellesley sailed, was very nearly lost in very bad weather, at the back of the Isle of Wight, in the night after quitting Spithead.

Hill's corps entered the Tagus on the 4th or 5th, having been seen by the vessel which brought the last accounts; so that by the 5th or 7th we shall have about 22,000 British troops in the neighbourhood of Lisbon, and whatever Portuguese troops they may have.

The plan of operations for the French will be to move Victor's corps from Badajoz to Abrantes; then cross the Tagus; and as soon as that corps is ready to move on towards Lisbon, to bring on the other two weaker corps from Oporto and Salamanca; and the whole to join in the neighbourhood of Santarem; unless, indeed, they should be certain that Cradock cannot move, in which case they will move down according as they may find it convenient.

As soon as the junction and co-operation of the three French corps shall be secure, they will detach from 5000 to 10,000 across the Tagus to the southern bank, where we have not a man, either British or Portuguese. They will post this corps upon the heights of Almada, which, you will recollect, are opposite Lisbon, and in their continuation command the harbour. As soon as they will have possession of this ground, the Admiral will find out that he cannot remain there with his ships of war; and the General, that he cannot embark his troops; and by this manœuvre alone the French will obtain possession of Lisbon, most probably before I shall arrive there. If they should not make this detachment, I have no doubt that Lisbon may be, and will be, defended; and I have long determined to fortify the heights of Almada, so as to be able to hold them with a small body of men, as the first step I should take upon my arrival.

You shall hear from me constantly.

To the Rt. Hon. J. Villiers.*   Lisbon, 23rd April, 1809.

I shall attend to your suggestion in respect to the Commanding officer of the artillery and chief engineer.

Upon considering the subject well, I think it best that Beresford should come here, unless he should apprehend any inconvenience to the public service from his absence from his corps, principally on the score of its discipline. I write to him on this subject; and shall be obliged to you if you will order a boat for him to Santarem.

To Marshal Beresford.   Lisbon, 23d April, 1809.

I arrived here yesterday, having had a passage of one week from Portsmouth. The fleet, having on board my horses, the 2 regiments of heavy dragoons, and some horses for the artillery, sailed, I believe, on the day after I did, and may be expected in a day or two. The 24th foot may likewise be expected from Jersey, and likewise a brigade of light infantry from England, and a regiment of hussars.

The expectation of the immediate arrival of some of these troops, and the consideration of the various different arrangements to be made, and which can be made only here, in respect to transport, commissariat, staff, the defence of Lisbon and the Tagus, and eventually the defence of the Eastern frontier, during the absence of the army to the northward, sup-

---

* Afterwards Earl of Clarendon.

posing it should be decided to undertake the expedition against Soult, will, I fear, detain me here for a few days; and it occurs to me that time will be saved, and much advantage will result from your being here. Accordingly, I wish that you could make it convenient to yourself to come here as soon as possible.

If, however, you should be of opinion that it would be inconvenient to the public service, on account of the state of discipline of the Portuguese troops, or for any other reason, that you should absent yourself from them; or if the journey should be inconvenient to yourself, I request you not to come; and I must only delay deciding upon those points of the subject on which it is advisable that I should have your opinion till we meet.

P. S. Pray let Cradock know if you should determine to come down.

To Lieut. Gen. Sir J. Cradock, K.B.   Lisbon, 23rd April, 1809.

Mr. Villiers will have informed you of my arrival here yesterday, and of the concurrence of my opinion with that which you appear to entertain in respect to the further movement to the northward.

I conclude you will have determined to halt the army at Leiria. I think that before any further steps are taken in respect to Soult, it would be desirable to consider the situation of Victor, how far he is enabled to make an attack upon Portugal, and the means of defence of the Eastern frontier, while the British army shall be to the northward; and eventually the means of the defence of Lisbon and the Tagus, in case this attack should be made upon this country.

All these subjects must have been considered by you, and I fear in no very satisfactory point of view, as you appear to have moved to the northward unwillingly; and I should be glad to talk them over with you, in order to be able to consider some of them, and make various arrangements which can be made only here. I have asked Beresford also to come, if he should not deem his absence from the Portuguese troops in their present state likely to be disadvantageous to the Portuguese service, and I have desired him to let you know whether he will come or not.

It might possibly also be more agreeable and convenient to you to see me here than with the army, and if this should be the case, it would be a most desirable arrangement to meet you here: I beg, however, that you will consider this proposition only in a view to your own convenience and wishes. If you should come down, I should be much obliged to you if you would bring with you the Adjutant and Quarter Master Generals, the Chief Engineer, the Commanding officer of Artillery, and the Commissary General.

To the Rt. Hon. J. H. Frere.*   Lisbon, 24th April, 1809.

I arrived here the day before yesterday, and I propose to take the command of the army in this country, as soon as I shall have communicated with Sir J. Cradock.

I conclude that Sir John has kept you informed of the movements of

---

* Mr. Frere was Ambassador to the Court of Spain, and as such accompanied the Central Junta wherever it went. It was at this time at Seville.

the French in the north of Portugal.   I do not find that there has been any material alteration lately in their position.   They have not passed the Vouga, to the southward, nor have they extended themselves into Tras os Montes since the loss of Chaves.   But they have made some movements towards the Tamaga, which divides Tras os Montes from Minho; and it is supposed they intend to acquire for themselves the option of retreating into Spain through Tras os Montes, if they should be pressed by the British troops.

I intend to move towards Soult, and attack him, if I should be able to make any arrangement in the neighbourhood of Abrantes, which can give me any security for the safety of this place during my absence to the northward.   I am not quite certain, however, that I should not do more good to the general cause by combining with Gen. Cuesta in an operation against Victor; and I believe I should prefer this last, if Soult were not in possession of a part of this country which is very fertile in resources and of the town of Oporto, and if to concert the operations with Gen. Cuesta would not take time which might be profitably employed in operations against Soult.

I think it probable, however, that Soult will not remain in Portugal when I shall pass the Mondego: if he does, I shall attack him.   If he should retire, I am convinced that it would be most advantageous for the common cause, that we should remain on the defensive in the north of Portugal, and act vigorously in co-operation with Cuesta against Victor.

In the first place, I do not know that, singly, I should be equal to the French force in Galicia; and I am convinced that a movement of the British force into that province, inasmuch as it would oblige the French to collect their force, would put an end for the moment to the war of the peasantry, which has hitherto been so successful, has been so distressing to the enemy, and, in fact, prevents them from doing all the mischief which their position would enable them to do.

An operation against Victor is attended by these advantages.   If successful, it effectually relieves Seville and Lisbon, and in case affairs should take such a turn as to enable the King's ministers to make another great effort for the relief of Spain, the corps under my command in Portugal will not be removed to such a distance from the scene of operations as to render its co-operation impossible, and we may hope to see the effect of a great effort made by a combined and concentrated force.

It is true, that Galicia and other parts, which might be relieved by a different and a more dispersed application of our force, will continue for some time longer in the possession of the enemy; but this must be recollected, that the relief of Galicia is certain, if this great effort, which I have supposed may be made, should be successful; and it is probable that relief procured by these means would be permanent.

I am convinced that the French will be in serious danger in Spain only when a great force shall be assembled which will oblige them to collect their troops; and this combined operation of the force in this country, with that under Gen. Cuesta, may be the groundwork of further measures of the same and a more extended description.

I shall be very much obliged to you if you will communicate to me any information you may have of the strength and position of the different French corps now in Spain.

To the Rt. Hon. J. Villiers.   Lisbon, 24th April, 1809.

I enclose my letter to Mr. Frere, which, you will observe, is important; and it is very desirable that it should not fall into the hands of the enemy, or that, if it does, he should not at an early period discover its contents. If you should think that the messenger is in any danger of being taken, it will be necessary, I should think, either to caution him particularly to destroy this letter, or to put it into cipher.

To Visct. Castlereagh.   Lisbon, 24th April, 1809.

Having heard from the Admiral that he intends to send the *Statira* to England at an early hour to-morrow morning, I shall not suffer that opportunity to pass by without writing to you, although I have but little to tell you.

I arrived here on Saturday, and found that Sir J. Cradock and Beresford had moved up the country to the northward with the troops under their command respectively, the former to Leiria, and the latter to Thomar. Sir J. Cradock does not, however, appear to have entertained any decided intention of moving forward; on the contrary, indeed, he appears, by his letters to Mr. Villiers, to have intended to go no farther, till he should hear that Victor's movements were decided; and, therefore, I consider affairs in this country to be exactly in the state in which, if I found them, it was the intention of the King's ministers that I should assume the command; and accordingly I propose to assume it as soon as I shall communicate with Sir J. Cradock. I have written to him and to Gen. Beresford, to apprise them that I conceive advantages will result from our meeting here, and I expect them both here as soon as possible.

In respect to the enemy, Soult is still at Oporto, and he has not pushed his posts to the southward farther than the river Vouga. He has nothing in Tras os Montes, since the loss of Chaves, of which you have been most probably apprised; but he has some posts on the river Tamaga, which divides that province from Minho; and it is supposed that he wishes to secure for himself the option of retreating through Tras os Montes into Spain, if he should find it necessary.

Gen. Silveira, with a Portuguese corps, is in Tras os Montes; but I am not acquainted with its strength or its composition.

Gen. Lapisse, who commands the corps which it was supposed, when I left England, was marching from Salamanca into Portugal, has turned off to his left, and has marched along the Portuguese frontier to Alcantara, where he crossed the Tagus, and thence he went to Merida, on the Guadiana, where he is in communication with, indeed I may say part of, the army of Victor. He has an advanced post at Montijo, nearer to the Portuguese frontier than Merida. Victor has continued at Medellin since the action with Cuesta. He is either fortifying himself at that post, or making an entrenched camp there. Cuesta is at Llerena, collecting a force again, which it is said will soon be 25,000 infantry, and 6000 cavalry, a part of them good troops. I know nothing of the Marques de la Romana, or of anything to the northward of Portugal.

I intend to move upon Soult as soon as I can make some arrangement on which I can depend for the defence of the Tagus, either to impede or delay Victor's progress, in case he should come in while I am absent. I should prefer an attack upon Victor in concert with Cuesta, if Soult was not in possession of a fertile province of this kingdom and of the favorite town of Oporto, of which it is most desirable to deprive him; and if any operation upon Victor, connected with Cuesta's movements, would not require time to concert it, which may as well be employed in dislodging Soult from the north of Portugal, and to bring the British army to the Eastern frontier.

If the light brigade should not have left England when you receive this letter, I trust that you will send them off without loss of time; and I request of you to desire the officer commanding them to endeavor to get intelligence as he shall go along the coast, particularly at Aveiro, and the mouth of the Mondego; and I wish that he should stop at the latter place for orders, if he should find that the British army is engaged in operations to the northward, and that he should not have already received orders at Aveiro. The 23d light dragoons might also receive orders to a similar purport. The hussars, I conclude, will have sailed before this time.

We are much in want of craft here, now that we are going to carry on an operation to the northward. Constant convoys will be necessary, and the Admiral does not appear to have the means in his power of supplying all that is required of him. The 24th regt. arrived this day.

To Visct. Castlereagh.   Lisbon, 24th April, 1809.

I have arranged to send the transports to Cork to bring here 1100 horses, of which 800 are supposed to belong to the 23rd light dragoons, and 300 to the Commissariat; but I have not been able to carry into effect that part of the arrangement which was settled in England in respect to these Commissariat horses, for their care on their passage; as the men of the English Commissariat, who were to have been sent to Ireland in the empty transports for this purpose, are with the army at Leiria, and the transports would be delayed for some days, if I were to detain them till they should return from the army.

I therefore beg leave to suggest to you to have directions given to Lieut. Col. Seymour,* of the 23rd light dragoons, to have 100 men with officers and non-commissioned officers of the 23rd, attached to the horses of the Commissariat, to take care of them on the passage from Cork to Lisbon.

To Vice Adm. the Hon. G. Berkeley.   Lisbon, 25th April, 1809.

I have the honor to inform you, that I received directions from the Secretary of State, to request you to send tonnage to Cork of the horse ships now in the Tagus, to convey to Lisbon 1100 horses under such convoy as you may think necessary.

* Afterwards Serjeant at Arms.

I shall be very much obliged to you if you would give directions upon this subject, in order to carry into execution the wishes of His Majesty's government.

To Visct. Castlereagh. Lisbon, 27th April, 1809.

I arrived here on the 22nd inst., and having communicated with Lieut. Gen. Sir J. Cradock to put me in orders on the 25th, I have assumed the command of the army.

The whole of the British army in Portugal are assembled at Leiria and Alcobaca, with the exception of the 2nd batt. 30th regt., in garrison at Lisbon; of the 16th light dragoons, on its march to join the army; and of the 2nd batt. 24th regt., the 3rd dragoon guards, and the 4th dragoons, just landed.

The corps of Marshal Soult is still in the north of Portugal, occupying the city of Oporto, with its advanced posts at Ovar. It is engaged with its left in an attack upon Gen. Silveira on the Tamaga, with a view to open the province of Tras os Montes, for its communication with Spain. The corps of Gen. Lapisse, which had advanced from Salamanca, and had threatened an attack upon the province of Beira, has marched along the frontiers of Portugal to Alcantara, where it crossed the Tagus; and it is now joined with that under the command of Marshal Victor, at Merida, upon the Guadiana. The corps of Marshal Victor has been upon the Guadiana, since the defeat of the Spanish army under Gen. Cuesta, with its advanced posts south of that river.

Gen. Cuesta is at Llerena; and I understand, by a communication from Mr. Frere to the Sec. of State, a copy of which has been sent here, that the Spanish government are taking measures to reinforce that General; and that he will move into Portugal, if Victor should take advantage of the absence of the British army engaged in operations to the northward of Portugal.

Under these circumstances, I have determined forthwith to move to the northward. I purpose to take with me 6000 Portuguese troops, and the whole of the British troops now in Portugal, with the exception of the 2nd batt. 30th regt., the 2nd batt. 24th regt., the brigade of infantry under the command of Major Gen. Mackenzie, and the 3rd dragoon guards, and 4th dragoons. These troops, with about 7000 Portuguese infantry and cavalry, will be left upon the Tagus to watch the movements of the enemy upon the frontier, and to guard the passages over the river, between Abrantes and Santarem.

As soon as the enemy shall have evacuated the north of Portugal, it is my intention to return to the Eastern frontier of the Kingdom, and to co-operate with the Spanish General, Cuesta, against the army of Marshal Victor.

G. O. Adj. Gen.'s Office, Lisbon, 27th April, 1809.

1. His Majesty has been pleased to appoint Lieut. Gen. Sir A. Wellesley, K.B., to be Commander of his Forces in Portugal, and his Excellency having arrived in this country to assume the command, all reports, applications, &c., are henceforward to be addressed to him through the usual channels.

To Visct. Castlereagh. Lisbon, 27th April, 1809.

Upon the arrival of Gen. Beresford at Lisbon on the 25th inst., he informed me that he had had some communication with a French officer, through the means of M. ——, at Oporto, which announced a disposition in the officers of Soult's corps to revolt, and to seize Soult and other principal officers of the army.

On the night before last, a French officer, by the name of ——, arrived here, accompanied by Major Douglas,* who had been sent by Gen. Beresford to the French advanced posts to confer with him; and I had yesterday an interview with this officer. He informed me that great discontent and dissatisfaction with the measures of Buonaparte prevailed throughout the French army, and particularly in the corps of Marshal Soult, which had suffered, and was still suffering, extreme distress; that dissatisfaction had long prevailed on various accounts, particularly the conscription, but had been greatly increased by a sense of the injustice of the measures adopted in respect to Spain, and the seizure of the king; and that a large proportion of the officers of the army of Soult were determined to revolt, and to seize the General and other principal officers of the army, supposed to be particularly attached to the interests of Buonaparte, if that army should be pressed by the troops under my command, so as to oblige Soult to concentrate in situations chosen with a view to their defence rather than with a view to their subsistence.

—— having met Major Douglas between the advanced posts of the two armies, and his communications having there appeared to the Major to be so important, that he thought it desirable that —— should see Gen. Beresford, he proposed that —— should come to Lisbon. I draw your Lordship's attention to this fact, as it removes a suspicion which might otherwise attach to the whole subject. The objects of these communications appear to be—first, to prevail upon us to press upon Soult's corps; and, secondly, to give to —— and two other captains of the French army passports to go to France.

In respect to the first of these objects, your Lordship is aware that I had adopted a plan of operations which would have effected it; and I must add, that in the different conversations with Major Douglas, Gen. Beresford, and me, ——, in pressing that plan upon us, advised us to watch the movements of the enemy on the left of the Tagus, while we should be engaged in operations to the northward. He was, at the same time, entirely ignorant of the situation of Victor, and of all the other French corps in Spain, excepting that of Ney.

In respect to the second object, I asked —— particularly the reason he had for wishing to go to France at all, and those he had for wishing to go before any blow should be struck. His answer was, that he wished to go in order to communicate to Generals —— ——, ——, and others dissatisfied with the existing order of things, the measures which the officers of Soult's army had in contemplation, and which would certainly be adopted if the army should be at all pressed by us; and that he wished to go at an early period, because it was certain that as soon as Buonaparte should receive intelligence of the event, he

* Lieut. Gen. Sir J. Douglas, K.C.B., then Lieut. Colonel in the Portuguese army.

would seize all suspected of being adverse to him, and would put an end to the hopes which were entertained that the same measures would become general throughout the French army.

In the existing situation of affairs in Portugal I have considered it proper to refuse to attend to these communications. I have therefore asked the Admiral to give to —— passports for himself and two other Captains of the French army to go to France by sea; in which —— says they will experience no difficulty, as Soult allows vessels of all nations to quit Oporto; and the Commanding officers of the regiments to which they belong, being parties to the plan of revolt, are desirous and have the power to permit them to go. I have pledged myself no further; and I have particularly desired Gen. Beresford, in delivering his passports to ——, to request that he will inform his friends in the French army, that he asked from me, and only obtained, passports to go to France; that I wish them success in the accomplishment of their objects; but that the line which I shall take upon them must depend upon the circumstances in which the French army shall stand at the moment the officers may seize their General.

I acknowledge that I do not entertain any hopes that I shall be enabled to effect more to the northward than oblige Soult to retreat from Portugal. If circumstances should enable me to do more, the question whether the operations against the French army ought to be carried to extremities, or they should be allowed to seize their General and place themselves under our protection, becomes one of greater difficulty; upon which I am desirous, if possible, of having the opinion of His Majesty's government.

Your Lordship will observe, that I have not thought it proper to discourage the disposition which appears to prevail among the French officers; at the same time that I have taken care not only not to pledge myself to any particular line of conduct, but that those concerned should understand that I do not consider myself pledged by anything that has passed. The successful revolt of a French army might be attended by the most extensive and important consequences; whereas their defeat, or what is a more improbable event, their surrender, would affect only local interests and objects, excepting that either of these events would add to the reputation of His Majesty's arms.

In the consideration and decision of this question much must depend upon the minute circumstances attending the situation in which each of the armies shall be placed at the moment; but I consider it my duty to give the earliest intelligence to His Majesty's ministers, in order, if possible, that I may have the advantage of their opinion, and His Majesty's commands, before I shall have to decide upon the line which I shall adopt.

To Visct. Castlereagh.   Lisbon, 27th April, 1809.

I have but little to add to my public dispatches of this date. I fully believe in the intentions of the French officers to revolt. The existence of this intention is confirmed by the recollection of what dropped from nearly every individual of the French army with whom I conversed when

I was in this country last year, and it is highly probable on other grounds. I doubt, however, whether it will be quite so easy to carry their intentions successfully into execution as their emissary appears to imagine; and I also doubt whether it follows of course, as is generally imagined by those with whom I have conversed here upon this subject, that the successful revolt of this corps would be followed immediately by that of others; and I am convinced that the mode proposed by ——, which will be explained to you by Col. Bayley, to accomplish that object, would not answer that purpose. It is, however, very certain, that the successful revolt of one French army would have a great effect, particularly in this part of the world; and would probably do more for Spain than Spain would ever do for itself. In case there should be an opportunity, I should not wait for a revolt, but shall try my own means of subduing Soult. If this army should revolt, or, indeed, at all events, I anxiously recommend to you to set all your emissaries to work in France. I have no doubt of the detestation of Buonaparte by the people of that country. There is a very clever fellow in communication with Mr. ——, who ought to be useful to you.

I shall be much obliged to you if you will get all the officers gazetted, who have been recommended for promotion, as serving in the Portuguese army. I shall set out for the army to-morrow morning.

To Lieut. Gen. Sherbrooke.   Lisbon, 27th April, 1809.

I have received your letter of the 25th, and I assure you that I derive great satisfaction from the renewal of our old connection and friendship; and that I am convinced I shall derive the greatest advantage from your advice and assistance.

It is my intention to advance forthwith upon Soult; accordingly, I request you, as soon as you shall receive this letter, to send an officer of the Q. M. G.'s department to Coimbra, to arrange the quarters there for the whole of the British army with you, including the 16th light dragoons, which are ordered forward, excepting Major Gen. Mackenzie's brigade, which you will find otherwise disposed of in this letter. The officer will arrange at Coimbra for the reception not only of the British troops, but of about 6000 Portuguese troops, including 350 Portuguese cavalry.

You will then commence your march on the 29th as follows : * Gen. Hill's corps, with the cavalry under Gen. Cotton, to Condeixa; Guards, and Stewart's brigade, German light dragoons, and one brigade of artillery, from Leiria to Pombal; the troops at Alcobaça to Leiria; and the troops at Caldas to Alcobaça.

On the 30th, Gen. Hill's corps, and Gen. Cotton's cavalry to Coimbra; Guards, Stewart's brigade, cavalry, and artillery, to Condeixa; Tilson's and Campbell's brigades of infantry, and one brigade of artillery, to Pombal; Gen. Murray's and Gen. Sontag's brigades to halt at Leiria; Gen. Cameron's brigade from Alcobaça to Leiria.

---

* Sir A. Wellesley, on joining the army, issued his instructions to the Q. M. G. for the movement of the troops, which the Q. M. G. circulated through the officers of his department to the officers commanding divisions, brigades, &c. Some of these instructions previous to important offensive movements and battles will be given.

On the 1st May, Guards, &c , cavalry and artillery, to Coimbra; Tilson's and Campbell's brigades and artillery from Pombal to Condeixa; Gen. Murray's and Gen. Sontag's brigades and artillery from Leiria to Pombal; Gen. Cameron's halt at Leiria.

On the 2nd May, Tilson's and Campbell's brigade and artillery to Coimbra; Gen. Murray's and Sontag's brigades and artillery from Pombal to Condeixa; Gen. Cameron's brigade from Leiria to Pombal.

On the 3rd May, Gen. Murray's and Sontag's brigades and artillery to Coimbra; Gen. Cameron's from Pombal to Condeixa.

On the 4th May, Gen. Cameron's brigade to Coimbra.

Gen. Mackenzie's brigade, and a brigade of 6 pounders, to march on the 29th to Ourem, where he will halt till he shall find that the Portuguese troops have passed on their march from Thomar to Coimbra. He will then march to Thomar. He shall receive further instructions from me for his guidance.

Since writing the above, I have received your letter of the 26th. I have ordered the 16th light dragoons to move to Leiria, having taken measures for supplying them with forage at Rio Maior, and having directed the Commanding officer to carry on 3 days' forage upon the backs of his horses. When they shall arrive at Leiria, I request you to order them on with any one of the divisions of infantry, and you will then reduce that division by one brigade, and add that brigade to Gen. Cameron's, which will move up the last. Gen. Cameron, having arrived at Alcobaça, need not make any alteration in this arrangement. He may march on the 29th from Alcobaça to Leiria, halt there on the 30th and 1st May, and move on the 2nd according to the arrangement.

I propose to leave this place to-morrow, and shall be at Leiria by the 29th, if possible, or at latest on the 30th, and I shall then go on to Coimbra. An Assistant Commissary must attend Gen. Mackenzie to Ourem, and he should take with him, if possible, 3 days' provisions. The troops marching forwards should also take with them 3 days' provisions, if possible; and, if that cannot be done, measures should be adopted, either to send that quantity after them, or to receive it on the road from Coimbra. A Commissary should likewise be sent to Coimbra, to prepare for the reception of the troops.

To the Junta of Spanish Estremadura.   Lisbon, 28th April, 1809.

I have had the honor to receive the representation which you addressed to me yesterday, and I assure you that I am not insensible to the dangers which threaten the southern provinces of Spain and the Kingdom of Portugal. With every disposition to meet and avert those dangers, I am concerned that I have it not in my power to do all that I wish; and, particularly as the security of the Kingdom of Portugal being the principal object entrusted to me, I cannot divert from it the forces which are necessary for the accomplishment of all the other objects which you have recommended to my attention.

You must be aware that the forces of this Kingdom are but in their infancy in respect to organisation, discipline, and equipment; and it is not with troops in this state that any reasonable expectation can be formed of success against the veteran and disciplined troops of France, notwithstanding that I have every confidence in the valor, the zeal, and the loyalty of the troops of Portugal. The safety of Portugal must therefore depend upon the exertions of the troops of His Majesty; and I cannot venture to employ their services out of this Kingdom, although ultimately for its advantage and safety as well as for the general advantage, till the enemy who has invaded Portugal shall have been removed.

There are some points, however, of your paper to which it is in my power to give immediate attention.

1st. A corps has been ordered to take the field from the garrison of Elvas, and to act, as an army of observation, in co-operation with a similar corps from the garrison of Badajoz.

2nd. The corps under the command of Sir R. Wilson is no longer in the neighbourhood of Alcantara, but has crossed the Mondego, and has approached the Douro. I doubt whether the corps under the command of Col. Le Cor is sufficiently strong to occupy Alcantara, but I shall inquire if it should be so ; and I shall be happy to have it in my power to comply with your wishes in this respect.

3rd. Upon this last point I must refer you to the commencement of this letter. I wish, and I hope soon to have, an opportunity of concerting operations with Gen. Cuesta, and it will give me pleasure if they should be satisfactory to the Junta of Estremadura.

To J. P. Boys, Esq., Dep. Paymaster Gen.   Lisbon, 28th April, 1809.

In order to obviate every inconvenience that might arise from the want of proper authority for granting warrants, for the regular payment of the subsistence for the troops who are, or may be hereafter stationed, at Lisbon, I have judged it expedient to authorise Lieut. Col. Walsh, of the 9th foot and Town Major of Lisbon, to grant warrants on Mr. Hunter, who will remain as Dep. Paymaster Gen. at Lisbon. You will therefore be pleased to direct him to pay all such warrants as may be regularly transmitted from Lieut. Col. Walsh, with the estimate which will accompany them, for the subsistence only of such corps or detachments as may require it. You will be pleased to take especial care that His Majesty's regulations are in all respects strictly observed.

To Lieut. Col. Walsh, Town Major of Lisbon.   Lisbon, 28th April, 1809.

As great inconvenience and delay to the service would arise to the troops stationed at Lisbon, and such as may hereafter arrive, unless some officer on the spot is duly authorised to issue warrants to the Dep. Paymaster Gen., who will be stationed at Lisbon, for the purpose of providing for their subsistence, I do hereby empower and authorise you to grant warrants for the subsistence of the troops, only upon the proper estimates being laid before you, strictly conforming to His Majesty's regulations upon this subject; and you will be pleased to cause the same to be duly examined, and keep a regular account of the number of warrants so issued, together with the amounts of each, in order that the same may be submitted to me from time to time, as opportunities may offer.

To Visct. Castlereagh.   Villa Franca, 29th April, 1809.

I write in the chance that this letter may still find the packet at Lisbon, to inform you that I have received a very bad report indeed of the state of the artillery horses lately arrived from England with the heavy dragoons, being very old, diseased, and out of condition. I shall receive it officially probably in a day or two, when I shall transmit it to England. In the mean time, I think it proper to acquaint you with the state of these horses, and to recommend that for that reason, as well as because it would be very desirable to attach a troop of horse artillery to so very large a body of cavalry as we shall have, that a troop of horse artillery should be sent out.

To the Rt. Hon. J. H. Frere.   Villa Franca, 29th April, 1809.

I received yesterday your letter of the 21st inst., together with one from Gen. Cuesta, and one from Don Martin de Garay. I send you a copy of the answer which I have written to the former, and my answer to the latter. According to my instructions, I think that I ought not to have any communication with the Spanish government excepting through you ; and if you should be of the same opinion, I request you to tell Don Martin that I can communicate with him only through you, and acquaint him with my sentiments as contained in the enclosed letter.

I hope that the Spaniards will adhere to their determination of acting upon the defensive, till I shall return to the eastward. They should reinforce Cuesta as much as possible. He has only 19,000 infantry and 1,500 cavalry, as he tells me in his letter of the 23d.

It will also be very desirable that Cuesta should observe the motions of the French if they should enter Alentejo, and follow them, if their object should be to invade Portugal, which, however, is very improbable. At all events, if they should invade Portugal, we shall not be without a force upon the Tagus, and in the passes in the mountains between Alcantara and Abrantes.

I recommend that Cuesta should observe Victor's movements in Alentejo, because it is not impossible that he might enter that province with a view to an invasion of Andalusia. It is very improbable, however, that in the present state of the French force in Spain, he will move at all, till he shall have heard of Soult.

P.S. In respect to the 40th regt., I certainly must have it ; but in the state in which affairs are at present I think it best that it should remain at Seville till I shall be able to fix upon a safe route for it.

To Don Gregorio Cuesta.   Villa Franca, 29th April, 1809.

I had the honor of receiving yesterday your Excellency's letter of the 23rd April, and I assure your Excellency that it will give me great satisfaction to co-operate with your Excellency, as far as it may be in my power, to defeat those forces of the enemy which threaten the cities of Seville and Lisbon.

Your Excellency must be aware of the state of the Portuguese army ; a commencement has only lately been made to organise and discipline it : and although I have the utmost reliance on the valor, the zeal, and the loyalty of the troops of Portugal, I cannot at this moment consider them in such a state of discipline as to confide to their exertions the safety of Portugal, especially committed to my care, against the further attempts which may be made upon it by the disciplined troops of France, which have already invaded, and are in possession of, an important part of this kingdom. Under these circumstances, my attention has necessarily been directed, in the first instance, to remove from Portugal the further evils with which both Spain and Portugal are threatened by Marshal Soult; and the greatest part of the army under my command is now on its march for that purpose. A small detachment of British troops, with one of Portuguese troops, will remain upon the Tagus, to watch the movements of the enemy, and to guard the passages of that river, in case the enemy should direct his attack upon this country.

If I should succeed in removing Marshal Soult from the north of Portugal, I intend to go forthwith with all the troops under my command (consisting of about 25,000, of which nearly 4000 will at that time be cavalry), to the Eastern frontier of Portugal, in the neighbourhood of Elvas; and I shall be happy to co-operate with you in any plan which may be agreed upon for the attack of Marshal Victor. In the mean time, a detachment of the garrison of Elvas has been directed to take the field, in co-operation with a similar detachment of the garrison of Badajoz, to act as a corps of observation in that quarter; but I cannot avoid taking this opportunity of recommending that this corps should not be exposed to the attack of the enemy, or to be cut off from the garrisons to which the parts of it respectively belong.

In the present situation of affairs, all that we can require is time; and that we should not lose our men, or any of the valuable positions which we still possess. In a short time we shall all be enabled to co-operate in a vigorous attack upon the enemy; and till that period shall arrive, it is not very material whether he acquires a little more of the open country, provided we do not lose any of the men who are destined to defend the valuable points and positions which remain in our hands.

Your Excellency is mistaken respecting the position of Sir R. Wilson's corps. He has been removed to the neighbourhood of the Douro, to confine himself to that quarter. I consider the position of Alcantara, however, to be so important at this moment, in respect both to the defence of Portugal and to our future designs upon Marshal Victor, that I shall give directions that it should be occupied by a Portuguese corps, if it should be possible to form one fit for that purpose. I shall be obliged to your Excellency, if you will give directions that any Portuguese or British corps, which may go to Alcantara, may be received there.

I have written to your Excellency a long letter in English, understanding that you have under your command officers in your confidence who can explain it to you, in which I have taken the liberty of giving my opinions with great freedom. I hope that your Excellency will receive them, as they are intended, as a mark of my sincere desire to be of use to you, as far as is in my power at present; which I hope and believe, from the situation of the enemy, I shall have still better opportunities of proving to you before much time shall elapse.

To Don Martin de Garay.   Villa Franca, 29th April, 1809.

I have had the honor of receiving your Excellency's letter of the 21st inst., and I am happy to find that the plan of operations which I had adopted for the troops under my command, immediately upon my arrival in this country, and upon which they have already marched, viz., to remove Marshal Soult from the north of Portugal, is approved of by the Supreme Junta. As soon as that operation shall be performed, it is my intention to collect the whole of the army under my command on the Eastern frontier of Portugal, and to co-operate by every means in my power with Gen. Cuesta in an attack upon Marshal Victor. In the mean time, I cannot sufficiently recommend a strict defensive position in all quarters. In the present situation of affairs, we have every reason to hope that in a short time we shall all be able to co-operate in a vigorous attack upon the only remaining force of the enemy; in which attack we have every reasonable prospect of success, if we do not lose any of the valuable positions which we still possess, or the men who defend them, in fruitless attacks of the enemy in the plains.

It cannot be a matter of much importance whether they possess, for a short time longer, more or less of the plains of La Mancha, provided the Spanish troops do not incur the risk of sustaining a fresh defeat by the superior cavalry of the enemy, and, by diminishing the strength and efficiency of the corps destined to defend the passes of the Sierra Morena, risk the loss of those important positions, and of all that remains that is valuable. I do not conceive that the enemy are now in a situation to undertake anything of importance, particularly till they hear of Marshal Soult; and if this be true, there is every prospect of ultimate success, if we should wait till all can join in the attack of Marshal Victor.

To the Rt. Hon. J. Villiers.   Villa Franca, 29th April, 1809.

I was in hopes that I should have seen you yesterday, but I was so much occupied, that I could not go to you, and I was not able to leave town till 3 o'clock: I shall be at Rio Maior this day.

I received yesterday a letter from Mr. Frere, of which I wished to communicate to you the enclosures, but I now send you copies of them. It is evident to me that the French, without the co-operation of Soult, are unequal to any attempt, so that I shall have time for everything; and it is likewise obvious that, for once, we are all agreed upon the general plan of our operations.

I likewise enclose to you letters from Cuesta, and from the Spanish minister, Don M. de Garay, to me, which I beg of you to return to me, and my answers, which I request of you to have copied, and send me the copies. I have sent my answer to Mr. Frere, because I think I ought not to have any communication with the Spanish minister, excepting through him. I likewise send you a letter from Edward Paget, who is expected.

In my hurry yesterday I forgot to speak to Bandeira respecting Mrs. Canning's orange trees; and I shall be much obliged to you if you will get them and send them to her.

To Lieut. Gen. Sherbrooke.   Leiria, 30th April, 1809.

I have just received your letter of the 30th: that by the returning dragoon on the mule did not reach me.

I am afraid I shall be obliged to stop here to-morrow, in order to give a little rest to my horses, which are not very well able to get on after being so long at sea : however, I shall get on if I can.

I wish the troops, &c. to live, while at Coimbra, on what that place can afford; as I wish to collect there all that the Commissary can bring forward.

I enclose a memorandum for an officer of the Q. M. G.'s department, whom I beg you will send as soon as possible to Figueira, at the mouth of the Mondego.

To Major Gen. Mackenzie.*   Leiria, 30th April, 1809.

I wish you to remain at Ourem till the 3rd May, as 2 squadrons of the 16th light dragoons will march into that town on the 2d; and I am afraid that you will experience inconvenience if you go there before they shall have passed through.   Your corps is destined to watch the movements of Marshal Victor, and to guard the passes into Portugal, while I shall be employed to the northward.

I have not yet had time to write your instructions, but I hope to be able to send them to you to-morrow or the day following.

To Major Gen. Mackenzie.   Leiria, 1st May, 1809.

The corps of troops placed under your command is destined to watch the movements of the enemy on the Eastern frontier of Portugal, and to guard the passes into this country on the right of the Tagus, during the period that the main body of the British army under my command will be employed on the Douro.   It will consist, besides the brigade of infantry and the artillery which marched from hence with you, of the 2d. batt. 24th regt., now on its march from Lisbon to Santarem; and of the 3d dragoon guards and 4th dragoons, lately arrived from England; and which corps will begin their march to Santarem and Golegao to-morrow.

Besides these troops, those enumerated hereafter have been placed under your orders by Field Marshal Beresford:

One batt. 1st regt.
One .. 3d ..
Two .. 4th ..
Two .. 13th ..
One .. 15th ..
3 squadrons of cavalry at Golegão.
2 squadrons of cavalry at Abrantes.
3 regts. of Militia at Abrantes.
3 regts. of Caçadores † at Abrantes and Villa Velha, under Col. Le Cor.
800 Yagers.
350 men collected from the late garrison of Oporto.

The enemy are collected on the Guadiana, with their head quarters at Merida, and their numbers are stated to be about 30,000 men.   They have in their front a Spanish army, with Gen. Cuesta, at Llerena, which

---

* Afterwards killed at Talavera.   † Light troops, 'chasseurs.'

army was defeated in the month of March, and has since been reinforced to the amount of 20,000 men. As the enemy did not pursue their advantage upon that occasion, and, from the contents of several intercepted letters, I judge that they do not consider themselves sufficiently strong to venture to penetrate into the province of Andalusia, till they can have the co-operation of Marshal Soult; on the other hand, I doubt whether they are sufficiently strong to make a detachment into Portugal, in order to try to communicate with Soult. By this measure they will expose themselves to be attacked, and will be attacked by Cuesta, who is receiving reinforcements. However, the object of the corps placed under your command is to guard against this possible, though not very probable, attempt; and I now proceed to communicate to you my notions of the probable line of attack of the enemy, and to suggest to you the different points of your defensive line.

If the enemy should invade Portugal, it will be either between the Tagus and the Guadiana, or north of the Tagus by Alcantara, or by both lines of attack. If he should make his attack between the Tagus and the Guadiana, he may endeavor to cross the Tagus at Villa Velha, at Abrantes, at Santarem, or even lower down, at Salvaterra. I understand that the river will not be fordable anywhere for a month, and therefore the enemy must intend to seize the boats in the river, if he should now make his attack by this supposed line. The civil government will be required to give directions, that, upon the first alarm, its officers may exert themselves to collect the boats, particularly on that part of the river below Abrantes; and you will do every thing in your power to assist them.

If they should succeed in crossing the river above Punhete, you will defend, as long as may be in your power, the positions on the Zezere. If you should find that they attempt the passage lower down, and are likely to succeed in effecting it, particularly in the neighbourhood of Salvaterra, you will leave the upper parts of the Tagus, and the positions on the Zezere, to be defended by the Portuguese light troops and militia; and you will take care to keep yourself, with the British troops, in such a position, in respect to the enemy, as that you shall have your communication open with Lisbon. If you should be under the necessity of retiring, you will do it gradually, defending every position that can be defended, particularly Villa Franca and Bucellas, Lumiar and Sacavem, &c. &c.; and you will adopt every measure in your power to gain time for me to come to your assistance.

If the enemy should direct his attack solely by the line of Alcantara, it will be necessary that you should carry your whole force into the mountains between Castello Branco and Abrantes, where I understand Col. Le Cor now is with his caçadores and yagers. You will find the positions in those mountains very strong; but they are turned by the new road from Capinho, near Covilhao, to Cardigos; and, if the enemy should take that road, you must defend the Zezere, as before pointed out.

In the view of rendering it more difficult for the enemy to make his attack north of the Tagus, I have requested Marshal Beresford to make arrangements for occupying Alcantara with a garrison; by which measure, as long as the river shall continue full, the enemy will be obliged to go

round by the bridge of Almaraz, and give you more time for your defensive arrangements. As Alcantara is not a very good post, you will
take care that the garrison is withdrawn, as soon as it shall have answered
the purpose of obliging the enemy to look for another passage.

From the circumstances which I have above mentioned respecting the
state of the enemy's force, it is not probable that they will attack by both
of the lines which are open to them. If they should, you will oppose them
in the mountains by the caçadores, yagers, and the militia, and keep your
regular troops on the right for the defence of the Tagus, in the first
instance, of the Zezere, and eventually to cover Lisbon.

I understand from Marshal Beresford that an officer of engineers is
employed in the construction of works to defend the passage of the Tagus
at Abrantes. You will urge the completion of those works; and you will
be so kind as to have the Tagus examined, with a view to discover in what
places it is likely to be fordable in the dry season, particularly between
Punhete and Salvaterra; and you will have works constructed for the
defence of the passage, in the first instance, at those places to which any
principal road leads on the other side. You will direct your Commissary
to correspond with the Dep. Commissary Gen. at Lisbon respecting supplies of provisions, if the country should not be able to afford you supplies
in sufficient quantities. As you will have your communication open by the
river, you cannot be in want. There is a depôt of military stores at Santarem, from which you will draw such supplies of that description as you
may require.

The persons employed at Badajoz and Elvas, and elsewhere on the
frontier, to give intelligence of the enemy's movements, will be directed
to correspond with you; and I shall have persons placed on the road
between your head quarters and me, for the purpose of keeping up a constant communication between us.

Besides the defence of the points referred to, it is very desirable that,
till their service should be otherwise called for, the assistance of our troops
should be given to discipline the Portuguese regular regiments. I request you to quarter the Portuguese regiments and the British regiments
as much as possible together; and urge the Commanding officers of the
latter to aid the former, as much as may be in their power, in training
and disciplining their soldiers. I need not point out the advantage which
must result from this mode of employing the leisure which it is probable
the troops will have, particularly to your corps, if the army should be
employed to the northward till the Tagus may become fordable.

P. S. In the enumeration of Portuguese troops which will be placed
under your command, I have omitted to mention 3 brigades of artillery at
Santarem. In case you should want any heavy ordnance for the batteries
on the Tagus, you will write to Mr. Villiers for it, and it will be sent up
the Tagus.

To the Rt. Hon. J. Villiers.   Pombal, 1st May, 1809.

I arrived here this day, and shall be at Coimbra to-morrow. I have
written Gen. Mackenzie's instructions, of which I shall send you a copy.
In the mean time it is very desirable that some arrangements should be

made to secure the boats upon the Tagus, as far down as Salvaterra, upon the first alarm of invasion. This can be effected only by means of the civil authorities of the country, and I shall be much obliged to you if you will concert measures with the government for that purpose.

Gen. Mackenzie may require heavy ordnance for the batteries which he will have constructed upon the Tagus; and I have desired him to write to you if he should require any, and I shall be obliged to you if you will apply to the government for what he may require. There is a report in the country that the French had forced the passage of the Tamaga on the 27th. I know Silveira still held his ground on the 26th.

To Major Gen. Mackenzie.   Coimbra, 2d May, 1809.

In explanation of that part of my instructions relative to the collecting of the boats on the Tagus, on the approach of the enemy, I beg it may be understood that the boats must be either destroyed or carried down the river below Salvaterra, where the river is broad enough to place them out of the reach of musketry from the opposite bank; and also to take the precaution of placing a guard over them.

To the Rt. Hon. J. Villiers.   Coimbra, 2d May, 1809.

I received your letter of the 30th April last night; and I now enclose you the copy of my instructions to Major Gen. Mackenzie, in which you will see that the point of attack by Salvaterra has been considered and means of defence suggested, and that all the measures ordered in those instructions have in view the ultimate defence of Lisbon itself, if Portugal should be invaded by a part of Victor's corps, during my absence to the northward. I should not be at all surprised if a small corps were pushed in; but nothing but a large one will answer to oblige Gen. Mackenzie to retire. If the government look well after the boats, the whole of Victor's army would not be able, at present, or I believe for a month to come, to cross the Tagus.

A garrison has been ordered into Alcantara. I agree with you about the 40th; and I enclose a letter for Mr. Frere, which I beg you to peruse and forward. I shall write to the Admiral respecting transports for this corps.

I understand that the corps which came from the neighbourhood of Caceres consisted of cavalry only, and returned to Merida. It is not impossible, however, that Victor, if obliged to remain on the defensive till he shall hear of Soult, will send a corps into Portugal to get intelligence of him; but no corps will make any impression by the Tagus at this season of the year, if the government will look well after the boats on that river; and a small corps will make no impression in an attack by Alcantara, supposing that they should anticipate us in the possession of that place. We mean to fortify all the fords on the river at and above Salvaterra; and you will observe the directions which I have given to Mackenzie on the subject; but we must have a little time.

I am obliged to you for your offer to procure me assistance to copy my dispatches; but I have plenty of that description. The fact is, that, excepting upon very important occasions, I write my dispatches without making a draft, and those which I sent to you were so written before I set out in the morning, and I had not time to get them copied before they were sent, which is the reason why I asked you to return me copies of them.

To Vice Adm. the Hon. G. Berkeley.   Coimbra, 2d May, 1809.

I received your letter of the 30th last night, and accept with pleasure your offer to send to Puerto de Sta Maria transports to convey the 40th regt. to Lisbon. I have written to Col. Kemmis orders to march to Puerto de Sta Maria; and I shall be very much obliged to you if, with the infantry transports, you will send also transports to convey round 100 horses and mules, in order that the regiment may be enabled to march immediately upon its arrival at Lisbon.

I am much obliged to you for the information which you send me of our convoy. I hope it will soon arrive, as it is much wanted. We have had very bad weather, yet I arrived here this day, and the troops will all be here by the 4th.

I give no credit to the report of the defeat of the French: they may have been ill treated in a skirmish of the advanced guards, but I doubt whether the main body on either side is inclined to fight. I understand that the French corps which had appeared at Caceres has returned to Merida.

To the Rt. Hon. J. H. Frere.   Coimbra, 2d May, 1809.

I arrived here this day, and the army will be collected in this town and neighbourhood on the day after to-morrow.

In making my arrangements for the defence of the Tagus, and of the frontiers on the north bank of that river, to be occupied by my detachments during my absence, I find that I shall be very bare of troops without the 40th regt.; and I shall feel still greater inconvenience from the want of them, when I shall return from the expedition to the northward, and shall move to the frontiers of Spain; as at that time I shall be obliged to send 2 battalions to Gibraltar, and detachments equal in strength to 2 more to England, according to the instructions which I have received, which must be obeyed as soon as the enemy shall have retired from Portugal. I am anxious, therefore, that the 40th regt. should be sent to me as soon as possible, more particularly as they can be of no use at Seville; and I avail myself of the offer of the Admiral to send transports to Puerto de Sta Maria to bring them to Lisbon. I shall be obliged to you to send to Col. Kemmis the enclosed orders to march to Puerto de Sta Maria, there to embark for Lisbon, and if you will ask the Spanish government to afford every facility for the march of the regiment under his command.

I have no news from this quarter. I understand that Soult has moved the greatest part of his force towards the Tamaga, I suppose with an intention of retreating through Tras os Montes into Spain.

To Col. Kemmis, 40th regt.   Coimbra, 2d May, 1809.

I beg that, as soon as it may be convenient after you shall have received this order, you will march with the regiment under your command, from

Seville to Puerto de Sta Maria, by such route as may be settled for you by the government of Spain; and you will there embark in transports which will have been sent round for the regiment, and will proceed to Lisbon, where you will receive further orders.

As it might be inconvenient to the officers of the regiment to part with the horses and mules which they may have, and as they would be unable to take the field immediately upon their arrival at Lisbon, if they should part with them, I have requested the Admiral to send to Puerto de Sta Maria transports to convey the horses and mules, as well as the regiment.

Memorandum of an arrangement for the Commissariat.   Coimbra, 2d May, 1809.

1. There shall be attached to each brigade of infantry, to each regiment of cavalry, to the artillery, and to head quarters, an Assist. Commissary, with a sufficient number of clerks, interpreters, &c.

2. The troops shall march from Coimbra, with 3 days' bread on their backs: the cavalry and artillery with 3 days' forage.

3. The Assist. Commissaries with brigades, regiments, &c., to have cattle tor their brigades and regiments for three days.

4. The Assist. Commissaries with brigades and regiments should likewise have with them bread for their brigades and regiments for 3 days.

5. This bread must eventually be carried on mules; but till mules can be provided to carry the whole, the mules now with the Commissariat should be divided among the brigades and Commissaries to carry a portion of the bread, and waggons to carry the remainder.

6. The Assist. Commissaries and others attached to brigades will, on their route through the country, do everything in their power to procure supplies. If they cannot procure them in time for the use of the brigades or regiments, to which they will be attached, they will order them to be prepared for the succeeding troops on the march, or they will order them to the next depot to be formed; and they will invariably report to the succeeding Commissary, and as soon as possible to the Commissary Gen., the success which they have had in procuring supplies.

7. All requisitions on the country must be made by the officers of the troops on the Assist. Commissaries, who will report these requisitions to the Commissary Gen. as soon as made.

Memorandum for the Commissary General on the expedition into the North of Portugal.
Coimbra, 2d May, 1809.

1. The troops will march in two principal columns, the right composed of about 6000 infantry and 1000 cavalry, by the route of Vizeu to Lamego; the left of about 20,000 infantry and 1400 cavalry, by the route of Vouga towards Oporto.

2. A depot for 6 days for 30,000 men, and 5000 horses, should be formed at Coimbra. This should be carried forward by the waggons of Coimbra, in its due proportions, to Vizeu and Vouga respectively; which waggons should commence their march 2 days after the troops shall have set out. These waggons should return as soon as they shall have performed this service, and fresh waggons procured at Vizeu and Vouga to carry on the supplies.

3. A Commissary to be sent to Vizeu to collect supplies for the column proceeding by that route. This column should set out from Vizeu with the same quantity of provisions as it has on setting out from Coimbra.

4. On the arrival of the troops at Vizeu, a Commissary to be sent forward to make arrangements for supplying the troops at Lamego on their arrival there.

5. On the —, a Commissary to be sent to Aveiro to prepare supplies of bread, forage, &c., for the troops at that place. This bread, &c., will be embarked at Aveiro, and carried by boats to Ovar, from whence the troops and brigade Commissaries should start with the same supply as from Coimbra. A depôt should be formed at Ovar, and kept up for the troops advancing on that line for 5 days, by which the troops should be supplied by carts hired at Ovar and in the neighbourhood, in their advance to and till their arrival at Oporto.

To the Rt. Hon. J. Villiers.   Coimbra, 3d May, 1809.

I am very much obliged to you for your letter of the 1st.

I shall send in a flag of truce to Soult, on the subject of the exchange of the British officers who are his prisoners, as soon as I shall be prepared to let him know in another manner that we are here.

I know nothing more that bears upon the subject on which Bayley is gone to England, excepting the greatest civility from the French officer at the outposts to Col. Trant, lately, when he had a communication with them by a flag of truce. One of the officers whom he saw was mentioned by my friend as being of his party. I do not understand from any intelligence that I have seen that any corps is coming to Alcantara. The movement from Truxillo, mentioned by Capt. Mayne, is of heavy cannon,

---

G. O.   Coimbra, 3d May, 1809.

1. Returns to be sent, by the General officers, and other individuals, entitled to bât men, and by the Commanding officers of corps, stating the number of natives of Portugal that have been hired, to serve in lieu of bât men, given by each corps, and of the names of the several officers in whose service they are employed.

2. Upon all occasions, when the army will march, it will be in one or more columns, on one or different roads, with a view to take up a position, or by separate battalions, brigades, or larger divisions, with a view to occupy certain cantonments. In the first case, the reserve artillery and stores, drawn, or carried by horses or mules, are to follow the troops; then the baggage of regiments, and individuals of each column, is to follow, arranged in the order in which the corps or individual will stand in the column; and lastly, the artillery and commissariat stores on carts, drawn by bullocks.

3. In the other cases, when battalions or larger divisions are to take up cantonments, the baggage of each division, going to a separate cantonment, is to follow that division, and is to be arranged in the order in which each corps or individual will stand in the order of march of the division to which he may belong.

4. On all occasions, the leaders of columns, whether composed of the whole army, or of smaller divisions, will halt, once in every hour and a half, for 5 minutes, to allow the men to fall out; and Commanding officers of companies will be held responsible if any man falls out of the ranks at any time during the march, excepting during these halts, or is absent from his company, at the end of it, upon any occasion, excepting sick and consequent inability to keep up.

5. If any man should be taken ill on a march, measures are to be taken for the care of him, according to the mode heretofore pointed out in the G. O., particularly paragraph No. 11, of the G. O. 24th April; and the Commanding officer of his company will send a non-commissioned officer with him to the nearest magistrate as therein pointed out.

6. When circumstances will oblige battalions, in rear of any column, to halt, the head of such column must not be halted without the special orders of the officer commanding the column, who will judge of the necessity of halting, according to the length of the
interval

to Merida, which, whatever may be the enemy's intention, cannot be destined for the invasion of Portugal by Alcantara. If, indeed, we occupied Alcantara, the heavy cannon might be intended to deprive us of that point; but the French are well aware that we do not occupy Alcantara, as Lapisse passed through that place very lately with his division.

I have not heard of any movement on the frontier, excepting that of the cavalry to Caceres, adverted to in my letter of yesterday.

You will have seen that I had alluded to the necessity of intelligence of the enemy's movements for Gen. Mackenzie, upon which subject, as well as others, I propose to make arrangements with Beresford as soon as he shall arrive. It would be well, however, if you could correspond with Gen. Mackenzie, and find out where he will have his head quarters from time to time, and ask Forjaz to desire his friends upon the frontier to write to Mackenzie. The latter, however, should receive this intelligence, and provide for his own security. Beresford will be here to-night.

To Lieut. Col. Trant.   Coimbra, 3d May, 1809.

I received in the night your letter of 8 P.M., and this morning that of 9½ P.M. In respect to the first, I have only to request that you will keep your position till I shall be in readiness, not only to move to you, but to push on to Oporto. In respect to the second, I beg you to convey the enclosed letter in any way you can to the Captain of the *Nautilus*.

As we shall have some troops at Mealhada, on the road to Vouga, to-morrow, on their march towards Vizeu; and as it is desirable your friends should not see more of our troops than is absolutely necessary, and should know nothing of our operations, I request you to bring or send

---

interval which will thereby be occasioned in his column, the necessity there is that the column should be well closed up, and the probability that from the nature of the impediments of the road, the head of the column will soon be halted, and give time to the rear to close up.

7. Two Assistant Provosts, in addition to those already appointed, are to be appointed; and Commanding officers of regiments and brigades will recommend such non-commissioned officers as they may think trust-worthy and capable of performing the duties which will be required from them; they will receive Ensign's pay and allowances.

8. Depôts are to be established at the following places, upon which subject the Commissary Gen. will receive directions, viz.:

Rio Maior, Leiria, Coimbra. An officer and 20 men of the 80th regt. are to be stationed at Rio Maior, and conduct the details of the duties there; the senior officer, in charge of the sick and convalescents at Leiria, is to conduct them at Leiria; and an officer will be established at Coimbra, for the same purpose.

9. These officers will correspond constantly with each other, and with the Q. M. G. of the army and Town Major at Lisbon.

10. Whenever stores or provisions are dispatched from Lisbon, the Q. M. G. is to be informed thereof, of the number of waggons or other means of conveyance on which they are laden, and of the route which they are directed to take, specifying by what stages. The Town Major is likewise to give notice of this dispatch to the officer at Rio Maior; this officer is to relieve the escort, and send it back to Lisbon, and is to report the arrival and the probable departure of the convoy to the Q. M. G. and the officer commanding at the next station; the officers stationed at Leiria and Coimbra are to do the same respectively.

11. Non-commissioned officers in charge of convoys will be held responsible for the conduct of the soldiers under their command on the march with convoys, and returning to their cantonments.

18. General Orders will be issued, at the Adj. Gen.'s office, at 10 o'clock precisely, every morning. The officers in the department and Majors of Brigade to be responsible that the Adjutants have them by 12.

them word to Martede, 3 leagues from hence on the road to Aveiro, and let me know at what hour they will be there.

To Lieut. Col. Trant.   Coimbra, 3d May, 1809.

I have just now received your letter of this day.   Lieut. Col. Douglas is gone to Aveiro to reconnaitre the road for me ; and I have sent the party of dragoons to join him, and I have desired him to take them into the town of Aveiro to-morrow night, for the purpose mentioned by you. If the dragoons should fall in with Col. Douglas, I have desired him to send to you at Agueda, and you need not go over to Aveiro ; but if the dragoons should not find Col. Douglas, and you should not hear from him, it will be necessary that you should go over to Aveiro to-morrow night, to meet them, and to receive the persons expected.   I have accordingly given instructions to the officer of the Staff, who will go with the dragoons to find Col. Douglas or you, and as soon as he shall find either, he will return.

I will meet you and your friends at Fornos, 1 league from hence on the road to Vouga, at the hour you shall name on the 5th.

P. S. Col. Douglas is not yet gone, and he shall take the dragoons; and you may do as you please, either go to Aveiro or not—only send him word.   You will do well to send away the dragoons as soon as you get out at Aveiro.

To Lieut. Gen. the Hon. E. Paget.   Coimbra, 4th May, 1809.

I have assembled the main body of the army at this place, with a view to an operation against Soult, for reasons into which it is unnecessary that I should enter at present, but which I shall detail to you when we meet; and we have a detachment of British and Portuguese troops on the Tagus, to watch Victor's movements, and to guard the passes into Portugal north of that river.   I should wish you to join this corps, and I recommend you to come up by Villa Franca, Rio Maior, Leiria, Pombal, and Coimbra. You will find forage at all these places, but at no others on the road.

If Gen. Fane should be with you, I wish him to join the brigade of heavy dragoons, which I have been obliged to leave with the corps upon the Tagus, on account of the want of forage upon the road to this place; and let Gen. Erskine come up to command the 1st hussars and 23d dragoons, which corps have been ordered into the Mondego, where they will be landed.

I shall put all this in orders as soon as I shall know who is arrived : in the mean time it will be convenient to all parties to know their destination. I hope to march on the 7th.

To the Rt. Hon. J. Villiers.   Coimbra, 4th May, 1809.

In the letter which I wrote to Gen. Paget, and sent to you from Villa Franca, I told him that I wished Gen. Erskine to join the brigade of heavy dragoons on the Tagus, if Gen. Fane was not come out; and I have every reason to be apprehensive that Gen. Fane will have been detained in England to attend Parliament, and I did not advert to Gen. Erskine's seniority to Gen. Mackenzie, over whom it would be inconvenient to place him at the present moment. In case that Paget should not have arrived, I enclose another letter for him, in which I have rectified this mistake; and in that case, I beg you to deliver the enclosed letter, instead of that transmitted to you from Villa Franca, which I will thank you to return to me.

Of course you will not say any thing upon this subject to any body. If Paget should have arrived without Fane, the inconvenience cannot be avoided, and we must make the best of it; and I really believe that I should have every reason to place confidence in Gen. Erskine, if he had been a little longer in Portugal. If you should have given the other letter to Paget, I request you to return the enclosed.

To the Rt. Hon. J. Villiers. Coimbra, 4th May, 1809.

Since I wrote to you yesterday, we have heard that the French had forced the bridge of the Tamaga on the 2d, and that Silveira had retired across the Douro to Lamego. The French also appear to have pushed a detachment across the Douro at Ambos dos Rios. On the other hand, we heard

---

G. O. Coimbra, 4th May, 1809.

1. The army will be brigaded, and stand in line, as follows, until further orders:

CAVALRY.

	14th Light dragoons . .	
	20th	Major Gen. Cotton.
	3d Lt. dragns. K. G. L. .	
	16th	
	Coldstream Guards, 1st batt.	
	3d do. 1st do.	Brig. Gen. H. Campbell.
	1 company 5th batt. 60th regt.	
1st brigade	3d or Buffs	
	66th	Major Gen. Hill.
	48th	
	1 comp. 5th batt. 60th regt.	
3d brigade	5 comps. 5th batt. 60th regt.	
	88th	Major Gen. Tilson.
	1st batt. Portuguese grenads.	
	87th	
5th brigade	7th	
	1st batt. 10th Portuguese regt.	
	53d	Brig. Gen. A. Campbell.
	1 company 5th batt. 60th regt.	
7th brigade	9th	
	2d batt. 10th Portuguese regt.	
	83d	Brig. Gen. Cameron.
	1 company 5th batt. 60th regt.	
6th brigade	1st batt. detachments . .	
	1st do. 16th Portuguese regt.	Brig. Gen. R. Stewart.
	29th	
4th brigade	2d batt. detachments . .	
	2d do. 16th Portuguese regt.	Brig. Gen. Sontag.
	97th	
	1 company 5th batt. 60th regt.	
2d brigade	27th regt.	
	45th	Major Gen. Mackenzie.
	31st	
K. G. L.	Brig. Gen. Langwerth . .	Major Gen. J. Murray.
	——— Drieberg . .	

2. Although this is to be the order of the line of battle, circumstances of ground and situation may render a deviation from it necessary.

3. The light infantry companies belonging to, and the riflemen attached to each brigade of infantry, are to be formed together, on the left of the brigade, under the command of a Field officer

from Oporto, that they are blowing up magazines of gunpowder, which looks like an immediate evacuation.

Since I wrote to you yesterday, I have received intimation that I am to see two persons to-morrow on the business on which Bayley went to England.

I had a conversation with Beresford last night, on a subject on which you spoke to me before I left Lisbon, viz., the settling the person who should have powers to sign for and bind the Portuguese government by his acts, if such a measure should be necessary; and I agree entirely with Beresford, that whether it be he or me, the Portuguese government must be the persons who shall decide. I wish, therefore, that you would arrange this matter with Forjaz; and I acknowledge that I shall not be sorry if they should decide either that I shall not bind them by any act of mine without Beresford's concurrence, or that Beresford alone shall bind them. Lest Forjaz should think that we have any

---

officer or Captain of light infantry of the brigade, to be fixed upon by the officer who commands it. Upon all occasions, in which the brigade may be formed in line, or in column, when the brigade will be formed, for the purpose of opposing an enemy, the light infantry companies and riflemen will be of course in the front, flanks, or rear, according to the circumstances of the ground, and the nature of the operation to be performed. On all other occasions, the light infantry companies are to be considered as attached to their battalions, with which they are to be quartered or encamped, and solely under the command of the Commanding officer of the battalion to which they belong.

4. An Assistant Commissary, with the necessary number of clerks, will be attached to each brigade of infantry, to each regiment of cavalry, to the artillery, and to head-quarters, to whom application must be made for provisions and supplies of all kinds required for the brigade, corps, or department, to which he will be attached. No requisitions must be made upon the country, excepting by the Commissary Gen., or his deputy or assistants, excepting in cases of necessity, in which small bodies of troops may be in upon their march, unattended by a Commissary, which case of necessity must always be clearly made out to the satisfaction of the Commander of the Forces.

5. All requisitions made contrary to this order, will be paid for by the Commissary, and the amount charged to the account of the officer who will have signed it.

6. The officers of the army must have observed the scarcity of all supplies, which our army requires in Portugal; at the same time that the discipline and efficiency of the troops depend upon their regular delivery. The Commander of the Forces trusts, therefore, the General officers of the army, and the Commanding officers of regiments, particularly those who may be detached, will communicate constantly with the officer of the Commissariat department attached to their brigades and regiments, and will advise and assist them as far as may be in their power in their endeavoring to procure supplies for the troops.

8. The pay of the officers who have been transferred to the Portuguese service, must be paid by the Paymaster of the regiment to which they belong, till it will have been notified in the Gazette, or in General Orders, that His Majesty has approved of their promotion.

9. Major Campbell, A. A. G., is appointed to act as Commandant of head quarters until further orders. Major Campbell will regulate all matters concerning the quartering, marches, and police of head quarters. Whenever the head quarters are to move, all persons concerned are to send an officer to the Commandant, for instructions relative to the moving of their baggage, &c., and for which a proper guard will be allotted by the Adj. Gen.

Officers belonging to head quarters will give strict injunctions to their servants in charge of their baggage, to have it ready at the place and time that shall be fixed by the Commandant; and they must be warned that all orders issued by him are to be implicitly obeyed, as he is answerable to the Commander of the Forces for the regular march of the baggage of head quarters, and conduct of those who accompany it.

13. Brigade's sick returns to be sent weekly, on Sunday morning, and monthly, on the 20th of every month, to the head of the Medical department of the army, by the staff surgeons attached to brigades; and in the absence of the staff surgeon, all his duties, as directed in G. O., are to be performed by the senior medical officer, of whatever rank.

notion of another Convention, I do not know whether it would not be advisable that you should state to him the object of our conferences with the person who came to Lisbon. However, that is a point on which your better knowledge of his discretion will enable you to form a more correct judgment than I can.

Beresford's corps marches to-morrow, and mine will move on the 7th, if we should find that Silveira has really retired, of which we have as yet no official accounts.

P. S. We are very much in want of money, and till we can bring our resources to bear, it will be a great convenience if you would give us back half of the sum of money which the Commissary lately advanced to you, and send it up to us as soon as possible.

To Capt. Dench, H.M.S. *Nautilus*.　　　　　　　　Coimbra, 4th May, 1809.

Col. Trant has communicated to me the intelligence you have transmitted to him, for which I am much obliged to you. You will much oblige me also if you will direct all convoys coming down the coast with troops or stores, to put into the Mondego, as I wish to land the troops in that river, with a view to the operations which I am about to carry on to the northward.

To Lieut. Gen. Sir J. Cradock, K.B.　　　　　　　Coimbra, 5th May, 1809.

I enclose copies of letters which I brought from England with me, relative to the relief of 2 regts. at Gibraltar, by 2 battalions from this army, which you will observe it appears to have been intended by the Sec. of State should have been made by sending, in the first instance, from hence the 2 regts. to relieve those coming from Gibraltar. These letters were written before the Sec. of State was aware of the situation of affairs in this country, and knew of the demand and pressure for troops; otherwise, I am convinced that he would have desired that the relief might be commenced by sending to this country from Gibraltar, at least one of the 2 regts.

What I have to request is that, if you should view this matter in the

---

G. O.　　　　　　　　　　　　　　　　Coimbra, 5th May, 1809.

2. Whenever an order is given for the troops to march on the following day, the Commissaries attached to those troops are to issue to them one day's meat, which is to be cooked on that night, for the following day, so that the troops on their arrival at their new ground, having carried their provisions for the day, will be sure to have them.

12. Those horses of the dragoons and artillery, which will eat the corn and forage of the country, are to feed with that description of forage only; the Commanding officers of dragoons and artillery will give directions that all their horses may be accustomed to the corn and forage of the country, by being fed at first, in the proportions of half English and half Portuguese corn and forage; then of two-thirds Portuguese and one-third English; and lastly of the whole Portuguese; the Commissary Gen. will make his issues accordingly, to cavalry and artillery.

13. The Commander of the Forces calls the attention of the General, field, and staff officers, to the foregoing order: it is very desirable that all horses should feed upon the forage of the country; and it is certain, that none will, unless they should by degrees be accustomed to it; he therefore recommends, that all the horses of the army should be fed in the proportions above directed for those of the dragoons and artillery. The Commissary Gen. will be pleased to attend to the requisition of any General, field, or staff officers, who may require a larger proportion of English forage for any particular horse, as far as his stores will allow.

same light I do, you would consent to send to Portugal, on your arrival at Gibraltar, one of the regts., in the room of which a regt. shall be sent from hence on its arrival. If you should consent to this arrangement, I would further request you to ask the Admiral to send forthwith to Gibraltar 1,500 tons of shipping to convey the regt. to Portugal.

To Dom Miguel Pereira Forjaz.*   Coimbra, 5th May, 1809.

I have received the letter which your Excellency has addressed to me, conveying to me the commission of Marshal General of the armies of Portugal, which the Regency, acting in the name of the Prince Regent, have conferred upon me.

I beg that you will do me the favor to present to the Regency my best acknowledgments for the great honor which they have conferred upon me, which I hope I shall merit by the zeal with which I shall endeavor to promote the interests and to provide for the security of the kingdom of Portugal; and I also request that you, Sir, will accept my thanks for the handsome expressions in which you have conveyed to me the pleasure of the Regency.

To W. Huskisson, Esq., Sec. to the Treasury.   Coimbra, 5th May, 1809.

I promised to let you know the state of our money concerns upon my arrival in this country, and I am concerned to have to give you so bad an account of them.

Instead of £400,000, which you and I expected from the accounts that I should have found in Portugal, I have found not quite £100,000, and this sum was in Spanish coins, which could not have been circulated in Portugal, excepting at a considerable loss, and without revealing to the dealers in money at Lisbon the fact of our want of money, which would have raised the expense of drawing bills excessively. I have therefore sent the Spanish gold to Cadiz to be exchanged for dollars; and I am now here with the whole army, about to proceed to the attack of Soult, with only £10,000, and with monstrous demands upon us.

The estimate of the expenses in Portugal amounts to about £200,000 *per mensem* upon a rough estimate. Of this sum, however, a large proportion, £50,000 *per mensem*, is paid by the Dep. Paymaster General, and ought to be drawn for by him on the Paymaster General. Another large proportion, the amount of which I do not know, is paid by the Ambassador, and ought to be drawn for by him; and the remainder of the expense properly defrayed by the Commissary Gen. I have desired this officer to send to the Treasury an accurate estimate of his demands under these three heads, that you may not conceive that, after having provided for the pay of the army, in the Army estimates, and for the subsidy to Portugal, you have besides to provide a sum for the military operations in this country, amounting to £2,500,000 *per annum*.

* One of the ministers of Portugal, through whom the communications and correspondence passed to the Government of the Regency of Portugal. Although in subsequent communications with Mr. Stuart, there are some remarks not complimentary to Dom M. Forjaz, ample justice followed a more intimate acquaintance with his merits, and the Duke of Wellington afterwards found Dom M. Forjaz to be the ablest man in the Peninsula (*see* 11 Oct. 1813).

You may depend upon it that I shall keep the expenses as low as possible. I have already made arrangements for sending home a quantity of transport and victualling tonnage; and as soon as I can look a little more about me, and if I should have some good fortune, I intend to send home the whole. I think, however, from all that I have heard of the possibility of procuring money for bills at Lisbon, at Cadiz, and at Gibraltar, to which last places we have sent, that it will be necessary that you should occasionally send specie here. I recommend that you should send £100,000 in silver to Portugal, as soon as possible after you shall receive this letter; and I will apprise you from time to time of the necessity which may exist for sending more. This advantage will certainly result from sending us money occasionally from England; viz., that of enabling us to command and keep down the expense of drawing bills in all the money markets, which advantage is no small one.

To Marshal Beresford.   Coimbra, 6th May, 1809, 1½ P.M.

I enclose a letter from Douglas: I have besides received a letter from him, stating that he will be this day in the neighbourhood of Mealhada with our friends. I have appointed him to be near Fornos, at half past 6 this evening. I likewise send you some letters from Trant. You have omitted to leave me a statement of the rations of your troops, or an account of the period to which they are victualled. You have also omitted to tell me where the interpreters attached to the brigades are to get horses and mules. I wish much to see Arentschildt.*

Your troops made but a bad figure this morning at the review. The battalions very weak, not more than 300 men; the body of men, particularly of the — regt., very bad; and the officers worse than any thing I have seen.

P.S. Mr. Rawlings has informed me that you have taken away 40 mules which he had got from the magistrates here. We must keep clear of each other in our requisitions, otherwise all will sink. If our Com-

---

* An officer of the Artillery K. G. L. in the Portuguese army.

G. O.   Coimbra, 6th May, 1809.

9. The Portuguese troops attached to the British brigades are to be victualled by the Assist. Commissary of brigades to which they are attached, and are to receive each man, 1½ lb. of bread, or 1 lb. of biscuit, and ½ lb. of meat *per diem*. Cavalry the same as the British cavalry.

11. The Commander of the Forces recommends the companies of the 5th battalion of the 60th regiment, to the particular care and attention of the General officers commanding the brigades of infantry, to which they are attached; they will find them to be most useful, active, and brave troops in the field, and that they will add essentially to the strength of their brigades.

Major Davy will continue to superintend the economy and discipline of the whole battalion, and for this purpose will remain with that part of the army which will be most convenient to him, with a view to that object.

The regimental surgeons of the brigades, about to march, will immediately report the number of sick they intend to leave behind to staff surgeon Morrell, charged with the duty of superintending them. An assistant surgeon from each regiment will remain with the sick, till they are properly given over, and one or more assistant surgeons per brigade, according to the numbers, will remain in Coimbra to take care of them.

Subsistence to the 24th inst. at the rate of 10d. per day, for every man, must also be left in the hands of the Brigade assistant surgeon.

missary is to supply the Portuguese troops when engaged in an operation of this kind, we must have all the supplies the country can afford.

To Major Gen. Mackenzie.   Coimbra, 6th May, 1809.

I have received your letter of the 3d.

You will receive with this letter a copy of all the orders issued to the army; and you will consider as applicable to yourself that order which allows one interpreter to every officer commanding a brigade, to which Portuguese troops are attached, and you will take an interpreter.

Gen. Beresford and the government at Lisbon have Spanish and Portuguese correspondents on the frontier, and there are officers employed to give intelligence to the Commander in Chief, respecting whom the Q. M. G. will write to you, and they are all directed to correspond with you.

I have written to Lisbon to request that there may be a daily post between Abrantes and this place, during the time that I am to the northward, and between this place and the army. In case you should have any thing very important to communicate, send off an *officer, post,* and his expenses shall be paid.

Gen. Beresford informed me that he had settled your relative situation with Gen. Miranda, and, as I understood him, had apprised you of the arrangement he had made.

In case of the approach of an enemy, you are to move the troops as you may think proper, without reference to him; but reporting to him for his information. Before the enemy shall approach, you are to suggest to him to make any movement of which you may be desirous. If he should make any difficulty about moving troops as you may wish, tell him that you make it in compliance with directions from me.

To the Rt. Hon. J. Villiers.   Coimbra, 6th May, 1809.

I enclose for your information a letter which I have received from Lisbon, relating to our communications. What appears to be the best is this: 1st, that there should be a daily post from Coimbra to Lisbon, and, *vice versâ,* through Thomar. 2dly, that there should be a daily post from Abrantes to Thomar, and *vice versâ;* by which means we shall be enabled to correspond, not only with Lisbon, but with Abrantes, Gen. Mackenzie's head quarters, daily. Pray arrange this matter with the government at an early period. My troops move to-morrow.

To Visc. Castlereagh.   Coimbra, 7th May, 1809.

I think it proper to draw your Lordship's attention at this early period to the state of the cavalry horses in Portugal; and I enclose a paper, containing an account of the number deficient at the present moment, and of the number unserviceable in each regiment. The deficiencies in the 3d

G. O.   Coimbra, 7th May, 1809.

4. The Commanding officers of regiments will make reports to the officers commanding brigades, at the moment they find any ammunition, of any man in the regiment they command, damaged or deficient, in order that requisition may be forthwith made to replace it, and that the requisitions may not be made out at a moment a corps is to march.

dragoon guards are stated to have been occasioned by the want of 40 horses to complete it, when that corps was sent from England, and by the loss of a transport, containing 26 horses, run down by one of H.M.'s ships on the passage; those in the 14th light dragoons, by the ordinary casualties of the service, and by glanders caught in the transports in which they came from England. Your Lordship will observe that the 14th light dragoons have cast no horses for 14 months, and they have now 64 horses unserviceable. As it is of the utmost importance to keep up the cavalry to its full numbers, and as no horses can be procured in Portugal, I take the liberty of recommending that a remount for each of the regiments, to the amount stated in the enclosed paper, may be sent from England at an early period.

In case your Lordship should think proper to attend to this recommendation, I further beg leave to recommend that the horses sent may not be those collected at the depôts of the regiments respectively, which I understand are generally too young for immediate service; but horses either drafted or purchased for the purpose, and of the description and in the condition to perform the services which will be immediately required of them.

To Visc. Castlereagh.   Coimbra, 7th May, 1809.

Before I left Lisbon I made arrangements for sending to England all the tonnage, containing provisions of every description, and 5000 tons of infantry transports, which quantity I intended, and do still intend, further to increase by the whole amount of the transports in Portugal, if I can either beat or cripple Soult.

I do not know whether this arrangement has been carried into execution, as the Agent of transports is the worst hand I have seen of that description, and you are aware that the transports are not solely under my directions. I write to inform you, however, what I intended; and to tell you that if you wish that I should arrange this branch of the service on the most economical plan for the public, you will send out Lieut. Fleetwood, whom I had with me last year in Portugal, to be Agent of transports in charge of the whole fleet. Commissioner George is well acquainted with him.

To Vice Adm. the Hon. G. Berkeley.   Coimbra, 7th May, 1809.

I have received your letters of the 4th and 5th, and I am very much obliged to you for the plans which you propose to adopt in aid of Gen. Mackenzie's measures for fortifying the Tagus, and for removing the boats from the river in the event of invasion by the enemy. The victuallers and other store ships are not yet arrived at Figueira; but the hussars are arrived there, under convoy of Capt. Mudge, and I have written to him to beg that he will land them.

I am much obliged to you for sending the horse transports for the use of the 40th regt. I do not know whether there are any transports for them at Cadiz; but as you will probably think it necessary to send convoy for them, you might probably send transports, if it is not certain that there are some at Cadiz. I am certain that Mr. Frere will consent to their departure from Seville.

I am much obliged to you for the orders which you have given to Capt. Grainger of the *Semiramis*. I had already sent out a schooner with a letter addressed to any officer going down the coast with a convoy having troops on board, to request him to put into the Mondego; and I expect the arrival of a brigade of light troops, as well as the 23d light dragoons and the hussars.

Gen. Beresford's corps moved the day before yesterday. My advanced guard marched this morning; and I hope that in a few days we shall be in possession of Oporto. I am afraid that the loss of the bridge of Amarante will prevent us from doing more than hurry the enemy out of Portugal.

To Capt. Mudge, R.N. Coimbra, 7th May, 1809.

I have received your letter of yesterday evening, and I am much obliged to you for the newspapers you have transmitted.

I shall be very much obliged to you if you will be so kind as to land at Figueira the troops which have come from England under your convoy, with the exception of the men of the 2d batt. 24th regt., whom I should wish to have sent to Lisbon, that battalion being stationed upon the Tagus.

As I have before had cavalry landed in the Mondego, I have reason to apprehend that you will experience difficulty in landing those which you have brought: the best mode of effecting our object we found to be to send into the river all the vessels whose draught of water would permit their passing the bar, where we experienced no difficulty in disembarking them. In respect to those vessels whose draught of water would not permit them to pass the bar, we disembarked the horses from them with the boats of the country, of which large numbers are to be found at Buarcos and Figueira, and thus took the horses across the bar in these boats, and landed them with ease.

To Marshal Beresford. Coimbra, 7th May, 1809.

Our friend came to Aveiro yesterday; and I saw him last night at a fire on the road between Fornos and Martede.

He says there are two parties now in the army: one, to seize at all events; the other, who wish to seize only in case the person persists in declaring himself King. He had two plans to propose: one, that we should endeavor to draw Soult into a snare, by persuading some of the people in this part of the country to address him to declare himself King, and even that I should write to recommend the same measure to him, as one most likely to pacify Portugal and Spain; the other, that we should make our dispositions, and attack forthwith, taking care to cut off their retreat by a strong corps upon the Douro, and even at Villa Real.

In respect to the measures proposed for my adoption, I declared that I could have nothing to do with them, as the inevitable result would be to deprive me of the confidence of the Portuguese. In respect to the attack, I told our friend that I would make it as soon as I could, but that the time must depend upon circumstances. He said that if Soult could be induced to declare himself King, the whole army of Laborde and Loison would declare against him, and *lead the army back into France.*

I could not exactly understand by what road the French were to march after having made good their retreat to Villa Real: he said, towards Benavente in Spain. However, it is not impossible that they might endeavor to pass the Douro and to go by Lamego, which place, indeed, our friend mentioned at one time, though he did not say where they were to go from Lamego. He showed me a paper very ably drawn up, as he said, by an officer of rank, pointing out their different lines of retreat, which states a decided preference for that of Villa Real, but to what point from Villa Real is not stated; and I observe that there are several roads which lead through Villa Real, to Braganza, to Chaves, &c. Our friend particularly cautioned me against the employment of too small a corps to cut them off at Villa Real. Now upon all this the question is, what we shall do? My opinion is, that we are not sufficiently strong in British troops to make such an attack upon Oporto as will oblige them to evacuate that town, and to post such a corps at Villa Real as will effectually cut them off. We must be content, therefore, with preventing them from crossing the Douro; and this can be done only by your being at Lamego as soon as possible, that is to say, by the 10th or 11th at latest.

I conceive that your corps will be at Vizeu on the 8th, and may be at Lamego on the 10th: if I make my attack on the outposts on the Vouga at Ovar and Oliveira on the 9th, as I intended, it will be known at Amarante on the morning of the 10th: the French are in strength at that point; and on the same day they may seize Lamego, supposing that to be their object. I propose, therefore, to delay my attack on the outposts till the 10th, in hopes to give you time to occupy Lamego and the banks of the Douro before the enemy at Amarante shall know of it.

In respect to your occupation of Villa Real, it would be a most important and decisive step if you could venture upon it, supposing the enemy not to have anticipated you; but I acknowledge that I should not like to see a British brigade, supported by 6000 or 8000 Portuguese troops, in *any but a very good post,* exposed to be attacked by the French army; and I must observe that they would have every facility, and probably time, to attack you at Villa Real before I could arrive in a situation to assist you, by breaking the bridges at Oporto and Amarante; and by defending the passages of the Douro and the Tamaga by rear guards. I therefore recommend to you not to occupy Villa Real, even if you should find the French have not anticipated you, unless you should know that the post is of such a description as that you will certainly be able to hold it for 2 or 3 or more days. In all this view of the case, the loss of the bridge of Amarante is a great misfortune, and is the greater from the manner in which it was lost. Our friend says it was carried by the French making two false attacks on the right, under cover of which they mined the barricade on the bridge, which was very strong, and blew it up in the morning at daylight; threw a column over it, which surprised the Portuguese asleep; and they were unable to blow it up as they had intended; and the French carried everything before them. He says that the French *courent sur les Portugais comme s'ils étaient des lièvres.* He says that the French have not lost above 200 or 300 men in all their attacks in Portugal, and advised me strongly not to put any trust in the Portuguese troops.

Some of the Colonels of your regiments have just been here to say that they cannot march, having no money to pay for the mules and muleteers attached to their corps to carry certain baggage. I have desired that money may be advanced to them, on the account of the Portuguese government, by our Paymaster Gen., which must be repaid ; but we ought to have had an account of all these wants before we took them.

To Visc. Castlereagh.   Coimbra, 7th May, 1809.

I met last night ——, for the first time since I had seen him at Lisbon. He told me that the French army was at this time divided into two parties : one, which intended to seize Soult at all events, and to carry into execution the plan he had before communicated to me ; the other, consisting of —— ——, and even those connected with Buonaparte, who were determined to seize Soult, if he should declare himself King of Portugal, of which he has manifested an intention. This latter party would then lead the army into France, where it is understood that Buonaparte wishes to have it. But —— thinks that if Soult was once seized, every thing would go on as *his* friends wished. He then made two propositions to me : one, that I should make my arrangements to attack them immediately, taking care to cut off their retreat into Spain ; the other, that, if I would not make my attack immediately, I should endeavor to prevail upon the inhabitants of some of the towns in Portugal with which I was in communication, to petition Soult to take upon himself the government of Portugal as King ; and that I should even go so far as to advise him myself to take that step as the most likely to secure the peace of Portugal and Spain, and to lead to the overthrow of Buonaparte.

In answer to these propositions, I told ——, as to the first, that I should certainly operate upon Soult as soon as I should be ready. In regard to the second, I told him that I could not take any measures to induce the people of Portugal to act as he proposed, without incurring the risk of leading them to believe that I was unworthy of their confidence. He then gave me a good deal of information respecting the strength, the position, and the plans of the enemy, and of the detestation of Soult generally prevailing in the army ; all of which was confirmed by M. ——, who came with him ; and I sent him back without his having seen any of our troops, or knowing that we had such numbers collected here.

I firmly believe what he says respecting the prevailing discontent, and I think it not improbable that ——, and others attached to Buonaparte, aware of it, and apprehensive of its effects, would turn it so far to account of Buonaparte, as to induce the army to seize their General, for being guilty of an ambitious abuse of his authority, and disobedience of the orders of the Emperor. And if they are really in a scrape, which I acknowledge I doubt, they would make use of this act, if possible, to induce us to allow them to go away. This is certainly the case if ——, ——, and others of that party knew of ——'s communications with us, which I cannot find out.

To the Rt. Hon. J. Villiers.   Coimbra, 7th May, 1809.

I enclose a copy of a letter which I wrote this day to Beresford, and a letter to Lord Castlereagh, in respect to Capt. ——, which is open for your perusal. Forward the latter to England, and return the former.

I have received your letter of the 5th. The measures proposed respecting the boats are very judicious. I shall be happy to receive any reinforcements sent to me; but I do not think I ought to ask for any. I have sent to Lisbon two officers of engineers with orders respecting the defence of Lisbon, the Tagus, Palmella, and Setuval. Elvas has, I understand, a garrison of 10,000 men, which ought to be sufficient; but I shall inquire upon that subject.

I have written a very fine letter on my appointment as Marshal.

I send, by this opportunity, a packet of army letters, and my dispatches for England, which I request you to forward by the first opportunity. I enclose a letter from Gen. Sherbrooke, which I beg you to peruse, and to act upon it as you may think proper.

To Visc. Castlereagh.   Coimbra, 7th May, 1809.

I have the honor to inform you, that, in conformity with the intention which I announced to your Lordship on the 27th April, I have assembled the army at this place, with the exception of the 2d batt. 30th regt., employed to garrison Lisbon, and the detachment on the Tagus, under the command of Major Gen. Mackenzie.

The whole were assembled here on the 5th inst., and, on the same day, a detachment consisting of one brigade of British infantry, and one squadron of British cavalry, and a corps of about 6000 Portuguese troops, infantry, cavalry, and artillery, moved towards Vizeu, under Gen. Beresford, in order to operate upon the enemy's left; while I shall move upon his right at Oporto, with the main body of the British army, and 2 battalions of Portuguese infantry. The British advanced guard commenced its march this morning.

The enemy remains nearly in the same positions, as well on the Eastern frontier, and in the northern provinces of this Kingdom, as he did when I wrote last. No alteration whatever, that I know of, has been made in the positions of the French army on the Guadiana; and the only difference in this quarter is, that the Portuguese General, Silveira, has been defeated upon the Tamaga, and the French have obtained the possession of the bridge of Amarante on the 2d inst. This acquisition is important, inasmuch as it affords them the facility of retreating through the province of Tras os Montes.

To Visc. Castlereagh.   Coimbra, 7th May, 1809.

My dispatch of this date will give you a notion of the state of affairs here. I think that I shall soon settle this part of the country in some way or other; and I shall then turn my attention entirely to Victor. I think it probable that Cuesta and I shall be more than a match for the French army on the Guadiana, and that we shall force them to retreat. The tenor of my instructions will then become important; and, unless they are altered, I shall be obliged to halt at the moment I shall have removed from the Portuguese frontier the danger by which it is threatened; possibly, at that time at which the continuance of my advance might be most important to the cause of the Spaniards. I wish the King's ministers to consider this point, and to give me a latitude to continue my operations in Spain, if I should consider them important to the Spanish cause and consistent with the safety of Portugal.

To the Rt. Hon. G. Canning.   Coimbra, 7th May, 1809.

My dispatches and letters to Lord Castlereagh will inform you of the state of affairs here. I think we are getting on, and that we may make something of the Portuguese army. We want arms, however, and caps for the men; and the pay of the officers must be increased.

Villiers informed me that he had written to you for permission to use the King's name in the grant of this increase of pay, which he appeared to think so important, as to induce him to delay the execution of the orders he had received to recommend the increase of pay to the government till that authority should reach him.

I acknowledge that, provided the increase of pay is granted, it is not of material importance whether the King's name is used, or not, in the grant. On principle, I should say it ought not, as the King can have no right to claim an interference in a domestic concern of this description in any mode excepting by advice, with which advice the officers of the army might not be made acquainted; but such is the state of the government of this country at present, that I conceive that they would feel such an interference but little, if at all; and it is better that Mr. Villiers should be gratified, even in this irregular wish, than that the measure should be delayed by any further consideration and discussion of it.

I therefore beg of you either to grant or refuse, as soon as possible, the authority for which Mr. Villiers has asked to use the King's name, in the grant of the increase of pay to the officers of the Portuguese army, which is really necessary on all grounds, but particularly in reference to the *régime* which has lately been adopted in respect to them.

To Capt. Mudge, R. N.   Coimbra, 8th May, 1809.

Since I wrote to you yesterday, I have heard that some men and horses for the 20th light dragoons are come out in the fleet under your convoy, which men and horses should go to Lisbon, as well as the detachment of the 24th foot, mentioned to you yesterday. Till I shall receive from the officer of the army a return of the troops in the convoy, I request that you will have disembarked only the horses and men in the 1st hussars, the men of the staff corps, and those of the 87th regt.

G. O.   Coimbra, 8th May, 1809.

3. The troops which will march are this day to receive meat for to-morrow, which must be cooked, and three days' bread and forage, for the 9th, 10th, and 11th inst. inclusive.

4. The Commissary General will take measures that the assistant commissaries, with brigades, may besides be provided with three days' bread and meat, according to the directions he has received.

5. The head quarters will be fixed to-morrow, at the Quinta de Graciosa, on the right of the road beyond Pio.

6. The baggage of head quarters will move in rear of the troops; officers belonging to it will receive instructions from the Commandant.

To Major Gen. Hill.   Coimbra, 8th May, 1809.

We halted yesterday to give Gen. Beresford time to get forward, and we shall proceed with our operations to-morrow.

You will receive from the Q. M. G. a paper, fully explanatory to you of all that it is intended you should perform; to which I have only to add, 1st, that you will find the boats ready for you at Aveiro, and will have to get boatmen only, in which Douglas, whom I send to you, will assist you: 2dly, that I mean you should bring up to-morrow night in such a place as that the enemy cannot discover you, in that part of the river or lake of which the banks are swampy: 3dly, that you should land your light infantry below the town, where it is certain the enemy never is, in order to secure the unmolested disembarkation of the remainder of your corps at Ovar, where it is possible the enemy may have a small patrole.

I recommend to you to cook a day's provisions at Aveiro for your men for the 10th, and to refresh your men at Ovar, while you are waiting there to learn the progress of Gen. Cotton with his cavalry. Having communicated with that General, you will then move from Ovar by the road which leads from Ovar to Feira, till that road meets the great road from Coimbra to Oporto. You will halt there till you shall be joined by the cavalry. My intention is to push the enemy as far as I can on the 10th, even into Oporto if possible.

To Vice Adm. the Hon. G. Berkeley.   Coimbra, 8th May, 1809.

I have the honor to acknowledge the receipt of your letter of the 6th, and I have given directions for the issue of bât and forage to the naval and marine officers employed to garrison the forts on the Tagus.

To the Senior Officer of H. M.'s Navy at Figueira.   Coimbra, 8th May, 1809.

I am in daily expectation of the arrival of a convoy of provisions and stores from Lisbon at Figueira, and as I purpose to move forward the army to-morrow, I shall be obliged to you, when the convoy shall arrive, to send them to Aveiro, where I shall transmit further directions for them.

G. A. O.   Coimbra, 8th May, 1809.

1. Lieut. Gen. Paget being arrived to-day, the army is to be divided as follows, till the other Lieutenant Generals attached to it will join.

        Guards . . . .
        Major Gen. Hill's . . . . . .   Right wing.
        Brig. Gen. A. Campbell's . . . . .
        Brig. Gen. Cameron's . . . . . .

with a brigade of heavy 6 pounders, and a brigade of light 6 pounders.

2.   The King's German Legion . . . .
        Brig. Gen. Suntag's . . . . . .   Left wing.
        Brig. Gen. R. Stewart's . . . . . .

with one brigade of 6 pounders, and one brigade of 3 pounders.

3. These wings will be formed into two or more lines, as circumstances may require, and brigades will be detached from them according to circumstances, to form advanced guards and reserves: there is to be no alteration in the orders of march to-morrow.

Memorandum. Orders will always be given out immediately on the arrival of head quarters at a new station; brigade majors will come provided with the addresses of their General officers.

The A.G. to Capt. de Sousa, A.D.C. to Marshal Beresford. 9th May, 1809.

The return of the Portuguese army, which is required by Lieut. Gen. Sir A. Wellesley, is to include the whole; specifying that part of it which is advancing under the immediate orders of Marshal Beresford.

The memorandums for the movements of the army were given by the Commander of the Forces to the Q.M.G., and circulated by him, as the General Orders were by the Adj. Gen., to the different corps and divisions of the army. The detailed instructions, however, of each day's march have not been introduced, but only those relating to strategical movements preparatory to active operations and battles.

Extracts from the instructions communicated by the Q. M. G. relative to the advance of the army towards Oporto.

‘ Coimbra, 8th May, 1809.

‘ The brigade commanded by Major Gen. Hill, which has been already ordered to be at Aveiro early on the 9th inst., will embark there the same day, on board the boats which will be prepared for it; so that the embarkation may be completed a little before the time of low water, which will be about 4 o'clock P.M. The brigade will then proceed towards Ovar; but orders are to be previously given for the boats to bring-to about 2 leagues short of Ovar, and there remain till slack water on the morning of the 10th, which will be about 4 A.M., when the whole will again proceed. The object of this delay is to prevent the enemy becoming aware of Gen. Hill's approach until the advanced guard of the column under Major Gen. Cotton, which is to march by the great road from Coimbra, shall have arrived near the French outposts.

‘ Gen. Hill will cause 3 companies of light infantry to be disembarked at a landing place which is on the western side of the Lake of Aveiro, about half a league from Ovar, with instructions to advance rapidly and possess themselves of the town and harbour, in order to facilitate the landing of the rest of the brigade.

‘ As Brig. Gen. Cameron's brigade, with a brigade of 6 pounders, is to be at Aveiro on the 10th inst., to follow Gen. Hill, the boats are to be sent back to Aveiro with the least possible delay, for the conveyance of these troops ; and precautions must be taken to prevent the escape of the boatmen, and to cause them to proceed direct to their destination.

‘ Gen. Hill will inform himself at Ovar respecting the roads which lead from that place towards the river Vouga, lest any event should occur to render it necessary to use them; a small detachment of Portuguese cavalry will be sent by the road leading from Angeja to Ovar, very early on the morning of the 10th, to join Gen. Hill, and he will be so good as not to move forward from Ovar, until he has certain intelligence of Gen. Cotton's troops having reached Oliveira on the Oporto road.

‘ Major Gen. Cotton will cause the cavalry to begin their march during the night of the 9th inst., or very early on the morning of the 10th, so that the head of the column may arrive by daybreak at the outposts of the Portuguese troops under the command of Col. Trant. The brigade of 3 pounder guns may either accompany the cavalry, or move with the nearest brigade of infantry, as Gen. Cotton may think proper. Brig. Gen. R. Stewart's brigade of infantry, with half a brigade of 6 pounders, will follow the cavalry. The King's German Legion, with half a brigade of 6 pounders, will follow Gen. R. Stewart's brigade ; and Major Gen. Murray will regulate the march of the legion, so as to be at hand to give efficient support to the troops in front.

‘ Major Gen. Cotton's first object will be to endeavor to surprise the enemy's advanced guard near Albergaria Nova. And when a junction shall have been effected with Gen. Hill, where the roads from Coimbra and Ovar meet, he will press the enemy ; and if an opportunity should offer for doing so, he will attempt to pass the bridge at Oporto with the French rear guard, or at all events endeavor to prevent, if possible, the destruction of the bridge. He will secure whatever boats may be found on the left bank of the river.

‘ Brig. Gen. Cameron's brigade, with a brigade of 6 pounders, will form on the Oporto road, 3 miles in advance of Coimbra, early on the morning of the 9th inst., and will march at 6 A.M. to cantonments at Murtede and adjacents. These troops will proceed on the 10th to Aveiro, there to embark and join Gen. Hill at Ovar.

‘ The brigade of Guards, with 1 brigade of 6 pounders, Brig. Gen. Alex. Campbell's brigade, and Brig. Gen. Sontag's brigade, will form, under the orders of Lieut. Gen. Sherbrooke, on the morning of the 9th inst., in rear of Gen. Cameron's brigade ; and will proceed at 6½ A.M. by the Oporto road, to Mealhada and adjacent villages. These brigades will continue their march on the morning of the 10th inst. at the same hour.

‘ All the troops are to be marched off by their right. The baggage of head quarters will precede the troops under Lieut. Gen. Sherbrooke.’

To the Rt. Hon. J. H. Frere.   Quinta de la Graciosa, 9th May, 1809.

I have just received your letter of the 4th, and I am very much obliged to you for having given me such immediate intelligence of the march of a French corps from Aragon, probably directed to the relief of Marshal Ney, or of Marshal Soult. I have not yet heard from any other quarter of the approach of this corps to the frontiers of Portugal, and yet we have garrisons in Chaves, Braganza, Ciudad Rodrigo, and Almeida. It is possible, therefore, it may have been stopped, or its destination altered. The troops under my command have commenced their operations against Marshal Soult, one column having marched by Vizeu towards Lamego, and another under my own command being on its march towards Oporto. This last will cross the Vouga, on which are the enemy's outposts, to-morrow morning.

I do not think that the intelligence which you have communicated to me, even if it were confirmed, should induce me to alter my plan, till the enemy's force from Aragon should be nearer to us.

In respect to Soult, I shall omit nothing that I can do to destroy him; but as he has lately forced the important point of the bridge of Amarante, and has since taken possession of Villa Real, I am afraid that it is not in my power, with the force which I have at my disposal, to prevent him retreating into Spain. The question will then remain for consideration, whether it is best for Portugal and the general cause that I should turn my attention to Victor's corps, and remain upon the defensive in the north of Portugal; or that I should follow Soult, or attack Ney in Galicia, and leave the east of Portugal on the defensive. The solution of this question will depend very much upon the extent of the enemy's force in Galicia and the Spanish provinces bordering upon the north of Portugal.

If the safety of Portugal should be seriously threatened in that quarter, you will see by my instructions I must consider that my principal object, and I must therefore remain in the north. If, on the other hand, nothing should remain in the Spanish provinces bordering on the north of Portugal, excepting the corps of Ney and Soult, I conceive I should act in the best manner for Portugal, and for the whole of the Peninsula, by co-operating in a plan to oblige Victor to retreat, or, if possible, in his defeat.

I fear that the letters which I have already written to Gen. Cuesta, and for Don M. de Garay, will have prevented you from making use of my name to induce the Junta Militar to adopt the plan of offensive operations in La Mancha; in the same manner as my promise to return to co-operate with Gen. Cuesta, after I should have obliged Soult to withdraw from the north of Portugal, has prevented you from promising that co-operation as a condition in case the Spaniards should carry on those proposed operations. My reason for recommending that defensive measures should be

G. O.   9th May, 1809.
3. The Commander of the Forces requests that attention may be paid to the order relative to soldiers marching out of the ranks, and he desires that the files may be counted, and if men are absent the roll shall be called of each company, when the men will reach their ground after a march, and absentees are to be reported to the officer commanding brigades.

adopted every where was, that the troops not absolutely necessary for defence in any point might be sent to reinforce Gen. Cuesta, who, by his own account, did not appear to me to be sufficiently strong to defend the important point which he occupies, and upon which all seems to me to depend.

An offensive operation in La Mancha might be of use to me and to the north of Spain, by diverting the French corps said to be destined for this quarter, and on its march from Aragon, if there should be no reserve in the neighbourhood of Madrid. Whether there should be such a corps or not, it might be fatal to Cuesta, to the seat of government, and to all the important interests in the south of Spain; and as the French would always have it in their power to draw towards Madrid the corps supposed to be on its march from Aragon, this offensive operation would give them but little uneasiness for the safety of that city. In this consideration of the subject I have supposed that this operation would be successful, which is by no means certain. However, upon all these points, the decision must turn upon an accurate knowledge of relative numbers, and of the position of corps, which I acknowledge I do not possess; and I ought to have refrained from giving Gen. Cuesta, or Don M. de Garay, through you, my opinion upon this subject. But I don't think I could, with propriety, have avoided informing Gen. Cuesta of my intentions, in case I should succeed in removing Soult from Portugal, or in defeating him.

I have just heard that the Marques de la Romana is in the neighbourhood of Monterey, and I shall endeavor to communicate with him there. If he should be at Monterey, it is possible that he has heard of the movement of the French corps from Aragon, and that he has drawn back towards the frontiers of Portugal.

To the Marques de la Romana.　　　　　Quinta de la Graciosa, ce 9 Mai, 1809.

Le Chevalier Wilson ayant fait savoir au Maréchal Beresford que vous étiez auprès de Monterey, je vous écris pour vous faire savoir que je suis en marche pour attaquer le corps du Maréchal Soult à Oporto; et que je passerai le Vouga demain. Le Maréchal Beresford est à present à Vizeu, et sera demain, ou le jour suivant, à Lamego. L'ennemi, ayant défait le corps du Général Silveira, a occupé le pont d'Amarante et la ville de Villa Real; c'est donc probable qu'il compte faire sa retraite, ou le long du Douro vers Zamora, ou par Braganza, ou par Chaves en Galice.

J'ai reçu aujourd'hui des nouvelles de Seville, du 4 de ce mois. Les armées des deux côtés sont postées comme elles l'ont été depuis un mois. M. Frere me mande qu'un corps, censé être de 16,000 hommes, a quitté l'Aragon le 14 du mois passé, et doit passer par Tudela le 16; son but est, à ce qu'on dit, de donner la main au Maréchal Ney. Je n'ai pas eu de nouvelles de ce corps; et je vous serai bien obligé de me faire savoir si vous en avez reçues.

To Marshal Beresford.　　　　　Quinta de la Graciosa, 9th May, 1809.

I enclose an extract of a letter which I have just received from Mr. Frere, announcing the march of a French corps from Aragon towards this part of the Peninsula.

Before I had received your letter of the 7th, I thought it possible that Soult might have heard of this corps, as Trant sent me a report this morning that the enemy had his whole force in Villa Nova and south of the Douro, where he was intrenching himself; but since the receipt of your letter, stating that Romana is at Monterey, I think it most probable that he has heard of the movement of this corps to reinforce Ney, and that he has withdrawn in consequence towards the frontiers of Portugal. Whether this corps is coming here, or wherever it may be going, I see no reason for altering our plan of operations, at least till we shall hear that they are nearer us; and therefore I shall cross the Vouga to-morrow morning, and lose no time in proceeding to Oporto.

The British troops who marched with you went away provided with bread for 6 days, and with meat and forage for 3 days, as did the Portuguese battalions in the British brigade, I believe. I have ordered the Commissary General to send for 6 days' of every thing from Coimbra for 10,000 men; besides that a Commissary is sent to Vizeu to prepare provisions for you.

I enclose a letter for Romana, which I beg of you to forward. I consider the letter I wrote to you the other day as entirely applicable to the present situation of affairs, unless indeed the enemy should really have crossed the Douro, and should intend to fight us on this side of the river. In that case you might cross and attack him at Villa Real, without risk of great loss; and therefore, and for every reason, I recommend to you to collect as many boats, high up, as you can lay your hands upon. If I can spare them, you shall have the cavalry after to-morrow. Send people to Braganza, Chaves, Ciudad Rodrigo, and even to Zamora, if you can, to transmit intelligence of this corps from Aragon.

To Marshal Beresford.   Convento do Grijo, 11th May, 1809.

If the French should weaken their corps about Amarante and Villa Real, so as to give you any reason to hope that you can do anything against them, then I wish you to attack them, and take any opportunity of getting possession of either of these points. But remember that you are a Commander in Chief of an army, and must not be beaten; therefore do not undertake anything with your troops, if you have not some strong hopes of success. I have a plan to reinforce that point also, if the French should cross the Douro, and pretend to defend themselves at Oporto by so doing.

To the Rt. Hon. J. Villiers.   6 A.M. 11th May, 1809.

I have just time to tell you, that we drove in the enemy's cavalry, and other posts, north of the Vouga, yesterday, and gained ground as far as Oliveira. We attempted to surprise the cavalry, which attempt failed, for causes into which it is not necessary to enter; and afterwards we did not do as much as we ought against the cavalry. With the infantry we gained a good deal of ground.

G. O.   Convento do Grijo, 11th May, 1809.

4. The Commander of the Forces calls the attention of officers commanding regiments and companies relative to the orders respecting the regularity of march, keeping their companies collected, not permitting their men to straggle. Lieut. Col. Doyle, of the 16th Portuguese, is referred particularly to this order.

I hope that we shall have finished with Soult before the reinforcements can arrive of which Frere has given intelligence. They tell me that the Portuguese riflemen, the students I believe, behaved remarkably well.

P. S. We took one piece of cannon.

To the Rt. Hon. J. Villiers.   6 P.M., 11th May, 1809.

I wrote to you this morning to apprise you of our operations of yesterday; I have now the pleasure to inform you, that we have been still more successful this day. We have completely beaten a corps of about 4000 infantry that was opposed to us in two affairs, first with its outposts, and afterwards itself. The corps engaged were the 1st battalion of detachments, 2 battalions K.G.L., and Col. Doyle's battalion of the 16th Portuguese regt. This last regiment behaved remarkably well. Recollect that in talking upon this subject, you do not forget to mention the name of the Colonel of the regiment, who was in the field I know, for I had given him a piece of my mind in the morning. Two squadrons of cavalry, one of the 16th and one of the 20th, under Charles Stewart, also did great execution.

The enemy showed but little cavalry, and made no great stand. Indeed Gen. Murray's movement with the German Legion upon their left flank, and that of the Portuguese battalion upon their right, would have made any troops quit their position.

I do not know whether they propose to give us another field day on this side of Oporto, but I should think not, as they did not show their cavalry this day. If they should do so, I shall have my whole corps upon them. This day I had only the advanced guard.

P.S. We have lost some few men killed and wounded, and have taken some.

To Visc. Castlereagh.   Oporto, 12th May, 1809.

I had the honor to apprise your Lordship on the 7th inst., that I intended that the army should march on the 9th from Coimbra, to dispossess the enemy of Oporto.

The advanced guard and the cavalry had marched on the 7th, and the whole had halted on the 8th, to afford time for Marshal Beresford with his corps to arrive upon the Upper Douro.

The infantry of the army was formed into 3 divisions for this expedition, of which 2, the advanced guard, consisting of the King's German Legion, and Brig. Gen. R. Stewart's brigade, with a brigade of 6 pounders, and a brigade of 3 pounders, under Lieut. Gen. Paget; and the cavalry under Lieut. Gen. Payne; and the brigade of Guards, Brig. Gen. Campbell's and Brig. Gen. Sontag's brigades of infantry, with a brigade of 6 pounders, under Lieut. Gen. Sherbrooke, moved by the high road from Coimbra to Oporto; and one, composed of Major Gen. Hill's and Brig. Gen. Cameron's brigades of infantry, and a brigade of 6 pounders, under the command of Major Gen. Hill, by the road from Coimbra to Aveiro.

On the 10th in the morning, before daylight, the cavalry and advanced guard crossed the Vouga, with the intention to surprise and cut off 4 regiments of French cavalry, and a battalion of infantry and artillery, cantoned in Albergaria Nova and the neighbouring villages, about 8 miles from that river, in the last of which we failed; but the superiority of the

British cavalry was evident throughout the day. We took some prisoners and their cannon from them; and the advanced guard took up the position of Oliveira. On the same day Major Gen. Hill, who had embarked at Aveiro on the evening of the 9th, arrived at Ovar, in the rear of the enemy's right; and the head of Lieut. Gen. Sherbrooke's division passed the Vouga on the same evening.

On the 11th, the advanced guard and cavalry continued to move on the high road towards Oporto, with Major Gen. Hill's division in a parallel road which leads to Oporto from Ovar. On the arrival of the advanced guard at Vendas Novas, between Souto Redondo and Grijo, they fell in with the outposts of the enemy's advanced guard, which were immediately driven in; and shortly afterwards we discovered the enemy's advanced guard, consisting of about 4000 infantry and some squadrons of cavalry, strongly posted on the heights above Grijo, their front being covered by woods and broken ground. The enemy's left flank was turned by a movement well executed by Major Gen. Murray, with Brig. Gen. Langwerth's brigade K.G.L.; while the 16th Portuguese regt. of Brig. Gen. R. Stewart's brigade attacked their right, and the riflemen of the 95th, and the flank companies of the 29th, 43d, and 52d of the same brigade, under Major Way, attacked the infantry in the woods and village in their centre. These attacks soon obliged the enemy to give way; and Brig. Gen. the Hon. C. Stewart led 2 squadrons of the 16th and 20th dragoons, under the command of Major Blake, in pursuit of the enemy, and destroyed many and took several prisoners.

G. O.   Oporto, 12th May, 1809.

The Commander of the Forces congratulates the troops upon the success which has attended their operations for the last four days, upon which they have traversed above 80 miles of most difficult country, in which they have carried some formidable positions, have beat the enemy repeatedly, and have ended by forcing the passage of the Douro, and defending the position they had so boldly taken up, with numbers far inferior to those with which they were attacked. In the course of this short expedition the Commander of the Forces has had repeated opportunities of witnessing and applauding the gallantry of the officers and troops, the activity and conduct of the 95th, and of the light infantry of the 29th, 43d, and 52d. The bravery of the 16th Portuguese regiment, the able movement made by Major Gen. Murray with the 1st and 2d batt. Hanoverian Legion, under Brig. Gen. Langwerth, and the gallant attack made by Brig. Gen. the Hon. C. Stewart, with a squadron of the 16th, and a squadron of the 20th light dragoons, under the command of Major Blake of the 20th, contributed essentially to the success of the attack on the enemy's advanced guard on the 11th, and the steady gallantry of the Buffs, 48th and 16th regts. under the command of Major Gen. Hill. The timely passage of the Douro and subsequent movement on the enemy's flank by Lieut. Gen. Sherbrooke, with the brigade of Guards and 29th regt., and the bravery of the 2 squadrons of the 14th light dragoons, under the command of Major Hervey, and led by Brig. Gen. the Hon. C. Stewart, obtained the victory, which has contributed so much to the honor of the troops on this day. The Commander of the Forces has to express his acknowledgments to Lieut. Gen. the Hon. E. Paget, for the manner in which he conducted the advanced guard on the 10th, 11th, and 12th, and in which he took up the position beyond the Douro, and he regrets the misfortune which has deprived him (he hopes only for a time) of his assistance.

To Lieut. Gen. Sherbrooke, Major Gen. Murray, Major Gen. Hill; to Brig. Gen. the Hon. C. Stewart; to Lieut. Col. De Lancey, Q. M. G.'s department, and Capt. Mellish, Adj. Gen.'s department, in the assistance they rendered Gen. Stewart, in his charge of the enemy's defeated infantry, on the 11th and 12th, and to Major C. Campbell, of the Adj. Gen.'s department, for the assistance he rendered Gen. Hill, on the defence of his post, and Brig. Gen. the Hon. C. Stewart in his charge on the enemy's infantry, on the 12th.

The Commander of the Forces also acknowledges the assistance he has received from the A. G. and Q. M. G., and the officers of these departments respectively, and to Lieut. Col. Bathurst and the officers of his personal staff.

On the night of the 11th the enemy crossed the Douro and destroyed the bridge over that river. It was important, with a view to the operations of Marshal Beresford, that I should cross the Douro immediately; and I had sent Major Gen. Murray in the morning with a battalion of the King's German Legion, a squadron of cavalry, and two 6 pounders, to endeavor to collect boats, and, if possible, to cross the river at Avintas, about 4 miles above Oporto; and I had as many boats as could be collected brought to the ferry, immediately above the towns of Oporto and Villa Nova. The ground on the right bank of the river at this ferry is protected and commanded by the fire of cannon, placed on the height of the Serra convent at Villa Nova; and there appeared to be a good position for our troops on the opposite side of the river, till they should be collected in sufficient numbers. The enemy took no notice of our collection of boats, or of the embarkation of the troops, till after the 1st battalion (the Buffs) were landed, and had taken up their position, under the command of Lieut. Gen. Paget, on the opposite side of the river. They then commenced an attack upon them, with a large body of cavalry, infantry, and artillery, under the command of Marshal Soult, which that corps most gallantly sustained, till supported successively by the 48th and 66th regts., belonging to Major Gen. Hill's brigade, and a Portuguese battalion, and afterwards by the first battalion of detachments belonging to Brig. Gen. R. Stewart's brigade. Lieut. Gen. Paget was unfortunately wounded soon after the attack commenced, when the command of these gallant troops devolved upon Major Gen. Hill.

Although the French made repeated attacks upon them, they made no impression; and at last, Major Gen. Murray having appeared on the enemy's left flank on his march from Avintas, where he had crossed; and Lieut. Gen. Sherbrooke, who by this time had availed himself of the enemy's weakness in the town of Oporto, and had crossed the Douro at the ferry between the towns of Villa Nova and Oporto, having appeared upon their right with the brigade of Guards and the 29th regt., the whole retired in the utmost confusion towards Amarante, leaving behind them 5 pieces of cannon, 8 ammunition tumbrils, and many prisoners.

The enemy's loss in killed and wounded in this action has been very large, and they have left behind them in Oporto 700 sick and wounded. Brig. Gen. the Hon. C. Stewart then directed a charge by a squadron of the 14th dragoons, under the command of Major Hervey, who made a successful attack on the enemy's rear guard.

In the different actions with the enemy, of which I have above given your Lordship an account, we have lost some, and the immediate services of other valuable officers and soldiers. In Lieut. Gen. Paget, among the latter, I have lost the assistance of a friend, who had been most useful to me in the few days which had elapsed since he had joined the army. He had rendered a most important service at the moment he received his wound, in taking up the position which the troops afterwards maintained, and in bearing the first brunt of the enemy's attack. Major Hervey also distinguished himself at the moment he received his wound in the charge of the cavalry on this day.

I cannot say too much in favor of the officers and troops. They have marched in 4 days over 80 miles of most difficult country, have gained many important positions, and have engaged and defeated 3 different bodies of the enemy's troops.

I beg particularly to draw your Lordship's attention to the conduct of Lieut. Gen. Paget, Major Gen. Murray, Major Gen. Hill, Lieut. Gen. Sherbrooke, Brig. Gen. the Hon. C. Stewart; Lieut. Col. Delancey, D. Q. M. G., and Capt. Mellish, A. A. G., for the assistance they respectively rendered Gen. the Hon. C. Stewart in the charge of the cavalry this day and on the 11th; Major C. Campbell, A. A. G., for the assistance he rendered Major Gen. Hill in the defence of his post; and Brig. Gen. the Hon. C. Stewart in the charge of the cavalry this day; and Brigade Major Fordyce, Capt. Currie, and Capt. Hill, for the assistance they rendered Gen. Hill.

I have also to request your Lordship's attention to the conduct of the riflemen and of the flank companies of the 29th, 43d, and 52d regts., under the command of Major Way of the 29th; that of the 16th Portuguese regt., commanded by Col. Machado, of which Lieut. Col. Doyle is Lieut. Colonel; that of the brigade of the King's German Legion, under the command of Brig. Gen. Langwerth; and that of the 2 squadrons of the 16th and 20th light dragoons, under the command of Major Blake of the 20th, in the action of the 11th: and the conduct of the Buffs, commanded by Lieut. Col. Drummond; the 48th, commanded by Col. Duckworth; and 66th, commanded by Major Murray, who was wounded; and of the squadron of the 14th dragoons, under the command of Major Hervey, in the action of this day.

I have received the greatest assistance from the Adj. Gen., and Col. Murray, Q. M. G., and from all the officers belonging to those departments respectively throughout the service, as well as from Lieut. Col. Bathurst and the officers of my personal staff; and I have every reason to be satisfied with the artillery and officers of engineers.

I send this dispatch by Capt. Stanhope, whom I beg to recommend to your Lordship's protection: his brother, the Hon. Major Stanhope, was unfortunately wounded by a sabre whilst leading a charge of the 16th light dragoons on the 10th inst.

Return of Ordnance captured on the 12th May, 1809.

Ten 12-pounders; twelve 8-pounders; eighteen 4-pounders; sixteen 3-pounders; two howitzers.

Return of the killed, wounded, and missing on the 10th, 11th, and 12th May, 1809.

	Officers.	Serjeants.	Rank & File.	Horses.	Total loss of officers, non-commissioned officers, and rank and file.
Killed	1	—	42	—	43
Wounded	17	1	150	—	168
Missing	—	—	17	—	17

To Marshal Beresford.   Oporto, 12th May, 1809.

I wrote to you at 12, to inform you that the enemy had left this town, excepting their small guards, and that my troops are passing over.

As soon as one battalion, the Buffs, had passed, the enemy made a most furious attack upon them, which they continued for about 2 hours. We threw over reinforcements as fast as we could; but the most we could do was to send over the remainder of Hill's brigade and the Portuguese battalion, which corps defended themselves most gallantly, and we ended by obtaining a complete victory. We have taken some pieces of cannon, how many I cannot say, many prisoners, killed vast numbers; and the infantry went off towards Valongo and Amarante in the utmost confusion. Some of the cavalry went the same way. I am much afraid that we shall not be able to march till the day after to-morrow.

I have received your letter of the 9th. Keep Villa Real if you can do so with safety, and depend upon my being close upon the heels of the French. I shall state my movements exactly as soon as I can.

To Capt. Grainger, R.N., off Oporto.   Oporto, 12th May, 1809.

I have the honor to communicate to you that the troops under my command have gained possession of the town of Oporto, after having defeated the enemy. And I have to request that you will have the goodness to allow Capt. Dench, of H. M. S. *Nautilus,* to convey my dispatches to England, and to communicate the information to the Lords Commissioners of the Admiralty.

To Maréchal Soult.   Oporto, ce 12 Mai, 1809.

Vous savez que vous avez laissé dans cette ville un grand nombre de malades et de blessés, dont vous pouvez être sur que je prendrai le plus grand soin, et qu'autant que je le pourrai, personne ne leur fera du mal. Mais vous avez oublié de laisser avec eux des officiers de santé pour les soigner. Je ne crois pas qu'on doive se fier aux officiers de santé de la ville d'Oporto; et je vous previens que je n'ai pas un plus grand nombre d'officiers de santé, qu'il ne me faut pour le service des troupes qui sont sous mes ordres.

Je vous prie donc d'en envoyer ici un nombre suffisant pour le soin de tous les malades et blessés de l'armée Française que vous avez laissés ici, et je vous promets que quand ils auront guéri les malades, ils vous seront renvoyés.

Vous avez quelques officiers et soldats de l'armée Anglaise, prisonniers de guerre, et je serai bien aise d'établir avec vous un cartel d'échange pour ceux de l'armée Française que j'ai en mon pouvoir.

To the Rt. Hon. J. Villiers.   Oporto, 13th May, 1809.

I informed you of our success on the 11th. We forced the passage of the Douro yesterday. The enemy attacked us upon the disembarkation of the first of our troops, and we completely defeated them with the loss of many men, guns, &c. All our troops were in Oporto last night. Paget, I am sorry to say, was wounded in the right arm, which was amputated, and he is doing well. Our loss has not otherwise been great. I shall send you a copy of my dispatch to England which I shall send from hence, if I can get the officer of the Navy to go with it.

P.S. Soult was in the action, and the enemy are off to Amarante. We follow them immediately.

Proclamation.

Arthur Wellesley, Commander of the British army in Portugal, and Marshal General of the armies of H. R. H. the Prince Regent.

Oporto, 13th May, 1809.

Inhabitants of Oporto! The French troops having been expelled from this town by the superior gallantry and discipline of the army under my command, I call upon the inhabitants of Oporto to be merciful to the wounded and prisoners. By the laws of war they are entitled to my protection, which I am determined to afford them; and it will be worthy of the generosity and bravery of the Portuguese nation not to revenge the injuries which have been done to them on these unfortunate persons, who can only be considered as instruments in the hands of the more powerful, who are still in arms against us. I therefore call upon the inhabitants of this town to remain peaceably in their dwellings. I forbid all persons not military to appear in the streets with arms; and I give notice that I shall consider any person who shall injure any of the wounded or of the prisoners as guilty of the breach of my orders.

I have appointed Col. Trant to command in this town till the pleasure of the government shall be known; and I have ordered him to take care that this Proclamation is obeyed.

To the Hon. B. Paget. Oporto, 13th May, 1809.

I am much concerned to have to inform you that poor Edward was wounded yesterday in the right arm, and that it has been necessary to amputate it. He is, however, doing remarkably well, and is in good spirits. He crossed the Douro with the first of the troops, who were afterwards attacked; and he was shot at an early period in the hand, and through the great artery of his arm, and was obliged to leave the field. I cannot express to you how much I regret the loss of his assistance, or how much the joy of the whole army on account of this success has been damped by the misfortune of him who has been the principal promoter of it. I hope, however, that he will soon recover.

To the Rt. Hon. J. Villiers. Oporto, 13th May, 1809.

I now enclose the copy of my dispatch to Lord Castlereagh, of which you will communicate such parts as you may think proper to the govern-

---

G. A. O. Oporto, 13th May, 1809.

1. The following troops are this day, or to-morrow morning early, to receive 3 days' bread for the 14th, 15th, and 16th, viz. the brigade of Guards, Brig. Gen. A. Campbell's, Brig. Gen. Cameron's, the cavalry, two brigades of light 6-pounders: the horses of the cavalry, artillery, staff, &c. are to receive 3 days' oats or Indian corn for the same time. The above mentioned corps are to march to-morrow morning at such hours, and according to routes which will be sent to them by the Q. M. G.; they are to cook meat this day for to-morrow.

2. Spare musket ammunition must be sent with these corps.

ment. I have written a short letter to Forjaz, containing the outline of our proceedings.

I have appointed Col. Trant to be Commandant of Oporto, and the troops under his command to be the garrison, till the orders of the government shall be given. I have also appointed the former Corregidor to be Corregidor till the orders of government should be known. It was necessary to make this appointment, in order to get the supplies which the place could afford. I have also issued a Proclamation, calling upon the inhabitants to leave any prisoners, and the sick and wounded, unmolested.

The government will of course receive copies of all these papers; and I shall be obliged to you if you will urge them to confirm these acts of mine, particularly the last.

Soult had arrested Capts. ——, ——, and the principal conspirators, on the 10th May. I have found the orders for their arrest and their being put ' *au secret.*' I have just learnt that Capt. —— has made his escape, and has come in. We took a Portuguese who was Commissary to the French. I believe he ought to be tried for treason. I enclose a letter found among Soult's papers.

To Major Gen. J. Murray.   Oporto, 13th May, 1809.

Information is just arrived that the enemy have burnt their artillery, and have retreated precipitately to the left, and are gone towards Valença and the Minho. I wish you immediately to send a patrole, either of cavalry or mounted riflemen, if you can get mules or horses, and endeavor to ascertain whether this information is correct, transmitting immediate intelligence to me, that I may take my measures accordingly. I hope to hear from you by 12 o'clock this night. I trust you will push your patroles, if possible, to Penafiel. Gen. Silveira is said to be at Amarante.

To the Bishop of Oporto.   Oporto, 13th May, 1809.

I cannot avoid taking the liberty of congratulating your Lordship upon the late successes of the army, which have had the effect of freeing this city from the oppression under which it has suffered from French tyranny. I am happy to have been instrumental in effecting this great object.

To H. R. H. the Duke of York.   Oporto, 13th May, 1809.

Although your Royal Highness unfortunately is no longer at the head of the army, I am convinced that you cannot but be interested in their success; and I therefore enclose to you the copy of a dispatch which I have written to the Sec. of State, giving an account of the operations of the troops under my command, up to yesterday. We failed in cutting off the enemy's cavalry on the morning of the 10th, principally from the badness of the roads leading to and from the bridge over the Vouga, which delayed the march in advance till so late an hour in the morning that we could not turn the position of the enemy unperceived; and I believe that the guide with the cavalry missed his road. The advanced guard of the infantry, however, in the course of that day, were in the rear of the enemy's cavalry, and they were saved from destruction only by going off at a great rate. The infantry were so near to them at Oliveira, as to go into the town at one end when they went out at the other.

On the 11th, the enemy tried their usual manœuvres with their sharp-shooters in the woods, but our troops and the Portuguese got the better of them; and the movement of Major Gen. Murray upon the flank was decisive of the whole position.

In the action of yesterday, our position was vulnerable only on the right. The left was completely defended by the fire of the artillery from the Serra convent, and the troops were posted in a field enclosed by a high stone wall, which defended their front from the fire of the enemy's artillery from the only height in the neighbourhood of the position; and this height was not sufficiently large to contain any body of the enemy's infantry. The pressure upon the right of our troops was strong till Major Gen. Murray made his appearance from Avintas. It is impossible to say what induced Soult to be so careless about the boats on the river, particularly near Oporto; or to allow us to land at all at a point so interesting to him as that which we occupied. I rather believe we were too quick for him, and that he had not time to secure the boats on all the points necessary to protect the retreat of his corps.

The troops have behaved remarkably well in every instance; and I cannot conclude this letter without telling your Royal Highness that the brigade of Guards are in every respect the example and the object of admiration of the whole army. They have not yet been engaged with the enemy; but I have no doubt but that they will acquit themselves as well in that respect as they do in all others.

To the Rt. Hon. the Commander in Chief.   Oporto, 13th May, 1809.

I cannot adopt a better mode of making you acquainted with the operations of the army under my command in this country, than by transmitting to you the copy of my dispatch of yesterday's date to the Sec. of State.

To Major Gen. J. Murray.   Oporto, 12¼ A.M., 14th May, 1809.

If I should find it to be decided that they have gone to Braga, I shall follow them that way, and move straight upon Braga immediately. Loison had, at Amarante and in the neighbourhood, 4500 men. If Silveira and Beresford united have been able to keep him in check, and to induce Soult to think that he could not retreat by the road which he intended to take, Loison must be lost, by leaving him in the hands of Beresford and Silveira. I therefore think the best thing for you, as well as for us to do, is to move upon Braga.

I shall be able, however, to decide better when I shall receive Mellish's report; in the mean time, I wish you to halt at Valongo till I can write to you after having received it; and inquire whether there is a road from Valongo to Villa Nova de Famelição by which guns or infantry can march.

To Major Gen. J. Murray.   Oporto, 14th May, 1809.

As Mellish reports that he saw fires in the direction of Penafiel, it is evident that there must be somebody still thereabouts; and I think it not impossible that Loison may have waited to cover the retreat of the others between Amarante and Penafiel. I wish you, therefore, particularly if this intelligence be confirmed by the reports of your aide de camp, to move towards Penafiel, and at all events to ascertain what is in Amarante this day. You might at the same time communicate with Beresford's corps, either by Amarante itself, or by a ford or ferry at Serra de Libe-ração, over the Tamaga, about a league to the southward; or from Pena-fiel by Ambos dos Rios, across the Douro, and thence to Beresford's quar-ters, which are between Amarante, Lamego, and Villa Real. The road to the ferry at the Tamaga stretches off at Castro, one league from Penafiel, where you will get on to Amarante. If you should find them gone, it would be most desirable that you should push for Chaves. From Braga, if the enemy have gone there, they must go out of Portugal either by Valença, or somewhere across the Minho, or by Chaves, as they came in. If they go by Chaves, which is not unlikely, when they find that you press them, you will intercept them at Chaves.

If your aide de camp should have sent you word that they are all posi-tively gone, Loison and all, towards Braga, move from Valongo towards Braga with your corps, and get on as far this day as you can. I send one column of the army by Ponte de Lima, and another by Braga. I shall go myself by Braga. If your artillery should impede your march on any of these roads, leave it, and order it back to Oporto.

P.S. Since writing the above, I have heard from Beresford, and there is every reason to believe he is at this time at Amarante.

To Marshal Beresford.   Oporto, 14th May, 1809.

The enemy are certainly off by Braga. Whether any of them still remain at or about Amarante is a point about which I am not yet certain. Mellish saw fires last night near Penafiel; therefore, it is not impossible but that Loison may have remained there last night to cover the retreat of Soult.

I have desired Gen. Murray, who is on that road, to ascertain that point; and if he finds from the report of his aide de camp, who went on when Mellish returned, that Loison is still there, he is to move on towards Amarante, to communicate with you, and to proceed to Chaves, by which movement that road into Spain will be cut off. If Loison is not there, Murray is to proceed to Braga, to join the rest of my corps, and I recommend to you to proceed to Chaves. Soult destroyed his guns and blew up his ammunition yesterday morning at about half a league on this side Penafiel, and then went off towards Braga. My troops are in march towards Braga and Ponte de Lima. I shall go towards Braga. I have just received yours of the 12th.

To the Rt. Hon. J. Villiers.   Oporto, 14th May, 1809.

I may as well make use of the time I am waiting here for the last re-ports from Gen. Murray, to apprise you of the result of the attempts in the French army to seize Soult.

On the 9th inst. Capt. —— was seized on his return to this place, after his last interview with me. His papers were likewise seized, among which were found the English passports, and he could not deny that he had had communication with me. I think it appears that he had been endeavoring to gain over the French Gen., ——, who revealed the secret to Soult. Capt. —— had formerly been aide de camp to Gen. ——, and he made Soult promise that he should have his life and liberty. Capt. —— had afterwards the weakness, at the persuasion of the Gendarmerie who had the charge of him, to reveal the names of some of his fellow conspirators, who were likewise seized. I have the original orders for their seizure and confinement ' *au secret.*' They were all marched away as prisoners after the battle of the 12th; and yesterday morning, Capt. —— having made an attempt to shoot the Captain de Gendarmerie, who, he thinks, contributed to deceive and induce him to reveal the names of his accomplices, escaped and came into Oporto. He escaped by the advice of Col. ——, of the dragoons, one of the principals of the conspiracy, who conceived that when Capt. —— should be gone, there would be no evidence against himself. Capt. —— says that he does not think that Soult will dare to injure —— or the others. From all this, it is evident that there was a conspiracy, and it is probable that it was extensive, and it has been put an end to, probably only for the moment, by the weakness, or indiscretion, or treachery of ——, who, Capt. —— says, mentioned the name of Gen. —— as one of the conspirators.

To the Rt. Hon. J. Villiers.   Oporto, 14th May, 1809.

You will have heard from Beresford that the movement upon the Douro has answered all the purposes we wished for it. Loison was stopped at Amarante.

Soult, finding this yesterday morning, destroyed his guns, and blew up his ammunition, about half a league on this side Penafiel, and went off towards Braga. My troops are in march towards Braga and Ponte de Lima.

I have desired Beresford to go to Chaves, at all events, to stop them by that road, and Murray to go there with the King's German Legion, if he should find that Loison still hangs about Amarante, and if he is not able to defeat him in the first instance.

Memorandum for Col. Trant.   Oporto, 14th May, 1809.

1. The 20th dragoons and a brigade of infantry are expected. If they should arrive here they must be ordered to Figueira, where they will receive orders to disembark.

2. All the guns left by the French in Oporto, whether French or Spanish; all those left in the neighbourhood of Penafiel, or elsewhere in the country, of which some will be brought in by Gen. Murray; are to be sent on board any of His Majesty's ships, the Captains of which will consent to take charge of them, and Col. Trant will take the receipt of the Captains for them.

3. The English vessels in the harbour of Oporto should be allowed to sail with their cargoes as soon as the Captains please, giving security, to the full amount of the value of ships and cargo, to answer such demands as His Majesty, or the government of Portugal, may have upon them ;

the former on account of salvage, or prize for his navy or army; the latter on the account of any claims which the laws of nations or the law of the country may give them.

To Vice Adm. the Hon. G. Berkeley.   Villa Nova, 15th May, 1809.

We have taken about 2000 sick, wounded, and prisoners, at and near Oporto; I should, therefore, be much obliged if you would send transports to take them to England. I think they should have 2 tons per man, as many of them are severely wounded. I don't wish to use the transports coming with the stores, &c. from Lisbon, as I shall want them to aid in the arrangement for my own movements.

To Vice Adm. the Hon. G. Berkeley.   Villa Nova, 15th May, 1809.

I have found at Oporto a considerable number of vessels, which I have directed Col. Trant, in concert with the senior officer of the Navy off Oporto, to take an account of; and I shall be glad if you would decide what is to be done with them, and let me know as soon as you can. Mr. Villiers will, of course, have acquainted you with our movements. We are now in pursuit of the enemy, who appear to be retiring towards Chaves.

To Visc. Castlereagh.   Villa Nova, 15th May, 1809.

In my secret dispatch, of the 27th ult., I apprised your Lordship that I had had certain communications with an officer of the French army, in respect to the discontent which prevailed against Marshal Soult. I have since had further communications with the same officer, with the details of which I proceed to acquaint your Lordship. Capt. —— met me within the posts of the British army, between Coimbra and Aveiro, on the night of the 6th inst., accompanied by M. ——, in the presence of Lieut. Col. Bathurst. He informed me that the discontent had increased, and that there were a larger number of officers who were determined to seize their General than when he had last seen me. He said, however, that they were divided into two parties, one discontented with Buonaparte himself, and determined to carry matters to extremities against him: the other, consisting of ——, ——, and others whom he had before mentioned, as attached to the cause of the Emperor, were dissatisfied with Soult's conduct, particularly with an intention which he was supposed to entertain to declare himself King of Portugal; and that they were determined, if he should take that step, to seize him and to lead the army back into France, where it was understood the Emperor wished to see it.

Capt. —— then urged me again to lose no time in pressing upon Soult, as the mode most likely to induce the more violent of the two parties to endeavor to accomplish their purpose. But he said that if my attack was likely to be delayed, it was desirable that I should endeavor to prevail upon some of the towns over which I was supposed to have influence, such as Coimbra, Aveiro, &c., to follow the example of Oporto, and petition Soult to take upon himself the government of the Kingdom, as King; and that I even should write to him to urge the adoption of this measure. In answer to this, I told him, that I certainly should make my

attack as soon as it was in my power, but that I could not fix any day, nor
state to him the plan of my operations; and that in respect to his propositions, regarding the measures to be adopted by me to induce Soult to
declare himself King of Portugal, they were quite out of the question;
that I could not risk the loss of the confidence of the people of Portugal
by doing what he desired in respect to the people of Coimbra, Aveiro, &c.,
nor my own character by writing the letter which he proposed I should.
I told him at the same time that I considered that, notwithstanding all that
had passed between him and me, I had a full right to take what steps I
pleased, even if the officers of the French army should seize their General.
He then went away, and M. —— returned with me to Coimbra, and confirmed all the statements which Capt. —— had made of the discontent of
the officers of the army.

I heard no more of Capt. —— till the 13th, the day after the capture
of Oporto, on which day the original orders for the arrest and secret
detention of Capt. ——, Col. —— of the —— dragoons, and Col. ——
of the —— regiment of infantry, were found among some papers sent to
me by the police of the town; the order for the arrest of the first bearing
date the 9th, and of the last two the 10th inst. In a few hours afterwards,
on the same day, Capt. —— came into Oporto, and informed me that, on
the night of the day he had returned from his last interview with me, he had
been arrested, and his papers had been seized, among which had been
found the 3 passports which I had given him. He said that he attributed
his arrest to the General of Division ——, a man of weak intellect, to
whom he had formerly been aide de camp, and on whom he had endeavored
to prevail, as he thought successfully, to join the party. Gen. —— had,
however, informed Soult of all the circumstances, requiring only his promise that —— should not be injured, and should retain his commission
and his military pretensions.

Soult examined him in presence of Gen. ——, respecting his accomplices, but he declined to name any, and he was sent back to prison in
charge of a Captain of Gendarmerie. This person prevailed upon him,
with promises of pardon and indemnity to all concerned, to consent to tell
Soult the names of his accomplices, which he did on the following night,
notwithstanding, as he says himself, similar promises in his own favor
made to Gen. —— had not been performed, and that as soon as he
had named Cols. —— and ——, immediate orders were sent for their
arrest and secret detention. They marched, in confinement, with the
army from Oporto on the 12th, and on the 13th, at 5 o'clock in the morning, Capt. —— made his escape, at the desire of Col. ——, from the
party of Gendarmes in whose charge he was detained. He now declares
that the conspiracy still exists, and that sooner or later it must burst forth
and fall heavily upon the head of the usurper; and he talked of the war
in Spain as being odious to the army and to the whole nation.

Capt. —— expressed a desire to return secretly to France, and to
bring to England his wife and family, she having, as he says, some property to enable him to live in England till the arrival of better times in
France. I told him that I would send him to England when an opportunity should offer to apply for permission to go to France; and I shall

have the honor of addressing him to your Lordship when the opportunity shall occur of sending him.

To Vice Adm. the Hon. G. Berkeley.   Ruivaes, 17th May, 1809.

I enclose a letter and its enclosures, which I have received from Mr. Cochrane Johnstone, and if it should appear to you, as it does to me, that some of the transports, viz., 8, could be at the present moment spared from the service, it is my opinion that the employment of them, in the manner proposed by Mr. C. Johnstone, would be a public benefit; at the same time, as I have told him that I should consider him chargeable for the freight from the time the transports shall leave Lisbon till they may arrive in England, the public will be released from the expense. If you should agree in opinion with me upon this subject, I would request you to write a line to Sir J. Sinclair, according to Mr. Johnstone's request, and send me back the enclosed letters from Mr. Johnstone to me, that I may make you an official application on the subject. If you should not deem it inexpedient to allow Mr. Johnstone to have the transports, it is certainly desirable that they should be sent to Cadiz at an early period.

Mr. Villiers will let you know how we are going on. If the weather had not rendered the roads so very bad, I think we should have overtaken Soult before now; as it is, he is out of his scrape.

To the Rt. Hon. J. Villiers.   Ruivaes, 17th May, 1809.

Beresford forced in Loison's posts to the eastward of Amarante on the 12th, while I was passing the Douro at Oporto; and on the morning of the 13th, Soult's advanced guard was surprised to find Loison leaving Amarante, when Soult was proceeding there to pass the Tamaga. Soult then destroyed all or the greater part of his guns near Penafiel, at 11 that morning, and marched towards Guimaraens, where he arrived on the 14th. Gen. Murray marched in pursuit of the enemy from Oporto on the 13th, and I heard, at about 5 that evening, of the destruction of the guns, and the alteration of the direction of the retreat. As soon as I had verified the accounts I had received, I directed Beresford upon Chaves; Murray to communicate with Beresford, if Loison still remained in the neighbourhood of the Tamaga; and with the greater part of my corps I moved to the northward, understanding that the enemy intended to direct his course towards the Minho.

I arrived at Villa Nova, about 3 leagues from the enemy, on the 14th, and I then was certain, from the movements of his corps about Braga, that

G. O.   Ruivaes, 17th May, 1809.

2. The troops will have observed the extreme difficulty of supplying them with bread in this part of the country, and the necessity that exists, that they should take care of that which is issued to them, and make it last for the time specified in General Orders; for want of attention to this object, and care of their bread, the best operations are necessarily relinquished.

3. On leaving Oporto, the troops had all bread to the 16th inclusive; some of them received bread at Villa Nova, and all one day's bread at Braga, and yet, in this day, they had none: the state of the provisions requires the continual superintendence of the Commanding officers of regiments, and of the General officers.

4. Till the army will be in a more plentiful country, the allowance of bread is to be 1 lb., and 1½ lb. of meat each man.

his object was Chaves or Montealegre; and I marched to Braga on the 15th; Gen. Murray to Guimaraens; Soult to Salamonde; and yesterday Gen. Murray joined me on the road to Salamonde, where we arrived in the evening, and had a little affair with the enemy's rear guard, in which we killed and wounded some, and took some prisoners. We should have had the whole rear guard if we had had half an hour more daylight; and, as it is, I understand that a large part of them were lost in crossing a narrow bridge over the Cabado, in the dark and in the hurry of their flight. The Guards only were engaged.

Soult is gone to Montealegre, Baptiste is upon one flank, and Silveira between him and Chaves, and I shall follow him to-morrow if he does not turn towards Chaves. He has lost every thing, cannon, ammunition, baggage, military chest; and his retreat is, in every respect, even in weather, a *pendant* for the retreat to Coruña. If I do not overtake him or intercept him, I shall at least have forced him into Galicia, in a state so crippled that he can do no harm, and he may be destroyed by Romana, if he has any force at all. We have got a good many prisoners, and more are coming in every hour.

Pray forward the enclosed letters. Our weather is terrible; it has rained almost incessantly since the 13th, which has rendered our pursuit very laborious and difficult. I only hope that the army will not lose their health.

To Visct. Castlereagh.   Montealegre, 18th May, 1809.

When I determined upon the expedition to the north of Portugal against Marshal Soult, I was in hopes that the Portuguese General, Silveira, would have been able to hold his post upon the Tamaga till he should be reinforced; by which, and by the possession of Chaves, the enemy's retreat would have been cut off, excepting across the Minho; and I intended, if successful, to press him so hard, that the passage of that river would have been impracticable. The loss of the bridge of Amarante, however, on the 2d inst., altered our prospects. I had then no hopes that Marshal Beresford, who marched towards the upper part of the Douro on the 5th, and arrived at Lamego on the 10th, would be able to effect more than confine the enemy on that side, and oblige him to retire by Chaves into Galicia, rather than by Villa Real into Castille. General Beresford, however, having obliged the enemy's posts at Villa Real and Mezam Frio to fall back with some loss, and having crossed the Douro, drove in Gen. Loison's outposts at the bridge of Amarante, and again acquired possession of the left bank of the Tamaga on the 12th, the day on which the corps under my command forced the passage of the Douro at Oporto.

Loison retired from Amarante on the morning of the 13th, as soon as he had heard of the events at Oporto of the preceding day, and met the advanced guard of the French army at a short distance from the town, which Gen. Beresford immediately occupied. I was unable to commence the pursuit of the enemy till the morning of the 13th, when the Hanoverian legion moved to Valongo, under Major Gen. Murray. On that evening I was informed that the enemy had, in the morning, destroyed a great proportion of his cannon in the neighbourhood of Penafiel, and had directed his march towards Braga. This appeared to be the probable result of the situation in which he found himself, in consequence of Gen. Beresford's operations upon the Tamga; and as soon as I had ascertained that the fact was true, I marched on the morning of the 14th, with the army in two columns, towards the river Minho. At the same time I directed Gen. Beresford upon Chaves, in case the enemy should turn to his right; and Major Gen. Murray to communicate with Gen. Beresford, if he should find, as reported, that Loison remained in the neighbourhood of Amarante.

On the evening of the 14th I was certain, from the movements of the enemy's detachments in the neighbourhood of Braga, that he intended to direct his retreat upon Chaves or Montealegre; and directed Gen. Beresford, in case of the latter movement, to push on for Monterey, so as to stop the enemy if he should pass by Villa de Rey. Gen. Beresford had anticipated my orders to march his own corps upon Chaves, and had already sent Gen. Silveira to occupy the passes of Ruivaes and Melgaço, near Salamonde, but he was unfortunately too late.

I arrived at Braga on the 15th (Gen. Murray being at Guimaraens, and the enemy about 15 miles in our front), and at Salamonde on the 16th. We had there an affair with their rear guard. The Guards, under Lieut. Gen. Sherbrooke and Brig. Gen. Campbell, attacked their position, and having turned their left flank by the heights, they abandoned it, leaving a gun and some prisoners behind them. This attack was necessarily made at a late hour in the evening.

On the 17th we moved to Ruivaes (waiting to see whether the enemy would turn upon Chaves or continue his retreat upon Montealegre), and on the 18th to this place. I here found that he had taken a road through the mountains towards Orense, by which it would be difficult, if not impossible, for me to overtake him, and on which I had no means of stopping him.

The enemy commenced his retreat, as I have informed your Lordship, by destroying a great proportion of his guns and ammunition. He afterwards destroyed the remainder of both and a great proportion of his baggage, and kept nothing excepting what the soldiers or a few mules could carry. He has left behind him his sick and wounded; and the road from Penafiel to Montealegre is strewed with the carcases of horses and mules, and of French soldiers, who were put to death by the peasantry before our advanced guard could save them. This last circumstance is the natural effect of the species of warfare which the enemy have carried on in this country. Their soldiers have plundered and murdered the peasantry at their pleasure; and I have seen many persons hanging in the trees by the sides of the road, executed for no reason that I could learn, excepting that they have not been friendly to the French invasion and usurpation of the government of their country; and the route of their column, on their retreat, could be traced by the smoke of the villages to which they set fire. We have taken about 500 prisoners. Upon the whole the enemy has not lost less than a fourth of his army, and all his artillery and equipments, since we attacked him on the Vouga.

I hope your Lordship will believe that no measure which I could take was omitted to intercept the enemy's retreat. It is obvious, however, that if an army throws away all its cannon, equipments, and baggage, and everything which can strengthen it, and can enable it to act together as a body; and abandons all those who are entitled to its protection, but add to its weight and impede its progress; it must be able to march by roads through which it cannot be followed, with any prospect of being over-taken, by an army which has not made the same sacrifices.

It is impossible to say too much of the exertions of the troops. The weather has been very bad indeed. Since the 13th the rain has been con-stant, and the roads in this difficult country almost impracticable. But they have persevered in the pursuit to the last, and have been generally on their march from day-light in the morning till dark. The brigade of Guards were at the head of the column, and set a laudable example ; and in the affair with the enemy's rear guard, on the evening of the 16th, they conducted themselves remarkably well.

To the Rt. Hon. J. Villiers.   Ruivaes, 19th May, 1809.

I received this morning, from Mackenzie, an account that the French had obtained possession of the bridge of Alcantara, to which I acknow-ledge that I do not give much credit. However, having finished yester-day, near Montealegre, my operations against Soult, finding that he had taken to the mountains and had gone towards Orense, and that I had no chance of impeding his progress or of overtaking him, I determined to set out immediately for the Tagus, and I shall not stop one day till I shall arrive there, if my horses can go on. The troops also will commence their march to the same quarter to-morrow, and some of them will be across the Mondego in a week. The weather is terrible : the troops have no shoes to their feet, and we have no bread.

I have just received your letter of the 11th. Let the light brigade and 23d dragoons land at Lisbon, if they should come there. I have given directions to the engineer whose business it is, respecting the defence of Lisbon. Gen. Blunt has nothing to do with these directions.

Notwithstanding the report of the Oporto merchant on board the *Nautilus*, Loison is alive and merry, and with the army.

The question of rank between the English and English-Portuguese officers is one of a very delicate nature; and it arises entirely out of the practice of giving to officers going into the Portuguese service a step of Portuguese rank beyond that which they held in the service of the King. The officers in the two services must rank according to the dates of their respective commissions; but English officers taking temporary Portu-guese commissions must rank, in respect to British officers, according to the date of the commission which they hold in the service of His Majesty. In future, I recommend that they should serve in the Portuguese army with the same rank as they have in that of the King. It is my opinion, the situation of these officers having advanced Portuguese rank will be an anomaly, but that cannot be helped.

I wish to God that Beresford would resign his English Lieutenant General's rank. It is inconceivable the embarrassment and ill-blood which it occasions. It does him no good ; and if the army was not most successful, this very circumstance would probably bring us to a stand-still.

To Major Gen. Mackenzie.   Ruivaes, 19th May, 1809.

I received this morning, near Montealegre, your letters of the 15th, the one announcing the approach of the French to Alcantara, and the other their being in possession of the bridge. I acknowledge that I do not give entire credit to the latter report: first, as you do not mention your authority; secondly, because they could not be in possession of the bridge without first taking the fort; and I think you would have heard of that misfortune, or the probability of its occurrence, before you heard of its

---

G. O.   San Pedro, 19th May, 1809.

2. The different brigades will leave, at Braga, such men as are unable to march, in charge of an assistant surgeon from each brigade, till an hospital can be established there.

Officers must be left at Braga, in charge of the sick of each brigade, in the proportion of one subaltern for 30 men, one captain and one subaltern for 100. A serjeant must be left in charge of the sick of each brigade, if the number left should be under 30, and a serjeant and corporal, besides the officer, for each 30 men above the number.

4. When bread cannot be delivered to the troops, they must have 2 lbs. of beef for their ration.

5. It is to be understood by the soldiers, that wine forms no part of their ration; it is given to them at the pleasure, and upon the responsibility, of the Commander of the Forces, and must be discontinued when circumstances prevent its being procured.

6. The ration of bread is to be increased to 1½ lb., by order from the officers commanding brigades, as soon as the assistant commissaries of brigades will report that they can make issues to that amount.

7. All horses, mules, bullocks, &c. taken from the enemy, are to be offered for sale to the Commissary General, who will buy them, if they should be found to answer for the cavalry, the artillery, or for commissariat purposes.

8. All purchases of captured horses, mules, &c. contrary to this order, will, in future, be considered null and void, unless they should be purchased by officers commanding troops or companies, with the knowledge and consent of the General officers commanding their brigades, for the purpose of carrying camp kettles, &c.

9. The officers commanding troops and companies will recollect, that although mules are given to them from the commissariat, at the commencement of the campaign, they have received an allowance from the public to purchase them, and it was expressly understood that they were to purchase others, if the mules given to them by the commissariat should be worn out.

10. As the Commander of the Forces has reason to believe many horses and mules are kept by even the soldiers of the army, and maintained by means entirely inconsistent with discipline and good order, he desires the officers commanding regiments and brigades to inquire into the number of horses and mules which are attached to the regiments under their command, and to enforce the immediate sale of those not allowed to be kept by the regulations of the army.

11. The Commander of the Forces is much concerned to learn, that the unmilitary practice of firing off their pieces in their quarters, which he had attributed entirely to troops not supposed to be so well disciplined as those of His Majesty, is to be attributed equally to those from whom he expected a better example.

12. The practice of firing off pieces by the soldiers in their quarters, or at all, but by order of their officers, is strictly forbid, and any man guilty of it, is to be punished for disobedience of orders.

13. The soldiers are to be accountable for the quantity of ammunition in their possession, and any man who shall be found to have made away with it, is to be tried and punished.

14. This is not the only irregularity of which the Commander of the Forces has to complain.

15. Under the pretence of taking horses from the enemy, the soldiers have taken them from Portuguese gentlemen, and have even gone so far as to take two horses belonging to the 16th light dragoons, which the Q. M. G. had at Ruivaes.

16. The attention of the officers, commanding regiments and brigades, is called particularly to the conduct of the soldiers under their command.

17. The officers of companies must attend to their men in their quarters, as well as on a march, or the army will very soon be no better than a banditti; if these practices are continued, he desires that officers, commanding brigades, will give directions that the rolls of companies may be called every hour, and all absentees may be punished. He is, besides, determined that those troops who plunder shall be in the rear instead of in the front of the columns.

consequence. However, my operations against Soult finished yesterday. I followed him as long as there was any corps that I thought was likely to stop or impede his march; and I discontinued the pursuit yesterday, after he had passed the Portuguese frontier on his road to Orense, finding that there were no longer any hopes of overtaking him. We beat his rear guard on the 6th at Salamonde, and should have cut it off, if we had had one hour more daylight. Our loss in this affair was trifling. I have come here this day in consequence of your letters, and I shall not stop until I reach the Tagus. The troops will to-morrow commence their march towards the same point, and before a week shall have elapsed some of them will be to the southward of the Mondego. If you should be menaced on the side of Alentejo, break up the bridge of Abrantes, and secure the boats upon the Tagus; and if you have had only half the rain that we have had, I defy the French to cross. If you are attacked only on the side of Alcantara, you have nothing to fear; the enemy cannot penetrate by that road, if vigorously opposed.

To Marshal Beresford.   S. Pedro, 19th May, 1809.

I enclose to you the information I have received from Major Gen. Mackenzie, in consequence of which I propose to leave this place immediately. It is very desirable that I should meet you as soon as possible. I shall be at Ruivaes this day, at Braga to-morrow, and at Oporto on the following day.

P.S. I have just received your letter of the 17th, and I beg you will not hurry the British brigade towards Abrantes, as I do not think the enclosed information renders that at all necessary.

To Visc. Castlereagh.   Braga, 20th May, 1809.

After I had determined to discontinue the further pursuit of Marshal Soult's army, and to return with the British troops to the south, I heard that Marshal Victor had broken up on the Guadiana, and had made an attack and had carried Alcantara on the 14th. A small garrison, consisting of the 2d batt. of the Lusitanian Legion, and the Idanha a Nova batt. of Portuguese militia, since the army marched to the northward, had occupied that place, which it was forced to evacuate, with some loss, in consequence of this attack. An attempt was made to blow up the bridge over the Tagus, which failed, and the enemy's cavalry crossed immediately.

My former dispatches will have apprised your Lordship of the measures which I had adopted, with a view to the defence of that part of Portugal, in case it should be invaded during the absence of the army to the north-

---

G. O.   Ruivaes, 20th May, 1809.

1. The Commander of the Forces calls the attention of the officers, commanding brigades and regiments, to the following extract of a letter from the Bishop of Braga; it points out forcibly the necessity which exists, that the officers of companies should attend to the conduct of the soldiers under their command, and in what manner want of discipline and good order must defeat the best combined operations.

2. The bread represented to have been irregularly seized by the soldiers in the rear, was intended for those at the head of the column, who have, therefore, been in want: commanding officers of regiments are held responsible for obedience to the G. O. of the 4th inst. relative to requisitions from the country.

ward; and I have now the honor to inform your Lordship that the army is in march to the southward, and the head of it will cross the **Mondego** before the end of this week.

To the Rt. Hon. J. Villiers.   Braga, 20th May, 1809.

I send you a letter to Mr. Frere, in which you will see a copy of my dispatch to the Sec. of State, containing an account of our late operations.

I have received your letters of the 14th and 15th. Your friend would have been very useful, if he had come a little sooner; as it is, I fear he will be of little use to us; but I shall talk to him.

You shall have the *Seminario* at Santarem for its original purpose.

The officers of the —— regt. must of course be released; but it would be proper to enable me to report that they have been tried and acquitted. What steps did Cradock take on this subject? I find that Alcantara is taken; but I shall soon be in Beira.

To the Rt. Hon. J. H. Frere.   Braga, 20th May, 1809.

Mr. Villiers will have made you acquainted with our first successes against Marshal Soult, and I now send you a copy of my dispatch to the Sec. of State, containing an account of their result. I am apprehensive, however, that these operations will not be satisfactory to our friends at Seville; at least if I may judge from Gen. Cuesta's letter of the 3d May to Don Anto. Cornel, which you have transmitted to me. I wish, however, to make a few observations upon that letter. In the first place my force did not, and does not at present, amount to the numbers stated by Gen. Cuesta; and of that force there were 5 battalions, with 3 regiments of cavalry, left to the southward; and one battalion, the 40th, at Seville. The force of 20,000 men and 4000 cavalry, which Gen. Cuesta notices, was what I supposed I should have to march into Spain, after the expedition to the northward should be completed, and included my reinforcements expected from England and from Gibraltar, which are not yet arrived.

You will see in the enclosed dispatch an account of the efforts I have made to intercept the enemy's retreat, and of the causes by which they were frustrated; but of this I am certain, that Soult will be very little formidable to any body of troops for some time to come. I did all that I could, and more than I said I should; but no efforts of mine could have prevented him from saving the remnants of his army. I shall not remark on the General's observations on former plans of operations, or upon our system being that of not exposing our troops, excepting to declare that I shall adhere to that system, as I did in the case of the detachments from the garrisons of Elvas and Badajoz, whenever I shall not see any clear advantage to be derived from exposing the troops.

Sir R. Wilson was withdrawn from Alcantara before I arrived in Portugal, for reasons with which I am unacquainted; but thinking the post of importance, I sent another detachment to occupy it, which I am sorry to say was beaten out of it on the 14th inst. by a French corps of 12,000 men. I am now on my return to the southward, and some of the troops will cross the Mondego by the end of the week.

To Major Gen. Mackenzie.   Convent of S. Terso, 21st May, 1809.

I have received your letters to the 18th, and I observe that the enemy has carried the bridge of Alcantara, with 10,000 or 12,000 men, and has advanced as far as Castello Branco. I do not think it clear, however, that a column will enter Portugal on the side of Alentejo; but if one should enter, and you have taken up the bridge at Abrantes, and secured the boats on the Tagus, I do not see what you have to apprehend from it at this season of the year, more particularly after the late heavy fall of rain. I beg, therefore, that you will not be too ready to give credit to the report that a column is invading Alentejo. 2dly, that if one should enter Alentejo, you will not be too ready to abandon your posts in the mountains towards Castello Branco, if you have taken up your bridge at Abrantes and have secured the boats. If no column should enter by Alentejo, or if you should have no reason to apprehend that it will be able to cross the Tagus, I must say that I consider your force, constituted as it is, fully equal to keep a corps of 12,000 French from entering by those passes.

You are in an error in supposing that the Portuguese troops will not fight. One battalion has behaved remarkably well with me; and I know of no troops that could have behaved better than the Lusitanian Legion did at Alcantara the other day; and I must add that if the Idanha a Nova militia had not given way, they would have held their post.

If the enemy should turn the passes, and come by the Estrada Nova, you are equally able to defend the Zezere, till I shall come up to your assistance. The head of the army will cross the Mondego by the 26th, so that I shall not be long separated from you. My opinion is that Victor cannot venture to invade Portugal with his whole force. It is probable that the corps which has crossed at Alcantara is a reconnaitreing party, sent in for the purpose of ascertaining what has become of Soult, what our force is, &c.; and if this be true, it will go from Castello Branco towards Guarda. If it does so, it will run the risk of never getting out of Portugal again.

P.S. The store at Santarem ought to be sent away forthwith, excepting a supply for your own corps for 4 days. It should be put in boats and kept below Salvaterra, ready to move up the river again if you should want it. From these boats you can keep up the store to 4 days for your corps.

I have just received your second letter of the 18th, which pleases me much better than the first. Look at your instructions, my dear Mackenzie, act boldly upon them, and I will be responsible for all the arrangements.

To the Rt. Hon. J. Villiers.   Convent of S. Terso, 21st May, 1809.

I have received your letter (no date), and I enclose the copy of a letter to Mackenzie, which contains my opinion upon all points.

I have written to desire that the hussars may be halted at Villa Franca, where the Commissary must take care to provide them with food and forage by water. The 20th light dragoons must return to Lisbon, and take care of their horses, and all the officers of the staff must resume their duties at the same place. It will not do to allow officers to volunteer their services for duty in the field when they are required in garrison; and I should and shall feel the greatest inconvenience from the absence of those officers from Lisbon, when I shall have to re-equip and refit the army.

As for Gen. Blunt's brigade, the Portuguese government must act as it pleases with its own troops. But surely when a plan has been well considered, it is best to adhere to it, till there shall be some reasonable ground for altering it: and I acknowledge that I have not yet seen any reason for believing that the force which has entered by Alcantara is too strong for Mackenzie, or that any force will enter by Alentejo; and yet I have received intelligence to the 18th, and when you wrote to me you had received it only to the 15th.

Mackenzie has no confidence in the Portuguese troops, and therefore for what reason increase their numbers under his command? I should prefer placing them at Villa Franca as a reserve, and to secure that entrance into Lisbon rather than at any other place, excepting their quarters at Lisbon itself.

To the Rt. Hon. J. Villiers.   Oporto, 22d May, 1809.

I received this morning your letter of the 19th, and 2 from Mr. Frere, one of the 15th, the other of the 19th.

I wrote to you that I wished the 23d light dragoons to land at Lisbon, if they should arrive there; but if they should arrive either here or at the mouth of the Mondego, I propose that they should land to the northward. I am much obliged to you for sending the officer to Almeida. He will be very useful in that quarter.

Mr. —— assured me, some days ago, that he had left at Lisbon blank bills upon the Treasury, to be filled up by the Dep. Com. Gen. I believe rather the truth to be, that we have been deceived by Mr. ——'s reports of the resources of money or bills to be found at Lisbon, and that, instead of large sums, they are very small and very difficult to get at. If we are to carry on war in this country, money must be sent from England. But, after all, I do not see why Gen. Mackenzie should have required a sum of money to have enabled him to move, more than I did with the army; and, as I told you, we had not above £10,000. I can give you no answer respecting the disposal of the arms at Lisbon. I expect Beresford here this day, or to-morrow, to confer with me upon our northern frontiers during my absence to the southward, and I shall prevail upon him to settle that point.

I have 4 brigades here this day, which will be across the Mondego on the 26th. Indeed I am not certain that I shall not have the whole army to the south of that river on that day. Remember that I did not receive the account of the attack of Alcantara till the morning of the 19th, near Montealegre, about 90 miles from hence. I rather think, however, from the accounts which Frere has sent of Cuesta's movements, that the French are not coming into Portugal, but are retiring northwards. They were not at Castello Branco on the evening of the 19th.

P.S. I cannot be certain of the subsistence of this army, unless the Portuguese government will let us have 300 or 400 good mules, with saddles and drivers. It is ridiculous that in Portugal that number cannot be found.

To the Rt. Hon. J. H. Frere.   Oporto, 22d May, 1809.

My letter of the 20th will apprise you of all that has occurred in this quarter, since I wrote to you on the 9th inst. I have returned here with the advance of the army, having done all I could or had to do to the northward, and having thought it necessary to move to the southward, in consequence of the threatened invasion of Portugal, by the attack and capture of Alcantara. The greater part of my troops will pass the Mondego on the 26th inst.

I am much obliged to you for your letters of the 15th and 17th. I acknowledge that I do not consider Lord Wellesley's appointment * a subject of congratulation to himself or his friends. I suspect that the task which will devolve upon him will be a most arduous one ; and that some time will elapse before he will be sufficiently *au courant des affaires* to be able even to form a judgment of its extent. I am truly concerned, however, that your removal should not be consonant to your own wishes.

To Don Gregorio Cuesta.   Oporto, 22d May, 1809.

I had the honor of writing to you from Villa Franca on the 29th of last month, in which letter I informed you that I was on the point of setting out with the army to attack Marshal Soult.

I have now to inform you, that, having collected my troops at Coimbra early in this month, I broke up from thence on the 9th, and marched in 2 columns towards the Vouga. We passed that river on the 10th, and surprised and drove in the enemy's advanced guard of cavalry. On the following day, the 11th, we beat the advanced guard of infantry, the division of Gen. Merle and other troops, and 4 or 5 squadrons of cavalry at Grijo; and on the 12th we forced the passage of the Douro, beat off the attack of the enemy upon our advanced guard which first crossed the river, and took possession of the town of Oporto, and a great proportion of the enemy's artillery. The enemy retired towards Amarante, and my advanced guard followed them on the morning of the 13th.

Gen. Beresford, who had broken up from Coimbra on the 5th May, with a British brigade of infantry, some battalions of Portuguese infantry, and 4 squadrons of cavalry, arrived at Lamego on the Douro, on the 10th and 11th; to which quarter Gen. Silveira had retired after the defeat of his corps, on the 2d inst., at the bridge of Amarante. Gen. Beresford drove in the enemy's posts from Villa Real and Mezam Frio on the 11th, and on the 12th drove in their outposts beyond the Tamaga, and thus cut off their retreat by the best road into Castille. The enemy, upon finding his retreat cut off, retired from Amarante on the morning of the 13th, and Gen. Beresford took possession of that town. The enemy then destroyed, near Penafiel, a great part of the artillery and baggage which he had carried with him, and marched by a mountain road, by Guimaraens,

---

* Sec. of State for Foreign Affairs.

towards the road from Braga to Chaves. My advanced guard followed him; and Gen. Beresford moved upon Chaves, detaching Gen. Silveira to seize the passes of Ruivaes and Melgaço; and I marched with the army direct upon Braga, as soon as I had ascertained the enemy's direction. I arrived there on the 15th, and followed the enemy to Salamonde on the 16th, where we beat his rear guard in the evening, and took from him a gun and some prisoners. He had crossed at Melgaço on that day.

I went to Ruivaes on the 17th, to ascertain whether he would retire upon Chaves, and I proceeded to Montealegre on the 18th. Gen. Beresford, finding that the enemy went upon Montealegre instead of Chaves, marched upon Ginzo, in Galicia, but the enemy had taken a mountain road towards Orense. I therefore discontinued the pursuit; and, on the 19th, having heard of the attack on Alcantara, by a corps of Marshal Victor's army, I determined to return to the southward, and I arrived here this day with a part of the British army.

I did every thing in my power to intercept the enemy; and although I did not succeed, I have the pleasure to inform your Excellency, that since I attacked him on the Vouga on the 10th inst., he has lost one fourth of his army, and the whole of his artillery and equipments. The road between this and Montealegre is strewed with baggage, and the carcases of men, horses, and mules; and he is gone into Galicia, very little able to do mischief to anybody. I hope to hear soon from your Excellency in what manner I can be useful to your operations. A part of the army under my command is upon the Tagus, near Abrantes, and the remainder which is here and on its march from the northward will be across the Mondego on the 26th, unless I shall hear that the corps at Alcantara is moving to the northward.

To Capt. Chambers, R.N.　　　　　　　　　　　　　　Oporto, 22d May, 1809.

If you have not yet sailed with the convoy under your orders, in consequence of my former request to that effect, I shall now be obliged to you to remain at Aveiro, as I have driven Marshal Soult beyond the frontiers of Portugal; and the army is now on its return to the southward, in consequence of information respecting the movements of Marshal Victor on the side of Alcantara; the provisions, stores, &c., are therefore likely to be wanted either at Aveiro or at Figueira.

To the Duke of Richmond.　　　　　　　　　　　　　　Oporto, 22d May, 1809.

I have just returned from the most active and severe service. I have been on the pursuit, or rather chace, of Soult out of Portugal. We should have taken him if Silveira had been one or two hours earlier at the bridge of Melgaço, or if the Captain of militia of the province had allowed the peasants, as they wished, to destroy it. We should have taken his rear guard on the 16th, if we had had a quarter of an hour's more daylight; but, in the dark, our light infantry pursued by the road to Ruivaes instead of by that of Melgaço. But as it is, I think the chace out of Portugal is a *pendant* for the retreat to Coruña. It answers completely in weather: it has rained in torrents since the 12th.

I am now moving the army as fast as possible to the Eastern frontier, by which a corps of Victor's army has entered. I hope soon to be able to force them out also. Remember me most kindly to the Duchess.

To the Marques de la Romana.   Oporto, ce 23 Mai, 1809.

Je viens de recevoir la lettre que vous m'avez écrite le 19 de ce mois; et comme on me dit que le brig *Attack*, qui me l'a apportée, va se mettre en mer tout de suite, je vous envoie la copie d'une lettre que j'ai écrite hier à M. le Général Cuesta, qui vous montrera de quelle manière l'armée Française, sous les ordres du Maréchal Soult, est rentrée en Galice. J'ai fait tout ce qui était en mon pouvoir pour couper totalement sa retraite, mais cela n'a pas été possible; et je n'ai discontinué la poursuite, que lorsque j'ai vu qu'il n'y avait plus moyen de couper l'ennemi, et qu'il ne m'était pas possible de l'attaquer. Je n'avais aucune nouvelle de l'état des affaires en Galice. Depuis que votre Excellence s'est séparée de l'armée Portugaise à Chaves, au mois de Mars, nous n'avions pas eu de vos nouvelles, et nous ne savions même pas où vous étiez.

J'avais promis au Général Cuesta, qui depuis un mois se tient sur la défensive auprès de Llerena, que j'irais co-opérer avec lui, aussitôt que les Français auraient quitté le nord du Portugal; mais n'ayant nulle espérance de pouvoir détruire l'armée de Soult, en continuant la poursuite, il était nécessaire que je la cessasse pour retourner donner du secours au Général Cuesta. Voilà les raisons qui m'ont déterminé à cesser la poursuite le 18 de ce mois; mais si je ne l'avais pas cessée ce jour-là, je l'aurais surement cessée le lendemain; car j'ai reçu le 19, les nouvelles que les Français avaient quitté leurs cantonnemens sur la Guadiana le 12 et le 13; qu'ils avaient attaqué un corps Portugais posté à Alcantara le 14, et qu'ils étaient en possession du pont d'Alcantara. Le Portugal était en même tems menacé par l'attaque d'un autre corps de 10 à 12 mille hommes qui avait suivi les premiers; et la défense du Portugal, qui m'est spécialement confiée, m'aurait obligé de cesser la poursuite du Maréchal Soult, aussitôt que j'aurais reçu ces nouvelles.

Vous me demandez de l'assistance pour la Galice et les Asturies, les deux provinces de l'Espagne que je reconnais être les plus intéressantes comme points militaires de la monarchie; mais en même tems, la Junte Suprême me demande des secours pour le Général Cuesta; et je crois que je pourrais combiner la défense du Portugal avec les secours qu'il me serait possible de lui donner, mieux que je ne le pourrais avec ceux que vous me demandez pour la Galice et les Asturies. Je vous envoie par cette occasion une lettre à votre adresse, que j'ai reçue hier au soir de Séville. M. Frere m'a dit, qu'elle contenait les dernières nouvelles reçues du Général Cuesta. Quand les Français se sont retirés de la Guadiana, ce Général s'est avancé du côté de Badajoz, et il était près de cette ville quand le courier a passé.

Je n'ai pas encore bien éclairé les mouvemens des Français. Ils ont attaqué Alcantara avec 10,000 à 12,000 hommes, et ils avaient, à ce que dit le Général Cuesta, un pareil nombre à Brozas. Ou ils se retireront de l'Estremadure, ou ils attaqueront le Portugal. J'aurai mon armée vers le Mondego, et s'ils se retirent, je ferai en sorte de couper toute communication entre les armées Françaises du nord, et celles qui se retirent du sud, et je ferai mon possible pour vous être utile, et pour leur faire du mal.

To Visct. Castlereagh.   Oporto, 23d May, 1809.

The bearer of this letter is M. ——, respecting whom I have written to your Lordship from this country.   He is now going to England, in consequence of the circumstances which I have lately communicated to you, and he has desired to be recommended to your Lordship.   He wishes to be permitted and to have the facilities given to him to return to France as soon as possible, in order that he may sell a property he has in France, before the accounts of the transactions in which he has been concerned shall be known to the government; and I shall be very much obliged to

---

G. O.   Oporto, 23d May, 1809.
1. The Q. M. G. will forthwith furnish a corps of mounted guides, to be under the immediate superintendence of an officer of the Q. M. G.'s department; this corps will receive the pay and allowances of cavalry, and the officers, non-commissioned officers, and privates, will be mounted on horses, or mules, found by the public.   The corps to be composed as follows: 4 officers receiving the pay and allowances of lieutenant; 4 officers receiving the pay and allowances of cornet; 6 serjeants; 6 corporals; 2 farriers; and 20 privates.

2. As the officers on the staff of the Adj. and Q. M. G.'s department are not allowed in Portugal to keep the same number of horses, which are allowed to officers in the same situations in other parts of the world, and, as it is necessary that the communications between the different divisions of the army should be kept up, in a great degree, through their means, they will be allowed to go post, and to charge for post mules when sent above 10 miles from head-quarters.

The bill for these charges must, however, be vouched by the signature of the head of the department, and further by a copy of the order to take the journey, specifying the distance.

3. As the General staff officers of the army experienced the greatest difficulty in getting their horses shod, whereby they are frequently disabled from the performance of their duty, the Commander of the Forces will allow of smiths from the corps of infantry being attached, by permission of the Commanding officers of the regiments to which they belong, to the officers hereinafter named, to shoe the horses of the General staff officers under their command, or in the neighbourhood of their stations, viz. Lieut. Gen. Sherbrooke; Major Gen. Murray; Major Gen. Hill.   These officers will each be allowed to draw forage for one mule to carry the implements and tools of the smith : the mule must be provided by those who will benefit by the establishment.   Two smiths are also to be attached in the same manner to the Commandant at head quarters, to shoe the horses of all the staff.

9. On the arrival of the army at Aveiro, where the ship with medical stores has been detained, every surgeon, whether staff or regimental, is immediately to renew and complete all deficiencies in any part of the original field equipment, directed in General Orders.

The Commissary Gen. will replace, on application, any of those public mules that have been so injured as to be unserviceable.

General officers, commanding brigades, are requested to facilitate, as much as possible, the conveyance of what has been ordered during the approaching march, as the succour of the sick, and the preservation of the wounded in the field, must, in a great degree, depend upon what regiments carry with them.

G. A. O.   Oporto, 23d May, 1800.
1. The Commander of the Forces has been informed, and, indeed, has observed, notwithstanding the orders issued by the late Commander of the Forces and himself, much of the private baggage of the army is moved upon bullock cars.   The officers must have felt the inconvenience which this mode of transporting their baggage must be to themselves personally.   It is scarcely possible that the baggage can keep up with them, even at present, and when the army will move in larger divisions, will become quite impossible.

The public inconvenience resulting from this mode of transporting private baggage is still greater.   The Commander of the Forces is aware that in forced marches, and in bad weather, it may happen that animals provided for carriage will knock up, but hopes that officers of the army will consider it as a determined measure, that no baggage is to be carried upon bullock cars, excepting those allowed by the late Commander of the Forces, and that those who have baggage to carry, must be provided with mules or horses.

your Lordship if you will give directions that these facilities may be given to him.

Your Lordship is fully acquainted with all that has passed between Capt. —— and me, and will judge how far he has any claim to a provision from the British government. Possibly it might be deemed good policy not to allow a man to starve who was engaged in a scheme which, if it had been successful, would have tended more than any other to the destruction of the power of Buonaparte. But exclusive of this general claim upon the bounty of the British government, —— is not without some which appear to me sufficiently strong. His plan was his own, and his communications with me were voluntary; but that which occasioned the discovery of the plan, and ruined him when it was discovered, was his first journey to Lisbon to meet me, and his second journey within our posts to Coimbra. He undertook the first of these journeys at the positive request of Lieut. Col. Douglas, who had been employed by Gen. Beresford to meet him at Ovar; and who, when he met him, found his communications so important, that he thought it desirable that —— should see Gen. Beresford, and he came the second time by my desire. I trust, therefore, that your Lordship will think that he has some claim upon the bounty of government, and that you will give him such an allowance as may enable him to live decently in England.

To the Rt. Hon. J. Villiers.   Oporto, 23d May, 1809.

There is nothing new this day. Beresford is on his return. I heard from him at Chaves on the 20th.

Upon the capture of Oporto we found here several English, some Danish, Swedish, and one or two French vessels, and a considerable quantity of property, some of which had been loaded in these ships; and another part, principally cotton, which the French had bought in different parts of the country, and had collected here in charge of the French consul. I wrote to the Admiral some days ago to recommend that he should order the Captain commanding off the port to send an officer on shore to take an account of the vessels and their contents, in concert with Col. Trant; and I received an answer yesterday from him, stating that he had desired his secretary to correspond with Col. Trant respecting these vessels. The most valuable part of this property is 3000 tons of wine, belonging, I believe, to the English merchants; upon which the Admiral, on the notion that all the property at Oporto is liable to be considered and dealt with by the rules of prize, thinks us entitled to salvage. My opinion is, that if we are entitled to it at all, we are entitled to the whole of the property: but the doubt which I entertain is, whether we have a right to any part of this property; and upon this doubt I wish to have your opinion. It appears to me, that Oporto being a Portuguese port, and the British army acting in this country as allies, or even as a subsidiary army to the government of Portugal, every thing taken in Oporto belongs to the government of Portugal; and must be dealt with as that government chooses, and not according to the rules which govern cases in which His Majesty's sea and land forces take a port or town from the enemy, which afterwards becomes a part of his own dominions.

I wish you to consider the question not only as one of civil law, but also in reference to the manner in which the Portuguese government would feel, if we were to consider the property which we found here in possession of the enemy as prize; for however glad I shall be that the success of the army should turn out to their benefit, as well as to their honor, and however convenient it might be to me to share in this benefit myself, I am very unwilling to be instrumental in forwarding such a claim, if it is to have the effect of putting our friends out of temper with us.

Since I began this letter I have received one from the Marques de la Romana; of which, and of my answer, I shall send you a copy. He was at Gijon on the 15th May, having about 9000 men in the Asturias, and 4000 or 5000 at Vigo. He wants my assistance to defend the Asturias.

To Capt. Mackinley, R.N.   Oporto, 23d May, 1809.

I have had the honor of receiving your letter of the 18th inst.; and I send one for the Marques de la Romana, which I beg of you to forward.

You have been informed, I believe, of the success which attended the operations of the troops under my command to the 12th inst. We pursued the enemy on the 13th, and every measure that was practicable was adopted to cut off the enemy's retreat into Galicia : but it was impossible; and he penetrated through the mountains to Orense, on the 19th and 20th, having lost, since I attacked him on the Vouga on the 10th inst., above the fourth of his army, all his cannon, ammunition, and equipments, and all his baggage, excepting what the soldiers and a few mules could carry. The road was strewed with the carcases of horses, mules, and French soldiers. I am now returning to the southward, in consequence of an attack threatened upon the Eastern frontier of Portugal by a corps of 12,000 men, which has taken Alcantara.

To the Rt. Hon. J. Villiers.   Oporto, 24th May, 1809.

This letter will be delivered to you by M. ———, whom I recommend to your protection and kindness. He is going to England, with an intention of returning to France as soon as possible, with a view to sell his estate before the government shall obtain a knowledge of transactions here in which he has been engaged. I have recommended him to Lord Castlereagh, and I shall be very much obliged to you if you will aid him in getting away from Lisbon, either in a ship of war or in the packet, as soon as possible.

G. O.   Oporto, 24th May, 1809.

2. The army being likely to go into huts at an early period, the Commander of the Forces is disposed to supply the officers with tents from the public stores, in the proportion of one tent for each field officer, and one tent for the officers of each company, and one for the staff; it will be necessary, however, that the officers, to whom these tents will be issued, shall provide means for the carriage, without increasing the demands for forage.

3. The officers commanding regiments will send to the Q. M. G., through the officers commanding their brigades, returns of the names of those officers who are desirous of having tents, stating the numbers required for the regiments under their command, according to the proportions above specified.

To the Rt. Hon. J. Villiers.   Oporto, 24th May, 1809.

I enclose you a memorandum which has been put into my hands by the Q. M. G., and I shall be very much obliged to you if you will apply to the government for the information which he asks in the first paragraph, and for the drawings and sketches required in the second.

We are sadly in want of shoes; and the carts upon the road from Lisbon to Coimbra have been so ill used, that I fear we cannot depend upon the communication; and if we could, I believe we should receive them sooner by sea. It will require 40 carts to bring up 20,000 pairs of shoes, which we want; and I shall be very much obliged to you if you will ask the Admiral to allow one of his ships of war to take them on board, and bring them as soon as possible to the mouth of the Mondego: we cannot depend upon the transports making way against the wind at this season. The Commissary at Lisbon will have orders to embark the 20,000 pairs of shoes, if you should tell him that the Admiral will send them to us; if not, he will send them by land.

To Major Gen. Mackenzie.   Oporto, 24th May, 1809.

It has occurred to me, that you may be in the neighbourhood of Gen. Cuesta, and that he may propose to you to make some movement in aid of his operations. You will recollect that your corps is destined to the defence of Portugal; and it must not be risked in any offensive operations. Gen. Cuesta's corps is by no means equal in point of strength to that of the French opposed to him; and it is not impossible that he may wish to strengthen himself by a co-operation or a junction with that under your command. All that is very well, as long as the defence of Portugal is the object; but I cannot be responsible for the safety, or for the risk, for an inadequate object, of the King's troops, in an operation with the Spanish troops under the command of Gen. Cuesta. If, therefore, Gen. Cuesta should press you to undertake any service beyond the line of your instructions, you will tell him that your corps is destined to defend a particular line of country, beyond which you cannot go without orders, so long as the French remain on the Tagus; and that in case they should move northward, you have orders, which I now give you, to join the British army.

P. S. The troops will be on the Mondego on the 26th and 27th.

To Brig. Gen. Alex. Campbell.   Oporto, 24th May, 1809.

The Adj. Gen. has communicated to me your letter of the 23d inst., reporting the conduct of Capt. the Marquez ——, in absenting himself from his battalion without leave on the 15th inst., and that you had put him in arrest.

I observe from the date that this offence was aggravated by being committed at a moment when the troops were in march in pursuit of the enemy. I am not disposed, however, to carry matters to extremities with the Marquez; and I beg that you will call him and the officers of the regiment to which he belongs before you, and point out to him the extreme impropriety of his conduct. You will particularly point out to him that all the exertions of Great Britain, and that all that the valor and discipline of British soldiers can effect, will not save Portugal and secure her independence, unless the people of Portugal exert themselves in their own cause; and that it is particularly incumbent upon the nobility and persons of great fortune and station to set the example of that devotion to the service of their country, and of that strict attention to the rules of military discipline and subordination, which can alone render any exertions useful, and lead to that success to which all must look forward with anxiety.

You will tell the Marquez that I hope that the lenity with which his fault has been treated upon this occasion will induce him to be more attentive to his duty; and that I expect from him exertions in the cause of his country, patience to bear the hardships of a military life, and submission to the rules of military discipline and subordination, in proportion as his rank, station, and fortune are superior to those of others of his countrymen in the service. You will then release the Marquez from his arrest.

To Marshal Beresford.   Quinta de la Mealhada, 25th May, 1809.

I was in hopes that I should have seen you at Oporto, and I stayed there till this morning. I shall be at Aveiro to-morrow. It is absolutely necessary that I should see you. I consider the north of Portugal to be now the most exposed part of the country, and we must make a good arrangement for its security before we move to the southward.

To Lieut. Gen. Sherbrooke.   Aveiro, 27th May, 1809.

I hope you will have a better passage than I had. My horses are not yet arrived.

In respect to Mr. G——, I am aware of his merits, and I shall be happy to do something for him. But it would not answer to promote an Assist. Commissary to be a Deputy Commissary, when we have already 4 Deputy Commissaries with the army; more especially as he was appointed by the Treasury only in 1807. Besides, with every sense of Mr. G——'s merits, I must have a longer experience of them, and a better opportunity of comparing them with the merits of others, than I have had in the short period since the troops took the field.

To the Rt. Hon. J. Villiers.   Aveiro, 27th May, 1809.

I received yesterday your letters of the 21st and 23d. In answer to the first, I have to inform you that I conclude Gen. Blunt will not order the 40th regt. from Lisbon, when that corps shall arrive there, till he shall receive directions from me. As soon as I can get my papers I propose to send the 30th regt. to Gibraltar, to relieve a part of that garrison; and I propose that the 40th shall do the duty at Lisbon, till I can get one of the

G. O.   Ovea, 26th May, 1809.

1. The Commander of the Forces begs that the officers commanding brigades will ascertain the number of men left behind, on the march, by each of the regiments under their command, from the time the army left Coimbra; and they will make a return of them to the Adj. Gen.'s office, stating the names of the officers commanding the companies from which those men have absented themselves.

younger corps down from the army to relieve the 40th. I also hope that Gen. Blunt will not order the 23d light dragoons from Lisbon, if that corps should arrive in the Tagus, without receiving directions from me.

I am concerned that I do not agree in opinion with you respecting the propriety of sending one regiment of dragoons to Castello de Vide; particularly not one which will have been but just landed. Neither officers, men, nor horses are, in the first days after their disembarkation, fit for any duty, and particularly not for that description of duty to be performed by one regiment of dragoons opposed to a whole army.

If mules could be got in the country for any purpose, I should wish to apply them to some other purpose besides the draught of two 3 pounders to be attached to the 23d dragoons. If such an equipment should be desirable, I shall have it in my power to supply it with horses.

I don't know what Beresford means by negotiation. In an intercepted letter from Victor to Marshal Jourdan, I believe, (for the copy sent to me was so faulty that I could not make out its contents, or to whom addressed,) he says that ' he will not make a certain movement,' (not described, but probably a retrograde one,) ' till a French negotiation should have brought to a close his negotiations with the Junta, of the success of which he had some hopes.' It is probable that the movement to which he referred was that lately executed upon Alcantara, so that the negotiation must have already been brought to a close. But if it were not, I should not think it advisable that we, in Portugal, should suggest any measures, in regard to negotiations, to the Junta of Seville, especially measures founded upon any thing so vague as the contents of an old intercepted letter.

In answer to your letter of the 23d, I have to mention that I had intended to move by Guarda, possibly Almeida, if the enemy had remained at Alcantara, and had pointed northward. But at present I intend to follow my original plan, and to assemble the army on the Tagus. From thence I shall act upon the north or south side of that river, as I may think proper. I hope, however, that the troops will be left in their stations, till I shall send them orders to move.

The foundation of all military plans is compounded of the situations of one's own troops, those of the allies, and those of the enemy; but if I cannot be certain even of my own, it is impossible for me to form, much less to execute, any military plan. I do not in general leave the troops idle, and you may depend upon it they will have enough to do before the campaign is over. Besides, you see that the reliefs from Gibraltar and England are to be executed, and the troops must not be moved without my direction.

I propose to send all the prisoners to England, excepting the Hanoverians, who will be allowed to enter the Legion.

The French broke a great number of their arms, and the Portuguese peasantry took and carried away the remainder.

I don't know what to do, or to recommend, in respect to the magistrates of the country. They are so very inefficient or remiss in the performance of their duty, that we are constantly stopped or thwarted, for

want of the assistance which we must require from them. I have now to
complain of the magistrates of this place and Ovar, for disappointing us
in the boat people necessary to attend the boats to transport the troops
across the lake. For want of boats and boatmen the troops are not so
forward on their march to the southward as I intended they should be.

To Lieut. Gen. Sir J. Cradock, K.B.   Aveiro, 27th May, 1809.

I have the honor to enclose a letter for you from the Sec. of State,
containing directions to send to Portugal from Gibraltar the 48th and
61st regts., as soon as corps could be sent from Portugal to relieve them.
I now send from Portugal the 2d batt. 30th regt., and I purpose to send
round to Gibraltar another battalion, as soon as one can be marched down
the country. In the mean time, I have requested the Admiral to send to
Gibraltar a sufficiency of tonnage for the conveyance of both the regiments;
and I hope that you will have no objection to detach from Gibraltar both
the regiments, in consideration of the urgency of the service in Portugal,
although only one battalion is now sent from Portugal to relieve them;
but you may depend upon it that the second battalion shall follow as soon
as possible.

To Vice Adm. the Hon. G. Berkeley.   Aveiro, 27th May, 1809.

Before I left England, I received directions from the Sec. of State, of
which I enclose a copy, to send to Gibraltar 2 battalions of infantry, to relieve 2 battalions of that garrison ordered to join the army in Portugal.
I propose that the 2d batt. 30th regt. shall be one of the battalions to go to
Gibraltar; and I have written to the commanding officer at Gibraltar to
request that, as soon as that battalion shall arrive there, he will send round
the 2 battalions destined for service in Portugal.

I shall therefore be much obliged to you if you will be so kind as to
give directions that tonnage for 2000 men may be prepared, to be sent
round to Gibraltar, on board of which transports the 2d batt. 30th regt.
will be ordered to embark, as soon as the 1st batt. 40th regt. shall relieve
them at Lisbon. I shall hereafter request of you to order tonnage for
another battalion to be sent to Gibraltar, as soon as I shall have been
enabled to decide which I shall send, from a comparison of their relative
fitness for service in the field.

To Lieut. Col. Gordon.   Coimbra, 27th May, 1809.

I have the honor to enclose a list of officers in the British army in
Portugal, who have been allowed, by the late Commander of the Forces,
to serve with the Portuguese army on the same terms with the officers
who were sent from England with Gen. Beresford to serve in Portugal.
I understand that all these officers have complied with the conditions on
which they were to be allowed to transfer their temporary services to the
Portuguese troops; and I beg you will submit their names to the Commander in Chief, to be promoted one step in rank. It is very desirable
that officers should be sent to replace them in the regiments to which they
belong

I also enclose a list of the names of officers permitted by the late Commander of the Forces to serve with the Portuguese army as Brigadier Generals. Sir R. Wilson, indeed, has been for a considerable time employed in that situation ; and I beg leave to recommend that these officers may be allowed to draw the pay and allowances of Brig. Generals on the British establishment.

To Brig. Gen. Cox, Governor of Almeida.   Cantanhede, 28th May, 1809.

I have received your letter of the 22d inst. I shall be very much obliged to you if you will take measures to obtain a knowledge of the movements and strength of the different French corps in the neighbourhood of Almeida, and write to me by every opportunity. The British army, having defeated and driven Soult out of Portugal, is now on its return to the south; and, if I should find that the object of the late movements of the French towards Alcantara is to retire northward, I shall turn towards Almeida.

I shall be obliged to you to let me know what quantity of provisions and military stores you have at Almeida ; whether those of both descriptions, left in the place last year by the British army, are still there, and in what state of preservation. Direct to me at Coimbra, where my quarters will be to-morrow.

To Major Gen. Mackenzie.   Cantanhede, 28th May, 1809.

You probably do not know that the hussars are a few stray ones belonging to the 1st regt., which landed at Lisbon, instead of Figueira with their regiment. The regiment is inefficient without them, as you may readily believe. Pray, therefore, let them be halted somewhere, till I can lay hands upon them to join them to their corps.

I have received your letters of the 24th and 26th. All that you have done is perfectly correct in every part. I should like to see Alcantara occupied again ; but it will not do to contest the point with the French army at Brozas. I think it probable that the people who were there on the 25th were only a patrole. The march of the army has been delayed in some measure for the want of shoes ; but our head is at Coimbra, and we are all in motion to the southward.

To Marshal Beresford.   Coimbra, 29th May, 1809.

I have had the honor of receiving your letter, enclosing one from Major Gen. ——, expressing the desire of that officer to be relieved from the command of the brigade placed under his orders, and to be allowed to return to England, if it is intended to employ his services, in future, in co-operation with the Portuguese troops. As the Commander in Chief of the British and Portuguese allied army in this country, it is impossible for me to engage to any officer that the troops under his command shall not be employed in concert or co-operation with any particular description of troops. In that capacity, I consider myself wholly and solely responsible that His Majesty's troops shall not be employed in improper situations, and the Major Generals, or other inferior officers, responsible only that they and those under them do their duty in the situation in which they may be employed.

I request you, therefore, to inform Major Gen. —— that he has my leave to resign the command of his brigade, and to go to England when he thinks proper; and that I desire he will deliver over the command to the senior officer of the brigade present.

To the Rt. Hon. J. Villiers.   Coimbra, 30th May, 1809.

I am very much afraid that I did not sufficiently explain myself on the

---

G. O.   Coimbra, 29th May, 1809.

The Commander of the Forces is much concerned to be obliged again to complain of the conduct of the troops; not only have outrages been committed by whole corps, but there is no description of property of which the unfortunate inhabitants of Portugal have not been plundered by the British soldiers, whom they have received into their houses, or by stragglers from the different regiments of the army. The Commander of the Forces apprehends that the interior discipline of the regiments is materially relaxed, and he therefore desires that the soldiers of every company, in each of the regiments, may be formed into as many squads as there are non-commissioned officers, each squad having in it one non-commissioned officer, who must be responsible for the conduct of the soldiers in his squad. The non-commissioned officers must always be quartered with the men of their squads.

On halting days an officer of each company must visit the quarters of the men of his company, 4 times each day, of which one must be at 8 o'clock in the evening. On marching days an officer of each company must visit the quarters, twice after the men have got into them, of which once must be at 8 o'clock in the evening. An officer must also visit the quarters of the company, before the soldiers march in the morning. The object of these visitings is to see that the soldiers conduct themselves regularly in their quarters, to ascertain whether there are any complaints by the landlords, and of whom, and that the men are in their quarters, instead of marauding in search of plunder. The officers of the companies, who will visit, must report to the Commanding officer that they have visited the quarters the number of times ordered, specifying the number. The Commanding officer will report daily to the officer commanding the brigade, that these visitings have been made. The officers must be quartered in the immediate neighbourhood of their companies.

The Commander of the Forces calls the attention of the officers commanding brigades and regiments to the orders given out, and repeated with a view to prevent the soldiers from straggling from their regiments on a march, which have hitherto been ineffectual. He desires that a report of absentees may be made after every march to the officer commanding the brigade; and the officer commanding the brigade will send this report, with a statement from what companies the men are absent, to the Commander of the Forces.

The use of carts to carry baggage of any description, is again positively forbid; and it is equally forbid to have guards with any baggage.

The hospital bedding and stores heretofore carried under charge of regimental surgeons, is to be sent into the hospital at Coimbra; there will be only one cart attached to each regiment, viz. that to carry men who may fall sick on a march; no guard whatever must be out of the ranks on a march, excepting those ordered by the General Orders.

No soldier must be employed to press carts or bullocks, for draught or food, excepting accompanied and directed by the assistant commissary of the brigade, or his deputy or clerk, except in cases of evident necessity; when the commanding officer of the brigade, in the absence of the assistant commissary, may direct that carts or bullocks for draught or food may be pressed, in which case an officer must command the party; and the officer commanding the brigade must report the circumstance as soon as possible, to head-quarters.

The circumstances which have occasioned these orders have given the Commander of the Forces the greatest concern; and he hopes, with the assistance of the officers of the army, to put an end to the disgraceful practices which have prevailed.

The people of Portugal deserve well of the army; they have in every instance treated the soldiers well; and there never was an army so well supplied, or which had so little excuse for plunder, if any excuse can in any case exist. But if the Commander of the Forces should not by these and other measures be enabled to get the better of these practices, he is determined to report to His Majesty, and send into garrison those corps who shall continue them; as he prefers a small but disciplined and well ordered body of troops to a rabble, however numerous; and he is resolved not to be the instrument of inflicting upon the people of this country the miseries which result from the operations of such a body.

The regulations of these orders are to be understood as applicable to the dragoons and the artillery, as well as the infantry.

subject of the rank of British officers in the Portuguese service. I have no pretensions to decide upon the question of difference which arises upon it; but when it is referred to me, I must give my opinion upon it, and I am concerned if it differs from yours. I have no desire that it should be decided by me: decide it yourself, or let it be referred to the ministers in England, and I shall act cordially upon any decision that may be passed upon it.

The practice has been to take a Captain from the British army to make him a British Major, and then to make him a Portuguese Lieutenant Colonel. A British Lieutenant is by the same process made a Portuguese Major; and Lieut. Col. Blunt and Lieut. Col. Campbell are made Portuguese Brigadiers over the heads of all the Colonels and all the senior Lieut. Colonels of the British army serving in Portugal. The rank thus given to these officers is not permanent, for they may return to the King's service to-morrow. They have not entered permanently into the Portuguese service. If they had, I should not have a word to say; but after having, during the service in Portugal, commanded their permanent superiors in the British service, they are to return to that service to be commanded by those superiors.

I don't dispute the rank of the Portuguese commission; on the contrary, I assert it; but I wish that an arrangement should be made which would satisfy the officers of this army respecting the rank they are to hold, in relation to their juniors in the British service who hold superior military rank in the Portuguese service.

It may be asked, Why are they to require satisfaction? to which I only answer, that men's minds are so constituted, that when they conceive they are injured, they are not satisfied until the injury is removed. Dissatisfaction on one subject begets it on others, and I should have (indeed I may say I have, for the first time) the pain of commanding a dissatisfied army.

If military rank and pre-eminence is an object (and it is an object on service in the field against the enemy, or it is none at all), these officers are injured by the temporary supercession of themselves by their juniors in the British service; and all that I ask is either that British officers entering the Portuguese service shall serve in the same rank which they hold in that of His Majesty, or, if superior rank should be given to them in the Portuguese service, it should be understood that, when they meet British officers of superior British rank to themselves, they are to receive their orders. The effect of this last arrangement would be to give for that moment Portuguese rank to the British officer who should thus exercise the command.

I mentioned Beresford's local rank only as an instance of the dissatisfaction unnecessarily created by such arrangements. It is of no use to Beresford; for, as Field Marshal and Commander in Chief of the Portuguese army, he must command everybody excepting the Commander in Chief

G. O. Coimbra, 30th May, 1809.
3. The ration of all the mules and horses with the army, is hereafter to be as follows:
14 lbs. of hay or straw.
12 lbs. of oats, or 10 lbs. of Indian corn or barley.

of the British army, and that by virtue of a special arrangement; and I observe that the same feeling exists respecting it in England, for it has virtually been done away, respecting all Major Generals senior to him, by a late order. The dissatisfaction, however, occasioned by the grant of this rank, is undoubted. It is the cause of the resignation of one General officer, —— who, by the bye, was by no means affected by it; and Major Gen. J. Murray, who will be a loss, is determined to resign, and go away, notwithstanding that, as I have above told you, the rank has now no effect with respect to him. But these two instances will be sufficient to show you in what manner dissatisfaction, once excited, works in a British army; and I must say that, from the highest to the lowest, dissatisfaction does now exist in the British army.

We are not naturally a military people; the whole business of an army upon service is foreign to our habits, and is a constraint upon them, particularly in a poor country like this. This constraint naturally excites a temper ready to receive any impressions which will create dissatisfaction; and when dissatisfaction exists in an army, the task of the Commander is difficult indeed. I am, therefore, most desirous that the reasonable grounds for it, which do now exist, should be removed; and I have pointed out one of two modes in which this object can be effected.

I cannot go to Lisbon, and cannot move from hence for 2 or 3 days; but I shall let you know my motions exactly.

To Don Gregorio Cuesta.   Coimbra, 30th May, 1809.

I wrote to your Excellency, on the 22d inst., an account of the operations of the army under my command, and I informed your Excellency that the army was in march towards this place. Its progress has been in some degree delayed by the badness of the weather and the roads, and the want of shoes; but the whole are in full march for this place, and will proceed, as fast as circumstances will permit, towards the Tagus, and I expect that all the reinforcements will have arrived by the time it reaches that river.

I now send to your Excellency's head quarters 2 officers in my confidence, Lieut. Col. Bourke,* of the Q. M. G.'s. department, and Lieut. Col. the Hon. H. Cadogan,† one of my aides de camp, in order to explain to your Excellency my intentions, and to ascertain those of your Excellency, with regard to the co-operation of the two armies under our command respectively, in an attack upon Marshal Victor, with the view to the destruction of his corps, if possible; or, if not possible, its removal from its threatening position on the frontiers of Portugal and of Andalusia.

Lieut. Col. Bourke will explain to your Excellency the points on which I wish to have information, which I request your Excellency to afford him.

Memorandum for Lieut. Col. Bourke, A. Q. M. G.   30th May, 1809.

If the two armies under Gen. Cuesta and Sir A. Wellesley are to co-operate in an attack upon Marshal Victor, the co-operation must be upon

---

* Lieut. Gen. Sir R. Bourke, K.C.B., afterwards Governor of New South Wales.
† Afterwards killed at Vitoria.

the principle of a junction; or of a co-operation with communication; or of a co-operation on separate lines previously combined and arranged.

If on the principle of a junction, where is it proposed that the armies should join?

If on the principle of a co-operation, with constant communication, by what points is the communication to be kept up?

If the operations of each army are to be separate and distinct, although previously combined, and it is proposed that the British army should act upon the right flank and rear of the enemy, what operations does Gen. Cuesta propose for his army?

What is the position at present occupied by the enemy, and his strength in it?

What are his lines of retreat from it, and what are the advantages and disadvantages attending each?

What support has the enemy's flank, and between him and Madrid?

What is the position occupied by Gen. Cuesta? What is his strength in infantry, cavalry, and artillery?

What number of days would be required for Gen. Cuesta to march from his present position to that occupied by the enemy, with a view to a combined attack upon him?

Is there any fortified position of which it would be necessary for Gen. Cuesta to possess himself and occupy, before he could join in the attack with advantage?

Are there any natural difficulties in the road?

What French corps, and of what strength, are on the left of Victor, and where situated?

How do these troops communicate with Victor?

Is their junction practicable, and if both were to withdraw, where could they join?

What is the strength of the corps under Gen. Venegas? and where is he situated?

How does he communicate with Gen. Cuesta?

Would it be possible to include this corps in the system of operations to be adopted against Victor?

Are the roads practicable for an army, leading along the Tagus, both north and south of that river?

What roads lead from the Tagus to the Guadiana, and what communication between one of these roads and the other?

To W. Huskisson, Esq., Sec. to the Treasury.   Coimbra, 30th May, 1809.

The distress, of which I gave you a sketch in my last letter, has been aggravated by its continuance, and by an accumulation of debt for all our supplies from that period to this.

I am convinced that £300,000 would not now pay our debts in this country. Pay is due to the troops, and we have not a shilling, or the chance of getting any. The money sent to Cadiz to be exchanged is not returned, and none can be procured at Lisbon for bills. In short, we must have money from England, if we are to continue our operations in this country. You should now send us £300,000 as soon as possible.

I believe that we have all been deceived respecting the supposed facility of procuring money at Lisbon for bills upon England. Where is the trade which is likely to supply a demand for bills to the amount of 2 millions a year? Is it to be believed, on the other hand, that the merchants of Portugal are sending their whole capital to England? And if they are, must there not be some limit to the amount of the demand for bills for this purpose? In short, Mr. —— has given you an erroneous view of the state of the money market at Lisbon, as he has to me upon many other subjects; he has availed himself of all that it could supply, and nothing now remains.

I trust that £100,000 will have been sent immediately after you received my last letter, and that you will send £200,000 more as soon as possible. I borrowed from the merchants of Oporto all that I could get; but the sum was very small indeed, and we are in the greatest distress.

The A.G. to Col. Peacocke, Lisbon.   May, 1809.

I am directed by the Commander of the Forces to acquaint you, in reply to your letter of the 3d inst., that Col. Donkin has been appointed by His Majesty to the staff of the army in Portugal; with which appointment he cannot presume to interfere. With regard to your wishes of being placed on the staff, his Excellency sees much difficulty in the arrangement, especially as there are Colonels senior to you in this army, serving with their regiments, whom the Commander of the Forces would not feel justified in not placing equally on the staff; and there are not brigades for all the General officers that are expected to join this army. Col. Donkin has received the Commander of the Forces' leave to go to England, and probably will not return.

The A.G. to Lieut. Olfermann,* 97th regt.   May, 1809.

I have not failed to lay your letter of yesterday's date before the Commander of the Forces, who has directed me to say that you must remain with your regiment, as none, under the rank of a captain, will be appointed Town Major of Oporto: and from your rank in the army you are ineligible for the situation of D. A. A. G. by the late regulations.

The A.G. to Lieut. Col. Walsh, Town Major, Lisbon.   May, 1809.

I have not failed to lay your letter of the 20th inst. before the Commander of the Forces relative to the officers of the — regt. who have been tried on suspicion of murdering a Spaniard, and acquitted thereof by the Portuguese civil power; and have in consequence received his Excellency's commands to signify to you his pleasure that the officers alluded to do not repair to their regiment, but that they are to be permitted to stay at Lisbon, where they will remain until further orders shall be received concerning them from England.

To the Rt. Hon. J. Villiers.   Coimbra, 31st May, 1809.

I have long been of opinion that a British army could bear neither success nor failure, and I have had manifest proofs of the truth of this opinion in the first of its branches in the recent conduct of the soldiers of this army. They have plundered the country most terribly, which has given me the greatest concern. The Town Major of Lisbon, if he has the orders, will show you, if you wish to read them, those that I have given out upon this subject. They have plundered the people of bullocks, among other property, for what reason I am sure I do not know, except

* See Note respecting this officer, 14th Oct. 1810.

it be, as I understand is their practice, to sell them to the people again. I shall be very much obliged to you if you will mention this practice to the ministers of the Regency, and beg them to issue a proclamation forbidding the people, in the most positive terms, to purchase any thing from the soldiers of the British army.

We are terribly distressed for money. I am convinced that £300,000 would not pay our debts; and two months' pay is due to the army. I suspect the Ministers in England are very indifferent to our operations in this country. I rather suspect that Sir J. Cradock has detained the *Surveillante* at Cadiz, and that this is the reason why that ship has not returned with the dollars in exchange for our gold.

To Vice Adm. the Hon. G. Berkeley.   Coimbra, 31st May, 1809.

I have had the honor of receiving your letter of the 29th. I am much obliged to you for the trouble you have taken, and the directions you have given, respecting the oats in the ships *Bellona, Enterprise,* and *Anne.* I have given directions to the Commissary Gen. to see that the arrangements which you propose respecting the cargoes of these ships should be executed forthwith, not only in respect to these, but in respect to all the victuallers, hay and oat ships, now in the port of Lisbon. The hire of store houses will be a much less heavy expense upon the public than that of victuallers, which may, of course, be sent back to England whenever you may think proper.

I have written to England to request that no more spirits or salt provisions might be sent out to Portugal. I propose to address you more fully hereafter respecting the future movements of the army; in the mean time, I have the honor to inform you, that it is now on its march towards Abrantes, on the Tagus.

To Vice Adm. the Hon. G. Berkeley.   Coimbra, 31st May, 1809.

I have received your letters of the 29th, to both of which I proceed to give you an answer. I proposed to you to limit the number of transports to 8; because at that time I had it in contemplation to send home only

---

G. O.   Coimbra, 31st May, 1809.

1. There being now 6000 pairs of shoes, the officers commanding brigades will direct the officers commanding regiments in their brigades, to make a requisition to the assistant commissary attached to the brigade, for the number of pairs of shoes they will require to complete the men; but no regiment is to require more than one pair of shoes for each man. These shoes are to be paid for at the rate of 6s. 6d. per pair.

2. The regiments are to make a requisition on the Q. M. G. for bill-hooks, in the proportion of 1 for every 10 men; these bill-hooks are to be carried by the soldiers under the straps of the knapsack, outside. The troops will very soon experience the use of them, and must take the greatest care of them; they must be produced by the men at every inspection of necessaries. A return of them must be made to the Q. M. G. once a month; and any deficiencies of the numbers not accounted for in a satisfactory manner, must be made good by the companies to which the bill-hooks have been delivered.

3. Those regiments in want of camp kettles, will make a requisition for them upon the Q. M. G.; deficiencies must however be accounted for in a satisfactory manner: in future a return of camp kettles must be sent to the Q. M. G. on the first of every month; likewise returns monthly of haversacks and canteens to him. The regiments will make a requisition for the numbers they now want to complete; a satisfactory account must be given of the deficiencies.

Mr. C. Johnstone's sheep, thinking, from his account, that the government of Spain would find the means of sending home those they intended to present to His Majesty. I entirely concur with you, however, that it is desirable to increase the number to 25, or more, as they can be spared from the service; and that, in fact, the expense on account of the public is discontinued from the time that they shall leave the Tagus.

I think that all the 3 months' infantry ships, and the horse ships of which you sent me the list the other day, may be sent home, or to Cadiz. Or, indeed, if you are desired to send home those you included in your list, you might send other horse ships to Cadiz for the sheep.

I am very much obliged to you for the trouble you have taken respecting the supply of beef for the Alentejo, as likewise for sending us our shoes, and all the assistance we have received from you. I am now about to move the army to the Tagus, and I have requested Capt. Chambers to come to the Mondego with his fleet, as soon as he can get out of Aveiro. My wish and intention were to send to Lisbon, by sea, the troops which are to go home when the relief shall come out; but from the accounts received this day by the *Parthian* from England, I think it not improbable that I shall be in Spain before the reinforcements, in infantry at least, can arrive. I should wish, however, Capt Chambers to remain in this quarter for a few days longer, till I shall have set every thing fairly in motion to the southward, and shall have closed my concerns in this quarter.

I have not answered your letter respecting the property captured at Oporto, because, just at the time that I received it, a doubt occurred to me whether, under the circumstances of the case, we ought to consider the property as prize, or the captors entitled to salvage for that part which belonged to British merchants. Oporto is a town belonging to the Prince Regent, and we, the army, could be considered only in the light of auxiliaries to His Royal Highness. Your ships would be considered in a different point of view; but I imagine that your right would be founded upon ours, and would arise from our success in a conjoint expedition. So that if we have no claim, you have none. The principle upon which all claims to prize are founded is, that the property captured from an enemy belongs to His Majesty, who gives it either by Act of Parliament, or by his Proclamation, in certain shares, to his navy and his army; but in this case, the property captured could not belong to His Majesty, but to the Sovereign in whose territory we were carrying on our operations, and to whom we were auxiliaries. Under these circumstances, I should doubt whether the King's Courts would condemn the property as prize, and whether the Act of Parliament, or the King's Proclamation, would operate upon it. However, I have desired Col. Trant to proceed in every respect, notwithstanding these doubts of mine, as your secretary has pointed out; viz., to have an account taken of every thing, to have copies taken of all papers, to seal them up, and make the Captains of the vessels give receipts for them, and to send every thing to England. I have also written to Villiers upon the subject.

You will have heard, I conclude, from the Captain of the *Parthian,* from Oporto. He has sent me word by Col. Elley,* that Adm. Young desired him to return immediately from Oporto, if I did not wish to detain him; and I have sent him word that I have no desire to keep him.

I have letters from England of the 16th, but no news. I hope that the defeat of the Austrians has not been so decisive as the French accounts would make it.

To Visc. Castlereagh. Coimbra, 31st May, 1809.

I have had the honor of receiving your Lordship's letter of the 15th inst., enclosing the extract of one from the late Commander of the Forces in Portugal, and the copy of one from the Master General, relative to the deficiency of supplies of ammunition. I believe that Sir J. Cradock did not intend to represent to your Lordship that there was any deficiency of ammunition in Portugal; I certainly have not experienced any : but that the difficulties of procuring conveyance, and of the communications, were such, as that the quantities which he had been enabled to bring forward for the use of the army in the field were not what he thought sufficient.

To Visc. Castlereagh. Coimbra, 31st May, 1809.

I request your Lordship will be pleased to give directions that a supply of 30,000 pairs of shoes for the use of the British troops may be sent to Lisbon at an early period. It is desirable that the storekeeper should give directions that these shoes should be of the best quality. I shall also be much obliged to your Lordship if you will give directions that 1,500,000 lbs. of biscuit may be sent to Lisbon for the use of the troops, and 3,000,000 lbs. of hay, and 3,000,000 lbs. of oats.

I have also to inform your Lordship, that from every information I have received of the probable supply of money for bills upon England, it is my opinion, that a sum amounting to not less than £300,000 ought to be sent to Lisbon at an early period.

To Visc. Castlereagh. Coimbra, 31st May, 1809.

I have the honor to inform your Lordship, that since my letter of the 20th inst., the enemy has withdrawn the corps which had taken possession of Alcantara on the 14th, and his army is concentrated in the neighbourhood of Caceres, between the Tagus and the Guadiana.

The Spanish army, under Gen. Cuesta, had advanced from its position at Llerena, upon receiving accounts of the enemy's march from the Guadiana, and the advanced guard had attacked a fortified post which the enemy still held at Merida. But, by a letter from Gen. Cuesta of the 20th inst., I find that he had discontinued the attack, owing to the difficulty of supporting it, in consequence of the swelling of the Guadiana. His head quarters were, by the last accounts, at Fuente del Maestre.

Gen. Mackenzie is in the mountains behind Castello Branco, and he has been directed again to occupy Alcantara, in such force as to be able to secure that passage over the Tagus. The army is in march towards this place; the leading brigades have already arrived here, and I expect the

* The late Lieut. Gen. Sir J. Elley, K.C.B.

whole in the course of a few days. The march has, in some degree, been delayed in consequence of the badness of the weather, and the general want of shoes by the troops, it having been impossible to bring up from Lisbon a sufficient supply. The arrangements, however, are all made for the early movement of the troops to the Tagus, and they will begin their march on the day after to-morrow.

To Visc. Castlereagh.   *Coimbra, 31st May, 1809.*

I have received your Lordship's letter of the 13th inst., relative to the officers of the British army allowed to serve in the army of Portugal, and I have the honor to inform your Lordship that I transmit by this opportunity, to the office of the Commander in Chief, lists of the names of officers, belonging to regiments in Portugal, who have been allowed to serve with the Portuguese troops. I hope that their names will be submitted to his Majesty for promotion for one step of rank at an early period.

I have to request your Lordship will give directions that all the officers who have been promoted for service with the Portuguese troops, as well of the original number of 24 as of the last number of 30, referred to by your Lordship in your dispatch of the 13th inst., may be ordered to Portugal without loss of time.

To Visc. Castlereagh.   *Coimbra, 31st May, 1809.*

I have but little to add to the contents of my public dispatches. You will hear officially from the Admiral respecting the discharge of transports. The Agent of transports has kept himself so much aloof from us, that I am not enabled to write to you accurately on the subject. I can only tell you in this way, that I have begged of the Admiral to send home all the 3 months' infantry ships, a great proportion of the cavalry ships, and all the victuallers, as I have desired that all the provisions and stores may be landed and put in store on shore. I shall also make arrangements to send home all the ordnance store ships, as soon as I can see the Commanding officer of artillery, who is not yet come up.

I shall soon be in Spain, and if Victor does not move across the Tagus, he will be in as bad a scrape as Soult. I hope to receive from you, before long, some orders respecting my conduct, supposing I should drive Victor away from the frontiers of Portugal, and should be required by Cuesta or the Junta to pursue him. We are getting on well, and I hope the government are satisfied with us. The army behave terribly ill. They are a rabble who cannot bear success any more than Sir J. Moore's army could bear failure. I am endeavoring to tame them; but if I should not succeed, I must make an official complaint of them, and send one or two corps home in disgrace. They plunder in all directions.

I have sent Col. Bourke and Col. Cadogan to Cuesta, to arrange a plan of co-operation in an attack upon Victor.

To Vice Adm. the Hon. G. Berkeley.   *Coimbra, 1st June, 1809.*

I have the honor to enclose two letters which have been transmitted to me by Col. Trant, relative to the horse transports sent to Oporto to convey to England the French prisoners, many of whom are sick and wounded.

I beg leave to recommend that infantry transports, to convey 1000 men, may be sent to Oporto, in addition to the horse transports already sent there, as many of the prisoners are not yet come in; and I learn from Col. Trant that there will be no room for above 600 of those now at Oporto in the horse transports. As it will be necessary to make some alteration in the horse transports to render them capable of containing the prisoners at all, and as this alteration will occasion expense, and some expense must be incurred, and inconvenience and delay occasioned, in order to refit the ships as horse transports, you will probably think it proper to order the alteration of the horse transports to be discontinued, and to send infantry transports for the whole. I beg leave to refer you to my letter of the 15th May for a statement of the tonnage required.

To Marshal Beresford.   Coimbra, 1st June, 1809.

I enclose a dispatch which I received yesterday from England, relative to the officers to be appointed to the Portuguese service. I wrote to Lord Castlereagh to request that all those already appointed by Sir J. Cradock and me might receive their promotion immediately; and that those appointed in England, as well of the first 20 as the last 30, might be ordered to join in Portugal without loss of time.

You have made use of Mr. M'Neal, the Commissary attached to Major Gen. Tilson's brigade, and have made him superintendent of your Commissariat. I cannot spare him to you: he is one of the best of his rank; and I am now obliged to employ him on another service.

Villiers will show you the dispatches from England respecting Capt. ——.

G. O.   Coimbra, 1st June, 1809.

1. The Commander of the Forces has been informed that the officers commanding companies, and other regimental officers, having been supplied with mules by the commissariat, by order of the late Commander of the Forces, for the carriage of camp kettles, of paymasters' books, and of the medicine chest, when the army took the field, have applied to have those mules exchanged.

The officers commanding companies, paymasters, and surgeons, must be aware that they receive an allowance from the public to furnish mules or horses for the carriage of camp kettles, books, or medicine chests; they are reminded by the orders of the 11th Oct., the 18th March, and 19th May, that these mules were given to them by the Commissariat only as an indulgence, and that they were to keep them up at their own charge; and under these circumstances it is impossible for the Commissary Gen. now to exchange them.

2. The mule attached to each regiment for the carriage of the intrenching tools, and placed by the orders of the 16th March in charge of the quarter-master, belongs to the public, and he must be exchanged by the commissary, if the exchange should be necessary (which it ought not to be). It is clearly understood, that although the camp kettle mules, and those for the books and medicine chests, are to be kept up by the captains, paymaster, and surgeons respectively, they must not be used for any purpose, excepting those for which they are exclusively allowed.

6. Although from circumstances it is at present impossible to supply the paymasters of regiments with money to the full amount of their estimates, and the captains of companies have not yet received the full amount of pay of their several companies for the last month, no reason exists why the accounts of the soldiers should not be settled to the 24th of the month of May, and the balances struck, which will be paid off as soon as the money shall come up.

8. An officer from the —, —, —, and — regts. to proceed forthwith by the road of Aveiro, Oporto, and Braga, to look for the men who have been allowed to straggle from those regiments, according to the return sent in to the Adj. Gen. s office, copies of which they are to be furnished with by the officers commanding the corps.

The Commander of the Forces trusts that more attention will be paid by the officers commanding companies to prevent the soldiers from straggling in future.

To the Rt. Hon. J. Villiers.   Coimbra, 1st June, 1809.

I enclose you the answer to my first dispatch respecting Capt. ——, which I received yesterday from England. I think that the ministers have taken nearly the same view of the subject which we have. I also enclose Lord Castlereagh's private letter upon the subject, in which you will see a prospect of another success in the West Indies. Pray return these papers.

I had written to the Admiral respecting the claim of the navy to share in any prize we should make at Oporto, long before I received your letter. In fact, if the frigates had not been stationed off the port, there was nothing to prevent the French from sending away any thing they pleased; and if we had any right, the navy must have it likewise. If I had been so inclined, it would have been impossible afterwards to dispute the claim of the navy, and to assert our own; and therefore all that I have done has been to apprise the Admiral of the doubts (I ought to say the certainty) I entertain, that none of us have any claim whatever. If you are decidedly of the same opinion, I think you had better say no more upon the subject, excepting to let the government know that there is a large property in cotton, &c. at Oporto.

I have desired that the guns belonging to the French should be embarked in the frigate, and sent to Lisbon; those belonging to the Portuguese, of which there are many fine brass guns, will be left in the arsenal at Oporto. The French have lost above 60 pieces of cannon in this expedition into Portugal.

To the Rt. Hon. J. Villiers.   Coimbra, 1st June, 1809.

Since I wrote to you this morning, I have received yours of the 30th. I shall stay here till the 5th, when I shall go by Thomar to Abrantes, and I shall be glad to see Col. Alava.* I do not mean, however, to allow any detachment of the British troops to move until the whole army is ready to support it.

I am concerned that any complaint has been made by the people of Oporto. The facts are these : It was represented to me upon my return to Oporto, after the pursuit of Soult, that the merchants and the Senate were not unwilling to assist us by a loan of money, we being at that time in want of every thing, particularly shoes, and not having one farthing. I asked Mr. Murray whether he thought the exposure of our distress at Oporto was likely to have a baneful influence on the money market at Lisbon; and having been told that it would not, I made known our temporary distress, first to the Senate, who immediately said they would advance us all that was in their power. I then applied to the merchants of the Wine Company, some of whom did not appear equally willing to assist us; upon which I said to them as I left the room, that I left them to consider of the statement I had made, and of my wish that they should assist us; and that all I could say was, that if they refused to assist our

---

* Don Miguel de Alava was subsequently attached to the staff of Lord Wellington, on which he remained until the end of the war. He was also with the Duke of Wellington at Waterloo. He was afterwards minister for the Court of Spain at the Court of St. James's. He resigned his diplomatic employment on the revolution of La Granja, and died in emigration at Bagnères, in July, 1843.

distresses with the money which we wanted, after all that we had done for them, the world, when the story should be told, would not believe it. This is the amount of the *dureté* which has been put upon them. I believe I did shame them into lending us a sum of money. After all, the sum borrowed at Oporto, for it was not levied, amounted to about £10,000, and this is what the government call ' severe.' I really believe that I saved for them property for which they will get a hundred times that amount; and if I had waited to attack Soult till I had had money sufficient to render this loan unnecessary (for which I may wait the next time my assistance is wanted), the expense of the support of his army would have been ten times the amount.

I am very much obliged for the papers which you have sent to the government respecting the conduct of their magistrates. I wait here till the greatest part of the army is gone by, as there are constant difficulties and distresses which must immediately be relieved; and I may as well be here as anywhere else; and my horses require rest.

To Marshal Beresford.   Coimbra, 2d June, 1809.

I have been endeavoring to form a corps of guides; that is to say, one of officers and non-commissioned officers, who should be interpreters between our people and those of the country, who must show them their roads. We have got some officers, but we want non-commissioned officers. I shall be very much obliged to you if you will allow us to have Jozé Bannas, corporal in the 2d company of grenadiers of the 13th regt., and 8 or 10 other serjeants, corporals, or steady soldiers, men of good character, who can speak either English or French, to make of them serjeants or corporals of guides. They will have with us the pay and allowances of British cavalry.

To J. Murray, Esq., Commissary General.   Abrantes, 3d June, 1809.

I shall be very much obliged to you if you will let me know, as soon as possible, what progress you make in procuring money.

You should send up here by water, without loss of time, all that you can get. We can do no longer without money.

I also request you to desire the Commissary at Lisbon to let the Com-

G. O.   Coimbra, 2d June, 1809.
3. The Order No. 2, of the 30th May, has not been attended to, no regiment having yet sent to the Q. M. G. any account of articles required from Lisbon. The earliest attention must be given to all orders. In this instance, the regiments may feel the greatest inconvenience for want of those articles in store at Lisbon, which it was the intention of the orders of the 30th May to supply, and which articles they cannot get by any other means.
4. Whenever sick are left in hospital at any place, the strictest attention must be paid, that officers and non-commissioned officers of each brigade are left in charge of them, according to the proportion ordered in G. O. of the 19th May, for the hospital at Braga.

G. O.   Coimbra, 3d June, 1809.
2. Whenever it is possible for the assistant commissaries of brigades to issue the quantity, cavalry must receive and carry 3 days' corn, and the infantry 3 days' bread.
3. The senior of the officers left in charge of the sick at the different hospitals must take the command of the whole, and correspond with head quarters; no convalescents must be moved from any hospital station without orders from head quarters.

missary at Abrantes know daily what is sent off. We much want the 10,000 pairs of shoes ordered, and the stores and baggage required in the Q. M. G.'s department, as well as the stores ordered for your own.

To Marshal Beresford.   Coimbra, 3d June, 1809.

I enclose a letter which Col. Fletcher has given me, which affords but a bad prospect of a defence for the Tagus. I think that if Capt. Chapman's facts are true, his arguments are unanswerable; and that it is very doubtful whether any heavy ordnance ought to be placed in the batteries on the upper Tagus. However, there can be no harm in constructing the batteries, and we can arm them with some guns of a small calibre, which would be of no use to the enemy, if they should fall into their hands.

To Brig. Gen. Howorth, R.A.   Coimbra, 3d June, 1809.

I have to thank you for the trouble you have taken about the captured ordnance. I did not trouble you upon this subject, because I was not aware that you would be under the necessity of remaining at Oporto. The barrels of gunpowder which you mention were sent by Great Britain for the service of Portugal, and must therefore be left at Oporto for the orders of Gen. Beresford.

To Major Gen. Cotton.   Coimbra, 3d June, 1809.

I enclose the copy of a letter transmitted to me by the Dep. Commissary Gen., and it is absolutely necessary that the cavalry should carry 3 days' corn for themselves, whenever it can be procured, as no carts can be allowed for this purpose.

The A.G. to Lieut. Col. Walsh, Town Major, Lisbon.   3d June, 1809.

In reply to your letter of the 31st ult., I am directed by his Excellency the Commander of the Forces to acquaint you, that he can decide upon no case of any officer having leave of absence, or not, without the regular certificate being forwarded for his inspection; and this power cannot be delegated to another, though it might, in a particular instance, be convenient.

The recovered men fit to join their regiments are to remain at Lisbon until further orders.

To Capt. Chambers, R.N.   Coimbra, 4th June, 1809.

I am concerned that you are still detained at Aveiro; and I apprehend that you will not get out for some days till there shall be an easterly wind.

As soon as you can get out, I should wish you to go to the mouth of the Mondego for the following objects:

1st. To receive into the transports a small detachment of the 3d hussars, who will have been dismounted.

2dly. To receive into the transports a certain quantity of stores not required for the use of the army.

3dly. To deliver to a Commissary, who shall be there to receive, 300,000 lbs. of bread, and 80,000 rations of oats. He will take charge of these stores, and embark them in schooners, which I have directed him to hire for this purpose.

In case there should not be in the victuallers a sufficient quantity of bread and oats to supply these deliveries, I shall be obliged to you if you will order their delivery from the empty transports and horse ships.

I shall be obliged to you to send the enclosed letter to any fleet of transports that may appear off Aveiro.

To Staff Surgeon ——.   Coimbra, 4th June, 1809.

I have received your letter of the 3d inst., and its enclosure. It is impossible for me to enter into a discussion with you on the propriety and expediency of the orders which you have received from the Dep. Inspector, and I have only to desire that you will obey them without loss of time.

To Lieut. Col. Walsh, Town Major, Lisbon.   Coimbra, 4th June, 1809.

I have just heard that Col. Roche was off Oporto on the 2d inst., in the *Swallow* sloop of war, charged with dispatches for me; that he was unable to land himself, being indisposed, and he was unwilling to send the dispatches on shore, and that he is gone with them to Lisbon.

I request you will get from Col. Roche the dispatches as soon as he shall arrive at Lisbon, and forward them to me. I shall be at Thomar on the 6th, and at Abrantes the 7th inst. I request you also to inform Col. Roche that I shall always be happy to see him, when he is able to come to me; but that it is desirable, when he has the charge of dispatches from government, he should adopt the most expeditious and the safest mode of conveying them to the persons to whom they are addressed, and not keep them at sea with a contrary wind for a longer period than is absolutely necessary.

To Lieut. Col. Framingham, R.A.   Pombal, 5th June, 1809.

I enclose the copy of a letter which I have written to the Commanding officer of the artillery at Lisbon, and the copy of another which I have written to the Dep. Commissary Gen. at Coimbra. In case you should think it desirable to add any other articles to those enumerated in my letter to be carried in the reserve artillery, or should think any additional number of wheels desirable, I beg that you will write for them yourself.

I hope that your horses on their arrival on the Tagus will not be in the unserviceable state in which you expect they will be. If they should be so, I must relinquish that important branch of our equipment, the British artillery; and I have requested Gen. Beresford to have some brigades of Portuguese artillery in readiness to join and do duty with the British army on its entry into Spain.

In respect to the reserve ammunition which has not yet come up, my opinion is, that the best thing to do is to embark it from Oporto for Lisbon; or if it should have marched from Oporto, to send it by boats from Coimbra to Figueira at the mouth of the Mondego, and have it in readiness to be embarked there in the store ships as soon as they shall arrive there from Aveiro.

I beg of you to communicate this opinion to Gen. Howorth.

To Lieut. Col. Fisher, R.A., Lisbon.   Pombal, 5th June, 1809.

I beg that, upon the receipt of this letter, you will send by water to

Santarem, in charge of an officer, and of a sufficient number of men, 50 spare wheels for light 6 pounder carriages and cars, and 20 spare wheels for heavy 6 pounder carriages and cars; likewise 60 rounds for each gun of the three 6 pounder brigades with the army, of round shot, with ammunition complete, and 30 rounds for each gun of spherical case shot, with ammunition complete. You will send a proportionate quantity of shells, with ammunition complete, for the 5½ inch howitzers in those brigades. You will also send 800,000 rounds of musket ammunition, 200,000 rounds of rifle, and 200,000 of carbine, to the same place, by the same conveyance.

I have written these orders in the notion that the depôt which had been formed at Santarem has been removed. If it has not, you will understand that the ammunition, &c. which I now require is in lieu of that which has hitherto been in reserve with the army to the northward, and which I apprehend cannot be brought back to the Tagus. If the depôt should still be at Santarem, you will understand that it need not be replenished, excepting to complete the quantities above ordered.

P. S. 100 horses arrived from England some days ago for the waggon train; and there are, I believe, about 200 horses at Lisbon of those sent out for the artillery about a month ago. I beg you will have all these horses examined, and that you will give orders that as many of them as are fit for artillery service, and in condition to take the field, may be sent in charge of proper officers, and by easy marches, to Santarem. You will give the Commissary notice of the march of the horses, that he may provide for them.

To C. Dalrymple, Dep. Commissary General.   Pombal, 5th June, 1809.

I was much concerned to learn, in conversation with Col. Framingham this morning, that the horses of the artillery are nearly destroyed, and that they will be unable to draw the artillery farther than the Tagus, owing to the want and irregularity of the delivery of food to them. As I cannot allow this important branch of the equipments of the army to be destroyed, without inquiring how it has occurred, I desire to know as soon as possible, what quantity of forage has been delivered for the use of the horses and mules attached to each of the brigades of artillery, and to the reserve artillery, on each day since the 5th May last.

The complaint of Col. Framingham, however, is not confined solely to the want of forage, but to the irregularity and delay, which, he says, prevails not only in the delivery of forage, but of all descriptions of provisions to the men under his command. I desire to know in what manner this has occurred. Surely where there has been no want either of provisions or forage, a very little arrangement in the Commissariat would insure their early delivery to the troops. The officers of the Commissariat will be responsible in an eminent degree if, owing to their want of capacity and management, I should lose the use of the British artillery.

I desire that most effectual measures may be taken to supply the horses of the artillery with forage hereafter. You will see in the G. O. some directions respecting the time of the day at which provisions and forage are to be issued to the troops.

To the Rt. Hon. J. Villiers.   Pombal, 5th June, 1809.

I have received your letter of the 2d. If the question respecting the rank which the officers of the British army are to hold among themselves is referred to me, I must decide it as I told you I would. If government should decide upon it, I shall act cordially upon their orders. I do not see how any military officer could determine upon the question which Trant referred to me. If our officers are to decide these questions upon British principles, they are British, and not Portuguese officers.

I have but one opinion respecting the expenses of the Portuguese army; every thing ought to be managed by them (that is to say, Beresford and their officers) in the best way for them. We ought to ascertain how much of the expense they could bear, and we ought to pay the remainder. My opinion is, that the militia, excepting those for whom there are arms, ought to be sent to their homes, the ordenanza to be dismissed, and the regulars kept in garrisons or cantonments, till they are clothed, armed, and disciplined: to take them into the field now, only removes the period at which they may be really useful; and we should take advantage of this period of peace for Portugal, to discipline the troops as they ought to be.

I shall be at Abrantes the day after to-morrow. If the French stay where they are, I must move as soon as possible to co-operate in dislodging them, but I doubt that I shall be able to quit the Tagus till the middle of the month.

I certainly recommended the officers you mentioned to Col. Gordon and Lord Castlereagh, by desire of Mrs. Villiers, and was informed they should be appointed, excepting Capt. ——, for the reason I stated. I shall write, however, to Col. Gordon respecting them.

To Vice Adm. the Hon. G. Berkeley.   Thomar, 7th June, 1809.

I have not yet been able to acknowledge the receipt of your letter of the 2d inst., having been constantly moving. By a note of the 24th May, from Sir J. Cradock, I find that he had prevailed upon Adm. Purvis to give him 1500 tons of the transports at Cadiz to bring one of the regiments from Gibraltar to Portugal, which will be so many taken away from the sheep concern; but I do not think that signifies much.

I informed you, in my official letter of this morning, of the detention of the *Port Mahon* and her convoy at Aveiro. I am seriously apprehensive that they will not be able to get out till after the next rainy season. If they should, however, I have begged Capt. Chambers to go to the mouth of the Mondego with his whole fleet, my wish being to form there a depôt afloat, in schooners, of 10 days' provisions, and oats for the whole army, as the victuallers with him do not now contain that quantity. I have asked him to give from the transports as much bread and oats as the Commissary may require. As soon as he shall have delivered these provisions, and shall have received on board the transports a few stores which we did not want, and which go down by water to Figueira from Coimbra, and some men of the 3d hussars, with their appointments, whom I wish to send by sea to Lisbon, I have requested Capt. Chambers to return to Lisbon. His probable detention, however, at Aveiro deranges these projects, and I must be satisfied with my depôt there, instead of at Figueira;

and I must find some other mode of sending down to Lisbon the spare stores, and the hussars and their appointments.

I have arranged to have every thing I want for the equipment of the army brought up the Tagus to Abrantes; and I am obliged to you for the offer of Capt. Shepherd's assistance. Our Commissariat is very bad indeed; but it is new, and will improve, I hope. You will have seen that Ney is in the Asturias. It is most desirable, however, to adopt every practicable mode of strengthening Vigo.

I doubt whether Sir W. Scott's opinion respecting the Danish ships in Lisbon would apply to the case of the Danish ships in Oporto. When we took Lisbon from the French, that city, and indeed the whole Kingdom of Portugal, had, in a manner, been ceded to them by the Prince Regent; at all events, they had established their government in it. We acted as principals in the expedition against Lisbon, which was considered as a port in the enemy's possession; and His Majesty ordered that every thing belonging to the French, and to the Russians, found there, should be considered as prize. But at Oporto they had had only a momentary possession; they had nothing else but that town, and the different points in the country occupied by their troops; and we acted only as auxiliaries to the Portuguese government. The state of all the parties, you will observe, was very different, and I should doubt whether, under these circumstances, Sir W. Scott's former opinion could be considered as applying.

To Vice Adm. the Hon. G. Berkeley.   Thomar, 7th June, 1809.

I have the honor to enclose you the copy of a dispatch, which I received in the night from the Sec. of State. It is my opinion, that transports for 3000 horses may, with safety, be sent to England as soon as you think proper to dispatch them

As government have called for so large a proportion of cavalry ships, I conclude that you will think it proper to order some, or all of that description ordered to Oporto, to receive the prisoners of war to go to England directly, either with the prisoners on board, or without the prisoners, if they should not have been embarked. I shall write to Col. Trant upon this subject; and desire him to attend to any instructions he may receive from you thereupon. It is necessary to have at Oporto 4000 tons of shipping, to carry home the prisoners of war : this is the number for which I asked in my letter of the 15th May; viz., transports for 2000 men, at 2 tons each man, on account of the number of sick and wounded there was among them.

In answer to a paragraph of your private letter of the 2d, and to your official letters of the 5th, upon this subject, which I received yesterday, I have to inform you, that the *Port Mahon* and her convoy are shut up in Aveiro. The late gales from the westward have increased the bar of that harbour to such an extent, that there is not upon it at present, I understand, more than 7 feet water; and I apprehend that some time will elapse before the bar will be again cleared. The ships under the convoy of the *Port Mahon* cannot therefore be reckoned as applicable either to the removal of the French prisoners from Oporto, or to the dispatch to England, in consequence of the orders of the Sec. of State of the 22d May, of which I enclose you the copies.

To Lieut. Col. Trant, Oporto.   Thomar, 7th June, 1809.

I think it probable that the Admiral will immediately require all the cavalry ships which he has lately sent to Oporto, to receive the prisoners of war to send to England without loss of time, in the shape of cavalry ships. You will, therefore, immediately discontinue your alteration of those ships, if you should have continued them after the receipt of Col. Murray's letter upon this subject. I have requested the Admiral to send you directions either to embark the prisoners in the cavalry ships, or not, as he may think proper, supposing that he should wish to send to England immediately the cavalry ships destined to convey the prisoners. You will therefore have the prisoners in readiness to embark in store ships at a moment's notice, if the Admiral should desire it; and, at all events, the ships in readiness to sail.

You will understand, however, that the prisoners must not be unreasonably crowded in these ships, and you will report to me what number will remain at Oporto, after you shall have sent those whom the Admiral may require you to send in the cavalry ships.

To Gen. Sir D. Dundas, K.B., Commander in Chief.   Thomar, 7th June, 1809.

I have the honor to acknowledge the receipt of your dispatch of the 13th May, relative to the appointment of officers in His Majesty's service, to serve with the Portuguese troops, under the command of Gen. Beresford.

It appears to be His Majesty's intention that the number of officers who should receive one step of British promotion, upon being permitted to serve with the Portuguese troops, should not exceed 24; and that 30 officers who were to be sent from England to serve with the Portuguese troops, and all who should be appointed from the army in Portugal for the same duties, should continue to hold in the British army the commissions which they had hitherto held; and to be allowed to serve with the Portuguese troops, with one step of advanced Portuguese rank, and the pay of the Portuguese commission in which they should serve with the Portuguese army.

The King's commands, as thus conveyed, differ, I believe, from what were understood to be the intentions of His Majesty's government by the late Commander of the Forces in Portugal, and from his practice, and from that which I have followed since the command has devolved upon me. He understood that the officers who should be allowed to serve with the Portuguese troops from the regiments of the army in this country, were to stand in the same situation, and were to accept their appointments in the Portuguese service upon the same conditions with the officers first appointed in England to serve with the Portuguese troops; and he, and I, since the command has devolved upon me, have allowed officers, of whose names I lately transmitted you lists, to serve with the Portuguese troops on those conditions. As but few officers have applied to serve with the Portuguese troops, even with the advantage of receiving one step of British promotion, I should have doubted whether any would be willing to serve in this manner, upon the advantage now held out to them, of receiving one step of Portuguese rank, which can be but local and temporary, together with the pay of the Portuguese rank in which they should be employed, if you had not transmitted me a list of the names of 30 officers who are willing to be so employed, upon the terms held out to them.

Upon this list, however, I beg to observe that it contains the names of some officers now in Portugal, who will refuse to serve with the Portuguese troops on the terms proposed. One of them, indeed, Capt. Fordyce, of the 81st, who is Brigade Major to Major Gen. Hill, and who has been recommended as an officer to serve with the Portuguese troops upon the more advantageous terms, which it was imagined here that it was intended we should hold out, has desired that he may not be employed with the Portuguese troops; and that he may not be considered as having expressed a wish to be so employed, unless he should receive one step of promotion in the British army; and that this promotion should be notified to the army in this country. I am convinced that no officers in this country will offer their services upon the terms which I now understand are to be held out to them.

There is one branch of these terms to which I wish to draw your particular attention and early decision. It is that part which gives to British officers one step of Portuguese rank above that which they hold in His Majesty's service. The Portuguese government claim a right which I believe cannot be refused to any independent state, of granting commissions in their army; and that the officers holding these commissions should rank, according to seniority of dates, with the officers holding commissions of the same denomination and rank in the service of other powers. Under the terms proposed to be held out to the officers of the British army in Portugal, to induce them to serve with the Portuguese troops, they are to receive one step of Portuguese rank above that which they hold in the British army; and as, under their Portuguese commission, they are to rank with British officers holding His Majesty's commission of the same denomination and rank, according to the seniority of dates, the result of this offer will be to give to all who accept of it local and temporary rank over the heads of their seniors employed on the same foreign service. This effect would not be felt if the British and Portuguese troops were not likely to serve together; but as they do and must serve together, it will be felt daily, and will give occasion to dissatisfaction and constant complaints. I have to mention upon this part of the subject, that this dissatisfaction has already existed; and I have been called upon to decide upon a complaint made in consequence.

The practice has been hitherto to give an officer, who had already been promoted, one step of British rank, to induce him to serve with the Portuguese army, and another step of Portuguese rank when he entered that service; thus making those promoted to be British Majors, Portuguese Lieut. Colonels, and giving them temporary and local rank over all the Majors of the British army.

In consequence of this dissatisfaction and complaint, I have already had some discussion with the British Ambassador and Marshal Beresford upon the subject; and I proposed either that British officers, appointed to serve with the Portuguese army, should have Portuguese commissions only of the same rank with those which they held from His Majesty; or that if they should hold superior Portuguese commissions, in a view to give them more extended command over the Portuguese troops, they should rank with British officers when they should meet them on service, only by the dates of their commissions in His Majesty's service. As, however, His Majesty's commands, as conveyed in your letter of the 13th May, recognise the principle of a British officer holding advanced Portuguese rank, and consequently a local temporary superior commission to those held by his seniors in the British service, I think it proper to delay giving any decision upon these complaints, and to refer the following points for your consideration and that of His Majesty's servants:

1st. Are officers in the Portuguese service to rank with officers in His Majesty's service, according to the dates of their several commissions?

2dly. If they are, is it intended that officers of the British army, who have been or shall be appointed to serve with the Portuguese troops, shall serve with a Portuguese commission of the same rank with that which they hold in the King's service, or with a Portuguese commission of a superior rank?

3dly. If with a Portuguese commission of a superior rank, in what manner is the relative rank of these officers to be settled with the rank of officers senior to them in the British service, although junior in reference to their Portuguese commissions?

4thly. If officers belonging to the British army in Portugal are not to serve with the Portuguese troops with advanced Portuguese commissions, what other encouragement is to be held out to them to induce them to accept of this employment?

To the Rt. Hon. J. Villiers.   Thomar, 7th June, 1809.

I send you a letter for Lord Castlereagh, containing one which I have received from Sir D. Dundas, which will surprise you not a little, and the copy of my answer to Sir David. Pray forward this letter, and every thing going up from the army by this occasion, by the first opportunity. If the French are off, which I hear they are, I shall go down to see Lord Wellesley.

To the Rt. Hon. the Secretary at War.   Thomar, 7th June, 1809.

I had the honor of receiving your letter of the 4th May this morning, and I beg to inform you, that it has been the practice hitherto in this army to make the soldiers pay 10*d.* *per diem*, when in hospital, leaving to them a residue of 2*d.* *per diem*, and to other ranks a proportionate sum. I have ordered that, from the 25th inst. inclusive, the hospital stoppage shall be for all ranks 9*d.*, leaving for each rank the daily net sum stated in the enclosure No. I. of your letter. I shall be obliged to you if you will let me know whether it is your intention that the directions contained in your letter of the 4th May should have a retrospect; and if so, from what period. The soldiers in Portugal receive a full ration from the Commissariat, and of course are liable to a daily deduction from their pay each of 6*d.*

To Visc. Castlereagh.   Thomar, 7th June, 1809.

I did not receive your dispatch of the 22d May, relative to the transports for the conveyance of 3000 horses, till this morning, although I heard on the 4th that Lieut. Col. Roche was off Oporto on the 2d, charged with dispatches for me, that officer having thought it proper to take the dispatches to Lisbon. I have now the honor to inform your Lordship that I wrote this morning to Adm. Berkeley, to apprise him of my opinion, that horse transports for the conveyance of 3000 horses might be sent to England immediately, without any inconvenience, and to request that he would dispatch them as soon as possible.

To Visc. Castlereagh.   Thomar, 7th June, 1809.

I have the honor to acknowledge the receipt of your Lordship's dispatch of the 13th May, relative to the appointment of British officers to serve with the Portuguese troops. I have likewise this day received one of the same date from the Commander in Chief, of which I enclose to your Lordship a copy, together with a copy of my answer to that dispatch; and I beg your Lordship's early consideration of, and decision on, the several points discussed in that dispatch.

To Marshal Beresford.   Thomar, 7th June, 1809.

You will be very much surprised at reading the enclosed from Sir D. Dundas, after seeing that which I before sent you from the Sec. of State; although, by the bye, upon a more attentive perusal of the letter, I think, that though inaccurately expressed, it does not differ from the former. I have sent Sir David the answer of which I enclose you the draft, and a copy of his letter and of my answer to Lord Castlereagh. I dine with Miranda to-day, and shall be at Abrantes to-morrow.

To Visc. Castlereagh.   Thomar, 7th June, 1809.

Since I wrote last, Marshal Victor has broken up from the neighbourhood of Caceres; has removed his head quarters to Truxillo; and has, I understand, passed a division of his army over the Tagus, by the bridge of Almaraz. It is probable that the whole are about to retreat. A part of the army of Gen. Cuesta was, by the last accounts of the 3d inst., on the Guadiana, near Medellin, and one division near Merida. The whole are, I understand, advancing towards that river. A part of the troops under my command have arrived upon the Tagus, at Abrantes, and the remaining 4 brigades are following them.

To Lieut. Col. Bourke, A. Q. M. G.   Abrantes, 8th June, 1809.

I write just to acknowledge the receipt of your letters of the 4th and 6th; that of the 6th, last night, at Thomar; that of the 4th, this morning, at the same place, as it had passed me on the road as I was coming from Coimbra. I shall forthwith take into consideration the different plans of operation proposed; and you may assure Gen. Cuesta that I shall co-operate in one or other of the modes suggested. I shall enter further into detail to-morrow, when I shall have had further time to consider of the subject.

I beg you to tell Gen. Cuesta that I have never received the plan of operations which he proposed for my consideration through Col. Alava. The troops have not yet arrived from the northward; and when they shall reach the Tagus, which will not be till the 11th or 12th, they will require a day or two's rest, before I can put them in motion again for a fresh operation. But this time will not be thrown away, as it may be very usefully employed in collecting supplies at Badajoz. Besides, I hope that by that time my reinforcements will have arrived from England; and it is not impossible but that I may be relieved from the restriction in my operations, which would prevent me from going to any distance in Spain. I beg also that you will inform Gen. Cuesta, that I have heard and believe that Marshal Ney, joined by Kellermann with 8000 or 9000 men, has invaded the Asturias.

I did not understand that the Marques de la Romana's troops had any action with the enemy; indeed I do not believe they were in the Asturias; but the Marques himself was at Gijon, from whence he embarked with his money, arms, ammunition, &c., and all the Spanish and English officers and the Governor; and he was going round to Vigo. In the mean time, if the French have obtained a footing in the Asturias, they have lost that

---

G. O.   Abrantes, 8th June, 1809.

1. The regiments will make a requisition upon the Commissary at Abrantes for a sufficient number of pairs of shoes to complete them to two good pairs each man : the period of the delivery of those shoes will be notified in G. O.; they will be paid at the rate of 6s. 6d. per pair. The regiments not already completed with bill hooks, canteens, haversacks, and camp kettles, according to the G. O. of the 31st ult., will make a requisition upon the Q. M. G., at Abrantes, for the same : the period of the delivery of those articles will likewise be notified in G. O.

2. Various complaints having been made to the Commander of the Forces, of the irregularity of the delivery of articles from the commissariat, the following rules are to be observed upon that subject in future:

3. When articles are delivered to troops from a general store, the Commissary Gen. must, if possible, have two or more stores for the delivery of each article, viz. forage, corn, wood, meat, bread, and wine.

4. He must signify to the Assist. Commissaries of brigades and regiments, at which store, and where situated, troops in the brigade or regiment will receive their supplies, and in what order by brigades, and at what hour, the supplies will be delivered to the troops of each brigade or regiment at each store.

5. In general, however, it is better the troops of each brigade or regiment should receive their supplies at the brigade or regimental store.

6. When the army will halt, a commencement must be made to make the deliveries at the commissaries' stores at daylight, and the delivery must be continued without interruption, till the whole of the troops to receive their supplies at such store shall have received them. The soldiers of each brigade or regiment will attend to receive the supplies at the hour appointed for them precisely, and not before.

7. The meat for the troops must invariably be delivered to them from a brigade or regimental store, and should be killed on the preceding night, or at daylight in the morning, when the army halts. When it marches, the order of the 5th of May comes in force, and the meat should be killed, delivered, and cooked, as soon as possible after the orders for marching are given out.

8. When the army marches, the Commissary Gen. should notify as soon as possible to the Assist. Commissaries of brigades and regiments of cavalry, where the store of each article of supply for the troops will be made to each brigade or regiment. The deliveries on marching days must commence as soon as possible after the troops reach their ground.

9. It is obvious, however, that on marching days it is still more important than it is on halting days, that the delivery should be made from a brigade or regimental, rather than a general store.

10. The Assist. Commissaries with regiments of cavalry and brigades must not be changed, unless the change is notified in G. O.

11. The Assist. Commissaries with brigades and regiments of cavalry must take care to obtain copies of all G. O. from the brigade majors or adjutants respectively. The Commissary Gen. is responsible that all other officers of the department, not attached to brigades or regiments of cavalry, have copies of the G. O.

which they had in Galicia, as I understand the Spanish troops were in possession of Lugo.

In proportion as the French spread themselves, they certainly do mischief in the country, which is always to be regretted, but they at the same time weaken themselves. I do not consider that the operations of Marshal Ney can have any effect upon the conduct of Victor, excepting probably to induce him to delay any measures he might have in contemplation, till Ney should reinforce him. This was the plan ordered by the Gallo-Spanish government to Victor, in an intercepted dispatch; but it is very obvious that Ney, Soult, and Kellermann will have more work upon their hands than they will be able to manage in the Asturias and Galicia: and if they should venture to detach, they will lose both those kingdoms; or if they do detach one or even two of these corps to the assistance of Victor, Gen. Cuesta and I shall still be strong enough for them.

To Major Gen. Cotton.   Abrantes, 8th June, 1809.

I enclose a letter which I have received from Mr. ——, a staff surgeon with this army, who had been sent to England during Sir J. Cradock's command, I conclude, not for his good behaviour, and who was lately sent out again. I have ordered him home again with the French prisoners, and *not* to return. In consequence of this, he thinks it proper to attack the characters of all his superiors.

I had not an opportunity when I was at Coimbra of visiting the hospitals there, although I did visit that at Oporto, and found it in excellent order. I shall be very much obliged to you if you will visit those at Coimbra, which are placed at the San Benito, Boa Ventura, and Trinidada convents, and let me know in what state you find them. I think it not improbable that there may be a want of beds, as, notwithstanding all those were given in which the regimental surgeons had with them, and many from the town, there were not so many from the latter as there might have been.

To the Rt. Hon. J. Villiers.   Abrantes, 8th June, 1809.

It is impossible to guess what the French are doing, our accounts are so very contradictory. However, I shall certainly move eastward as soon as I can. In the mean time, it is most desirable that I should see Lord Wellesley, if he shall arrive before the troops shall be ready to march. He comes in the *Donegal*, Capt. Malcolm; and if you will send me off a messenger the moment that the ship appears in the offing, I will go down to Lisbon, by the Tagus, as soon as I shall receive your letter, and I shall be back again in a very short time.

To Vice Adm. the Hon. G. Berkeley.   Abrantes, 9th June, 1809.

I have just now received your letter of the 7th; and I conclude that about this time you will have received mine of the 7th, respecting the horse transports. I see no occasion for retaining the gun boats in the river at present; and I conceive that one armed transport at Villa Nova will be sufficient to keep the country boats in that part of the river under our control.

To Lieut. Col. Bourke, A. Q. M. G.   Abrantes, 9th June, 1809.

Since I wrote to you yesterday I have fully considered the different plans suggested in your letters to the Q. M. G. of the 4th and 6th, upon which I am now about to give you my opinion. It appears to me that it will be very difficult, if not impossible, to cut off the enemy's retreat by any movement upon either of his flanks, made by detachments from either of the armies. In the event of the junction, as proposed, we must expect that Marshal Victor will fall back and cross the Tagus at Almaraz and Alconeta, and probably some of his infantry at Arzobispo.

Adverting to the difficulties of approaching the Tagus at all, and those of the passage after the Tagus should have been reached by the combined armies, I think it nearly certain that the Marshal would be able to defend the passage with a part only of his force, while with another part he would beat one or both the detachments which would have been sent round his flanks. Indeed, that detachment which, according to the proposed arrangement, should have been sent from La Serena to Talavera, being between the corps of Victor and Sebastiani, could hardly escape. At all events, these detachments on the two flanks appear to me to be too weak to produce any great effect upon the movements of Victor. That which would oblige him to retire would be the collection of force in his front; and he would be under no embarrassments respecting his rear from the efforts of these detachments. This objection would appear more forcible by entering into a calculation of the marches of these detachments, compared with those of the British army from hence.

I conclude that Gen. Cuesta would not wish to detach either of his divisions, till the British army should be well advanced towards the frontier; and if this should be the case, it will be found that we should be at Merida, the enemy possessing a knowledge of our position, before the division detached to the left would be at Alcantara, or that detached to the right would have made two marches through the mountains. The enemy would thus have his retreat open, annoyed only by whatever pressure we might make on his rear guard. According to this reasoning, it would appear that we should effect nothing by the junction, excepting to oblige the enemy to retire across the Tagus, with a certain degree of risk to two Spanish divisions. But it will also be attended with some inconvenience to ourselves.

I shall now suppose that we should be able to cross the Tagus, and that the enemy would not attempt to defend the passage of that river, having the knowledge that the great body of our force was collected on the south side of the river; the inconvenience which I apprehend in that case is the want of provisions and forage in Estremadura, between the Tagus and Guadiana. The enemy has been in that country above 2 months, and we understand has suffered some distress latterly; and we know that where they suffer distress, we are not likely to find any quantity of provisions and forage on our march through the country.

A magazine formed at Badajoz would be little able to supply the troops on the rapid march which they would have to make across from the Guadiana to the Tagus. I have no objection to incur the risk of this inconvenience, if it is to answer any good purpose; but as the consequence of this junction will be only to oblige the enemy to retreat across the Tagus, it will be better, in my opinion, to produce this effect by another mode equally certain of producing it, with this additional advantage, that no risk will attend it; that the enemy, after having crossed the Tagus, cannot stand to defend the passage of that river, and that there is no reason to believe that any of the troops will suffer from the want of provisions.

In regard to the plan proposed, that the British army should cross the Tagus at Alcantara, and co-operate from thence in an attack upon Victor, it appears to me to be equally inefficient with the other, with this addition to it, that as there is no road along the south bank of the Tagus, according to your answers to my queries, the two armies would be separated, and therefore each comparatively weak; while my appearance at Alcantara would not affect the enemy's line of retreat, as I must go down as far as Caceres before I could turn towards the Tagus again.

Of the 3 propositions made to me, I decidedly prefer that which takes the British army to Plasencia. By this movement, if it should be concealed from the enemy for a sufficient length of time, we must cut off his retreat by the bridge of Almaraz, and possibly by Arzobispo and Talavera.

If it should not be concealed, at all events the enemy cannot pretend to defend the Tagus. It is unattended by risk, as both armies are, I conceive, sufficiently strong to defend themselves separately against any attack which Victor might make upon them; and the probability of want is lessened for both armies, as we shall be in a country which has hitherto been untouched; and the Spanish army, having only themselves to supply in Estremadura, will incur less risk of want than if we also were to be supplied from the same resources.

Another plan has occurred to me by which we should turn the enemy's left flank, and that is, to reinforce Vanegas's corps from the right of Gen. Cuesta to such an extent as to enable him to beat Sebastiani, and then to bring Vanegas's army upon the Tagus about Talavera; or if that cannot be done, for Gen. Cuesta to move himself, with his whole army, by La Serena, and through the mountains to Talavera, leaving me to occupy, with the British army, the ground in the enemy's front.

I suggest these last plans only because an operation upon the enemy's left appears to be preferred to an operation upon his right and rear at the Spanish head quarters; but I conceive there are the following objections to both plans: to the first, that the detachment could not be made to Vanegas, till I should be so near as to give the enemy a knowledge of my position; and to the second, there is the same objection, that Gen. Cuesta could not move till I should be ready to occupy his ground; and that he would in fact place himself, when weak in artillery, between the two French armies. But I acknowledge that I have this further objection to all attempts upon the enemy's left, viz., that they do not afford a chance of cutting off his retreat, as those upon the right do; as, supposing they should be successful and the Spanish army in possession of Talavera, there will be nothing to prevent the retreat of the French army from the bridge of Almaraz, by Plasencia and the Puerto de Baños.

I am much concerned that it is not in my power, with the instructions under which I act, to enter into any great system of co-operation with the

Spanish armies. I can never admit, however, that (although, from circumstances, it is not in my power to do all I could wish) a great and important object will not have been attained by the removal of Marshal Victor from the imposing position which he occupies, menacing the seat of government of Portugal, as well as of Spain, even though he should be able to retire with all his artillery and stores. This, however, I consider to be quite impracticable, unless he has already commenced to send a part of them to the rear, which you appear to think he has not.

I request to hear from you as soon as you shall have obtained the opinion of Gen. Cuesta upon the different points contained in this letter. The first movements will be to be made by me, whatever plan may be adopted; and you may assure the General that I shall not lose a moment, and shall move as soon as I shall have given my troops a few days' rest, and shall have supplied them with shoes and other articles which they require, after the marches which they have lately made.

P.S. I request you to get for me all the information you can of the roads in the country north of the Tagus, and of the course of the Tietar, the passages of that river, &c.

To the Rt. Hon. J. H. Frere.   Abrantes, 9th June, 1809.

When I was enabled, by the flight of Soult from Portugal, to return to the southward, I sent Lieut. Col. Bourke to the head quarters of Gen. Cuesta, to converse with him on the different plans of operations which we might adopt; and I gave him certain queries, of which you will find copies enclosed, the answers to which would give the information I required to make up my own mind on the points under consideration.

I enclose to you copies of the letters which I have received from Col. Bourke, and of my answer of this day, in which you will see the line of operations I prefer.

I shall be very much obliged to you if you will apply to the Junta for orders to the magistrates about Plasencia, or, indeed, in all parts of Spain to which I may go, to assist me, as far as may be possible, with supplies of provisions and forage; and with carriages and mules which I may require for the movement of the army.

I understand that when Sir J. Moore was in Spain last year, the Commissaries of his army received the supplies of provisions and forage which they required for the British troops from the Officers of the Hacienda; and probably some arrangement of the same kind would facilitate the supply of the British troops in this campaign.

To the Rt. Hon. J. Villiers.   Abrantes, 9th June, 1809.

It is necessary that some arrangements should be made respecting the carriage of our letters by the post, as nothing can be more irregular than the communication is at present. My wish was to have a daily communication by post between Lisbon and the army, when it was engaged in operations to the northward, by Thomar, and one from Abrantes to Thomar, by which arrangement we should have been able to communicate with you and with Gen. Mackenzie every day. I don't believe the post has ever gone oftener than 3 times a week, and no arrangement was made for the line to Abrantes.   Mackenzie was 13 days before he received a letter written by me on the 13th May ; and very lately letters dispatched from Coimbra did not arrive for 6 days, and had been round to Lisbon. I imagine that by far the best mode of proceeding in future would be :

1st. To have a daily post between the army and Lisbon.

2dly. To have a daily communication from Abrantes, by Thomar and Coimbra, to Oporto.

3dly. That we should either pay for our letters, as other people do, or that we should make up a packet at head quarters daily, which should be forwarded by either or both those lines, and pay a certain sum for the conveyance of each of those packets.   In short, let us adopt any mode to insure a speedy and safe communication.

To Don Gregorio Cuesta.   Abrantes, 10th June, 1809.

I received last night, from Col. Alava, your letter of the 27th May ; and I am happy to find, from a perusal of it, that the plan of operations for the British troops, which Col. Bourke will have informed you that I preferred in consequence of the directions which I gave him in a letter of yesterday's date, is that which you at that time recommended, with the exception that I shall not send a detachment of British troops to Alcantara. This post will, however, be occupied by a detachment of Portuguese troops, who will make the demonstrations upon the enemy's flank which you are desirous should be made by a detachment placed at Alcantara.

I should with great pleasure comply with your desire, and place at Alcantara a British detachment, if it were not desirable, on many accounts, to keep the British army as much concentrated and collected as possible. Indeed, it is only by keeping them in a collected state that we can hope to derive from them that service which they are capable of rendering.

I beg leave to congratulate your Excellency upon the success of Gen. Blake in Aragon, and upon that of the Austrian armies in Italy.

G. O.   Abrantes, 10th June, 1809.

1. The baggage of the army is immediately to be disembarked from the transports in the Tagus, and to be placed in stores at Lisbon ; each regiment will, as soon as possible, send to Lisbon an officer, or a careful non-commissioned officer, to superintend the removal of the baggage belonging to the regiment, to the storehouse allotted to receive it ; these officers and non-commissioned officers will report themselves, on their arrival at Lisbon, to the A. Q. M. G. stationed there, and will receive his directions respecting the storehouse to be allotted for the baggage of the regiment, the means of removing it from the transports to the storehouse, and those for arranging it there.

2. After the baggage shall have been placed in the storehouses at Lisbon, it must be in charge of one non-commissioned officer or steady private soldier of each regiment, who is to be left there, and all the other officers and non-commissioned officers sent to Lisbon respecting baggage must return to join the army.

Memorandum. Should any regiment have officers or non-commissioned officers at Lisbon, who can perform the duty relative to regimental baggage, for the purpose of officers commanding regiments will send instructions to them, agreeable to the G. O., from hence, and there will be no occasion for regiments to detach persons for the above duty.

As the cisterns in the town of Abrantes are all sealed and closed up, with a view to the preservation of the water which they contain, for the purpose of the fortification which is to be erected here, the soldiers must not touch them ; several of the cisterns having been already broken open by the soldiers, notwithstanding that they were sealed and locked up. The officers commanding regiments are requested to visit the quarters occupied by their corps, to see that all the cisterns are again locked up and sealed, and a sentry must be placed over each.

The troops must bring from the river the water which they require.

To Vice Adm. the Hon. G. Berkeley.   Abrantes, 10th June, 1809.

I have had the honor of receiving your letter of the 8th inst. I agree entirely in opinion with you that it is expedient that the baggage of the army should be landed, and placed in storehouses at Lisbon; and I have given directions to the Q. M. G. to have a proper store hired for that purpose, and orders to the army to send proper persons down to Lisbon to remove the baggage from the transports, and arrange it in the storehouses.

I shall be obliged to you if you will direct the Agent of transports to communicate with the A. Q. M. G. at Lisbon upon this subject, and to land the baggage, when the latter shall signify to him that the officers sent to Lisbon by the different regiments are prepared to receive it.

To Col. Peacocke, Lisbon.   Abrantes, 10th June, 1809.

I request you will desire the commanding officer of the 40th regt. to make all the arrangements for taking the field with his regiment at a short notice, as I shall move them to join the army as soon as other troops ordered to Lisbon shall approach that city.

The officers commanding companies, the Paymaster, and the Surgeon, must provide themselves with mules for the carriage of the camp kettles of their companies, of their books, and of the medicine chests respectively; and a requisition must be made upon the Commissary for one mule to carry the intrenching tools. Requisitions must likewise be made upon the Q. M. G.'s department for bill hooks, haversacks, canteens, and camp kettles, to complete the battalion; and the officers will apply to the Q. M. G. for such number of tents as they may require, according to the orders recently given out upon that subject.

I expect the 48th and 61st regts. from Gibraltar, to which corps you will give the same orders immediately upon their arrival as I have above directed you to give to the 40th regt.; and the same to the 43d, 52d, and 95th regts., and the 23d light dragoons, expected from England. The officers of the 5 last mentioned regiments of infantry will probably be in want of money to equip themselves for the field; and you will therefore inform the officers commanding them to send to head quarters, as soon as possible after they shall land, returns for their bât and forage, if they should not already have received that allowance this year; and you will convey to the Dep. Paymaster Gen. at Lisbon my desire that he will advance to the Paymasters of regiments such sums, on account of this allowance, as they may find it necessary to demand, and that I shall send the warrant for its payment without loss of time.

You will take care that the corps as they arrive shall receive copies of all the G. O. which have been issued to the army.

To the Rt. Hon. J. Villiers.   Abrantes, 10th June, 1809.

I enclose a memorandum, which I have drawn in concert with Beresford, for an arrangement of the Portuguese Commissariat. If you should approve of it, I shall write to the Treasury to prevail upon them to alter the absurd instruction which I enclose, which they have given to Mr. Murray, respecting the Portuguese Commissariat. It would appear from this, and from the instruction of the Commissary of Accounts, that they intended that the Portuguese Commissary should settle accounts before the Board of Auditors, than which no idea could be more absurd.

The reason of the 6th clause is that I have received instructions to issue to the Portuguese troops no stores of any description, it being intended that all they should receive should be through you, and by way of subsidy. This cannot be easily effected; at the same time, that to omit or delay to issue the stores might be attended by the most serious inconveniences. I was, therefore, desired to get your receipt for all stores which I should issue to the Portuguese troops, and, of course, your bill for the value.

The A.G. to Brig. Gen. H. Campbell, brigade of Guards.   10th June, 1809.

The Commander of the Forces having been pleased to accept the resignation of the Provost Marshal of the army, has directed me to acquaint you that he is desirous of conferring this appointment upon such serjeant of the Guards as you may select, who, in your judgment, will discharge the duties of the situation with activity and zeal. You will be pleased to acquaint me, without loss of time, of the name of the non-commissioned officer you can recommend, and you will direct him to repair to head quarters, reporting himself on his arrival to me, when he will receive further orders.

To Brig. Gen. Howorth, R.A.   Abrantes, 11th June, 1809.

I enclose a letter that I have received from Lieut. Col. Fisher, which I beg you to return to me as soon as you shall have taken a copy of it.

In respect to the wheels, I conclude that Col. Robe will improve the arrangement made by Lieut. Col. Fisher by my orders, by ordering up to Santarem the carriages as well as the wheels of the two 6 pounder brigades.

I request you to make your own arrangements respecting the 231 horses and 26 mules, which I believe will be at Santarem to-morrow, or next day, for the service of the Royal artillery; and make them known to the Q. M. G., that he may direct them to be carried into execution. In order to enable you to do this more effectually, I mention to you that I have reason to believe that there will be some difficulty in getting higher up the river, by water, than Valada, which place is 3 leagues below Santarem, and that it may expedite the business if you should determine to draw up your gun carriages by land from Valada. The reserve stores might come as far as Santarem by water.

G. O.   Abrantes, 11th June, 1809.

2. When the army is in cantonments, the following rules are to be observed in respect to quarters : the allotment of the quarters of any considerable corps of the army is to be made by the officer commanding it, through the A. Q. M. G. attached to the corps, or, in his absence, through any other officer of his staff; no individual is to take quarters for himself, or change them without the authority of the officer commanding in the cantonments. The staff and other unattached officers are to be quartered by the A. Q. M. G. of the corps of the army to which they belong, or the officer acting for him. Regimental officers are to take their quarters in the street or district allotted to their respective corps : but when a regiment is placed in any public building, which does not afford accommodation for officers, such as are not ordered to remain with the men will have quarters allotted to them. All regulations respecting quarters in the town or village where the head quarters of the army are established, are to be made by the Commandant at head quarters.

3. All men able to march, whether convalescents from the hospital at Lisbon, or men lately arrived there from England, who have arms and accoutrements, will be ordered to join their regiments.

To Lieut. Col. Bourke, A. Q. M. G.   Abrantes, 11th June, 1809.

Since I wrote to you yesterday, I have received from England authority
' to extend my operations in Spain, beyond the provinces immediately
adjacent to the Portuguese frontier,' and I beg you to discuss with Gen.
O'Donoju the operations which it may be expedient that the combined
armies should carry on after we shall have forced Victor across the Tagus.
My opinion is generally that the 2 armies ought to keep so near each
other as to afford to each other mutual support, and to be able to form a
junction in case the enemy* should receive reinforcements ; but that in
other respects we ought to keep separate, for the convenience of subsistence, &c. ; that I should take the left, and endeavor to place myself between
Victor and the French corps in Galicia ; that neither of the armies ought
to go to Madrid, but rather to direct their march upon Segovia ; thus
threatening the enemy upon his right, cutting off his communication with
the French corps in Galicia, and hurrying him back upon the Ebro.

I only throw out these general notions for consideration. I am not sufficiently acquainted with the country to be able positively to decide that
this plan would be the best : of course, that must depend upon the strength
and position of the Spanish corps, which may and ought to be brought to
bear upon the French, as well as upon the positions they may take up, and
upon the natural difficulties which may exist in the country, to impede
the retreat of the enemy, of which we might take advantage.

To Don Gregorio Cuesta.   Abrantes, 11th June, 1809.

I have the honor to inform you that I have just received a report from
the officer commanding at Alcantara, dated the 10th, stating that a division of the enemy's troops, with 7 pieces of cannon, had just made an
attack upon his post, and that he had, in consequence, blown up the bridge.
I am induced to believe, from a report which I have received, that the
messenger who carried the letter from your Excellency to the Commanding officer at Alcantara, in which you advised him not to destroy the
bridge, fell into the hands of the enemy, and was put to death. The officer
commanding at Alcantara has not, I believe, received your letter ; and, if
it be true that it fell into the hands of the enemy, it is probable that this
attack has been made to bring about the destruction of the bridge.

To the Rt. Hon. J. H. Frere.   Abrantes, 11th June, 1809.

I enclose the copy of a letter which I have received this morning from
England, and the copy of one which I have, in consequence, written to
Col. Bourke.

I should now be ready to move into Spain in 2 or 3 days if I had any
money : but the distress in which we are from want of that necessary
article will, I fear, render it impossible for me to move till I shall receive
a supply. I have, however, reason to expect money from Cadiz in exchange
for Spanish gold, which I sent there in the *Surveillante* about 6 weeks
ago, and a supply from England.

To the Rt. Hon. J. Villiers.   Abrantes, 11th June, 1809.

I received last night your letter of the 9th. Till I learned by Lord

Burghersh's letter of the 9th, received this morning, that Lord Wellesley had deferred his departure from England for a few days, I thought it probable that the Admiral and you would have determined not to come up, in the expectation that I should go down to you: this arrival being now, however, more than ever uncertain, I think there is a chance that I shall see you on Tuesday or Wednesday. I need not tell you how happy your arrival will make me.

I regret to learn that you think of quitting us. I recollect your mentioning this intention when I was at Lisbon, which gave me great concern, which concern has increased from the experience I have had of the good you have already done, and from the expectation which I had that you would have it in your power to do still more good. I do not know under what engagement you undertook your present office, but I am very certain that government will find nobody who can execute what is still to be done so well as yourself.

My dispatches from England announce a reinforcement of 7 battalions, besides Craufurd's corps, for which I believe I may thank you; and I have besides authority to extend my operations beyond the provinces immediately adjacent to the Portuguese frontier, provided 'I shall be of opinion that my doing so is material to the success of my operations, and not inconsistent with the safety of Portugal.' So that the ball is now at my foot, and I hope I shall have strength enough to give it a good kick. I should begin immediately, but I cannot venture to stir without money. The army is 2 months in arrears; we are over head and ears in debt every where; and I cannot venture into Spain without paying what we owe, at least in this neighbourhood, and giving a little money to the troops.

You might as well keep the corporal and the dragoons.

To Major Gen. Mackenzie.   Abrantes, 11th June, 1809.

I am very much obliged to you for all your letters, and that of this morning. I am sorry that you feel the general distress for want of money; but we shall get some in a day or two, and all that comes shall be given to your corps. I have desired that Mr. Downie* may draw upon Mr. Dalrymple for 10,000 dollars, to pay the supplies collecting at Castello Branco for the army.

I beg you will let Mr. Downie know that he is a Commissary, and his business at Castello Branco is to collect supplies; and that I am much surprised and highly displeased with him for quitting his station and the business on which he was employed, to move forward to Alcantara, where a few shots were fired, *to see what service he could render there;* as if he could render any so important as that upon which he was employed by me. I thought he had seen too much service to have been so inconsiderate.

As to yourself, I think you had better stay where you are. Beresford is going to Castello Branco in a day or two, to organize his Portuguese troops, and you had better remain at Sobreira.

---

* Then in the Commissariat department. Afterwards Sir J. Downie, Lieut. Gen. in the service of Spain. He was a very gallant soldier. He died when holding the distinguished command of Captain General of Andalusia, and Alcayde of the Alcazar at Seville.

To Visc. Castlereagh.   Abrantes, 11th June, 1809.

I think it proper to draw your Lordship's attention to the want of money in this army. The troops are nearly 2 months in arrear, and the army is in debt in Portugal a sum amounting to not less than £200,000. I know of no resource to answer these demands, excepting a sum amounting to less than £100,000 expected from Cadiz in dollars, in exchange for Spanish gold, sent to Cadiz about 6 weeks ago, it not being current in Portugal.

There is no reason to expect any large sum for bills of exchange on England, negotiated at Lisbon, Cadiz, or Gibraltar: and I conceive that the expenses in this country, including those of the ordnance, the advances to the Portuguese government, the pay of the army, and the extraordinaries, will not fall short of £200,000 *per mensem*. The whole of this sum ought, for some months at least, to be sent in specie from Great Britain, otherwise the operations of the army will be cramped for want of money.

To Visc. Castlereagh.   Abrantes, 11th June, 1809.

Marshal Beresford has represented to me, in urgent terms, the want of officers of superior rank to command the Portuguese troops, on whom he can rely, of which I am fully aware; and he has expressed a desire that I should request your Lordship would urge the Commander in Chief to send out the officers of whose names I enclose a list, to serve in Portugal, in the ranks set opposite to their respective names. This arrangement is not likely to supersede any officer now serving with the British army serving in Portugal.

Marshal Beresford has also desired to have the assistance of a certain number of medical officers, which appears to me to be equally necessary with that of officers to command the troops. He has desired that I would recommend Dr. Fergusson, who has served in St. Domingo, as the fittest person, from his experience and other qualifications, to be the medical superintendent, and that he should have the assistance of 10 or 12 staff surgeons.

I forward a list of arms and military equipments, principally for cavalry, which Marshal Beresford is desirous of having for the use of the Portuguese troops.

40,000 knapsacks, 5000 saddles and bridles, 6000 carbines, 6000 swords, 4000 pairs of pistols, 2000 rifles, 5000 saddle bags.

To Lieut. Col. Walsh, Town Major, Lisbon.   Abrantes, 12th June, 1809.

300 horses belonging to the Irish Commissariat will have arrived from Cork in the fleet which brought out the 23d dragoons; and I desire that these horses may be landed, as well as the 23d dragoons, and given in charge to the officers and men of those troops of the Waggon Train which are at Lisbon. Care must be taken that none of these horses, or of those of the 23d, are put into the infected stables at Lisbon.

To Lieut. Col. Seymour, 23d light dragoons.   Abrantes, 12th June, 1809.

I have every reason to hope that this letter will find you at Lisbon, and probably with a great part of your corps disembarked. I am particularly anxious that your horses should join the army in a condition for service, and in that view I recommend your attention to the following objects:

1st, to their shoeing: the greater the number of sets of spare shoes and nails the better.

2dly, you should at an early period accustom the horses to eat barley, or Indian corn and straw. We find that by giving them half barley and half oats, and by degrees diminishing the proportion of oats, they soon eat the former as well as the latter. The same with hay and straw. I shall take care that, when you get your route for marching, you shall not be made to go marches of too great length. Some of the stables at Lisbon are infected by glanders; and, indeed, at all events, it is desirable that after the first day or two you should have your horses picketed rather than placed in stables.

To Dom Miguel Forjaz.   Abrantes, 12th June, 1809.

I am very much obliged to you for the communication of the arrangement made for the command of the troops at Oporto, which I conceive to be a very good one; and I shall be very much obliged to the Regency, if they will allow Col. Trant to command in that town under the orders of Marechal de Campo Bacellar, as long as there may be any French prisoners, or any English sick and wounded there, or any stores belonging to the English army.

To Lieut. Col. Trant.   Abrantes, 12th June, 1809.

I have received your letters of the 9th inst. I have no doubt whatever of your readiness to take the field in an advanced position, if Gen. Beresford or I should order you to do so. But I trust that without receiving those orders you will not think of stirring from Oporto. The Marechal de Campo Bacellar has been appointed by the Regency to command in the district of Oporto; you are to continue to command in the town.

The directions which you have given to the transports to cross the bar are perfectly proper. I wish that you had ordered all, whether having on board wounded, or prisoners in health. I wish to have a return of the number of guns we have taken belonging to the enemy. You must allow the cotton to go to Lisbon according to the directions, taking an account of it, and a receipt of the person to whom you deliver it.

To Lieut. Col. Bourke, A. Q. M. G.   Abrantes, 12th June, 1809.

I have just received your letter of the 10th inst. I enclose you intelligence which I have received from the Junta of Plasencia, which would tend to prove that the enemy are retreating; and the movement upon Alcantara of the 10th, whether made with a design to destroy the bridge

---

G. O.   Abrantes, 12th June, 1809.

1. When bedding is required for the sick, whether regimental or general hospitals, and it cannot be supplied by the general stores, the surgeon in charge of the hospital must make a requisition in writing for what he requires to the commissary of the brigade, or the Commissary Gen.; the officer of the commissariat will make a requisition upon the magistrate of the place, for what will thus be required by the surgeon; the surgeon will give his receipt for the bedding delivered to him, and he will be responsible to return the whole of the bedding to the magistrate who procured it.

or not, does not look like a settled plan to attack Gen. Cuesta immediately. I cannot, however, avoid urging you to repeat my recommendation to Gen. Cuesta to avoid a general action with the enemy till I shall be able to co-operate with him.

To the Rt. Hon. J. H. Frere.   Abrantes, 12th June, 1809.

I have just received your letter of the 9th.

I am much flattered by the notion entertained by some of the persons in authority at Seville, of appointing me to the command of the Spanish armies. I have received no instructions from government upon that subject; but I believe that it was considered an object of great importance in England, that the Commander in Chief of the British troops should have that situation, but one more likely to be attained by refraining from pressing it, and by leaving it to the Spanish government themselves to discover the expediency of the arrangement, than by any suggestion on our parts.

I concluded that you had been made acquainted with the wishes of government upon this subject, and had seen copies of my instructions. But if you had no knowledge of the wishes of government, I do not conceive that your insinuations upon the subject are likely to have any effect, excepting to forward the object of government, even though the opinion of ministers be well founded, viz., that that which will prevent the accomplishment of this object is the jealousy of the Spanish government.

I assure you, that after Soult had passed the bridge of Melgaço, near Ruivaes, there did not exist the smallest chance of surrounding him. Indeed, if Silveira had been in time to break that bridge, Soult might have turned to his right. When an army is reduced to the state in which his was, it is impossible to overtake it; and surrounding it is out of the question. I might have followed them another march or two into Galicia; but since the Marques de la Romana's departure from Chaves, we had no knowledge of the state of affairs in Galicia, excepting that Vigo was in possession of the Spaniards; and I did not see any reason to believe that the Spanish peasantry could stop Soult more effectually than the Portuguese peasantry had been able to do.

I shall be very glad to have with the British army a division of Spanish cavalry, and that the Duque de Alburquerque shall command it; but till we can remove Victor from his position, I think that I ought not to ask for any reinforcement which is to diminish Cuesta's force.

I shall be much obliged to you if you will not ask for Spanish rank for Col. —— and Col. ——. I have great difficulty in settling the question arising from the Portuguese rank granted to British officers, which difficulties would be increased in cases in which Spanish rank should be granted. It is better that the officers of the two armies should rank according to the dates of their commissions respectively, and that Spanish rank should not in future be granted to any British officers, excepting by the application of the British Commander in Chief, through the Ambassador.

To Visc. Castlereagh.   Abrantes, 12th June, 1809.

I have the honor to acknowledge the receipt of your Lordship's dispatch of the 25th ult., in which your Lordship conveys to me, by His Majesty's commands, an authority to extend my operations in Spain beyond the provinces immediately adjacent to the Portuguese frontier.

It does not appear to be quite certain that Marshal Victor has retired, or has made any preparatory arrangements with a view to withdraw from the province of Estremadura; and the accounts which we receive of his movements are so contradictory, that I am not enabled to give your Lordship any positive opinion upon the subject, or any satisfactory statement of facts which might enable you to form your own.

Upon my arrival at Coimbra, in the end of last month, I dispatched Lieut. Col. Bourke and Lieut. Col. Cadogan to Gen. Cuesta's head quarters, with a view to arrange with him a plan of co-operation for the British and Spanish armies; with a view also to attack Victor, and to oblige him to retire from the menacing position which he had assumed in relation to the seats of government of Portugal and Spain. I propose now to extend the objects of this co-operation, Gen. Cuesta having expressed himself but little satisfied with the limits which I had assigned to it: but I fear that I must delay making any movements whatever till the army shall receive a supply of money.

To Lieut. Col. Bourke, A. Q. M. G. Abrantes, 13th June, 1809.

I have just received your letter of the 11th inst., the contents of which have induced me to alter my plan, and to consent to carry on my operations between the Tagus and the Guadiana. Notwithstanding that, I am convinced that the most effectual mode of destroying the French army would be to adopt the line which I at first proposed; more particularly, if Gen. Cuesta could be prevailed upon to place his army in a situation of security, till the British army should be so far advanced on its march as to render it impossible for the enemy to attack the Spanish army without being exposed to certain destruction. But this concession will answer no purpose, unless Gen. Cuesta will secure his position. I cannot march till I shall get shoes for the troops from Lisbon, and some money. Indeed, the troops are not yet all arrived from the northward; and it is obvious that, till I shall be upon the Guadiana, the Spanish army will not be in that state of security, only because Gen. Cuesta does not choose to make it secure.

As to the plan of attack mentioned in the General's letter, it is too loose for me to be able to give any opinion upon it; as far as I can understand it, it labors under the disadvantage of separating the combined armies, and placing the French army between them, without having the advantage of cutting off the enemy's retreat, which is the plan I had proposed. My opinion was, and is, that if I had once gained the bridge of Almaraz, (Gen. Cuesta having placed his army in security,) the enemy would have been in our power: they could not have attacked him with any prospect of success, and they could not have attacked me without the certainty of having him upon their backs. According to the proposed plan, they will have it in their power to attack either army separately; and their retreat is always open, excepting so far as it may be impeded by Marshal Beresford's corps. This plan will obviously not answer.

If I am to go upon the Guadiana, which I certainly will do, if Gen.

Cuesta persists in thinking it the best plan, the two armies must co-operate more closely; otherwise, I fear the weaker of the two may be defeated. I have no objection to taking any share of the action that may be allotted to me; but I am convinced, that, if the Spanish army separates itself from us, as proposed, at the distance of 10 or 15 leagues, with rivers and mountains between us, they will be defeated, and we shall see nothing of the enemy. I shall be obliged to you if you will make a suggestion to Gen. Cuesta in this view of the case.

I shall also be much obliged to you if you will obtain for me, as soon as possible, an account of the roads leading from Badajoz and Montijo to Caceres, how far they pass from the enemy's position at Montanches, Torremocha, and Alcuescar; an account of the roads from Merida to Caceres, from Merida to Truxillo, from Medellin to Truxillo; whether there are any roads or communication between the roads from Merida and Medellin to Truxillo and Caceres, respectively, and the roads from Badajoz and Montijo to Caceres. I beg you also to let me know what is the nature of the country about Caceres, Montanches, Torremocha, and Alcuescar, and also about Truxillo.

G. O. Abrantes, 13th June, 1809.

The senior officer in charge of the sick at Oporto and Coimbra, will once a week send by the post to head quarters, a return of the sick, specifying the number of recovered men able to march.

The Commanding officers of those regiments of the army, to the men of which clothing is due, will report to the Q. M. G. whether the clothing is arrived at Lisbon, and where.

1. Whenever 40 men at either hospital are sufficiently recovered to be able to march, an order and a route will be sent for their march by easy stages.

2. They are to take with them, at setting out, 3 days' bread in biscuit, which they are to keep by them as a reserve.

3. The Commissary Gen. will arrange that they shall be fed at the different halting places.

4. An officer must be sent in command of every detachment of 40 men, and 2 officers if the number should amount to 80, and so on; 1 officer for every 40 in addition; 1 non-commissioned officer must be sent for every 20 sick; and the commanding officer at the hospital must make arrangements that other officers and non-commissioned officers should take charge of the remaining sick of the brigade, in charge of which such officer or non-commissioned officer has been left at the hospital.

5. The senior officer at the hospital will report to the Q. M. G. the departure of the recovered men; and officers commanding the party of recovered men must report their progress to head quarters by every opportunity.

6.   *   *   *   *   *   *

7. The Commander of the Forces requests that olive and other fruit trees may not be used by the troops in hutting, except in case of evident necessity.

8. If the country in the neighbourhood of the several cantonments should afford materials fit for hutting, the Commander of the Forces is desirous that the troops should be moved into huts as soon as possible; the officers commanding brigades will make arrangements accordingly. The tents will be delivered to the officers who have made requisitions for them, under the orders of the 24th May, as soon as they shall arrive from Lisbon.

9. All Commissariat and other persons who have Portuguese dragoons attached to them, are to send the dragoons to Abrantes immediately, reporting to the Adj. Gen. that they have done so.

10. The Commander of the Forces is concerned to have to announce to the army that private ——, of the 53d regt., has been wounded, and has probably died of the wounds he received from some peasants in the neighbourhood of Coimbra; and that corporal —— and private —— have probably met with the same fate: this is one of the consequences of the irregularities of which the soldiers have been guilty, which have had the effect of turning into enemies a people who were grateful for the benefits which they had received from the British nation, and manifested their gratitude by affording to the soldiers every comfort and assistance which was in their power.

The Commanding officers of brigades and regiments are particularly requested to point out to the soldiers the consequences of their irregularities.

To Don Gregorio Cuesta.   Abrantes, 13th June, 1809.

I have the honor to inform your Excellency, that I have received accounts from Gen. Viana at Monção on the Minho, stating that the enemy had made an attack on the 7th inst., with 2000 men and 5 pieces of cannon, on the Spanish troops under the Conde de Norona, and that they had been repulsed with loss. I beg to congratulate your Excellency upon this fresh instance of the steadiness and bravery of the Spanish army.

I acquaint your Excellency, in another letter, of my intention to co-operate with you in an attack upon the enemy between the Guadiana and the Tagus; and I have only to recommend to your Excellency to keep your troops in their strong positions till I shall be in a state to give them assistance.

To Don Gregorio Cuesta.   Abrantes, 13th June, 1809.

I have had the honor of receiving your Excellency's letter of the 11th inst.; and, as I find that your Excellency prefers that I should co-operate with you in an attack upon the enemy between the Tagus and the Guadiana to an endeavor, by the army under my command, to intercept the enemy's retreat across the Tagus, by the march of this army to Plasencia, and thence to Almaraz, I shall comply with your Excellency's desire, and shall direct my march upon Badajoz as soon as I am able to move my troops. I request your Excellency will, in the mean time, give directions that preparations may be made to supply this army with provisions at Badajoz. Notwithstanding that the great body of the British troops will co-operate with your Excellency between the Tagus and the Guadiana, a body of British and Portuguese troops, under the command of Marshal Beresford, will move by Plasencia on the line which I had before proposed to take with the British army.

To the Rt. Hon. J. H. Frere.   Abrantes, 13th June, 1809.

I send you copies of the letters I have received from the Spanish head quarters, and of those which I have written to Gen. Cuesta and Col. Bourke this day. Col. Bourke's letter explains so fully the situation of Cuesta's army, and my letter to him is so explicit upon the dangers of his position; the small chance there is that I shall be able to serve him, unless he should take up a strong position till I can come to his assistance; and upon the advantages of the operation which I had proposed; that I do not think it necessary to trouble you further upon the subject. I can only say, that the obstinacy of this old gentleman is throwing out of our hands the finest game that any armies ever had; and that we shall repent that we did not cut off Victor when we shall have to beat the French upon the Ebro. With such a letter, however, as Col. Bourke's before me, I could not but yield the point to Gen. Cuesta, which I hope will convince the Spanish government of my sincere desire to be of service to them.

To the Rt. Hon. J. Villiers.   Abrantes, 13th June, 1809.

I have the honor to enclose to you a letter which I have received from Brig. Gen. Langwerth, in which he encloses the proceedings of a Court of Inquiry, on the circumstances attending the absence of a corporal and

2 private soldiers from an escort of Commissariat carts, on their march from Aveiro to Coimbra. It is obvious that one of the private soldiers has been wounded; it is probable that all 3 have been put to death by the peasantry of Murtede. I am sorry to say, that, from the conduct of the soldiers of the army in general, I apprehend that the peasants may have had some provocation for their animosity against the soldiers; but it must be obvious to you and to the government, that these effects of their animosity must be discouraged, and even punished; otherwise it may lead to consequences, fatal to the peasantry of the country in general, as well as to the army. The government may depend upon my exertions to keep the troops in order, and that I shall exert all the power which the law has placed in my hands to punish those who may be guilty of any outrages. The discovery and proof against the soldiers guilty of them is, however, a matter of considerable difficulty, as the law now stands; and it is rendered more difficult by the unwillingness of the inhabitants of the country to come forward to give their evidence on oath before a Court Martial. Probably this evil might be remedied, or removed, either by the circulation of a proclamation or a circular letter to the country magistrates, by the government, calling upon the people to come forward with their complaints against the soldiers, and to prosecute them to conviction before a Court Martial. What I have now to request is, that strict inquiry may be made respecting the circumstances of the probable death of the 3 soldiers of the 53d regt. at Murtede, that those who put them to death may be discovered and brought to trial.

The A.G. to Lieut. Col. Walsh, Town Major, Lisbon.   13th June, 1809.

The Commander of the Forces has been made acquainted, by me, with the commendable reasons that induced you to urge your removal from Lisbon for active service in a regiment. But under your long experience and your attention to the arduous duties of the situations you now fill, I am directed to acquaint you that, consistent with the good of the public service, his Excellency cannot agree to your removal from it. He will bear in mind, I am persuaded, your views at a proper opportunity, and I shall not fail to call your services to the Commander of the Forces' recollection.

To Lieut. Col. Bourke, A. Q. M. G.   Abrantes, 14th June, 1809.

I have received your letter of the 12th, and one from Gen. Cuesta. The enclosed, to Mr. Frere, contains a copy of his and my answer, and of the enclosure in the letter.

I acknowledge that I entertain no apprehensions that the French will attack Gen. Cuesta: I am much more afraid that they are going away, and strengthening themselves upon the Tagus. Indeed, I understand that they have fortified the Puerto de Mirabete. If this be true, their design is obvious; and the only way to defeat it is to adopt the plan I originally proposed.

P.S. I wish you would hint to Gen. O'Donoju, that if the French should attack Gen. Cuesta, and he should be beaten, he will be highly responsible for omitting to place his army in a good position.

To Don Gregorio Cuesta.   Abrantes, 14th June, 1809.

I have had the honor of receiving your Excellency's letter of the 12th inst. My letter of yesterday's date will have apprised your Excellency that, in compliance with your desire, I intended to march towards Badajoz, in order to co-operate with your Excellency in the attack of the enemy in the manner which you preferred. Your Excellency may depend upon it that I shall not delay the march of the troops for one moment after I shall have it in my power to move them; and I beg leave to refer your Excellency to Col. Alava for a detailed account of the circumstances which must prevent my march at the present moment.

From the enclosed paper, I should judge that the enemy had not concentrated his force, and that he had no intention of attacking the army under the command of your Excellency. But if your Excellency has reason to believe that the enemy has adopted the measures to which you refer, and has concentrated his force, your Excellency will, doubtless, have deemed it expedient to concentrate the Spanish army, to receive his attack in a position which, from its strength, will give your troops every advantage We have nothing now to apprehend, excepting that a misfortune may happen to one army before the other can join it, or shall be in a position to co-operate with or give it assistance; and I feel confident that when your Excellency shall have considered the situation in which I stand at this moment, the absolute necessity which exists that I should delay my march till all my troops shall have joined, and till I shall have received all that I require, you will deem it most for the general benefit to place your army in a secure position till I can move to your assistance, which you may depend upon my doing as soon as it shall be in my power.

To the Rt. Hon. J. H. Frere.   Abrantes, 14th June, 1809.

I enclose the letters received this day from the Spanish head quarters, and copies of my answers.

One of the great difficulties which I have in moving is the want of money; however, I have reason to expect that will be removed at an early period, either by the arrival of the *Surveillante*, from Cadiz, with £100,000, or by that of a vessel from England, with a similar sum. The arrival of either would enable me to march forthwith, as I have reason to expect the shoes and other necessaries every moment.

It has occurred, however, to Mr. Villiers, who is here, and to me, that the Spanish government, which is so much interested in my early advance, might be able to lend me £100,000 in specie, to be repaid out of the first money that may arrive from England for the army. If they will do so, and will send the money to Badajoz, I shall move forthwith.

To Visc. Castlereagh.   Abrantes, 14th June, 1809.

I have had the honor of receiving your Lordship's dispatch of the 26th May, in which you have notified that His Majesty had ordered 7 battalions of infantry therein named to proceed to Portugal, to reinforce the army under my command. I request that those battalions may be ordered to Lisbon. I propose to send to England the 2 battalions composed of detachments, as soon as the other troops shall arrive in Portugal, and a detachment of the 3d German hussars immediately. I have drafted from these last the few horses they had, and given them to the 14th light dragoons, which regiment your Lordship will have observed was incomplete in horses at the commencement of the campaign, and sustained some loss in the actions of the 10th, 11th, and 12th May.

I have arranged with the Admiral to send to Cork forthwith horse transports to convey one regiment of cavalry, 800; one troop of horse artillery, 200; and artillery horses, 300; in the whole 1300 horses. I request your Lordship will order such of the above mentioned troops and horses as may be destined for Portugal to proceed to Lisbon. The 23d light dragoons having arrived, the 20th will proceed to Sicily as soon as there shall be transports ready for them.

The A.G. to Brig. Gen. R. Stewart.   14th June, 1809.

I herewith enclose an order for the ammunition required by your letter of yesterday for the 1st batt. detachments. At the same time I am desired to direct that those men who have lost their ammunition may be regimentally tried and punished, and that you will call upon Lieut. Col. Bunbury to state if the officers of companies have regularly examined their men's ammunition every day, agreeable to G. O.: if not, that he will report the names of the officers to you, to be transmitted to me for his Excellency's information, in order that they may be noticed for neglecting instantly to demand ammunition for the men of their companies, which was expended so long ago as it is stated to have been used.

To Vice Adm. the Hon. G. Berkeley.   Abrantes, 15th June, 1809.

I have the honor to inform you that I have received the orders of His Majesty's Sec. of State to send to Gibraltar the 2d batt. 9th regt , to relieve one of the regiments, for which transports have been ordered to that garrison; and I shall be much obliged to you if you will give directions that transports may be prepared to convey the 2d batt. 9th regt. to Gibraltar as soon as that corps shall arrive at Lisbon.

I have also received the directions of the Sec. of State to send to Cork horse transports, containing stalls for 1300 horses, to convey to Portugal one regiment of dragoons consisting of 800 horses, 300 horses for the service of the artillery, and one troop of horse artillery, 200.

To J. Murray, Esq., Commissary General.   Abrantes, 16th June, 1809.

I am happy to hear of the arrival of the *Surveillante.*

You will do quite right to refer to the Lords of the Treasury the charge of Mr. Duff of a per centage upon the exchange of the gold for dollars. I have settled with Mr. Villiers that he is not to have any of the money which has arrived in the *Surveillante*, or that is disposable at the present moment.

The Paymaster at Lisbon and the Paymaster of Artillery must have those sums *which are absolutely necessary, and no more,* as they will be in a place where some money can always be procured; and the bills drawn upon Lisbon must be paid. I do not think any demands can be more

G. O.   Abrantes, 15th June, 1809.

6. A board of field officers of King's German Legion will sit at Barquinha without loss of time, under the directions of Brig. Gen. Langwerth, to report upon the shoes of the brigade reported unfit for service.

7. A division of apothecary's stores having arrived at head quarters, surgeons of regiments are immediately to complete their field panniers with whatever has been directed, by requisitions to the Inspector of hospitals at head quarters.

pressing than those of the service of the army; and I conceive that no demands ought to be paid, or no money left for the Paymaster Gen., or others, which will reduce the sum to be brought here to a smaller amount than £110,000; you will, therefore, take measures to have that sum sent up to the army without loss of time.   This will be £50,000 in addition to the £60,000 which you tell me in your letter of the 15th was coming up.

To Col. Donkin.*   Abrantes, 16th June, 1809.

I received last night your letter of the 11th, upon which I shall take an opportunity of writing to you fully in a day or two.

I trouble you now upon a subject which has given me the greatest pain: I mean the accounts which I receive from all quarters of the disorders committed by, and the general irregularity of, the — and — regts.   I have ordered a provost to Castello Branco to put himself under your orders, and I hope you will not fail to make use of him.   I beg that, on the receipt of this letter, you will call on the Commanding officers of the — and — regts., and apprise them of the concern with which I have heard these reports of their regiments; and of my determination, if I should hear any more of them, to send their regiments into garrison, and to report them to His Majesty as unfit for service in the field, on account of irregularity of conduct and disorder.   I desire that, upon the receipt of this letter, the — and — regts. may be hutted outside of the town of Castello Branco, if there should be wood in the neighbourhood, not fruit trees, and the rolls to be called every hour, from sunrise till 8 in the evening, all officers, as well as soldiers, to attend.

The number of men absent from these regiments in consequence of their late marches is scandalous; and I desire that an officer from each of them may go back immediately the whole road by which the brigade has moved since the 5th May, in search of the missing men.   Those missing on the late march and ground between Guarda and Castello Branco must be sent on immediately to Castello Branco; and those missing on the former march must be collected at Guarda, and afterwards brought up by the officers to the regiment when they shall return through that town.   I beg to have reports from you of the state of the arms, ammunition, &c. of these regiments, and to hear whether the roll calls above ordered are regular, and are attended by all the officers.   Non-commissioned officers and soldiers absent must be punished.   I beg to know whether the brigade has received all the orders.

To Visc. Castlereagh.   Abrantes, 16th June, 1809.

I beg you to see a letter which I have written to the Commander in

* The late Lieut. Gen. Sir Rufane Donkin, K.C.B.

G. O.   Abrantes, 16th June, 1809.

1. Two more assistant provosts will be appointed; commanding officers of brigades will please to send in recommendations of men capable of filling the situation: one of the assistant provosts is to repair to the camp near Abrantes, and to report himself to the officer commanding the camp.   He will patrol round the neighbourhood of it, and will take up all stragglers and marauders; two dragoons are to be attached to this provost, and to be relieved daily.

Chief, enclosing one from Gen. —— to Marshal Beresford, in which that officer objects to being employed on service with the Portuguese troops, and my letter to Marshal Beresford on that subject, allowing that officer to go to England. I only hope that Gen. —— will not be placed on the staff of the army anywhere else.

The A.G. to Lieut. Col. Arentschildt, 1st hussars, K.G.L.   16th June, 1809.

In reply to your letter of yesterday's date, I am directed by the Commander of the Forces to acquaint you that you will perceive by the orders and regulations that captains of troops, paymasters, and surgeons of regiments are to make good the losses of mules allotted for the carriage of camp kettles, medicine chests, and paymasters' books. The mules given by the Commissariat for these purposes in the first instance, is only an additional favor to the regiment by the Commander of the Forces. With respect to the carriage of the spare and broken saddles, as they are a concern belonging to the Colonel, the public cannot provide a carriage for them. The mules therefore, above the number, must be returned to the Commissariat. With regard to the mules, captains of troops, paymasters, and surgeons must, out of what is allowed them, defray the expenses of their own shoeing.

To the Junta of Badajoz.   Abrantes, 17th June, 1809.

I have had the honor of receiving your 2 letters of the 16th inst., and I am very sensible of the attention which you have paid to the wants of the army under my command. It is my intention to march by the route of Castello Branco and Coria, towards Plasencia and the banks of the Tietar, and I request you to give directions that provisions may be prepared in that quarter for 30,000 men and 6000 horses, including those of the cavalry, artillery, and military equipages.

To Lieut. Col. Gordon, Military Secretary.   Abrantes, 17th June, 1809.

I enclose a memorial which has been given into my hands by Major Davy, which I beg you to lay before the Commander in Chief.

I believe that H. R. H. the late Commander in Chief had intended to promote all the Majors commanding battalions in the late service in Portugal; and certainly, if the services of any battalion could give to their Commanding officer a claim to promotion, the conduct and services of the 5th batt. 60th foot entitled their Commanding officer to this advantage. I have had every reason to be satisfied with their conduct again upon this occasion, and I shall be very much obliged to you if you will recommend Major Davy to the favorable consideration of the Commander in Chief.

I likewise enclose a memorial from Mr. Thompson, Inspector of Hospitals to this army, who prays, what appears to be a matter of justice, that his appointment of Inspector may be notified in the gazette.

To Major Gen. Mackenzie.   Abrantes, 17th June, 1809.

I have received your 2 letters of the 16th. I do not think it necessary to make any movement in consequence of the intelligence of the passage of the Tagus by the enemy. There is no doubt, I believe, now, that Victor is retiring; and I conclude that the troops mentioned in the enclosures of your letters are some strong parties which have crossed the Tagus in the places referred to. I propose that the whole of the army should move forward in a few days, when the money shall have arrived to pay them;

but I do not like to move any part of the force till the whole shall be prepared to follow.

To Visc. Castlereagh.   Abrantes, 17th June, 1809.

I have received your letter of the 31st May.

My correspondence with Gen. Cuesta has been a very curious one, and proves him to be as obstinate as any gentleman at the head of any army need be. He would not alter his position even to ensure the safety of his army, because he supposed that this measure might be injurious to him-

---

G. O.   Abrantes, 17th June, 1809.

1. The Commander of the Forces has been much concerned to receive reports of the misconduct of the soldiers left behind, in all the hospitals, particularly at Oporto; and he desires that in future, whenever an hospital is established, the following regulations will be observed :

' When soldiers are dismissed from the hospital as convalescents, they are, if possible, to be quartered in the same building; if that should not be possible, they are to be quartered on the inhabitants of the house in which the hospital is established ; in either case the officers in charge of the men left behind in hospital are to attend, and to put in execution the Orders of the 29th ult. relative to visiting the soldiers in their quarters.

' 2. No convalescent must ever be permitted to appear out of his quarters in the streets of the town, excepting with his side arms, and dressed according to the orders of his regiment. As soon as a sufficient number of convalescents are strong enough, a guard must be mounted daily, of which patrols under a non-commissioned officer must be sent during the night to take up all soldiers straggling from their quarters after hours. Convalescents must parade with their arms twice a day, once in the morning, and in the evening at sunset; all officers being present at each parade. After the evening parade, the soldiers are to be marched to their quarters, and none are to be permitted to appear in the streets after that hour.

' 3. All officers left in sick quarters, in any town where an hospital is established, are to be considered as belonging to the hospital until they shall have recovered, and are to do duty according to their respective ranks with the officers left in charge of the sick men in hospital, till they shall be ordered to join the army.

' 4. The officer commanding at each of the hospitals, including that of Lisbon, will report to the Adj. Gen. that these orders have been carried into execution, along with the weekly report ordered to be made by the G. O. of the 13th June. Copies of these orders are to be sent to all the hospitals, and a copy to be left by the Adj. Gen. wherever an hospital may be left in future.

' 5. When the army, or any portion of it, in future requires green forage, commissaries, or, if there should be no commissary, the quartermaster of the regiment, under the orders of the General or commanding officer, will make a requisition upon the magistrate for it, and will point out to him the field or place from whence it can be provided ; the magistrate is then to have it cut ; forage is to be delivered to the troops by the commissary, in rations, according to the ordered proportions. A guard will be left in the field, in charge of the remainder of the forage, after the commissary has made his delivery. If there should be no magistrate, or if the magistrate should refuse to consent to deliver or cut the green forage, or if it should be necessary on any account the troops should cut it for themselves, the commissary of the brigade or regiment, accompanied by an officer of the Q. M. G.'s department, or if there should be none with that division of troops, by the quartermaster of a regiment, and if possible by the magistrate of the place, or the occupier of the ground, or by some inhabitant of the country, is to proceed to value the field, and to estimate the number of rations of forage it contains. Having done this, the commissary is to allot the field in its due proportions to the quartermasters of the different regiments to be supplied with forage from it; parties of fatigue from those regiments, under the command of an officer, are to proceed and cut and carry away the forage thus allotted to them. For all green forage required, the usual receipts must be given.

' 6. The commissary of each division, brigade, or regiment, on his arrival in any place near which he understands the troops to which he is attached are to halt more than one night, must take immediate and effectual measures to ascertain the number of ovens in the neighbourhood ; and if they should be insufficient to supply the troops to which he is attached with bread, he will take care that a sufficient number are built forthwith.

' 8. No man of the brigades in huts must be allowed to quit the lines of his regiment without being dressed with his side arms, according to the orders of his regiment.'

self, notwithstanding that this alteration would have been part of an operation which must have ended in the annihilation of Victor's army if he stood our attack, or, in his retreat through the mountains to Arzobispo, with the loss of all his cannon and baggage if he went away.

I hope I acted right in giving way, more particularly as the operation was to be carried on in Spain, and the argument urged to me was, that the safety of Cuesta's army depended upon my compliance. The best of the whole story is, that Cuesta, in a letter of the 27th May, which I did not receive till after I had written to him to propose my plan of operations, proposed to me the same plan with very little alteration. I hope that notwithstanding Col. Roche's delay, and the partiality which the Admiral has for the employment of the horse transports in all services, the horse transports will have arrived in time. It is desirable that all the transports for horses, as well as those for infantry, should have a thorough cleaning; for I have reason to believe that some of the former in particular are infected.

To Visc. Castlereagh.   Abrantes, 17th June, 1809.

I have received information that the French withdrew their post which they had at Merida, and their outposts in front of Medellin, and there is every reason to believe that their whole army is retiring across the Tagus and towards Madrid. The Spanish troops under Gen. Cuesta took possession of Merida, and crossed the Guadiana at Medellin.

I have had a discussion with Gen. Cuesta, respecting the plan of operations to be carried on by the British and Spanish armies in the attack of Marshal Victor. We had every reason to believe that the French army consisted of about 27,000 men, and that the defeat and retreat of Soult had deprived Victor of all support; and that the Spanish army consisted of 30,000 men, of which 7000 were cavalry; and the combined British and Portuguese force, which I was in hopes I should have been enabled to march upon this expedition, would have amounted to about 24,000 men, of which nearly 4000 would have been cavalry.

The only practicable retreat for the French army was by the bridge of Almaraz, and my proposition to Gen. Cuesta was, that he should remain with the Spanish army, in a position in which, if attacked, he could have the advantage, such as that by which he had so long kept in check the French armies, until I should move by Castello Branco and Plasencia to Almaraz, and cut off the only practicable retreat which the French had to Madrid.

It appears by the correspondence of Lieut. Col. Bourke, that Gen. Cuesta had by no means a good position on the Guadiana; and the Colonel expresses in strong terms his apprehensions and those of Gen. O'Donoju, that if the Spanish army should be attacked in that position, it would be defeated. At the same time Gen. Cuesta could not be prevailed upon to draw farther back towards the Sierra Morena, although it was obvious that the consequence of any movement which should place the Spanish army in security, while I should move round the enemy, would be, most probably, to cut off their retreat; and he pressed me in the most earnest terms to join the British army to that under his command upon the Gua-

diana. Finding it impossible to induce Gen. Cuesta to improve his position, and that serious apprehensions were entertained for his safety, I
consented to forego the execution of the plan which I preferred, and I
promised to march to Badajoz as soon as I should be enabled to move, by
the arrival of money from Cadiz or from England, and as the army had
had a few days' rest, and had received a supply of shoes. In the mean
time the French army having retired, probably upon hearing of the arrival
of this corps upon the Tagus, I proposed to continue on the right bank of
that river, and to move towards Plasencia.

The money expected from Cadiz arrived at Lisbon on the day before
yesterday, and I propose to commence my march as soon as it shall reach
the army.

P.S. Since writing the above, I have received letters from Gen. Cuesta
and Lieut. Col. Bourke, of the 16th. The General was to move his head
quarters to Merida on this day; his advanced guard is at Alcuescar and
Albala. Gen. Cuesta now wishes me to march by Plasencia.

To Visc. Castlereagh.   Abrantes, 17th June, 1809.

I cannot, with propriety, omit to draw your attention again to the state
of discipline of the army, which is a subject of serious concern to me, and
well deserves the consideration of His Majesty's ministers.

It is impossible to describe to you the irregularities and outrages committed by the troops. They are never out of the sight of their officers, I
may almost say never out of the sight of the Commanding officers of their
regiments, and the General officers of the army, that outrages are not committed; and notwithstanding the pains which I take, of which there will
be ample evidence in my orderly books, not a post or a courier comes in,
not an officer arrives from the rear of the army, that does not bring me
accounts of outrages committed by the soldiers who have been left behind
on the march, having been sick, or having straggled from their regiments,
or who have been left in hospitals.

We have a Provost marshal, and no less than 4 assistants. I never
allow a man to march with the baggage. I never leave an hospital without a number of officers and non-commissioned officers proportionable to
the number of soldiers; and never allow a detachment to march, unless
under the command of an officer; and yet there is not an outrage of any
description which has not been committed on a people who have uniformly
received us as friends, by soldiers who never yet, for one moment, suffered
the slightest want, or the smallest privation. In the first place, I am convinced that the law is not strong enough to maintain discipline in an army
upon service. It is most difficult to convict any prisoner before a regimental Court Martial, for I am sorry to say that soldiers have little regard
to the oath administered to them; and the officers who are sworn ' well
and truly to try and determine, *according to the evidence,* the matter before
them,' have too much regard to the strict letter of that administered to
them. This oath, to the members of a regimental Court Martial, has
altered the principle of the proceedings of that tribunal. It is no longer
a court of honor, at the hands of which a soldier was certain of receiving
punishment if he deserved it; but it is a court of law, whose decisions are

to be formed according to the evidence, principally of those on whose actions it is constituted as a restraint. But, admitting the regimental or detachment Court Martial, as now constituted, to be a control upon the soldiers equally efficient with that which existed under the old constitution of a Court Martial, which my experience tells me it is not, I should wish to know whether any British army (this army in particular, which is composed of 2d battalions, and therefore but ill provided with officers) can afford to leave with every hospital, or with every detachment, 2 captains and 4 subalterns, in order to be enabled to hold a detachment Court Martial. The law in this respect ought to be amended; and when the army is on service in a foreign country, any one, 2, or 3 officers ought to have the power of trying criminals, and punishing them *instanter*; taking down all proceedings in writing, and reporting them for the information of the Commander in Chief on their joining the army. Besides this improvement of the law, there ought to be in the British army a regular provost establishment, of which a proportion should be attached to every army sent abroad. All the foreign armies have such an establishment: the French *gendarmerie nationale*, to the amount of 30 or 40 with each of their corps; the Spaniards their *policia militar*, to a still larger amount; while we, who require such an aid more, I am sorry to say, than any of the other nations of Europe, have nothing of the kind, excepting a few serjeants, who are taken from the Line for the occasion, and who are probably not very fit for the duties which they are to perform.

The authority and duties of the Provost ought, in some manner, to be recognized by the law. By the custom of British armies, the Provost has been in the habit of punishing on the spot (even with death, under the orders of the Commander in Chief) soldiers found in the act of disobedience of orders, of plunder, or of outrage. There is no authority for this practice excepting custom, which I conceive would hardly warrant it; and yet I declare that I do not know in what manner the army is to be commanded at all, unless the practice is not only continued, but an additional number of Provosts appointed.

There is another branch of this subject which deserves serious consideration. We all know that the discipline and regularity of all armies must depend upon the diligence of the regimental officers, particularly the subalterns. I may order what I please; but if they do not execute what I order, or if they execute it with negligence, I cannot expect that British soldiers will be orderly or regular.

There are two incitements to men of this description to do their duty as they ought; the fear of punishment, and the hope of reward. As for the first, it cannot be given individually; for I believe I should find it very difficult to convict any officer of doing this description of duty with negligence, more particularly as he is to be tried by others probably guilty of the same offence. But these evils of which I complain are committed by whole corps; and the only way in which they can be punished is by disgracing them, by sending them into garrison and reporting them to His Majesty. I may and shall do this by one or two battalions, but I cannot venture to do it by more; and then there is an end to the fear of this punishment, even if those who received it were considered in England as disgraced persons rather than martyrs.

As for the other incitement to officers to do their duty zealously, there is no such thing. We who command the armies of the country, and who are expected to make exertions greater than those made by the French armies, to march, to fight, and to keep our troops in health and in discipline, have not the power of rewarding, or promising a reward, for a single officer of the army; and we deceive ourselves, and those who are placed under us, if we imagine we have that power, or if we hold out to them that they shall derive any advantage from the exertion of it in their favor.

You will say, probably, in answer to all this, that British armies have been in the field before, and that these complaints, at least to the same extent, have not existed; to which I answer: 1st, that the armies are now larger, their operations more extended, and the exertions required greater than they were in former periods; and that the mode of carrying on war is different from what it was; 2dly, that our law, instead of being strong in proportion to the temptation and means for indiscipline and irregularity, has been weakened, and that we have not adopted the additional means of restraint and punishment practised by other nations, and our enemies, although we have imitated them in those particulars which have increased and aggravated our irregularities. And, finally, that it is only within late years that the Commanders in Chief abroad have been deprived of all patronage, and, of course, of all power of incitement to the officers under their command.

It may be supposed that I wish for this patronage to gratify my own favorites; but I declare most solemnly that, if I had it to-morrow, there is not a soul in the army whom I should wish to promote, excepting for services performed.

I have thought it proper to draw your attention to these subjects, which I assure you deserve the serious consideration of the King's ministers. We are an excellent army on parade, an excellent one to fight; but we are worse than an enemy in a country; and take my word for it, that either defeat or success would dissolve us.

To the Duke of Richmond.   Abrantes, 17th June, 1809.

I have been waiting here ever since I wrote to you last, for money, and to give the troops some rest after the marches they had had to the northward. The money is arrived at Lisbon, but has not yet reached the army; and I shall be ready to march in a day or two. In the meantime Victor has retreated, I conclude, upon hearing that we have arrived upon the Tagus.

The Spanish army crosses the Guadiana this day, and when I move I shall march upon Plasencia. I rather believe that Joseph must evacuate Madrid.

To Major Gen. Mackenzie.   Abrantes, 18th June, 1809.

The enemy are retiring across the Tagus; and it is not by any means probable that they will make any offensive attempt upon our post at Alcantara, though not at all unlikely that they might push a patrole that way to ascertain the strength of the corps by which we hold that point. It is very desirable, however, that the greatest part of Col. Mayne's corps should be placed at Zarza la Mayor, with a view to look to the valley of Plasencia, and that Alcantara should be held by a small force only; but let it be under the command of an officer who will not take fright when the enemy look at him from the other side of the river.

The late movements of the enemy have induced an alteration of our plans. I propose to move the whole British army into the vale of Plasencia, as soon as I can get from Lisbon what I want, which is principally money; and the Portuguese troops, with the exception of the legion which remains with me, are to go to the northward with Marshal Beresford. I do not understand from your letter that the 2 Portuguese battalions have moved to Zibreira. If they should not have gone there, they must not be moved; and, indeed, I conceive the position at Zarza la Mayor to be but little exposed, and not to require much immediate support. If they have been moved, it does not much signify; they can march to the north from thence.

The 87th and 88th regts. are at Castello Branco. The hussars were halted at Thomar, when it was imagined that we should be obliged to go into Spain, between the Tagus and the Guadiana; but they will now be ordered to move on to Castello Branco. But until the British troops are paid, I wish none of them to be moved forward.

To Lieut. Col. Bourke, A. Q. M. G.   Abrantes, 18th June, 1809.

I have received your letters of the 14th and 16th, and one from Gen. Cuesta of the 16th. I send copies of all these papers, and of my answer of this day, to Gen. Cuesta, in the enclosed to Mr. Frere, which I beg you to forward.

The money from Cadiz is arrived at Lisbon, and I expect it here every moment. I also expect the shoes and other necessaries for the army, which have been an unaccountably long time upon the river. I shall

---

G. O.   Abrantes, 18th June, 1809.

2. The Commander of the Forces is concerned, from reports which have been lately made to him of the practice of some of the regiments in the army, to be obliged to desire the captains of companies to inspect the arms, ammunition, and flints, in possession of the soldiers of their companies at every parade with arms, and particularly on the march, which takes place on the morning of a march.

4. As the weather will now admit of the troops hutting, and they can therefore move together in large bodies, brigades are to be formed into divisions as follows:

Guards	
Brig. Gen. Cameron's brigade	} 1st Division.
Hanoverian Legion	
Major Gen. Hill's brigade	} 2d Division.
Brig. Gen. R. Stewart's do.	
Major Gen. Mackenzie's brigade	} 3d Division.
Col. Donkin's do.	
Brig. Gen. A. Campbell's brigade	} 4th Division.
Col. Peacocke's do.	

Lieut. Gen. Sherbrooke will take the command of the 1st division; the senior General officers of brigades will respectively take the command of the division in which their brigades are placed, till the other Lieut. Generals will join the army.

The brigades in divisions are to be formed from the right, as placed in this order:

The divisions will stand in one or more lines, in respect to each other, as will be ordered at the time.

An Assist. Adj. Gen. will be attached to the officer commanding the division; an Assist. Provost will also be attached to each division.

wait for none of the reinforcements, although I expect to hear at every moment of the arrival of 5000 excellent infantry, and a troop of horse artillery; but I shall march as soon as the money and the shoes arrive, which cannot be in less than 2 or 3 days.

In respect to yourself, I wish you to join the army; but it is very desirable that I should have an officer at Gen. Cuesta's head quarters, who can talk to him and Gen. O'Donoju confidentially; and I propose to send Col. Roche there, who is lately come from England. I should wish you to stay till Col. Roche will arrive, unless you are very anxious to return; in which case you will desire Cadogan to stay till he shall be relieved by Col. Roche. I cannot omit taking this opportunity of expressing to you how much I am satisfied with all the communications I have received from you, and with the manner you have performed the service on which I sent you.

To Dom Miguel Forjaz.   Abrantes, ce 18 Juin, 1809.

Comme les nouvelles arrivées disent que les Français devaient entrer à Orense le 14 de ce mois, et comme les Gouverneurs du Royaume voudraient savoir les dispositions qui ont été faites pour la défense du Portugal, j'ai l'honneur de vous faire savoir que toutes les troupes Portugaises sont en marche pour arriver sur le Douro, et que le Maréchal Beresford, qui va à Lisbonne, ira au nord du Royaume pour se charger du commandement.

Quoique les Francais s'avancent sur Orense, je ne crois pas qu'ils aient l'intention d'envahir le Portugal par la Galicie. Ils n'ont pas une force suffisante pour cet objet, sans abandonner la Galicie et les Asturies entièrement; et s'ils abandonnent la Galicie, la force qu'ils auraient envoyée dans le Portugal serait surement perdue. Le Maréchal Victor s'étant retiré pour passer le Tage à Almaraz, je compte marcher sur Coria à Plasencia; mais je serai toujours en communication avec le Portugal, et je tournerai à gauche, si je trouve que l'ennemi envahit encore ce pays-ci.

To Don Gregorio Cuesta.   Abrantes, 18th June, 1809.

I had the honor to receive last night your Excellency's letter of the 16th. I agree entirely with your Excellency, that the best line for the march of the British army is by Plasencia, towards the banks of the Tietar, and I propose to put the troops in movement to that quarter as soon as it shall be in my power.

To Marshal Beresford.   Abrantes, 19th June, 1809.

I enclose a letter for Lord Castlereagh, in respect to the ordnance and military stores you require. It appears to me that you have omitted to require carriages for the carronades; and you might as well alter your letter and ask for them. I also think you had better have another copy made of the list of intrenching tools required, and leave out the remarks at the end. You can get the plank and timber in Portugal. I also think that you might get artificers' tools, iron wedges, coils of rope, junk, iron, steel, tarpaulins, chests of tools, sand bags, ballast baskets, in Portugal, and you had better omit them in your list altogether; as it only swells it, and will delay the transmission of other articles more necessary to you.

P. S. When you shall have made these alterations, forward the letter to Lord Castlereagh.

To Visc. Castlereagh.   Abrantes, 19th June, 1809.

I have the honor to enclose a letter which I have received from Marshal Beresford, detailing the articles of ordnance and military stores which it is necessary should be supplied as soon as possible to this country. I am convinced that these articles are necessary, in order to get this country in a proper state of defence, and I request your Lordship to have them sent at an early period.

G. O.   Abrantes, 19th June, 1809.

2. The Commissary Gen. will take care that all regimental baggage and stores lodged in the stores at Abrantes, for which he will give his receipt, are sent to Lisbon by water, and lodged in the regimental stores of the regiment to which it belongs; and his officers at Lisbon will take the receipt of the non-commissioned officer in charge of the regimental stores at Lisbon, for it.

5. There are so many complaints and references respecting the mules attached to regiments, that it is necessary again to state in Orders the principles on which they are given. Each regiment of infantry, consisting of 10 companies, has 15 mules, of which one for each company is allotted to carry the company's camp kettles, one to carry the surgeon's instruments, and one to carry the paymaster's books. Captains of companies, paymasters, and surgeons, each of whom has received £10 bât money, and is bound to keep up those mules, which were originally given to them by the commissariat, as a matter of favor by the late Commander of the Forces. One mule is attached to each regiment of infantry to carry the intrenching tools, and is, by different orders, to be in charge of the quarter-masters of regiments.

The Commander of the Forces desires that the commissaries in each brigade will see the intrenching tool mules in charge of each brigade this afternoon, and that they will hereafter see them once a week.

The mules allotted for the carriage of intrenching tools are the public property, and must be kept up at the public charge.

Each regiment of cavalry has 14 mules, 8 for carrying camp kettles, 1 for the surgeon, 1 for the paymaster, respectively, having received bât money for, and liable to keep up; besides these, a regiment of cavalry has 1 mule for the veterinary surgeon, 1 for the serjeant armorer, 1 for the serjeant saddler, and 1 for the intrenching tools.

These last four are the property of the public, and must be kept up at the public expense; they must be taken care of by the persons for whose use they are provided, respectively; and the Commanding officers of regiments will give directions that one of the quarter-masters may take charge of the mule for the intrenching tools. The assist. commissaries, with regiments of cavalry, will see these public mules attached to regiments of cavalry this afternoon; and in future they will inspect them once a week.

Commanding officers of regiments of cavalry and infantry are requested to give particular directions to the quartermasters, and others in charge of the public mules, to take the greatest care of them, and to see that they are applied to no other use than that for which they are allowed; as in many instances the commissary was under the necessity of supplying the regiments with hired mules to carry camp kettles, surgeons' chests, and paymasters' books, of which the public have been paying the hire ever since. The Commissary Gen. is requested, as soon as possible, to supply the officers with purchased instead of hired mules.

6. The captains, surgeons, and paymasters of regiments, which have lately arrived, or may hereafter arrive, in Portugal, from Great Britain or Ireland, or the islands, and which have received the allowance called embarkation money, are to provide themselves with mules, for the carriage of camp kettles, paymasters' books, or surgeons' chests, respectively; and the captains, paymasters, and surgeons of those regiments which arrived from Gibraltar, and have not received the allowance called embarkation money, will be allowed each £20 to purchase a mule for their service.

x 2

The A.G. to ———.   19th June, 1809.

Your several letters have been laid before the Commander of the Forces, and I am directed to thank you for the accurate information they contain, which has been interesting. In expressing his disapprobation of an officer going from one line of duty, which has been prescribed, to another, he did not mean to do it with severity, but only to apprise you, as well as the army at large, that he cannot countenance this being at any time done. If permitted, you must yourself perceive what disorder would arise. Zeal is highly commendable, but it may be carried too far.

To Brig. Gen. Cox, Governor of Almeida.   Abrantes, 20th June, 1809.

I am very much obliged to you for your letter of the 17th, which I received this morning.

I shall give directions that provisions, bread, flour, and corn, principally, and some military stores, for the use of the British army, may be sent to Almeida, and I shall be obliged to you to have them taken care of when they may arrive there. They shall go in a regular manner, and not as the barrels of pork, in charge of the serjeant of the 5th K. G. L. These appear to me to have wandered to Almeida, not knowing where they were to go.

I shall be obliged to you for any intelligence you may have it in your power to send me. Marshal Victor has retired from the Guadiana, I conclude upon hearing of our arrival upon the Tagus, as part of his army has crossed the Tagus, at Almaraz. Gen. Cuesta has crossed the Guadiana, and his head quarters were on the 18th at Majadas. The British army will move in a day or two towards Plasencia, by Castello Branco and Coria.

I shall be much obliged to you if you will forward the enclosed letter to the Junta of Ciudad Rodrigo.

To the Junta of Ciudad Rodrigo.   Abrantes, 20th June, 1809.

I have had the honor of receiving from your Excellencies an account of the sums due at Ciudad Rodrigo, and in the neighbourhood of that city, for articles received by the British army, when under the command of Sir J. Moore. It is my wish to pay these sums immediately; but as it will be difficult to transport the money to Ciudad Rodrigo, I should be glad, if equally convenient to your Excellencies, to pay it to any agent you might appoint to receive it at Lisbon. If, however, this mode of payment should be inconvenient to your Excellencies, I shall send a gentleman to Ciudad Rodrigo to pay the demand.

To Don Gregorio Cuesta.   Abrantes, 20th June, 1809.

As Lieut. Col. Bourke has concluded the business on which I sent him to wait upon your Excellency, and as he fills a station in this army of

---

G. O.   Abrantes, 20th June, 1809.

1. When the troops march with a route, it must be invariably specified, in the route, where they are to get provisions; and they are to receive provisions according to what is stated in the route. The commissaries attached to brigades and regiments of cavalry must not issue provisions to troops marching with a route, unless it is specified in the route that they are to do so.

2. As the supply of cattle is not now plenty, all the troops in the huts, and towns of Abrantes and Punhete, and the neighbouring cantonments, will be supplied with salt meat for a few days.

which it is desirable that he should resume the duties, I have written to him to request that he will return; and I send Col. Roche with this letter, with whom I understand you are acquainted, and who has received marks of your favor. As it may be convenient to your Excellency that a British officer should attend at your head quarters, in order to communicate to me your wishes, and to explain to your Excellency such circumstances as I may have to communicate, I wish Col. Roche to remain with you to accomplish these objects.

To Vice Adm. the Hon. G. Berkeley. Abrantes, 21st June, 1809.

Having received the orders of the Sec. of State to send the 20th light dragoons with their horses to Sicily, I shall be much obliged to you if you will give directions, that transports may be prepared for them, and that a convoy may be allotted to take them to Sicily, as soon as they shall be embarked. The A. Q. M. G. at Lisbon will acquaint the Agent of transports with the number of men and horses to be embarked. I have also received the directions of the Sec. of State to send to England by the first opportunity a detachment of the 3d hussars, K. G. L., without their horses; and I shall be obliged to you if you will give directions that this detachment, of the strength of which the A. Q. M. G. will acquaint the Agent of transports, may be embarked in any of the empty transports returning to England.

I have sent orders to Lisbon that the 48th and 61st regts. may join the army as soon as they are prepared to march, by being provided with the mules, &c. which they require. I have directed that they may proceed by water as far as Valada; and I shall be very much obliged to you if you will give directions that such assistance in the way of boats as the Navy can afford may be given to them.

To Vice Adm. the Hon. G. Berkeley. Abrantes, 21st June, 1809.

I received last night your letter of the 19th. I fancy the 27th regt. was obliged to march, because the Commissary could not procure boats for their conveyance, and that they could not procure boats because they have, till lately, had no money to pay the boatmen. I shall be very happy to receive any suggestions from you through Major Berkeley, on this or any other subject.

I have written to you about the 20th dragoons, the hussars, 48th and 61st regts.

Lord Castlereagh, in a letter to me, expresses some anxiety respecting the employment of the horse ships in the transport of the sheep. I am very sensible of the pains you have taken to establish for us a good water communication with Lisbon, which is indeed a most desirable object.

P.S. I enclose a report from the A. Q. M. G. at Lisbon respecting the

G. O. Abrantes, 21st June, 1809.

6. The General Hospital at the Convent of S. Antonio, at Abrantes, being now ready for the reception of sick, the surgeons of regiments may send such of their patients there as are not likely to do well in cantonments; but they are previously to be inspected by the staff surgeon of the divisions, as none can be received into the general hospital without his approving signature.

mode of disembarking horses in the Tagus. The officers of the cavalry have before mentioned the same subject, which deserves attention and requires reform. Probably the best thing to do would be to put the horses into our own flats, or the large country boats, from the transports.

To Marshal Beresford.   Abrantes, 21st June, 1809.

I have considered of the means of supplying you immediately with intrenching tools, and I find that I can give you what is stated in the enclosed paper, marked No. 2 in pencil, if Villiers will give a receipt for them; and as to the first you received for this place, I enclose the receipt of the officer of Engineers here for them, which Villiers ought to keep.

P.S. I signed an order similar to the enclosed, No. 3, for the tools given to Capt. Patton.

To Lieut. Col. Bourke, A. Q. M. G.   Abrantes, 21st June, 1809.

I received in the night your letter of the 19th inst. Col. Cadogan has informed me of your objects respecting yourself; and although I shall be sorry to lose your assistance at this critical moment, when you have shown that you are so capable of assisting me materially, I can do no more than express my regret at your departure. It is impossible for any man to pretend to give an opinion upon the feelings which induce you to take the step which I so much regret. Before you leave Gen. Cuesta's head quarters, however, I wish you to get information for me upon some points, by which my operations, and indeed those of all the Spanish corps which will co-operate with us, must in a great measure be guided.

I enclose a paper containing queries, on which I wish you to obtain as much information as you can from Gen. O'Donoju. If the two corps under Victor and Sebastiani should join, my opinion is, that they will give battle on this side of Madrid; more particularly if there should be any position in the country which would afford them any advantage. I should rather suspect this to be their intention, as I observe that the French corps in Galicia have not yet made any movement, which would induce me to believe that they intend to evacuate that country; and yet, if Victor and Sebastiani withdraw beyond Madrid, the French corps in Galicia must leave that kingdom, otherwise Victor and Sebastiani will not be able to hold their ground.

The first queries are directed to the possibility of an action on this side of Madrid. If they do not fight on this side of Madrid, where will they find a position north of that city? The next queries are directed to that point.

Lastly, they will certainly defend the Ebro as long as they can; and the last queries are directed to this point.

My object in these inquiries, is to be able to make up my own mind, and to recommend to the Spanish officers such a disposition of our forces, at an early period, and to combine our march in such a manner, as that, whenever we may have to attack the enemy, we shall not have to halt, and alter our disposition immediately in his front, and thus give him a knowledge of our intentions. It is true that I have had no great encouragement to recommend any thing to the Spanish officers, but still I shall not fail to communicate to them my opinion upon the plan for our operations.

My determination upon the line of march which I shall take from Plasencia must depend much upon the answers to these queries. For many reasons I should think it best to take the line which would lead me nearest to the Portuguese frontier, particularly if the enemy are likely to retire to the Ebro. If Gen. Cuesta had not determined to pass with his corps on the other side of Madrid, my opinion is, that his corps, as well as Venegas', ought to leave that city on their right; that the pressure of the whole army ought to be on the enemy's right; and our object to be, in hurrying them from Madrid, to cut off their communication with the corps in Galicia. However, if Gen. Cuesta and Venegas leave Madrid upon their left, I must march by the Escurial, or insulate myself entirely from them.

Memorandum of Queries. *Abrantes, 21st June, 1809.*

1. When the French corps under Victor and Sebastiani shall join near Toledo, and be reinforced probably by the French garrisons in Toledo and Madrid, is there any defensive position they could take up? Is such a position afforded by the Guadarama or the Manzanares, throwing their left upon the Tagus?

2. What is the nature of the country between the Guadarama and Manzanares? What the nature of the banks of those rivers, particularly the upper part of the former? What the nature of the banks of the Tagus between them? Any fords or other passages?

3. Are there any roads leading from Plasencia or Talavera, and of what description, to the upper part of the Guadarama?

4. Supposing the enemy to retire beyond Madrid, upon being threatened with an attack by the 3 combined corps, under Gens. Cuesta and Venegas and myself, could the mountains of Castille afford him any defensive position?

5. What position would be most probably taken up by the French army in those mountains?

6. What are the commonly used passages through them from the southward, in the whole extent of their range?

7. What the nature of the country on this side? and of the different passages through them?

8. What the nature of the country after passing them?

9. Supposing the enemy to retire at once to the Ebro and take up his position upon that river, his object would be most probably to secure his communication with France. With that view what position would he take up?

10. Is the Ebro fordable in the whole length of its course?

11. Where the principal passages?

12. The nature of the banks generally?

13. The nature of the country on both sides?

14. What Spanish corps are there in Valencia, Murcia, Aragon, and Catalonia, which might be brought to co-operate in a general movement upon the enemy?

To Brig. Gen. Campbell.   Abrantes, 21st June, 1809.

I have received and perused the proceedings of the General Court Martial, of which you are President, on the trial of * * * *, private soldier of the 29th regt. of foot, ' for mutiny, and for attempting to shoot Ensign ——, of the 88th regt.,' and I am concerned that I cannot agree in opinion with the Court, that the prisoner ought to be acquitted.   Differing as I do in opinion with the Court Martial, it is my duty to state the grounds of that difference of opinion, and to request that the Court will revise their sentence.

It appears that the detachment of troops to which Ensign ——, of the 88th regt., and private * * * *, belonged, were on their march towards Leiria; and that on the 4th May, between Carvalhos and Leiria, Ensign ——, in consequence of orders from his superior officer, Lieut. F——, of the 36th regt., endeavored to keep order in the detachment, and pushed, and even struck * * * *, who, among other soldiers, was pressing forward to the front, out of his place in the ranks.   That the offence having been repeated, he repeated the chastisement; and that then the soldier went to the rear, muttering something which Ensign —— could not understand, loaded his firelock, and came again to the front, threw his firelock from his right hand into the left, and was in the act of firing at Ensign ——, when he was stopped by private L——, of the 88th regt.

It appears by the evidence of serj. T——, of the 88th regt., that * * * * repeatedly refused to form in his place in the ranks, which was the cause of Ensign —— striking him.

It appears by the evidence of private P——, of the 50th regt., that the prisoner loaded his piece on the road; and the prisoner declares himself that he loaded it (though for a different purpose) on ' that day' on the march, and it appears by the evidence of other witnesses who saw the charge drawn that it was loaded with ball cartridge; and by that of serj. T—— that the piece was primed; and that he, the serjeant, as ' acting serjeant major of the detachment, had never heard of any order given to load, nor did it ever come under his observation that any pieces were loaded.'

It appears by the evidence of Ensign ——, that private * * * * having loaded his piece, had it on the recover, when he turned round and saw him.   Serj. T—— saw him ' coming up nearly as fast as he could walk, with his firelock nearly in the position of the port.   Some person, when he came near to Ensign ——, called out to him (Ensign ——) to take care, as that man's piece (meaning the prisoner's) was loaded.   The witness then saw the prisoner bring his firelock nearly to the level, when it was seized.'

It appears by the evidence of private L——, of the 88th regt., that he saw the prisoner ' coming from the rear, with his firelock nearly at the position of the charge, with his thumb upon the cock; that the prisoner was going at the time faster than the other men;' and it appears that this same L——, of the 88th regt., was the person who, having been called to by the other men, seized his firelock, and prevented the prisoner from executing his purpose.

From this statement of the evidence, I conceive the crime of mutiny, refusing to obey the officer's orders, and that of attempting to shoot Ensign ——, to be clearly made out; and there is no contradiction whatever of the evidence, no justification and no pretence stated on the part of the prisoner, excepting that he heard that day on the march that the French were in the neighbourhood. But there is one circumstance stated in evidence which tends to confirm the proof of the crime; and that is, the fact that the soldiers of the detachment, at the time, believed that it was the intention of private * * * * to shoot Ensign ——. From the length of time which has elapsed, and the variety of occurrences which have taken place since the 4th May, they might have forgotten some of the circumstances that occurred, which, by being now related, might have thrown light upon the transaction; but the Ensign, the serjeant, and the private L——, agree in that fact, that the soldiers of the detachment, who saw private * * * * come up, imagined that he was about to endeavor to kill Ensign ——, and they put the Ensign on his guard. This fact tends to confirm all the other evidence.

In respect to the fact stated to me by your surgeon, that private * * * * is insane, I have to observe that there is no proof whatever of its existence. It might not be necessary to prove it, the prisoner being acquitted; but if the Court should agree in opinion with me, upon the revision of their sentence, that the prisoner ought to be convicted of one or both of the crimes charged against him, it will be necessary that means should be taken to ascertain whether he is insane.

To the Rt. Hon. J. Villiers.   Abrantes, 21st June, 1809.

I received last night your letter of the 20th. I am much concerned to hear of the distress of the Portuguese troops; more particularly as it is out of my power to relieve it at present, excepting by the repayment of those sums of money which our troops received from their Paymaster Gen.; and of any sums (I know of none) that we are said to have received from the provincial treasuries. If I give any of the money I now command, not only will the British army be unable to move, but it must starve where it now is, as *I cannot get either supplies, or boats or carts to move supplies from Lisbon, without money.*

The British government appear to me to have undertaken more in this country than they can manage; and I am concerned that I have it not in my power to make up for the deficiency of supplies which they have furnished for the service.

I have asked for £200,000 every month, in which sum I have included the estimate of a sum of £40,000 a month required by you for the Portuguese troops. If you should require more, the supply must be increased in proportion; this in addition to the money which can be got at Lisbon, Cadiz, and Gibraltar, for bills. Besides this a sum of money must be sent from England to pay the arrear due to the Portuguese government. I expect from England £100,000, of which sum you may take £50,000 for the Portuguese government, when it shall arrive; but I cannot allow any more to be allotted for this service, or any of the money which may be got for bills at Lisbon or elsewhere, without exposing to want, or even imminent risk, the King's troops under my command.

Mr. —— is arrived, but is so unwell that I cannot speak to him   He has always had a gentleman at Lisbon charged with the business of nego- tiating his bills; another at Gibraltar, and another at Cadiz.   The mis- fortune is that this gentleman, like many others attached to this army, does not appear to me to be very equal to the performance of the duty which he has undertaken.

To W. Huskisson, Esq., Secretary of the Treasury.   Abrantes, 22d June, 1809.

Upon referring to the instructions of the Treasury to the Commissary Gen. with this army, it appears to me to have been understood by their Lordships that it was intended that the Commissariat attached to the Por tuguese army was to be conducted under the orders of the Commander in Chief of the British army, and its expense to be defrayed by the British government; and upon this ground I imagine that their Lordships thought proper to order the Commissary Gen. to furnish the Commissary Gen. of the Portuguese army with instructions; and that the accounts of the latter should be examined by the Commissary of Accounts attached to the British army.   I request you, however, to apprise their Lordships, that the Portuguese army have long had a Commissariat adapted to the nature of the country, and managed by persons who have long been employed in its management, probably at less expense to the government than it would be managed under rules established by their Lordships' authority.   All that is required is the assistance of some persons belonging to the British Commissariat, to conduct the business under the Portuguese government according to the rules established for that branch of their service; and to make rules to prevent the clashing of the officers of the Commissariat of 2 armies acting in the same country, and for the mutual payment for supplies furnished by the one to the troops of the other nation.

I have the honor to enclose an arrangement, which I propose should be adopted on this subject, if it should meet their Lordships' approbation. I have submitted it to the Ambassador and to Marshal Beresford, who entirely concur in it; and I have ordered Dep. Com. Rawlings to place himself under the directions of Marshal Beresford, in order that he may superintend the Portuguese Commissariat under this arrangement.

There are 2 points which require an explanation in the arrangement: the one, the difference of the price of the ration; the other, the mode of payment for magazines delivered by the British Commissariat for the use of the Portuguese army.

The cause of the difference of price is that the Portuguese ration is smaller than that delivered to the British soldiers; and I have arranged this mode of paying for magazines, because I have understood it to be the wish of His Majesty's government, that all stores delivered to the Portu- guese government should be in the way of subsidy, and should reach them with the knowledge and through the means of the Ambassador. If their Lordships should approve of this arrangement, it will be neces- sary that they should cancel the 30th article of the Instructions to the

Commissary Gen. and the 35th of the Instructions to the Commissary of Accounts.

Memorandum of an arrangement for the Portuguese Commissariat.

Abrantes, 10th June, 1809.

1. The Portuguese Commissariat, whether superintended by a British Dep. Commissary or by a Portuguese Commissary, must be solely and exclusively under the direction of the Portuguese government and the Commander in Chief of the Portuguese army.

2. When the British and Portuguese armies shall be joined, or when the troops of the one nation shall pass through the cantonments occupied by the other, the Commissary Gen. of the Portuguese army will communicate with the Commissary Gen. of the British army respecting the proportion of the supplies of the country to be allotted for the Portuguese Commissariat, and the quarters from whence to be drawn. The arrangements upon these occasions must necessarily be made by the Commissary Gen. of the British army.

3. The requisitions upon the country for mules, horses, carriages, and boats, are to be regulated in the same manner.

4. When the detachment of the troops of the one nation shall act with the army of the other, the Commissaries are to pay for the rations they will receive at the following rates; that is to say, the Portuguese Commissary Gen., for every ration issued to the Portuguese troops, 9*d.*; and the British Commissary Gen., for every ration issued to the British troops, 1*s.* Rations to horses and mules to be paid for each at the rate of 2*s.*

5. When the British Commissary Gen. shall receive magazines or supplies of any description from the Portuguese Commissariat, he is to pay the Portuguese Commissary for them, at the rate at which the same description of supplies can be purchased in the country at the same time.

6. All magazines and supplies of every description, given by the British Commissary Gen. to the Portuguese Commissariat, are to be delivered under the orders of the British Commander in Chief; and the receipt of the Ambassador must be taken for them, and his bill upon the Lords of the Treasury for the amount of the value.

The value to be settled according to the price of the same articles in the country at the time.

To Visc. Castlereagh. Abrantes, 22d June, 1809.

I judge from your letter to me, from one which I have received from the Admiral, and from a letter from Cooke to your brother, that government are not pleased with our having allowed the transports to go to Cadiz to take to England the Merino sheep ; and as I was, I believe, the first mover in this business, in Portugal at least, I wish to let you know what I did, and from what motive.

Mr. C. Johnstone wrote to me a letter, which I received at Ruivaes, about a month ago, to tell me that he had got the sheep in question, but that he was afraid that he should lose them, unless we could lend him some of our transports to carry them home early in the summer. At this time I saw clearly that we should not want the transports in order to evacuate Portugal; and I sent Mr. Johnstone's letter to the Admiral at Lisbon, and told him that I thought all the 3 months' transports might be sent home; and that as it was certainly a national object to get home the Spanish sheep, I saw no objection to allow 8 of the 3 months' infantry transports to go to Cadiz to convey them home, on condition that Mr. Cochrane Johnstone should pay for their hire from the time they should sail from the port of Lisbon for this purpose.

Mr. Frere afterwards made a requisition for transports to carry home 2000 sheep for His Majesty; and the Admiral having represented this circumstance to me, and having stated that 8 transports could carry only a small number of sheep, I consented to his sending 25 of the 3 months' ships. I fear that the Admiral sent horse ships instead of infantry ships on this service, which arrangement might be inconvenient. But if he sent infantry ships, I acknowledge that having received instructions to send home 3 months' ships as soon as I thought they could be spared, without risk to the King's troops, in order to save the expense of their hire to the public, I thought I could not better answer that purpose than to get rid of the expense at Lisbon instead of in England, by consenting to an arrangement which would accommodate an individual, and was likely to be advantageous to the public. I must add, at the same time, that I am not even acquainted with Mr. Johnstone.

To Lieut. Col. Gordon, Military Secretary.   Abrantes, 22d June, 1809.

I have the honor to enclose a letter (No. 1) which I have received lately from Staff surgeon ——: in consequence of which, not having had an opportunity of visiting the hospitals at Coimbra, when I passed through that town, I directed Major Gen. Cotton, who was still there, to visit them, and make a report on the state in which he found them. I have the honor to enclose his report (No. 2).

I trouble you with these papers, not because I am apprehensive that the Commander in Chief, or the head of the Medical department in England, should listen to the reports of any inferior officer to the prejudice of his superior. If we are fit to be trusted with the charge with which we are invested, our characters are not to be injured by defamatory reports of this description. But I am aware that there are not wanting in England channels for circulating defamation of this kind; and I am desirous of laying before the Commander in Chief, in the most authentic form, the original complaint, and the real state of the case as it was found to be upon inquiry.

I understand that Staff surgeon —— was sent home some time ago, by the late Commander of the Forces in Portugal, in consequence of a complaint from the head of the Medical department here, and because he is a person of that description of temper with which no other person could agree. Notwithstanding that he was sent home by Sir J. Cradock, he was sent back by the Medical department in England to this country; and, considering that it was still desirable that Mr. —— should not serve with the army in Portugal, I lately ordered that he should return to England, with the sick and wounded prisoners of the French army. This drew from him a remonstrance, to which I paid no attention, excepting to desire him to obey the order he had received, and then it appears that he commenced his inquiries into the conduct of his superior officer, Dep. Inspector Fergusson. In respect to this gentleman, I must say that I never saw him till I met him on my arrival in this country, and that I have had every reason to be satisfied with his conduct. In respect to Mr. ——, I shall be obliged to the Commander in Chief if he will prevent his being sent back to Portugal.

To the Rt. Hon. J. H. Frere.   Abrantes, 22d June, 1809.

I enclose my late letters from Col. Bourke, and my answers, and the copy of a letter from Gen. Cuesta.

I am sorry that Col. Bourke is coming from the Spanish head quarters; and I fear that I shall lose his assistance altogether, as he wishes to go to England, and even to retire from the service.

To Marshal Beresford.   Abrantes, 22d June, 1809.

I enclose you a letter from Fletcher. You will probably be able to discover the cause of the discontinuance of the works at Lisbon. If you have no workmen, however, you cannot want our officers; and I should wish to have them again.

To the Rt. Hon. J. Villiers.   Abrantes, 22d June, 1809.

I am concerned to forward to you an account of another British soldier put to death by the inhabitants of the country in the neighbourhood of Santarem, upon which I beg to refer you to my letter of the 13th inst. I am concerned to add that 2 soldiers of the 7th regt. were wounded in this neighbourhood a few days ago, by 2 inhabitants of the country; and that I have reason to fear that others, now missing from the camp near this place, have been killed by them.

To Visc. Castlereagh.   Abrantes, 22d June, 1809.

I have the honor to inform your Lordship that I have ordered the detachment of the 20th light dragoons, which has been in Portugal, to embark for Sicily, with all their horses; and that I have ordered to England, by the first opportunity, the detachment of the 3d hussars, which was left in Portugal when the regiment marched into Spain last year. I have drafted the horses from the 3d hussars to the 14th light dragoons.

The 1st batt. 48th regt., and 1st batt. 61st regt., are arrived at Lisbon; and the 2d batt. 30th regt. are gone to Gibraltar. The 2d batt. 9th regt. are ordered to Gibraltar to replace the 61st.

I propose to send to England the 2 battalions of detachments, as soon as I shall be joined by Col. Robert Craufurd's brigade.

To J. Murray, Esq., Commissary General.   Abrantes, 22d June, 1809.

I conceive that it is consistent with your instructions, and at all events it is desirable, that you should procure as much money at Gibraltar as you can for bills upon England, at the rate of exchange of Lisbon, or at any other reasonable rate. I conceive that you ought to endeavor to make the merchants pay the freight, but not to insist upon this as a *sine quâ non*, as it is most important to get money in any way.

To Visc. Castlereagh.   Abrantes, 22d June, 1809.

When I wrote you last I was in hopes that I should have marched before this time, but the money is not yet arrived. Things are in their progress as they were when I wrote on the 17th. The French are continuing their retreat; Sebastiani has also fallen back towards Toledo; and Venegas has advanced, and Cuesta had his head quarters at Truxillo on the 19th.

I am apprehensive that you will think I have delayed my march unnecessarily since my arrival upon the Tagus. But it was and is quite impossible to move without money. Not only were the officers and soldiers in the greatest distress, and the want of money the cause of many of the disorders of which I have had reason to complain; but we can no longer obtain the supplies of the country, or command its resources for the transport of our own supplies, either by land or by water. Besides this, the army required rest after their expedition to the frontiers of Galicia, and shoes, and to be furbished up in different ways; and I was well aware that if necessity had not obliged me to halt at the present moment, I should have been compelled to have made a longer halt some time hence. To all this add, that, for some time after I came here, I believed the French were retiring (as appears by my letters to your Lordship), and that I should have had no opportunity of striking a blow against them, even if I could have marched.

I hope that you will attend to my requisitions for money; not only am I in want, but also the Portuguese government, to whom, Mr. Villiers says, we owe £125,000. I repeat that we must have £200,000 per month from England, till I write to you that I can do without it; in which sum I include £40,000 per month for the Portuguese government to pay for 20,000 men. If the Portuguese government are to receive a larger sum from Great Britain, the sum to be sent to Portugal must be proportionably increased. Besides this, money must be sent to pay the Portuguese debts and our debts in Portugal. There are, besides, debts of Sir J. Moore's army still due in Spain, which I am called upon to pay. In short, we must have £125,000; and £200,000 per month, reckoning from the beginning of May. It is very extraordinary that I have not received a line from Huskisson upon this subject, notwithstanding that I wrote to him upon it early in May.

P.S. I hope you will send the remount horses soon. I have given to the 14th and 16th 95 horses from the Irish Commissariat, and I believe I shall give some to the other regiments. This arrangement, and the draft from the 3d hussars, will keep up the regiments for a short time. But it is inconceivable how fast both the horses of the cavalry and artillery fall off. When horses, as well as men, are new in war, I believe the former are generally the sacrifice of their mutual inexperience. I hope we shall profit by the experience acquired in the expedition to the northward, and that we shall be able to keep up the regiments rather better in future.

The A. G. to Major Aylmer, 24th regt.   22d June, 1809.

I have the Commander in Chief's directions to desire that the men of the 45th, 87th, 88th, and 31st regts. now in town, or who will join you from camp the day after to-morrow in the morning, are to proceed under your command, by a route you will receive from the Q. M. G., to join their regiments. They are to receive provisions for 3 days here, except wine, and at Corticada to carry them to Castello Branco.

You are to march the detachment every morning at 4 o'clock. You are to go at the rate of 2¼ miles an hour; to halt for 5 or 10 minutes at the end of every hour and a half; to keep every man up, and the men regularly formed. You will make the officers and non-commissioned officers march with their respective divisions on the march, and you will make the officers responsible that no man shall fall out of the ranks.

You will report to me in detail, on your delivering over the detachments to their regiments, that you have obeyed these orders; likewise any absent men.

To Marshal Beresford. Abrantes, 23d June, 1809.

I have received your letter of the 21st. The question respecting Silveira's advance is a very delicate one: in the first place, it involves the Portuguese troops necessarily in the desultory operations of Romana in Galicia; secondly, there is no ground for calculating relative force or numbers, on which any solid plan of operation could be founded. In the same letter in which Romana asks for these reinforcements, he tells you that he wants every thing, arms, ammunition, and provisions; and yet he wants you to unite yourself to this deficiency of means, to carry on an operation in Galicia. You can only lose by entering into it. At the same time, I think that Spain has some claim upon Portugal, on the ground of Cuesta's operations, when Portugal was threatened by the French corps at Alcantara. It may be said that we shall remunerate these claims by our advance into Spain at present; but I think we ought to do more than is expected from us.

I am decidedly adverse to our engaging in the loose, desultory operations in which Romana appears to delight. They can answer no purpose excepting to disorganise your troops; they will not answer to us even the ends to which he appears to aspire; for when we come to engage in them, it will very soon be found that we are doing nothing. My opinion is, that you should call upon Romana to state what his object is, and what his means of accomplishing it, and what the force of the enemy opposed to him. You might tell him that our intention was to remain on the defensive in the north of Portugal, and to employ the time in the discipline and organization of the troops which should elapse while the British army would be engaged in co-operation with Gen. Cuesta, in forcing the enemy to evacuate the south of Spain.

That these objects, from which we shall not depart, may be combined with his, and we may consistently be able to give him assistance; provided his objects and means are clearly explained and defined. If you get from him a clear explanation upon these points, and that all he intends is to hold a little of Galicia, I see no objection to your giving him the assistance of 2 or 3 battalions and some squadrons under Silveira, which would as effectually cover Portugal in Galicia as in Portugal itself. But it will be rank madness to enter upon an offensive plan in Galicia at present; and indeed I conceive that we must make up our minds to lose

G. O. Abrantes, 23d June, 1809.

4. D. A. A. Gs., D. A. Q. M. Gs., majors of brigades, and aides de camp, will be allowed forage for 3 horses and 1 mule from the date hereof.

for future operations the corps which Silveira will, under this arrangement, have under his command. We certainly derive some advantage from Romana and his operations, but I conceive none that would compensate for the loss of the discipline and organization of our troops. I cannot but observe that it is curious that Romana should now call for assistance, when he stated to me that he found the Portuguese army so undisciplined, and in such a state of disorganization, that he incurred the risk of a quarrel between the two nations by staying with them; and therefore he quitted them without further notice, as he appears to intend to do now.

Do as you please about my aide de camp. The best thing for him would be to consider his promotion to the rank of Lieut. Colonel of Militia as one step, viz., that of Captain; and now to give him the rank of Major in the Line. However, do as you like, and adhere to your own rules. Col. Peacocke is gone to command at Lisbon: I shall send you a copy of the instructions given to him. Our money, which left Lisbon on the 15th, is not yet arrived!

To J. Murray, Esq., Commissary General.   Abrantes, 23d June, 1809.

I have just received your letter of this day's date, respecting the supplies of money to be procured at Gibraltar.

There is no doubt but that the most advantageous mode for the public will be to negotiate bills at Gibraltar, as it is probable that those who prefer to buy bills at Lisbon will send their money there, so that you will have the advantage of both modes. It is true, however, that if the merchants at Gibraltar send their money to Lisbon, the exchange at Gibraltar will very soon rise to the Lisbon rates. I recommend to you to send to Gibraltar your bills, to be negotiated by your assistants there. I do not believe you have authority to give your assistant the power of drawing on the Treasury; and if you had, I do not see what would be gained by negotiating his bills instead of yours.

To Col. Peacocke, Lisbon.   Abrantes, 23d June, 1809.

As there is at Lisbon a Portuguese Lieut. General in command of the troops, it is necessary that you should lay before him all orders that you will receive from me relating to the British troops and establishments at that place, and report to him all measures that you may take in consequence.

To Col. Donkin.   Abrantes, 23d June, 1809.

I have received your letter of the 21st. I am delighted with your account of the 5th batt. 60th regt. Indeed every thing that I have seen and known of that excellent corps has borne the same stamp.

I am astonished that it did not occur to the Commanding officer of the 2d batt. —— regt. that their armorer would be useful to the corps on service, and that he could be of no use any where without his tools. I am really ashamed of such ignorance in a British officer of what it is necessary to attend to, to enable his men to be of any use whatever. Let the armorer be ordered to join the regiment forthwith. I am afraid I have no arms to give this corps. Let me have an official report upon their accoutrements, that I may send it to England. You must let me know the exact quantity of ammunition which the 2d batt. —— regt. requires, and it shall be supplied. But it is really necessary to impress upon the minds of the officers the necessity of looking after the arms, accoutrements, and ammunition of their companies and regiments daily, otherwise they will do nothing against the enemy. I shall try to borrow armorers, but I doubt whether the artillery have any We have no arms or accoutrements. I approve of your discontinuing the hourly roll calls; and you may discontinue them entirely when you th proper.

I have sent provisions to Castello Branco. The regiments have made requisitions for shoes, I presume, in the quantities they want. Those for which they have made a requisition will be delivered to the officers, who, I conclude, will be here this day, under the G.O. of the 20th.

P.S. If I had known that the 2d batt. —— regt. had been in so bad a state, I should have sent them to Gibraltar instead of the 9th; and if they do not soon improve, I shall still send them there : an unserviceable regiment is of no use here.

I see that the hussars are arrived at Castello Branco. If you find that you cannot forage them in a body in that town, separate them into half squadrons, and put half a squadron in each village in the neighbourhood, either forward or backward, or on your flanks. They must eat green forage if they cannot get dry, according to my orders of the 17th June.

Keep the forge carts, and let all the shoeing work go on at Castello Branco.

2d P.S. Since writing the above I have received your letter of the 19th. Measures shall be taken to send to your brigade the bill hooks, intrenching tools, and the camp stores wanting to complete, according to their requisitions on the Q. M. G. made under the G. O. of the 8th June.

Let Lieut. Col. Talbot's squadron of the 14th be put into the place where it is most likely to get forage and corn, reporting to me where it is.

All the men belonging to your brigade which are here shall march tomorrow morning.

To Major Gen. Cotton.   Abrantes, 23d June, 1809.

I wish that you and Hill should be made Lieut. Generals in Portugal, but as this promotion will remove you from your brigade of cavalry, I do not like to recommend it without your own consent. I shall be much obliged to you, therefore, if you will let me know what you feel upon the subject. With your objects in the cavalry I should recommend you not to move. Payne has just been here about your forage. We could move one regiment to Torres Novas, and get the other upon the river; but this would not get you grain : and if you went to Golegão, you would be in an unhealthy situation. Besides, it would be a move which I conceive it desirable, for your shoeing, &c., to avoid just at this moment.

They have blundered the business of our grain in such a manner that I do not know whether we shall get it; but I shall make arrangements this day to send you the first which comes. I refer you to the G. O. of the 17th inst. respecting green forage. There is no want of it about Thomar :

in its present state it is nearly as good as hay and oats together, and you must cut whatever you want. In the mean time I shall send you grain as soon as any can be procured.

To the Rt. Hon. J. Villiers.   Abrantes, 23d June, 1809.

I am sorry to have to inform you that Lieut. B——, of the 66th, was shot in a duel some days ago, as is supposed, by Lieut. D——, of the same regiment. I enclose you the report of persons who viewed the body of Lieut. B—— after he was dead, and the proceedings of a court of inquiry into the circumstances which occasioned the duel. Capt. M——, Lieut. D——, &c., are now in arrest; and if the government of the country think proper to order that they should be tried by the tribunal of the country, they shall be given up: if not, I shall give directions that they may be tried by a General Court Martial.

P.S. I beg you will return the enclosed original papers.

To Visc. Castlereagh.   Abrantes, 23d June, 1809.

I omitted to inform your Lordship yesterday, that, having received a letter from Gen. ——, in which he has, in my opinion, sufficiently retracted his erroneous military notion, as stated in his letter of the 10th May to Gen. Beresford, I have consented to allow him to continue with the army, and have re-appointed him to command a brigade.

The A.G. to Brig. Gen. A. Campbell.   23d June, 1809.

I am directed by the Commander of the Forces to acquaint you, in reply to your letter and enclosure from ——, that he cannot, under present circumstances, grant leave of absence to officers, under very urgent affairs, unless the nature of the affairs is stated, so as to enable his Excellency to judge of the imperious necessity of the case.

The A.G. to Col. Donkin.   23d June, 1809.

In reply to your letter enclosing the Court Martial on ——, of the —th regt., I am directed by the Commander of the Forces to say, that he cannot but think his punishment essentially necessary for the very reason you state as an inducement to remit the same. It is general example that is wanting and desired; and if British soldiers have imbibed such ideas, and have permitted their morals to be so corrupted, as not to know there is harm in absolute robbery, his Excellency thinks it is a most lamentable reflection for him in the command of this army. The Commander of the Forces regrets the sentence was not put in execution, as awarded, by the drummers of the garrison under your orders; but, notwithstanding, he has ordered the same to be carried into effect to-morrow at camp.

Memorandum for the Officer commanding the Artillery.   Abrantes, 24th June, 1809.

It is desirable, with a view to the future operations of the army, to form a depôt at Almeida, consisting of 1,200,000 rounds of musket ammunition, 200,000 rounds of rifle, 800,000 rounds of carbine, and 200,000 of pistol ammunition, and 100 rounds for each gun of the four brigades of 6 pounders, and the brigade of 3 pounders, which will move with the army; besides such stores as the officer commanding the artillery may deem necessary in a forward station of this description.

The mode in which this depôt must be formed is, that the stores must be embarked in a schooner or schooners at Lisbon, with the necessary number of conductors of stores and artillerymen to take charge of the stores and proceed to Oporto. From Oporto they must go in boats by the Douro to Lamego, and from Lamego in carts to Almeida, by a route which the Q. M. G. will furnish.

Directions will be sent to Col. Trant to give every assistance to forward the stores by boats to Lamego, and to have carts procured at Lamego to move the stores from thence to Almeida, and to furnish a guard of Portuguese troops to accompany them.

To Marshal Beresford.   Abrantes, 24th June, 1809.

I have written to you fully about Silveira's operations ; and I have now to answer your letter of the 22d inst. in respect to the soldiers of the Buffs. I certainly ordered all soldiers absent from the Buffs to join, upon a representation from Col. Muter. The form and words of the order I know nothing about ; but people are not unwilling to detain men when they have them ; and I dare say the order was peremptory. I gave the order because the men have now been absent from their regiment 3 months, because that time was full long enough to drill any thing on which they could have been employed, and because men of that description are now wanted by the Buffs to drill their own recruits lately come

---

G. O.   Abrantes, 24th June, 1809.

1. The frequent irregularities which occur on the march of detachments of convalescents, or recruits to join their regiments with the army, render it necessary to publish the following regulations :

2. All detachments must march by a route from the Q. M. G.'s department, in which they will be named, the places at which such detachments will receive provisions, and from whom.

3. The Commanding officer of each detachment on its march, must take care to send forward notice to the person from whom the provisions are to be received, of the arrival of the detachment, and of its strength.

4. It is to be understood that when 2 or more days' provisions are issued to the troops, they are not to receive at the same time, 2 or more days' wine. It has already been frequently explained in orders, that wine forms no part of the soldier's ration ; it will be delivered to them when it can be procured, and when it cannot they must go without it.

5. When a detachment will move, the soldiers must be formed into divisions, and officers and non-commissioned officers must be posted to each division.

The orders of the 29th May must be particularly attended to by the officers posted to divisions ; and they must exert themselves to prevent the repetition of the complaints which are so disgraceful to the army.

6. A detachment must universally march at daylight in the morning ; the officers and non-commissioned officers must march with the divisions to which they are posted, and must prevent the soldiers falling out of the ranks and straggling. The detachments must march at the rate of 2¼ miles an hour ; one halt must be made for 5 or 10 minutes at the end of every hour and a half.

7. Officers commanding detachments are to report their progress to head quarters by every opportunity.

8. A communication between head quarters and all parts of Portugal is to be carried on through Lisbon : all officers, having occasion to write, must send their letters by post, under cover, unless specially ordered to do otherwise, to the town major, Lisbon, from whose office a courier will be dispatched daily to head quarters.

9. Whenever an officer is sent from any of the hospitals, or Lisbon, in the command of a detachment of convalescents or recruits, he is to be furnished with a copy of these orders, and on his arrival at head quarters, he will report specially that the orders in the 3d, 5th, and 6th articles of this day's orders have been carried into effect.

10. The number of horses, for which staff officers are allowed to draw forage, having been increased by the orders of the 23d inst., it is to be understood that they are to do all duties required from them by means of their own horses, unless when required to go and return from a place at a greater distance from their station than 20 miles.

out. I particularly struck out of the list of men, to be called in, Col. Blunt's *servant*; but when the Commanding officer represented to me that he had more servants than were allowed by the orders of this army, or by the standing orders of his regiment, I could not avoid ordering the overplus to join their corps.

I propose to give the best drilled of the 7 battalions coming to Portugal, in order to assist in your drills, and to call off all the other privates and serjeants you have got.

Col. Campbell, of the ———, came to me the other day, and wanted to join his regiment, saying he had accepted his command in the Portuguese service only at the moment Portugal was threatened by invasion, and that he wished now to resign it. I refused to allow him to do so: but if the question of rank should be settled, as I expect it will, it may probably be proper to allow him to resign the command of his brigade.

Nothing detains me now but the non-arrival of the money. It will hardly be believed, and I am ashamed to tell it, that the money which left Lisbon on the 15th of this month is not yet arrived ! !

To Major Gen. Mackenzie.   Abrantes, 25th June, 1809.

I have received your letter of the 23d. I beg that you will let Mr. Downie know that I am perfectly satisfied with the activity with which he has done his duty, and sensible of the advantage, in a military point of view, which I have derived from his late reconnaissance into the vale of Plasencia.

My objection to his conduct was founded upon his own report, written in pencil on the letter from Col. Grant, upon the military principle, that the only proper place for any military officer was that to which he was

G. O.   Abrantes, 25th June, 1809.

2. Paymasters of regiments at Abrantes and in the huts, and all officers of the army, or others to whom any money is due, whether on account of claims for losses, which claims have been before the Board of Claims, for horses shot for the glanders, or on any other account, are to call on the Paymaster Gen. this afternoon, where the former will receive payment for the subsistence of their respective regiments to the 24th June, and all the latter what may be due to them.

4. The accounts of the soldiers of the army to the 24th June must be settled and signed, and balances paid on this day and to-morrow, and those in camp; to those at a distance on the following days. General officers commanding brigades are requested to see this order carried into execution.

7. The troops in the huts are this day to apply to the Q. M. G. for orders on the Commissary Gen.'s stores, for the camp kettles, canteens, haversacks, and bill hooks, for which they have made requisitions under the orders of the 8th inst.; Gen. Sherbrooke's division will receive the same articles as they will pass through Abrantes on the 27th; the same articles will be sent to Gen. Cotton's brigade, and the infantry of Major Gen. Mackenzie's division.

8. The allowance of intrenching tools is to be only 5 spades, 5 shovels, 5 pickaxes, and 5 felling axes, for each battalion of infantry; 8 spades, 8 shovels, 4 pickaxes, and 4 felling axes for each regiment of cavalry; and the requisitions will be corrected accordingly.

9. The Deputy Inspector of hospitals will give directions for the formation of the hospitals at Abrantes, upon the principle that all the men likely to continue sick for any length of time are to go to a general hospital, which is to be formed under the care of a sufficient number of surgeons of each brigade.

10. The Commander of the Forces is under the necessity of again requesting the attention of all the officers of the army to the strict obedience of the orders issued, particularly to those respecting supplies of provisions, carts, boats, &c. It is again positively forbid to any officer to stop supplies going to any part of the army, or to press boats, or carriages, excepting under the directions of a commissary. The commissariat drivers attached to the artillery at Abrantes, and all the other stations of the army, must this day be delivered over to the Commissary Gen. or his assistants.

ordered. However, I am not irreconcileable upon this or any other subject; and I am quite convinced that Mr. Downie did what he thought best for the service, and that a gentleman who feels a censure so sorely will take care not to incur the risk of receiving another.

To Marshal Beresford.   Abrantes, 25th June, 1809.

When I wrote to you yesterday I had not referred to Stewart. I find now that, notwithstanding I had observed the irregularity of Col. Blunt having 3 servants from the ranks, I specially directed that none of them should, and not one of them has been ordered to join.

Your ammunition that is here will be of use to us, and I propose to take it. I shall give you in return 200,000 rounds of musket ammunition, and if you choose to have it at Aveiro, I can give you an order upon a transport in that harbour for that quantity.

The A.G. to the Rev. N. S. Seymour, Lisbon.   25th June, 1809.

I am directed by the Commander of the Forces to acquaint you, in reply to your letter, that it will be necessary to know the dates of the several appointments of chaplains before they can be inserted in Orders. When you favor me with these, there shall be no delay on my part.

With regard to your wish of remaining at Lisbon, the Commander of the Forces directs that one chaplain must remain there to do all duty in the city, and at the hospital, and at Belem: all the remaining chaplains must join the army. The senior chaplain must fix on the chaplain that is to remain at Lisbon.

To Brig. Gen. Cox, Governor of Almeida.   Abrantes, 26th June, 1809.

I have had the honor of receiving your letter of the 23d inst. I have directed the Commissary Gen. to have prepared and laid in store at Almeida a quantity of biscuit for the British army, and the Commanding officer of the artillery to send there a quantity of ammunition and military stores. I request you to receive into the fort of Almeida what may be lodged there for our use.

P.S. I have likewise received your letter of the 21st.

To Lieut. Col. Bourke, A. Q. M. G.   Abrantes, 26th June, 1809.

I have received your letters of the 21st and 23d; and I have the pleasure to inform you the army will march to-morrow morning, the money having arrived yesterday; the advanced guard will be at Zarza la Mayor on the 2d July, and the infantry of the army on the 4th and 5th. There will be some difficulty in moving the cavalry on account of the want of forage; and one regiment has not yet arrived from Lisbon. But the whole will move forward to Plasencia as soon as possible: indeed I do not propose to make any halt till I shall arrive at that place. I strongly recommend to Gen. Cuesta to risk nothing till I shall be at hand to give him assistance.

To the Rt. Hon. J. H. Frere.   Abrantes, 26th June, 1809.

I enclose the last two letters I have received from Col. Bourke, and my answer of this day.

I shall not go into Spain as strong as I could wish, or as I expected, as 3000 men are not yet arrived. But I think it better to move with the troops I have, having received the money, than to delay my march for one moment after I am enabled to commence it.

I conclude that Col. Bourke has given me the character which he has heard of Señor ——; but I beg you will believe that if I should find it correct, I shall be convinced you had no knowledge of this character when he was sent; and, at all events, I shall have no prejudice against Señor ——.

I shall be very much obliged to you if you will send me any topographical or geographical information respecting Spain which can be procured at Seville. I particularly wish to have 2 copies of Lopez's maps, which I request you to send me by any messenger who may come.

To Visc. Castlereagh.   Abrantes, 26th June, 1809.

I have the honor to enclose a letter from Brig. Gen. the Hon. C. Stewart, in which he desires that Major Waters * should be attached to the department of the Adj. Gen. of the British army. I am equally aware with Brig. Gen. Stewart of the advantages which the public would derive

* The late Major Gen. Sir J. Waters, K.C.B.

G. O.   Abrantes, 26th June, 1809.

1. The Commander of the Forces desires that the troops should always march at daylight, in order that they may reach the ground at as early an hour as may be practicable; he is also desirous that they should hut every day; and it is to be understood that they are to hut invariably where there is wood conveniently situated, in reference to water. This wood, however, must not be olive trees, or other valuable fruit trees.

2. The order (No. 5 of the 3d May) in respect to men taken sick on the march, referring to the order (No. 11 of the 24th April) by the late Commander of the Forces, is countermanded; the Commander of the Forces being convinced that, from circumstances, it is impossible to carry it into execution.

3. In future, the General officers commanding divisions and brigades will direct, that men taken sick upon a march may be carried on till orders will be given for forming a general or brigade hospital.

4. The huts at present occupied by Major Gen. Tilson's brigade are to be occupied as hospitals by the sick of the different regiments to be left in brigade hospital.

5. The staff surgeons attached to divisions will make the distribution of the huts to the different brigades, and will order a sufficient number of surgeons from each brigade, to remain in the huts to attend the sick. This order is not to prevent the surgeons of those brigades which have already got hospitals in the town of Abrantes from continuing to occupy them. Surgeons of regiments are to make requisitions on the purveyor's stores for bedding for the sick, in the proportion of a blanket for every patient in the huts.

6. A sufficient number of officers and non-commissioned officers from each brigade are to be left in charge of the sick at Abrantes, according to the orders of the 19th May and 2d June.

7. The officers commanding companies are at all times to leave with the surgeons in charge of hospitals in which the men are left, the amount of the hospital stoppages of 9d. per diem for each man left behind, from the day the men will enter the hospital to the following 24th of the month, as soon as possible after the 24th of every month. The surgeons in charge of hospitals are invariably to send to the paymasters of regiments, by the mode of conveyance pointed out in the orders of the 24th inst., the account of stoppages for the men of each regiment who have been in the hospital under their charge since the 24th of the preceding month, according to the printed form. No accounts of stoppages must be sent to England in future.

8. A few tents having arrived, those officers who have made known their wishes to have them under the orders of the 24th May, No. 3, are to apply to the Q. M. G., who will give orders upon the Commissary Gen. for them.

9. Complaints having been made by the Lieut. General commanding the cavalry, by Brig. Gen. Fane, and by Lieut. Col. Lord E. Somerset, commanding the 4th dragoons, to which regiment Assist. Commissary —— is attached, of his neglect of duty, of incapacity to perform his duty, and of his making false reports to Lieut. Col. Lord E. Somerset; Assist. Commissary —— is dismissed from his office as Assist. Commissary. Mr. —— is to be released from arrest, and is to quit the army.

from the employment of the services of Major Waters with the department of the Adj. Gen. ; but as Major Waters has been promoted to the rank of Major, in order that he may serve with the Portuguese troops, I have considered myself precluded, by the principle on which British officers were allowed to serve in the Portuguese army, from selecting any officer so allowed and promoted for that purpose for any staff situation in this army. Upon looking over the list of the officers appointed to the Portuguese service, particularly the first appointed, your Lordship will observe the names of some whom it would be most desirable to employ upon the staff of the British army.

Adverting to your Lordship's recent directions to me to employ Major Roche, of the Portuguese service, with the Spanish armies ; and observing that Major Carroll is still employed with the Marques de la Romana, I should wish to know whether I am to understand that I am at liberty to employ Major Waters, or other officers appointed and promoted to serve in Portugal, in any other manner excepting with Portuguese troops ?

To Visc. Castlereagh.   Abrantes, 26th June, 1809.

As Lord W. Bentinck is employed, I imagine, in Germany, and Gen. Spencer's health is in such a state as to prevent him from joining, and Gen. Paget must necessarily be absent for some time, it is desirable that I should have some officers appointed to be Lieut. Generals in Portugal, to take the command of divisions.

Gens. Cotton and Hill, two Major Generals of this army, are senior to Gen. Beresford; and it would be desirable that they should be made Lieut. Generals in the Peninsula, if only to place them in their proper situations in the British army relatively with that officer; and indeed I am obliged already to employ Gen. Hill in the command of a division of infantry. If Major Gen. Murray had not quitted the army, because he did not choose to serve with it, Gen. Beresford, having been made a Lieut. General in Portugal, although junior to him, I should likewise have requested your Lordship to have him appointed as Lieut. General.

To Marshal Beresford.   Abrantes, 27th June, 1809.

The money having arrived, the army marches this day. I have received from you 3 letters of the 24th, and one of the 25th.

I shall speak to Col. Fletcher respecting the employment of Capt.

G. O.   Abrantes, 27th June. 1809.

3. A guard of 1 serjeant and 6 dragoons from Brig. Gen. Fane's brigade to be attached to the Paymaster Gen.'s mules during the march ; they are to report themselves and receive instructions from the Paymaster Gen. ; 1 corporal and 2 private dragoons to be attached to the provost guard, which, with all the prisoners, will move with the head quarters of the army.

10. Assist. Commissary —— having expressed his concern for the neglect of duty of which he has been guilty, and Lieut. Gen. Payne having expressed a desire his conduct should be looked over upon this occasion, and that he should be reinstated in his office ; the order of yesterday respecting him is countermanded, and he is to return to his duty as assist. commissary attached to the 4th dragoons.

The Commander of the Forces, however, hopes Mr. —— will show by his attention to his duty in future, that he merits the indulgence of Lieut. Gen. Payne; and he hopes that the example of the dismissal of Mr. —— for the neglect of duty, will operate as an example to all the officers of the commissariat.

Chapman with the army; but I rather believe that his business having been interrupted in consequence of the terror occasioned by Victor's movement to Alcantara, he has not finished what I sent him upon. If, however, we should not want him at Lisbon, I shall call him to the army, as you do not require his services, and you shall keep at Lisbon the Lieutenant of the Germans.

I should wish you to delay, if possible, all arrangements respecting the rank of the English officers till I shall receive the answer to my letter of the 7th inst. I think it probable that none of the officers whose names are mentioned in the letter from the Commander in Chief, of the 1st June, will come out before that answer shall arrive. But if they should, at least if they are all of the same stamp with Col. ——, you would be much better without them, as he is the person who was obliged by Sir J. Moore to retire from the —th regt., for incapacity in the last campaign.

If Mr. Rawlings has not been already directed to place himself under your orders, he shall be so in the G. O. of this day. I shall speak to the Commissary Gen. respecting the 3 clerks to be appointed assistants, and you shall have them, if he can spare their services. Mr. Belson shall be ordered this day to place himself under your orders.

I don't recollect whether I sent home the return for your saddles. If I did, the letter went to yourself, I believe. I think you had better send to Cooke, in a private letter, the amended return which was sent home by me. Tell Cooke also to take care that your saddles are made with narrow trees. I shall order Capt. ——, of the 9th, to place himself under your orders.

——'s conduct appears, by your account of it, to be very bad. These people are so much accustomed to trick, that they cannot refrain from it; and they have recourse to it now to acquire popularity, in the same manner as they did formerly to acquire Court favor. There is only one line to be adopted in opposition to all trick; that is, the steady straight line of duty, tempered by forbearance, lenity, and good nature.

The government having published ——'s letter, you can have nothing to say to him upon that ground. But you ought to call upon the government to furnish you with the original, or with official copies of the reports from —— which they have published. You ought then to call —— to account: 1st; for having made any report to the government instead of to you, his superior officer: 2dly; for the difference between his report to government and his reports to you: and 3dly; for his deviations from the truth in his reports to government, in respect to his operations, at which you were present. Having received his answers upon these subjects, you ought to publish an order to forbid any officer to make a report to any superior authority, excepting through the medium of his immediate Commanding officer; and you ought to point out the variations, the inconsistencies, and the falsehoods in the report made by ——, as the cause of the order at that moment. I think that by these means you will give a check to the propensity of these gentlemen to endeavor to acquire popularity at your expense, by trick and falsehood. I would insert in this order, or in the correspondence, no severity or asperity, only a plain and short abstract of the facts.

I have not got (but I will get) a return of our medical gentlemen at Lisbon; you shall have all the assistance of this kind that I can give you. I think that the French are drawing out of Galicia, and it is not impossible but that they may take a look at Braganza as they pass by. I conclude that that place is dismantled, as all the other Portuguese places are.

You are acquainted with my opinion respecting the position for your corps, in case the enemy should move to his left; that is, that you move to your right upon an inner and of course a smaller circle, being convinced that they are moving from Galicia into Castille. You have done quite right, therefore, to halt your corps upon the Douro, at Coimbra and Guarda. In respect to the place for assembling them, you must recollect that your object is twofold; first, to organize and discipline your troops; next, to observe the motions of the enemy, and to cover and secure, by your appearance, your numbers, and your reputation, the entrance into Portugal, which may at the moment be threatened by the enemy. In choosing your position, you should take care not to put yourself too forward towards the enemy, otherwise you may be interrupted in your measures for obtaining your first object; and indeed you may put to risk the security which you might give to the country if you were at a greater distance from them.

In respect to me, I conceive that, at present, whether you march a day or two farther one way or another, it can make but little difference to my operations. You must depend very much upon the movements of the French. If they should hang about the Guadarama in strength, I must move that way; if not, I shall certainly go upon Segovia, and, in doing so, I shall try to keep as near the Portuguese frontier as possible.

I have already told you that you shall have the best of the new battalions coming out. Would you like the 2d battalion of your own regiment? I shall likewise try to send you some riflemen.

To Visc. Castlereagh.   Abrantes, 27th June, 1809.

The money for which I have been waiting arrived here on Sunday, and the army has marched forward. Our advanced guard will enter Spain at Zarza la Mayor, on the 2d July.

The French retired from Almaraz on the road towards Madrid on the 24th; and Gen. Cuesta was at the bridge of Almaraz on the same day, and was making arrangements to cross the Tagus. Sebastiani was retiring towards Toledo. He was, on the 22d, at Madridejos, and Venegas at Villarta.

It is unfortunate that I could not march 10 or 12 days ago; but just to show you the uncertainty of all communications in this country, and, probably, the deficiencies of our Commissariat, I shall mention that the money which arrived on the 15th at Lisbon, and was sent off immediately, did not arrive here till late on the 25th. It is the same with every thing else. On the day I determined to move into Spain from Abrantes I ordered every thing that could be required for the army, and I have not had occasion to add to or to alter the original order; yet the articles ordered are not yet arrived, notwithstanding that there is a water communication from Lisbon, and officers and others come up in 5 days. I believe much of this delay and failure is to be attributed to the want of experience of our Commissariat; much to the want of money, and to our discredit in Portugal, on account of our large and long owed debts; and something to the uncertainty and natural difficulties of all the communications in Portugal.

We shall not go into Spain quite so strong as I could wish; but when Craufurd's brigade arrives, I think we shall have nearly 20,000 R. and F. of infantry, and about 3000 cavalry. I shall desire that a weekly state may be sent to your Lordship, that you may see how we really stand; for I observe it is frequently imagined in England that armies are much stronger than they really are, and expectations are formed which cannot be realised. It is a most difficult task to keep up numbers, particularly of cavalry, in this country and climate. The brigade of heavy cavalry, which has not yet done a day's duty, is obliged to leave here nearly 100 horses; and the brigade which has been to the northward is so much reduced, that they are happy to take 110 horses of the Irish Commissariat. I hope, therefore, you will send us the remount as soon as you can.

The A.G. to Dr. Thompson, Lisbon.   27th June, 1809.

I am directed by the Commander of the Forces to acquaint you that the General Hospital Staff and hospital stores of the army are nearly exhausted by the formation of so many hospitals; and that the army is now marching forward without a disposable Medical officer, or a blanket to cover a sick man. I have, therefore, to call your constant attention to the wants of this army, both as to Medical Staff and hospital stores, as also proper officers of the Purveyors' department; and it is essentially necessary that the different demands made by the Inspector Gen. here, and the supplies he has pointed out, should be forwarded to their destination with the utmost expedition.

To Major Gen. Mackenzie.   Corticada, 28th June, 1809.

The Commanding officer of the 24th regt. has, I am sure, contrary to your orders, and certainly contrary to mine, left the sick of his regiment here, without money, without non-commissioned officers, and without giving them over to the officer of the 31st regt., left here in charge of the sick of the 31st. The 24th regt. have money, I know, in advance, for the subsistence of the regiment to the 24th July; and I desire, as soon as possible after the receipt of this, that officers may be sent over here with subsistence for the sick of their companies to the 24th July, at 9*d. per diem*, according to the G. O.; and that these officers should deliver their men regularly over to the charge of the officer of the 31st, left with the sick of the brigade; likewise the proportion of non-commissioned officers ordered to be left with all sick, according to the G. O.

I shall be very much obliged to you if you will let me know any cause that may have come to your knowledge for the desertion by its inhabitants, and plunder, even to gutting, of Cardigos.

To Col. Peacocke.   Corticada, 28th June, 1809.

I have desired that Col. R. Craufurd's brigade, consisting of the 43d, 52d, and 95th, may move to join the army as soon as they may be equipped and in readiness to march, as also a troop of horse artillery, expected at Lisbon from England. In moving these troops, you will, of course, use the water communication as far as Valada, if Col. Craufurd should approve of it.

It occurs to me that it might be a convenience to the horses of the horse artillery, particularly just after they are landed, if the artillery, and carriages, and stores belonging to the troop were sent up by water, even as far as Abrantes. But, in doing this, great care must be taken to provide for the payment of the boatmen the whole way up to Abrantes; and that proper measures are adopted at Valada to transship the artillery carriages, &c., from the large boats used in the lower parts of the Tagus, to the smaller ones used in the upper parts. If you will speak to the Admiral on this subject, I am convinced that he will give you every assistance; and you will allow Col. Craufurd to decide whether they shall move by land or by water, if the artillery should come out and are to march with him; or the Commanding officer of the troop, if they should come out and are to march alone.

Besides the troops above mentioned, I expect from Ireland and the islands 7 battalions of infantry, one regiment of cavalry, one troop of horse artillery, and 300 artillery horses. You will direct the battalions of infantry to equip themselves immediately for the field, according to the orders of the army. You will send me up the returns for bât and forage, if they should not already have received that allowance this year; and you will direct the Paymaster Gen. at Lisbon to make such advances upon it as the officers of the regiments may require to put themselves in a state of equipment fit to take the field. I desire that these regiments may be encamped on the high ground immediately above and behind Belem, where they are to remain in readiness to move till I shall send them further orders. You will inspect each of them on their arrival, and make a particular report on their state as soon as possible, in order that I may determine whether I shall call them to the army or not.

The cavalry and horse artillery expected are likewise to send up their bât and forage returns, but I do not at present intend to call these corps immediately into the field. I beg that the stables at Belem, Alcantara, &c., may be washed, painted, and whitewashed, for the reception of those horses and of the 300 horses of the artillery. All these are to remain at Lisbon till further orders.

To W. Huskisson, Esq., Secretary of the Treasury.   Corticada, 28th June, 1809.

The money which had been sent to Cadiz to be changed arrived at Lisbon on the 15th, and with the army on the 25th; and we marched yesterday, having been obliged to halt nearly 3 weeks for want of money. Our distress for every thing has been very great indeed, and has been produced by the want of money. After all, the sum which we have received, and that which we have lately got for bills upon England, will not do more than pay the army their arrears to the 24th of this month, and to keep in hand a sum of about £30,000 to begin with in Spain, leaving all our debts in Portugal unpaid. I trust that you will have attended to my first requisition for £100,000, and that that sum will arrive soon, and that you will have made arrangements to send to Portugal £200,000 every month.

It will be better for government, in every view of the subject, to relinquish their operations in Portugal and Spain, if the country cannot afford to carry them on. The gentlemen of the Commissariat are very new in their business, and I am not without grounds of complaint of their want of intelligence; but I believe they do their best, and I shall not complain of them. I dismissed one assistant, Mr. ——, 2 days ago; but I have cancelled the order for his dismission, upon his promise of greater exertion in future, and upon the request of the General officer who had complained of him.

We shall want some more assistants with the reinforcements coming out: there are several sick at Lisbon, and as our operations extend, we are obliged to detach the Commissaries to a greater distance.

To Major Gen. Mackenzie.   Sarzedas, 29th June, 1809.

I am sorry to tell you that I have passed a broken cart, laden with intrenching tools and other baggage, belonging to the 31st regt., in charge of a serjeant's guard, in the pass on this side of Sobreira Formosa. A mule is allowed for the intrenching tools of each regiment, which ought to be employed in no other manner. If he is sick, it might be excused putting the intrenching tools on a cart; but the cart ought not to have been loaded with three times more baggage than it could carry; and, above all, no guard ought to have been left with any baggage. The serjeant of the guard is taken sick, and is at the river at the bottom of the pass.

Whenever an order is disobeyed, an officer must be sent to set matters right again. I therefore request you to send an officer of the 31st, with a cart, to bring up the intrenching tools and the sick serjeant, and nothing else, and then to return to-morrow with the party to Castello Branco. I shall be obliged to you to tell the Commissary, that, having put on the carts 3 casks of flour instead of 2, a great number of the carts have broken down between Sobreira Formosa and this place. I request, that immediately on the receipt of this note he will send off 20 empty carts, with an officer of the Commissariat. He will meet at the river at the foot of the pass the officer of the 31st, in charge of the convoy, who will let him know where the different carts have broken down, and where the casks of flour are; and I beg that only 2 casks may be placed on each cart.

As you have so many men absent who are not likely to join you till to-morrow, I have no objection to your halting to-morrow at Castello Branco, if the Commissary should think that he can give you another day's provisions, without interfering with the supply of three days for the other divisions, as they shall come up. If, however, that supply should be likely to run short, you must march according to your route. Col. Donkin's brigade might as well halt if you do, if it can be done without inconvenience, as I observe they have many things behind. I shall be at Castello Branco to-morrow.

To J. Murray, Esq., Commissary General.   Castello Branco, 30th June, 1809.

I have received information that the *Rosamond* has brought from England about 300,000 dollars (£65,000); and the *Niobe* £60,000 in Spanish doubloons, £50,000 in Portuguese gold coin, and £50,000 in dollars, making a total of £225,000.

I beg that the disposal of this money may be made as follows: the £60,000 in Spanish doubloons are to come up to the army in charge of Brig. Gen. R. Craufurd's brigade. I desire that an efficient arrangement may be made to supply carts or mules to move this money. The loads must not be made too large, not more than 200lbs. for a mule; and the drivers must receive rations in the same manner as soldiers, deducting 6*d.* for each ration from their pay. If they should require rations of forage for their cattle they must have it; but a proportionate reduction must be made in the rate of their hire.

Mr. Villiers must have for the use of the Portuguese government such sums as he may require, not exceeding £80,000, which may be paid him in the Portuguese gold coin, or in dollars, in their proportion in the military chest: and I beg that you will give directions that £50,000 of the sum which will remain in the chest be employed in the discharge of the debts due on the road from Oporto to Coimbra, Leyria, Thomar, and Abrantes. The remainder, or £35,000, must remain in the military chest at Lisbon till I shall give further directions for its disposal.

I beg that you will continue to make every exertion in your power to procure money for bills upon England, at Lisbon, Cadiz, and Gibraltar; and that you will give me a return every Monday of the sums received for those bills, at any of the three places.

P.S. I enclose a letter from the Junta of Castille, from which it appears that they have deputed Don Ant. Palacios and Don Vicencio Ibarra to receive the sum of money due to the town of Ciudad Rodrigo by Sir J. Moore's army. I beg that you will give directions that this sum be paid to those gentlemen at Lisbon, when they shall ask for it.

To Vice Adm. the Hon. G. Berkeley. Castello Branco, 30th June, 1809.

His Majesty's principal Sec. of State having intimated to me the wish of His Majesty's servants, that I should send home the transports now in the Tagus, if I should not require their services, I have the honor to inform you that it is my opinion that all the transports now in the Tagus may be sent home without inconvenience, with the exception of 5000 tons of transports for infantry, of the coppered ships.

I some time ago gave directions to the Commanding officer of the artillery, and to the Commissary General, to have disembarked from the ordnance store ships, victuallers, &c., and to put in store at Lisbon, all the ordnance and military stores, provisions, forage, &c. &c., which were in those ships, and destined for their departments respectively; and I have called upon these gentlemen this day to let me know what progress has been made in the execution of those orders. It is my opinion that all those store ships and victuallers, as soon as their contents shall be disembarked, may be sent home, as well as the transports to which I have above referred.

To the Rt. Hon. J. Villiers. Castello Branco, 30th June, 1809.

I arrived here this day, and shall go on the day after to-morrow. I find that £225,000 have arrived in the *Rosamond* and the *Niobe.* I have desired that £80,000 of this sum be paid to you in the proportions of gold and dollars as they are in the military chest at present. I have allotted

£50,000 to pay part of our debts in the north; £60,000 to be sent to us into Spain, in Spanish doubloons; and £35,000 to remain in the chest in Lisbon.

To Visc. Castlereagh.   Castello Branco, 30th June, 1809.

I received your letter of the 11th yesterday. I am much obliged to you for the reinforcements you have sent, and you may depend upon it that I shall make the best use of them in my power; but none are yet arrived, excepting the 23d light dragoons. It is impossible to say how we shall stand in point of numbers when these troops arrive, till I shall see a return of their numbers. But nothing is more fallacious than a return such as you have sent me. It contains an enumeration of no less than 11 battalions not arrived, of 2 gone to Gibraltar, and of 2 (the detachments) ordered home, and of the 20th light dragoons, ordered and gone by this time to Sicily; and it omits, on the other hand, 2 battalions, the 48th and 61st, arrived from Gibraltar. The mischief of these returns is that they never convey an accurate notion of the strength of the army. According to your account I have 35,000 men; according to my own, I have only 18,000; and the public will not be satisfied either with you or me, if I do not effect all that 35,000 men are expected to do. Including officers, who ought to be counted, I make no doubt that I shall have before long more than 35,000 men; but from all these returns a deduction (of 10 in 100 ought always to be made for sick, and then you may come nearly to the mark.

I enclose an abstract of the last return I have received of Victor's army, which shows the comparative numbers of effectives and total. I hope that our effectives will never be so much reduced in comparison with our total as that is. But surely it must be admitted that if our army is now only 18,000, and hereafter to be called 35,000 R. and F., the French army ought to be calculated in the same manner; and yet neither you nor I shall be forgiven by those who will see your return, if I do not now perform deeds which might with justice be required from 35,000 men.

If I am to have the 57th from Gibraltar, you should send an order to the Governor to send that corps to Portugal in exchange for one which I shall send to Gibraltar to relieve it.

I enclose you an abstract of the last return of the Portuguese forces which I have received. Of this number we pay for 20,000 men £480,000, or, I believe, £500,000 per annum. My belief is, that the Portuguese government cannot go on unless Great Britain will assist them with a million.

The Portuguese army is not yet in a state of discipline, or organized as it ought to be for service. I have settled with Beresford, that he shall collect all that part of it not required for garrisons in a camp on the most exposed frontier, for the double purpose of watching the enemy's movements, and disciplining his officers and troops. If he can get them together for 2 or 3 months they will be a fine army, and probably very useful. But in order to effect this object they must be kept clear of the desultory operations of Romana, and other Spanish chiefs in Galicia. Besides these troops, called regulars, there is an army of militia, amounting, I believe, to 30,000 men. They are divided into battalions of 1000 each. We propose to discipline the whole of these by 600 at a time, in reliefs of 200 each; and when the whole are disciplined, to call out the whole in camps of 8000 or 10,000 men, at a season of the year in which the country can spare the labors of the men, and perfect them, and then send them to their homes till they may be wanted. I conceive that, exclusive of the militia, the Portuguese army will be 50,000 men when complete. The question is in what way this force ought to be employed.

There is no doubt but that that part of the Portuguese force which is not required for internal purposes ought to be employed against the common enemy in Spain, if that addition of force is likely to be of any avail. But if circumstances should bring the contest in Spain to that state that, notwithstanding all our efforts, the enemy should still be superior to us in the field, I should then have doubts of the expediency of marching the Portuguese troops beyond their own frontier.

These doubts turn upon a view of the military operations which it would be expedient to adopt in that case throughout the Peninsula, which I think should be founded upon strong reserves in parts of Spain as well as of Portugal, and by means of which the contest would be infinitely prolonged, even if it should ever be in the enemy's power to make the conquest. They are also founded upon my apprehension that great length of time must elapse before we can make the Portuguese sufficiently good troops to retire before a superior enemy; and my opinion is that they, as well as we, should be lost before we could enter the frontiers of Portugal.

I enclose the copy of a letter which I have written to the Admiral, by which you will observe that you will have home the ships in the Tagus of all descriptions, excepting 5000 tons of infantry coppered transports; and I propose to keep horse transports for 300 horses, when they shall return from Ireland, in case I should have occasion to move horses by sea.

To Brig. Gen. R. Craufurd.   Castello Branco, 1st July, 1809.

I am glad to find, by a letter which you have addressed to the Adj. Gen. on the 28th, that you arrived on the 28th June. You do not mention the troop of horse artillery, and I therefore conclude it is not come with you. You will find orders at Lisbon upon all points on which you can require them.

I beg that if the troop of horse artillery should not be ready to march when your brigade will be ready, you will not wait for them.

We have here two battalions composed of detachments from all the regiments which composed the army under the command of the late Sir J. Moore, and among others, of the 43d, 52d, and 95th; of which three I enclose a return. I believe that these men belong, generally, to the 2d battalions of those regiments. I propose to send these battalions of detachments down to Lisbon immediately, in order that they may embark for England, if I should find that the enemy do not make a stand on this

G. O.   Castello Branco, 1st July, 1809.

2. Great care must be taken when rye is given to the horses that they are not watered 2 hours before, or 2 hours after they are fed; the same rule should be observed when they are fed with Indian corn or barley.

side of Madrid, in a position which I understand they can occupy near Talavera de la Reyna. I beg that you will inquire from the Commanding officers of the 43d, 52d, and 95th, whether they wish that the officers and men belonging to these regiments respectively should be detained in Portugal, and of course, with the army to join the regiments; or whether I shall send them down to Lisbon to go home with the other detachments.

To Lieut. Col. Roche.   Castello Branco, 1st July, 1809.

I have just received your letter of the 29th. The British army are in full march towards the frontier, and no time shall be lost in collecting them at Plasencia.

In the present situation of affairs my opinion is, that Gen. Cuesta should establish his bridge at some point on the Tagus below the junction with the Tietar, to which there would be a road on each side of the Tagus, in order to enable me to move to his assistance if it should be necessary, or he to mine. He will be the best judge of the exact situation for the bridge. If Gen. Venegas' corps can be put in a secure position in or about its present situation, it ought for the present to be kept where it is, because it threatens Toledo and Madrid, and the enemy's rear, in case he should advance against Gen. Cuesta and me. If Gen. Venegas' corps cannot be put in security where it is, it ought either to fall back into the mountains, if it is apprehended that the enemy entertain designs to march towards Cordova and Seville by the road of La Carolina; or, if those apprehensions are not well founded, it ought eventually to be brought in communication with the corps of Gen. Cuesta. Upon the whole, I prefer for Gen. Venegas' corps, at present, a strong position near the situation in which it is, as being most likely to keep the enemy in check till I shall be up; but if such a position cannot be found, it ought to be put in security, by being obliged to fall back to its old position in the mountains. You will communicate these my sentiments to Major Gen. O'Donoju.

To Major Gen. J. Erskine.   Castello Branco, 1st July, 1809.

I am much concerned to hear of your continued indisposition, and I am seriously of opinion that you ought to lose no time in going to the coast, and even to England, if you should not recover. No man likes to withdraw from an army in the situation in which we stand at present; but you ought to consider that your health is in such a state as to render it impossible for you to do a day's duty, and you must be a burthen to yourself and to every body else.

I have sent a carriage to bring you in to Castello Branco; but I strongly recommend to you to set off on your return to Lisbon as soon as you are able.

I cannot conclude without expressing my concern to lose your assistance; but I am convinced that, if you were to stay, you would be unable to afford me any, and that you will become worse instead of better.

To the Military Sec. to the Commander in Chief.   Castello Branco, 1st July, 1809.

I have the honor to enclose extracts of the orders which I have issued, containing appointments of officers to the Staff, till the pleasure of His

Majesty should be known, and other arrangements which require the confirmation of authority. I shall explain such appointments and arrangements as appear to me to require explanation.

1. When I arrived in Portugal, Capt. Cooke was D. A. Q. M. G.; and before I left England, I had recommended that he should be D. A. A. G., to which appointment I understood the Commander in Chief had consented. I found, however, that his name was omitted in the list of the officers of the department which I received from your office: this omission I concluded was a mistake, and I appointed Capt. Cooke to act as D. A. A. G., which department he preferred to that of the Q. M. G. I have since found, by a letter received from the Commander in Chief, that Capt. Cooke is appointed D. A. Q. M. G.; but I propose to keep him in the department of the Adj. Gen., which he prefers, and for which he is most fit, till I shall receive your answer to this letter.

2. I likewise found Capt. Vernon Graham in the department of the Adj. Gen., and I continued to employ him in it as a D. A. A. G.; and I appointed Capt. Mellish to be D. A. A. G.

3. At that time Lieut. Col. Elley, Capt. Cockburn, and Capt. Ompteda, of those officers whose names are in the list received from your office, were not in Portugal. Lieut. Col. Elley has since arrived; but Lieut. Col. Darroch and Major Tidy have gone home.

4. I apppointed Capt. Reynett, of the 52d, to be D. A. Q. M. G., because I had recommended him to the Commander in Chief, by desire of the Q. M. G., and understood that his appointment had been approved of, and he had left England before the letter was written which ordered him to join his regiment.

5. The letter from the Commander in Chief, of the 5th June, also directs the appointment of Capt. Maw to be D. A. Q. M. G., which appointment I had made on the 6th May, 1809, having found Capt. Maw doing duty with the department on my joining the army, and that his services were then necessary. Capt. Maw has since returned to England.

6. The following officers, whose names appear in the list of the department as furnished from your office, are not in Portugal, Major Blaquiere and Major Northey; and the following are employed with the Portuguese service: Capt. Hardinge,* Capt. Le Mesurier, and Capt. Waller. Capt. Gomm was ordered to join his regiment. I have therefore thought it necessary to appoint Capt. Mercer, Capt. Doyle, and Capt. Humphries, to be D. A. Q. M. Gs. I found Lieut. Merganthal doing duty with the Q. M. G.'s department when I took the command of the army, and as he was useful in it, I continued him in his situation.

7. The appointment of Assist. Provost marshals, I am sorry to say, is but too necessary; and I trust that the allowance granted to them by the order of the late Commander of the forces in Portugal, viz., Ensign's pay and allowances, by his orders of the 14th April, and the allowance to purchase a mule, given by me, will be approved of by the Commander of the forces.

8. When the army went upon the expedition to the northward, it was deemed expedient to attach a battalion of Portuguese infantry to each of 4

---

* Lieut. Gen. Sir H. Hardinge, K.C.B.

British brigades, and an interpreter was attached to each of the Commanding officers of these brigades. This expense has been discontinued since the Portuguese battalions have been detached from these brigades.

9. The order of the 7th May, attaching Mr. Cussan and Mr. Andrade to the office of the Q. M. G., was issued with a view to the formation of the corps of guides, respecting which the order was finally issued on the 23d May, 1809.

This corps is essentially necessary in all operations in Portugal. It is most difficult to obtain any information respecting roads, or any of the local circumstances which must be considered in the decisions to be formed respecting the march of troops; and this difficulty obliged me last year, and all those who have since conducted operations in this country, to form a corps of this description.

The object is not only to have a corps whose particular duty it will be to make inquiries, and have a knowledge of roads, but to have a class of persons in the army who shall march with the heads of columns, and interpret between the officers commanding them and the people of the country guiding them, or others from whom they may wish to make inquiries.

10. The order of £10 bât money to Surgeons and Paymasters of regiments of the 10th and 23d June was issued to enable them to keep up a mule to carry the Surgeon's medicine chest and Paymaster's books, respectively.

11. I appointed Col. Peacocke to be a Colonel on the Staff, as he was the senior Colonel of the army, with the exception of Col. Anson, who declined the appointment; and there was a brigade of infantry which had no Commanding officer. Since the appointment of Gen. Anson to be a Brig. General, by His Majesty, Col. Peacocke is gone to command the British troops at Lisbon, where it was necessary to station an officer of rank.

12. I appointed Col. *Baron* Low to be a Brig. General, as he was the senior Colonel of the Legion present; Brig. Gen. Drieberg was gone to England for the recovery of his health, and Col. *Baron* Low was senior as a Colonel to many officers who are Brigadiers in this army.

13. I appointed Mr. Leslie Melville and Mr. Head to be Assist. Commissaries, and to be attached to the Portuguese troops, upon the recommendation of the Ambassador, and because the appointment was necessary.

14. Lieut. Carlos de Tamm, appointed a D. A. Q. M. G., is an officer of Portuguese Engineers, who had been very useful to the Q. M. G., and whose services were still necessary to him.

To the Rt. Hon. the Commander in Chief.   Castello Branco, 1st July, 1809.

I have the honor to enclose a letter which I have received this day from Col. Donkin, who commands the brigade of infantry in which the 5th batt. 60th regt. is serving, to which Lieut. ――, to whom these papers relate, belongs.

In addition to the complaints contained in these papers of the conduct of Lieut. ――, I have to mention that that officer waited on me last night with a letter from the Adj. Gen., authorising him to serve with the Portuguese troops; and he desired that I would permit him to join them. I declined doing so, as I wished to wait for an answer to the letter which I had addressed to you on the 7th June, before I should allow any other officer to join and do duty with the Portuguese troops; and Lieut. —— then told me that he was very sorry that he could not do duty with his regiment, as he was unwell.

I beg to recommend that officers, particularly belonging to regiments doing duty in Portugal, should not be permitted to serve with the Portuguese troops, unless they should be recommended by the officers commanding the regiment to which they belong.

To the Rt. Hon. J. H. Frere.   Castello Branco, 1st July, 1809.

Lieut. Col. Bourke has returned to the army, and I shall hereafter communicate to you the detailed information which he has brought to me, in answer to the queries which I had sent him. In the mean time, I enclose the copy of a letter just received from Lieut. Col. Roche, and my answer. I should not be surprised if we were to have a battle on this side of Madrid.

To Visc. Castlereagh.   Castello Branco, 1st July, 1809.

The enemy's corps, commanded by Marshal Victor, have continued their retreat from the Guadiana across the Tagus at Almaraz, and along that river towards Talavera; while the corps commanded by Sebastiani have likewise retired towards the Tagus. The retreat of both these corps has been gradual, and they have sustained no loss; although the former has been followed by the army of Gen. Cuesta, and the latter by that of Gen. Venegas.

Gen. Cuesta's advanced guard crossed the Tagus at Almaraz, on the 26th June, and the main body were to follow as soon as the bridge of boats should be completed. Gen. Venegas' corps were, on the 22d, the last day on which I heard of them, at Villarta.

The British army broke up on the 27th June from the camp and' cantonments on the Tagus, and are on their march into Spain by Zarza la Mayor towards Plasencia. The advanced guard will be at Zarza la Mayor on the 3d.

I have the honor to inform your Lordship that I have heard that Gen. R. Craufurd arrived at Lisbon with his brigade on the 28th June.

To the Rt. Hon. J. H. Frere.   Castello Branco, 1st July, 1809.

I have just received intelligence from Oporto, stating that the *Resistance* had passed by, having been at Coruña, which place and Ferrol were in the possession of the Spaniards. I have a letter from the Marques de la Romana, from Orense, of the 25th, in which he states that he had heard reports that the enemy had evacuated Coruña.

To Visc. Castlereagh.   Castello Branco, 1st July, 1809.

Since I closed my dispatch to your Lordship of this day's date I have heard from Col. Roche, who has relieved Col. Bourke at Gen. Cuesta's head quarters. It appears that Joseph Buonaparte had arrived at Toledo on the 22d, with a corps consisting of about 5000 men, and he had crossed the Tagus, and had proceeded as far as Mora to join Sebastiani, apparently with a view to fall upon the corps of Venegas. He had, however, returned to Toledo, as I understand Col. Roche, with Sebastiani's corps and the troops he had brought with him, and he was on his march towards Talavera, where the French were in considerable strength.

The whole of the army of Gen. Cuesta had crossed the Tagus at Almaraz, on the 29th, excepting three divisions, amounting to 10,000 men, which were higher up the river, at and in the neighbourhood of Arzobispo, on the left bank; and his advanced posts were at Navalmoral, on the right bank, and he occupied some villages still nearer to Talavera. The General had determined, however, upon hearing of the collection of the French troops at Talavera, to recross the Tagus; and Col. Roche expected that that operation would be completed by that night. I have recommended to Gen. Cuesta to throw his bridge over the Tagus at a place below the junction of the Tietar with that river, in order that I may join him, or he may join me, if the enemy should move against either of the corps, and that Venegas' corps should be kept in a place of security near Villarta, in which position he threatens Toledo and Madrid, and the enemy's rear, in the event of his moving to this quarter.

To Brig. Gen. Cox, Governor of Almeida.   *Zibreira, 2d July, 1809.*

I enclose a letter which I request you to forward to the Duque del Parque. The advanced guard of the British army will enter Spain to-morrow morning at Zarza la Mayor. It is understood that the French armies are collecting at Talavera, and that King Joseph has joined them with 5000 men. Gen. Cuesta therefore repassed the Tagus, I understand, at Almaraz, on the 29th June.

To the Duque del Parque.   *Zibreira, 2d July, 1809.*

I have had the honor of receiving the letter which your Excellency addressed to me, in which you have informed me of your intention to depute two gentlemen whom you have named to receive the sum of money due on account of the British army to the town of Ciudad Rodrigo.

I shall be obliged to your Excellency if you will direct those gentlemen to proceed to Lisbon, the British Commissary at that city having received instructions to pay the money.

To the Marques de la Romana.   *A Zibreira, 2 Juillet, 1809.*

J'ai reçu hier la lettre que votre Excellence m'a écrite d'Orense le 25 du mois passé, et je vous félicite sur l'évacuation prochaine de la Galicie par l'armée ennemie. J'ai reçu hier les nouvelles qu'ils avaient évacué la Corogne et Ferrol, dont les Espagnols étaient en possession; mais je ne crois pas qu'il y ait des troupes Anglaises de ce côté-là. Je crois plutôt que l'ennemi a été obligé d'évacuer la Galicie par la nécessité de ses affaires en général.

Le Général Cuesta avait passé le Tage à Almaraz à la poursuite de l'armée de Victor, qui s'était repliée du côté de Talavera de la Reyna. Mais, ayant reçu des nouvelles le 29 du mois passé qui lui donnaient lieu de croire que l'ennemi rassemblait toutes ses forces à Talavera, et que le Roi Joseph avait joint l'armée Française avec 5000 hommes; le Général Cuesta avait l'intention de repasser le Tage ce jour-là. Je n'ai pas eu de ses nouvelles depuis le 29 du mois passé. Le Général Sebastiani avec son corps est, je crois, à Talavera, avec le corps de Victor et les 5000 hommes ci-dessus nommés.

Le Général Venegas est à Villarta avec son corps. L'armée Anglaise est en marche pour entrer en Espagne par Zarza la Mayor, Coria, et Plasencia; l'avant-garde sera à Zarza demain matin.

Je ne crois pas que Ney et Soult envahissent le Portugal encore; mais s'ils y entrent, ils y trouveront le Maréchal Beresford avec l'armée Portugaise.

To Don Martin de Garay. Zarza la Mayor, 3d July, 1809.

I have had the honor of receiving your Excellency's letter of the 29th June. When I was about to march the British army into the north of Portugal, I wrote to Gen. Cuesta and to your Excellency on the 29th April, recommending a defensive system for the Spanish armies on the frontiers of Andalusia. I gave this recommendation, not because the continuance of the Spanish armies on the defensive was likely to prevent the enemy from interrupting the operations of the British army; for it was obvious to me, as it must be to your Excellency, that the best mode of preventing the enemy from undertaking such an operation would have been for the Spanish armies to act upon the offensive; but I recommended that Gen. Cuesta and Gen. Venegas should continue on the defensive till I should be able to return to their assistance, from a conviction, that although the army under the command of each was more numerous than that opposed to it, yet the armies of the enemy were more inured to war; and I promised to return and give that assistance which would render the contest more advantageous, at least as soon as I should have settled affairs to the northward. According to my promise, I did return, as soon as Marshal Soult was driven out of Portugal; and my march into Spain has been delayed till this moment, only on account of the want of some necessaries, without which the army could not move; and it did move, without waiting for its reinforcements, on the day after its wants were supplied. I have the pleasure to inform your Excellency, that the advanced guard passed the frontier this day; the army will follow to-morrow and the following days; and no time shall be lost in placing ourselves in communication with Gen. Cuesta.

I shall be much concerned if, in the intermediate time, the enemy should fall with his whole concentrated force on Gen. Cuesta or Gen. Venegas. But as both these Generals are aware of the superiority of the enemy's strength, and the former, in particular, is aware of my near approach to him, I conclude that each of them will have placed themselves in such a situation as that the misfortune which your Excellency apprehends cannot occur.

To J. Murray, Esq., Commissary General. Zarza la Mayor, 3d July, 1809.

I have received your letter of the 1st. It is necessary that your measures, adopted both at Gibraltar and Cadiz, to procure money for bills upon England, should be much more extensive than you have stated them to be. Your agents at those places and at Lisbon should have unlimited power of drawing upon the Lords of the Treasury; otherwise some money may be directed into other channels; and I know that we have no chance of receiving supplies of money in future, excepting for our bills upon England. Claims for deliveries of provisions must not be paid, of course, unless the receipts for the deliveries should be produced. It may be proper to allow those claims, upon a consideration of the particular circumstances in which the deliveries were made by the Commander of the Forces. But the safe rule for your Commissariat is to reject, in the first instance, all claims not duly vouched by receipts.

To the Rt. Hon. J. H. Frere.   Zarza la Mayor, 3d July, 1809.

I enclose the copy of a letter which I have received from Don M. de Garay, and my answer, which I beg of you either to send to that gentleman, or to communicate to him its purport.

I don't think that Don Martin has made a correct or a fair reference to my letter of the 29th April to Gen. Cuesta and himself; nor does he act very fairly in attributing to me the misfortune which may possibly befall Gen. Cuesta or Gen. Venegas. I have repeatedly warned Gen. Cuesta of the danger to which he was exposed till I should join him.

To Lieut. Col. Roche.   Zarza la Mayor, 4th July, 1809.

I have just received your letter of the 3d. I shall be obliged to you to send me to Coria, where I shall be on the 6th, the particulars of the intelligence acquired by the intercepted letters from Victor to King Joseph.

I am glad that Gen. Venegas has put himself in safety. I shall be very much obliged to you if you will endeavor to obtain for me an accurate account of the course of the Alberche, the nature of its banks, the depth of water, &c., particularly low down towards Talavera; whether there are many bridges over that river besides that which has been broken up, or fords, or ferries, the nature of the roads leading to such passages on both sides the river, through what towns they pass.

I shall also be obliged to you if you will mention to Gen. O'Donoju, that I think it would be very desirable, if possible, to get some intelligent person to examine the lower part of the Alberche and the enemy's position upon that river. Till the post of cavalry, mentioned by you, and the infantry which they must have at Talavera, are driven in, it will be impossible to employ an officer in this reconnaissance, unless in disguise. I also request you to mention to Gen. O'Donoju, that I conceive it will be desirable to occupy the Puerto de Baños with the Spanish infantry, which I understand are at Plasencia, as soon as I shall arrive at that city with the British army: they will strengthen our whole position, while we are engaged in our operations against Victor.

To the Rt. Hon. J. Villiers.   Zarza la Mayor, 4th July, 1809.

I received this day your letters of the 29th June and 1st inst. I think you had better employ the physician you mention with the Portuguese troops; I am afraid that he would not answer for us.

I shall appoint Mr. Lees to the Commissariat, and Mr. Melville shall go back to the Pay office, if the Paymaster Gen. requires his services.

I think that I shall not want either of the gentlemen you recommend as my aide de camp, for I have as many as I want; and I read Spanish, and always enter my answers in English.

I shall have the officers tried by a General Court Martial; but I should wish to have a line from you officially upon the subject.

G. O.   Zarza la Mayor, 4th July, 1809.

1. The A. A. Gens. and brigade majors of those divisions and brigades stationed in the neighbourhood of head quarters, must attend at the Adj. Gen.'s office for orders, at 10 o'clock precisely.

2. The brigade majors will attend at the A. A. Gs. of divisions to receive the division orders, at half past 11 o'clock, and at 1 the brigade majors must give out the orders to the adjutants of regiments, which must be given out to troops and companies, and read to the soldiers at evening parades.

3. In case circumstances should prevent the brigade majors from issuing the G. O. to the adjutants of regiments before 3 o'clock on any halting day, they are to receive and issue on that day only the orders requiring immediate execution, of which the General officers commanding brigades are to make the selection, and on the following day the other orders of general regulations.

4. All orders received by the adjutants of regiments must at the first parade, or earlier if necessary, be read to the troops.

5. On marching days the A. A. Gs. and brigade majors stationed near head quarters will attend at the Adj. Gen.'s office for orders, as soon as the troops reach their ground.

6. All orders requiring immediate execution issued on marching days must be given to the adjutants, and read to the troops as soon as possible.

7. The G. O. will be sent from head quarters to divisions at a distance by the first opportunity; those requiring immediate execution must be issued and read to the troops as soon as received; the others, if not received by the General officer of the division before 2 P.M., are not to be issued till the following day.

8. The A. A. Gs., or the brigade major of the division or brigade at a distance to which the G. O. will have been sent, must send to the Adj. Gen. by the first opportunity, a receipt for the orders received, specifying the numbers of each day.

9. When pass orders will be sent, directions will be written on the back of them, stating whether they are to be circulated by the person who will have carried them from head quarters, or to the officers respectively to whom they will have been addressed.

10. Every officer to whom they are addressed must sign his name on the paper on receiving them, and insert the hour of the day at which they reached him.

11. As pass orders invariably must require immediate execution, they must be issued and read to the troops without loss of time.

12. The numberless mistakes which have occurred, and the many instances of neglect and disobedience of orders issued referring to the health, subsistence, or the convenience of the troops, render it necessary not only to observe the early circulation of orders, but if possible, obedience to them and their early and prompt execution.

13. The obedience to orders of general regulations must depend upon the attention of General officers commanding brigades, and Commanding officers of regiments, and their determination to enforce regularity and discipline, but obedience to them requiring execution can be secured by other means.

14. Accordingly the Commander of the Forces desires that officers commanding regiments shall report to the General officer commanding the brigade, that the G. O. requiring the performance of any duty, or the execution of any arrangement, have been obeyed.

15. The General officers commanding divisions and brigades will take care to notify to the troops, to what day they have received bread upon every issue.

17. The Commander of the Forces requests the attention of General officers commanding divisions and brigades to the G. O. of the 4th and 5th of March, by the late Commander of the Forces, relative to the use of the mules allowed for carrying camp kettles, in any service excepting the carriage of camp kettles.

18. The consequence of loading them with other baggage is, that they are unequal to carry the kettles which they are given to convey, and the loads are so ill put on that they fall from the mules, and the camp kettles do not arrive from the march till after the hour at which they ought to be used by the troops.

20. General, staff, and other officers are requested to put their names on the doors of the houses in which they are quartered.

We are advancing towards Plasencia, where, I think, the army will be collected by the 12th. Cuesta is upon the Tagus; but whether on the right or left bank I cannot say. I heard on the 29th that he intended to pass again to the left bank, as he had heard that King Joseph had arrived at Toledo with 5000 men, and that the whole French army was collecting at Talavera. Venegas is at Villarta with his army. I should not be surprised if we had to fight a battle for the possession of Madrid.

I don't think it quite certain that the *Donegal* has passed Lisbon. Lord Wellesley was not expected at Portsmouth, on the 18th June, till the middle of that week, which would have brought us to the 23d or 24th; and it is not probable that he would have passed by on the 29th. The *Resistance* passed Oporto on the 28th, and most probably Lisbon on the 29th, on her way to Messina.

To Vice Adm. the Hon. G. Berkeley.   Coria, 5th July, 1809.

It is desirable that the transports lately arrived from Ireland and the islands should be sent back to England, as well as those respecting which I wrote to you on the 30th June, reserving, of those last arrived, tonnage for infantry to carry 2000 men, of the 2 battalions of detachments which I propose to send back from the army, and to England, as soon as I shall have ascertained exactly the movements and intentions of the enemy. This tonnage is in addition to the 5000 tons mentioned in my letter of the 30th June. I am also of opinion that the transports which brought out the horse artillery ought to be sent home as soon as possible.

To the Rt. Hon. J. Villiers.   Coria, 6th July, 1809.

Since I wrote to you last I find that Cuesta has passed, and is on the left bank of the Tagus. The French have crossed the Alberche, near Talavera, where they have a good position. They have detached across the Tagus; and I believe King Joseph himself is gone in pursuit of Venegas, who has retired towards the passes of the Sierra Morena, so that all is safe till we shall arrive. I shall be at Plasencia on the 8th. The whole army will be there on the 12th, Craufurd excepted.

P. S. I believe that the northern French were at Zamora in the beginning of the month. I have reason to think they are moving from thence to Valladolid. Franceschi has been taken with his 2 aides de camp, riding post between Toro and Tordesillas, on his road to Valladolid; and I understand that a division of troops was in march at no great distance from the place where he was taken, in the same direction.

To Marshal Beresford.   Coria, 6th July, 1809.

I received your letter of the 2d last night. I have done every thing you have recommended respecting our new troops; that is, I have ordered them to encamp near Lisbon for some time.

G. O.   Zarza la Mayor, 5th July, 1809.

1. The Commander of the Forces desires that it may be considered as a standing order, that the troops are not to quit their lines, unless dressed according to the orders of their regiment, with their side arms; excepting when on fatigue duty, in which case they must be in charge of an officer, or non-commissioned officer, according to their numbers.

I am ordered positively to give you nothing; particularly neither ordnance nor military stores, as every thing of that kind was to be given in the way of subsidy. I am willing, however, to assist you, if Mr. Villiers will give me a receipt, or will authorise any one else to give me a receipt for the articles delivered. If Mr. Villiers should decline to do this, to which, by the bye, he has consented both in conversation and by letter to me, I cannot allow you to have any thing, even though I do not want what is essentially necessary to you. If the service should fail in consequence, the fault is not mine.

I have written to the Commandants of Abrantes and Castello Branco, to beg them to assist our convoys with escorts of militia. Our battalions are so lamentably weak, that this is necessary.

I observe, from a letter from Col. Cox, that the Duque del Parque is disposed to annex conditions to the permissions you have asked to encamp within the Spanish frontiers, a compliance with which will defeat the great object of collecting your army.

To the Junta of Plasencia.   Coria, 6th July, 1809.

I have had the honor of receiving the letter of the Junta of Plasencia, dated the 4th inst.; and I am very sensible of the attention and kindness of the Junta in their expressions in their letter to me, as well as in their proclamation to the people under their government. I shall, on my part, do every thing in my power to maintain the discipline of the army; and I have no doubt but that the people of Plasencia will have no reason to complain of the troops; and, in order that they may put the inhabitants of the towns, through which they pass, to as little inconvenience as possible, they construct huts for themselves, and lodgings will be required only for the General officers and officers of the Staff.

To Vice Adm. the Hon. G. Berkeley.   Coria, 6th July, 1809.

I have received your letter of the 2d. I believe there is no doubt that all the French have withdrawn from Galicia, and Kellermann's corps from the Asturias. They were in some strength at Zamora in the beginning of July, and I have some reason to believe were to move towards Valladolid. This looks like a general retreat. I am much obliged to you for the trouble you have taken about our boating.

To Dep. Paymaster Gen. Boys.   Plasencia, 8th July, 1809.

The Q. M. G. has communicated to me your letter of the 5th, which has astonished and disappointed me not a little. I cannot understand why you did not move at an earlier day, after I had quitted Abrantes; nor for what reason you did not make known to me, at an earlier period, the difficulties in procuring conveyance for the military chest, if these difficulties prevented its removal. I beg that, upon your arrival within the Spanish frontier, you will take measures for moving at least two stages in a day, in order to join head quarters; from whence you are not in future to separate yourself without my orders.

To the Commissary General.   Plasencia, 8th July, 1809.

I enclose the copy of a letter which I have received from Mr. Boys, which has surprised and disappointed me not a little. You must have been aware, indeed Mr. Dalrymple was repeatedly informed, that I waited only for money to commence my advance into Spain, as I was determined that the army should not be reduced in that country to the difficulties under which it had labored in Portugal for want of money. Yet I am sorry to observe that Mr. Boys, who, I expected, would have left Abrantes a day or two after me, does not come away till the 5th, nine days after I had set out; and then, instead of bringing with him all the money in his possession, he brings only about £23,000, out of which sum I know that he would have to pay £5000 or £6000 to the Paymasters of the regiments which had been stationed at Castello Branco, and who had omitted to send in their estimates before I quitted Abrantes.

Thus, then, the object for which I stayed so long at Abrantes has been defeated, and the promise which I have made to the Spanish authorities upon the frontier, viz., ' that ready money should be paid for the supplies furnished to the British troops,' will be violated; and the Commissaries will experience all the difficulties in procuring supplies, and the troops will suffer the distress for the want of them, which we suffered in Portugal. All these evils would have been avoided if Mr. Boys had been supplied with 30 carts, which is the largest number that would have been required to draw £60,000 in silver, which I believe is the utmost of the sum he had in the military chest at Abrantes.

It is impossible that any man can pretend that Portugal, or even the neighbourhood of Abrantes, could not supply 30 carts for this service. I cannot and nobody can believe, that, if proper measures had been adopted, a sufficient number of carts could not have been procured to remove the treasure at an early period; and I now beg that, immediately upon the receipt of this letter, you will wait upon the Commissary at Abrantes, and tell him that I desire he will employ parties of the militia at that place to bring in carts in sufficient numbers to remove, not only the money, but the provisions and stores which you have received directions to remove. You will then adopt efficient measures to have the drivers of the carts fed and paid during their march; and you will send off every thing without loss of time. It is necessary that positive orders should be given not to put more than 600 lbs. on any cart, and that a certain number of spare carts should accompany the convoy.

I hope that efficient measures have been adopted to secure the arrival of the £60,000 in Spanish gold with Gen. R. Craufurd, and that I shall not be disappointed there also.

To the Officer of Royal Artillery at Castello Branco.   Plasencia, 8th July, 1809.

I learn from the Dep. Paymaster Gen. that he has been unable to move the military chest from Abrantes for want of carts, and I beg that, upon the receipt of this letter, you will call upon the magistrate at Castello Branco to supply as many carts as he can get, and you will employ the artillerymen under your command to press them. You will then send them under escort of the artillerymen under your command to Abrantes by the road of Villa Velha. After taking the carts to Abrantes the artillerymen may return, as there are escorts at Abrantes for the money as well as for the ordnance stores, &c. The number of carts wanted for the money is 30; but I doubt not but others are required to move the ordnance stores.

To the Officer commanding the Royal Artillery.   Plasencia, 8th July, 1809.

It is desirable that all the horses, belonging to the artillery in different parts of Portugal, should be ordered to be collected at Lisbon, with the exception of those attached to Capt. Baynes' brigade at Castello Branco.

It is desirable that a 9 pounder and a 6 pounder brigade should be equipped for the field with these horses, and should be encamped upon the high ground behind Belem with the seven battalions of infantry now there; and I beg that you will give directions accordingly.

In case this letter should not find you upon the road, I send a duplicate of it to the officer commanding the artillery at Lisbon, through the Commissariat at that station, in order that he may take measures to carry these orders into effect.

To Col. Peacocke, Lisbon.   Plasencia, 8th July, 1809.

I enclose a letter for the officer commanding the artillery, which I beg of you to peruse and deliver to the officer commanding the artillery at Lisbon. Although I have thus given directions that the strength of the body of troops in the camp at Belem should be augmented, I beg that you will understand that they are to move; but not till I shall send orders for their movement, after I shall have received from you and from the General officers commanding them a report of their state, such as I directed should be made in my letter to you of the 28th June.

I beg that you will communicate this letter to Major Gen. Lightburne and to Brig. Gen. Catlin Craufurd, who, I conclude, command these troops.

To the Rt. Hon. J. H. Frere.   Plasencia, 8th July, 1809.

I have arrived here with the advanced guard of the British troops. The army which was with me on the Tagus will be here on the 9th and 10th, having marched some of them from the neighbourhood of Santarem since the 27th of last month. The distance is not far from 200 miles. The cavalry and part of the infantry lately arrived will be up in 2 or 3 days afterwards.

I am going over to see Gen. Cuesta the day after to-morrow, and I shall return here on the 12th. I shall write to you from his quarters.

You will have heard that Gen. Franceschi is taken, with dispatches from Soult to King Joseph, and other interesting papers. I have seen the purport of these papers; but I shall be very much obliged to you if you will send me copies of the originals, which have been sent to Seville, as well as Gen. Franceschi and his aides de camp.

To Lieut. Col. Roche.   Plasencia, 8th July, 1809.

I have received your letter of the 6th. I have this day received from Almeida the purport of the letters taken from Gen. Franceschi's possession, of which I have given to Lieut. Col. O'Lawlor a copy to forward to Gen. Cuesta, who may not have received them.

From these it appears that Soult has evacuated Galicia, and come to Zamora, solely with a view to give repose and to refit his army, and that he intends to plunder Braganza and to threaten Portugal; and he has detached a small corps under Col. Guipé, the precise object of whose operations is not stated. Ney remains, and must remain, in Galicia. I beg that you will tell Gen. O'Donoju that I have no apprehensions for Portugal. Braganza must be plundered, and that we cannot help; but I have taken measures to prevent any serious impression being made upon Portugal. I think, however, that the corps under Col. Guipé may be destined to pass through the Puerto de Perales or the Puerto de Baños, to endeavor to ascertain what is going on in this quarter. The latter will be occupied on the 11th inst., but it is very desirable that some measures should be taken to occupy the Puerto de Perales, from whence the enemy could equally and most effectually annoy my communications with Portugal.

I propose going over to see Gen. Cuesta on the 10th, to stay with him the 11th, and to return on the 12th.

To the Rt. Hon. J. Villiers.   Plasencia, 8th July, 1809.

Beresford will have communicated to you the accounts which he has received from Gen. Cox of the capture of Gen. Franceschi and his aides de camp, and of the letters taken on his person. From these letters it appears to me that Soult has been obliged to come out from Galicia to Zamora solely for the purpose of giving repose to and refitting his army; that he intends to plunder Braganza, which I conceive we cannot well prevent, and by his position, as well as by his movements, to threaten Portugal; that Ney remains in Galicia, in which kingdom he is to fortify certain points, and to occupy them with his troops.

You are aware that Beresford is about to collect his army upon the frontier, somewhere south of the Douro; and I defy Soult to do him or Portugal any injury as long as his army is in its present situation, or by any amelioration of its situation which can be produced in a short period of time. He may be able to plunder Braganza, or any other village; but I trust that the Portuguese government will have firmness sufficient to look at the great objects of the war, and not to disturb our plans or operations by calling for detachments to protect trifling objects upon the frontier; which detachments, after all, will not be able to effect any of the objects which the government would have in view in calling for them. Beresford's army on the frontier of Portugal will protect that country, and will add much to the strength of my left flank. Hereafter it will be able to accomplish more important objects; and, in the mean time, I do not think it much signifies whether a village more or less is plundered.

I arrived here this day. It is said that King Joseph has crossed the Tagus with some of Victor's cavalry and infantry, and the reinforcement he brought with himself, and is gone to join Sebastiani's corps, which will thus amount to 30,000 men; and that his intention is to beat Venegas, who has 20,000 men, and then to penetrate to Seville by Cordova. Victor remains near Talavera with the remainder of his army, it is said, in great distress for provisions.

I enclose the copy of a letter which I have received from Mr. Boys, and the copy of one which I have in consequence written to the Commissary Gen. I shall be very much obliged to you if you will mention to the government the great inconvenience which the army has felt, ever since its arrival in Portugal, for the want of the assistance of the Civil government to procure the supplies it has required, particularly of carriages and mules. For the latter I have written to you, I believe, not less than 10 letters; but they have not yet assisted the British army with one, and the magistrates of the country have rather prevented than aided us in procuring carts.

I hope that now that we have left the country more attention will be paid to our demands, and that I shall not want that which alone I shall require from Portugal, the means of moving the money and ordnance stores which I shall want from Lisbon. I shall be obliged to you if you will send to Beresford the observations contained in the first part of this letter.

To Marshal Beresford.   Plasencia, 9th July, 1809.

I have received your letters of the 4th and 5th. I have not forgotten either the Puerto de Baños or the Puerto de Perales, and have called upon Cuesta to occupy both. The former is already, and the latter will be so in a day or two. I have no apprehension that Soult will be able to do any thing for some time with his whole corps, but I think that that column ought to be watched. Your position in this view of the enemy's

---

G. O.   Plasencia, 9th July, 1809.

1. All the officers belonging to regiments which are in huts, must be encamped with the men, excepting those whose health requires that they should remain in houses: applications for quarters for those officers must be made through the General officer commanding the brigade, to the officer of the Q. M. G.'s department with the division, or with head quarters.

2. The officer of the Q. M. G.'s department with divisions, must quarter the General officers and their staff as near to their divisions and brigades as possible.

3. All officers, whether of the staff or regiments, requiring quarters at head quarters, must apply to Capt. Kelly, of the Q. M. G.'s department; and all officers requiring quarters at the head quarters of any division must apply to the Q. M. G. of the division. No officer, excepting those of the department of the Q. M. G., employed in this branch of the service, must apply for quarters to the magistrates.

4. As commissaries have been appointed to supply all and every part of the army, to whom every individual, entitled to provisions and forage, can apply for what he requires, no application excepting by the commissaries must be made by any officer or soldier, or other persons attached to the army, to the magistrates of the country for any article whatever.

5. A General Court Martial will assemble to-morrow morning, at 11 o'clock, for the trial of such prisoners as will be brought before it.

Major Gen. Mackenzie, President.

	Field Officers.	Captains.	Subalterns.
Major Gen. Mackenzie's brigade	1	2	1
Major Gen. Hill's division	2	1	2
Brig. Gen. Campbell's do.	1	3	1
Total . .	4	6	4

The name of the officer appointed to act as Dep. Judge Advocate will be sent in the course of the day to the President.

All evidences to proceed immediately to head quarters who have been permitted to march with their divisions, and to report themselves to the Adj. Gen.'s office.

operations will materially aid our left. I believe that the enemy do not know now where we are.

In respect to your officers, I have no objection to your appointing them to regiments, if you think you can do so without inconvenience hereafter. All that I say is that the decision of the Commander in Chief and of government upon my letter of the 7th June must be final, and must be carried into execution.

I have not yet been able to obtain a return of our camp stores. As soon as I can get a return, I will spare you what can be given without inconvenience to the British troops; but I must have Mr. Villiers' receipt for every thing.

I should have thought that the arrangements which I had made for paying Mr. Villiers £80,000 of the money lately arrived would have enabled you to have taken the field. I am going to Cuesta's camp, and I shall write to you again when I return.

To the Rt. Hon. J. Villiers.   Plasencia, 9th July, 1809.

I have received your letter of the 5th, and I am perfectly satisfied with any notice taken by the government of the present acts of enmity committed by the people of Portugal on the troops, which I fear that the latter deserve but too well.

We must have some general rule of proceeding in cases of criminal outrages by British officers and soldiers, by which the individuals guilty of them may be brought to early punishment. As matters are now conducted, the government and I stand complimenting each other, while no notice is taken of the murderer; and the example of his early trial and punishment is lost to the troops.

The artilleryman who has committed the murder at Cascaes must be tried according to the laws of the country, or for a military offence under the Articles of War. My opinion is that he, and all guilty of similar offences, ought to be tried (I mean tried in earnest, and not as the officers of the —th were tried) according to the laws of the country; but if the government prefer that we should take cognizance of these offences, as being of a military nature, we will do so at once in every case; but they must assist us in obliging the witnesses to come forward and give their testimony on oath, to which I find they have great objections.

A. G. O.   Plasencia, 9th July, 1809.

The Commander of the Forces having arranged with the magistrates of the different districts and towns in Spain, that the officers, soldiers, and others belonging to the army, are to be furnished with what they require, at the market prices of each place where they may be quartered, makes known to the troops, that the magistrates will cause to be put up, in the square or market place of each town or village, a list of the various articles of provisions, &c. &c. with their prices annexed to them: and in case any of the inhabitants should demand a higher price than that fixed, the soldiers are to complain to their officers, stating what inhabitants attempted to impose upon them, and the commanding officer of the regiment is to make known the soldier's complaint to the magistrates of the town, who will take proper measures on the occasion.

The soldiers are not, however, to attempt to take things by force, or on their own terms, under pretence that large prices have been demanded from them. Heads of departments and persons attached to head quarters, in addition to putting up their names on the doors of their quarters, will always, on their arrival in a new quarter, immediately send their addresses to the Adj. Gen., and to the Commandant at head quarters.

I have been working ever since I have been in Portugal to effect the object proposed by government in respect to the carts; but the army commenced ill before I arrived, and I have never been able to get it right since. I shall most readily come into any measure proposed by government to remedy the horrible abuses and hardships now existing, and occasioned entirely by the mode in which carts are taken for the service of the British army. Let me see the plan of the government before they promulgate it. I have directed that the money borrowed from Quintella at Oporto be repaid to him at Lisbon.

The A.G. to Capt. ——, *and Lieut.* ——, — *regt.*   9th July, 1809.

I am to acquaint you that a General Court Martial will be assembled to-morrow morning at Plasencia, before which you are to be tried, ' For being second in a duel fought on the 19th June last, in the camps near Abrantes, between Lieut. —— and Lieut. ——, of the — regt.' You will please to inform me of the evidences you mean to produce, in order that they may be warned by the Dep. Judge Advocate.

The A.G. to Brig. Gen. Lightburne and Brig. Gen. C. Craufurd.   9th July, 1809.

I am directed by his Excellency the Commander of the Forces to acquaint you that he has been induced to order the second battalions lately arrived from England to remain for a certain period encamped near Lisbon, in order that they may be most minutely looked into and attended to, and brought forward into such a state of discipline as will render them more capable of taking the field with credit and honor to themselves, when they shall be ordered to join the army. I am, therefore, to call your earnest and particular attention, as well to the exercising and forming of the men of these battalions, as to their health, diet, and general conduct. And his Excellency desires that you will transmit to me for his information regular returns and reports of the progress of the different corps, together with such other circumstances as are necessary to remark upon, by every courier that leaves Lisbon for the head quarters of the army.

In order, however, to afford the Commander of the Forces the most exact information of the actual state of the corps, he has directed me to desire you will make immediately a half yearly inspection or review return, conformable to the form directed in the G. O. of the army, of each corps under your command, and transmit them to head quarters without loss of time.

It is his Excellency's further pleasure that the men are exercised at daylight in the morning for such time as may be necessary, as also that they have another parade at sunset every evening; and he hopes the greatest exertion on the part of the officers will be used to render these different battalions in all respects fit for field service.

P.S. Lieut. Col. Walsh, Town Major, receives every day's G. O., and you will please to ascertain they are correctly taken by the different regiments and made known to the men.

To Major Gen. O'Donoju.   Plasencia, 13th July, 1809.

We arrived here last night, and Col. O'Lawlor has this day communicated to me your letter of the 12th, with the information from your officers sent on a reconnaissance towards the Alberche, for which I am much obliged to you.

G. O.   Plasencia, 13th July, 1809.

1. Such regiments as have bakers who can bake biscuit, are immediately to send a list of their names to Mr. Dep. Com. Gen. Dalrymple, and to the Adj. Gen.'s office, and the bakers are to attend at the Dep. Com. Gen.'s this evening, at 7 o'clock.

2. The attention of the General officers is called to the orders of the 8th June, respecting the delivery of provisions by the Commissaries, and the Commander of the Forces begs to have from them a report that those orders have been complied with.

I desired Sir R. Wilson to write to you respecting the 2 battalions of infantry; and I shall be very much obliged to you if you will tell Gen. Cuesta that I have ordered Sir Robert to march on the 15th, and that it is desirable that the battalions should go to-morrow to El Toril, or at all events next day to Majadas, to communicate from thence with Sir Robert, whom I will desire to leave orders for them at El Toril. I have desired Sir Robert to move thus early, in order that he may cover and assist the Commissaries whom I am about to send into the Vera de Plasencia, to endeavor to draw some subsistence from thence.

Sir Robert tells me that the road by Majadas, Talayuela, and the Venta de San Julian, is a good one for artillery. I have sent an officer to examine it as far as Oropesa, and I expect his report to-morrow. If it should turn out to be good, it would probably be most convenient that I should march by that road; and I shall be obliged to you if in the mean time, till I shall receive the officer's report, which I shall communicate to you, that you will ask Gen. Cuesta whether he thinks that any inconvenience will result from my being so far from him when he shall cross the Tagus. If he does, I shall go by the road originally fixed. We shall have some difficulty in getting all the bread we shall require at this place, but I still hope that we shall do.

To Marshal Beresford.   Plasencia, 13th July, 1809.
I have received your letter of the 7th.

Dr. Fergusson writes to Mr. Thompson, to desire that you may have a certain proportion of medicines, for which Mr. Villiers must give his receipt.

I am sorry that I cannot allow any officers to take soldiers as servants from the British regiments in this army. You will observe that the late Commander of the Forces gave orders that officers belonging to regiments in this army should have Portuguese bâtmen and servants, for the hire of which he gave them an allowance; and it would be rather an extraordinary circumstance if I were to allow soldiers as servants to officers not belonging to regiments in Portugal, particularly when the Commander in Chief in England, by their own account, consented to their bringing servants with them from their regiments. I therefore return their application.

In respect to the commissions for your officers, the question is exactly whether the commission by the local government will give their authority equally with that given to others by the Prince. If it will not, they ought to have the Prince's commission.

I don't think I should do you much good in giving you any part of our Commissariat. Nothing can be worse than it is; and I should recommend to you to take the Portuguese Commissariat, and do the best you can with it.

I wish you would desire your Commissaries, and others employed, not to take carts from the neighbourhood of the Tagus for the service of the Portuguese army, and to give up to the British Commissary at Abrantes above 200 carts, which are collected at Thomar for the use of the Portuguese army. You will recollect that to take carts in our neighbourhood is inconsistent with our arrangements for the 2 Commissariats.

In consequence of this seizure of the carts for the Portuguese army, we cannot move our ammunition or our money from Abrantes.

To the Rt. Hon. J. H. Frere.   Plasencia, 13th July, 1809.

I received your letter of the 8th, at Gen. Cuesta's head quarters, to which I went on the 10th, in order to settle the plan of our future operations. I stated to the General my opinion that the principal attack upon the enemy's posts on the Alberche ought to be made by the united force of the British army and the Spanish army under his command; that it would be desirable to detach a corps consisting of 10,000 men, on our left, towards Avila, to turn the enemy's right; and that Venegas, after having driven Sebastiani's corps across the Tagus, by which alone he is understood now to be opposed, should turn to his right, across the Tagus, either at Aranjuez or at Fuentidueña, and threaten Madrid by the enemy's left.

The General proposed that I should make the projected detachment to Avila from the British army, which I declined, on the ground that the British troops, to act with advantage, must act in a body; and that I thought that the detachment might with more propriety and advantage be made from the Spanish army, which already appeared to me to be more numerous than was necessary for the operations on the Alberche, or than would be found convenient in reference to its state of discipline.

I then proposed that this Spanish detachment should march by the Puerto de Baños, that by Arenas and the Puerto del Pico being deemed impracticable for artillery. Gen. Cuesta, however, declined making any large detachment from his army; but offered to send 2 battalions of infantry and a few cavalry, to join Sir R. Wilson's Portuguese brigade, and march upon Arenas, and thence upon Escalona on the Alberche, in communication with the left of the British army. He adopted, however, the remainder of the plan proposed, which we shall begin to carry into execution on the 18th inst.

Gen. Cuesta having declined to send any large detachment to the quarter proposed by me, I of course have no opportunity of requesting that the Duque de Alburquerque should have the command, to which I certainly should have been disposed, as well on account of your recommendation as from his own character.

To the Rt. Hon. J. H. Frere.   Plasencia, 13th July, 1809.

I have received your letters of the 8th; and you will see in the accompanying letters an account of my endeavors to prevail upon Gen. Cuesta to make a detachment upon Avila, and eventually upon Segovia. I agree with you in thinking that such a detachment would be a great advantage in a military point of view, and it might be attended by the political advantages to which you refer.

In order to enable you to endeavor to attain the political advantages, I write the accompanying letter; but I must at the same time inform you that I do not consider the movement to be *necessary* as a military measure; nay, that to order it at present, when we have settled our operations, might be very inconvenient, and would certainly create delay; and I conceive it would excite a jealousy of me in the mind of Cuesta which does not appear now to exist. The General received me well, and was very attentive to me; but I had no conversation with him, as he declined to speak French, and I cannot talk Spanish.

I settled the plan of operations with Gen. O'Donoju, who appears to me to be a very able officer, and well calculated to fill his station. It is impossible for me to say what plans Gen. Cuesta entertains. The general sentiment of the army, as far as I can learn it from the British officers, appears to be contempt of the Junta and of the present form of the government; great confidence in Cuesta, and a belief that he is too powerful for the Junta, and that he will overturn that government. This sentiment appears to be so general, that I conceive that the Duque de Alburquerque must entertain it equally with others; but I have not seen the Duque, as he was at Puente del Arzobispo.

I acknowledge that I conceive that the Junta would gain but little by the change of the person in whose hands the command should be placed; that person, in the existing state of the government, must be formidable to them, particularly if he should be successful; and if this be true, I do not know whether there are not some advantages to be derived from the employment of Cuesta. By dividing the troops into different armies they may certainly diminish the danger; but this security can only be temporary, for in proportion as the French concentrate their troops, the Spanish armies must do so likewise; and they must, when together, be under one head, and this head will be an object of fear and danger to the Junta.

I don't know what your opinion is of O'Donoju: he is certainly an able man, and I think that if it is your opinion that he can be trusted, I could talk confidentially to him; and if I did not guide their measures, and prevent all mischief, either by Cuesta or others, I should at least obtain a knowledge of their real designs.

I have no reason to complain; on the contrary, I have reason to be satisfied with Señor —— ——. He only appears to me to be too anxious to obtain a knowledge of our plans; but I don't know whether I ought to attribute this appearance of anxiety in him to my prejudices against him or to his desire to make his own employment of more importance, to his curiosity, or to his wish to make himself useful. A man in his situation must have a foreknowledge of all our intended operations, and if he is not honest, he has it in his power to do us much mischief. —— —— has certainly the mind and manners of an *intrigant*, and he comes from a part of Spain, of which the people are most likely not to be inimical to the French. Besides the anxiety of —— —— to obtain a knowledge of our plans from me, I have heard him making inquiries respecting the strength of corps from others, with the result of which inquiries he certainly had no concern.

Upon the whole I am not quite sure that it would not have been better to send me 8 or 10 Spanish Assist. Commissaries to act with mine, and that the Junta should have given general orders throughout the country that my requisitions should be attended to.

To the Rt. Hon. J. Villiers.   Plasencia, 13th July, 1809.

I have received your letters of the 6th and 7th. I did not understand, when I desired Mr. Murray to pay you £80,000, that you had already received £35,000, otherwise I should certainly have confined the supply to you to £45,000; but as I ordered that you might have £80,000 out of the sum of money arrived from England, which sum I then thought and still think can be spared from the demands of the army, I desire Mr. Murray to give you the sum of £80,000 besides £35,000 which you have received, making a total of £115,000.

When I reflect that the largest sum you have ever stated to be necessary for you is £125,000, I hope that I may say that the wants of the Portuguese army, in money, have been well supplied by us; and I wish I could say, with equal truth, that our wants in mules, carriages, provisions, &c., for which we are ready to pay, had been equally well supplied by them; or that they had been supplied at all. Seven or 8 regiments of infantry are at this moment waiting at Lisbon for want of 12 mules for each regiment, to be purchased by the officers, to carry camp kettles, medicine chests, &c. &c.!

In respect to further supplies of money for the Portuguese troops, I must regulate them from time to time, by the knowledge I shall have of the state of the treasury at Lisbon, Cadiz, and Gibraltar; and of the wants of the British army; that being, in every possible case, the object to be attended to in the first instance. As far as I can arrange it you shall feel no inconvenience from delay in the issue of money to your orders, which money can be given from the British military chest. But I must consider the British army in the first instance; and you must attribute any inconvenience which may result from the delay, not to me, but to those who have evidently undertaken to accomplish objects which they are not able to reach, from the want of pecuniary means. I send you a dispatch from Mr. Frere, which I beg you to put up in a cover and forward to Mr. Canning.

P.S. I shall answer your letter of the 7th to-morrow morning.

To the Rt. Hon. the Judge Advocate General.   Plasencia, 14th July, 1809.

I have the honor to enclose the proceedings of a General Court Martial on the trial of private * * * *, of the — regt., for mutiny and for attempting to shoot Ensign ——, of the — regt., of which crime the Court at first acquitted him; but upon a revisal of its sentence, under my direction, the Court found him guilty, and sentenced him to be shot.

The Court at the same time represented to me that private * * * * was insane, and they entered into an inquiry upon this subject, of which I likewise enclose the proceedings, as well as the report of Dep. Inspector of Hospitals, Fergusson, on private * * * *'s health, and a memorial from private * * * * to myself.

I am desirous of receiving His Majesty's commands respecting the execution of the sentence of the General Court Martial on private * * * *

G. O.   Plasencia, 14th July, 1809.

4. When a brigade of artillery will be detached with a division of infantry, the officer commanding must give directions to the Commissary of one of the brigades of infantry to provide the artillerymen, drivers, and horses, with provisions and forage.

To Brig. Gen. Cox, Governor of Almeida.   Plasencia, 14th July, 1809.

I have received your letter of the 9th.   I request you to have each man that you may find belonging to the British army clothed and fed.   Send me from time to time a list of their names, and of the regiments to which they belong, and I shall send you directions how they are to be disposed of; and an account of the disbursements made for each man, and I shall have the money reimbursed to you.   I am obliged to you for the orders you have given to the Assist. Surgeon and party of the 87th regt.

I don't think that Soult is able to attack Ciudad Rodrigo, although it is not impossible that he may annoy the frontier.   He has no artillery, and is not well provided with arms.

To Marshal Beresford.   Plasencia, 14th July, 1809.

I have received your letters of the 8th and 9th.   I had already received from the Duque del Parque the extract from Soult's letter, of which I have since received copies from Seville.   The latter are much more full and important than the former, particularly as they relate to Portugal; and I send you the extracts of what is written on this subject.

I don't believe that Ney has quitted Galicia; at least we have not heard that he has; and you will see that Soult ordered him to remain there.   Soult can certainly do nothing against Portugal, for he is in a most miserable state, without arms, artillery, ammunition, shoes, &c.   But if Ney withdraws from Galicia, Romana must in some manner be brought into play.   Your plan for him appears to be a good one, and will, I hope, keep all in check till we shall have decided our affairs with Victor.

I have given orders that you may have 1000 camp kettles, including the 70 without crates.   Villiers must give his receipt for them.   I shall write for your great coats and clothing.   I see no objection to your giving your English officers the bât and forage of their English rank, and 2 months' advance of their regimental English pay.

To Vice Adm. the Hon. G. Berkeley.   Plasencia, 14th July, 1809.

I have had the honor of receiving your letter of the 5th, relative to the disembarkation of the ordnance and stores; and, having conversed on the subject with the Officer commanding the artillery, it appears to me that it would be expedient to retain in the Tagus the ships (11) named in the margin, with the ordnance and stores on board; and that the stores in the other ships, of which you enclose me a list, should be disembarked, with the exception of those on board the *Richmond*, No. 321, which stores are to be left in that ship; and that she, with her stores on board, and those ships from which the stores shall be disembarked, should be sent home as soon as may be possible.

To the Rt. Hon. J. Villiers.   Plasencia, 14th July, 1809.

I have perused Dom M. Forjaz's paper respecting carts, &c., upon which I will send him some observations as soon as I shall have conversed upon the subject of it with the Q. M. G. and the Commissary Gen.   In the mean time I beg you will inform Dom M. Forjaz that the greater part of what he has recommended has already been carried into execution.

The A.G. to Col. Donkin.   14th July, 1809.

In reply to your memorandum on the return of the sick left at Castello Branco,
I am desired to observe that the Commander of the Forces' intention is, that the
G. O. should be strictly complied with, which have been issued for the superintendence of the sick. The proportion of officers to be left with sick men was fixed
by the G. O. of the 19th May, viz. one subaltern for every 30 men of each brigade; consequently, by the return, your brigade should leave 2 officers; and
indeed you have almost the proportion of 100, which requires a Captain. Gen.
Mackenzie's brigade should have left a subaltern; and I have written to that officer
to direct one to be sent. Gen. Cameron's and Hill's brigade should likewise have
left a subaltern, and 2 shall proceed to Castello Branco forthwith; and the attention of the General officers above mentioned shall be called to the neglect of
former orders. With reference to your application relative to Capt. M'Gregor,
the Commander of the Forces directs, that, besides him, a subaltern from your
brigade shall be sent to remain at Castello Branco until further orders.

It appears by the enclosed, Gen. Cameron's brigade did leave an officer; therefore there must be a mistake in your report of not one officer being left behind.

To Lieut. Gen. Sherbrooke.   Plasencia, 15th July, 1809.

I enclose a letter which has been forwarded to me by Dep. Commissary
Gen. Dalrymple from Mr. Commissary ——, containing an account of
transactions at Castello Branco, which does not differ materially from that
which you gave me of the same transactions.

I am not astonished that you and the General officers should feel
indignant at the neglect and incapacity of some of the officers of the
Commissariat, by which we have suffered and are still suffering so much;
but what I have to observe, and wish to impress upon you, is, that they

---

G. O.   Plasencia, 15th July, 1809.

1. In consequence of the representations of the Lieut. General commanding the cavalry,
of the insufficiency of the allowance of the veterinary surgeons, and farriers of the regiments
of dragoons, an additional allowance of 3d. for each horse per month to the former, and
$\frac{1}{2}d.$ per day for each horse to the latter, will be given.

2. Extract of a letter from the Deputy Inspector of Hospitals to his Excellency the
Commander of the Forces.

' Many men have lately been sent to the hospital, both here and elsewhere, in a state of
the utmost filth, some with no shirts at all, and others with only one that had not been
washed for any discoverable length of time; greater attention to cleanliness and the state
of the men's necessaries seems therefore called for in some brigades of the army, and bath-
ing whenever practicable at an early hour in the morning, but at no other time, ought to
be universally practised during the hot season. The worst species of contagious fever is
infallibly generated among the troops by the neglect of personal cleanliness; new killed
meat without salt is very prejudicial; and the mode of issuing and conducting the rations
has been productive of much annoyance, exhaustion, and disappointment, and consequently
of diseases to the soldiers.'

3. The Commander of the Forces is concerned to state, that he has found those soldiers
who were sent into hospitals in the shameful state reported by the Inspector of hospitals,
belonged to the 24th, 31st, and 45th regts., and the German Light Dragoons; and he
desires that more attention may be paid to the men's necessaries by the officers in future.

4. It is very desirable that the officers commanding companies should endeavor to procure salt in sufficient quantities for their men, and that the officers commanding regiments
should, if possible, make some arrangement for supplying the men with breakfast.

7. The army will march on the 17th, and all the arrangements must be made in the
course of this day and to-morrow, for leaving in the general hospital such men as it will
not be possible to move; subsistence to the 24th July must be left for such men as may be
sent to general hospitals, and officers for the sick, in each brigade, according to the proportion in the G. O. 18th May. Commanding officers of regiments will send this day to
the Adj. Gen., before 7 o'clock P.M., a return of carts attached to their regiments.

8. The Commissary Gen. will this day make his arrangements with the Assist. Commissaries of brigades and regiments, to deliver to the troops at Plasencia, to-morrow, 4 days'
bread, viz. 17th, 18th, 19th, and 20th inst.

are gentlemen, appointed to their office by the King's authority, although not holding his commission; and that it would be infinitely better, and more proper, if all neglects and faults of theirs were reported to me, by whom they can be dismissed, rather than that they should be abused by the General officers of the army. Indeed, it cannot be expected that they will bear the kind of abuse they have received, however well deserved we may deem it to be; and they will either resign their situations, and put the army to still greater inconvenience, or complain to higher authorities, and thereby draw those who abuse them into discussions, which will take up, hereafter, much of their time and attention.

I don't enter into the grounds you had for being displeased with Mr. ——, which I dare say were very sufficient; but I only desire that, in all these cases, punishment may be left to me, who alone can have the power of inflicting it.

To Visc. Castlereagh.   Plasencia, 15th July, 1809.

After I had written to your Lordship, on the 1st inst., King Joseph Buonaparte crossed the Tagus again, and joined Sebastiani with the troops he had brought from Madrid, and with a detachment from Marshal Victor's corps, making the corps of Sebastiani about 28,000 men, with an intention of attacking Venegas' corps. Venegas, however, retired into the mountains of the Sierra Morena, and Col. Lacy, with his advanced guard, attacked a French corps in the night, and destroyed many of them. The French troops then again returned to the Tagus, which river King Joseph had crossed with the reinforcement which he had taken to Sebastiani's corps; and this last corps, amounting to 10,000 men only, was on the left bank of the Tagus, about Madridejos, in front of Venegas, who was again advancing. The last accounts from this quarter were of the 8th. The French army under Victor, joined by the detachments brought by King Joseph from Sebastiani's corps, and amounting in the whole to about 35,000 men, are concentrated in the neighbourhood of Talavera and on the Alberche.

Gen. Cuesta's army has been in the same position which I informed your Lordship that it had taken up when I addressed you on the 1st inst.

The advanced guard of the British army arrived here on the 8th, and the troops which were with me on the Tagus arrived by the 10th. The 23d light dragoons arrived yesterday, and the 48th and 61st regts. will arrive to-morrow.

I went to Gen. Cuesta's quarters at Almaraz on the 10th, and stayed there till the 12th, and I have arranged with that General a plan of operations upon the French army, which we are to begin to carry into execution on the 18th, if the French should remain so long in their position.

The Spanish army under Gen. Cuesta consists of about 33,000 men (exclusive of Venegas' corps), of which 7000 are cavalry. About 14,000 men are detached to the bridge of Arzobispo, and the remainder are in the camp under the Puerto de Mirabete. The troops were ill clothed, but well armed, and the officers appeared to take pains with their discipline. Some of the corps of infantry were certainly good, and the horses of the cavalry were in good condition.

I have the pleasure to inform your Lordship that the 7 battalions of infantry from Ireland and the islands, and the troops of horse artillery from Great Britain, arrived at Lisbon in the beginning of the month. Gen. R. Craufurd's brigade are on the march to join the army, but will not arrive here till the 24th or 25th.

To Visc. Castlereagh. Plasencia, 15th July, 1809.

I have nothing to add to my public letter of this date. I enclose to you the last state of the army, with such remarks upon it as may be useful to you. I have but a bad account of the corps arrived from Ireland and the islands; and I have been obliged to leave them still at Lisbon, till they can get mules and other means to enable them to move; and I have desired the officers to take advantage of that time to put them in a state fit for service.

The A.G. to Capt. ——, Lieut. ——, Assist. Surg. ——, — regt. 15th July, 1809.

I am directed by the Commander of the Forces to acquaint you that, agreeable to orders received from England, in which is pointed out that, by the 15th section of the Mutiny Act, a power is reserved to Courts Martial to proceed against persons who have been acquitted of any crimes or offences by the civil magistrates for military offences committed by them; it has, therefore, been determined to bring you before a Court Martial, to be held at the head quarters of the army, as soon as you shall join it. A copy of the charge to be preferred against you I herewith enclose, and it will be necessary for you to send me a list of the evidences you mean to produce in your own behalf. If there should be any Portuguese, or persons in a civil capacity, at Lisbon, whom you may wish to call upon, their expenses to the army and back will be defrayed. You will be pleased, on receipt of this, to set out for the head quarters of the army accordingly, reporting to me your arrival. I have in my possession the authenticated copy of your acquittal by the civil power at Lisbon of the murder, and also that of the Court of Inquiry.

To Major Gen. Mackenzie. Plasencia, 16th July, 1809.

I have perused the proceedings and sentence of the General Court Martial, of which you are President, on the trial of ——, private in the — regt., for striking Ensign ——, of the — regt., and I am concerned that I cannot agree in opinion with the General Court Martial in respect to their sentence, and that I must request them to revise it.

There appears to be no doubt of the guilt of the prisoner ——; and the question remains for consideration whether any circumstances have appeared upon the trial which ought to prevent the Court from passing upon —— the sentence of death.

The only justification that can be alleged is that Ensign —— ' collared the prisoner ——' to take him to a place of confinement, for it does not

G. O. Plasencia, 16th July, 1809.

3. When the Commissary Gen. is unable to issue wine to the troops, either on account of the scarcity of the article, or of the difficulty of issuing it, he must not interfere in any manner with the sale of wine where the troops may be quartered, or in the neighbourhood. The Provost Marshal and his assistants will in that case take care that order is preserved in the wine houses.

G. A. O. Plasencia, 16th July, 1809.

The A. A. G. of the division in which the brigade is that furnished the guards this day, will be responsible that they join their corps in the morning before they move off, except the ammunition guard at the artillery park and the provost guard, which remains as heretofore.

appear in any part of the evidence that —— was struck by Ensign ——, But supposing he was struck by the officer, as it appears he was by the serjeant, it is no justification for the crime of the greatest magnitude that a soldier can commit, and committed, I observe, in this instance, after previous repeated threats. A soldier has modes of redress for violence committed upon him by his officer, without threats and blows; and the General Court Martial cannot intend, by their sentence, to give currency and sanction to an opinion that a soldier can be justified, by any circumstances, in threatening and striking his officer.

I am the more anxious that the General Court Martial should revise their sentence upon this occasion, because I am concerned to state that several instances have occurred lately of soldiers having struck officers and non-commissioned officers in the execution of their duty.

To Major Gen. O'Donoju.   Plasencia, 16th July, 1809.

The officer who was sent out to examine the road by Majadas and Talayuela has reported that it will answer for artillery; so that, in consequence of your letter, we shall march by it. My head quarters will be, on the 18th, at Majadas; on the 19th, Centenillo; and on the 20th at Oropesa. I am sorry to say that we shall march but ill provided with many articles which we require, owing to the deficiency in the means of transport in our possession; and this country is either unable or unwilling to supply them. I have sent a Commissary to Gata and Ciudad Rodrigo, but he has not been able to procure one mule; and I fear that he will not be more successful at Bejar, as there appears a general disinclination to give that assistance to the army which every army requires, more particularly in a country unprovided with magazines or strong places.

Nothing shall prevent me from carrying into execution the arrangements which I settled with Gen. Cuesta when I had the pleasure of seeing him, although to do so will be attended with the greatest inconvenience, on account of the deficiency of the means of transport, which I then hoped that this country and Ciudad Rodrigo would have afforded; but I think it but justice to the army under my command, and to His Majesty, to determine that I shall undertake no new operations till I shall have been supplied with the means of transport which the army requires; and but fair and candid towards Gen. Cuesta to announce to him this determination at the earliest moment. The British army does not require much assistance of this description; none for the baggage of individuals; and what is wanted is to be applied solely to the transport of provisions, ammunition, money, and medical stores. All countries in which an army is acting are obliged to supply these means; and if the people of Spain are unable or unwilling to supply what the army requires, I am afraid that they must do without its services.

I shall be obliged to you if you will lay this letter before Gen. Cuesta for his information, and tell him that I shall send a copy of it to Mr. Frere for the information of the government. I beg you at the same time to inform Gen. Cuesta that I am convinced Señor L. de Torres and Col. O'Lawlor have done every thing in their power to procure for the army the means of transport which we have required.

To the Rt. Hon. J. H. Frere.   Plasencia, 16th July, 1809.

I enclose the copy of a letter which I have written to Major Gen. O'Donoju, which I beg of you to communicate to the government.

It is impossible for me to express to you the inconvenience and risk which we incur from the want of means of conveyance, which I cannot believe the country could not furnish if there existed any inclination to furnish them.

I cannot but observe, however, that although to me, personally, there has been much civility from all classes of the inhabitants since I came into Spain, this has not been the case with the army in general. The officers complain, and I believe not without reason, that the country gives unwillingly the supplies of provisions we have required, and I have been obliged to promise that they shall be replaced from our stores in Portugal; and we have not procured a cart or a mule for the service of the army. This does not look promising; and I shall certainly not persevere if our prospect of good treatment does not improve.

P.S. We really should not be worse off in an enemy's country; or, indeed, so ill, as we should there take by force what we should require.

To C. Flint, Esq.   Plasencia, 17th July, 1809.

The Spaniards took Gen. Franceschi and his two aides de camp, Capts. Antoine and Bernard, on their way from Zamora towards Tordesillas and Madrid; and I saw these gentlemen at Zarza la Mayor, on their journey to Seville, about a fortnight ago. Gen. Franceschi was very anxious that his wife and family should be informed that he was alive, as well as his aides de camp, and not likely to be hurt, although a prisoner. I shall be much obliged to you, therefore, if you will convey to Madame Franceschi de Somme this intelligence through Holland, according to the address, ' *Madame Franceschi de Somme, Rue Ville l'Evêque, à Paris.*'

To the Rt. Hon. J. Villiers.   Plasencia, 17th July, 1809.

I sent you my last dispatch to Lord Castlereagh, which will have apprised you of our intended operations. The infantry moved this morning, and the whole army will be across the Tietar to-morrow, in order to carry into execution the plan of operations concerted with Cuesta.

Mr. Murray is not come up; but as soon as I shall see him, and shall get from him an exact account of the states of our supplies of money, I propose to desire him to give directions that one-sixth of all the money which may arrive from England, and which may be procured for bills at Lisbon, Cadiz, and Gibraltar, may be paid to you for the use of the Portuguese government, your demand being about one-sixth of the estimated expenses.

We do not yet know what the French are doing. The intelligence from Gen. Cuesta looks like a retreat; that from other quarters, as if they intended to fight us on the Alberche.

To Marshal Beresford.   Plasencia, 17th July, 1809.

The infantry of the army moved this day, and the whole will cross the Tietar to-morrow, to co-operate with Cuesta in an attack upon the French upon the Alberche. It is not quite certain yet whether they intend to retire, or to wait for us, but I am inclined to think they will do the former.

I have ordered Gen. Lightburne, and the 2d batt. 5th regt., and 2d batt. 58th regt., to be prepared to obey any orders they may receive from you. Having been in camp for a fortnight, at Alcantara (Lisbon), I conclude that they are now prepared to move. I have ordered the other troops to join me by Abrantes, and I shall be obliged to you if you will arrange that this brigade, which is to join you, should proceed by any other road. You must take care of their subsistence on the road; and I beg you to recollect that they are young troops, unaccustomed to war, and I shall be obliged to you if you will not march them more than 3 or 4 leagues in a day. They will be subsisted to the 24th Aug., before they leave Lisbon.

I asked Cuesta to secure for me the passes of Baños and Perales, and he has occupied the former, but has left the latter to be occupied by the Duque del Parque. I wish that you would send somebody to see how the pass is occupied, and that, at all events, you should have an eye to that pass. It will make me quite secure, and will render me the greatest service that, in their present situation, the Portuguese troops could render. I don't think that the French would like to venture through that pass in the existing situation of their affairs. The bridges of Alcantara and Almaraz being irreparable, they would be in a *cul de sac*, and would have no *exit*, excepting through a desert on the frontier of Portugal.

P. S. If you don't like to have ——, you may leave him at Lisbon.

To Vice Adm. the Hon. G. Berkeley.   Plasencia, 17th July, 1809.

I have had the pleasure of receiving your letter of the 10th inst. I do not understand to what use Dom M. Forjaz could apply the articles which he has demanded from the naval stores. I rather believe, however, that he would require two good cables to be passed across the river, one ahead, the other astern of the boats, to which the boats are fastened head and stern by other ropes. This is the more approved mode of fixing a bridge, particularly in a river liable as the Tagus is to sudden rises and falls.

I have not yet sent off the 2 battalions of detachments, and shall not send them till I shall be more certain of the movements of the enemy. It is probable that it will be so late in the season before they could arrive at Abrantes, that they would experience much delay and inconvenience in embarking in boats before they could reach Valada.

I am glad to find the accounts confirmed which we had received of the evacuation of Ferrol and Coruña by the French troops.

To Major Gen. O'Donoju.   Majadas, 18th July, 1809.

The British army crossed the Tietar this morning, and I have my head quarters at this place. I hear that an officer passed at Bazagona last night, with a letter for me from Gen. Cuesta, and through the army this morning, but he missed me, and I have not yet seen him. I imagine from the dust I saw near Almaraz, that the Spanish army crossed the Tagus this day.

I shall probably meet you at Oropesa, but, if I should not, I mention now, that I think it would be desirable that we should revise our plan for the attack of the enemy, so far as goes to the separation of the two armies. When at Escalona, I shall be 9 leagues from you, and the enemy will have been perfectly acquainted with my movements, which will have been made along his front. It appears to me, that we ought to concentrate our attack, and both armies to cross the Alberche at or near the same place. As long as we are together, no accident can happen to either; when separate, we are both liable to be attacked by the enemy's whole force, and it does not appear to me that any object will be gained by our separation.

To the Junta of Plasencia.   Majadas, 18th July, 1809.

I was much concerned that I was not at home when you did me the honor of calling upon me last night; and I have now the honor of acknowledging the receipt of the letter which you wrote to me.

I am much gratified to learn that I have given you satisfaction during my residence at Plasencia, and that you have no cause for complaint of the conduct of the British troops. A certain degree of inconvenience must be felt by the inhabitants of every town near which an army is stationed, and I did every thing in my power to alleviate that which you would feel from the neighbourhood of the British army.

Upon my entrance into Spain, I certainly expected to derive that assistance in provisions and other means which an army invariably receives from the country in which it is stationed; more particularly when it has been sent to the aid of the people of that country. I have not been disappointed in the expectations I had formed of receiving supplies of provisions, and I am much obliged to the Junta for the pains they have taken upon that subject, and I am convinced that they did every thing in their power to procure for us the other means we required, although I am sorry to say we did not receive them.

To Major Gen. O'Donoju.   Centenillo, 19th July, 1809.

I have received your paper from Col. O'Lawlor, for which I am much obliged to you. We shall be at Oropesa to-morrow. I agree with nearly all that you suggest; I wish you and Gen. Cuesta, however, to consider of the suggestions contained in my note of yesterday.

When the enemy shall retire over the bridge of the Alberche, near Talavera, it is probable that he will destroy it. The question will then arise, whether the river can be crossed there with artillery; if it cannot, in my opinion, the greatest part, if not the whole, of both armies, ought to attack by San Roman, where I understand the river is fordable for artillery; otherwise, while a part of our united army, or the British troops for instance, may be engaged with the whole of the enemy's force on the left bank of the Alberche, the Spanish army may be *hors de combat* on the right bank, by being unable to ford the river, or to repair the bridge. This would be the case, supposing the lower part of the river not to be fordable for artillery; but supposing it is so, I still think that the two armies ought to co-operate with each other, as near as possible, in order to throw our whole concentrated force upon the enemy, and insure a victory to your new troops.

When we shall cross the Alberche the engagement will have begun, the enemy will have assembled his force, and the distance of 3 leagues between the Spanish and British armies will be too much, and will expose both to some risk.

I wish you to consider these points, and I will meet you to-morrow at Oropesa, or at Montalban, if that place shall be more convenient to you, if you will name the hour.

To the Rt. Hon. J. Villiers. Centenillo, 19th July, 1809.

I have only now received your letter of the 13th, and I am glad that I have had it in my power to gratify you with the £80,000. As soon as I shall see the Commissary Gen., I shall desire him to arrange that you shall have one-sixth of all the money we procure for bills, &c., from England, and I can do no more.

It is not my fault if tne British government have undertaken in Spain and Portugal a larger concern than they can find means to provide for.

I must take measures to prevent the British troops from suffering want; and I think I provide very handsomely for the Portuguese subsidy, which amounts to one-sixth of our estimated expense, by allotting to it one-sixth of our supply, whatever it may be. I cannot do more, and cannot give you an unlimited power of taking money from the Commissary at Lisbon.

Col. —— is mad : neither he nor we have any thing to do with the expenses of the Vice consul; and he knows that the Commissary Gen. must pay the expenses of transporting the troops.

I have nothing new from hence. The Spanish army has crossed the Tagus, and I believe that the French are still in the same situation. King Joseph is certainly gone to Madrid.

To Don Gregorio Cuesta. Talavera de la Reyna, 23d July, 1809.

I have the honor to inform your Excellency that 2 divisions of British infantry, and one brigade of British cavalry, will cross the Alberche to-morrow morning at 4 o'clock, and will proceed to the attack of the right of the enemy's position on the heights near Cazalegas. Two divisions of British infantry, and 2 brigades of British cavalry, will remain in reserve on the plain on the right of the Alberche, with their left on the wood near the Duque de Alva's palace, to act in support of the other British divisions, or otherwise, as circumstances may require.

G. O. Oropesa, 20th July, 1809.

The Commander of the Forces wishes that the corps should be as strong as possible, and that no man should be left with baggage whom it is not absolutely necessary to leave in care of it.

The men's arms to be particularly examined this afternoon by the officers; every man must have a good flint, and the dust must be well cleaned from the locks and touch-holes. The Commander of the Forces desires that the unmilitary practice of firing in the neighbourhood of the lines may be discontinued by the troops.

The commissaries must give receipts or pay for whatever they may receive from the inhabitants of the country. The time of the Commander of the Forces yesterday was occupied in hearing complaints of the commissaries having taken different articles of provisions without giving receipts for them, and he trusts that he will have no further ground for noticing this disobedience of orders.

I understand it to be settled by your Excellency, that a Spanish division of infantry and cavalry is to cross the Alberche in a centrical point, between the bridge and the wood in which the Duque de Alva's palace is situated, nearly at the time the British divisions will commence their attack upon the enemy's right; and that nearly at the same time another Spanish division of infantry and cavalry, and strongly supported by artillery, is to attack the bridge over the Alberche. I also understand that your Excellency intends that a large division of infantry, and the great body of the Spanish cavalry, should be in reserve in the plain behind the Alberche.

Having been this evening on the left bank of the Tagus to examine the enemy's position on that side, I am of opinion that great facility will be given, and eventual success will attend, the attack of the bridge over the Alberche, if a battalion with four 6 pounders were this night sent over the Tagus, with directions to the Commanding officer to place himself, and use his artillery, first on the flank of the enemy's defences of the bridge, and secondly, as the Spanish troops will advance, on the left flank of his position on the heights. I am of opinion that if the guns are unlimbered, and taken over by hand, there will be no difficulty in getting them across the bridge over the Tagus, and that they can be at their station in the evening. If your Excellency wishes it, I will send an English officer with them to show where they ought to be stationed.

To Lieut. Gen. Sherbrooke.   Talavera de la Reyna, 24th July, 1809.

I find that Gen. Stewart is gone forward with 2 squadrons of hussars, and he followed the enemy to Sta Olalla, where the rear guard was in force, and he is returning to El Bravo, which is about 2 leagues forward from Cazalegas, where I understand that he has some thoughts of leaving the 2 squadrons. You will be the best judge whether they ought to remain there, and will give your own directions upon that subject. I also

G. O.   Oropesa, 21st July, 1809.
The army will march to-morrow morning; the regiments to be in the ranks as strong as possible.

The army will parade this evening, in marching order, at 5 o'clock, on the right of the high road from Oropesa towards Talavera de la Reyna, to be seen by Gen. Cuesta; the infantry and artillery formed in one line from the left, in the following order:

The 4th division with its left at the point near Oropesa, pointed out by the Commander of the Forces.

Major Gen. Hill's division.

Lieut. Gen. Sherbrooke's division.

Third division.

Lieut. Gen. Payne will receive directions from the Commander of the Forces where to form the cavalry.

The troops will be at open ranks, and will present arms, and officers salute; drums and bands to play a march; each regiment, by word of command from its own commanding officer, when the General will approach its left.

The Commander of the Forces desires that mules, which will bring the provisions, may be allowed to go away as soon as the provisions will be delivered, and those who bring them will have got their receipts; the most serious inconvenience has already resulted from the detention of those mules.

G. O.   Talavera de la Reyna, 22d July, 1809.
One third of each regiment to remain accoutred in their lines, and the whole must be on the alert.

Officers commanding regiments are to keep their officers with their companies.

find that Gen. Cuesta is advancing with his army upon Sta Olalla, and I think it more than probable that he will be in a scrape, and will send to you to move to his assistance. I beg that you will not move till you shall hear from me.

P.S. The Commissary sends you 5000 rations of bread, which I shall be obliged to you if you will divide among the troops of yours and Mackenzie's divisions and Anson's brigade.

To Lieut. Gen. Sherbrooke.   Talavera de la Reyna, 24th July, 1809.

I have just received your letter of 4 P.M., and I have learnt from Gen. Stewart that he has left the 2 squadrons at Sta Olalla. As the Spanish armies are there, they can be of no use, and I am sure will be much better with their regiment. You will therefore do well to draw them in in the morning.

To the Rt. Hon. J. H. Frere.   Talavera de la Reyna, 24th July, 1809.

I conclude that Gen. Cuesta apprised the government of the success of the first operations of the combined armies. We intended to attack the enemy this morning at daylight in his position on the Alberche, and all the arrangements were made and the columns formed for that purpose; but the enemy retired to Sta Olalla in the course of last night. Gen. Cuesta has since marched to Cevolla; and I do not know whether he intends to halt there, or what are to be his future operations.

I have been obliged to intimate to him, since my arrival here, that I should consider that I had performed the engagement which I had made with him as soon as I should have removed the enemy from the Alberche, and should thereby have given him possession of the course of the Tagus, and should have laid open to him the communication with La Mancha and with Gen. Venegas' corps, and that I could attempt no further operation till I should be made certain of my supplies, by being furnished with proper means of transport and the requisite provisions from the country.

This intimation has become still more necessary within the last 2 days, in which I am concerned to say that, although my troops have been on forced marches, engaged in operations with the enemy, the success of which I must say depended upon them, they have had nothing to eat, while the Spanish army have had plenty; notwithstanding that I have returns of engagements made by the alcaldes of villages in the Vera de Plasencia to furnish this army before the 24th of this month with 250,000 rations.

I certainly lament the necessity which obliges me to halt at present, and will oblige me to withdraw from Spain, if it should continue. There is no man that does not acknowledge, even Gen. Cuesta himself acknowledges, the justice and propriety of my conduct in halting now, or in eventually withdrawing; and I can only say, that I have never seen an army so ill-treated in any country, or, considering that all depends upon its operations, one which deserved good treatment so much.

It is ridiculous to pretend that the country cannot supply our wants. The French army is well fed, and the soldiers who are taken in good health, and well supplied with bread, of which indeed they left a small magazine behind them. This is a rich country in corn, in comparison

with Portugal, and yet, during the whole of my operations in that country, we never wanted bread but on one day on the frontiers of Galicia.
In the Vera de Plasencia there are means to supply this army for four
months, as I am informed, and yet the alcaldes have not performed their
engagements with me. The Spanish army has plenty of every thing, and
we alone, upon whom every thing depends, are actually starving.

I am aware of the important consequences which must attend the step
which I shall take in withdrawing from Spain. It is certain that the
people of England will never hear of another army entering Spain after
they shall have received the accounts of the treatment we have met with;
and it is equally certain that without the assistance, the example, and the
countenance of a British army, the Spanish armies, however brave, will
never effect their object. But no man can see his army perish by want
without feeling for them, and most particularly must he feel for them
when he knows that they have been brought into the country in which
this want is felt by his own act, and on his own responsibility, and not by
orders from any superior authority. I shall be obliged to you if you will
make known to the government my sentiments upon this subject.

I have reason to believe that the enemy are in full march towards
Madrid. They had their rear guard in Sta Olalla this day; and I have
just heard that Gen. Cuesta was marching to that place instead of to
Cevolla. I am only afraid that he will get himself into a scrape: any
movement by me to his assistance is quite out of the question. I advised
him to secure his communications with Venegas and the course of the
Tagus, while measures should be taking to supply the British army with
means of transport. If the enemy should discover that we are not with
him, he will be beaten, or must retire. In either case he may lose all
the advantages which might have been derived from our joint operations,
and much valuable time, by his eager desire to enter Madrid on an early
day. The enemy will make this discovery to-day, if Cuesta should risk
any attempt upon their rear guard at Sta Olalla.

To the Rt. Hon. J. H. Frere.   Talavera de la Reyna, 24th July, 1809.

I find Gen. Cuesta more and more impracticable every day. It is impossible to do business with him, and very uncertain that any operation
will succeed in which he has any concern. O'Donoju expresses himself to
be heartily tired of him, and has declared that he will quit him at the first
moment he is unsuccessful. He has quarrelled with some of his principal
officers; and I understand that all are dissatisfied with him, for the manner in which he has conducted his operations near this place. He contrived to lose the whole of yesterday, in which, although his troops were
under arms, and mine in march, we did nothing, owing to the whimsical
perverseness of his disposition; but that omission I consider fortunate, as
we have dislodged the enemy without a battle, in which the chances were
not much in our favor. His want of communication with his officers of
the plan settled with me for the 22d, and his absence from the field, were
the cause that we did the French but little mischief on that day; and of
these circumstances his officers are aware.

Upon the whole, I understand that there is a material change in the sentiments of the army respecting him; and I am told (although I cannot say that I know it to be true) that if the government were now to deprive him of the command, the army would allow that their order should be carried into execution. However, I think that the government, before they take this step, ought to have some cause for removing him, the justice of which would be obvious to every body, or they ought to be more certain that their order would not be resisted by the army than I have it in my power to make them.

To Visc. Castlereagh.   Talavera de la Reyna, 24th July, 1809.

According to the arrangement which I had settled with Gen. Cuesta, the army broke up from Plasencia on the 17th and 18th inst., and reached Oropesa on the 20th, where it formed a junction with the Spanish army under his command.

Sir R. Wilson had marched from the Venta de Bazagona on the Tietar, with the Lusitanian Legion, a battalion of Portuguese caçadores, and 2 Spanish battalions, on the 15th. He arrived at Arenas on the 19th, and at Escalona on the Alberche on the 23d.

Gen. Venegas had also been directed to break up from Madridejos on the 18th and 19th, and to march by Tembleque and Ocaña to Fuentidueña on the Tagus, where that river is crossed by a ford, and thence to Arganda, where he was to arrive on the 22d and 23d.

The combined armies moved on the 22d from Oropesa, and the advanced guards attacked the enemy's outposts at Talavera. Their left was turned by the 1st hussars and the 23d light dragoons, under Gen. Anson, and directed by Lieut. Gen. Payne, and by the division of infantry under the command of Major Gen. Mackenzie, and they were driven in by the Spanish advanced guard under the command of Gen. Zayas and the Duque de Alburquerque. We lost 11 horses by the cannonade from the enemy's position on the Alberche, and the Spaniards had some men wounded.

The columns were formed for the attack of this position yesterday, but the attack was postponed till this morning, by desire of Gen. Cuesta, when the different corps destined for the attack were put in motion. But the enemy had retired at about one in the morning to Sta Olalla, and thence towards Torrijos, I conclude, to form a junction with the corps under Gen. Sebastiani. I have not been able to follow the enemy as I could wish, on account of the great deficiency in the means of transport with this army, owing to my having found it impossible to procure even one mule or a cart in Spain.

I enclose the copy of a letter which I thought it proper to address upon this subject to Major Gen. O'Donoju, the Adj. Gen. of the Spanish army, as soon as I found that this country could furnish no means of this description; and I have since informed Gen. Cuesta, that I should consider the removal of the enemy from his position on the Alberche as a complete performance on my part of the engagement into which I had entered with him in his camp on the 11th inst., as that operation, if advantage was duly taken of it, would give him possession of the course of the Tagus, and would open his communication with La Mancha and with Venegas.

Within these 2 days I have had still more reason for adhering to my determination to enter into no new operation, but rather to halt, and even to return to Portugal, if I should not be supplied as I ought, as, notwithstanding His Majesty's troops have been engaged in very active operations, the success of which depended no less upon their bravery and exertions than upon the example they should hold out and the countenance they should give to the Spanish troops, they have been in actual want of provisions for these last 2 days; and even if I should have been willing, under such circumstances, to continue my co-operation with Gen. Cuesta, I am unable to do so with any justice to the troops. Gen. Cuesta is, I believe, fully sensible of the propriety of my determination, and I understand that he has urged the Central Junta to adopt vigorous measures to have our wants supplied. It is certain that at the present moment the people of this part of Spain are either unable or unwilling to supply them; and in either case, and till I am supplied, I do not think it proper, and indeed I cannot, continue my operations in Spain.

I ought probably to have stipulated that I should be supplied with the necessary means of transport before the army entered Spain. I did require and adopted the measures necessary to procure these means, which I conceived would have answered, considering the large supplies of the same kind which the army under the command of the late Sir J. Moore had procured; and as I could not engage to enter upon any operations in Spain which should not be consistent with the defence of Portugal, I did not think it proper to make any stipulation for the advantage of the troops, which stipulation after all did not appear necessary, in order to enable me to procure what I wanted.

I have great hopes, however, that before long I shall be supplied from Andalusia and La Mancha with the means which I require, and I shall then resume the active operations which I have been compelled to relinquish.

To Major Gen. O'Donoju.　　　　　Talavera de la Reyna, 25th July, 1809.

It is difficult to guess what are the enemy's ultimate objects. That which he has immediately in view is evidently to join with Sebastiani, who would have been in a bad scrape if we had beaten Victor yesterday. I think also that they must have some troops at Madrid, probably Suchet's corps, to oppose Venegas. He, I conclude, is by this time pretty well advanced towards, if not at, Arganda.

I am doing every thing in my power to procure for the army means of transport and provisions. I hope I have got some of the former, which may reach me in 3 or 4 days, and in the mean time I may get something to eat. We are still in great distress for provisions, which I don't see any very early prospect of relieving.

I should recommend to Gen. Cuesta to be very cautious in his movements, particularly of the main body of his army, and to direct his march rather to the right towards Toledo than to the left towards Madrid.

I have 2 divisions of infantry and 2 regiments of cavalry at Cazalegas and Brujel, and Sir R. Wilson at Escalona; the rest of the army here. I should not be surprised if the enemy, when joined, were to offer us battle again, particularly if they have any thing at Madrid to oppose Venegas.

To Major Gen. O'Donoju.   Cazalegas, 25th July, 1809.

I have just returned from Cevolla, where I heard that Gen. Cuesta was about to retire across the Alberche. I have ordered Gen. Sherbrooke to remain here with his corps till to-morrow 'morning, at all events, unless he should be hard pressed by the enemy.

I think that, supposing the Spanish army should cross the Alberche, it would be desirable to occupy and fortify the sand hills on the left bank of that river, near the bridge. But it would probably be best not to cross the river this evening, but to let the troops halt on this side, holding the heights with your advanced guard; and give us time till to-morrow morning to consider of the position in which it would be most expedient to place the combined armies to receive the attack which it is to be hoped the enemy will make upon us. No position can be worse than that which we occupied before the French retired; but I propose to make a further reconnaissance this afternoon, and I think I shall be able to propose one to the General which will answer our purpose.

Pray do not give up the sand hills on the left side of the bridge.

To Lieut. Gen. Sherbrooke.   Talavera de la Reyna, 25th July, 1809.

I have reason to think that the enemy are drawing together their forces between Torrijos and Puebla de Montalban, by which position they threaten the right of our position by Cevolla. I do not know that there are any Spanish troops at that place, the whole Spanish army being, as I believe, at Sta Olalla. I wish therefore that you would this night send 2 squads. of hussars to Cevolla, and desire them to report all extraordinaries to you as well as to me. I think also that you should order Mackenzie to join you at daylight in the morning; for if I should find that Cevolla is not occupied by the Spanish army to-morrow morning or this night, I shall send either one or both of your divisions to that place. Cevolla is about one league and a half from you to the south east towards the Tagus.

To the Duke of Richmond.   Talavera de la Reyna, 25th July, 1809.

We formed a junction with the Spanish army under Gen. Cuesta, on the 20th, at Oropesa; and on the 22d our advanced guards drove in the enemy's outposts at this place. We were to have attacked him in his position on the Alberche yesterday morning; but Victor retired in the night, and is gone towards Toledo, I believe, to join himself with Sebastiani. Whether they will offer us battle again when joined, or will retire to the northward, I cannot tell. We have certainly closed upon Madrid on both sides, with Venegas' corps of 20,000 men at Arganda, and Sir R. Wilson's Portuguese and Spanish corps of 4000 at Escalona; and I think the question whether they will offer us battle or not depends upon their means of defending Madrid, without the assistance of their main army. I think, however, that, with or without a battle, we shall be at Madrid soon: and I think it best for the Spaniards that they should never fight any general action.

The A.G. to Brig. Gen. C. Craufurd. 25th July, 1809.

I have the honor to acknowledge the receipt of the different reports of the regiments inspected by you, which have been laid before the Commander of the Forces. I am directed to acquaint you that his Excellency was desirous of having not only these, but the regular review returns of each regiment, according to the form in the regulations of the army. The 1st is the field return; 2d, that of the whole regiment, accounting for every man, showing his age, size, &c.; 3d, the return of clothing, arms, and accoutrements. As I presume the regiments have the forms of these returns, I do not send them, but request they may be made out and forwarded immediately.

The A. G. to Col. Donkin. 25th July, 1809.

In reply to your letter of the 20th inst., I am directed by the Commander of the Forces to acquaint you that he does not know of any instance where Colonels on the staff have been allowed aides de camp. They were not permitted in the last campaign in Spain to Cols. Langwerth and Dreiberg, then Colonels on the staff; a Brigade Major to the brigade being all that was allowed.

To Major Gen. O'Donoju. Talavera de la Reyna, 26th July, 1809.

I have just received your letter of last night. I have not heard of the biscuit you mention; but if I should get that, I am ready to join you immediately. I rather believe, however, that you are mistaken respecting this business. I am now going to look out for some position near Cevolla, in case the enemy should advance, as I think that upon the Alberche is very bad.

I am of opinion that the best thing which can happen would be that the enemy should attack us. I shall support Gen. Cuesta, as far as is in my power, whether he moves to Cevolla or retreats here.

To Lieut. Gen. Sherbrooke. Talavera de la Reyna, 26th July, 1809.

In a note which you wrote me yesterday, at half past 4, you mention some biscuit taken from the enemy at Maqueda. I know nothing of the circumstances attending this capture, which I conclude are referred to in the letter from Sir R. Wilson, which ought to have been, but was not, in the packet. Pray send it to me as soon as possible, or, if you have mislaid it, let me know its purport.

To Lieut. Gen. Sherbrooke. Talavera de la Reyna, 27th July, 1809, past 9 A.M.

As soon as you shall receive this, you may withdraw across the river. Leave Mackenzie's division and the cavalry at their old position in the wood, and come yourself with the Germans to the town. If you have no enemy near you, it does not much signify where you cross the river; if you have an enemy near you, I recommend you to cross at a ford nearer the bridge, and at a greater distance from the heights, than the ford is at which you first crossed.

P.S. I desired Murray to look this morning for such a ford as I have above described, and to have it shown you.

To Visc. Castlereagh. Talavera de la Reyna, 29th July, 1809.

Gen. Cuesta followed the enemy's march with his army from the Alberche, on the morning of the 24th, as far as Sᵗᵃ Olalla, and pushed forward his advanced guard as far as Torrijos. For the reasons stated to your Lordship in my dispatch of the 24th, I moved only 2 divisions of infantry and a brigade of cavalry across the Alberche to Cazalegas, under the command of Lieut. Gen. Sherbrooke, with a view to keep up the communication between Gen. Cuesta and me, and with Sir R. Wilson's corps at Escalona.

It appears that Gen. Venegas had not carried into execution that part of the plan of operations which related to his corps, and that he was still at Daymiel, in La Mancha; and the enemy, in the course of the 24th, 25th, and 26th, collected all his forces in this part of Spain, between Torrijos and Toledo, leaving but a small corps of 2000 men in that place. This united army thus consisted of the corps of Marshal Victor, of that of Gen. Sebastiani, and of 7000 or 8000 men, the guards of Joseph Buonaparte, and the garrison of Madrid; and it was commanded by Joseph Buonaparte, aided by Marshals Jourdan and Victor, and by Gen. Sebastiani.

On the 26th, Gen. Cuesta's advanced guard was attacked near Torrijos, and obliged to fall back; and the General retired with his army on that day to the left bank of the Alberche, Gen. Sherbrooke continuing at Cazalegas, and the enemy at Sta Olalla. It was then obvious that the enemy intended to try the result of a general action, for which the best position appeared to be in the neighbourhood of Talavera; and Gen. Cuesta having consented to take up this position on the morning of the 27th, I ordered Gen. Sherbrooke to retire with his corps to its station in the line, leaving Gen. Mackenzie with a division of infantry and a brigade of cavalry as an advanced post in the wood, on the right of the Alberche, which covered our left flank.

The position taken up by the troops at Talavera extended rather more than 2 miles: the ground was open upon the left, where the British army was stationed, and it was commanded by a height, on which was placed *en échelon*, as the second line, a division of infantry under the orders of Major Gen. Hill. There was a valley between the height and a range of mountains still farther upon the left, which valley was not at first occupied, as it was commanded by the height before mentioned; and the range of mountains appeared too distant to have any influence on the expected action. The right, consisting of Spanish troops, extended immediately in front of the town of Talavera, down to the Tagus. This part of the ground was covered by olive trees, and much intersected by banks and ditches. The high road leading from the bridge over the Alberche was defended by a heavy battery in front of a church, which was occupied by Spanish infantry. All the avenues of the town were defended in a similar manner. The town was occupied, and the remainder of the Spanish infantry was formed in 2 lines behind the banks on the road which led from the town, and the right to the left of our position. In the centre, between the 2 armies, there was a commanding spot of ground, on which we had commenced to construct a redoubt, with some open ground in its rear. Brig. Gen. Alex. Campbell was posted at this spot with a division of infantry, supported in his rear by Gen. Cotton's brigade of dragoons and some Spanish cavalry.

At about 2 o'clock on the 27th, the enemy appeared in strength on the left bank of the Alberche, and manifested an intention to attack Gen.

Mackenzie's division. The attack was made before they could be withdrawn; but the troops, consisting of Gen. Mackenzie's and Col. Donkin's brigades, and Gen. Anson's brigade of cavalry, and supported by Gen. Payne with the other 4 regiments of cavalry in the plain between Talavera and the wood, withdrew in good order, but with some loss, particularly by the 2d batt. 87th regt., and the 2d batt. 31st regt., in the wood. Upon this occasion, the steadiness and discipline of the 45th regt., and the 5th batt. 60th regt., were conspicuous, and I had particular reason for being satisfied with the manner in which Major Gen. Mackenzie withdrew this advanced guard. As the day advanced, the enemy appeared in larger numbers on the right of the Alberche, and it was obvious that he was advancing to a general attack upon the combined armies. Gen. Mackenzie continued to fall back gradually upon the left of the position of the combined armies, where he was placed in the second line in the rear of the Guards, Col. Donkin being placed in the same situation farther upon the left, in the rear of the King's German Legion.

The enemy immediately commenced his attack, in the dusk of the evening, by a cannonade upon the left of our position, and by an attempt with his cavalry to overthrow the Spanish infantry, posted, as I have before stated, on the right. This attempt entirely failed. Early in the night, he pushed a division along the valley on the left of the height occupied by Gen. Hill, of which he gained a momentary possession; but Major Gen. Hill attacked it instantly with the bayonet, and regained it. This attack was repeated in the night, but failed; and again, at daylight, on the morning of the 28th, by 2 divisions of infantry, and was repulsed by Major Gen. Hill. Major Gen. Hill has reported to me, in a particular manner, the conduct of the 29th regt., and of the 1st batt. 48th regt., in these different affairs, as well as that of Major Gen. Tilson and Brig. Gen. R. Stewart. We lost many brave officers and soldiers in the defence of this important point in our position; among others, I cannot avoid mentioning Brigade Major Fordyce and Brigade Major Gardner; and Major Gen. Hill was himself wounded, but I am happy to say but slightly. The defeat of this attempt was followed about noon by a general attack with the enemy's whole force upon the whole of that part of the position occupied by the British army.

In consequence of the repeated attempts upon the height upon our left, by the valley, I had placed 2 brigades of British cavalry in that valley, supported in the rear by the Duque de Alburquerque's division of Spanish cavalry. The enemy then placed light infantry in the range of mountains on the left of the valley, which were opposed by a division of Spanish infantry, under Lieut. Gen. Bassecourt.

The general attack began by the march of several columns of infantry into the valley, with a view to attack the height occupied by Major Gen. Hill. These columns were immediately charged by the 1st hussars, K. G. L., and 23d light dragoons, under Brig. Gen. Anson, directed by Lieut. Gen. Payne, and supported by Brig. Gen. Fane's brigade of heavy cavalry; and although the 23d dragoons suffered considerable loss, the charge had the effect of preventing the execution of that part of the enemy's plan. At the same time, he directed an attack upon Brig. Gen. Alex. Campbell's position in the centre of the combined armies, and on the right of the British. This attack was most successfully repulsed by Brig. Gen. Campbell, supported by the King's regiment of Spanish cavalry, and 2 battalions of Spanish infantry, and Brig. Gen. Campbell took the enemy's cannon. The Brig. General mentions particularly the conduct of the 97th, the 2d batt. 7th, and of the 2d batt. of the 53d regts.; and I was highly satisfied with the manner in which this part of the position was defended.

An attack was also made at the same time upon Lieut. Gen. Sherbrooke's division, which was in the left and centre of the first line of the British army. This attack was most gallantly repulsed by a charge with bayonets by the whole division; but the brigade of Guards, which were on the right, having advanced too far, were exposed on their left flank to the fire of the enemy's batteries, and of their retiring columns, and the division was obliged to retire towards the original position, under cover of the second line of Gen. Cotton's brigade of cavalry, which I moved from the centre, and of the 1st batt. 48th regt. I had moved this last regiment from its position on the height as soon as I observed the advance of the Guards, and it was formed in the plain, and advanced upon the enemy, and covered the formation of Lieut. Gen. Sherbrooke's division.

Shortly after the repulse of this general attack, in which apparently all the enemy's troops were employed, he commenced his retreat across the Alberche, which was conducted in the most regular order, and was effected during the night, leaving in our hands 20 pieces of cannon, ammunition, tumbrils, and some prisoners.

Your Lordship will observe, by the enclosed return, the great loss which we have sustained of valuable officers and soldiers in this long and hard fought action with more than double our numbers. That of the enemy has been much greater. I have been informed that entire brigades of infantry have been destroyed; and indeed the battalions which retreated were much reduced in numbers. I have particularly to lament the loss of Major Gen. Mackenzie, who had distinguished himself on the 27th, and of Brig. Gen. Langwerth, of the King's German Legion, and of Brigade Major Beckett, of the Guards.

Your Lordship will observe that the attacks of the enemy were principally, if not entirely, directed against the British troops. The Spanish Commander in Chief, his officers and troops, manifested every disposition to render us assistance, and those of them who were engaged did their duty; but the ground which they occupied was so important, and its front at the same time so difficult, that I did not think it proper to urge them to make any movement on the left of the enemy while he was engaged with us.

I have reason to be satisfied with the conduct of all the officers and troops. I am much indebted to Lieut. Gen. Sherbrooke for the assistance I received from him, and for the manner in which he led on his division to the charge with bayonets; to Lieut. Gen. Payne and the cavalry, particularly Brig. Gen. Anson's brigade, to Major Gens. Hill and Tilson, Brig. Gens. Alex. Campbell, R. Stewart, and Cameron, and to the divisions and brigades of infantry under their command respectively; particularly to the 29th regt., commanded by Col. White; to the 1st batt. 48th, commanded by Col. Donellan; afterwards, when that officer was wounded, by Major Middlemore; to the 2d batt. 7th, commanded by Lieut. Col. Sir W. Myers; to the 2d batt. 53d, commanded by Lieut. Col. Bingham; to the 97th, commanded by Col. Lyon; to the 1st batt. of detachments, commanded by Lieut. Col. Bunbury; to the 2d batt. 30th, commanded by Major Watson; the 45th, commanded by Lieut. Col. Guard; and to the 5th batt. 60th, commanded by Major Davy.

The advance of the brigade of Guards was most gallantly conducted by Brig. Gen. H. Campbell; and, when necessary, that brigade retired and formed again in the best order. The artillery, under Brig. Gen. Howorth, was also throughout these days of the greatest service; and I had every reason to be satisfied with the assistance I received from the Chief Engineer, Lieut. Col. Fletcher; the Adj. Gen., Brig. Gen. the Hon. C. Stewart; the Q. M. G., Col. Murray; and the officers of those departments respectively; and from Lieut. Col. Bathurst, and the officers of my personal Staff.

I also received much assistance from Col. O'Lawlor, of the Spanish service, and from Brig. Gen. Whittingham, who was wounded in bringing up the 2 Spanish battalions to the assistance of Brig. Gen. Alex. Campbell.

Return of Ordnance captured from the enemy at the battle of Talavera.

15 pieces of cannon, of various calibre.
2 howitzers.
2 tumbrils, with ammunition complete.

Return of the numbers of killed, wounded, and missing at Talavera de la Reyna on the 27th and 28th July, 1809.

	Officers.	Serjeants.	R., and F.	Horses.	Total loss of officers, non-commissioned officers, and R. and F.
Killed	40	28	789	211	857
Wounded	195	165	3553	71	3913
Missing	9	15	629	159	653

Memorandum upon the battle of Talavera.*

The position was well calculated for the troops which were to occupy it. The ground in front of the British army was open, that in front of the Spanish army covered with olive trees, intersected by roads, ditches, &c. The Spanish infantry was posted behind the bank of the road leading from Talavera to the left of the position.

The German Legion were on the left of the position in the first line. I had intended this part for the Guards; but I was unfortunately out, employed in bringing in Gen. Mackenzie's advanced guard, when the

* See Appendix to this volume for the French report of the battle of Talavera : Maréchal Jourdan au Maréchal Soult. Bargas, 30 Juillet, 1809 (p. 82 b).

troops took up their ground. The 5th and 7th battalions of the Legion did not stand their ground on the evening, and in the beginning of the night of the 27th, which was the cause of the momentary loss of the height in the second line. Gen. Sherbrooke moved his division, which was the left of the first line, to support Gen. Hill's attack, in order to regain the height; and it was difficult to resume in the night the exact position which had been first marked out; and in fact, on account of these circumstances, we had not that precise position until after the enemy's attack upon the height at daylight in the morning had been repulsed.

G. O.   Talavera de la Reyna, 29th July, 1809.

1. The Commander of the Forces returns his thanks to the officers and troops, for their gallant conduct in the 2 trying days of yesterday and the day before, in which they had been engaged with, and beaten off, the repeated attacks of an army infinitely superior in number. He has particularly to request that Lieut. Gen. Sherbrooke will accept his thanks, for the assistance he has received from him, as well as for the manner in which he led on the infantry under his command to the charge of the bayonet. Major Gen. Hill and Brig. Gen. A. Campbell are likewise entitled in a particular manner to the acknowledgments of the Commander of the Forces, for the gallantry and ability with which they maintained their posts against the attacks made upon them by the enemy.

The Commander of the Forces has likewise to acknowledge the ability with which the late Major Gen. Mackenzie (whose subsequent loss the Commander of the Forces laments) withdrew the division under his command from the out-posts, in front of the enemy's army, on the 27th inst.; as well as to Col. Donkin for his conduct on that occasion.

The Commander of the Forces likewise considers Lieut. Gen. Payne and the cavalry, particularly Brig. Gen. Anson and his brigade, who was principally engaged with the enemy, to be entitled to his acknowledgments; as well as Brig. Gen. Howorth and his artillery, Major Gen. Tilson, Brig. Gen. R. Stewart, Brig. Gen. Cameron, and the brigades under their commands, respectively. He had opportunities of noticing the gallantry and discipline of the 5th batt. 60th, and the 45th, on the 27th, and of the 29th and 1st batt. 48th, on that night, and on the 28th, of the 7th and 53d; and he requests their commanding officers, Major Davy, Col. Guard, Col. White, Col. Donellan, Lieut. Col. Sir Wm. Myers, and Lieut. Col. Bingham, to accept his particular thanks.

The charge made by the brigade of Guards under the command of Brig. Gen. H. Campbell, on the enemy's attacking column, was a most gallant one; and the mode in which it was afterwards covered by the 1st batt. 48th, was most highly creditable to that most excellent corps, and to their commanding officer, Major Middlemore. The Commander of the Forces requests Col. Fletcher, the chief engineer, Brig. Gen. the Hon. C. Stewart, A. G., Col. Murray, Q. M. G., and the officers of those departments respectively; and Lieut. Col. Bathurst and those of his personal staff, will accept his thanks for the assistance he received from them throughout these trying days.

2. The bakers of the different brigades, who have already been employed by the Com. General, will be sent immediately to his stores to receive his directions under a non-commissioned officer of Brig. Gen. Cameron's brigade, to parade at the Commander of the Forces, to receive instructions from Major Campbell, A. A. G.

3. Two camp kettles to be immediately sent from every regiment, for the wounded men in the general hospital at Talavera.

4. Commanding officers of regiments and brigades will direct that all arms, collected in the field of battle, may be sent in by a proper escort to such artillery stores as Brig. Gen. Howorth shall point out.

In the return of killed, wounded, and missing, directed to be sent in yesterday, attention must be paid to specify the same in two distinct returns, one of the 27th, and one of the 28th; as also to state the names of the officers killed, wounded, and missing, mentioning whether slightly or severely.

All prisoners and deserters to be sent to the Provost Marshal.

The names of the General and staff officers, killed, wounded, and missing, to be specified in the returns called for; these returns must be sent in to the Adj. Gen.'s office before 8 o'clock to-morrow morning at the latest.

G. P. O.   Talavera de la Reyna, 29th July, 1809.

The Commander of the Forces calls the attention of officers commanding brigades and regiments to prevent the practice of the soldiers firing off their muskets in camp; such men, whose arms cannot be drawn, must be regularly paraded, and their firelocks discharged at the same time.

The advance of the Guards to the extent to which it was carried was nearly fatal to us, and the battle was certainly saved by the advance, position, and steady conduct of the 48th regt., upon which Gen. Sherbrooke's division formed again.

The ground in front of the Spanish troops would not have been unfavorable to an attack upon the enemy's flank, while they were engaged with us, as there were broad roads leading from Talavera and different points of their position, in a direct line to the front, as well as diagonally to the left : but the Spanish troops are not in a state of discipline to attempt a manœuvre in olive grounds, &c., and if they had got into confusion, all would have been lost.

G. O. Horse Guards, 18th Aug. 1809.

The Commander in Chief has received the King's commands to notify to the army the splendid victory obtained by his troops in Spain, under the command of Lieut. Gen. the Rt. Hon. Sir A. Wellesley, on the 27th and 28th of the last month, at the battle of Talavera de la Reyna.

His Majesty is confident that his army will learn, with becoming exultation, that the enemy, after escaping by a precipitate retreat from the well concerted attack with which Sir A. Wellesley, in conjunction with the Spanish army, had threatened him on the 24th July, concentrated his force, by calling to his aid the corps under the French General Sebastiani, and the garrison of Madrid, and thus reinforced, again approaching the allied army on the 27th July; and on this occasion, owing to the local circumstances of its position, and to the deliberate purpose of the enemy to direct his whole efforts against the troops of His Majesty, the British army sustained nearly the whole weight of this great contest, and has acquired the glory of having vanquished a French army double its numbers, not in a short and partial struggle, but in a battle obstinately contested on 2 successive days (not wholly discontinued even throughout the intervening night), and fought under circumstances which brought both armies into close and repeated combat.

The King, in contemplating so glorious a display of the valor and prowess of his troops, has been graciously pleased to command that his Royal approbation of the conduct of the army serving under the command of Lieut. Gen. Sir A. Wellesley shall be thus publicly declared in General Orders.

The Commander in Chief has received the King's commands to signify, in the most marked and special manner, the sense His Majesty entertains of Lieut. Gen. Sir A. Wellesley's personal services on this memorable occasion, not less displayed in the result of the battle itself than in the consummate ability, valor, and military resource, with which the many difficulties of this arduous and protracted contest were met and provided for by his experience and judgment.

The conduct of Lieut. Gen. Sherbrooke, second in command, has entitled him to the King's marked approbation : His Majesty has observed, with satisfaction, the manner in which he led on the troops to the charge with the bayonet, a species of combat which on all occasions so well accords with the dauntless character of British soldiers.

His Majesty has noticed with the same gracious approbation the conduct of the several General and other officers. All have done their duty ; most of them have had occasions of eminently distinguishing themselves, the instances of which have not escaped His Majesty's attention.

It is His Majesty's command, that His Royal approbation and thanks shall be given, in the most distinct and most particular manner, to the non-commissioned officers and private men. In no instance have they displayed, with greater lustre, their native valor and characteristic energy; nor have they on any former occasion more decidedly proved their superiority over the inveterate enemy of their country.

Brilliant, however, as is the victory obtained at Talavera, it is not solely on that occasion that Lieut. Gen. Sir A. Wellesley and the troops under his command are entitled to His Majesty's applause. The important service effected in an early part of the campaign by the same army, under the command of the same distinguished General, by the rapid march on the Douro, the passage of that river, the total discomfiture of the enemy, and his expulsion from the territory of one of His Majesty's ancient and most faithful allies, are circumstances which have made a lasting impression on His Majesty's mind, and have induced His Majesty to direct that the operations of this arduous and eventful campaign shall be thus recorded, as furnishing splendid examples of military skill, fortitude, perseverance, and of a spirit of enterprise, calculated to produce emulation in every part of his army, and largely to add to the renown and to the military character of the British nation.

To the Rt. Hon. J. Villiers.   Talavera de la Reyna, 29th July, 1809.

The enemy having collected all the troops he had in this part of Spain, attacked us here on the 27th. The battle lasted till yesterday evening, when we beat him in all parts of our line; and he retreated in the evening and night, leaving in our hands 20 pieces of cannon, ammunition, waggons, prisoners, &c. The battle was a most desperate one. Our loss has been very great, that of the enemy larger. The attack was made principally upon the British, who were on the left; and we had about two to one against us; fearful odds! but we maintained all our positions, and gave the enemy a terrible beating. The Spanish troops that were engaged behaved well; but there were very few of them engaged, as the attack was made upon us.

I have received your letters of the 19th and 22d July. I shall send the Commissariat an extract of your letter respecting the want of bills; it is strange that there should be any want of this kind. I rather believe that a Commissary, Mr. Nelson, has been sent to Ciudad Rodrigo, to settle our accounts and pay our debts there, notwithstanding that 2 gentlemen have been sent to Lisbon for the same purpose. I shall write also to the Commissary Gen. upon this subject.

The demands of the Portuguese upon our funds are so very large, as well on account of debts as of subsidy, that I do not know how to answer them; but I will see what can be done in respect to this debt on bills. I wish that you would give government a hint privately that they have embarked on too wide a scale, and that the funds which they have provided cannot supply us and the Portuguese subsidy, and Sir John Moore's old debts in Portugal and Spain.

P.S. I shall send you my dispatch, and one to the Regency to-morrow.

To Lieut. Col. Gordon, Mil. Sec.   Talavera de la Reyna, 29th July, 1809.

I beg that you will do me the favor of recommending Major Middlemore* to the particular protection of the Commander in Chief. He commanded the 1st batt. 48th regt., after Col. Donellan was wounded, during the greater part of the advance of that corps, which tended so much to the final success of the action yesterday, by covering and enabling Gen. Sherbrooke's division to form again. He is, besides, an excellent officer, and if his conduct then did not, I would almost say, demand promotion, his uniform good conduct and attention to his duty would do so.

To the Rt. Hon. J. H. Frere.   Talavera de la Reyna, 29th July, 1809.

I have to inform you, that the enemy having collected all their forces in this part of Spain, made an attack upon the combined armies on the day before yesterday, which lasted till a late hour yesterday. Their principal efforts were directed against the British troops, which were upon the left of our position; but they were repulsed in all their attacks with considerable loss, and they retreated during the night, leaving in our hands 20 pieces of cannon, some ammunition, tumbrils, prisoners, &c. Our loss has been very large indeed, as may well be imagined, con-

* Lieut. Gen. Middlemore, C.B., commanding the troops in the West Indies.

sidèring that, during 2 days and a night, we were attacked by a body of French troops of more than double our strength. But a reinforcement of 3000 men has joined the army this morning, which will, I hope, make up in some degree for our loss of men : that of officers is, I am afraid, irreparable.

I am well satisfied with the conduct of the Spanish officers and troops who had an opportunity of assisting us. Bassecourt's division was of great use to us in covering our left flank on a mountain. The regiment of cavalry, I think called the King's, made an excellent and well timed charge upon our right, and the Duque de Alburquerque, who was in the rear of our left, showed throughout the day the utmost readiness to do what I wished. Two pieces of cannon, 8 pounders, which I borrowed from Gen. Cuesta, were likewise very useful to us.

I beg that you will apprise government of these circumstances. I shall send you a copy of my dispatch to the Sec. of State as soon as I shall have time to write it.

To Marshal Beresford.   Talavera de la Reyna, 29th July, 1809.

I have received your letters of the 19th, 23d, and 26th July, the last by Sewell, who will give you an account of the manner in which we have been engaged for the last 2 days.

I have given directions that the debts of the British army at Ciudad Rodrigo may be paid, which, I trust, will re-establish confidence in that quarter. A Commissary is gone there, which measure was, I believe, necessary; at the same time that I believe 2 Spaniards are gone to Lisbon to settle the account. The debt will, however, be positively paid, if I can get any obedience to my orders. I shall communicate with Gen. Tilson, respecting the demand upon him at Guarda.

I shall endeavor to let you have some blankets, and will let you know how many. I send you the decision of the Commander in Chief, received this day, on my letter of reference of the 7th June. You will now appoint your officers as you may think proper.

Your position now becomes more important to me than ever it was. The result of the battles of the 27th and 28th must show the enemy that they have nothing to hope from a general action, and they must and will endeavor now to act upon my communications with Portugal, by the troops which they are re-organizing to the northward. What I should wish to see would be a good communication between you and Romana, upon the eastern frontier of Portugal, for your mutual security, that of my left, and the safety of Portugal, Ciudad Rodrigo, &c.

If this was once settled, and I shall work with the Junta upon it, while you may do the same by Romana, you might place yourself where you pleased, the enemy would not like to venture through the passes into Estremadura, having me on one side of him, and you and Romana on the other, or into the *cul de sac*, Portugal. You and Romana would be thus most useful to the general cause; and in proportion as your armies should become disciplined, you would aid in driving them north, if they should not be disposed to go that way after what they received yesterday. Their loss was immense, but ours was so likewise.

My intention now is to get Cuesta to follow them, particularly if they should have detached a corps this morning to oppose Venegas, who, I believe, entered Toledo yesterday; and I shall follow as soon as my troops are a little rested and refreshed, after 2 days of the hardest fighting I have ever been a party to. We shall certainly move towards Madrid, if not interrupted by some accident on our flank.

If you cannot arrange a good communication and understanding with Romana, with a view to these specified objects, you must look to your own security and that of Portugal, rather than to mine, and to the benefit of the common cause; and if, while I am operating in the common cause, I cannot, from any circumstances, be secured as I ought to be, I must give up the common cause, and seek for security by turning round and attacking the army which may attempt my flank, leaving Cuesta to manage his affairs as he can.

These are my general opinions upon this subject; you must decide yourself upon the details. A position which would prevent the enemy from attacking the Puerto de Baños with a large force (for there is a small Spanish corps now taking care of it) would be most useful to me. If you and Romana communicated and understood each other well, you might take each a position which, at the same time, would cover Portugal and Ciudad Rodrigo. But if you do not understand each other, you are not, I believe, sufficiently strong to be of much use to me.

I shall try and prevail upon the Junta to give you some Spanish cavalry.

I shall send you a copy of my dispatch to the Sec. of State. Apprise the Duque del Parque and the Marques de la Romana of our success of yesterday and the day before.

To the Duke of Richmond.   Talavera de la Reyna, 29th July, 1809.

You will see the account of the great battle we fought yesterday. Our loss is terribly great. Your nephew is safe. His horse was shot under him on the 27th. Almost all my staff are either hit or have lost their horses; and how I have escaped unhurt I cannot tell. I was hit in the shoulder at the end of the action, but not hurt, and my coat shot through.

Tom Burgh's son * was hit by a cannon shot in the arm, but, what is extraordinary, not much hurt.

I will enclose a plan if I can get one; but I send you a memorandum which will throw some light upon my dispatch.

Tell Lady Edward that I received her letters, &c., last night, and gave them to Lord Edward, who is very well. Remember me kindly to the Duchess and all the little girls.

To the Rt. Hon. J. H. Frere.   Talavera de la Reyna, 30th July, 1809.

We have received this morning accounts that the enemy are threatening the pass of the Puerto de Baños, which leads to Plasencia, in which object if they should succeed, they would cut off my communication with Portugal, and may otherwise do us infinite mischief.

I have long had in view this operation of the enemy, and, upon my

* Major Gen. Lord Downes, K.C.B.

arrival at Plasencia, I prevailed upon Gen. Cuesta to place in the Puerto de Baños a small corps, under the command of the Marques de la Reyna. I had also desired Gen. Beresford long ago to collect the Portuguese army on the frontier of Portugal; by which measure not only would he have protected that country and Ciudad Rodrigo, but he would have saved my left flank by the security which he would have given to the passes through the mountains into Estremadura.

I am afraid, however, that Gen. Beresford is, unfortunately, not strong enough for the enemy in that quarter. He will not be able to collect more than 10,000 to 15,000 men, of which only 600 are cavalry, and the troops none of them of the best description; whereas the enemy have, on the Duero and in the neighbourhood, not less than 20,000 men, being the remains of the corps of Soult, Ney, and Kellermann.

From your knowledge of my instructions, it must be obvious to you, that my first duty is to attend to the safety of Portugal; and I must do nothing which can be deemed inconsistent with that object. At all events, if my flank and communication with Portugal are not secured for me while I am operating in the general cause, I must move to take care of myself, and then the general cause must suffer. It appears to me, however, that by a better and more combined arrangement of our forces, we shall be able to effect all our objects.

1st. I would recommend that the Marques de la Romana, who has, as I understand, 25,000 men in arms somewhere near Fermoselle, at the junction of the Tormes and the Duero, and the Duque del Parque should be ordered by the Central Junta, without loss of time, to communicate and come to an understanding with Marshal Beresford, to whom I have already given directions on this subject, and that they should direct their efforts to the following specific objects: To secure the frontiers of Portugal; to secure the city of Ciudad Rodrigo; to secure the passages into Estremadura through the mountains, and, consequently, my left flank.

2dly. I should recommend that the government should adopt measures to reinforce these combined armies with cavalry. The Duque del Parque has one regiment, that of La Reyna, but there ought to be 3000 or 4000.

G. O. Talavera de la Reyna, 30th July, 1809.

2. The Commissary Gen. is to attend to the requisitions of the Inspector of hospitals, for provisions and other articles for the sick and wounded. The brigades to appoint officers and non-commissioned officers to take charge of the sick and wounded in general hospital, in proportion to their numbers, according to the G. O.

3. These officers and non-commissioned officers are to be selected from those who have slight wounds which are likely to detain them at Talavera, at the same time that they are not likely to be confined to their houses for any length of time.

A field officer to be appointed to superintend the military arrangements of the general hospital; he will report to the Adj. Gen. what sentries will be necessary, and what guards will be required to furnish them. The 1st division to furnish the field officer.

4. General officers commanding brigades are desired to attend to the early and precise execution of all orders relating to the care of the sick and wounded, and to have reports made upon them according to the G. O. 4th July.

5. General officers commanding divisions and brigades are desired this day to see that all the soldiers are supplied with ammunition and flints, &c. It is recommended to officers commanding regiments to have the accoutrements of the killed and wounded men collected, which are lying about the ground. They will report to the Q. M. G. the numbers collected, in order that arrangements may be made to procure storehouses for them at Talavera.

If these measures were adopted, the enemy would not venture to move into Estremadura, as he would expect to be opposed in front, and attacked in his rear, by our combined Spanish and Portuguese force, whose original position might, in the first instance, be calculated only to give security to the frontiers of Portugal and to Ciudad Rodrigo.

By degrees, as we should be enabled to get on in this quarter, and as the Spanish and Portuguese troops under the Marques de la Romana and Beresford would be disciplined, we might look further, and make them act on the offensive in the general cause.

I shall be obliged to you if you will take these suggestions into consideration, and convey them to the government, if you should approve of them; but I hope they will lose no time in sending their orders, as the object is of importance.

The A.G. to Lieut. Col. White, 29th regt.   30th July, 1809.
I have presented the French standard, taken by the 29th regt. on the 28th inst., to the Commander of the Forces; and I am directed by his Excellency to return it to you, that it may remain in possession of the 29th regt. as a testimonial of their gallant conduct.

To Major Gen. O'Donoju.   Talavera de la Reyna, 31st July, 1809.
Adverting to the intelligence which has been received of the movements of a French corps towards the Puerto de Baños, I cannot avoid requesting that you would press his Excellency Gen. Cuesta to detach towards that quarter, on this night, a division of his infantry with its guns, and a Commanding officer upon whose exertions and abilities he can rely.

I certainly never should have advanced so far, if I had not had reason to believe that that point was secure; and I still think that the movements of Gen. Beresford with the Portuguese army on the frontier, or that of the Duque del Parque from Ciudad Rodrigo, combined with the natural difficulties of the country, and the defence by the Marques de la Reyna, may delay the enemy's advance till the arrival of this division. At all events this division will not be missed here, and it will be in a situation to observe the enemy, if he should have crossed the mountains before the arrival of the division. But if the division should arrive in time, it will perform a most important service to the common cause, as it will preclude the necessity of my adopting more effectual measures to re-establish and secure my communication with Portugal, which measures must tend to delay the execution of all our plans against the great body of the enemy.

P.S. I have to observe that his Excellency is equally interested with me in preventing this irruption into Plasencia, as the enemy's first step will certainly be to interrupt his Excellency's communication with Seville by the bridge of Almaraz.

To Major Gen. O'Donoju.   Talavera de la Reyna, 31st July, 1809.
I have just received intelligence from a man of the 60th regt., who was taken prisoner on the 28th, that the enemy are in the villages on the other side of the Alberche; and I think it would be desirable to adopt, at an early period, some mode of ascertaining this point, by the observation

of officers or peasants or others, from this side of the Alberche, and from the other side the Tagus.

In addition to the official letter which I have written to you this morning, respecting the advance of the enemy through the Puerto de Baños, I cannot but observe to you that the situation of both armies will become very critical in such an event. There is but one way to avoid it, besides stopping the enemy's advance through the Puerto de Baños, and that is, to urge on the advance of Gen. Venegas towards Madrid, by a line as distant and as distinct from that adopted by the combined armies as may be possible. The enemy must then detach from his main body to oppose him, and the main body will in that case be so much weakened as to enable us to attack it without disadvantage, or, if that measure should be preferable, to enable the combined armies to detach a sufficient corps to beat the army which is supposed to be advancing through the mountains of Plasencia.

I shall be obliged to you if you will explain these my sentiments to Gen. Cuesta.

To the Rt. Hon. J. H. Frere.   Talavera de la Reyna, 31st July, 1809.

I have the honor to enclose the copy of a letter which I have received from Don M. de Garay, upon which I request of you to convey to him the following observations.

I shall be very much obliged to him if he will understand that I have no authority, nay, that I have been directed not to correspond with any of the Spanish ministers; and I request that he will in future convey to me through you the commands which he may have for me. I am convinced that I shall then avoid the injurious and uncandid misrepresentations of what passes, which Don M. de Garay has more than once sent to me, apparently with a view of placing on the records of his government statements of my actions and conduct which are entirely inconsistent with the truth, and to which statements I have no regular means of replying.

As soon as my line of march into Spain was determined upon, which you and Don M. de Garay are aware was not till a very late period, I sent to procure means of transport and other supplies at the places in which I considered it most likely I should get them, namely, Plasencia, Ciudad Rodrigo, Gata, Bejar, &c.; and as soon as I found that I had failed, I wrote to Gen. O'Donoju, on the 16th July, a letter, of which you have, and of which I know the government have, a copy, in which I told him that, as I had not received the assistance I required, I could undertake for no more than the first operation, which I had settled with Gen. Cuesta in my interview with him on the 11th. It is therefore an unfounded assertion that the first account that the government received of my intentions not to undertake any new operations was when they heard that I had left Gen. Cuesta alone to pursue the enemy.

The statement is not true, for, although I disapproved of Gen. Cuesta's advance of the 24th and 25th, which I knew would end as it did, I did support it with two divisions of infantry and a brigade of cavalry, which covered his retreat to the Alberche on the 26th, and his passage of that river on the 27th: and supposing the assertion to have been true, and that

Gen. Cuesta was exposed to be attacked by the enemy when alone, it was his fault and not mine ; and I had given him fair notice, not only by my letter of the 16th July, but frequently afterwards, that I could do no more.

It is not a difficult matter for a gentleman in the situation of Don M. de Garay to sit down in his cabinet and write his ideas of the glory which would result from driving the French through the Pyrenees ; and I believe there is no man in Spain who has risked so much, or who has sacrificed so much, to effect that object as I have. But I wish that Don M. de Garay, or the gentlemen of the Junta, before they blame me for not doing more, or impute to me beforehand the probable consequences of the blunders or the indiscretion of others, would either come or send here somebody to satisfy the wants of our half starved army, which, although they have been engaged for 2 days, and have defeated twice their numbers, in the service of Spain, have not bread to eat. It is positively a fact that, during the last 7 days, the British army have not received one third of their provisions ; that at this moment there are nearly 4000 wounded soldiers dying in the hospital in this town from want of common assistance and necessaries, which any other country in the world would have given even to its enemies ; and that I can get no assistance of any description from the country. I cannot prevail upon them even to bury the dead carcasses in the neighbourhood, the stench of which will destroy themselves as well as us.

I cannot avoid feeling these circumstances ; and the Junta must see that, unless they and the country make a great exertion to support and supply the armies, to which the invariable attention and the exertion of every man and the labor of every beast in the country ought to be directed, the bravery of the soldiers, their losses and their success, will only make matters worse and increase our embarrassment and distress. I positively will not move, nay, more, I will disperse my army, till I am supplied with provisions and means of transport as I ought to be.

To Lieut. Col. Gordon, Mil. Sec.   Talavera de la Reyna, 31st July, 1809.

I have the honor to enclose a memorial to the Commander in Chief from Capt. Mellish, who is an A. A. G. with this army. I beg leave to recommend Capt. Mellish in the most particular manner to the attention of the Commander in Chief, as an officer whose activity, ability, and attention to his duty upon all occasions deserve, and have obtained, the approbation of all those with whom he has served.

To W. Huskisson, Esq., Sec. to the Treasury.   Talavera de la Reyna, 1st Aug. 1809.

I have received your letters of the 8th June and 19th July. The supplies of money have come very opportunely, and I hope that you will contrive to supply us with all you can afford. You are certainly mistaken in England respecting the sums of money to be procured at Lisbon, Gibraltar, or Cadiz, for bills. They are not near so large as you imagine ; and, indeed, till the money arrived from England, and that which had been sent to be changed arrived from Cadiz, the sum we procured for bills was trifling indeed. If circumstances should prevent government from supplying us with money, it ought to become a question with them whether they should keep us here, for we can do nothing without money; and, indeed, our existence in this country, unless supplied with sufficient quantities, would become very precarious.

I do not know what we can do more than we have done to draw to our net all the money which is to be got for bills at Gibraltar, Cadiz, and Lisbon, unless, indeed, we were to insist that none of the British authorities, excepting the Commissary Gen., should draw bills at the two former places, as we have done at Lisbon, and thus leave the market to him alone; and, of course, to him the charge of providing supplies for the expenses at Gibraltar and those at Cadiz. We might not get more money by this mode of proceeding, as I believe we now get all that there is, but we might get it at rather a cheaper rate.

On the other hand, it must be observed, that as the Commissary Gen. of this army would, under this arrangement, be obliged to furnish supplies of money for the expenses of Gibraltar and Cadiz, he would be obliged to keep the treasuries at those places full to the extent of the regular demands upon him, and thus we might not get the resource from those places which we may expect under the existing arrangement. We feel very much in this manner the inconvenience of the heavy demands on the Commissary Gen. at Lisbon, for services not altogether of a military description. But we could not get on at all there, if any body but the Commissary Gen. were permitted to draw a bill.

To Major Gen. O'Donoju.   Talavera de la Reyna, 1st Aug. 1809.

We have got 13 pieces of French artillery, which I wish to give over to the Spanish army; the other 7 you have already got. I shall be obliged to you if you will urge Gen. Cuesta to desire the Commanding officer of the Spanish artillery to receive charge of them from the Commanding officer of the English artillery.

We want 90 artillery horses to complete the number required to draw the guns we have in the field. Could you give us any assistance in this way, either in draught horses or mules? During the action of the 28th, many of the horses of our dragoons and of the artillery strayed, and were taken possession of by the stragglers from the Spanish army who were in the rear of the town. I see English horses, with short tails, in possession of many of the Spanish troops; and I shall be very much obliged to you if you will urge Gen. Cuesta to give an order that all persons having in their possession English horses, or horse appointments, such as saddles, bridles, &c., should take them to the English cavalry lines forthwith.

I also understand that, on the morning of the 29th, when our officers and soldiers were engaged in collecting the wounded and in burying the dead, the arms and accoutrements of both were collected and carried away by the Spanish troops. The consequence is, that, as our soldiers recover in the hospital, we shall have no arms or accoutrements for them. I shall be very much obliged to Gen. Cuesta if he will give orders that all English arms and accoutrements of infantry may be lodged at the convent of San Geronimo.

We are much in want of medical assistance for the attendance of the wounded in the hospital; and I have been obliged to send there all those who ought properly to do duty with the regiments in the field. This cripples our operations much; and I shall be very much obliged to you if you will urge Gen. Cuesta to apply to the government for the assistance of at least 40 or 50 surgeons as soon as possible, who shall be paid at the same rate as the hospital mates in the British service.

To Visc. Castlereagh,   Talavera de la Reyna, 1st Aug. 1809.

Since I last had the honor of addressing you on the 29th July, the enemy have continued to keep a rear guard of about 10,000 men on the heights on the left of the Alberche, and I imagine that the whole army is still in the neighbourhood. It is difficult, however, to ascertain the fact, owing to the great deficiency of intelligence in the Spanish army.

On the 30th we received intelligence that provisions had been ordered for a French corps of 10,000 or 12,000 men, on the road from Alba de Tormes towards Bejar, in the Puerto de Baños, which affords the best road through the range of mountains which separates Plasencia and Estremadura from Castille. I had hoped that this pass had been effectually secured by the Spanish troops, otherwise I certainly should not have moved from Plasencia; and I had taken the further precaution to secure that point, as well as the frontier of Portugal, by directing Marshal Beresford to assemble the Portuguese army in the neighbourhood of Ciudad Rodrigo, within the Spanish frontier.

I am apprehensive, however, that the Marshal, although he was at Ciudad Rodrigo, had not been able to collect his troops in time; and as I cannot prevail upon Gen. Cuesta to detach a sufficient force to secure that important point, I am apprehensive that this French corps will pass through the mountains into Estremadura in our rear. These circumstances, combined with the extreme fatigue of the troops, the want of provisions, and the number of wounded to be taken care of, have prevented me from moving from my position.

Brig. Gen. R. Craufurd arrived with his brigade on the 29th, in the morning, having marched 12 Spanish leagues in a little more than 24 hours. Gen. Venegas' corps arrived upon the Tagus on the 28th and 29th; and he attacked Toledo with a detachment under Brig. Gen. Lacy, and moved himself to the bridge of Aranjuez.

To Visc. Castlereagh.   Talavera de la Reyna, 1st Aug. 1809.

When I addressed you this morning I had not received the report from the outposts. It appears that the enemy withdrew the rear guard which was posted on the heights on the left of the Alberche last night at 11 o'clock, and the whole army marched towards Sᵗᵃ Olalla, I conclude, with an intention of taking up a position in the neighbourhood of the Guadarrama, with a view to be able to throw their whole force upon Venegas, or upon this army, if either should move towards Madrid.

To Visc. Castlereagh.   Talavera de la Reyna, 1st Aug. 1809.

My public letters will give you some idea of our situation. It is one of some embarrassment, but of which I think I shall get the better, I hope, without fighting another desperate battle, which would really cripple us so much as to render all our efforts useless. I certainly should get the better of every thing, if I could manage Gen. Cuesta; but his temper and disposition are so bad, that that is impossible.

Venegas' movement will probably relieve our front. I think it probable also that the French will not like to press through the Puerto de Baños, having Beresford's army on their rear, and a victorious army in their front; and, indeed, that point would be quite secure, if I could prevail upon Gen. Cuesta to reinforce his troops at Bejar, so as to secure that point as I had understood it to be.

We are miserably supplied with provisions, and I do not know how to remedy this evil. The Spanish armies are now so numerous that they eat up the whole country. They have no magazines, nor have we, nor can we collect any; and there is a scramble for every thing.

I think the battle of the 28th is likely to be of great use to the Spaniards; but I don't think them yet in a state of discipline to contend with the French; and I prefer infinitely to endeavor to remove the enemy from this part of Spain by manœuvre to the trial of another pitched battle. The French, in the last, threw their whole force upon us, and although it did not succeed, and will not succeed in future, we shall lose great numbers of men, which we can but ill afford. I dare not attempt to relieve ourselves from the weight of the attack by bringing forward the Spanish troops, owing to their miserable state of discipline, and their want of officers properly qualified. These troops are entirely incapable of performing any manœuvre, however simple. They would get into irretrievable confusion, and the result would probably be the loss of every thing.

I have received your Lordship's letter of the 11th July, for which I am much obliged to you. I hope that your expedition will succeed. I guessed the point to which it was directed.

To the Rt. Hon. J. H. Frere.   Talavera de la Reyna, 2d Aug. 1809.

The state in which our men in hospital are from want of sheets and shirts induces me to request of you to prevail upon the government to have 5000 or 6000 of each sent here from Seville without loss of time: 200 mules would carry the whole, and I will pay for them.

I have seen a letter from the government to Gen. Cuesta, stating that they had determined to send us a large quantity of salt beef. If, instead of salt beef, they would form in this neighbourhood a magazine of 300,000 or 400,000 lbs. of biscuit, they would enable us to get on and to take advantage of our successes.

G. O.   Talavera de la Reyna, 2d Aug. 1809.

2. The soldiers plunder the inhabitants bringing in provisions, notwithstanding the repeated orders given upon the subject, and the knowledge which they all have, that this practice must tend to their own distress.

3. The Commander of the Forces desires that particular attention may be paid to former orders, requiring that no soldier should quit his lines, excepting on fatigue, in charge of an officer or non-commissioned officer, unless he is dressed according to the standing orders of his regiment with side-arms.

The rolls must be called in camp every two hours, and commanding officers of brigades will give directions what proportion of officers of each regiment are to be present. The Provost and his assistants must patrole the neighbourhood of the camp constantly, and the assistants must relieve each other.

To Gen. O Donoju.   Talavera, 2d Aug. 1809.

The officer who will have the honor of delivering this letter to you is Col. Mackinnon, of the Guards, who is stationed at Talavera in charge of the British hospital. I shall be very much obliged to you if, during my absence, you will allow him to communicate with you upon the wants of the hospital, and if you will apply to Gen. Cuesta for such assistance as he may require, particularly of parties of men on fatigue to assist in cleaning the hospital.

I do request you to communicate to Lieut. Col. Mackinnon, in confidence, any movement that the General may wish to carry into execution the orders which I have given him to remove the hospital, in case the General should think it proper to fall back.

The A.G. to Lieut. Col. Mackinnon.   2d Aug. 1809.

I am directed by the Commander of the Forces to acquaint you that you are appointed to remain at this place, having the superintendence of the sick and wounded in hospital, also the convalescents and troops that are left at Talavera.

A letter is herewith enclosed for Gen. O'Donoju, of the staff of the Spanish army, which contains the Commander of the Forces' request that he will apprise you, from time to time, of Gen. Cuesta's intentions, more particularly if, from any unforeseen event, the General should find himself under the necessity of withdrawing from Talavera. Should this occurrence arise, which can hardly be looked forward to, the Commander of the Forces directs that you will use your utmost exertions not only to bring off the guard of troops placed over the hospitals, as stated in the margin, but also all officers and convalescents or sick men that it is possible, by procuring transport or otherwise, to move; and that you will direct your march on the bridge of Arzobispo from that to Truxillo and Merida: on your way thither, further orders would, in the above case, reach you. Recurring to such an event, it would be necessary that the Commissary who remains with you should be left with the sick unable to be moved, as also the necessary medical attendance for them; and you will not fail to write such a letter, which you will leave with the Commissary, to the officer commanding the enemy's troops, as would insure ours such treatment as is ever shown by British troops to those who fall into their power. The manner in which Sir A. Wellesley has always considered the troops of the enemy, may be forcibly urged.

Gen. O'Donoju will be likewise requested to afford you every assistance for your interior arrangements of the sick in hospital; and it is hoped, through his interference, that you will obtain what you require from the Junta.

A copy of the G.O. for the regulation of hospitals is herewith enclosed. Officers commanding regiments have been directed to see that officers of companies leave pay for their men up to the 24th Aug., in addition to which £500 has been left with the Commissary of accounts. I beg to receive an exact return, as early as possible, of the sick men, &c., at Talavera.

To Marshal Beresford.   Oropesa, 3d Aug. 1809.

The movement of Soult through the Puerto de Baños has deranged all our plans, and I am obliged to return to drive him out. I think you might be able to assist us materially in effecting this object, or probably even to cut off his retreat entirely.

We understand that he arrived at Plasencia on the 1st, and I have not yet heard that he has moved from thence; but I shall desire the officer who will take you this to procure for you all the intelligence he can up to the latest moment. I intend to go to Navalmoral to-morrow, and if I should find that Soult is still at Plasencia, I hope to be at that place by the 6th or 7th.

We are miserably off, however, for provisions, and it is possible that I may be obliged to halt a day, to endeavor to procure a day's bread for the men. If we should find Soult at Plasencia, he will endeavor to retreat by the Puerto de Baños, or by that of Perales, or he may make a run for Portugal. I think that you may stop him for me either in Perales or Baños. You cannot do much if he goes for Portugal, where we must make other and more extensive arrangements. I wish you, therefore, if you can, to occupy Baños and Perales as soon as possible after you shall have received this letter. I rather think that there is a point not far from Plasencia, intermediate between the two passes, which effectually commands the road to either from Plasencia. If this should be the case, which you will find out at Ciudad Rodrigo, I recommend you to occupy that point.

To the Rt. Hon. J. H. Frere.   Oropesa, 3d Aug. 1809.

Notwithstanding the anxiety which I felt, the pains which I took, and the assurances which were given to me respecting the security of the Puerto de Baños, Gen. Cuesta received intelligence yesterday morning, that the French corps which had threatened that point had passed through unopposed, and had entered Plasencia on the 1st, at about 2 o'clock. I had at last prevailed upon the General to detach a sufficient corps to defend the Puerto, which marched yesterday morning; but after the evil was done, he became equally sensible with myself of the important advantage which had been gained by the enemy, and he came to me to propose that half of the army should march immediately to set the matter right again. I told him that if by half of the army he meant half of the Spanish and English corps, I could not consent to the proposal, and that I would either stay or go with my whole corps. He then desired that I would choose, and I offered to go. My reason for this preference is, that I think that I shall effect the operation, probably without contest, in a shorter time than he could, and with much more certainty; and that I can bring to bear upon this point, not only all the Spanish troops in the neighbourhood, but the Portuguese army, which are collected not far from Ciudad Rodrigo.

It is possible that the enemy, who by last night's accounts appeared to be occupied by Sir R. Wilson's appearance again, near Escalona, may not hear of my departure before I shall be upon my return; or, what I think more probable, from his movements towards Escalona, and his having Victor's head quarters at Maqueda, that he intends to re-enter Estremadura that way, despairing of success by the way of Talavera: thus at the same time to turn that position, and give a hand to Soult, who, I conclude, will endeavor to advance by the Tietar. If, however, I should be mistaken in this conjecture, and the enemy should discover that I am gone, and should move upon Gen. Cuesta in full force, he must only retire until he shall again join me. In the meantime, with all these movements, we are horribly distressed for provisions. The soldiers seldom get enough to eat, and what they do get is delivered to them half mouldy, and at hours at which they thught to be at rest.

I enclose to you the copy of an intercepted letter which Sir R. Wilson sent to me this morning. I am induced to suspect that it was put in his way purposely. The senator who was at Vitoria on the 21st, with such important intelligence, would have been at Madrid long ago, and we should have heard of his arrival. There are rumours, however, among the deserters, of the preliminaries of peace having been signed.

To Major Gen. O'Donoju. Oropesa, 3d Aug. 1809.

I arrived here a little after 12, but have received no intelligence of the enemy. There is no dust forwards; and I understand that we have a Commissary at Navalmoral, who would probably have moved if he had heard of the enemy on this side of the Tietar. I have written to Gen. Bassecourt to recommend to him to halt to-morrow at Cèntenillo, and to patrole the roads in the Vera de Plasencia, as well as in his front.

The movements of the enemy which Sir R. Wilson announced in his letter of last night, which I gave you this morning, induce me to think that he will not endeavor again to force his way through the valley of Talavera; but that he intends to be in readiness to aid Soult by Escalona, between the Alberche and the Tietar. If I should be correct in this notion, Gen. Cuesta may be induced to give up his position at Talavera, and then my hospital there will be placed in a state of risk. This gives me much uneasiness. At all events, in the present state of our operations, it appears to me that the hospital is too far advanced at Talavera, and I am very desirous of removing it farther back.

I wish that you would mention this subject to Gen. Cuesta, and request him, from me, to make a requisition in the country south of the Tagus, for carts to remove the hospital. It is impossible to hope to be able to remove it at once. Indeed, to attempt it might destroy the men whom we wish to save; but by first fixing upon an intermediate station, at no great distance from Talavera, we might soon remove the whole from thence, and afterwards by degrees to the place to be ultimately fixed upon for the hospital.

I cannot avoid again taking this opportunity of recommending that Gen. Venegas should be ordered to keep the enemy in a state of alarm for the safety of Madrid, by the road of Fuentidueña and Arganda, as the only one by which he can oblige the enemy to keep his forces divided. This is really necessary, till we shall have our rear clear and secure again.

To Major Gen. O'Donoju. Oropesa, 3d Aug. 1809.

I have just received your letter of this day and its enclosures. I acknowledge that I do not conceive the enemy are likely to attack you or to harass me, as they say they will, for some time, and I wish that Gen. Cuesta had remained a little longer. Sir R. Wilson must give you notice if they break through at Escalona; and you are in time if you march when you find the enemy making that movement, or breaking up for a forward movement from Sta Olalla. You see that Joseph, with Sebastiani's corps, is, or rather was, at Bargas. At all events, I conceive that it will be desirable that you should delay your march till morning, and send off your wounded, commissariat, baggage, &c., before you, and that you should halt in the wood where the venta is, till the wounded shall have arrived at Arzobispo, and your baggage be here.

Depend upon it, you are mistaken in Soult's strength; and that Victor, without Sebastiani and the King, who cannot move while Venegas is where he is, can do us no harm.

P.S. I conclude that you will take care to establish a strong post at Arzobispo, and destroy the bridge at Talavera.

To Gen. Bassecourt.   Oropesa, le 3 Août, 1809.

Je suis arrivé ici avec l'armée Anglaise, ayant l'intention d'arrêter les progrès du corps Français que l'on dit être entré à Plasencia par le Puerto de Baños. Je vous serai bien obligé de me faire savoir si vous avez quelques nouvelles de ce corps. Comme ce corps là est plus fort que celui que vous avez sous vos ordres, il me paraît que vous êtes trop en avant de moi. Je vous conseille donc de faire halte demain à Centenillo; j'irai à Navalmoral si je le puis, et vous serez à 2 ou 3 lieues de distance. Si l'ennemi connaît nos mouvemens, il tâchera de passer par la Vera de Plasencia à l'autre côté du Tietar. Il ne peut pas y mener son canon, mais je vous prie d'avoir l'œil sur cette route.

To Major Gen. O'Donoju.   Oropesa, 3d Aug. 1809.

I have just heard that the enemy was coming into Navalmoral this afternoon, and I also understand that your officer at Almaraz was prepared to break the bridge upon the first appearance of the enemy. This being the case, what does Gen. Cuesta propose to do? I think it probable that he would be able to drive off Soult if he is alone, or even with Ney; but you know much time must elapse before your bridge would be repaired, if it could be repaired at all; and it would not be pleasant to fight a general action with the whole French army, with the river at our back, and no means of passing it. We cannot fight here without holding Calera, which appears to me to be impracticable, and, therefore, what I would recommend is, that the whole army should assemble at this side of the bridge of Arzobispo. I have written to Gen. Bassecourt to recommend that, as soon as he shall receive my letter, he should march either to this place or to La Calzada.

To Gen. Bassecourt.   Oropesa, le 3 Août, 1809.

Je viens de recevoir la nouvelle que l'ennemi est entré cet après-midi à Navalmoral.

Je crois que le Général Cuesta a marché cet après-dîner à 3 heures, et il m'informe que l'ennemi est en force des deux côtés. Je vous conseille donc de marcher aussitôt que vous aurez reçu cette lettre à la Calzada ou à cette place. Si vous allez à la Calzada, envoyez un officier pour prévenir nos patrouilles.

To Marshal Beresford.   Oropesa, 3d Aug. 1809.

Since I wrote you the letter which goes with this I have received a letter from Gen. Cuesta, which gives me reason to believe that it is possible that Ney may be with Soult; and he so far thinks that Victor will be of the party, that he breaks up from Talavera, leaving there my hospital, and follows me. Under these circumstances, it is difficult for me to say what I shall do.

The Spaniards will certainly retire across the bridge of Almaraz, and in that case, with Ney and Soult before me, and Victor, and probably the King, behind me, I cannot go to Plasencia. However, if I find my front weak, that is the line I shall take; and I wish you to be prepared to stand behind Soult if he should be alone. If Ney should be with him, you will do best to go with your army, as soon as you can, to Castello Branco, and defend the passes.

The A.G. to the officer commg. sick at Oropesa.   3d Aug. 1809.

I am directed by the Commander of the Forces to desire that you will forthwith march with all the men you can remove from the hospital, together with the officers who have them in charge, to the Puente del Arzobispo, which you will cross, and endeavor to accommodate them on the other side, until you receive further directions. You will probably be joined at the bridge by the sick, &c. from Talavera, under the command of Col. Mackinnon, of the Guards, whose orders you will follow. A Commissary will be directed to accompany you, to procure what may be necessary for the men. Such men as cannot be removed will remain here, under a proper medical attendant, who will receive further instructions.

The A.G. to Dr. Franck, Inspector of Hospitals.   3d Aug. 1809.

It is the Commander of the Forces' directions, that such of the men in hospital here, as are capable of being moved, should march this night, under charge of the officer commanding the convalescents, and such other officers as are appointed to the sick, to the Puente del Arzobispo, which bridge they are to pass, and remain on the other side in such accommodation as can be got, until further orders; they will be joined there by Col. Mackinnon and the sick from Talavera, from whom they will receive orders. A Commissary will proceed with them. The remainder of the sick that cannot be moved, will remain here with a proper medical attendant, who will receive further instructions.

The A.G. to the Dep. Commissary General.   3d Aug. 1809.

I am directed by the Commander of the Forces to desire that an officer of your department may proceed this night with the convalescents from hence to the bridge of Arzobispo, where they will meet the sick from Talavera. The Commissary will then remain, to provide in the best manner he can for them, till further orders.

To Major Gen. O'Donoju.   Puente del Arzobispo, 4th Aug. 1809.

I have received the letter containing Gen. Cuesta's congratulations upon the honor conferred upon me by the government, and I beg that you will do me the favor to congratulate his Excellency upon the honor conferred upon him.

I beg you, at the same time, to inform him, that not having found any good position on the right of the Tagus, and having heard that he had ordered his army to pass the river, I have ordered that under my command to pass the river likewise. If he should be attacked before we should make our ulterior dispositions, it would not make half an hour's difference: I wish, however, that the General would carry into execution the plan agreed upon this morning, and fall back on the Tagus.

To the Rt. Hon. J. H. Frere.   Puente del Arzobispo, 4th Aug. 1809.

I wrote to you yesterday a letter, which I now send to you, since which time the appearance of our affairs has changed for the worse.

After I had written to you, I learned that the enemy had arrived at Navalmoral, by which movement he acquired possession of Almaraz, and that the bridge at that place was destroyed by the Marques de la Reyna, who had retired thither from Baños. Shortly afterwards I received a letter from Gen. O'Donoju, in which he informed me that the French corps which had entered by Baños consisted of 30,000 men, being composed of all the troops which had been in the north of Spain; and that Gen. Cuesta, being apprehensive that I was not strong enough for them, and moreover, having reason, from the contents of intercepted letters and the reports of Sir R. Wilson from the neighbourhood of Escalona, to apprehend that the enemy intended to press upon my rear, while I should be engaged in front, and that he should be cut off from me, had determined to march from Talavera yesterday evening. Thus my security was gone, and nearly 1500 of my wounded soldiers were left behind. It then became a subject of serious consideration what I should recommend to the General to do. We could not regain the ground of the bridge of Almaraz without a battle, and, in all probability, we should have had to fight another with 50,000 men before the bridge could be re-established, supposing we had succeeded in the first. We could not stand at Oropesa, where we were, the position being but an indifferent one, and liable to be cut off, by Calera, from this place, its only point of retreat. I preferred and recommended the latter: 1st, from a consideration of the losses which we, the English, must have sustained in these successive contests, without the chance of being able to take care of our wounded. 2dly, from the consideration that if it were true that 30,000 men had been added to the French forces in this part of Spain, it was quite impossible for us to act upon the offensive. A diversion must be made in favor of the armies in this quarter, by the movement of some other body towards Madrid, which will draw off a part of their forces to oppose it, and then we may resume the offensive. 3dly, in order that these operations and battles should be successful, it was necessary that the marches to be made should be long, and made with great celerity. I am sorry to say that, from the want of food, the troops are now unequal to either the one or the other; and it is more than probable that Victor would have been upon our backs before the first action between Soult and me could have been concluded.

Upon the whole, therefore, I am convinced that the measure which I have advised is the wisest, and likely to lead to the best, if not to the most brilliant, result.

As usual, Gen. Cuesta wanted to fight general actions. Now that all the troops are removed from Castille, Romana and the Duque del Parque ought to be directed to make some demonstrations towards Madrid, which would now relieve this front. I understand that, besides the 50,000 men, there will be a corps of 12,000 employed to observe Venegas.

The A.G. to Dr. M'Dowall. 4th Aug. 1809.

I am directed by the Commander of the Forces to desire that you will remain at Oropesa, taking charge of the sick and wounded that cannot be removed from hence. If it should so happen, that, by the falling back of Gen. Cuesta's army, the enemy should enter this place, it will then be your duty to represent to the officer in command the uniform good treatment that prisoners have received from British soldiers, and you will claim for the sick all that protection and care their case requires. You will explain how very anxious his Excellency the Commander of the Forces feels on this subject; and that he places confidence in the humanity and liberality of the enemy now, especially as Sir A. Wellesley has ever treated the French prisoners with every care.

A sum of money will be left you, together with the men's pay to the 24th Aug.

To Lieut. Col. Sir R. Wilson.   Peraleda de Garbin, 5th Aug. 1809.

It is difficult for me to instruct you when every letter I receive from you informs me that you are farther from me, and are carrying into execution a plan of your own. The last instructions I gave you were to communicate with, and of course follow the motions of, the Spanish army. The day before yesterday Gen. Cuesta abandoned Talavera, and arrived on the morning of the 4th at Oropesa, on the ground that Soult and Ney, joined, had come through Plasencia, that I was not strong enough for them, and, moreover, that he was threatened on his left flank and in his front. Soult was then at Navalmoral, and the bridge at Almaraz was taken up. In my opinion there remained for us but one line to adopt, Gen. Cuesta's intelligence being correct, and that was to withdraw across the bridge of Arzobispo, and re-establish as soon as possible our communication with Seville and with Lisbon. I have done so. The General is, I understand, still at Arzobispo, having drawn in his advanced guard from Talavera. You will do well to march, directly that you will receive this, by Calera to Arzobispo, and there cross the river and send word to Gen. Cuesta that you are coming there, that he may not break the bridge before you arrive. I doubt whether you would find your way through the mountains of the Vera at present.

P.S. You should have followed the movements of Gen. Cuesta here.

To Marshal Beresford.   Mesa de Ibor, 6th Aug. 1809.

After I had written to you on the 3d, and I had fully considered our situation, I thought it best to retire across the Tagus, by the bridge of Arzobispo, to take up the line of that river, and to move the British army as soon as possible, to secure the passage of Almaraz. Soult arrived that day at Navalmoral, and had therefore possession of the road to the bridge, which was either taken up, or, if not taken up, the enemy might have destroyed it. I was not certain that Ney was not with Soult; and I was certain that, if not with him, he was at no great distance from him: we should, therefore, have had a battle to fight to gain the road to Almaraz, for Plasencia was then out of the question: and if Victor had followed Cuesta, as he ought, most probably another battle, before the bridge would have been re-established, with the whole French army, and, if unsuccessful, I should have been obliged to retire over one bridge, supposing that I had been able to re-establish the bridge at Almaraz at all. Then it was to be considered that Cuesta having left Talavera, the bridge of Arzobispo was open to the enemy's enterprise; and if he had destroyed it, and we had failed in forcing Soult at Navalmoral, we were gone.

To all these considerations, add that it was evident to me that we must take up the defensive, if Soult and Ney were come through the Puerto de Baños; and although you will believe I gave up with reluctance the fruits of our victory, and of all our toils and losses, I did not hesitate, and do not repent that I crossed the Tagus at Arzobispo; and your letter has confirmed my opinion of the propriety of that proceeding.

I should have written to you sooner, only that I considered my second letter of the 3d to be likely to keep you in safety, which was all I wished for; and I did not like to trust a second letter to the chance of falling into the enemy's hands. I propose now to take up the position of Almaraz, to give my troops some rest and some food, both of which they want, and to see what the enemy will do. My opinion is, that they will invade Portugal, in order to draw us away, and you will do well to put yourself in a situation to defend the passes.

I am concerned to hear of the desertion of your troops. Is there no remedy for it? I was sure that the Commander in Chief's decision upon my letter would induce all the officers to quit the Portuguese service.

To Major Gen. O'Donoju.   Deleytosa, 7th Aug. 1809.

I arrived here this morning. The whole army has passed over the worst part of the road. One division is still at Mesa de Ibor; but all the artillery is by this time at Campillos. The advanced guard is upon the Tagus, opposite Almaraz. I have sent an Engineer to look at the river, to examine and settle what defences it will require, which I shall have constructed forthwith; and I will replace the bridge. I shall want some Spanish artillery, of heavy calibre, however, to arm these batteries; and for this, as for other reasons, I would recommend to Gen. Cuesta to take early measures for sending the greatest part, if not the whole, of his heavy artillery through the mountains, as soon as he can; as well as his Valencian and Catalonian carts, which travel through these mountains with great difficulty, and can be of no use to him where he is.

I shall this day, if I can get it copied, or to-morrow, send you a report on the Tagus, from the bridge of Talavera to that of Almaraz, from which you will see an account of the banks, mill dams, and fords. It would appear from this report, that the enemy would not find it difficult to throw over the river some light infantry between you and us, which we might find inconvenient in the interruption of our communication, if in nothing else; I therefore recommend to you to have a division of infantry at Mesa de Ibor, if only with the object of keeping up the communication between the two armies; but I have also observed that this is a very strong post indeed, and in case of any accidents upon your right, it would effectually secure your retreat.

To Brig. Gen. R. Craufurd, at Mirabete.   Deleytosa, 8th Aug. 1809.

I intended going to see you this day, but there are so many points to be arranged here, that I must defer my visit till to-morrow. The measures to be adopted at your post upon the Tagus depend so much upon our general situation, that it is impossible to enter upon them at all without explaining our whole situation, with which I am about to trouble you.

From all that I learn, the enemy have brought, or are bringing through the Puerto de Baños to Plasencia, all the troops they had in Castille. Gen. Beresford, in a letter of the 4th, from Almeida, tells me that they have now none left in Castille, and that the number sent through amounts to 34,000 men. This would make the French force in this part of Spain about 70,000 men. They will either press us upon our right with this body, and force their way to Cordova; or they will try again the game of diversions, and detach a large corps into Portugal, in order to make us separate from the Spaniards. I do not think it likely that they will endeavor to force the passage of the Tagus. Indeed, success at any point above Almaraz would not be of much use to them, for they could not march an army by any road excepting that by which we have come, and which might be easily defended. That which we have to guard against, then, is, 1st, a march into Portugal; 2dly, an attempt upon the right of the Spaniards to force their way to Cordova.

It might be hereafter convenient that we should re-establish the bridge at Almaraz, but that is out of the question at present. Even if a tempting opportunity of striking a blow were offered to us, we require rest and food for men and horses before we could take advantage of it.

In a view either to the march into Portugal, or to the defence of the passage of the Tagus at Almaraz, my opinion is, that the following arrangements ought to be adopted : 1st; we ought to break up the bridge over the channel on the right bank, preserving the planks, and bringing them over to the left bank : 2dly; we ought to separate the boats of the bridge tied to this side : the boats might be removed to the dry creek just below the passage, and the beams and planks to the hill behind the passage : 3dly; we ought to construct works upon those points of the ground which would best enable us to defend the passage.

By the adoption of these measures, we should be enabled to defend the passage, if the enemy should attempt to force it; and, on the other hand, if we should find that the enemy move towards Portugal, and that we are obliged to move that way, the Spanish division, which will be at Mesa de Ibor, will take your place in security, and we shall have it in our power to burn the materials of the bridges; or, if it should turn out to be expedient to cross the river, we can easily re-establish them.

I am in hopes that, to-morrow, I shall be able to send you some guns. I shall, this afternoon, send you an Engineer and tools for the construction of such works as may be necessary. I understood that there were Spanish artillery at the batteries of the bridge; but I have been misinformed on this, as well as on other subjects. I have written to Gen. Cuesta, to desire that Spanish artillery of a heavy calibre may be sent to defend the passage at Almaraz. I have ordered provisions to be sent to you. I have hopes that after this day we shall receive our regular rations.

To Don M. de Garay.   Deleytosa, 8th Aug. 1809.

I have had the honor of receiving the letter which your Excellency did me the honor of writing to me on the 31st July, in which you have expressed the approbation of the Central Junta of the conduct of the British army under my command, in the action of the 29th July. I am very sensible of the value of the approbation of the Central Junta, and I beg that you will convey to them my respectful acknowledgments.

I am particularly flattered by the confidence they have reposed in me,

in appointing me one of the Captains General of the Spanish armies; and
I have this day written to His Majesty's Principal Sec. of State, to request
him to lay before His Majesty this testimony of the approbation and confidence of the Central Junta, and to request His Majesty's permission for
me to accept the commission in the Spanish army with which the government are pleased to honor me. Until His Majesty's answer shall be received, I shall be happy to render the government every service that may
be in my power.

To Don M. de Garay.   Deleytosa, 8th Aug. 1809.

I have in a separate letter expressed my acknowledgments to the government for the honor they have done me in appointing me a Captain General
in the Spanish army, and I have now to return them my thanks for the
horses which they have been pleased to present to me in the name of His
Majesty King Ferdinand VII. In respect to the pay attached to the rank
of Captain General, I hope the government will excuse me if I decline to
become a burden upon the finances of Spain during this contest for her
independence.

To Visc. Castlereagh.   Deleytosa, 8th Aug. 1809.

I apprised your Lordship on the 1st inst. of the advance of a French
corps towards the Puerto de Baños, and of the probable embarrassment of
the operations of the army, which its arrival at Plasencia would occasion;
and these embarrassments having since existed to a degree so considerable
as to oblige us to fall back, and to take up a defensive position on the
Tagus, I am induced to trouble you more at length with an account of
what has passed upon this subject.

When I entered Spain, I had a communication with Gen. Cuesta,
through Sir R. Wilson and Col. Roche, respecting the occupation of the
Puerto de Baños and the Puerto de Perales; the former of which it was
at last settled should be held by a corps to be formed under the Marques
de la Reyna, to consist of 2 battalions from Gen. Cuesta's army, and 2
from Bejar; and that the Puerto de Perales was to be taken care of by
the Duque del Parque, by detachments from the garrison of Ciudad Rodrigo. I doubted the capacity of the garrison of Ciudad Rodrigo to make
the detachment to the latter, but so little as to the effectual occupation of
the former, that in writing to Marshal Beresford on the 17th July, on this
subject, I desired him to look to the Puerto de Perales, but that I considered Baños secure, as appears by the extract of my letter, which I enclose.

On the 30th intelligence was received at Talavera that 12,000 rations
had been ordered at Fuente Roble for the 28th, and 24,000 at Los Santos
for the same day, for a French corps, which it was believed was on its
march towards the Puerto de Baños. Gen. Cuesta expressed some anxiety
respecting this post, and sent me a message, to propose that Sir R. Wilson
should be sent there with his corps. Sir Robert was on that day at Talavera, but his corps was in the mountains towards Escalona; and as he
had already made himself very useful in that quarter, and had been near
Madrid, with which city he had had a communication which I was desirous
of keeping up, I proposed that a Spanish corps should be sent to Baños

without loss of time.   I could not prevail with Gen. Cuesta, although he certainly admitted the necessity of a reinforcement when he proposed that Sir R. Wilson should be sent to Baños; and he was equally sensible with myself of the benefit to be derived to the cause from sending Sir Robert back to Escalona.   At this time we had no further intelligence of the enemy's advance, than that the rations were ordered; and I had hopes that the enemy might be deterred from advancing by the intelligence of our success on the 28th; and that the troops in the Puerto might make some defence; and that, under these circumstances, it was not desirable to divert Sir Robert from Escalona.

On the 31st, however, I renewed my application to Gen. Cuesta, to send there a Spanish division of sufficient strength, in a letter to Gen. O'Donoju, of which I enclose a copy, but without effect; and he did not detach Gen. Bassecourt till the morning of the 2d Aug., after we had heard that the enemy had entered Bejar; and it was obvious that the troops in the Puerto would make no defence.

On the 2d, we received accounts that the enemy had entered Plasencia in 2 columns.   The Marques de la Reyna, whose 2 battalions consisted only of 600 men, with only 20 rounds of ammunition each man, retired from the Puerto and from Plasencia, without firing a shot; and went to the bridge of Almaraz, which he declared that he intended to remove.   The battalions of Bejar dispersed without making any resistance.   Gen. Cuesta called upon me on that day, and proposed that half of the army should move to the rear to oppose the enemy, while the other half should maintain the post at Talavera.   My answer was, that if, by half the army, he meant half of each army, I could only answer, that I was ready either to go or to stay with the whole British army, but that I could not divide it. He then desired me to choose whether I would go or stay; and I preferred to go, from thinking that the British troops were most likely to do the business effectually, and without contest; and from being of opinion, that to open the communication through Plasencia was more important to us than to the Spanish army, although very important to them.   With this decision Gen. Cuesta appeared perfectly satisfied.

The movements of the enemy in our front since the 1st had induced me to be of opinion that, despairing of forcing us at Talavera, they intended to force a passage by Escalona, and thus to open a communication with the French corps coming from Plasencia.   This suspicion was confirmed in the night of the 2d by letters received from Sir R. Wilson, of which I enclose copies; and before I quitted Talavera on the 3d, I waited upon Gen. O'Donoju, and conversed with him upon the whole of our situation, and pointed out to him the possibility that, in the case of the enemy coming through Escalona, Gen. Cuesta might find himself obliged to quit Talavera before I should be able to return to him; and I urged him to collect all the carts that could be got, in order to remove our hospital.   At his desire, I put the purport of this conversation in writing, and sent him a letter to be laid before Gen. Cuesta, of which I enclose a copy.

The British army marched on the 3d to Oropesa, Gen. Bassecourt's Spanish corps being at Centenillo; where I desired that it might halt the next day, in order that I might be nearer it.   About 5 o'clock in the evening I heard that the French had arrived from Plasencia at Navalmoral, whereby they were between us and the bridge of Almaraz. About an hour afterwards, I received from Gen. O'Donoju the letter and its enclosures, of which I enclose copies, announcing to me the intention of Gen. Cuesta to march from Talavera in the evening, and to leave there my hospital, excepting such men as could be moved by the means he already had, on the grounds of his apprehension that I was not strong enough for the corps coming from Plasencia; and that the enemy was moving upon his flank, and had returned to Sta Olalla, in his front.

I acknowledge that these reasons did not appear to me sufficient for giving up so important a post as Talavera, for exposing the combined armies to an attack in front and rear at the same time, and for abandoning my hospital, and I wrote the letter of which I enclose a copy. This unfortunately reached the General after he had marched; and he arrived at Oropesa shortly after daylight on the morning of the 4th.

The question what was to be done was then to be considered. The enemy, stated to be 30,000 strong, but at all events, consisting of the corps of Soult and Ney, either united, or not very distant from each other, and supposed by Joseph Buonaparte and Marshal Jourdan to be sufficiently strong to attack the British army stated to be 25,000 strong, were, on one side, in possession of the high road to the passage of the Tagus at Almaraz, the bridge at which place we knew had been removed, although the boats still necessarily remained in the river. On the other side, we had reason to expect the advance of Victor's corps to Talavera, as soon as Gen. Cuesta's march should be known; and after leaving 12,000 men to watch Venegas, and allowing from 10,000 to 11,000 killed and wounded in the late action, this corps would have amounted to 25,000. We could extricate ourselves from this difficult situation only by great celerity of movement (to which the troops were unequal, as they had not had their allowance of provisions for several days), and by success in 2 battles: if we were unsuccessful in either, we should have been without a retreat; and if Soult and Ney, avoiding an action, had retired before us, and had waited the arrival of Victor, we should have been exposed to a general action with 50,000 men equally without a retreat. We had reason to expect that as the Marques de la Reyna could not remove the boats from the river at Almaraz, Soult would have destroyed them. Our only retreat therefore was by the bridge of Arzobispo; and if we had moved on, the enemy, by breaking that bridge while the army should be engaged with Soult and Ney, would have deprived us of that only resource. We could not take up a position at Oropesa, as we thereby left open the road to the bridge of Arzobispo from Talavera by Calera; and after considering the whole subject maturely, I was of opinion, that it was advisable to retire to the bridge of Arzobispo, and to take up a defensive position upon the Tagus.

I was induced to adopt this last opinion because the French have now at least 50,000 men disposable to oppose to the combined armies, and a corps of 12,000 to watch Venegas; and I was likewise of opinion that the sooner the defensive line should be taken up, the more likely were the troops to be able to defend it. Accordingly I marched on the 4th, and crossed the Tagus by the bridge of Arzobispo; and have continued my route to this place, in which I am well situated to defend the passage of Almaraz, and the lower parts of the Tagus. Gen. Cuesta crossed the river on the night of the 5th, and he is still at the bridge of Arzobispo.

About 2000 of the wounded have been brought away from Talavera, the remaining 1500 are there; and I doubt whether, under any circumstances, it would have been possible or consistent with humanity to attempt to remove any more of them. From the treatment some of the soldiers wounded on the 27th, and who fell into the hands of the enemy, experienced from them, and from the manner in which I have always taken care of their wounded who have fallen into my hands, I expect that these men will be well treated; and I have only to lament that a new concurrence of events, over which, from circumstances, I had and could have no control, should have placed the army in a situation to be obliged to leave any of them behind.

To Visc. Castlereagh.   Deleytosa, 8th Aug. 1809.

I have but little to add to my public dispatch of this date, which I hope will justify me from all blame in the eyes of His Majesty's ministers, excepting that of having trusted the Spanish General in any thing. We should have been safe, if I could have prevailed upon him to occupy Baños, as it ought to have been; and we should have avoided the disgrace of the loss of the hospital, if he had sent away Gen. Bassecourt on the night of the 30th or on the morning of the 31st, or if he had maintained his post at Talavera. As it is, I really believe that I have saved the whole of both armies, by determining to retire to Arzobispo, and taking up the line of the Tagus, as soon as I found the enemy at Navalmoral, and that Gen. Cuesta had irrevocably quitted Talavera.

We have now in Estremadura the whole host of Marshals, Soult, Ney, Mortier, Kellermann, Victor, and Sebastiani, and the King and 5000 men from Suchet. Beresford writes me on the 4th from Almeida, that 34,000 men had gone by Baños to Plasencia, and that none but sick remained in Castille. I have recommended to the Junta to set Romana, the Duque del Parque, and the guerrillas to work towards Madrid.

What will the French do, now that they have got together their force? They will either attack the right of the Spanish army under Venegas, and push forward by Cordova; or they will try another diversion, and invade Portugal by Castello Branco; or they will try and force the passage of the Tagus at Almaraz, where alone the passage can be of any use to them. In any of these cases we have our retreat open; and in case of the invasion of Portugal by Castello Branco, I have ordered Beresford to move his corps to the right towards Castello Branco, while I shall move into Portugal, and cross the Tagus at Abrantes.

I beg you will do what you think best with my dispatch and its enclosures: either publish the whole, or a part, keeping back the enclosures; or let a statement be drawn up from the dispatch. At all events I request you to show the whole dispatch and enclosures to my brothers Pole and Henry, and send a copy to the Duke of Richmond.

I wish you to observe the statement of the French operations made by Jourdan to Soult; and see how accurately they were informed of all our

movements and intentions. Observe particularly that Victor knew positively on the 23d that we were to attack him on the 24th. He could have
known this only by intelligence from our camp, because none of the troops
moved preparatory to the attack till after dark, when Bassecourt's division moved to Cardiel; and indeed Victor began his retreat that night,
before Bassecourt commenced his movement from Talavera; and yet it is
pretended that the French have no intelligence in Spain. Charles will
tell you how much we are distressed for provisions.

To the Duke of Richmond.   Deleytosa, 8th Aug. 1809.

Since I wrote to you last the enemy have introduced a large corps,
supposed to be 30,000 men, into our rear by Baños and Plasencia; in
consequence of which, and of a train of mismanagement by the Spaniards,
we have been obliged to withdraw, and to take up the defensive line of
the Tagus. I have desired Lord Castlereagh to send you a copy of my
dispatch and its enclosures, if he should not publish it, which will make
you acquainted with every thing. We were in a bad scrape, from which
I think I have extricated both armies; and I really believe that, if I had
not determined to retire at the moment I did, all retreat would have been
cut off for both.

To the Rt. Hon. J. Villiers.   Deleytosa, 8th Aug. 1809.

I enclose my public and private letters to Lord Castlereagh, which will
apprise you of the exact situation of affairs in this quarter. All is now
safe, and I should feel no anxiety on any subject if we had provisions:
but we are almost starving.

I enclose a memorandum which I gave to Col. Murray some days ago
for a supply of articles to be brought from Lisbon. I shall be very much
obliged to you if you will desire the government to arrange with the
Commissary Gen. for the stages by which these articles are to be carried
by the carts from Lisbon to Badajoz.

To Marquis Wellesley, Ambassador at the Court of Spain. Deleytosa, 8th Aug. 1809.

I have received your Excellency's letter of the 31st, from Cadiz. I
conclude that Mr. Frere will make your Excellency acquainted with the
general situation of affairs in Spain.

I have the honor to enclose a copy of my dispatch of this date to the
Sec. of State, which will make you acquainted with the circumstances
which have rendered it necessary for the armies to take up a defensive
position behind the Tagus. I have already apprised Mr. Frere in a
private letter of my opinion, that it would be necessary to put in motion
the Marques de la Romana's or the Duque del Parque's force, or some
other in the north of Spain, to induce the enemy to weaken his force in
Estremadura, before the armies could resume offensive operations. In
the mean time it is necessary that many arrangements should be adopted
to enable the troops to take advantage of any success they may have in
an offensive operation, or even to maintain their defensive positions. I
shall endeavor to detail these in this dispatch, with my reasons for thinking them absolutely necessary.

The first of these is the formation of magazines of provisions and forage, principally biscuit, cattle, and barley, at reasonable distances in the rear of the armies.

This part of Spain is but thinly inhabited, and but ill cultivated in proportion to its extent and its fertility, and it is nearly exhausted. As now equipped, the armies, amounting to not less than 60,000 mouths, and 16,000 to 18,000 horses, depend entirely for their daily supply of provisions upon the country, which does not contain a population in an extent of many square miles equal to the numbers of the army, and of course cannot produce a sufficiency for its subsistence. It is necessary, therefore, to send to great distances for supplies, which are procured with difficulty; consequently, the troops are ill fed, and not regularly; and very frequently receive no food at all.

The next arrangement to be made is, to supply the armies with means of transport, not only to move forward the magazines when that may be necessary, which means should be specially attached to the magazines; but also means of transport to enable the army to communicate with the magazines, or to send to any part of the country for supplies of provisions or forage. 3000 or 4000 mules would effectually answer the first object; and I should consider the British army well supplied with what it would require, if it had 1500 mules and about 100 of the Valencian or Catalonian mule carts.

These measures are equally necessary for the Spanish and the British armies. No troops can serve to any good purpose unless they are regularly fed; and it is an error to suppose that a Spaniard, or a man or animal of any country, can make an exertion without food. In fact, the Spanish troops are more clamorous for their food, and more exhausted if they do not receive it regularly, than our own are.

The other points to which I shall draw your attention are referrible to the state of the Spanish troops. My opinion is, that an exertion ought to be made immediately to clothe them in the national uniform. By the adoption of this measure, the practice which prevails, I am sorry to say, very generally, of throwing away their arms and accoutrements and running away, and pretending to be peasants, would be discontinued. Large bodies could not change their clothing or the distinctive marks of dress in a soldier; and it is probable that, as they would not only find no security, but rather increase their danger, by throwing away their arms and accoutrements in their flight, the State would not so frequently sustain the loss of these valuable articles.

Another advantage which would result from the more general use of the national uniform is, that it would be in the power of the General to punish the troops who misbehave before the enemy, in the manner most likely to affect the feelings of Spaniards, viz., by disgrace. When a number of peasants are collected together with arms in their hands, and in the garb of peasants, it is difficult to fix a mark upon those corps or individuals who have behaved ill, which shall point them out as objects or execration to the whole community: and yet it is acknowledged that a punishment of this description would have ten times the effect of that which was lately carried into execution in the Spanish army on account of the misbehavior of some corps in the battle of Talavera, viz., the putting to death every tenth man, of the number who ran away, and a third or fourth of the officers ! If the whole army wore the national uniform, it would be possible to disgrace those who should misbehave, either by depriving them of it, or by affixing some mark to it, which would tend more effectually than any thing else to prevent a repetition of these misfortunes. It is difficult to describe to your Lordship the extent to which this practice prevails. Whole corps, officers and men, all run off upon the first appearance of danger; and I doubt not, if the truth could be ascertained, that the army of Gen. Cuesta, which crossed the Tagus 36,000 or 38,000 strong, does not now consist of 30,000, although it has not lost 500 men in action with the enemy.

The plan of operation which I should recommend for the Spanish nation is one generally of, defence. They should avoid general actions, but should take advantage of the strong points in their country to defend themselves and to harass the enemy. Their principal army should be collected on the Tagus, if they can hold that river; or farther back if they cannot: and wherever they can form a body of troops, or the guerrillas of the country can be put in motion, they should be employed upon the enemy's communications, and should be pushed on even to Madrid.

To Marquis Wellesley.   Deleytosa, 8th Aug. 1809.

I have the honor to acknowledge the receipt of a letter, dated 3d inst., from Mr. Frere. I shall be very much obliged to your Lordship if you will urge Don M. de Garay to adhere to the rule laid down for the government of my communications with the Spanish ministers by His Majesty's commands; and on all future occasions to make known to me the wishes of the Spanish government through the English Ambassador. I am aware that it is difficult, if not impossible, to drive the Spaniards from a false assertion, or a sophistical or bad argument; and I consider it but of little importance what remains in their own archives, if what they write is confined to them. But as those who have the honor of serving His Majesty are liable to misrepresentations and unfounded calumnies of every description, I am desirous of avoiding to give those who circulate these calumnies respecting my actions those grounds for them, which they would find in Don M. de Garay's dispatches to me, by requiring that he should adhere to the rule which His Majesty has laid down for my government.

I am happy to find that the Junta have taken measures to supply the armies. Your Lordship will receive my sentiments, upon the permanent arrangements to be adopted for this purpose, by the courier who will deliver this letter. In the mean time I must inform your Excellency, that if the government have not already made great exertions to supply us, and if we do not experience the immediate effects of these exertions, by receiving a plentiful supply of provisions and forage, we must move away in as many detachments as there are roads from hence to the frontiers of Portugal. I assure your Excellency, that, since the 3d, the army has had no bread till yesterday, when about 4000 lbs. of biscuit were divided among 30,000 mouths. The army will be useless in Spain, and will be entirely lost, if this treatment is to continue; and I must say, that if any efficient measures for our relief had been adopted by the government when they first received the accounts of our distresses from the want of provisions, we ought before now to have received the benefit of them. There is this day again no bread for the soldiers. I must, at the same time, do the late British minister the justice to declare that I do not conceive that this deficiency of supplies for the army is at all to be attributed to any neglect or omission on his part. It is to be attributed to the poverty and exhausted state of the country; to the inactivity of the magistrates and people; to their disinclination to take any trouble, excepting that of packing up their property and running away when they hear of the approach of a French patrole; and to their habits of insubordination and disobedience of, and to the want of power in, the government and their officers.

To Marquis Wellesley.   Deleytosa, 8th Aug. 1809.

I have the honor to enclose a letter which I have received from Don M. de Garay, conveying to me the approbation of the Junta of the conduct of the British troops in the actions of the 27th and 28th July, and the information that the Junta had been pleased to appoint me a Captain General of the Spanish army.

I conceive that I cannot with propriety accept this commission without the consent of His Majesty, and I have accordingly written a letter to Don M. de Garay, by which I have made the acceptance of the commission conditional upon His Majesty's pleasure. This, however, may be considered offensive to the Junta, or your Excellency may have reasons unknown to me, which might induce you to wish that I should not decline the acceptance till His Majesty's pleasure should be known, although it is necessary that the offer should be considered as referrible to His Majesty. I have therefore written a second letter; and I beg your Excellency to decide which of them you will send to Don M. de Garay. I likewise enclose a third letter to Don M. de Garay, in which I have accepted the horses presented to me by the Junta in the name of King Ferdinand VII., but have declined to accept the pay of a Captain General. I shall be obliged to your Excellency if you will send this letter also to Don M. de Garay.

To Marquis Wellesley.   Deleytosa, 8th Aug. 1809.

The public dispatches which I transmit with this letter will give you a full and faithful picture of the state of affairs here. You have undertaken an Herculean task; and God knows that the chances of success are infinitely against you, particularly since the unfortunate turn which affairs have taken in Austria.

I wish I could see you, or could send somebody to you; but we are in such a situation that I cannot go to you myself, and I cannot spare the only one or two people, to converse with whom would be of any use to you. I think, therefore, that the best thing you can do is to send somebody to me as soon as you can; that is to say, if I remain in Spain, which I declare I believe to be almost impossible, notwithstanding that I see all the consequences of withdrawing. But a starving army is actually worse than none The soldiers lose their discipline and their spirit. They plunder even in the presence of their officers. The officers are discontented, and are almost as bad as the men; and with the army which a fortnight ago beat double their numbers, I should now hesitate to meet a French corps of half their strength. Send somebody, however, by the road of Merida and Truxillo, at both of which places he must hear of me.

Au Général en Chef de l'armée Française.   Deleytosa, 9 Août, 1809.

Le sort de la guerre a mis dans vos mains un nombre d'officiers et de soldats Anglais qui sont blessés. Ils sont braves, et ils méritent les attentions et les soins de tous ceux qui estiment la bravoure. J'ai l'honneur de vous les recommander; et je vous prie encore de me permettre d'envoyer à Talavera, pour en avoir soin, des officiers qui ne seront pas censés être prisonniers, et auxquels il sera permis de retourner quand les officiers et soldats blessés seront un peu rétablis. Je vous prie aussi de me permettre d'envoyer aux officiers blessés des petites sommes d'argent, qui leur seront sûrement nécessaires.

Je vous fais des réclamations au nom de l'humanité; et j'ai encore des droits à les faire, ayant toujours bien soigné les soldats Français que le sort de la guerre a mis dans mes mains, et même fourni de l'argent aux officiers.

Au Général Kellermann.   Deleytosa, 9 Août, 1809.

Le sort de la guerre a mis dans les mains du Commandant en Chef de l'armée Française des officiers et des soldats blessés de l'armée Anglaise dans la bataille qui s'est donnée dernièrement à Talavera. J'écris au Commandant en Chef de l'armée Française, pour lui recommander ces

---

G. O.   Deleytosa, 9th Aug. 1809.

1. As the troops composing the army in Spain have not received their rations regularly since the 22d July, it is not just that the full price of the ration should be stopped from the soldier's pay: from the 23d July. therefore, the stoppage from the soldier's pay, on account of his rations, is to be only 3*d*., until the supplies are such as it will be possible to make regular deliveries of provisions. The Commander of the Forces will hereafter give notice of the period at which the full price of the rations is to be charged to the men: this order is applicable to the troops composing Gen. R. Craufurd's brigade, only from the 30th July inclusive, and to the troops of Horse Artillery only from the 3d Aug.

2. The Commander of the Forces desires that the roll may be called in camp every two hours, and the officers commanding divisions will give directions what proportion of officers are to attend.

3. The soldiers themselves render the difficulties of the moment greater than they would otherwise be by their irregularity, as they seize and plunder the mules coming in with provisions, by which the good and regular soldiers of the army are deprived of their just share of them.

4. The Provost Marshal will ascertain by what roads provisions are coming in; he will take care that his assistants patrole those roads constantly, and any man caught in the act of plundering provisions coming to the army is to be punished on the spot, as such a heinous offence deserves.

5. Soldiers must not quit their lines unless dressed with their side-arms, excepting when on fatigue; all soldiers on fatigue must be under the command of an officer or non-commissioned officer.

6. The practice of taking roots and vegetables without paying for them must be entirely discontinued; if roots or vegetables are required, they must be taken by regular parties formed under the command of an officer, who must take care and is responsible the owner of the ground is paid for what is taken.

soldats, et pour le prier de me permettre d'envoyer à Talavera pour en avoir soin des officiers, qui ne seront pas censés être prisonniers de guerre ; et auxquels il sera permis de s'en retourner à l'armée quand les blessés seront rétablis. Je le prie aussi de me permettre d'envoyer des petites sommes d'argent aux officiers.

Ayant l'honneur de vous connaître, j'ose réclamer vos bons offices auprès du Commandant en Chef de l'armée Française, et vous recommander mes blessés. Si c'est le Maréchal Soult qui commande, il me doit tous les soins qu'il peut donner à ces braves soldats, car j'ai sauvé les siens, que le sort de la guerre a mis dans mes mains, des fureurs de la populace Portugaise, et les ai bien soignés. D'ailleurs comme les deux nations sont toujours en guerre, nous nous devons récriproquement ces soins que je réclame pour mes blessés, et que j'ai donnés toujours à ceux que le sort a mis dans mes mains.

To Major Gen. O'Donoju. Deleytosa, 9th Aug. 1809.

I am desirous of sending Lieut. Col. Waters, who will deliver this letter to you, with a flag of truce to the head quarters of the French army, with letters to the Commander in Chief, respecting the English wounded left at Talavera. I shall be very much obliged to you if you will apply to Gen. Cuesta, that he may be permitted to pass the Spanish outposts and return again. Col. Waters will show you the letters with which he is charged.

To Major Gen. O'Donoju. Deleytosa, 9th Aug. 1809.

I have heard that the Spanish head quarters were yesterday at Peraleda de Garbin; that the enemy's cavalry passed the river by the ford of Azutan, but that Gen. Bassecourt still held possession of the bridge of Arzobispo: and that the Spanish head quarters were to be moved last night to Mesa de Ibor.

I shall be very much obliged to you if you will make me acquainted with Gen. Cuesta's movements, his present situation, and his future intentions. As it is impossible for us just at present to make use of the bridge of boats at Almaraz, I have desired Gen. Craufurd to take the boats out of the water, and to remove them to a place where they will be protected from the effects of the enemy's fire. The bridge over the little stream is left standing, as Gen. Craufurd found the water so shallow, that it was a matter of indifference whether the bridge was there or not. The pontoon carriages are at the river side, and it would probably be desirable that the mules should be sent there also, in order to move them with greater facility, if necessary, for the defence of the passage at Almaraz.

In respect to the bridge of Arzobispo, the only view in which I think it would be advisable to destroy it is, that you might prevent the enemy from bringing his artillery against your posts at Mesa de Ibor, and in the mountains, which I conclude you will continue to hold. But upon this point the first question is, whether the enemy can bring artillery from the bridge of Talavera, along the left bank to Arzobispo? the next, whether they can bring artillery across the ford at Azutan, or any other ford above Arzobispo? If they can, it is hardly worth while to destroy the bridge of Arzobispo ? If they cannot, it is an object of importance to the defence of your posts in the mountains that it should be destroyed.

It is very clear to me that there is no difficulty in moving artillery of any dimensions from Arzobispo to the Ibor; and that being the case, the destruction of the bridge would depend upon the possibility of moving the artillery on the left bank to Arzobispo. If you should be obliged to withdraw your posts from Arzobispo, I conclude that you will take care of your right flank, towards the Puerto de San Vicente.

P.S. Gen. Beresford, who is in the Puerto de Perales, informs me that the Duque del Parque occupies the Puerto de Baños. The enemy have no troops in Castille, and have passed 34,000 men from thence through the Puerto de Baños. All were through by the 3d inst.; Soult, Ney, Mortier, and Kellermann command these corps; some of them returned yesterday to Plasencia.

To Marquis Wellesley.   Deleytosa, 9th Aug. 1809.

I have not received any communication from Gen. Cuesta since the morning of the 6th (when at Peraleda de Garbin I saw Gen. O'Donoju), until I received this morning from Lieut. Col. Roche a letter, of which the enclosed is a copy. I did not even know that Gen. Cuesta had moved his head quarters from the bridge of Arzobispo, much less that any disaster had happened to his troops, even to the limited extent stated by Lieut. Col. Roche. About 3 o'clock this day, however, the Duque de Alburquerque arrived here and informed me, that the French cavalry had surprised the Spanish outposts at the bridge of Arzobispo, by crossing the river at a ford immediately above the bridge, at half past one; that the Spanish troops had given way, and that the French had possession of the bridge, of the cannon destined to its defence, and of 5 pieces belonging to the Duque's division which were left behind.

The Duque de Alburquerque states his belief that the French were in Peraleda de Garbin this morning, where your Excellency will have observed that Gen. Cuesta's head quarters were yesterday afternoon. Gen. Cuesta has since sent me a message by one of his aides de camp and Col. Roche, from whom I understand that the General had not, to the moment of their departure from Mesa de Ibor at 10 o'clock in the morning, brought any of his artillery or of his carriages across the Ibor.

On this side that river there is a high mountain, up which it is impossible to draw artillery, excepting by the assistance of men; and it is obvious that, unless the General has saved Peraleda de Garbin, and the positions between the Ibor and that village, the Spaniards must lose their artillery, although they may hold the position of the Mesa de Ibor. I enclose to your Lordship the copy of a letter which I wrote to Gen. O'Donoju on the 7th, and of another which I have just dispatched to him; but I acknowledge that I am apprehensive that the Spanish army will lose, or rather has lost, its artillery before this time. I can do nothing to assist them; and, indeed, in any case, it would have been impossible for me to do any thing for their assistance, excepting by persuading Gen. Cuesta to adopt early measures to pass his heavy artillery over the Ibor.

To Brig. Gen. R. Craufurd.   Deleytosa, 9th Aug. 1809.

I have just received your letter, and conceive that you have done quite right in not destroying the little bridge. I have written to Gen. Cuesta respecting mules to draw the pontoon carriages. I have not yet been able to send you guns, as our horses were so much fatigued by the passage of the defiles. I hope I shall be able to send you some this evening.

I find that the Spanish head quarters were yesterday at Peraleda de Garbin, and I think it probable that they may have moved last night to Mesa de Ibor.

The French cavalry had crossed yesterday at a ford at Azutan, above Arzobispo; but the Spanish division under Bassecourt still held the bridge. I intended going to see you this morning, but I do not like to be out of the way till the Spanish army is landed somewhere.

To Brig. Gen. R. Craufurd.   Deleytosa, 9th Aug. 1809.

The Spanish advanced guard was surprised yesterday at the bridge of Arzobispo, in the middle of the day, and gave way, leaving in the enemy's hands the cannon for the defence of the bridge, and 5 pieces belonging to the Duque de Alburquerque's division. Cuesta's head quarters were then at Peraleda de Garbin, and he moved them last night to Mesa de Ibor. He has now his advanced guard on the high ground on the right bank of the Ibor, the main body on the left bank, and the enemy have not this day pressed the advanced guard. The artillery and carriages of the Spanish army were still at 4 this morning in the low ground on the Ibor; and it is not improbable that if the enemy should attack and drive in the advanced guard, they will take the whole of it. In this case I am convinced that the Spanish army will disband. If they would make any exertion to get their artillery out of the Ibor this night, they ought to be able to defend themselves on the Mesa de Ibor, and possibly will do so. If, however, I should find that they retire from that strong post, either by being beaten from it, or from any other cause, it will be very obvious to the whole world that they cannot fight for themselves. My intention is, in that case, to collect the British army at Jaraicejo; to send you orders to fall back upon that place; and then to march the whole to Truxillo, and thence by the high road to Badajoz and Elvas.

I think it will be desirable for you to have an eye upon the road by which you marched from Mesa de Ibor to Romangordo; as, should the enemy carry the Mesa de Ibor, it is not impossible that they might push something that way, which would lie very awkwardly upon your flank as you would draw out of the Puerto.

I have desired the Spaniards to occupy Val de Casas, as part of their position at Mesa de Ibor, but I hardly expect they will. The guns will go to you in the morning.

The A.G. to Col. Mackinnon.   9th Aug. 1809.

I am directed by the Commander of the Forces to desire that you will proceed to move the 1st division of sick and wounded to-morrow, agreeable to route, which you will receive from the Q. M. G.; such carts and cars as you have in your possession must carry as many of the bad cases as they afford conveyance for; the remainder must remain until further conveyance arrives, and is sent to the convent, which, it is hoped, will be procured in the course of to-morrow. You will move as large a proportion of the slight cases as you can with the 1st division. It is the Commander of the Forces' direction, that no commissaries' mules are to go with the sick and wounded, as they are imperiously wanted for other services. Should any be at the convent, they are to return to the Commissary Gen. at Deleytosa.

You will please to inform me of the number of men you march with the 1st division, as also the number that remain with the 2d, and under whose command.

To Don Gregorio Cuesta.   Mesa de Ibor, noon, 10th Aug. 1809.

Having been down to the Ibor, I observed, that although the whole of the artillery, and the carriages of your Excellency's army, have crossed the river, they are not yet brought up the hill. Your Excellency will find the mules and horses quite incapable of drawing them up; and that to attempt it by their means will destroy them. I should therefore recommend to your Excellency to employ working parties of 300 or 400 men each, of the troops, who would complete the work in a few hours. It will also be necessary that your Excellency should send a battalion to the river at the bottom of the hill at Campillos, as there is on that hill, near the river, a turn in the road, at which all the guns must be unlimbered; and they can be drawn past that turn by hand only by the troops. I mention these circumstances, as, having passed through the defiles with the British artillery, I am acquainted with the mode in which the passages of your Excellency's carriages will be facilitated.

I conclude that your Excellency will occupy the right of the Ibor in strength, till your artillery shall have passed through the defiles; afterwards, I should conceive that one division of infantry, with the advanced guard at Mesa de Ibor, one division at Campillos, one division at Fresnedoso, and the main body with the cavalry at Deleytosa, would secure the right flank of the combined armies. By repairing the road from Deleytosa to the river at the bottom of the hill of Campillos, before referred to, and particularly by an alteration of the turn near the river, artillery may be employed in the defence of all these posts, with the certainty of being able to withdraw it, while the enemy can employ none in the attack.

I propose to move the head quarters of the British army to-morrow morning to Jaraicejo, in order to make room for the cavalry of your Excellency's army which has come through the defiles.

To Marquis Wellesley.   Deleytosa, 10th Aug. 1809, 6 P.M.

I have been this day to Gen. Cuesta's head quarters, at the Mesa de Ibor. The whole of his artillery and wheel carriages had crossed the Ibor; and about one half of the whole appeared to me to have been brought up the mountain on this side of the Ibor at 12 o'clock.

The enemy's light troops were in Peraleda de Garbin, those of Gen. Cuesta at Bohonal. The enemy has made no movement since yesterday morning. The General complained of his distress for provisions, which, indeed, is equally felt by all the troops. The horses of the British cavalry and artillery suffer much from the want of barley. We have lost many hundreds of the former, and above 200 of the latter, by the use of other grains, not having been able to procure barley (the only wholesome food for horses in this country) for the horses of the British cavalry and artillery, notwithstanding that the Spanish cavalry have been plentifully supplied.

I have also to mention to your Excellency, in order to point out the description of assistance which is given to us in this country, that having applied for a remount of cavalry of only 100 mares, (which cannot be used by the Spanish cavalry, as they ride stallions,) I have not got one, or even an answer from the government on the subject; and having asked Gen. Cuesta, after the battle of Talavera, to assist me with 90 mules, to draw the British artillery, in lieu of those lost in the action, he refused to give me any, notwithstanding that there were hundreds in his army employed in drawing carts containing nothing. The consequence is, that I shall now be obliged to send back to Portugal one, if not two, brigades of artillery drawn by bullocks, if I should be able to procure these animals; if I should not, I must destroy them.

P. S. In stating to your Excellency the wants of this army of draught for the artillery, and the means adopted to supply it, I beg to observe that I have endeavored to purchase both horses and mules; but I cannot procure them in sufficient numbers. I also wish to draw your Excellency's notice to the fact, that Gen. Cuesta has within these two days lost 11, and, if I am rightly informed, 20 pieces of artillery, the mules and horses attached to which were not lost, for the Duque de Alburquerque offered to make over to me the mules attached to 5 pieces which he had lost; but Gen. Cuesta has taken them.

To Lieut. Gen. Payne.   Jaraicejo, 11th Aug. 1809.

I have just heard so melancholy a report of the state of the squadron which has been with Gen. R. Craufurd, on the Tagus, that I request you to relieve the squadron there every day, and to send with them a day's forage. You should recollect the artillery horses in your distributions of forage. If they are starved, we shall be knocked up more effectually than if the horses of the cavalry were so. Pray let them have a portion of your barley.

To Brig. Gen. R. Craufurd.   Jaraicejo, 11th Aug. 1809.

I have moved my head quarters to this place. The infantry of the army are in the wood behind it. The Spanish army, to which I paid a visit yesterday, were at Mesa de Ibor. All their guns and carriages were on this side of the Ibor, and about half of them up the first hill from the river. The French troops had not passed Peraleda. The Spanish light troops were at Bohonal.

I have written to Gen. Payne, to desire that he would relieve the squadron with you every day; and I shall desire the Commanding officer of artillery to do the same by the horses of the artillery. They shall take forage with them for the day they will stay with you.

We have reports here of columns of the enemy's troops marching towards Plasencia. Have you seen any thing of the kind?

G. O.   Jaraicejo, 11th Aug. 1809.

The army are desired to attend particularly to the orders relative to the watering their horses, until two hours before or after feeding.

To Don Gregorio Cuesta.   Deleytosa, 11th Aug. 1809.

I have had the honor of receiving your Excellency's letter of the 10th inst., and I am concerned that you should conceive that you have any reason to complain of the conduct of the British troops; but when troops are starving, which those under my command have been, as I have repeatedly told your Excellency since I joined you on the 22d of last month, and particularly had no bread whatever from the 3d to the 8th inst., it is not astonishing that they should go to the villages, and even to the mountains, and look for food where they think they can get it. The complaints of the inhabitants, however, should not have been confined to the conduct of the British troops: in this very village I have seen the Spanish soldiers, who ought to have been elsewhere, take the doors off the houses which were locked up, in order that they might plunder the houses, and they afterwards burnt the doors. I absolutely and positively deny the assertion, that any thing going to the Spanish army has been stopped by the British troops or Commissaries.

On the 7th, when the British troops were starving in the hills, I met a convoy of 350 mules, loaded with provisions for the Spanish army. I would not allow one of them to be touched, and they all passed on. Gen. Sherbrooke, on the following day, the 8th, gave a written order to another convoy, addressed to all British officers, to allow them to pass through the army unmolested. Yesterday I met on the road, and passed, not less than 500 mules loaded with provisions for the Spanish army; and no later than yesterday evening, Major Campbell, my aide de camp, gave an order to another large convoy, addressed to all British officers and soldiers, not to impede its progress. I also declare to your Excellency most positively, on the honor of a gentleman, that the British army has received no provisions since it has been at Deleytosa, excepting some sent from Truxillo, by Señor L. de Torres; and I call upon the gentleman, who has informed his friend that biscuit addressed to the Spanish army has been taken by my Commissaries, to prove the truth of his assertion.

But this letter from your Excellency brings the question respecting provisions to a fair issue. I call upon your Excellency to state distinctly, whether it is understood by you that the Spanish army are to have not only all the provisions the country can afford, but all those which are sent from Seville, I believe, as much for the service of the one army as of the other.

I beg you to let me know in reply to this letter, whether any magazines of provisions have been formed, and from whence the British troops are to draw their provisions.

I hope that I shall receive satisfactory answers to these two questions to-morrow morning. If I should not, I beg that your Excellency will be prepared to occupy the post opposite Almaraz, as it will be impossible for me to remain any longer in a country in which no arrangement has been made for the supply of provisions for the troops; and in which it is understood that all the provisions which are either found in the country, or are sent from Seville, as I have been informed, for the use of the British army, are to be applied solely and exclusively to the use of the Spanish troops.

In regard to the assertion in your Excellency's letter that the British troops sell their bread to the Spanish soldiers, it is beneath the dignity of your Excellency's situation and character to notice such things, or for me to reply to them. I must observe, however, that the British troops could not sell that which they had not, and that the reverse of the statement of your Excellency upon this subject is the fact, at the time the armies were at Talavera; as I have myself witnessed frequently in the streets of that town.

P.S. I send Col. O'Lawlor with this letter, who knows the truth of the facts stated in it respecting the convoys which have been forwarded, and respecting the supplies received here from Truxillo.

To Don Gregorio Cuesta. Deleytosa, 11th Aug. 1809, 8½ A.M.

I have the honor to inform your Excellency, from the reports which I have received from my post on the Tagus opposite Almaraz, that within these two days the river has fallen from 18 inches to 2 feet, and that it is now fordable in two places above that where the bridge of pontoons was fixed.

To Don Gregorio Cuesta. Jaraicejo, 11th Aug. 1809.

I have to inform your Excellency that as Mr. Commissary Richardson was coming from Truxillo, with bread and barley for the British army, he was pursued by a body of Spanish cavalry, which contrived to get from him all the barley. He secured the bread, a small part of which, however, the Spanish cavalry forced him to give up, but for which he made the non-commissioned officer sign the receipt which I enclose. Unless it should be understood by your Excellency that all the bread baked in the country, and all that is sent from Seville, and all the barley, are to be appropriated exclusively to the use of the Spanish troops, I should hope you will take measures to punish this act of outrage, and prevent its recurrence in future.

To Don Gregorio Cuesta. Jaraicejo, 11th Aug. 1809.

I have the honor to enclose to your Excellency a letter which I have just received from the Junta at Plasencia, which is now stationed at Talavan, stating that the enemy have returned towards Plasencia.

I have sent to our outposts to ascertain the fact. The enclosed letter having been addressed to me, as well as to your Excellency, I have taken the liberty of opening it.

Memorandum.

Plan of Operations to be adopted in case the Enemy's columns now on their march towards Plasencia, should enter Portugal, sent to Mr. Villiers, Marshal Beresford, and Brig. Gen. ——. Jaraicejo, 12th Aug. 1809.

1. Marshal Beresford's corps is already ordered to fall back upon Castello Branco when necessary, where, or on the road to which place, he will probably find the British brigade under the command of Major Gen. Lightburne. The Marshal will naturally take the road from Castello Branco by Sobreira Formosa, throwing a small corps by the road of Perdigão; the enemy probably will take the road by Fundão and by the tops of the hills, which comes into the other road at Cardigos. The Marshal will in this case have an opportunity of delaying the enemy at the ravine at Cardigos.

2. From Cardigos they may move direct upon Abrantes, or they may move by Villa de Rey, and across the Zezere upon Thomar. Here, therefore, we must have a fresh combination for our defence.

3. Brig. Gen. —— has been ordered to halt at Abrantes, if his orders should find him there; at Niza, if they should find him south of the Tagus; or at Castello Branco, if north of the Tagus. He should be ordered to proceed to Abrantes, wherever he may be; if at Castello Branco, he should proceed by Villa Velha, and should destroy the flying bridge and all the boats at that place. This, however, must be done in communication with Marshal Beresford.

4. From Abrantes he should proceed to S. Domingo, and defend the passage of the Cades, in case the enemy should take the direct road to Abrantes from Cardigos, instead of that by Villa de Rey towards Thomar.

5. Marshal Beresford will in this case go to Villa de Rey, and defend the passage of the Zezere.

6. If Gen. —— should find himself obliged to retire, he will throw himself into Abrantes, which place he will maintain at all events as long as possible; and with this view he will give immediate directions, and will take measures that a large quantity of provisions should be brought up the hill into the town.

7. It is possible that at this season of the year the Tagus may be fordable at Villa Velha, and the enemy, instead of turning to his right and taking the road by the hills, called the *Marquez d'Alorna's*, may turn to his left, and cross the Tagus at Villa Velha. In that case, Marshal Beresford and Gen. —— will join their corps at Abrantes as soon as possible. They will take up the bridge at Abrantes, keeping the boats and the materials under the hill below the town.

8. It is to be observed, that the object of all these operations is only to gain a few days of time to enable the British army to return from Spanish Estremadura. Every day's delay would therefore be of importance.

9. It would be very desirable that Marshal Beresford should reinforce Brig. Gen. —— with a brigade of artillery, and a squadron of dragoons for patroles.

To Marshal Beresford. Jaraicejo, 12th Aug. 1809.

I have put in the form of a memorandum nearly what I stated to Hardinge yesterday, of which I send you one copy, and another to —— : of course you will make such alterations in this plan as may appear to you most expedient upon a view of the situation of affairs upon the spot; understanding always that I wish that Gen. —— should join me at Abrantes, if the enemy should operate upon the north of the Tagus; and that I wish you and —— to be ready to throw yourselves upon his back, while I shall attack him in front, if he should cross at Villa Velha, and remain in Alentejo.

I have not yet heard that they have passed Plasencia; as soon as I do I

A. G. O. Jaraicejo, 12th Aug. 1809.

Commanding officers of regiments are to report immediately to the Adj. Gen. the names of all officers who have absented themselves, without leave, since the 25th of last month, in order that their names may be published in the Orders of the Army, and that they may be ordered to the army in arrest.

shall move, and shall not halt till I shall reach Abrantes. I understand that the 3 divisions which had passed to Plasencia are not strong, and I think are composed of the troops of Soult and Ney's corps. Mortier is certainly still at Arzobispo.

Memorandum for the Commissary Gen.   Jaraicejo, 12th Aug. 1809.

1. The store at Abrantes, according to the return of it given to me yesterday, is much too large, particularly in biscuit and flour, and it ought forthwith to be reduced to the amount of 300,000 rations of flour.

2. This should be done by sending down, in boats to Santarem or Valada, in the first instance, all the overplus.

3. Orders should be forthwith sent to Abrantes to commence upon this operation without loss of time, care being taken that the boat people are paid, to secure the return of the boats.

4. Boats should likewise be sent up from Lisbon, Santarem, and Valada, as soon as possible, to aid in the removal of the stores; and regular passports must be made to the boat people, in order to secure their regular service.

5. After the flour and biscuit shall have been removed, the oats and barley should be reduced to a supply of 6 days for the horses, &c., of the army by the same means; and the salt meat to 90,000 lbs.

To Don Gregorio Cuesta.   Jaraicejo, 12th Aug. 1809.

I have the honor to enclose a copy of a letter which I received last night from Col. Waters, whom I had sent with a flag of truce on the preceding day, the 10th. Your Excellency will observe that there are no troops nearer than the bridge of Arzobispo, and but few there.

I have to inform your Excellency that I learnt last night from my posts upon the Tagus, that the enemy have been moving in corps of considerable strength for the last 3 days towards Plasencia. I do not know that any troops now remain at Navalmoral or at Almaraz.

To the Rt. Hon. J. Villiers.   Jaraicejo, 12th Aug. 1809.

Since I wrote to Lord Castlereagh, on the 8th inst., letters which I sent for your perusal, the Spaniards have been surprised at the bridge of Arzobispo, which they lost, together with from 10 to 20 pieces of cannon.

They have since that day been employed in getting their army through the mountains, which they have not yet accomplished.

We have occupied the bridge of Almaraz, with the army, first at Deleytosa, then at this place, in the rear of that point.

Our wounded are gone to Truxillo, and I propose to move them from thence to Elvas, where I shall establish the hospital.

The French have been moving since the 9th towards Plasencia. They have gone in three divisions, none of them of great strength, the first only about 4000 men. I have not yet received intelligence whether they have passed Plasencia, and I can therefore form no decided opinion respecting their intentions. I think, however, that if they meditated a serious attack upon Portugal, they would not have moved off by daylight in sight of our troops; and I therefore suspect that these movements are intended only as a feint to induce us to separate from the Spaniards, to secure that kingdom.

In case, however, the intention to invade Portugal should be serious, I have drawn up a memorandum of the plan of defence to be adopted, of which I enclose you a copy. I have sent a copy to Marshal Beresford, and another to Gen. —— ——, through Gen. Leite, by this messenger; but it is desirable that you should also send them copies of this paper, by a trusty person, without loss of time. I shall know this night whether the enemy have passed Plasencia : if they shall have done so, I shall march to-morrow, and I shall not halt until I reach Abrantes. I trust, therefore, that the government will be under no alarm for the safety of Portugal.

Our Commissary has collected at Abrantes an unreasonable quantity of provisions and stores. I have given him directions to reduce the magazines there to a reasonable extent, by sending down the overplus by water. I shall be obliged to you to urge the government to give him every assistance in boats of a light draught, to navigate the upper part of the river; as I propose in the first instance, in order to make shorter work of it, to remove the overplus only as far as Santarem or Vallada, from whence we can get it, when I please, either up or down the river. I shall be obliged to you if you will read the memorandum which is sent to Mr. Dunmore and Mr. Murray by the messenger who will go this night.

In case the enemy should enter Portugal, I should wish the troops at Lisbon to remain at that station, till they shall receive orders from Marshal Beresford or me to move; and I do not propose to move them, at all events, farther than Villa Franca.

We are starving, and are ill treated by the Spaniards in every way : but more of this hereafter. There is not a man in the army who does not wish to return to Portugal.

To Marquis Wellesley.   Jaraicejo, 12th Aug. 1809, 8 A.M.

I have the honor to enclose to you the copy of a letter which I received yesterday morning from Gen. Cuesta, and a copy of my answer. I have not since heard from the General, but I transmitted to him yesterday afternoon a report which I received from Mr. Commissary Richardson, who was coming from Truxillo to the British army with bread and barley, and was stopped and deprived of all his barley and a small part of his bread, by a detachment of Spanish cavalry.

I understand there was a firing of cannon and musketry in the neighbourhood of the Mesa de Ibor, yesterday morning about 8 o'clock. But I conclude that it was an affair of no consequence, and probably the Spanish posts firing at a French patrole, as I learn from Lieut. Col. Waters (whom I had sent in to the French Commander in Chief with a flag of truce relating to our sick and wounded), from Val de Casas on the 10th, that there were no French troops on this side of the bridge of Arzobispo, excepting those immediately at the bridge.

The enemy have been in motion for the last 3 days, viz., the 9th, 10th, and 11th, in large columns towards Plasencia, from which movement I conclude that they are either jealous of the position of the Duque del Parque's troops or of those of Gen. Beresford in the mountains of Baños and Perales; or that they propose to invade Portugal, in order to draw me out of Spain. In either case it is obvious that they do not intend to make a serious attack at present on the south of Spain. I shall know during this day which course they have taken from Plasencia; and if they have moved towards the frontiers of Portugal, I must follow them. Indeed the experience of every day shows the absolute necessity that the British army should withdraw from this country.

It is useless to complain, but we are certainly not treated as friends, much less as the only prop on which the cause in Spain can depend. But besides this want of good will, which can easily be traced to the temper and disposition of the General commanding the Spanish army, and which ought to be borne with patience if there was any hope of doing good, there is such a want of resource in the country, and so little question of bringing forward what is to be found, that if the army were to remain here much longer it would become totally useless. The daily and increasing loss of horses in the cavalry and the artillery, from a deficiency and badness of the food, is really alarming; and the Spanish cavalry having begun to intercept the small supply of food for horses which we could procure, this evil must increase.

The A.G. to Col. ——.   12th Aug. 1809.

I have laid your letter and enclosure before the Commander of the Forces, who has perused them with attention, and has directed me to acquaint you that he really does not understand what you have to complain of in Brig. Gen. ——'s orders. Those respecting soldiers on their march appear to his Excellency to be directed solely to carry into execution, in a most effectual manner, the G.O. frequently recalled to the recollection of the officers of the army, but imperfectly executed. Under these circumstances, the Commander of the Forces does not see of what you complain, and begs you will specify more distinctly, for he cannot remove your brigade, without the smallest reason, from Brig. Gen. ——'s division.

With respect to your wish of having a leave of absence on account of your health, the Commander of the Forces has no objection to your going to the rear, provided you send a sick certificate.

To Don Gregorio Cuesta.   Jaraicejo, 13th Aug. 1809.

I have had the honor of receiving your Excellency's letter of the 11th. The plan which your Excellency proposes of placing all the supplies in a magazine, to be formed at Truxillo, and to divide them between the two armies in proportion to the strength of each, would answer perfectly if it were practicable. But your Excellency must be aware that many articles of provisions are received by your Excellency's army which do not pass through Truxillo, and could not be brought there without great inconvenience and delay, and could never appear in the accounts of the magazines; and that other supplies could easily be turned off from Truxillo without my having any knowledge of the fact.

The British army receive no provisions of which Sr. Lozano de Torres has not a knowledge; and your Excellency has it in your power to give him such orders as you may think proper, both as to the formation of the magazine, and the share which the British troops shall have of it.

When the British army entered Spain I had reason to expect, and I expected, that a great effort would be made to afford us subsistence, at least for payment, and those means of transport, and other aids, without which your Excellency is well aware no army can keep the field. Your Excellency also knows how these expectations have been fulfilled. Since I joined your army the troops have not received, upon an average, half a ration, and on some days nothing at all; and the cavalry no forage or grain, excepting what they could pick up in the fields, of an unwholesome description, by the use of which hundreds of horses have died. I can procure no means of transport, and your Excellency knows that I have been obliged to leave some ammunition in the mountains, of which you have possession; and if I now move, I must leave behind me two thirds of the small quantity of ammunition I have got, having been obliged to allot the Portuguese carts, which have moved it hitherto, to the purpose of removing the wounded soldiers.

The fire of the enemy, and the badness and scarcity of food, have destroyed many of my artillery horses; and I have asked, but in vain, for some assistance of this description. The consequence is that I shall be obliged to destroy many guns, when I shall move from hence. I have not received even an answer to the request I made to have a remount for the cavalry of only 100 mares, which would be entirely useless to the Spanish cavalry.

Under all these circumstances, your Excellency cannot be surprised that I should think that the British army has been neglected and ill treated; or at the determination which I now communicate to you, that whatever may be the consequences to the valuable interests to which you refer in your letter, I shall march them back into Portugal, if they are not more regularly and more plentifully supplied with provisions and forage, and with the means of transport, and other aids which they require. I have to observe, that whether I put this determination into execution or not, the evil consequences that you apprehend to the valuable interests to which you refer, must equally follow; as the army will be unable and unfit to perform any operation, if the privations which it has suffered are still to continue.

I request your Excellency to give orders to the troops you have sent to Truxillo not to prevent the officers and soldiers of the British army from buying what they want there. The troops have had no salt or other necessary articles for some time, and it is desirable that they and their officers should be allowed to buy at Truxillo what that place can afford.

To Marquis Wellesley.   Jaraicejo, 13th Aug. 1809.

I have the honor to enclose an answer which I have received from Gen. Cuesta, to the letters which I addressed to him on the 11th inst., with my reply of this date. The plan which he proposes of dividing between the two armies, in proportion to their numbers, all the provisions received at Truxillo, however specious in appearance, would be fallacious in practice, and would probably starve the British army. It would not be difficult to forbid the convoys of provisions coming from Seville from going to Truxillo; and it is probable that the supplies of provisions from Seville do not amount to one fourth of the consumption of both armies, the remainder being supplied by the country, in which, of course, the Spanish army has the preference.

An arrangement of this description is impracticable in execution, even if the Commissaries of the two armies would act fairly by each other; but this is not to be expected; every Commissary will do the best he can for the troops to which he is attached, and many articles must be procured in the country which will not be brought to account in the magazine of Truxillo. In short, my Lord, it comes to this; either the British army must be fed and supplied with the necessaries which they require, or I shall march them back into Portugal, whether that Kingdom is invaded or not by the French corps which has moved within these few days towards Plasencia.

I have received Mr. Frere's private letter of the 10th, in which he has enclosed the copies of a correspondence that he has had with Don M. de Garay, on the subject of the evacuation of Talavera by Gen. Cuesta.

I observe from these papers that Gen. Cuesta had given the Junta reason to believe, that when I marched from Arzobispo, on the 5th, I intended to return to Portugal : and that he prevailed upon me to take up the position of Almaraz, by a message through Gen. O'Donoju and Lord Macduff*. I beg to inform your Excellency, that although Gen. O'Donoju and Lord Macduff did come to me at Peraleda de Garbin on the 6th, Gen. Cuesta knew, on the 4th, my opinion respecting our future operations, and my determination to secure as soon as possible the important points of the Mesa de Ibor and Campillos, which if the enemy had seized on his arrival at Almaraz, the combined armies could not have extricated themselves from the mountains.

I have also another observation to make upon this correspondence. My letters to Mr. Frere of the 3d and 4th were given to the General to be sent to Arzobispo on the 4th; yet it appears that they were not transmitted till after the General had written, on the 6th, his account of the supposed success of the mission of Gen. O'Donoju and Lord Macduff; and Mr. Frere did not receive them till the 10th.

P.S. I beg to mention to your Excellency, that the troops have received, this day and yesterday, only half an allowance of bread, and the cavalry no forage excepting what they can pick up in the fields. The troops suffer considerably from want of salt, and neither officers nor soldiers have had any wine for the last fortnight.

In case I should move, I must leave behind me two thirds of the small quantity of ammunition I have remaining, having been obliged to give all the Portuguese carts, which had hitherto carried the ammunition, to move the wounded, and not having been able to procure in this country means of transport for any thing. Surely, my Lord, the Junta have had time, since the 17th of last month, to supply the wants of the army with which they were then made acquainted.

Memorandum.   Jaraicejo, 13th Aug. 1809.

From the orders sent to —— yesterday, of which a copy is enclosed, he will see how important it is that an officer should strictly obey the orders which he receives ; and having obeyed them, that he should patiently wait for further orders. He could not suppose that he was forgotten; or that the depôts at Castello Branco, or Abrantes, were forgotten ; or that any of those points respecting which he has taken upon himself to give orders, such as the march of the 11th regt., and of the artillery from Lisbon, &c., had not

---

* The Earl of Fife, then serving in the Spanish army.

been attended to at head quarters; or that means did not exist for communicating the orders upon them which might be necessary.

The orders given yesterday contain a detailed plan for the defence of Portugal, combined of the operations of different corps, and the whole founded upon a supposition that they were in certain situations ordered for them; and that they would find, particularly Marshal Beresford's corps, a depôt of provisions at Castello Branco, which would have supported it while at and in the neighbourhood of that place, and while passing through the mountains to the rear.

In consequence of ——'s orders and arrangements, all this now becomes a matter of doubt; and the enemy being in force at Plasencia, it is uncertain, not only whether there will be troops to oppose him in the stations supposed, if he should invade Portugal, but whether there will be magazines of provisions to support those bodies of troops whose commanders may have obeyed their orders. If it should be possible, it is still wished that the orders of yesterday may be carried into execution; and —— will understand that his movements and orders have involved him in a very serious responsibility.

To Marshal Beresford. Jaraicejo, 14th Aug. 1809.

Arbuthnot arrived last night, and has communicated to me your opinion that it is best that I should not move towards Portugal, which agrees so far with mine as this, that I do not consider the enemy's movement towards that Kingdom to be so decided, as to render such a movement on my part necessary or proper. I think, however, that you are mistaken respecting the amount of the force which you suppose to be at, and in the neighbourhood of Plasencia. We know that they moved to that quarter 4000 or 5000 men on the 9th; another column was seen on its march towards the same quarter on the 10th, and was supposed by Col. Donkin, who saw it, to be 10,000 men. Gen. R. Craufurd, who saw the tail of the column, did not think it was more than 5000; and another column was seen in march in the same direction on the 11th, which the officer of the German artillery, who saw it, said was three hours in passing one point, but which Gen. Craufurd also saw, and did not think more than 5000 men. The number, therefore, at Plasencia must be between 15,000 and 25,000 men, of which many are cavalry. I believe the whole corps of Ney and Soult are in that quarter. Mortier is certainly between Almaraz and Arzobispo.

The question is, what is their object in going to Plasencia? They may not be aware of the inefficiency of all the troops collected and scattered on the frontiers of Estremadura; and they may apprehend that we shall play them the same trick, on the same ground, that they have played us.

Sir R. Wilson's march from the neighbourhood of Talavera, through the mountains to Bejar, must have astonished them; and as they have set down his troops at 15,000 men, they may wish to guard against his enterprises. Their right would certainly be very insecure, if all these troops were efficient; and if the French believe them to be efficient, the occupation of Plasencia is easily accounted for. But as I find the French perfectly informed of every thing, excepting, indeed, the amount of Sir

2 E 2

R. Wilson's corps, I should be inclined to believe that the occupation of Plasencia is founded upon some more solid view than one of defence for their right, against the enterprises of the troops on the different points on the frontier of Estremadura. At the same time, I do not think it certain that the corps assembled at Plasencia is intended to invade Portugal. In the first place, alone and unsupported, it is not in sufficient strength: in the next place, if an invasion of Portugal had been determined on as a measure of the campaign, they would not have marched in open day, in the presence of our troops.

We know that the great object of the French, and that which has probably induced them to bring this large corps from the north of Spain, is to separate the English from the Spaniards; and I think it most probable that the principal object in the occupation of Plasencia is to distract our attention, and probably to induce us to withdraw. The object of keeping open the communication with Castille is not improbably connected with the above stated. The forces on both sides in Estremadura are now so equally balanced in point of numbers, being about 70,000 men on each side (including Venegas' and ours, and excluding your corps, &c.), that I do not think the French can look to any solid offensive operation in any quarter. On the other hand, if we should undertake any, they will again throw the corps occupying Plasencia on our backs, and take their chance of what might be done by the troops of the allies in different parts of the frontier of Estremadura. If they should undertake an offensive operation, it will probably be on the right upon Venegas, and in that view of their plan, the corps occupying Plasencia would be very inconveniently situated for any operation which we might undertake in this quarter by way of diversion in his favor. Upon the whole, therefore, I am inclined to think that Plasencia is occupied as the right of the French army in Estremadura, rather than as a point on the march towards Portugal.

In whatever way it is occupied, I conceive that you cannot be better placed than at Zarza la Mayor. At Moraleja you might be turned, and cut off by the cavalry and light infantry from Zarza, there being a road and a ford direct from Coria to Zarza, impracticable for artillery, good for light infantry, and bad for cavalry. As a military position, you would be in a better one on the other side of the river, which forms the boundary of the two Kingdoms, and you might equally draw your provisions from Zarza la Mayor, which is a fertile country that has not been exhausted.

Whether Portugal is to be invaded or not, my opinion is, and I wish, that Gen. —— should recross the Tagus, where he was ordered to halt. If Portugal is to be invaded, he will then be in his place according to the defensive plan proposed by me, of which one copy went to you by a messenger yesterday, and another the day before through Gen. Leite: and as in that case you will only have to retire, your retreat would be more likely to be embarrassed, than aided, by this additional body of infantry. If Portugal is not to be invaded, I shall want Gen. —— to join me; and as he cannot cross the Tagus any where above Vella Velha, it is best that, in either view of the case, he should be sent there without loss of time. The 11th regiment must join him; and let him remain at Niza till he shall receive orders from me, or from you, supposing Portugal to be invaded. Let him get up the money and the other articles he was bringing with him to the army, to Niza.

I have still to trouble you respecting various detachments of convalescents belonging to this army, who are marching about in different directions, and who have already acquired the name, as I doubt not they will soon the manners, of battalions of detachments. If any of these are at Zarza la Mayor, I beg you to send them across the Tagus at Alcantara, in detachments of such a size daily, as that they may get over the river in one day. Let them collect at Alcantara, and march from thence by the enclosed route to join the army. If you should find the enemy advancing, you will of course stop these detachments from passing the river, and will send orders to those already passed to commence their march, and I shall take care of them afterwards. Those of them which shall not have passed must in this case retire into Portugal with you.

All the detachments of convalescents which have not passed Castello Branco, must join Gen. ——, and pass the Tagus with him at Villa Velha. There is only one small boat at Alcantara ; I understand there are 2 at Alconeta, but this last place is nearer to Galisteo than it is to Zarza ; and the road to it is not absolutely impracticable for artillery. It would be desirable, therefore, to endeavor to remove the boats from Alconeta to Alcantara ; if only for the purpose of passing over our men. Indeed the boats ought to be removed from thence at all events. No carriage can cross at Alcantara, and only one horse at a time.

To Lieut. C. Ellis, 40th regt., at Talavan.   Jaraicejo, 14th Aug. 1809.

I have not heard from you since you left this, which I attribute to the deficiency of your means of communication. I request you to spare no expense either in procuring the earliest and most certain intelligence of the enemy's movements, or in transmitting it to me in the speediest manner. Keep the bearer with you till you shall have occasion to send. He is a Portuguese messenger.

To Senor Lozano de Torres.   Jaraicejo, le 14 Aout, 1809.

Le Colonel Waters, qui vous donnera cette lettre, vous montrera le précis d'une correspondance que j'ai eue avec les Generaux Cuesta et Eguia, sur les besoins de l'armée Anglaise, et sur les moyens que l'on a proposés pour y remedier. Je l'ai nomme avec M. Wemyss pour faire un arrangement avec des officiers nommes par le Commandant en Chef Espagnol de concert avec vous ; ils vous montreront les memorandums que je leur ai donnés, et je vous prie de les aider de vos conseils et de votre assistance.

To Gen. Eguia.   Jaraicejo, 14th Aug. 1809.

I have had the honor of receiving your Excellency's letter of the 13th, and I beg leave to congratulate you upon succeeding to the command of the Spanish army. I assure your Excellency that I have every desire to adopt any arrangement which can tend to facilitate the procuring and distribution of supplies to the combined armies ; and I am fully convinced of your Excellency's desire to relieve the wants and remove the inconvenience which the British army has already suffered during its operations in Spain.

I must observe to your Excellency, however, that with every confidence in the good faith with which an arrangement made by you will be carried into effect on your part, I am apprehensive that from the nature of the proposed arrangement it is impracticable of execution. But at your Excellency's desire, I have sent Lieut. Col. Waters, of the Staff, and Mr. Wemyss, of the Commissary General's department, to Truxillo, where they will meet any officers who may be appointed by you, and in concert with Senor L. de Torres, the Intendant employed by government with the British army, will settle such an arrangement as may be practicable. These officers will likewise be charged to communicate to those whom you appoint, the particulars of the other wants of the British army.

Memorandum for Lieut. Col. Waters.   Jaraicejo, 14th Aug. 1809.

1. The number of rations required daily by the British army is now 25,000 for men, and 6000 for horses, &c

2. It appears to me that it will be difficult to settle any plan by which the contents of any magazine could be issued to the two armies in proportion to their numbers, because both armies may, and the Spanish army certainly does, draw provisions and forage from some quarters besides the magazine which is formed at Truxillo. The British army now get their bread only from Truxillo; therefore, any arrangement which should throw all the bread baked at, or which may be brought to, Truxillo, into a magazine to be divided in proportions between the two armies, would be unjust towards the British, and would probably starve it.

3. If, however, any arrangement can be adopted by which this difficulty can be got over, I shall have no objection to it in respect to bread, and no objection whatever in respect to barley.

4. In respect to meat, as that is to be got in all parts of the country, it would be best to leave the supply as it is, in the hands of the Commissaries of the different nations.

5. At least 1000 beasts of burthen are required for the British army.

6. 100 carts, each to carry 600 lbs., are required to carry the ammunition left at Deleytosa.

7. 100 good draught mules or horses are required to draw the British artillery.

8. 300 mares are required to remount the British cavalry.

9. Payment will be made on the spot for such of these animals as shall be purchased, and the regular and usual hire paid for those which shall be hired.

To Marquis Wellesley.   Jaraicejo, 14th Aug. 1809.

I received yesterday, from Gen. Cuesta, the letter of which I enclose your Excellency a copy, in which he informs me that he has resigned the command of the army, on account of his increasing infirmities. It appears that he had a paralytic stroke on the night of the 12th, which deprived him of the use of his left leg, and he cannot now walk.

I likewise enclose the copy of a letter which I have received from, and of my answer to, Gen. Eguia, the present commanding officer of the army. The letter to which he refers, as having been written by me, is that addressed to Gen. Cuesta, and of which I transmitted a copy to your Excellency yesterday. I have not yet heard that the enemy have made any alteration in their position at Plasencia. It appears that they have thrown their posts forward towards Banos by some accounts, as well as towards Coria and Galisteo.

To Gen. Eguia.   Jaraicejo, 15th Aug. 1809.

I have had the honor of receiving your letter of the 14th inst., relative to our future operations.

The last accounts which I have received of the enemy state that, on the 12th, they attacked the Puerto de Banos with a large corps of infantry, cavalry, and artillery, where they were opposed by Sir R. Wilson's corps, which had retreated from Talavera to the hills, and had arrived at Banos on the 11th. The enemy carried the Puerto after a contest which lasted the whole day, and Sir Robert writes from Colmenar on the 12th, at night. My opinion is, that notwithstanding the strength of his reinforcements, the enemy is not strong enough to undertake any offensive operations; but that if he should undertake any against the right of the combined armies, I mean the Spanish corps with Gen. Venegas, the French corps at Plasencia, supposing it to remain there, will be well situated to impede any operations which we in this quarter might undertake, in order to make a diversion in his favor.

The first object for our attention should be to get provisions for the men and horses of the army. The horses of the British army are now so much reduced from want of food, that they are scarcely able to march the distance which it is necessary they should march to relieve their outposts, much less to undertake any hostile or forward movement, while the arrangements for procuring food and collecting magazines are making.

I have already stated to Gen. Cuesta, in a letter of the 10th inst., which I understand has been communicated to you, the defensive positions that, in my opinion, the armies ought to occupy in this quarter.

When they may be prepared to carry on more active operations, my opinion is, that they ought to be directed on the right of the enemy, at Plasencia; and it might be possible to bring the corps of Marshal Beresford to co-operate in the plan. But I fear that nothing can be expected, either from the Duque del Parque, who is too weak, or from the Marques de la Romana, who appears to have been still at Coruna on the 3d of this month.

To Marquis Wellesley.   Jaraicejo, 15th Aug. 1809.

I received from Marshal Beresford this morning a letter, stating that the enemy's corps which had gone to Plasencia had, on the 12th, attacked and carried the Puerto de Banos. This point was defended by Sir R. Wilson's corps, and, I believe, by a detachment from the garrison of Ciudad Rodrigo. Sir R. Wilson had retired from the neighbourhood of Talavera by the hills of the Vera de Plasencia, and had arrived at the Puerto de Banos on the 11th. He writes from Colmenar on the 12th, at night.

I do not understand that the enemy had made any movement from Plasencia since the 12th. His patroles were yesterday on the Tagus, in the neighbourhood of Talavan, and of the Puente del Cardenal. Marshal Beresford was yesterday between Moraleja and Zarza la Mayor.

I have the honor to enclose the copy of a letter which I received yesterday from Gen. Eguia, and the copy of my answer this day. I have just received your Excellency's dispatch of the 13th. Your Excellency will observe from my letter to Gen. Eguia, that the Marques de la Romana was still at Coruna on the 3d August, and probably even at a later period. There is no chance, therefore, of a diversion being made by his army in favor of the operations of the troops in Estremadura; and your Excellency will observe that the attempt of the Duque del Parque to hold only the Puerto de Banos, although aided by Sir R. Wilson's corps, the assistance of which he had no reason to expect, has entirely failed.

I consider the answer of the Junta to the note of your Excellency, in respect to the supplies of provisions for the army, and to the means of transport required, to be very unsatisfactory. The army cannot exist in the shape of an army, unless those supplies and means are provided; and the Junta have been already informed by me, that if Spain, or rather that part of Spain under their government, which in fact now comprises the whole Kingdom, excepting those parts of Estremadura, Castille, and Aragon, occupied by the enemy's troops, cannot, or is unwilling, to make the exertion which is necessary in order to secure those supplies and means, Spain must do without the services of the British army.

In respect to Marshal Beresford's corps, which the Junta are so desirous should be brought forward, I have to observe, that the Marshal has equal reason with myself to complain of the deficiency of supplies of provisions and other assistance, since he has been in Spain. But this army is the only disposable force of Portuguese troops which exists, and is all that Portugal has to depend upon for its defence. It is not in a very efficient state for offensive purposes, as it wants cavalry, is but newly raised, and but imperfectly trained and disciplined. The object in collecting it upon the frontier was to train and discipline it, and at the same time to defend the frontiers of Portugal, and to give an *appui* to my left flank; and the government of Portugal willingly concurred in its quitting the frontier for these objects. But I doubt whether the government of Portugal would consent, or that I could recommend that they should consent, to the employment of this corps in an operation in Castille, giving up the defence of their own frontier, which is menaced with an attack, at the call of the government of Spain, who do not appear willing or capable of making any exertion for themselves. Accordingly your Excellency will observe, that in the different letters that I have written in which I have recommended movements towards Madrid, I have never mentioned Marshal Beresford's corps, knowing that its services could not be, at present, spared at a distance from the Portuguese frontier; and that the Portuguese government would not allow it to move to any distance.

To Marquis Wellesley.   Jaraicejo, 15th Aug. 1809.

I understand from one of our Commissaries, who was very near the bridge of Arzobispo on the day the Spaniards were surprised there, that vast numbers fled from thence, throwing away, as usual, their arms and clothing. I think that it would be desirable to take early measures to ascertain what the existing strength is of each of the armies, particularly that of Cuesta, for I suspect that by these desertions it is much weakened, although it has not lost 500 men in action.

I think that the French have in Estremadura and Toledo about 70,000 men, and we (including Venegas and excluding Beresford) may have about the same number, if Cuesta is not reduced below 30,000 by desertion. I do not think the French are sufficiently strong, with these relative numbers, to undertake an offensive operation; and it is probable that things will remain as they are, unless I can strike a blow upon the right of their line, until their reinforcements shall arrive from France.

There are advantages and disadvantages attending the positions of each of the armies. The French have the advantage of an early communication from their right at Plasencia, to their left in La Mancha, and they can collect their whole army without any difficulty at any one point. On the other hand, our defensive position is the easiest; and the possession of the bridge of Almaraz, and of the mountains between that point and the bridge of Arzobispo, protects the country behind the Tagus, from Toledo nearly to Abrantes, as the enemy cannot penetrate with cannon at any point between Almaraz and Toledo; and the passage of the river is nearly impracticable for an army between Almaraz and Abrantes, excepting, probably, at Villa Velha, in Portugal, and with difficulty at the ferry of Alconeta.

I believe also that Venegas' position in the mountains of the Sierra is so strong, that it cannot be attacked, excepting by a very superior force. We should still, however, be in a difficult position in respect to the corps at Plasencia, supposing it to remain there, should Venegas be attacked, and we were required to make a diversion in his favor in this quarter.

In the expectation that we shall receive such a requisition at some time or other; or if by the arrival of food, &c., I should ever be enabled to make a forward movement, I am preparing to repair the Puente del Cardenal on the Tagus, between this and Plasencia, in order to be able to strike a blow there.

To the Rt. Hon. J. Villiers.   Jaraicejo, 15th Aug. 1809.

I shall be very much obliged to you if you will give directions to somebody to purchase and send us by a courier the medicines, and in the quantities enumerated in the enclosed letters. Let the Commissary General pay for them.

There is nothing new. The French at Plasencia appear to have pushed towards the Puerto de Banos, where they beat Sir R. Wilson, and I believe a corps of the Duque del Parque, on the 12th; Sir Robert had retired through the hills from Talavera, which is the reason that he was at Banos on the 12th.

The A.G. to Major Gen. Hill.   15th Aug. 1809

I am directed by the Commander of the Forces to desire that you will let Capt

——, — regt., know that the owner of property has a right to take his property, which has been stolen from him, wherever he may find it; that this is a fair and just principle which prevails in all civilised countries, and must be applied to the case of the horse in question. It is certainly true that many horses are stolen, and afterwards sold; and the right of property, in many horses of the army, may not rest upon better grounds than those Capt. —— has to the horse of Lieut. ——: but this is no reason why a just and fair principle, universally acknowledged and adopted, should not be applied when a case occurs to which it is exactly applicable. The Commander of the Forces, therefore, directs that Capt. —— shall immediately deliver up the horse to Lieut. ——; and you will be pleased to report to me the execution of this order.

To Gen. Eguia.   Jaraicejo, 16th Aug. 1809.

I have had the honor of receiving your letter of the 15th, and I am much obliged to you for the intelligence contained in it. There is nothing new in this quarter.

I enclose an extract of a letter from the Lieut. General commanding the British cavalry, in consequence of which I have been obliged to move the cavalry farther to the rear, towards Caceres, in order that they may be enabled to procure forage, no longer to be obtained in the neighbourhood of this place.

I had the honor some time ago to beg of Gen. Cuesta that he would send some guns of heavy calibre to occupy the batteries which have been thrown up at the Puente de Almaraz. These guns have not yet arrived, and I must beg leave again to renew my application, and to request that 8 guns may be sent there as soon as possible.

['Aldea del Obispo, 15th Aug. 1809. We have only received one day's issue of barley since our arrival here, and that did not exceed 4 lb. per horse!']

To Marquis Wellesley.   Jaraicejo, 16th Aug. 1809.

I have the honor to enclose a copy of a report which I received last night from the officer commanding the British cavalry, in consequence of which I have ordered him to move towards Caceres, to endeavor to procure food for the horses, but where he will be nearly 30 miles distant from the army.

The enemy have made no movements of any importance in this quarter. They have had their patroles at the Puente del Cardenal, and the people of the country believed that they intended to attempt to repair that bridge. I had intended to repair the bridge myself, in case it should have been desirable to move upon the enemy's right at Plasencia, and had given directions for the collection of materials for that purpose; but the report which I received last night of the want of forage for the cavalry, and the consequent necessity of moving them to a distance, has put that operation out of the question; and I have now ordered that the Puente del Cardenal

G. O.   Jaraicejo, 16th Aug. 1809.

1. The soldiers are again positively prohibited to plunder bee-hives; any man found with a bee-hive in his possession will be punished.

2. The rolls to be called in camp every two hours: the officers commanding divisions will settle what number of officers of each regiment are to attend.

3. The Provost must patrole in the neighbourhood of the camp, and every man found out of his lines without his accoutrements, and not dressed as a soldier ought to be, is to be punished.

Men sent on fatigue will be under the command of an officer, or non-commissioned officer.

may be effectually destroyed, so as to render its repair impossible. I received this morning from Gen. Eguia, the report of the defeat of Gen. Venegas' corps on the 11th.

To Gen. Eguia. Jaraicejo, 18th Aug. 1809.

I am sorry to have to inform your Excellency that the British army under my command have this day no bread, instead of receiving the plentiful supply of which your Excellency announced the arrival in the conversation which I had with you yesterday. I trust that your Excellency will have taken measures to occupy, in this night, the posts in the neighbourhood of Almaraz.

To Gen. Eguia. Jaraicejo, 18th Aug. 1809, 6½ p.m.

I have had the honor of receiving your Excellency's letter and its enclosures of this day's date, respecting the provisions in the magazine at Truxillo for the use of the British army; and as the soldiers have not received their provisions for this day, and there does not appear to me to be a sufficiency for the consumption of to-morrow, I shall, however unwillingly, carry into execution the intention I announced to you yesterday. I trust, therefore, that you will have ordered troops to relieve my outposts on the Tagus, if you still propose to hold that position.

To Gen. Eguia. Jaraicejo, 18th Aug. 1809.

I have had the honor of receiving your Excellency's letter in reply to mine of this morning.

I have frequently complained to the government and to the late Commander in Chief, and, as I thought, to you, in conversation yesterday, that I must retire into Portugal to seek for food, if food should not be supplied to the British army in Spain; and I particularly specified to your Excellency the number of rations of each description of food that the British army required.

Your Excellency is much mistaken in supposing that I intended to remain in my position, if I should receive a portion of the supplies to be collected at Truxillo for the use of the armies, although I might be convinced that such portion would be allotted honorably and with good faith. That which obliges me to move into Portugal is a case of extreme necessity, viz., that description of necessity which an army feels when it has been starving for a month, when it wants every thing and can get nothing; and as I stated to your Excellency yesterday, this necessity has now become so urgent, that I must either move into Portugal, where I know I shall be supplied, or I must make up my mind to lose my army, unless I am made certain, not only of a portion of the supplies which may be sent to Truxillo, but of a sufficiency of bread and corn for the troops and horses daily. I hope, therefore, that your Excellency will occupy the posts on the Tagus this night. But if you should not do so, I can only say that my troops shall be withdrawn from them to-morrow night, whether relieved or not.

To Marquis Wellesley. Jaraicejo, 18th Aug. 1809.

I have the honor to enclose different reports, which I received yesterday, of the measures taken by the Spanish officers and troops to prevent the British army from foraging.

The foraging parties to which these reports relate were necessarily obliged to go to a distance of 4 and 5 leagues (from 16 to 20 miles) in order to procure the forage they required; which, with the distance they would have to return, appears to be sufficient work for the parties and their horses: but when, having performed this work, they are deprived of the forage by the Spanish cavalry, it must be obvious that the equipments of the army must be ruined. I understand that similar outrages were committed on the foraging parties yesterday, but I have not yet had the official reports of them. Gen. Eguia did me the honor of calling upon me yesterday, when I communicated to him these reports, and he promised that the evils complained of should be redressed. I desired him, however, to prepare to occupy, in the course of the night, the posts in the neighbourhood of the bridge of Almaraz, as it was impossible for me to remain any longer in this part of the country, suffering as the army does, from wants of every description.

In my last letter I apprised your Excellency of the wants of the cavalry, and of my having been obliged to remove them to the neighbourhood of Caceres to look for food. In my conversation yesterday with Gen. Eguia, I found that the Spanish cavalry had, every day, received some barley, although not an entire ration. The enclosed reports will show to your Excellency in what manner this same cavalry, which occupies every village in the neighbourhood of this army, supplies itself with straw. The British army has no bread for this day, the troops receiving, in lieu of that necessary article, half a pound of flour, or one-third of their ration for each man; notwithstanding Gen. Eguia told me yesterday that on this day, and always in future, arrangements would be made to supply both infantry and cavalry with their full rations of provisions and forage.

More than a month has now elapsed since I informed Gen. Cuesta that if the British army were not supplied with means of transport and with provisions, not only I would not co-operate in any forward movement beyond the Alberche, but that I could not remain at all in Spain; and the General informed me that he had sent a copy of my letter to the Supreme Central Junta; and indeed I sent a copy of it to Mr. Frere.

In the course of this month, if proper measures, or indeed if any measures had been adopted, supplies might have been forwarded to us from the most distant parts of Andalusia; but we have not received a mule or a cart, or an article of provision of any description, under any order given or arrangement made by the government: so that when I march I shall be obliged to leave behind my ammunition, and 6, and probably 12 pieces of cannon; and I assure your Excellency most solemnly, that since the 22d of last month the horses of the cavalry and artillery have not received 3 regular deliveries of barley, and the infantry have not received 10 days' bread. Under these circumstances, I can remain no longer in Spain; and I request you to give notice to the government that I am about to withdraw into Portugal.

I have no doubt but that the government have given orders that we should be provided as we ought to be; but orders, I have to observe, are not sufficient. To carry on the contest with France to any good purpose, the labor and services of every man and of every beast in the country should be employed in the support of the armies; and these should be so classed and arranged as not only to secure obedience to the orders of the government, but regularity and efficiency in the performance of the services required from them. Magazines might then with ease be formed and transported wherever circumstances might require that armies should be stationed. But as we are now situated, 50,000 men are collected upon a spot which cannot afford subsistence for 10,000 men, and there are no means of sending to a distance to make good the deficiency.

The Junta have issued their orders to supply the deficiencies of means of transport as well as of provisions; but from want of arrangement there are no persons to obey their orders, and this army would perish, if I should remain, before the supplies could arrive.

I hope your Excellency and the government will believe that I have not determined to go till.it has become absolutely necessary. I assure you that there is not a General officer in this army who is not convinced of the necessity of my immediate departure.

To Marshal Beresford.   Jaraicejo, 19th Aug. 1809.

I received last night your letter of the 17th. The principle on which I have acted respecting Gen. —— is this: neither he nor you, nor both joined, could do any thing effectual against the enemy, unless in co-operation with me.

In co-operation with me, your force, without Gen. ——'s, was fully sufficient to do any thing that might be required from it. There was, therefore, no reason whatever why Gen. —— should not be placed in the situation most convenient for the performance of those services that it was most probable would be required from him; which were, either to join me, or to be employed in the defence of Portugal, according to the plan proposed in my memorandum. But, in fact, it has for some time been very obvious to me, that I was unable to undertake any offensive operation of any description. The want of provisions and means of transport is so great, that I can move neither artillery nor ammunition, and the troops and horses having been starved for the last month, neither are equal to any exertion; and no means exist here of refreshing the one, or of giving even the necessary food to the other.

Supposing, then, that Gen. ——'s assistance would have been necessary to you in any offensive operation which we might have undertaken in concert, which I think it would not, it was pretty obvious, from the state of this army, that such offensive operation would not be undertaken. Your line must have been to retire towards Portugal; and in this operation, Gen. ——, having only infantry, would in those plains have done you more harm than good. Besides this, Gen. ——'s disobedience of orders, although well intended, was positive, and committed with his eyes open; and as his corps was useless at Zarza la Mayor, and in your retreat might have embarrassed you, I was not sorry, by ordering him back to the position which he had quitted, to show him and the army that I must command and they must obey.

I agree with you in thinking that the enemy will not now invade Portugal; and I also agree with you in thinking that it is desirable that your troops should have rest and leisure; and that a serious endeavor should be made to organize, discipline, and clothe them, for which, indeed, there has hardly yet been time. I concur with you also in the choice you have made of the position from Abrantes to Leiria, for your purpose: I should wish you, however, if possible, to leave Abrantes and the course of the Tagus to us, for the reasons which I am about to detail to you.

After having made an effort to maintain myself here, I find it quite impossible. We are starving, our men falling sick, and we have nothing to give them in the way of comfort for their recovery; and our horses are dying by hundreds in the week. We have not had a full ration of provisions ever since the 22d of the last month; and I am convinced that in that time the men have not received 10 days' bread, and the horses not 3 regular deliveries of barley. We have no means of transport, and I shall be obliged to leave my ammunition on the ground, on quitting this place. We now want 1800 horses to complete the cavalry!!! and 200 or 300 for the artillery. Under these circumstances, and seeing no prospect of an amelioration of our situation, which gets worse and worse every day, I have determined to withdraw towards the frontiers of Portugal, and I shall begin my march to-morrow. My intention is to put myself along the frontier, with the right towards Elvas; there are some large towns there, which will subsist us; and, at all events, there is a store at Abrantes, which will supply us for a great length of time. In order, however, that we may be able to draw our resources from this store, as well as what we want from Lisbon, it is necessary that we should have the command of all the resources in carriages, &c., which Alentejo and the banks of the Tagus can afford. Now if you should occupy Abrantes, we shall interfere with each other; and for this reason, I request you to put your right at Thomar.

I have not been well for these 3 or 4 days, which is the reason why I have not written to you. But I now send De Sousa* with this.

I think that the circumstances in which the world, and this Peninsula in particular, will be placed in a short time, call upon you to report, at an early period, the actual progress which has been made, and the prospects which exist of forming an army in Portugal. The desertion of the troops, the prospects of stopping that evil, the means and their efficiency of supplying the vacancies which it occasions, would be prominent points in such report. I think we owe this to government, at an early period, in order to enable them to determine how far they will go in expense, and how much they will risk in an army to maintain Portugal in the existing situation of the world.

A great deal has been done, and government may be supposed to have acted rightly in sending their troops when they did, and in saving Portugal when the French were involved in the Austrian contest. But the question becomes one of a different description, that contest being finished; and I think that government will be assisted in their decision very much by the prospect which you may be able to hold out of the existence of a Portuguese military force.

* The Conde de Villa Real.

To Gen. Eguia.   Jaraicejo, 19th Aug. 1809.

I have had the honor of receiving your Excellency's letter of this day's date, and I feel much concerned that any thing should have occurred to induce your Excellency to express a doubt of the truth of what I have written to you. As, however, your Excellency entertains that doubt, any further correspondence between us appears unnecessary ; and accordingly, this is the last letter which I shall have the honor of addressing to you. Although your Excellency has expressed a doubt of the truth of what I have written to you, I entertain none of what your Excellency has written to me ; and I am well convinced that your Excellency has given orders, and that all the contents of the magazine at Truxillo will be given to the British troops, even though the Spanish troops should want food. But notwithstanding these orders, and an obedience to them, the British troops are still in want. Yesterday they received but one third of a ration, and that was in flour; this day they received only half a ration, likewise in flour; and on neither of these days have the horses of the army received any thing. These deficiencies arise not from the want of orders by your Excellency, or of your faithful execution of your promises to me, but from the want of means in the country, and from the want of arrangement by the government in the adoption of timely measures to supply the wants which they were informed long ago existed. But to whatever cause the deficiency of means of supplying the troops with provisions may be attributed, it is obvious that it exists.

According to the return of the state of the magazine at Truxillo, sent to me by your Excellency yesterday, it did not contain a sufficiency to feed the British army even for one day. This being the case, the wants of the army must continue ; I must lose men and horses daily ; and therefore, in order to save the army, I must remove to a country in which I know that I shall get food, and other assistance which I require. Whatever your Excellency may think of the truth or falsehood of my assertion, I repeat, that want, and the apprehension of its further consequences, are the only reasons for my quitting Spain.

I have the honor to inform your Excellency, that besides the ammunition left at Deleytosa, I shall be obliged to leave here another large quantity, from the want of means of moving it. I shall send an officer to Deleytosa to-morrow, to deliver to the officer whom you may appoint to receive it, the ammunition which is there ; and if you will send an officer here in the course of the day, he shall receive charge of the ammunition which will be left here, if your Excellency wishes to have these articles ; if you should not wish to have them, I propose to destroy them, as I have no means of moving them from hence.

P.S. I have just received your Excellency's second letter of this date, enclosing one of the 16th from the Minister of War at Seville. The Minister has been entirely misinformed of the actual situation of the French armies. A large corps has marched to Salamanca ; another is at Plasencia; Marshal Mortier, with a part of Victor's corps, is at Talavera, Oropesa, and Arzobispo; and the remainder of Victor's corps, with Sebastiani's, is in La Mancha. Marshal Beresford is on the frontiers of Portugal, near Salvaterra. Under these circumstances there might be an opportunity of striking a blow with advantage; although no permanent good could be produced, till the corps of the Marques de la Romana, or some other corps, could be brought forward. But the Minister of War forgets that we have no food; that our cavalry, from want, are scarcely able to move from their ground; that our artillery horses are not able to draw the guns; that I have no means of moving; and that I am actually obliged to leave here my ammunition from the want of means of moving it; and, above all, that the soldiers are worn down by want and privations of every description.

It is extraordinary that the Minister did not advert to these circumstances, which have been frequently laid before him; or that, adverting to them, he should have proposed to me any operation of any description, to which he must have known that I was unequal: but his having omitted to advert to them sufficiently accounts for their continued existence.

The A.G. to Lieut. Gen. Sherbrooke.   19th Aug. 1809.

I have laid before the Commander of the Forces the statement herewith returned from the paymaster of the 83d regt., and I am directed to acquaint you that it must be submitted to the consideration of the first Board of claims that may be ordered to sit. With respect to the public money that has been lost, the Commander of the Forces has been pleased to direct that the same shall be made good immediately, so that the corps should suffer no inconvenience; and the paymaster of the 83d regt. will apply to the Military Sec. for an order on the Paymaster Gen. for the money.

To Señor Don L. de Calvo.   Jaraicejo, 20th Aug. 1809, 8 A.M.

I have had the honor of receiving your letter of the 19th from Truxillo, to which I write this reply, notwithstanding that I hope to have the pleasure of seeing you at Truxillo in the course of this morning.

I must first beg leave to inform you, that I have no motive for withdrawing the British army from Spain, whether of a political or military nature, excepting that which I have stated to you in conversation, viz., a desire to relieve it from the privations of food which it has suffered since the 22d of last month; privations which have reduced its strength, have destroyed the health of the soldiers, and have rendered the army comparatively inefficient.

You gave me assurances yesterday, which you have repeated in your letter, that these privations shall not continue; that in 3 days there shall be plenty of provisions; and that in the mean time we shall have all that the magazine at Truxillo contains. In answer, I have to observe to you, that I have received the same assurances from every Spanish Commissioner who has been employed with the British army; each in his turn has disappointed me; and although your rank is higher, and your powers are greater than those of the other Spanish officers who have been with me, I acknowledge, that in a case so critical as that of a starving army, I feel no confidence in your assurances; and I give no credit to the accounts of

G. O.   Truxillo, 20th Aug. 1809.

4. Officers commanding corps will give particular directions that the men having charge of cars are not to load them above 600 pounds weight, the utmost they can carry; the consequence must be, if this order is not complied with, that cars must break down, and cannot now be replaced.

the existence of resources said to be upon the road (in what place not known), or of any others in the magazine at Truxillo. In respect to the magazine at Truxillo, according to the accounts of its contents yesterday evening, which I received last night, it does not contain enough to feed the British army one day only; and the provisions for the Spanish army must be likewise drawn from it.

You tell me that the British troops shall have every thing, and the Spanish nothing. To which I reply, that its execution is utterly and entirely impracticable, and is certainly very inconsistent with what has hitherto taken place. Till lately, the Spanish troops have received their rations regularly, while he British troops were starving. I am not so well aware of the manner in which the Spanish troops have been lately supplied, but I know, from the best authority (the Commander in Chief of the Spanish army), that the Spanish cavalry were receiving at least half a ration of barley, while the British cavalry had none: and I imagine that they have been well supplied with other provisions, as I have in my possession a letter from yourself, stating that you had ordered to the Mesa de Ibor, for the use of the Spanish army, all the provisions required for the British army by Mr. Downie, the British Commissary, and provided by the town of Guadalupe and its neighbourhood. I cannot, therefore, give credit to the execution of any plan which shall go to give provisions to the British army, to the exclusion of the Spanish troops; and I conceive the proposal to have been made to me, only as an extreme and desperate measure to induce me to remain in Spain. But supposing the plan to be capable of execution, I could not give my sanction to it. The Spanish army must be fed as well as the British army, otherwise neither will be of much use in the positions which they have hitherto occupied.

If the Spanish army is to be fed, (and it cannot be otherwise,) the magazine at Truxillo will be found not to be equal to one third of the demand of the British army for one day, according to the official return of its contents yesterday, which I received last night. But, besides provisions, the army requires other assistance, for which I have called in vain; and for the want of which I am now obliged to leave behind me my ammunition, and to deliver it to the Spanish Commander in Chief.

I am fully aware of the consequences which may follow my departure from Spain: not that I apprehend those to which you have referred; for, in point of fact, there is now no enemy in our front. But I am not responsible for these consequences, whatever they may be. Those are responsible for them who, having been made acquainted with the wants of the British army more than a month ago, have taken no efficient measures to relieve them; who have allowed a brave army, that was rendering gratuitous services to Spain, that was able and willing to pay for every thing it received, to starve in the centre of their country, and to be reduced by want almost to a state of inefficiency; who refused or omitted to find carriages to remove the officers and soldiers who had been wounded in their service, and obliged me to give up the equipment of the army for the performance of this necessary duty of humanity.

I have one more observation to make, in reply to your letter, in respect to the requisitions made by the British Commissaries for provisions in the villages. There is but one Commissary now so employed, and he is at Caceres. Indeed, all the villages in this neighbourhood are occupied by the Spanish troops, and it would be useless to send a British Commissary to endeavor to procure any thing from them. But I shall be obliged to you to state where is this Commissary? Supposing the report made to you to be founded in fact, surely, while the British army is starving, it may be allowed to a Commissary to endeavor to obtain some relief for the troops for whom he is bound to provide, paying for what he receives.

To Señor L. de Torres.   Jaraicejo, le 20 Août, 1809.

Je suis fâché d'avoir à vous annoncer que je me mettrai en marche demain pour la frontière de Portugal. Malgré les efforts que vous avez faits, malgré les représentations que depuis un mois j'envoie au gouvernement, mes soldats ne reçoivent pas leurs rations.

Hier ils n'ont eu qu'une demi livre de farine, aujourd'hui que trois quarts d'une livre, et les chevaux absolument rien. J'ai perdu dans la dernière semaine 100 chevaux de la cavalerie et beaucoup de l'artillerie. On ne me donne point de moyens de transport, et je suis obligé de laisser ici et à Deleytosa, et de donner à l'armée Espagnole, mes munitions. Je regrette cette nécessité, je l'ai évitée aussi longtems que j'ai pu : vous avez fait tout ce qui était en votre pouvoir, j'ai fait des représentations au gouvernement, et malgré tout, nous mourons de faim, et je ne peux plus rester. Je vous verrai demain à Truxillo.

To Vice Adm. the Hon. G. Berkeley.   Truxillo, 21st Aug. 1809.

I have received your letter of the 15th, and I am very much obliged to you for the trouble you have taken respecting the army. I have written to Mr. Murray, to desire him to buy the mules and bullocks to be had in Barbary. But I should think it desirable that they should be landed at the mouth of the Guadiana, or probably at Lisbon, instead of Cadiz, in consequence of the change in our situation. Mr. Villiers will apprise you of the circumstances which oblige me to quit Spain. I am very much obliged to you for the trouble you have taken to explore the navigation of the Tagus for us.

To the Rt. Hon. J. Villiers.   Truxillo, 21st Aug. 1809.

I have received your letters of the 14th and 16th.

The principle upon which I founded my calculation of one sixth of the supply we should receive, being allotted to the Portuguese government, was founded upon a comparison of your demand with the estimates of the whole expense of the army.

Your demand was stated to be £40,000 : the estimate of the total expense £240,000 ; of which sum, £40,000 was the sixth part; and I thought it fair that you should have the sixth of the supply, whatever that might be. You object to the calculation of the estimate; into which objection I cannot enter, as I have not seen the estimate, and only know that its total amount is £240,000 *per mensem*, calculating your demand at £40,000 *per mensem*. But as the demand of the Portuguese troops is only for their pay, and that for the British troops includes all extraordinaries, even ordnance, I am not surprised that the estimate for the whole expense of 30,000 men of the latter in the field should be £200,000, and the expense of the pay of the former only £40,000.

It appears by a paper enclosed in your letter of the 14th, that the monthly expense will run nearer £50,000 than £40,000, taking the exchange at *par*, which is the fair way of calculating. This will increase the estimate of the monthly expense in Portugal to £250,000, of which your demand will be one fifth; and according to what I think the first principle on which I decided before, one fifth, instead of one sixth of the monthly supply, ought to be allotted to you. It appears, however, that you object not only to the calculation of the sixth, but also to that mode of supplying the Portuguese government the money they ought to have.

I have to observe, that government having undertaken upon the Peninsula more than their funds will allow them to perform, we, who are to carry the services into execution, must either starve one service to feed the other; or we must allot to each service its due proportion of the funds in our power, calculated upon the amount of the demands of each.

I cannot suffer the British army to be starved, in order that the Portuguese army may be paid; nor is it proper that the engagement to the Portuguese government should be violated in order that the expenses of the British army should be paid. The measure, therefore, which I have adopted, with the amendment of a fifth, instead of a sixth, appears to me, on the whole, to be the best. But if you should not approve of this measure, the only one to which I can give my consent is, that I should decide from time to time what sums of money can, with convenience, be allotted to the Portuguese government. This, however, leaves that government exposed to the inconvenience which must always result from the arbitrary decision of any individual. I beg of you, therefore, to decide whether you will take a fifth of the supply, or leave the sum to be given at my discretion. In either case I shall give directions that you may be apprised, on the 15th and 30th of every month, of the sum disposable for the Portuguese government; and you will give directions that it may be drawn in one sum from the military chest at Lisbon, and you will give your bills, for the sum you shall have received, upon the Sec. of State. I mention this, because Mr. Murray has expressed a desire that his office may be freed from all accounts between Mr. Bell and individual officers, and the Paymaster Gen. of the army.

I am much obliged to you for the trouble you have taken respecting the supplies to be sent to us to Elvas. You will see by the dispatches which I send with this, that I am going towards that quarter. Any mules that can be got would be of great use to us; but as we shall run the province of Alentejo very hard in carriages for some time, it would be desirable not to push it too hard in mules at the same time.

To Marquis Wellesley.   Truxillo, 21st Aug. 1809.

I did not march from Jaraicejo till yesterday, not having been able to arrange, till that moment, for the removal of the sick of the army, to remove whom has taken every carriage and every mule we had to carry the remainder of our reserve ammunition and the stores in the commissariat, and I have given over the ammunition to the Spanish General. We have not received any assistance of any description from the country, or from the agents of the Spanish government.

I have the honor to enclose to your Excellency copies of letters which I have received from Gen. Eguia, and copies of my answers. Your Excellency will observe in Gen. Eguia's letter to me of the 19th inst. a very injurious, improper, and unfounded assertion, that I made use of the want of provisions as a pretext for withdrawing from Spain; and that it was a false one, for that there were plenty of provisions for the army. I assure your Excellency, that on that very day the troops in my camp at Jaraicejo received only ¾ lb. of flour, and the cavalry and the other horses of the army no forage excepting what they could pick up. Until this insulting assertion was withdrawn, it was impossible for me to continue any correspondence with Gen. Eguia, after I should have replied to his letter, which I hope I did with the temper which became my situation and character.

Your Excellency will observe, that in his reply to me he has either misunderstood or affected to misunderstand that part of his former letter to which I referred; and he has, in fact, left the charge of making use of a false pretext where it stood; and I have, therefore, not given him any reply upon that or any other subject on which he has addressed me. Your Excellency will likewise find an insinuation of the same kind in a letter from Don L. de Calvo, dated the 19th inst., of which and of my answer of the 20th I enclose copies. These letters contain nearly the substance of a conversation which I had with Don L. de Calvo on the evening of the 19th; and I assure your Excellency that at the moment Don L. de Calvo was writing his letter from Truxillo, stating the contents of the magazine at that place, on which statement he founded his insinuation that I was withdrawing from Spain upon a false pretext, Lieut. Col. Waters delivered to me a return of the contents of the magazine, made up to the evening of the 19th, from which it appeared that it did not contain a sufficiency to feed the British troops even for one day; and if the magazine had contained a sufficiency of food, there were no means of transport to remove it to the positions which the troops occupied.

Your Excellency will recollect, that in my correspondence with Gen. Cuesta, and with Gen. Eguia, I stated the difficulty of settling any arrangement for the division of the magazine to be formed at Truxillo, for the proportion of the strength of the two armies, because probably both armies, but certainly the Spanish army, would draw provisions from other quarters, which provisions would not go through the magazines; to which answers were given, calling upon me to rely upon the honor and good faith with which the arrangement to be made should be carried into execution.

I now beg to refer your Excellency to the enclosed copy of a letter, of which I have the original in my possession, from the alcalde of Guadalupe to Mr. Commissary Downie, that he had received the directions of Don L. de Calvo, which he had obeyed, to send to Mesa de Ibor, the head quarters of the Spanish army, *the provisions which Mr. Downie had ordered, and which had been procured for the use of the British army, to be sent to the magazine at Truxillo!* This is the honor and good faith with which the arrangement respecting the magazine at Truxillo was to be carried into execution! And this Don L. de Calvo is the gentleman in whose assurances I was to place confidence (as if I had not already gone far enough in confidence in the assurances of the agents of the Spanish government!) that all the contents of the magazine at Truxillo should be given to the British troops to the exclusion of the Spanish army, and that every thing which the army required, of every description, was on the road from Seville.

I find that it is intended to justify the Spanish government for their neglect of us, by circulating a report that my complaints of want of supplies, of means of transport, and I might have added, of the common attention and even of acts of humanity towards the army, and particularly towards the wounded, were mere pretexts.

This plan has been carried into execution so far that Senor L. de Torres, the Spanish superintendent attached to this army, declared publicly, yesterday, that he could prove that the British army, instead of wanting food, had received double rations ever since it arrived in Spain; and yet this same gentleman has expressed to me in the most indignant terms, more than once, the shame he felt, as a Spaniard, on account of the manner in which we had been treated, and the privations which we were made to endure; which expressions he acknowledges this day.

These reports and insinuations against me may do very well for the people of Seville: but the British army will not soon forget the treatment it has received; and I know that there is not a General officer in it, and I believe not an officer or soldier, who does not think that I should have neglected its interests, and even should have risked its existence, if I had delayed its departure for another day.

I have the honor to enclose a copy of my dispatch of this date to the Sec. of State.

P. S. By a letter from Marshal Beresford, I learn that he also has been distressed for provisions. He informs me that the Marques de la Romana was still at Coruña on the 5th inst.

P. P. S. I beg to draw your Excellency's attention to a fact which has occurred here this day. Your Excellency will observe that Don L. de Calvo boasted in his letter of the 19th inst., that he had here, at command, means of transport to carry provisions to the British army, and its detachments, not less than 30 miles from hence, and the quantity not less than 100,000lbs. in weight daily. Some sick had been sent here from Jaraicejo who had not been considered in the arrangement made for the removal of the sick, and 6 carts to remove them were wanting, which were required last night from Senor L. de Torres, another deputy from the Junta, and living with Don L. de Calvo. These 6 carts have not been given, and I have removed these sick in the best manner I could.

Just to show to your Excellency the difference of the manner in which we were treated in Portugal, I mention that Gen. Leite, having heard, by accident, that our wounded were going to Elvas, prepared to receive them. and the preparations for the hospitals' were actually made unsolicited, before the officer who was charged to make them arrived with my

letter to Gen. Leite, to communicate my wish to establish the hospital at
Elvas. In the same manner I must mention that stores, for which the
orders did not reach Lisbon till the 12th, will be at Elvas on the 26th;
and yet Lisbon is farther from the army than Seville is, and the means of
transport in Portugal not half what they are in Spain.

To the Duke of Richmond.   Truxillo, 21st Aug. 1809.

Starvation has produced such dire effects upon the army, we have suffered so much, and have received so little assistance from the Spaniards,
that I am at last compelled to move back into Portugal to look for subsistence. There is no enemy in our front of any consequence: Ney is
gone back into Castille; Soult is at Plasencia; Mortier at Oropesa, Arzobispo, and Navalmoral; Victor's corps is divided, being half of it at
Talavera, and half in La Mancha with Sebastiani. They cannot say we
were compelled to go therefore by the enemy, but by a necessity created
by the neglect of the Spaniards of our wants.

To Visc. Castlereagh.   Truxillo, 21st Aug. 1809.

When I marched from Talavera on the 3d inst. with a view to oppose
the French corps, which we had heard had passed through the Puerto de
Baños, and had arrived at Plasencia, Sir R. Wilson was detached upon the
left of the army towards Escalona; and before I marched on that morning
I put him in communication with the Spanish General Cuesta, who, it had
been settled, was to remain at Talavera. I understand that Gen. Cuesta
put Sir Robert in communication with his advanced guard, which retired
from Talavera on the night of the 4th. Sir R. Wilson, however, did not
arrive at Velada till the night of the 4th, having made a long march
through the mountains; and as he was then 6 leagues from the bridge of
Arzobispo, and had to cross the high road from Oropesa to Talavera, of
which the enemy was in possession, he conceived that he was too late to
retire to Arzobispo, and he determined to move by the Venta de San
Julian and Centenillo, towards the Tietar, and across that river towards
the mountains which separate Castille from Estremadura.

Some of Sir R. Wilson's dispatches having missed me, I am not aware
by which of the passes he went through the mountains, but I believe by
Tornavacas: he arrived, however, at Banos on the 11th, and on the 12th
was attacked and defeated by the French corps of Marshal Ney, which,
with that of Soult, returned to Plasencia on the 9th, 10th, and 11th; that
of Ney having since gone on towards Salamanca.

I enclose Sir R. Wilson's account of the action; he has been very
active, intelligent, and useful, in the command of the Portuguese and
Spanish corps, with which he was detached from this army. Before the
battle of the 28th July he had pushed his parties almost to the gates of
Madrid, with which city he was in communication, and he would have
been in Madrid, if I had not thought it proper to call him in, in expectation of that general action which took place on the 28th July. He afterwards alarmed the enemy on the right of his army; and throughout the
service has shown himself to be an active and intelligent partisan, well
acquainted with the country in which he was acting, and possessing the

confidence of the troops which he commanded. Being persuaded that his retreat was not open by Arzobispo, he acted right in taking the road he did, with which he was well acquainted; and although unsuccessful in the action which he fought, which may be well accounted for by the superior numbers and description of the enemy's troops, the action, in my opinion, does him great credit.

To Visc. Castlereagh.   Truxillo, 21st Aug. 1809.

I have the honor to enclose the copy of a letter which I received on the 4th inst., from Don M. de Garay, the Spanish Minister of State, conveying to me the intention of the government to appoint me a Captain General in the Spanish service, with the pay of that rank; and presenting me with 6 Andalusian horses in the name of King Ferdinand VII.

My wish was to lay this mark of the approbation of the Spanish government before His Majesty, and to delay to accept it till His Majesty's pleasure should be known; but it occurred to me that this mode of proceeding might not be understood at Seville, and that the Spanish government might be displeased at the temporary refusal of the honor they conferred upon me, that it might interfere with political objects, which the British Ambassador might have in view, at the same time that I make the acceptance referrible to the subsequent pleasure of His Majesty. I therefore wrote two answers to this part of Don M. de Garay's letter (of which I enclose copies), leaving it to Lord Wellesley to deliver that which he thought proper, in a letter to his Lordship, of which I enclose a copy; and I enclose the copy of his Lordship's answer, stating that he had delivered the second letter. I accepted the horses which the government intended to present to me in the name of King Ferdinand VII.; but declined to accept the pay of Captain General in another letter to Don M. de Garay, of which I enclose a copy.

To Visc. Castlereagh.   Truxillo, 21st Aug. 1809.

I wrote, some days ago, a letter to the French Commander in Chief, which I sent to him by Lieut. Col. Waters, to request his care and attention to the wounded officers and soldiers of the British army who had fallen into his hands, in return for the care and attention which I had paid to the French officers and soldiers who had fallen into my hands at different times; and that he would allow money to be sent to the officers; and that officers, who should not be deemed prisoners of war, might be sent to superintend and take care of the soldiers, till they should recover from their wounds, when these officers should be sent to join the British army. I received a very civil answer from Marshal Mortier, promising that every care should be taken, and every attention paid to the British officers and soldiers who were wounded; but stating that he could not answer upon the other demands contained in my letter, having been obliged to refer them to the Commander in Chief.

Since the receipt of this letter, Mr. Dillon, the Assist. Commissary, has arrived from Talavera, having been taken prisoner near Cevolla, on the 27th July, previous to the action, and having been allowed to come away.

He reports that the British officers and soldiers who were wounded are doing remarkably well; and are well fed and taken care of; indeed he says, preferable to the French troops.

I propose to send Lieut. Col. Waters with another flag of truce to-morrow evening, and a letter to the Commander in Chief of the French army, requesting that a sum of money, which I shall send, may be given to the officers; and I shall endeavor to establish a cartel of exchange as soon as possible.

To Visc. Castlereagh.   Truxillo, 21st Aug. 1809.

Gen. Cuesta moved his head quarters from the neighbourhood of the bridge of Arzobispo, on the night of the 7th inst., to Peraleda de Garbin, leaving an advanced guard consisting of 2 divisions of infantry, and the Duque de Alburquerque's division of cavalry, for the defence of the passage of the Tagus at this point. The French cavalry passed the Tagus at a ford immediately above the bridge, at half past one in the afternoon of the 8th, and surprised this advanced guard, which retired, leaving behind them all their cannon, as well as those in the batteries constructed for the defence of the bridge. Gen. Cuesta then moved his head quarters to the Mesa de Ibor on the evening of the 8th, having his advanced guard at Bohonal. He resigned the command of the army on the 12th, on account of the bad state of his health, and the command has devolved upon Gen. Eguia. The head quarters of the Spanish army are now at Deleytosa.

It appears that a detachment of Venegas' army had some success against the enemy in an attack made upon it in the neighbourhood of Aranjuez on the 5th inst.: Gen. Venegas was then at Ocana, and he had determined to retire towards the Sierra Morena; and after the 5th, he had moved in that direction. He returned, however, towards Toledo, with an intention of attacking the enemy on the 12th inst.; but on the 11th, the enemy attacked him with Sebastiani's corps, and 2 divisions of Victor's, in the neighbourhood of Almonacid. The action appears to have lasted some hours; but the French having at last gained an advantage on Gen. Venegas' left, he was obliged to retire, and was about to resume his position in the mountains of the Sierra Morena.

On the 9th, 10th, and 11th, large detachments of the French troops, which had come from Plasencia, returned to that quarter; and on the 12th, they attacked and defeated Sir R. Wilson in the Puerto de Baños, on their return to Salamanca. It appears now, that the French force in this part of Spain is distributed as follows: Marshal Victor's corps is divided between Talavera and La Mancha; Sebastiani's is in La Mancha; Marshal Mortier's at Oropesa, Arzobispo, and Navalmoral; Marshal Soult's at Plasencia; and Marshal Ney's at Salamanca.

From this distribution of their forces, it is obvious that they do not intend, at present, to undertake any offensive operation: if any, it will be upon the right in La Mancha; at the same time that if the combined armies were in a situation to be enabled to undertake any thing, they would experience great difficulty in the operation, and might be exposed to the same misfortune as that which stopped them lately and deprived them of the fruits of their victory at Talavera. But, from what follows, your Lordship will observe, that the British part of the army, at least, is incapable of undertaking any thing ; and that the distress for want of provisions, and its effects, have at last obliged me to move towards the frontiers of Portugal, in order to refresh my troops.

In my former dispatches, I have informed your Lordship of our distress for the want of provisions and means of transport. These wants, which were the first cause of the loss of many advantages after the 22d July, which were made known to the government, and were actually known by them on the 20th of last month, still exist in an aggravated degree, and have produced all the evil effects upon the health and efficiency of the army which might have been expected from them.

Since the 22d of last month, when the Spanish and British armies joined, the troops have not received 10 days' bread; on some days they have received nothing ; and for many days together only meat, without salt : frequently flour instead of bread, and scarcely ever more than one third, or at most half, of a ration. The cavalry and the horses of the army have not received, in the same time, three regular deliveries of forage, particularly of barley, the only wholesome subsistence for a horse in this country ; and the horses have been kept alive by what they could pick up for themselves, for which they have frequently been obliged to go from 12 to 20 miles' distance, particularly lately.

During a great part of this time, at least till the 4th or 5th of this month, I know that the Spanish army received their regular rations daily : after they lost the bridge of Arzobispo, I believe they were in want for some days ; but since they have come through the passes of the mountains, I know, from the best authority, that of Gen. Eguia, that the Spanish cavalry have been supplied daily with at least half a ration of barley, and I believe the troops have received their regular allowance of bread.

The consequence of these privations upon the British army has been the loss of many horses of the cavalry and artillery. We lost 100 in the cavalry last week ; and we now want 1000 horses to complete the 6 regiments of dragoons, besides about 700 that are sick, and will probably be fit for service only after a considerable period of rest and good food. The horses of the artillery are also much diminished in numbers, and are scarcely able to draw the guns.

The sickness of the army, from the same cause, has increased considerably ; particularly among the officers, who have fared no better than the soldiers ; and have had nothing but water to drink, and frequently nothing but meat without salt to eat, and seldom any bread, for the last month. Indeed, there are few, if any, officers or soldiers of the army who, although doing their duty, are not more or less affected by dysentery, and the whole lie out, and nothing can be got for them in this part of the country.

To these circumstances I must add, that I have not been able to procure means of transport of any description since my arrival in Spain. I was obliged to employ the largest proportion of the carts in the army, whether they carried money or ammunition, to convey the wounded soldiers to the hospital at Elvas ; and the ammunition which was laid down at Mesa de

Ibor and Deleytosa was delivered to the Spanish General. The few carts which remained in the army were required to move the sick we have at present, and I have been obliged to leave behind me the remainder of the reserve ammunition, which I have also given to the Spanish troops; and if I had waited longer, I should not have been able to move at all without leaving the sick behind. Under these circumstances, I determined to break up on the 20th from Jaraicejo, where I had had my head quarters since the 11th, with the advanced posts on the Tagus, near the bridge of Almaraz, and to fall back upon the frontiers of Portugal; where I hope I shall be supplied with every thing I want.

I have given your Lordship only an outline of the distresses of the army. You will find the details of them in my correspondence with the British ministers at Seville, copies of which, I conclude, they will send home to the Foreign office.

Your Lordship will observe, that from the dispersed situation of the French army, and the losses the enemy has sustained, the Spanish troops are not likely to suffer any inconvenience from our absence; but I assure your Lordship that if I had been certain that the enemy could and would attack the Spaniards on the day after my departure, I could not, with justice to the army, have remained any longer; and there is not a General officer in the army who has not repeatedly represented the lamentable and neglected situation in which we were placed, and the absolute necessity which existed that I should withdraw from Spain altogether.

To Visc. Castlereagh.   Truxillo, 21st Aug. 1809.

My dispatches of this date will give you an unpleasant account of our situation in this country, than which nothing indeed can be worse; we want every thing and can get nothing; and we are treated in no respect as we ought to be; and I might almost say not even as friends. However, I acknowledge that I go with regret, and I wish that I had been able to stay a little longer, not that I think I could have done much good, for I am convinced that we should not have been able to resume the offensive.

Our own cavalry and artillery are very low indeed; Cuesta's army is much weakened. I understand that it has lost 10,000 men since it crossed the Tagus, although not 500 in action; whole corps, officers and all, have disbanded and gone off. If we could have fed, and have got up the condition of our horses, we might probably, after some time, have struck a brilliant blow upon Soult at Plasencia; or upon Mortier in the centre; but till there should be a force in the centre of Spain capable of keeping in check Ney's corps, and probably Soult's, or of alarming Joseph for Madrid, or till we could put a force in Baños on which we could depend, we could not hope to make any progress with the offensive in this quarter.

The Marques de la Romana, who alone has numbers, has neither cavalry nor artillery, and cannot venture to quit the mountains; and he, I understand, was still at Coruna on the 5th; and we could depend upon nothing excepting British to keep Ney, and eventually, Soult, out of Estremadura, after what I have seen of Spanish troops.

I shall not now answer your letter respecting the discipline of the army, notwithstanding that I am more than ever convinced that something is necessary to be done.

The A.G. to Major ——, *Capt.* ——, *Lieut.* ——, *— regts., Lisbon.*   21st Aug. 1809.

Having laid your letter of the 16th inst. before his Excellency the Commander of the Forces, I am directed to acquaint you that it was with no little surprise he learned of your having, with other officers, proceeded to Lisbon without applying for leave through the regular channels. Such instances of impropriety on the part of officers who happen to be wounded in action cannot fail, in the course of a campaign, to be in the highest degree prejudicial to the good discipline, regularity, and order of the army. He very much doubts whether the order, as you mention, was ever given by Col. —— ; at all events, it must have been done entirely on his own responsibility, and as such, would naturally have been reported by him. His Excellency desires you will, together with all officers who have behaved with this shameful irregularity, proceed immediately to the general hospital at Elvas, reporting your arrival there to me, for his information, as also yourself to the Inspector of hospitals.

Au Marechal Mortier, Duc de Trevise.

Au Quartier General de l'armee Anglaise,
ce 22 Août, 1809.

J'ai eu l'honneur de recevoir la lettre que vous m'avez écrite, et je vous suis bien oblige de la promesse que vous m'y faites d'avoir soin des blesses de l'armee Anglaise, qui vous sont tombés dans les mains. M. le Commissaire Dillon est aussi arrive il y a quelques jours, et m'a fait grand plaisir en m'apprenant les bontes que vous avez pour ces braves officiers et soldats.

Je vous envoie encore le Col. Waters, a qui j'ai donné 139 onces d'Espagne ou 500 livres sterling ; et je vous serai bien oblige si vous voulez permettre que cette somme soit donnee au plus ancien des officiers Anglais, avec ordre de la distribuer parmi les autres officiers et les chirurgiens qui sont prisonniers. Je vous prie aussi de permettre qu'il m'envoie un mémoire, avec les noms de ceux auxquels il aura donne l'argent, et la somme qu'il a donnee a chacun. Je vous serai bien oblige si vous voulez laisser partir sur sa parole tout officier qui sera suffisamment retabli ; et si vous voulez etablir un échange, je m'engagerai a faire renvoyer en France autant du meme rang d'officiers et de soldats que vous me renverrez, et vous nommerez ceux qui retourneront en France.

To Marquis Wellesley.   Miajadas, 22d Aug. 1809.

I have this day had the honor of receiving your Excellency's dispatch of the 20th inst. My former letters will have apprised your Excellency that I was aware that Marshal Ney's corps was gone to Salamanca. In respect to the intelligence from Gen. Venegas, it appears to me that the enemy have no intention to make any progress in that quarter beyond the foot of the mountains. If they entertained any intention of proceeding farther, they would have gone in greater strength.

Whatever may be the enemy's designs in that quarter, my former dispatches must have convinced your Excellency that I was unable to co-operate in any movement in this quarter, which should have for its object to draw the enemy from La Mancha, or indeed in any movement of any description, excepting that which I am now making ; having no provisions, no stores, no means of transport ; being overloaded with sick ; the horses of the cavalry being scarcely able to march, or those of the artillery to draw the guns; and the officers and soldiers being worn down by want of food, and privations of every description.

The Spanish ministers cannot have adverted to what I have frequently repeated to them through different channels since the 17th of last month, viz.: that if I were not supplied with what I required, not only I could not co-operate in any forward movement, but must withdraw from Spain: or they could not give credit to the existence of the wants of the British army; or they must believe me to be so exceedingly desirous of serving them, that whatever might be the consequences to the army, I should make it march and fight so long as two men should remain together. Nobody feels more disappointed and hurt than I do, that so little attention has been paid to the demands which I have frequently made; and whatever may be the consequence of the steps which I have been compelled to take, I am in no manner responsible for them.

I have now proceeded 3 marches to the rear from Jaraicejo since the 20th, and have not met a supply of any description on its way to the army; so that if I had remained at Jaraicejo so long, it would have been the 26th before the army would have received any of the supplies from Seville; and yet Don L. de Calvo undertook that the army should be fully supplied on every day after the 19th, and was much surprised that I had no confidence in his promises of the arrival of supplies, respecting the progress of which upon the road, or even of their quitting Seville, he had no information.

To Marquis Wellesley.   Merida, 24th Aug. 1809.

I have not lost a moment in replying to your dispatch which I received in the night. I think you will agree with me in opinion that it is best that I should have no more communication with the Spaniards, although it is by no means necessary, nor do I intend, to hurry into Portugal.

I have just heard that the Junta have ordered Gen. Eguia to move to the rear. I do not understand from his letters to Col. O'Lawlor whether that movement is to be made with or without my sanction; but I have desired Col. O'Lawlor to say that I have written to Seville to express my disagreement in opinion with the person who proposed the movement, and to recommend to Gen. Eguia not to move till we hear further. If he should not think of commencing his movement till to-morrow, I shall be in time to stop him.

G. O.   Medellin, 23d Aug. 1809.

1. Officers commanding divisions and brigades will be pleased to take measures to prevent the women and followers of the army buying up the bread which is prepared for the soldiers' rations: this practice, carried on in the irregular manner as it is at present, must ultimately prejudice the soldiers, and prevent the regular supply of bread.

G. P. O.   Medellin, 23d Aug. 1809.

The women of the army must be prevented from purchasing bread in the villages within 2 leagues of the station of any division of the army; when any woman wants to purchase bread, she must ask the officer of the company to which she belongs for a passport, which must be countersigned by the Commanding officer of the regiment. Any woman found with bread in her possession, purchased at any place nearer than 2 leagues, will be deprived of the bread by the Provost, or his assistants; as will any woman who goes out of camp to purchase bread without a passport. Women who will have been discovered disobeying this order, will not be allowed to receive rations.

I believe you were not aware how we stood with the Spaniards with respect to any agreement, when you wrote to me your private letter of the 22d. In fact, we are under no agreement to furnish any troops.

To Marquis Wellesley.   Merida, 24th Aug. 1809.

I had the honor of receiving last night, at Medellin, your Excellency's dispatch, marked C, and dated the 22d inst.

From all that I have heard of the state of the government of Seville, I am not surprised that they should have been astonished and alarmed, when they heard that I had at last determined to adopt the measure which I had so frequently informed them I should adopt. Although I was desirous to avoid, as long as possible, withdrawing into Portugal, and certainly remained in the position upon the Tagus so long as it was practicable, and longer probably than was consistent with the anxiety which I have always felt for the welfare and comfort of the troops placed under my command, I am of opinion that, having been compelled to withdraw, it becomes a question for serious consideration, whether any circumstances should now induce me to remain in Spain, and to hold out hopes of further co-operation with the Spanish troops, to be decided on grounds very different from those which were to lead to a decision whether, being joined in co-operation with the Spanish army, I ought or ought not to separate from them.

I beg to lay my ideas upon that point before your Excellency, and to request the aid of your superior judgment to enable me to decide upon it, in the manner which will be most beneficial to the national interests. When the two armies were joined, this implied engagement existed between them, that so long as the operations were conducted by mutual consent, they were to continue in co-operation; and I should not have considered myself justified in separating from the Spanish army, unless Portugal should evidently have required the protection of the British army; or unless the Spanish army should have been under the necessity of adopting a line of operation, to follow which would separate me from Portugal; or, unless driven, as I was, to separate by necessity; or, unless the Spanish army had again behaved so ill, as a military body, as it did in its shameful flight from the bridge of Arzobispo. I conceived this last case would have made it so notorious that it was necessary for me to separate, that I had determined that it should induce a separation equally with the occurrence of any of the other three; and I should have stated it broadly and fairly, as my reason for withdrawing the British army from all communication with a body endowed with qualities as soldiers in a degree so far inferior to themselves.

Your Excellency will observe that my conduct in continuing with the Spanish army would have been guided by a fair view of our reciprocal situation, and by a consideration of what they might understand to be an engagement to act with them, so long as it was consistent with the order I had received, 'to consider my army applicable to the defence of Portugal' with which orders the Spanish government are fully acquainted. At the present moment, however, I have been compelled to separate from the Spanish army; and the question now is, whether I shall place myself in co-operation with them again.

The first point which I should wish your Excellency to consider is the difference of the reasoning by which the decision of this question must be guided, from that which I have above stated would have guided, and did in fact guide me in the decision of the other. In that case I considered the armies to be under an implied engagement to each other, not to separate excepting on certain defined or easily definable grounds; but in this case there is positively no engagement of any description. There is none in the treaty between His Majesty and the Spanish government: there is none expressed or implied by me. Indeed, the argument would lead the other way: for His Majesty, having offered the Spanish government the services of his army upon certain conditions, the conditions were refused; and it must have been understood that His Majesty would not give the aid of his army; and accordingly His Majesty has never ordered, but has only permitted me to carry on such operations in Spain as I might think proper, upon my own responsibility, and as were consistent with the safety of Portugal.

The question then comes before me to be decided as a new one, whether I shall again join in co-operation with the Spanish army. I must here take into consideration, as I did upon the first occasion, the objects of such co-operation, the means which exist of attaining those objects, and the risks I shall incur of loss to my army, and of losing sight of Portugal; for the defence of which country the British army has been sent to the Peninsula.

The object held out in your Excellency's dispatch, and which I consider as only the first and immediate object (for I am convinced your Excellency must look to offensive operations as soon as the means shall be prepared for them), is the defence of the Guadiana. Upon this point I must inform your Excellency that, in my opinion, the Guadiana is not to be defended by a weaker army against a stronger. It is fordable in very many places, and it affords no position that I know of; and the result of withdrawing the Spanish army from its present position to that which has been proposed to your Excellency for them, would be to expose them to be defeated before I could assist them.

The Spanish army is at this moment in the best position in this part of the country, which they ought to hold against any force that can be brought against them, if they can hold any thing. As long as they continue in it, they cover effectually the passages of the Guadiana, which they would not cover by the adoption of any other position; and their retreat from it, in case of accident, must always be secure. There is no chance of their being attacked by superior numbers. I have reason to believe that Soult, as well as Ney, has passed through the mountains into Castille; and there remain only Mortier's corps, and 2 divisions of Victor's in Estremadura; the total of which force cannot amount to 25,000 men.

The subsistence of the Spanish army in their present position, particularly now that we have withdrawn, cannot be very difficult. Upon the whole, then, I recommend that they should continue in their present position as long as possible, sending away to Badajoz the bridge of boats, which is still opposite to Almaraz.

According to this reasoning, it does not appear to be necessary, and it is not very desirable, that the British army should be involved in the defence of the Guadiana.

But it might be asked, Is there no chance of resuming the offensive? In answer, I have to observe, that at present I see none, and hereafter certainly none. Your Excellency is informed of the history of the causes which led to the late change in our operations, from the offensive, after a victory, to defensive. The same causes would certainly exist if we were to recommence our operations. The French have as many troops as we have; indeed I am not certain that they are not now superior to us in numbers, as they are certainly, at least to the Spanish army, in discipline and every military quality. Unless we could depend upon the troops employed to keep the passes of the mountains, we could not prevent the French corps in Castille from coming upon our rear, while those in Estremadura and La Mancha would be in our front. But I certainly can never place any reliance upon the Spanish troops to defend a pass; and I could not venture to detach from the British army, British troops in sufficient numbers to defend the passes of Banos and Perales. Even if we could, however, by the defence of those passes, prevent the enemy from attacking us in the rear, we could not prevent him from penetrating by the passes of Guadarrama or Avila, and adding to the numbers in our front.

To this add, that there are no troops in the north of Spain which could be employed to make a diversion. Blake has lost his army; the Marques de la Romana is still in Galicia; and he cannot venture to quit the mountains, having neither cavalry nor artillery; the Duque del Parque has very few troops; and, as he has shown lately, he does not like to risk them at a distance from Ciudad Rodrigo.

But I come now to another topic, which is one of serious consideration, and has considerable weight in my judgment upon this whole subject, and that is the frequent, I ought to say constant, and shameful misbehavior of the Spanish troops before the enemy. We in England never hear of their defeats and flights; but I have heard of Spanish officers telling of 19 and 20 actions of the description of that at the bridge of Arzobispo, an account of which has, I believe, never been published.

In the battle of Talavera, in which the Spanish army, with very trifling exceptions, was not engaged, whole corps threw away their arms, and ran off *in my presence*, when they were neither attacked nor threatened with an attack, but frightened, I believe, by their own fire. I refer your Excellency for evidence upon this subject to Gen. Cuesta's orders, in which, after extolling the gallantry of his army in general, he declares his intention to decimate the runaways, an intention which he afterwards carried into execution.

When these dastardly soldiers run away, they plunder every thing they meet; and in their flight from Talavera, they plundered the baggage of the British army, which was at the moment bravely engaged in their cause.

I can easily conceive the unwillingness of officers in command, or acting with troops, to report their misbehavior in presence of the enemy, for where the troops misbehave no honor can be acquired; and in this way I account for the numerous histories we have of the bravery of the Spanish troops. I have found, upon inquiry and from experience, the instances of the misbehavior of the Spanish troops to be so numerous, and those of their good behavior so few, that I must conclude that they are troops by no means to be depended upon; and then the question again arises, whether, being at liberty to join in co-operation with those troops or not, I ought again to risk the King's army?

There is no doubt whatever, but that every thing that is to be done must be done by us; and certainly the British army cannot be deemed sufficiently strong to be the only acting efficient military body to be opposed to a French army consisting of not less than 70,000 men.

Upon every ground, therefore, of objects, means, and risks, it is my opinion that I ought to avoid entering into any further co-operation with the Spanish armies; and that, at all events, your Excellency should avoid holding out to the government any hope that I would consent to remain within the Spanish frontier, with any intention of co-operating in future with the Spanish troops.

At the same time I see the difficulty in which the government may be placed. Their army may be seized with one of those panic terrors to which they are liable, and may run off and leave every thing exposed to instant loss. To which I answer, that I am in no hurry to withdraw from Spain. I want to give my troops food and refreshment, and I shall not withdraw into Portugal, at all events, till I shall have received your Excellency's sentiments upon what I have submitted to your judgment. If I should withdraw into Portugal, I shall go no farther than the frontier (but to this I should not wish to engage); and I shall be so near, that the enemy will not like to venture across the Guadiana, unless he comes in very large force indeed, having me upon his flank and his rear. I shall in effect, therefore, be as useful to the Spanish government within the Portuguese frontier as I should be in the position which has been proposed to your Excellency; and indeed more useful, as I expect that the nearer I shall move to Portugal, the more efficient I shall become; at the same time that by going within the Portuguese frontier, I clear myself entirely of the Spanish army; and shall have an opportunity hereafter of deciding whether I shall co-operate with them at all, in what manner, and to what extent, and under what conditions, according to the circumstances of the moment.

P. S. Since writing the above, Lieut. Col. O'Lawlor has received a letter from Gen. Eguia, stating that he has received orders from the government to retire upon Villa Nueva de la Serena, in consequence of the movement made by the troops under my command. If he should retire so far, it will be necessary that he should fall back still farther to Monasterio, having no position upon the Guadiana.

I have also to observe to your Excellency, that even if I should remain in Spain, it will be impossible for me to take up the position which it has been proposed to your Excellency that I should take up; as, in case of the further retreat of the Spanish army, I should find it difficult to get back into Portugal. Indeed, at all events, the best way for me to cover the Guadiana and Seville is by a position on the enemy's flank.

To Visc. Castlereagh.   Merida, 25th Aug. 1809.

I received by Mr. Hay, on the day before yesterday, your letter of the 4th Aug., and having for some time past turned my mind very seriously to the consideration of the points to which it relates, I am not unprepared to give you an opinion upon them.

The information which I have acquired in the last two months has opened my eyes respecting the state of the war in the Peninsula; and I shall just state a few facts which will enable the King's ministers to form their own opinions upon it.

I calculate the French force in the Peninsula now to consist of about 125,000 men: of this number, about 70,000 are in this part of Spain; St. Cyr's corps, about 20,000 men, are engaged in the siege of Gerona; Suchet's, about 14,000, in Aragon; and the remainder are employed in different garrisons, such as Avila, &c., and in keeping up the communication with France: all of which, if necessary, are disposable for the field. These 125,000 men are exclusive of the garrisons of Pamplona, Barcelona, &c. &c. These troops, you will observe, are all in Spain; and against this force the Spaniards have, under Venegas and Eguia, late Cuesta's army, about 50,000 men; Romana, the Duque del Parque, and every thing to the northward, about 25,000; Blake may have gotten together again about 5000 or 6000; and I believe there is nothing in Aragon and Catalonia, excepting an armed population.

Thus, the Spaniards have not, at the end of 18 months nearly, after the commencement of the revolution, above 80,000 men, of which the composition and quality will be found still more defective than the numbers are deficient to carry on the contest with the French even in their present strength. To these numbers add all the troops we can bring into the field at present, which are about 25,000 men, and about 10,000 Portuguese, and you will see that the allies are, at this moment, inferior in point of numbers only to the enemy in the Peninsula. However, in this account of the troops of the allies, I do not reckon many garrisons and towns occupied by both Spaniards and Portuguese; nor do I reckon the French garrisons. I count only those men on both sides who can be brought into the field to fight.

In respect to the composition of these armies, we find the French well supplied with troops of the different descriptions and arms required; viz., infantry, artillery, and cavalry, heavy and light. Cuesta's army had about 7000 cavalry, Venegas' about 3000, and there may be about 2000 more cavalry distributed throughout Spain. The English have about 2500 cavalry left, and the Portuguese army may have 500 or 600. Probably, if all this cavalry were efficient, and could be divided as it ought to be, it might be sufficient, and might be found more numerous than that of the French in the Peninsula: but you will observe that all the cavalry is now

---

G. O.   Merida, 25th Aug. 1809.

3. The army must not take forage for themselves, but must get it from the Commissary according to the usual mode, by sending in returns of the number of animals for which forage is required, and receiving from him the regular rations; or if forage cannot be provided in that mode, and it is necessary it should be taken from the fields, it must be taken according to the G. O. of the 17th June, 1809.

in the south, and Romana's army (which it is most important to bring forward, as unless it is brought forward the allies can never make any impression on the French to the southward) has neither cavalry nor artillery, and cannot quit the mountains; neither has the Duque del Parque more than one regiment, or Blake more than the same number.

I come now to the description of the troops, and here I am sorry to say that our allies fail us still more than they do in numbers and composition. The Spanish cavalry are, I believe, nearly entirely without discipline. They are in general well clothed, armed, and accoutred, and remarkably well mounted, and their horses are in good condition; I mean those of Eguia's army, which I have seen. But I have never heard any body pretend that in any one instance they have behaved as soldiers ought to do in presence of an enemy. They make no scruple of running off, and after an action are to be found in every village and every shady bottom within 50 miles of the field of battle. The Spanish artillery are, as far as I have seen of them, entirely unexceptionable, and the Portuguese artillery excellent.

In respect to the great body of all armies, I mean the infantry, it is lamentable to see how bad that of the Spaniards is, and how unequal to a contest with the French. They are armed, I believe, well; they are badly accoutred, not having the means of saving their ammunition from the rain; not clothed in some instances at all, in others clothed in such a manner as to make them look like peasants, which ought of all things to be avoided; and their discipline appears to me to be confined to placing them in the ranks, three deep at very close order, and to the manual exercise.

It is impossible to calculate upon any operation with these troops. It is said that sometimes they behave well; though I acknowledge that I have never seen them behave otherwise than ill. Bassecourt's corps, which was supposed to be the best in Cuesta's army, and was engaged on our left in the mountains, at the battle of Talavera, was kept in check throughout the day by one French battalion: this corps has since run away from the bridge of Arzobispo, leaving its guns; and many of the men, according to the usual Spanish custom, throwing away their arms, accoutrements, and clothing. It is a curious circumstance respecting this affair at Arzobispo (in which Soult writes that the French took 30 pieces of cannon), that the Spaniards ran off in such a hurry, that they left their cannon loaded and unspiked; and that the French, although they drove the Spaniards from the bridge, did not think themselves strong enough to push after them; and Col. Waters, whom I sent in with a flag of truce on the 10th, relating to our wounded, found the cannon on the road, abandoned by the one party, and not taken possession of, and probably not known of, by the other.

This practice of running away, and throwing off arms, accoutrements, and clothing, is fatal to every thing, excepting a re-assembly of the men in a state of nature, who as regularly perform the same manœuvre the next time an occasion offers. Nearly 2000 ran off on the evening of the 27th from the battle of Talavera (not 100 yards from the place where I was standing), who were neither attacked, nor threatened with an attack, and who were frightened only by the noise of their own fire : they left their arms and accoutrements on the ground, their officers went with them ; and they, and the fugitive cavalry, plundered the baggage of the British army which had been sent to the rear. Many others went whom I did not see.

Nothing can be worse than the officers of the Spanish army ; and it is extraordinary that when a nation has devoted itself to war, as this nation has, by the measures it has adopted in the last 2 years, so little progress has been made in any one branch of the military profession by any individual, and that the business of an army should be so little understood. They are really children in the art of war, and I cannot say that they do any thing as it ought to be done, with the exception of running away and assembling again in a state of nature.

I really believe that much of this deficiency of numbers, composition, discipline, and efficiency, is to be attributed to the existing government of Spain. They have attempted to govern the Kingdom in a state of revolution, by an adherence to old rules and systems, and with the aid of what is called enthusiasm ; and this last is, in fact, no aid to accomplish any thing, and is only an excuse for the irregularity with which every thing is done, and for the want of discipline and subordination of the armies. People are very apt to believe that enthusiasm carried the French through their revolution, and was the parent of those exertions which have nearly conquered the world ; but if the subject is nicely examined, it will be found that enthusiasm was the name only, but that force was the instrument which brought forward those great resources under the system of terror which first stopped the allies ; and that a perseverance in the same system of applying every individual and every description of property to the service of the army, by force, has since conquered Europe.

After this statement, you will judge for yourselves, whether you will employ any, and what strength of army, in support of the cause in Spain. Circumstances with which you are acquainted have obliged me to separate myself from the Spanish army, and I can only tell you that I feel no inclination to join in co-operation with them again, upon my own responsibility ; and that I shall see my way very clearly before me indeed, before I do so ; and I do not recommend you to have any thing to do with them in their present state.

Before I quit this part of the subject, it may be satisfactory to you to know that I do not think matters would have been much better if you had sent your large expedition to Spain, instead of to the Scheldt. You could not have equipped it in Galicia, or any where in the north of Spain. If we had had 60,000 men, instead of 20,000, in all probability we should not have got to Talavera to fight the battle, for want of means and provisions. But if we had got to Talavera, we could not have gone farther, and the armies would probably have separated for want of means of subsistence, probably without a battle ; but certainly afterwards. Besides, you will observe that your 40,000 men, supposing them to be equipped and means to exist of feeding them, would not compensate for the deficiency of numbers, of composition, and of efficiency in the Spanish armies ; and that supposing they had been able to remove the French from Madrid,

2 G 2

they could not have removed them from the Peninsula, even in the existing state of the French force.

I now come to another branch of the subject, which is Portugal itself. I have not got from Beresford his report upon the present, and the probable future, state of the Portuguese army; and therefore I should wish to be understood as writing, upon this part of the subject, liable to corrections from him.

My opinion is, and always has been, that the mode of applying the services of the English officers to the Portuguese army has been erroneous. I think that Beresford ought to have had the temporary assistance of the ablest officers the British service could afford; that these officers ought not to have been posted to regiments in the Portuguese army, but under the title of 'Adjutants' to the Field Marshal, or any other, they ought to have superintended discipline, military movements, and arrangements of all descriptions, wherever they might be: fewer officers would then have answered his purpose, and every one given to him would have been useful; whereas many (all in the inferior ranks) are, under existing arrangements, useless. Besides this, the selection of officers sent out to Portugal for this service has been unlucky, and the decision on the questions which I sent to England on the 7th June has been made without reference to circumstances, or to the feelings or opinions of the individuals on whom it was to operate; and just like every other decision I have ever seen from the same quarter, as if men were stocks and stones. To this, add that rank (Portuguese rank, I mean) has been given in the most capricious manner. In some instances, a man not in the army at all is made a Brigadier General; in others, another who was the senior of the Brigadier General when both were in the army, is a Lieutenant Colonel; then a junior Lieutenant Colonel is made a Brigadier General, his senior a Colonel, and his senior a junior Colonel; and there are instances of juniors being preferred to seniors in every rank; in short, the Prince Regent of Portugal is a despotic prince, and his commissions have been given to British officers and subjects in the most arbitrary manner at the Horse Guards; and the answer to all these complaints at the Horse Guards must be uniform, nobody has any right to complain; the Prince Regent has a right to give to any body any commission he pleases, bearing any date he chooses to assign to it. The officers of this army have to a man quitted the Portuguese service, as I said they would, and there is not an officer who has joined it from England who would not quit it if we would allow him; but here we keep them: so much for that arrangement.

The subject upon which particularly I wished Beresford to report, was the state of the Portuguese army in respect to its numbers. The troops have lately deserted to an alarming degree; and, in fact, none of the regiments are complete. The Portuguese army is recruited by conscription constitutionally, very much in the same manner with the French army; but then it must be recollected, that, for the last 50 years nearly, the troops have never left their province, and scarcely ever their native town; and their discipline, and the labors and exertion required from them, were nothing. Things are much altered lately, and notwithstanding that the pay has been increased, I fear that the animal is not of the description to bear up against what is required of him; and he deserts most terribly.

The military forces stationed in the provinces enabled the civil government to carry into execution the conscription; but, under present circumstances, the military force is, upon principle, as well as necessity, removed to a distance. The civil government has been so frequently overthrown in all parts of Portugal that it can hardly be said to exist; and there is another circumstance which I am afraid cramps its operations, particularly those operations which are to put a restraint upon the people, and that is, that they are all armed, and they defy the civil magistrate and the government who order them to march as conscripts, whose authority is unsupported by a sufficient military force. I am, therefore, very apprehensive that Beresford will find it impossible to fill his ranks: however, as I said before, I should wish government to delay making their minds up on this part of the subject till I shall be enabled to send them Beresford's report, for which I have called.

The next point in this subject is, supposing the Portuguese army to be rendered efficient, what can be done with it and Portugal, if the French should obtain possession of the remainder of the Peninsula? My opinion is, that we ought to be able to hold Portugal, if the Portuguese army and militia are complete. The difficulty upon this sole question lies in the embarkation of the British army. There are so many entrances into Portugal, the whole country being frontier, that it would be very difficult to prevent the enemy from penetrating; and it is probable that we should be obliged to confine ourselves to the preservation of that which is most important, the capital.

It is difficult, if not impossible, to bring the contest for the capital to extremities, and afterwards to embark the British army. You will see what I mean, by a reference to the map. Lisbon is so high up the Tagus that no army that we could collect would be able at the same time to secure the navigation of the river by the occupation of both banks, and the possession of the capital. One of the objects must, I fear, be given up, and that which the Portuguese would give up would be the navigation of the Tagus; and, of course, our means of embarkation. However, I have not entirely made up my mind upon this interesting point. I have a great deal of information upon it, but I should wish to have more before I can decide upon it.

In the mean time I think that government should look to sending back at least the coppered transports, as soon as the grand expedition shall have done with them; and as they receive positive intelligence that Napoleon is reinforcing his armies in Spain: for you may depend upon it, that he and his Marshals must be desirous of revenging upon us the different blows we have given them; and that when they come into the Peninsula, their first and great object will be to get the English out.

I think the first part of my letter will give you my opinion respecting one notion you entertained, viz., that the Spaniards might be induced to give the command of their armies to a British Commander in Chief. If such offer should be made to me, I shall decline to accept it till I shall receive His Majesty's pleasure; and I strongly recommend to you, unless you mean to incur the risk of the loss of your army, not to have any thing to do with Spanish warfare on any ground whatever in the existing state of things. In respect to Cadiz, the fact is this, that the jealousy of all the Spaniards, even of those most attached to us, respecting Cadiz, is so rooted, that even if the government should cede that point (and in their present difficulties I should not be surprised if they were to cede it) to induce me to remain in Spain, I should not think any garrison which this army could spare to be safe in the place.

If you should take Cadiz, you must lay down Portugal, and take up Spain; you must occupy Cadiz with a garrison of from 15,000 to 20,000 men, and you must send from England an army to be employed in the field with the Spaniards, and make Cadiz your retreat instead of Lisbon. You ought, along with Cadiz, to insist upon the command of the armies of Spain. I think you would certainly be able in that case to get away your troops, secure the Spanish ships, &c.

But you see from the facts in the commencement of this letter, how little prospect you have of bringing the contest to the conclusion for which we all wish.

I shall be very glad if you will send us the remount horses, and any regiment of dragoons that is to come, as soon as possible; the best thing to do then, probably, would be to draft the horses of one of the regiments to complete the others, and send that regiment home dismounted. It would be very desirable also to send us 600 or 700 sets of horse appointments.

To Marshal Beresford.   Merida, 26th Aug. 1809.

I am very much obliged to you for the orders which you have given respecting the convalescents of the British army, and the stores belonging to the flying artillery, which you found at Castello Branco. In respect to Gen. Lightburne's brigade, if you do not want it, order him to go to Abrantes to occupy the huts in front of that town, and to report to head quarters.

I have been for some time very anxious respecting the description of officers who have been sent to you from England. I have always been of opinion that the most advantageous mode of using the English officers, who should be sent to Portugal, would have been not as regimental officers, but as a description of staff, unknown, I believe, to all armies excepting the French. They should have been called 'Adjutants,' or 'Adjutants General to the Field Marshal,' and he should have placed them where he pleased, to superintend the discipline of individual corps, the movements or operations of armies, or any other operation, and their power should have been supreme, wherever he should think proper to employ them.

The officers to be employed in this manner must have been the best the British service could afford, probably so like black swans, that the service could afford very few of them; but fewer would have been required, and the service of all would have been efficient; whereas I suspect that the service of many of those you have got is not worth the expense, and that as the Portuguese will have become acquainted with their ignorance and inefficiency, their respect for them will diminish. I recommend to you to turn this notion of mine in your mind, and see whether you could not engraft upon the present system, a system such as that which I have suggested to you. For instance, supposing that from among your officers of all ranks you were to select from 12 to 20 of the best to be employed, with any title you pleased, in the manner which I have proposed. Almost upon recollection, I could name 12 who might be so employed with advantage; some of whom are now of no use in the subordinate situations in which they are placed, and the use of the others is extremely limited.

The great objection to this plan is, the jealousy it would create among the Portuguese military. I should doubt, however, whether that jealousy would be greater than it is under the existing arrangement; and I think in reason it ought not to be so great: at all events, this system would have the advantage of being efficient, your eye and directions being everywhere; whereas the other, with the instruments you have to work with, cannot be so.

The A.G. to Col. Peacocke, Lisbon.   26th Aug. 1809.

I herewith enclose certificates of leave of absence for Capt. ——, — light dragoons, and Lieut. ——, — dragoons, as also for Major ——, — regt.; but you will acquaint the latter officer his application for leave should have been made through you.

With regard to your having the permission, on certified emergencies, to allow officers to proceed to England, the Commander of the Forces by no means approves of it.

To J. Murray, Esq., Commissary General.   Merida, 27th Aug. 1809.

As the army is about to return into Portugal, I wish you very much to turn your mind to the state of its conveyances, upon which I am about to give you my opinion. The lines with which it is most important it should communicate are the direct line from Elvas to Lisbon, and that from Elvas to Abrantes. I request you, therefore, as soon as possible to communicate with the officers of the Portuguese government, respecting conveyances upon these roads, to be established upon the following principles:

1st. That every carriage required should carry 600 lbs., and shall go a certain number of days' journey, at a certain price, when it shall be invariably relieved, and be allowed to go home.

2dly. That these stages shall be fixed in reference to the conveniences of the country in assembling the number of waggons required, and that whenever —— days' notice is given to the proper office at Lisbon or Abrantes respectively, that any number of waggons are wanted, they shall

---

G. O.   Merida, 27th Aug. 1809.

4. The Commander of the Forces begs to call the attention of the officers of the army to the orders of the 29th May, 1809. General officers commanding divisions and brigades are requested to have the orderly books of those regiments examined which arrived in Portugal since the 1st May last, and they will have inserted in them, and read to the soldiers, all orders of regulations, if any there be, which have not been issued to them.

8. Commanding officers of regiments are referred to the G. O. (No. 3, of the 31st May), requiring them to send in returns of bill-hooks, camp kettles, &c.

9. As shirts and shoes for the army are on the road from Lisbon, Commanding officers of regiments are requested, as soon as possible, to send in returns to the Q. M. G. of the number of shirts and pairs of shoes they will require to complete each man with two good shirts and two good pairs of shoes.

be ordered to be prepared, and shall be ready at the different stages upon the road.

But besides these conveyances, which will be required to keep up the communication between the army and Abrantes and Lisbon, respectively, it will be necessary to have with and attached to the army from 300 to 400 waggons with bullocks.

It appears to me that the best mode of procuring these last will be to contract for them with one of the great Portuguese contractors at Lisbon. The terms of this contract may either be to supply the drivers with provisions, and the cattle with forage, or not   But I should prefer the first; and you may engage to pay for these carts once a fortnight, keeping them a fortnight in arrear.   The contractor to keep a person with the army to manage these carts, and no cart to be paid for which is not furnished with a native driver.

I wish you to communicate with Mr. Villiers on these points, and request his assistance in both objects.

To Marquis Wellesley.   Merida, 28th Aug. 1809.

I am anxious to receive your Excellency's sentiments on the points discussed in my dispatch of the 24th inst., No. 14, as it will be necessary that I should make early arrangements to draw out of Portugal the supplies of ammunition, stores, and necessaries for the troops, which I have reason to believe are already collected at Elvas. Having been able to separate the army, the troops have received their regular rations since the 25th inst., with the exception of the horses of the cavalry.

I have to inform your Excellency, however, that none of the supplies, either of provisions or means of transport, which Don L. de Calvo informed me, and the Spanish ministers informed your Excellency, were so near the army, have yet reached Merida, which is at least four marches from Jaraicejo ; and I entertain doubts whether any of them were even ordered, till your Excellency presented your first note to the ministers.

The officers and troops are still very unhealthy, and I fear that I shall find it difficult to remove them from hence to Elvas, where the British hospital is established, for want of carriages, and I can get none here. The loss of horses also continues to be very great, on account of the necessity of giving them wheat instead of barley.

The A.G. to Lieut. Col. Mackinnon.   28th Aug. 1809.

I have to acknowledge the receipt of your letter of the 25th from Elvas, together with its enclosures ; and I am directed by the Commander of the Forces to desire you will make me a particular report whether the number of men returned 'fit for duty,' are actually in a state to join their regiments. This number seems to exceed 1200 ; and it appears most extraordinary that so large a proportion of soldiers should have gone to the rear on such very slight cases, and some probably without being at all ill, as to be so rapidly fit for duty. You will call upon Capt. ——, — regt., to explain the reason of his proceeding to Lisbon, without leave ; and you will please to direct him immediately to join his battalion, unless a medical certificate is sent, stating his inability.

The A.G. to Brig. Gen. Baron Low, K.G.L.   29th Aug. 1809.

I have the honor to acknowledge the receipt of your letter of the 28th inst., and beg to inform you that it was not intended that the men in question should be received by the officer commanding the Legion against his consent. You will be pleased, therefore, to give directions that these men are sent to the Provost, who will take them in charge until an opportunity offers of sending them to Lisbon, and from thence to the Isle of Wight.

To Marshal Beresford.   Merida, 30th Aug. 1809.

I received yesterday your letter of the 27th. I know of no change of circumstances which ought to occasion an alteration of the plan you had fixed upon for your troops; and having once concurred in that plan, and having nothing to communicate to you from this quarter, I have not written to you for some days.

I should like to have Sir R. Wilson on this side the Tagus in our front. We must have somebody within the Spanish frontier; and we ought to have with this army some troops belonging to the country. Sir Robert is much liked here, and I should prefer him to anybody else: I should wish you, therefore, if you can spare him, to send somebody else in front of the Portuguese army to Castello Branco and Penamacor; but if you wish to keep Sir Robert, I shall not ask for him. Upon trial, I rather think the Portuguese are better than the Spaniards; at all events, with their English officers. My plan now is to remain on the defensive, and not to enter into any plan of co-operation with the Spanish army of any description (unless ordered from England) till I shall see defined objects and corresponding means to effect them.

As affairs are now settled, the French have more troops that they can bring into the field than we have, including Romana, who, from the want of artillery and cavalry, cannot quit the mountains. To this add, that the Spanish troops have no discipline, that they are not efficient, that they are defective even in the spirit of troops: that they cannot be depended upon for any operation of any description, and that they want means of all kinds; and I believe it will be admitted, that unless I undertake, with 25,000 British troops, to conquer Spain, I must either be satisfied with maintaining myself in Portugal as long as I can, or I must make up my mind to take upon my own shoulders the disgrace of the certain failure which must attend the military operations in Spain.

You and I might make a very pretty little expedition into Castille, which we might concert with the military section of the Junta, and we should have the promise of all the Generals for their hearty co-operation. The French would then put 10,000 men at Almaraz, 5000 at Arzobispo, and 5000 at Toledo, which would effectually keep in check the Spanish army, and they would collect about 50,000 men in Castille to oppose us. There would thus be an end to this expedition.

You shall have Mr. Rawlings whenever you please, and any other assistance that I can give you in that line: but we have lost some commissaries, and others are sick; and we are much less efficient in that branch than we were when I gave you this assistance before, although the demand for the service of commissaries is greater on account of the increased numbers of troops.

In respect to the officers of cavalry, I can only say that when an officer applies to me to go into the Portuguese service, I must in such case inquire whether he can be spared from his regiment. We have lost many officers, and a very great proportion are sick, and if I were now called upon to answer, I should say that this army can spare none of any description; but I should wish to delay giving any answer till the request shall be made by any individual, when his particular case and the demands of his regiment will be considered.

I think the complaints of B—— and C—— exceedingly unreasonable, ridiculous, and improper. I do not see any greater objection to making an officer of an English gentleman than to making an officer of a Portuguese gentleman. They could not object to the latter, and yet they do to the former. I am not quite certain whether —— is not the best appointment that has been made by the Horse Guards; and he is one of those I should recommend to you to use, as I pointed out in my last letter. As for ——, his conduct is more extraordinary and improper than that of the others, and whatever may be done respecting them, he cannot be allowed to quit the service, for he got a step of promotion in the King's service to induce him to go into the Portuguese service. It would be a curious circumstance if he were to say, 'Now that I am an English Lieut. Colonel and a Portuguese Colonel, the Portuguese government shall not exercise the prerogative it has always exercised over the army, of making any gentlemen they pleased officers of any rank.'

I think that we ought to have at Villa Velha a bridge instead of a flying bridge. The only operation that the French can undertake, which can do Portugal any permanent mischief, is the siege of Ciudad Rodrigo, and we must all move to prevent its success. The movement would be much accelerated by having a bridge there instead of a flying one. I should not be surprised if they undertook this operation, for they can really do nothing else.

To Marshal Beresford.   Merida, 30th Aug. 1809.

I received yesterday your letter of the 24th, and last night that of the 28th. All your couriers have either gone, or will go to you this day. I dispatch one whenever I have any thing material to say to you; but when there is no alteration on my side the country, and none wished for on your's, I do not think it necessary or proper to put the public to the expense (no small one) of sending a courier. When you do not hear from me, you may depend upon it there is no alteration since the last letter.

I omitted in my letter of yesterday to recommend to keep your cavalry at Lisbon, or, at all events, somewhere upon the Tagus, or the Mondego, where they could draw their supplies from the sea, or from a distance. We must look to the operations which we may have to carry on in the advanced season of the year, to the necessity which may exist of assembling large bodies of troops between the Mondego and the Tagus; and we should take care of the resources in that part of the country, particularly the straw. I beg you, therefore, to keep your cavalry out of it; and if you have occasion to move them through it, let it be in small bodies, and by different routes.

P.S. I wish that you would make out for government a report on the present state of the Portuguese army and militia, stating particularly the prospect which exists of keeping the former complete in numbers.

To W. Huskisson, Esq., Secretary to the Treasury.   Merida, 30th Aug. 1809.

I have received your letter of the 6th inst. You will have learned with great satisfaction that the market for bills has been much more productive of money lately at Lisbon, as well as at Cadiz and Gibraltar, than we had found it, or had reason to expect it would be on my first arrival in Portugal; and I am convinced that we shall be able to go on without drawing any more specie from England, at least till you shall know the result of Mr. C. Johnstone's speculation.

I shall take care that you shall have from Mr. Murray all the information you require respecting our demands.

I believe the greater part of the world will lament that I was not detained a little longer at Abrantes, and they will not quarrel with me for waiting for money, which I knew would alone procure the supplies which I have since found could not be procured even for ready money.

I wish that the eyes of the people of England were open to the real state of affairs in Spain, as mine are; and I only hope, if they should not be so now, that they will not purchase the experience by the loss of an army. We have gained a great and glorious victory over more than double our numbers, which has proved to the French that they are not the first military nation in the world. But the want of common management in the Spaniards, and of the common assistance which every country gives to any army, and which this country gives most plentifully to the French, have deprived us of all the fruits of it. The Spaniards have neither numbers, efficiency, discipline, bravery, nor arrangement, to carry on the contest; and if I could consent to remain in Spain, its burthen and the disgrace of its failure would fall upon me.

To the Rt. Hon. J. Villiers.   Merida, 30th Aug. 1809.

I received last night your letter of the 26th, containing that which you forwarded from Pole*.

I had hoped that I had at last settled the share which the Portuguese government were to have of all the supplies which we should receive; but the government at home having interfered, as appears by the enclosed letters, we are as far from a settlement as ever.

The object of this interference is certainly to prevail upon the Portuguese government to take this silver in bars for more than it is worth in the market of Lisbon; for, with all our grandeur, we are not above turning a penny in an honest way when we can. I shall write to Mr. Murray, to desire that the silver in bars may be disposed of according to your orders; and I conclude that it will defray all the demands on account of the Portuguese troops till the end of September, and of course that you will not have occasion to make any demands upon us till the beginning of November. However, you will let me know if I am mistaken on the subject.

* The Hon. W. Wellesley Pole, Earl of Mornington.

I had ordered the £15,000 to be paid immediately, but I shall now of course countermand that order.

I do not know what can be done to Oporto. It appears to me that it cannot be defended, excepting by an army in the field; and whether the army should be assembled for the defence of that place only, or for the defence of any other part of Portugal which may at the same time be threatened, must be a question to be determined by those who are to consider of the general defence of the country at the moment it is menaced. It is very obvious, however, that the lines at Oporto did more harm than good, and would do more harm than good again, if they were not to be defended by a good army. Those who are attached to Oporto, or to any other situation, may think that an army cannot be better employed than in the defence of that important city, or in that of the situation to which they are attached; and may be of opinion that a portion of the army ought to be allotted to defend the lines which ought to be immediately constructed. But I cannot agree in these opinions; and at all events Beresford, being in the command of the Portuguese army, must be consulted, and give his opinion upon this subject.

A partisan like Baptiste may do a great deal of good; but, if my memory does not fail me, Baptiste is the most useless of that description of persons. He was upon the frontiers of Portugal when I was in pursuit of Soult; and he certainly not only did nothing, but kept out of the way, although he might have done much. At all events, there is now no enemy upon the Portuguese frontier, particularly north of the Douro, the scene with which Baptiste is best acquainted.

To J. Murray, Esq., Commissary General.   Merida, 30th Aug. 1809.

I have received from England a copy of the orders from the Treasury to you of the 5th inst., relative to the disposal of 209,909 ounces of silver in bars, and of 17,948 ounces of gold coins, consigned to you by H. M. S. *Fylla**.

You will be so kind as to hold the silver above mentioned at the disposal of Mr. Villiers, for the purposes of the Portuguese government, and you will not pay the sum of £15,000 on account of bills in the hands of that government, which I directed you to pay; and you will discontinue all payments to Mr. Villiers until you shall receive further directions from me. I shall send directions respecting the gold coin upon a future occasion. I shall be very much obliged to you if you will make out, as soon as possible, the estimate directed to be sent in the last paragraph of the letter from the Treasury, and I request you will transmit it to me before you send it home.

I am very desirous of knowing what progress has been made in paying for the supplies, &c., received by the army at Coimbra and in the north of Portugal; and what sum still remains due in that quarter or elsewhere, on account of the army under my command.

In answer to your letter of the 12th, I have to inform you that I had settled with Mr. Villiers that Mr. Bell should draw upon you for a net sum, with the amount of which I would acquaint him on the 1st of every

---

* One of the ships of war taken at Copenhagen.

month. Mr. Bell's drafts are, however, now entirely stopped, and there is no occasion for troubling you with detailed instructions upon that subject, till the period at which they may be recommenced.

I conclude that all the demands at Ciudad Rodrigo are not unsupported by vouchers, and it appears to me that Mr. Nelson ought to have been supplied with money to. pay those which were regular and would have been admitted.

In answer to your letter of the 22d, I have to inform you that I conceive it would be desirable to exchange the French gold coins, referred to in the enclosure therein, for Portuguese gold coins.

To Marquis Wellesley.   Merida, 30th Aug. 1809.

I enclose you a Gazette and a bulletin of the 11th, which I received last night. I have received no letters, excepting one from Pole, in which he informs me that it is understood in England that the Emperor did not approve of the armistice concluded by the Archduke, and that peace between Austria and France was not considered certain. He also tells me that my letter of the 24th July to the Sec. of State (of which I enclose a copy) had been received, and that the government approved of my determination to quit Spain, if I should not be supplied as I ought to be.

I am very anxious to receive your answer to my letter of the 24th. The troops which had marched by the road of Caceres had not, by some accident, received the notification of my intention to halt here; and being ill provided on that road, they have pushed on for the frontier of Portugal. The army is therefore, at this moment, separated at a greater distance than it ought to be under any circumstances, more particularly under the circumstances of the retreat of the Spanish army from their posts on the Tagus. I am not informed when that retreat is to be made, but I believe this day; and if it should be so, I must either bring the British troops again out of Portugal, and have the army in a more collected state, or I must move those which I have detained here, waiting for your answer to my letter of the 24th, towards the frontiers of Portugal. Not having the benefit of your opinion, I shall adopt the latter, as being in conformity with my own, which has been strengthened by reflection since I wrote to you.

The A.G. to Mr. ——, Assist. Commissary Gen.   30th Aug. 1809.

I have laid your letter and enclosures before the Commander of the Forces, who approves of the delinquents having been lodged in jail; but very much regrets either Mr. —— or yourself should have expressed any wish that should prevent their being treated with the utmost rigor of the law, and I am therefore directed by his Excellency strongly to animadvert on this mistaken lenity on your part.

The A.G. to Mr. ——, Assist. Commissary Gen.   30th Aug. 1809.

I am directed by the Commander of the Forces to acquaint you, that he has seen with very great regret a declaration of yours, at the bottom of a deposition of the circumstances of a robbery which occurred, and in which you lost your property. If you meant by the expression of such a wish to show mercy, his Excellency thinks you very little consider the fate of unfortunate soldiers in this army who may fall into the hands of villainous wretches, who live in this country by plunder. The Commander of the Forces desires that you may in future let the law take its course, and never interfere in a manner that may be so prejudicial to the interests of the army in this country.

The A.G. to Brig. Gen. Howorth, R. A., and Brig. Gen. Fane.   30th Aug. 1809.

I am directed by the Commander of the Forces to call your attention to the horses that may die or be destroyed in your brigade, and to state that it is essential for the health of the army that all dead horses should be, as soon as possible, buried, or removed beyond the ground the troops occupy. It would be of great advantage if you would be pleased to fix upon a proper spot, as remote as possible from your lines, where all horses might be brought previous to their being destroyed, or dragged there if dead ; and if you would issue orders to the artillery and gunner drivers, that a certain proportion of them are to assist in burying at such place their own horses, as it is impossible for the infantry parties on this duty to get through the numerous demands that are on all sides for burying horses, offal, &c., often not knowing the spot where the dead lay, from the general inattention on this head. The Commander of the Forces has enjoined me to call this circumstance especially to your notice.

To Marquis Wellesley.   Merida, 31st Aug. 1809.

The Spanish government having lately sent forward a large number of shirts and sheets, for which I had applied through Mr. Frere, for the use of the hospitals, I shall be very much obliged to your Excellency if you will give directions that I may be furnished with an account of the expense of these articles, stating to whom I shall order payment to be made for them. The persons who brought them have run away with their mules, and I am apprehensive that I shall be obliged to leave here the shirts and sheets; but that is no reason why the Spanish government should not be paid for them.

After I had written to your Excellency on the 28th inst., 9 carts arrived here from Seville, loaded with biscuit for the use of the British army ; and the carts are marked as intended for our service. It is very desirable that I should be informed by the government on what terms these carts are to be received into the service, whether to be purchased or hired, and at what rates. I propose now to employ them in the removal of the men who have been lately taken ill, to the hospital at Elvas; but if the Spanish government should be of opinion that when the British army shall be in Portugal, it ought not to enjoy the advantage of the means of transport which have been procured for it in Spain, these carts shall be sent back, notwithstanding that if the government and people of Portugal had acted upon the same principle when the British army entered Spain, the army could not have made one march within the Spanish territory.

I am very anxious to receive your Excellency's sentiments upon the points which I submitted to you in my letter of the 24th (No. 14). That part of the British army (the cavalry particularly) which had moved by the road of Caceres, having been pressed for provisions, and not having, by some accident, received the notification of my intention to halt here for some days, had marched on, and has actually arrived within the Portuguese frontier. In the mean time the Spanish army has, I understand, marched to take up its position behind the Guadiana, and will probably arrive at La Serena this day. This being the case, it is necessary that I should get the British army in a more collected state, either in Portugal or within the Spanish frontier; and as the opinions contained in my dispatch (No. 14) of the 24th inst. are strengthened by reflection, since I addressed it to you, I propose to commence moving towards Badajoz on the day after to-morrow, unless I should in the intermediate time receive from your Excellency a communication of your sentiments which shall occasion an alteration of my opinion.

The pontoon bridge which had been on the Tagus, near Almaraz, arrived here last night on its way to Badajoz. I cannot avoid taking this opportunity of drawing your Excellency's attention to the ease with which all the services of this description, required for the Spanish army, have been performed, at the same time that nothing could be done, in the most urgent requisitions of service, as well as of humanity, for the British army.

When the guns were taken from the enemy in the battle of Talavera, there was no difficulty about drawing them off; when the British army laid down its ammunition for want of the means of conveying it, there was no difficulty about transporting it; and there has been none in providing the means to remove the pontoon bridge from the neighbourhood of the Tagus, at Almaraz, to Badajoz. Yet the application of these means, at any period, to the service of the British army, would have relieved many of the difficulties under which we laboured, and would certainly have prevented the separation from the Spanish army at the moment at which it was made.

But I beg your Excellency to observe, that among all the offers which were pressed upon me to divide the contents of the magazine of provisions at Truxillo, to take what I pleased from it, nay, to take the whole, even at the risk of starving the Spanish army, offers of which I knew and explained, and have since been able to prove, the fallacy, not one was made to assist the British army with a cart or a mule, or any means of transport, which abounded in the Spanish army.

To Lord Burghersh.   Merida, 1st Sept. 1809.

I received last night your letter of the 26th. I lament as much as any man can the necessity of separating from the Spanish armies; but I was at last compelled to go, and I believe that there was not an officer in the army who did not think I stayed too long.

I don't understand what ———— means by my having departed from the old principles of war. The fault I committed consisted in trusting at all to the Spaniards, who I have since found were entirely unworthy of confidence; but even admitting that I knew they were so, which I think I prove I did not, unless it is asserted that I had and could have no communication with Portugal, excepting through Plasencia, I do not see how I departed from any old principle of war. Now, I say, I had established, before Soult came in by Plasencia, and I have now, a shorter and better communication with Lisbon than that by Plasencia. So far for ————'s criticisms.

In respect to yourself, I think you will do well, and I should be glad, if you would journey through Granada, Murcia, and Valencia, and send me accounts how they are going on there; what forces they have; whether they are raising any; what numbers they consider necessary and are determined to keep for their own defence; and what numbers they consider applicable to the general purposes of the country.

I shall have the British army upon the frontiers of Portugal and Spain, with my head quarters either at Badajoz or at Elvas.   I move to-morrow.

To Marquis Wellesley.   Merida, 1st Sept. 1809.

I have the honor to acknowledge the receipt of your Excellency's private letter of the 29th Aug., containing a copy of Don M. de Garay's note of the 25th Aug., and of your Excellency's answer of the 28th, and of your dispatch (marked D) of the 30th, and of your dispatch (marked separate) of the same date.

I am happy to find that your Excellency concurs with me in the opinions which I laid before you on the 24th ult., and I propose on to-morrow to commence my movement from this place.   I intend that the greatest part of the army shall remain within the Spanish frontier, if I should be able to maintain it in that position; and I shall apprise your Excellency of the exact positions which I shall occupy, and hereafter of any change that I may think it necessary to make.   My reason for wishing not to engage to remain on the Portuguese frontier is, that the principal magazines of the British army are at Abrantes, Santarem, and Lisbon; and notwithstanding the good will of the Portuguese government, and the inclination of the people to give us every assistance in their power, Alentejo being a poor country, I might find it impossible to maintain the whole army at such a distance from the magazines, as the positions which they will occupy on the frontier.   Besides, I think it is desirable that the Spanish government should be induced to look into and acquire an accurate knowledge of their real situation, compared with that of the enemy; and that they should be induced to make such an exertion as should at least provide for their defence by their own means.   On this account, and as I think I ought not to involve His Majesty's army in any system of co-operation with the Spanish troops, for the reasons stated in my dispatch of the 24th ult., I beg to decline accepting the honor, which the government have offered to confer upon me, of the command of the corps of 12,000 men, to be left in this part of the country.   I could not have accepted this command under any circumstances, without His Majesty's permission, excepting for the time that I should have considered myself authorised by the instructions of His Majesty's ministers, or should have been enabled by circumstances to continue in co-operation with the Spanish army; but having been obliged to separate from them, and considering it advisable that the British army should not at present enter upon any system of co-operation with them again, I cannot take upon myself the command of any Spanish corps whatever.

In respect to offensive operations in future, it is desirable that the means, actually existing in Spain, of the French and of the allies, should be reviewed, and the advantages which each party possesses in the use of those means should be weighed.   I estimate the French force in Spain, disposable for service in the field, to amount to 125,000 men, well provided with cavalry and artillery; in which number I do not include the garrisons of Pamplona, Barcelona, &c. &c. I include, however, the corps commanded by St. Cyr and Suchet, which I calculate to amount to 32,000 men, employed in Aragon and Catalonia; and the remainder, being above 90,000 men, are in Castille and Estremadura. Of this number 70,000 men are actually in the field, in the corps of Victor, Soult, Ney, Mortier, and Sebastiani; and the remainder are employed in garrisons, as at Madrid, el Escurial, Avila, Valladolid, &c., and in keeping up the communications with those places; every man of whom might be brought into the field if occasion required. In these numbers I do not include sick and wounded, but found my calculations upon what I knew were the numbers of the French army before the battle of Talavera, deducting a loss of 10,000 men in that battle.

Your Excellency will observe that there are 7 French corps in Spain. I believe there were originally 8, for Suchet's is the 8th corps; and each corps, composing in itself a complete army, ought to consist of from 30,000 to 40,000 men. Against this force the Spanish government have about 50,000 men in the two corps of Eguia and Venegas; Blake may have collected again 6000 men; and the Marques de la Romana has 15,000, of which number 1500 have no arms. The Duque del Parque has 9000 men in the garrison of Ciudad Rodrigo, but he is unwilling to detach them. Besides these numbers, the British army may be reckoned from 20,000 to 25,000 men.

I am aware that there are troops in Spain besides those which I have above enumerated, but they are not in any manner and cannot be considered disposable for the field. The plan of operations must be founded upon the relative numbers above stated. But besides considering the numbers, it is necessary to advert to the composition and to the state of efficiency of these different armies. The French corps are, as I have already stated, each a complete army, having, probably, a greater proportion of cavalry, and certainly of artillery, than they ought to have for the existing numbers of their infantry; and they are well disciplined, excellent troops.

The Spanish corps of Venegas and Eguia have probably between them not less than 10,000 cavalry, which is more than their proportion, and they are well provided with artillery. But the corps of Romana has neither cavalry nor artillery, and, for want of those arms, is unable to quit the mountains of Galicia. The Duque del Parque is unable, if he were willing, to assist him with what he wants. Blake's corps, I believe, consists only of infantry. Both infantry and cavalry are comparatively undisciplined; the cavalry are tolerably well clothed, well armed, accoutred, and mounted; but the infantry are not clothed or accoutred as they ought to be, notwithstanding the large supplies of clothing and accoutrements sent out from England. With these relative numbers, and adverting to the state of discipline and efficiency of the different armies, it would appear impossible to undertake an offensive operation with any hope of success; more particularly adverting to the local difficulties with which the allies would have to contend, and the advantages of the enemy.

The enemy has it in his power to collect his whole force in Castille and Estremadura at any point north of the Tagus, and can dispose of the parts of it in the front or rear of the armies of the allies, as he may think proper.

The allies must move upon the enemy in two distinct corps at least. There can be no military communication between the corps assembled in this part of Estremadura, and that which would advance from La Carolina through La Mancha, on account of the chain of mountains on the whole of the left bank of the Tagus, from the Puerto de Mirabete to the bridge of Toledo. The only communication which these two corps can have is by the right bank of the river from Almaraz and by the bridge of Toledo, and it is obvious that a battle must be fought with the enemy's whole force, and won by one of the two corps, before that communication can be established.

This consideration was the reason that, in the late operations, the march of Venegas was directed upon Ocana and Fuentiduena and Arganda. It was impossible to join with Venegas before a battle should be fought with the enemy's whole force by one of the armies; and it was thought best to order Venegas to adopt such a line of march as should be most distant from the combined armies, in relation to which and the combined armies, the enemy could not have taken up a centrical position from which he could have had the choice of attacking either. The enemy would thus have been forced either to detach to oppose Venegas, or, if he had kept his whole force collected to fight the combined corps advancing from this side, he would have lost Madrid, and his retreat would have been cut off. Venegas did not, however, obey the orders he received, I believe in consequence of directions from the Junta. Instead of being at Arganda, close to Madrid, on the 23d, he did not approach the Tagus till the 28th, when he was kept in check at Toledo by 2000 men, while the enemy's whole army were engaged at Talavera. These circumstances will show your Excellency the difficulty which attends the position of the allies; and indeed ought to have some influence with the Spanish government in the distribution of their troops at present.

The French having 70,000 men disposable in Castille and Estremadura, may employ them either in opposing the advance of the allies from this side, who could not bring more than from 50,000 to 55,000 to oppose them; or they would detach 20,000 to oppose Venegas, and meet the allies with 50,000. The whole would thus be kept in check, even if it could be hoped that one or both corps would not be defeated.

The Marques de la Romana, the Duque del Parque, Blake, &c., could afford no relief from their embarrassing circumstances, having no artillery nor cavalry to enable them to enter the plains of Castille. But even if these first difficulties could be overcome, and the French armies should retire to the northward, the numbers of the allies would be found still more unequal to those of the enemy. The corps of St. Cyr and Suchet would then take their places in the operations, and the Spanish armies would have no corresponding increase. These difficulties, however, are of a nature not to be overcome by the means at present in the power of the Spanish government; they must increase their forces, and clothe, equip, and discipline their troops, before they can reasonably attempt any offensive operation against the French ; and in the mean time, it becomes a question how the troops ought to be disposed of.

From what I have already stated, your Excellency must observe the importance of their having a strong Spanish corps in this part of Estremadura. The British army must necessarily be the foundation of any offensive operation the Spanish government can undertake; and it is obvious that the place of this army must be on the left of the whole issuing from the frontiers of Portugal.

If the Spanish corps, which is to act with the British army, should be weak, their operations must be checked at an early period; and in that case I should apprehend that the operations of the large Spanish corps directed from La Carolina would not be very successful. But the prospect of these offensive operations may be considered too distant to render it reasonable to advert to them in a disposition of the Spanish army which is about to be formed, and I should therefore suggest other grounds for recommending that the army in Estremadura should not, if possible, be weakened.

Your Excellency has observed that Soult entertains a design of attacking Ciudad Rodrigo : which design, I understand, was discussed and recommended by a council of war held some time ago at Salamanca. The success of this enterprise would do more mischief than the French are capable of doing in any other manner. It would completely cut off the only communication the Spanish government have with the northern provinces; would give the French the perpetual possession of Castille, and would most probably occasion the loss of the Portuguese fort of Almeida. I should be desirous of making every exertion to save Ciudad Rodrigo ; but if Estremadura should be left with only 12,000 men, it must be obvious to your Excellency that Seville, as well as Portugal, will be exposed, while I should be removed from this part of the country.

I am much afraid, from what I have seen of the proceedings of the Central Junta, that in the distributions of their forces they do not consider military defence and military operations, so much as they do political intrigue and the attainment of trifling political objects. They wish to strengthen the army of Venegas, not because it is necessary or desirable on military grounds; but because they think the army, as an instrument of mischief, is safer in his hands than in those of another; and they leave 12,000 men in Estremadura, not because more are not, or may not be deemed necessary in any military view of the question, but because they are averse to placing a large body under the Duque de Alburquerque, who I know that the Junta of Estremadura have insisted should be employed to command the army in this province. I cannot avoid observing these little views and objects and mentioning them to your Excellency ; at the same time that I lament that the attention of those who have to manage such great and important affairs as those are which are intrusted to the management of the Central Junta, should be diverted from great objects to others of trifling importance.

I cannot conclude this letter without adverting to the mode in which Don M. de Garay, in his note to your Excellency of the 25th ult, disposes of the Portuguese troops, without having had one word of communication with the Portuguese government, or any body connected with it, respecting them. In fact those troops have been equally ill, indeed I might say worse, treated than the British troops, by the officers of the Spanish government, and were at last obliged to quit Spain for want of food; and I shall no more allow them than I shall the British troops to enter Spain again, unless I should have some solid ground for believing that they would be supplied as they ought to be.

It is a curious circumstance respecting Marshal Beresford's corps, that the Cabildo of Ciudad Rodrigo actually refused to allow them to have 30,000 of 100,000 lbs. of biscuit, which I had prepared there, in case the operations of the army should be directed to that quarter, and for which the British Commissary had paid; and they seized the biscuit on the ground that debts due to the town of Ciudad Rodrigo by the British army under the command of the late Sir J. Moore had not been paid; although one of the objects of the mission of the same Commissary to Ciudad Rodrigo, was to settle the accounts and discharge those debts! Yet this same Cabildo will call for assistance as soon as they shall perceive the intention of the enemy to attack them; having seized, and holding probably in their possession at the moment, the means which, if lodged as directed in the stores at Almeida, would enable me effectually to provide for their relief.

To Lieut. Col. Sir R. Wilson.   Lobon, 2d Sept. 1809.

I received last night your letter of the 30th; and I conclude that before now you must have received mine of the 27th, which I sent to Castello Branco

I have no further intelligence to give you from this quarter; I am going to take up my ground upon the frontier, where I shall remain till I see what the enemy will do.

I beg that as soon as possible after you shall receive this letter, you will write to the Duque del Parque, and tell him that if the enemy should attack Ciudad Rodrigo, I shall strain every nerve to relieve the place; that I trust he has aided my Commissary whom I sent some time ago, to have a large quantity of biscuit prepared for the British army, which ought to be lodged in the stores of Almeida; as upon that supply my ability to relieve the place will principally depend.

Gen. Beresford informed me that the Cabildo of Ciudad Rodrigo had seized my biscuit in payment of debts due by Sir J. Moore's army, notwithstanding that one of the objects of the Commissary's mission to Ciudad Rodrigo was to settle the accounts and pay those debts. I hope that the Duque del Parque will see that justice is done to us on this score; and that at all events the biscuit will be sent to Almeida, otherwise I may find it difficult to collect my army in that quarter.

I am convinced that the operation in which the enemy are most likely to succeed, and that which would do us and the common cause most mischief, is the siege of Ciudad Rodrigo; and it is not unlikely that they will undertake it. I wish you, therefore, to remain where you are, to watch their movements with a view to that operation, and send me constant intelligence of them. It is not unlikely that Soult may, if he entertains that design, endeavor to drive you off your ground : maintain it as long as you can, and then secure for me the boats at Villa Velha by sending Col. Grant with one battalion to take them out of the river, on this side. You will retire with the remainder of the troops towards Sarzedas, into the passes of the mountains.

Keep me regularly informed of the enemy's movements, and depend upon my not losing a moment in going to your assistance, and do not let Col. Grant take up the flying bridge at Villa Velha till the last moment, making it certain, however, that he secures the boats for my passage. Keep the Spanish battalions upon your left till you shall hear further from me. I have ordered your guns to join you.

P.S. I send a duplicate of my letter of the 27th. I recollect your mentioning an intention of sending us some horses for the artillery, but we never received one. However, if you sent them, I shall pay for them, notwithstanding that I think it most probable they, as well as other things, fell into the hands of our worthy allies! The horses you say you have now sent have not arrived. When they do arrive, they shall likewise be paid for, if they should be deemed fit for the service of the artillery. Let me know the price of the first, and when you shall send them, that of the last.

To Lieut. Col. Sir R. Wilson.   Badajoz, 3d Sept. 1809.

I am afraid that I wrote to you more positively than I intended on the 27th to cross the Tagus. The fact is, that I imagined you would receive that letter long before you would reach Castello Branco. Indeed, I did not know that Beresford had ordered you there; and I intended that your further progress towards me should be very much guided by the directions you should receive from him, upon which I have written to him. I conclude, however, that you will have received my letter of yesterday this day, and that you will return to Castello Branco. But if you should not have done so, I now beg you to return, as I consider the enemy's movement north of the Tagus by far the most worthy of attention.

G. O.   Badajoz, 3d Sept. 1809.

As the Commander of the Forces proposes that the troops shall remain in the stations in which they are now or will shortly be placed as long as circumstances will permit, he desires that the officers commanding regiments will send to Lisbon, as soon as possible, an officer belonging to the regiment under their command respectively, in order to get from the regimental stores such articles of clothing, accoutrements, and necessaries as the soldiers require. The names of the officers sent upon this duty are to be sent in to the Q. M. G.; these officers, on their arrival at Lisbon, are to report themselves to the A. Q. M. G. stationed there, and are to give him a list of the articles which they will have been directed to send up to their regiments, specifying the weight of the whole, and, as far as possible, of each article. They will likewise report to him the day on which the articles required will be ready to quit Lisbon, and they will obey such directions as they will receive from this officer respecting the transport of the baggage, whether by land or by water. The A. Q. M. G. at Lisbon, having received from the officers before mentioned the returns of the baggage required for their regiments and the weight, will make requisitions upon the Commissary for boats, and carts to transport it to the army, taking care to allow no more to be put on each cart, drawn by 2 bullocks, than 600 lbs. weight. The officer in command of the troops at Lisbon will give such assistance of fatigue parties to the officers going down for baggage as they may have occasion for.

Such sick men as cannot march must be sent to the hospital at Elvas.

To Lieut. Col. Roche.   Badajoz, 3d Sept. 1809.

I have received your letters of the 30th Aug. and 1st inst. I beg that you will continue to communicate to me all the reports you may hear, and every thing that occurs. It does not much signify whether they turn out to be true or false. I shall always be able to judge of their probable truth or falsehood from other accounts.

To the Conde de Montijo.   Badajoz, 3d Sept. 1809.

I had the honor of receiving your Excellency's letter this morning.

I am much concerned that the Central Junta should conceive they have any reason to complain of your Excellency, and that your Excellency should have incurred their displeasure. Your Excellency must be aware that, being strangers in this country, and employed as allies of the government, it is impossible for us to interfere in any matter between government and individuals; or in any concern in the country, excepting that in which we are especially employed, viz., to carry on the war against the common enemy.

To Marquis Wellesley.   Badajoz, 3d Sept. 1809.

I have received from Lord Castlereagh copies of Mr. Sec. Canning's dispatches to your Excellency, dated 12th Aug.; and I have been directed by his Lordship to lay before your Excellency my opinion on the points referred to in those dispatches.

The letters which I have had the honor of addressing to your Excellency on the 24th Aug. and 1st Sept. (Nos. 14 and 15) will have apprised you of my opinion on the first point referred to by Mr. Sec. Canning, viz., the prospect of success in offensive operations against the enemy; which opinion I should equally entertain, even though the British army could be increased to 40,000 instead of 30,000 men, as long as the Spanish armies shall continue of the limited numbers, in the undisciplined and inefficient state, and ill composed as they are at present.

Your Excellency has before you in my dispatch of the 1st Sept. (No. 17) the detailed information upon which I formed my opinion, upon which you may form your own, if the information should be found correct; if it should be found materially erroneous, it may be corrected.

In the existing state of the forces of the enemy and the allies in the Peninsula, it would be difficult for the British army, if not impossible, to connect the defence of Portugal with that of Spain; and quite impossible, unless great improvements should be made in the mode of supplying armies in Spain. Hereafter, when it is probable that the existing relative numbers of the armies will be altered to the advantage of the enemy, it will be quite impossible for the British army to connect with the defence of Portugal that of the south of Spain.

The British government have determined to defend Portugal; but if the army should be hereafter detained to defend the south of Spain, instead of Portugal, I conceive it will be absolutely necessary that the Commanding officer of the British troops should have the command of the Spanish army; that we should have a garrison in Cadiz; and that the most efficient measures should be adopted to secure supplies and means of transport for the allied armies.

To Dom Miguel Forjaz. Badajoz, 3d Sept. 1809.

I have the honor to acknowledge the receipt of your Excellency's letter of the 31st Aug., and I am very sensible of the kindness with which the Governors of the Kingdom of Portugal have uniformly received every service which the troops under my command have been enabled to render to the common cause.

I request you to assure their Excellencies that whatever position I may take, or in whatever operation I may engage, I shall pay due attention to the interests of the Spanish nation, with which the safety of Portugal is so strongly united ; and that I shall render such assistance to Spain as circumstances will permit me.

I am infinitely obliged to the government for their kindness to the troops : the whole army acknowledge the uniform good treatment they have received from the government and the people of Portugal, and I shall adopt some mode of acquainting the troops of the favor and good-will of the Governors of the Kingdom towards them upon their return to Portugal ; but I request the Governors of the Kingdom not to ask me to accept of the present which they have desired to make to the troops, which, at the same time that it would give a superfluity of provisions, would waste the resources of the country of which the army stands so much in need.

With the permission of the Governors of the Kingdom, I will settle with Gen. Leite the mode in which I shall convey to the troops the approbation of their good conduct by the Governors of the Kingdom, of which I hope their Excellencies will approve.

To Marquis Wellesley. Badajoz, 3d Sept. 1809.

I enclose to your Excellency the copy of a letter which I have received from Dom M. Forjaz, Sec. of State at Lisbon, and the copy of my answer. I beg to draw your Excellency's attention to that part of the former in which it is desired that I should as far as possible extend the assistance of the British army to Spain.

To Marshal Beresford. Badajoz, 4th Sept. 1809.

You will have seen a copy of the intercepted letter from Soult, and I should not be surprised if the French were to carry into execution the plan proposed by him, of attacking Ciudad Rodrigo. The success of this scheme would do them more good, and the allies more mischief, than any other they could attempt ; and it is most likely of all others to be successful. I hear that they have withdrawn their troops from La Mancha, which is the first step towards any operation on this side, and that they are collecting provisions and means at Talavera. If this intelligence be true, they intend something against the Spaniards in this quarter, against Ciudad Rodrigo, or against us. The last is the least probable ; the first not very likely. If they should show against Ciudad Rodrigo, we must strain every nerve to save it. I shall march from hence with all the troops, and we must have something upon the Tagus at Abrantes and lower down. What can you produce in the field upon my left from Thomar, Leiria, Coimbra, &c.? and what can you leave upon the Tagus?

I have ordered Sir R. Wilson to stay north of the Tagus, and watch Soult's movements closely. If I leave this to move upon the covering army of Ciudad Rodrigo, the enemy will most probably follow me from the Tagus into Portugal, leaving in this part of the country a corps to watch and keep in check the Spanish army. The troops which they may, in that case, send into Portugal, will not be very numerous, but still they may do mischief.

To Brig. Gen. R. Craufurd.   Badajoz, 4th Sept. 1809.

I halted at Merida some days, in consequence of some letters which I received from Lord Wellesley, expressing a desire that I should remain within the Spanish frontier, at least for a time; with which desire I have complied so far as to place the right of the army at Talavera Real, Hill's division at Montijo and La Calzada, and the heavy brigade of cavalry at Merida, where they will get forage. This alteration has induced me to change your situation to Campo Maior. I should put you in front on the other side, only that I think the movement we shall next make will probably be across the Tagus.

The enemy appear to entertain a design of attacking Ciudad Rodrigo. Soult proposes this operation in a letter to the King, which we have in-

---

G. O.   Badajoz, 4th Sept. 1809.

4. The Commander of the Forces requests the attention of the General officers commanding divisions and brigades to the G. O. of the 4th July, respecting the early obedience to orders.

10. The soldiers in the hospitals must not be allowed to straggle about the towns in which the hospitals are stationed, and all men found at the distance of one street from the hospital must be tried and punished for the disobedience of orders. The rolls of the hospital must be called once every hour, in the presence of an officer, or such number of officers as the Commanding officer at the hospital will appoint to attend to the roll calling.

11. All men absent from roll calling, to be tried and punished for disobedience of orders.

12. The soldiers in hospital, or convalescent at the station where the hospital is, and victualled by the Commissary, or on the route to join their regiments, are not to receive wine, unless directions in writing should be given by the medical officer that they are to receive it; and the medical officer is particularly desired not to give those directions unless in cases in which it may have appeared to him that the soldiers have conducted themselves as they ought in the hospital, and in such a manner as to secure their early recovery.

13. As comforts for the sick can now be got, the regimental hospitals are to be established upon the plan ordered by His Majesty's regulations, and the soldiers are to be under the usual stoppage while in hospital.

G. A. O.   Badajoz, 4th Sept. 1809.

The Commander of the Forces is concerned to hear that last night several soldiers came into the town of Badajoz, and plundered a bakery and the houses of several individuals of bread. This continued misbehavior of the soldiers gives the Commander of the Forces the greatest concern; and he is determined, however difficult it may be, to put a stop to it. The rolls are to be called in the different corps of the 4th division every hour till further orders: and the Commander of the Forces desires that no soldier whatever may be allowed to quit his lines on any account, excepting in charge of an officer.

The Provost must punish all those found disobeying this order. A guard must be placed at the gate of the town of Badajoz, and all soldiers attempting to pass in are to be made prisoners, and sent to the Provost guard. The Provost will forthwith turn out of the town all soldiers who may be in it.

tercepted; and I think it not improbable that they may attempt it. If they should attempt it, we must make an effort to prevent its success; and I know of none that would have the effect, excepting a movement to that quarter. If, however, I should be mistaken, and the enemy should come this way, we could put you in front before the army would be collected.

You will be better supplied at Campo Maior than at Castello de Vide. I have given directions that your Commissary should be supplied with money. His want of it, hitherto, is to be attributed entirely to the Dep. Commissary General, as there is more money with the army than we know what to do with; and we ought to pay in ready money for every thing we receive.

To J. Murray, Esq., Commissary General.   Badajoz, 4th Sept. 1809.

I cannot avoid taking this opportunity of urging you to join the army as soon as possible. I have not had the pleasure of seeing you, from causes which I am aware you could not control, and which I exceedingly regret, since the month of June last, at Coimbra; and the army has suffered the greatest inconvenience from your absence. Indeed, it is so great, that if I should find your absence is likely to be of much longer continuance, I shall consider myself obliged to make arrangements for doing the duty of the Commissariat, which shall be exempt from these inconveniences.

To Brig. Gen. Alex. Campbell.   Badajoz, 4th Sept. 1809.

I am very sorry indeed to lose you, and particularly so that the bad appearance of your wound obliges you to go; but that cannot be avoided, and you must do every thing in your power to re-establish your health entirely. I will give you any letter you please; but it will only subject you to the mortification of a disappointment, and me to that of making another request in vain in favor of a person who deserves the King's favor.

To the Rt. Hon. J. Villiers.   Badajoz, 4th Sept. 1809.

I have received your letter of the 31st Aug. I am very much obliged to you for the pains you uniformly take to make, in England, a favorable impression of the measures and operations which I conduct. I now enclose you my dispatches of this date to the Sec. of State. You will see that I have received the copies of the dispatches to Lord Wellesley of the 12th, and these may be worth your perusal, as they will show you the view which I, and, I believe, he takes of the situation of affairs in the Peninsula.

We are very anxious to hear of Lord FitzRoy's arrival in England; and if the answer to the dispatches should arrive by an English messenger, pray forward them by a Portuguese or Spanish messenger, unless the English *gentleman* should engage to come as fast as the other. The last was 4 days on his road to this place, which another would have come in 30 hours at most.

To Visc. Castlereagh.   Badajoz, 4th Sept. 1809.

Having continued the march of the army from Truxillo, after I had written to you last, I was induced to halt for a few days at Merida, in consequence of a letter of the 22d Aug., which I received from Lord Wellesley, a copy of which will go to you by this occasion; and I have since occupied such positions with the troops as will enable them to subsist, and to get the necessary refreshments with ease; at the same time that I have it in my power to collect them in a short space of time.

I have ordered Brig. Gen. C. Craufurd to join the army with the 11th and 57th, and 4 of the battalions arrived from Ireland; and that the horse artillery, and the horses for the artillery recently sent from Cork, should come up from Lisbon.

The enemy have continued nearly in the same positions since I addressed your Lordship on the 21st Aug. Marshal Ney is at Salamanca; and there appears to be another French corps in Old Castille, which I believe is the 6th corps, under the command of Gen. Kellermann. Marshal Soult is at Coria, with his advanced posts at Moraleja and Zarza la Mayor; but he has not with him more than from 6000 to 8000 men. Marshal Mortier is at Arzobispo; and two divisions of Victor's corps are at Talavera, and the remainder in La Mancha with the 4th corps, hitherto called Sebastiani's.

I have heard that the French are again retiring from La Mancha; but I have no authentic account of that movement. If they should retire from thence, it is possible that they may make the attempt upon Ciudad Rodrigo, which Soult has recommended to the King, in a letter which has been intercepted; and as I consider success in this enterprise to be more likely to be mischievous to Portugal than any other they could undertake, and would prevent the future co-operation of the troops from Portugal with Spain, in case circumstances should hereafter render that co-operation possible, I propose to do every thing in my power to prevent the execution of this plan; and I shall move for that purpose as soon as I shall find, from the disposition of the enemy's troops, that they really intend it.

I have apprised the Duque del Parque that I propose to exert myself for his relief; and I have urged him to hold out as long as he can. The Spanish head quarters have been moved from Deleytosa to Truxillo, partly in consequence of their finding it difficult to support their army in the exhausted country upon the left bank of the Tagus, and partly on account of orders received from the Junta to detach the greatest part of the army to La Carolina, leaving only 12,000 men in Estremadura. They still occupy La Mesa de Ibor and the Puerto de Mirabete, opposite Almaraz, in which last post they relieved our troops on the 20th.

I have communicated to Lord Wellesley, as your Lordship will see, my opinion of the danger which may attend this disposition of their forces; and I have urged the government to make an exertion to maintain their strong position upon the Tagus, but I doubt whether my remonstrance will have any effect; and I expect that if the enemy should make an attack upon Ciudad Rodrigo, he will possess himself of the Tagus, and probably of the Guadiana, nearly to this place, at the same time.

To the Rt. Hon. the Judge Advocate Gen.   Badajoz, 4th Sept. 1809.

I have the honor to enclose the proceedings of a General Court Martial, of which Major Gen. Tilson is President, on the trial of Mr. ——, paymaster of the — regt., upon which I am desirous of receiving His Majesty's pleasure. I must at the same time inform you that Major Gen. Tilson has communicated to me the wish of the General Court Martial that I should recommend Mr. —— to His Majesty's mercy.

When I marched from Talavera on the 3d Aug. to oppose the progress of the French troops which had entered Estremadura from Castille, by Plasencia, the paymasters of several of the regiments remained at Talavera to supply with money the officers left in charge of the sick and wounded in the hospital, and they were to join their regiments at Oropesa in the evening. In the course of that day the Spanish General, Cuesta, determined to break up from Talavera, and having apprised the officer in charge of the British hospital of this intention, he gave notice of it to the British officers at Talavera, and made arrangements for moving across the Tagus at Arzobispo the sick and wounded that could be moved. The paymasters of several of the regiments belonging to this army, instead of joining their regiments at Oropesa on that evening, proceeded to Arzobispo with the sick and wounded, from whence they continued their progress till they reached Elvas, in Portugal, not waiting for the sick and wounded after they had crossed the Tagus.

I conceived that there was so little ground for this conduct, because, in fact, the army was never in any manner pressed in its movement across the Tagus; and as it is so reprehensible, even if the strongest grounds existed for apprehension that the retreat would have been pressed, I determined to bring to trial, before a General Court Martial, every paymaster who had so conducted himself. As, however, these gentlemen are not educated in the military profession, as it appears that Mr. —— had a sum of money in his charge, and as the apprehensions he entertained were equally felt by all the gentlemen in the same situation, and, above all, as the Court Martial has recommended him, I beg leave to recommend Mr. —— to His Majesty's gracious mercy.

To Visc. Castlereagh.   Badajoz, 4th Sept. 1809.

I have had the honor of receiving your Lordship's letter of the 12th, in which you have enclosed a copy of Mr. Sec. Canning's letters of the same date to Lord Wellesley; and I now enclose to your Lordship copies of a correspondence that I have lately had with Lord Wellesley upon the points to which Mr. Sec. Canning's dispatches relate, which will give the King's ministers all the information that they wish to have. Lord Wellesley had before desired that I would send home copies of this correspondence.

I have to request your Lordship's attention to the offer which was made me of the command of a Spanish corps of 12,000 men, to be left in Estremadura, while the rest of the Spanish army should march to La Carolina. As this offer was necessarily connected not only with the renewal of the co-operation of His Majesty's troops with the Spanish army, which your Lordship will see I did not deem expedient, but with that renewal in a

defensive system, which could have answered no end, excepting again to
involve the British army in the Spanish operations, I deemed it expedient
to decline to accept it.   I have but little doubt, however, that if circumstances should at any time render it advisable in the opinion of His
Majesty's ministers to co-operate with the Spanish troops, either in offensive or defensive movements, not only the government, but the army, will
be desirous that the officer who shall be trusted by His Majesty to command his troops should command the whole.

When I entered Spain, I had reason to believe that I should be joined
by a Spanish army, in such a respectable state of discipline and efficiency
as that it had kept in check, during nearly 3 months after a defeat, a
French army, at one time superior in numbers, and at no time much inferior.   The enclosed letters will show how the fact stands; and I can
now account for the inactivity of the French army under Marshal Victor,
after the defeat of the Spanish army at Medellin, only by attributing it to
his desire to avoid risking an advance towards Seville, till Marshal Soult
should have secured his right by the conquest of Portugal, and the possession of Lisbon.

I had likewise reason to believe that the French corps in the north of
Spain were fully employed; and although I had heard of the arrival of
Marshal Soult at Zamora on the 29th June, with a view to equip the remains of his corps, which appeared to be in want of every thing, I did
not think it possible that a French corps, consisting of 34,000 men, under
3 Marshals, could have been assembled at Salamanca without the knowledge of the Governor of Ciudad Rodrigo, or of the Junta of Castille;
that these corps could have been moved from their stations in Galicia, the
Asturias, and Biscay, without setting free for general operations any
Spanish troops which had been opposed to them; or without any other
inconvenience to the enemy than that of protracting to a later period the
settlement of his government in those provinces; and that they could have
penetrated into Estremadura without a shot being fired at them by the
troops deemed sufficient to defend the passes by the Spanish General.

All these occurrences, however, with the diminished numbers of the
Spanish troops in consequence of desertion, and their general relative in-
feriority to the enemy in point of numbers, in consequence of the occurrences before referred to, have made such an alteration in the state of
affairs, that I conceive I shall be justified in having declined to co-operate
again with the Spanish armies.   I do not conceive that reinforcements
which should increase this army to 40,000 men, or even to a larger
amount, would make any material difference in the state of affairs in
Spain.

I believe that the estimate of the enemy's force, which the enclosed
letters contain, is nearly correct, as I conclude from what the enemy has
done in respect to Galicia and Asturias, that he would weaken his force
in Aragon and Catalonia, in proportion as he should find the allies, and
particularly the British army, enabled to press him in this quarter; at the
same time that no benefit would result to the general cause from the
enemy's weakness in Catalonia and Aragon, excepting the repose which
the people of those provinces would enjoy from the absence of the enemy's

troops, and the delay in the settlement of the enemy's government among them. But if the enemy should, contrary to my expectation, not remove the troops from Aragon and Catalonia, in case he should be pressed in this quarter, but should rather retire to the Ebro, I conceive that no force which Great Britain could afford, with all that Spain could bring forward, under existing arrangements, would be able to dislodge the enemy from that position.

To Visc. Castlereagh.   Badajoz, 4th Sept. 1809.

I have received your letters of the 12th, and I am happy to find that the King's ministers approved of my conduct up to the 24th July. I hope that they will approve of my subsequent measures.

I send you by this occasion a copy of a correspondence that I have had with Lord Wellesley, which will give the government my opinion upon the points referred for his and mine in Mr. Canning's dispatches of the 12th. They are nearly of the same purport with my last letter to you.

There is only one point in that letter which I wish to alter, and that relates to the garrison required for Cadiz. Upon further inquiry, I find that there are means in Cadiz of putting in security from a *coup de main* by the inhabitants 4000 or 5000 men; and I should think that number sufficient to give us a footing there, of which we might take further advantage by throwing in more troops, if we should find it expedient.

Observations on Mr. Sec. Canning's Dispatch of the 12th Aug. to Marquis Wellesley.
           Badajoz, 5th Sept. 1809.

In co-operation with the Spanish armies, or in conjunction with them.

A British army of 30,000 men, or even of 40,000 men, would not be sufficient in co-operation, or in conjunction with the Spanish armies, to effect the deliverance of the whole of the Peninsula, by the expulsion of the French armies now in Spain. The foundation of this opinion is to be found in my dispatches of the 24th Aug., 1st and 3d Sept.

How far a force of 30,000 or 40,000 men would be enabled to make head, or, in other words, to carry on defensive operations against the augmented force which Buonaparte may be enabled to direct against Spain, would depend upon the extent of that force, and upon the extent of the defensive system to be adopted. 30,000 or 40,000 men would not be able to defend both the south of Spain and Portugal.

In the existing state of the Spanish armies, I doubt whether a British army could defend the south of Spain against the attack which an augmented French force would make upon that country. It is certain, however, that 30,000 British troops, or even a smaller force, could get off from Cadiz or Gibraltar.

The separate defence of Portugal, and that Portugal will be best defended.

Portugal will certainly be best defended by confining the British force within the limits prescribed by my existing instructions.

With a reasonable prospect of success ; if he shall think that Portugal would be best defended in the end, &c.

In the present state of the Spanish and Portuguese armies, and adverting to the deficiency of supplies and means of transport in Spain, it would be difficult to connect the defence of Portugal with that of the south of Spain, with 30,000 or 40,000 British troops, even against the French force now in the Peninsula.

The next question which will then arise, &c.

In case the British government should enter upon any plan of operations connected with the Spanish armies, they should insist: 1st, upon having a garrison in Cadiz: 2dly; upon having the command of the armies in the hand of the officer commanding the King's army: 3dly; upon the adoption of a system throughout all the provinces under the government of the Junta, which would ensure to the armies all the supplies and means of transport which the country could produce.

All horses, mules, asses, carts, &c., in every district, should be numbered and registered, with the owner's name, place where to be found, &c.; and all should be liable to be called for, and should be produced under a heavy penalty, when called for for the use of the army.

With a view to prevent the recurrence of these inconveniences, &c.

In the same manner wheat, barley, straw, flour, bullocks in every district, should be registered, and the owners should be obliged to produce the quantities registered for the service of the army when called for.

This ought to be the law of the country, and should be extended to all districts from which the enemy's troops should withdraw.

These arrangements, with the system proposed by Lord Wellesley for forming magazines, which these arrangements would enable the government to carry into effect, would give the government and the army the command of the supplies in the country.

Cadiz would be essentially important.

It is obvious that our operations in Spain must be defensive; that they cannot be connected with Portugal; that we must have a retreat upon Cadiz; and that that retreat cannot be secure, unless Cadiz is in our hands. I am convinced, however, that the Spanish government will never cede Cadiz.

Sine qua non. If the command is not to be in the British General.

I conceive this is a point not to be urged too soon. Let government make up their mind definitively, whether they will defend Portugal or the south of Spain. I should not be surprised if the advantage of the possession of the fleets of Spain, and the certainty that the army could be embarked at Cadiz, which is not, in the Tagus, quite clear, should induce our government to prefer the operation in the south of Spain to that in Portugal. If that should be the case, we might find it difficult to obtain the command for the British General, if a Generalissimo should have been appointed.

To Marquis Wellesley.   Badajoz, 5th Sept. 1809.

I have had the honor of receiving your Excellency's letter of the 4th inst., marked E. I considered my dispatches of the 24th Aug., and 1st and 3d inst., as containing my opinion upon all the points referred to in Mr. Sec. Canning's dispatch to your Excellency of the 12th Aug.; and accordingly I sent copies of those dispatches to England yesterday, with a letter to Lord Castlereagh, of which I enclose a copy. I have, however, now written in the margin of the copy which your Excellency has sent me of the dispatch of the 12th Aug., from Mr. Canning, answers upon those points on which I understand from Mr. Wellesley that your Excellency wishes for my opinion.

The A.G. to Lieut. Col. Mackinnon, Elvas.   5th Sept. 1809.

I am directed by the Commander of the Forces to reply in answer to your letter respecting the convalescents at Elvas, and you will be pleased to order that those men, who are actually fit for duty, shall forthwith proceed with their officers to join their respective regiments, by the routes that I here enclose from the Q. M. Gen. You may retain such men for guards as are absolutely necessary: it is desirable that they should be as few able men as will be sufficient for that duty.

The A.G. to Brigade Major ——.   5th Sept. 1809.

I have the Commander of the Forces' directions to acquaint you that he cannot accord you the leave you desire; and in any future applications you may make, you will address yourself, through the General officers commanding your brigade and division, to me, to be laid before his Excellency for his approval.

The A.G. to Capt. ——, *D.A.A.G.*   5th Sept. 1809.

In answer to your letter of the 30th ult., I have to acquaint you, from the Commander of the Forces, that it will be necessary, previous to your obtaining leave to go to Lisbon, that a statement of your ill health should be certified by a Board of Medical officers at Elvas, and requiring that you should proceed to Lisbon on the above account.

To Marshal Beresford.   Badajoz, 7th Sept. 1809.

I shall be very much obliged to you if you will inquire what has

---

G. O.   Badajoz, 7th Sept. 1809.

1. Notwithstanding the repeated orders given out upon the subject, the soldiers of the 4th division of infantry plundered bee-hives, in the neighbourhood of Badajoz, on the day before the division marched from that place; it is impossible these outrages can be committed daily, and that this last outrage in particular could have been committed without the officers obtaining some knowledge of it. The officers with the army do not appear to be aware how much they suffer in the disgraceful and unmilitary practices of the soldiers, in marauding and plundering every thing they lay their hands upon. The consequence is, the people of the country fly their habitations, no market is opened, and the officers, as well as the soldiers, suffer in the privation of every comfort and every necessary, excepting their ration, from the neglect of the former, and the criminal misconduct of the latter. The Commander of the Forces has done, and will continue to do, every thing in his power to put an end to these disgraceful practices; but it is obvious that all his efforts must be fruitless, unless the officers of the army, generally and individually, exert themselves for the same object.

2. The practice of seizing and detaining carts has been prohibited by the G. O. of the army; but it still continues to such an extent as to render it difficult, if not impossible, to supply the troops with what they require, and if persevered in will again cut off the communications with the sources of supply. Commanding officers of divisions, brigades, and regiments are referred to the G. O. of the 25th June, No. 10.

3. All carts now with any department, regiment, or individual to which a driver is attached (whether drawn by mules or bullocks), are to be forthwith allowed to return to their homes, the Commissary paying them their hire for the time they have been employed.

4. Regiments or departments which have carts without drivers are to retain them.

5. Commanding officers of regiments are to report to the officers commanding brigades what number of carts with drivers each will have sent away, and what number of carts without drivers each will have retained, under these orders. Commanding officers of brigades will transmit these reports, in the usual channel, to the Q. M. G. Heads of departments are to make a similar report to the Q. M. G. These orders are not intended to apply to the covered carts drawn by mules lately sent from Seville, nor to any carts actually engaged in the performance of any service, until that service shall have been completed. In future, when carts are required by regiments or departments, application is to be made for them to the Commissary Gen., according to the orders of the 25th June, No. 10
6. The

become of M. Veron de Farincourt, a lieutenant in the French service, who was taken prisoner by Silveira at Chaves.

I have latterly no accounts of the enemy; but I still think Ciudad Rodrigo his most probable object, and that in which he is most likely to succeed. I gave you the command of our magazines at Castello Branco, when you had troops there. Now that you will have none, you cannot want them, nor those at Villa Velha, and yet your Commissaries have got fast hold of them, particularly the last, and will not give them up. Pray, therefore, desire them to give up to our Commissaries immediately every thing at Castello Branco and Villa Velha.

To Brig. Gen. Cox, Governor of Almeida.   Badajoz, 7th Sept. 1809.

I have received your letter of the 30th Aug.   I am much concerned

---

6. The Commander of the Forces has observed that camp kettles are, in some instances, carried upon carts, a practice which is positively contrary to orders, and must be exceedingly inconvenient and prejudicial to the troops. He begs that the officers commanding brigades and regiments will see that regiments are properly provided with the means of carrying camp kettles without loss of time.

7. The officer in command of the hospital at Elvas, and the officer commanding at Lisbon, will take care that every soldier joining the army from either of those places is supplied with two good shirts, and two good pairs of shoes, which will be supplied by the Commissary upon his requisition. The officer or non-commissioned officer, in charge of the hospital of the soldier requiring the necessaries, will make the requisition, specifying in it the soldier's name, the regiment and company to which he belongs, and the number of shirts and pairs of shoes he requires : this must be given in in duplicate; one copy of which must be sent to the regiment, and the other delivered to the Commissary. The officer or non-commissioned officer, in charge of the soldier requiring the necessaries, is to sign the receipt of the necessaries at the bottom of both copies of the requisition, when they will have received them from the Commissary.

8. When officers may be in such a state of health as to render it necessary that they should quit the army, they must send to head quarters a certificate that the state of their health requires removing; this certificate will be sent to the Inspector of hospitals, and a board of medical officers will be ordered to assemble to consider of the necessity of this removal; and unless this board should certify that removal is necessary, it will not in any case be permitted. In the same manner, if the medical attendant on any officer, either with the army or at out-quarter, should think his return to England necessary, he will certify it to the board ordered to consider of the case.

9. The Commander of the Forces cannot avoid to take this opportunity of observing that when an officer is separated from his regiment in the performance of his duty, or by unavoidable circumstances, it is his first duty to endeavor to join, when the duty shall have been performed, or the circumstances shall no longer exist, which occasioned his separation from his regiment; this is peculiarly his duty, and most probably would be an object to every officer in this army, at a moment when the army might be supposed to be involved in difficulties. From the excellent character which Lieut. ———— bears, and from his former services and good conduct, the Commander of the Forces believes with the Court Martial that he was desirous of joining his regiment. That which has occurred to him, however, and the fact which is notorious to the whole army, if any effort had been made to join it, it must have been successful, should be a warning to all officers in the situation in which Lieut. ———— found himself, not to listen to the senseless reports which invariably prevail on the flank and rear of all armies, but to endeavor seriously to join their regiments; at all events, not to go farther to the rear till the necessity for so doing will have become evident and urgent.

10. It is directed that particular attention may be paid by the regiments of the army to sending in their weekly states and monthly returns correct. There have been of late so many mistakes and alterations in men and horses unaccounted for, that almost invariably the states have been returned to the regiments prior to the possibility of making out the general state of the army. This occasions not only trouble, but considerable delay. In addition to the due examination of the returns by the Commanding officer previous to his signature, and his comparing them with the former to see that they correspond, brigade majors and assist. adj. gens. of divisions must strictly compare and examine all states sent in ; the latter will be held particularly responsible for forwarding correct states.

that you should have any trouble with our soldiers, whose trip from Talavera to Almeida appears as extraordinary as many other of their feats.

We have so many officers sick and wounded, that it would be difficult now to spare one from this army to do the duty which you propose should be done by a British officer to be stationed at Almeida. I would therefore request you to continue to take the trouble of doing it, and to draw upon the British Paymaster Gen. at Lisbon for any money you may disburse for this, or for any other service for the British army; and if you will make your drafts payable at a fortnight's sight, and give me notice of them, I shall take care that they are duly honored. If you cannot get money at Almeida for your bills, I will send you some, and request you to let me know what sum. I shall be obliged to you to send me an account, from time to time, of the sums you may have disbursed, stating the name of the soldier to whom given, his regiment, and the company to which he belongs.

We have suspected for some time past that the enemy intended to attack Ciudad Rodrigo, which we must strain every nerve to prevent. Send me the earliest intelligence, by the quickest means of conveyance, of any of the movements in that quarter which may give you reason to believe that they really entertain, and are about to carry that design into execution. If they should move heavy artillery from Valladolid, Burgos, or Madrid, it may be considered certain.

Let me have all the information you can acquire of the roads leading from Castello Branco to Ciudad Rodrigo; and particularly whether it is possible to go with the guns on any road without passing by Guarda between Guarda and the Puerto de Perales. Sir R. Wilson is at Castello Branco, watching the enemy's motions.

To J. Murray, Esq., Commissary General.   Badajoz, 7th Sept. 1809.

Since I wrote to you on the 30th Aug., having learned from Mr. Villiers that much time will elapse before the silver lately arrived from England can be coined, and that the Portuguese government will suffer great inconvenience if he should not be able to make the usual payments on account of the subsidy, I request you will by return of post inform me what sums of money you have received at Lisbon between 1st and 31st Aug. on account of bills on England, negotiated at Lisbon, Cadiz, or Gibraltar; and what sums you have received from England or elsewhere, exclusive of the bullion and gold coin lately arrived in the *Fylla*, in order that I may direct you what sum you are to pay to Mr. Villiers.

To J. Murray, Esq., Commissary General.   Badajoz, 7th Sept. 1809.

I enclose a letter which I have received from Adm. Berkeley, regarding the mules purchased for the army at Tangier; and I beg that, upon the receipt of this letter, you will take the most efficient measures, not only to pay for the mules which may have been purchased at Tangier, but to have them received and taken care of at their landing place, and thence brought up to the army.

I likewise enclose an extract of a letter from Adm. Berkeley, pointing out what he conceives would be a satisfactory mode of paying for these mules; upon which I have only to observe, that if you should adopt this mode, to which I see no objection, it is desirable that you should authorise your agent at Gibraltar to grant the bills in payment for the mules, instead of the paymaster at Gibraltar, with whom this army has no concern; and that as this is a business of some magnitude and expense to the public, I think it desirable that you should send somebody to Tangier more likely to be a good judge of a mule than the Agent of transports, upon whose receipt the payment should be made. But it must be clearly understood that payment must be made for all mules received by the Agent of transports before your agent shall have arrived at Tangier.

To Col. Roche.   Badajoz, 7th Sept. 1809.

I have received your letter of the 4th. I beg that you will tell Gen. Eguia that I consider it as very irregular that any sealed letter should pass his front from the enemy to any body in this army; that those which have arrived lately related solely to the wounded officers and soldiers, and to a proposal which I had made to exchange them; and that I beg that, in future, he will be so kind as to open any letter which may come to his posts, and which may be sealed. I should send for his perusal those which have come lately, only that I have been obliged to make a reference to Lord Wellesley upon them, and have yet to answer them. Let me hear from you constantly, and all reports.

Do you want money for your messengers, or other purposes?

P. S. If you have any opportunity, you may tell M. V. de Thevenon that I will inquire about his friend, M. V. de Farincourt, and will let him know the result. I request you to mention to Gen. Eguia that there are 2 battalions, one of Seville, the other of Merida, still with Sir R. Wilson, who is employed watching the movements of the enemy towards Ciudad Rodrigo; and I shall be obliged to Gen. Eguia if he will inform me what shall be done with them. These 2 battalions are much in want of pay, having received none for some time; and if Gen. Eguia wishes it, I shall order that some may be advanced to them.

To Vice Adm. the Hon. G. Berkeley.   Badajoz, 7th Sept. 1809.

I have the honor to acknowledge the receipt of your Excellency's letter, and I am much obliged to you for your intentions to send a transport to convey to Lisbon the recovered men of the 27th regt. As these men have been removed to Gibraltar, I conclude Adm. Purvis will not have had it in his power to send them round.

I have directed the Commissary Gen. to adopt the most early and efficient measures to pay for the mules purchased for the army at Tangier, and have desired him to follow the mode proposed in your letter, with this difference, that his agent at Gibraltar is to give his own bills on the Lords of the Treasury on the production of the receipts of the Agent of transports for the mules, instead of the bills of the Paymaster Gen. at Gibraltar, who has no concern whatever with this army. As this is a business of some magnitude, and likely to be expensive to the public, and is very important to the army, I have also thought it proper to desire the Commissary Gen. to send an agent of his own to Tangier, in whose judgment of a mule he can confide, upon whose receipts the payment may be made. I have thought it proper to give this direction, in order to avoid the complaints of the mules and references which I should hereafter have made to me; but I have directed that all the receipts of the Agent of transports should be taken up, and the value of the mules paid at Gibraltar till the Commissary's agent shall arrive.

To the Rt. Hon. J. Villiers.   Badajoz, 7th Sept. 1809.

I have the honor to acknowledge the receipt of your Excellency's letter of the 1st inst., enclosing an extract of one from Mr. Sec. Canning, respecting the practicability of procuring at Lisbon certain articles of ordnance and military stores, required for the use of the Portuguese troops. You will observe that these articles were required by Marshal Beresford, who is now at Lisbon, and is more capable than I am of giving you accurate information of the urgency of the want of each article, and of the capacity of the city of Lisbon to supply any, and what part of the demand. I think it very desirable, however, that a part at least of the demand of each article should be supplied from England, as soon as the Ordnance can prepare it.

To the Rt. Hon. J. Villiers.   Badajoz, 7th Sept. 1809.

Conceiving that, upon the receipt of the bullion, you would not require your fifth, I had desired Mr. Murray not to pay it to you; but I now write to him to desire that he will let me know how much you are entitled to for last month; and as soon as I shall receive his answer, I shall give orders that it may be paid to Mr. Bell. I shall inquire respecting the serjeant of the 43d; but, from the complexion of the case, I suspect that it will not be possible to do any thing for him.

To Marquis Wellesley.   Badajoz, 7th Sept. 1809.

I have the honor to enclose a memorandum stating the positions occupied by the British army, for your Excellency's information.

Badajoz	Head Quarters and the artillery.
Merida	{The brigade of Heavy cavalry and troop of Horse artillery.
Montijo, Puebla de la Calzada .	One division of Infantry.
Talavera Real . . .	One division of Infantry, and a brigade of artillery.
Near Badajoz . . .	One division of Infantry.
Campo Maior . . .	One division of Infantry.

1 squadron of Cavalry in each of the following towns: Alburquerque, La Roca, Montijo, Talavera Real, Badajoz, Elvas, Campo Maior, 2 in Olivenca, and 4 in Villa Vicosa.

To Marquis Wellesley.   Badajoz, 7th Sept. 1809.

I wrote to the Commander in Chief of the French army some days ago, to propose that some of the wounded officers in the hospital at Talavera de la Reyna should be exchanged for French officers in our possession: in answer to which proposition I have received a letter from Marshal Soult, in which he proposes to exchange some of them for Gen. Franceschi, Capt. Antoine, and Lieut. Bernard, who were lately taken on the road from Zamora to Valladolid, and are now prisoners at Seville.

I think it is not improbable that the Spanish government, adverting to the manner in which the British officers in the hospital at Talavera have become prisoners of war, might not be disinclined to allow Gen. Franceschi, and the other officers with him, to be at liberty in exchange for some, and to facilitate the general exchange of all the British officers; and I shall be very much obliged to your Excellency if you will exert your influence with the Spanish government, in order that this arrangement may take effect.

To Marquis Wellesley.   Badajoz, 7th Sept. 1809.

I shall feel very much obliged to you if you will desire Armstrong, or Forbes, to send me copies of the accounts which the government receive from Venegas, &c., and of the enemy's movements and operations in their front, as from them I shall be able to judge in some degree what are their designs.

At present I have no intelligence whatever, excepting the nonsense I receive occasionally from ——, as the Spaniards have defeated all my attempts to obtain any, by stopping those whom I sent out to make inquiries. It is very desirable, however, that I should have the means of forming an early judgment on their designs, that I may move early to defeat them; and that I should know that they do not design any operation immediately, as it is desirable that I should go to Lisbon for a few days, if I can venture to quit the army; and I should wish also to go towards Seville to see you.

The A.G. to Col. ——, Lisbon.   7th Sept. 1809.

In reply to your letter addressed to the Military Secretary, which, upon a point of discipline, should have been addressed to this department, I am directed by the Commander of the Forces to acquaint you that you will call upon Capt. —— to give in charges against Dr. ——, who must be brought to trial before a General Court Martial, which will be ordered to assemble at Lisbon.

The A.G. to Lieut. ——, Queen's regt.   7th Sept. 1809.

I have the Commander of the Forces directions to acquaint you that you are to be tried by a Court Martial, which is ordered to assemble to-morrow at Lieut. Gen. Payne's quarters here at 12 o'clock, upon the following charge : 'For having struck a sentinel of the Portuguese guard at Elvas whilst in the execution of his duty, wresting his bayonet from him, and throwing it over the ramparts of the town.' You will be pleased to appear before the Court at the above mentioned hour, when your trial will be proceeded upon.

The A.G. to Col. Peacocke, Lisbon.   7th Sept. 1809.

I have the Commander of the Forces directions to acquaint you that you will be pleased to order the officers who have absented themselves from the army, without leave, immediately under arrest, and send them up to the head quarters of the army, reporting themselves to me. I enclose you a list of such as I have selected.

I have also to inform you that all officers who should be sufficiently recovered from sickness or otherwise, to be able to take their duty, should proceed and join their regiments without delay.

To Marshal Beresford.   Badajoz, 8th Sept. 1809.

I have just received your letter of the 3d, and I am glad to find that you agree with me in opinion respecting the mode in which British officers might have been employed with the Portuguese army to the greatest advantage. It appears, however, that we differ in opinion on two points respecting these officers : one, that it would have been necessary in that case that all of them should have been of high rank ; the other, that it would have been impossible to use any of them at present in the manner in which I had proposed.

In respect to the first point, I have to observe, that according to my notion, they would have derived all their authority from you, as the head of the army ; and as being your adjutants, acquainted with your sentiments, conveying your orders, and representing your authority ; and they would have required no rank to perform the duties of their situation. In respect to the use of them at present, I agree with you that Blunt or Campbell might be very much surprised and annoyed to see Douglas or Warre act as viceroy over them; but there is no occasion to send them to Blunt or Campbell. I should send them to govern Silveira, or Miranda, and people of that description; and I should employ the drills to superintend those like Machado and others, of whom you have many. The English officers employed regimentally, and who may be of more use than I supposed them to be, could have no objection to this employment of their juniors; not to command them, but to superintend the conduct of those who do and must command them.

We are mistaken if we believe that what these Portuguese and Spanish armies require is discipline, properly so called. They want the habits and spirit of soldiers ; the habits of command on one side, and of obedience on the other ; mutual confidence between officers and men ; and, above all, a determination in the superiors to obey the spirit of the orders they receive, let what will be the consequence, and the spirit to tell the true cause if they do not. In short, the fact is, there is so much trick in the Portuguese army, and the kind of subaltern character they have given you as officers is so little likely to check it, or to make you acquainted with the true state of things, that I despair of seeing matters upon a proper footing till you shall be able to superintend almost personally all branches of the service.

I have sent you all the letters which I have received from England regarding the Portuguese service. Did you send me an official letter respecting the pay of the officers? I don't recollect it.

G. O.   Badajoz, 8th Sept. 1809.

The Commander of the Forces has heard with much concern that persons employed at Lisbon in landing stores for the army have landed goods liable to pay duty, under pretence that they were for the use of the troops. The Commander of the Forces is determined to disgrace and punish those who shall be found out to have been concerned in those scandalous transactions ; and in order to prevent them in future, he desires that when any articles are to be landed from any ship in the Tagus for the use of the troops, the officer at the head of the department, for whose service they are to be landed, is to give one day's previous notice to the officer commanding at Lisbon of this intention, stating particularly the ship from which in the river, and the place to which on shore, the articles are to be taken, and, as far as may be possible, the denominations and quantities of the articles to be landed.

The Commanding officer at Lisbon is immediately to convey this notice to His Majesty's ambassador at Lisbon, in order that he may make such communications on the subject to the government as he may think proper. In case the government may think proper to order it, customhouse officers are to be allowed to attend in the ship, in the boats conveying the articles from the ship to the shore, and in the store house, in order to see that the goods are conveyed to their destination according to notice given.

I send you the regulation which we have received, and according to which I shall invariably act in respect to the issue of bât and forage money.

I intended to leave to your decision whether Sir R. Wilson should remain north of the Tagus, or should come to this side, and I thought I had so expressed myself in my letter to him. But upon referring to my letter to him, I find that he might have considered what I stated as a wish that it might be practicable for him to come to this quarter as an order for him to come across the Tagus; and he marched accordingly. I stopped him, however, and he is gone back to Castello Branco.

I have ordered Gen. C. Craufurd to join the army, the brigades and divisions of which I want to arrange, preparatory to any fresh operations.

You shall have Capt. White of the 27th. Don't you think Golegão high up for your cavalry? I think that before the winter is over we shall have to assemble between the Tagus and the Mondego the whole of the British and Portuguese army; and I want to save the resources of the country, particularly the straw, barley, and India corn, for that movement, which will decide the fate of Portugal.

I would eat up every thing at Lisbon, because we can always import or bring down by the river what we want, and preserve every thing at a distance. If we cannot use it or remove it, we can easily burn it.

To the Rt. Hon. J. Villiers.   Badajoz, 8th Sept. 1809.

I have received your letter of the 5th, and I enclose a copy of the order which I have issued respecting the smuggling transactions at Lisbon.

We ought to pay for the couriers certainly, and I enclose a warrant for the money, addressed to the Commissary General at Lisbon, where it will be received.

It is an extraordinary circumstance that I cannot receive an answer from the 14th dragoons respecting the discharge of Kelly; I write, however, again.

The soldiers of the army have permission to go to mass, so far as this: they are forbidden to go into the churches during the performance of divine service, unless they go to assist in the performance of the service. I could not do more, for in point of fact, soldiers cannot by law attend the celebration of mass, excepting in Ireland. The thing now stands exactly as it ought; any man may go to mass who chooses, and nobody makes any inquiry about it. The consequence is, that nobody goes to mass, and although we have whole regiments of Irishmen, and of course Roman Catholics, I have not seen one soldier perform any one act of religious worship in these Catholic countries, excepting making the sign of the cross to induce the people of the country to give them wine. Although, as you will observe, I have no objection, and they may go to mass if they choose it, I have great objections to the inquiries and interference of the priests of the country to induce them to go to mass. The orders were calculated to prevent all intrigue and interference of that description; and I was very certain, that when the Irish soldiers were left to themselves either to go or not, they would do as their comrades did, and not one of them would be seen in a church. I think it best that you should avoid having any further discussion with the priests on this subject; but if you should have any, it would be best that you should tell them what our law is, and what the order of this army. Prudence may then induce them to refrain from taking any steps to induce the Roman Catholic soldiers to attend mass; but if it should not, and their conduct should be guided by religious zeal, I acknowledge, that however indifferent I should have been at seeing the soldiers flock to the churches under my orders, I should not be very well satisfied to see them filled by the influence of the priests, taking advantage of the mildness and toleration which is the spirit of that order.

I enclose a complaint from Dr. Forbes, of his servant, who is in custody, Col. Walsh knows where. It is very desirable that some steps should be taken to punish this man. Although we have reason to be satisfied with the Portuguese nation in general, there are many individual instances of this kind of conduct, and it is very desirable that the people of the country should know that they cannot be guilty of it with impunity; probably they would send the delinquent to me to be disposed of as a follower of the army.

In respect to the complaints you have sent me of the conduct of detachments, they are only a repetition of others which I receive every day from all quarters of Spain and Portugal; and I can only lament my inability to apply any remedy.

In the first place, our law is not what it ought to be; and I cannot prevail upon government even to look at a remedy.

2dly; Our military courts having been established solely for the purpose of maintaining military discipline, with the same wisdom which has marked all our proceedings of late years, we have obliged the officers to swear to decide according to the evidence brought before them, and we have obliged the witnesses to give their evidence upon oath. The witnesses being almost in every instance common soldiers, whose conduct this tribunal was constituted to control, the consequence is, that perjury is almost as common a military offence as drunkenness and plunder; and when the soldiers are brought before a General Court Martial upon serious questions, in which they formerly told the truth on their oath, (oaths, and the breaking of oaths, being so common,) the truth can never be ascertained.

3dly; The people of Spain and Portugal, ready enough to complain, and in the first to claim payment for the outrages committed by the soldiers, and in the last to assign these outrages as an excuse for not doing what they are ordered, have invariably declined to prosecute, and have omitted to appear as evidence against the soldiers. Only 2 days ago, I was obliged to convey my sentiments in plain terms to the Governor of this place, and to Gen. Leite; the former of whom, having confined 3 soldiers for an outrage, respecting which he made a formal complaint, wanted me to excuse them from punishment; and the latter having complained of, and indeed placed in confinement, an officer and a soldier who had attacked and disarmed a sentry at Elvas, wished that I should take no further notice of this outrage.

I have made inquiries respecting the officer of the cavalry stated to have committed outrages at Thomar, but I am very well convinced that the person who has complained of him will not appear to substantiate the complaint when called upon, any more than the other gentleman will to substantiate the complaint against the Commissary or the Inspector of Hospitals. Under these circumstances, how can discipline be maintained? It is a curious circumstance, that notwithstanding I have been aware of the necessity, and have determined to execute any man founa guilty or in the act of plunder, I have not yet executed one; although I really believe that more plunder and outrage have been committed by this army, than by any other that ever was in the field : to this add, that I have not less than 7 or 8 Provosts, other armies having usually 2.

I know nothing about Capt. Chapman's promise of stores from the Engineer department. I have been positively ordered not to give the British stores, and I must obey those orders, excepting in cases in which I shall see the necessity of giving them, and shall be convinced that they can be spared. Besides this, Beresford ought to make the application, if the stores are required.

P.S. In respect to the complaints that the British soldiers have taken all the beasts off the road to Castello Branco, it is positively false; I passed that road in June last, before any of the troops passed, and there were neither men nor beasts upon it.

The A.G. to Col. Walsh, Town Major, Lisbon.   8th Sept. 1809.

I have laid your letter and several enclosures, relating to the correspondence between you and Col. Peacocke, before the Commander of the Forces, and am directed to remark that his Excellency's time cannot be taken up with examining into trivial complaints and grievances between two officers placed in situations to assist each other in carrying on the public service; and it is much beneath them to be catching at opportunities of doing each other ill service. It is impossible that the business at Lisbon can be carried on if Col. Peacocke and you transact every thing by letter when personal communication is so much more easy and satisfactory. The Commander of the Forces desires this may be understood with regard to the other point. You certainly did no more than your duty in acquainting the A. Q. M. G. that the men of the 9th and 20th were ready to proceed to Gibraltar. They are to go the first opportunity. The Commander of the Forces hopes to hear no further of such trifling complaints as your last letter is filled with.

The A.G. to Lieut. Gen. Payne.   8th Sept. 1809.

I have laid your letter and enclosure before the Commander of the Forces, and am directed to acquaint you that if the question respecting the rank of Capt. Bishoffshausen and Capt. Aly had occurred in any regiment excepting one belonging to the Legion, he would have decided that Capt. Aly was the senior in the regiment; but as the 1st hussars form a part of the Legion, the rank of which may be guided by different rules from those which prevail in the British national service, his Excellency will refer the question for the consideration of H. R. H. the Duke of Cambridge, Colonel of the Legion. In the mean time Capt. Bishoffshausen must continue to command the squadron, and be considered as the senior captain.

To Visc. Castlereagh.   Badajoz, 9th Sept. 1809.

I have the honor to acquaint your Lordship that Mr. Dillon, an Assist. Commissary, was taken by the enemy on the 26th July. He was told that it was not the custom to consider either Surgeons or Commissaries as prisoners of war; but that, as the British troops in Calabria had taken and detained a M. Hébert, a French Commissary, he, Mr. Dillon, could only be allowed to return in exchange for that gentleman.

I have herewith the honor to enclose the *Cartel d'Echange* which Mr.

Dillon brought with him; and I beg to observe, that M. Hébert is called *Intendant Général de la Régie des Vivres*, and is therefore of a much higher rank than an Assist. Commissary. If, however, His Majesty's government chose to admit the principle of not considering either Surgeons or Commissaries as prisoners of war, M. Hébert should be sent back with a notification of the admission of this principle; otherwise I imagine they will not allow Mr. Dillon to be exchanged for a person of so much superior rank. In the mean time I have ordered Mr. Dillon to do his duty until I receive your Lordship's answer.

The A.G. to Thos. Keate, Esq., Surg. Gen., London.   9th Sept. 1809.

The Inspector of hospitals, Dr. Franck, has referred your letter of the 13th ult. to his Excellency Sir A. Wellesley, and I am directed by him to acquaint you that with whatever views the Medical board may have sent the instructions of the 12th Aug., which your letter conveys, his Excellency is of opinion they will fully agree with him on the impropriety of those orders being now carried into effect; indeed it would be totally impracticable without a manifest suffering of the British army. The battle of Talavera having produced so great an addition to the hospitals of this army, and the army having nearly 10,000 sick, make it impossible, with proper justice to the medical officers now belonging to it, to attend to all the patients, and a greater supply is certainly required here. You will therefore see how little any medical assistance can be spared. Dr. Franck has in consequence been directed to suspend taking any measures, in consequence of your letter, until he hears further from you.

To Brig. Gen. Alex. Campbell.   Badajoz, 10th Sept. 1809.

I am concerned that it is necessary that you should go home, and I enclose you letters for Lord Castlereagh and Sir D. Dundas, which I hope may be of use to you, but I fear will not be so.

To Major Gen. J. Murray.   Badajoz, 10th Sept. 1809.

I am very much obliged to you for your letter of the 21st Aug. I do not know any thing of Mr. ——; indeed I never heard his name; and I can scarcely believe that my brother Henry would have employed him or any body else, as agent to me or the army, without informing me of it. I should suspect that Mr. —— is a trading Prize agent, who is very willing to interfere in any prize case which may offer itself to his attention, without any direct authority from any of the parties concerned in the prize.

I considered well, when I was at Oporto, the whole question of the claim of the army to the property at Oporto, and I discussed it with the Admiral, and the result was a conviction on my mind that we have no

G. O.   Badajoz, 9th Sept. 1809.

1. Staff Surgeons of divisions, Surgeons of brigades, regimental Surgeons, and Assist. Surgeons, having charge of regimental sick, are directed to pay particular attention to the G. O. respecting the hospital department. The Inspector of hospitals has not been able to obtain correct returns of the regimental medical staff and of the sick, from the circumstance of the orders of the 13th Aug. not having been obeyed.

2. Weekly returns of sick are to be transmitted every Sunday morning to the Inspector of hospitals, and monthly returns every 20th, in which will be specified the names of regimental surgeons and assist. surgeons, whether present or absent, and how employed; also hospital mates, who may be attached to regiments, must be included in the returns; the general and regimental hospital staff will transmit to the Inspector of hospitals' head quarters their names, and dates of their commissions from the time of their entrance into the service.

claim whatever, either to prize or salvage. I should be glad to be convinced that we were mistaken, but I am pretty certain we were not so ; indeed so certain, that I have never taken an opinion upon the subject, although I desired Col. Trant to take an account of the property found at Oporto.

G. O.   Badajoz, 10th Sept. 1809.
2. The Commander of the Forces has much pleasure in publishing to the officers and troops the following copy of a letter from the Secretary of State, conveying His Majesty's approbation of their gallant conduct in the late action of Talavera.

Visc. Castlereagh, one of His Majesty's principal Secretaries of State, to his Excellency Lieut. Gen. Sir A. Wellesley, K.B.

Downing Street, 21st Aug. 1809.
Sir, Your letters of the dates referred to in the margin * have been received and laid before the King.

That of the 29th of July, which reports the result of an attack made on the combined British and Spanish armies, near Talavera de la Reyna, on the 27th and 28th ult., by the united corps of Victor and Sebastiani, and the troops from Madrid, has been received by His Majesty with the utmost interest and satisfaction.

The nature of the position occupied by the Spanish army, and the deliberate purpose of the enemy to direct his whole efforts against the troops of His Majesty, as it has thrown upon the British army nearly the entire weight of this great contest, has afforded them an opportunity of acquiring for themselves the important glory of having vanquished the French army of more than double their number, not in a short or partial struggle, but in a battle obstinately contested in two successive days, not wholly discontinued even throughout the intervening night, and fought under circumstances which brought the mass of both armies into close and repeated combat.

The King, in contemplating so glorious a display of the valor and prowess of his troops, has commanded me to declare his Royal approbation of the conduct of his whole army.

His Majesty has directed me to signify in the most marked and especial manner to you his gracious sense of your personal services on the ever-memorable occasion, not less displayed in the glorious result of the battle itself, than in the consummate ability, valor, and military resource with which the many difficulties of this arduous and protracted contest were met and provided for by your tried experience and judgment.

The conduct of Lieut. Gen. Sherbrooke has entitled him to the King's entire approbation. His Majesty has observed with satisfaction the manner in which he led on the troops to the charge with the bayonet, a species of attack which, on all occasions, so well accords with the dauntless character of British soldiers.

His Majesty has noticed with the same gracious approbation the conduct of the several General and other officers; all have done their duty, most of them have had occasion of eminently distinguishing themselves; the instances of which, as reported by you, have not escaped His Majesty's attention.

In signifying to the officers of the army in public orders His Majesty's approbation and thanks, it is His Majesty's pleasure that they be extended in the most distinct and particular manner to the non-commissioned officers and men; on no occasion have they displayed with greater lustre the inestimable qualities which they possess as soldiers, nor have they on any former occasion more nobly sustained the military character of the British nation.

In acknowledging the services of the brave army under your command, His Majesty cannot refrain from those expressions of sorrow and regret with which his Royal mind has been affected, at observing the great number of gallant officers and soldiers who have fallen at the battle of Talavera. His paternal feelings derive their best consolation, on this occasion, from the persuasion that bravery so distinguished, and exertions so heroic, cannot but have obtained for their country the most important and lasting advantages ; and, whilst the security and glory of his own Empire have been confirmed by the achievements of his troops, His Majesty trusts that their efforts will not prove unavailing, under Divine Providence, in the defence of the rights and liberties of the Spanish nation.

His Majesty has directed a medal to be distributed to the General and other officers commanding corps, in commemoration of the victory of Talavera; and has further commanded, that his Royal approbation of the services of his gallant troops in Spain should be published in General Orders to the whole of the British army.

* 29 July : 1 Aug.

The principles upon which prize questions rest, are; 1st; What is captured belongs originally to His Majesty. 2dly; That by various Acts of Parliament, and his proclamation, His Majesty has granted to the navy and army, in certain shares, the property captured from an enemy. 3dly; This property must be condemned as prize in the Court of Admiralty.

In the case of Oporto, we were acting as allies to the government of Portugal, in the territories belonging to that government, and a large property was taken from the enemy, which had been private, but which the enemy had converted into public. The territory was that of our ally, and the property was within it; and of course the property belonged to the power which possessed the territory. Neither the English acts of parliament, nor the King's proclamations, could operate upon it; much less could the King's courts, without a fresh act of violence, viz. that of removing the property from Oporto to England, make it the subject of their discussions and decisions. In respect to salvage for English vessels, and property taken from the enemy in the port of an ally, the question depends upon the wording of an act of parliament which I have not by me, but I understand that the claim can be successfully resisted.

In respect to the relative claims of army and navy, the facts are as follows. The army attacked and beat the enemy out of Oporto, there being at that time off the port two of His Majesty's ships, belonging to Adm. Berkeley's squadron. The business was done by the army, but there is no doubt but those ships and the Admiral have a right to share in any benefit resulting from the capture; and, on the other hand, the army have a right to share with the navy. These are the facts, and my opinion upon them, but I may be wrong; and I should be sorry if the army were to lose any advantage to which they are entitled by any error of judgment of mine. I shall therefore be obliged to you if, in concert with Greenwood, you will take law opinions upon the different points contained in this letter; and if those opinions should be favorable to the right of the army, either to the property captured, (of which I desire Col. Trant to take an account,) or salvage for the British vessels and property recovered from the enemy, I shall further request you to employ some proper person to assert the right of the army, either in concert with the Agent employed by the navy, or otherwise, as you may think best.

I shall also be obliged to you, if you will desire Greenwood to write to my brother Henry, and ascertain from him whether he employed Mr. —— in any manner; I would write to him, but I do not know where he is; and it is as well that you and Greenwood should know how this matter stands, and what kind of man this Mr. —— is, before you proceed any further.

I regret that you were not with us at Talavera; your presence would have been most useful. You will be sorry for poor Langwerth.

To Marshal Beresford.   Badajoz, 12th Sept. 1809.

I received last night your letter of the 8th regarding the rations of your aides de camp, upon which I have only to reply, that doubtless you and your aides de camp are entitled to all allowances as a British Lieut. General and his aides de camp.

In respect to forage, the invariable rule is, that no officer shall draw for more than he requires; and the application of that rule to yourself, to the case of yourself and your aides de camp, would bring it to this: that receiving forage from the Portuguese Commissariat, you ought not likewise to receive it from the British.

I am, however, disposed to settle the matter in any way that may be agreeable to you and your aides de camp; but I think the best way of arranging the business would be, if the Portuguese Commissaries have no forage at Lisbon, or none of the description that you and your aides de camp require, that I should order the Commissary Gen. to deliver from his stores at Lisbon to the Portuguese Commissary, certain quantities of forage, for which Mr. Villiers will pass his receipts, according to the Commissariat arrangement settled between you and me. It is impossible for me to attach to you an English Commissary to supply you and your aides de camp with forage, and I think it would be irregular that you or they should receive forage from our Commissaries when you are at Lisbon, and not at any other time: I think, therefore, that the arrangement above

---

G. O.   Badajoz, 11th Sept. 1809.

2. The Commander of the Forces cannot, however, avoid to observe that unfortunate catastrophe which has occurred, and the circumstances which have brought these serjeants to trial before the General Court Martial, originated in disobedience of orders, repeatedly given out in orders.

3. The use and object of a sick-cart to any regiment is to carry the men, or the arms of the men who may be taken ill on the march; and, in order to accomplish this object, the cart ought to be with the regiment, and not 2 days' march in the rear: if a cart is to be employed to carry sick men, it should equally accompany the regiment, in which case, if the cattle which draw it should be tired, application might be made to the Commissary for fresh cattle, and, at all events, no cart carrying sick should be left without some medical officer attending it: besides this, the Commander of the Forces observes that the pay-master's books, and probably other articles belonging to him, were left upon this cart, which is positively contrary to orders, other means being provided to carry the paymaster's books; and he desires that the Commanding officer of the 2d batt. 28th regt. will call on the paymaster to account for his books being upon this cart, and will report whether he is now furnished with a horse or mule to carry his books.

4. The occurrences which have been the subject, and have been brought out before this General Court Martial, point out forcibly the necessity that the officers of the army should obey strictly the orders they receive.

5. The means of transport and conveyance are so scarce in this country, that unless the regulations respecting them are strictly obeyed the army cannot be served; and most particularly it cannot be served if every officer and non-commissioned officer is to do as he pleases, and take what he pleases by force of arms, wherever he may meet it.

G. A. O.   Badajoz, 12th Sept. 1809.

The 4th division having again in three instances plundered bee-hives, notwithstanding the orders of the 7th inst., the regiments of that division are forthwith, upon the receipt of this order, to be turned out and placed under arms, and they are not to quit their arms till one hour after sunset, when they are to be sent to their huts, and sentries placed round the camp to prevent all men from straggling; and they are to be put under arms again to-morrow morning, at an hour before sunrise, and to stand by their arms till an hour after sunset, and so on day after day, till the soldiers shall have been discovered who have been guilty of these outrages, which, it is repeated, cannot be committed without the knowledge of the officers and non-commissioned officers of the regiments. When the regiments shall be under arms, men must be sent on fatigue for water, for their provisions to cook, &c. &c. under charge of officers and non-commissioned officers, in proportion to the strength of the parties, who must be brought back to the lines as soon as the work required for them shall have been performed.

Col. Kemmis will report whether the orders of the 4th inst., requiring that the rolls should be called in the 4th division every hour, have been obeyed. This order is not intended to apply to the 11th regt.

proposed would answer best. By the bye, writing about receipts reminds me that we ought to have receipts from Mr. Villiers for the provisions you received at Castello Branco.

In respect to forage and provisions for all the other officers attached to the Portuguese army, excepting you and your aides de camp, I have no more to say to those concerns than I have to their pay.

It is unfortunate that all these questions were not considered and decided when first the arrangement was made of bringing them to this country. I should think, however, that the best thing to do would be to settle with Mr. Villiers what rations of provisions each British officer shall receive, and you should get it from the Portuguese Commissariat. If you want those provisions from the British stores, you shall have them upon Mr. Villiers's receipt: but I can much less undertake to find Commissaries to furnish with provisions each British officer serving with the Portuguese army, than I can to find a Commissary to supply you and your aides de camp with forage.

You are mistaken in supposing that, because these officers pay for their rations, they are entitled to receive them from the British Commissariat. If they do pay, the sum is carried to account by the person who pays them, with whom we and our Commissariat have nothing to do. In respect to forage, they are no more entitled to it from the British Commissariat than any other Portuguese officer.

I positively refused leave of absence to Col. ——, telling him that I could not interfere with any officer in the Portuguese service. He has gone, therefore, without leave. I shall write to Lord Wellesley about him; but I should think that he will find it impossible to force him to return to Portugal.

I shall recommend your friend for an Ensigncy. Should you prefer a Cornetcy for him, I may be able to give him one. I have also received your letter of the 8th, respecting Ciudad Rodrigo. I think that the French have not had, since they entered Spain, so good an opportunity of attacking Ciudad Rodrigo as at the present moment. The arrival of Romana's force, if it is good for any thing, may indeed make some difference; at all events, it will give us an opportunity of collecting a very large force in that quarter, which may disturb them a little. I think, however, that things are so nearly balanced in this part of Spain between strength of position and numbers, that neither party can do the other much mischief just at present; and I believe the French are of the same opinion, which is the cause of their inactivity.

I shall be very much obliged to you if you will desire your Adj. Gen. to send me a copy of his last monthly return of all the troops in Portugal, including militia, with an additional column specifying where the corps are; likewise a copy of his general monthly return every month. And I request you also to desire D'Urban to write me a line to let me know when any of the corps are moved from the stations at which they appear to have been by the monthly return.

I have sent you all the letters that I have received from England respecting officers to be sent out for the Portuguese army. I have likewise received your letter of the 8th, respecting Romana's movements. He is to be here on the day after to-morrow, when I shall know more of what his objects are. His movements now appear very unaccountable.

I heard some time ago of the retrograde movements of the French; but on the next day there was a contradiction of them, which possibly had not reached Lisbon when you wrote. I think it very improbable that they will materially weaken their force in this part of Spain.

To Marquis Wellesley.   Badajoz, 12th Sept. 1809.

I have received intimation from Marshal Beresford that Col. ——, of the Portuguese service, is now at Seville, being absent from his regiment without leave, and being indebted to the Portuguese government in a large sum of money, of which he has given no account. I conclude that the usual means have been adopted by Marshal Beresford to induce Col. —— to return to his duty in Portugal; but as they have failed to produce their effect, and as this gentleman is one of His Majesty's subjects, and in the service of his ally the Prince Regent, I request your Excellency to urge the Spanish government to have him sent into Portugal without loss of time, or to my head quarters at this place. I know that Col. —— is absent from his regiment without leave, as I refused to give him leave.

To Col. Peacocke.   Badajoz, 12th Sept. 1809.

I have had the honor of receiving your letter of the 9th inst., and its enclosures.

I desire that the troops in Lisbon and Belem may receive salt provisions twice a week, till those provisions shall be consumed which have been reported as likely to become unfit for use if kept much longer. The women and children of the officers and soldiers of the army are entitled, the former each to half a ration, the latter to a quarter of a ration daily: and I see no objection to extending these allowances to the wives and children of clerks and others employed in the public departments, provided they are English born. If the clerk be Portuguese, it may be very necessary and proper to give him his rations, but it cannot be necessary to his wife and children, and I desire that this practice may be discontinued.

I conclude that the rations drawn by the lady, to whom you refer, as an officer's wife, are for the wives of other officers or soldiers, and if so they are perfectly regular; if not, they must be discontinued: and, at all events, forage must not be allowed to the horse of an officer's lady residing at Lisbon. I beg that you will understand that I am desirous of giving to the wives of the officers and soldiers of the army every indulgence to the fullest extent allowed by His Majesty's regulations; but I can suffer no abuse, and every appearance of abuse must be checked immediately.

The officers of the army are allowed to draw rations in the field for servants not soldiers, paying for the same; and I conceive the same indulgence may be extended to their families residing at Lisbon for English servants, but not for Portuguese.

I beg that you will communicate this letter to the Commissariat department.

To Vice Adm. the Hon. G. Berkeley.   Badajoz, 12th Sept. 1809.

I have received your official letter of the 9th, relative to the Danish ships at Oporto, and the only official answer I can give is, that I have nothing to do with those ships.

However, I must mention to you that I have desired that a legal opinion might be taken in England respecting the right of the navy and army to the property captured at Oporto; and it would probably be desirable that we should not lose hold of these ships till we know what that opinion is. I have scarcely any doubt, however, for the reasons I have before stated to you, that we have no right to any of the property; and if you should be of the same opinion, I shall write you an official answer to your letter of the 9th, to the purport above stated.

To the Rt. Hon. J. Villiers.   Badajoz, 12th Sept. 1809.

Before I left Lisbon, Madame da Silva gave me a list containing the names of persons who, she said, were detained in France, and who, I believe, were the Bishops and other deputies called out of Portugal by Buonaparte, under pretence of settling a government for that country; and she begged that if I had an opportunity I would interest myself in their favor, and have them sent back. Upon looking at the list, however, I found it contained the names of the Marquez d'Alorna and others, who are certainly traitors; and I wrote to her to say that I could have nothing to do with them.

Nearly at the same time a prisoner, who had made his escape, brought in two letters from the Marquez d'Alorna, which Sir R. Wilson sent to me; and Senhor Sodré having perused them, and told me that they were only common letters to his wife and to one of his friends, I sent them to Madame da Silva to be delivered to her. Madame da Silva had more sense than Sodré, and discovered something in the letters which he had not perceived, and wrote me that she would not deliver them without hearing further from me. Upon which I wrote to her to beg to have the letters again, and I now enclose them to you with their translations.

Beresford wrote to me some time ago to desire to have these letters; at that time they were in Madame da Silva's hands, and you are the most proper person to determine what is to be done with them.

P.S. I have settled your money concerns as you wish, and only wait to hear from the Commissary Gen. to let you know how much you may now draw for. I send this by an English messenger, and I wish him to be detained at Lisbon ready to sail, till my dispatches shall arrive, when he must go home. I propose to send by him duplicates of my dispatches of the 8th, as I fear that Stanhope, not having arrived in England on the 26th, has been taken. Can the enclosed direction be the Bishop of Castello Branco?

To the Duke of Portland.   Badajoz, 12th Sept. 1809.

I am very much obliged to your Grace for your kind letter of the 22d Aug., and highly flattered by your good opinion.

His Majesty's most gracious acceptance of my services, and his notice of the troops under my command, have been most gratifying to me; and I hope that I shall not prove myself undeserving of the honor which he has manifested a disposition to confer upon me at your Grace's suggestion.*

To Visc. Castlereagh.   Badajoz, 12th Sept. 1809.

I am very much obliged to you for your kind letter of the 20th Aug., as well as for the mark of the King's approbation, which your friendship for me has induced you to suggest to your colleagues to recommend to the King to confer upon me. I can only promise to do my best to prove myself not undeserving of the King's favor and of the partiality of my friends. It has been most gratifying to me to read the proofs which you sent me, that the King's mind corresponded with the wishes of my friends upon this occasion ; and I have great hopes that he will not be dissatisfied with subsequent transactions in this country, although they are of a different nature from those of which he had marked his approbation in a manner so gracious towards me.

I am more than ever convinced that if I had not taken the steps I did, as detailed in my dispatches of the 8th and 21st Aug., I should have lost the army ; whereas it is now acquiring strength daily.

I send by this opportunity duplicates of the letters and dispatches sent on the 8th, as I fear that the *Britannia*, in which Stanhope went, who had charge of them, may have been taken, as he had not arrived in London on the 26th Aug.

We shall be glad to receive the 1st dragoons and the remount for the cavalry. I am besides endeavoring to purchase horses here. The regiments conceive that they have more horses at the recruiting quarters than are to be sent out to them. The 4th dragoons, in particular, which will only receive 45, have many more, as well as the 16th. I am also much obliged to you for the recruits.

I wish very much that some measures could be adopted to get some recruits for the 29th regt. It is the best regiment in this army, has an admirable internal system, and excellent non-commissioned officers ; but for the want of a second battalion, and somebody to attend to its recruiting, it is much reduced in numbers, by losses in the actions of Roliça and Vimeiro, in the expedition to the north of Portugal and at Talavera.

What shall I do with the horse transports now in the Tagus, and those coming ?

I am very much obliged to you for your kindness about Hill and other officers. Hill deserves every thing that can be done for him, and I should be glad to see him honored as he deserves.

* The Duke of Portland, K.G., First Lord of the Treasury, to Lieut. Gen. the Hon. Sir A. Wellesley, K.B.   London, 22d Aug. 1809.

To congratulate you on your victories would be so feebly to express my sense of your services, that I must indulge, in the first instance, the gratitude which I feel to be due to you, and request your acceptance of my best thanks for the credit as well as the service you have done to your country, which I trust will make all the impression which it ought to do on the minds of all descriptions of persons in the Kingdom.

Nothing could be more gracious than the King's acceptance of your services, or more immediate and decisive than his approbation of the suggestion of creating you a Viscount. Long may you enjoy that honor, and be placed for the advantage and honor of your country in those situations which may enable you to add to your own.

The A.G. to Brig. Gen. Fane. 12th Sept. 1809.

I am directed by the Commander of the Forces to request your attention to the inaccuracy with which the regiments in your brigade transmit their returns. Their last dates have been twice sent back, and the inaccuracies marked upon them, so that they may be especially corrected; but they have been returned without alteration or explanation. I have, therefore, to desire that, if the officer who makes out the returns does not see that both men and horses in the last returns are unaccounted for, he will proceed immediately to head quarters, that he may furnish, by personal communication, the necessary explanation. If, on the contrary, the omissions are perceived, may I beg you to give the officers commanding regiments and the Brigade Major a caution that these mistakes do not occur again, as it is inconceivable the trouble that it occasions in this department.

To the Duke of Richmond. Badajoz, 13th Sept. 1809.

I have received, and thank you for, your letter of the 18th Aug. I am glad that you were satisfied with our battle, and I hope that you will have been so with our subsequent operations. I find that my dispatch of the 8th Aug. did not get home, in which I gave an account of the causes and circumstances of our retreat across the Tagus, a copy of which, with its enclosures, I desired might be sent to you; but I have sent a duplicate of it this day, and a copy of it will go to you. Pray observe in Jourdan's letter to Soult the accurate knowledge the French had of all our movements. I have since heard that they had messages going between them and their spies in the Spanish army throughout the days of the 27th and 28th; but this I can scarcely credit. Soult says that we are covered with glory; but that if we had remained 2 days longer we must all have been prisoners; and I am afraid we must, or have been destroyed.

The army are recovering, and we shall be in high order again. The French have done nothing for the last month, and I believe meditate nothing, excepting possibly the siege of Ciudad Rodrigo, the success of which I shall prevent, if the Spaniards will hold out for a few days.

Lord Edward has been unwell for some time : he has been living with me, and is now much better. He has had the common dysentery, aggravated by a slight fit of the gout. The latter has gone, and the former is getting better every day.

The last accounts I had of Lord Chatham were of the 20th Aug. He had then, I think, gone the full length of his success. It was impossible to make any head on the continent against one army collecting in his front and another in his rear in Holland.

Pray, remember me kindly to the Duchess and Lady Edward, and all the children.

P.S. I send by this occasion a plan of the battle of Talavera, which is not very correct; but it will serve to give you a notion of it.

To Lieut. Col. Gordon, Military Secretary. Badajoz, 13th Sept. 1809.

Accounts have been received, to which I give full credit, although they are not of a nature on which I can found an official report, that Lieut. Col. Donellan, 48th regt., is dead.

I cannot avoid, upon this occasion, again drawing the attention of the Commander in Chief to the claims of Major Middlemore.* The 48th

* See note, p. 378.

regt. distinguished itself at the battle of Talavera, particularly when the command devolved upon Major Middlemore; and I hope that the claims of an officer senior to him, who is already a Brevet Lieut. Colonel, and to whom this commission can be no object, as he never joins his regiment, or does any duty with this army, will not be preferred to the substantial claims of Major Middlemore. I know nothing of Major Middlemore, excepting as a soldier on service; and I should not recommend him if I did not believe that his promotion would give general satisfaction, and that he really deserves it.

To the Junta of Estremadura.   Badajoz, 13th Sept. 1809.

I have had the honor of receiving your letter of the 12th inst., enclosing one addressed to me by the inhabitants of Puebla la Calzada, in which they desire that I should remove the troops which are quartered in that town.

In consequence of the desire expressed by the Central Junta to the British ambassador at Seville, I consented to allow the British army to remain within the Spanish frontier; and I distributed it in such a manner as that the country should not find it difficult to feed the troops, and that I should have it in my power to assemble the army without loss of time, in case the movements of the enemy should render that measure necessary. Accordingly, 3 battalions have been quartered at La Calzada, because there is no wood in the neighbourhood in which the troops would find shelter, excepting olive or other fruit trees which I wished not to destroy; but if there had been wood and water, I should have preferred to have hutted the troops in the wood, as I have done at Talavera Real and in this neighbourhood. It appears, however, that the inhabitants of La Calzada, although with the most patriotic sentiments, and with the utmost devotion to the cause of their country, complain of the inconvenience which they feel from having these troops quartered upon them. They enumerate the provisions with which the troops are supplied: but they have forgotten to state that they are regularly paid for every thing they give.

In answer to this complaint of inconvenience, I must observe, that the inhabitants of this country, and Spaniards in general, have formed a very erroneous estimate of the nature of the contest in which they are engaged, if they suppose that it can be carried on without inconvenience to every individual in the country. Not only it cannot be carried on without personal inconvenience, but unless every individual shall devote himself, his property, and every thing he can command, not in words and professions only, but in fact, to do what government shall order, there can be no success; and the best combined operations must fail.

Having made these observations, I must inform you, that I cannot easily alter the distribution which I have made of the troops; and either the town of La Calzada must continue to suffer the trifling personal inconvenience of having these troops within their town, or the Spanish nation and the province of Estremadura must suffer what the Central Junta will, I believe, consider a greater evil.

To the Rt. Hon. J. Villiers.   Badajoz, 13th Sept. 1809.

I beg that you will send off Mr. Shaw with the letters and dispatches sent down this night. Every thing appears so quiet that I may venture in a few days to go to Lisbon, where I want to look about me a little, and decide finally upon our plan of operations, in case Portugal should be invaded in the autumn or winter.

To Visc. Castlereagh.   Badajoz, 13th Sept. 1809.

Affairs have remained nearly in the same state in which they were when I addressed you on the 4th inst. The enemy has not moved, and the Spanish head quarters still continue at Truxillo. Gen. Venegas has, I understand, again moved forward into La Mancha, the enemy having retired towards Toledo.

The army under the command of the Marques de la Romana has moved from Galicia through Portugal, and is arrived in the neighbourhood of Ciudad Rodrigo, where it is to be under the command of the Duque del Parque; the Marques de la Romana being on his way to Seville, and expected here to-morrow.

I understand that this corps consists of about 13,000 men.

The A.G. to Major Aird, Royal Waggon Train.   13th Sept. 1809.

I have laid your letter of the 9th inst., together with its enclosures, before the Commander of the Forces. By a reference to the G. O. of the 5th Feb., of which I send a copy, you will perceive the two troops of the Irish Commissariat corps that came to this country with Sir A. Wellesley are incorporated in the Royal Waggon Train, and have increased that corps to 12 troops. With regard to the Irish Commissariat Train having their troops at a different establishment from the Royal Waggon Train, it can be of no consequence, as you are only to consider the establishment of the Royal Waggon Train as that which is to direct your corps.

With respect to the question of serjeants: if those men who have been attested as such cannot be reduced for misconduct, they may be dismissed, and their places filled by other men of the corps; however, there probably are few of these. It would nevertheless be advisable for you to refer to the head quarters of your own corps for precise instructions, if any difficulty of establishment should still exist.

To Lieut. Col. Roche.   Badajoz, 14th Sept. 1809.

I received this day your letter of the 11th. The French Major has not yet made his appearance.

Gen. Eguia's plan is rank nonsense. I send you the newspapers: you will see how Gen. Cuesta is abused for nothing.

G. O.   Badajoz, 14th Sept. 1809.

1. The orders of the 12th inst. respecting the plunder of beehives by the troops of the 4th division are countermanded; the plunderers having been discovered and ordered for trial.

2. The Commander of the Forces is always concerned when he is obliged to order any measure of severity towards the troops; he is concerned that the disorders of which frequent complaints are made are committed by a few; but unless the good soldiers, and the officers and non-commissioned officers in particular, exert themselves to prevent these outrages, and discover the perpetrators when they are known to them, the whole army must suffer in character, as well as the privations which are the invariable consequence of plunder by the troops.

3. The cavalry have been distributed in their present quarters principally with a view to their being fed with facility, and in order that the horses might recover their condition. In order to insure this object, it is desirable that they may not be used as orderlies to carry letters, and the Commander of the Forces prefers infinitely to pay for messengers to the use of the cavalry in this manner. If it should be necessary, however, at any time to send a dragoon with a letter, in consequence of the impossibility of procuring a messenger, the Commander of the Forces desires that his rate may be confined to the walk of his horse, unless in a case of very urgent necessity, which may require the early delivery of the letter.

To the Rt. Hon. J. Villiers.   Badajoz, 14th Sept. 1809.

I enclose some letters which I have received from Mr. Phillips, a gentleman who has lately imported wheat and barley to Lisbon, the latter of which has been bought from him by the Commissary Gen.; and the former, it appears, is wished for by the Portuguese government: but they and Mr. Phillips cannot agree upon the mode of payment. Why should not the bills in the hands of the Portuguese government be used for this purpose; Mr. Phillips taking them at par? or if the Portuguese government prefer it, I will order Mr. Murray to give Mr. Phillips bills for the wheat; but in this case the Portuguese government must give credit for these bills at the price of the day. In short, the wheat being wanted by the Portuguese government, settle with Mr. Phillips for the payment of it in any manner you please, and I will carry into execution any thing for which you may engage, and let Mr. Phillips go to England. I enclose a letter for him.

To Marshal Beresford.   Badajoz, 15th Sept. 1809.

I have the honor of acknowledging your letter of the 12th inst., relative to the mode of paying British officers attached to the Portuguese service, with Portuguese rank, in which you have enclosed a copy of your letter to me of the 12th July, a part of which related to the same subject. I transmitted that letter to the Commander in Chief in England, as soon as I received it, but have never received any decision on its contents, excepting that contained in his Excellency's letter to me of the 15th, in answer to mine of the 7th June, from Thomar, of both of which you have copies. It is desirable, however, indeed necessary, that the mode of paying the British officers in the Portuguese service should be fixed; and I would suggest the mode detailed in this letter to your consideration, and that of Mr. Villiers; and that, if you should approve of it, it should be immediately carried into execution.

In the mean time I shall make a report on the subject to the Sec. of State; and if His Majesty's government should not approve of the arrangement which has been made, it can be altered, and any other adopted which they may direct; and it can be applied with ease to the payments which may have been made, under the arrangement which I now propose for your consideration.

It appears that the principle on which His Majesty's government have proceeded, in the assistance which they have given to Portugal, is to consider the expense of each particular description of assistance in the light of a subsidy; and it has been accordingly settled, that those British officers serving with the Portuguese army, to whom British advanced rank has been granted, shall be paid by an officer employed under the directions of the Ambassador. The same principle must be applied to the payment of British officers serving with Portuguese rank. These officers have, generally, commissions in His Majesty's service, of which they are to receive the pay; they are also to receive the ordinary British field allowances of their rank; and they are to receive the Portuguese pay and allowances of their Portuguese commissions. Some of them, the brigadiers and major generals, are to receive the British staff pay and allowances of those ranks, besides their regimental pay.

I think it probable that His Majesty's government would not consider the regimental pay or the half pay of any of these officers in the light of subsidy. They are lent from the ordinary establishment of the army to the Portuguese service ; and, whether employed in this or any other manner, they must equally receive their pay. But that is a question which need not be decided at this moment. The government will not have an opportunity of considering it, and may settle whether this expense should be considered as subsidy, or should be charged against the several regiments to which these officers belong.

The field allowances to all ranks, and staff pay, must evidently be considered as subsidy, upon the principle which His Majesty's government have already settled in respect to British officers serving in Portugal holding advanced British rank. Whether the Portuguese pay to be given to these officers is to come from the British or Portuguese government is, in my opinion, a question of trivial importance, and will at all events be open for the decision of the King's government. Till they shall decide it, and if it should be decided that the British government are to defray this expense, it must be considered in the light of subsidy, in the same manner with the other heads of expense which I have before discussed.

The measures, then, which I have to recommend to your consideration, and that of Mr. Villiers, are ;

1st ; To appoint Mr. Bell to be the Paymaster of the British officers serving with the Portuguese troops with Portuguese rank.

2dly ; That they should be directed to draw from him the British regimental or half pay to which they may be respectively entitled, according to the forms, and supported by the vouchers, required by His Majesty's regulations : so that, if it should be ultimately decided that these payments should be made by the ordinary channels, Mr. Bell will experience no difficulty in recovering from the agents of the several regiments to which the officers belong, and from the Paymaster of the half pay, respectively, the sums which he may have advanced.

3dly ; That Mr. Bell should pay these officers the British field allowances of their respective ranks, according to the custom of the army, and the orders lately issued ; and all staff pay in the same manner as he now pays the officers attached to the Portuguese service holding advanced British rank. In these regiments, the officers will of course give in separate abstracts.

4thly ; That Mr. Bell should pay these officers their Portuguese pay of their respective rank, for which they must furnish him with the vouchers, &c., required by the Portuguese government, in order that no difficulty may be experienced in recovering this money from the Portuguese government, if it should be determined that they are to defray this expense.

5thly ; That Mr. Bell should be directed to keep an account of the payments made to each officer, under these several heads.

If you and Mr. Villiers should concur with me in what I have proposed for your consideration, you can give orders that it should be carried into immediate execution ; and I shall write upon the subject to the Sec. of State, in order to obtain the final decision of government upon all points of doubt.

To Marshal Beresford.   Badajoz, 15th Sept. 1809.

I enclose applications from an officer for leave to be aide de camp to a General officer in the Portuguese service. I do not know what you have determined upon this subject. It appears to me, however, that it is desirable that a British General officer in the Portuguese service should have the assistance of Portuguese staff officers. An English ensign can be of little use to him, or to any body else.

I hope that my official answer of this date will be satisfactory to you, respecting the payment of your officers. I have received your private letters of the 11th and 12th. I shall speak to Mr. Murray respecting the assistance to be given to you in Commissariat officers. I shall take an opportunity of looking at the Portuguese troops at Elvas, while I am in this part of the world.

I wish that you would speak to Villiers seriously about the augmentation of the pay of the officers in the Portuguese army. Time is going apace : in 3 months we may have to fight for Portugal; and Great Britain will be much disappointed if, notwithstanding the pains taken, and the expense incurred, the Portuguese army should do nothing. I think much depends upon this increase of pay. The King's ministers will say that we desired that the measure might be recommended to the Regency by our Ambassador, and it will not be known that no answer has ever been given upon a reference made upon this subject. Supposing, however, it should be known that this reference has been made, is it upon a point of such consequence in the case that a measure of vital importance at present should be any longer delayed for the answer to it? My opinion is, and always has been, not only that it is of no importance, but that upon principle the measure proposed by Villiers, viz., that the King's name should be used in the communication to be made to the Portuguese army, is wrong. If this be true, Villiers takes upon himself a serious responsibility in delaying any longer to make the recommendation to the Portuguese government; and although he does not mind responsibility in cases in which he can do good, he should consider that he takes it in this instance to delay a beneficial measure for an object of, at least, doubtful advantage. I wish that you would urge these topics with him, and beg him to let us have these points settled.

I want to save the forage between the Tagus and the Mondego for our probable future operations. Can't you get forage for your cavalry, and exercise ground about the south banks of the Tagus, at Aldea Galega, &c. ?

You should write to Mr. Canning about the clothing sent out to you.

The name of the French officer, respecting whom I wish you to inquire, is M. Véron de Farincourt, who was taken at Chaves by Silveira.

I am a little annoyed about the situation of Romana's troops. It is a great object with the French to destroy his corps; and I think it not improbable that they may make a dash at them. He will find no shelter in Ciudad Rodrigo, and he must consequently take to Portugal. How must he feed in that country? Where shall we find food for 40,000 or 50,000 men, that we shall have between the Tagus and the Mondego, if the French should make an attempt upon Ciudad Rodrigo? I have ordered magazines upon the Mondego and the Douro, but we must look a little after these cormorants of Romana, in case they should fly into Portugal.

You ought to send somebody to Almeida, or authorise Cox, in case he finds them flying into Portugal, to fix upon the stations to which they are to go; and let the magistrates have orders to obey Cox's directions to provide for their subsistence at those stations. As to payment for the same, I conclude that is out of the question.

P.S. Unless Romana's people cross the Douro immediately, or unless they have wings, they will not be able to pass over that river when followed by the French.

To Marquis Wellesley.   Badajoz, 15th Sept. 1809.

This letter will be delivered by the Marques de la Romana, whom I beg to introduce to you. You will find him more intelligent and reasonable upon Spanish affairs than most Spaniards; I have found him more so than any that I have seen. He is in some degree alarmed that the Junta should treat him ill, even arrest his person, on account of some conduct of his towards the Junta of Galicia and Asturias. I do not know the details of that conduct, but it cannot be intended to do much mischief, for you see that he has quitted the country and brought away his army, of which he has given up the command. You are, however, aware of the connexion which he has with the ministers and people in England; and on the whole I am convinced, that if you can prevent the Junta from laying violent hands upon him, at least till they shall have convicted him upon trial of evil intentions, you will do a good thing.

P.S. I don't take up my title till I receive the Gazette, or some notification of it which is authority.*

To M. le Capitaine Victor de Thévenon.   Ce 16 Septembre, 1809.

Vous croirez à peine que quoique j'aie une communication journalière

---

* The notification of Sir A. Wellesley's elevation to the Peerage was received on the 16th Sept.; dated 26th Aug. 1809, by the titles of Baron Douro of Wellesley, and Viscount Wellington of Talavera.

G. O.   Badajoz, 16th Sept. 1809.

1. The Commander of the Forces cannot avoid to take this opportunity of calling upon the field officers of the regiments in particular, and all the officers in general, to support and assist their Commanding officer in the maintenance of discipline, and in the preservation of order and regularity in their corps.

2. The officers of the army are much mistaken if they suppose that their duty is done when they have attended to the drill of their men, and to the parade duties of the regiment: the order and regularity of the troops in camp and quarters, the subsistence and comfort of the soldiers, the general subordination and obedience of the corps, afford constant subjects for the attention of the field officers in particular, in which, by their conduct in the assistance they will give their Commanding officer, they can manifest their zeal for the service, their ability and their fitness for promotion to the higher ranks, at least equally as by an attention to the drill and parade discipline of the corps.

3. The Commander of the Forces desires that the principle of the order of the 29th May, given out at Coimbra, which requires that officers should be quartered near the companies, may be applied to the encampments, that the tents of the officers may be placed near those of the men under their command, and that the situations of the field officers may be pitched upon by the quarter master of the battalion.

4. The Commander of the Forces desires that all officers and soldiers of the army will understand, that the Spanish and Portuguese soldiers are entrusted with the performance of duties when sentry, equally with British soldiers in the same situation; and that any resistance to a Spanish or Portuguese sentry, and particularly any violence committed upon him, upon any assumed superiority of character, by any British officer or soldier, will be punished as such a breach of military discipline shall deserve.

avec le Quartier Général de l'armée Espagnole, je n'ai su qu'aujourd'hui que vous y attendez la réponse de la lettre que vous m'avez apportée de la part du Commandant en Chef de l'armée Française.

Je vous en fais mes excuses, et je vous prie de retourner à M. le Maréchal Duc de Dalmatie, et de lui dire, avec mes complimens, que je suis bien fâché de ne pouvoir, quant à présent, lui donner réponse sur le Général Franceschi, qui est à Seville, parceque je n'ai pas reçu de réponse à la lettre que j'y ai écrite sur son compte, mais que j'aurai l'honneur de lui écrire aussitôt que je recevrai la réponse.

Je n'ai pas reçu non plus la réponse que j'attendais à la lettre que j'ai écrite à Lisbonne sur M. Véron de Farincourt; mais je vous enverrai de ses nouvelles si je peux en avoir. Je vous prie encore d'excuser la peine que je vous ai donnée en vous faisant attendre si long-temps, et de croire que vraiment je ne savais pas que vous étiez au Quartier Général Espagnol; et je comptais renvoyer ma réponse par un officier Anglais.

To Lieut. Gen. Sir J. Sherbrooke, K.B.   Badajoz, 16th Sept. 1809.

Upon considering the charge against Ensign —— of the ——, which is founded solely upon his having crossed the bridge at Merida; and the second charge, which is founded solely upon his writing the enclosed letters, I think them so frivolous, that I shall be very much obliged to you if you will call before you Gen. ——, the Commanding officer of the regiment, and Ensign ——, and inform them that I consider the first charge as frivolous, and the second as groundless; and therefore, that I have ordered Ensign —— to be released from his arrest. At the same time, I beg you to point out to Ensign —— that I will not allow him to disobey any order of his Commanding officer, however trifling; and that the next time he errs, he shall certainly be brought to trial.

P.S. I understand that 8000 rations of biscuit are gone to you this day.

To Vice Adm. the Hon. G. Berkeley.   Badajoz, 16th Sept. 1809.

I have had the honor of receiving your letter of the 11th inst., and I have desired Mr. Murray to send an agent to Tangier by the route pointed out by you.

I am concerned that so much difficulty is experienced in landing the mules at the mouth of the Guadiana; but if that difficulty should be found to be of a nature to prevent their being landed there, I would request that they might be brought to Lisbon, rather than be landed in any part of the Spanish territories, from the knowledge I have of the impossibility of procuring in Spain any means of taking care of the mules, or of bringing them to join the army.

To the Rt. Hon. J. Villiers.   Badajoz, 16th Sept. 1809.

I enclose a correspondence which has passed between one of the officers of the Commissariat and Gen. Leite, respecting some biscuit which was left by the British troops at Elvas last year, and is now in Fort La Lippe. The most convenient way of settling for supplies received by the British troops would be to pay for them in money; and if stores are to be transferred by the British Commissariat to the Portuguese government, they should be settled for as proposed by my Commissariat arrangement, approved by you and Beresford.

I shall be very much obliged to you if you will inquire whether the account between the Junta de Viveres and our Commissariat has really been settled in the manner stated by Gen. Leite ; and if it has, whether it has been done by order of government; whether any balance is due by us on the account, and, in short, how the account stands. If it has not, it would be desirable that, by way of example, this small store of biscuit should be given over to us ; and we ought to settle the account immediately, and pay the balance.

The sum of money received in the last month of August for bills, and in all modes, amounts to £158,000, of which sum the fifth, or about £32,000, are at your disposal, at the Commissary General's office. Of this sum you have already, I understand, received a part. This sum of £158,000 is exclusive of the money arrived in the *Fylla*, amounting to £150,000 and more, the silver belonging, I understand, exclusively to the Portuguese government.

P.S. This is the first time I have signed my new name. Would the Regency give me leave to have a *chasse* at Villa Viçosa?

To Marquis Wellesley.   Badajoz, 16th Sept. 1809.

I enclose an extract of a letter which I received yesterday from Col. Roche, from the Spanish head quarters at Truxillo; and I beg to draw your Excellency's attention to the cause stated for the movement of the troops, viz. *the want of provisions;* notwithstanding that I was urged 3 weeks ago to remain with the British army, even in front of Truxillo and was informed that there were provisions in sufficient quantities for both armies.

I likewise enclose a letter which I have this day received from Lieut. Gen. Sherbrooke, from Talavera Real, being the report made to him yesterday by the Commissary attached to his division of infantry. As long as the Spanish armies are suffered to continue in the state of indiscipline and disorder in which they are at present, it will be impossible to continue in their neighbourhood; as they not only consume the provisions of the country, but will not allow the villagers to supply to the British troops those provisions which they require, and which the Spanish troops do not want.

I have communicated the enclosed letter to the Junta of Badajoz, and have requested them to adopt measures to supply Gen. Sherbrooke's division from hence; and I beg your Excellency to inform the Spanish government that if, in consequence of this new disposition, or the irregularities of the Spanish troops, and the failure of supplies from this town, I shall be obliged to move Gen. Sherbrooke's division of infantry into Portugal, I shall likewise move the whole army within the Portuguese frontier, as I cannot, with propriety, separate the different parts of it so much as they would be separated by leaving a part in Spain.

To Marquis Wellesley.   Badajoz, 16th Sept. 1809.

I enclose some Madrid newspapers, which I received from Col. Roche, solely because he has desired I should send them, and not because I think they contain any thing interesting, excepting that they afforded ground for belief that the armistice was not broken off, but rather was renewed: nor was peace signed at a late period in the month of August.

A packet has arrived at Lisbon, bringing accounts that the troops are returning from the Scheldt, without attacking Antwerp or the fleet, but retaining possession of Walcheren.

To the Junta of Estremadura.   Badajoz, 17th Sept. 1809.

I have had the honor of receiving your letter of the 16th inst., respecting the means of supplying the British army with bread; and I have requested the bearer of this letter, Mr. Murray, the Commissary Gen., to wait upon you to settle the quantities of flour which shall be furnished from the British magazines at Abrantes, the price which shall be paid for it, and the mode of paying the expense of its transport from Abrantes to Badajoz. Mr. Murray will then give you the orders on the storekeeper at Abrantes for the quantities of flour which it will be settled that you should have.

To Marshal Beresford.   Badajoz, 17th Sept. 1809.

I have had the honor of receiving your letters of the 13th inst., respecting the losses of horses and baggage by British officers employed in the service of H. R. H. the Prince Regent of Portugal; and I beg to propose for your consideration, and that of Mr. Villiers, that the claims for losses by these individuals should be decided upon according to the mode pointed out in His Majesty's regulations, under your directions; and that those claims reported to be well founded should be discharged by Mr. Bell, and the accounts for the disbursements on this account be made in the same manner as is pointed out in my letter of the 15th inst. for the field allowances of the same description of persons.

To Marshal Beresford.   Badajoz, 17th Sept. 1809.

I think that you will be satisfied with my decision respecting the claims of your officers for losses. I return your letter respecting the vacancies, to which I think you will do well to add a recommendation of the successors to each. This recommendation will not interfere with the grant of the request; at the same time that if it is granted, you will enjoy the benefit of it some months sooner than you would otherwise.

I thought I had written to you some time ago about Capt. ———; at all events, I stated in a late letter my opinion of the small degree of service which an English aide de camp would have it in his power to render to a General officer employed with the Portuguese army.

In respect to bât and forage to officers who have not had the Com-

G. O.   Badajoz, 17th Sept. 1809.
3. Officers who require quarters at any of the stations of the army, or at head quarters, are to apply to the officer of the Q. M. G.'s department at such stations, or to Capt. Kelly, at head quarters, for billets, and are not on any account to apply themselves to the magistrates. Capt. Kelly at head quarters, and the officers of the Q. M. G.'s department at the other stations of the army, will keep a register of the names of the officers for whom they procure billets, stating the name of the owner of the house on whom the billet is procured, so that it may always be known what officers have been quartered in each house.

mander in Chief's leave to serve with the Portuguese army, the rule which I have laid down, and which is applicable to all extra aides de camp and staff without pay serving with this army, is, that officers who have not had the Commander in Chief's permission to join the army are not to have the bât and forage of the rank or situation in which they may be serving. If this rule should be applied to Col. Grant and Sir M. Gerrard, it would decide against their claims. However, I do not see why it should.

It is an object to government, and to the Commander in Chief, to persuade officers to serve in the Portuguese army; and, besides, as I am authorised to allow officers to serve with it, I conceive I may as well allow one on half pay as one on full pay. If I allow one to serve with the Portuguese army, with which it is an object to government that he should serve, I may venture to relax a rule which I have made myself with regard to officers serving with this army without the leave of the Commander in Chief. I think, therefore, you may give Col. Grant and Sir M. Gerrard their bât and forage allowance.

To the Rt. Hon. J. Villiers.   Badajoz, 17th Sept. 1809.

I enclose an application which has been made to me by Dr. Franck, Inspector of Hospitals, for additional accommodation for the sick at Lisbon, for which I request you to apply to the government. I understand that the Convent of S. Benito can be given to us without inconvenience, being occupied by a very small detachment of Portuguese troops. If the government should consent to give this accommodation, I shall be obliged to you if you will announce it to Col. Peacocke.

To Marquis Wellesley.   Badajoz, 17th Sept. 1809.

I have the honor to enclose the extract of a letter which I have received from Col. Roche, giving an account of the state of the Spanish army, which I am sorry to say is, I believe, too well founded. In justice to Col. Roche I must add, that before I joined Gen. Cuesta's army, he wrote to me an account of its state, to which I was not inclined and did not pay any attention at that time, but which I afterwards found to be a true account in every respect.

I beg to draw your Excellency's attention to the exposed situation of this province and Andalusia, and even of Seville itself, if the want of provisions or any operation should oblige me to quit my present position. A corps, consisting nominally of 10,000 men, are very unequal to the defence of the Guadiana, or of the positions in the Sierra Morena; yet that is all that these valuable interests will have to depend upon.

The A.G. to Lieut. Col. Fenwick, 34th regt.   17th Sept. 1809.

I have the honor to acquaint you, that his Excellency the Commander of the Forces has been pleased to appoint you to relieve Lieut. Col. Mackinnon, of the Coldstream Guards, in charge of the general hospital at Elvas. You will, therefore, proceed to that place, and receive from Lieut. Col. Mackinnon such instructions, &c., as may have been sent to him from time to time.

The A.G. to Lieut. Col. Walsh, Lisbon.   18th Sept. 1809.

I have to request you will furnish the brigade under the orders of Lieut. Col.

Pakenham, now at Abrantes, with copies of all such orders of general regulation as will be necessary for their guidance, and that a copy of the G.O. may be, in future, regularly forwarded to them from your office.

To Marquis Wellesley.   Badajoz, 19th Sept. 1809.

Campbell has shown me the paper which Armstrong has sent him, containing the information of the numbers of the French army, which had been communicated to you by the Frenchman sent to Seville by Col. Roche, tending, I rather think, to prove that this person cannot be depended upon.

The estimate which I made of the French force in Spain included only effectives; if the sick and wounded are included it would amount to 30,000 or 40,000 more. In order to explain this point to you, I enclose an abstract of the return of Marshal Victor's army for the month of May, of which you will see that the effectives were 29,321, and the sick 10,024, or rather more than one third; and rather less than one fourth of the total, which was 44,958. These proportions being taken for the whole, would give between 30,000 and 40,000 sick for the whole French army : and I must observe, that there must have been more than 12,000 sick in the hospital at Madrid, after the battle of Talavera, which certainly added 8,000 wounded to the number. Viewing the state of the French army in another light, I think I shall show the accuracy of my own estimate, and the probability that the sick amount to between 30,000 and 40,000 in addition.

When the French army entered Spain, it consisted of 8 corps, each of which consists generally of between 30,000 and 40,000 men. Victor's, we see, was in May 45,000; and Soult's and Ney's were each, I know, between 32,000 and 35,000 men. Supposing the 8 corps upon an average to have been 25,000, the total numbers would be 200,000; and, I believe, 220,000 is the number Buonaparte is supposed to have had in Spain last year. Of these he withdrew his Guards, but I believe nothing else. If this be true, let us see where the French have since lost any men. They lost some at Coruña, some in Portugal, and, accordingly, we find Ney's corps about 14,000 or 16,000 men, and Soult's about 8,000 or 10,000. They lost some at Zaragoza; some in different battles fought on their entrance into Spain, a few at Medellin and in La Mancha. But there has been no great catastrophe to carry off thousands; and it is going a great way to admit that they have lost, in killed, prisoners, and deserters, 50,000 men since they entered Spain last year. But admitting that they have lost between 40,000 and 50,000 men, there would still remain between 150,000 and 160,000 to be accounted for; and I should say that they have 125,000 effective, and between 30,000 and 40,000 sick and wounded, throughout Spain.

I hear that Soult is collecting his corps at Plasencia, but I attribute this movement to the arrival of the Marques de la Romana's troops at Ciudad Rodrigo, and their subsequent movements towards Perales and Baños. I do not find that the French are making any preparations for the siege of Ciudad Rodrigo, and I cannot conceive what they are about. I am apprehensive, however, that the movement of the troops from this province into

G. O.   Badajoz, 19th Sept. 1809.
    4. The Commander of the Forces cannot avoid to take this opportunity of drawing the attention of the army to the unworthy conduct of these soldiers, who have plundered the stores on their way to the army, for the use of their comrades, over which they were placed as a guard.

La Mancha will be fatal, if any circumstances shall occur to oblige me to move from hence.

P.S. I am very anxious to have an answer respecting the exchange of Gen. Franceschi.

The A.G. to ———, Assist. Commissary Gen.   19th Sept. 1809.

I am directed by the Commander of the Forces to inform you, that his Excellency has perused your correspondence on the subject of a mare belonging to the 3d dragoon guards lately in your possession. His Excellency is surprised, in the first place, that you should assert that the mare was ever in the possession of the enemy, the assertion being entirely without proof or foundation of any description : 2dly ; that you should have thought that you had any right to keep and use (even for a moment) a horse belonging to a regiment of dragoons, when it was claimed by that regiment and by Lieut. Gen. Payne : and, 3dly ; his Excellency expresses equal astonishment that you should have denominated the conduct of Lieut. Gen. Payne (in demanding the mare) indelicate, as if there was to be any delicacy in demanding the King's property, which has been so long withheld after repeated applications.

His Excellency directs me to say that he is happy to find that the mare was returned upon his intimation of his opinion that it ought to be ; but he cannot avoid to express what occurs to him upon the perusal of the papers upon the subject.

The A.G. to Col. Peacocke, Lisbon.   19th Sept. 1809.

I have it in command from his Excellency the Commander of the Forces to acquaint you, that his notice has been drawn to an order given out by you, in which Lieut. Col. Walsh has been suspended from the execution of the duties of his office of Town Major. His Excellency desires you will be pleased to observe that Lieut. Col. Walsh was appointed to do the duties of Town Major and of Inspector of Convalescents by Lieut. Gen. Sir J. Cradock, and has been continued in the performance of them by him ; and that he conceives Sir J. Cradock agreed with him in not considering the two duties as incompatible with each other. The Commander of the Forces is very certain that if the duties are incompatible, Lieut. Col. Walsh ought to have the choice which of the offices he would retain ; and should he retain that of Town Major, his Excellency does not know who could replace him in charge of the detachments. His Excellency further directs me to add that he cannot avoid observing the frequent disputes about nothing in which Col. Walsh and yourself are involved, and which never occurred when Brig. Gen. Blunt commanded in Lisbon : he cannot, therefore, attribute them to Lieut. Col. Walsh ; and as they take up much of the public time and attention upon matters which the Commander of the Forces considers of trifling importance, he, therefore, cannot but desire that they may be discontinued, and that, at all events, the garrison order of the 14th Sept. 1809, may be countermanded.

To Col. Peacocke.   Badajoz, 20th Sept. 1809.

I have this morning received your letter of the 15th, and having yesterday communicated to you, through the Adj. Gen., my opinion respecting Lieut. Col. Walsh's situation, I might now save you the trouble of the perusal of a second letter upon the same subject ; only that it appears to me that you have entirely mistaken the nature of Lieut. Col. Walsh's appointment and employment, as commanding the detachments and convalescents at and in the neighbourhood of Lisbon. There would be no reason for having at that place an officer in his situation, if there was not an infinite detail in drawing the pay, and the payment, and in keeping the accounts of the men of not less than 50 regiments, of which those detachments are composed.

Lieut. Col. Walsh was appointed to do this duty principally; and although it was and is intended that he should likewise superintend the conduct and the discipline of these men personally, the performance of that part of the duty by him is not so necessary as the accurate performance of that first mentioned; more particularly as there are other officers of the rank of Field officer at Lisbon and Belem in a state of convalescence, each of whom is obliged to assist in the performance of this duty. I consider that Lieut. Col. Walsh, in his line, has rendered very essential services to the army; and I am so little disposed to allow him to be removed from either of his offices, of which he has, till you took the command, done the duty in a satisfactory manner, that if these complaints should continue, I shall be under the necessity of making an entirely new arrangement at Lisbon, however disagreeable it may be to me.*

The regulations do not allow you a brigade major, or an aide de camp, and I regret that I cannot allow you either. You have the assistance of a Town major and a Town adjutant, which must be deemed sufficient.

To the Rt. Hon. J. Villiers.   Badajoz, 20th Sept. 1809.

You will have found that I had ordered your proportion of the money received in the month of August to be issued to you as soon as I learned its amount. From your letter, however, I fear that the sum which will have been received by Mr. Bell will not have proved sufficient for your wants at the present moment; and if this should be the case, as we have now more money than we immediately want, you shall have as much more as you please, after I shall hear from you.

I cannot yet fix the day for my departure for Lisbon; first, because I do not think the enemy's movements sufficiently decided to enable me to say that I can go with safety; and, secondly, because I have not been well for above a month, and have still hanging upon me a low fever which I cannot shake off. Soult has, however, collected his corps at Plasencia, most probably because Romana's army has come to Ciudad Rodrigo, and has spread into the mountains of Perales and Gata, and even, it is said, of Baños; and it is probable that in a day or two he must make a decided movement one way or the other. As soon as I shall ascertain what that is, if it does not require our interference, I shall set out, and I think it probable that the journey may do me good.

The Portuguese head quarters must accommodate matters a little. I am willing to give every thing to the Portuguese army that our stores and means can afford; but it must be done in the way of subsidy to the Portuguese government, according to the mode which I have repeatedly pointed out. Half the business of the world, particularly that of our country, is done by accommodation, and by the parties understanding each other; but when rights are claimed, they must be resisted, if there are no grounds for them: when appeal must be made to higher powers there can be no accommodation; and much valuable time is lost in reference which ought to be spent in action. I have never refused any thing that has been

* See letter to Dom M. Forjaz, 16th Aug. 1813, expressing the favorable opinion of Major Gen. (now Gen. Sir Warren) Peacocke's conduct, in the discharge of the duties of his command at Lisbon.

asked for the Portuguese government which our stores could afford; I have invariably given my time and attention to frame the modes in which all assistance could be given, and all difficulties occasioned by the orders under which we act could be overcome; but when, instead of adopting these modes, what is wanted is claimed as a right, I must resist every claim of that description, not founded upon the King's regulations; or, if they are persisted in, I must appeal to England.

I shall write to Madame da Silva to remove any uneasiness she may feel about the letters : she is either decidedly honest, or she is a terrible rogue.

To Brig. Gen. the Hon. G. Anson. Badajoz, 21st Sept. 1809.

I have perused the proceedings of the General Court Martial of which you are President, on the trial of ——, Paymaster of the —— regt., which I am desirous that the Court should revise, as it appears, to me that one very material point for their inquiry has not been investigated. It appears that Mr. —— thought proper, for the security of his money, to move from Talavera on the evening of the 3d Aug., with the sick and wounded, and that he considered it dangerous to endeavor to join the army and his regiment, which was at Oropesa, 2 leagues distant from Arzobispo, and that he knew the army was there. The point into which I conceive the General Court Martial ought to inquire is, whether Mr. —— did really remain with the hospital. Did he put himself under the directions of Col. Mackinnon? Did he ever ask information from him or from the superior officers of the army with the hospital respecting the position of his regiment?

This inquiry will make it appear to the Court that, on the 5th Aug., the hospital was within 2 miles of the —— regt., and that on the 7th Aug. it was with the head quarters at Deleytosa. The inquiring into these points may probably induce the Court to alter their sentence; but if it should not, I beg leave to suggest to them to revise it so far as to omit the word 'privately,' preceding the word 'reprimanded;' as I conceive that a private reprimand is so difficult to define or to execute, that the commanding

G. O. Badajoz, 21st Sept. 1809.

1. When regimental hospitals are to be established in any division of the army, they must be formed in the manner pointed out in His Majesty's regulations ; and the soldiers who go into regimental hospitals must be under a stoppage of 9*d.* *per diem,* which must be paid to the regimental surgeon, or other person in charge of the hospital, and accounted for in conformity with those regulations.

2. This stoppage is intended to enable the surgeon to subsist the soldier in regimental hospital, as well as to provide him with those comforts which his situation will require ; but as it may happen that the divisions may be placed in situations in which there is no market, and the surgeons of regiments would find it impracticable to purchase food for the soldiers in hospital, General officers commanding divisions are in such case requested to order the commissaries attached to their divisions to supply the regimental surgeons with such proportion of a ration for each man in hospital as they may think proper, for which regimental surgeons will make a daily requisition on the commissary ; and the regimental surgeons are to pay for each of these rations such proportion of 6*d.* as that they will receive will bear to the whole ration of the soldier.

3. These sums are to be paid to the commissary, and the account closed by the regimental surgeons, on the 25th of every month, for all that he will have received from the 25th of the preceding month, to the 24th of the current month.

4. The soldiers are to pay 6*s.* for each pair of shoes received from the Commissary Gen., and 6*s.* 7*d.* for each shirt. The Commissary Gen. will make known to the Paymaster Gen. as soon as possible, what number of each have been delivered to each regiment, in order that the price may be stopped from the regiment, and the soldiers may pay for them in the muster ending on the 24th inst.

officer, charged with the execution of the sentence, will require instructions upon the subject. I have also to observe that privacy is inconsistent with every just notion of punishment.

To Vice Adm. the Hon. G. Berkeley.   Badajoz, 21st Sept. 1809.

I have the honor to acquaint you that Lieut. Col. Bathurst, the Mil. Sec., has received an application from Capt. Collins of the Royal Marines, claiming the allowance of bât and forage, as a field officer, for himself, and that of Captain for the adjutant.

I beg leave to remark, that in consequence of the late regulations respecting the bât and forage allowance, these claims are totally inadmissible; but if you should consider Capt. Collins as having been appointed Commandant of a battalion of seamen and marines, during the time he served on shore, he might be entitled as such to 2 additional rations of forage; and if Mr. Paxton was considered as adjutant, he might be entitled to £5 baggage money instead of £3. 15s., which he received as a subaltern; but he could not draw in both situations. If you should be of opinion that they are entitled to these additional allowances, the warrant can be sent back to head quarters and altered.

To Marquis Wellesley.   Badajoz, 21st Sept. 1809.

I received this morning your letter of the 19th, and your dispatches, Nos. 4 and 5, and I sent forward the messenger with them to Lisbon.

I do not know whether it is worth while to make the misrepresentation, by the Marques de Malespina, of what passed between him and me, the subject of a dispatch, of which you will judge from what follows.

Malespina came to me with Lord Macduff, who has taken the Spanish cause under his protection, and they produced a letter from Gen. Eguia, quoting one from Don A. de Cornel, stating that the British Ambassador had settled that a defensive position should be taken up on the Guadiana; and they desired me to arrange the positions to be occupied by the troops in concert with them. I answered, that I could not enter upon such an arrangement, as I did not conceive that the position was a good one. Lord Macduff then said, ' What! will you not carry into execution an arrangement settled by the British Ambassador?' To which I answered, that the arrangement, as stated in Don A. de Cornel's letter, was not that suggested by the British Ambassador, of whose note I had a copy in my possession; that he had suggested that certain positions should be occupied on the Guadiana, by the two armies, if I consented to remain in Spain, and provided that certain arrangements were adopted to supply the troops with provisions, means of transport, &c.; that I did not think I could remain in Spain; and that the conditions regarding provisions and means of transport had not been fulfilled; and therefore that the proposal, in respect to the position, must be considered as never having been made; and I recommended Gen. Eguia to keep his army in its position on the Tagus as long as he could, but, at all events, until he should receive further orders.

Although the Duque de Alburquerque is *proné* by many, among others by Whittingham and Frere, and is feared by the Junta, you will find him out. I think the Marques de la Romana the best I have seen of the

Spaniards. I doubt his talents at the head of an army; but he is certainly a sensible man, and has seen much of the world.

To Visc. Castlereagh.   Badajoz, 21st Sept. 1809.

Since I addressed you on the 13th inst., Marshal Soult has collected his corps at Plasencia; but I have not heard that the enemy have made any movements in any other quarters. I conclude, therefore, that this assembly of Soult's corps is to be attributed to the arrival of that lately under the command of the Marques de la Romana in the neighbourhood of Ciudad Rodrigo; and to the subsequent movements which I understand it has made into the mountains of Perales and Gata, and even as far as Baños.

Gen. Eguia's head quarters have been moved from Truxillo to La Serena; and I understand that the whole of the Spanish army, which has hitherto been in Estremadura, with the exception of 10,000 men, are to march to La Carolina. The 10,000 men are to remain in Estremadura under the command of the Duque de Alburquerque. I am apprehensive that this disposition of the Spanish forces may be attended by bad consequences, if the British army should be obliged to quit its present position.

To Visc. Castlereagh.   Badajoz, 21st Sept. 1809.

I have nothing to add to my public letter of this date.

The 1st dragoons, nearly the whole of the remount for the cavalry, and the recruits for the infantry, are arrived at Lisbon.

I have ordered the battalions of detachments to Lisbon, having taken from them the men belonging to the regiments of which we have one battalion in this country, and I shall send the remainder to England.

To the Junta of Estremadura.   Badajoz, 22d Sept. 1809.

I am concerned to have to state to you that the supplies of bread for the British army, although much separated for the convenience of the country in furnishing it with subsistence, are very scanty and by no means regular. I conclude from these circumstances that the people of this part of Estremadura are either unable or unwilling to supply what is required for the troops under my command, notwithstanding that they are paid regularly, and in ready money, for every thing they furnish; but, from report, I am induced to apprehend that the failure on their part proceeds from want of inclination. Still, whatever may be the cause of deficiency, I now inform you that I propose to withdraw the army from Spain entirely, on the first day there may be any failure or deficiency in the supplies of provisions to the troops.

G. O.   Badajoz, 22d Sept. 1809.

3. The Commander of the Forces cannot avoid to express his regret upon losing the services of the two battalions of detachments, which are about to join their corps in England. He will not flatter them by saying that he has not had, upon several occasions, reasons to be dissatisfied with their conduct, in their quarters, their camps, and on their marches; but they have uniformly sustained, in an exemplary manner, the character of the regiments to which they belong, and of British soldiers, in the field against the enemy; and he trusts that the few, of whose conduct he cannot but complain, even upon this occasion, will discontinue and forget their bad practices and habits, upon their return to their regiments; and that they will endeavor to become an example of orderly and regular conduct in their quarters, as they must ever be of gallantry and discipline in the field.

To Marquis Wellesley.   Badajoz, 22d Sept. 1809.

I have received intelligence from Almeida of the 18th, and from Castello Branco of the 21st, which gives me reason to apprehend that the Duque del Parque has risked an action with the enemy's forces collected at Salamanca, of the result of which there can be no doubt.

I do not think it follows that the enemy will undertake the siege of Ciudad Rodrigo because he has been successful in this action, unless he knew of the march of the Marques de la Romana's corps, and its destination for that quarter, and has waited to commence his operations upon Ciudad Rodrigo till he shall have defeated and dispersed it. This has long been a favorite object of the enemy, which I am afraid he has at last been enabled to accomplish, by that fatal imprudence and presumption which induce Spanish officers to push forward their troops in situations in which they must be attacked; and by the national pride which prevents them from making a timely retreat, when threatened by an attack from an enemy superior in numbers, as well as in every military quality. I should certainly move immediately, if my movement was not likely to expose the city of Seville to imminent danger, under existing arrangements. Therefore, although I am still determined to make an exertion to save Ciudad Rodrigo, I propose to delay my march till I shall be certain that the enemy intends to make an attack upon that place. As far as I can learn, it does not appear that he is equipped for such an enterprise.

I have the honor to enclose to your Excellency copies of two letters which I have written, the first lately, and the last this day, to the Junta of Estremadura, from which you will observe that want may again oblige me to change my position. I propose, however, to remain upon this frontier of Portugal as long as it shall be in my power.

I have given the Junta of Estremadura orders on the British magazines in Portugal, for a quantity of flour, very nearly equal to what the British army has consumed in this part of the province, and have agreed to pay for the carriage of it; and yet the people are unable or unwilling to continue to furnish the necessary supplies to the troops.

To Marquis Wellesley.   Badajoz, 22d Sept. 1809.

I am very uneasy respecting that part of your note to Don M. de Garay, and of your dispatch, No. 5, which recommended the assembly of the Cortes; not that I do not think the line which you have taken upon this question will give great satisfaction in England, but because I fear that the Cortes may be worse than any thing we have had yet.

I acknowledge that I have a great dislike to a new popular assembly. Even our own ancient one would be quite unmanageable, and, in these days, would ruin us, if the present generation had not before its eyes the example of the French revolution; and if there were not certain rules and orders for its guidance and government, the knowledge and use of which render safe, and successfully direct its proceedings. But how will all this work in the Cortes, in the state in which Spain now is? I declare that if I were in Buonaparte's situation, I should leave the English and the Cortes to settle Spain in the best manner they could; and I should entertain very little doubt but that, in a very short space of time, Spain must fall into the hands of France.

At the same time I must agree with you in thinking that affairs are now in so desperate a situation that they cannot be worse; that there is a real want of men of common capacity in Spain, in whose hands any form of government, intended for vigorous action, could be placed with any hope that their powers could be used to the public advantage; and that the Cortes, with all their faults, and the dangers attendant upon such an assembly, will have at least this advantage, that they will have the confidence of the country, and the prejudices of their countrymen of the lower class in our favor, and against France; your remark being perfectly well founded, that there is no prejudice or jealousy of us anywhere in Spain excepting by the government. But, in order to enjoy common safety under such an assembly as the Spanish Cortes, the rules and orders for their proceedings and internal government ought to be well defined, and to be, if possible, a part of the constitution of the assembly. Great care should also be taken in their formation, to protect them from the effects of popular fury in the place of their sitting; but still, with all these precautions, I should prefer a wise Bourbon, if we could find one, for a Regent, to the Cortes.

I wish you would add to your note of the 8th Sept. advice that the Junta, appointed to consider of calling the Cortes, should suggest rules for their proceedings, and to secure the freedom of their deliberations; as, in case of accidents, it will show that the rock upon which such a machine was likely to split was not unforeseen.

To W. Huskisson, Esq., Secretary to the Treasury.   Badajoz, 22d Sept. 1809.

The recent promotion of Mr. Rawlings to be a Dep. Commissary has occasioned the enclosed application from Acting Dep. Commissary Boyes, whose services I am induced to rate very highly. In the campaign of 1808, in Portugal, as well as on the march of the troops into Spain last autumn, and in the operations in the north of Portugal in the spring of this year, and in the late service in Spain, the exertions of Mr. Boyes have been conspicuous, and I cannot but consider him most deserving of the promotion he solicits. I have also to recommend to their Lordships that Assist. Commissary Aylmer and Assist. Commissary Gauntlett should be promoted to be Acting Dep. Commissaries, as being those of the Assist. Commissaries who have shown most ability and activity, and have given most satisfaction.

I observe that their Lordships have lately promoted Acting Assist. Commissary Coffin to be an Assist. Commissary, who, I have no. doubt, will prove himself worthy of their Lordships' favor; but he has hitherto been employed with the Commissary Gen., and has never done any duty with the army. I therefore beg leave to recommend to their Lordships' favor, to be made Assist. Commissaries, Acting Assist. Commissary Haynes, Acting Assist. Commissary Downie, and Acting Assist. Commissary Wemyss. The first and last mentioned have performed their duty in a most satisfactory manner, and Mr. Downie has been employed on duties which belong to a Dep. Commissary rather than to an Acting Assistant.

To Visc. Castlereagh.   Badajoz, 23d Sept. 1809.

I enclose an estimate of the expenses in Portugal for the months of September, October, and November; and of our probable means, from which you will see that our finance is in a more flourishing state than it was some months ago. A copy of this paper will go to the Treasury.*

I also enclose a paper,† marked No. 1, which I have extracted from the

---

* Estimate of the probable demands on the Military chest in Spain and Portugal, from the 25th Aug. to the 24th Nov. 1809, inclusive.

	£.	s.	d.
SERVICE:			
Ordinaries	118,000	0	0
Ordnance	18,150	0	0
Portuguese subsidy	150,000	0	0

EXTRAORDINARIES:	£.	s.	d.			
Arrears of debt	50,000	0	0			
Provisions	175,000	0	0			
Forage	55,000	0	0			
Transport	26,000	0	0			
Purchase of horses and mules	10,000	0	0			
General hospital	3,000	0	0			
Forage money	30,000	0	0			
Staff and Commissariat pay and salaries	12,900	0	0			
Contingencies	6,000	0	0	367,900	0	0

Total . £654,050 0 0

		£.	s.	d.
Amount per month, one third of the above, or		218,016	13	4
To which is to be added one third of the loss on Bills, as per contra		17,000	0	0

Total expenditure per month . £235,016 13 4

Estimate of the probable means of providing for the services stated in the preceding estimate.

	£.	s.	d.
Balance remaining in the military chest on the 25th Aug. about	250,000	0	0
Amount of bar silver and Spanish gold coin received by H.M.S. *Fylla*, estimated at	150,000	0	0

Probable amount of Bills to be negotiated	At Lisbon	£345,000	0	0			
	Cadiz	75,000	0	0			
	Gibraltar	90,000	0	0			

Total . £510,000 0 0

	£.	s.	d.			
Subject to a loss which, computing the dollar to be raised on an average at 5s. sterling, would amount to 10 *per cent.*, or	51,000	0	0	459,000	0	0

Total . £859,000 0 0

---

† No. 1. Estimate of the expense of the British army in Portugal for a month, taken from the estimate of all the expenses in Portugal for the months of Sept., Oct., and Nov.

	£.	s.	d.
SERVICE:			
Ordinaries	39,334	0	0
Ordnance	6,050	0	0

EXTRAORDINARIES:	£.	s.	d.			
Provisions	58,334	0	0			
Forage	18,334	0	0			
Transport	8,667	0	0			
Purchase of horses and mules	3,334	0	0			
General hospital	1,000	0	0			
Staff and Commissariat salaries	4,300	0	0			
Bât and Forage money	5,000	0	0			
Contingencies	2,000	0	0	100,969	0	0

Total for one month . £146,353 0 0

Total for one year . £1,756,236 0 0

estimate, showing the real monthly expense of the army in Spain and Portugal, striking from the account the Portuguese subsidy and the arrear of debt; the first of which cannot be called the expense of the army, nor the other a part of the monthly expense of this army. It is a claim upon our funds, occasioned partly by our own and partly by Sir J. Moore's former poverty; and it is very properly included in the estimate, although rated rather highly. But it cannot be called a part of the expense occasioned by this army.

I likewise enclose a paper, marked No. 2,* showing what I conceive

---

* No. 2. Estimate of the expense of the army now in Spain and Portugal, if it were in England.

	£.	s.	d.
Ordinaries, as by the estimate for Spain and Portugal[a] . . .	39,334	0	0

Difference of pay 6d. *per diem* now stopped for provisions for
    1,919 serjeants.
      728 drummers.
  33,602 R. and F. of cavalry and infantry.

	£.	s.	d.
36,249 men for 30½ days[b]	27,639	0	0
Forage for 2620 horses of the cavalry at 2s. a day, for 30½ days .	7,991	0	0
Beer money for 36,249 men of the cavalry and infantry for 30½ days .	4,607	0	0
Difference of price of bread and meat for 36,249 men for 30½ days, the former taken at ¾d., the latter at ¼d. a day for each man . .	4,607	0	0
Marching money for 36,249 men, supposing the whole to move 6 days in the year, or ½d. a day each month	830	0	0
Additional General and staff officers in England, when the army would return, with forage for their horses	2,000	0	0
Ordnance, as by the estimate for Spain and Portugal . . .	6,050	0	0

Difference of pay for serjeants   90
           Drummers   26
           R. and F.   2,252
           Artificers   49

	£.	s.	d.
2,417 at 6d. a day, now stopped for provisions for 30½ days . . .	1,842	0	0
Forage of 1148 horses of the artillery, at 2s. a day each horse for 30½ days	3,502	0	0
Beer money for 2417 men of the artillery for 30½ days . . .	307	0	0
Difference of the price of bread and meat for the same . . .	307	0	0
For one month . .	99,016	0	0
× 12 = for one year .	£1,188,192	0	0

Add Barrack allowances.
    Allowance for cleaning arms, 2s. 9d. each man.
    Allowance for altering clothing, 2s. 6d. each man, not given abroad.

	£.	s.	d.
Amount of the expense of the British army in Spain and Portugal for one year	1,756,236	0	0
Amount of the same in England	1,188,192	0	0
Difference by having the army in the field .	£568,044	0	0

[a] In this sum are included some few expenses which would not be incurred in England, but on the other hand, sums are subtracted from the amount which would not be subtracted in England; such as stoppage for rations from the pay of officers, stoppage for servants not soldiers, &c., into the detail of which I have not the means of entering; but I think the Ordinaries could not be far short of this amount.

[b] The calculations are all made for 30½ days, in order to bring out more nearly the expense for the year; the estimate of the expense in Portugal and Spain being calculated for 92 days, of which, in Paper No. 1, I have taken the third.

would be the expense of this army if it were at home, from which you will observe that the difference is not much more than £500,000 *per annum;* and I really believe that if I could include all home expenses it would not be so much. You will observe that I have not taken into the account the expense of transports, which, however, you are aware is now almost nothing; or of the provisions and forage which we have here. I have no account of the former; and these and the expense of the victuallers must be carried against the army in the field. In respect to the forage and provisions, however, you will observe that in the estimate for the expense for 3 months, the Commissary Gen. estimates the full price of the provisions and forage which the army will consume; and if it should consume any of that in its own magazines, it will be a saving of so much upon the estimate.

With the exception of salt meat, I believe that the expense of forage and provisions is nearly the same in this country as it is in England; and I therefore conceive that the estimate covers the expense of the purchase of these articles in England, and there remains to be charged only that of their transport to Lisbon. In this view of the subject, the forage and provisions, like the shoes and boots, and articles of that description, for which we should be obliged to pay here, may be considered in the light of so much money.

To Vice Adm. the Hon. G. Berkeley.   Badajoz, 23d Sept. 1809.

I am much obliged to you for your letter of the 19th, and for the information you gave me respecting the harbour of Faro; and I shall therefore direct the Commissary Gen. to make arrangements for receiving and forwarding to the army the mules which may be landed there.

I am in daily expectation of the mules which were landed at the mouth of the Guadiana; and when they arrive, I will let you know whether they are good. I will also send an officer to examine and report upon the navigation of the Guadiana, from Badajoz to Mertola, and from Mertola to the mouth of the river; but there is reason to believe that it is not navigable from Badajoz to Mertola.

To Marshal Beresford.   Badajoz, 24th Sept. 1809.

I have received 2 letters from you of the 19th, and 2 of the 22d.

I shall inquire of Gen. Howorth whether any wheels can be given to you; but I should think not, as we have been hard run ourselves. Would our wheels fit your axletrees?

Shall I send to England a copy of my letter to you, regarding the payment of the English officers? I have written to Villiers respecting the increase of pay for the Portuguese officers.

I should not select the senior, but the officer most likely to be useful, in recommending for promotion.

I shall certainly go down to Lisbon as soon as I can. I stay here only till I see the result of the collection of troops at Plasencia and Talavera.

There never was any thing like the madness, the imprudence, and the presumption of the Spanish officers, in the way they risk their corps, knowing that the national vanity will prevent them from withdrawing them from a situation of danger, and that, if attacked, they must be totally destroyed. A retreat is the only chance of safety for the Duque del Parque's corps; but instead of making it, he calls upon you for cavalry. My opinion, founded upon Soult's position, and the patroles and movements he has made, is, that he has collected his force at Plasencia, because he did not think it possible that the Duque del Parque would risk his corps as he has done, excepting in concert with some operation of mine, which Soult has certainly put himself in an attitude to resist. If this conjecture be correct, what must be the presumption of the Duque del Parque!

I have ordered magazines to be prepared upon the Douro and Mondego, to assist in providing these vagabonds if they should retire into Portugal, which I hope they will do, as their only chance of salvation. This will give us an interval of decided tranquillity, and I shall then go to Lisbon.

To the Rt. Hon. J. Villiers.   Badajoz, 24th Sept. 1809.

I desired Beresford to speak to you respecting the increase of pay to the Portuguese officers, because it appeared to me that you had adopted a decided opinion upon that subject, which it was not very likely I should shake by a letter. It appears from his answer that I entirely misunderstood your objection to recommend the increase of pay to the Portuguese officers; and I now find that, notwithstanding that I think the objection a

---

G. O.   Badajoz, 24th Sept. 1809.

1. The mistakes made in the returns and states sent from many of the regiments of the army are so frequent and so glaring, that the Commander of the Forces apprehends that the proper mode of keeping an account of their men is neglected, or is not known in those regiments. The foundation of all states and returns is the roll, and morning and evening states of the troop or company, in which every man absent ought to be accounted for by name, including casualties, till struck off the strength by order of the Commanding officer of the regiment.

The weekly and other states called for from regiments are made up of the totals of the states of each troop or company, which totals should be entered in the regimental weekly or monthly state book; and at the bottom the names of all men making any alteration from the preceding state should be entered by companies.

2. No state should be ever sent in without being made to tally with the last state sent in; and it may be certain that if the second state, whether weekly or monthly, does not account for every man returned in the first, there has been an error, which ought to be investigated, and rectified before the state is sent in.

4. The Commander of the Forces is convinced that either those regiments have never known the proper mode of making out a return, or that their interior economy has been lately entirely neglected.

5. He requests the General officers commanding brigades to inspect accurately the books of the regiments of their brigades, and to see in what manner they make out their states, whether the absent men of each troop or company are accurately accounted for by name on the rolls, and on the morning and evening states at every parade, and that they will look particularly into the interior economy of the regiments under their command.

6. The Commander of the Forces wishes the commanding and other officers of the regiments, particularly the field officers, to recollect that there is a great deal to do to keep their regiments in order upon service, besides attending to the parades and drills of the men.

7. The Commander of the Forces desires that Col. Peacocke will pay attention to the state of discipline (meaning by that word, habits of obedience to orders, subordination, regularity, and interior economy) of the 2d batt. 83d regt., and 2d batt. 87th regt., lately ordered to Lisbon, as well as to their parade discipline and drill.

8. The Commander of the Forces deems it but justice to the two battalions of Guards to state that their returns have in every respect been as accurate, as the conduct of these excellent corps has been regular and exemplary in every other respect. The returns of the Legion and of the regiments of cavalry are also very accurate.

very solid one, and that it is very probable that you will not succeed in obtaining the object, you are so kind as to say that you will propose it, if I should think it desirable that it should be proposed.

I acknowledge that I think it ought to be proposed, and strenuously urged upon the Portuguese government to increase the pay of their officers. How can it be expected that, in a country in which the expense of the necessaries of life is higher than in England, men will serve as officers upon the pay which our serjeants and even soldiers receive? Whatever may be eventually the fate of Spain, Portugal must be a military country; and it is certain that it cannot become so till the gentry of the country enter the army as officers, and this they will never do as long as the pay continues upon the existing footing.

If we do not succeed in carrying the measure, the French will carry it for us; and on every ground, I believe, there is no doubt that it ought to be adopted. But all this is not exactly applicable to the question for consideration; which is, whether you should now propose the increase to the Portuguese government, notwithstanding their repugnance to it, founded as it is upon their want of means? My opinion is, that we, who are charged with the defence of this country, should not be justifiable if we neglect to propose to the Portuguese government, or to our own, any measures which we may think it advisable to adopt, with a view to the defence of Portugal; and that this is a most essential one no man can doubt. But I conceive that this proposition to the Portuguese government is the first step to be taken to procure from the British government the means to provide for the expense, at least for a time. The British government can have no official knowledge of the deficiency of the means in Portugal to provide for this essential expense, till the subject shall have been discussed with the Portuguese government, and they shall have stated the deficiency; and that will be the time to press the British government to provide for this expense. Upon every ground, therefore, I should recommend to you to lose no time in urging the measure upon the Portuguese government.

To the Rt. Hon. J. Villiers.   Badajoz, 24th Sept. 1809.

I heard some time ago that a detachment of Spanish cavalry, under the Principe de Anglona, was to march through Portugal to Ciudad Rodrigo; and being aware of the manner in which the Spaniards are disposed to treat the Portuguese government, I hinted to Col. O'Lawlor, who is employed here by the Spanish Commander in Chief, that it was desirable that I should be informed of the strength of this corps, otherwise that it might incur the risk of being but ill supplied. I enclose a letter which he has this day sent me, from which it appears that this cavalry was about to enter Portugal without giving notice to any body, and unprovided with a Commissary, and of course without money or means of any description. I have desired Col. O'Lawlor to tell the Prince that he must halt till I shall receive an answer from the Portuguese government.

I enclose a route, by which I propose that this corps of cavalry shall march in 4 divisions; and I shall be very much obliged to you if you will explain to the Portuguese government the circumstances of this march, and will desire them to give orders that means may be provided for them at the stages pointed out in this route. I request them also to let me know when the means will be provided, that I may then allow the Principe de Anglona to commence his march. I have given Col. O'Lawlor a hint about the necessity that this corps should have a Commissary.

To Brig. Gen. Cox, Governor of Almeida.　　　　　　Badajoz, 25th Sept. 1809.

I have had the honor of receiving your letters of the 18th and 21st inst., but not that of the 15th, which you state to have written.

So long as the Duque del Parque continued his operations without requiring the assistance of the British or Portuguese troops, I considered it my duty to refrain from making any observations upon them; but as his Excellency has required the aid of Marshal Beresford, I request you to communicate to him the following observations, as the foundation of my determination to decline giving him the assistance which he has required.

Upon a consideration of all the information which I have been able to acquire of the relative state of the armies of the enemy and of the allies in the two Castilles and Estremadura, I am convinced that the enemy are superior to the allies not only in numbers of men for service in the field, including even the corps which Marshal Beresford can bring forward; but, adverting to the composition of the Spanish armies; the want of cavalry by some, of artillery by others; the want of clothing, accoutrements, ammunition, and arms; and the want of discipline in all; the enemy must be considered as superior to the allies in efficiency, to a greater degree even than he is in numbers. These circumstances, and the absolute deficiency of means to enable us to continue our operations, were the causes of our being obliged to put ourselves on our defence, after we had gained a great victory at Talavera; and they have not altered for the better since that period.

But, besides these advantages, I must observe that the enemy enjoys others, which bear particularly upon the operations proposed to be carried on by the Duque del Parque. The enemy, from the nature of the position of his troops, can draw a part or the whole of them to any quarter he pleases; whereas the operations of the different corps of the allies must necessarily be insulated, and each of them for a time must be exposed to be defeated. For instance, there is nothing to prevent the enemy from throwing upon the Duque del Parque's corps, aided, I will suppose, by Marshal Beresford's, the whole of the corps of Soult, Ney, and Kellermann; and even if I had the inclination, I have not the means, and could not possibly be in time to prevent their destruction.

In the same manner this army, if I were to expose it in a forward position, would be liable to the same misfortune: and the Spanish army in La Mancha equally so. It follows, then, that if any operation is to be undertaken by any one of these corps, or if any one of these corps is to be placed in a position in which it is liable to be attacked by the enemy, all the other corps in Castille, Estremadura, and La Mancha should cooperate, otherwise the separate corps must be defeated; and upon this supposed general co-operation, I have already shown that the allies have neither numbers, nor efficient troops, nor means of carrying into execution any plan of co-operation. The consequence of undertaking such a plan would be, that after a battle or two, and some brilliant actions by some, and the defeat of others, and the loss of many valuable officers and soldiers, the allies would be obliged to resume again the defensive positions which they ought never to have quitted. Under these circumstances, I have determined that, although I shall make an effort to prevent the enemy from carrying into execution his design of obtaining possession of Ciudad Rodrigo, I shall not give any assistance to enable the Duque del Parque to maintain the forward position which he has taken up.

I have already shown that the assistance of Marshal Beresford's corps will not enable him to maintain it; and I am very well convinced that this is not the mode by which the enemy can be prevented from undertaking the siege of Ciudad Rodrigo. The mode in which the Duque del Parque can most effectually prevent the enemy from undertaking that operation is to place his corps in such a situation as that the enemy cannot attack and defeat it without a long previous preparation, which will give time to other troops to come to his assistance, and cause a march in which the enemy himself may be exposed to defeat.

The best mode of preventing an attack, or at all events the success of an attack of the enemy on Ciudad Rodrigo, is not to expose to defeat the troops which must ultimately co-operate in its defence, but to place that corps in such a position, that it cannot be attacked without risk to the enemy, and from which it can with ease co-operate with other corps which must be put in motion, if Ciudad Rodrigo is to be saved. I shall not take upon me to say what position the Duque del Parque ought to take up; but I am very certain that his corps and Beresford's joined would not prevent the junction of the enemy's forces in Castille; that the consequence of this junction must be the defeat of the allies if they should remain in an advanced position, and the certain loss of Ciudad Rodrigo, and other misfortunes, none of which can occur under any other probable, or even possible concurrence of circumstances.

To Vice Adm. the Hon. G. Berkeley.   Badajoz, 26th Sept. 1809.

The 2 battalions of detachments from regiments now in England, which have been for some time doing duty with this army, are now on their march to Lisbon, and I wish to send them to England as soon as may be convenient after their arrival there. I have directed the A. Q. M. G. at Lisbon to wait upon your secretary with a return of their numbers, as soon as he shall have received it; and I shall be much obliged to you if you will give directions that tonnage may be allotted for the conveyance of these troops to England; and they shall embark, and sail as soon as you may think proper.

G. O.   Badajoz, 26th Sept. 1809.
2. The Commander of the Forces refers the officers of the medical staff to the G. O. of the 7th Sept. (No. 8), in which they will find detailed the mode in which medical boards must be ordered, and the certificates by which it must be preceded. He will notice no reports of medical boards that are not held in conformity with the mode pointed out in that order.

To Marquis Wellesley.   Badajoz, 26th Sept. 1809.

I am anxious to receive, if possible, the answers of the Junta respecting the payment for the shirts and sheets which they sent to us; also respecting the payment for the carts, and whether we are to keep the carts; and also respecting the exchange of Gen. Franceschi.

Gen. Eguia has lately been guilty of a most unwarrantable act. I have had occasion to send different flags of truce on the subject of the wounded officers and soldiers; and the letters which I have written have invariably been opened, and have been submitted to the inspection of the Spanish Commander in Chief. The answers of the French officers have also been unsealed, and have been seen by the Spanish Commander in Chief; excepting 2 letters, one from Marshal Soult to me, proposing the exchange of Gen. Franceschi; another from Gen. Kellermann to Gen. Stewart, which was, in fact, a private letter, and related to horses and other private concerns. Gen. Eguia represented through Col. Roche that these letters were sealed, and through the same channel I made him acquainted with their contents, and desired that if in future any sealed letters were sent into the Spanish lines from any French officer, they might be opened and read at the Spanish head quarters.

Notwithstanding this explanation, with which I understood Gen. Eguia was satisfied, he detained the officer who brought Gen. Kellermann's letter, under pretence of waiting for my answer, which I never intended to give, as in fact Gen. Kellermann was not Commander in Chief, and it was of no use to write to him again.

I heard of the detention of this officer on the 15th, from the Marques de la Romana, and immediately wrote him a letter to apologize for it, which I sent open to Col. Roche, that Gen. Eguia might see it. Notwithstanding this circumstance, I learn from Mr. Knight, who arrived here yesterday, that this officer is still detained at Deleytosa, and that they will not allow him to depart. The consequence of this conduct must be a cessation of all intercourse between me and the French on the subject of our prisoners, and the continuance and aggravation of their captivity. I shall be obliged to you if you will mention this circumstance to the Spanish government. I would write to you an official dispatch, only that I think it is too bad to become the subject of a public dispatch; and that if it were to be known in England, it would create such an irritation against Gen. Eguia and the Spaniards in general, that they would not easily remove it.

I must mention, that, besides the 2 letters to which I have above referred that came sealed through the hands of Gen. Eguia, there was another addressed to the Adj. Gen. of the army, from the Chef d'Etat Major of Victor's corps, which came sealed through the hands of Venegas, and was forwarded by you.

To Marquis Wellesley.   Badajoz, 26th Sept. 1809.

I have the honor to enclose the copy of a letter which I have received from Brig. Gen. Cox, dated the 21st, and a copy of a letter which I wrote to that officer yesterday.

I apprehend that the troops which reconnaitred the position of the

Duque del Parque on the 18th, were only a small detachment from Ney's corps at Salamanca, and that if the Duque should have allowed his troops to continue at Villa Vieja, they would have been seriously attacked and defeated.

The accounts which I have recently received of the state of the French force in Estremadura and New Castille, prove that I underrated it in the estimate which I made of it about a month ago, and communicated to your Excellency. It appears that the corps of Soult, Mortier, Victor, and Sebastiani consist of 65,000 men, and the King's guards, which are 1000. Besides these troops, there are in Old Castille the corps of Ney and Kellermann, which cannot be reckoned at less than 20,000.

To the Rt. Hon. J. Villiers.   Badajoz, 26th Sept. 1809.

Some time ago Col. Seymour, of the 23d light dragoons, who is still very unwell, and who has obtained leave to go to England, sent me the enclosed letter, and the resignation of his commission, which I likewise enclose. I can easily conceive the feeling which induced Seymour to resign at the moment he did; and I should certainly wish that his wife should enjoy all the advantage to be derived from this act; and I have acted in such a manner as to secure it to her. At the same time, I should consider it a great misfortune, in the event of Seymour's recovery, if he were to be lost to the service, in a view both to himself and the public; and I have always determined, if he should recover before he left Portugal, to give him the option again, whether he would retire or not. I understand that he is not yet so well as I expected he would be; but it is more than probable that his health will be considerably re-established before his arrival at Lisbon, or, at all events, before his embarkation.

I wish you, therefore, upon his arrival at Lisbon, to tell him that I am willing to give him an option then to receive back his resignation; but if you should think him so ill as that he might die on the passage, and his wife might lose the benefit of his resignation if he were now to take it back, I beg you will tell him that he shall have the option of recalling his resignation when he shall arrive in England, and that I will take no steps upon it till I shall have heard from him after his arrival. If he should not take back his resignation, or if he should be so ill as that you think it proper to leave it to his option to have it back when he shall arrive in England, I beg you to return the enclosed papers.

To Marquis Wellesley.   Badajoz, 27th Sept. 1809.

I have received your letter of the 24th by Col. Stopford,* and I enclose a memorandum in answer to the notes of the Duque de Alburquerque and Don M. de Garay.

I consider the mode in which they have been communicated as private, and therefore adopt this mode of replying to them; but it will be easy to turn this memorandum into a dispatch, if you should prefer to have them considered in that mode.

I shall write a dispatch respecting Malespina's statement; but I should wish to have a copy of it, as well as of your note of the 8th Sept. I do

---

* The late Lieut. Gen. the Hon. Sir E. Stopford, G.C.B., then of the 3d Foot Guards.

not doubt that the force left in Estremadura does not exceed 8000 infantry and 900 cavalry, and you have been made acquainted with the exact extent of it, because the Duque de Alburquerque, who is appointed to command it, is interested in making known the truth. But they have lied about the cavalry ordered to the Duque del Parque; instead of being 4000, there are only 1200 horses drawing rations, of which number it could not be expected that above 800 would appear in the field.

Then they have sent this cavalry in such a manner. They never mentioned the intention of its march through Portugal to the Portuguese government, to me, or to any body connected with them: I heard of it by accident, and desired that it might be recommended to the Principe de Anglona to make me acquainted with his march, in order that I might assist him; and I then found out his numbers, and that he had no Commissary with him, no money, and no means of any description. Under these circumstances, I could not take upon me to order the Portuguese magistrates to supply him; and I sent an express to Lisbon, with a request that the government would take measures that he might be supplied on his march.

The Spanish government are really too bad! Surely troops are never sent into any foreign country without having some communication with the government or officers of that country; or without a Commissary attending them, or money to pay for what they receive! Is the English General, or are the Portuguese magistrates to act as Commissaries to the Spanish troops? and to have the honor of paying for their supplies?

I had no doubt that what has turned out would be the result of the expedition of the Scheldt.

P. S. I have considered it best to write a dispatch on the notes of Don M. de Garay, which I forward.

To Marquis Wellesley. Badajoz, 27th Sept. 1809.

I have had the honor of receiving the copy of the note addressed to your Excellency on the 23d inst. by Don M. de Garay, enclosing the copy of a note from the Duque de Alburquerque, addressed to Don A. de Cornel, which your Excellency enclosed in your private letter of the 24th inst. Both these papers refer to the operations of the British army, each of them upon different principles; and I shall now endeavor to reply to both.

The Duque de Alburquerque confines his demand to a requisition that I should engage to remain in the position at present occupied by the British army, or in some other which he proposes I should occupy on the Guadiana, but which he has not described, for 25 or 30 days, during which time he hopes to form an army capable, not only of defending the position on the Tagus, but of undertaking active operations against the enemy; or, in other words, that I should protect the formation of this army. In answer to this proposition, I have to observe, that I have no intention of quitting the position I at present occupy, unless obliged to do so by the want of food, or by some operation by the enemy which may endanger the safety of Portugal; or may expose the British army to a risk which I might not think it expedient that it should incur.

My opinion is, that if the Duque del Parque does not expose his corps to be destroyed, which corps does not consist of 20,000 infantry and 2000 cavalry, as is stated by Don M. de Garay, but of about 10,000 infantry, armed and equipped for service, and 1000 cavalry, as I am informed by good authority, the enemy have not the power of undertaking any offensive operation without exposing some one or other of his corps to be defeated under very disadvantageous circumstances; and that if this misfortune is avoided, the season will pass over, the river Tagus will fill, and even the small corps left in Estremadura will be found capable of defending its post; and no disadvantage will have resulted from the gross error which has been committed in weakening the force in Estremadura, in order to strengthen that in La Mancha.

The government have been repeatedly informed, that if any serious attempt were made by the enemy to obtain possession of Ciudad Rodrigo, I must make an effort to save that place, which would necessarily remove the troops under my command from this quarter: and they were told that it was probable that the attempt upon Ciudad Rodrigo would be accompanied by an attack upon the Tagus, and upon the Guadiana; on which ground I recommended that they should not weaken their force on the Tagus. The collection of troops at Talavera, if the account be well founded, of which I have received no information, looks very like the execution of the whole of the plan according to which the government have been informed that the enemy would most probably proceed, if they really intended to attack Ciudad Rodrigo; and I now only request of them to consider the situation in which their affairs will stand, with their whole army collected in La Mancha, if, as is probable, the enemy should force not only the Tagus, but the Guadiana, and even the passes of Monasterio; thus placing himself between the main body of their army and the city of Seville.

The Spanish government do not like to hear of their weakness in comparison with the enemy; and in order to conceal it from themselves, I imagine, it is that they bring forward such propositions as that contained in Don M. de Garay's note of the 23d inst.

The communications formerly made to the Spanish government of the intentions which I had, in respect to the employment of the British troops under my command, might have saved him the trouble of forwarding the note from the Duque de Alburquerque, as he must know that I should be unwilling, nay, that I could not enter into the engagement which the Duque required I should, as the condition on which he should assume the command of the army in Estremadura. But the propositions in Don M. de Garay's note are still more extraordinary than those contained in that received from the Duque de Alburquerque. He must be aware that the government have adopted no measures to support this army at Merida, or in any other part of Spain; that if I were now to collect it, even at this place, it must starve; and yet he proposes not only that I should collect it at Merida, but that I should move it forward into the Vera de Plasencia, in order to prevent Soult from falling upon the Duque del Parque, in a paper, in which he informs your Excellency that the enemy had collected his whole force at Talavera. Thus, the British army, unprovided with supplies or means of transport, and supported by only 8000 Spanish troops, is to move into the Vera de Plasencia, exposed to the attack of the whole French army, in order to save the Duque del Parque; who requires only prudent management on his own part, not only to save his own army, but to place affairs on such a footing, as to render it very improbable that the enemy will be able to undertake any thing of importance. The mere statement of such a proposition is a sufficient answer to it, and I shall not trouble your Excellency by any further consideration of it.

To Marquis Wellesley. Badajoz, 27th Sept. 1809.

I have had the honor of receiving your Excellency's dispatch of the 24th, marked (G.), enclosing a note from Don M. de Garay, regarding certain mares which have been supplied by the Spanish government for the use of the British army; and I shall be much obliged to your Excellency if you will give directions that the 130 mares may be sent to this place, where they will be received and taken care of by British dragoons. It is desirable that I should be informed of the day on which they are likely to arrive here; that I should know the price to be paid for them, and to whom it is wished that the money should be paid.

To Vice Adm. the Hon. G. Berkeley. Badajoz, 28th Sept. 1809.

I write to tell you that the first detachment of mules is arrived, and that they are considered so good, that I have desired the Commissary Gen. to purchase an additional number of 200 at the same place, for which I shall be obliged to you if you will afford him the same facilities.

The cattle are not quite so good, and they are dear; and as we experience no difficulty in procuring cattle in Spain or Portugal, I think it will be better to discontinue the purchase in Africa, at least for the present.

To Marquis Wellesley. Badajoz, 28th Sept. 1809.

There is one part of the case which I had under consideration yesterday, to which I did not advert in either of my letters, because it is one of such real difficulty, that I did not know what to recommend; and that is, what line of operation shall be recommended for the troops assembled in La Mancha, in case the enemy should combine for an attack upon Ciudad Rodrigo, an attack upon the Tagus, the Guadiana, and the positions in the rear.

If the Spanish troops were of the same description, or nearly of the same description, with those opposed to them, I should, by all means, let them move direct upon Madrid. If the French should have broken the bridges at Toledo and Aranjuez, as I imagine that these bridges, any more than those at Almaraz and Alcantara, cannot be repaired, let them go by Ocaña, Fuentidueña, and Arganda. But, unfortunately, this assembled corps in La Mancha, which, I understand from Stopford, the government call 60,000 men, would be stopped by Sebastiani's corps of 12,000. I suspect that it does not consist of 30,000, from what I have heard from Roche, and from the accounts I have received from various quarters, of the number of soldiers met with on all the roads, quitting the army. But whether it consists of 30,000 or 60,000, no dependence can be placed on its operations, if at all opposed by the French; and therefore, in playing for such a stake as Seville is, I should prefer the more certain game, and should recommend that, if the enemy are decidedly and seriously determined to carry on the proposed operation, a part of the army assembled in La Mancha, that part of it which belonged to Estremadura, should be thrown into the passes of Monasterio.

I think, however, that there is reason to doubt the truth of the intelligence received of the collection of troops at Talavera. You received the intelligence about the 23d or 24th, and the French must have brought their troops there by the 20th. They could not remain at Talavera, as the country is completely exhausted, the town has been plundered, and the inhabitants have fled. They must have commenced their operations and have struck their blow immediately, and I must have heard of it before this time. I have heard of no movement of any description. If they really did move troops from Toledo to Talavera, I think it most probable that it was a defensive movement, of the same description with those which they appear to have made on the right of their line, between the 15th and 20th, which movements I attribute to a notion which they entertained, and in my opinion very justly, that the Duque del Parque could not have risked his corps in the manner he did, excepting in concert with me, and in expectation of my co-operation. Soult certainly collected his troops at Plasencia, and from the disposition of his outposts, I should imagine must have expected that I would endeavor to cross the Tagus above Alcantara, and he has made no movement since. It might be advisable, however, to frighten the gentlemen at Seville with their own false intelligence; and prevail upon them to re-enforce Estremadura, which, I am convinced, is the measure most likely to give a quiet autumn and winter; during which time, if the gentlemen should be overturned, any thing that succeeds may form an army capable of doing something in the spring; or, at all events, capable of defending themselves, and of making the final conquest of the country most difficult, if not impossible.

To the Rt. Hon. the Commander in Chief.   Badajoz, 28th Sept. 1809.

I beg leave to draw your attention to the enclosed letter from the Commissary Gen., relative to a claim made by certain officers to an allowance for shoeing mules employed in the carriage of camp kettles, Surgeons' chests, and Paymasters' books in this army, claimed under an order issued by the late Commander of the Forces, of which a copy is enclosed.

This order appears to have been founded on the principle of the circular letter of the 11th June, 1804, from the Sec. at War, pages 424 and 425 of the printed Regulations; but as the grant of the allowance appears inconsistent with the late regulations respecting bât and forage, and as I wish to have the attention of the Treasury drawn to that part of their late order, which prohibits the issue of 'preparation money,' I think it best to adopt this opportunity of obtaining orders upon the whole subject of the mode of procuring carriage for camp kettles, &c., in Portugal and Spain.

When the army landed in Portugal last year, the regiments having received the allowance called 'preparation money,' including £20 bât money for each company, and £10 for the Surgeon; the Captains of companies,

Surgeons, and Paymasters were obliged to supply mules for the carriage of the camp kettles, medicine chests, and Paymasters' books.

When the army subsequently marched into Spain, the late Commander of the Forces, Lieut. Gen. Sir J. Moore, upon a representation of the Captains, that the mules which they had purchased were unequal to the performance of the service, directed the Commissary Gen. to supply a mule for each company, one for the carriage of the Surgeon's chest, one for the carriage of the Paymaster's books, and one for the carriage of intrenching tools, under different orders, of which I enclose copies. The late Commander of the Forces in Portugal, Lieut. Gen. Sir J. Cradock, at the opening of the campaign in Portugal, likewise issued orders, of which I enclose copies, directing the Commissary Gen. to supply the regiments with mules for the carriage of camp kettles, medicine chests, Paymasters' books, and intrenching tools; but shortly after my arrival in Portugal, having found that this mode of supplying mules for the carriage of camp kettles, regimental medicine chests, and Paymasters' books of regiments of infantry, and for the medicine chest of the Veterinary surgeon, for the serjeant armourer, and the serjeant saddler of regiments of cavalry, was not only a great expense to the public, but an intolerable burden and drain upon the means of equipment for the army, I reverted to what I conceived had been the original intention of government; and considering the ' preparation money,' including £20 bât money for companies, as the price the public allowed for the purchase of these mules, and £10 in the annual bât and forage money for each company, as the sum allowed for the keeping them up, I threw the whole expense of their purchase and of keeping them upon the Captains of troops and companies, the Surgeons and regimental Paymasters; and gave £20 bât money to the Captains, Surgeons, and Paymasters of those regiments which had not received the ' preparation money.'

The ' preparation money ' has since been struck off, and the whole question respecting the mode of procuring carriage for the camp kettles, Surgeons' chests, and Paymasters' books, is again at large; and, indeed, the measures which I had ordered require revision on other grounds. The camp kettles, Paymasters' books, Surgeons' chests, and intrenching tools in regiments of infantry, and the same articles and the medicine chest for the Veterinary surgeon, and implements for the serjeant saddler, and the serjeant armourer, in regiments of cavalry, are articles necessary for the troops, which must always be with them; the expense of carrying which the public must pay. The mode adopted under the system of preparation money, and enforced by me, has been of the nature of a contract with the Captains of troops and companies, Paymasters, and Surgeons; but I must observe that it is a contract in a manner forced upon those who enter into it, and which is highly disadvantageous in this country to the contractors.

I have no reason to believe that those officers did not take care of the animals employed in the service by the Commissariat, under the orders of the late Commander of the Forces, excepting the general reason that the officers seldom take such good care of that which does not, as of that which does, belong to them; and yet the losses of mules on this service, and the consequent demands for them, were so frequent and so heavy as to cramp the operations of the army, by diverting the means of equipment from other important objects, which was one reason why I altered the system. I have since found that the Captains of companies, in particular, have replaced the mules employed in carrying the camp kettles, many of them twice, and some of them three times, since the troops took the field in April.

It is scarcely possible to purchase a mule capable of performing this service for a less sum than from £18 to £25 ; and I am conscientiously convinced that all have been losers already ; and yet only a few months have elapsed of the 4 years which, according to the principle of the letter of the 11th June, 1804, these animals ought to last. In fact, that order, as well as others relating to an army in the field, apply only to the state of the service in England, and not at all to that in foreign countries.

I should therefore beg leave to recommend that for this army, at least, an allowance of £20 bât money should be made with each of the two issues of bât and forage money to the Captains of troops and companies, Surgeons, Paymasters, and others obliged to furnish mules for the public service, to enable them to purchase and keep up mules for the carriage of camp kettles, medicine chests, Paymasters' books, Veterinary surgeons' chests, serjeant saddlers', and serjeant armourers' implements, and that an allowance of one dollar per month shall be made, to pay for shoeing these mules, for saddles, halters, &c., and that the £10 bât money allowed to Captains of troops and companies in the bât and forage allowance should be withdrawn.

To Brig. Gen. R. Craufurd.   Badajoz, 29th Sept. 1809.

I have been for some time very anxious respecting a part of what forms the subject of your letter of the 26th ; I mean the camp kettles ; and I am much obliged to you for your opinions on the subject. Faulty as is the existing mode of carrying the camp kettles, it is more efficient than that of which it is the substitute in this country ; and I have written a letter to England, which I hope will have the effect of making the allowance for keeping up the mules more equal to the object for which it was granted than it has been hitherto. There is much to be said on both sides of the question respecting the description of kettle which the soldiers ought to have ; and as the iron kettle is the best for cooking, and lasts longest ; and moreover, as the use of that description and size of kettle requires the employment of fewest men in cooking, the choice between them resolves itself into this point, which is most likely to be carried with certainty, so as to give the soldier at all times the use of a kettle.

In deciding upon this question, much depends upon the care which officers take of their men, and the degree of minute attention which they give to their wants. In a regiment well looked after, it is certain that the tin kettles would answer best, as the officers would oblige the soldiers to take care of them, and regimental arrangements would be made to provide for the casual increase and diminution of numbers occasioned by men coming out of and going into hospital, returning from detachment, &c. ; and in actions they would be prevented from throwing them away ; and care would be taken that the carrier of the kettle should, above all other men, not straggle or stray behind his regiment till the hours for cooking should be past, or get drunk and lose the kettle. But in two thirds of the regiments of this army such care would not be taken; and whether the regiment would have kettles or not would depend upon that most thoughtless of animals, the soldier himself, and I should very soon hear that there were none.

According to the existing system, bad as it is, the care of the camp kettles is not only the business of the bâtman of the company, but of all the bâtmen of the regiment and of the brigade. The officer of the bag· gage guard is particularly interested, as with the kettles he loses the mule; and the officers commanding the regiments and the brigade are not inattentive to the subject. I think also that the practical effect of this system must improve as the army becomes more experienced in the field.

Upon the whole, therefore, I prefer the iron kettles to the tin for general purposes; but I have no objection to try the latter in some of our best regiments, in order to see how the experiment may answer.*

I agree with you about the expediency of allowing the Captains of companies to ride. The forage required for this purpose is no object, as forage for 200 or 300 mules cannot be very difficult to procure. The objection I think is the increased number of bâtmen and servants which will be taken out of the ranks, which becomes an object of the greatest consequence.†

To the Rt. Hon. J. Villiers.   Badajoz, 29th Sept. 1809.

I received yesterday your letter of the 26th inst., and I instantly sent off to the Principe de Anglona to desire him to begin his march.

I am afraid I misunderstood you respecting the measures which you intended to adopt regarding the additional pay to the Portuguese officers. I thought that you did not propose to take any step whatever till you should be authorised to use the King's name in the communications to be made to the Portuguese army upon the subject; notwithstanding that you had authority from England to go the full length of all the arrangements which were necessary in order to carry the measure into effect. It appears, however, that you have no authority from England with respect to the expense, and you must be satisfied with empty remonstrances to the Portuguese government, which I fear will not answer the purpose.

I have seen Lord Wellesley's dispatches, Nos. 4 and 5, and forwarded them to you.

I have determined not to press for the convent of St. Benito, and shall be obliged to you if you will tell Col. Peacocke that I desire he will take any other building which may be found convenient for the hospital. I shall write to him, but I request you to mention the subject, lest I should not have time to do so by this messenger.

That foolish fellow the Duque del Parque has been endeavoring to get his corps destroyed upon the frontier; but I find that he has retreated, and is now in safety, I hope. I have written to Cox a long letter to be com-

---

* This experiment was tried, with a favorable result, by the regiments of the Light division, and tin cooking kettles were afterwards ordered for the other divisions of the army. They were carried on the march alternately by the men of each mess. When tents were issued to the army in 1813, they were carried on the camp kettle mules. (See G. O. 1st March, 1813.)

† This permission, with the restriction as to bâtmen, but without the allowance of forage, was afterwards extended to the subaltern officers, who after long and otherwise fatiguing marches, sometimes in presence of the enemy, had important duties to perform.

municated to him, in which I have given him my opinion, and explained my determination not to stir a foot to save him from the consequences of his own imprudence, although I will make every effort to save Ciudad Rodrigo, if the enemy should attack that place.

To Col. Peacocke.   Badajoz, 29th Sept. 1809.

I have reason to believe that several men belonging to regiments of this army are detained at Lisbon very improperly, and I wish that, without loss of time, you would have an inspection of all the soldiers at Lisbon, and that you would send to the army those coming under the following descriptions.

1st. All soldiers attending physicians, or surgeons of the hospital, as servants or bâtmen.

2d. All recovered soldiers, excepting such as are absolutely necessary to attend the hospital as orderlies, after providing as many men of that description as can be got from among the convalescents not able to march, and other men who must from circumstances remain at Lisbon.

It is to be observed that the men of one regiment must not be employed as orderlies to men of other regiments in the hospital; and if there should not be a sufficient number of men of any particular regiment to attend the sick belonging to it as orderlies in hospital, men must be supplied for that purpose by the troops in garrison, and not by convalescents or recovered men belonging to other regiments with the army.

3d. All servants and bâtmen belonging to officers at Lisbon, which officers did not bring their servants or bâtmen with them by permission of the commanding officers of their regiments.

4th. Soldiers serving as servants or bâtmen with officers' wives who have not the permission of the commanding officer to detain them.

I beg that you will inform the Inspector of Hospitals at Lisbon that I do not propose to persist in the requisition to have the convent of St. Benito as an hospital; and that I desire that he will fix upon any other building which it may be convenient to the Portuguese government to allow us to have.

To Marquis Wellesley.   Badajoz, 29th Sept. 1809.

I this day received a letter from Brig. Gen. Cox, at Almeida, stating that on the 23d inst. the Duque del Parque, having had reason to believe that the French intended to attack him at San Felices, where he had been since the 18th inst., had moved to Campillo and Ituero in the neighbourhood of Ciudad Rodrigo.

To Visc. Castlereagh.   Badajoz, 29th Sept. 1809.

The Duque del Parque having been appointed to command the corps lately under the orders of the Marques de la Romana, which within these few days had arrived through Portugal in the neighbourhood of Almeida and Ciudad Rodrigo, immediately commenced offensive operations against the French troops in Old Castille, and on the 16th and 17th had his advanced guard at Villa Vieja in front of San Felices; and on the 18th collected his corps at that place.

It appears that the enemy advanced from Salamanca and reconnaitred the Duque's position on the 18th, and there was some skirmishing between the light troops, and on the 19th the Duque del Parque returned to San Felices, where he remained till the 23d; on which day having heard that the enemy were in movement from Salamanca to attack him, the Duque retired to Campillo and Ituero in the neighbourhood of Ciudad Rodrigo, on the left of the Agueda. In the mean time the Duque has urged us to give him the assistance of Portuguese or English troops; but as I did not perceive any benefit likely to result from his desultory but imprudent operations; and as it was obvious that he was risking the loss of his army and of any troops that might be sent to his assistance, without having any object, as long as the others of the allied armies were necessarily obliged to remain upon the defensive, I communicated to him my determination to give him no support in the position which he had assumed, although I should make every effort to save Ciudad Rodrigo, if the enemy should manifest a design to attack that place.

I cannot form an opinion whether the Duque del Parque's corps is now in safety; but I am convinced that if it should be lost, and if the fall of Ciudad Rodrigo should be the consequence, these unfortunate events must be attributed to the presumption and imprudence with which the corps was risked, which, if it should be safe, must prevent the enemy from undertaking any thing against Ciudad Rodrigo, unless he should draw such a force from Estremadura as will allow me to cross the Tagus, without incurring the risk of losing great objects in this quarter during my absence.

The dispatch from Marshal Beresford of the 26th inst., which I forward by this occasion, will show your Lordship how important it is that the Portuguese troops should be kept in tranquillity for some time. The same circumstances render it desirable that the Spanish troops should also be kept in tranquillity, if the officers would take the same advantage which Marshal Beresford is disposed to take of the enemy's inactivity.

The movements which I reported in my last which had been made by Marshal Soult were evidently defensive; and I conclude that he could not believe that the Duque del Parque would risk his corps in Old Castille, excepting in concert and in expectation of co-operation with me. I judge from the movements of his troops, and the positions of his advanced guards, that Soult expected that I should endeavor to cross the Tagus above Alcantara; and yet the first certain intelligence I received of the Duque del Parque's position was on the 25th, after the enemy had reconnaitred his position at Villa Vieja on the 18th. The other armies are nearly in the positions as reported in my last dispatch.

It has been reported, I believe without foundation, that the enemy had collected a corps at Talavera about the 20th; but as no movement has been made in that quarter, I conclude that if a corps was collected at Talavera, it was with the same defensive views with which I suppose Soult to have collected his corps at Plasencia.

To the Rt. Hon. J. Villiers.   Badajoz, 1st Oct. 1809.

I received yesterday at Elvas your letter of the 28th, and one to Lord

Wellesley, containing your dispatch of the 25th to Mr. Canning, which I forwarded by Mr. Geddes as soon as I had perused it.

I can account for the arrangement of the Regency, as far as I am concerned, only by the desire manifested in the government of Brazil to weaken the British influence over the army in this country, by a division of the authority placed over it. However, the persons who formed this arrangement appear to me to be entirely ignorant of the national character of Englishmen; and particularly of the character of those who were the objects of this arrangement, in thinking that by such means they would effect their views.

I cannot conceive what can have induced our government to recommend the Marquez das Minas and the Marquez Monteiro Mór to the government of Brazil, particularly without your concurrence. I imagine they are both as inefficient as I should certainly be; for I do not understand the internal politics of Portugal, nor do I see how I am to find time or opportunity to acquire a knowledge of them.

I have received a letter from the Prince Regent, appointing me the Marshal General of his army, with all the power and privileges held by the Duque de Lafoes; and I believe that is what I had before, and it was certainly as much as was necessary, or as I could manage; and I do not see any reason for altering our arrangements and the practice under the old appointment, even though the new one may be different.

To Marquis Wellesley. Badajoz, 1st Oct. 1809.

I enclose a letter and some papers which I have received from Don A. de la Vera, which I request your Excellency to lay before the Spanish government. This gentleman was governor of Merida when the head quarters of the British army were at that place (to which situation he had been appointed by Gen. Cuesta), and I must add that he took more pains to supply the wants of the British army than any other officer in the Spanish service with whom I have yet met; and I therefore wrote to him a letter from Merida, upon the movement of the troops, to acknowledge his exertions.

The government have, however, since appointed another person to command at Merida, from whom the same assistance has not been received, and by whom the same exertions have not been made, as I am informed by Gen. Fane, whose brigade of cavalry has continued there.

To Marshal Beresford. Badajoz, 3d Oct. 1809.

I have received your letter of the 29th Sept., regarding Brig. Gen. ——. I do not know what you can do respecting him; I conclude that he must

---

G. O. Badajoz, 1st Oct. 1809.

1. The Commander of the Forces observes that the women of the regiments have come up from Lisbon along with the clothing, to the great inconvenience of the army, and to their own detriment; and as they travel on the cars, they delay and render uncertain the arrival of the regimental clothing for the troops, and defeat all the arrangements for bringing it up to the army.

2. The Commander of the Forces desires that Col. Peacocke will prevent the women from leaving Lisbon with the clothing and regimental baggage; and the officers and non-commissioned officers coming up from Lisbon in charge of clothing are desired to prevent the women from travelling on the cars.

go; but you should make a strong representation on his conduct to the Horse Guards. In respect to Col. ——, I will state to you what I have done with officers of the British army going home on their private affairs. I have invariably obliged them to declare what their business was, and have fixed the period of their return; and if they do not return in time, I propose to bring them to a Court Martial for being absent without leave.

In respect to officers who are sick, their sickness is first certified by a surgeon, and the certificate is sent to head quarters; a Medical Board is then ordered upon them, which board reports whether such officer is so ill as to require leave of absence, and whether it is necessary that he should quit Portugal. By these means I have detained many in the country, and I shall have their services as soon as they are tired of Elvas, Caldas, &c.

I think the French are as much disposed to remain in tranquillity as we are to allow them to remain so; and I shall certainly go to Lisbon in a few days.

To Lieut. Gen. Sir J. Sherbrooke, K.B.　　　　　　Badajoz, 5th Oct. 1809.

I received last night a letter, of which I enclose a copy, containing the King's commands to invest you with the Order of the Bath, which I shall carry into execution with great pleasure, either to-morrow or next day, if you will come over here. Let me know which day will be convenient to you, that I may make arrangements to do the business in a suitable manner. Send me over the insignia and any papers you may have received with them. Bring with you the General officers and staff of your division, and the commanding officers of the battalions of Guards.

I forwarded your letter to Capt. Boothby, and will do all in my power to have him set at liberty; but the Spaniards are behaving so ill upon this, as well as other subjects, as I will explain to you when we meet, that I am not certain I shall be able to effect any thing.

To Marshal Beresford.　　　　　　Badajoz, 5th Oct. 1809.

I received last night your letter of the 2d, and I propose to set out for Lisbon on Sunday, being obliged to stay till that day, in order to invest Gen. Sherbrooke with the Order of the Bath on Saturday.

I have not heard from the Portuguese government respecting the changes in the government of Lisbon. As far as the military government is concerned, I do not think that the Prince's letter has made any material alteration in the state of things; and I need not assure you, that as far as that letter or any other orders may have increased my powers, they shall be uniformly exerted to forward your views for the amelioration of the Portuguese service. You must only inform me in what manner I can do so, and you will find me disposed to do every thing in my power.

I regret the departure of Villiers much. My brother will do every thing in his power; but we shall miss Villiers often, and particularly in our moments of difficulty. As I go with my own horses, I shall not be at Lisbon till Wednesday.

To Marquis Wellesley.   Badajoz, 5th Oct. 1809.

On the 3d Sept. last, Marshal Mortier sent in to the Spanish advanced posts, opposite Almaraz, Capt. V. de Thévenon, aide de camp to Gen. Brayer, charged with letters to me, relating to the wounded officers and soldiers belonging to the British army left at Talavera de la Reyna. It was impossible for me to reply to these letters, as they related to a *cartel* for an exchange, upon which it was necessary that a reference should be made to the Spanish government, to which they have to this day given no answer; and I had concluded that the French officer who had brought the letters had been sent back, as is usual in such cases, from the outposts.

I was informed, however, on the 15th Sept., that he was at the Spanish head quarters, detained for an answer from me; and I immediately desired Col. Roche to inform Gen. Eguia that I was unable at that moment to return an answer to the proposition of the French Commander in Chief, and that I requested that Capt. Thévenon might be allowed to depart forthwith. This request was made, but Capt. Thévenon has been still detained; and I received yesterday a letter from Marshal Mortier, of which I enclose your Excellency a copy, in which he states that he has received information that Capt. Thévenon has been removed to Seville; and he complains, with reason in my opinion, of this gross violation of the laws and customs of war among civilized nations.

In consequence of the receipt of this letter, I have again written to Gen. Bassecourt, by Capt. the Hon. A. Gordon, my aide de camp, to urge him to send back Capt. Thévenon forthwith, if he should be with the Spanish army; and if he should have been sent to Seville, I request your Excellency to claim him, as being evidently under my protection as the officer commanding the British army, and to remonstrate against the measures which have been adopted respecting this officer, by those acting under the authority of the Spanish government.

The least of the evils which must result from them, if not now set right, must be to put an end to all communication between the commanding officer of the French army and me, respecting the British officers and soldiers who are in their hands, every one of whom is wounded: and if the Spanish government will but consider the manner in which they received their wounds, the circumstances which have occasioned their captivity, the degree to which this misfortune may be aggravated, and the space of time during which it may be lengthened by this interruption to the communication between the Commanders in Chief of the French armies and me, they will be probably disposed to discountenance the measures which have been adopted by the Spanish Commander in Chief; and if Capt. Thévenon should have been sent to Seville, to order that he may be brought to me without loss of time.

To Gen. Bassecourt.   Ce 6 Octobre, 1809.

La lettre que vous m'avez envoyée de la part de M. le Maréchal Mortier contenait la demande que M. le Capitaine Thévenon, qui m'avait apporté une lettre des avant-postes Francais le 3 du mois de Septembre, soit renvoyé tout de suite, et M. le Maréchal fait des remontrances bien fondées sur sa détention et sur son envoi à Seville, dont il a reçu des nouvelles.

Je ne peux pas croire qu'il ait été envoyé à Seville, surtout quand j'avais prié, par l'entremise du Colonel Roche le 16 Septembre, qu'il fût renvoyé tout de suite à l'armée Française; et je suis étonné qu'on l'ait détenu un moment après que j'ai fait savoir, par le Colonel Roche, que j'enverrais la réponse à la lettre que le Capitaine Thévenon m'avait apportée par les mains d'un officier Anglais. Je vous prie, Monsieur, de renvoyer le Capitaine Thévenon avec le Capitaine Gordon, mon aide de camp, qui aura l'honneur de vous présenter cette lettre, s'il est toujours au quartier général de l'armée Espagnole; et s'il n'y est pas, je vous prie de faire savoir au Capitaine Gordon où il est, et pourquoi il est détenu, afin qu'il puisse faire cesser les inquiétudes de M. le Maréchal Mortier sur son compte.

To Gen. Bassecourt.   *Ce 6 Octobre, 1809.*

La détention du Capitaine Thévenon, dont je vous écris aujourd'hui, est vraiment une violation des lois de la guerre, qui peut avoir des suites très inconvenantes; et j'espère que vous le renverrez tout de suite; ou s'il n'est pas avec vous, que vous me ferez savoir où il est.

Je serais bien aise d'avoir avec vous une communication constante, et je vous prie de me faire savoir dans quelle situation vous vous trouvez, quel nombre de troupes vous avez, et si je peux vous être utile à quelque chose. Le Capitaine Gordon vous montrera les lettres dont il est chargé pour le Maréchal Mortier et le Capitaine Thévenon, et je vous envoie ci-incluse une copie de celle que vous m'avez envoyée hier de la part du Maréchal Mortier.

To Maréchal Mortier, Duc de Trévise.   *Ce 6 Octobre, 1809.*

Je viens d'avoir l'honneur de recevoir la lettre que vous m'avez adressée le 29 Septembre, et je suis, je vous assure, bien surpris et fâché d'entendre que M. le Capitaine Thévenon ne soit pas retourné à l'armée Française.

J'ai entendu, par hasard, le 16 du mois de Septembre, qu'il attendait au quartier général de l'armée Espagnole la réponse d'une lettre qu'il m'avait apportée, que je croyais être de la part du Maréchal Duc de Dalmatie; et je lui ai écrit ce jour là une lettre dont je vous envoie ci-incluse la copie; et par l'entremise d'un officier Anglais, qui est auprès du Commandant en Chef de l'armée Espagnole, j'ai prié son Excellence qu'il fît partir M. le Capitaine Thévenon tout de suite, et j'ai cru qu'il était parti jusqu'à ce que j'aie reçu votre lettre du 29 Septembre.

J'écris aujourd'hui une lettre au Commandant en Chef de l'armée Espagnole, dont je vous envoie la copie, pour renouveler mes instances que M. le Capitaine Thévenon soit renvoyé avec mon aide de camp, le Capitaine Gordon, qui aura l'honneur de vous présenter cette lettre; et j'écris encore une lettre au Capitaine Thévenon, dont je vous envoie la copie. Je fais aussi des remontrances au gouvernement Espagnol sur sa détention jusqu'à présent en cas qu'il soit envoyé à Seville, ce que je ne saurais croire; et je vous assure, M. le Maréchal, que je ne cesserai mes efforts pour le faire renvoyer, que lorsque je saurai qu'il est arrivé à l'armée Française.

J'envoie par le Capitaine Gordon quelques lettres pour les officiers Anglais qui sont blessés, et de l'argent, que je vous prie de leur faire remettre.

To the Rt. Hon. J. Villiers.   Badajoz, 6th Oct. 1809.

Although I think your successor is well chosen, I regret exceedingly that we are to lose your assistance at this moment, in which it may be most important to Portugal that we should have it. I conclude that you will not go till Henry shall arrive, and we shall have time to talk over and settle many matters.

I propose to leave this for Lisbon on Sunday, and I shall arrive there on Tuesday, if you can send 2 or 3 carriages, or 5 or 6 horses, to meet me early on that day at Pegões. I also request you to let me know at Monte Mór o Novo on Monday, if possible, at what hour the tide will answer best, and at what hour *I must be* at Aldea Galega on Tuesday, in order to cross the Tagus to Lisbon, and I shall be obliged to you if you will order boats to Aldea Galega to take me over.

I have looked over the estimate of the expenses of the British government in Portugal, which I think for the next 3 months will be about £205,000, including £50,000 for you: you ought, therefore, to have one fourth of our receipts; and as we received in September £183,728, I have ordered Mr. Murray to pay to Mr. Bell £45,932, which I beg you to desire him to receive for September.

Stupidity must have been the cause of my misunderstanding you respecting the increase of pay for the Portuguese officers.

To Marquis Wellesley.   Badajoz, 6th Oct. 1809.

Since I addressed your Excellency yesterday, I have received through Ciudad Rodrigo a letter from Gen. Kellermann, in which he has requested that his aide de camp, M. de Turenne, who had been made prisoner by a Spanish patrole near Tordesillas, might be sent back to him in exchange for an English officer who has been allowed to return on his parole, and who will go back to the French army if the exchange should not be completed. I learn from Ciudad Rodrigo, that M. de Turenne is on his road to this place, in order that the Central Junta may signify their pleasure respecting him, as the Duque del Parque did not consider himself authorised to consent to this proposed exchange. I shall be very much obliged to your Excellency, if you will request the consent of the government to place M. de Turenne at my disposal. I do not ask them to consent to the exchange of M. de Turenne for the British officer sent back by Gen. Kellermann, as I do not consider that officer of equal rank with the French officer; but if the Spanish government should consent to place him at my disposal, I hope to be able to liberate a British officer of equal rank, and thus to commence the work of setting free our prisoners.

I cannot avoid taking the opportunity of drawing your Excellency's attention to the inconvenience which is the result of the delay of government giving answers to these requests. A month has elapsed since a proposition was laid before them to allow Gen. Franceschi, &c., to be exchanged for British officers. An answer in the negative would have been preferable to the delay in giving any answer, as upon that negative I might have founded a negotiation for a *cartel* of exchange on other grounds; whereas, the delay in giving any answer has been, that the greater number of British officers taken in the hospital at Talavera, all those the state of whose wounds permitted their removal, or who are ever likely to be able to render any service again, have been sent to France, and it is well known that they will not be set at liberty during the war.

To the Rt. Hon. G. Canning.   Badajoz, 6th Oct. 1809.

I received your letter of the 15th regarding the exchange of Major Fotheringham, and in case I should be able to settle a *cartel*, I shall not forget your wishes in favor of that officer. I had proposed a *cartel* to the French Commander in Chief, to which he agreed, and proposed that Gen. Franceschi, who was taken by, and is in the possession of, the Spaniards, should be included in it. This proposition did not appear to me to be unreasonable, considering the circumstances under which it happens that the French have any officers of ours in their hands; and, indeed, if the French officers in the power of the Spaniards were not to be included in the *cartel*, we should have none to exchange for ours, as we gave up to the Spaniards, and sent to Seville, all the prisoners we took both previous to and during the battle of Talavera. I accordingly requested Lord Wellesley to ask the Spanish government to allow Gen. Franceschi to be exchanged; but although more than a month has elapsed since this request was made to them, he had not been able to obtain an answer. The whole business is therefore at a stand; and, in the mean time, our officers are being moved off to France.

To the Mil. Sec. to the Commander in Chief.   Badajoz, 6th Oct. 1809.

In consequence of the uniform good conduct of the 45th regt. since they have been under my command, I beg to recommend Lieut. Urquhart, the senior Lieut. of that regiment with this army, to the company in the 47th regt., which the Commander in Chief has been pleased to appropriate for such Lieut. of this army as I should recommend. I beg also to recommend Ensign Ouseley, the senior Ensign, to be Lieut. *vice* Urquhart.

To Visc. Castlereagh.   Badajoz, 6th Oct. 1809.

The French corps under Marshal Ney did not pursue the Spanish corps under the Duque del Parque in their movements related in my dispatch of the 29th Sept., but returned immediately towards Salamanca: and the Duque remains encamped in the neighbourhood of Ciudad Rodrigo.

Marshal Soult moved his corps on the 1st inst. from Plasencia towards Talavera, and I understand they have passed Navalmoral; so that no attack can be intended in this quarter.

The Spanish corps which lately marched from Estremadura under Gen. Eguia have arrived at La Mancha, and have joined the corps hitherto under the command of Gen. Venegas; and the whole are now under the orders of Gen. Eguia, with their head quarters at Daymiel. This collection of troops in La Mancha, combined probably with the distress for the want of provisions in Plasencia, may have occasioned Soult's movement from that place.   Gen. Bassecourt continues to command the Spanish corps in this province, and has his head quarters at Deleytosa.

To Visc. Castlereagh.   Badajoz, 6th Oct. 1809.

I have received your letters of the 9th and 12th by Lord FitzRoy Somerset, and I am very much obliged to you for the care you take of me, and for all your kindness.

In answer to your letter of the 12th, I think I can already tell you that there is no occasion for taking further precautions for the safety of this army, at least till affairs shall be settled in Germany, and it shall be seen whether Buonaparte can turn his whole attention to the Peninsula, than to send to Lisbon that part of the coppered tonnage of the country which can be spared from service elsewhere.

I think it desirable that that tonnage should be kept in the Tagus, if not inconvenient to the service, for these reasons : 1st ; it gives confidence to our own officers and troops : 2dly ; whenever it does become necessary seriously to think of embarking, this country will not be alarmed by seeing the collection at Lisbon of a large fleet of transports.   They will have become accustomed to the sight of the ships ; the arrival of a few more will, if noticed at all, make no impression upon them, and the operations of the native troops will be carried on, and the exertions of the people made, without the suspicion that we intend to leave them to their fate. I do not mean to say that we ought, in any case, to deceive them ; on the contrary, they ought to be distinctly apprised that the King would not risk the loss of his army by capture by the enemy, but that we should not quit them until the last moment ; and that the period would depend very much upon their own exertions.   Still, however, the lower orders would suspect our intentions ; and the arrival of a large fleet of transports at the moment of danger and exertion would excite their suspicions, and probably paralyse their exertions in their own defence.   At the same time, all these reasons for keeping the coppered transports in the Tagus are worth nothing, if they are wanted elsewhere, or if any expense or inconvenience would be occasioned by the measure.

I am going to Lisbon on Sunday, all being quiet ; and I hope in a short time to be able to make a report on the defence of Portugal which will be satisfactory to government.

To the Rev. W. Elliott.   Badajoz, 6th Oct. 1809.

I have had the pleasure of receiving your letter of the 24th Aug., and I am much obliged to you for the satisfaction you express upon the success of the army at the battle of Talavera.

I would, with great pleasure, forward your wishes in favor of your son, but, as he is only a Lieutenant, it is impossible to employ him on the staff consistently with an obedience to the King's regulations.   I shall not forget your wishes, however, if he should become eligible, and an opportunity of gratifying them should offer.

Pray remember me kindly to Mrs. Elliott, and all friends at Trim.

To Visc. Castlereagh. Badajoz, 7th Oct. 1809.

I have the honor to report to your Lordship that I have ordered the 2 battalions of detachments to embark and to proceed to England as soon as transports shall be furnished for their reception, with the exception of the detachments belonging to regiments of which one battalion is serving in this country, which I have directed to join and to be incorporated in such battalion.

To M. le Capitaine Thévenon, A.D.C. Ce 8 Octobre, 1809.

Je viens de recevoir une lettre du Maréchal Mortier, Duc de Trévise, par laquelle j'apprends que malgré les instances que j'avais faites au Commandant en Chef de l'armée d'Estremadure le 16 Septembre, quand je vous ai écrit la dernière fois, vous êtes toujours détenu aux postes Espagnols; et même Monsieur le Maréchal m'informe que l'on vous a envoyé à Séville. Je ne sais pas pourquoi on vous a détenu, et comme je ne crois pas qu'on vous ait envoyé à Séville, je vous écris cette lettre pour vous faire savoir que j'ai renouvelé mes instances auprès du Commandant en

---

G. O. Badajoz, 7th Oct. 1809.

1. A Board of Claims is to be assembled at Campo Maior, consisting of * * * * *, for the consideration and decision of all claims of officers and soldiers of the army, for losses sustained up to the 1st Oct.

The claims sent to the military secretary will be referred to this board for their consideration and decision.

2. The principles on which such claims are to be considered and decided are as follows : no claim for a loss can be allowed which has been occasioned by a disobedience of orders, or by neglect or omission in the party claiming for the loss, or his servant or bât men.

No claim can be allowed for a loss sustained by the ordinary occurrences of the service, such as deaths of horses or mules of fatigue, occasioned by the ordinary marches of the army, the loss of accoutrements and necessaries in hospital, or by the breaking down of carts, fatigue of oxen, &c. &c.

3. As the principle on which the compensation for losses by the public is founded, is that the claimant may replace his loss, and the public may not lose his services; claims for losses on behalf of officers or soldiers who are dead cannot be admitted.

4. As the officers of the army have been restricted in the amount of their baggage by different orders by the late and by the present Commander of the Forces, it would be inconsistent with every principle on which compensation for losses is granted, and with the practice of former boards of claims, if the full amount of the value of the whole of an officer's baggage (as allowed by His Majesty's regulations) was granted to replace the baggage allowed to be carried, or actually carried by any officer on the service, in Spain or Portugal.

5. The value of the whole and of the different proportions of officers' baggage lost, is to be rated at two-thirds of the sum allowed by His Majesty's regulations.

6. The claims for regimental baggage, accoutrements, and horse appointments lost, are likewise to be considered as decided upon by the board upon the same principles.

7. But it is to be observed that clothing, accoutrements, and horse appointments lost, can be paid for according to the practice of the service, only when they shall be replaced by new, and then only three-fourths of the price.

8. The Commander of the Forces is concerned to be obliged to notice that, notwithstanding repeated orders upon the subject, and particularly the G. O. of the 4th May, the officers of the army continue to give receipts for articles of provisions and forage, notwithstanding that other arrangements are made for their supply.

9. Those officers marching up from Lisbon, in particular, either alone or with detachments, have taken up articles of provisions and forage upon their own receipts, contrary to the orders given them in their routes, and notwithstanding that there is a commissary at every stage, at which it is specified in their route that they are to receive the provisions and forage for themselves and their detachments.

10. This repeated disobedience of all order defeats every arrangement which can be made for the regular supply of the troops, and gives the Commander of the Forces the greatest concern. He is determined to carry into execution his order of the 4th May, and
he

Chef de l'armée d'Estremadure, pour qu'il vous fasse partir tout de suite; et que j'envoie aujourd'hui au gouvernement Espagnol des remontrances sur votre détention jusqu'à présent.

J'envois cette lettre et le duplicat à celle que je vous ai écrite le 16 Septembre, par mon aide de camp, le Capitaine Gordon, et je vous prie de me faire savoir s'il vous faut quelque chose, en quoi je puis vous être utile.

Je vous préviens que votre ami M. de Farincourt existe, et se porte bien. Il est dans les mains de la Régence de Portugal, et je suis bien assuré qu'il est bien traité. Mais comme vous vous intéressez à son sort, je tâcherai de le faire renvoyer à l'armée Française en échange pour un officier Anglais ou Portugais, et en attendant je lui ferai donner de l'argent et tout ce qu'il lui faut.

To J. Murray, Esq., Commissary General.   Lisbon, 11th Oct. 1809.

I observe that the regiments have seized upon the Seville carts, which they are using for private purposes, and in all probability we shall lose

---

he gives notice that every officer who shall make a requisition, and give a receipt for any article of supply, will be called upon to account for his having done so; and if his act should have been in disobedience of orders, or unnecessary, such officer will have to pay for the supplies for which he will have given a receipt.

11. In case any officer or non-commissioned officer should have occasion to make a requisition and sign a receipt for any article of supply delivered by any of the magistrates of the country, the requisition and receipt must be made out according to the following form, and can always be procured in print from any of the commissaries.

FORM.

Return of
for
from the   to the   18

	No. of Persons.	No. of Horses.	No. of Mules.	No. of Oxen.
Total				

REMARKS.

Received from   at | In Figures. |

(N.B. The quantities to be written in words at length; no erasure or interlineation to be allowed.)

— lbs. of bread   . . . .
— lbs. of meat   . . . .
— pints of wine   . . . .
— lbs. of barley   . . . .
— lbs. of Indian corn . . . .
— lbs. of straw   . . . .
— lbs. of wood   . . . .

For which I have signed triplicate receipts.   * * * *
(Signature of the officer Comm⁵.)

their services from hard and bad usage. I have this day given an order upon the subject, which I hope will have the effect of putting a stop to this pernicious practice; and in the mean time I beg you to give orders to your commissaries to get possession of these carts, and not to allow them to be used excepting for public purposes.

The carting business appears to go on with tolerable regularity upon the road, but you must take care to keep your commissaries at Estremoz, Monte Mór o Novo, and Aldea Galega, supplied with money. I think it would be an improvement of our system, and indeed would be but fair towards the Estremoz cart owners, to hire carts at Badajoz to relieve there those from Estremoz, and to carry to the regiments which are beyond Badajoz whatever might be brought up for them.

To Lieut. Gen. Payne.   Lisbon, 11th Oct. 1809.

I arrived here yesterday, and I saw the 1st dragoons, in the streets, and I think that in my life I have never seen a finer regiment. They were very strong, the horses in very good condition, and the regiment apparently in high order.

I met upon the road at Arrayolos a cart belonging to the Commissariat, one of those hired at Seville, and marked as belonging to the army, and drawn by 4 mules, and escorted by a dragoon, and upon inquiry from him I found that ' it was a cart belonging to the — light dragoons, which was drawing Major ———'s baggage.'

1st, I do not know what business the — light dragoons have with a cart belonging to them, after the repeated orders which have been given upon the subject, and particularly with one of those Seville mule carts, which I had taken much pains to procure for the army, and am endeavoring to retain in our service.

2dly, If a regiment has a cart, it must not be employed in carrying the baggage of an officer, and particularly must not be sent 100 miles from the regiment in order to carry his baggage. Major ——— must have

---

G. O.   Lisbon, 11th Oct. 1809.

1. The Commander of the Forces is apprehensive that his orders, respecting the returning of carts in the possession of the regiments of the army, have not been understood, as they have not been obeyed; he now desires, that upon the receipt of this order, the officers commanding regiments will send to the commissary of the brigade or division, in which the regiment is placed, all carts in possession of the regiments to which native drivers are attached.

2. In future, if any regiment should retain a cart after it shall have performed the special service for which it has been supplied to the regiment, the hire of such cart for the number of days it will be so detained will be charged against the subsistence of the regiment.

3. The officers commanding brigades will report to the Q. M. G., on the 18th inst., whether this order has been obeyed.

4. The carts with oxen or mules without native drivers are to be retained in the service of the regiments which have them, and these regiments are to send to the Q. M. G. a monthly return of them on the 1st of every month.

5. The officer commanding the cavalry will take care that each detached squadron of the cavalry receives and carries into execution this order.

6. The clothing and other regimental stores received by the different regiments of the army are to be delivered out to the soldiers as soon as possible after they shall be received, as it will be impossible to provide carriages to remove them in case any movement should be made.

7. The officers commanding brigades will report to the Q. M. G. that this order has been obeyed on the 5th day after each regiment shall have received clothing or stores.

known that he ought to provide means to carry his baggage himself, and not call upon his regiment to provide them for him, and send them to Lisbon.

3dly, I am surprised that Major ——— should have stayed so long from his regiment since his arrival in Portugal, and that he should only now have joined it.

I wish you to notice these circumstances to the — light dragoons. I shall publish an order, and give directions to the Commissary Gen. respecting carts.

To Lieut. Gen. Sir J. Sherbrooke, K.B.   Lisbon, 11th Oct. 1809.

I arrived here last night, and I understand that a packet is come in, and if the report of its arrival be correct, this shall go to you to-night, with the contents of the packet for the army. I have not yet heard any news.

I send an order to be published relating to carts, which, notwithstanding all the orders upon the subject, the regiments still retain, much to the public inconvenience.

From what I have seen on the road, I should hope that all the clothing is gone from hence, and will be with the regiments before the end of the week, and that the blankets will soon follow. I conclude that the rain of Monday morning will have induced you to put the troops in quarters.

Memorandum.

According to the desire expressed by Mr. Villiers, I proceed to give my opinion on the points referred to in his dispatch to the Sec. of State, dated 2d Oct. 1809.

11th Oct. 1809.

Mr. Villiers is certainly misinformed respecting the state of the British army, a knowledge of which can be acquired from the returns better than from any reports.

The measure of drawing it towards the Portuguese frontier, and of dispersing it in some degree, has answered completely in recruiting the strength of the cavalry and the artillery; and the reinforcements which have been sent of horses for the artillery, and the arrival of the 1st dragoons, have rendered both those branches equally efficient as when the army marched into Spain in June.

Both officers and soldiers of the infantry have been sickly, as all persons are in these climates in the months of September and October, particularly an army which had previously suffered much from fatigue and privation. Many men have been and are still sick in some of the divisions; in others the men are not extraordinarily unhealthy, adverting to the season; and, upon the whole, the sick list, including wounded prisoners and others, does not exceed 7800 men out of 33,000. The infantry of the army are also stronger in numbers than when it entered Spain in June, from the arrival and junction of the reinforcements.

The omission, then, 'to take any further advantage of the present moment,' must not be attributed to 'the loss, the fatigue, and the sickness of the troops,' but to the conviction of their General that the French were superior not only in discipline, efficiency, and composition, but in numbers for the field also, to the allies in the two Castilles and Estremadura.

The grounds of this conviction are explained in two dispatches to the Ambassador at Seville, dated the 24th Aug. and 1st Sept., and in a dispatch to the Sec. of State, of the 4th Sept., the whole of which have been seen by Mr. Villiers.

The mode in which the enemy would bring this superiority of numbers to bear upon the operations of the allies is likewise detailed in those dispatches; and, till I shall see a great alteration for the better in the situation of the allies, I must consider it certain that the result of any offensive operation on their part must be defeat of their plan, if not of one or more of their armies.

I might refer to the same dispatches for an opinion regarding the effect which might be produced on the Peninsula by the introduction into operation of a corps of 20,000 fresh British troops. But it will save time and trouble to refer to the dispatch from the Sec. of State to Lord Wellesley, of the 12th Aug., in which it will be seen that it is positively stated that that number of men could not be spared from the service in Great Britain and Ireland.

In respect to the army and armament of the people in Spain and Portugal, there is no man more aware than I am of the advantage to be derived from those measures, and if I had not reflected well upon the subject, my experience of the war in Portugal and in Spain (in Portugal, where the people are in some degree armed and arrayed, and in Spain, where they are not) would have shown me the advantage which an army has against the enemy when the people are armed and arrayed, and are on its side in the contest. But reflection, and, above all, experience, have shown me the exact extent of this advantage in a military point of view; and I only beg that those who have to contend with the French will not be diverted from the business of raising, arming, equipping, and training regular bodies, by any notion that the people, when armed and arrayed, will be of, I will not say any, but of much, use to them.

The subject is too large for discussion in a paper of this description, but I can show hundreds of instances to prove the truth of as many reasons why exertions of this description ought not to be relied on. At all events, no officer can calculate upon an operation to be performed against the French by persons of this description; and I believe that no officer will enter upon an operation against the French without calculating his means most anxiously.

I rather believe Mr. Villiers is misinformed respecting the desertion of the German troops in the French service; they do desert, certainly, when the British army is near them, and so do the French, but not in the numbers supposed. I believe, however, that they would desert in greater numbers if the Spanish peasants did not murder every thing in the shape of a French soldier found at any distance from the lines; and Gen. Cuesta had already adopted measures to encourage desertion, by preventing these murders, by offering and giving a reward for every soldier belonging to the enemy brought in alive. At the same time I must add, that although the German troops, in particular, had a good opportunity of deserting when the British army was at Talavera, very few of them availed themselves of it.

With respect to the proposed increase to the armies of the allies, by raising independent legions, I most readily concur with such good authority, in recommending the adoption of any measure by the allies which will have the effect of giving them an army in a short space of time. Before, however, the measures now in progress are abandoned, it would be desirable to consider well whether those recommended will be more efficient, and particularly to ascertain the difference between them. The measures now in progress consist in raising and training regiments of infantry, cavalry and artillery, upon the old and understood establishment of Spain and Portugal; those recommended are to raise legions. A legion is, I understand, a corps consisting of one, two, or more battalions of infantry, and a proportion of cavalry and artillery; and these troops must be equally clothed, armed, organized, and trained with the others.

I do not believe that any advantage will be gained by training the troops in a legion, instead of in a battalion or a brigade; and I am afraid that some inconvenience and delay would be experienced in raising legions instead of battalions and regiments, at least in Portugal, as the conscription for the latter is perfectly understood by the provinces, and it must be taught them for the former. If it should be thought that the number and composition of troops in a legion are convenient for the service, although both numbers and composition are undefined and perfectly arbitrary, I have to observe, that the mode of raising and training men by battalions and regiments now in use, affords equal or even greater facilities for the employment of any numbers of any composition upon any service, as there is nothing to do but to compose brigades and divisions of any numbers of infantry, cavalry, and artillery, that may be deemed expedient, and the object is attained. But the proposal to form legions, as contained in Mr. Villiers's dispatch, does not apply solely to the mode of raising and training soldiers, or to the composition of bodies for service, but affects also the employment of small bodies of troops rather than large bodies, against the enemy in the Peninsula.

I entirely concur with Mr. Villiers that independent small bodies, operating upon the enemy, may be extremely useful, when those operations are connected and carried on in concert with those of a large body of troops, which at the moment occupy the whole of the enemy's attention and the operations of all his troops. But when, from circumstances, the enemy is relieved from the pressure of the operations of the larger body, and can turn his attention to those of the legion or smaller body, the smaller body must discontinue its operations, or be destroyed. I should therefore doubt the expediency of the adoption of a military system, which must be attended with these effects. In Spain, and possibly in Portugal, officers might be found capable of commanding these small independent corps. In the Spanish service, in particular, there are officers very capable of commanding brigades, and divisions, and independent corps: where the Spaniards fail is in the lower ranks of their officers, and in their soldiers; but if there were ten legions in the service of the allies, instead of one legion, they would not effect any one of the objects which Mr. Villiers proposes for their operations, unless they should join together under one head, and become an army, like any other of equal numbers; or unless their operations were carried on in concert with, and were protected by, those of a larger body, capable by its numbers, its composition, and its efficiency, of taking up the attention of the enemy. The partial warfare which is the object of Mr. Villiers's dispatch to recommend, and of the system of raising legions to carry it into execution, cannot be carried on against the enemy in the position occupied by him to the end of September, without the certain loss of the corps employed in carrying it on, having previously failed in attaining any one object.

With respect to the British army acting in separate corps for the same object, the commander of each being independent of the other, it is inconsistent with the practice of all armies, and particularly the French army; and it is to be apprehended that, although the employment of 50,000 men, or even a smaller body, in two or more corps, might, under circumstances, be advisable, the distinctness and independence of commands must be prejudicial to the service.

To Brig. Gen. Slade.   Lisbon, 12th Oct. 1809.

I have perused the proceedings of the General Court Martial, of which you are President, on the trial of Lieut. ——, of the — regt., for 'most unofficerlike and ungentlemanlike conduct, in being concerned in an affray which took place in the city of Lisbon, on the night of the 3d of March last, 1809,' of which crime the Court have *honorably* acquitted him; and I request you to re-assemble the General Court Martial, and to desire them to revise this sentence.

It appears that the affray in which the Court have found that Lieut. —— was concerned originated in a brothel, in which Lieut. —— was with other officers; and although his conduct in the affray might have been distinguished by his activity to quell it, and merits the acquittal which the Court have sentenced, I should not do my duty by them or by His Majesty, who has intrusted me with the power of confirming their sentence, if I did not draw their attention to the use of the term *honorably*, which it contains.

It is difficult and needless at present to define in what cases an honorable acquittal by a Court Martial is peculiarly applicable; but it must appear to all persons to be objectionable, in a case in which any part of the transaction, which has been the subject of investigation before the Court Martial, is disgraceful to the character of the party under trial. A sentence of honorable acquittal by a Court Martial should be considered by the officers and soldiers of the army as a subject of exultation; but no man can exult in the termination of any transaction, a part of which has been disgraceful to him; and although such a transaction may be terminated by an *honorable* acquittal by a Court Martial, it cannot be mentioned to the party without offence, or without exciting feelings of disgust in others: these are not the feelings which ought to be excited by the recollection and mention of a sentence of honorable acquittal.

I believe that there is no officer upon the General Court Martial who wishes to connect the term honor with the act of going to a brothel; the common practice forbids it, and there is no man who unfortunately commits this act who does not endeavor to conceal it from the world and his friends. But the honorable acquittal of Lieut. ——, as recorded in this sentence, which states that he was concerned in an affray, which is known to have originated in a brothel, will have the effect of connecting with the act of going to a brothel the honorable distinction which it is in the power of a Court Martial to bestow on those brought before them on charges of a very different nature, by the sentence which it may pass upon them. I therefore anxiously recommend to the General Court Martial to omit the word *honorably* in their sentence.

To Lieut. Gen. Sir J. Sherbrooke, K.B.   Lisbon, 13th Oct. 1809.

The packet arrived only this morning, and I now send the letters for the army by a messenger. There does not appear to be any news, but a change of the ministry is probable.

I shall mention what you wish in my dispatch to the Sec. of State. You have done quite right, and what I expected about the troops. I send to the Adj. Gen. some orders, Courts Martial, &c., and answers upon the applications for leave. I am very anxious to throw as many impediments in the way of people leaving the army as is possible, and therefore I have ordered the certificates, medical boards, &c. &c.; but if you know any body who really requires change of air, do not hesitate about letting him go.

I intended that Pakenham should command Campbell's brigade during his absence, till Cole should arrive; he now wishes for another arrangement, however, about which I write to him. I intended that Kemmis should remain at Badajoz with the 27th and the 40th, and Pakenham would, as senior officer, have been in command of Olivença as well as of Campbell's brigade.

To Lieut. Gen. Payne.   Lisbon, 13th Oct. 1809.

I have received orders to draft the horses of the 23d dragoons into the other regiments, and send the men home; which measure I propose to carry into execution as soon as I shall join the army. I beg you to turn your mind to the arrangements to be adopted in order to carry this measure into execution. That which I think of is, to bring the whole of the 23d to Villa Viçosa, there to divide and allot the horses to the different regiments, and let the regiments have at Villa Viçosa a certain number of dismounted men to take charge of the horses they shall receive.

I conclude that we must transfer with the horses some of the appointments belonging to the 20th dragoons. Let me have all this arrangement cut and dried by the time I shall return. Could you not contrive to give some of the horses of the 23d to the heavy cavalry? I enclose a bit of a letter of the 23d from Lady Liverpool.

To the Rt. Hon. J. Villiers.   Lisbon, 13th Oct. 1809.

I have the honor to acknowledge the receipt of your letter of the 12th; and as I am convinced of the necessity of having an additional piece of ground at Lisbon for the burial of the dead, I will give directions that the expense of the ground you mention may be paid, till I shall hear from your Excellency that other arrangements have been made for paying for it.

To Dom Miguel Forjaz.   Lisbon, 15th Oct. 1809.

I have had the honor of receiving your letter of the 12th inst., conveying to me, by desire of the Regents of the Kingdom, the copy of a memorial from Don Evaristo Perez de Castro, on the part of the Spanish government, in which he desires the co-operation of the Portuguese corps on the frontiers of Castille, with the Spanish corps under the command of the Duque del Parque.

From the numbers and position of the enemy in Castille and Estremadura, and from the superior discipline, composition, and efficiency of their troops, compared with those of Spain, I have long been of opinion that the operations of the war must necessarily be defensive on the part of the allies; and that Portugal at least, if not Spain, ought to endeavor to avail herself of the period during which the enemy was likely to leave this country in tranquillity to organise, discipline, and equip her army. These objects, which are most essential, cannot be accomplished unless the troops are kept for some time longer in a state of tranquillity; and I conceive they are much more important to the cause, not only of Portugal, but of the allies, than success in any desultory expedition against the French corps stationed at Salamanca.

But success against this corps would not be certain, even if the Portuguese troops were to co-operate in the expedition; and, at all events, if the troops of the allies should be successful, their success must be confined to the few days which might elapse before the French corps would be reinforced; when the allied troops must retire, having failed in their object, having incurred some loss of men, and, above all, having lost time which may and ought to be usefully employed in equipping, and in the formation of the troops. On these grounds I do not recommend to the government of the Kingdom to give the assistance required on the present occasion.

To Marquis Wellesley.   Lisbon, 15th Oct. 1809.

I apprised your Excellency in my letter of the 5th that I had sent my aide de camp, Capt. A. Gordon, to Gen. Bassecourt to urge him to send back forthwith to the French head quarters Capt. Thévenon, the officer respecting whom I wrote to you on the 5th, and I now have the honor to enclose the answer to my request which I have received from Gen. Bassecourt, and Capt. Gordon's report of his mission.

After the request which I made to the Spanish government through your Excellency, I acknowledge that the refusal to consent to my request, coming from the Minister of the War department, surprised me, as I imagined that I had some claims to the favorable consideration of any request of mine to the Spanish government. But when I consider that this officer came into the Spanish lines under my protection, to bring me a letter on a subject equally interesting to the Spanish government as to myself, and as I have a right to claim him, unless it should be established as a principle that the commanding officer of the British forces is not to hold any communication with the French Commander in Chief, relating to the officers and soldiers who are prisoners of war, I am still more astonished that the refusal to allow this officer to depart, upon my request, should have proceeded from the government.

The pretences for detaining him, as stated in Gen. Bassecourt's letter, are as idle as the detention of him is improper and ungracious towards me personally. It is said that he crossed the river by swimming; upon which I have to observe that it was probable he could not cross the river in any other manner opposite the Spanish posts. He was sent with a letter to me by his commanding officer; and the Spanish troops being on one side of the river, and the French on the other, he could deliver the letter only by crossing the river, and it is probable at that place he was obliged to swim. But if his passage was irregular, he might have been sent back, and might have been ordered to bring his letter to the place at which the Spanish Commander in Chief chose to receive it; or if there had been any thing irregular in his conduct, it might and ought to have been mentioned when he first arrived at the Spanish head quarters. But not a word is said against the mode in which this officer entered the Spanish lines, nor is any complaint made of his conduct in answer to two different requests made by me that he should be sent back to the French head quarters; and these objections to his return are discovered at Seville by the Minister in the War department, 6 weeks after this officer had arrived, and had been detained in the Spanish lines.

The other objection to his return is that, during his residence at the Spanish head quarters, he may have acquired a knowledge of the positions of the Spanish army, and that it was therefore imprudent to allow him to· return to his own army. This objection is equally futile with the other, for in point of fact this gentleman has been in confinement ever since his arrival at the Spanish head quarters, and can have obtained no knowledge of any thing of importance. But it is a curious circumstance that the arrival of the French officer at the Spanish head quarters, which is to be attributed to the ignorance of duty in the officer at the Spanish outposts; and his detention there, which is to be attributed to the injustice of the Spanish Commander in Chief, and of the Spanish government, should now be stated as reasons for a further detention, for continued injustice and violation of the laws and customs of war, and for a continuation of an indignity upon the commanding officer of the British forces in Spain.

The objection to the knowledge acquired by this officer of the nature of the positions of the Spanish army is futile in another point of view, and cannot apply to his being delivered over to me. Reasons might exist why he should not be sent back by the way he came, or even by the way of Arzobispo; but none can exist for refusing to deliver him to me, and to allow me to send him to the French lines by some other road

I beg to draw your Excellency's attention to this subject, which is of importance, not only because the conduct of the Spanish government upon this occasion may put an end to all communication between the French officers and me, regarding the British officers who are prisoners of war; and may be the cause of their detention in captivity throughout the war between Great Britain and France, unalleviated by any communication with their friends, or by the receipt of money or other assistance or comforts, but on account of the principles which this conduct would establish, and the temper which it shows now exists in the Spanish councils.

I believe that when the armies of two powers are acting in concert, it has never been understood that the Commander in Chief of the one could prevent the correspondence of the Commander in Chief of the other with the enemy, upon subjects not only not inconsistent with the objects of their co-operation, but upon one equally interesting to both parties.

In respect to the subject of this correspondence, I have to inform your Excellency that no suspicion could have been entertained, as I desired the Spanish Commander in Chief to open and read all the letters which passed through his posts, whether sealed or otherwise. If this principle is to be adopted; if barbarities such as are committed by both sides, in the warfare between the Spanish and French nations, are to be extended to the British troops; and if our prisoners are to be treated in the manner in which it appears from Capt. Gordon's letter that the French prisoners in the hands of the Spaniards are to be treated, it will become still more difficult than it is for a British army to give any assistance to the cause of Spain.

The temper which the refusal to liberate this officer has manifested may be perhaps only personal towards me, although I had hoped that I had established some claim for consideration by the Spanish government. At all events, I cannot believe that the government is favorably inclined to the British army in thus throwing impediments in the way of the release of wounded officers and soldiers from captivity, who were wounded in the service of Spain, and who were made prisoners only in consequence of a movement made by the Spanish army.

I entreat your Excellency to make a representation on this subject to the Spanish government; and if it should not be successful, I shall be under the necessity of making a report upon it to the Sec. of State, to be laid before the King.

P.S. I beg to call your Excellency's attention to Capt. Gordon's report of the Spanish army, which was stated to your Excellency to consist of 12,000 men.

To Lieut. Gen. Sir J. Sherbrooke, K.B.　　　　　　　　Lisbon, 16th Oct. 1809.

As I am sending a dispatch to Lord Wellesley on the extraordinary conduct of the Spanish government in respect to Capt. Thévenon, I avail

---

G. O.　　　　　　　　　　　　　　　　　Badajoz, 16th Oct. 1809.

The Commander of the Forces cannot avoid to draw the attention of the army in particular to the circumstances of Capt. ——'s case, and to urge them to avoid misfortunes similar to those he has met with, by avoiding the places in which they originate. The Commander of the Forces will not aggravate the distress which Capt. —— must feel, by entering into further particulars; but in pursuance of the sentence of the General Court Martial, he hereby reprimands him for his conduct, at Lisbon, on the night of the 3d March, 1809.

G. O.　　　　　　　　　　　　　　　　　Badajoz, 17th Oct 1809.

8. ——, having been tried by a General Court Martial, is to be released from his close arrest, but is to continue at Lisbon in arrest at large till further orders, and in to show himself daily at the Town Major's office.

The Commander of the Forces is always concerned when he is obliged to place an officer in close arrest; but if officers break their arrest and conceal themselves, and quit the situation pointed out for their residence, they must expect that the Commander of the Forces will use the power which he has to compel them to conduct themselves as British officers ought.

myself of the opportunity to acknowledge the receipt of your letter of the 13th. I shall write to England respecting Capt. Christie's exchange, but I must have the original cartel given to him by the French officer. I hope to be at Badajoz next Sunday, as I intend to leave this on Friday.

To J. Murray, Esq., Commissary General.　　　　　　　　　Lisbon, 16th Oct. 1809.

I return you the papers you had left me. The whole of the demands of which they are the vouchers ought to be paid; those which I have approved of ought to be charged to the public, and a list should be made of those of which I have not approved, and the individuals whose names appear to the vouchers ought to be called upon to account for having signed these receipts; and it ought particularly to be inquired into, whether they could have received the articles from the Commissariat or any officer belonging to it; or whether, under the orders in their route, their provisions for that day were not already supplied. I think it probable that the result will be that the whole ought to be charged to the public; but in the mean time the inquiry will prevent further irregularities. I observe that many of these irregular receipts are signed by Commissaries, and others in the Commissariat department; and I beg that you will let these gentlemen know that if they should give receipts irregularly drawn, or improperly signed, in future, the articles shall be paid for, but the amount shall be charged to their private account.

The objection I have to allowing payments to be made to others, excepting to the parties who supplied the articles for which payment is required, is, that it is probable that the vouchers have been sold; and the consequence of this system must be to raise the price of all articles upon the public. I am therefore very averse to encourage the practice of the purchase and sale of vouchers for the supply of articles for the British army, although I am well aware of the convenience that would result as well to the parties as to the service, if the agents and assignees of the parties could be paid for the supplies at Lisbon, instead of on the spot where the supplies are furnished. I am however disposed to adopt your recommendation, and will authorise the payment for supplies to the assignees of the party who has furnished them, in every case in which it shall appear to you that the transaction is a fair one, and that the assignee is the real agent of the party claiming the debt, and not the purchaser of a voucher or vouchers at a low price, from the person who furnished the supplies.

There is one mode in which you will be able to form a judgment upon this subject, and that is, by the party having only a few or many debts assigned to him: if only one or a few, it is probable that he may be a real agent; if many debts, he is certainly a purchaser of vouchers.

To Lieut. Gen. Sir J. Sherbrooke, K.B.　　　　　　　　　Lisbon, 19th Oct. 1809.

I received yesterday your letters of the 10th, 15th, and 16th. Mr. —— has not behaved very well to you, for he should have told you that I had already refused him leave to establish himself, or to go to Lisbon. However, you did quite right in allowing him to go.

The regiments have all of them required so many carts to carry clothing and baggage, much of which I am persuaded they cannot want, and I shall be obliged to carry back again to Lisbon, that the country cannot produce carts sufficient to carry up other articles wanted by the army. They will go, however, in time; and I give orders that the medicines, at all events, shall be sent up to the army forthwith. These medical gentlemen should, however, give us some more notice, and not come and report that their medicines are expended, the first time they notice the probability of a want.

Desire Mr. Hancock to state what induced him to separate from the sick to go to Lisbon. I send answers upon the different points referred to in yours of the 15th, to the Adj. Gen.

I dread a removal of the sick to Lisbon: the last cost us many men, and they must go on bullock carts: the next will cost us more in consequence of bad weather.

Desire Col. de Lancey * to take a ride over to Estremoz, and see whether he could find accommodation for any at that place or Evora. If he cannot, we must send them to Lisbon, but we had better wait till the ten days' rain shall be over.

To J. Murray Esq., Commissary General. Lisbon, 19th Oct. 1809.

I have received your letter of the 15th inst. The carts which will be hired to attend upon the army ought not to be employed on the road of communication between Lisbon and Badajoz, but should do the business with the army itself, the means adopted for the communication with Lisbon being very likely to answer perfectly.

I think there are objections to Mr. Ogilvie's arrangement. The difference of rates for working days and halting days, and for carts with and without rations, opens the door for disputes, which must protract the settlements of accounts, and in the end the public will pay the highest rate. It would be much better at once to give rations, and to fix a price, whether they work or not, and pay that price once a week. I am concerned to observe from Mr. Ogilvie's letters that his operations are cramped; nay, that the price of articles is increased from his want of money.

In respect to the supplies at Portalegre, you must expect that the General officers will interfere with your magazines and arrangements until your officers are so diligent and expert in the performance of their duty, as to make it certain that the troops and horses shall get their food regularly, if it is to be got in the country. If the General officers (Gen. Payne particularly) had not exerted themselves, in the late campaigns in Spain and Portugal, the troops and horses must have died of want; and I doubt not that ascertained want at Villa Viçosa, or apprehension of want, is the cause of Gen. Payne's order upon Portalegre. You will recollect that your contractor drew all the supplies from Villa Viçosa for the troops, &c. at Elvas.

I enclose a letter which has been put into my hands by Mr. Villiers, and I request you to adopt immediate measures for the settlement of this account, and the payment of the debt to the Junta de Viveres. I beg you also to desire Mr. Dunmore to take up from the Portuguese govern-

* Assist. Q. M. Gen. He was mortally wounded at Waterloo.

ment bills given to them by Mr. Erskine for £15,000, according to the
directions I before gave you upon that subject.

To Dom Miguel Forjaz.   Lisbon, 19th Oct. 1809.

I have had the honor of receiving your letter of the 17th inst., in which
you enclose, by desire of the governors of the Kingdom, a letter from
Don E. Perez de Castro, Chargé d'Affaires of Spain.

The object of this note is to obtain from their Excellencies, on the
part of his Royal Highness, a positive and definite answer, at what time
the troops of Portugal shall co-operate with those of Spain, within the
Spanish territory, against the common enemy in the Peninsula; and the
governors of the Kingdom have been pleased to desire to have my opinion
before they order that an answer should be sent to this note.

In the letter which I had the honor of addressing your Excellency on
the 15th inst., I informed you of the circumstances which render it un-
advisable, in my opinion, to enter upon any operation with the Portuguese
troops at present; and it would be difficult for me, or for any person, to
point out the precise period at which an alteration of those circumstances
will take place.

Besides this alteration of circumstances, as referrible to the state of the
Portuguese troops, and to the state and position of the enemy's troops in
Castille and Estremadura, I have to observe that it is desirable that other
objects should be accomplished, and other arrangements made, before the
Portuguese troops can enter with propriety upon operations in Spain.

1st, It is desirable that it should have an army with which it can co-
operate, on some defined plan of operations, which all parties will have
means, and will engage to carry into execution, as far at least as any person can engage to carry into execution any particular military operation.

2dly, It is desirable, nay, it is necessary, that some means should be
pointed out, and fixed, by which the Portuguese troops are to be subsisted
while they shall remain in Spain, so that they may not starve, as they did
when they were in that country lately, and may not be obliged by want
of food to retire.

When decided answers shall be given upon these points, I have no
doubt that I shall be enabled to tell their Excellencies the governors of
the Kingdom that they have an army in a state to be sent into Spain.

To Lieut. V. de Farincourt.   Ce 20 Octobre, 1809.

Je vous envoie une lettre de la part de votre ami le Capitaine Thévenon, à qui j'avais donné connaissance de votre sort, quoique vous ne soyez
pas sous ma charge. Je vous envoie aussi 40 piastres pour lesquels je
vous prie de m'envoyer votre reçu, et je vous préviens que le gouvernement Portugais m'a fait la grâce de consentir à la prière que je lui ai
faite de vous laisser retourner à l'armée Française en échange pour un
officier Anglais qui a été renvoyé par le Général Kellermann. Comme
il n'est pas possible que vous passiez ou par le Portugal ou par l'Espagne
sans escorte, le Maréchal Beresford vous préviendra quand l'escorte sera
prête, et vous donnera la lettre que je lui ai envoyée pour le Général
Kellermann et votre cartel d'échange.

Au Gen. Kellermann.   Ce 20 Octobre, 1809.

J'ai reçu les deux lettres que vous m'avez fait l'honneur de m'écrire, et je suis bien sensible aux bontés que vous avez eues pour les officiers Anglais qui ont passé par votre quartier général. Je suis fâché que vous croyez avoir à vous plaindre de quelques uns d'entre eux ; mais si vous examinez l'action qu'ils ont commise, vous verrez qu'ils n'ont pas tant tort que vous l'imaginez.

Les officiers Anglais qui ont donné leur parole, et qui jouissent en conséquence d'un peu de liberté et de l'aisance que les lois et coûtumes de la guerre donnaient autrefois aux prisonniers de guerre, ne violeront jamais

---

G. O.   Badajoz, 20th Oct. 1809.

1. Complaints having been made of the irregularity and difficulties which exist in quartering officers in Lisbon, owing to the disobedience of the G. O. of the late Commander of the Forces, of the 14th March last, these Orders are again published, and the attention of the officers of the army is again called to them.

2. Officers now quartered in Lisbon are forthwith to return to the A. Q. M. G., at Lisbon, their names, stating where they are quartered ; and the A. Q. M. G. will make out a general list of the officers and their quarters, and will deliver it to the Superintendent of the police.

3. Officers who will omit to give their names and places of abode to the A. Q. M. G., according to this order, will be considered as having quitted the house in which they were billeted, others will be billeted on the house, and the officer, who will be guilty of this omission, will be obliged to hire a lodging.

4. In future all officers moving from one place to another, in Portugal or Spain, are to have a route from the Q. M. G.'s department, which is to specify where the officer is to halt each day.

5. The officers of the Q. M. G.'s department, who will grant these routes upon application for them, will keep copies of them ; and the officers, who will receive them, will send them to the Q. M. G. on their arrival at their destination.

6. Officers applying for a route to quit Lisbon are to return their billets to the A. Q. M. G., who will forthwith send them to the Superintendent of the police.

' G. O.   Lisbon, 14th March, 1809.

' Representations having been made to the Commander of the Forces on the subject of the inconvenience sustained, both by the inhabitants and officers of the army, from want of better arrangements regarding billets, his Excellency finds it necessary to establish the following regulations :

· 1. All General officers and heads of departments will apply, and receive their billets, from the D. Q. M. G.

' 2. All other officers are to receive their billets from the Town Major.

' 3. No officer quitting Lisbon is to retain his quarters, but he must give back his billet to the department from which he has received it, whether the D. Q. M. G. or Town Major.

' 4. No officer is on any account to select any particular house, nor to choose his own quarters ; all that they can expect is, that each shall be provided with a quarter suitable to his rank.

' 5. Colonels will be entitled to four rooms, Field officers three, Captains two, Subalterns one room for each. Staff officers will have quarters allotted them according to their comparative rank they hold in their several departments, civil or military.

' 6. No officer, under the rank of a General officer, is to require more than two servants' beds at the most.

' 7. No officer is on any account to deliver over his billet to another.

' 8. No billet is to be exchanged for any officer of any rank, without previous application to the D. Q. M. G. If the officer applying be under the rank of a General officer, he is to apply through the Town Major, who will presently explain to the D. Q. M. G. the cause of the application.

' 9. No officer whatever has any pretensions to look for or require any thing more than his lodgings, where he is billeted.

' 10. The Town Major, in applying to the Intendant General for billets, is to specify the several ranks for which they are required ; and if they are for Staff officers, he will indicate the comparative rank held by them.

' All officers whatever who have got into houses without regular billets, are to send in their names to the D. Q. M. G., that billets may be either made out for the present quarters they now occupy, or other quarters allotted to them.'

la parole qu'ils ont donnée ; et je puis vous assurer que s'il y en avait un dans le cas d'avoir commis cette action, je le renverrais tout de suite à l'ennemi, s'il osait m'approcher. Mais ceux que vous gardez prisonniers sous les gardes, qui n'ont aucune perspective qu'une longue captivité, s'échapperont quand ils pourront, malgré que vous les traitiez avec des égards. Soyez sûr, M. le Général, qu'il vaudrait bien mieux leur donner la parole à tous, et que l'honneur d'un officier Anglais vaut bien mieux que tous les gardes et sentinelles au monde.

Votre aide de camp, M. de Turenne, est prisonnier du Commandant en Chef de l'armée Espagnole en Castille, et il a été envoyé à Seville. Il a passé avant que je n'aie su qu'il était prisonnier ; mais j'ai eu de ses nouvelles, et il se porte bien. J'ai fait la demande au gouvernement Espagnol de me faire la grâce de consentir à son retour à l'armée Française, en échange pour le Lieut. Cameron, mais je n'ai pas encore reçu de réponse. Vous pouvez être sûr que je ferai tout en mon pouvoir pour vous rendre le Lieut. de Turenne, et que si je n'ai pas de succès dans cet objet-là, je tâcherai au moins d'adoucir son sort. En attendant que je reçoive la réponse du gouvernement Espagnol, je renvoie le Lieut. Louis Véron de Farincourt en échange pour le Lieut. Cameron, et je renverrai le Lieut. de Turenne en échange pour quelqu'autre, aussitôt que j'aurai la réponse du gouvernement Espagnol.

Cartel of exchange.

Head quarters of the British army, 20th Oct. 1809.

Cartel of exchange between Lieut. Cameron of the 79th regt., taken by the French army at Talavera, (and sent in to the British army, on a cartel of exchange with Lieut. de Turenne, aide de camp to Gen. Kellermann,) and Lieut. L. Véron de Farincourt of the 2d light infantry of the French army, taken by the Portuguese army at Chaves, and now in confinement at Lisbon.

The above mentioned exchange with Lieut. de Turenne not taking effect, Lieut. Cameron of the 79th is exchanged for Lieut. L. V. de Farincourt. In consequence thereof, Lieut. Louis V. de Farincourt is authorised to join the French army ; and all officers commanding English, Portuguese, and Spanish troops, are requested to allow him to pass to the French army without molestation.

Lieut. V. de Farincourt will show this cartel of exchange to the Commander in Chief of the French army.

Memorandum for Lieut. Col. Fletcher, commanding Royal Engineers.*

Lisbon, 20th Oct. 1809.

In the existing relative state of the Allied and French armies in the Peninsula, it does not appear probable that the enemy have it in their power to make an attack upon Portugal. They must wait for their rein-

---

* ' The plan was altered after this memorandum was written, as it was found that the plain of Castanheira could not be occupied with advantage; the right was therefore thrown back on Alhandra. But this memorandum is the foundation on which the whole work was commenced and completed. It was written after a detailed reconnaissance of the ground, and a personal visit to every part of it.'

forcements; and as the arrival of these may be expected, it remains to be considered what plan of defence shall be adopted for this country.

The great object in Portugal is the possession of Lisbon and the Tagus, and all our measures must be directed to this object. There is another also connected with that first object, to which we must likewise attend, viz.; the embarkation of the British troops in case of reverse.

In whatever season the enemy may enter Portugal, he will probably make his attack by two distinct lines, the one north, the other south of the Tagus; and the system of defence to be adopted must be founded upon this general basis.

In the winter season the river Tagus will be full, and will be a barrier to the enemy's enterprises with his left attack, not very difficult to be secured. In the summer season, however, the Tagus being fordable in many places between Abrantes and Salvaterra, and even lower than Salvaterra, care must be taken that the enemy does not, by his attack directed from the south of the Tagus, and by the passage of that river, cut off from Lisbon the British army engaged in operations to the northward of the Tagus.

The object of the allies should be to oblige the enemy as much as possible to make his attack with concentrated corps. They should stand in every position which the country could afford, such a length of time as would enable the people of the country to evacuate the towns and villages, carrying with them or destroying all articles of provisions and carriages, not necessary for the allied army; each corps taking care to preserve its communication with the others, and its relative distance from the point of junction.

In whatever season the enemy's attack may be made, the whole allied army, after providing for the garrisons of Elvas, Almeida, Abrantes, and Valença, should be divided into three corps, to be posted as follows: one corps to be in Beira; another in Alentejo; and the third, consisting of the Lusitanian legion, 8 battalions of caçadores, and 2 of militia, in the mountains of Castello Branco.

In the winter, the corps in Beira should consist of two thirds of the whole numbers of the operating army. In the summer, the corps in Beira and Alentejo should be nearly of equal numbers.

I shall point out in another memorandum the plan of operations to be adopted by the corps north and south of the Tagus in the winter months.

In the summer, it is probable, as I have above stated, that the enemy will make his attack in two principal corps, and that he will also push one through the mountains of Castello Branco and Abrantes. His object will be, by means of his corps south of the Tagus, to turn the positions which might be taken up in his front on the north of that river; to cut off from Lisbon the corps opposed to him; and to destroy it by an attack in front and rear at the same time. This can be avoided only by the retreat of the right centre, and left of the allies, and their junction at a point at which, from the state of the river, they cannot be turned by the passage of the Tagus by the enemy's left.

The first point of defence which presents itself below that at which the Tagus ceases to be fordable is the river of Castanheira, and here the army should be posted as follows :—10,000 men, including all the cavalry, in the plain between the Tagus and the hills; 5000 infantry on the left of the plain ; and the remainder of the army, with the exception of the following detachments, on the height in front, and on the right of Cadafoës.

In order to prevent the enemy from turning, by their left, the positions which the allies may take up for the defence of the high road to Lisbon by the Tagus, Torres Vedras should be occupied by a corps of 5000 men ; the height in the rear of Sobral de Monte Agraço by 4000 men; and Arruda by 2000 men.

There should be a small corps on the height east by south of the height of Sobral, to prevent the enemy from marching from Sobral to Arruda ; and there should be another small corps on the height of Ajuda, between Sobral and Bucellas.

In case the enemy should succeed in forcing the corps at Torres Vedras, or Sobral de Monte Agraço, or Arruda; if the first, it must fall back gradually to Cabeça de Montachique, occupying every defensible point on the road ; if the second, it must fall back upon Bucellas, destroying the road after the height of Ajuda ; if the third, it must fall back upon Alhandra, disputing the road particularly at a point one league in front of that town.

In case any one of these three positions should be forced, the army must fall back from its position as before pointed out, and must occupy one as follows :

5000 men, principally light infantry, on the hill behind Alhandra ; the main body of the army on the Serra de Serves, with its right on that part of the Serra which is near the Cazal de Portella, and.is immediately above the road which crosses the Serra from Bucellas to Alverca ; and its left extending to the pass of Bucellas. The entrance of the pass of Bucellas to be occupied by the troops retired from Sobral de Monte Agraço, &c., and Cabeça de Montachique by the corps retired from Torres Vedras.

In order to strengthen these several positions, it is necessary that different works should be constructed immediately, and that arrangements and preparations should be made for the construction of others.

Accordingly, I beg Col. Fletcher, as soon as possible, to review these several positions.

1st. He will examine particularly the effect of damming up the mouth of the Castanheira river ; how far it will render that river a barrier, and to what extent it will fill.

2d. He will calculate the labor required for that work, and the time it will take, as well as the means of destroying the bridge over the river, and of constructing such redoubts as might be necessary on the plain, and on the hill on the left of the road, effectually to defend the plain. He will state particularly what means should be prepared for these works. He will also consider of the means and time required, and the effect which might be produced by sloping the banks of the river.

3d. He will make the same calculations for the works to be executed on the hill in front, and on the right of Cadafoës, particularly on the left of that hill, to shut the entry of the valley of Cadafoës.

4th. He will examine and report upon the means of making a good road of communication from the plain across the hills into the valley of Cadafoës, and to the left of the proposed position, and calculate the time and labor it will take.

5th. He will examine the road from Otta by Abregada, Labrugeira to Merciana, and thence to Torres Vedras; and also from Merciana to Sobral de Monte Agraço. He will also examine and report upon the road from Alemquer to Sobral de Monte Agraço.

6th. He will entrench a post at Torres Vedras for 5000 men. He will examine the road from Torres Vedras to Cabeca de Montachique; and fix upon the spots, which to break up, might stop or delay the enemy; and if there should be advantageous ground at such spots, he will entrench a position for 400 men to cover the retreat of the corps from Torres Vedras.

7th. He will examine the position at Cabeça de Montachique, and determine upon its line of defence, and upon the works to be constructed for its defence, by a corps of 5000 men; of which he will estimate the time and the labor.

8th. He will entrench a position for 4000 men on the two heights which command the road from Sobral de Monte Agraço to Bucellas.

9th. He will entrench a position for 400 men on the height of Ajuda, between Sobral and Bucellas, to cover the retreat of the corps from Sobral to Bucellas; and he will calculate the means and the time it will take to destroy the road at that spot.

10th. He will construct a redoubt for 200 men and 3 guns at the windmill on the height of Sobral de Monte Agraço, which guns will bear upon the road from Sobral to Arruda.

11th. He will ascertain the points at which, and the means by which, the road from Sobral to Arruda can be destroyed.

12th. He will ascertain the labor and time required to entrench a position which he will fix upon for 2000 men to defend the road coming out of Arruda towards Villa Franca and Alhandra, and he will fix upon the spot at which the road from Arruda to Alhandra can be destroyed with advantage.

13th. He will construct a redoubt on the hill which commands the road from Arruda, about one league in front of Alhandra.

14th. He will examine the æstuaries at Alhandra, and see whether, by damming them up at the mouths, he could increase the difficulties of a passage by that place; and he will ascertain the time and labor and means which this work will require.

15th. He will fix upon the spots, and ascertain the time and labor required to construct redoubts upon the hill of Alhandra on the right, to prevent the passage of the enemy by the high road; and on the left, and in the rear, to prevent by their fire the occupation of the mountains towards Alverca.

16th. He will determine upon the works to be constructed on the right of the position upon the Serra de Serves, as above pointed out, to prevent the enemy from forcing that point; and he will calculate the means and the time required to execute them. He will likewise examine the pass of

Bucellas, and fix upon the works to be constructed for its defence, and calculate the means, time, and labor required for the execution.

17th. He will calculate the means, time, and labor required to construct a work upon the hill upon which the windmill stands, at the southern entrance at the pass of Bucellas.

18th. He will fix upon spots on which signal posts can be erected upon these hills, to communicate from one part of the position to the other.

19th. It is very desirable that we should have an accurate plan of the ground.

20th. Examine the island in the river opposite to Alhandra, and fix upon the spot, and calculate the means and time required to construct batteries upon it to play upon the approach to Alhandra.

21st. Examine the effect of damming up the river which runs by Loures, and calculate the time and means required to break up the bridge at Loures.

To Visc. Castlereagh.   Lisbon, 20th Oct. 1809.

I enclose a letter from Marshal Beresford, dated the 11th inst., containing an application from Lieut. Col. Cox, who is acting as a Brigadier General in the Portuguese service, to be permitted by His Majesty to accept the commission of Brigadier General in Spain, to which the Central Junta have promoted him from that of Colonel, which he had before accepted by His Majesty's permission, and I request your Lordship to recommend the application of Brig. Gen. Cox to His Majesty's approbation.

I likewise enclose a letter, of the 11th inst., from Marshal Beresford, relative to the wish felt by many British officers, who have been appointed to serve with the Portuguese army, to return to England to join their regiments, the gratification of which wish has hitherto been resisted here on the ground that the officers having voluntarily accepted employment in a service on which they were consequently ordered by His Majesty, they could not be permitted to relinquish it without His Majesty's orders.

If this principle should be approved of, there will still remain for consideration the case of Lieut. Col. Macdonell of the 78th,* and other officers promoted in His Majesty's service, after they had received orders to serve and had arrived in Portugal. His Majesty might have thought it fit to allow Major Macdonell to serve in Portugal, but when that officer is promoted to be a Lieut. Colonel, and the command of a British regiment would probably devolve upon him, it might be inconvenient to His Majesty's service to allow him to remain in Portugal. I therefore request to be made acquainted with the wishes of His Majesty's government upon cases of this description.

I likewise enclose a letter from Marshal Beresford, of the 19th inst., relative to Brig. Gen. —— and Col. ——, who have absented themselves from the Portuguese service without leave, and who, it appears, cannot be punished for this misconduct, as they are not in His Majesty's service. I beg leave to recommend that, in future, persons of this description

* Lieut. Gen. Sir James Macdonell, K.C.B.

may not be sent to serve in Portugal, for reasons referrible to the sensations which the employment of them creates in the Portuguese service; as well as because no means exist of punishing the military disorders and irregularities of which they may be guilty, of the kind committed by Brig. Gen. ⸻ and Col. ⸻. In respect to these gentlemen, I should also beg leave to suggest, that they may not in future be employed in England in the capacity of Inspecting Field officers, &c.

To Visc. Castlereagh.   Lisbon, 20th Oct. 1809.

I enclose a letter from Marshal Beresford, of the 16th inst., in which he desires that Capt. Trant, who is acting as a Colonel in the service of Portugal, may not lose his situation on the permanent Staff of the Q. M. G. while so employed. If Capt. Trant should be obliged to make the option, whether he would return to his duty at the Horse Guards or remain in Portugal, he must choose the former, and this country will lose the services of an officer who has made himself most useful, and who may hereafter be most usefully employed here.

I hope, therefore, that this consideration, as well as the recollection of the engagement held out to officers to induce them to serve in Portugal, that their situation in the service of His Majesty should not be altered for the worse, will induce your Lordship to urge the Commander in Chief to allow Capt. Trant to retain his appointment in the Q. M. G.'s department.

To Visc. Castlereagh.   Lisbon, 20th Oct. 1809.

I enclose a letter from Marshal Beresford, relative to the want of clothing and accoutrements by the Portuguese troops, which I beg leave to urge may be sent out without loss of time.

I also beg leave to recommend to His Majesty's government the adoption of the measures proposed by Marshal Beresford, to apprise the officers in this country to what extent and to what periods their requisitions will be complied with. It would also be advisable that the articles provided in England for the use of the Portuguese army should be submitted to the inspection of a board of officers previously to their being sent from England.

To Visc. Castlereagh.   Lisbon, 22d Oct. 1809.

I came here a few days ago, in order to be better enabled to form a judgment on the points referred to in your Lordship's dispatch of the 14th Sept., upon which I hope to be able to make a report in the course of a few days.

Since I addressed your Lordship on the 6th inst., I have received accounts that the enemy have collected a corps upon the Tagus, near Toledo, supposed to consist of 30,000 men, with which they have invaded La Mancha.

Gen. Eguia, who commanded the Spanish troops in that quarter, consisting of his own corps, which had been in Estremadura, and that of Gen. Venegas, retired to La Serena, where he was on the 16th inst., and the enemy had not manifested any intention of attacking him.

Soult's corps was, by the last accounts, at Oropesa and Arzobispo, and Mortier's at Talavera; and I conclude that the movement of the whole to their left has been occasioned by the invasion of La Mancha. Ney's corps is still at Salamanca, and the Duque del Parque is near Ciudad Rodrigo. He has lately been reinforced by about 800 cavalry, which had been detached from the army of Estremadura, and by the corps of Ballesteros,* which had been in the Asturias, and consisting of about 7000 men. This corps attacked Zamora on its march southward, but was repulsed, and its march was then directed through Portugal.

I imagine that the late invasion of La Mancha by the French has been occasioned solely by their desire to prevent the Spanish army under Gen. Eguia from enjoying the resources of that province.

To Lieut. Gen. Sir J. Sherbrooke, K.B.   Lisbon, 25th Oct. 1809.

I returned here yesterday, and this morning received yours of the 23d. My horses are gone upon the road, and I shall certainly set out on Friday morning, and shall be at Badajoz on Sunday.

You may depend upon my doing every thing in my power for Capt. Boothby; but having no prisoners in our own hands, and not being able to prevail upon the Spanish government even to give an answer relative to the different propositions made by the French generals for cartels of exchange, I have it not in my power to do much. I think, however, that I may now be able to do something, as the Portuguese government have given me the disposal of all the prisoners in their possession, respecting whom I shall write to Soult as soon as I reach Badajoz. Release Lieut. ——. I send an order to that gentleman.

To Marshal Beresford.   Lisbon, 25th Oct. 1809.

The Portuguese government having placed at my disposal the French prisoners now in confinement in the castle of Lisbon, I request that you will be so kind as to convey the enclosed letter and sum of money to Lieut. V. de Farincourt. I beg you also to send him under an escort to Almeida as soon as may be convenient to you, with the enclosed cartel of exchange, and the letter to Gen. Kellermann; and desire Brig. Gen. Cox to forward him likewise under an escort to the head quarters of the Duque del Parque, and to request the Duque to have him sent to the first French post with his letter, and his cartel of exchange.

To Marquis Wellesley.   Lisbon, 25th Oct. 1809.

I have not been able to quit this place yet; but propose to set out on Friday, and I shall be at Badajoz on Sunday. It will afterwards take a day or two to post my horses on the road towards Seville, and I shall not be able most probably to set out for that place till Tuesday or Wednesday. I suspect that, in this case, I shall be too late to see you; but if you should have been delayed at Seville so long, and if you will write me a line to Badajoz, which I shall receive on Sunday, I shall be happy to go to you. I shall expect to find the carriage at Fuente de Cantos. I have been prevented from answering your last dispatches by the business which I have had here.

* This name so written in MS., and as it was generally written and printed at the time, although in his letters to Lord Wellington this officer signs 'Vallesteros.' B and V in many Spanish words are indiscriminately written, and the difference in pronunciation is not to be distinguished.

To Marshal Beresford.

Lisbon, 26th Oct. 1809.

Col. Fletcher writes to have a corps of militia consisting of 600 men at Torres Vedras, a corps consisting of 500 men at Sobral, and a corps consisting of 800 men at St. Julian, in order to furnish working parties to complete the works at these places respectively, and I shall be obliged to you if you will give orders accordingly.

To Vice Adm. the Hon. G. Berkeley.

Lisbon, 26th Oct. 1809.

I have the honor to enclose an extract of a letter which I have received from the Sec. of State, relative to the defence of this country, in the event of the enemy's armies in Spain being reinforced to such a degree as to render the possession of Portugal doubtful.

In case the enemy should make a serious attack upon Portugal, his object, as well as that of the allies, would be the possession of the city of Lisbon. The British army would necessarily have another object, viz., a secure embarkation, after the possession of the city of Lisbon should be evidently lost.

The line of frontier of Portugal is so long in proportion to the extent and means of the country, and the Tagus and the mountains separate the parts of it so effectually from each other, and it is so open in many parts, that it would be impossible for an army, acting upon the defensive, to carry on its operations upon the frontier without being cut off from the capital. The scene of the operations of the army would therefore most probably be considerably within the frontier, whether their attack be made in winter or in summer; but if it should be made in summer, when the Tagus is fordable in many places, at least as low down as Salvaterra, the scene of the operations of the army would necessarily be lower down than that point. It is probable, also, that in the event of the enemy being enabled to invade this country in force, he will make his principal attack by the right of the Tagus; but he will employ one corps upon the left of that river, with the immediate object of embarrassing, if not of preventing, the embarkation of the British army, and of precluding the use of its navigation by the allies. I should wish, then, to be assisted with your opinion respecting the possibility of embarking the army in its transports, and bringing them away from the following places, in the event of a defeat by the enemy in the field which should oblige the British army to evacuate the country, and which of course supposes that they would be pressed by the enemy.

1st, Peniche. I conceive that I should be able to hold this place during any length of time that might be necessary for an embarkation; but, from what I have above stated, you will observe that in the event of the attack being made between the months of June and November, when the Tagus is fordable, the operations of the army would be carried on in a part of the country which would be cut off from Peniche, and the retreat to that place would be impracticable.

2dly, Paço d'Arcos on the Tagus. I could not pretend to hold the high ground which commands Paço d'Arcos without occupying it with at least 20,000 men, which, in the circumstances stated, would possibly be the total amount to be embarked.

2 o 2

3dly, The two bays to the eastward of St. Julian. I could hold St. Julian and the Bugio for at least 8 days, and could cover an embarkation to be made in these bays, particularly in that immediately under St. Julian, and protect the passage of the fleet out of the river. In deciding upon all projects of embarkation in the Tagus, I beg of you to advert to the probability that the enemy, if in sufficient force, may and will occupy the ground on the left of the river from Almada to Trafaria; and that you will consider how far it will be practicable, if it should be necessary under these circumstances, to remain in the Tagus with the fleet of transports.

4thly, Setuval. I could hold the ground which would cover the embarkation and protect the passage of the fleet out of Setuval for 8 days: but it must be observed respecting this place of embarkation, that an enemy's corps on the left of the Tagus might, if in sufficient strength, render it impracticable to reach it with a beaten army. It is also to be observed, that if the army, after its defeat, should be able to embark in boats and cross the Tagus, to go to Setuval, it might equally embark in boats to go to the transports in the Tagus, and a long and fatiguing march would be avoided.

To Col. Peacocke. Lisbon, 26th Oct. 1809.

I am concerned to be obliged to inform you, that it has been mentioned to me that the British officers who are in Lisbon are in the habit of going to the theatres, where some of them conduct themselves in a very improper manner, much to the annoyance of the public, and to the injury of the proprietors and of the performers. I cannot conceive for what reason the officers of the British army should conduct themselves at Lisbon in a manner which would not be permitted in their own country, is contrary to rule and custom in this country, and is permitted in none where there is any regulation or decency of behaviour. The officers commanding regiments, and the superior officers, must take measures to prevent a repetition of the conduct adverted to, and of the consequent complaints which I have received; or I must take measures which shall effectually prevent the character of the army and of the British nation from suffering by the misconduct of a few.

The officers of the army can have nothing to do behind the scenes, and it is very improper that they should appear upon the stage during the performance. They must be aware that the English public would not bear either the one or the other, and I see no reason why the Portuguese public should be worse treated. I have been concerned to see officers in uniform, with their hats on, upon the stage during the performance, and to hear of the riots and outrages which some of them have committed behind the scenes; and I can only repeat, that if this conduct should be continued, I shall be under the necessity of adopting measures to prevent it, for the credit of the army and of the country.

I beg you to communicate this letter to the commanding officers of the regiments in the garrison of Lisbon, and to the commanding officer of the detachments of convalescents, and desire them to communicate its contents to the officers under their command respectively.

Indeed, officers who are absent from their duty on account of sickness might as well not go to the playhouse, or at all events upon the stage, and behind the scenes. I beg you also to take such measures as may appear to you to be necessary to prevent a repetition of this conduct.

To Lieut. Col. Torrens, Mil. Sec. to the Commander in Chief.   Lisbon, 26th Oct. 1809.

Lieut. Col. Waters is proceeding to England by my leave, with Major Gen. C. Stewart, who is going for the recovery of his health; and I cannot allow him to depart without adopting this mode of recommending him, in the strongest manner, to the Commander in Chief. Although attached to the Portuguese army, he has made himself extremely useful to the British army, by his knowledge of the languages of Spain and Portugal, by his intelligence and his activity. I have employed him in several important affairs, which he has always transacted in a manner satisfactory to me; and his knowledge of the language and customs of the country has induced me to send him generally with the patroles employed to ascertain the positions of the enemy, in which services he has acquitted himself most ably.

It would be most desirable to have Col. Waters exchanged from the Portuguese service to the line, and to send him out here again on the establishment of the A. G. or Q. M. G., as the regulations do not allow of his being promoted.

I have come down here to arrange our future operations in Portugal, and I shall return to the army to-morrow.

To Col. Roche.   Estremoz, 28th Oct. 1809.

I am very much obliged to you for your letters of the 21st and 22d inst., which I received this morning. I am now on my road from Lisbon to Badajoz, where I shall arrive to-morrow. The head quarters of the army are still there, and the army in, and in the neighbourhood of, that town.

I beg that you will tell Gen. Areyzaga that I congratulate him upon the prospect of his appointment to the command of the army of La Mancha; and that nothing will give me greater pleasure than to communicate with him, in the most unreserved manner, upon all points relating to the service. All that I can promise him is, my real opinion on all points on which he may require it; and I shall be most happy if I can be of any use to him.

I do not think the French are now strong enough to make a serious attempt upon the Sierra Morena, particularly if the Spanish army is as strong as you suppose it is. If the French do make such an attempt, I trust the Spaniards in La Mancha will follow the example of those in Castille, and will maintain their position, and drive back the enemy. That is the mode of warfare for which they are best suited, and which I trust they will at last adopt. Large masses, in strong positions, which will give them an opportunity of acquiring a system of discipline, at the same time that the French can do them no harm, and will be exposed themselves to the attacks of the Spanish detachments, and of the guerrillas, which, under the protection of these masses, and while the enemy's attention would be taken up by them, might operate on their flanks and rear; this is the system which I have always recommended, for which the country and people are particularly well calculated. Small detachments, operating alone, will not answer. It is a mistake to suppose that the French were beat out of Galicia by a force of this description: in fact, they beat themselves out of Galicia.

1st, Soult invaded Portugal, where he lost the greatest part, and destroyed the efficiency of the remainder of his army; nearly about the same time Ney invaded Asturias with a great part of his army. The absence of these troops enabled the English navy and the Spaniards to form an establishment at Vigo, from which Ney was unable to dislodge them when he returned from Asturias; then he could not keep his army together without getting it re-equipped, and giving it some repose, and for these purposes he marched into Castille; and Romana's army having come out of the Asturias, and being reinforced by the troops collected at Vigo, and the insurrection being general, Ney was obliged to evacuate Galicia. That is the history of these operations. But if it were true that a partisan war, as it is called, had obliged the French to evacuate Galicia, it happens that Galicia is a country peculiarly favorable for the operations of that description of war, and others in Spain are not. But, as I have above shown you, the evacuation of Galicia was occasioned by remote events, with which the partisan war in that country had no connexion; and was occasioned immediately by the collection in that country of a mass of troops superior in numbers to the French remaining in the province, under the protection of which the partisan war may have been carried on to advantage.

I take the trouble of setting you right upon this point, because I must do you the justice to say that your opinions and reports, upon all points relating to the Spanish armies, have been much more correct than any others that I have seen or heard, most particularly those which you gave me before I joined Gen. Cuesta's army in July last; and I should be sorry that you were misled upon a point of this description.

I write to Gen. O'Donoju by this occasion. I should be very glad if he would come to me, if circumstances should enable me again to enter Spain, particularly in co-operation with any Spanish corps; but, till that shall happen, I think he will do better to remain with the army, or at Seville.

In respect to your money affairs, I wish that you would send me an order upon the Treasury, drawn in favor of J. Murray, Esq., Commissary Gen., for any sum that you may require, which shall be left for you at the British Ambassador's at Seville. As you have the power of drawing upon the Treasury, it is more regular that you should receive your money upon your drafts, than that your name should appear in my contingent bill.

P.S. I observe, in one of your letters to Lord Wellesley, a complaint of Gen. Eguia, of my having sent. Col. Colborne * to Gen. Venegas. The answer is short and easy. When Col. Colborne went to Gen. Venegas, that General was in command of the army of La Mancha. It was never intended to send him to an officer when *not in command* of an army. He

* Lieut. Gen. Lord Seaton, G.C.B.

arrived at Gen. Venegas' head quarters before the army of Estremadura joined; and when that army joined, there was an end of his commission.

To Lord Burghersh.   Estremoz, 28th Oct. 1809.

I received this day your letter of the 18th inst., from Granada, and that in which you enclosed the paper to which you had referred in the former, and I am very much obliged to you for the interesting information which those letters contain.

It is obvious that the longer and the more intimately we become acquainted with the affairs of Spain, the less prospect do they hold out of any thing like a glorious result. The great extent of the country, the natural difficulties which it opposes to an enemy, and the enmity of the people towards the French, may spin out the war into length, and at last the French may find it impossible to establish a government in the country; but there is no prospect of a glorious termination to the contest.

I have been at Lisbon to settle some business there, and am now on my return to Badajoz, where I shall arrive to-morrow. My head quarters have been there since the beginning of September, and there they are likely to remain.

The French army in Estremadura and Castille is too strong for us to hope to make any impression upon it by any offensive operation, and we have only to wait till our allies shall be sufficiently strong and efficient to attack the enemy, or till the enemy shall attack them. There is a corps of 30,000 men now in La Mancha, which has forced Eguia's and Venegas' armies to retire to La Carolina. Soult and Mortier are at Talavera and at Oropesa, and Ney at Salamanca. The corps of the latter was defeated a few days ago by the Duque del Parque, in an attack which they made upon him in the position of Tamames, near Ciudad Rodrigo. The Spaniards took one piece of cannon, and killed and wounded some men, and drove off the French.

I understand that Franceschi is confined in the Alhambra at Granada. I wish that you would try to see him, and tell him that I am endeavoring to prevail upon the Spanish government to consent to his exchange; but hitherto I have had no success. Give him, however, any money he may want, and let me know what you give him.

To Major Gen. O'Donoju.   Badajoz, 30th Oct. 1809.

I received the letters which you were so kind as to write to me some time ago, and I should have answered them before now, if I had had an opportunity of writing to you: but our communication with your part of the world is very difficult, and opportunities for it occur but seldom, or I should long ago have thanked you for your kindness.

Col. Roche has communicated to me a very flattering wish which you have expressed to join my head quarters; and I assure you that I am fully aware of the benefit which I should derive from your assistance, and of the value of the sentiments towards me which have induced you to express that wish.

Under existing circumstances, however, I conceive that it would be more advantageous for you not to come near me; but if circumstances should ever enable me again to co-operate with a Spanish army, I shall hope for your assistance, and I shall call for it without any further ceremony.

It will give me great pleasure to hear from you sometimes; and I will let you know what passes in the quarter in which I may be, whenever an opportunity may offer.

To Marquis Wellesley.   Badajoz, 30th Oct. 1809.

I have had the honor of receiving your Excellency's dispatch (marked I) of the 17th inst., containing a copy of your note to Don M. de Garay, of the 8th Sept., and a copy of his note in answer to your Excellency of the 3d Oct.

I am not surprised that Don M. de Garay should endeavor to attribute to the irregularities of the English Commissariat the deficiencies of supplies by means of transport experienced by the British army in its late service in Spain. I am not disposed to justify the English Commissaries where they deserve blame; but I think it only justice to them to declare that the British army is indebted to their exertions for the scanty supplies it received. From some of the statements contained in Don M. de Garay's note, it would appear that the British army had suffered no distress during the late service; others have a tendency to prove that great distress was suffered by both armies at a very early period; particularly the quotation of a letter from Gen. Cuesta of the 1st Aug., in answer to a complaint which I am supposed to have made, that the Spanish army and their prisoners were better supplied than the British army. The answer to all these statements is a reference to the fact that the army suffered great distress from want of provisions, forage, and means of equipment; and although that distress might have been aggravated, it could not have been occasioned, by the inexperience or the irregularity of the English Commissariat.

I know nothing of the orders which Don M. de Garay states were sent by the government to the different Provincial Juntas, to provide provisions and means of transport for the British army, on its passage through the different towns in the provinces. If such orders were sent, it is obvious that the Central Junta, as a government, have no power or influence over the Provincial Juntas and magistrates to whom their orders were addressed, as they produced no effect; and the supplies, such as they were, were procured only by the requisitions and exertions of the English Commissaries. But it is obvious from Don M. de Garay's account of these orders, that the Central Junta had taken a very erroneous view of the operations to be carried on by the army, and of the provision to be made for the troops while engaged in those operations; the government provided by their orders for the troops only while on their passage through the towns; relying upon their immediate success, and making no provision for the collection in one body of not less than 50,000 men, even for one day. At the same time that they were guilty of this unpardonable omission, which paralysed all our efforts, they rendered that success doubtful by countermanding the orders given to Gen. Venegas by Gen. Cuesta; and thus exposing the combined armies to a general action with the enemy's concentrated force. The effect of their orders will appear more fully in the following detail.

As soon as the line of my operations in Spain was decided, I sent a Commissary to Ciudad Rodrigo to endeavor to procure mules to attend the army, in concert with Señor Lozano de Torres; that city and its neighbourhood being the places in which the army commanded by the late Sir J. Moore had been most largely supplied. Don M. de Garay expresses the astonishment of the government that the British army should have entered Spain unprovided with the means of transport, notwithstanding that, a few paragraphs preceding this expression of astonishment, he informs your Excellency, in the name of the government, that they had given orders to the Provincial Juntas of Badajoz and Castille (at Ciudad Rodrigo), and the magistrates, to supply and provide us with those means, which of course they must have been aware that we should require. No army can carry on its operations if unprovided with means of transport, and the British army was, from circumstances, particularly in want at that moment.

The means of transport commonly used in Portugal are carts drawn by bullocks, which are unable, without great distress, to move more than 12 miles in a day, a distance much shorter than that which the state of the country in which the army was to carry on its operations in Spain, and the nature of the country, would oblige the army to march. The number of carts which we had been able to bring from Portugal was not sufficient to draw our ammunition, and there were none to carry provisions.

Having failed in procuring at Ciudad Rodrigo and in the neighbourhood the means of transport which I required, I wrote to Gen. O'Donoju on the 16th July a letter, in which, after stating our wants, and the failure of the country in supplying them, I gave notice that if they were not supplied, I should discontinue my co-operation with Gen. Cuesta after I should have performed my part in the first operation which we had concerted, namely, the removal of the enemy from the Alberche; and that if not supplied as I required, I should eventually withdraw from Spain altogether. From this letter of the 16th it will appear that I called for the supplies, and gave notice that I should withdraw from Spain if they were not furnished, not only long previous to the retreat across the Tagus of the 4th Aug., but even previous to the commencement of the operations of the campaign.

Notwithstanding that this letter of the 16th July was communicated to the Central Junta both by Mr. Frere and Gen. Cuesta, the British army

---

G. O.   Badajoz, 30th Oct. 1809.

1. A certain number of blankets having arrived, they are for the present to be issued to the infantry at the rate of one for two men; the commanding officers of regiments will make requisitions accordingly upon the Q. M. G. for them, and the Q. M. G. will take measures for issuing the blankets without loss of time to the troops at the several stations.

2. These blankets are to be considered as articles of regimental necessaries, and are to be carried by the men to whom they are delivered, who are to be accountable for them, and to produce them at every weekly inspection of necessaries; as soon as a large quantity of them shall arrive from Lisbon, a sufficient number will be issued for one blanket to each soldier.

3. The General Court Martial, of which Brig. Gen. R. Craufurd is president, is dissolved.

has to this day received no assistance of this description from Spain, excepting 20 carts which joined at Merida, 10 on the 30th Aug., and 10 on the 1st Sept. ; and 300 mules of about 500 which were hired at Bejar, and joined at a subsequent period. None of the mules stated to have been hired and dispatched to the army from Seville, or by Eguia or Cevallos, or the 2 brigades of 40 each, or the horses, have ever joined the British army ; and I conclude they are with the Spanish army of Estremadura, as are the remainder of the 10 brigades of carts (100), which were intended and are marked for the British army. But none of these mules or carts, supposing them to have been sent from Seville for our use, reached Estremadura till after the 21st Aug., the day on which, after 5 weeks' notice, I was obliged to separate from the Spanish army.

It is not true, therefore, that my resolution to withdraw from Spain, as then carried into execution, ' was sudden,' or ought to have surprised the government, nor does it appear to have been 'perilous,' from what has since occurred in this part of Spain. I ought probably on the 16th July to have determined to suspend all operations till the army should be supplied with the means it required ; but having on the 11th July settled with Gen. Cuesta a plan of operations to be carried into execution by the armies under the command of Gen. Venegas, Gen. Cuesta, and myself, respectively, I did not think it proper to disappoint Gen. Cuesta. I believed that Gen. Venegas would have carried into execution that part of the plan of operations allotted to his army, although I was afterwards disappointed in that expectation; and I preferred that the British army should suffer inconvenience rather than that Gen. Venegas' corps should be exposed alone to the attack of the enemy ; and above all, I was induced to hope that I should be supplied. Accordingly, I marched on the 18th July from Plasencia, the soldiers carrying on their backs the provisions to the 21st, on which day a junction was formed with Gen. Cuesta's army; and from that day to the 24th Aug. the troops or their horses did not receive one regular ration. The irregularity and deficiency both in quality and quantity were so great, that I considered it a matter of justice to the troops to remit to them during that period half the sum usually stopped from their pay for rations.

The forage given to the horses was picked up for them by their riders, wherever they could find it, and was generally wheat or rye, which are considered unwholesome food; and the consequence was, that, exclusive of the loss by engaging with the enemy, the army lost in the short period of five weeks not less than 1500 horses.

I have no knowledge of what passed between Gen. Cuesta and Señor L. de Torres and the Intendant of provisions of the Spanish army. I never saw the latter gentleman excepting twice ; the first time on the 22d July, when he waited upon me to claim for the Spanish army 16,000 rations of bread, which had been brought into Talavera and had been sent to my quarters, and which were delivered over to him, notwithstanding that the British troops were in want; and the second time on the 25th July, when he waited upon me also at Talavera to desire that the ovens of that town might be delivered over for the use of the Spanish army; they having moved to Sta Olalla, and the British army being still at Talavera. This request, which was not complied with, is an example of the preference which was given to the British troops while they were in Spain.

The orders stated to have been given by the Central to the Provincial Juntas and magistrates were not more effectual in procuring provisions than in procuring means of transport. In the interval between the 15th and 21st July, the British Commissaries had made contracts with the magistrates of the different villages in the Vera de Plasencia, a country abounding in resources of every description, for the delivery at Talavera, on different days before the 24th July, of 250,000 rations of provisions. These contracts were not performed; the British army was consequently unable to move in pursuit of the enemy when he retired on that day; and I conclude that the French army have since subsisted on these resources.

The British army never received any salt meat, nor any of the rice or other articles stated to have been sent from Seville for their use, excepting to make up the miserable ration by which the men were only prevented from starving, during the period to which I have adverted; nor was it attended ' by the troops of biscuit bakers;' nor did it enjoy any of the advantage of their labors; nor was the supposed magazine of 400,000 lbs. of biscuit ever formed. These are notorious facts which cannot be disputed, to the truth of which every officer and soldier in the army can bear testimony.

I assure your Excellency, that not only have the supplies furnished to the army under my command been paid for, whenever the bills for them could be got in, but the old debts, due to the inhabitants for supplies furnished to the army under the command of the late Sir J. Moore, have been discharged; and I have repeatedly desired the Spanish agents, and others acting with the army, and the different Juntas with which I have communicated, to let the people know, that all demands upon the British government which could be substantiated would be discharged.

I beg to refer your Excellency to my dispatches of the 21st Aug., No. 12, for an account of the state of the magazine at Truxillo, on the 20th Aug.; and of the state of the supplies of provisions and forage at that period. Lieut. Col. Waters had, by my desire, made an arrangement with the Spanish Commissariat for the division of the magazine at Truxillo between the 2 armies; and he, as well as I, was satisfied with the principle and detail of that arrangement. But if the British army received only one third of a ration on the 19th Aug., and only one half of a ration on the 20th, not of bread, but of flour; if the horses of the army received nothing, and if the state of the magazine at Truxillo was such at that time as to hold out no hope, not of improvement (for it was too late to wait for improvement), but of a full and regular supply of provisions and forage of all descriptions, I was justified in withdrawing from Spain. In point of fact, the magazine at Truxillo, which, under the arrangement made by Lieut. Col. Waters, was to be the sole source of the supply to both armies, did not contain, on the 20th Aug., a sufficiency to supply one day's demand upon it.

But it is said that Don L. de Calvo promised and engaged to supply the British army; upon which I have only to observe, that I had trusted too long to the promises of Spanish agents; and that I had particular reason for want of confidence in Don L. de Calvo; as, at the moment he was assuring me that the British army should have all the provisions the country could afford, in preference to, and to the exclusion of, the Spanish army, I had in my possession an order from him (of which your Excellency has a copy), addressed to the magistrate of Guadalupe, directing him to send to the head quarters of the Spanish army provisions which a British Commissary had ordered to be prepared and sent to the magazine at Truxillo, to be divided between both armies, in conformity with the agreement entered into with the Spanish Commissaries by Lieut. Col. Waters.

As the state of the magazine at Truxillo was the immediate cause (as far as the want of provisions went) of my withdrawing from Spain, I beg to observe to your Excellency, that I was not mistaken in my opinion of its insufficiency; as, if I am not misinformed, Gen. Eguia's army suffered the greatest distress in the neighbourhood of Truxillo, even after that part of the country and the magazine at Truxillo had been relieved from the burthen of supporting the British army.

In respect to the conduct of the operations in Spain by the Spanish General officers, many things were done of which I did not approve, some contrary to my expectations, and some contrary to positive agreement.

Don M. de Garay has stated that the orders to the Marques de la Romana were framed in conformity with suggestions from Marshal Beresford; and thence he infers that the operations of that corps were approved of by me.

The Marques de la Romana was still at Coruña on the 5th, and I believe as late as the 9th Aug.; and the armies of Estremadura retired across the Tagus on the 4th Aug. This reference to dates shows that there was, and could have been, no connexion in the operations of those different armies. In fact, I knew nothing about the Marques de la Romana's operations; and till I heard on the 3d Aug. that Marshal Ney's corps had passed through the mountains of Estremadura at Baños, and was at Navalmoral, I did not believe that that part of the enemy's army had quitted Astorga; or that the Marques was at liberty, or had it in his power to quit Galicia.

Marshal Beresford's corps was collected upon the frontiers of Portugal in the end of July, principally for the purpose of forming the troops; and it was hoped that he would keep in check the enemy's corps under Soult, which was at Zamora, and threatened Portugal; that he would act as a corps of observation in that quarter, and on the left of the British army; and I particularly requested Marshal Beresford to attend to the Puerto de Perales. But I never intended, and never held out any hope to the Spanish officers, that the corps under Marshal Beresford could effect any operation at that period of the campaign; and never was a party to any arrangement of an operation in which that corps was to be concerned.

In the cases in which measures were carried on in a manner of which I did not approve, or which I did not expect, or contrary to positive agreement, those who acted contrary to my opinion may have been right; but still they acted in a manner of which they were aware I did not approve:

and the assertion in the note that all operations were carried on with my concurrence, is unfounded.

I expected from the communications I had with Gen. Cuesta, through Sir R. Wilson and Col. Roche, that the Puerto de Baños would have been effectually occupied and secured; and, at all events, that the troops appointed to guard that point, upon which I was aware that all the operations, nay the security, of the army depended, would not have retired without firing a shot.

It was agreed between Gen. Cuesta and me, on the 11th July, that Gen. Venegas, who was under his command, should march by Tembleque, Ocaña, and Fuentidueña to Arganda, near Madrid, where he was to be on the 22d and 23d July, when the combined armies should be at Talavera and Escalona. This agreement was not performed; and the consequence of its non-performance (which had been foreseen) occurred, viz., that the combined armies were engaged with the enemy's concentrated force. I have heard that the cause of the non-performance of this agreement was, that the Central Junta had countermanded the orders which Gen. Venegas had received from Gen. Cuesta; of which countermand they gave us no notice. I shall make no observation upon this proceeding, excepting that the plan of operations, as agreed upon with me, was not carried into excution by Gen. Venegas in this instance.

It was agreed by Gen. Cuesta, on the 2d Aug., that when I marched against Soult on the 3d, he should remain at Talavera; that agreement was broken when he withdrew from Talavera, in my opinion without sufficient cause. And it is also my opinion that he ought not to have withdrawn, particularly considering that he had the charge of my hospital, without my consent.

I do not conceive, that if Gen. Cuesta had remained at Talavera, it would have made any difference in the result of the campaign. When Soult added 34,000 men to the numbers already opposed to the combined armies in Estremadura, the enemy were too strong for us; and it was necessary that we should retire across the Tagus. But if Gen. Cuesta had held the post at Talavera according to agreement, I should have been able to remove my hospital; or, at all events, to know the exact situation of every individual left there, and I think that other disadvantages might have been avoided in the retreat.

When adverting to this part of the subject, I cannot avoid observing upon the ambiguity of language used in the note respecting the assistance afforded by Gen. Cuesta to remove the English hospital from Talavera; that assistance amounted to 4 carts on the 3d Aug. at Talavera, and 2 carts on the 4th Aug. at Oropesa. In the subsequent removal of the wounded, and of those subsequently taken sick, we had absolutely no assistance from the Spanish army, or the country. We were obliged to lay down our ammunition, which was delivered over to the Spanish army, and to unload the treasure, and employ the carts in the removal of the wounded and sick. At Truxillo, in particular, assistance which could have been afforded was withheld on the 22d and 23d Aug.; Don L. de Calvo and Señor L. de Torres being in the town.

In respect to the refusal to make movements recommended by me, I am of opinion, that if Gen. Bassecourt had been detached towards Plasencia on the 30th July, when I recommended that movement, and if the troops had done their duty, Soult would have been stopped at the Tietar, at least for a sufficient length of time to enable me to secure the passage of the Tagus at Almaraz; and here, again, the hospital would have been saved. He was not detached, however, till the 2d; and then, I understand from Don M. de Garay's note, that it was Gen. Cuesta's opinion that the movement was useless.

It could not have been considered useless by Gen. Cuesta on the 30th, because the proposition for making a detachment from the combined armies originated with himself on that day; and it could not have been considered useless even on the morning of the 2d; as, till the evening of that day, we did not receive intelligence of the arrival of Soult at Plasencia. A reference to the date of the period at which the General considered this detachment as useless would have been desirable.

I cannot account for the surprise stated to have been felt by Gen. Cuesta upon finding the British army at Oropesa on the morning of the 4th Aug. The army had left Talavera on the morning of the 3d, and had marched to Oropesa, 6 leagues, or 24 miles, on that day; which I conceive a sufficient distance for a body of men which had been starving for many days before. The accounts received on the evening of the 3d, of the enemy's position at Navalmoral, and of his strength, and of Gen. Cuesta's intended march on that evening, leaving my hospital to its fate, were sufficient to induce me to pause and consider our situation; and at least not to move before daylight on the 4th; shortly after which time Gen. Cuesta arrived at Oropesa.

Upon considering our situation at that time, it was evident to me that the combined armies must retire across the Tagus; and that every moment's delay must expose them to the risk of being cut off from their only remaining point of retreat. A battle, even if it had been successful, could not have improved our situation: two battles, or possibly three, must have been fought and gained before our difficulties, resulting from the increased strength of the enemy in Estremadura, could be removed. I did not consider the British army at least equal to such an exertion at that moment. It is unnecessary to make any observation upon the Spanish army; but the occurrences at Arzobispo a few days afterwards showed that they were not equal to any great contest.

Don M. de Garay complains of the alteration in the line of our operations, and of the sudden changes in the direction of our marches, to which he attributes the deficiency of supplies, which, in this part of the note, he is disposed to admit that the British army experienced. I know of but one alteration in the plan of operations, and in the direction of the march, which was occasioned by the circumstances to which I have just referred. When intelligence was first received of the arrival of the enemy at Plasencia, and of the retreat without resistance of the corps appointed to guard the Puerto de Baños, my intention was to move towards Plasencia, to attack the enemy's corps which had passed through the Puerto. That intention was altered only when I heard of the numbers of which that corps consisted; and when I found that, by Gen. Cuesta's movement from

Talavera, the rear of the army was not secure, that the only retreat was liable to be cut off, and that the enemy had it in their power, and at their option, to join, or to attack us in separate bodies. It could not be attributed to me that this large reinforcement was allowed to enter Estremadura, or that we had not earlier intelligence of their approach.

The Puerto de Baños was abandoned without firing a shot by the Spanish troops sent there to guard it; and the Junta of Castille, if they knew of the collection of the enemy's troops at Salamanca, sent no notice of it; and no notice was, in fact, received till accounts came that the enemy had ordered rations at Fuente Roble and Los Santos; and they arrived on the following day. But when the enemy marched into Navalmoral in Estremadura in such strength, and the post at Talavera was abandoned, the Central Junta will find it difficult to convince their country and the world that it was not expedient to alter the plan of our operations, and the direction of our march.

But this alteration, instead of aggravating the deficiency of our supplies, ought to have alleviated our distresses, if any measures had been adopted at Seville to supply the British army in consequence of my letter of the 16th July. The alteration was from the offensive to the defensive; the march was retrograde; and if any supplies had been prepared and sent, the army must have met them on the road, and must have received them sooner. Accordingly, we did meet supplies on the road; but they were for the Spanish army; and, although our troops were starving at the time, they were forwarded untouched to their destination.

I have sent to Marshal Beresford a copy of that part of Don M. de Garay's note which refers to the supplies for the Portuguese army under his command, upon which he will make his observations, which I propose to forward to your Excellency. I shall here, therefore, only repeat, that the want of magazines, and the apathy and disinclination of the magistrates and people in Spain to furnish supplies for the armies, even for payment, were the causes that the Portuguese army, as well as the British army, suffered great distress from want while within the Spanish frontier.

Till the evils, of which I think I have reason to complain, are remedied; till I shall see magazines established for the supply of the armies, and a regular system adopted for keeping them filled; and an army upon whose exertions I can depend, commanded by officers capable and willing to carry into execution the operations which may have been planned by mutual agreement, I cannot enter upon any system of co-operation with the Spanish armies. I do not think it necessary now to enter into any calculations to show the fallacy of Don M. de Garay's calculations of the relative numerical strength of the allies and of the enemy in the Peninsula: if the fallacy were not so great, as I am certain it is, I should be of the same opinion respecting the expediency of co-operating with the Spanish troops. But if the British and the Portuguese armies should not actively co-operate with them, they will at least do them no injury: and if Don M. de Garay is not mistaken, as I believe he is, in his calculations of numbers; and if the Spanish armies are in the state of efficiency in which they are represented to be, and in which they ought to be to invite our co-operation, the deficiency of 36,000 men, which the British and

Portuguese armies might add to their numbers, can be no objection to their undertaking immediately those operations which Don M. de Garay is of opinion would give to his countrymen the early possession of those blessings for which we are contending.

To J. Murray, Esq., Commissary General.   Badajoz, 31st Oct. 1809.

The Chief Engineer, Lieut. Col. Fletcher, is desirous to have stores prepared, as stated in the enclosed papers, at the stations therein mentioned, to which I have annexed a memorandum, stating the places at which it will be most convenient to prepare them.

I recommend that application should be made to Col. Fletcher for a return of the different articles he requires.

Stores required by the Chief Engineer from the Commissary General.	Memorandum.
1. 3000 palisades, to be provided at Torres Vedras.	Nos. 1 and 2 can be provided easily at Torres Vedras, where there is plenty of wood.
2. 1500 fascines, at Torres Vedras.	
3. 3000 palisades, } at Sobral. 4. 1500 fascines, }	Nos. 3 and 4 can be provided also at Torres Vedras, and carried to Sobral with ease.
5. 13,000 palisades, } at Lisbon. 6. 7,000 fascines, }	Nos. 5 and 6 may be made in any part of the course of the Tagus, or of the coast of Portugal, which may be found most convenient, and kept in store at Lisbon, and to be sent where the Engineers may want them.

To Lieut. Col. Fletcher, Commanding R.E.   Badajoz, 31st Oct. 1809.

I enclose the copy of a letter which I have written to the Commissary Gen. upon the subject of your 2 memorandums respecting materials. You will see that the largest number of your articles will be collected at Lisbon, from whence you can dispose of and distribute them as you please. The delay will only be one tide, which will be more than compensated for by leaving to the Commissary Gen. the whole course of the Tagus and of the coast of Portugal.

Au Gen. Bassecourt.   Badajoz, 31 Oct. 1809.

Le Capitaine Gordon, mon aide de camp, vous montrera les lettres dont je l'ai chargé pour les Maréchaux Soult et Mortier; et je vous prie de le laisser passer par les avant postes Espagnols pour les délivrer.

Au Gen. Bassecourt.   Badajoz, 31 Oct. 1809.

J'ai reçu la lettre que vous m'avez fait l'honneur de m'adresser, à laquelle j'aurais répondu plutôt si je n'avais pas été à Lisbonne la semaine passée. Votre position est bien intéressante, et deviendra plus assurée tous

---

G. A. O.   Badajoz, 31st Oct. 1809.

3. The Commander of the Forces requests the officers commanding divisions will make their divisions march a distance of not less than 3 leagues in marching order twice a week, besides the formations which the nature of the ground may induce them to make in the course of the march. The officers commanding the cavalry and artillery will also, by frequent exercise, prevent the horses from losing the habit of marching.

5. The Commander of the Forces desires that the officers commanding brigades of artillery will distinctly understand, that he holds them responsible for the condition of the artillery horses attached to their brigades, and they will take measures that the officers and men of the gunner drivers do their duty by taking proper care of them.

les jours, surtout si on vous renforce comme l'importance de la position l'exige : en tout cas je vous prie de me donner constamment de vos nouvelles ; et je vous assure que rien ne me donnerait plus de plaisir que de pouvoir vous être utile, en cas que vous fussiez attaqué par l'ennemi. Je partirai pour Seville demain matin ; mais je serai de retour dans quelques jours.

To the Rt. Hon. J. Villiers. Badajoz, 31st Oct. 1809.

When I was lately at Lisbon, I had some discussion with the Regency respecting the necessity of establishing magazines for the support of the Portuguese armies, and I found that the great difficulty which they would experience in doing so was the want of money. Among other plans to provide for this deficiency, the government proposed that an advance should be made to them of the monthly sum they receive from Great Britain, for the payment of 20,000 men ; and as the maintenance of these men with provisions is included in the amount of the sum ; and as this is the season in which the provisions ought to be purchased, I beg leave to recommend to your consideration the expediency of making an advance to the Portuguese government of the sum due to them on account of the expenses of 20,000 men, for the month of November, as soon as possible.

I find, upon inquiry, that the Commissary Gen. can, without inconvenience, advance the money for this payment ; and I have desired him to hold £50,000 at your disposal, besides the sum for October, if you should think proper to attend to this recommendation.

To the Rt. Hon. J. Villiers. Badajoz, 31st Oct. 1809.

I find, upon inquiry, that your share of our receipts for October is £47,000; and, besides this sum, I have desired Mr. Murray to pay Mr. Bell £50,000 for November, making a total of £97,000 ; and I wrote to you the public letter this day, suggesting that you should make an advance of one month's subsidy for the purpose of purchasing magazines for the Portuguese army.

I have also looked into the state of our affairs, in order to ascertain how far we could advance money on account of the bill to be drawn by the government on Sr· de Sousa for £100,000, on which subject you are to write to me ; and I find that I can allow of an advance on that account immediately for £50,000, and of the second £50,000 by the 20th Nov., provided the £80,000 coining at the mint are placed at the disposal of the Commissary Gen. I think that, as we shall now advance the full amount of the subsidy for November, at least £50,000 out of the £80,000 ought to be placed at our disposal. If this is not done, it may distress us to advance the second £50,000 on the 20th Nov.

I enclose a letter respecting the effects of an officer which have been seized in the house of a person suspected of disaffection, and who has fled. Pray make the necessary applications, that Capt. —— may have his effects again.

To Visc. Castlereagh. Badajoz, 31st Oct. 1809.

The Spanish corps under the Duque del Parque was attacked on the

19th inst. by a considerable part of the French corps (lately Ney's) commanded by Gen. Marchand, in a position which the Duque had taken up at Tamames, near Ciudad Rodrigo. The French corps consisted of 10,000 infantry, and 1200 cavalry; and, after a very vigorous attack, they were repulsed with considerable loss, and retired upon Salamanca, leaving one piece of cannon in the hands of the Spaniards. The loss of the Spanish troops was about 200 killed, and 400 wounded: that of the enemy much more considerable. The Spanish infantry are stated to have conducted themselves well in this action, but the cavalry otherwise; and indeed they had lost in the commencement the Spanish flying artillery, which was afterwards recovered by the infantry.

The post of Tamames is noted throughout the country for its strength; and I understand that it was well occupied by the Spanish troops, and that throughout the action the Duque del Parque distinguished himself. He was joined, on the following day, by the corps of Ballesteros; and he moved forward on the 25th, and took possession of Salamanca, which the enemy abandoned, retiring upon Toro and Zamora.

The corps of Gen. Eguia, which is under the temporary command of Areyzaga, who has lately come from Catalonia, has retired to La Carolina, and the French are in possession of the whole country to the foot of the mountains, but they have made no attack to force the passes.

All has continued quiet in this quarter, and I have not heard that the enemy's corps at Oropesa and Talavera have made any movement to their right, in consequence of the failure of Gen. Marchand's attack upon the Duque del Parque.

To Visc. Castlereagh.   Badajoz, 31st Oct. 1809.

Although I think it probable that you are out of office, I enclose you two interesting papers that I have lately received, which I think will give you some notion of the state of affairs in Spain, and the presumption of the Spanish character; and I beg you will give them to your successor. One is a letter from Lord Burghersh, whom I sent lately into the south-eastern provinces to see what they were doing; whether they were forming an army; whether they had one, &c. &c.: the other is from Capt. Ruman, an officer employed to obtain intelligence from the frontier.

Burghersh's is an exact description of the state of affairs in nearly every province of Spain; Ruman's shows what a Spanish General thinks and says, when he has had a little success. If he does not mind what he is about, this same gentleman will have Soult upon one side of him, through the Puerto de Baños, and Marchand and Kellermann on the side of the Douro. I have warned him of his danger, however, by Baños, and have urged him either to secure the Puerto, or to destroy the road effectually, and thus shut the door to all communication between Castille and Estremadura.

Au Maréchal Mortier, Duc de Trévise.   1 Nov. 1809.

Je vous prie d'avoir la bonté de permettre qu'on donne l'argent, que j'envoie par mon aide de camp, le Capitaine Gordon, aux officiers Anglais, prisonniers de guerre, et les médecines aux officiers de santé.

Je n'ai rien pu faire pour le Capitaine Thévenon ; mais je vous assure que je n'omettrai nulle occasion de faire prévaloir auprès du gouvernement Espagnol les droits de la guerre, et j'espère qu'avant peu de tems on vous le renverra. J'ai fait renvoyer le Lieut. de Farincourt, du 2ᵉ d'infanterie légère, en échange pour le Lieut. Cameron, renvoyé par le Général Kellermann. Il passe par la Vieille Castille.

Au Maréchal Soult, Duc de Dalmatie.   1 Nov. 1809.

J'ai des excuses à vous faire de ce que votre lettre du 26 Août n'a pas encore reçu de réponse ; mais avant de vous en envoyer une je voulais faire tous mes efforts pour faire consentir le gouvernement Espagnol à faire l'échange du Gén. Franceschi, en quoi je suis fâché de vous dire que je n'ai pas réussi. En attendant cependant je vous envoie une liste d'officiers Français que je pourrais vous renvoyer en échange pour ceux de l'armée Anglaise, dont je vous envoie une liste (No. 2) ; si ceux dont les noms sont dans cette dernière sont trop éloignés, je vous prie de m'en envoyer d'autres des mêmes rangs.

Je me rappelle parfaitement la lettre que j'ai eu l'honneur de vous écrire au moment de votre départ d'Oporto ; et je crois vraiment que vous n'êtes pas au fait des circonstances dans lesquelles sont les officiers et soldats qui étaient vos prisonniers en ce moment-là. Après que j'ai reçu votre lettre du 26 Août, j'ai demandé compte de sa conduite à un de ces officiers, et je vous envoie la copie de la lettre qu'il m'a écrite, qui en même tems qu'elle le justifie entièrement, montre que votre confiance peut-être abusée, et que vous ne pouvez pas être sûr que les ordres bienfaisants, que vous donnez pour le traitement de vos prisonniers, sont obéis par ceux chargés de leur exécution. En lisant cette lettre, et connaissant les circonstances du moment, je dis que c'est la garde qui a quitté les prisonniers, et non pas les prisonniers qui ont quitté la garde. Mais en tout cas, quand on met des officiers prisonniers sous la charge d'une garde, excepté pour leur sureté personnelle, on doit s'attendre qu'ils s'en iront quand ils pourront ; et si on ne leur a donné nulle liberté sur parole, on ne peut pas dire qu'ils ont oublié les lois de l'honneur en s'en allant. Je vous assure que le meilleur moyen de garder les officiers, c'est de leur accorder la parole, et je vous promets que si j'en trouve un qui l'ait oubliée, je vous le renverrai.

Pour ceux-ci la question est simplement si un officier ou soldat, une fois prisonnier, doit l'être toujours jusqu'à ce que son échange soit fait ; et si cette question est décidée dans la négative, selon l'usage de tous les jours, ces Messieurs ne peuvent plus être considérés comme prisonniers. Mais en tous cas, c'est à vous à décider ce que vous ferez, si jamais le sort de la guerre les place en vos mains, et je suis bien sûr que vous les traiterez comme vous le devez.

P. S. Le Lieut. V. de Farincourt du 2ᵉ· régiment d'infanterie légère est renvoyé en échange pour le Lieut. Cameron, renvoyé par le Général Kellermann.

To Visc. Castlereagh.   Badajoz, 1st Nov. 1809.

I have the honor to enclose returns of the provisions and all kinds of

2 P 2

stores, in charge of the Commissary Gen., for the use of the army under my command.

To Lieut. Gen. Sir J. Sherbrooke, K.B.   Seville, 3d Nov. 1809.

I arrived here yesterday, and in the evening I received your letter, enclosing one from Col. Donkin, to which I shall give an answer at another period. There is no news here, excepting that the French have retired from La Mancha, and again crossed the Tagus. I doubt the last part of this intelligence; if it is true, it is possible that this movement has been occasioned by the partial business of the Duque del Parque, in Castille, and his subsequent movement towards Salamanca. It is necessary, however, that we should be prepared for all events; and I shall be much obliged to you if you will desire the sick cases requiring carriages, in Hill's division and in the heavy brigade of cavalry, to be removed to Elvas without loss of time.

I had desired the Commissary Gen. to employ 30 carts in removing 200 of the sick of Hill's division, before I quitted Badajoz; and I shall be obliged to you if you will desire him to send the remainder of his covered carts to Merida, to remove the sick from thence; and to continue the removal from the quarters of Hill's division, as long as there may be a man in them whose case is such that he could not march away, if we should be obliged to assemble the army.

To Lieut. Gen. Sir J. Sherbrooke, K.B.   Cadiz, 7th Nov. 1809.

I have received your letter of the 2d, and I shall be at Badajoz again on Sunday to dinner. I am obliged to you for reminding me to put in orders the leaves of absence given to different officers, which I will arrange as soon as I shall return to the army.

In regard to Gen. Cole's aide de camp, he must be put in orders, whether he is on the establishment or supernumerary. If the latter, he will draw no pay, and no bât and forage, unless the Commander in Chief should have given permission to Gen. Cole to bring him to Portugal; in which case he will have the bât and forage only. But no Major General can draw pay for more than one aide de camp.

I have been induced to come on here, partly to arrange money matters with Lord Wellesley, and partly by curiosity to see this place. I shall leave it on the day after to-morrow. One good has resulted from my journey, viz., that the Junta have given me an answer respecting the exchange of Franceschi and Turenne, and have released the officer they held in confinement at Deleytosa. So that we may now hope to get away some of our officers.

To the Rt. Hon. J. Villiers.   Badajoz, 13th Nov. 1809.

I received on the 11th your letters of the 27th Oct., and of the 5th and 8th of this month, and I now send you an official answer to the first. In respect to the last, I am glad to find that you still remain with us, and I hope that you will determine to stay till your successor shall arrive. I left Lord Wellesley at Cadiz, on Thursday. He was to embark and sail on Friday; but I am not certain that he carried his intentions into execution. I returned here yesterday evening.

It is best that it should be understood that the whole of the sum of £80,000, coining at the mint, should be paid to the Commissary Gen.; and if you should hereafter require more than your fifth for the Portuguese troops, you must have what you require. The debts due to the Portuguese government shall be paid as soon as they shall produce the vouchers. Of course you will take as much of the chest as you please.

To the Rt. Hon. J. Villiers.   Badajoz, 13th Nov. 1809.

I had the honor of receiving on the 10th inst. your letter of the 27th Oct. in which you have enclosed an extract of one from S^r. de Sousa, the Prince Regent's minister in London, to the Patriarch, relative to a sum of £100,000 sterling in S^r. de Sousa's hands, for the use of the government of Portugal. This resource was one of those mentioned to me by the Regency, when I was at Lisbon, as being applicable to the purpose of purchasing provisions, to be laid in magazines for the Portuguese army; and the only difficulty appeared to me to consist in realizing the money in Portugal. It was imagined that S^r. de Sousa would experience equal if not greater difficulty than the Treasury had experienced in procuring specie to export to Portugal; and it was apprehended that the government of Portugal would not be able to get money at Lisbon for their bills drawn upon S^r. de Sousa.

These difficulties are, I conclude, the reason for which you have desired tnat the Commissary Gen. should advance money on the credit of the sum belonging to the Portuguese government, in the hands of S^r. de Sousa; and having, in consequence of the conversations I had with you on this subject when at Lisbon, reviewed the state of the funds of the army, and considered the possibility of assisting the Portuguese government to realise in Portugal the sum of £100,000 in the hands of S^r. de Sousa, I have to inform you that the Commissary Gen. can advance, without inconvenience, the whole or any part of the sum of £100,000, for which you may chance to call, for the use of the Portuguese government; but that it is impossible for him, either himself to advance money for a bill drawn by the Portuguese government or S^r. de Sousa, or to lend the credit of his name and office to the bill drawn by the Portuguese government, to enable them to get the money from other persons.

I should imagine, however, that you will experience no difficulty in arranging the mode in which the Portuguese government should repay in England the extent of the assistance which you may think proper to afford them on the credit of the sum of money in the hands of S^r. de Sousa.

To the Earl of Liverpool, Secretary of State.*   Badajoz, 13th Nov. 1809.

I have the honor to enclose cartels of exchange which have been given to Capt. Christie and Ensign Sandilands, of the Coldstream Guards, by the French Commander in Chief; and I request your Lordship to have the

---

* A change of Ministry had taken place, and the Earl of Liverpool became Secretary of State for War and Colonies, *vice* Viscount Castlereagh, until June 1812, when he was succeeded by Earl Bathurst.

officers named in these papers sent to France; that is to say, Lieut. C. M. Guiot, of the French navy, in exchange for Capt. Christie, and Lieut. A. R. Dorfemille, of the 11th regt. of infantry, in exchange for Ensign Sandilands.

The A.G. to Col. Kemmis, commg. 4th div.   13th Nov. 1809.

I am directed by his Excellency the Commander of the Forces to acquaint you, that he is pleased to remit the punishment awarded by the General Court Martial to ———, — regt.; but his Excellency desires it may be intimated to him that he is induced to show this lenity, entirely on account of his good character, and in the hope it will serve as a warning to him, and prevent his being guilty of the like crimes in future.

The A.G. to Lieut. Col. Arentschildt, 1st hussars, K.G.L.   13th Nov. 1809.

I am directed by the Commander of the Forces to return the annexed certificate of the loss of a horse which belonged to Cornet Baring, and to inform you, that as the horse did not die until 5 weeks and 4 days after the action, it cannot be considered as if the horse was actually shot in action, and therefore the claim for the same must be sent in to the Military Secretary, as directed by this day's order. I am further directed to observe, that it is not for Cornet Baring to certify that the horse died in consequence of the wound, but for the veterinary surgeon; and if you, therefore, will send in the claim of Cornet Baring, accompanied by the necessary vouchers from you and the veterinary surgeon, it will be laid before a Board of claims, which will consider whether an indemnification will be granted to Cornet Baring or not.

The A.G. to Lieut. Col. Fenwick, Elvas.   13th Nov. 1809.

I have laid your letter before his Excellency the Commander of the Forces, and am directed to acquaint you, that whatever sentries may be necessary for the hospital, they will be found by the Portuguese troops; and he will write to the General commanding at Elvas, requesting he will give orders for the furnishing them, as his Excellency does not approve of more men being with the general hospital than is absolutely necessary for the attendance on the sick; and he trusts that such discipline will be maintained in the hospital as to insure obedience to the orders the Portuguese sentries may receive.

The A.G. to Brig. Gen. R. Craufurd.   13th Nov. 1809.

Referring to Capt. Cotton's letter, — inst., desiring permission to make use of damaged ammunition for practice, which letter I have had the honor of laying before the Commander of the Forces, I have been directed to signify to you in answer, that his Lordship approves of your expending, for practice, as much ammunition as you may think proper, reporting from time to time to this office the quantity expended.

The A.G. to Lieut. Gen. Hill.   13th Nov. 1809.

Having had the honor of laying before the Commander of the Forces your letter of the 26th ult., and its enclosures from Assist. Surgeon ———, of the 2d batt., — regt., explanatory of his motive for quitting Talavera de la Reyna, where he had been left in charge of the sick and wounded, I have received his Lordship's commands to desire that you will be pleased to warn Mr. ——— to prepare to return to Talavera de la Reyna, as he appears, from his own account, to have taken advantage of the liberty afforded to him by the French Commander in Chief to make his escape.

The A.G. to Lieut. Gen. Sir S. Cotton, Bart.   13th Nov. 1809.

Having had the honor of laying before the Commander of the Forces your letter of the 1st inst., enclosing letters from Lieut. Col. ——— and Lieut. Col. ———, of the — dragoons, and a medical certificate of the ill state of health of Lieut. Col. ———, I have received his Lordship's command to signify to you in answer that he has granted leave of absence to that officer to proceed to England for 3 months from this date, on his private affairs; and leave of absence to Capt. ——, of the — dragoons, to proceed to England on his private affairs. Capt. —— is to return to Portugal by the first packet which will leave England in January.

The Commander of the Forces has directed me to express his surprise that, when the — dragoons was under orders for foreign service for many months before it left England, Lieut. Col. —— and Capt. —— should not have settled any family affairs they might have to arrange before they embarked.

To the Earl of Liverpool.　　　　　　　　　　　　　Badajoz, 14th Nov. 1809.

I delayed to reply to Lord Castlereagh's dispatch of the 14th Sept., till I should be able to go to Lisbon, and should have ascertained, on the ground, the possibility of defending the Kingdom of Portugal, from which I was prevented till late in October by the movements of the armies in the neighbourhood of Ciudad Rodrigo; and the report required by his Lordship has been further delayed by a necessary reference to the opinion of Adm. Berkeley on some of the points of the inquiry, and by my journey to the south of Spain to communicate personally with Lord Wellesley, previous to his departure for England.

From all I have learned of the state of the enemy's force at present in the Peninsula, I am of opinion, that unless the Spanish armies should meet with some great misfortune, the enemy could not make an attack upon Portugal; and if events in Spain should enable the enemy to make such an attack, the force at present in Portugal is able to defend that country.

If in consequence of the peace in Germany the enemy's army in the Peninsula should be largely reinforced, it is obvious that the enemy will acquire the means of attacking Portugal, not only in proportion to the extent of his reinforcements, but in proportion as the arrival of those reinforcements may have an effect upon the public mind in Spain, and may induce persons, now in hostility with the enemy, to submit to his usurpation, and thus enable him to employ troops in active operations which are at present employed only on the defensive, in keeping up the communication between his armies, or in guarding certain interesting and important points in the country.

Even in this case, however, I conceive that till Spain shall have been conquered, and shall have submitted to the conqueror, the enemy will find it difficult, if not impossible, to obtain possession of Portugal, if His Majesty should continue to employ an army in the defence of this country, and if the improvements in the Portuguese military service should be carried to the extent of which they are capable.

The extent of the army which it would be necessary that His Majesty should employ in Portugal ought to be 30,000 effective men, in aid of the whole military establishment of Portugal, consisting of 3000 artillery, 3000 cavalry, 36,000 regular infantry, and 3000 caçadores and the militia. I have lately ascertained, as nearly as possible, the expense to Great Britain of this British army in Portugal, which I find amounts to £1,756,236 *per annum*. It must be observed, however, upon this point that these troops, if employed elsewhere abroad, would cost an equal sum; and if employed in Great Britain or Ireland, would cost £1,188,192, or £568,044 less than they would in Portugal or Spain. In this calculation I have not included the expense of transports to attend upon this army.

This is an expense which must be incurred for a British army employed on any service abroad, and in the circumstances now under consideration must be incurred for the army employed in Portugal. But it is probable that the larger part, if not the whole of the transports, which it would be necessary to attach to the army in Portugal, would be on the public service if the army were at home.

In respect to the Portuguese army, the public now incur an expense of about £600,000 *per annum*, being the expenses of 20,000 Portuguese troops, and the pay of the British officers employed with the Portuguese army : but I conceive that other expenses must be incurred in order to put the Portuguese army in the state in which it ought to be for this impending contest. The expense which in my opinion must be incurred at present by Great Britain, in addition to that already incurred, is that of an increase of pay to the officers of the Portuguese army, without which it is vain to hope for much exertion from them. The officers of the Portuguese army have for many years done little or no duty. Their country having, with trifling and short exceptions, been at peace since the year 1763, they were generally throughout their service employed in the same garrison, if they remained with their regiments ; or they lived with their families at home. Besides these advantages, I believe that the abuses which had crept into the service afforded them others, of no small amount ; and they were certainly enabled to maintain themselves upon this low pay, as officers ought, in a country in which all the necessaries of life are dearer than they are in England.

It is scarcely necessary to point out the alteration in their situation produced by the appointment of Marshal Beresford to command the Portuguese army. All the abuses which existed in the service have been done away ; and a regular system of discipline has been established, requiring the attention and attendance of all the officers with their regiments ; and the situation of the country, and the duties required from the army, have necessarily removed the regiments from their fixed stations, and have increased to a very large amount the necessary expenses of the officers.

Your Lordship will observe, from what I shall have to lay before you in a subsequent part of this dispatch, that it is absolutely impossible for the Portuguese government to bear the expense of this augmentation of the pay of the officers of the army. As far as I have been able to learn their sentiments, they feel the necessity for it ; but are unwilling to give orders that it should be carried into execution, till they shall be certain that they possess the means of defraying the expense.

I enclose a paper stating the actual pay of each rank in the Portuguese service, with the proposed increase, the expense of which will amount to about £130,000 *per annum*. Adverting to the miserable situation in which those officers now are, compared with that of the British, the Spanish (whose pay has been very largely increased), and the French officers, with whom they are liable to meet on service ; and the severe, but necessary discipline which has been introduced into their army ; and to the service which will be required from them, I cannot avoid recommending that His Majesty should furnish the Portuguese government with a sum sufficient to defray the expense of this augmentation of pay during the war.

I am not aware of any other specific head of expense, the means of which it would be desirable that Great Britain should furnish, in order to enable the Portuguese government to support the impending contest. I cannot avoid, however, drawing your Lordship's attention to the general state of the finances of this government, of which I have obtained a knowledge, in consequence of the confidence reposed in me, with His Majesty's consent, by the Prince Regent.

The estimated expense, civil and military, of the government of Portugal for the year 1809 is 14,679,250 dollars. The estimated revenue is 8,447,500 dollars; thus leaving a deficiency of 6,221,750 dollars. The revenue, the heads of which we estimated, actually received and expected to be received by the end of the year, amounts to 7,031,927 dollars; and the sums have been received in this year, which cannot be expected in future, making a total receipt, in 1809, of 8,607,337 dollars, leaving a deficiency of 6,070,000 dollars. The public servants on the civil and judicial establishments, the interests of debts, and other ordinary expenses of the government, have been paid only in part; and the necessary expenses only, such as the army, and some civil expenses, equally important to the existence of the state, have been defrayed.

The assistance afforded by Great Britain amounts to about £500,000 *per annum*; and the remainder, about £900,000, is a deficiency which cannot be made good in Portugal. It is obvious that it becomes more probable every day, that this deficiency of revenue will fall upon the means allotted for the support of the army. Very lately, His Majesty's servants and officers in this country were obliged to consider of means to be afforded immediately to enable the Portuguese government to collect magazines for the support of their army; without which, they must have disbanded a part of their force, and the whole would have been in a state of inefficiency at the moment at which their services would be called for.

It does not appear to me to be practicable to diminish the expenses, or to increase the revenue of the country, or to raise money by loans on its own credit.

In respect to the revenue, I have to observe, that the country is so much impoverished by the events of late years, and by the emigration of the Court to Brazil, that the inhabitants are not able to pay the taxes already imposed upon them; and the produce of the Customs, which was formerly the principal branch of the revenue, is almost reduced to nothing, owing to the transfer of the Brazil trade from Portugal to Great Britain.

This transfer, if an advantage to Great Britain, as it is evidently and materially disadvantageous to Portugal, would appear to give to Portugal a claim for some assistance in this moment of difficulty, in addition to that which the policy of His Majesty has induced him to afford to the government to support their military establishment. Probably a sum of £300,000 *per annum*, in addition to the expense of the increase of pay to the officers, to enable the government to defray the expense of forming and maintaining the magazines, for the support of the Portuguese army; or an engagement by the British government to maintain 10,000 additional troops, which would cost about £250,000 *per annum*, leaving the expense of the magazines upon the government, would enable them to get through the difficulties of the moment; but I am convinced from what I have seen of the state of the Portuguese finances, that without some assistance of this description, the whole will sooner or later fail; and all the trouble taken, and all the expense hitherto incurred, will have been thrown away.

In respect to the embarkation of the British army in the event of failure in the contest which we may expect in Portugal, I have the honor to enclose the copies of a correspondence which I have had with Adm. Berkeley upon that subject, and I have no doubt that we should be able in that case to embark, and bring away the British army, not including the horses of the cavalry and of the artillery

In respect to these, I would submit to your Lordship, that it should be decided that they should not be brought away from the Peninsula. In the event of an embarkation after a defeat, it would be impossible to bring them away; and in any other event, if the transports which should be employed should be retained only three months in the service, their expense for each horse will amount to £30, after deducting the expense of transporting the man, for whom provision must still be made, whereas the original purchase money of the horse would be only 25 guineas. It is true that many of the horses are worth more money; but others, after long service in this country, would be useless in England; and if the army should not be forced to embark by adverse circumstances, it is probable that the horses would be sold for more than it would cost to take them home.

I would therefore recommend to the government to provide transports only for the conveyance of the better horses belonging to officers, which could not be replaced without large expense to themselves, or to the public. In the event of the evacuation of Portugal by the British army, either at the present moment or after a defeat, I am not aware of any measures which could be adopted, which would enable the Portuguese government to continue to hold the country for the Prince Regent.

Although I consider the Portuguese government and army as the principals in the contests for their own independence, and that the success or failure must depend principally upon their own exertions, and the bravery of their army, (and I am sanguine in my expectations of both from them, when excited by the example of British officers and troops), I have no hope of either, if His Majesty should now withdraw his army from the Peninsula; or if it should be obliged to evacuate it by defeat. I have no doubt that the immediate consequence of withdrawing from the Peninsula would be the possession of Lisbon by the enemy, probably without contest, and that other consequences would follow, affecting the state of the war not only in Portugal, but in Spain.

If, therefore, it should be thought advisable now to withdraw from Portugal; or if, eventually, the British army should be obliged to withdraw, I would recommend to His Majesty's government to consider of the means of carrying away such of the Portuguese officers and troops as should be desirous of emigrating, rather than to continue by their means the contest and the defence of Portugal.

To the Earl of Liverpool.   Badajoz, 14th Nov. 1809.

I wrote to you an official letter this day, in answer to one from Lord Castlereagh of the 14th Sept., which will probably satisfy you upon all the points referred to by your Lordship in your private letter of the 20th Oct. However, as the arrangement of the questions * contained in that letter may be more convenient to you than those in Lord Castlereagh's dispatch, to which mine is an answer, which were of a general nature, and as every consideration of this interesting subject is desirable, I proceed to give you answers to the questions contained in your letter.

In answer to the first question, my opinion is, that if the Spaniards are commonly prudent, if they do not adventure themselves too far forward to obtain possession of the capital before the enemy shall receive his reinforcements, and to gain a momentary popularity for the cause, it must be a very large reinforcement indeed which would give the enemy the military possession, much larger that which would lead to the complete subjugation of the country.

In answer to your second question, my opinion is, that the enemy ought to make the possession of Portugal their first object, when their reinforcements shall arrive in Spain. I do not think they will succeed with an army of 70,000, or even of 80,000 men, if they do not make the attack for 2 or 3 months, which I believe now to be impossible. I conceive not only that they may, but will make the attack before they will subdue the north of Spain. The centre of Spain, or Old Castille, is already subdued; and indeed that country, at all times, in all wars, has been in the possession of the army which was strongest, particularly in cavalry.

In answer to your third question, my opinion is, that the enemy have neither the means nor the intention of attacking Portugal at present, and that they would be successfully resisted. I am likewise of opinion that when they shall receive their reinforcements, they can be successfully resisted.

You will find a complete answer to your fourth question in my dispatch of this date. I am convinced we could embark after defeat.

I enclose the last weekly state of the army, which will show you its strength. Included in the sick and absent are the wounded at Talavera, about 1500 in number, and about 1700 convalescents at Lisbon and Elvas, which will reduce the number of sick to about 6000 men upon an army of about 30,000. We are now, as I believe the whole world is, very sickly; but in all times and places the sick list amounts to at least 10 men in the

* Questions put to Lieut. Gen. Visc. Wellington in Lord Liverpool's private letter of the 20th Oct. :

1st. As there is every reason to believe that peace has been concluded between France and Austria, and that the whole military efforts of France will probably in a short time be directed in consequence of this event against Spain, what is the chance of these efforts proving successful; I mean their leading, with partial exceptions, to the complete subjugation of the country?

2d. Would the French be likely to make a serious attack upon Portugal before they had acquired a tolerably quiet possession of every part of Spain north of the Sierra Morena? Are they likely to be able to spare an army sufficient for this purpose, before the north and centre of Spain are subdued?

3d. If a serious attack is made by the French upon Portugal, what is at present the prospect of successful resistance?

4th. If resistance is not likely to prove ultimately successful, how far would the British army be endangered, and its embarkation be likely to be prevented, by delaying to withdraw it till the French had penetrated in force into Portugal?

100, or 3000 upon 30,000 men.   In order, therefore, to give us an efficient operating army of 30,000 men, you should send us 3000 men soon.   We ought also to have 1000 men to occupy the castle of Lisbon, and another 1000 to make up for the deficiency in the return, which will be occasioned by the departure of the 23d light dragoons, and probable losses by death between this time and the period in which we shall have the contest, making in the whole 35,000 rank and file, besides the prisoners at Talavera, still in the return.

I would besides recommend a relief of our bad second battalions.   There are really many in this army that are quite unfit for service in respect to composition and discipline; and they, as well as the old regiments, are made worse by the constant change of the officers.   At this moment, there are not less than 60 officers quitting the battalions in this army, with which they have served and have acquired some experience, to join other battalions of the same regiment in some other part of the world.   The worst of this arrangement is, that the officers who go are the oldest, and probably the best of their respective ranks; and they are replaced by others, without experience, who have no knowledge of their men or of their duty, or of the orders and regulations of this army, and the whole must be taught to them; and it is not less expensive to the public than it is prejudicial to the service, as the travelling expenses of each of these officers to and from their battalions are paid by the public.

It is besides very necessary that some effectual measures should be taken to increase the Medical staff, not with gentlemen of rank, but with hospital mates.   The duty of the general hospitals in every active army ought to be done by the general Medical staff, and the regiments ought to have their surgeons and assistants entirely disengaged for any extraordinary event or sickness that may occur.   We have not now one surgeon or assistant with each regiment, instead of three, the others being employed in the hospitals instead of hospital mates, and we have always been equally deficient.   Indeed, one of the reasons which induced me to cross the Tagus on the 4th Aug., instead of attacking Soult, was the want of surgeons with the army, all being employed with the hospitals, and there being scarcely one for each brigade; and if we had had an action, we should not have been able to dress our wounded.

I entirely concur with you, and wish you every success in the measures you are taking for forming a government, and I hope you will not allow yourself to be diverted from them by any circumstances whatever.   If you are beaten you cannot help it, but do not give up unnecessarily.

To Brig. Gen. Cox, Governor of Almeida.   Badajoz, 15th Nov. 1809.

I have received your letter of the 8th inst., for which I am much obliged to you.   I have spoken to the Commissary Gen. respecting Mr. Cooper, and have desired him to direct that gentleman, with your permission, to construct temporary storehouses to cover our stores and provisions at Almeida.   It will not answer to leave them in the open villages.

To Marshal Beresford.   Badajoz, 15th Nov. 1809.

I returned here on the Sunday, and received yesterday your letters of the 9th, 10th, and 11th. I had before received that which you wrote to me on the 31st Oct.

I have no doubt that Buonaparte has come to some kind of an arrangement with Austria; but I suspect, from the mode in which it has been announced, and from the speech of the Arch Chancellor to the Senate, on the 22d Oct., of which I have seen an extract, received through Catalonia, that the arrangement is not of a permanent nature; at all events we must go on with every thing as if it was permanent, and matters are so proceeding.

I wish you could see a dispatch which I have written to Lord Liverpool, which I send to Mr. Villiers to be transmitted to England by the packet which ought to sail on Sunday.

There is no doubt that you must have the power of approving the sentences of Courts Martial exclusively in your hands, and you should so settle before you quit Lisbon.

I order Lieut. Pigot, 5th regt., and Ensign Elgie of the 97th regt., and Ensign Power, 97th regt., to place themselves under your orders. I shall recommend Mr. J. Beresford Dunlop for an ensigncy.

The rule in the British army is, that officers allowed by the Commander in Chief to serve with any General officer, as extra aides de camp, receive bât and forage; those serving in that situation, without his permission, do not receive it. I have one of this description in my family. Is Capt. —— your aide de camp, by permission of the Commander in Chief?

I do not know what to say to Capt. Arentschildt's claim. According to the principle laid down, and the practice, he ought to receive his pay and British allowances, and the pay of his Portuguese rank, and no more. I suppose Sir J. Cradock gave him 10s. a day when he employed him at Oporto, and I do not know how Capt. Dickson comes to have received this allowance; but it is obvious that it is extra, and that it cannot be granted without a deviation from the principle fixed for all others.

In respect to Gen. Hamilton, his case is one deserving serious consideration; and if you continue to wish to make him a Lieut. General, I must refer it home. I think that you have mistaken the case. A General officer comes out appointed by the Commander in Chief in England to serve in Portugal with the Portuguese troops, in a certain rank, with the British pay and allowances of that rank. An officer of the Line comes to serve with one step of Portuguese advanced rank, with the Portuguese pay of that advanced rank, and the British pay of his British commission. So far as to the pay; if you promote Gen. Hamilton to be Lieut. Gen. in the Portuguese service, you must give him British Lieut. General's pay and allowances, or you will deviate from the rule laid down for General officers.

But this is not the only objection that I have to your proposal. You do not appear to me to advert to the great difficulties under which we shall labor in consequence of the advanced rank of the British officers in the Portuguese service when the 2 armies shall come to act together, which must be done, if the Portuguese army is to render any service. You do not recollect the difficulty I had even with your own advanced rank, certainly occasioned by misconceptions and prejudices; but still it existed, and will exist in a still stronger degree, at a most critical moment, in relation to Gen. Hamilton's rank, if he is now to be taken from the bottom of the list of Major Generals to be made a Portuguese Lieut. General, and in that capacity to command all the Major Generals in the British service serving with this, or in the same army. You also forget the motives which induced you and me to agree that I should recommend Gen. Hamilton to be a Major General in Portugal, viz.; that he was at the top of the list of Colonels, and that there was nobody in this army who could object to his promotion. Pray look how many there are who will object to his promotion to be a Lieut. General.

If, however, after perusing this letter, you should still be desirous that the promotion should be made, I will send it home to England, to have him appointed to be a Lieut. General to serve with the Portuguese troops, in the same manner as he was appointed a Major General to serve with those troops; but I must at the same time state my reasons for thinking the appointment inexpedient.

I understand that the Duque del Parque has retired to the mountains, and had his head quarters at Bejar on the 8th.

I have ordered a General Court Martial to assemble at Lisbon for the trial of your servant. You have not sent a crime against him, or his name, or the list of evidences; but I shall endeavor to make out a crime, and to recollect his name, and the whole shall go up with this letter.

Have you heard at Lisbon of a naval victory in the Mediterranean? We hear of it from Catalonia, and I think the report is well founded. We also hear that the siege of Gerona is raised, which I believe to be true, and that this event is connected with the naval victory. The object of the French fleet was certainly to relieve Barcelona; and it is probable that, having failed in that object, they think it preferable to employ Augereau's army in the relief, even at the risk of losing the immediate possession of Gerona, to losing Barcelona.

P.S. Madame Fortunati d'Elvas has begged me to apply to you to appoint her son, Antonio d'Aguilar, an officer; he has been 7 years a cadet in the 8th regt. of cavalry, and always doing duty with his regiment.

To the Junta of Estremadura. Badajoz, 15th Nov. 1809.

The Commissary Gen. of the British army, Mr. Murray, has communicated to me a correspondence which he has had with you relating to supplies for the British army, and to orders which have been issued in the different villages to prevent the sale of supplies to the British Commissaries who have been sent to purchase; copies of which orders have been communicated to you. I have already had occasion to explain to you my sentiments and intentions upon this subject. Spain is either unable or unwilling to furnish supplies of provisions and forage, on payment, for the armies necessary for her defence; and as in either case it is impossible for me to risk the existence of His Majesty's army, in a country so situated, I announce to you, therefore, my intention, upon the first failure of these supplies, which are necessary for them, to remove the troops into a country in which I know they will be supplied.

To Bart. Frere, Esq.* Badajoz, 15th Nov. 1809.

I have the honor to enclose a letter which I have received from Marshal Beresford, in answer to that part of Don M. de Garay's note of the 3d Oct., which relates to the Portuguese troops, while lately in Spain. I beg leave to recommend that you should transmit this paper to Lord Wellesley.

I have received information that orders have been given in the villages in this province, to prevent the sale of forage and provisions to the British Commissaries employed to purchase those articles for the use of the British army; and the Commissary Gen. has informed me that he apprehends an immediate scarcity on this account, and that the Junta of Estremadura have omitted to adopt any of the measures which he has proposed, to prevent the evil effects of the orders to which I have above referred, or to relieve him from the apprehension which he entertains of a scarcity of supplies. I have therefore this day addressed a letter to the Junta, of which I enclose a copy, which I request you to lay before the government, and to inform them that I shall be under the necessity of drawing nearer to my magazines, if there should be any failure of supplies in this part of the country.

To Bart. Frere, Esq. Badajoz, 15th Nov. 1809.

I am much obliged to you for your letter of the 12th, and the intelligence which it contains. I give credit to the report of the naval victory, as well as to another report in circulation here, that the siege of Gerona is raised, and I think that the fact which it states is connected with the naval victory. The French fleet having been directed to relieve Barcelona, it is probable that the army of the siege of Gerona is now destined for the same purpose, the fleet having failed.

The A.G. to Col. Peacocke, Lisbon. 15th Nov. 1809.

Enclosed, I have the honor of transmitting to you 2 certificates of ill health; and I am directed by the Commander of the Forces to desire that you will be pleased to order a Medical board to assemble at Lisbon for the purpose of examining and of reporting upon the state of health of the officers therein mentioned. You will be pleased to transmit me the proceedings of the Board.

To Marshal Beresford. Badajoz, 16th Nov. 1809.

I have ordered the General Court Martial for the trial of ——, your servant; but we ought to have here his crime, which should be signed by the Adj. Gen., and sent back from hence to the President of the Court Martial. This ceremony, which ought to be gone through, would delay the meeting of the Court probably till Wednesday, which might be inconvenient to you; and if that should be the case, I have desired that the town Major should sign the crime, and send it to the President or Judge Advocate, and the trial shall commence on Monday. It is desirable, how-

* On the departure of Marquis Wellesley, and previous to the arrival of his successor, the Hon. H. Wellesley, as Ambassador to the Court of Spain, Mr. Bart. Frere was appointed and acted as Minister Plenipotentiary.

G. O. Badajoz, 16th Nov. 1809.

8. The Commander of the Forces requests the officers commanding regiments will take care that the officers who have lately joined this army, are made acquainted with all the G. O. which have at different times been given out.

ever, that if not very inconvenient to you, I should see the crime, and that the Adj. Gen. should sign it before —— is tried upon it.

The Duque del Parque is in the Puerto de Baños with his whole force, and the frontier of Portugal is open ; and the enemy's corps in Old Castille consists, as the Duque reports, of 36,000 men. I think that this does not signify, and that the enemy can at present do nothing ; but probably it might be well to put your corps on the frontier on their guard.

To the Rt. Hon. the Commander in Chief.　　　　　　Badajoz, 16th Nov. 1809.

I have availed myself of the presence of Col. Pakenham, of the 7th Fusiliers, in this country, to employ him as an assistant in the department of the Adj. Gen. ; and he is now doing the duty of that department, in consequence of the absence of Brig. Gen. the Hon. C. Stewart, for the recovery of his health. As the office of D. A. G. has never been filled up, and as Col. Pakenham is the senior of all the officers doing duty in the department, and is well qualified for it, I beg leave to recommend him to be appointed D. A. G.

To the Rt. Hon. the Commander in Chief.　　　　　　Badajoz, 16th Nov. 1809.

I have the honor to enclose a letter which I have received from the Inspector of hospitals with this army, and a list of promotions in the Medical department, which he has recommended, and of which I have approved.

I beg leave to observe, however, that although I believe these promotions are well merited, and that it is necessary to make them, that which this army wants, principally, is an additional number of hospital mates. There is not a sufficient number of officers of this description to do the duties of the General hospitals ; the regimental surgeons and their assistants are therefore necessarily employed in the General hospitals ; and the regiments are not attended as they ought to be at all times, but particularly at this season, on service, by the due and regular proportion of regimental Medical staff.

To Lieut. Col. Torrens, Mil. Sec.　　　　　　　　　Badajoz, 16th Nov. 1809.

Having received certain information of the death of Lieut. Col. Donellan, of the 48th regt., on the 1st Sept., at Talavera, I have to request that you will again submit to the favorable consideration of the Commander in Chief my strongest recommendation of Major Middlemore to succeed to the Lieut. Colonelcy of the 48th regt.*

I also beg leave to request that the promotion may be given in that regiment, as recommended in Major Middlemore's letter, which I had the honor to transmit on the 26th Sept. I also beg to recommend Mr. Martin Lima to succeed to the vacant Ensigncy, from the date of Lieut. Col. Donellan's death, as Mr. Lima had been gazetted in the 61st regt., which appointment was done away in consequence of the circumstances attending the death of Capt. Scott, whose succession was not allowed to be given in the 61st regt.

* See page 378.

To the Adj. Gen. of the Forces.   Badajoz, 16th Nov. 1809.

I have had the honor of receiving your letter of the 23d Oct., announcing the arrival of remount horses for the cavalry in this country, and I shall make the best arrangements in my power to have men at Lisbon, belonging to each of the regiments, to take care of the horses on their arrival. So large a proportion of the men of the dragoons, however, are now sick, and so many of the horses of each of the regiments are still unfit for service, that I fear that I shall reduce the effective cavalry of the army lower than it ought to be, unless I should retain in Portugal, to take care of those horses on their arrival, a part, at least, of the 23d dragoons.

I propose, therefore, to detain a detachment of the 23d dragoons, from which regiment the horses have been drafted, according to the orders of the Commander in Chief; sending home the greater part of the officers and men of that regiment immediately; and I shall send home the remainder as soon as the other regiments of cavalry shall have so far recovered from the sickness which now prevails in the army, as to enable them, without reducing the numbers of effective cavalry, to take charge of them all.

I understand from Lieut. Gen. Payne that there are many men in the 23d dragoons who are desirous of volunteering their services into the other regiments, and I shall be much obliged to you if you will let me know whether the Commander in Chief will permit me to allow them to be transferred to the regiments of cavalry with their own consent. Lieut. Gen. Payne has reported to me that all the regiments are in want of horse appointments; and I beg leave that the Colonels may be directed to send out 50 sets of horse appointments for each of the regiments without loss of time.

To the Earl of Liverpool.   Badajoz, 16th Nov. 1809.

I have the honor to transmit, for your Lordship's information, the returns of the stores and provisions remaining in His Majesty's magazines in Portugal on the 1st Nov.

To the Earl of Liverpool.   Badajoz, 16th Nov. 1809.

The corps which had been defeated by the Duque del Parque at Tamames having been joined by the corps under the command of Gen. Kellermann, which had been for a considerable time at Valladolid, and other reinforcements having been sent from New Castille and Estremadura through the Puerto del Pico, the Duque del Parque retired from Salamanca in the beginning of this month, and on the 8th his head quarters were at Bejar, at the entrance of the Puerto de Baños, which pass was occupied by the troops under his command. The enemy's troops in Old Castille, supposed to amount to 36,000 men, are under the command of Marshal Mortier.

Since I wrote to Lord Castlereagh on the 31st Oct., the Spanish army under Gen. Areyzaga, which was at that time at La Carolina, has moved forward into La Mancha; and on the 10th inst., the date of the last accounts which I have received of their operations, their head quarters were at Los dos Barrios, not far from Ocaña, at which place there was a French corps under Sebastiani; and there was another French corps under

Marshal Victor at Yevenes, between Toledo and Consuegra. The Spanish army under Gen. Areyzaga will probably have fought a general action before this time.

The Spanish troops still remaining in Estremadura have been placed under the command of the Duque de Alburquerque.

To Brig. Gen. R. Craufurd.   Badajoz, 17th Nov. 1809.

I delayed answering your letters of the 3d Nov. till I should have an opportunity of considering with Murray our long list of officers in the Q. M. G. department; and the result of our consideration is, to tell you that I am happy to have it in my power to appoint Capt. W. Campbell to be an Assistant, and that he shall be attached to the 3d division of infantry.

I have desired the Commissary Gen. to provide the palliasses for the hospital, according to your desire. He has spoken to the Commissary of your division upon the subject this morning, and has directed him to pay for them. I shall be much obliged to you if you will give him every assistance in your power to get them made.

I had not time before I went to Lisbon to see the troops of your division; and if not inconvenient to you, I shall go over to-morrow to Campo Maior for that purpose. I shall be there at 9 o'clock. I must, however, return here to dinner.

To Bart. Frere, Esq.   Badajoz, 17th Nov. 1809.

I have received your letters of the 13th and 14th inst., for which I am much obliged to you.

I do not understand the Duque's retreat from his position. He never apprised me of it. It is very desirable that Alava, and Whittingham as soon as he is able, should be sent to the Duque de Alburquerque, who, although he does not want spirit, is deficient in other qualifications for a commander, which his confidence in those officers can alone supply.

I am most anxious about Areyzaga's corps, the fate of which must be decided before this time. If he should fail, the situation of the Duque del Parque will become critical. I have put Marshal Beresford upon his guard respecting the frontier of Portugal, into which, however, the enemy will not attempt to penetrate till he shall be reinforced.

P.S. I shall be much obliged to you, when Col. Elley shall pass through Seville, if you will use your influence with the government that he may be allowed to look at the mares which I understand have been collected, 190 in number, for the British army.

To Lieut. Col. Roche.   Badajoz, 19th Nov. 1809.

I have received your several letters to the 13th, and I am much obliged to you for them. Matters are in a critical situation in your quarter, and I wish that they may turn out well; but that does not appear very probable.

I do not understand how Gen. Areyzaga could think that I was to co-operate with him. I can co-operate in nothing of which I have no knowledge, or, indeed, I might say, which is not concerted with me; but not only was this plan not concerted with me (if there ever was any plan at all), but the whole system on which it is founded and proceeds is known to be directly contrary to my opinion, and the advice I have repeatedly given.

To Bart. Frere, Esq. Badajoz, 19th Nov. 1809.

I have received your letters of the 15th and 17th. It appears to me, that Areyzaga's corps is in a very critical situation. I fear it must be defeated, and if it should be defeated, the Duque del Parque and the Duque de Alburquerque will be lost. You will observe, that there is in Old Castille a superior enemy's corps, which has obliged the Duque del Parque to retire to the mountains, and his head quarters were at Bejar on the 11th. The government have now ordered him to move into the valley of the Tagus, there to join the Duque de Alburquerque, who is to cross the Tagus, and the united armies are to move to Talavera.

It is not necessary to advert to the period in which this movement will be made, as a diversion in favor of Areyzaga; but I beg you to observe, that the Duque del Parque, when joined with the Duque de Alburquerque at Talavera, will be in relation to the enemy, and to Areyzaga, precisely in the situation in which the combined armies under Cuesta and myself were in the beginning of August, in relation to the enemy and to Venegas; with this difference, that at that time Venegas could have crossed the Tagus at a ford at Fuentidueña, and Areyzaga, I am afraid, cannot do so now; and the Duque del Parque has not gained a victory, and is not half so strong as we were.

I think it possible, and indeed probable, that the enemy's troops in Old Castille may pass through the mountains at the Puerto del Pico, instead of at the Puerto de Baños. If they do, the Duque del Parque may be able to retire with great difficulty by the bridge of Arzobispo. In a view of his retreat, which I consider inevitable, unless Areyzaga should defeat the enemy now opposed to him, and should obtain possession of Madrid, which is very improbable, I have spoken to the General here respecting the bridge of Almaraz. He tells me that they have no money, even to commence the equipment of it; that they want certain articles, such as rope, &c., which they can get only from Seville; that the government are aware of these wants; and that if they had every thing required, a week would elapse before the bridge could be ready; and I know that it would take another week for the bridge to reach the point in the river at which it ought to be placed. I believe, however, that they have some 6 or 8 boats in readiness, and I mean to urge the General to have them sent off, so that the Duque del Parque may have the means of constructing a flying bridge, and may have that road in some degree open to him, if he should have it in his power to take it.

I consider the affairs of Spain to be at this moment in a worse situation than I have yet known them to be. The Duque del Parque is in the greatest danger; at all events, he will scarcely be able to return to Castille, but I believe that that is not intended. It is impossible for me to do any thing for their relief, supposing there were means of subsisting such bodies of troops as will be in the valley of the Tagus, and other circumstances should occur in inducing me to think it expedient to join the Duque del Parque and the Duque de Alburquerque. I have no means of crossing the Tagus excepting at Arzobispo; the road to which bridge, at this season of the year, is scarcely practicable for an army; and it is more than probable that, if I should attempt it, I should lose my equipment. If I were to move towards Truxillo in order to be at hand to give them assistance, I fear that I should embarrass them by the consumption of provisions, more than I should have it in my power to aid them. But even this movement to Truxillo is not provided for in any manner. Upon these points I shall write to you officially in answer to Don F. de Saavedra.

In answer to your letter of the 15th, I have to observe, that I know of no reason that Gen. Areyzaga had for saying that the British army would co-operate with him. I think it most probable, that on the 10th he began to discover the difficulties of his situation, which could only be aggravated by his continuing to advance; that he therefore determined not to advance; and that he gave out to his army our expected co-operation as the reason for the discontinuance of his advance.

I agree entirely in opinion with you, that it is desirable that we should have the means of knowing exactly what is passing in Catalonia; and that it is desirable that some English officers should be sent there without delay; and that you could not make a better selection than Major Campbell of the artillery. But I would suggest to you that Catalonia is Gen. Doyle's station, and that it might interfere with Lord Wellesley's plans and instructions, if you were to send another officer to that quarter. I would therefore recommend to you to send Gen. Doyle, with such instructions as you may think proper to give him. These officers were formerly under my directions, having been sent out under orders from the Sec. of State for the War department. But when Lord Wellesley arrived, he brought orders with him for them to report to him, and since that time I have had no communication with any of them, excepting Col. Roche.

I have had no letter whatever from the Duque de Alburquerque, but I hear that he has moved towards the bridge of Arzobispo.

Since writing the above, I have received your second letter of the 15th by the hand of Capt. Silvertop. I am convinced that the Marques de la Romana never gave any assurance to Areyzaga of the nature described in Col. Roche's letter of the 11th. Indeed, it appeared to me that the Marques de la Romana did not approve of Areyzaga's movement more than I did.

I do not know Col. ——, and cannot recommend him to the government for employment. Generally speaking, it is desirable that the Spanish government should not employ British officers without the consent of the King, and as (between ourselves) I have not heard a very good character of this Colonel, I consider it desirable that you should rather discourage them from employing him.

To Bart. Frere, Esq.   Badajoz, 19th Nov. 1809.

I received last night your letter of the 17th inst., containing the copy of Don F. de Saavedra's note of the 16th, addressed to you, in which he has required the co-operation of the British army with the troops under the Duque del Parque, ordered on the same day to break up from Bejar, and to march into Estremadura to form a junction with those under the Duque de Alburquerque, likewise ordered to cross the Tagus; when both corps are to advance to Talavera de la Reyna, and there endeavor to create a diversion in favor of the Spanish corps under Gen. Areyzaga, now in La Mancha.

The intelligence received from La Mancha, of as late a date as the 13th of this month, would tend to point out the inutility of these movements as a diversion in favor of Gen. Areyzaga, who at that time was one fortnight at least in advance of the Duque del Parque. This officer cannot receive his orders until the 19th, and will not be at Talavera till the 25th or 26th. If at that moment Gen. Areyzaga should have been defeated, or if he should have been thrown on the defensive, or if he should have been checked by the difficulty of crossing the Tagus at this season of the year, the corps assembled at Talavera, which it is reasonable to suppose will be followed from Old Castille by the enemy's troops, that were already superior in that quarter, and were supposed by the Duque del Parque to amount to 36,000 men, will be in a situation of imminent danger, from which it can be extricated only by an immediate and well-concerted retreat across the Tagus.

I should naturally wish to avoid being concerned in these operations, which not only have not originated in any plan concerted with me, but are decidedly contrary to the opinion I have invariably given since I was obliged to retire with the British army after a victory, from being involved in a situation nearly similar to that in which the Duque del Parque will find himself. These operations are, I believe, the result of no fixed plan, but the consequence of an operation imprudently commenced by one corps, to endeavor to extricate which corps from its difficulties, the whole will now be in a state of imminent risk; and I feel so strongly the situation in which all these troops are involved, that if there were any means prepared to enable the army under my command to cross the Tagus; and if there was the most distant chance that I should be able to subsist the army while engaged in this expedition, I should immediately put it in motion to endeavor to save the troops of our allies. You are, however, aware of the difficulty which the Duque de Alburquerque, and before him Gen. Bassecourt, experienced in procuring subsistence for a few thousand men on the left bank of the Tagus; and you will conceive how much the difficulty and distress will have been increased on the right bank, the country being exhausted in a still greater degree, the army being more numerous, and no arrangements whatever having been made to collect magazines for their support, or to supply the deficiencies of provisions in the country. I am at the same time convinced, that nothing that I could do could prevent the necessity of a retreat; and I beg to refer you to my dispatches to Lord Wellesley (No. 17), dated Merida, 1st Sept., for the detail of my opinion of all plans of co-operation between a corps in La Mancha and troops in Estremadura.

These dispatches, and the accounts of the situation of the combined armies in the beginning of August, will point out to you more clearly the grounds of this conviction, which induces me to think that I should rather increase than diminish the embarrassments of the Spanish troops, if I were to approach them. I beg you, therefore, to inform Don F. de Saavedra that I do not think it expedient to move the British army upon this occasion. With respect to the blame that will be transferred to us for the misfortunes which there is reason to apprehend will be the result of these operations, I am too much accustomed to receive blame for the actions of others to feel much concern upon the subject, and I can only endeavor not to deserve any for my own.

The A.G. to the officer commg. — regt.   19th Nov. 1809.

I am directed by the Commander of the Forces to put you in possession of the annexed papers, forwarded by Lieut. Col. ——, of the 2d batt. — regt., representing the unparalleled proceedings of an officer of your corps. His Lordship has commanded me, in explicit terms, to state, that in his life he never perused a more insulting, more ungentlemanlike, or a more unprovoked letter than that addressed by Lieut. —— to Capt. ——, whilst it appears the former was under arrest for another offence at the very time he committed that at present submitted to consideration. You are, as officer commanding the — regt., to give the within letter of Col. —— and a copy of his own letter to Lieut. —— for perusal, in order that he may reflect on his past conduct. Call on Lieut. —— to deliver into your hands a written acknowledgment of his offence towards Capt. ——, in which he will solicit the pardon of that officer : this apology, it is to be understood, will be made public. You will give Lieut. —— one hour to comply with this desire ; and in the event of his declining so to do, you are to put that officer under close arrest.

The A.G. to Brig. Gen. Baron Low, K.G.L.   19th Nov. 1809.

In acknowledging the honor of your letter of the 18th inst., which has been submitted to the Commander of the Forces, I am to request you will give instructions for the suspension of Lieut. ——'s pay, if possible, from the period of his absence till further orders. I am further commanded to order a Medical person to inspect that officer, and have instructed Col. Peacocke, who commands at Lisbon, that in the event of Lieut. ——'s proving ill, he is to require him to keep his house; on the other hand, should that officer appear to be in health, Col. Peacocke is to order him in close arrest, and send him to the army for absenting himself from duty without just cause. These, my directions, I have been particularly instructed to communicate to you.

To Marshal Beresford.   Badajoz, 20th Nov. 1809.

I enclose a letter from the magistrates at Ceclavin, with the copy of a receipt given for shirts by an officer of the Legion. I shall be obliged to you if you will take measures to have the money paid for these shirts, which I conclude has been stopped from the men. I believe that the money had better be paid to our Commissary Gen. at Lisbon.

Areyzaga has been brought to a stand in La Mancha ; he marched to Los dos Barrios on the 9th, about a league from Ocaña. I believe he lost 2 pieces of cannon in an attack he made upon a French corps at Ocaña. He remained at Los dos Barrios 3 days, and marched on the 13th to his right, towards Zarza.

The government have begun to take the alarm, and have, in a letter of the 16th from Seville, ordered the Duque del Parque, who was still at Bejar on the 11th, to pass the mountains into Estremadura, and join the Duque de Alburquerque at Talavera ; who is likewise ordered to cross the Tagus. At Talavera their united armies are to create a diversion for Areyzaga. He was in danger on the 13th, and they may arrive at the place in which they may draw the enemy's attention, on the 26th or 27th!!!

The French, in the mean time, are collecting all their force in New Castille and Estremadura, to fall upon Areyzaga ; and they have, besides, 36,000 men in Old Castille, with which they had overpowered the Duque del Parque, and had obliged him to retire to Bejar. The Duque del Parque and the Duque de Alburquerque, when they shall arrive in Estremadura, as they will certainly be followed by the enemy from Old Castille, will be precisely in the situation in which I was in the beginning of August; and must retire if they can. They will have the troops of the left of the French army in their front, and those of the right in their rear ; and ten to one they are lost. This will be the case, if Areyzaga should be defeated between the 13th and 26th ; or even if the state of the Tagus, in this season of the year, and the destruction of the bridges by the enemy should stop him ; or if he should by any cause be thrown upon the defensive, nothing can save these two corps but a victory by Areyzaga, and the possession of Madrid ; which are the most improbable of events. Thus you see how matters stand in Spain ; the government had literally no plan, excepting to urge or allow Areyzaga to ' *buscar el enemigo ;*' and then, when they found he was in a scrape, they go near to lose all, that they may say that they endeavored to save him.

They have written to me to desire I will move, but they have no means prepared for me to cross the Tagus; no means of subsistence forward from thence ; no magazine formed, or preparation made of any description. I would try to save the destruction of every thing if there were any means of subsistence forward ; but there are none; and I should only add to their distress by the additional consumption of provisions. In whatever way these circumstances turn, whether the Duque del Parque be destroyed, or effect his retreat across the Tagus, it is very obvious we shall be much affected by them in Portugal.

It is probable that as soon as the Duque's corps are disposed of, the enemy will turn his attention to Ciudad Rodrigo, and the frontiers of Portugal. I intend, therefore, in a few days, that is to say, as soon as I can disembarrass the advanced divisions of the army of their sick, which I have begun, to put the army in march to cross the Tagus. I think I shall leave one division upon the Tagus ; for if the Duque del Parque and the Duque de Alburquerque are destroyed, which is not unlikely, and, indeed, is pretty certain, unless the enemy should enter Estremadura by the Puerto del Pico, instead of by the Puerto de Baños, we must expect that the enemy will immediately cross the Tagus, and we must make our arrangements for the defence of Portugal, according to the plan we settled when I was at Lisbon, to be adopted when the enemy's reinforcements should arrive in Spain. In respect to the re ainder of the army, I should put the right in Guarda, and the left towards Viseu, and your troops might be in second line behind us.

Murray will write to D'Urban * more fully, as well upon this disposition as upon the route that the army will take, which it probably might be necessary to clear a little for us.

P.S. Pray make Villiers acquainted with the contents of this letter.

* Gen. Sir B. D'Urban, G.C.B., then the Q.M.G. of the Portuguese army.

To Vice Adm. the Hon. G. Berkeley.   Badajoz, 20th Nov. 1809.

I shall be very much obliged to you if you will be so kind as to give directions that transports may be prepared to convey to England, as soon as they may be ready to be embarked, a detachment of the 23d light dragoons, with officers, horses, &c.; of the exact strength of which, the A.Q.M.G. at Lisbon will acquaint your secretary.

To the Rt. Hon. J. Villiers.   Badajoz, 20th Nov. 1809.

In reference to the conversation which I had with you and Marshal Beresford, relative to the situations of Lieut. Col. Cox and Lieut. Col. Trant, and the expenses incurred by those officers in the command of Almeida and Oporto respectively, I beg leave to recommend that the staff pay of each should be made equal to that of a Brigadier General in the British service; and that you should pay each of them such a sum as, in addition to the pay they receive from the Portuguese government, will make up the pay and allowances of a British Brigadier General.

To the Rt. Hon. J. Villiers.   Badajoz, 20th Nov. 1809.

The enclosures in my dispatches to England, relative to the French fleet, will have relieved you from any anxiety respecting its operations. I understand that all which came out have either been taken or destroyed.* I consider it very desirable, however, to put the Bugio in a proper state of repair; and I am very glad that this work has been thought of, and that the repairs will be effected. We must, however, have a small guard in the tower as soon as it shall be in a state of repair, upon which subject I shall write to Col. Peacocke.

I am concerned to hear that the rule respecting the packets cannot be adhered to. It is most convenient to the army and to my public business; and I acknowledge that I do not see the necessity of breaking through a rule to send off a packet every Sunday, if there should be one in the Tagus, because it is necessary at this moment to send away 2 or 3 together, in order that there may be packets on the other side of the water. However, it is no business of mine, and I shall accommodate myself to any plan that may be adopted.

In respect to the Talavera club, before I consent to belong to it, I must see who are the society; and possibly it might be well to look a little into the character of those who constituted it at Lisbon. If the officers who first went down to Lisbon from the army, they are people who ought not to be countenanced on any account, as they in fact deserted; and each of them, as he comes up, is in arrest, and he is obliged to give an account of himself.

I do not know what to think of the Peace. At first, upon a misrepresentation, or rather a misconception, of the meaning of the *Moniteur* of the 22d Oct., by a Spanish agent on the frontiers of France, I thought the account was not true. Upon seeing the paper in question, I do not

---

* Three sail of the line and a frigate were driven ashore between Cette and Frontignan, on the 23d Oct. 1809, by the advanced squadron under Rear Admiral, now Sir G. Martin, G.C.B.

think there is more reason to doubt of the peace with Austria, than there is to doubt the truth of any of the transactions mentioned in the *Moniteur*. Buonaparte may be sick, and it will certainly take some time before he can reinforce his armies in Spain to any large extent. I know there is great discontent in the French army, and I also know that if the officers choose to have any communication with us, means and opportunities are not wanting; and if they do not make use of them, I must be convinced that they do not choose to communicate upon that subject, and to touch upon it would only do more harm than good. If an opening should be made by them, you may depend upon it that I shall avail myself of it.

I refer you to my letter of this date to Beresford for information on the state of the military operations.

To Vice Adm. the Hon. G. Berkeley. Badajoz, 20th Nov. 1809.

The news which I sent to Mr. Villiers on Thursday, of which you probably may have received still further details, will have relieved you from the anxiety you felt respecting the Toulon fleet. But at all events, I am glad you have adverted to the state of the tower of Bugio, upon which I had already spoken to Col. Fletcher, and which must be put in order.

I am concerned that you should meet with any difficulties with the Portuguese officers in effecting any measures for the public service; but I hope when Dom M. Forjaz shall understand what is required, and for what object, that he will enforce your wishes. We must, however, have matters put on such a footing, as that we shall have no difficulties when the moment of contest shall arrive.

Plan for removing the sick from the out stations of the Army to the Hospital stations at Elvas and Estremoz, sent to Dr. Franck, Inspector of Hospitals, to the Commissary General, and to the officers commanding at Elvas and Estremoz.

Badajoz, 20th Nov. 1809.

50 men, of such cases as the medical gentlemen at Elvas shall conceive can be moved with least injury, to be sent to Estremoz every third day, till 250 shall have been sent. 50 men to be sent to Elvas daily from the regimental hospitals of the corps at Badajoz, Talavera, Lobon, and Montijo, till 400 shall have been sent.

The sick at Talavera, Lobon, and Montijo, to be brought the first day to Badajoz, where preparations will be made for their reception, and the next day to Elvas. The Commissary Gen. is to send 10 covered carts to Elvas this day, to make the removal of the sick from thence. 10 covered carts to be employed at Badajoz to remove the sick from thence to Elvas. 5 at Montijo, and 5 at Lobon and Talavera, to remove the men from those stations respectively to Badajoz.

The Inspector of hospitals will arrange that a medical gentleman shall accompany each convoy of sick; and the officers commanding stations will take care that a proper proportion of officers and non-commissioned officers accompany them, according to the general order of the 13th June, 1809.

The surgeons will of course return as soon as they shall have delivered over the sick to the person appointed to take charge of them at the hospital or elsewhere, according to the orders of the Medical Inspector.

The officers commanding at Elvas and Estremoz respectively will determine whether the officers and non-commissioned officers are to remain, according to the proportions of each which he has with the hospital, and which he may require.

The Commissary Gen., the Inspector of hospitals, and the officer commanding at the hospital at Elvas, will communicate upon the execution of this plan.

A copy of this paper to be immediately sent to the Commissary Gen., the Inspector of hospitals, and commanding officer at Elvas.

The Inspector of hospitals to give his directions for the removal of the sick from Talavera, Lobon, and Montijo to Badajoz, and from Badajoz to Elvas.

To the Sec. of the Treasury.   Badajoz, 20th Nov. 1809.

I enclose a letter, received from the Commissary Gen., which has been laid before me by Lieut. Col. Bathurst, my military secretary, upon which I beg to be acquainted with the pleasure of the Lords of the Treasury. It relates to the article in the instructions of the Commissary of accounts, which requires that the signature to all receipts and vouchers passed by him should be testified by two witnesses; which article the Commissary of accounts with this army has applied to the contingent accounts of staff officers.

I beg to know whether it is the intention of their Lordships that this article should be so applied. Upon this point I should observe to them, that it will be very inconvenient to staff officers to procure the signature of two witnesses to every payment they may make; and in very frequent instances I apprehend that it will be quite impossible. But if it should be their Lordships' pleasure that their rule should extend to these accounts, I would beg leave to submit that it cannot with justice or propriety be extended to those for expenses incurred before the rule was known.

The rule is not observed in the War office, where the contingent accounts of staff officers serving in Great Britain are passed; and the officers who have made the payments, of which the vouchers are now considered imperfect, had no knowledge whatever that they would be required to produce the signature of two witnesses to the payments they had made, and it would be quite impossible at present to procure them.

It is very desirable that I should receive their Lordships' decision upon this subject, as well as upon the letters which I have had the honor of addressing to them, of which the dates are in the margin.

To the Earl of Liverpool.   Badajoz, 20th Nov. 1809.

Some time ago Mr. Villiers sent me the copy of a dispatch to Mr. Canning of the 2d Oct., on several military subjects on which he suggested that I should give my opinion to government; and I wrote a memorandum upon the dispatch, which I did not send home, as, from the conversation I had with Mr. Villiers, I doubted whether he had sent home his dispatch. When I was afterwards at Seville with Lord Wellesley, he expressed a desire that I should send home the memorandum; and I now enclose the dispatch and memorandum,* in case Mr. Villiers should not have sent home the former. If he should have done so, it may be desirable that the latter should be in the office.

It occurs to me that you may not understand one part of my dispatch of the 14th, relative to the estimate of the expenses of the army. You will find it explained in a letter to Lord Castlereagh, of the 23d Sept.,† which you had better see, if you should not have already perused it.

To the Rt. Hon. J. H. Frere.   Badajoz, 21st Nov. 1809.

I return your maps, excepting those of Toledo, La Mancha, and Madrid, which, with your permission, I shall detain for some time longer, as they are not in the collection which I got from Richard Wellesley.

To the Earl of Liverpool.   Badajoz, 21st Nov. 1809.

I beg to draw your Lordship's attention to the frequent paragraphs in the English newspapers, describing the position, the numbers, the objects, and the means of attaining them, possessed by the armies in Spain and Portugal. In some instances the English newspapers have accurately stated, not only the regiments occupying a position, but the number of men fit for duty of which each regiment was composed; and this intelligence must have reached the enemy at the same time it did me, at a moment at which it was most important that he should not receive it.

The newspapers have recently published an account of the defensive positions occupied by the different English and Portuguese corps, which certainly conveyed to the enemy the first knowledge he had of them; and I enclose a paragraph recently published, describing the line of operation which I should follow in case of the occurrence of a certain event, the preparations which I had made for that operation, and where I had formed my magazines. It is not necessary to inquire in what manner the newspapers acquire this description of information; but if the editors really feel an anxiety for the success of the military operations in the Peninsula, they will refrain from giving this information to the public, as they must know that their papers are read by the enemy, and that the information which they are desirous of conveying to their English readers is mischievous to the public, exactly in proportion as it is well founded and correct. Your Lordship will be the best judge whether any and what measures ought to be adopted to prevent the publication of this description of intelligence. I can only assure you that it will increase materially the difficulty of all operations in this country.

The A.G. to Dr. Franck, Inspector of hospitals.   21st Nov. 1809.

Having submitted your letter of the 19th inst., and enclosures of the 16th, to the consideration of the Commander of the Forces, I am directed to convey to you his Excellency's opinion, that Mr. —— 's answer has by no means been satisfactory;

---

* See page 544.   † See page 516.

and it is his Lordship's wish that you clearly explain to the Purveyors that they will be held strictly accountable for the loss sustained by the regiment in this manner. I have been directed to ascertain the state of the registry of soldiers' accoutrements and necessaries, which ought to be systematic in all hospitals, when, on receipt of his Lordship's final orders on this head, I shall further communicate with you.

The A.G. to Lieut. Col. Fenwick, Elvas.   21st Nov. 1809.

Representations having reached the Commander of the Forces, that confusion has occurred, and much loss has been sustained by regiments, by an irregular mode of issuing arms and accoutrements out of the several hospitals, I am directed to require you to examine the registry at Elvas hospital, equally to ascertain whether it is carried forward with system, as to observe whether, heretofore, arms and accoutrements have invariably been issued to those soldiers who delivered them into store. In such instances as they have been otherwise disposed of, you will be pleased to report the authority. I take this occasion to request you will impress on all officers in charge of stores of this description, that they will be held by his Lordship strictly responsible for any loss or deficiency of such stores from their respective trusts.

To the Rt. Hon. J. Villiers.   Elvas, 25th Nov. 1809.

I enclose dispatches for Lord Bathurst, which will show that I was not a false prophet, unfortunately.* Pray send them home immediately.

I have been at Villa Vicosa since Wednesday, and do not understand the Duque del Parque being at Salamanca. He was ordered on the 16th to Talavera. If he is still in Castille I shall not be able to go to Beira till I shall know the final result of the dispersion of the Spanish army.

To Lieut. Col. Roche.   Badajoz, 26th Nov. 1809.

I received last night at Elvas your letter of the 22d, for which I am much obliged to you. I acknowledge that I have never expected any other result from the march of Gen. Areyzaga, and I am not at all surprised at what has happened. The folly will appear in a still stronger light, if, after all that has occurred, the French should be unable to penetrate into Andalusia, which I really believe will be the case, if Gen. Areyzaga should be able to collect any proportion of his scattered forces.

We are still here. The Duque de Alburquerque has been unable to carry into execution the orders sent to him by the government, and he is at Arzobispo. The Duque del Parque moved from Bejar towards Salamanca, as soon as he found that the French corps which had reinforced Ney had marched to Madrid, and he did not receive the orders sent to him; so that these 2 corps are safe for the present.

To Vice Adm. the Hon. G. Berkeley.   Badajoz, 26th Nov. 1809.

I received last night your letter of the 22d, at Elvas, and as the orders of the Admiralty are positive, my opinion is, that you had better not send home the 23d light dragoons till you shall hear further from England, and I can only assure you that there can be no inconvenience in the delay. I am certain, however, that the meaning of the order was only to put an end to the former order, which required that the transports should be

---

* The total defeat of the Spanish army under Gen. Areyzaga, at Ocaña, on the 19th Nov. (See pp. 593, 594, 595, 597, 598, and 599.)

sent home; and indeed it is obvious that you would not be wrong in employing the transports in carrying home troops, which must go home eventually, and which I have received orders to send home. However, as I said before, there is no inconvenience in their remaining for a short time; and obedience to an order is always right.

I am much obliged to you for the account of the tonnage which you have sent me. It would be very desirable if the agent would transmit to Col. Murray a list of the ships, with their marks, and the tonnage of each; and would apprise him from time to time of any alteration of their numbers, as it would enable us at any time to make the arrangements for embarking, so far as they may depend upon us.

To Bart. Frere, Esq.   Badajoz, 26th Nov. 1809.

I received last night, at Elvas, your letters of the 23d and 24th, and as I conceived it possible that your dispatches might arrive in time to go to England by the packet, which would sail from Lisbon this day, I forwarded them immediately by the Spanish messenger who brought them.

I have not yet received your letter of the 22d. You are aware that I have expected the unfortunate result of Gen. Areyzaga's expedition which has occurred: it will be a strong proof of his folly, if the French should, after all, be unable to penetrate into Andalusia; and I am very well convinced that this will be the case, if Gen. Areyzaga should be able to collect any proportion of his scattered forces. The destruction of this army, however, renders it most important that I should cross the Tagus.

If the enemy cannot penetrate into Andalusia, they may, at least, be very certain that the Spanish army of La Carolina cannot do them any harm for some time to come; and it is reasonable to suppose that they will now direct their efforts seriously to establish their government in Old Castille, in order that they may be prepared to take every advantage of their reinforcements, when they shall arrive, or that they may even push on their operations during the winter. Nothing will contribute so much to check them as the British army upon the frontier, and indeed, at all events, the necessary defence of Portugal will oblige me to move to that quarter during the fine weather in the month of December. I wish, therefore, that you would urge the government to make up the Duque de Alburquerque's corps to 20,000 men as soon as possible, which might be done without inconvenience, by drawing to this quarter, from the Duque del Parque's army, the number required during the time that I shall be in motion to the northward, or even before I shall commence my march.

P.S. Since writing the above, I have received your letter of the 22d.

To **** *****   Badajoz, 26th Nov. 1809.

It always gives me great concern to be under the necessity of refusing compliance with a request made to me by an officer of the army under my command; and I might have hoped to have been spared this concern by one who must know that I should be happy to gratify him if it were in my power; and who must be aware that it is not only unusual, but absolutely without precedent, that any officer should ask, much less obtain leave of absence from the army while on foreign service on any account, excepting on that of sickness or of business, the neglect of which might be materially prejudicial to the officer who requests the leave.

I repeat, that I cannot give leave to any officer whose health does not require his return to England, or who has not business to transact which cannot be done by another, and cannot be delayed. You cannot bring forward either of these pleas. Your health is good; and as for your business, I know of none that can require your immediate return which would not have required that you should have remained in England when you left it six months ago. I trust that I shall be spared the pain of again refusing you.

To Lieut. Col. ——.   Badajoz, 27th Nov. 1809.

I have had the honor of receiving your letter of the 19th Nov., and I should have great pleasure in recommending you to the Spanish government for employment in the Spanish service, if I had the pleasure of your acquaintance, or if you had been recommended to me. Under existing circumstances, however, I must decline to recommend you to the Spanish government.

To Col. Don M. de Alava.*   Badajoz, 27 Nov. 1809.

J'ai recu hier votre lettre du 25 ; et je vous écris en Français, comme je n'entends pas l'Espagnol, ni vous l'Anglais.

J'ai fait prier le gouvernement de renforcer l'armée du Duc d'Alburquerque jusqu'au nombre de 20,000 hommes, et je lui conseille en tout cas d'occuper la position de Fresnedoso, la Mesa de Ibor, Roman Gordo, et las Casas del Puerto, dans laquelle l'ennemi ne peut pas le forcer et ne voudra pas tenter de l'attaquer ; et il pourrait mettre sa réserve à Deleytosa, et son quartier général, s'il le veut, à Truxillo. L'ennemi ne peut pas non plus le tourner, excepté par Ciudad Real, et il faudrait d'abord avoir les moyens de forcer non seulement les passages de Despeña Perros, &c., mais un corps assez nombreux pour soutenir l'attaque du Duc en dos, pendant qu'ils auraient à pousser l'attaque par Monasterio en front. Ils ne tenteront pas cette manœuvre.

L'avantage que le Duc gagnerait en occupant la position indiquée est qu'il conservera pendant l'hiver toute l'Estremadure qui serait envahie, s'il passe la Guadiana. D'ailleurs, il ne pourrait pas tenir sa position sur cette rivière, et il serait obligé de se retirer à la Sierra Morena. Si l'ennemi fait la tentative de passer le Tage quand je serai en Estremadure, je communiquerai avec le Duc pour le battre ; mais je crois, selon le plan que j'ai proposé au gouvernement, que je passerai vers la frontière de la Vieille Castille, où la guerre va devenir plus vive après ce qui s'est passé dans la Manche.

To the Duque de Alburquerque.   Badajoz, 27th Nov. 1809.

I have had the honor of receiving your Excellency's letter of the 24th

* Don Miguel de Alava was afterwards attached, by the Spanish government, to the head quarters of Lord Wellington until the end of the war, and also in the subsequent campaign of 1815. He was Spanish Minister at the Court of St. James's in 1835, and died at Bagnères in July, 1843.

inst., and I have to inform you that it is not in my power to enter into any arrangement with your Excellency to defend the banks of the Guadiana.

I should rather recommend to your Excellency to defend the passage of the Tagus opposite Almaraz, and the passes in the mountains at the Mesa de Ibor, Fresnedoso, &c.; and if the enemy should attempt to penetrate into Estremadura by that route, whilst I shall remain in this province, I shall be happy to have the honor of communicating with your Excellency respecting the means of attacking him.

To Brig. Gen. R. Craufurd.   Badajoz, 27th Nov. 1809.

I have received your letter relative to the advance of money for the Captains of companies, upon which subject I had intended to adopt a rule before I heard from you. There is no doubt but that a great part, if not the whole of the subsistence of each regiment ought to be issued in advance on the 25th of every month, to the regimental Paymasters; and it has not hitherto been issued, principally because it was inconvenient to the regimental Paymasters and the Captains to receive it. It is, however, necessary to the regularity of accounts, and to the obedience to the orders of the Paymasters Gen. by their deputy, that the month's pay should be advanced to the regimental Paymasters, and should be received by them; and I intend that it shall be so from this time forward.

Capt. Wells, 43d, shall be paid the pay of a D.A.Q.M.G., while acting as secretary to the Board of Claims, and he shall be notified as such in Orders to-morrow.

I shall consider the case of Gen. ——'s chargers, and shall send you an answer upon it when I shall have had time to look at the Regulations.

To Marshal Beresford.   Badajoz, 27th Nov. 1809.

I enclose a memorandum which I have received from Brig. Gen. Victoria, who appears a good kind of a man; and I shall be obliged to you if you can make it convenient to promote his son, who appears to have been superseded by a British officer.

To Marshal Beresford.   Badajoz, 27th Nov. 1809.

I have received your letters of the 19th, 22d, and 24th inst. Lieut. Bourke shall be put in orders to place himself under your command, and Arbuthnot may keep serjeant Robinson.

I can't supply you with blankets, indeed I have not as many as I wanted for my own troops. I enclose, however, a letter which I received from England last night, relative to the supplies of clothing, &c., which you have required.

In respect to our meeting between the Mondego and the Estrella mountains, it would be best to defer it till the end of your northern tour; as I cannot well quit the army till I shall know what shape things will take after the defeat of the army in La Mancha.

I think the French will carry the greatest part of their force into Old Castille, and endeavor to settle their government in that province. To penetrate into Andalusia is, in my opinion, even now, not in their power.

I never know to what regiment the Horse Guards will appoint an officer whom I recommend for a commission, and I am therefore unwilling to send Mr. Dunlop to any particular regiment, lest he should not be posted to it. You had better, therefore, keep him for a few days longer, in the course of which time I must receive an account of his appointment. I dislike to have any thing to do with —— ——; but as you wish it, let an official application be sent from Capt. Arentschildt to be put, in point of allowances, on the same footing as Capt. Dickson.

If you should make Gen. Hamilton Inspector Gen. of the Infantry, you will of course recommend for him such allowance as the officer filling that office has had and ought to have : but I am decidedly of opinion that he cannot receive more pay as a General officer upon the Staff, whether Portuguese or British, than that fixed for him by the Commander in Chief, viz., that of a Major General.

You will have heard, probably, that I had pressed upon the government your proposition to add regimental staff to the regiments, to which they were not inclined; and I enclose the translation of my letter upon that subject. It occurs to me that you might in some degree provide for the expense of this arrangement, by abolishing the color bearers; and having the colors carried by Ensigns, as in the British service. I suggest this arrangement for your consideration.

You will have seen that I have recommended that our government should provide for the increase of pay to the officers, and should give even further pecuniary assistance, which I think will be complied with.

In respect to our movement, you may depend upon it that I will disturb you as little as possible. All I shall ask is, probably, that some of your battalions should leave their cantonments on the high road and go into the villages in the neighbourhood, off the road, for a few days, while we shall be passing; which will require neither time nor carriages, as your troops will return to their quarters when we shall have passed. Murray will write more particularly on this subject to Col. D'Urban. I think that you will be full near enough to us in the positions you at present occupy. Indeed, it might be more convenient to all parties if you were more distant.

I send an order to Col. Fisher to give you 3000 stand of arms; I must send you the others from Elvas, unless you should wish to have them there. Let me know your wishes upon this point.

Let me have an official report respecting the detention of M. V. de Farincourt at Ciudad Rodrigo.

You did not enclose ——'s application to be appointed a Brig. General. I don't understand what he means by it.

The officers who have presented a memorial claiming an increase of pay have carried the principle, that words break no bones, as far as it is possible ; and I must say that the greatest part of my time is taken up in resisting applications of this description. They have misstated the principle on which they were appointed to serve with the Portuguese army, and have omitted to give any one reason why the agreement under which they engaged to serve in the Portuguese army should be departed from, excepting that they wish to have a little more money in their pockets; which is equally applicable to the situation of every other officer in the army.

I enclose you the copy of a dispatch of the 7th Nov., from Lord Liverpool, in answer to three of yours of the 11th and 19th Oct., and the copy of one of the 14th Nov., relative to Trant and Cox's rank, to which you will observe, by another dispatch, that the King consents.

I likewise enclose the extract of a letter of the 13th, from Sir D. Dundas, relative to the appointment of additional field officers to the Portuguese army. You will observe that Hawkshaw is to be promoted, *vice* Patrick. In respect to the other two, it does not appear quite clear, from the General's letter, whether he means that I am to recommend them from the British army under my command exclusively, or to include officers serving with the Portuguese troops. I rather believe the latter; and if you are of the same opinion, I wish you would fix upon two now serving with the Portuguese troops, with Portuguese advanced rank and pay, either Captains or Majors, or one of each, to be promoted; and I shall be glad if they should belong to the regiments in this army, in order that those regiments may have the benefit of the promotion in succession. However, you must be guided in this last point by your own views of what is right and fair to others.

To the Earl of Liverpool.   Badajoz, 27th Nov. 1809.

I have had the honor of receiving your Lordship's letter of the 2d inst., in which you have enclosed the copy of one from Mr. Villiers; and in case I should have any opportunity of communicating with the German corps in the service of the enemy, I shall attend to your Lordship's instructions.

It is impossible for me to say what number of Germans were enlisted at Oporto and Ciudad Rodrigo from the enemy's troops, because I did not command His Majesty's troops in this country at the time; but I did in the months of July and August last, and I have no recollection of the arrival of any German deserters from the Escurial, much less of 160. Neither do I recollect the circumstance of a battalion being in treaty to join us, when the British army was in the neighbourhood of that of the enemy in July and August.

The German troops were at and in the neighbourhood of Toledo, with few exceptions; some few then deserted, but not in such numbers as to deserve serious attention; and adverting to the encouragement they had from the Commander in Chief of the Spanish army, and to the facilities afforded to them by our neighbourhood and their own position, I was rather inclined to be of opinion that as a body, or even in very large numbers, they were not desirous of quitting the French service. At the same time, the commanding officers of the German regiments in the British service were not anxious to receive them as recruits, in which they were not wrong, as most of the few they did receive have since deserted from them; and, upon the whole, I did not think there was any ground for a belief that any measures which I might adopt to encourage or facilitate desertion from the enemy's German troops would have an effect at all proportionate to the expense of them.

The A.G. to Col. Peacocke, Lisbon.   27th Nov. 1809.

I have the honor to acknowledge the receipt of your letter, 24th inst., and enclosures from Lieut. Crompton, 9th foot. His Excellency has directed me in reply to communicate, that although it would have gratified him to continue in a staff situation an officer who has afforded you satisfaction, yet his Lordship cannot sanction the disobedience of an order issued by His Majesty's command.

To the Rt. Hon. J. Villiers.   Badajoz, 28th Nov. 1809.

I have the honor to enclose a letter, which I have received from the Superintendent General of the custom houses of the province of Alentejo, relative to wine purchased in Portugal for the use of that part of the British army stationed in Spain.

If the wine purchased for the consumption of that part of the British army stationed in Portugal is liable to the duty in question, it appears perfectly reasonable that the wine exported to Spain for the use of the army should not be exempt from the payment of the same ; but if the wine consumed in Portugal should not pay duty, I hope that the government will so far take into consideration the inconvenience which the troops who are in Spain will suffer, as to allow that which is exported for their use to be exported duty free.   As it might be inconvenient to allow this wine to remain under sequestration until the answer to the references made shall arrive, I have written to the Superintendent of the custom houses in Alentejo to request him to allow the wine to pass into Spain, under the engagement which I have given to pay the duties, if the government of Portugal should decide that they must be paid.

To Marshal Beresford.   Badajoz, 28th Nov. 1809.

We are much in want of boots, and I shall be very much obliged to you if you will be so kind as to give over to the Commissary Gen. at Lisbon 500 pairs of the 2500 which were sent out for the Portuguese troops, and desire him to forward them to Badajoz without delay.

To the Earl of Liverpool.   Badajoz, 28th Nov. 1809.

I have received your letter of the 1st inst., and I assure you that nothing can be more satisfactory to me than to renew my public communications with you.   I am convinced that I shall always receive from you that fair protection, support and assistance to which an officer is entitled when he acts fairly by the public, and all the friendship and kindness which I have been accustomed to receive from you in another situation.

I trust that my public and private letters on the subject of the war in the Peninsula, and of Portugal in particular, will have been satisfactory to you and to the government. You see that I agree entirely in opinion with you, not only that we cannot in good policy give up the Peninsula, but that we may be able to continue the contest in Portugal with success, and that we shall finally bring off our army.   During the continuance of this contest, which must necessarily be defensive on our part, in which there may be no brilliant events, and in which, after all, I may fail, I shall be most confoundedly abused, and in the end I may lose the little character I have gained ; but I should not act fairly by the government if I did not tell them my real opinion, which is, that they will betray the honor and interests of the country if they do not continue their efforts in the Peninsula, which, in my opinion, are by no means hopeless, notwithstanding the defeat of Areyzaga.

Lord Castlereagh's misfortunes have given me the greatest concern. His kindness to me has been unbounded; and I shall always be happy to hear of any thing that can tend to his honor or satisfaction.

To the Duke of Richmond.   Badajoz, 28th Nov. 1809.

I enclose a letter which I have lately received from —————, and the copy of my answer. He wanted to impose a promise upon me, which he would afterwards have urged you, and probably would have urged me to request you, to perform; but I think my letter will put an end to all prospect of success on this subject.

The army has been very sickly lately, but I hope that the cold weather, which has now set in, has operated a permanent change for the better.

The troops, allies as well as enemies, are nearly in the positions which I took up in August; and if the Spaniards had not taken it into their heads that they could fight a general action, and had not lost an army of 50,000 men, defeated by half the number of French, in La Mancha, on the 19th of this month, I really believe that the war in Spain and Portugal would have ended in some arrangement advantageous to the world. I don't yet despair, as it is impossible to say what may be the result of this defeat. If the troops should collect again, and they will only manage them with prudence, I hope that we may yet keep up the ball in the Peninsula sufficiently long to tire out Buonaparte.

I was at Villa Viçosa (the family seat of the Dukes of Braganza) some days ago, and I shot with ball 10 head of deer in 3 days. The park in which they were is immense, and, I dare say, did not contain less than 5000 head, many of them red deer. This is pretty good sport.

I conclude that you will go to Pole's this winter. Remember me most kindly to the Duchess.

To Bart. Frere, Esq.   Badajoz, 29th Nov. 1809.

Capt. Silvertop, late of the 14th dragoons, has expressed a desire to serve with the Spanish army, and that I should recommend him to you for that purpose. Capt. Silvertop has been strongly recommended to me by the Commanding officer of the 14th light dragoons, under whose command he served; and I shall be very much obliged to you if you will recommend him to the government.

To the Earl of Liverpool.   Badajoz, 29th Nov. 1809.

We are much in want of the lower class of medical assistants with this army, such as assistant surgeons and hospital mates: so much so, that if I were obliged to move, I should not have with the regiments nearly a sufficient number to do the duty; and those attached to the hospitals have more duty to perform than they can well manage, particularly now that the disorders are so violent. I shall be very glad if an effort can be made to send us some hospital mates. We should have at least 30, to put us in this respect in the state in which we ought to be.

To the Governor of Badajoz.   Badajoz, 29th Nov. 1809.

I have the honor to acknowledge the receipt of your Excellency's letter to Lieut. Gen. Sherbrooke of the 24th inst., relative to certain outrages committed by English soldiers, in resistance of the authority of a sentry. One of the soldiers principally concerned in this affray is wounded, and has not yet recovered from his wounds. There was also a non-commissioned officer with the men in question, whom I have ordered into confinement; and they shall be tried for this offence as soon as the wounded man shall be sufficiently recovered to stand his trial, and punished according to the sentence of the Court Martial. I assure your Excellency that nothing gives me more concern than these outrages, which I invariably punish when they come to my knowledge. I consider a sentry as a depositary of the public authority at his station, and that all men, however high in rank, are bound to obey the orders he has to give them.

I think it proper, however, to inform your Excellency, that the orders given to the sentries in this garrison are not uniformly the same, or that care is not taken to make them understand their orders in the same manner, as I have myself experienced, particularly lately; and it is not astonishing that ignorant people, as soldiers are, should be disinclined to obey orders given by a sentry, which they may believe are dictated by caprice, and have not been received from superior authority. I do not mention this subject by way of excuse for these soldiers, whose conduct has been inexcusable, but to draw the attention of your Excellency to this fact.

G. O.   Badajoz, 29th Nov. 1809.

1. As some doubts have been entertained respecting the order of the late Commander of the Forces of the 16th March, respecting the hire of native servants instead of bât men from the ranks, it is published again for general information.

2. Extracts from the G. O. by Lieut. Gen. Sir J. Cradock, K.B., dated 16th March, 1809:

'The Commander of the Forces being desirous of rendering the army in the field as effective as possible, directs that no soldier whatever acting as a servant to an officer, shall appear in any other dress than his uniform; and on a march he is to carry his arms and accoutrements.

'The servants of regimental officers to be in the ranks on the march, and the Commander of the Forces calls on the General and other officers in command, strictly to enforce this order.

'With a view to diminish as much as possible requisitions on regiments for soldiers as servants, Lieut. Gen. Sir J. Cradock authorises any officer who is entitled by the usage of the service to appear mounted, and keep a horse, to hire a servant as bât man, in lieu of a soldier, for which he will be allowed at the rate of 1 dollar per week, and a ration; but it is to be distinctly understood that this allowance is not to be extended to any persons attached to this army, who by the custom of the service are not usually entitled to soldiers to wait on them; and whenever it is drawn, an effective soldier is to be thereby restored to the army.

'The following will be the scale for the number allowed to each rank:

	Number of bât men or servants each.
'Commander of the Forces	4
Lieutenant General	3
Major and Brigadier Generals, and heads of departments . . .	2
All other officers, Regimental and Staff	1

'These men will be paid by the Dep. Com. Gen. monthly, on regular pay lists being transmitted every 25th, certified by the Paymasters of corps, and approved by commanding officers of battalions.

'The returns for the General Staff officers to be made out by departments, and to be certified by the heads of each. Those of General officers and their families to be certified by the General officers: a form may be had of the Dep. Com. Gen.

'The Commander of the Forces most strongly recommends it to all the General officers of the army, to return immediately any bât men they may have to their corps, and to direct their Staff to do the same; at all events, no officer of any rank is to employ more than one soldier of this army to attend upon him, whether he acts as his personal servant or bât man.'

3. The officers of the army will observe that the intention of this order was, to allow the hire of a native servant instead of a bât man, or servant from the ranks, to the officers entitled, by the custom of the service, to have bât men and servants from the ranks.

4. Field

I have also to acknowledge the receipt of your Excellency's letter respecting the conduct of a person in the service of Gen. Payne; and if your Excellency will do me the favor to send him to me, his conduct shall be inquired into, and he shall be punished.

To the Earl of Liverpool.   Badajoz, 30th Nov. 1809.

The Spanish army in La Mancha, which I reported to your Lordship in my dispatch of the 16th Nov. were on the 10th inst. at Los dos Barrios, not far from Ocaña, moved on that night to attack a French corps which was in Ocaña.

It appears that the Spanish Commander in Chief was not aware that the French corps in Ocaña consisted of 5000 infantry as well as of 800 cavalry : and he made his first attack with the Spanish cavalry only, supported by the infantry, which were repulsed with some loss of men, and,

---

4. Field officers of regiments are entitled each to a servant and bât man ; and of course to draw the allowance for each, if they should not have the service of them.

5. The captains each a servant, and a bât man for their company. Subaltern officers, adjutant, quarter master, paymaster, surgeon, and assistant surgeon, each a servant ; and the surgeon a bât man for the medicine chest mule ; the paymaster one for the mule to carry his books, and the quarter master one for the mule carrying the intrenching tools.

6. The General and other officers on the Staff who have not bât men from the regiments, are to draw the allowances allotted to each.

7. It has never been the custom of the service to allow soldiers from the ranks to attend upon the officers of the Commissariat, or the medical Staff ; and the orders of the 16th March cannot be considered as relating to them.

8. The Commander of the Forces requests that particular attention may be paid to the form of the account which must be sent in, claiming payment for these bât men, and that the General officers, heads of departments, and commanding officers of regiments, who are to certify these bills, will not certify them for any officer who has a servant from the ranks to attend upon him.

9. The allowance of wood for the troops in camp or cantonments is to be as follows :

Daily to each non-commissioned officer and private soldier . 3 lbs.
.. to each subaltern and regimental Staff . . . . . . 12 lbs.
.. to each captain . . . . 21 lbs.
.. to each Field officer . . . . 30 lbs.

The officers upon the Staff are to draw according to their rank in the army. The officers of the Commissariat and medical Staff are to draw each the proportion of wood allotted to the officer of corresponding rank in the army.

As the General officers have Staff, &c. attached to them, their allowance of wood is unlimited ; but as the supply of wood in this country is very small, and it is very difficult to be procured, the Commander of the Forces requests the General officers of the army will observe the utmost economy in the expenditure of wood, and that they will take measures that the quantities of that article supplied for their use are applied solely for that purpose, and not stolen or applied to the use of the owner of the house in which they are quartered.

G. A. O.   Badajoz, 29th Nov. 1809.

1. Officers commanding brigades of artillery are requested to give directions, that when the horses attached to their guns are sent to water, or to exercise, they may be marched regularly under the command of an officer of the gunner drivers ; an officer of the gunner drivers should likewise attend all horse parades.

2. The Commander of the Forces requests the officers commanding regiments to explain to both officers and soldiers of the battalions under their command, that it is equally criminal to resist a Spanish or Portuguese sentry or guard, as it is to resist either belonging to the British army.

A guard or sentry must be understood at all times to be charged with the execution of the orders of a competent authority at the place in which either may be stationed, or may be found, and must not be resisted on any account.

Guards or sentries may mistake their orders, or may execute them improperly, and in these cases complaints must be made ; but on no account must they be resisted.

as I have understood, of 2 pieces of cannon. The French maintained their position in Ocaña till 3 in the morning, when they retired one league from the town towards Aranjuez; and at daylight they retired to that town, and the Spanish army took up its quarters again at Los dos Barrios. They remained there till the 13th, when they moved to their right to Sta. Cruz de la Zarza; and on the 18th they returned to Los dos Barrios, with an intention of attacking a French corps of about 25,000 men, including 5000 cavalry, which was advanced from Aranjuez towards Ocaña. Gen. Areyzaga found, however, that it was most probable that the enemy would attack him before he should be prepared to make his movement, and he formed his army in the plain in the rear of Ocaña to receive their attack on the morning of the 19th inst. The enemy advanced in three columns, with one of which they took possession of Ocaña; and having overthrown the Spanish cavalry on the right of their position, they broke the Spanish infantry of the right wing, which was thrown into confusion; and the left wing of the army, which was likewise threatened with an attack by the right column of the enemy, retired without firing a shot.

The loss of the Spanish army upon this occasion has been considerable. Not less, I understand, than 55 pieces of cannon have fallen into the enemy's hands, together with the military chest, the provisions, baggage, clothing, &c., of the army. The head quarters were, on the night of the 19th, at Tembleque, and on the 22d at La Carolina. A corps of Spanish dragoons, consisting of 1000 men, under Gen. Bernay, which had not been in the action at Ocaña, and which were ordered to Madridejos to cover the retreat of the fugitives from the battle, also dispersed on the 20th, on hearing of the advance of a detachment of the enemy's cavalry; and on the 24th, the date of the last accounts from La Carolina, only 500 cavalry of different regiments had assembled at Manzanares, and very few of the defeated army had arrived at La Carolina.

The advanced parties of the French cavalry had not passed Villarta as late as the 21st; and by the accounts from La Carolina of the 24th, it appears that the enemy had not advanced any farther. It is supposed that the fugitives from the battle of Ocaña have gone generally into Murcia and Valencia.

Besides the corps consisting of 25,000 men, commanded by the King and Marshal Soult, with which Gen. Areyzaga was engaged on the 19th inst., it is understood that another corps, under Victor and Sebastiani, was to cross the Tagus at Fuentidueña, and fall upon the right of the Spanish army. The enemy also occupied Talavera de la Reyna with 10,000 men. It appears that, between the 12th and 14th, they withdrew from Old Castille the reinforcements which they had sent into that province from Estremadura, in consequence of the Duque del Parque's success at Tamames; but I should doubt whether these troops were engaged in the operations against the Spanish army commanded by Gen. Areyzaga.

The Duque del Parque, who I reported to your Lordship in my letter of the 16th inst., had his head quarters at Bejar, continued in that situation till the 17th, when hearing of the evacuation of Castille by the reinforcements which had been sent from Estremadura, he advanced again; and I understand from the last accounts that a detachment from his corps was again in possession of Salamanca. This possession, however, can be but momentary, as it must be expected that the enemy will take advantage of the defeat of the army under Gen. Areyzaga, to reinforce their troops in Old Castille to such an extent as to establish their government in that province.

The corps under the Duque de Alburquerque, which had been directed to cross the Tagus at the bridge of Arzobispo, and to co-operate with the corps under the Duque del Parque, which had been ordered to pass through the mountains at Baños, and to proceed to Talavera de la Reyna, to create a diversion in favor of Gen. Areyzaga, is at Peraleda de Garbin, near the bridge of Arzobispo, which is occupied by the Duque de Alburquerque's advanced guard.

I have the honor to enclose the copies and extracts of a correspondence which I have had with Mr. Frere, on the subject of the co-operation of the British army with the corps of the Duque de Alburquerque and the Duque del Parque, in this plan of diversion.

Adverting to the opinions which I have given to His Majesty's ministers, and to the Ambassador at Seville, it will not be supposed that I could have encouraged the advance of Gen. Areyzaga, or could have held out the prospect of any co-operation by the British army.

The first official information which I had from the government, of the movement made by Gen. Areyzaga, was on the 18th, the day before his defeat; and I gave the answer on the 19th, regarding the plan, of which I now enclose the copy. I was at Seville, however, when the General commenced his march from the Sierra Morena; and in more than one conversation with the Spanish ministers and members of the Junta, communicated to them my conviction that Gen. Areyzaga would be defeated.

The expectation, however, of success from this large army, stated to consist of 50,000 men, was so general and so sanguine, that the possibility of disappointment was not even contemplated; and, accordingly, your Lordship will find it was not until the 16th that the government began to think it necessary to endeavor to make a diversion in favor of Gen. Areyzaga; and it is probable that it was thought expedient to make this diversion only in consequence of the fall of the General's own hopes, after his first trial with the enemy on the night of the 10th inst. It is impossible for me to express any opinion on the probable consequences of this defeat, till I shall know its exact extent, and in what numbers and in what state the Spanish troops will re-assemble.

I am anxious to cross the Tagus with the British army, and to station it on the frontiers of Old Castille, from thinking that the point in which I can be of most use in preventing the enemy from effecting any important object, and which will best answer for my future operations in the defence of Portugal. With this view I have requested Mr. Frere to urge the government to reinforce the Duque de Alburquerque's corps, in order to secure the passage of the lower part of the Tagus: and although the state of the season would render it desirable that I should make the movement at an early period, I do not propose to make it till I shall see more clearly the consequences of the late defeat, and some prospect that the city of Seville will be secure after I shall move.

To the Earl of Liverpool.   Badajoz, 30th Nov. 1809.

In addition to the official documents which I have forwarded to you in my dispatch of this day, I enclose the copy of a private letter of the 19th to Mr. Frere, in which I have pointed out more in detail the consequences of the operations which had been proposed to me by the government, and the difficulties which would attend, indeed I may say the impossibility of their execution.

I understand that the people of Seville are informed of my opinions upon the late expedition; and that they have expressed an anxious desire that the government should attend to what I should recommend to them in future.

To the Earl of Liverpool.   Badajoz, 30th Nov. 1809.

I enclose the copy of a letter from the Admiralty to Adm. Berkeley; in consequence of which I have recommended to the Admiral not to send transports to England with that part of the 23d light dragoons which I intended to send home immediately. I am convinced that the order could not be intended to prevent the use of the transports for the service of the army; and particularly not to transport troops to England, which in case of the evacuation must go thither. But as I have made a reference to the Commander in Chief respecting the 23d light dragoons, I was not sorry to detain them a little longer.

As I know the Admiralty are very quick in dispatching orders, I was not sure what might have passed in the Cabinet to occasion this order; and upon the whole, I thought it best and safest, and liable to no inconvenience, to recommend an obedience to its letter. It is desirable, however, that, as soon as possible, we should have some latitude given to us respecting the disposal of the transports in the Tagus.

To the Rt. Hon. J. Villiers.   Badajoz, 30th Nov. 1809.

I beg you to read my dispatches, which I have desired Capt. Canning to deliver to you, and to refer you particularly to that which contains an answer to one from Lord Liverpool, on the subject of the German deserters, in which it appears you had written a dispatch to England. I wish that you had done me the favor to have referred the authority to me, on which you founded your report, before you sent it home; as I could have proved to you that it was incorrect, not only in those statements which related to transactions supposed to have taken place while I commanded the army, but that it was equally incorrect respecting the 500 Germans stated to have deserted upon a former occasion. Several people in England have given credit to this statement, supported as it now is by your authority; and it is supposed that I have neglected the important means pointed out of diminishing the strength of the enemy's forces. Now, I must tell you a secret upon this subject, the truth of which can be proved by the inspection of our returns by any body who will take the trouble of looking at them, and that is: supposing the story of the desertion of the Germans to be true, and that 160 entered the British army without my knowing any thing about it, we have lost more Germans by desertion from our army than the French have from theirs.

I have received your letter of the 26th, and I am much obliged to you for the packet arrangement. I was at Villa Viçosa last week, and did not write to you by the messenger who took the army letters to Lisbon.

I have again spoken this day to the Commissary Gen. respecting the French gold, and he will write to Mr. Dunmore respecting it. I think we ought not to send this coin to our officers at Madrid, as it is probable that they would experience as much difficulty or loss in passing it as we should here or at Lisbon; and I think the small sums we are permitted to send them ought to be in the coins which they could pass with the greatest advantage.

I am afraid that it would be inconvenient to us to give to you the whole sum of £100,000 at once, as our supplies have lately failed us a little; but Mr. Murray has directions to pay to your order £50,000 whenever you please; and £50,000 more you shall have in a fortnight afterwards.

P.S. The death of Lord Lansdowne, which, if it has not already occurred, must occur, I understand, very shortly, is a political event of the greatest consequence, and I think very likely to have very extensive effects upon the affairs of the present moment.

To Marshal Beresford. Badajoz, 30th Nov. 1809.

I have received your letters of the 26th and 29th.

The Duque del Parque has advanced, because, whatever may be the consequence, the Spaniards always think it necessary to advance when their front is clear of the enemy, whatever may be the ultimate consequences of their advance. He will retire again in a terrible hurry, as soon as he shall find that Areyzaga is destroyed, and that the French are again reinforcing Castille, and mean to destroy him.

I wish I knew what was likely to be the final result of the action at Ocaña, and could cross the Tagus. The next important event will certainly occur in that quarter. You should warn your battalions on the frontier, that they may not be surprised.

P.S. I have begged Villiers to show you my dispatches.

To Major Gen. the Hon. G. L. Cole. Badajoz, 30th Nov. 1809.

I enclose the copy of a letter which I have lately received from the Sec. at War, respecting certain accounts of the — regt., which have not been transmitted to the War office, and a copy of a letter which has been written to the commanding officer of that regiment, by my desire, and of his answer.

As the Sec. at War has directed that the cause of the non-transmission of these accounts may be particularly inquired into, I beg that you will assemble a Court of Inquiry, to consist of yourself and three of the senior field officers of the 4th division, (not including any of the — regt.,) and that you will inquire into, and especially report on, the cause of deviation from established rule in the 1st batt. — regt., noticed by the Sec. at War.

To Vice Adm. the Hon. G. Berkeley. Badajoz, 30th Nov. 1809.

I have had the honor of receiving your letter of the 23d inst., and I have sent directions to the officer commanding at Lisbon, specifying those carriages belonging to the Waggon Train which are to be landed and received into store at Lisbon, as being likely to be of use to the army; and those which are to be sent back to England. I shall be much obliged to you if you will give directions that the last, 30 in number, may be embarked in an empty victualler, to be returned to England.

To the Rt. Hon. the Paymaster General.   Badajoz, 30th Nov. 1809.

I have received your letter of the 31st Oct., in which you have desired that, in the case mentioned in a letter to your Deputy with this army, a copy of which you have enclosed, I shall allow Mr. Dep. Paymaster Gen. Hunter to return to England.

As it is not probable that the army will be immediately concentrated in Portugal, and as the head quarters will certainly not be established at Lisbon, I do not propose to make the alterations which you had directed in the expectation of the occurrence of these events.

To Lieut. Col. Torrens, Mil. Sec.   Badajoz, 30th Nov. 1809.

I have to request that you will submit the enclosed memorial to the favorable consideration of the Commander in Chief; and I beg leave to recommend Major Coghlan, 61st regt.,* in the strongest manner, as an officer most deserving of the promotion he solicits.

To Bart. Frere, Esq.   Badajoz, 1st Dec. 1809.

I enclose some papers which have been put into my hands by the Commissary Gen. of the British army. A person, by the name of ——, was employed as Commissary of the cavalry at Merida, and in consequence of some suspicion of the propriety of the charges in his accounts, the Commissary Gen. went there and removed him from his situation. Upon further inquiry, it appeared, that among other improprieties, he had been guilty of receiving 5 *per cent.* from the dealers in different articles furnished to the troops on payment of their demands, and that the Junta had a knowledge of this circumstance; and yet it appears that after his dismissal from his situation at Merida by the Commissary Gen., the Junta wrote the letter to have him replaced, of which I enclose the copy.

I do not know whether the government have any and what authority over the Provincial or Municipal Juntas. If they have, it is obvious that this Junta of Merida is entirely undeserving of their confidence.

To Bart. Frere, Esq.   Badajoz, 2d Dec. 1809.

The officer who will have the honor of delivering this letter to you is

---

* Major Coghlan had been wounded and left at Talavera, and had escaped from prison on his march towards France. He was soon afterwards promoted to be Lieut. Colonel of the 61st, in the command of which regiment he was shot through the heart at the battle of Toulouse, on the 10th April, 1814. Lieut. Col. Coghlan lived, in person, mind, and conduct, the model of a British officer; and died, where he had often distinguished himself, at the head of his regiment, in the moment of victory. He was buried, under fire, in a temporary grave, on the position captured from the enemy; but, on the 12th, was removed to the Protestant cemetery in Toulouse, where all the officers of the army then in Toulouse paid the last tribute of respect to his remains.

Sir W. Myers,* the Lieut. Col. of the Fusiliers, who is going to Seville for a few days; and I beg leave to recommend him to your attention.

To Bart. Frere, Esq.   Badajoz, 2d Dec. 1809.

I have just received your letter of the 30th, and I shall forward your dispatches to Lisbon by the first opportunity.

You did quite right to open the letter from Col. Roche; and I beg that you will peruse any that he may send to you in future which may be addressed to me.

A letter from Col. Alava, of the 29th, informs me that the Duque's army consists only of 10,000 infantry and 600 cavalry; and from the movements of the enemy, of which he has given me an account, I have no doubt but that they are about to reinforce their army in Castille, when they will certainly strike a blow of importance. I should not be surprised if they were to endeavor at the same time to amuse me in this quarter. The reinforcement of the Duque's corps, therefore, becomes a measure of the greatest importance and urgency; and if it can be done in time, I should hope that the enemy will derive no substantial advantage from their late success in La Mancha, excepting that which they have already acquired in the defeat of so large a body of men.

There are two battalions in this garrison, that of Merida, and that of Seville, which were brought from Portugal to reinforce the Duque's army, but have been detained here, I believe, contrary to orders.

P.S. I do not know why the bridge of Arzobispo should not be destroyed: if that were done, every thing on this side of the Tagus would be in safety and tranquillity during the winter, as the enemy have no bridge, nor any means of moving one; time would be afforded to organize and discipline an army in Estremadura; and, at all events, I might commence my march across the Tagus immediately.

To Col. Malcolm.   Badajoz, 3d Dec. 1809.

I am very much obliged for your letter of the ——, which I received about a month ago, and which I thought so interesting, and the sentiments it contained on the situation of affairs at Madras so well deserving the attention and consideration of the King's servants, that I sent it to Lord Harrowby, who was at that time President of the Board of Control. I have not received any answer from him, nor do I know what has been determined, particularly respecting the state of affairs at Madras. But I understood generally that Sir G. Barlow's conduct had been approved; but that it was not intended to confirm the suspension of all the officers who had been suspended by him.

You cannot conceive how much I have felt for what has passed on the Madras establishment. I scarcely recognise in those transactions the men for whom I entertained so much respect, and had so much regard, a few years back; and I can only lament that they, and the army, and the affairs of that Presidency in general, have been so much mismanaged. These transactions, and their causes, prove that it is not always the man

* Afterwards killed at the battle of Albuera, on the 16th May, 1811, in command of the Fusilier brigade. He was an officer of great promise.

who has the character of being the best natured, and one of the easiest disposition, who will agree best with those placed in authority over him, or those with whom he is to co-operate. They owe their origin to the disputes of the persons in authority in India, that is to say, between the Governor and the Commander in Chief. Both, but principally the latter, looked for partisans and supporters; and these have ended by throwing off all subordination, by relinquishing all habits of obedience, and almost by open resistance. Nothing can be more absurd than the pretext for this conduct.

Col. Munro's * opinion might be erroneous, and might have been harsh towards his brother officers; but not only he ought not to have been brought to a Court Martial for giving that opinion, but he ought to have been brought to a Court Martial if he had refrained from giving it, when he was called upon by the Commander in Chief to make him a report on a subject referred to his official consideration. The officers of the army are equally wrong in the part they have taken in the subsequent part of the question, which is one between the Governor and the Commander in Chief, whether the former had a right to protect Col. Munro from the acts of the latter, upon which question no man can have a doubt who has any knowledge of the Constitution of Great Britain, and particularly of that of the Indian governments. I, who have arrived pretty nearly at the top of the tree, should be the last man to give up any point of military right or etiquette. But I have no doubt whatever, not only that it was the right, but that it was the duty of the Governor in Council to interfere to save Col. Munro; and that if he had not done so, and the public had sustained any loss or inconvenience from his trial, or if the public attention had been drawn to the injustice of his trial, the Governor would have been severely responsible for the omission to perform his duty.

So far for my opinion upon the main points of the question. As for the others, the conduct of officers upon the addresses, the orders issued, the resolutions entered into, the resignations of their offices, &c. &c., they are consequences of the first error; that is, of persons in authority making partisans of those placed under them, instead of making all obey the constituted authorities of the state. This conduct in the officers of the army would have been wrong even if the cause had been just, and the Commander in Chief had wished to screen Col. Munro from the persecution of the government: and it is really not worth while to take up my time in describing, or yours in perusing, a description of the folly, the inconsistency, or the breaches of discipline and subordination contained in all those documents. I have so much regard for the Madras army, to which I owe much, that I would sacrifice a great deal to have it in my power to restore them to that state of discipline, union, and respectability in which I left them in the year 1805; and I assure you that I shall rejoice most sincerely when I shall hear that their good sense and good temper have predominated over their feelings of party and their prejudices.

I am very much obliged to you for your account of Persian affairs. I understand that an ambassador has passed Gibraltar, on his way to

* Col. John Munro.

England; but the question is, on what terms this concession on the part of Persia has been obtained. I am entirely ignorant of all this, and I only wish that you had been the instrument of making this arrangement.

You will have heard of all that has passed in this country, and I will not, therefore, trouble you with a repetition of the story. The battle of Talavera was certainly the hardest fought of modern days, and the most glorious in its result to our troops. Each side engaged lost a quarter of their numbers. It is lamentable that, owing to the miserable inefficiency of the Spaniards, to their want of exertion, and the deficiency of numbers even of the allies, much more of discipline, and every other military quality, when compared with the enemy in the Peninsula, the glory of the action is the only benefit which we have derived from it. But that is a solid and substantial benefit, of which we have derived some good consequences already; for, strange to say, I have contrived, with the little British army, to keep every thing in check since the month of August last; and if the Spaniards had not contrived, by their own folly, and against my entreaties and remonstrances, to lose an army in La Mancha about a fortnight ago, I think we might have brought them through the contest. As it is, however, I do not despair. I have in hand a most difficult task, from which I may not extricate myself; but I must not shrink from it. I command *an unanimous army*; I draw well with all the authorities in Spain and Portugal; and I believe I have the good wishes of the whole world. In such circumstances one may fail, but it would be dishonorable to shrink from the task.

Pray remember me kindly to all friends in the East Indies. I do not mention names, as I do not know whom you have with you; but I assure you that I have the most affectionate recollection of them all, and that nothing gives me greater pleasure than to hear of their prosperity.

P.S. You will have seen that your father in law * distinguished himself in the battle of Talavera. He was wounded, and is gone to England; but he is now quite well, and I expect his early return to the army.

To Major R. Barclay.   Badajoz, 3d Dec. 1809.

I will not send away the letters which I have been writing to Malcolm and others without giving you a few lines to assure you of my constant remembrance and friendship. I have seen with concern the accounts of transactions at Madras; but it has given me unfeigned pleasure to find that your name has not been mixed up in any of them. I should have been vexed if any body, so nearly connected officially and in friendship with me while I was in India, had been concerned in such folly.

I don't pretend to give you an account of affairs here. We have had hard work, and shall have still harder; but I don't despair. I have an *unanimous* army; I agree well with all the authorities in Portugal and Spain; and I believe I have the good wishes of the whole world.

The battle of Talavera was the hardest fought of modern times. The fire at Assye was heavier while it lasted; but the battle of Talavera lasted for 2 days and a night. Each party engaged lost a fourth of their numbers!!! Pray remember me to all friends, particularly to Symonds.

* Lieut. Gen. Sir Alex. Campbell, K.C.B.

P.S. Pray how does Salabut Khan get on? Though he did call me a
——, because I would not allow him to eat pork, I cannot avoid being
anxious about him.

To Bart. Frere, Esq.   Badajoz, 5th Dec. 1809.

I write by desire of Mr. Dillon, to inform you that he is employed by
contract with the Commissary Gen. of the army, to make at Seville, and
to forward to Elvas, for the use of the British, 400,000 lbs. of biscuit.

To Bart. Frere, Esq.   Badajoz, 6th Dec. 1809.

I have had the honor of receiving your letters of the 2d and 3d, to
which I had intended to reply by a detailed statement of my sentiments
respecting the operations to be adopted by the corps of the Duque del
Parque and the Duque de Alburquerque; but this morning has brought
me accounts of the defeat of the former on the 28th Nov.; and that the
latter had withdrawn from his position on the 2d inst., by order of government; which order must have been sent at the time Don F. de Saavedra
wrote the note to you of the 2d. It is useless for me, therefore, to trouble
you with my ideas upon operations which can no longer be carried into
execution. I must act according to my own views of what will be best
for the general cause; and I propose, therefore, to commence my march
to cross the Tagus without loss of time.

To Bart. Frere, Esq.   Badajoz, 6th Dec. 1809.

Six weeks have elapsed since the French Gen. Kellermann released
Lieut. Cameron, of the 79th regt., on condition that Lieut. de Turenne,
his aide de camp, who had been taken prisoner by the guerrillas in Castille, should be released in exchange. Lieut. Cameron had arrived at the
British head quarters, and I applied to the government through the
Ambassador, Lord Wellesley, that Lieut. de Turenne might be placed at
my disposal; to which application, after the delay of a considerable period
of time, I received a refusal; and I then applied to the Portuguese
government, and received their consent to the release of Lieut. V. de
Farincourt in exchange for Lieut. Cameron. I directed Marshal Beresford to send that officer from Lisbon to the outposts of the Spanish army
with his cartel of exchange; and I have now the honor to enclose a report
which I have received from Marshal Beresford of the steps he had taken

G. O.   Badajoz, 5th Dec. 1809.

The conduct of Lieut. ——, the officer of the barrack guard of the — regt., in interfering with his guard between Lieut. —— and the Spanish guard, was still more improper than the conduct of Lieut. ——; and its indiscretion was equally manifested
with its impropriety, as he was very shortly obliged to withdraw from all interference, by
the superior numbers of the Spanish guard.

The officers and troops in Badajoz are to understand that they are quartered in this town
only because it is a convenient station in the line of cantonments occupied by the army;
but they are no part of the garrison of the fort, and have nothing to do with its duties.

The guards which are mounted by the British troops are solely for regimental or brigade
purposes, and for the security of the stores of the army over which they are placed: they
have nothing to say to the safety of the place or its police, as connected with its security.

The Commander of the Forces adopts this mode of expressing his disapprobation of the
conduct of Lieuts. —— and ——, of the — regt. He desires, however, that these
officers may be released from their arrest, as he hopes that what he has above stated will
prevent them as well as others from being guilty of such conduct in future.

to carry my orders into execution, and of the circumstances which have prevented him from completing them; and I have further to inform you, that, from later accounts from Almeida, I understand that, notwithstanding Marshal Beresford's remonstrance, Lieut. V. de Farincourt, and the Portuguese officer in whose charge he was placed, are still detained at Ciudad Rodrigo.

It is scarcely necessary to animadvert upon the impropriety of this conduct, which has been so frequently repeated by different officers in different parts, that it is hardly possible to believe that it is not countenanced by the government.

I have hitherto omitted to make any representation to the Sec. of State upon this subject, from a desire to avoid bringing under the view of His Majesty circumstances which are calculated to give him so much pain. But I can no longer omit to perform this duty, unless Lieut. V. de Farincourt should be forthwith allowed to proceed from Ciudad Rodrigo, and reparation should be made for the insults to the Portuguese officer sent in charge of him.

It must be obvious to the government, that they cannot with propriety claim a right to prevent any of the allies from communicating with the General officers in command of the enemy's troops on the subject of the relief to be afforded to, and the exchange of, their prisoners; and that the result of this claim, and of the exercise of it in the manner in which it has been exercised, must be to increase the difficulty of giving them any aid, and to alter the disposition of the officers and soldiers of the army, and of all the people in England, to give their cause every assistance in their power.

To Bart. Frere, Esq.   Badajoz, 6th Dec. 1809.

In reference to Lord Wellesley's dispatch, marked R, of the 10th Nov., in which he enclosed the account of sums due to the Spanish government for certain shirts and sheets supplied for the use of the British hospitals, I have the honor to enclose the reports of the Commissary Gen., and of the Purveyor Gen. of Hospitals of the British army. From these reports, it would appear that the first transmitted from Seville only reached the British army; and that the articles found in the bales did not correspond in number with the statement contained in the paper forwarded by Lord Wellesley, of which I enclose a copy. I conclude that the second transmiss was received by the Spanish army; but we certainly received only one.

I shall be obliged to you if you will let me know to whom I am to pay for the shirts and sheets which we have received.

To Bart. Frere, Esq.   Badajoz, 6th Dec. 1809.

I shall not detain the messenger by any addition to my official letters of this day, excepting to lament that a cause which promised so well a few weeks ago should have been so completely lost by the ignorance, presumption, and mismanagement of those to whose direction it was intrusted.

I declare that if they had preserved their two armies, or even one of them, the cause was safe. The French could have sent no reinforcements which could have been of any use; time would have been gained; the state of affairs would have improved daily; all the chances were in our favor; and in the first moment of weakness occasioned by any diversion on the continent, or by the growing discontent of the French themselves with the war, the French armies must have been driven out of Spain. But no! Nothing will answer excepting to fight great battles in plains, in which their defeat is as certain as is the commencement of the battle. They will not credit the accounts I have repeatedly given them of the superior numbers even of the French; they will seek them out, and they find them invariably in all parts in numbers superior to themselves.

I am only afraid, now, that I shall be too late to save Ciudad Rodrigo; the loss of which will secure for the French Old Castille, and will cut off all communication with the northern provinces, and leave them to their fate. I wonder whether the Spanish officers ever read the history of the American war; or of their own war in the Dutch provinces; or of their own war in Portugal.

To the Rt. Hon. J. Villiers.　　　　　　　　　　Badajoz, 6th Dec. 1809.

I have received your letter of the 3d, and I am much concerned that any thing I wrote in mine should have hurt you in the least. I am thoroughly convinced that you have uniformly acted towards me in the fairest and the kindest manner, and if my letter to which you refer expressed any other sentiment, it contained that which I did not, and could not, mean to express.

You certainly never communicated to me the information on which you founded your dispatch of the 2d Oct., although you did the dispatch itself. This dispatch refers only to the general subject of the foreigners in the service of France, and expresses your opinion that much might be done to distress France, by inducing those foreigners to desert from the armies in Spain, without reference to any particular facts or information upon which the last part of the opinion was founded. If I had known at the time that the last part of your opinion was founded upon reports, I should have requested you not to send home those reports, as they would make an impression injurious to me upon false grounds, with the same freedom that I complained that this impression had been made certainly very unknowingly by you. You never could suspect that the whole of the report made to you was without foundation; and you naturally imagined that the facts were known to me, and that, from an erroneous opinion of mine, I had neglected this mode of annoying the enemy. You were quite right in bringing that subject before the government, and you were more in the right under the conception that I had neglected the subject entirely. But what I lamented was that I had not an opportunity of showing you that I had not neglected the subject, and that you were misinformed as to the facts, before you sent home. I agree entirely with you upon the whole of this subject; and you may depend upon it that, whenever I shall have an opportunity, I shall encourage the desertion of the foreigners from the army as much as may be in my power.

I am convinced that, in all your recommendations to government, you act fairly upon your own opinions, and it gives me the greatest satisfaction at all times to concur with you. Men in your situation and in mine, however, must look at all questions with a very different view; which difference of view is, I believe, the main cause of any difference of opinion which may appear to exist between us. In my situation, I am bound to consider not only what is expedient, but what is practicable, and no General officer in these days can venture, even in a confidential dispatch to a minister, to speculate upon advantages of any description which it is not practicable to accomplish. If he ventures upon such speculations, the tables are immediately turned upon him ; and although none of the conditions or requisites of his speculation may have been performed, he is asked for what reason he did not acquire those advantages which he had described in his dispatches. Besides that, I conceive that acting as I do confidentially with ministers, and acquainted as I am with their means, the employment for them, and the difficulties of all descriptions which in these days they have to contend with, I should not act fairly by them if I were to speculate in my dispatches upon advantages which would result if certain measures were adopted, which measures I know it to be out of their power to adopt.

This principle applies strongly to the question of the increase of the force in this country. I am perfectly aware that 40,000 men are better than 30,000; and that the sickness of the army, and other circumstances, may prevent my having 30,000 men for the field, out of the number for which I have called. But upon this point I beg to refer you to Mr. Canning's dispatch to Lord Wellesley of the 12th Aug., in which the whole question of the means of increasing the force in the Peninsula is fully canvassed, and the amount disposable for that purpose is decidedly stated. With the knowledge of these facts and opinions by the government, would it be fair, or indeed honest, in me to call for a man more than I thought absolutely necessary for my purpose?

In respect to the last part of your letter, I adverted to the subject of money for the Portuguese government at all, only because the Sec. of State in his letter to me, to which mine is an answer, point by point, refers to the assistance of all descriptions required to be given to Portugal, and the expense of that assistance. I had already called for arms, clothing, &c. &c., in different dispatches, and in the last I stated money.

If I have calculated the deficit in the Portuguese resources of the year 1809 erroneously, I have been misled by the papers which the Portuguese government have given me; and by a paper you gave me yourself at Abrantes, in which the deficit is stated at about £900,000.

I never pretended to cover a deficit of £900,000 with a subsidy of £300,000, but having stated the totals of the receipt, and of the expenditure as given to me, I stated the deficit, and upon what branches of the service it fell, and was likely to fall hereafter, all as stated to me officially; and as a measure of relief (a *practicable measure*, in my opinion, for I never will recommend any other), I recommended that the King's servants should assist them with £300,000. I said nothing of the extent of the relief this loan would afford, nor did I pretend any thing so absurd as that it would cover the deficit; all I hoped for was, that it would prevent the deficit from falling upon the military establishments, and those connected with them. If I had asked for £900,000, I should not have got a shilling, and I think it more than probable that I shall get the £300,000 besides the pay for the officers.

In respect to the effect of the advance of this sum upon Portuguese finance, or upon other exertions, I acknowledge that I for one am not sanguine enough to believe that any exertion Portugal can make, under existing circumstances, can increase her resources in any great degree.

The first step for any country in the situation of Portugal to take, is to collect in some reasonable degree the taxes already existing, before they add to the numbers of them; and I believe it will be very difficult for Portugal, with an enemy at the door, and having been in the possession of the French, and without a government, to pretend to make an efficient collection of the taxes already imposed on the people. The only resource that remains, then, is to prevail upon the English ministers to assist Portugal, with what? not the amount of the deficit, for that they cannot do, but with as large a sum as I think they have at their disposal, which, if it will not do every thing, will be of some use.

To the Rt. Hon. J. Villiers.   Badajoz, 7th Dec. 1809.

I have received your letter of the 3d, regarding Col. Handel; and I do not see any objection to his being sent here. I forward with this Mr. Frere's and my dispatches, which I beg you to peruse, and send them to England by the packet.

P.S. I enclose a petition upon a matter in which I have no concern, to which I request you to have such an answer sent as you may think proper.

To Vice Adm. the Hon. G. Berkeley.   Badajoz, 7th Dec. 1809.

I have had the honor of receiving your letter of the 30th Nov. Adverting to the orders you have received from the Admiralty, and to the opinion which I have communicated to you upon those orders, and to the detention of the 23d light dragoons in consequence of them, I cannot request you to send to England an additional transport for the accommodation of the officers of the army returning for their health, much less for that of officers returning to England on account of their private affairs; however desirous I am to accommodate officers as far as the public service will allow. When transports or other vessels return to England or Ireland, I shall be very much obliged to you if you will allow accommodation to be afforded in them, in the first instance, to such officers as are obliged to return on account of their health; and next, to those who may go on their private affairs: but I cannot request that any vessel may be sent on purpose for their accommodation. I did not write to you or Mr. Villiers by the messenger to whom you refer.

To Vice Adm. the Hon. G. Berkeley.   Badajoz, 7th Dec. 1809.

I have answered by this opportunity your letter of the 30th Nov. In case of necessity, I will take care of the boats upon the Tagus; but I have in contemplation an arrangement which I shall propose to the government on this subject, which I hope will have the effect of securing all we wish for.

I am much obliged to you for your attention to the Bugio. We shall have in readiness at Cadiz, by the 15th of the month, and at Gibraltar, at about the same time, sums of money, for which I shall be very much obliged to you if you will send a vessel. Probably she had best go first to Gibraltar; but that must depend very much upon the state of the wind.

To Lieut. Gen. Leite. Badajoz, 7th Dec. 1809.

I have for some time been desirous of having an opportunity of reviewing the corps in the garrison of Elvas, comprising the brigade of Brig. Gen. Victoria; and with your permission I shall be glad to see them at 10 o'clock on Monday, at any place between this and Elvas which you may fix upon.

To the Earl of Liverpool. Badajoz, 7th Dec. 1809.

I shall be very much obliged to you if you will urge the transmission at an early period of the blankets, clothing, and other stores ordered for the Portuguese army; as upon their arrival will depend in a great measure the numbers of them which we shall have for duty, and their efficiency.

In your last letter upon this subject, you referred only to 10,000 suits of clothing; this was the last demand made, when it was supposed that 20,000 suits were coming out. But as all these 20,000 were useless, and orders have now been given to send some of them elsewhere, I hope that you will have ordered out 20,000 suits in addition to the 10,000.

I also hope your Lordship will have made an exertion to send us out hospital mates. You can have no idea of the difficulties to which I am reduced in moving the army from its present quarters, for want of medical assistance; and if, unfortunately, the troops should be sickly in their new quarters, or on their march, I do not know what is to become of them. It is very desirable that a few hospital ships should be attached to this army. I understand that there are some in the service in England, which might be sent out; and in case of the necessity for embarking, they would be exceedingly useful to us. I also hope that your Lordship will have your eye upon us; and if you should find that we are likely to be hard pressed in Portugal, that you will reinforce the squadron in the Tagus.

To the Earl of Liverpool. Badajoz, 7th Dec. 1809.

I have the honor to enclose a return of stores, which I request your Lordship will be pleased to cause to be sent out to Lisbon as soon as possible, for the use of the army under my command.

Memorandum of articles of camp equipage required from England.

Badajoz, 2nd Dec. 1809.

Cavalry.	Number.
Sets of forage cords, four to a set	1500
Water buckets	500
Hair nose bags	3000
Picket {Ropes	500
Poles	1500
Mallets	200

3000 corn sacks; these being no longer considered as regimental necessaries.

To the Earl of Liverpool.   Badajoz, 7th Dec. 1809.

The Duque del Parque's corps, which, in my dispatch of the 30th Nov., I informed your Lordship had moved forward from Bejar on the 17th, upon finding that the enemy's troops in Old Castille had been weakened, had advanced as far as Alba de Tormes on the 21st, with his advanced posts between Carpio and Fresno. These were attacked at Carpio on the 23d by a large corps of cavalry and infantry from Valladolid; but the enemy was repulsed, notwithstanding that the Spanish cavalry behaved in the most dastardly manner. The Duque del Parque, after this affair, advanced as far as Fresno, from whence he retired again on the 26th, and I have no further authentic account of his operations, excepting what is contained in the enclosed extract of a letter from Mr. Frere, of the 6th inst.

The accounts which I have received from Col. Cox, at Almeida, state that the army was defeated on the evening of the 28th, and had dispersed; but Col. Cox communicated only the reports, usually exaggerated on these occasions, which he had received, but none of them from authentic sources.

I enclose copies of letters which I wrote in the months of Sept. and Oct., upon the plan of operations proposed for the Duque del Parque's corps, which was reinforced by the junction of Ballesteros' corps, of from 7000 to 10,000 men, after those letters were written, which will serve to point out the difficulty and risk to which any corps is exposed in operations in that country.

The last accounts which I have received from La Carolina are dated the 1st inst., at which period but very few of the remains of the dispersed army had come in; and many of those who had come in were without arms. I understand, however, that 8000 men had gone to Cuenca, where Gen. Echavarri had taken the command of them. The French had not continued the pursuit; but many of their troops had re-crossed the Tagus at Toledo, and some of their corps had marched into Old Castille, and others had come to Talavera and Oropesa.

I had urged the Spanish government to augment the army of the Duque de Alburquerque to 20,000 men, in order that it might occupy, in a sufficient manner, the passage of the Tagus at Almaraz, and the passes through the mountains leading from Arzobispo to Truxillo, in which position they would have covered effectually the province of Estremadura during the winter at least, and would have afforded time and leisure for preparations for further opposition to the enemy; and I delayed the movement which I have long been desirous of making to the northward of the Tagus, till the reinforcements could be sent to the Duque de Alburquerque, which I had lately recommended should be drawn from the army of the Duque del Parque.

During the discussions upon this subject, the government have given orders to the Duque de Alburquerque to retire with his corps behind the Guadiana, to a position which he cannot maintain; thus leaving open the road into Estremadura, and incurring the risk of the loss of that province, whenever the enemy choose to take possession of it. As it is very desirable that the British army should neither be involved in a contest for the security of Estremadura, nor should have the discredit of retiring from the province when it shall be attacked, I am obliged to commence immediately the movement which I had so long projected to the north of the Tagus.

The defeat, dispersion, and almost annihilation, as an armed body, of the army of La Mancha, and the probable loss of arms by the army under the Duque del Parque, induce me to draw the attention of the King's ministers to this important subject. From all that I hear of the army in La Mancha, defeated on the 19th Nov., I believe that the greater number of the soldiers have returned to their homes ; but the war has drawn so little hitherto upon the population of Spain, that I have no doubt that the government will be able again to collect men for a fresh army ; but they certainly have not in their possession, and cannot acquire without assistance from Great Britain, the means of arming them.

His Majesty's ministers must be the best judges of the propriety of affording this assistance ; and I must observe that such is the nature of the government and of the people of Spain, of the officers who command the armies, and of the soldiers who serve in them, that I cannot be certain that the same misfortunes would not again occur, if the government had the means of putting another army in the field ; and I cannot devise means by which His Majesty might be secured against this improvident waste of the resources and assistance which he might still be disposed to supply to the Spaniards.

I would venture to suggest, however, that if in the course of the winter the Spanish government should so far get the better of the consequences of the late defeats as to be able to collect again the officers and men of an army, it would be a source of great regret if means of arming them were wanting at the moment in which they should be ready, and should be required to take the field ; and it would be more particularly to be regretted, if recent events should have occasioned such an improvement of the government as has been long wished for in this country ; and if the situation of affairs in other parts of Europe should prevent the enemy from sending such a reinforcement to his armies in Spain as at once to put an end to the contest. I would therefore recommend that such a supply of arms as can be afforded should be sent out in the first instance to the Tagus, to be under the direction of His Majesty's minister at Seville, who should order them round to Cadiz, and dispose of them as he might deem best for His Majesty's service.

To Bart. Frere, Esq. Badajoz, 9th Dec. 1809.

I have had the honor of receiving your letter of the 6th inst., and I have

G. O. Badajoz, 8th Dec. 1809.

5. The Commander of the Forces requests that on the march which the army is about to make, the officers will attend to the orders of the 4th May, Nos. 5 and 6, and to the G. O. of the 7th Oct., Nos. 8, 9, 10, and 11, relating to the mode of making requisitions upon the country. In addition to these orders, the Commander of the Forces desires that when any officer finds himself in the situation to be obliged to take articles of provisions or forage from the country upon his own receipts, he will report to his commanding officer that he has done so, specifying particularly the date, the place, and the articles for which he has given his receipt. The commanding officer will send this report to the Assist. Com. attached to the brigade, regiment, or division of the army to which the officer belongs.

since received accounts of the army in Old Castille to the 3d inst.; from which it appears that although the army under the Duque del Parque has suffered considerably, and was not on the 3d in a state fit to perform any service, numbers of the troops still remain with it, and it may be re-established by care and attention to the wants of the troops, and rest.

Recent events in La Mancha, as well as in Old Castille, must have shown the Spanish government that it is desirable that they should avoid general actions in plains. Admitting that the Spanish infantry, in its present state, is able to contend on equal terms with the French, it is obvious that the cavalry is not so; and without that arm an army is incomplete, and enters upon every operation under very considerable disadvantages. It is not fair or just to the cavalry to attribute their conduct in the different actions which have been fought lately to want of spirit. They are people of the same description with the other soldiers of the army, and must partake of the same feelings. It is, in fact, want of discipline. Undisciplined cavalry have always conducted themselves in the same manner, in all countries; and in the first years of the revolutionary war, the French themselves suffered frequently the same disasters from the flight and misbehaviour of their cavalry. The want of discipline in the cavalry is an evil to which time alone can apply a remedy; and in the mean time it is probable that the experience of the whole war, and particularly of their recent misfortunes, will have pointed out to the government the only system of war which their troops are at present capable of undertaking, and for which their country is well adapted.

I would strongly recommend to them, if they should be able to collect their troops again, to form their armies in large masses, for the occupation and defence of the many strong and important positions which the country affords; to support these armies by magazines; and while they will draw the attention of the great bodies of the enemy, who are well aware, particularly from what occurred lately at Tamames, that the Spanish troops cannot be attacked with impunity, or with small numbers, in a strong position, the parties of guerrillas, &c., may carry on their operations upon the enemy's communications, and upon his flanks. If this system should be adopted, the enemy must turn these positions, if he should not attack them: this must take time, must alter the nature of his operations, must oblige him to form magazines for the support of his army, and increase the difficulty of all he undertakes.

I would now recommend to the government to form a corps of 20,000 men, under the Duque de Alburquerque, and to place it at Truxillo, Deleytosa, &c., occupying the Mesa de Ibor, and the other positions which defend the passes in the mountains between Arzobispo and Deleytosa. The bridge of Arzobispo ought also to be broken down, if in our power, as being entirely useless for an offensive operation by the allies, and only facilitating the attack of the Puerto de Mirabete, opposite Almaraz, by the enemy, if he should be in possession of that bridge, and should wish to force a passage that way. This will effectually secure the province of Estremadura. The remainder of the Duque del Parque's troops should be collected in the mountains near Ciudad Rodrigo, and by degrees extend themselves as far as the Puerto del Pico, destroying all the roads through those mountains, and thus preventing the enemy from passing through them.

I propose to collect the British and Portuguese armies between the Mondego and the Serra d' Estrella, communicating by their right with the Duque del Parque, if this plan should be adopted. If, however, the Duque de Alburquerque should be withdrawn from Truxillo, &c., it is obvious that a part of the British and Portuguese army must be on the Tagus.

According to this plan, we shall have a large force upon the left of the allied armies, capable at any time of extending into the plains of Castille, and upon the enemy's communications; and before the enemy can venture to make a serious invasion of the south of Spain with any very large force, he must dislodge the force which we shall have upon the frontiers of Castille; unless indeed he should have in Spain a disposable force sufficiently large for both objects at the same time.

I am not acquainted with the means which the government have of reforming their armies, and particularly of arming their troops, who must now require large numbers of arms. But in case they should have it in their power to collect an army again, after their late defeats, the plan, of which I have above suggested the general outline and some of the details, appears the best calculated for the circumstances of the moment. It is founded upon experience of past misfortunes, and upon a general knowledge of the country. It will keep the contest in existence; and if successful, will prevent the enemy from extending himself. It will give Spain the chance of accidents, and of a change in the affairs of Europe; and if any circumstance should oblige the enemy to weaken his force in Spain, or should even prevent him from feeding its strength with reinforcements; or if time should improve the military system and means of the Spanish nation, it may lead to the results for which we all wish.

The British troops have begun their march this morning; but some time will elapse before they are withdrawn from Merida, Montijo, &c.

MEMORANDUM OF OPERATIONS IN 1809.

(See letter to Lord Liverpool, p. 653 : Badajoz, 19th Dec. 1809.)

[The Notes to this Memorandum are in the Manuscript.]

Badajoz, 9th Dec. 1809.

The British army, intended for the service in Portugal and Spain, was complete in the end of April, with the exception of one brigade of infantry not arrived, and some troops expected from Gibraltar, when relieved by others to be sent from Portugal. Sir Arthur Wellesley landed at Lisbon on the 23d April.

At that time the French had got possession of Zaragoza. Marshal Soult held Oporto and the northern provinces of Portugal. The battle of Medellin had been fought on the 29th March; and Gen. Cuesta was endeavoring to recover from its effects, and to collect an army again at Monasterio, in the mountains of the Sierra Morena. The French, under Marshal Victor, were in possession of the Guadiana, and had their advanced posts as forward as Los Santos. Sebastiani was at Ciudad Real, and held in check the army of La Carolina, at that time under the command of Gen. Venegas, consisting of about 12,000 men. Ney was in possession of Galicia; Salamanca was held by a small detachment of French troops; St. Cyr was in Catalonia with his corps of 25,000 men; and Kellermann, who had succeeded to Bessières in the command of the 6th corps, was at Valladolid. Mortier,* with his corps, and the Duc d'Abrantes, with the 8th corps, at Zaragoza.

The Portuguese army was totally disorganized, and nearly annihilated; and the Spanish troops were scarcely able to hold their positions in the Sierra Morena.

The Marques de la Romana, who had been with his corps on the frontiers of Portugal, near Chaves, from the period of the embarkation of the British army at Coruña, in the month of January, till the month of March, had moved from thence when Soult invaded Portugal by Chaves, and afterwards moved towards the Asturias with his army, and went himself into that province.

Sir J. Cradock gave the command to Sir A. Wellesley on the 27th April; and on the same day the orders were given for the collection and march of the troops, preparatory to the attack of Soult at Oporto.

Soult was driven from Oporto on the 12th May, and on the 18th he entered Galicia, closely pursued by the British and Portuguese troops, having lost all his cannon, his military chest, many stands of arms, baggage, &c. &c., and bringing with him not more than 8000 men of his corps.†

In the mean time the following events had occurred in other parts. Ney, in conjunction with Kellermann, had invaded the Asturias, which province they entered on the beginning of May; the Marques de la Romana having escaped from Gijon in a sloop of war. The inhabitants of Vigo, aided by Capt. Mackinley of the *Lively*, had taken possession of that town; and in the absence of Ney and Soult from Galicia, had pushed their parties as far as Lugo, which town they had attacked. Marshal Victor repassed the Guadiana about the 12th or 13th May, and detached a division across the Tagus at Alcantara on the 14th. This division retired again in a few days, probably as soon as it had heard of the success of the 12th against Soult; but Sir A. Wellesley having discontinued the further pursuit of Soult on the 18th of May, and having on the 19th received the accounts of the passage of the Tagus of this division, immediately gave orders for the return of the troops to the southward, and set out himself.‡

The leading troops arrived at Coimbra, on the Mondego, on the 26th May; but Sir A. Wellesley, having in the mean time heard that the French division which had passed the Tagus at Alcantara had recrossed that river, discontinued the rapidity of the march which he had at first ordered, and the British troops did not arrive on the Tagus till between the 7th and 12th June.§ They halted here till the 27th June, partly to receive supplies of money, and of shoes and other articles of equipment wanting, and

---

* I rather believe that Mortier had moved from Zaragoza; but some time elapsed before he arrived in Old Castille.
† See letters to the Sec. of State 18th May.
‡ See dispatch to the Sec. of State 20th May.
§ See dispatch to the Sec. of State 31st May.

to give rest to the men and horses after the rapid marches they had made to the frontier of Galicia and back again. It was also desirable to receive the reinforcements of the 48th and 61st regts. expected from Gibraltar, and the 23d light dragoons arrived from England, before any further operations were entered upon.

During this time the French brought Ney's corps out of Asturias back into Galicia; and on the 6th June they made an attempt, in conjunction with a detachment from Soult's corps, to obtain possession of Vigo. In their attempt upon the bridge of San Payo they failed entirely; and Soult failed equally in all his endeavors to bring to action on the river Sill the corps of the Marques de la Romana, which had again in the beginning of the month of June assembled near Orense upon the frontiers of Portugal.

The Marques de la Romana having retired from Orense towards Vigo, Soult determined to withdraw from Galicia altogether, leaving Ney's corps alone in that province;* and he marched in the end of June to Zamora, on the Duero, in order to re-equip and refit his army. Ney, finding himself too weak to maintain Galicia when alone, also evacuated that province in the middle of July, and posted himself at Astorga. †

As soon as Victor found that the British army had arrived upon the Tagus, he began to retire from Estremadura on the 14th and 15th June; and he finally crossed the Tagus at Almaraz on the 24th June, 2 days before the British army broke up from Abrantes, &c., to march to Plasencia. ‡

* See the letters from Soult to King Joseph intercepted upon Gen. Franceschi.

† After the perusal of these details, and of Soult's letter to King Joseph, can any man doubt that the evacuation of Galicia was occasioned by the operations of the British troops in Portugal ? Soult retired from Portugal in such a state that he could do nothing till he was re-equipped, for which purpose he went to Zamora, leaving Ney in Galicia, and directing him to hold the province. Ney finds himself too weak to hold his ground, and goes to Astorga, and the province remains in the possession of the Marques de la Romana (who had been too weak to engage Soult's corps singly, even in its reduced and crippled state), and of the British seamen and others in the garrison of Vigo.

‡ One of the *cries* against Sir A. W. has been for delaying his march from Abrantes to so late a period, which was declared to be owing to some disputes with Gen. Cuesta about command, or some other trifling object. During the halt at Abrantes, a discussion was carried on with Gen. Cuesta, through Lieut. Col. Bourke, not about command or any other trifling object, but about the future operations of the two armies. The whole correspondence went to Mr. Frere, and is probably in the office of the Sec. of State for Foreign affairs. But I believe no man who knows what an army is, that the people and animals composing it are men and beasts like others, who require rest after great fatigues in a hot climate, and that carriages in an army, and other articles of equipment, require repair and to be replaced, after a long journey over bad roads, such as had been made from the Tagus to Galicia and back again in little more than a month, will believe that the halt upon the Tagus for one fortnight was too long. Besides, the army could not march without money. A supply reached Abrantes on the 25th; and the moment it was received the march was ordered, and commenced on the 27th.

But the pith of this *cry* is, that in consequence of this delay upon the Tagus, Victor escaped from Estremadura. Let any man trace Victor's operations from the middle of May till the end of June, when he finally crossed the Tagus, and he will see that they were guided by the intelligence he received of those of the British army. He sent a corps across the Tagus, and repassed the Guadiana himself, when he found the British army gone to Oporto to attack Soult; he withdrew that corps again when he heard of the result of the attack of Soult at Oporto; he began to retire across the Tagus on the 14th and 15th June, when he found the British army arrived upon the Tagus at Abrantes; and he withdrew his troops from Merida, and completed the evacuation of the southern Estremadura, and crossed the Tagus on the 24th June, when he found that the British army was about to march to Plasencia. If these facts are all true, and they are all recorded in the official reports of the day, what difference could it have made in Victor's situation if Sir A. W. had moved from Abrantes a few days sooner ? Only that Victor would have retired across the Tagus a few days sooner than he did !!!

Kellermann's corps evacuated Asturias and Biscay, and returned to Valladolid; and Mortier's corps was at Leon. Suchet, having defeated Blake at Belchite on the 18th June, had returned to Zaragoza; and the corps of St. Cyr was employed in the blockade of Gerona.

The Spanish army under Gen. Cuesta, which had been reinforced with cavalry and infantry, and had been refitted with extraordinary celerity since the action of Medellin, had advanced from Monasterio in the middle of May, when Victor had crossed the Guadiana to support the division which he had detached over the bridge of Alcantara; and Gen. Cuesta made an attack upon a fortified post which the enemy had left at Merida. In this attack he did not succeed; the enemy maintained their post at Merida, and Gen. Cuesta had his head quarters at Fuente del Maestre till the end of June, when the enemy evacuated Estremadura, and passed the Tagus at Almaraz, upon hearing of the arrival of the British army upon that river at Abrantes.

In the end of June Gen. Cuesta fixed his head quarters at the Puerto de Mirabete, opposite Almaraz, having a division of his army at Arzobispo. Thus, then, in the end of June, the Spanish army under Cuesta was upon the Tagus; the French, under Victor, at Talavera de la Reyna; Sebastiani had retired from Ciudad Real, and had arrived near Toledo; and Venegas' corps, which had likewise been reinforced, had advanced into La Mancha. The French had evacuated Galicia, with the exception of Ney's corps, which left that province at a later period, and arrived at Astorga in the middle of July. Mortier was at Leon, Soult at Zamora, Kellermann at Valladolid, Suchet at Zaragoza, and St. Cyr engaged in the blockade of Gerona. The British army broke up from Abrantes, &c., on the 27th June, to march to Plasencia, in order to co-operate with the Spanish troops in an endeavor to drive the French from the south of Spain.

The Commanding officer of the King's troops in Portugal is alone responsible for this operation, for which the motives were various. 1st, adverting to the general state of the war in Spain, as well as in Germany, it appeared to be desirable to make an effort at that time in Spain. 2dly, the means appeared to be adequate to the object in view. Gen. Cuesta had under his immediate command 38,000 men, and Gen. Venegas 18,000; and the British army was not less than 20,000 men, besides Gen. R. Craufurd's brigade, which had landed at Lisbon on the 28th June, and was to commence its march to join the army immediately. Against these troops were to be opposed 28,000 men under Victor, and 12,000 under Sebastiani; and whatever the King could bring from the garrison of Madrid, and his guards.

It was not known till the beginning of July that even Soult had evacuated Galicia, in a state, as appears by the intercepted letters taken on Gen. Franceschi, very unfit for service; nor that Ney had quitted that province and gone to Astorga, till late in July;* and Mortier and Kellermann were supposed still to be in the Asturias and Biscay.

The difficulties of the operation were calculated; but it was supposed that the orders of the Spanish government would furnish the means of

---

* I do not think we were certain of Ney's evacuation of Galicia till he entered Estremadura, in August.

transport and provisions that were or might be required, as they had expressed the greatest anxiety for the co-operation of the British troops. The means of transport were known to exist in the country, and the harvest about to be reaped, it was imagined, would have afforded an abundance of provisions.

The troops which broke up from Abrantes and the neighbourhood on the 27th June, reached Plasencia between the 7th and 10th July, on which day Sir A. Wellesley went over to the Puerto de Mirabete, to confer and concert a plan of operations with Gen. Cuesta. The objects of the plan were to bring into operation upon the enemy, at the same time, the British army and the two Spanish corps, under Cuesta and Venegas, in such a manner as to prevent the enemy from bringing his concentrated force to bear upon either.

It was impossible for the corps of Cuesta and Venegas, issuing from the defensive positions which they had occupied in Estremadura and La Mancha respectively, to join, or to have any military communication in this operation, excepting by Talavera and the bridge of Toledo;* and it was obvious that unless the enemy should be alarmed for the safety of Madrid by one of the corps, he would fall with his whole collected strength upon the other. It was necessary to divide the attention of the enemy as much as possible, and to choose such a line of march for each corps as to prevent the enemy from opposing the march of either by natural obstacles, or by any thing excepting detachments from his own concentrated force.

Gen. Venegas was therefore ordered by Cuesta to direct his march by Tembleque, Tarancon, and Fuentidueña to Arganda, where he was to be on the 22d July, the day appointed for the arrival of the combined British and Spanish armies at Talavera. By passing by Fuentidueña, Gen. Venegas could have crossed the Tagus at a ford, and nothing could have prevented his arrival at his station but the opposition of the enemy. This was all that was wished for; at the same time that, if he had been opposed by a corps too strong for him, his retreat was always open to the mountains of Cuenca; and the enemy could not have followed him in strength, and could not have undertaken any operation against La Carolina, pressed as they would have been on the other flank by the combined armies.

The only corps with which it was supposed that the combined armies would have had to engage, were the corps of Victor, Sebastiani, and the King. The other French corps in Spain were understood to be otherwise occupied; and, at all events, it was conceived that the occupation of the Puerto de Baños by Gen. Cuesta's detachment, and of the Puerto de Perales by the garrison of Ciudad Rodrigo, and by the position of Marshal Beresford's corps on the frontiers of Portugal, would have prevented the enemy from penetrating into Estremadura by the passes in the rear of the army.†

Sir A. Wellesley returned to Plasencia on the 12th, and found that the hopes were disappointed which he had formed of drawing from Ciudad Rodrigo, and other places in Castille, the means of transport which he had

---

* See dispatch to Lord Wellesley 24th Aug. from Merida, describing the difficulty of such an operation.

† See dispatch to the Sec. of State 8th Aug.

required,* and which had been supplied by those places in the preceding year to the army under Sir J. Moore. He still considered it necessary, however, to carry into execution the plan of operations agreed upon with Gen. Cuesta, as he was unwilling to disappoint that General ; and as Gen. Venegas' corps, which it was supposed would have commenced its operations, would have been exposed to risk ; and, moreover, Sir A. W. expected that the army would have been supplied with provisions from the Vera de Plasencia till it should be supplied with means of transport from Seville, for which Gen. Cuesta had written, or from La Mancha. Sir A. W., however, gave notice that he should co-operate only in the first operation,† which should put Gen. Cuesta in possession of the passage of the Alberche, and of the course of the Tagus, and should enable him to communicate with Gen. Venegas, until the wants of the British army should be supplied.

A part of the British army, consisting of about 1000 Portuguese troops under Sir R. Wilson, (and which corps had been reinforced by 2 Spanish battalions,) was to march according to the plan through the Vera de Plasencia, on the left of the combined armies, to Escalona, on the Alberche. This corps marched on the 15th July, and the British army, according to the plan agreed upon, commenced its march on the 17th and 18th July ; the 23d light dragoons and 48th regt. having joined the army while it was at Plasencia, and the 61st being expected to join on the 18th.

Sir R. Wilson arrived at Escalona on the 22d, and the combined armies at Talavera on the same day ; and they drove in the enemy's outposts. On the 23d ‡ arrangements were made, and the British army had marched and was in column near the Alberche to attack the French corps of Victor, posted on the heights beyond the river; but Gen. Cuesta preferred to delay the attack till the following morning ; and when the troops were formed on that morning at daylight, it was found that the enemy had withdrawn during the night. Gen. Cuesta then continued his march in pursuit of them to Sᵗᵃ Olalla ; but they had gone to Torrijos, and thence even farther, to Bargas. The main body of the British remained at Talavera ; with a division of infantry at Cazalegas to keep up the communication with Gen. Cuesta ; and another at Cardiel, on the Alberche, to keep up the communication with Sir R. Wilson at Escalona.

* See letter to Gen. O'Donoju 16th July, enclosed in dispatch to the Sec. of State 24th July.
† See letter to Gen. O'Donoju 16th July.
‡ See dispatch to the Sec. of State 24th July.
All the discussions upon this subject, and the misrepresentations, show the difficulty cf serving the British public, and the small degree of satisfaction which any foreign officer has in co-operating with the British troops. Gen. Cuesta chose to delay the attack to the 24th, for which delay there were not wanting good and valid reasons; but no such reasons are conceived, or are allowed to exist. A lie is invented and circulated, viz.; that the 23d was Sunday, and then Sir A. W. is abused for being the author of the lie. There was, however, one curious circumstance attending this transaction, which shows the nature of the war in Spain, and the deficiency of intelligence by the Spanish General officers, and that is, that although Sir A. W. suspected it on the evening of the 22d, and made preparations accordingly, it was not positively ascertained till the morning of the 23d that the whole of the French army was at Cazalegas; and yet the vedettes of the outposts were within shot of each other, and the narrow river of the Alberche alone divided the armies !!! The French must, in the night of the 23d, have acquired from our army the knowledge of our intended attack.

The scarcity of provisions had been so great since the 20th, owing to the failure of the magistrates and inhabitants of the Vera de Plasencia to perform the contracts into which they had entered with a British Commissary, to supply at Talavera 240,000 rations before the 24th, that the British army was totally unable to move.* The armies remained on the 25th in the positions taken up on the 24th, and the enemy collected all his force at Bargas.

It appears that Gen. Venegas had not obeyed the orders he had received, to direct his march upon Fuentidueña and Arganda.† The enemy therefore had no apprehension from his operations, and they collected their whole force to oppose the combined armies. They attacked Cuesta's outposts at Torrijos on the morning of the 26th, and drove them in; and Gen. Cuesta retired with his army on that day to the left bank of the Alberche, the British division still remaining at Cazalegas, the division at Cardiel having joined; and on the 27th Gen. Cuesta crossed the Alberche, and took up his position near Talavera; and the British troops retired from Cazalegas, one division remaining as an outpost in the woods opposite the enemy's position on the Alberche, the other going to its position near Talavera.

A general action being obviously to be expected on the 26th, Sir R. Wilson was ordered from Escalona to join the army with his corps, through the mountains by Marrupe. The enemy attacked the outposts in the woods on the 27th, which retired to the position occupied by the army; and on that night, and on the 28th, followed the battle of Talavera.‡ The enemy retired in the evening and during the night of the 28th, and took up a position, with a rear guard of 10,000 men, on the heights of Cazalegas, beyond the Alberche. The British army and Spanish armies, which had been joined on the evening of the 29th by Gen. R. Craufurd's brigade of infantry, remained on the field of battle of Talavera, with their advanced posts, consisting of Gen. Craufurd's brigade, in the woods, nearly in the place in which they had been on the 27th.

On the 29th, Gen. Venegas went to Aranjuez, and made an attack upon a post of about 2000 men, which the enemy had left at Toledo. The King with the reserve, therefore, and Sebastiani's corps, went to oppose his advance, while Victor was left to watch the combined armies.

On the 31st, Sir R. Wilson's corps, which had been called to the army when the general action was expected, and had arrived at Marrupe, returned towards Escalona; and the enemy's rear guard at Cazalegas retired on the same night, and went to Maqueda.

On the 30th, accounts had been received by Gen. Cuesta that rations for a corps of 12,000 men had been ordered at Fuente Roble, north of the Puerto de Baños; and for 24,000 men at Los Santos, near the same place; supposed to be for the corps of Soult, which was known to have

---

* See dispatch to the Sec. of State 24th July. There is no doubt that if these contracts had been performed the British army would have been at Madrid on the 27th July. Would matters have been improved by their going there, the French having at this time brought into that part of Spain all their troops, amounting to not less than 90,000 men?

† This failure by Gen. Venegas is to be attributed to orders which he had received from the Central Junta!

‡ See the dispatches to the Sec. of State 29th July, and 8th Aug.

been at Zamora in the end of June, and for which equipments had been called for by Soult. It was expected, however, that the troops in the Puerto would make some resistance, and would stop their march; or that Soult might have been induced to desist from it by the position of Marshal Beresford's corps, or by the accounts he would have received of the victory at Talavera on the 28th July.

It has already been stated that the Portuguese army in April was totally disorganized, and nearly annihilated; at the same time it had been necessary to employ the few men who were in the service in the expedition against Soult, and in the defensive measures adopted for the security of the western frontier, when the army marched on that expedition.

When the British army was about to enter Spain in the end of June, there was no longer any danger for the north of Portugal; and it was desirable that advantage should be taken of the leisure which this security afforded, to collect in one camp the disposable part of the Portuguese army, in which Marshal Beresford should have an opportunity of forming and organizing the troops.

A camp on the frontiers of Beira, between Ciudad Rodrigo and Almeida, was considered the best situation for this purpose; and it had this additional recommendation, that the Portuguese corps, to which a British brigade was to be added, principally for the purpose of example, would protect the only vulnerable part of the Portuguese frontier which was exposed to attack; added to the security of the left of the British army; and, above all, protected the passage into Estremadura by the Puerto de Perales. From this situation, also, this Portuguese corps could have been brought with advantage in a subsequent part of the campaign, when it was hoped that the troops would be formed; but it was neither intended nor expected that Marshal Beresford's corps should co-operate, except as above stated, in the first operations of the months of July and Aug.

Notwithstanding the hopes entertained that Soult's march might have been stopped, or that he might have been induced to desist from it, it was desirable, as Gen. Cuesta had not confidence in the exertions of the troops in the Puerto, that they should be reinforced; but he declined to reinforce them, and persisted in his refusal to do so till the morning of the 2d Aug., when he detached Gen. Bassecourt with his division for that purpose. In the mean time the troops in the Puerto had retired without firing a shot, and had gone to the bridge over the Tagus at Almaraz, which they took up; and Soult entered Plasencia unresisted on the 1st Aug.*

It was then necessary to take decisive measures to re-establish the communication with Portugal, and for this purpose the British army marched on the morning of the 3d to Oropesa, leaving Gen. Cuesta's division in charge of the post at Talavera, and of the hospital.† On that day, for the first time, Gen. Cuesta received accounts, apprising him of

---

* See dispatch to the Sec. of State 8th Aug.
† It will scarcely be believed that the French were able to collect the three corps of Ney, Soult, and Mortier, at Salamanca, and to make preparation there for this march, and that the Junta of Old Castille, sitting at Ciudad Rodrigo, knew nothing about it! And yet this is a fact.

the real strength of the army which Soult had brought with him into Estremadura, which consisted of 34,000 men, and he imagined that the British corps was not equal to a contest with such numbers. He there-fore immediately determined to withdraw from Talavera, and to join the British army at Oropesa; and thus he lost the hospital, and exposed the combined armies to be attacked in front and rear at the same time.

Soult's army arrived at Navalmoral on the evening of the 3d; and in this position stood between the combined armies and the bridge of Almaraz, which it was supposed was removed, but most probably was, or it might have been, easily destroyed. The only retreat which remained was by the bridge of Arzobispo. There was a direct road to this bridge from Talavera de la Reyna, by Calera, and another direct from Naval-moral, each of them passing at not less than 10 or 12 miles' distance from Oropesa, the station at which the combined armies were assembled on the morning of the 4th inst.

Besides these circumstances attending the only retreat the armies had, it was to be observed that the enemy had now collected in Estremadura all the disposable force which he had in Galicia and Castille, with the exception of the corps of Kellermann, which still remained at Valladolid : 34,000 men were known to be added to the force already opposed to the combined armies; and it was obvious that they must retire across the Tagus, and take up a defensive position on that river. Accordingly, the British army having halted at Oropesa on the night of the 3d, marched early on the 4th to Arzobispo, and immediately crossed the Tagus; and the Spanish army, which had marched from Talavera on the night of the 3d, halted during the early part of the day of the 4th at Oropesa, and marched, and arrived at Arzobispo on the evening of the 4th.

On the 5th, the British army continued its march, and the advanced guard was placed upon the Mesa de Ibor, to secure that passage; and on the 6th the army arrived at the Mesa de Ibor, and the advanced guard at the Casas del Puerto, on the Tagus, opposite Almaraz; and on the 7th the head of the column of the army arrived at Deleytosa, which place was reached on the 8th and 9th by the rear divisions.*

The Spanish army in the mean time crossed the Tagus on the 5th, and the head quarters were removed to Peraleda de Garbin on the 7th, leaving an advanced guard at the bridge of Arzobispo; which was surprised on the 8th, and lost many men, and 30 pieces of cannon.†

* This is the history of our giving up the *post of honor*, as the French call it, to the Spaniards. In fact, the British army was necessarily the left throughout the operations; and could not change that disposition without giving up the defence of Portugal. Besides that, all these operations, from the morning of the 4th, were carried on against the inclina-tion of Gen. Cuesta; and the retreat being necessary, Sir A. W. could not have made it, or have forced Cuesta to make it, if the British army had not begun it. Another circum-stance is, that the bridge of Arzobispo was not reckoned the post of honor. The Mesa de Ibor, till the evening of the 5th, was the point, the loss of which was most apprehended.

† See dispatch to the Sec. of State 21st Aug.
The French made much more of this affair than they ought. Nothing could behave worse than they did, excepting the Spaniards. They ought to have annihilated the Spanish army, but they were afraid to follow them, and did not even know that they had taken the greatest part of the cannon; they had not even patrolled the ground 3 days afterwards, when Col. Waters went to Mortier with a flag of truce from them. See dispatch to Lord Wellesley of the 9th Aug. for the detail of this surprise; and of the state of the Spanish army afterwards.

On the 11th Aug. the head quarters of the British army were transferred to Jaraicejo, leaving Deleytosa open for the Spanish army, to which place their head quarters were removed on the 13th; Gen. Cuesta having resigned the command of the army on the 12th.

While this was going on on the left, Gen. Venegas was attacked at Aranjuez by Sebastiani and the King on the 5th;* in which action he had some success. But he then resolved to retire to the Sierra Morena, and actually marched as far as Tembleque.† He then altered this resolution, and he returned to Almonacid on the 11th, where he was attacked and defeated, with the loss of 4000 men.‡ He then retired into the mountains of the Sierra Morena.

When the French evacuated Old Castille in the end of the month of July, to collect their armies in Estremadura, the Duque del Parque, the Commandant of Ciudad Rodrigo, sent a detachment from his garrison to take possession of Salamanca. This circumstance, and the probable early arrival of Romana's corps in Old Castille from Galicia, and the certainty that the position taken up by the allied armies was of such a nature, that no effort which they could make would dislodge them from it, induced the enemy to march the corps of Soult and Ney to Plasencia on the 9th, 10th, and 11th; and to send the latter into Castille through the Puerto de Baños, on the 12th Aug.§ Ney there fell in with, and defeated Sir R. Wilson's detachment; which, after the combined armies had retired from Talavera and Oropesa to Arzobispo, had been unable to reach the latter place; and had marched through the Vera de Plasencia, and the Puerto de Tornavacas; and was on its march when Ney passed through the Puerto de Baños. Thus, in the middle of August, Ney was at Salamanca; Kellermann at Valladolid; Soult at Plasencia; Mortier at Oropesa and Arzobispo; Victor at Talavera and Toledo; and Sebastiani in La Mancha: while the British army was at Jaraicejo; Gen. Eguia at Deleytosa (Gen. Cuesta having resigned); and Gen. Venegas at La Carolina, in the Sierra Morena.

On the 20th Aug., the British army, having suffered from extreme distress of provisions, broke up from its positions at Jaraicejo and the Casas del Puerto,‖ the latter of which was occupied by the Spanish troops; and it moved with its head quarters to Badajoz, on the 3d Sept., and occupied a position on the frontiers of Spain and Portugal, in which, while it would give protection to both countries, it would be enabled to subsist with ease; and it would be possible to give the troops the refreshments they required, as well as the clothing and equipments which they wanted; and it has remained in that position.¶ The Portuguese army,

* † ‡ § See dispatch to the Sec. of State 21st Aug.
‖ See dispatches to the Sec. of State 21st Aug.; and to Lord Wellesley of the 12th, 13th, 15th, 16th, 21st, and 22d Aug.
¶ There never was a position better calculated than this was for the purposes of defending Spain and Portugal.
The French had from the end of August not less than from 70,000 to 90,000 men disposable; they have since destroyed 2 armies of Spaniards which it was thought proper to expose to their attack; and yet they have not been able to advance, or to gain any solid advantage beyond that of destroying the Spaniards.
The fact is, that the British army has saved Spain and Portugal during this year. The Spaniards have no army now that is complete, excepting 13,000 men under the Duque de

under Marshal Beresford, also withdrew nearly about the same time within the Portuguese frontier, and went into cantonments.*

In the mean time the Spanish army of Estremadura was reduced to the number of 6000 men at Deleytosa; and Gen. Eguia commenced his march with the remainder towards La Mancha in the middle of September. Nearly about the same period 13,000 men of the corps of the Marques de la Romana arrived in the neighbourhood of Ciudad Rodrigo, from Galicia; and the command was taken from the Marques and given to the Duque del Parque.† The Duque immediately put himself at their head, and marched to Villa Vieja,‡ and threatened the French posts towards Salamanca; but the enemy having reconnaitred him, and having drawn in all their detachments with a view to attack him, the Duque del Parque retired from Villa Vieja on the 23d, to the neighbourhood of Ciudad Rodrigo.

The forward movement by the Duque del Parque, which the French conceived to be connected with a movement to be made by the British army, and with the march of Gen. Eguia into La Mancha, induced Soult to abandon Plasencia on the 1st Oct.; § and he moved to Oropesa. The Duque del Parque then occupied the strong position of Tamames, on the Castille side of the Puerto de Baños; in which he was attacked on the 19th Oct. by Gen. Marchand, in the command of Ney's corps,‖ Ney having gone to France; and the French were defeated, with the loss of one piece of cannon. The Duque del Parque was joined on the following day by Ballesteros' division of the Marques de la Romana's corps; and he then marched forward, and took possession of Salamanca on the 25th, the enemy having retired towards the Duero.

These events in Old Castille induced the enemy ¶ to withdraw some of the troops from Estremadura; and an army was collected there, consisting of Ney's, Kellermann's, and a part of Mortier's corps, amounting to 36,000 men, under the command of Marshal Mortier. The arrival of these troops in Old Castille obliged the Duque del Parque again to retire; and he arrived at Bejar, where he placed his head quarters on the 8th Nov. The movement of Gen. Eguia into La Mancha from Estremadura, in the middle of September, induced the French to move a large corps of

Alburquerque, in Estremadura; and yet nothing can be done by the French after all their victories. What would have been the relative state of the two contending parties, if the Spaniards had been tolerably prudent, and had acted as they were advised to act?

The advantage of the position of Badajoz was, that the British army was centrically posted, in reference to all the objects which the enemy might have in view; and at any time, by a junction with a Spanish corps on its right, or a Portuguese or Spanish corps on its left, it could prevent the enemy from undertaking any thing, excepting with a much larger force than they could allot to any one object.

* The Portuguese army would have been ruined if they had remained longer in the field; they wanted clothing, and every description of equipment; they were raw recruits, detested serving in Spain, where they were ill treated; and deserted in large numbers in the short time they were in that country. There are now good grounds for hope that something will be made of them. See Marshal Beresford's letter to Sir A. Wellesley, 26th Sept., included in a dispatch to the Sec. of State, 29th Sept.

† See dispatch to the Sec. of State 13th Sept.
‡ See dispatches to the Sec. of State 21st and 29th Sept.
§ See dispatch to the Sec. of State 6th Oct.
‖ See dispatch to the Sec. of State 31st Oct.
¶ See dispatch to the Sec. of State 16th Nov.

30,000 men under Victor, into that province;* when the Spaniards retired
to the Sierra Morena, and the French again withdrew their troops to the
Tagus.

But the events which had occurred in Castille in October, particularly
the battle at Tamames, induced the Spanish government to believe that a
favorable opportunity offered for obtaining possession of Madrid; and
they directed Gen. Areyzaga, who had, in October, taken the command of
the army of La Mancha, to move forward and push for the possession of
Madrid. He marched on the 3d Nov., and reached Los dos Barrios, near
Ocaña, on the 10th.† He made an attack upon a French corps of 5000
men, which occupied that town on the night of the 10th,‡ in which he
lost some men and horses; and the French made good their retreat. He
then moved to Sᵗᵃ Cruz de la Zarza on the 13th, where he remained till
the 18th; and having heard of an enemy's corps in his front, at Arganda,
which was about to pass the Tagus on his right at Fuentidueña, while
there was another corps of 25,000 men at Aranjuez and Ocaña, he returned to Los dos Barrios, and prepared to attack the French corps in his
front. He found, however, on the morning of the 19th, that the French
were likely to anticipate his attack; and he formed his army, consisting
of 50,000 men, in the rear of Ocaña. The French attacked him with
25,000 men, and completely defeated and dispersed the Spanish army,
taking 55 pieces of cannon. The head quarters arrived at La Carolina on
the 22d; and very few men had been collected on the 28th. The French
did not pursue farther than Villarta.

In the mean time, the Duque de Alburquerque, who had assumed the
command of the army of Estremadura, in the beginning of November,
marched to Arzobispo, when the French collected their troops on the
Upper Tagus to oppose Areyzaga. The French also, with the same view,
drew out of Old Castille, on the 13th and 14th Nov., a part of the troops
which they had sent into that province to oppose the Duque del Parque.
The Duque, upon finding Old Castille weakened, moved forward from
Bejar on the 17th Nov., and arrived at Alba de Tormes on the 28th,§
with his advanced guard at Carpio. It was there attacked by a French
corps assembled from Valladolid, &c., but the French were repulsed with
some loss. The Duque then moved forward to Fresno; but retired again
on the 26th, in consequence of orders from the Junta. By this time,
also, the French had reinforced again their corps in Old Castille; and the
Duque was attacked on the 27th and 28th on his retreat, and at Alba de
Tormes, and suffered considerably. He continued his retreat, however,
towards Ciudad Rodrigo and the mountains; and on the 29th, when
within 2 leagues of Tamames, the troops were alarmed by the appearance of 30 dragoons in their rear, and dispersed. There was no enemy,
however, at hand to take advantage of this panic; and it was expected that
they would be collected again. While this was going on in Old Castille,
the Junta ordered the Duque de Alburquerque to fall back with his corps

---

* See dispatch to the Sec. of State 22d Oct.
† See dispatch to the Sec. of State 16th Nov.
‡ See dispatch to the Sec. of State 30th Nov.
§ See dispatch to the Sec. of State 7th Dec.

on the Guadiana; and thus to give up the position of the Puerto de Mirabete, on the Tagus, and the Mesa de Ibor.*

These circumstances, and the necessity that the British army should be north of the Tagus, when the enemy's reinforcements should arrive, induced Sir A. Wellesley to put the British army in motion to cross that river immediately. He had long had that movement in contemplation, and had given notice of it to the Junta.†

The A.G. to Col. Peacocke, Lisbon.   10th Dec. 1809.

His Excellency desiring to afford the officers commanding corps every means of information relative to the non-commissioned officers and soldiers now absent from their respective regiments, I am commanded to desire you will call for, and forward to this office, as soon as possible, a nominal return of the non-commissioned officers and soldiers of the army in the general and convalescent hospitals at Lisbon.

I do request you will desire that soldiers of the same battalion shall in succession be placed in this return, under a heading of the number of the regiment, the more easily to enable extracts to be forwarded to the corps to which they relate, that being the final object in calling for this return.

The A.G. to Lieut. Col. Fenwick, Elvas.   10th Dec. 1809.

I have had the honor to receive and submit your letter of the 8th inst. to the consideration of the Commander of the Forces.

His Excellency, conceiving your request therein to be reasonable, has directed me to order Major Lindsay, of the 39th regt., to relieve you from the command of the Elvas station; but you will of course continue to superintend the public duties there till the arrival of Major Lindsay, when you will put that officer in possession of every instruction and document which may aid him in the conduct of the charge transferred. On the completion of these directions you will be pleased to rejoin your battalion.

The A.G. to Col. Peacocke, Lisbon.   11th Dec. 1809.

Adverting to the numerous representations which have reached head quarters respecting the conduct of the troops at Lisbon, and particularly the — regt., the Commander of the Forces has not without the utmost concern observed the frequent breaches of discipline, and failure even of common honesty in the soldiery. As these transgressions clearly show general want of order in the corps to which these soldiers belong, you are to call on the officers commanding regiments to exert

---

* This position is the most important in the country, to the province of Estremadura and the south of Portugal. If this position is held, the enemy cannot cross the Tagus to any efficient purpose, between the bridge of Toledo and Villa Velha, in Portugal. The position could not well be lost if the Spaniards would destroy the bridge of Arzobispo, as Sir A. Wellesley has frequently advised.

† The object in occupying this proposed position, is to be at the point of defence of Portugal; to divert the attention of the French from the south of Spain when they shall receive their reinforcements, and thus give time to the Spanish government to repair their losses. The filling of the rivers, and the destruction of the roads, will, with a very few troops, be a sufficient defence in the winter for the south of Spain. The same events which might impede the march of the British army to the north of Portugal, if longer delayed, would be fatal to Portugal, and might be so to the British army, if the enemy were to be able to invade that kingdom during the winter. It is absolutely necessary, therefore, to cross the Tagus immediately; and it may be depended upon, that the enemy's first effort upon receiving his reinforcements will be upon the troops north of the Tagus. The contents of this Memorandum must show the great use the British army has been to Spain and Portugal. Since they arrived in April, the French have destroyed three Spanish armies, Blake's, Areyzaga's, and Del Parque's; and yet they can do nothing. They have been obliged to evacuate the north of Portugal, Galicia, South Estremadura, and they hold but part of La Mancha: and also to keep their force concentrated in Old Castille, and about Madrid. If the Spaniards had not lost 2 armies lately, we should keep up the ball for another year. But as it is!—but I won't despair!

themselves, and by their example and orders unite the energy of the officers under their command, which is required for the suppression of those disorders, as also for the improvement of their several regiments.

I am further commanded to request you will express to Major ——, of the ——, his Excellency's disappointment at the apparent little advantage the corps under his command has derived from being at Lisbon, to which station it was removed purposely to afford every means of improvement. You will, besides, convey to Major —— the observation, that his credit and responsibility in command require his immediate exertion to correct and improve his battalion, the conduct of which in particular has occasioned the displeasure of the Commander of the Forces.

You will be pleased to direct the company rolls of that regiment to be called every hour during the day, till further orders, when no individual whatever is to be absent, those on duty only excepted.

The A.G. to Lieut. Gen. Sir J. Sherbrooke, K.B.   12th Dec. 1809.

I have had the honor to submit your letter of the 11th inst. and enclosures to the consideration of the Commander of the Forces. I am commanded to request you will communicate to Major ——, that his Excellency observes Ensigns —— and ——, of the — regt., have not presented such a case as to warrant the passing over the offence of which they have been guilty.

It appears these officers have committed a violent assault upon an inhabitant of Arroyo, who proposes to refrain from further complaint provided the officers in question will compensate him for the injury they have done. Before these gentlemen applied for pardon for their military offence in this instance, they should have been enabled to say they had positively satisfied the individual whom they had wantonly injured, and not have made the satisfaction to the individual dependent on the pardon to be granted them. Such conduct would have manifested the contrition which is the ground of their request for forgiveness, but under existing circumstances his Excellency cannot listen to their application.

To Lieut. Gen. Leite.   Badajoz, 13th Dec. 1809.

I understand that the surgeons of the Portuguese military hospital at Elvas have no objection, and have it in their power, to take charge of 300 sick of the British army; and as it would be a material convenience to the army to have that number of patients taken care of by those gentlemen, I shall be very much obliged to you if you will give your permission to have them removed to the Portuguese hospital, and there accommodated and taken care of, upon the usual allowances, which the Purveyor Gen. of the British army will pay.

To Bart. Frere, Esq.   Badajoz, 13th Dec. 1809.

I have just now had the honor of receiving your letters of the 9th and 11th inst.

Upon the destruction of the bridge at Arzobispo, I beg that you will observe to the government that that bridge affords the only passage across the Tagus, and road for the invasion of the province of Estremadura, there being none for an army from the bridge of Talavera, from that of Puebla de Montalban, or from that of Toledo, excepting from the last, by the circuitous road by Ciudad Real.

The road from Arzobispo to Deleytosa, it is true, is exceedingly bad, but still it is not impracticable; and the advantage of the destruction of the bridge would be, that in case the enemy should be desirous of forcing the passage of the Tagus at Almaraz, and of establishing a bridge there, which is the best, and indeed the only good passage for an army invading

Estremadura, he could not have a corps of troops in the mountains of the Mesa de Ibor, &c., and upon the right flank of the corps employed in the defence of the Puerto de Mirabete, as he had last winter when Gen. Cuesta was obliged, on that account only, to retire from the Puerto. If the enemy should by these means be prevented from forcing the passage of the Tagus at Almaraz, there is no passage for an army till he would arrive at Villa Velha, in Portugal, a distance which it is probable that he would find it difficult to move his bridge. This bridge of Arzobispo, like that of Almaraz, Alcantara, del Cardenal, and del Conde, is so high, that if once effectually destroyed, it cannot be repaired by temporary means during the war; so that the security its destruction would give would be permanent, while the Tagus should continue full; and at all events the evils of war would be removed from a numerous class of people inhabiting the hills between Deleytosa and Talavera de la Reyna. I therefore most earnestly recommend the destruction of this bridge.

To Bart. Frere, Esq. Badajoz, 13th Dec. 1809.

I enclose a letter which I received last night from Mr. Villiers, upon which he has desired that I should communicate to you my opinion. I acknowledge that I am not sufficiently acquainted with the local situation of Galicia to be able to give any opinion upon the necessity or expediency of fortifying those posts at all, or in preference to others. There is no man better acquainted with that province than the Marques de la Romana, or who knows better than he does how important it is in the present state of affairs to keep the enemy out of it, or how to effect that object.

To Major Davy, 5th batt. 60th regt. Badajoz, 13th Dec. 1809.

I have perused your letter of the 10th inst. to Col. Bathurst, relative to the charge exhibited by Lieut. —— against Capt. —— ; and I am glad to find, that although Capt. —— did return —— —— as Paymaster's clerk from Oct. 1808, to March, 1809, and drew an allowance for him in that capacity, but neither employed him nor paid him as such, he did so with the knowledge and permission of his commanding officer, Major ——, and that he paid the sum which he received in the name of

A. G. O. Badajoz, 13th Dec. 1809.

1. The Commander of the Forces is concerned to notice the continued and repeated disobedience of orders by the officers of the army, in pressing mules and carts, and in taking articles from the country upon their own informal receipts. He is concerned to be obliged to resort to measures to enforce obedience to his orders, and he now directs that Capt. ——, of the —— regt., may be put in arrest by the commanding officer of the hospital at Elvas, for taking away mules belonging to the Commissariat at Badajoz, contrary to orders; his crime will be sent to him by the Adj. Gen., and he is to proceed forthwith to Badajoz.

2. The Commander of the Forces calls the attention of the officers of the army to the following order, by the late Commander of the Forces in Portugal:

Extract from General Orders, by Lieut. Gen. Sir J. Cradock.

' The army is referred to the Orders of the 14th March (see p. 555), on the subject of quarters, which General officers are requested to impress on the troops under their command; and it is to be clearly understood that cover is all that any officer has a right to expect, and he has no pretensions to ask for either bed or furniture; when such articles are supplied, it is a matter of civility on the part of the owner, and must be received as a favor, and not as a right.'

This principle has been before laid down in General Orders, and must be extended throughout this Kingdom.

—— —— to serjeant ——, who did the duty of Paymaster's clerk. Capt. —— has therefore entirely cleared himself from any corrupt or improper motives in this transaction; and I shall certainly not gratify the malicious spirit by which Lieut. —— appears to be actuated in bringing forward this charge, by submitting the conduct of Capt. —— to any further inquiry.

I beg, however, to draw your attention, and that of Capt. —— and Major ——, to the impropriety of the whole of this transaction, and to a reflection on the risk which every officer incurs who allows himself to be involved in such. It affects the foundation of every military return, and exposes His Majesty and the public to frauds of every description; and such a transaction must positively never be repeated.

If it were necessary to employ and pay one man for the performance of the duties usually allotted to two, under the regulations of the Service, application should have been made to the Commander of the Forces, at the time, for permission so to do, but on no account ought his pay to have been drawn in the name of another.

I have also read your letter to the Adj. Gen. of the 10th inst., and I desire that you will direct the Paymaster of the 5th batt. 60th regt. to pay out of the subsistence of Lieut. ——, to Capt. ——, for the 12 pairs of shoes, the price of which has been awarded to him by the Court of Inquiry, of which Capt. —— was President, held on the 9th Nov., Lieut. —— receiving the shoes, and disposing of them as he may think proper.

I desire, also, that you will inform Lieut. —— that I will not order a Court Martial to be assembled for the trial of Lieut. ——, on the charge exhibited against him by Lieut. —— on the 10th inst.; the subject of that charge having already been incidentally before the General Court Martial.

I desire, however, that you will put Lieut. —— in arrest, 'for unmilitary and unofficerlike conduct, in disturbing the peace and harmony which ought to subsist among the officers of the 5th batt. 60th regt., contrary to the orders and warning given to him by the Commander of the Forces.'

You will keep Lieut. —— in arrest with the regiment, as I know enough of the character and past conduct of that officer to be suspicious that his late conduct is to be attributed to a desire to leave his regiment during the time it may be actively employed.

To the Rt. Hon. J. Villiers.   Badajoz, 13th Dec. 1809.

I received last night your letter of the 9th.

I am obliged to measure the assistance which I give the government by the state of our means and our own wants, and I am always sorry when it cannot be to the extent wished for by you, or by them. I cannot give the order for the second £50,000 for them, till I shall see my way through the difficulties of our own situation.

We are now on our march towards the Mondego; and as the government are at the same time forming their magazines, which ought to have been formed 6 weeks ago, when I consented to advance the money, it stands to reason that we shall get neither provisions nor means of transport, if we have not money to pay for them. The first money must be supplied to us, and they shall have their £50,000 in the second instance, paid to them in such manner as can be afforded from the military chest. I always feel much concern when any transaction of this kind cannot be carried into execution according to your wishes; but I have it not in my power to collect larger sums of money (particularly coin) than we have got, and are getting daily, not only at Lisbon, but at Cadiz and Gibraltar; and you are mistaken if you suppose that the assurances which I have repeatedly given you to the same purport are not founded in fact. I write to government upon this occasion to point out the necessity of some assistance in money, particularly if they intend to afford further assistance to the Portuguese government.

I forward by this occasion Mr. Frere's and my dispatches for your perusal; and I shall send to Mr. Frere your letter in respect to Galicia. I should doubt, however, whether the Spanish government have the means of defraying the expense of fortifying these posts; and if they have, whether they have the means of garrisoning them.

I expect to leave this in a few days; but you may as well continue to send any communications you may have to make by the road of Elvas, as I can always turn them to the road of Abrantes.

To the Earl of Liverpool.   Badajoz, 13th Dec. 1809.

I beg that your Lordship will be so kind as to give directions that the £100,000 in specie, for the use of the British army, may be sent to Portugal as soon as possible, and another sum of £100,000 in the course of the month of January.   Some difficulty has been experienced lately in procuring money for bills upon England at Lisbon, as well as at Gibraltar and Cadiz; and at the same time that the transmission of specie will relieve the inconvenience which otherwise would be felt from the want of money, it will probably have the effect of inducing persons to come forward again with their money for bills of exchange, and will probably lower in some degree the rate of exchange.   I have also to inform your Lordship, that in case His Majesty's government should think it proper to give any pecuniary assistance to the Portuguese government, in consequence of my dispatch of the 14th Nov., it will be necessary that specie should be sent from England to the amount of such assistance.

I am convinced that it would tend materially to increase the sums procured for bills in England, if the communication by the packets was more regular than it is.   His Majesty's minister at Lisbon has lately fixed on a day in every week on which the packet shall be dispatched; and it would be very desirable if the same arrangement were adopted at Gibraltar and Cadiz, and corresponding measures adopted in England, to secure the regular dispatch, at fixed periods, of the packets for those places and Lisbon.

The A.G. to the officers commg. at Lisbon and Elvas.   13th Dec. 1809.

I am commanded to refer you to the enclosed copy of a letter received from Major Coghlan, commanding 61st regt., with the foundation for which, so far as relates to the hospital establishment under your superintendence, you will make the subject of a specific report.   I am directed to observe that staff medical officers are on no occasion entitled to servants from the ranks. His Excellency further requires you will from time to time inspect the state of regiments and brigades, detachments of which may be at the station under your command, having at the same time in mind the relative number of officers, non-commissioned officers, and soldiers specified in the G.O., 19th May, No. 3, as necessary to take charge of and attendance on the sick. When the hospital list shall decrease by their becoming convalescent, such proportion of officers and non-commissioned officers are to be warned to move with them to regimental duty the first convenient opportunity, so as to leave at the hospital station only the number of officers and non-commissioned officers averaged by the regulations above referred to.

The A.G. to Col. Peacocke, Lisbon.   13th Dec. 1809.

I have had the honor to receive and lay before the Commander of the Forces your application of the 10th Dec. His Excellency permits you to recommend an officer eligible to fill the staff situation which will become vacant by the embarkation of Lieut. Crompton, conceiving your selection may best answer the service and the wishes you have expressed.

To the Earl of Liverpool.   Badajoz, 14th Dec. 1809.

The enemy has not made any forward movement either in Old Castille or La Mancha since I addressed your Lordship on the 7th inst.; but I understand that they are employed in reinforcing their corps in the former province.

The Spanish Commanders in Chief are endeavoring to collect their dispersed troops again; with what success I am not enabled accurately to state; but I am apprehensive that the loss of arms and accoutrements by both the armies lately defeated will be found to be immense.

The British army is on its march across the Tagus, and towards the frontiers of the province of Beira; and I shall move my head quarters as soon as the rear divisions shall arrive in this town. The number of sick in the army is still very large; but the diseases of the soldiers have not lately been so violent as they had been, nor so fatal; and I hope that the movement of the army will be beneficial to their health. I shall be obliged to your Lordship if you will give directions that at least 30 hospital mates may be sent to Portugal for the service of this army as soon as possible.

The A.G. to Major Lindsay, Elvas.   15th Dec. 1809.

In reply to your letter of the 14th inst., which has been submitted, I am commanded by his Excellency to observe, that the establishment of a British guard in a Portuguese garrison is irregular, unless that guard shall be understood to be under the immediate command of the Governor of the garrison. Should the Portuguese guard neglect the duties appointed to it, by suffering the soldiers to straggle from hospital, or by any other omission, you are to make a report of the same to the Governor, but you are not to order a British guard. Under the circumstances, however, of the Portuguese not exactly understanding the duties possibly required of them in the adjacent of the general hospital, it is recommended you should establish a system of orderly non-commissioned officers and privates for the exterior duties of your post, by which greater regularity and attention to instructions may be attained.

The A.G. to Major Lindsay, Elvas.   16th Dec. 1809.

The Inspector of hospitals has represented that the establishment of Villa Viçosa requires a military commandant. If you have not already done so, you will nominate the most eligible officer under your orders to that command. I have to observe, the officer you select must not be under the rank of captain, and that all reports and returns from Villa Viçosa must be equally forwarded through you, as those of Estremoz. You will require the officers commanding the out stations to sign all returns, which after inspection you will countersign, so as to preserve the chain of responsibility. I have been delayed some time in sending hospital regulations, in the expectation of receiving from Dr. Franck the hospital instructions which have been referred to in Mr. ———'s letter, when he requested that hospital tickets specifying the number of firelocks, accoutrements, and proportion of necessaries should be forwarded with each sick man. As it is his Excellency's wish to complete these instructions, I beg you will send me the order alluded to, if possible, in the course of this day.

The A. G. to the Commissary General.   16th Dec. 1809.

In reply to your note of yesterday, and annexed letter from Mr. Assist. Commissary ———, I have by his Excellency been directed to request you will impress on that officer that obedience to orders is his first duty. It appears also to the Commander of the Forces, that those persons to whom the public was indebted would willingly have come 5 or 6 leagues for payment of their demands, and that the reasons given for detaining escorts without authority have proved entirely unsatisfactory.

To the Earl of Liverpool.   Badajoz, 17th Dec. 1809.

I have the honor to transmit for your Lordship's information, returns of the stores and provisions in the magazines in Portugal on the 1st Dec. 1809.

To the Earl of Liverpool.   Badajoz, 17th Dec. 1809.

I beg to draw your Lordship's attention to His Majesty's regulation which prohibits the issue of their subsistence to the officers and soldiers who may be made prisoners of war; and I have to request permission to allow the issue of their subsistence to those officers and soldiers who may escape from the enemy, or who may be exchanged in the Peninsula.

The French General officers have in general behaved remarkably well to the British officers and soldiers who fell into their hands in consequence of the march of the Spanish army from Talavera de la Reyna in the month

G. A. O.   Badajoz, 14th Dec. 1809.

The Commander of the Forces is happy to find that the circumstances respecting the conduct of Capt. ———, — regt., did not occur as they were represented to him by the officer of the Commissariat department, Mr. ———; and that he is therefore enabled to release that officer from his arrest, notwithstanding that an irregularity was committed by the soldiers under his command. Capt. ——— is therefore released from his arrest, and is to join his regiment.

G. O.   Badajoz, 17th Dec. 1809.

1. The officer commanding the general hospitals at Elvas, Estremoz, and Villa Viçosa, is to appoint a Board of officers at each of those places to examine the arms, accoutrements, clothing, &c. belonging to soldiers now in hospital, or who have been discharged from the hospital, or have died, which articles may be in the possession of the Purveyor Gen. at the present moment.

This Board is to make a register of these articles by regiments, inserting in the register the marks or names on each article. Of this register one copy must be given to the Purveyor Gen., and one copy forwarded to the Adj. Gen.'s office, to be communicated to the several regiments.

2. The A. Q. M. G. at Elvas must be one of the members of this Board.

3. The Purveyor Gen. must be particularly careful in keeping the register of arms, &c. brought by the soldiers to the general hospital in future, in obedience to His Majesty's regulations of the 31st March, 1800.

4. In order to enable the Purveyor Gen., or his deputy, to obey this order, the officers commanding regiments are invariably to send with a soldier to the hospital, whether general, brigade, detachment, or regimental, a ticket made out in the following form :

To

of August last; and in many instances they have supplied the officers with money. I have also sent them sums amounting to £1200, of which I have the acknowledgments; and recently £500, but I have not received the detailed distribution either of those sums or of the sums which have been advanced to the British officers by the French General officers.

It is obvious that these last mentioned sums must be repaid; and I have

---

To the Purveyor of His Majesty's hospital at

SIR,

Please to receive into the hospital the following men of the

dated   the   day of   18

FRONT.	Men's names.	Troop or company.	Disease, and how long ill.	N.B. This must be signed by one commanding officer, besides the surgeon or his mate, as underneath.
				Capt. ——
				Lieut. ——
				Cornet ——
				Ensign ——
				Surgeon ——
				Surg. Mate ——

Return of arms, accoutrements, and necessaries, sent with him or them.

REAR.	Men's names.	Troop or company.	Necessaries.										Clothing.				Arms and accoutrements.								
			Shirts.	Shoes.	Stockings.	Brushes.	Black balls.	Combs.	Great coat straps.	Stock and clasp.	Gaiters.	Knapsack.	Cap and tuft.	Coat.	Waistcoat.	Breeches.	Great coat.	Fusil or halbert.	No. or mark on ditto.	Musket.	No. or mark on ditto.	Bayonet and scabbard.	Sling.	Bayonet belt.	Pouch belt, and pouch.	Haversack.	Canteen and strap.
		TOTAL .																								

5. When men are sent to a general or detachment hospital by any regiment, the officer commanding must report to the General officer commanding the brigade whether this order has been obeyed.

6. The Purveyor Gen., or the Medical officer, in charge of the arms, accoutrements, &c. in any hospital, must report immediately any instance in which obedience to this order may have been neglected, otherwise he will be considered responsible for all loss and damage of arms and accoutrements of soldiers in hospital.

7. The officer commanding at Lisbon will give directions that these orders, respecting the formation of the registry, &c. may be carried into execution at the general hospital at Lisbon.

lately requested, that the French General officers will let me know where and in what manner they wish they should be repaid; and I request your Lordship to instruct me in what manner these sums, as well as those advanced by me to the British officers, prisoners of war, are to be charged to the public in the first instance; whether in the army extraordinaries, or to the Transport office.

To the Earl of Liverpool.   Badajoz, 17th Dec. 1809.

I enclose an application which I have received from an officer in the service of Spain, Charles, Marquis d'Espagne,* to transfer the service of himself, and of the corps under his command, from the service of Spain to that of His Majesty, in case of the failure of the Spanish nation to effect the objects for which they are contending. From what I have heard of the Marques de España, I believe him to be one of the best of the Spanish officers; and I am desirous of receiving the directions of His Majesty's government respecting the answer to be given to his proposition.

In the event of the failure expected in the enclosed letters, it is probable that I shall receive many offers of the same description with the enclosed; and I beg to receive the instructions of His Majesty's government regarding the answer to be given to those officers.

To J. Murray, Esq., Commissary General.   Badajoz, 17th Dec. 1809.

Having considered the letter from Mr. Sampayo to you dated the 12th inst., enclosing copies of two letters from Mr. Rawlings to Mr. Sampayo, dated the 6th and 8th April, it is obvious to me that the letters from Mr. Rawlings, who acted under the direct authority of the late Commander of the Forces, must be deemed to be contracts with Mr. Sampayo for the supply, at certain prices, of the articles therein mentioned for the service of the troops, into which contract Mr. Rawlings was fully competent to enter; and the army, when commanded by me, and when you were their Commissary Gen., enjoyed the advantage of them. Under these circumstances, it appears to me that you ought to pay Mr. Sampayo according to the prices fixed in Mr. Rawlings's letters, as long as he continued to supply, under their authority, any of the articles to which they refer.

Adverting to the circumstances of the country, at the time the letters in question were written by Mr. Rawlings, and to the fact that the army, although numerous, was but ill provided with Commissaries, and that it was therefore necessary to employ a contractor, it does not appear to me that the bargains were improvident, or that the prices are large; and they are certainly not so large as those paid by Mr. Erskine for the same articles. But I do not conceive that the largeness of price has any thing to do with the question. The letters from Mr. Rawlings being considered of the nature of a contract, of which his successor availed himself, the prices agreed to by that contract must be paid.

The A.G. to Lieut. Col. the Hon. H. King, 5th regt.   17th Dec. 1809.

Dr. Franck having through this office submitted to the Commander of the Forces your letter of the 6th inst., I am commanded to require you to comply with the object of the Inspector's requisition, by ordering Assist. Surgeon ——, of the 2d

* Don Carlos de España.

batt. 5th regt., forthwith to repair to Elvas station. I have to observe, however, that to obviate such misunderstanding hereafter, as also to preserve the command and responsibility of officers in charge of corps, the instructions of the Inspector general of hospitals, so far as relate to regimental medical officers, are henceforward to be notified through the Adj. Gen.

To Lieut. Gen. Hill.   Badajoz, 18th Dec. 1809.

In the arrangements for the defence of Portugal, I shall form 2 principal corps, both consisting of British and Portuguese troops, the largest of which will be to the northward, and I shall command it myself; and the latter will be for the present upon the Tagus, and hereafter it may be moved forward into Alentejo, and I will not make any arrangement either as to the troops that are to compose it, or as to the officer who is to command it, without offering the command of it to you.

At the same time I shall not separate you from the army and from my own immediate command, without consulting your wishes; and I shall be glad to hear from you upon this subject as soon as possible, as the arrangements for quartering and disposing of the troops depend upon your decision upon this point. You will therefore send back either a messenger, if you can get one, or an officer, with your answer as soon as possible. I send your letters, arrived by the English mail.

To Lieut. Col. Carroll.*   Badajoz, 18th Dec. 1809.

I have had the honor of receiving your letter of the 4th inst., and I am much obliged to you for the details of the late events in Castille which it contains.

I had already received from Mr. Frere, and from other quarters, accounts of the proceedings of the army of Castille between the 17th and 20th Nov., both inclusive; to which I had been induced to give credit, adverting to the authority from which they had reached me. These differ in some respects from your account, which I attribute to the difference of the view of the same transactions taken by different people; but they have stated one material fact which you have omitted, upon which I beg to have your report.

I have been informed that the army dispersed on the 29th, when within 2 leagues of Tamames, upon hearing a report that the French dragoons were following them, notwithstanding that in point of fact only 30 dragoons did make their appearance. If this fact be true, it is desirable that you should have reported it; and indeed as the reports of officers, employed as you are, are the foundation of the measures adopted by His

* Lieut. Gen. Sir W. P. Carroll, K.C.H., then in the service of Spain.

G. O.   Badajoz, 18th Dec. 1809.

1. In order to prevent the inconvenience which the army would suffer from the absence of the officers of the Staff, the Commander of the Forces has determined that all officers belonging to the departments of the A. G. and Q. M. G. of the army in Spain and Portugal, who shall be absent from the Peninsula, on any account, except that of having been wounded, shall cease to receive their Staff pay and allowance in 2 months from the period of their embarkation, although they will continue on the list of their respective departments, and will return to their duties in them, when they will rejoin the army.

The A. G. and Q. M. G. will attend to this order in making up the abstracts of their several departments.

Majesty's government, and upon which I must found the operations of the army under my command, it is most desirable that they should be correct and full in every particular; and should give those who may read them an accurate notion of the events to which they relate.

To Vice Adm. the Hon. G. Berkeley.   Badajoz, 19th Dec. 1809.

I received yesterday morning your letter of the 13th inst. The greatest part of the army will be carried forward to the frontier of Castille; but some will remain upon the Tagus, to whom the boats you mention will be of use.

I am very much obliged to you for thinking of the transports at Salvaterra, which will be a great convenience to us, as well as the gun boats. Indeed, upon this last subject, I shall have to trouble you more at length as soon as Col. Fletcher and I shall have settled the defence of our positions to be taken up on the Tagus, in the event of the invasion of the country by the enemy.

I have written to the government respecting the boats on all the rivers, but particularly on the Tagus; to which letter I have as yet received no answer. The plan which I have proposed to them is:

1st; That the names of the owners of all boats, their sizes, &c., should be registered in the village or district in which the owners reside, and the boats numbered.

2dly; That the name of the owner of each boat, and of the village to which he belongs, and the boat's number, should be marked on each boat.

3dly; That the owners of boats should be made responsible, under a heavy penalty, to remove their boats to whatever point they should be directed by the magistrate of the village or district, at a moment's notice. The magistrate of the village or district would of course receive his orders from the government or their officers.

I have recommended an arrangement upon the same principle respecting the carts throughout the country.

P. S. I wait here to see the last of the troops out of Spain; and then I shall move to the northward without stopping.

To the Earl of Liverpool.   Badajoz, 19th Dec. 1809.

I have just received your letter of the 21st Nov. I sent by the last post to Mr. Sydenham, for the use of Pole principally, and of Lord Wellesley, a narrative * of the description you wish to have; and I desired him to show it to nobody else, lest it should get into print. I have now written to request him to let you have a copy of it; and you will communicate it to whomsoever you please; only I beg that it may not be printed. You will find it will answer your purpose perfectly; and I have referred in the margin to the official documents and authorities from which I drew it up. I am glad to find that the government are getting on well.

To the Earl of Liverpool.   Badajoz, 19th Dec. 1809.

I have had the honor of receiving your Lordship's dispatch of the 22d

* See Memorandum of Operations in 1809: Badajoz, 9th Dec. 1809, p. 631.

Nov., enclosing copies of the dispatch from Lord Bathurst to Mr. Villiers, No. 10, and of the separate dispatch, No. 1, regarding the payment of the Portuguese troops.

I have no copy of the original instructions from Mr. Canning to Mr. Villiers upon this subject; nor of the estimate of the expense of the Portuguese troops, upon which was founded the charge against the British government for the payment first of 10,000 and latterly of 20,000 men. I have viewed this subject possibly erroneously, but I have always considered that it was the intention of His Majesty's government to afford certain assistance to Portugal; the extent of which was to be measured by the exertions which Portugal should make in the cause; and by the information which should be received of the wants of that country. Upon this principle I conceive it was that the pecuniary assistance to be given to Portugal was made to depend first upon that country having 10,000 men, and afterwards upon having 20,000 men in her service. But the objects of His Majesty's government in Portugal were not confined to the 20,000 men, for the payment of which His Majesty was disposed to advance the means.

The greatest anxiety was likewise felt and expressed for the reestablishment of the Portuguese army; and, with a view to attain this desirable object, His Majesty allowed one of his generals, Gen. Beresford, to enter into the Portuguese service, to command the Portuguese army, and several of the officers of his army to serve in that of Portugal on various terms.

His Majesty likewise allowed me to accept the commission of Marshal General from the Prince Regent, in order that I might have the general superintendence over all the troops serving in Portugal. Under these circumstances, Gen. Beresford and I (as far as I have had any concern with them) have not limited our attention solely to the 20,000 men (no further than to take care that there were 20,000 men actually in the service before His Majesty's government were called upon to pay for that number), but have considered the whole Portuguese army in all its parts to be equally objects of our attention. The mode in which the business is done is, the Ambassador pays a certain sum monthly, being the estimated expense of 20,000 men, to the Portuguese government, and all the Portuguese troops without distinction are paid by the officers of the Portuguese government. I do not believe that the sum paid by the Ambassador to the Portuguese government is adequate to defray the expense of the 20,000 men; and it would be difficult to define accurately the amount of the expense of any particular number of men, being part of an army, the whole employed in the same country, some in garrison, and others in the field. There would besides be difficulties in paying this selected body, and arrangements must be made to provide for the exclusive command of these troops; and they must in fact be separated from the remainder of the Portuguese army, although the whole would serve in the same country, and possibly in the same operation.

This selected body (supposing the Portuguese government should be inclined to make such, into which part of the subject it is not my province to enter) would have no advantage in point of equipment or efficiency over other parts of the army; and indeed I believe in some respects would labor under disadvantages. The whole Portuguese army now receive the best assistance the means supplied by Great Britain and by Portugal can afford them. If that part of the army paid by Great Britain were alone to receive the assistance of equipments and other supplies furnished by Great Britain, it would want those which Portugal can afford, unless purchased for them at the expense of Great Britain; at the same time that that part which would be at the charge of Portugal would want many articles which Great Britain alone can supply. The effect of the arrangements, as far as regards equipments, would have been, that we should have had 20,000 equipped about as well as the whole army are at present; and the remainder very imperfectly equipped.

Thus, upon the whole, the arrangement of separating 20,000 men of the Portuguese army, to be paid, equipped, &c. &c., by Great Britain, would, if it had been originally intended by His Majesty's government, have been impracticable; and even if it could have been successful, it would have given a smaller and a less efficient force for the general cause in the existing contest on the Peninsula than that which we have at present, and at a larger expense. But, whatever might have been the consequences of adopting any other system than that upon which we have acted in Portugal, it is evidently impracticable now to alter that upon which we have been proceeding to the present moment.

In respect to the expense of the system which has been adopted, I have no copy of the estimate which was transmitted by the Ambassador to the Sec. of State, and I am not enabled to state accurately its extent. It may be classed, however, under the following heads :

1st; the pay and provisions for 20,000 men; which I had, upon recollection of the estimate, considered to be £500,000 *per annum*, or something more than £20,000 per month for each 10,000 men.

2dly; the pay and allowances of the British officers in the Portuguese service, which I estimate will amount to £100,000 *per annum*.

These officers are paid at different rates from the Portuguese officers, and upon principles settled by the Commander in Chief in England; and they have received their pay from Mr. Bell, who was appointed their paymaster by the Ambassador, with the consent of the Sec. of State. I enclose the copy of a letter which I wrote some time ago to Gen. Beresford, a copy of which has already been transmitted to England, which will explain the principles on which this part of the business is conducted.

The third head of expense is that of ordnance and military stores, arms, ammunition, clothing, and equipments of all descriptions required by the Portuguese army, a part of which has been furnished by Great Britain. I have no knowledge of the prices of these articles, and can furnish no estimate of the expense.

In a dispatch which I addressed to your Lordship on the 14th Nov., I stated to your Lordship the general situation of the finances of Portugal, and my opinion respecting the assistance which ought to be given to that country in order to provide for its defence, in answer to a dispatch which I had received from Lord Castlereagh upon that subject.

It is obvious that the sum with which I proposed that Portugal should be assisted will not make good the deficiency in the revenues, but is that which may prevent the deficiency from falling upon the army; and I have further to observe, that if the whole of the sum which I proposed in that dispatch should be given to Portugal, it will not amount to that which Great Britain would probably have to pay upon a fair estimate of the expense of 20,000 men.

Your Lordship may be convinced that I have not exaggerated the financial and other difficulties with which Portugal has to contend; and I must add, that if it be the policy of His Majesty's government to support the contest in the Peninsula, and to extend the assistance of Great Britain to Portugal, that country deserves that assistance, not only by the confidence reposed in His Majesty's servants and officers, but by the exertions which the government are disposed to make in their own cause; the whole of their revenue being employed in defraying the expenses of their troops, and of such establishments as are necessary for the support of the armies. But if Great Britain cannot afford this expense, and if the arms, clothing, and equipments required cannot be sent to Portugal, at least as soon as the enemy can send into the Peninsula the reinforcements to his armies, the contest must be carried on with manifest disadvantage.

To the Earl of Liverpool.   Badajoz, 19th Dec. 1809.

I have received your letter of the 21st Nov., regarding the provinces of Aragon, and Catalonia, and Valencia, which I agree entirely with you in thinking very interesting, although we have but little information upon them. I had lately sent Lord Burghersh into that part of Spain, and I forwarded to Lord Castlereagh his report from Granada, which I desired him to communicate to his successor. I have lately received a letter from him from Valencia, an extract of which I enclose, but I have desired him to make me a more full report.

The officers who had been employed in Spain by Lord Castlereagh were under the orders of the Commanding officer in Spain and Portugal; but when Lord Wellesley arrived, he brought with him orders from Lord Castlereagh to place themselves under the directions of the Ambassador at Seville, and I have had nothing to say to them since. Lieut. Col. Doyle * was the officer stationed in Catalonia, and I believe that he had to be sent down by Blake to Seville upon some business, after the defeat of his army at Belchite, and he has not since returned; and I understand from Mr. Frere that he expects instructions from England. If, however, I should find that he does not return to that quarter, I shall send there an officer. But Col. Bourke, who is certainly well qualified, is in England; and Sturgeon,† who is a clever fellow, and I should think also qualified for such a mission, cannot well be spared from the army. Generally speaking, these officers have not been of much use. In my opinion, they do not make accurate or useful reports of what passes in the quarters in which they are stationed, with the exception of Roche, of whom I must say, that although he was the friend of Cuesta, his reports were from the

* The late Lieut. Gen. Sir Charles Doyle, K.C.H.
† Lieut. Col. Sturgeon, killed in an affair near Vic Bigorre, in the south of France, in March, 1814.

beginning of a nature to discourage me from having any thing to do with him; and I found them upon experience to be perfectly well founded.

I should doubt very much the expediency of having any thing to do with the war in Aragon and Catalonia, excepting by assistance of arms, ammunition, and money, and probably squadrons on the coast. The French authority is in a manner established in Aragon; there is no regular resistance to it, and all that is done is by partisans, who do a great deal of good; but their operations are of such a nature, that we could have no connexion with them, excepting probably by encouraging them with money. In Catalonia, the resistance is more general and regular; but still the people are of a description with which your armies could not co-operate with any prospect of success, or even of safety. You see what Burghersh says of the Somatenes;* and it is notorious that the Catalans have at all times been the most irregular, and the least to be depended upon, of any of the Spaniards.

There is this to be added against any partial operation in Catalonia, such as the siege of Barcelona, or the co-operation in an attempt to relieve Gerona, that the seat of it is so near to France, and to the road by which reinforcements must come, that the British army or detachment would be in danger of being cut off, or at all events of being obliged to make an early and a hurried embarkation. In such a case, the army would suffer more by the disgrace of the failure and retreat than it could possibly gain even by the greatest success. If we had here a few thousand men to spare, it might be possible now to arrange with Blake (who is, I believe, the best of the Spanish officers) an expedition for the single object of relieving Gerona, which is a most interesting one to the whole Spanish nation. But the fall of Gerona must be decided, or the army engaged in the siege must be reinforced so as to render such an attempt hopeless, long before the men could arrive from England, supposing you could spare them.

To J. Murray, Esq., Commissary General.   Badajoz, 19th Dec. 1809.

I have the honor to enclose the copy of a letter which I wrote to the Sec. of the Treasury in the month of June last, in which I submitted to their Lordships the enclosed memorandum of an arrangement for conducting the duties of the British and the Portuguese Commissariats, as far as they were to be connected; to which letter I now enclose their Lordships' answer. I beg that the duties of the British and Portuguese Commissariat may in future be conducted according to the tenor of this arrangement; and that you will consider the 30th article of your instructions, and the 35th article of the instructions to the Commissary of Accounts from the Treasury, as repealed.

To Lieut. Col. Roche.   Badajoz, 19th Dec. 1809.

I have received your letters of the 12th and 14th. By this time the Seville gazette will have acquainted you with the motives which I had for moving the British army across the Tagus. In fact, the first effort of the enemy, when he shall receive his reinforcements, must be to possess himself of the course of the Tagus; and he can never venture to push

* The armed peasantry in Catalonia.

himself into the south of Spain till that object shall be accomplished. On this account, I had long determined to move to the frontiers of Castille in the fine weather in the month of December; and the army is now in march to that quarter, and I shall set out in 3 or 4 days, when I have seen the last of the troops out of Spain.

The Spaniards ought to defend the Despeña Perros with the force they have; but they go to the plains to be beaten, and thus cow the troops who would otherwise defend themselves in the mountains.

The A.G. to Officers commanding Divisions, Cavalry, and Artillery. 20th Dec. 1809.

I have received Lord Wellington's commands through the Military Sec. to give in a return of officers commanding corps at the battle of Talavera, including those who commanded the light companies of brigades, where those companies acted independently as belonging to light battalions. The officers who succeeded to temporary command of battalions from the original leaders being either killed or wounded are also to be noticed.

To enable my compliance with his Excellency's desire, I have to request you will be pleased to put me in possession of returns to this effect, so far as relates to the division under your command, which I am anxious should come under your inspection, to avoid a possibility of omitting any name that of right should stand in this honorable record.

This return being required without delay, I beg those of the 1st division may be sent to Abrantes.

To the Rt. Hon. J. Villiers. Badajoz, 21st Dec. 1809.

I send you my dispatches to Lord Liverpool, open for your perusal, and those of Mr. Frere.

I have given directions to the Commissary Gen. this day to order Mr. Dunmore to pay you £20,000 of the remaining £50,000 for the Portuguese government; and I hope that the state of our funds will enable me to advance the remainder of the money in a few days.

I set out on the 25th; but I request you to allow the messengers to come as usual till I shall write to turn them off to Abrantes.

To the Earl of Liverpool. Badajoz, 21st Dec. 1809.

The enemy have moved forward in force in La Mancha; and on the 15th they had a corps at Sta Cruz, at the foot of the hills, with their advanced posts within a league of Despeña Perros, the principal pass through that part of the Sierra Morena.

The French corps most advanced was Victor's, supported by that of Mortier; and Sebastiani had marched on the left towards Cuenca, in order to disperse the Spanish corps which had collected there under Gen. Echavarri, after the battle of Ocaña.

The Spanish army had collected again at La Carolina to the amount of 24,000 infantry; besides the corps at Cuenca, said to amount to 8000, there were 6000 cavalry. Col. Roche, from whom I have received the accounts, considers the estimate of 16,000 infantry with arms, and 3000 cavalry mounted, to be exaggerated; but I have seen other accounts, which state that larger numbers of infantry have their arms, and that the whole of the 6000 cavalry are mounted. This army ought certainly to be able to defend the passes of the Sierra Morena, if the enemy should attack them. I should imagine, however, from the delay of their attack, of which I have heard nothing for the last 2 days, that they do not propose at present to effect more than to oblige the Spaniards to withdraw from the low country into the more unhealthy climate of the mountains.

By the last accounts from Old Castille, it appears that the enemy still remained upon the Tormes. They had collected a large corps in that part of the country, which was under the command of Gen. Kellermann, with which they were watching the movements of the Duque del Parque. The corps d'armée, which was Soult's, is at and in the neighbourhood of Talavera de la Reyna.

The British army is still upon its march, and I expect that the leading divisions will arrive upon the Mondego in the course of 3 or 4 days. I propose to set out from hence on the 25th inst.

The weather has been remarkably fine, and I hope that it will continue till the army shall reach its new position. The health of the troops is much improved; and there are now many convalescents in the hospitals at Elvas and Estremoz nearly sufficiently strong to join their corps.

To the Earl of Liverpool.   Badajoz, 21st Dec. 1809.

I wish to draw your attention to the list of the General officers of this army; and I believe you will admit that, with some exceptions, there never was an army so ill provided. I may say to you in confidence, that I think, if I succeed in executing the arduous task which has devolved upon me, I may fairly say that I had not the best instruments, in either officers or men, which the service could have afforded.

That, however, to which I wish principally to draw your attention is the state of health of Sir J. Sherbrooke. He is at times quite incapable of doing any thing; and he very lately told me that he could not pretend to serve through another summer, and that he must go in April next at latest. The only officers I know of fit to succeed him are Gen. Graham, Gen. Oakes, or Sir G. Prevost. I have put their names down as being all senior to Gen. ——; but if none of them should come, and Gen. —— should be drawn home, there are then Lord W. Bentinck, Gen. Paget, and Sir B. Spencer.

One great difficulty, however, in all arrangements of this description arises from Gen. Beresford's rank in the Portuguese army. I have hitherto succeeded, and I hope I shall still succeed, in keeping down discussions on that subject; but still there is no denying that a Portuguese Marshal and Commander in Chief commands every body excepting the Commanding officer of the British army, and *that* by stipulation; and although there is no senior officer excepting Gen. Beresford who would have accepted, at the time he did, the charge which he has undertaken, his rank occasions heart-burnings, and may occasion difficulties in bringing officers to this army.

But, besides an officer to fill Gen. Sherbrooke's place, we want others to command brigades and posts in the country. I must sometimes allow General officers to go home for their health or on account of their private affairs; and we have not upon such an occasion one to spare. I wish, therefore, you could think of sending me some. Gens. Dyott, Leith, Picton, Meade, Houstoun, Nightingall, I should like to have; but Gen.

Meade is employed, and I fear that Gens. Houstoun and Nightingall would not like to come.

P. S. I beg you will observe that it will be very awkward to send any body here to supersede Gen. Sir J. Sherbrooke before he should be ready to go. When you shall have fixed upon the person, therefore, and will let me know his name, I will consult Gen. Sherbrooke again, and fix the time when his successor shall come out.

To Bart. Frere, Esq.   Badajoz, 22d Dec. 1809.

I was very much obliged to you for your letter of the 17th; and I forwarded your dispatch to Lord Bathurst to Mr. Villiers, according to your desire. I have since heard that the French had again withdrawn from the position at the foot of the Sierra Morena; which I always thought probable, particularly when they should hear of the movement of the British army towards the frontiers of Castille. Owing to the care of the Junta of Badajoz, and that of the Supreme Junta, in publishing my letter to the former, the enemy must have known of this movement at an early period.

I shall go on Monday : I shall write to you whenever I have any thing interesting to communicate; and I shall be glad to hear from you when convenient to you to write. I think it would be very desirable if the Spanish government would establish a regular *parte* * three times a week from Seville to the British army, as far as Elvas; from which place I shall prevail on the Portuguese government to provide for the carriage of the letters. The expense of sending messengers is enormous : but I should have no objection to defray the expense of the *parte*. Will you endeavor to establish it ?

I have received a letter from Lord Liverpool, in which he desires me to send an officer into Catalonia, in order that we may have some accurate knowledge of the state of affairs in that province. What have you done about Col. Doyle in respect of this province? I shall not send any body there till I shall hear again from you.

From accounts which I have from Almeida, I am apprehensive that the War department have not sent orders to Ciudad Rodrigo that Lieut. de Farincourt may be released and sent forward. I shall be obliged to you if you will again mention the subject to Don F. de Saavedra.

To Major Gen. Whittingham.†   Badajoz, 22d Dec. 1809.

I am concerned to hear that the state of your wound has obliged you to go to Gibraltar; but I wish that while you are in that part of the Peninsula, you would take an opportunity of seeing or writing to Gen. Venegas on the subject of the defence of Cadiz. I hope that the enemy are still very far from being able to undertake the siege of that important post. If they should not be so, it is most satisfactory to the whole world to see the defence of it intrusted to such a man as Venegas; and although we ought all to have, and have the utmost confidence in his abilities, I know

_____

* The Spanish and Portuguese term for *estafette* or post.
† Lieut. Colonel, the late Lieut. Gen. Sir S. Whittingham, K.C.B., was then a Major General in the service of Spain.

too much of these affairs not to be certain that the defence of a place of this description is always vigorous and well conducted in proportion to the extent of the preparations made for it, and the length of time which the operations required have been foreseen and have been provided for.

Although I am one of those who are of opinion that the English ought to have nothing to say to Cadiz, yet it cannot be denied that it is a point in the defence of which we are most materially interested, and in which we must co-operate at least with our Navy. Cadiz depends for many articles, and I believe some of the necessaries of life, upon its communication with the sea, in which the most material aid can be given by the British Navy; if, indeed, their co-operation is not deemed essentially necessary for the salvation of the place. Now we all know the length of time which a naval equipment of this description takes; which will not consist only in ships of war and armed craft, but in victuallers, water vessels, &c., which must be fitted up for the purpose. I should, therefore, recommend to Gen. Venegas, at an early period, to turn his mind to a calculation of his probable wants of this description, and to have them communicated to the British government in time, in order that all the preparations may be made, and that the assistance required may be given at the moment it is wanted. I have every confidence, not only in the patriotism and honor, but in the military abilities of Gen. Venegas; and I am convinced he will adopt every measure which prudence and skill can suggest for the defence of the place intrusted to his charge; but having lately visited this famous fortress, I took an opportunity of looking at it, although not so much as I could have wished, or as I should have done, if I had not known that some of the inhabitants might have felt a jealousy of my curiosity.

It occurs to me, however, that it would be most important to Cadiz to finish the work which has been commenced on the isthmus between Cadiz and the Isla de Leon; and I would even go farther, and would recommend the construction of another strong work at the Torre de Ercole, which would secure the communication with the Isla de Leon, and would much impede the advance of the enemy towards the main body of the place. The defence of and communication with the Isla de Leon is a most important consideration for any body who is to conduct the defence of Cadiz itself; and the works constructed, and the troops employed in the defence of this Isla and the approaches to it, would be materially aided, and their retreat to Cadiz covered and secured, in case of accidents, by the construction of the proposed work at the Torre de Ercole.

These are the points to which in particular I would draw the attention of Gen. Venegas, if I were likely to see him; but as that is not probable, I beg you either to see or write to him, and to communicate to him the sentiments which I have above written to you.

To the Rt. Hon. J. Villiers.   Badajoz, 22d Dec. 1809.

I am concerned to be obliged to make any complaint of a *protégé* of yours, but I must say that I think I have some cause to complain of Mr. ——. He was appointed by me to the Commissariat in June, and on the 11th July he writes a letter to the Lords of the Treasury, in which he gives them to understand neither more nor less than that the Commissary Gen., and all his officers, as well as myself, are either knaves or fools ; and that he can save thousands upon thousands to the public, by some new mode he has discovered of supplying the troops with bread. He disclaims, at the same time, any intention of making a charge against any of us!

Now, I must say that, if Mr. —— has made any discovery upon this subject, it was his duty to apprise me of it ; and at least to try whether our failure to save the public these thousands upon thousands was to be attributed to knavery or folly, before he wrote to the Treasury upon the subject.

To J. Murray, Esq., Commissary General.   Badajoz, 24th Dec. 1809.

I beg that you will deliver over to the officers of the Spanish Commissariat, appointed by the Duque de Alburquerque, or by the Junta of Badajoz to receive it, all the wheat, flour, and barley which you have purchased in this country, and which you have not the means of removing from Spain ; and you will take the receipts of those officers for the quantities you will deliver to them, which I will forward to His Majesty's minister at Seville, in order that he may receive the value of these articles from the Spanish government. It will be necessary that you should settle with the Junta of Badajoz the price which the Spanish government shall pay for these articles ; and I request you to take measures accordingly, in concert with Col. Alava, who is employed here by the Duque de Alburquerque.

To the Senate of Estremoz.   Elvas, 25th Dec. 1809.

I have received your memorandum relative to the conduct of the British officers at Estremoz, which has given me much concern ; and I wish that you had mentioned either the names of the officers who have conducted themselves in this shameful manner, or had described their persons, or the regiments to which they belong, or had even mentioned the days on which they passed through Estremoz. It is almost useless to complain of an injury if the name of the person behaving ill is not mentioned. However, I have given orders to the military commanding officer of the hospital to make arrangements upon this subject, which I hope will prevent complaints in future.

To J. Murray, Esq., Commissary General.   Badajoz, 25th Dec. 1809.

I have perused the agreement into which you entered yesterday with the Junta of Badajoz, by my desire, respecting the price to be paid for the wheat, flour, and barley left in this country by the British army, viz. 52 *reals* for each *fanega* of wheat and flour, and 48 *reals* for each *fanega* of barley, in which I fully concur. These prices are not so large as those which you have paid in the country for the same articles; but it must be observed that this large price was probably occasioned by the large demand for the supply of the British army, and that the army having marched, and the demand having ceased, the price must fall.

A larger price might possibly be got by the sale of the articles by auction : but this mode (if the government were disposed to allow of it) would be objectionable at this moment, considering that all the supplies of the country are required for the armies, and that a part of those which we have purchased, the superabundance of which are now to be disposed of, have been procured by the influence of the government. It is besides to be observed that if these articles were to be sold by auction, or in any manner by retail, it would be necessary to leave in the country, to superintend the sale, certain officers of the Commissariat, whose services cannot be spared from the army. I therefore sanction the arrangement which you have made.

To the Rt. Hon. J. Villiers. Badajoz, 27th Dec. 1809.

I have received your letter of the 24th, and I am much concerned that you did not detain my dispatch relative to the Portuguese troops, which was written under a mistake. I understood the arrangement to be as I stated it; but this mistake is one among many proofs that a man should never venture upon an official statement, upon any subject, without having official documents before him. I do not now understand how you check your payments, or whether you pay for 17,000 or 20,000 men. However, this is no business of mine; and I don't wish to have any concern in it, or in the office which you have chalked out for me. You had much better stay and see the game out yourself. I write to you now principally about your money concerns. The Portuguese government wanted £150,000 from us at the end of October to make up a sum to lay in magazines for their army, which, according to a plan suggested by Forjaz, was to be advanced as follows: the pay of 20,000 men for November in advance, and £100,000 on account of a draft on De Sousa in London. This proposition was made when I was at Lisbon in October, and I would not give a positive answer to it till I arrived at Badajoz, and could see the Commissary Gen.

I wrote to you a letter on the 31st Oct., in which I consented to advance the whole sum on account of November's subsidy, and your fourth for October, making altogether £97,000, which you received; and also the £100,000 on account of the draft on De Sousa in two payments, provided the £30,000 bar silver was placed at the disposal of the Commissary Gen. Refer to this letter. Thus you see you have had your subsidy for November, and £70,000 out of the £100,000. I think I shall be able to give you the other £30,000 in a few days. I should certainly have been able to give it, if the Mint had not been extraordinarily slow in coining the silver. I do not see any breach of engagement in all this transaction, excepting in the delay to pay the last £30,000, which may fairly be attributed to the delay in the coinage of the bar silver.

I am glad to find that the government are disposed to aid Portugal with money, but I have informed them that they must send out money; nothing else will answer.

I believe that the Admiral has had the batteries armed. It does not signify one pinch of snuff; we can disarm them in 5 minutes.

I made a dash at De Mello; and I am very glad to find that the government have done upon this subject what they ought.

P.S. As for Mr. ——, I only beg that he will not write letters to the Treasury on subjects which he does not understand.

To Bart. Frere, Esq.   Gafete, 27th Dec. 1809.

I have the honor to enclose the copy of a letter from Brig. Gen. Cox, commanding at Almeida, to Marshal Beresford, together with the enclosures marked Nos. 8, 9, 10, relative to the return of Lieut. V. de Farincourt to Almeida, after a detention in confinement at Ciudad Rodrigo for 6 weeks, —— having received orders from the Spanish government not to allow him to proceed to join the French army by that route.

It is evident to me, that —— had not received the orders which he states that he had received; or that the orders of the contrary tenor were not sent, which Don F. de Saavedra assured you had been sent, as mentioned to me in your letter of the 9th inst. The respect which I have for the character of Don F. de Saavedra induces me to hope that it may turn out that he has not deceived you.

I consider that the feelings of His Majesty, and of the public in general, are so much interested in favor of the brave officers and soldiers who are in the hands of the enemy, only because they were wounded in fighting the battles of Spain, that I cannot any longer delay reporting for His Majesty's information, the unusual difficulties which the Spanish government and officers have thrown in the way of every communication between the French Generals and me which had for its object either the relief or the exchange of these unfortunate persons. I must at the same time do the people of Spain the justice to say, that these difficulties are as inconsistent with their wishes as they are with their interests, or with humanity; as they have done every thing in their power to relieve these officers and soldiers, and have assisted such of them who have escaped from captivity, as much as has been in their power in their passage through the country.

To Dom M. Forjaz.   Gafete, 27th Dec. 1809.

I have had the honor of receiving your letter of the 20th Dec., in which you have enclosed the copy of a letter from the Corregidor of Coimbra, and the copies of a correspondence between that magistrate and an Assist. Commissary of the British army. I am concerned to learn that there exists a scarcity of provisions in that part of the country in which the troops have not been collected since the last harvest; and I had hoped, and still hope, that the scarcity is not so great but that the measures which I have adopted in the British army for the regular settlement of accounts, and early payment for supplies received from time to time from the country, will have the effect of procuring for the troops that assistance in provisions which they may require, and which every country in which an army is obliged to act must afford. However, not relying solely upon the effect of these measures, magazines for the use of the British troops have been fixed on the Mondego and the Douro, to aid in the supply of the demand for provisions.

The other points in your letter being referrible to His Majesty's government, I beg leave to request that you will communicate with His Majesty's minister at Lisbon upon them, from whom alone you can receive an answer. I beg leave to inform you, however, that you are mistaken in supposing that the measures which had been proposed when I was at Lisbon in October, with a view to assist the Portuguese government in collecting magazines of provisions, have not been carried into execution, as far as the funds of the British army were to be employed in giving that assistance.

The assistance to be given consisted in £150,000 sterling, of which £50,000 sterling were to be in advance on account of the pay, &c., of the 20,000 troops; and £100,000 on account of a sum of money expected from S^r. de Sousa in England.

The first mentioned £50,000 were paid immediately; that is, in the end of October. Of the £100,000, £50,000 were paid when the money was demanded, in the beginning of December, by Mr. Villiers; and of the other £50,000, £20,000 have since been paid. The whole sum would have been paid on demand if the silver could have been coined at the Mint in time; and if my expectation of receiving money on account of bills upon England had not been disappointed. But I have no doubt that I shall be enabled to order the issue of the remaining £30,000 on this account in a short time.

As the Governors of the Kingdom may be desirous of having my opinion on the points adverted to in your letter of the 20th inst., notwithstanding that they can receive from Mr. Villiers alone any decisive answer, I proceed to communicate it for their information.

I have not the estimate of the expense of the troops on which is founded the calculation of the monthly sum to be paid by the British government for the 20,000 men; but I have always understood that the expense of provisions for these 20,000 men was included in the estimate. If my understanding on this subject be correct, the British government will not be disposed to defray the expense of forming magazines for these troops, when they already pay the expense of their provisions in the monthly sum paid by His Majesty's minister at Lisbon to the Portuguese government. But although the British government will not defray the expense of the formation of magazines for the Portuguese army, it may be thought that the state of the supplies of grain in Portugal may require the assistance of Great Britain. Upon this point I am concerned to add, that from what I see of the prices of provisions in England, and from what I have heard of the produce of the last harvest, I have reason to believe that Great Britain could not afford any considerable export of grain to Portugal, excepting what may be necessary for the British army, in addition to the magazines now in Portugal, in order to aid the supplies which the army must continue to receive from the country; and it will be necessary that this country should look to a supply from the Western Islands, from the Mediterranean, and from America.

I have no doubt that this supply can be procured with money; and that His Majesty's government will be disposed to exert their influence to procure for Portugal every assistance of this description. But it will be necessary that the importers of this grain should be certain of a sale; and that the purchase should not be refused by the government, as in the late instance of the wheat imported into Lisbon by Mr. Phillips, of which the late Minister of Finance declined the purchase, notwithstanding the offer made by me to facilitate it as much as was in my power.

This circumstance will appear still more extraordinary, now that it is stated that there exists a scarcity in the country, of which the Minister of Finance must have had a knowledge at the time.

To Vice Adm. the Hon. G. Berkeley.   Gaviaõ, 28th Dec. 1809.

I have received your letter respecting the boats, &c., and I have given directions to the Commissary Gen. according to your suggestions.

I omitted to answer a part of a former letter from you, which related to the period at which vessels should be sent to Cadiz and to Gibraltar for the money for the army, upon which I wished to have some discussion with the Commissary Gen. before I gave you an answer. He says, what indeed I know to be true, that it is impossible for him to fix the periods at which his agents at those places will have money in their hands. This depends entirely upon the money market, and very much upon the periods of the sailing and of the arrival of the packets. I have written to England upon this subject, to endeavor to have regularity established in those communications, which will, I hope, tend to the relief of our pecuniary difficulties in some degree, as well as give us such a knowledge of the state of the money markets as to enable us to fix the periods at which vessels should be sent to bring our money away from Cadiz and Gibraltar.

To Bart. Frere, Esq.   Gaviaõ, 28th Dec. 1809.

I enclose a letter which Brig. Gen. Cox has written to Marshal Beresford, with its enclosures, being a proposition from the Duque del Parque, that a certain quantity of biscuit which he had heard was in the magazines at Almeida should be placed at his disposal, in order to provide, as he says, for any sudden movement which the army under his command might be obliged to make. I think this proposition rather extraordinary, particularly considering the person who makes it, who refused to allow Marshal Beresford to have a quantity of biscuit from Ciudad Rodrigo, although actually purchased and paid for by a British Commissary ; and considering the whole of his conduct towards the British and Portuguese army. However, I am not disposed to consider offences of this description, when the safety of an army is at stake. The biscuit in question was lodged at Almeida by my direction, in order to

---

G. O.   Gaviaõ, 28th Dec. 1809.

The Commander of the Forces requests that the officers commanding divisions will direct the officers of the Q. M. G.'s department attached to them respectively to arrange with the magistrates of the different towns and villages in which the troops may be cantoned, in what houses General officers, Field officers, captains, and subalterns, respectively, shall be quartered; and the officers are to be quartered according to this arrangement.

The Commander of the Forces is concerned to notice that complaints of the conduct of some of the officers of the army to the inhabitants of Portugal have already reached him, and he is convinced that it must be of those who have lately joined the army, and were not partakers of the kindness with which the whole army were treated by the people of this country at the commencement of the campaign.

There is no doubt that by civility and good treatment the officers of the army will receive from the inhabitants of Portugal again all the assistance and kindness which they can afford, and the Commander of the Forces is exceedingly anxious that the people of this country should not be brought by the misconduct of the army to detest those who are sent here to assist them in the defence of their country. He particularly desires that the officers on the Commissariat and medical Staff will pay attention to these orders, and that the Com. Gen. will send a copy of them to each of the commissaries who are detached.

enable me to draw the British army to that quarter, in case the enemy should have attacked Ciudad Rodrigo.

From the accounts which I have received of the state of the supplies in that part of Portugal, I have reason to believe that it will be very inconvenient to allow the Spanish army to have any part of this magazine; and if I should find this to be the case, it cannot be expected that I should allow the Duque del Parque to have it. Neither will I allow him to have it, in order to enable him to undertake an operation of the same description with that in which he lately nearly lost his army. But if I should find that the British or Portuguese army do not want the magazine, or if it can be replaced, I shall have no objection to afford the Spanish army the assistance which I can give them.

The situation of the army under the Duque del Parque, however, deserves the serious consideration of the government. If they begin already to require the assistance of the British and Portuguese magazines, their distress will be very great before the winter is over, and some serious steps ought to be taken for their relief. With this view, I would recommend to the government to send money into Estremadura, without which it will be impossible for the Junta of that province to forward to the Duque del Parque the supplies of provisions which I know it has in its power, as the British army gave them a considerable quantity solely upon their receipts.

I would also recommend that fast sailing and well equipped vessels should be sent from Cadiz to the mouth of the Mondego, loaded with biscuit, and whatever else this army may require. Unless the weather should be very bad, the cargoes can be landed at Buarcos, at about a league from Figueira, from whence the Mondego affords water carriage to within 20 leagues of Ciudad Rodrigo; and I should think there would be no difficulty in sending carriages from Ciudad Rodrigo to draw up the provisions from the landing place. I suggest this plan in case want of money, or any other cause with which I am unacquainted, should prevent the government from supplying this army from Estremadura.

To the Earl of Liverpool. Gaviaõ, 28th Dec. 1809.

I have the honor to enclose the copy of a letter which I have received from Marshal Beresford relative to the refusal of His Majesty's government to supply the Portuguese cavalry with arms, and relative to the want of muskets and accoutrements in Portugal for the militia. I beg to refer your Lordship to my dispatch of the 14th Nov., upon the subject of the assistance which I expected from the whole Portuguese regular army and militia in the contest in which we are likely to be engaged in this country.

I likewise enclose the translation of a letter which I have received from Dom M. Forjaz, the Sec. of State for the War department of the government of Portugal, upon the distress of this country for the want of provisions, and the copy of my answer. It is probable that Mr. Villiers will address His Majesty's ministers upon the subjects to which these letters relate.

I believe that Portugal has never produced a sufficient quantity of grain for its consumption; but from all the information I have received, I have no reason to believe that the harvest has failed this year; and the part of the country in which the scarcity is stated to exist is among the most fertile and best cultivated in Portugal. I conceive, therefore, that the difficulty in procuring provisions, if it exists, is to be attributed to the want of money by the government. In fact the Portuguese government have, since the restoration, been in the habit of taking provisions from the inhabitants of the country without paying for them, or even settling accounts. The people now conceal their provisions, and refuse to continue to furnish supplies, and the troops are distressed; and this concealment of the supplies of the country, and refusal to furnish them, and the distress for want of provisions suffered by the troops, will continue till the revenue shall be brought nearer to the necessary expenditure of the country.

These statements will show your Lordship the difficulties of the situation of this country, which must be felt more or less by the British army employed in co-operating in its defence, and can be alleviated only by the prompt and efficacious assistance of His Majesty's government. Portugal has no expectation of pecuniary or other assistance from Brazil, or from any of its foreign possessions; there is no manufacture of arms in this country; and it must depend for its means of defence upon the supplies which Great Britain will afford.

His Majesty's government must be the best judges whether it is proper to continue the war in the Peninsula; and whether the best mode of opposing the enemy in the Peninsula is by an exertion to create a military force in Portugal. But it is evident that we shall fail in producing the exertion of which this country is capable, and which the government and inhabitants are certainly willing to make, for want of means, unless His Majesty's government should be able to assist Portugal with money as well as with arms, and the other equipments, for which I have sent to England requisitions at different times.

To the Earl of Liverpool.   Gaviaõ, 28th Dec. 1809.

The enemy withdrew from La Mancha about the 18th inst., without having made any attempt to attack the passes of the Sierra Morena; and their object in their late expedition must have been to oblige the Spanish troops to withdraw from the plains into the more unhealthy climate of the hills. I think also that there is reason to believe that they had heard about that time of the march of the British army across the Tagus, as a letter from me to the Junta of Badajoz, apprising them of this intended move-ment, and written in the beginning of December, had been very indiscreetly published, first in the Badajoz newspaper, and afterwards in that of Seville. It is probable that the receipt of this intelligence, and that of a serious insurrection in Biscay, had induced the French to withdraw their troops again from La Mancha.

I have not heard that the troops in Castille have been reinforced, or have materially altered their position since I last addressed your Lordship. The Duque del Parque is still in the neighbourhood of Ciudad Rodrigo; and I understand that his troops are suffering the greatest distress for the want of provisions. He has collected again a force amounting to 20,000 men.

I have heard that Gerona has fallen, but not from authority on which I can place reliance.

To the Earl of Liverpool. Gaviaõ, 28th Dec. 1809.

I have to request that 1500 pickaxes and mattocks, and 300 felling axes, may be sent to Lisbon, for the use of the British army.

To Col. Peacocke. Gaviaõ, 28th Dec. 1809.

I shall be to-morrow at Abrantes, on the 30th and 31st at Thomar, and on the 1st Jan. at Leiria. You will send your messengers accordingly.

To the Earl of Liverpool. Gaviaõ, 29th Dec. 1809.

Since I closed my dispatch of yesterday, I have received intelligence on which I rely, stating that Gerona had surrendered on the 11th inst.

To Col. Don M. de Alava. Pombal, ce 2 Janvier, 1810.

J'ai reçu à Abrantes le 29 du mois passé votre lettre du 27, pour laquelle je vous suis bien obligé.

Par les nouvelles que nous venons de recevoir de Londres du 20 Déc., il paraît que c'est l'intention de Buonaparte de venir lui-même en Espagne. Il en a parlé dans son discours au Sénat; et Berthier est déjà nommé Major Général de l'armée d'Espagne, qu'on dit devait être renforcée de 100,000 hommes. Mais dans son discours au Sénat il ne parle plus de conquête en Espagne, mais des moyens sages et de la modération. Il ne viendra pas ici pour cela.

Je vous serai bien obligé, si vous avez quelque chose à me communiquer que vous croyez pouvoir intéresser le corps d'armée que j'ai laissé sur le Tage à Abrantes, si vous voulez envoyer votre lettre sous cachet volant adressée au Général Hill à Abrantes; ou, si vous le préférez, d'avoir la bonté de lui écrire.

L'armée du Duque del Parque est dans la Sierra de Gata. Il veut emprunter de la cavalerie Anglaise pour aller attaquer l'ennemi.

To Bart. Frere, Esq. Pombal, 2d Jan. 1810.

I received at Abrantes, on the 29th, your letters of the 26th, for which I am much obliged to you. I now send you some letters from England, which were enclosed to me.

I have no news for you, excepting to tell you that I have received a letter from Col. Carroll, from Viseu, dated the 30th Dec., in which he informs me that the Duque del Parque proposes to force his way into Galicia; and he has proposed that I should lend him 2000 cavalry, to enable him to act offensively against the enemy. His army was, on the 24th, in the Sierra de Gata; head quarters at San Martin de Trebejo. I think that Gen. Doyle ought to go to Catalonia without loss of time, and to transmit to us every intelligence he can procure.

To Lieut. Gen. Hill. Pombal, 2d Jan. 1810.

I enclose a return of the number of artificers which Capt. Patton requires at Abrantes, in order to enable him to complete the works at that place, which are very important in every point of view. I shall be obliged to you if you will assist him with as many (not exceeding the numbers of each description stated in the enclosed paper) as you can afford from the British troops under your command.

I request you to read the enclosed letter to Lieut. Col. Grant, of the Lusitanian legion, and desire the magistrate at Abrantes to forward it to him to Castello Branco. I also request you to desire the messenger to leave the enclosed letter for Gen. Payne at Portalegre, if he should not already have come from thence to Abrantes.

To Lieut. Gen. Payne.　　　　　　　　　　　　　　　Pombal, 2d Jan. 1810.

I am much concerned that you have been stopped on your march by so troublesome a companion as the gout, but I hope that you will soon recover.

I shall make inquiry respecting the cause of the want of forage at Portalegre. Repeated starving, in the midst of plenty, is too bad.

Among other reinforcements coming out are the 13th light dragoons, which will give us more cavalry in this country than we could feed with convenience, or than, according to present appearances, we shall require. However, there is no harm in having them at Lisbon, and there they shall remain for the present.

You will see by the letters from the Horse Guards, of which I have requested Lieut. Col. Bathurst to transmit you copies, that there is no objection to our detaining, for the present, a part of the 23d light dragoons, but that they must not be allowed to enlist with any other regiments. You will also observe what the Commander in Chief directs respecting the men of the 2d hussars K.G.L.

To the Rt. Hon. J. Villiers.　　　　　　　　　　　　Pombal, 2d Jan. 1810.

I have received your letters of the 25th and 26th; and I send by this messenger copies of the dispatch and letter which I received from the Sec. of State, respecting the additional subsidy to be paid to the Portuguese government. I conclude that you will have received a counterpart from Lord Wellesley, or from Lord Bathurst; but lest you should not, I hope that you will make the necessary communication to the Portuguese government, founded upon the enclosed dispatch.

I have requested Beresford to send you a plan for the augmentation of the pay of the officers of the army, the expense of which will be defrayed by this subsidy of £130,000 sterling. I shall not write to the Portuguese government upon this or upon the other part of the subject, till I shall hear that you have communicated with them; and then only to urge and support the measure which you will propose.

I have not seen the Commissary Gen. since I received your letter, nor shall I see him till I shall be at Coimbra to-morrow; but I know that he can give the Portuguese government provisions only in the way in which he can give them money, by depriving the British troops of them.

I believe there never was any officer, but certainly never a British officer, placed in so difficult a situation as I am in. Every body looks for British assistance in every thing: money, stores, provisions, and all that keep an army together, are required by both Spaniards and Portuguese; and they and the British nation, and even the government, conceive that I have all at my command, and that I have only to say the *word* to supply all their wants, and satisfy all their demands. The fact is, however, that I have not more than enough for my own army, and I have received the order of the government to give nothing. I can suggest no means of procuring the money required to keep the armies together, excepting that government should send money out. I have told them so repeatedly; and I have lately requested Lord Liverpool to send out £200,000. God knows whether it will arrive or not!

As soon as I shall see the Commissary Gen., I will let you know what your proportion is of our receipts of December, and will give an order that it may be issued to you.

You see the dash which the Common Council of the city of London have made at me! I act with a sword hanging over me, which will fall upon me whatever may be the result of affairs here; but they may do what they please, I shall not give up the game here as long as it can be played.

To the Earl of Liverpool. Pombal, 2d Jan. 1810.

I have received your letter respecting the transmission of the weekly states, which shall go to you regularly. The Horse Guards, however, might at any time have given the government any information which they could want regarding the state of the army.

I have lately had a return made out showing the total loss of the army in dead since I took the command in April last; which is only 4500 men, including the battle of Talavera, &c. Besides which, there are 1500 prisoners. This is about one third of the loss which the French compute that they suffered in about the same period of time.

I see that the Common Council of the city of London have desired that my conduct should be inquired into; and I think it probable that the answer which the King will give to this address will be consistent with the approbation which he has expressed of the acts which the gentlemen wish to make the subject of inquiry; and that they will not be well pleased. I cannot expect mercy at their hands, whether I succeed or fail; and if I should fail, they will not inquire whether the failure is owing to my own incapacity, to the blameless errors to which we are all liable, to the faults or mistakes of others, to the deficiency of our means, to the serious difficulties of our situation, or to the great power and abilities of our enemy. In any of these cases, I shall become their victim; but I am not to be alarmed by this additional risk, and whatever may be the consequences, I shall continue to do my best in this country.

I wrote to you the other day about General officers. I only beg you not to send me any violent party men. We must keep the spirit of party out of the army, or we shall be in a bad way indeed.

To Vice Adm. the Hon. G. Berkeley. Coimbra, 3d Jan. 1810.

I have received your letter of the 26th Dec., and I really knew so little of the origin and progress of the enforcement of the claim of the army to the salvage of the British ships at Oporto, and particularly of the employment of Mr. ——, that I do not know what answer to give you. It appears, or rather Mr. —— says, that my brother Henry employed him to enforce the claim of the army, which I think very improbable, as he certainly has never said or written one word to me upon the subject; and Mr. Greenwood has written me no answer to the letter which I wrote to

Gen. J. Murray, and in which I required that he should find out what directions my brother had given.

1 You have the copy of my letter to Gen. Murray upon this subject, in which you will see how little I knew of Mr. ——, and particularly what I thought of the claim of the navy. I have now had no answer to that letter which can satisfy me respecting Mr. ——'s character, or respecting the propriety of my sending him any directions which might have the effect of sanctioning all his first proceedings, and the expenses which he will charge for them. I think, therefore, that I ought to begin to act for the army from the commencement, either in conjunction or in concert with you; but, before I take this step, I should wish to have an opportunity of talking over the subject with some of the General officers interested in the case, whom I shall have an opportunity of seeing in a few days. My opinion is, that Mr. —— has proceeded without any authority. If I know my brother well, I am convinced that he would not have authorised his proceedings without consulting or informing me of them, particularly in a case in which an army is concerned. Gen. Murray is not in town, and has not had an opportunity of ascertaining this most important point. In respect to the Danish ships, I have written to Col. Trant, to desire that he will not prevent their sailing whenever or wherever you may think proper to order them, taking from the captains security for the vessels and cargoes, in case they should be deemed prizes. You are already aware of my opinion upon this part of the question; and I much fear that the whole will be considered as property in a neutral port.

If the Duke of Richmond has acted as you say he has, of which I know him to be very capable, he has behaved most handsomely towards Lord Wellesley.

I am glad that you concur in the measures which were adopted respecting De Mello. I think that we have put an end to all the plans for resigning commissions by common consent, &c. &c., and that we shall go on very quietly in future. The Marquez das Minas is much mistaken if he supposes that any thing he can do can shake the English in Portugal. We have done, we continue to do, and I hope shall still do much good in Portugal; and the benefit of the King's protection is too well appreciated by the Portuguese in general, and the general confidence in us too strong, to be shaken by any line he can take; and he had much better take care of himself, than attempt to injure Marshal Beresford, or the English interest.

I am much obliged to you for the offer of your boat. I could not quit Badajoz till the whole army had left Spain, and I was obliged to be in this quarter as soon as possible after they commenced arriving here; so that I had no time to go to Lisbon while the troops were on their march, which I should otherwise have wished to have done.

To Lieut. Gen. Sir J. Sherbrooke, K.B.   Coimbra, 3d Jan. 1810.

I arrived here this day, having been detained at Badajoz till the 25th, and having stopped one day at Thomar to see the Portuguese troops. I received your letter of the 30th yesterday morning, at Leiria.

Gen. Bacellar is not to collect at Viseu the recruits levied in Beira; but they are to go to Abrantes; the horses likewise.

I shall be with you in a few days; but I am obliged to stop here to settle all the affairs of our supplies, which I still hope will be sufficient. The money for the army will be here to-morrow; and I wish you would order the paymasters of your division to come here as soon as they please, to receive the balance due on their estimates to the 24th Dec. I would send the money on, only that the Paymaster's department have marched with me, and are in some degree knocked up. You shall have barley also, as well as money, I hope, before long.

P.S. I send the letters for your division. Pray forward the messenger with my letter for Gen. Craufurd, at Celorico or Pinhel.

To Brig. Gen. R. Craufurd.   Coimbra, 3d Jan. 1810.

I arrived here this day, having been detained at Badajoz till the 25th Dec.

On your arrival at your station, I request you will communicate with Brig. Gen. Cox at Almeida, and obtain from him all the information you can of the enemy's force, position, &c., upon the frontier. I request also that you will endeavor, through Gen. Cox, to communicate with Capt. Ruman, who is employed to get intelligence on the frontiers of Castille, and desire him to send you all his reports, directed to me, which you will of course peruse. I shall desire Col. Carroll, who is employed with the Duque del Parque's army, to write to you constantly. You will also endeavor to establish for yourself any other sources of intelligence which you may think fit, the expense of which I shall defray.

We have a store of provisions in Almeida, from which you will draw what you may require, if it should be necessary; but do not use it unless it be absolutely so. Your Commissary will find Torre de Moncorvo to be a very fertile district. I shall desire Mr. Murray to send him a supply of money, which I observe is the best persuasive to the people of the country to give their supplies.

I wish that you would desire Capt. Campbell, and any other officers in your division who are capable of it, to examine the course of the Coa, which runs by Almeida, and to report upon it; and likewise the course of the Agueda, if the position of the enemy should allow it. I will defray the expenses of the latter while employed on this service.

I shall be here for some days, in order that I may arrange every thing relating to our supplies; and hereafter I shall fix my head quarters at Viseu, and shall go forward to pay you a visit.

P.S. Do not work the hussars at Pinhel by sending them with letters. I should prefer to pay a messenger. Gen. Sherbrooke's division is at Viseu, and towards Celorico and Trancoso. The 4th division will be at Celorico, Guarda, and Pinhel.

To the Earl of Liverpool.   Coimbra, 3d Jan. 1810.

Having communicated to the King's minister at Lisbon my dispatch to your Lordship of the 19th Dec., relative to the arrangements under which His Majesty pays for 20,000 Portuguese troops, I find that I so far mis-understood that arrangement, and misinformed your Lordship, as that there are certain regiments in the Portuguese service, as per margin, which are understood to be paid by Great Britain. But the money is paid to the Portuguese government for the expenses of these regiments, and by the Portuguese government through their officers to the troops. The Portuguese government also defray all the expenses of the troops which the grant from His Majesty is intended to cover.

This arrangement was made before I arrived in Portugal, and I never had any official information of it; and I knew only that the Portuguese government received about £500,000 in payment of the expenses of 20,000 men, which resource is carried to account in the statement which I transmitted of their finance in my dispatch of the 14th Nov.

I have received your Lordship's dispatch of the 15th Dec. I cannot with propriety make any communication to the Portuguese government on the part of His Majesty, and I have therefore sent to the King's minister at Lisbon a copy of the dispatch, in order that he may make the necessary communications upon it to the Portuguese government. He will, I doubt not, endeavor to make such an arrangement with the Portuguese government for the distribution of the aid which His Majesty is pleased to give them as will be satisfactory to His Majesty's government; and I shall do every thing in my power to prevail upon the Portuguese government to adopt the arrangement which Mr. Villiers will propose, and to facilitate its execution.

In my dispatch of the 14th Nov., I intended to state £500,000 (the pay, &c. of 20,000 men) as the whole pecuniary resource received by the Portuguese government from Great Britain. Besides this sum, the expense of the pay and allowances to the British officers lent by His Majesty to the Portuguese government, amounting to about £100,000, is paid by Great Britain, making in all an expense of £600,000, which His Majesty incurred in aid of Portugal at the time I wrote that dispatch.

Effective strength.

No. 1	1356
2	1355
3	857
4	1544
7	1261
10	1449
11	1535
13	1275
14	1252
15	1128
16	1515
19	1351
	15,878

Chasseurs.

No. 1	627
3	589
4	624
	1,840

Total.
17,718

To Bart. Frere, Esq.   Coimbra, 3d Jan. 1810.

I received this morning your letter of the 29th Dec. The Marques de la Romana, and you, must be better judges of the wants of the respective provinces and armies of Spain for arms than I can be; and I concur entirely with you and him in the proposed distribution of the 10,000 stand expected from England, viz., 6000 stand to the Duque de Alburquerque's army, and 4000 stand to Valencia and Catalonia.

To the Rt. Hon. J. Villiers.   Coimbra, 4th Jan. 1810.

Since I wrote to you yesterday, I have seen the Commissary General, and the only mode which occurs to us in which we can assist the Portuguese government with more money than we have already given them, or with provisions, is by giving bills upon England, for any cargoes of provisions which they may purchase from merchant importers. It is important, however, that they should observe that we are purchasing in this manner; and that they should take care to avoid all competition with us, which would only have the effect of raising the price upon both parties.

I send you my dispatches open for your perusal.

I have seen several Portuguese battalions on my road through the country, and I am happy to inform you that some of them are in very good order, and all of them very forward in discipline. They are, in general, ailing; principally for the want of those articles of clothing, appointments, and necessaries, which all soldiers require in order to keep them healthy.

To Col. Peacocke.   Coimbra, 4th Jan. 1810.

I have been informed by the Sec. of State to the government of Portugal that certain officers in the garrison of Lisbon lately went in a masonic procession through the streets of the city, from the citadel to the British factory. I have no doubt but that this act was innocently committed by those concerned in it; but I have to inform you that the procession, the insignia, and the existence of Free-masonry, are contrary to the law in Portugal; and adverting to circumstances which have recently occurred at Lisbon, and to the reports in circulation of the causes of the confinement of different individuals by the government, I should have believed it impossible that it was not already known that these proceedings were illegal, if the persons concerned in them were not British officers. I am informed that this procession was most offensive to many persons in Lisbon, who are at least equally attached to the laws of the country as we are to those of our own; and that nothing prevented the expression of the general indignation by a riot, excepting the respect for the British character, and the hope entertained by the majority of the people that the violation of the law was to be attributed to ignorance of its provisions.

I beg of you to communicate the contents of this letter to the Commanding officers of regiments, and principal officers of the army at Lisbon, and that you will state to them my wish that the meeting of the masonic lodges in their corps, and the wearing of all masonic emblems, and all masonic processions, may be discontinued during the time they may be in Portugal.

To Lieut. Col. Torrens, Military Secretary.   Coimbra, 4th Jan. 1810.

I enclose a representation of Colin Campbell's case, which he has sent me; and I shall be obliged to you if you will lay it before the Commander in Chief.

You are aware how much I am interested in his promotion; and I shall be very much obliged to you if you will urge the Commander in Chief to promote him, either by brevet or otherwise, upon an early occasion.

To the Earl of Liverpool.   Coimbra, 4th Jan. 1810.

In my progress through Portugal to this place I have had opportunities of seeing 15 regiments in the Portuguese service, and I have great pleasure in informing your Lordship that the progress of all these troops in discipline is considerable; that some of the regiments are in very good order; and that I have no doubt but that the whole will prove a useful acquisition to the country. The troops are in general unhealthy, owing principally to the want of those articles of clothing and necessaries, without which all soldiers must suffer in the winter. But it is to be hoped that the early arrival of these articles from England will put a stop to this sickness.

The pains taken by Marshal Beresford, and all the British officers serving under his command, to bring the Portuguese army to the state in which it now is, are highly deserving of His Majesty's approbation.

To the Earl of Liverpool.   Coimbra, 4th Jan. 1810.

There has been no material alteration in the position either of the allied armies, or of the enemy, since I addressed you on the 28th of last month. It appears that the enemy had left 10,000 men in La Mancha to observe the Spanish corps in the Sierra Morena; and that a great part of the enemy's force in that part of Spain had moved to the northward by the road of Guadalaxara.

Gen. Areyzaga had, by the last accounts, collected 24,000 infantry, the whole of them armed. I cannot ascertain the number of mounted cavalry. I understand that he had proposed to the government another movement into the plains of La Mancha to attack the French.

The Duque del Parque's army is in the Sierra de Gata, much reduced in numbers, and in great distress for want of provisions.

To Bart. Frere, Esq.   Coimbra, 6th Jan. 1810.

I enclose the copy of a letter which I have received from Col. Carroll, expressing the desire of the Duque del Parque that I should lend him the British cavalry to aid in another offensive operation against the enemy in Castille; and expressing his Excellency's intention to move his army to the frontiers of Galicia; to which I have returned the answer of which I enclose the copy.

I also think it proper to communicate to you the copy of a letter written by the Duque del Parque to the Junta of Estremadura on the 24th Dec., the day on which Col. Carroll informed me of his Excellency's intention to move towards Galicia, announcing to the Junta of Estrema-

---

G. A. O.   Coimbra, 5th Jan. 1810.

1. As the profession of Free-masonry is contrary to the law of Portugal, the Commander of the Forces requests that the meetings of the lodges existing in the several corps, the use of masonic badges and emblems, and the appearances of the officers and soldiers in masonic processions may be discontinued, while the troops will be in this country. The Commander of the Forces is convinced, that the officers and soldiers of the army will feel the necessity of obeying the laws of the country which they are sent to protect, and that they will show their respect for the attachment of the people of Portugal to their own laws, by refraining from an amusement which, however innocent in itself, and allowed by the law of Great Britain, is a violation of the law of this country, and very disagreeable to the people.

2. The officers of the army are informed, that the government of Portugal have lately issued a decree, by which they have called upon all persons having horses of a description fit for the Portuguese cavalry, to send them to certain depôts formed for their reception, without loss of time; and as the government have been informed that some of the horse dealers and others have offered their horses for sale to the officers of the British army, the Commander of the Forces wishes to warn the officers of the army, those persons who shall thus dispose of them will be guilty of a breach of the law of the country; and that the purchasers of the horses of this description, after the date of the decree in question, will be liable to lose the horses they shall have purchased. Horses fit for cavalry service are 15 hands.

dura that he had taken a position in the Sierra de Gata, with a view to protect the province of Estremadura against the incursions of the enemy.

To Lieut. Col. Carroll.   Coimbra, 6th Jan. 1810.

I have had the honor of receiving your letters of the 24th and 30th Dec. and 2d Jan., to which I should have replied sooner, if I had not expected to have the pleasure of seeing you here; but as I am concerned to observe from your letter of the 2d that you are indisposed, I now proceed to reply to the requests made by the Duque del Parque.

It appears that his Excellency is desirous of undertaking another offensive operation against the enemy in Old Castille, for which purpose he requires the assistance of the British cavalry. I beg you to inform his Excellency that I remain at this moment of the same opinion which I had the honor of communicating to him through Brig. Gen. Cox on the 25th Sept. last, regarding the proposed offensive operations, which opinion recent events in Castille and La Mancha have only tended to confirm; and that the British cavalry is only sufficient for the purposes of the British army, and that I cannot allow it to be employed with any other body of troops.

To Col. Don M. de Alava.   Coimbra, ce 6 Janvier, 1810.

J'ai reçu seulement ce matin votre lettre du 29 Décembre. Je vous prie de dire au Duque de Alburquerque que je n'ai point d'armes dans ce pays-ci, mais qu'on en attend d'Angleterre à Cadiz tous les jours; et que j'ai écrit à M. Frere pour le prier d'en donner 6 mille à l'armée du Duque de Alburquerque, ce qui est arrangé. Je n'ai rien de nouveau ici.

To Lieut. Col. Carroll.   Coimbra, 6th Jan. 1810.

I have had the honor of receiving your letter of the 2d inst.; and as you are employed with the Spanish army under the command of the Duque del Parque, principally with a view to make the government, and His Majesty's servants and officers employed in Spain and Portugal, acquainted with the operations of that army, I can but recommend to you to place yourself in such a situation upon all occasions, as that you may have the best opportunity of procuring information which will enable you to give those to whom you will report a correct idea of the transactions to which your reports relate.

I am convinced that you will attribute this recommendation to my earnest desire that your reports may be of a nature to enable His Majesty's government, and his servants and officers in the Peninsula, to found their measures upon them.

To the Rt. Hon. J. Villiers.   Coimbra, 6th Jan. 1810.

I received in the night your several letters of the 1st and 3d inst., and the Commissary Gen. has shown me your letter to him, requiring £300,000 for the Portuguese government. It is needless to tell you that we cannot give one dollar of the sum. It is very obvious to me that Great Britain has undertaken more than she can afford in this country. I will not pledge the British government to pay money for Portugal, which I am not certain that I shall be able to pay; nor will I allow a

British Commissary to go into the market with a semblance of British credit, which is afterwards to be supported by Portuguese money. I have always said that we were going beyond our means in this country, and the truth is now discovered; and I must find out measures to bolster up the deficiency of money and of credit by the Portuguese government. I have written to England for money, which is the only resource.

I have no objection to any gentleman dedicating to me his work; but I cannot give my formal sanction to his doing so without reading and considering the work, and seeing whether it is of a nature to deserve that recommendation to the public. I have not leisure for this, and I therefore return the gentleman's paper.

The government wrote to me respecting the masonic procession; and I enclose the copy of a letter to Col. Peacocke, and of an order which I have issued upon that subject. I also enclose the copy of a letter which I have written upon it to Dom M. Forjaz. It is very irregular that he should write to me upon matters exclusively relating to the British troops. He ought to write to you upon these subjects.

To the Earl of Liverpool.   Coimbra, 6th Jan. 1810.
Having observed a considerable difference in the reports transmitted by Col. Carroll of recent events in Castille, and those transmitted by others of the same events, I have the honor to enclose a correspondence which I have had with that officer on the subject.

Although I have no longer any control over the officers thus employed to report the operations of the Spanish armies, I trust that my interference in this affair will be approved of; as it must be of the first importance to His Majesty that the information furnished to his government, and his servants and officers in the Peninsula, should be accurately correct.

To Vice Adm. the Hon. G. Berkeley.   Coimbra, 9th Jan. 1810.
I have had the honor of receiving your letter of the 4th inst., and I am much obliged to you for the measures you have adopted respecting the boats for Abrantes, and the transport to be anchored in the Tagus. Villa Nova is the point in the river used in the communication with the great body of the army, and probably it would be most convenient that the transport should be anchored there. The officers and couriers, however, who go by land, do not pass by Villa Nova.

The Commissary Gen. has already received my directions to make as much use as may be possible of the harbour of Figueira for the communication; and he has in the service a certain number of schooners for that purpose. Doubts are entertained in this part of the country, whether the harbour of Figueira can be used even by these schooners throughout the winter; but probably you have better information upon it than we can have. From all that I know, however, of the state of this harbour, I should doubt whether it would be possible at this season of the year to make use of it to remove the sick to Lisbon.

To Vice Adm. the Hon. G. Berkeley.   Coimbra, 9th Jan. 1810.
I am very much obliged to you for your attention to our probable

wants, and I will apply to you when we shall require your assistance. I fear it is now too late in the season to make use of any of the harbours for our communications, excepting so far as we have already got a depôt at the mouth of the Mondego.

I rear that the couriers would lose much time by going to S. Martinho, which is at least 8 leagues from the road, and no post horses on the line; the whole between Leiria and Lisbon being only 20 leagues, with post horses conveniently stationed; and there does not appear any prospect of our wanting to communicate with any of the posts on the coast.

To Col. Murray, Q. M. G.   Coimbra, 9th Jan. 1810.

I have perused the letter which you have sent to me from Major Sturgeon, of the Staff corps, relative to the means of procuring information at Ceclavim; and I beg that you will tell Major Sturgeon that I am willing to make the following arrangement for that purpose:

1st; To give ———— ———— 100 dollars a month for all the information which he will give, so long as I shall find this information to be at all founded on fact, or useful. If he should accept this offer, he shall receive the money on the 1st of every month from the commanding officer at Almeida, as long as I shall continue to pay it.

2dly; If he should bring any information of an important nature upon which I can rely, and I should find it to be true, I shall reward him in proportion to the value of the information.

3dly; Besides the 100 dollars *per mensem* mentioned in the 1st article, 4 dollars shall be paid for every letter, containing information, sent either to Lieut. Gen. Hill at Abrantes, or to Brig. Gen. Cox at Almeida.

If ———— ———— should accede to these propositions, Major Sturgeon will let me know it, in order that I may give the necessary directions to Lieut. Gen. Hill to pay for the letters according to the 3d article. I should also wish ———— ———— to send his letters to Lieut. Gen. Hill at Abrantes, as well as those for me at Almeida.

P.S. Lieut. Gen. Hill knows that he may expect letters from this person, and I have desired him to pay 4 dollars for each letter.

To Marshal Beresford.   Coimbra, 9th Jan. 1810.

I have the honor to enclose complaints which I have received of the conduct of Capt. ————, of the Lusitanian legion. If these complaints are well founded, Capt. ———— is a very improper person to be employed as an officer in the Portuguese army; and if he has threatened or forced a British sentry on duty, in whatever character, I imagine that a General Court Martial will not deem him a fit person to be an officer in His Majesty's service.

I recommend to you, therefore, that, if you should see sufficient cause in the enclosed papers, you should advise the Regency to dismiss him from the Portuguese service, that you should order him into arrest, and to report himself to Lieut. Gen. Hill at Abrantes, who will have my directions respecting the disposal of him.

To Lieut. Gen. Payne.   Coimbra, 9th Jan. 1810.

Circumstances may render it necessary that Lieut. Gen. Hill's division
of infantry, and other Portuguese troops, should move forward again to
Portalegre: in which case, I should wish to have them joined and supported by Brig. Gen. Slade's brigade of cavalry, and I accordingly request
that you will order this brigade to march, if you should receive a requisition to do so from Lieut. Gen. Hill.

To Lieut. Gen. Hill.   Coimbra, 9th Jan. 1810.

In case you should find that the enemy advance towards the Mesa de
Ibor and Truxillo, and the Duque de Alburquerque should retire with
the Spanish army under his command towards the Sierra Morena, I beg
that you will move forward with the troops specified in the margin * to
Portalegre. You will issue your own orders to the Portuguese corps,
who have directions to obey you; and you will, when you require the
British cavalry, send the enclosed letter to Lieut. Gen. Payne, at Santarem,
who will give orders to Gen. Slade's brigade of dragoons to follow you.
The object of this movement will be to enable you to check the enemy's
plans upon the frontiers of Portugal.

The enclosed reports of the frontier, from the Guadiana to the Tagus,
will show you that these plans must be confined between Arronches and
Campo Maior; or, at all events, between Campo Maior and Portalegre,
and that in this line he will have the fortresses of Badajoz, Elvas, and
Campo Maior, which is to be occupied on one flank, while you will be
in his front. The fort of Marvaõ, in front of Portalegre, is also to be
occupied. In case, however, that you should find that the enemy is in too
great strength for you, you will retire by the road of Gafete, and Gaviaõ,
to Abrantes. Having the magazine at Abrantes, you will be in no want
of provisions. Portalegre is also a large town, well supplied with provisions and forage.

The Lusitanian legion (2 battalions) and a brigade of Portuguese
militia are at Castello Branco, and in that neighbourhood; and I beg that
you will as soon as possible ascertain the mode in which the bridge at
Villa Velha is taken care of; and if you should find it necessary to retire
to Abrantes, you will take effectual measures to have that bridge taken
up, and the boats either destroyed or removed below Abrantes.

I shall hereafter take an opportunity of instructing you more fully regarding several points requiring your attention.

To Lieut. Gen. Leite.   Coimbra, 9th Jan. 1810.

Marshal Beresford will write to you to request that you will make all
the preparatory arrangements without loss of time for occupying the
forts of Campo Maior, Marvaõ, and Ouguela; and that you should place
a garrison in each of those places, as soon as you shall receive intelligence

* The 2d division of British infantry, Col. Campbell's brigade of Portuguese infantry
from Thomar, Brig. Fonseca's from Torres Novas, one brigade of British artillery, 2 brigades of Portuguese artillery from Chamusca, Gen. Slade's brigade of British cavalry at
Santarem, Gen. Seddon's of Portuguese cavalry at Salvaterra, and Gen. Madden's, still
at Lisbon.

that the enemy have possession of the Mesa de Ibor and Truxillo. Lieut. Gen. Hill, who commands the corps d'armée formed upon the Tagus, has directions to move with his corps to Portalegre, as soon as he shall receive intelligence of the same event.

To Bart. Frere, Esq. Coimbra, 9th Jan. 1810.

I have received your letter of the 3d inst., relative to the communication which you had had with Don A. de Cornel respecting the orders which he had sent to the Duque del Parque regarding Lieut. de Farincourt.

I observe that you mention on the 1st Jan. to Don F. de Saavedra, that you had the preceding night received a letter from me (I conclude that of the 27th Dec.), stating ' que le Lieut. de Farincourt, après avoir été détenu 6 semaines aux arrêts, avait été renvoyé de Ciudad Rodrigo à Almeida, sous prétexte que le Duque del Parque n'avait pas le pouvoir de le laisser passer.' If you will refer to the Duque del Parque's letter to Gen. Cox, enclosed in mine of the 27th Dec., you will see that the Duque del Parque not only had not the power, but that he had received orders not to allow any exchange to be made by that route.

From what I have seen latterly of ———— ————'s mode of transacting public business, particularly from the letters which I sent you on the 6th Jan., I am inclined to believe that the falsehood which is manifest in this transaction is his. It is obvious, also, that ———— ———— had deceived his own colleague.

The A.G. to Major Lindsay, Elvas. 9th Jan. 1810.

I have the honor to acknowledge your note accompanying the hospital states of the 4th inst. The Commander of the Forces approves of the indulgence you have granted to Lieut. Evatt, 57th regt.; but to enable the regulations on this head to be as closely followed as circumstances will allow, you are requested not to grant longer than one fortnight's leave on similar occasions, leaving to the judgment of a Medical board at Lisbon whether a prolongation of that leave be necessary. In reference to your communication of the 30th ult. and annexed reports, I return herewith an order for the delivery into His Majesty's ordnance store of the spare arms that appear, on the face of those reports, to be in the possession of the purveyors of Estremoz and Elvas hospitals. As there may be some mistake, I have to request you will look over the return, No. 2, of regiments that gave in to the purveyors' stores a greater proportion of arms than belonged to soldiers received into hospitals. I wish to be particular on this subject, as, in the event of the case so appearing, it will be necessary to make a specific report of the fact.

I send the routes you have requested for the recovered men of Estremoz and Villa Viçosa stations; it appears necessary that these 100 men should assemble at Elvas, to obtain the directed proportion of provisions, and from thence to proceed by the route, on which the Q. M. Gen. and Commissary Gen. have made arrangements for their reception. His Excellency rather desires a report of men esteemed fit to move, previous to their being allowed to march: you will therefore in future at least average numbers in your report of recovered men, to enable the issue of routes.

To Major Gen. J. Murray. Viseu, 12th Jan. 1810.

Since I wrote last, I have had a further correspondence with Adm. Berkeley, respecting the claims of the navy and army to the salvage of British vessels, and to the prize of other property found at Oporto when that place was captured, and the employment of ———— and ————,

and as the interests of so many are concerned in the measures to be adopted on the subject, I thought it proper to ask the opinion of Sir J. Sherbrooke before I answered the Admiral's letter, or decided upon the subject to which it referred. For my part, I never entertained any doubt but that the claim of the navy employed in the blockade of the Douro was as good as that of the army, to any advantage resulting from the operations; and having communicated to Sir J. Sherbrooke all that has passed upon this subject, he concurs with me in opinion, that it is not advisable, nor would it be proper, after all that has passed, to contest the right with the navy. I have accordingly written a letter, of which I enclose a copy to Adm. Berkeley, relative to that point, and the employment of ——— and ———, to which I wish to draw your attention.

It is a most extraordinary circumstance that these gentlemen should have been employed in this case; and that I should not have received one line from my brother Henry or Greenwood respecting their employment. But as it is, and as you approve of them, I certainly cannot consent to dismiss them and to employ the agents of the navy. As both parties, however, have the same object in view, it is reasonable, and will save expense, that they should act in conjunction.

To Vice Adm. the Hon. G. Berkeley. Viseu, 12th Jan. 1810.

Since I wrote to you from Coimbra, I have had an opportunity of talking with Gen. Sherbrooke respecting the state of the prize question at Oporto, and we are both agreed upon the following points:

1. That whatever may be the nature of the right of the army, either to salvage for the English vessels in the harbour at the time Oporto was taken, or to the prize of the remainder of the property, the right of the

---

G. O. Viseu, 12th Jan. 1810.

1. All officers wishing to go to any part of the country by post, must apply for a passport; if at head quarters, to the Commander of the Forces; if at any of the cantonments of the army, or at Lisbon, Elvas, &c., to the General officer commanding the division, or to the commanding officer at Lisbon, Elvas, &c. respectively; to whom blank passports will be transmitted for this purpose.

2. When the commissary attached to any division detached from head quarters, wishes to send a courier by post, he is to apply to the commanding officer of the division for a passport, who will grant it if he should concur in the expediency of sending the courier. The Commissary Gen. will apply for passports for the same purpose to the Commander of the Forces.

3. Persons belonging to the English army will not be supplied with post horses at any of the post stages, unless they should produce these passports for post horses of the Commander of the Forces.

4. When soldiers are sent to the general or any detachment hospital, their ammunition is to be delivered into store to the officer commanding the artillery, with the division in which the regiment is placed, with a return of the quantity so delivered in; which the officer commanding the artillery with the division is to direct the commissary of artillery to receive. The commanding officers of regiments are to adopt means for the preservation of the ammunition of soldiers in regimental hospitals.

5. The Commander of the Forces desires that the shooting of bullocks may be discontinued, as being a great waste of ammunition.

6. The government of Portugal having expressed their desire to give the troops a double allowance of wine on 3 days, as a demonstration of their satisfaction upon the return of the army to Portugal, a double allowance for each man is to be issued by the commissary on the 18th inst., being Her Majesty's birth day, on the 21st Jan., and on the 28th Jan.

7. The officers commanding regiments are informed, that they must not allow either officers or soldiers to absent themselves from their regiments without leave from the Commander of the Forces.

navy is equal; and that it will not be proper for us to contest that right; but on the contrary, by a concurrence with you, to facilitate the decision on the claims of both.

2. That as it appears that ———— and ———— have been employed to assert the claim of the army to salvage for the British vessels, and generally to the prize at Oporto, although without the direct authority of myself, or of any body authorised by me to employ them, it will not be reasonable or fair to discharge them from such employment in order to give it to others. Therefore we propose that ———— and ———— shall continue to be employed as the agents for the army, so long as they shall give satisfaction to Major Gen. Murray, to act in conjunction and co-operation with your agents for the general good of the captors.

I hope that what I have above stated will be satisfactory to you, and I beg you to forward the enclosed letters to Gen. Murray, and to apprise him of the consideration which Gen. Sir J. Sherbrooke and I have given to this subject, and of our determination upon it.

To Marshal Beresford.   Viseu, 13th Jan. 1810.

I take advantage of a courier for you from Lisbon to transmit you copies of two letters which I have written to Mr. Villiers, containing propositions for the supply of provisions for the Portuguese army in future; which, if they should be adopted, will, I hope, prevent all distress by the troops while they shall be within the Portuguese territory.

I am anxious to receive from you the plan of the country between the Tagus and the Mondego.

To Brig. Gen. Cox, Governor of Almeida.   Viseu, 14th Jan. 1810.

As I am going round the cantonments occupied by the British army, I propose to take that opportunity of seeing you at Almeida, where I think I shall be on Wednesday or Thursday next.

I shall be very much obliged to you if you will send to Capt. Ruman at Bejar, and let him know that I am going to Almeida, and that I shall be glad to see him there on Wednesday or Thursday, if possible.

To Lieut. Gen. Hill.   Viseu, 14th Jan. 1810.

Since I wrote to you on the 9th, it occurs to me, that in case the rain should fall heavily, you may experience some difficulty in moving, in the event for which your instructions provide; and as the enemy will also experience the same difficulty, probably even in a greater degree, I wish you to have constant information of the state of the roads from Abrantes towards Portalegre; and if you should find them to be so bad as to render your movement difficult, you will postpone it till the return of the dry weather shall have improved them again.

In the movement of the cavalry it will be necessary to take care that they have stables, particularly if the weather should be bad, to which I beg you to advert. I believe there is stabling for a brigade at least, at Portalegre; but if there should not be enough at that place, you must separate your cavalry till you shall want them, as it will not answer to keep the horses out of doors in the wet season.

To the Rt. Hon. Sir D. Dundas, K.B.   Viseu, 14th Jan. 1810.

I have the honor to enclose the list of officers entitled to receive medals, as being present in the battle of Talavera, according to the principles contained in your letter of the 20th Nov. 1809.

I have included in the list Lieut. Cols. Framingham and Robe of the Royal artillery, and Major Hartmann of the Royal Hanoverian artillery, for the reasons stated in the enclosed letter from those officers; and I have added, at the bottom of the list, the names of officers commanding corps in the battle of rank inferior to Lieut. Colonel, as I have reason to believe that hopes were entertained, in consequence of the Sec. of State's letter, a copy of which I have the honor to enclose, that this honorable distinction would be conferred upon all officers, of whatever rank, who had commanded corps upon that occasion.

I have likewise the honor of enclosing letters which I have received upon this subject from Brig. Gen. Howorth, Col. Robe, and Major Hartmann; and from Major Gwynn, of the 45th regt.; also from Brig. Gen. Howorth, with an enclosure from the Captains commanding brigades of artillery.

P.S. I have also the honor to enclose a letter from Lieut. Gen. Sir J. C. Sherbrooke, stating the claim of Lord Aylmer, A. A. G.

To the Rt. Hon. J. Villiers.   Viseu, 14th Jan. 1810.

I have only this day received your letter of the 9th inst. No expression in any letter of mine ought to have, or can have, the effect of binding you in any manner; and I only mean that what I write should bind myself.

A proposition was made, that from the funds at the disposal of the Commissary Gen. of the army, we should give £300,000 for the use of the Portuguese government, in addition to the monthly payments called 'Aids.' I call all the money that can be raised by bills on England at Lisbon, Cadiz, and Gibraltar, and all that is sent from England, funds at the disposal of the Commissary Gen. of the army; and finding from experience of the past that the funds are not sufficient to answer the regular demands made upon them, and that those demands must increase, I cannot engage that the Commissary Gen. shall give one dollar of the additional and extra demand of £300,000 now made upon him. I cannot engage that this money shall be paid in Portugal in 2, or 3, or any number of months, because I do not believe that the funds at the disposal of the Commissary Gen. of the army will enable him to perform that engagement without distressing other services, which cannot bear delay in payment; and as to its payment in England, I have nothing to say, and never had any thing to say, to that part of the question.

What I object to is, engaging to pay the money in Portugal now or at any future time, and giving bills to be negotiated at Lisbon, Cadiz, or Gibraltar, either now, or at any future time; because both these modes of supplying the money must affect the funds at the disposal of the Commissary Gen. for the support of the British army. I might, however, have saved myself the trouble of writing, and you that of reading this letter, as I think it probable that the propositions made to you in my letters of the

9th and 12th* inst. will have settled the whole question; but lest they should not, I send this letter.

I wish I could convince you that every shilling that can be raised in any manner is raised and applied for the public service in the best manner in my power. If it be true that we raise every shilling that can be got for a bill or any thing else; and if what we get is not sufficient for our ordinary demands, it must be obvious that we cannot promise to raise £300,000 for the Portuguese government; or, what is the same thing, to pay them £300,000 in addition to the ordinary aids, without breaking our promise, or distressing other services. If we grant bills to be negotiated at a future period, we anticipate our funds; as we throw into the market bills which will certainly be negotiated, and will as certainly keep out of the market others which would be granted by the Commissary Gen. in the usual course.

I think that this discussion about money, that the distress which we have felt ever since I arrived here, and that the increasing demands upon the funds we have at our disposal, must tend to convince you that Great Britain has undertaken a larger concern in Portugal than she has the means of executing.

I have no objection to communicate to you the return of the army, or to say, that in its present state it is not sufficient for the defence of Portugal; but the troops are recovering their health daily, the reinforcements from England are expected, and if l can bring 30,000 effective British troops into the field, I will fight a good battle for the possession of Portugal, and see whether that country cannot be saved from the general wreck. I do not mean to say that more troops would not be desirable; but it must be obvious to you; 1st, that the government could not give more; and if I thought 30,000 men sufficient, I should not have acted honestly by them if I had not told them what I thought the lowest number that could do the business: 2dly; that we could neither feed nor pay more consistently with the performance of our engagements, without an increase of our pecuniary means from England; that is, an increase of coin sent out, which all my communications forbid me to expect to receive.

You have seen all the dispatches that I have ever written to England, and know, as well as I do, how far they have confirmed what I wrote on the 14th Nov. Circumstances have certainly altered materially since that letter was written; but the question for me is, have they altered in such a manner as to induce me to think that with 30,000 men, which I have reason to believe I shall have in the course of a few weeks (together with the Portuguese army, which, by the bye, is better than I ever expected it would be, and wants only to be equipped as it ought), I shall not be able to save Portugal, or, at all events, to sell the country dearly?

I think that if the Spanish armies had not been lost, and if the Spaniards had made good use of their time, very large reinforcements indeed would have been necessary to enable the French even to attack us. As it is, have we

* The drafts of these letters are missing from the papers of the Duke of Wellington. Search has been made, unsuccessfully, for the original letters among the papers of the late Earl of Clarendon; as also among the archives of the Foreign office in Downing Street, and those of Her Majesty's Legation at Lisbon.

now no chance? Ought we to withdraw from the Peninsula, and give up the whole (for when we withdraw we shall give up the whole) an easy prey to the conqueror? Will 10,000 men more, which will distress our means, supposing that Great Britain can afford to supply them, compensate for the loss of these Spanish armies, and put us in the situation in which my dispatch of the 14th Nov. supposed we ought and should stand?

I conceive that the honor and interests of the country require that we should hold our ground here as long as possible; and, please God, I will maintain it as long as I can; and I will neither endeavor to shift from my own shoulders on those of the ministers the responsibility for the failure, by calling for means which I know they cannot give, and which, perhaps, would not add materially to the facility of attaining our object; nor will I give to the ministers, who are not strong, and who must feel the delicacy of their own situation, an excuse for withdrawing the army from a position which, in my opinion, the honor and interest of the country require they should maintain as long as possible. I think that if the Portuguese do their duty, I shall have enough to maintain it; if they do not, nothing that Great Britain can afford can save the country; and if from that cause I fail in saving it, and am obliged to go, I shall be able to carry away the British army.

I am afraid that I can't allow Cooke to remain with Mr. Casamajor, unless he should resign his situation on the staff.

To Vice Adm. the Hon. G. Berkeley.   Viseu, 15th Jan. 1810.

In a dispatch which I lately received from England, Lord Liverpool desires me to make him acquainted with the state of the transports in Portugal; what number of men they will contain; and whether any additional number could be got in Portugal in the event of the army leaving this country. It is probable that you will have received directions upon these subjects from the Admiralty, and will have reported upon them.

Col. Murray received one return, signed by Mr. Fleetwood, of the number of transports, and of the number of men each could contain; but since that return was sent, I believe that other transports have arrived, of which we have no account; and it would be very desirable that Mr. Fleetwood should let us know, from time to time, any alteration that may occur in the number of transports, and their capacity for holding men, in order that I may be able to give answers upon these subjects, as well as for other reasons. I shall be much obliged to you to let me know whether you think that any vessels could be procured in Portugal, in the event of an embarkation of the army. My opinion is, that in the event of our being obliged to withdraw, government ought to endeavor to bring off as large a proportion of the Portuguese army as possible, which is becoming so good as to be worth the expense of removing them. They would be very useful at all events in South America; and probably all the vessels which could be procured in Portugal ought to be applied to their use. At all events, it is desirable that we should have some general idea of what this country could do in the way of shipping, in the event supposed of an evacuation either forced or otherwise.

To Marshal Beresford.   Viseu, 15th Jan. 1810.

I conceive that it would be very desirable to call out that part of each regiment of militia which is armed, as soon as possible, placing at Almeida, Elvas, and Abrantes, and Valença, those destined to be the garrisons of those places respectively, and at some convenient place within their own district the other regiments. We shall call out the remainder of the men of each regiment of militia as soon as we shall get arms for them. Those regiments in the neighbourhood of Lisbon must continue to be employed in our works. I wish that you would write to the government upon this subject without loss of time.

I see that the head of the Duc d'Abrantes' corps passed Paris for Spain in the middle of December; and as Portugal will be liable to attack as soon as they arrive in Spain, it would be the worst species of economy to delay to be so far prepared, as the militia can prepare us for the attack. I also beg you, without loss of time, to fix upon the troops with which we are to occupy the batteries on the Zezere; and to order them to the neighbourhood of their several posts. Do you propose to occupy Alfaiates and Monsanto? I see that those places are armed, and I should think it desirable to occupy with militia every place of that description, giving to each place a good commandant, if possible. I am going round the cantonments of the British army.

To Lieut. Gen. Hill.   Viseu, 15th Jan. 1810.

I have omitted to mention to you that I have ordered to Santarem £10,000 a week from Lisbon, for the use of your corps, and of the cavalry. We calculate that the pay of the troops will take £15,000 a month, and the remainder of the sum, or £25,000 a month, will be for the Commissary General's department.

Let me know if there is any spare musket ammunition at Abrantes belonging to the Portuguese. There is plenty of gun and musket ammunition belonging to the army at Elvas.

To the Earl of Liverpool.   Viseu, 15th Jan. 1810.

The enemy have made no movement of importance since I addressed you on the 4th inst. I understand that they threaten an attack upon the kingdom of Valencia with their left; at the same time that the corps in La Mancha has been strengthened in some degree, as well as that at Toledo, and at Talavera de la Reyna. They are employed in fortifying the Retiro at Madrid, and the ancient castle of Toledo.

I conclude that the movement of the troops to the northward by Guadalaxara was made with a view to the intended attack upon Valencia; and that they will still further strengthen their corps in that quarter, when they shall have completed their works at Toledo and Madrid. The enemy's troops in Old Castille continue to occupy the same positions upon the Tormes, and have not been strengthened.

The Spanish armies remain nearly in the same situation as when I addressed your Lordship on the 4th inst. The Duque del Parque has requested me to afford him the assistance of the British cavalry to commence an offensive operation upon the enemy in Old Castille, the object of which was to enable him to cross the upper Duero, and to remove the corps under his command to the frontiers of Galicia. I have had no intimation from the government of their wish that the Duque del Parque should make this movement; and, at all events, I have declined to allow the British cavalry to co-operate in it, for the same reasons that I have uniformly objected to any partial offensive operation upon the enemy since they had collected their forces in the centre of Spain; as well as for others. As the Duque del Parque, however, has made preparations to cross the Douro at Torre de Moncorvo, within the Portuguese frontier, I imagine that he will move his corps in that direction, whatever may be the wishes of the government; and notwithstanding that in a letter which he wrote to the Junta of Badajoz on the same day that he desired my assistance to move to the frontiers of Galicia, he assured that body that he had taken a position on the frontiers of Estremadura with a view to defend that province.

The British army have arrived in their cantonments on the frontiers of Beira. We occupy Guarda, Pinhel, Celorico, and Viseu, with 3 divisions of infantry and a regiment of cavalry; Gen. Hill's division of infantry is at Abrantes, and the remainder of the British cavalry on the Tagus, between Abrantes and Santarem. I have left them on the Tagus, on account of the want of forage, and of stables in this part of the country.

I have made this disposition of the army with a view to form of the whole British and Portuguese armies two principal corps; one for the defence of the provinces south of the Tagus, which will consist of Gen. Hill's division of British infantry, 2 brigades of Portuguese infantry, one brigade of British, and 2 brigades of Portuguese cavalry, one brigade of British, and 2 brigades of Portuguese artillery; and the other of 3 divisions of British infantry, and all the Portuguese infantry not employed in garrisons, and the British cavalry, and the British and Portuguese artillery.

The Portuguese troops are cantoned in the rear of the British troops, with which they are destined eventually to act. The Lusitanian legion, and some Portuguese militia, occupy Castello Branco, and the mountains between the Tagus and the Mondego.

To Col. Wilson.* Guarda. 17th Jan. 1810.

In case the enemy should enter Portugal by the route of Zarza la Mayor, I beg of you to attend to the following instructions. If the enemy should be in such force as to oblige you to withdraw from Castello Branco, you will do so gradually by the road of Sarzedas, Sobreira Formosa, Corticada, and Cardigos, occupying and maintaining every defensible post as long as it may be in your power. You will send one of the battalions of militia on your right by the road of Perdigão, and another on your left by the Estrada Nova; and you will give each of them the same directions, and endeavor to communicate with each on your retreat, observing always that the defence of the Estrada Nova is very important, as the enemy, by that road, may cut you off at Cardigos. Before you quit Castello Branco, you will take measures to send away or destroy the provisions, magazines, &c.

* Lieut. Gen. Sir J. Wilson, K.C.B. and K.T.S.; then in the Portuguese service.

I beg you will communicate to Gen. Hill, commanding the troops in Abrantes, these instructions. You will also apply to him for provisions to support your troops in the mountains. You will apprise Gen. Hill if the enemy should move in strength by the Estrada Nova, in order that he may take measures to occupy the batteries of the Zezere, between Villa de Rey and Thomar.

To Lieut. Gen. Hill.   Guarda, 17th Jan. 1810.

Col. Wilson will communicate to you the instructions which I have sent him by this opportunity, applicable to the movements of the enemy towards Baños, and the possible invasion of Portugal by Castello Branco, or by the Estrada Nova. In case they should make this movement, it will be necessary that you should take measures to occupy the bridge, or Barca over the Zezere, between Villa de Rey and Thomar; and you can do this only by ordering there, in case it should be necessary, one or both of the regiments of Campbell's brigade of Portuguese infantry from Thomar. However, before the necessity for occupying this post will, I hope, occur, I shall put means in your power of occupying it, which will leave at your disposal this brigade of Campbell's for the other objects of your instructions of the 9th inst.

P.S. If the enemy should enter by Castello Branco, you will of course have preparations made to destroy all the bridges on the Zezere, as soon as the troops in the mountains shall have passed, excepting that at Punhete, which you must keep for your own communications.

To Vice Adm. the Hon. G. Berkeley.   Viseu, 22d Jan. 1810.

I have received your letter of the 13th inst., and I beg to assure you that I am at all times happy to be favored with your sentiments, or with any information which you think worthy of attention.

Marshal Beresford has had some communication with the government respecting the future treatment of Senhor de Mello, and he appeared to be rather of opinion that it was expedient that he should be released from his arrest, provided the government would consent to publish all that had passed upon the subject.

I am much concerned that you should imagine that measures are adopted for the supply of this army that occasion an useless expense which might be avoided. If ever there was an officer at the head of an army interested (personally I may say) in keeping down the expenses of the army, it is myself; for I am left wholly to my own resources, and am obliged to supply the wants of the allies, as well as of the British army, from what I can get; and if I fail, God will, I hope, have mercy upon me, for nobody else will. But besides economy in the expenditure of money, I must be certain of efficiency in the supply of necessaries for the troops; and it will not do for me to depend for what I want upon the navigation of the sea upon the coast of Portugal, during the winter, by victuallers and transports, or upon the passage of the bar of the Mondego by square rigged vessels, at a season when all the people of the country agree in stating that the bar can scarcely be passed by a schooner drawing little water.

When I landed there in the finest season of the year, in August, vessels drawing more than 8 feet water could not pass the bar, and that at high water at spring tides. In the winter season, there is more difficulty in passing the bar; and I conclude that vessels even of that draft of water cannot now enter the Mondego. For this reason I sanctioned the employment of the schooners. If, however, you are decidedly of opinion that they can enter the Mondego, I am sure nothing will give me greater satisfaction than to avail myself of your offer, to send these transports and victuallers; and I desired the Commissary Gen. to instruct his Deputy at Lisbon to make application to you to send some of the stores required for the army in its present station, by transports or victuallers.

I beg you to observe that I am held severely responsible for all failures, as well of supplies as of every thing else; and I have given the Commissary Gen. these directions in the confidence that your information respecting the Mondego is authentic, and that transports and victuallers can enter that river with greater facility in winter, than I know from experience they can in summer.

I have also received your letter of the 15th, respecting Mr. Phillips. This gentleman has been employed by the Treasury to purchase corn in the Mediterranean for the army; and I have received orders to take his corn if it should be wanted, and he should be disposed to let us have it, at as cheap a rate as we can get it elsewhere, and not otherwise. Now, I do want Mr. Phillips's corn, and he is disposed to let me have it at as cheap a rate as I can get it elsewhere, and moreover to receive payment for it in the manner most convenient for the public interests. I have accordingly directed that agreements may be made for the purchase, and I have made arrangements for the disposal of this corn, the disappointment of which will be inconvenient. Under these circumstances, you will probably think it proper to order that the embargo may be taken off the corn in question, and you will see that it is in Mr. Phillips's power to settle for the freight in a manner that will be satisfactory to you. I know nothing of this transaction of Mr. Phillips's excepting what I have above stated to you: but from circumstances which have come to my knowledge, I believe that he has been confidentially and extensively employed by government, on various occasions, in the same manner as at present.

I have already troubled you at too much length, or I think I could account to your satisfaction for the offer of a quantity of wheat for sale in the market at Lisbon, which wheat Mr. Murray (and the government of Portugal, strange to say!) had really declined to purchase, and for his drawing bills upon the produce of the expected sale of this wheat.

To Vice Adm. the Hon. G. Berkeley.   Viseu, 22d Jan. 1810.

I am much obliged to you for the information respecting the mules purchased at Tangier, and I have directed the Commissary Gen. to be prepared to receive them at Lisbon.

To J. Murray, Esq., Commissary Gen.   Viseu, 22d Jan. 1810.

I have the honor to enclose the extract of a letter which I received yesterday from Gen. Payne, by which I have the mortification to learn that, notwithstanding the sacrifices which I have made of the services of the cavalry, and the risks I incur in order to place them in a situation in which the horses might receive forage without difficulty, they have been worse supplied in their present quarters than they have yet been.

I observe, from the last returns which I have of the state of the stores, that there were in store at Abrantes, on the 1st Dec. last, 89,000 lbs. of hay; at Santarem, 30,000 lbs.; and at Villa Nova, 852,000 lbs.

The country on the banks of the Tagus, from Santarem to Punhete, has always been considered the most plentiful for cavalry; and the Portuguese government had always a large body of cavalry at Santarem, as well as at Golegaö. There has been no cavalry in that part of the country since the last harvest; and it is not to be believed that the country should have been so exhausted by the passage of the British army only through Punhete, as that it could no longer supply the wants of the horses of the cavalry. But if that country was exhausted for straw, that of the left bank of the Tagus, and the market of Lisbon, were not; and the stores at Lisbon contained, on the 1st Dec., 671,000 lbs. of hay. I should imagine that forage for the horses of the cavalry might have been procured by water carriage from any, or from some, of these quarters, by any arrangement, as well as from Abrantes, Santarem, or Villa Nova.

You were informed, on the ——, by the Q. M. G., of the proposed distribution of the British cavalry; and you were a party to many conversations I had at Badajoz, about that time, with the Q. M. G., relative to the necessity of placing the British cavalry in cantonments on the Tagus, with a view to the supply of forage, hay particularly, for the horses. I beg to know what orders you gave, and what arrangements you made, and on what dates, and to whom, to insure the accomplishment of these objects, or any supplies for the cavalry in their quarters.

I also desire to know who gave Mr. —— leave to go to Lisbon. He was informed by me on the 29th Dec., if he had not received information before, of the distribution of the cavalry, and of their want of hay particularly; and he ought to have made arrangements for their supply before he quitted his station, even if he had leave to do so.

I make these inquiries, because the bad condition of the horses of the British cavalry is a serious evil at the present moment, which may lead to the most important and unfortunate consequences; and I am determined that the government shall know how the public are served; and all the most important arrangements and objects are disappointed by the inefficiency or neglect of the officers of the Commissariat.

The A.G. to Col. Peacocke, Lisbon. 22d Jan. 1810.

In reply to your letter of the 15th inst., which I have had the honor to receive and submit, it has so far met his Excellency's approbation, together with the extract of transactions, 30th Oct. date, relative to Belem station.

You are authorised to permit the arms, accoutrements, &c. of the sick to be kept in depôt store, instead of being placed in charge of the purveyor; but this departure from general rule is alone to be considered an exception relating to Lisbon hospital, arising from the probability of constant variation in the establishment, and the great relief, under such circumstances, which an affixed depôt may afford.

It is the Commander of the Forces' desire, that you arrange your detachments

2 Y 2

in conformity to the brigading of regiments in the army, which you can now easily execute by the return of the army forwarded to you from Coimbra.

To Marshal Beresford.   Viseu, 23d Jan. 1810.

I returned yesterday from my tour of the quarters of the army.

While at Guarda, I received intimation of the enemy's movements in Old Castille towards the frontiers of Estremadura; and I judged it desirable to give instructions to Col. Wilson respecting the measures to be adopted by him for the defence of the country between Belmonte and the Tagus, and for his retreat. I enclose the copy of his answer, from which I find that he has only 750 men, in 2 battalions of the Lusitanian legion, and no militia; although I conceived that the former were at least as strong as they are stated to be in the last return which I have of the Portuguese army, and that the latter were a good brigade of 3 battalions.

We ought to have in those mountains at least 5000 men, with a brigade of artillery, of which 1700 or 1800 regular infantry, 200 or 300 cavalry, and the rest militia; and I wish you would make arrangements as soon as possible for that purpose. With that number we shall do there pretty well, particularly as I find that the Estrada Nova has batteries upon it, and that the use of it can be successfully impeded by breaking it up. I propose to have it broken up forthwith, as it can never be of any use to the country or to us, and may be very useful to the enemy. Besides this force in the mountains, I conceive that we ought to allot 2 regiments of infantry, and 3000 militia, and 200 or 300 cavalry, for the defence of the Zezere. With this force, that line, and the communication between Hill's corps and the army, would be tolerably secure.

The corps for the defence of the Zezere might be stationed at Thomar for the present; and I shall hereafter give the officer whom you will fix upon for the command of it detailed instructions for his guidance. Till you shall have fixed upon the troops to occupy this line, I have desired Hill, in case he should find that the enemy make a movement towards Castello Branco or the mountains, not to move Campbell's brigade from Thomar, even though he should be induced, under his instructions, to move into Alentejo.

I am sorry to tell you that I think you will be disappointed in your expectations from the garrison of Almeida. The 8th regt. have neither arms, accoutrements, clothing, discipline, nor numbers; the other two are not clothed and armed as they ought to be, their numbers are incomplete, and their discipline and appearance by no means equal to the others of the army that I have seen. It is evident to me that the 8th regt. will be of no use to Cox, or any body else, during this campaign; and it is also clear that he must have one good regiment with his militia. Pro-

G. A. O.   Viseu, 23d Jan. 1810.

The Commander of the Forces desires that the Brigade Major, of Major Gen. Lightburne's brigade, will send to the A. A. G. of the 4th division a return, stating the dates and numbers of the several G. O. received by that brigade; which the A. A. G. will examine, and he will send to the brigade any G. O. which they may not already have received.

The Commander of the Forces desires the attention of Major Gen. Lightburne to all these orders.

bably the best plan would be to move the 8th regt. somewhere to the rear. It would also be necessary to move one of the other regiments from Almeida to make room for the militia, as Cox's garrison is already so full that he has not room for his troops. At the same time the regiment to be moved will be badly off for clothing, as Cox says that neither the 12th nor the 24th can be clothed for 2 months by any exertion he can make.

I shall be very much obliged to you if you will let me know how the camp kettles of your troops are to be carried in the field, and how they are now equipped for this purpose; likewise in what manner they are to be supplied with ammunition, and how carried.

I also wish to know how the brigades with Hill are to be fed, if he should draw them out of their quarters. Have they Commissaries attached to them ? Are these Commissaries supplied with money, or directions where to get provisions, or must we supply them from our magazines ?

Probably the best mode of providing for the defence of the Zezere, till we shall finally arrange every thing, would be to consider the 5 regiments of caçadores under Le Cor as applicable to that service, and to let Hill still have Campbell's brigade. When you can give 2 regiments for this service, we may take the caçadores for this corps of the army.

P.S. When shall you be back, and fix yourself in your quarters? Since writing the above, Gen. Bacellar has been here, and has informed me of his intention to move the militia to Almeida immediately. I have recommended him to halt them till further orders from you, as it is impossible for the place to hold them and the regiments of the line also ; and you must determine what you will do about them after reading the account which this letter contains of their state.

To Major Gen. J. Murray.   Viseu, 23d Jan. 1810.

Since I wrote to you on the 12th inst., I have received a letter from Adm. Berkeley, which renders it desirable that I should trouble you again in respect to our claims, on account of the operations at Oporto. It is the determined intention of Sir J. Sherbrooke and myself to forego all opposition to the claims of the navy to a share of the advantage resulting from those operations, and it follows therefore that the King's proctor must be employed for the navy and army conjointly.

We conceive, however, that although ———— and ———— have been employed without any direct authority from me, or any person authorised by me, they have acted for the best, and deserve remuneration. We therefore mean that they should be the agents for the army, and that they should have that remuneration which will belong to them in that character.

To Vice Adm. the Hon. G. Berkeley.   Viseu, 23d Jan. 1810.

I have consulted Sir J. Sherbrooke on the contents of your letter of the 15th, respecting the employment of ———— and ———— on the part of the army in their claim for salvage of the British vessels found at Oporto.

I am perfectly aware of what you state, that Mr. Bishop must be the proctor for both army and navy in their claims, either for salvage or prize, on account of their operations at Oporto; and accordingly you will observe that in my letter to Major Gen. Murray, of the 12th inst., and to you of the same date, I mention —— and —— only as agents for the army; and Mr. Bishop, being the King's proctor, who must act as such for both; and Mr. Cooke being the agent for you. Mr. Greenwood is not the agent for the army. However, to obviate all difficulties, I enclose another letter for Gen. Murray, of which I request your perusal.

To Col. Don M. de Alava.　　　　　　　　　　　Viseu, ce 23 Janvier, 1810.

J'ai reçu vos lettres du 10, 12, et 13, pour lesquelles je vous suis très obligé. J'en aurais eu la réception plutôt si je n'avais pas été sur la frontière. Je ne sais pas ce qu'on va faire dans La Mancha; mais je ne crois pas qu'on eût rassemblé un si grand corps si on n'avait pas quelque dessein, et si on n'attendait pas les renforts tout de suite.

Je vous envoie une lettre de la Payno; je vous prie de recommander son fils au Duque de Alburquerque. Dites lui, en même tems, que j'ai répondu à la Payno que je pensais que de recommander un officier à un général, pour être son aide de camp, était presque la même chose que de recommander une demoiselle à un homme pour être son épouse.

Je suis content que le Marquis de la Romana a quitté la Junta. Elle ne peut pas durer.

To Bart. Frere, Esq.　　　　　　　　　　　Viseu, 23d Jan. 1810.

I received, on the day before yesterday, your letters of the 5th, 7th, 9th, 10th, and 14th Jan., for which I am very much obliged to you. I had been on a tour on the frontier, which is the cause of my not having received them sooner.

If Gen. La Buena should come here, I shall receive him with politeness, and hear what he has to say, and then refer him to you for his answer. If you and the Spanish ministers had agreed that it was desirable to send an officer to me, to confer upon a general plan of operations, I should have entered upon such a conference; but as it is, I conceive that I am precluded by the King's commands from having any communication with him, excepting to hear what he has to say to me, in the same manner as I should be obliged to receive and read any letter which the Spanish ministers might write to me.

The enemy have collected their troops in Old Castille, in the neighbourhood of Alverca, not far from Miranda del Castañar. They have some troops in Bejar; and I conceive that they have made this movement upon hearing of our arrival upon the frontier. I have not received any positive intelligence of the arrival of reinforcements; but I should think that some of them must have entered Spain, otherwise the enemy would not have ventured to collect so large a corps as it appears they have collected in La Mancha.

P.S. I request you to let Col. Roche know where we are. I have just received the report, of which I enclose a copy. This may be a part of the reinforcements expected from France. However, the Spaniards take such bad care of their posts, and have so little intelligence, that it is difficult to say by what troops this blow has been struck.

To Col. Peacocke. Viseu, 24th Jan. 1810.

I have reason to believe that certain regiments, intended to reinforce this army, as well as recruits for several of the regiments already composing it, will shortly arrive at Lisbon; and I beg that you will convey to the officers commanding these regiments and detachments of recruits, respectively, the following orders for their guidance :

If they should be under the command of a General officer, you will give him this letter, which he will consider in the same light as if addressed to himself.

The baggage of these several regiments is to be left in one of the transports which have brought out the regiments, to be fixed upon by the A.Q.M.G. at Lisbon, in concert with the Agent of transports. One non-commissioned officer, or steady man, belonging to each regiment, must be left in this transport in charge of this baggage; and he must have a list of the packages or cases left in his charge.

The regiments are to be landed immediately, and to be quartered in the most convenient manner in convents, barracks, or otherwise, in Lisbon or Belem; and the officers commanding regiments are, without loss of time, to direct the officers under their command to equip their companies and themselves for the carriage of their camp kettles, and the baggage of the officers. You will take care to give the Commanding officers of the regiments copies of the general orders upon these several subjects.

If the Paymasters of regiments should not have received in England the bat and forage, and if they should require money to make the necessary advances to the officers to purchase the mules, &c., which they will require, you will desire Mr. Hunter to make such advances on account as may appear to be necessary.

The Commanding officers of regiments will make the necessary requisition upon the Dep. Commissary Gen. at Lisbon for the mules to carry the intrenching tools, to be under the charge of the quarter master; and upon the A.Q.M.G. for canteens, haversacks, bill hooks, &c., in the usual proportion and force; blanket for each man, according to the G.O. of the 30th Oct. 1809.

The recruits for each regiment, under charge of the officers of the regiment who will probably have been sent out with them, are to remain at Lisbon till reports shall have been sent to, and orders received from, head quarters for their march. In the mean time they are to be equipped with canteens, haversacks, bill hooks, blankets, &c., and be prepared to march at short notice.

G. A. O. Viseu 24th Jan. 1810.

3. As the distance which the army is from Lisbon, makes it impossible to procure money in time to discharge the amount of the estimates in advance as required by the regulations, and as the consequence of the discharge of the balances due to the soldiers on the 24th of each month, for the month then ending, would be, that for a month the officers commanding companies would have no money in hand to supply those necessaries which the soldiers should require;

The Commander of the Forces desires that in future the accounts of the soldiers are to be settled on the 24th of every month, according to the regulations of the service, and the balances struck, but the balance is not to be paid to the soldiers till the 24th of the following month; that is to say, the balance due to the soldiers on the 24th Jan. not till the 24th Feb., and thus in succession from month to month.

An alteration in conformity to this order must be made in the certificate of payment at the bottom of the monthly return of regiments.

The Dep. Commissary Gen. must be required to supply carts for the conveyance of their camp kettles till they shall join their regiments to which they respectively belong, when the carts will be dismissed, and their camp kettles will be carried in the usual manner.

The baggage brought out with these recruits is to be placed in the stores of the regimental baggage of their respective corps.

If any horses should arrive for the regiments already in Spain and Portugal, they are to be placed in charge of the officers and men who have come out with them, of the dragoons belonging to the several regiments who are already at Lisbon, and of the officers and men of the 23d light dragoons, till the orders of the officers commanding the cavalry for their further disposal shall have been received. The baggage brought out with these horses is to be placed in store with the regimental baggage of the regiments for which the horses are destined.

If a regiment of dragoons should arrive, it must be disembarked and placed in the barracks at Belem or Lisbon, leaving its baggage in one of the transports, according to the orders above given for the disposal of the baggage of regiments of infantry; and this regiment of dragoons must be equipped, according to the general orders on this subject, and prepared to move.

Orders will be sent from head quarters for the movement of all these troops, when reports shall be received that they are equipped and ready to move.

To Vice Adm. the Hon. G. Berkeley.   Viseu, 24th Jan. 1810.

In view to the possible necessity of evacuating Portugal, I have for some time considered it desirable that the baggage of the army should be embarked in the transports which the government had sent to the Tagus for their reception; and it has occurred to me that the moment at which this measure can be adopted, without being misunderstood by the public, and without creating alarm, is that at which the reinforcements for the army shall have arrived from England.

I have accordingly desired the Q.M.G. to give directions that the baggage of the several regiments may be embarked as soon as the reinforcements shall arrive; and, in order that the baggage may be put in the ships in which the regiments would be placed, in case they were to be embarked in reference to their strength, the number of officers, &c., I have desired the Q.M.G. to make out a list of the ships in which it is desirable that the baggage of the regiments should now be placed.

I have the honor to enclose the arrangement, framed by the Q.M.G. from the list of transports which you transmitted to him; and I shall be obliged to you if you will give directions to the Agent of transports to carry the proposed measure into execution, as therein proposed, in concert with the A.Q.M.G. at Lisbon.

I have also to inform you that, with the same views, I have directed that the baggage belonging to the regiments expected from England should be left in one of the ships which have brought each from England, under an arrangement to be made by the A.Q.M.G. at Lisbon, and the Agent of transports, which I request you to sanction.

I shall be much obliged to you if you will give directions that one man may be victualled in each of the ships which will receive the baggage, in order that it may be properly taken care of.

To Lieut. Gen. Hill.   Viseu, 24th Jan. 1810.

I have received your letters of the 20th. Gen. Leite, who writes to you, is the commanding officer of Elvas, and Col. Brito de Mozinho is employed by the Portuguese government at Badajoz to collect and transmit intelligence to them. They are both persons deserving of credit, and as far as their means of acquiring intelligence go, they may be depended upon. I desired them to write to you, as well as Col. Alava and the Duque de Alburquerque, and the Superintendent of the Post office at Badajoz, who has very frequently early intelligence of the enemy's movements. Besides these persons, I should recommend to you to send to reside in some of the towns on the frontier some intelligent officer, with directions to correspond with the magistrates of the towns in advance; to communicate to you the intelligence which he shall receive, and to come off to you himself, if he should find that the enemy cross the Tagus, or penetrate through the hills to Truxillo.

I do not doubt that the Duque de Alburquerque has made the disposition of his force, which is stated in Brito's paper of the 18th Oct., which I return to you; so that you see that the Spaniards do not propose to defend the Mesa de Ibor, and that their troops in Estremadura will retire to Badajoz if the French should advance in that quarter.

The Portuguese corps ought to have a Commissariat attached to them, and I believe each brigade has a Commissary; but I believe they have no magazines, and no money to purchase supplies in the country. I have no doubt, therefore, that you will be obliged to assist them with provisions from the magazines at Abrantes, &c.; and I enclose you a paper, containing an arrangement under which these supplies are to be given to them, supposing that you should think it proper to give them.

In respect to the bridges of Villa Velha, Abrantes, and Punhete, there is a Bridge master at Abrantes who has charge of them all; and if you will speak to him, he will adopt measures to have them put and kept in complete repair; and if he should say that he cannot do so for want of money, you will advance him some for this purpose, letting me know the amount. I beg you to write to Col. Wilson to desire him to post a guard at Villa Velha, over the bridge there, and to send an officer there yourself to ascertain the means of preserving it on the one hand, or of destroying and removing the boats on the other.

The officers of the Staff corps are already employed in very important duties, from which they cannot be diverted without great public inconvenience. I recommend that you should have a person whom you can trust at Montalvao, on the bank of the little river Sever, particularly if you should receive intelligence that the enemy have passed the Mesa de Ibor; as I think it not improbable that they might endeavor to push a party of cavalry along the Tagus, and across the Sever, however difficult the passage, in order to surprise the guard at Villa Velha, and seize the bridge, of which it is of the utmost importance to them to deprive us, and to possess themselves. If you should employ an officer upon this or any other service out of the line of his duty, you will pay him, while so employed, 3 dollars *per diem.*

Since I wrote to you from Guarda, I have heard of no further movements of the enemy in Castille, and I am pretty certain that they have their hands too full at present to be able to molest us. I find, however, that the 3 regiments of militia, which I thought were at Castello Branco, are not embodied (but one ordered out), and that the Lusitanian legion is much less efficient than I supposed it was ; and upon the whole this part of the frontier is but very ill protected, and its defence but very ill provided for. It will soon be better, however. In the mean time, this state of things renders necessary an alteration in your instructions ; and accordingly I beg that if you find that Col. Wilson cannot maintain himself in the passes of the mountains, on account of the insufficiency of his force to defend them, you will not advance from Abrantes, even though the enemy should enter Estremadura ; and if you should have advanced, and you should afterwards find that Col. Wilson cannot maintain himself in the passes of the mountains, you will retire upon Abrantes, in the same manner as you are directed to do in your instructions of the 9th, in case you should think the enemy in Estremadura too strong for you.

I do not recollect that there is any magazine of ours now at Portalegre, and certainly there ought to be none ; but if there should be one, you will give orders that it may either be removed to Abrantes or Marvao, or be destroyed, if, when the time comes, you should determine either not to advance to Portalegre, or to retire from thence after having advanced. It is of the utmost importance that no magazine of ours should fall into the hands of the enemy, and indeed that all the provisions in the country should, if possible, be removed out of their reach.

I believe I have now answered all the points in your several letters ; and although this is written in a private form, you will consider it in every respect as an official instruction and authority.

To the Earl of Liverpool.   Viseu, 24th Jan. 1810.

I am not yet enabled to answer that part of your letter of the 15th Dec. which relates to the transports in the Tagus, as I have not yet received from the Admiral the information which I must have to enable me to answer your questions. I rather believe, however, that the transports now in the Tagus will not hold more than 22,000 men ; and if the army should embark, the remainder would be to be received by the men of war ; the number of which last in the Tagus will, I conclude, be vastly increased whenever the moment comes at which we may be forced to evacuate Portugal.

I also wish to draw your attention, and that of the government, to the possibility that a large proportion of the Portuguese army might be induced to evacuate the country with the British army. The Lusitanian legion were originally enlisted on the principle of serving in all parts of the world ; but they have since been filled up by men taken in the usual manner by requisition. The subject is one of that delicate nature, that it is impossible to ascertain the sentiments of the soldiers in general on the subject of embarkation, so as to form any estimate of the numbers that would be likely to embark in the case supposed. I understand, however, that in a late instance of the march of a brigade towards the coast, it was reported that the regiments composing it were about to embark, and no apprehension or disapprobation was expressed by the soldiers; and it is generally believed by the English officers in the army, that if nothing occurs to shake the confidence in us as a military people, the majority of the officers and soldiers of the army will evacuate the country with us, if we should be fairly obliged to evacuate it.

I wish government to turn their attention to this subject; and if they should determine to carry them off, to be prepared to a certain degree to carry that determination into execution. They are certainly now in a state to be highly useful any where; and will not be useless to the enemy if left in Portugal. He will soon find French officers to officer them completely; and the discipline we have given them may yet be turned against us. I also conclude that if the contest should be at an end in the Peninsula, government will not allow the colonies to pass into the hands of the French. These troops, if of no use elsewhere, will be of the greatest service on the continent of South America, for the general cause, as well as for the service of their own Prince.

I cannot tell you what effect the King s recent kindness, as communicated to me in your dispatch of the 15th Dec., has had on the Portuguese government, because Mr. Villiers not having received any instructions on the subject from the Sec. of State for Foreign affairs, no communication has yet been made to the Portuguese government; and thus one month has been lost. Indeed we have received no intelligence from England of any kind since the 20th of last month.

It would be very desirable if the packets were dispatched regularly from Falmouth, even though it should not be convenient to the ministers to write. The newspapers at times contain intelligence which it is desirable we should have; and as I before informed your Lordship, the regularity of the dispatch of the packets to and from England would contribute essentially to facilitate the raising of money by bills. This, our only resource, is become most important. The credit of the British government has been stretched to the utmost; and notwithstanding that we have paid large sums on that account, many debts still remain due on account of Sir J. Moore's army.

The people of Portugal and Spain are tired out by requisitions not paid for, of the British, Spanish, Portuguese, and French armies; and nothing can now be procured without ready money. I hope, therefore, not only that every facility will be given to our getting money by bills upon England, but that some money will be sent out according to the requests for it which I have made to your Lordship.

It would also be very desirable if an early answer was sent to the requisitions sent home for supplies, whether for the British or the Portuguese armies; stating only whether they would be complied with in the whole, or to what extent, and in what probable period. This is desirable, particularly in the case of the recent requisitions of arms for the militia of Portugal. If we cannot have them, we should know it, in order that we may make other arrangements, and employ in another manner the men who will not be armed; and narrow our system in proportion to the deficiency of our means in time. Corresponding communications ought upon every occasion to be made to the Ambassadors at Seville and Lisbon; for your Lordship knows, that, with my instructions, I can have no communication with the Spanish or Portuguese ministers, excepting through the medium of His Majesty's ministers at these courts respectively, unless upon subjects purely Portuguese, with the Portuguese government. I also wish the Treasury to send me an early answer respecting a reference made to them many months ago regarding the mode of carrying the camp kettles of the army. The subject is trifling in comparison with others, but still it is of importance, and affects in many instances the efficiency of a most important branch of the equipment of the soldiers.

I am concerned to tell you, that, notwithstanding the pains taken by the General and other officers of the army, the conduct of the soldiers is infamous. They behave well generally when with their regiments, and under the inspection of their officers, and the General officers of the army; but when detached, and coming up from hospitals, although invariably under the command of an officer, and always well fed and taken care of, and received as children of the family by the housekeeper in Portugal, they commit every description of outrage. They have never brought up a convoy of money that they have not robbed the chest; nor of shoes, or any other article that could be of use to them, or could produce money, that they do not steal something. I have never halted the army for 2 days that I have not been obliged to assemble a General Court Martial; and a General Court Martial was assembled during the whole time the army was at Badajoz. At this moment there are 3 General Courts Martial sitting in Portugal for the trial of soldiers guilty of wanton murders, (no less than 4 people have been killed by them since we returned to Portugal,) robberies, thefts, robbing convoys under their charge, &c., &c. I assure you that the military law is not sufficiently strong to keep them in order; and the people of this country have almost universally such an affection for the British nation, that they are unwilling to prosecute these unworthy soldiers in cold blood for the injuries they have received from them, at the distance of time which must elapse before the soldier can be brought to trial; although ready enough to complain and prosecute when smarting under the injury. Then the truth can never be got from themselves. Perjury is as common as robbery and murder; and the consequence of swearing them to tell truth before a regimental Court Martial is, that they invariably commit perjury when examined before a General Court Martial, where formerly the sanction of an oath was seldom given to falsehood. But upon the whole of this important subject, I refer you to my letter to Lord Castlereagh of the 17th June last.

I certainly think the army are improved. · They are a better army than they were some months ago. But still these terrible, continued outrages give me reason to apprehend that, notwithstanding all the precautions I have taken, and shall take, they will slip through my fingers, as they did through Sir J. Moore's, when I shall be involved in any nice operation with a powerful enemy in my front.

To the Earl of Liverpool. Viseu, 24th Jan. 1810.

The enemy have continued to augment their corps in La Mancha, having assembled there, according to the last accounts which I have received, the whole of the corps of Soult, Mortier, Victor, and Sebastiani; and the reserve, which usually attends the King's person, who has likewise himself gone into that province. They had left only a small detachment of Soult's corps at Talavera de la Reyna, and the neighbourhood; and one from Mortier's, at Toledo; and the left of their army, which had been at Cuenca, and even at Teruel, in Valencia, had returned into La Mancha by El Bonillo. Gen. Echavarri had made good his retreat from Cuenca to Hellin. With this army, well provided with artillery, they threatened an attack on the passes of the Sierra Morena, from Montizon to Almaden; but I have reason to believe that no attack was made so late as the 14th of this month. The Spanish troops under Gen. Areyzaga were posted in the passes of the mountains for their defence; but Col. Roche, from whom I have a letter of the 12th, did not expect that they would be able to maintain themselves.

The French troops in Old Castille collected about the 15th of this month, and marched to the neighbourhood of Miranda del Castanar, with a division in Bejar. It is probable that the object of this movement was to keep the Duque del Parque's corps in check in case he should attempt to move towards Talavera de la Reyna by Plasencia; and to provide for their own communication with the troops in La Mancha in the event of the British army making any offensive movement. This French corps consists of about 20,000 men. The Duque del Parque's corps is in the same situation as when I addressed your Lordship on the 15th inst.

I have not heard of the arrival of any reinforcements from France; but I think it probable that some of the troops expected have passed the frontiers of Spain, otherwise the enemy would not venture to collect so large a part of his force in La Mancha.

I have also received accounts that a small Spanish corps of about 500 men was surprised at Alcanices, not far from Braganza, on the 15th inst., by a body of French cavalry, which it is probable had but lately entered Spain.

The A.G. to Major Williamson, A.A.G. 24th Jan. 1810.

I have his Excellency's command to place you at the hospital station at Coimbra, it being found absolutely necessary to attach an officer of the department to that establishment, to aid in the conduct of those arrangements which must relate to every part of the army.

You will hold yourself in readiness to move on the arrival of Major Ponsonby and Capt. Cotton, to the first of whom you will transfer the documents of the division; and when you have reached Coimbra, you will be pleased to communicate with me.

The A.G. to Col. Peacocke, Lisbon. 24th Jan. 1810.

Assist. Surgeon Whimper, Coldstream Guards, having renewed an application for leave to refit, has drawn his Excellency's attention to his escape from the enemy. You will be pleased to call on that officer to detail by what means he was enabled to effect, and what situation he was in at the time he made his escape; viz., whether prisoner at large, on a species of parole, or closely confined; and whether he received any previous supply of money or otherwise, from the French General previous to his departure. Till the receipt of this information, the Commander of the Forces cannot further decide on Mr. Whimper's application.

To Capt. Ruman.   Viseu, 25th Jan. 1810.

I am very much obliged to you for the pains which you have taken in procuring intelligence of the enemy's movements, which become every day more interesting to us. I request you in future to transmit your reports to Brig. Gen. Cox, at Almeida, who will forward them to me; and I beg of you to adopt modes of transmitting them which you may be certain will be expeditious and sure.

You will apply to Gen. Cox at Almeida for any money that may be necessary to enable you to make these disbursements, as well as any others that you may think necessary to make in order to extend your means of early information. I think that you might be able to extend your correspondence even beyond the Douro, by disbursing money; and I have no objections to pay for what is authentic, and comes at an early period.

To Brig. Gen. Cox, Governor of Almeida.   Viseu, 25th Jan. 1810.

I have received your letters of the 21st and 22d, for which I am much obliged to you.

I cannot conceive that the French would venture to draw all their troops to the south of the Tagus, if the reinforcements for the army had not passed the frontier. However, we shall know more upon that subject; in the mean time I shall order up some of the British cavalry, and I will try if we cannot do something.

I have ordered Capt. Ellis to Almeida with instructions to assist you in procuring, arranging, and forwarding information of the enemy's movements in Castille; and I have directed 2 Spanish officers of the Q. M. Gen.'s department to place themselves under your directions, and to correspond with you, and I herewith enclose a letter for Capt. Ruman upon the same subject, which I beg you to peruse and forward to him. I have likewise desired Lieut. Col. Bathurst to send you £500 to be expended in procuring intelligence, of which sum I request you to keep a separate account.

I request that you will direct these several officers in what channel to conduct their inquiries, and in what manner the most expeditious to communicate to you the result. You will supply them and Capt. Ruman with such sums of money as they may require, and as you shall think reasonable for both purposes of acquiring and conveying intelligence to you. Capt. Ellis will assist you in arranging and forwarding this intelligence to Gen. Craufurd, Gen. Cole, and me; and in order to enable you to send it off in a certain and expeditious manner, I have ordered some hussars to Almeida and Pinhel, and there are detachments of guides at Celorico and Mangualde, as also between Celorico and Mangualde.

The officers should extend their correspondence as far as possible along, and north of the Douro, and direct their inquiries to every object, the march of every detachment, the names of the officers commanding corps of troops, the formation of magazines, collection of depots of ordnance and stores, fortifications of posts, &c. In case a man of —— —— should write any letter to me, or to you at Almeida, give the bearer of it 4 dollars, and forward it to me.

To tne Rt. Hon. J. Villiers.   Viseu, 25th Jan. 1810.

While I was absent on the frontier, I received several letters from you which remain unanswered; and I have this morning received your letters of the 19th and 21st, that of the 20th having reached me 2 days ago.

In respect to Capt. Smyth, if he is in the 3d batt. 95th regt., he does not belong to the army in Portugal, and I cannot appoint him to the staff without the special permission of the Commander in Chief. I conceived it was Capt. Smyth's wish to return to England, and stretched a point to allow him to do so; for the evidence was by no means clear that he had been removed from the 11th regt., which belongs to this army, to the 3d batt. 95th, which does not.

In answer to your letter of the 19th, I have only to repeat what I have said before, viz., that I know of no mode in which our funds can be increased, either at Lisbon, Cadiz, or Gibraltar; that every thing that I can conceive would raise a shilling has been resorted to; and the supplies from Gibraltar and Cadiz, as well as from Lisbon, are diminishing rather than increasing.

You appear to be satisfied with the exertions which have been made at Lisbon, although you state that £50,000 might be procured on a loan, through the means of Mr. Sampayo. Your letter is the first intelligence I have received upon this subject; and I can only say, in answer to it, that I shall have inquiry made respecting this loan: and if I should find the transaction to be of a description that the Commissary Gen. ought to enter into, I will authorise him to make the loan. But although you express a general satisfaction with the measures adopted at Lisbon, with which you are acquainted, you are not satisfied with those, and you desire 'increased activity' at Cadiz and Gibraltar, although you have no knowledge of the measures which have been adopted there. Now, I, who have that knowledge, who have superintended these transactions from the commencement, am convinced that it is impossible to get another shilling for bills upon England at either place. These transactions are most judiciously managed at Cadiz by Mr. Duff, the Consul General. At Gibraltar there is some difficulty in getting money, as not only the army in Portugal, but the fleet in the Mediterranean, the army in Sicily, the officers of Malta and Gibraltar, are supplied with money for bills upon England, negotiated at the same place by different persons. The state of the money there also has some influence over that of Cadiz; and even if I could find reason to disapprove of the conduct of the Commissary General's agent at Gibraltar, which I cannot, I do not see how I could increase the funds received from Gibraltar, by any arrangement I could make, or by any 'increased activity.'

In respect to the expenditure of the money received, I believe there is no man who doubts that the first and principal object of my attention, and of that of every British officer, must be the British army, and afterwards the allies whom His Majesty has bound himself to support. The nature and constitution of the British army absolutely requires that it should be regularly paid. It cannot plunder or take what it wants upon requisition like the French army, because it is not sufficiently numerous; and all the necessaries, and much of the food of the soldiers, depend upon their regular payment. I believe I have gone farther than any officer in withholding this payment, excepting Lord Hutchinson in Egypt; but there it must be observed that the troops received a description of ration which they could, and did, barter with the natives for the other articles which they required. The British army in Portugal has been sometimes 2 months, and is invariably one month, in arrear, notwithstanding the King's orders and regulations, and the customs and necessities of the service; and at this moment I have not as much money as will supply the pay of the troops.

Under these circumstances, it is useless to enter into the old discussion, whether we got £80,000 or you got £50,000, or under what head it was advanced. We agree that the British army must be the first object; and until the British government, who have entered into all these arrangements upon a clear and distinct view of their expense, and upon information repeated over and over again of the inadequacy of the funds placed at my disposal to meet the expense, shall adopt efficient measures to increase those funds, the difficulties under which we labor must continue to exist, and must increase.

The mention of 'increased activity' in the supply of these funds has suggested to me the notion of taking the whole out of the hands of the Commissary Gen. Let the minister at Lisbon or at Seville undertake the management of the money concerns of the government in this part of the world; let them draw all bills; and let me have no more to do with the subject than to give in regular estimates of the funds required monthly for the army under my command, and receive the money, in the same manner as other officers who have been employed in similar situations.

In answer to your official letter of the 15th, and to part of your letter of the 19th, and to that of the 21st, I have to inform you that, in concurrence with Marshal Beresford, I believe the Junta de Viveres, as a Commissary Gen., to be very inefficient; and I am also certain that a great part of the money which is placed at their disposal to pay for provisions is employed (perhaps necessarily) in paying salaries and establishments. I know from experience that the Portuguese army could not be in the distress which it suffers from the want of provisions, if only a part of the provisions it receives from the country were paid for; and the object of my proposition was to insure the disposal of the fund supplied by Great Britain to that purpose, and no other. If this proposition had been adopted through your interference, in the simple form in which it was made, I should have followed it up by another which I should have made and have pressed upon the Portuguese government, viz., that they should allot a certain sum of money out of the revenues of the country, to be expended in provisions for the troops; and that this sum also should be placed at the disposal of Marshal Beresford monthly.

I do not mean to say that, with these arrangements, they would have done every thing that was necessary to pay for the provisions of the troops, but at least they would have done something; one third, one half, or two thirds would have been paid for, and the country would have continued to supply what was wanted. But this proposition, instead of being adopted in the simple form in which it was made, is understood to be a design to overturn the Junta de Viveres, and substitute in its place a new system of Commissariat; a correspondence of volumes passes upon it; a fortnight has elapsed since it was made, and nothing is done ; a proposition is made that I should take into the hands of the British Commissary Gen. the supply of the provisions for 30,000 Portuguese troops, for which he has neither establishment, nor funds, nor any facilities to enable him to execute the task ; and thus, fortnight after fortnight, month after month, passes in discussions, instead of in making efficient arrangements to resist the very serious attack with which this unfortunate country is threatened.

My suggestion to you was simply this : that that portion of the money paid by Great Britain for provisioning 20,000 or 30,000 men should be placed at Marshal Beresford's disposal, to be applied as he should think proper in the payment for provisions, through ' *the Commissaries of the Portuguese army ;*' that is to say, through the officers of the Junta de Viveres, or the Commissary Gen. Marshal Beresford would have selected the parts of the country which had been most pressed to make these payments ; and the plan, if adopted, would have secured this object, viz., that every shilling would have been expended for provisions, instead of in salaries and establishments.

As far as Marshal Beresford is concerned, the detail of business would have been trifling, and no more than we are all obliged to enter into ; and probably much less than that into which he is now obliged to enter, from the daily complaints of scarcity from non-payment, which he forwards to the government. The Commissaries, to whom the Marshal would have ordered the issue of the money, would have been accountable to the Junta de Viveres for its due application, according to the Marshal's orders. Their receipt for the money would have been the charge, and their account of the disposal their discharge with their masters, the Junta de Viveres ; and there is neither complication, confusion, nor competition in any part of the plan, but merely the substitution of Marshal Beresford for the Junta de Viveres in the selection of the places where the bills for provisions shall be paid, and where they shall not ; in the same manner as I make the same selection for my own army in almost every case. So much for one of my suggestions for the relief of the distress of the Portuguese army for want of provisions ; and now for the other, the formation of magazines. In order to effect this object, the Portuguese government required money, I suppose, to buy provisions. I have twice offered to buy and pay for grain, and to lodge it in their stores ; once in September, and in my official letter to you of the 9th inst. ; and this same government, with a starving army, without a shilling in their treasury, and with the enemy upon their frontier, will not take it !

It is convenient to me to buy Mr. Phillips's grain (which, by the bye, he will sell at as cheap a rate as any other can be got), because he will take payment for it in bills upon the Treasury, which he engages not to negotiate at Lisbon, Cadiz, or Gibraltar ; and this grain is in fact tantamount to so much money introduced into the military chest. It will probably not be convenient to purchase the grain of another dealer, because he will come into the money market with his bills. But no ! after a fortnight's consideration, this suggestion is not adopted ! But no other plan is adopted, or even proposed. The army is still starving ; no magazine of any kind is formed ; and as far as that goes, we are just where we stood in October last.

However, I have done with the Portuguese government. I have performed my duty by them in suggesting practicable and efficient measures for the relief of the great distress under which they labor. My letters of the 9th and 12th Jan. will always relieve me from any blame for the misfortunes which must be the consequence of this mode of proceeding; and from this time forward I shall not write a line excepting in answer to those questions which may be put to me, or those propositions which may be forwarded for my consideration.

After this explanation of the plan contained in my letter of the 12th Jan., which I conceive is fully developed in the letter itself, and which is misunderstood only because the Junta de Viveres and the government choose not to understand it, it is scarcely necessary that I should give any further reply to your letter of the 21st. The Commissary Gen. has neither establishment nor means to undertake to feed 30,000 Portuguese troops. I have made an arrangement under which we can assist, and do assist, the Portuguese troops and Commissariat with provisions and magazines when they require them; but I can do no more.

In answer to your letter of the 20th, I have to inform you that Senhor Botelho is already employed under the Commissariat, in a manner in which we think he will be useful. We should suffer inconvenience if we were to remove him from that employment; and he could be of no use to us in that which he has chalked out for himself. There is also a letter from you that I have mislaid, relating to Mr. S—— I cannot give him leave of absence until he shall be relieved. Mr. A—— belongs to a division in the army, and must join it as soon as his health will permit.

The A. G. to Dr. Franck, Inspector of Hospitals.   25th Jan, 1810.

In forwarding to you the enclosed papers, I am directed to communicate to you, on their purport, that the Commander of the Forces finds with dissatisfaction, that his conjecture relative to the reports of Medical boards proves too well grounded; that the reports are not founded upon an examination of the state of health of the officer produced before the board, of the existing symptoms of his case, and of a communication with the medical gentleman who has attended, but rather upon the wish expressed by the officer himself. This inference will be obvious to you, in comparing the tenor of the report of the Medical board on the case of Capt. ——, and the correspondence between Capt. —— and Dr. ——.

These papers are transmitted for perusal, that you may be convinced his Excellency's accompanying commands are necessary; that you warn the medical officers of the army, that the duty which they are called upon on these occasions to perform is most important to the public as well as to individuals, and that it is expected they will, conscientiously, perform that duty without bias.

To Gen. Bacellar.   Viseu, 26th Jan. 1810.

With a view to the future operations of the allied armies, and to the communication between the different corps on this frontier, and on the Tagus, it is desirable that the road should be repaired from Ponte da Murcella to Espinhal by Venda Nova, S. Miguel, Foz d'Arouce, and Corvo; also, that the road should be repaired from Ponte da Murcella to Almeida, by Louroza, Galizes, and Pinhanços, to Celorico and Pinhel.

I request you to give directions to the several magistrates that these roads may be repaired forthwith, and inform them that I shall send an officer along the road in the course of a short time to see what has been done in consequence of these directions, and that I hope I shall find that they will have obliged the inhabitants of the country to do their duty.

To Vice Adm. the Hon. G. Berkeley.   Viseu, 26th Jan. 1810.

I have had the pleasure of receiving your letter of the 20th inst., and I have desired Col. Murray to write to Lieut. Fleetwood for any further information that may be necessary regarding the transports. I have already more than once stated to government my opinion, that in case of our being hard pressed in this country, it was absolutely necessary that you should have a reinforcement.

In respect to the use of Peniche in an embarkation of the army, I refer you to my letter written to you in October, from which you will observe, that the probable course of our operations will preclude the use of that port as one of embarkation for the British army. I think, however, we might maintain a garrison in Peniche for some time, even after we should have evacuated Portugal with the army : which would answer various purposes, as well for the fleet, which would of course be employed in the blockade of the Tagus, as for other objects which I have in contemplation.

I do not know what to make of the Portuguese government: I cannot bring my mind to doubt their good intentions; but you will scarcely believe, that, although their army is starving, and they have no money to buy provisions, they have hesitated and indeed refused to adopt two propositions made by me which would have relieved all their difficulties, and would have given them magazines. I have done with them.

It is very extraordinary that I have not the slightest recollection of the person who you say was arrested at Badajoz.

To Lieut. Gen. Payne.   Viseu, 27th Jan. 1810.

I have received your letter of the 13th, and I am equally surprised and annoyed at the failure of all our measures for the re-establishment of the heavy cavalry. This failure is, however, to be attributed entirely to Mr. ——, of whom I shall make a formal complaint to the Treasury, as soon as I shall receive the Commissary Gen.'s report, and I shall suspend him from his office till their pleasure shall be known.

It is so inconvenient, and indeed the army is exposed to so much risk, having the cavalry at such a distance, that I cannot consent to the arrangement you propose for the dragoons, more particularly as, by a little exertion by the Commissaries, we shall find no difficulty in feeding them in their present quarters; and I have ordered the direct road to be repaired, which, instead of placing them at the distance of 7 or 8 marches from the army, will bring them within three, of which only one will be forced. If the cavalry had been in order, and had recovered as I had reason to expect they would, I might now strike a blow of essential importance. However, it cannot now be helped. Mr. —— shall be punished, and I hope the next commissary will do his duty better.

G. A. O.   Viseu, 27th Jan. 1810.

The passports for post horses sent to the officers commanding divisions, &c. are to be used only to procure post horses for couriers and others whom it may be necessary to send by post upon the public service, or for officers to whom the officers in whose hands the passports are lodged choose to give permission to travel by post.

I have great objections to the increase of the ration : in the first place, I strongly suspect foul play in those heavy regiments at the time the officers were sickly, and I have never heard any sufficient reason why the horses of the heavy dragoons, the ——— in particular, which never moved after August, should be in such bad condition, when all the other horses of the army were in such fine order, and most particularly the Hussars, K.G.L. Besides, it would be ridiculous to order 12 lbs. of hay or straw for a ration for horses, in answer to a report stating that they could not be provided with more than half of 10 lbs.

Considering that the cavalry do no work, and that they are all in stables, and adverting to the very excellent condition in which the horses of the hussars are which have been most worked, and which I am sorry to say are now frequently fed upon rye, I cannot but be apprehensive that there is some deficiency of attention to stable duties. I should recommend to you, therefore, to call the attention of commanding officers of regiments to this subject, and to resume the use of the currycomb and brush universally, if they should not be able immediately to supply themselves with the hair gloves which you preferred.

I shall be very much obliged to you if you will have all the spare appointments with the regiments sent to Lisbon, so that when the cavalry shall be able to move, it may move light. I rather think that I shall very shortly draw the 16th up to Coimbra.

You will be sorry to hear that I lost 3 horses the other day, smothered in the stable, which had caught fire ; 2 of which were my black and the chestnut.

To the Duque del Parque.   Viseu, 27th Jan. 1810.

I have had the honor of receiving your Excellency's letter, in which you have informed me of your intention to move the army under your command across the Tagus, of the possibility that some of the divisions may pass through Portugal ; and you have expressed a desire that the magistrates and others in authority in Portugal may be directed not to throw any impediment in the way of the march of those troops, but may assist them as much as may be in their power with provisions, &c., for which payment is to be made.

I regret that your Excellency has not stated particularly the strength and composition of the divisions which will pass through Portugal, or the route which they will take, as the country through which they will probably direct their march is one but ill provided with supplies, and has been much exhausted by the march of troops in the course of the last year ; and although the directions have been given of which your Excellency was desirous, I am apprehensive, that unless further and more detailed arrangements are made for the supply of your troops on their march through Portugal, they will experience great distress for want of provisions.

To Major Gen. the Hon. G. L. Cole.   Viseu, 27th Jan. 1810.

I enclose a letter to Col. Wilson, which I request you to peruse and to have forwarded to him. You will observe that the Duque del Parque is about to move his army across the Tagus. It will be desirable, therefore, that you should have a post of observation at Alfaiates, to watch the Sierra de Gata, &c.

To Lieut. Gen. Hill.   Viseu, 27th Jan. 1810.

I send you the duplicate of a letter to Col. Wilson, which I beg you to peruse and forward to him. I think, that in order to preserve order at the bridge of Villa Velha, it is desirable that you should send there a company of British infantry under the command of a steady officer. I have no doubt that the Duque del Parque means to cross the Tagus at that place with his whole army.

To the Earl of Liverpool.   Viseu, 27th Jan. 1810.

I send home, by the vessel which will take this, Lieut. V. de Farincourt, of the *2me regt. d'infanterie legere* of the French army, with a cartel of exchange for Lieut. Cameron of the 79th regt., who was taken prisoner by the French on the 27th July, and was sent into Portugal by Gen. Kellermann from Valladolid. Upon the occasion of sending this officer to England, and of requesting that he may be sent to France, as soon as may be practicable, I think it proper to explain the reasons which have induced me to send him by this mode of conveyance.

I am concerned to have to inform your Lordship that since the British officers and soldiers were made prisoners in the hospital at Talavera, the Spanish government have thrown every obstacle in their power in the way of their being exchanged, and of every communication between the enemy's Generals and me, which had for its object either their exchange, or their relief by money or otherwise.

As the French prisoners taken in the battle of Talavera, and during the operations in Spain, were given in charge to the Spanish General at the time they were taken, I had no prisoners in my power to exchange for the officers and soldiers taken in the hospital.

Marshal Soult, however, proposed an exchange of prisoners, provided Gen. Franceschi, who had been taken in Old Castille in June, should be included in the cartel. This proposition having been referred to the Spanish government, they gave no answer to it for 3 months, and at length refused to agree to it.

They then, in the month of September, detained Capt. Thevenon, an aide de camp of Marshal Mortier, who had been sent into the Spanish posts with a letter for me, which was open: first, under pretence that it was necessary that he should wait for an answer; and afterwards, when I remonstrated against his detention, and declared that the letter required no answer, they detained him under the pretence that he had passed the Tagus at Almaraz, where they did not choose to receive flags of truce, although he was received at this same place with his flag by the officer commanding the Spanish outposts. After repeated remonstrances, they at length, in November, allowed Capt. Thevenon to return to the French army, having detained him in close confinement for nearly 2 months.

In the month of September, Gen. Kellermann sent Lieut. Cameron of the 79th regt. into Portugal from Valladolid, with a cartel of exchange for Lieut. de Turenne, his aide de camp, who had just been made prisoner in Old Castille. I immediately requested the Spanish government, through the Ambassador, to place Lieut. de Turenne at my disposal, which, after some delay, they refused; and I then prevailed upon the Portuguese government to allow Lieut. V. de Farincourt, who had been taken at Chaves, and was a prisoner at Lisbon, to be exchanged for Lieut. Cameron.

In order to avoid the difficulties which I had experienced in communicating with the enemy's Generals regarding the prisoners, by the frontier of Estremadura, I determined to send Lieut. de Farincourt at once into Old Castille, and he was attended by a Portuguese officer, Capt. Gill, 24th regt., who was to conduct him to the French outposts.

On their arrival at Ciudad Rodrigo, however, both were stopped, and Lieut. de Farincourt was put in confinement, and Capt. Gill was insulted and ill treated. Brig. Gen. Cox, who commanded at Almeida, remonstrated upon this conduct, but in vain; and at length when I was informed of it, on the 6th Dec., I wrote to Mr. Frere to request that he would make remonstrances on the subject; to which letter I received a reply on the 9th, a copy of which I enclose, stating that the orders had been sent to Ciudad Rodrigo to permit Lieut. de Farincourt to proceed to the French outposts. I found, however, by a letter from Brig. Gen. Cox to Marshal Beresford, dated the 18th Dec., of which I enclose the copy, not only that these orders had not been sent, but that the Duque del Parque stated that he had received others of a contrary tenor, and that Lieut. de Farincourt and Capt. Gill were sent back into Portugal.

The correspondence then ensued between Mr. Frere and me, of which I enclose the copies, from which it is evident not only that the Duque del Parque had not received the orders under which he assured Gen. Cox that he acted, but that Don A. de Cornel had deceived his colleague Don F. de Saavedra. The result of this conduct, however, is an impossibility of having any communication with the enemy's Generals, which has for its object either the relief or the exchange of the British officers and soldiers who were made prisoners, only because they were wounded in fighting the battles of Spain.

The A.G. to the Dep. Paymaster General.   27th Jan. 1810.

I do myself the honor to enclose a general account of sums expended by Major Lindsay, commanding the hospital station, Elvas, up to the 15th inst. inclusive, from the amount received by him for public service. The vouchers of this disbursement are in shape of regimental charges, which, on being checked, correspond with the sums contained in the annexed account. These have been forwarded to the head quarters of each battalion, and you will be so good as to take the remaining steps to reimburse the public for the general advance. The next period brought into account will be up to the 24th Jan. I am anxious to learn from you, whether this mode of carrying on the extra accounts of the hospitals appears to you correct, or whether there is any other system you should prefer.

You will suspend all pay and allowances from Capt. ——— till further orders, in consequence of that officer's delay in accounting for public money advanced on similar service.

To the Rt. Hon. J. Villiers.   Viseu, 28th Jan. 1810.

I have received your letter of the 23d inst., to which I do not lose a moment in replying.

Of course, the Commissary Gen. shall be directed to do whatever you desire him in the way of bills for you, and I expect to receive from you an official letter upon the subject. But I have already apprised you of the inconvenience to our finances of assisting the Portuguese government with bills drawn upon British credit. Although the bills, which you now propose should be granted, are for such sums that they cannot be themselves converted into cash, yet the government are to draw for smaller sums upon the holders of these English bills, which sums, if not disposed of in this way, would be in the market for the Commissary General's bills. However, having said thus much, and having frequently explained to you the inconvenience (which would now amount to an impossibility of remaining in the country) which must result from any interruption to our supplies of money, I have only to add that the bills shall be sent by return of the post, or of the messenger which shall bring an official letter from you, desiring that the Commissary Gen. may grant them.

To Col. Peacocke.   Viseu, 29th Jan. 1810.

I have the honor to enclose the proceedings of the General Court Martial, on the trial of ——— ———, camp follower, not a soldier, which I had thought proper to transmit to be laid before His Majesty for his confirmation; and a letter I have received from the Judge Advocate Gen., from which it appears that it is necessary that the members of the General Court Martial should be re-assembled. I have issued orders that they may re-assemble at Lisbon on the 8th Feb.; when, if they should all have arrived, or as soon after as the members shall have arrived, you will communicate to the Court the letter from the Judge Advocate Gen., and desire them to revise their sentence upon the prisoner ——— ———.

To J. Murray, Esq., Commissary General.   Viseu, 30th Jan. 1810.

I enclose the copy of a letter received from the Sec. of State in Portugal, by which an arrangement is made to place the boats on the rivers Tagus, Mondego, and Douro, under the orders of certain officers in the different districts, with a view to their being registered, and to their being removed out of reach in case the enemy should invade the country. I also enclose a letter received from the same gentleman, in which he desires that all applications for boats on any of those rivers may be made to the officers of the districts respectively charged with the arrangement and management of them.

I desire that in all cases boats, as well as carriages, may be procured for the service of the British army, by the sense of interest in the parties who may have them to hire, owing to the regularity of the payment of the hire of the boats and carriages. But if at any time, either owing to the pressing nature of the service, or to the large demand for boats or carriages, or to any other cause, it should be necessary to press or em-

---

G. A. O.   Viseu, 28th Jan. 1810.

The Commander of the Forces is desirous that all men who are sick and require carriage should be removed to the general hospital established at Coimbra from the several cantonments of the army once a week, according to arrangements and directions sent by the Q. M. G. and Inspector of Hospitals to the officers of the Q. M. G.'s department, and Medical Staff attached to the different divisions of the army. The General officers are requested to see those directions, and have them carried into execution.

bargo boats or carriages, you will direct the officers of the Commissariat to make application for those which they require to the officer of the Portuguese government charged with the management of the boats or carriages in the district in which they may be required.

To the Rev. S. Briscall, Chaplain to the Forces.   Viseu, 30th Jan. 1810.

I have perused the letter from the Sec. at War which you left with me, and I have great satisfaction in availing myself of this opportunity of testifying my sense of the assiduity, regularity, and propriety with which you have performed the duties of your situation, and with which you have conducted yourself since you have been attached to this army; and I hope that this certificate will have the effect of giving us the benefit of your continuance with us.

To Major Gen. the Hon. G. L. Cole.   Viseu, 30th Jan. 1810.

As I am going away for a few days upon a reconnaissance towards Torres Vedras, I wish to state in writing what I before told you in conversation when I saw you at Guarda.

I do not wish to lose possession of the Coa, although I do not mean to contend for it, if the enemy should collect a large force evidently with the intention of making a serious invasion of Portugal. If that should be the case, and you should deem it necessary, you will in concert with Gen. Craufurd withdraw from the Coa, and collect your division and the hussars from Guarda, Trancoso, &c., to Celorico, where also, in the case of necessity supposed, you will find Gen. Craufurd's division. If the same necessity should continue to exist, as I do not mean to defend the Mondego at Celorico, I should wish the troops to fall back gradually upon Pinhancos, where Sir J. Sherbrooke will be, in the case supposed, with his division and other troops. I conclude that you have posts upon the upper Coa, at Castello Bom, at Ponte de Sequeiros, at Rapoula de Coa, and also at Alfaiates, in consequence of my last letter.

To Brig. Gen. Cox, Governor of Almeida.   Viseu, 30th Jan. 1810.

I received last night yours of the 28th, and Col. Grant's letters of the 23d and 24th. The enemy carried the Sierra Morena on the 20th, on which day their head quarters were at La Carolina. You may depend upon it that the whole of Ney's and Kellermann's corps are in Castille.

To Bart. Frere, Esq.   Viseu, 30th Jan. 1810.

I have had the honor of receiving your several letters of the 16th, 17th, 19th, 20th, and 21st inst., for which I am much obliged to you. I had already received accounts of the enemy's having obtained possession of the pass of La Carolina.

I am perfectly aware of the advantage which the general cause would derive from the movement of the British army into Castille, if it be true

G. O.   Viseu, 30th Jan. 1810.

2. The officers of the army who have soldiers for their servants, should be particularly cautious not to give them orders, the execution of which are breaches of discipline and good order, and not to expose them in a state of intoxication to the temptation of committing offences, which must lead to the punishment of the soldier.

that the enemy's reinforcements have not yet entered Spain. I should doubt, however, the truth of the report, which states that only 8000 have arrived, both on account of the time which has elapsed since they passed Paris, and because the enemy has hitherto acted with so much caution, that I do not believe he would incur the risk of collecting at the Sierra Morena the large force which has lately been collected in that quarter, if the near approach and the expected early arrival in Castille of the reinforcements did not remove all chance of danger from this measure.

But these conjectures respecting the probable period of the arrival of the reinforcements would not prevent me from making a movement into Castille if the enemy was not at the present moment in greater strength in that province than I can bring into the field. Their force consists of Ney and Kellermann; and although it extends from Zamora to Avila and Valladolid, and even to Burgos, there is no doubt that they could collect it before I could make any impression upon any part of it.

The convalescents of the British army have only now commenced to join their regiments. The reinforcements have not yet arrived from England; and even if I should draw in the division placed upon the Tagus, which would expose the rear to some risk, particularly if the movement had the effect of relieving the southern provinces of Spain, I could not bring 20,000 men into the field.

The Portuguese army is well disciplined, and will soon, I hope, be a valuable addition to our force; but at present these troops are so sickly from the want of clothing and necessaries not yet arrived from England, and from the distress which they have suffered throughout the winter for provisions, owing to the deficiency of money to buy them, that the consequence of moving them from their quarters in this season would be the annihilation of that army, and would occasion the disappointment of all hopes of service from them, not only hereafter, but even in the operation which I should now undertake in the hope of their assistance. I have therefore, with great reluctance, given up all thoughts of moving at present.

The Duque del Parque has received his orders to cross the Tagus, and informed me on the 24th that he was about to carry them into execution. I am afraid that the person charged with the defence of Ciudad Rodrigo is a very improper one, and not very likely to do his duty. As this place is a most important one, I shall be much obliged to you if you will make inquiry respecting this person's character, and urge that he may be relieved by one more deserving of confidence on account of his talents and experience.

To Lieut. Col. Torrens, Military Secretary.   Viseu, 30th Jan. 1810.

I shall esteem it a great favor if you will tell Sir D. Dundas that I am very much obliged to him, but that I have no wish to be removed from the 33d regt., of which I was major, and lieut. colonel, and then colonel.*

I must say, however, that my friend, the late Sec. at War, made it the least profitable of all the regiments of the army, and, I believe, a losing concern, having reduced the establishment at once from 1200 to 800, when it consisted of above 750 men; and I had to pay the freight of the clothing to the East Indies, and its carriage to Hyderabad, about 500 miles from

* An offer had been made to remove Lord Wellington to a regiment with 2 battalions.

Madras. With all this, I have the reputation of having *a good thing* in a regiment in the East Indies!

To the Earl of Liverpool.   Viseu, 30th Jan. 1810.

I have the honor to enclose the returns of stores in His Majesty's magazines in Portugal up to the 1st Jan. 1810.

Return of provisions, wine, spirits, and forage remaining in His Majesty's magazines in Portugal on the 1st Jan. 1810.

Provisions, Wine, and Spirits.	Biscuit	1,792,160
	Flour	1,099,134 } lbs.
	Salt meat	1,797,190
	Wine	26 pipes.
	Rum	113,990 gallons.
Forage.	Oats	1,444,640
	Barley	1,286,385
	Wheat	87,070
	Indian corn	212,551 } lbs.
	Beans	1,660
	Bran	5,100
	Hay	1,372,304

J. MURRAY, Commissary General.

Return of Q. M. Gen.'s stores remaining in His Majesty's magazines in Portugal.

1900 Flanders tents	Soldiers' tents.
1900 Flanders poles	
1838 Iron collars	
6000 Mallets	
124,600 Pins	
724 Poles and cases	Camp colours.
431 Flags	
595 Powder bags.	
1060 Drum cases.	
698 Hatchets.	
785 Bill hooks.	
3493 Flanders kettles.	
264 Picket ropes.	
5 Pickaxes.	
453 Hair nose bags.	
461 Packsaddles with crooked haucums.	
264 Bridles and chain collars.	
167 Ammunition boxes.	
19 Medicine panniers.	
16 Tarpaulins.	
15½ Vals. marq. tents	Hospital.
14½ Sets of poles	
70 Bags of mallets and pins	
3 Reels and Lines.	
200 Langrels.	

626 Tin kettles.
335 Kettle bags.
604 Tin canteens.
6699 Wood canteens.
5286 Canteen straps.
43 Felling axes.
14,020 Havresacks.
2235 Blankets.
542¾ Sets of forage cords, 4 to a set.
106 Bundles of blankets.
735 Picket poles.
1 Knapsack.
618 Sets of bedding.
5 Shovels.
5 Spades.
149 Casks of accoutrements.
2 Cases of nails.
75 Mule halters.
34 French tent poles.
20 Small water casks.
13 Cases of buttons.
9 Cases of officers' swords.
99,062 Pairs of shoes.
45 Bales of army clothing.
10 Baskets.
400 Palliasses.

J. MURRAY, Commissary General.

To the Earl of Liverpool.   Viseu, 30th Jan. 1810.

I have the honor to enclose a return of the transports in Lisbon on the 21st Jan. 1810.

I shall attend to your Lordship's instructions of the 3d inst., in case it should be necessary to embark the army from Portugal. Your Lordship will observe, however, from the course of the enemy's recent operations, which will be reported to you by this occasion, the probability that he will proceed in the first instance to endeavor to complete the conquest of the south of Spain; and in the event of succeeding in that object, so far as to obtain possession of Cadiz, I conclude that it is not wished that I should, in case of the evacuation of Portugal, proceed with the army embarked in its transports off Cadiz.

I also beg to draw the attention of His Majesty's government to a fact respecting the harbour of Cadiz which has been stated to me, and which deserves their attention, and further inquiry from the officers of the navy, as being likely to influence their measures respecting Cadiz, even supposing that place should hold out till after the time at which the British army should evacuate Portugal. I understand that the channel by which large ships are obliged to enter and go out of the port of Cadiz lies to the northward, and is protected and commanded by the fire of the batteries on that side of the harbour, and by no means by that of the fort of Cadiz itself. These batteries had not been destroyed, or even disarmed, when I was at Cadiz in November, and I have not heard that they have yet been disarmed, although I have suggested through a third person to Gen. Venegas the expediency of disarming them, if he expected from the British navy any assistance in the defence of the place. Whether these batteries are destroyed and disarmed or not, it is obvious that if the only channel, which can be used by large ships, is on the north side of the entrance, the enemy will have the command of it during any operations which may be carried on at Cadiz.

To the Rt. Hon. J. Villiers.   Viseu, 30th Jan. 1810.

I have just received your letter of the 25th Jan., desiring that I will state to Dom M. Forjaz in what way I wish the government to act in respect to provisions. I beg to refer you to many letters which I have written to you in respect to provisions for the Portuguese army, particularly to my official letters of the 9th and 12th Jan.

In respect to the money concerns, and all the points on which I have ventured to give them advice, I beg to refer you to my dispatches to them; in which you will see that they have not adopted any one measure that I have recommended to them, either for the improvement of their financial concerns, or for the support of the efficiency and authority of their government, or for the efficiency of their army. I propose to send these last letters home, in order to show that I at least advised them as I ought.

It was impossible for Mr. Phillips, or any other dealer, to depend upon the changes of determination in the Portuguese government; and I ordered the Commissary Gen. to take his wheat, which I was very sure would be required sooner or later. I do not know what advantage the Junta de Viveres would derive from making the bargain themselves, more particularly as Mr. Phillips gives the wheat at the lowest price at which wheat of the same kind can be purchased. I have desired the Commissary Gen. to give all that shall be purchased from Mr. Phillips to the person you will order to receive it, upon getting your receipt, either for so much wheat, specifying the cost, according to the Commissariat arrangement, or for so much money, being the price to be paid to Mr. Phillips.

In respect to the difficulty mentioned in your letter of the 26th, I hope that Adm. Berkeley will see the propriety of taking off the embargo he has laid upon the corn, as there is no doubt that the Commissary Gen. can settle Mr. Phillips's debt to the Transport office in the mode pointed out by you. I certainly understood from Mr. Phillips that he had in the harbour of Lisbon as much as three million pounds of wheat, and some barley, which he engaged to give for bills upon England, not to be negotiated at Lisbon, Gibraltar, or Cadiz, excepting a small sum of money required at Lisbon for expenses incurred there. I imagine that Mr. Phillips has not deceived me.

I have also received your letter of the 26th inst., stating your belief that more money might be obtained at Cadiz for bills; and I am happy to find that you propose to send a person there to see whether 'greater activity and exertion' would not procure more money. It appears to me, that as Mr. Duff gets half *per cent.* for all he gets, he has as great a stimulus for 'activity and exertion,' if these qualities could procure money for bills any where, as any agent can have. However, your secret agent will report to you the state of the case; and I trust that if you should find that we are not well served there, you will take the management of the whole money concern into your own hands.

It is desirable, however, that, until you shall have been convinced by the inquiries of your secret agent, that Mr. Duff does not manage the business to advantage, our existing arrangements at Cadiz should not be disturbed.

To Brig. Gen. R. Craufurd. Viseu, 31st Jan. 1810.

I am going for a few days to look about me at Torres Vedras; but you will continue to direct every thing to me here, and Gen. Sherbrooke will read and forward to me your communications.

I don't think that the enemy is likely to molest us at present; but I am desirous of maintaining the Coa, unless he should collect a very large force, and obviously intends to set seriously to work on the invasion of Portugal. If that should be the case, I do not propose to maintain the Coa, or that you should risk any thing for that purpose; and I beg you to retire gradually to Celorico, where you will be joined by Gen. Cole's division. From Celorico I propose that you should retire gradually along the valley of the Mondego, upon Sir J. Sherbrooke's division, and other troops which will be there. If you should quit the Coa, bring the hussars with you.

I mention this in writing in case of accidents during my absence, which, however, I do not think likely to occur.

P.S. If you should withdraw from the Coa, bring with you the 12th Portuguese regt., which is in the villages on your right, having been sent out of the garrison of Almeida.

To Col. M'Mahon.* Viseu, 31st Jan. 1810.

I received your letter of yesterday's date. I had received directions from the Commander in Chief to give you leave of absence if you were indisposed, which I am happy to find is not the case; and you must be aware that the situation of affairs in Portugal will not allow of your absence at present.

* Lieut. Gen. Sir T. M'Mahon, Bart., K.C.B., then commanding a brigade of infantry in the Portuguese army.

Marshal Beresford informed me that he intended to move your brigade from Lamego, but he did not state to what place; and I request of you, when you shall receive his orders, to make known to Lieut. Gen. Sir J. C. Sherbrooke, who will be here, their purport, and at what time you will carry them into execution.

To Lieut. Gen. Sir J. Sherbrooke, K.B.   Viseu, 31st Jan. 1810.

I enclose you a memorandum of the points to which I wish you to attend in case the enemy should collect in our front for the purpose of attacking us during my absence. I think that you had better not have any communication with Gen. Bacellar, or any of the Portuguese officers, on the points in this memorandum previous to the time at which it will be necessary to execute them.

I have desired Campbell to give you all letters for me from the front, which you will open and then forward to me by a messenger whom I have desired should be sent from Viseu every evening, if there should be any letters for him to carry.

P.S. Enclosed I send you my route as far as I have settled it: Feb. 1, Coimbra; 2, Leiria; 3, Alcobaca; 4, Obidos or Caldas; 5, Torres Vedras.

Memorandum, left with Lieut. Gen. Sir J. Sherbrooke, K.B.   Viseu, 31st Jan. 1810.

The object of the position at present occupied by the army is:

1st; to defend the entrance into Portugal at the probable point of attack by the enemy.

2dly; to be in the situation to act offensively for the relief of Ciudad Rodrigo, if the enemy should make an attack upon that place, and it should be deemed expedient to make any movement for its relief.

3dly; to be in the situation to act offensively upon a more extensive scale in Castille, by way of diversion for the allies, if the relative state of the forces of the enemy and of the allies should permit such an operation without risk to the British army.

The 3d division, at Pinhel, occupies the lower part of the Coa, and the cavalry have posts of observation even upon the Agueda. The 4th division has a post at the bridge of Castello Bom, at Ponte de Sequeiros, and at Rapoula de Coa, the principal passages over the upper Coa. This position is perfectly secure from surprise, more particularly as Gen. Cole has been directed to have another post of observation at Alfaiates; the Duque del Parque's army, which was in the Sierra de Gata, being ordered to cross the Tagus into Estremadura.

It is desirable that we should not lose possession of the Coa, particularly to a small corps; but as I have no intention to maintain the possession of the Coa if the enemy should collect a large army in that quarter, Gen. Cole and Gen. Craufurd will retire with their divisions and the hussars, &c., if they should find that the enemy has collected a large army, and cross the Mondego to Celorico.

When the enemy shall begin to collect for this operation, Gen. Sherbrooke will cross the Mondego by Ponte de Fiaes; the troops at Mangualde by Ponte de Palheiros, and the whole will proceed to Pinhancos, which is 6 leagues in rear of Celorico

If the enemy should continue to advance, Gen. Cole and Gen. Craufurd will retire gradually by the valley of the Mondego, as will Gen. Sherbrooke, till the whole shall assemble at Ponte da Murcella, holding the height of Moita as an advanced post.

When Gen. Sherbrooke shall make his movement across the Mondego, he is to send orders to the Portuguese troops at Coimbra to march to Ponte da Murcella, or to the villages in the rear of the Serra de Saboga; to Gen. Blunt, at Figueira, to march his brigade to Coimbra, and thence to Mealhada; or direct to Mealhada, if there should be a road, from whence he is to occupy the pass between Mealhada and Martagoa, near the convent of Busaco; to the Portuguese troops at Leiria to move up to Ponte da Murcella.

Gen. Blunt must have with him a Portuguese brigade of artillery from Condeixa, and the remainder of the Portuguese artillery must be ordered to the Ponte da Murcella.

The 6 and 9 pounders in the British reserve artillery must be embarked in boats on the Mondego at Coimbra, and sent up to Foz d'Alva, and the horses will move direct to Ponte da Murcella.

Gen. Bacellar must be directed to order all the boats on the Mondego to go below Foz d'Alva; to have all the bridges on the Mondego broken up; viz., between Fornos and Juncal, Ponte Novo; near Villa Franca, Ponte de Cabra, Ponte de Palheiros, Ponte Novo; near Carvalhal, Ponte de Fiaes; and to order out and collect the militia and the ordenanza, to move the former across the Criz, and to employ the latter in annoying the enemy in every situation in which it may be practicable; to destroy the bridge near Fail over the Viseu; also the Ponte Pedrinha, over the river d'Asno, and that at Ferreroz, over the same river.   He should likewise direct the owners of carts and carriages in the country evacuated, of which he has the list, and the inhabitants, to move off with their property towards Oporto.   The British magazine at Foz Dao, upon the Mondego, should be moved to Foz d'Alva, upon the same river.

There is a brigade of Portuguese infantry at present at Lamego, under the command of Col. M'Mahon, which, however, were to be moved farther to the rear, and I do not recollect to what station.   If they should not be moved before the necessity of collecting the army should occur, they must march from Lamego by Viseu, to the Ponte de Fiaes, on the Mondego, where they will cross that river, and they are to be in the rear of Gen. Sherbrooke's division at Pinhancos.   If they should have marched, they must receive directions, in the case supposed, to proceed by Coimbra to the villages in the rear of the Serra de Saboga.   Col. M'Mahon is directed to let Gen. Sherbrooke know when he shall receive orders to march, and to what point.

To Lieut. Gen. Hill.   Viseu, 31st Jan. 1810.

I received this morning your letter of the 29th inst.   I had already, when I wrote to you, thought of sending some cavalry to Montalvao. But adverting to the difficulty of feeding them any where, and to the expediency of keeping the regiments collected, I preferred, in the first instance, that you should send to Montalvao only an officer.   When the enemy shall pass the Tagus, or penetrate the mountains, however, it may be desirable to station some cavalry at Montalvao; and you will then send either British or Portuguese, as you may think proper.

In respect to the bridge at Villa Velha, its preservation is important, either to enable me to cross the Tagus to you, by the shortest route, certainly, for some of my divisions; or to enable you to cross the Tagus by the shortest road to some stations in which I might require your assistance, and it might be consistent with other objects for you to give it to me. We know from experience, that but few troops could pass the river at a time by means of a flying bridge, and these only with great inconvenience. I am aware of the difficulty of removing the boats of that bridge, and of the probable chance of failure, and, therefore, I recommend that you should at once make up your mind to destroy them, when it shall be necessary; and that you should fill them with combustibles, or take such other measures as you may think necessary to insure that object in a short space of time. If the boats should be destroyed, I will, of course, pay for them.

I am going to-morrow to make a reconnaissance towards Torres Vedras, &c., and I enclose my route, and request you to write to me to those places, if you should have any thing important to communicate. I will apprise you of my further movements.

To the Earl of Liverpool.   Viseu, 31st Jan. 1810.

The enemy's troops, which I informed you in my dispatch of the 24th inst. had been collected in La Mancha, with the exception of Marshal Soult's corps, which I have reason to believe has been detached to the left, obtained possession of the Despena Perros, the principal pass in the Sierra Morena, on the 20th inst., on which night their head quarters were fixed at La Carolina.

I have not yet received an account of the mode in which they effected this operation. They had made different movements along the whole front of the Sierra, from Montizon to Almaden, between the 14th and 20th, and had penetrated with their right as far as Hinojosa, and afterwards to Pozo Blanco. I have also reason to believe that they had gained ground on their left and in the centre, which it was important for the Spaniards to hold; but that no opposition was given, or even a shot fired in all these operations, which have ended in the possession by the French of the passes of the Sierra Morena.

Since the 20th, the French advance had been near Cordova, probably from their right at Pozo Blanco, but had retired again; and I have not received intelligence of the movement of the head quarters from La Carolina. Neither have I heard of the movements of the Spanish army under Gen. Areyzaga since he quitted La Carolina on the 20th.

The Duque de Alburquerque, after leaving 4500 men on the Guadiana, destined to form the garrison of Badajoz, which troops entered Badajoz on the 26th inst., intended to interrupt the operations of the right of the French army, by making an attack upon them by Agudo. The French, however, having possession of that point, and having already pushed their patroles as far as Hinojosa through the mountains, he was apprehensive that he should be too late unless he passed them likewise; and he went by Guadalcanal and Cantillana to Carmona, where he was on the 24th.

The Duque del Parque was ordered by the Central Junta on the 21st to cross the Tagus, and move into Estremadura to join the Duque de Alburquerque's corps. I learned from him, by a letter of the 24th, that he proposed to carry this order into execution; but I have not yet heard that he had moved.

My last accounts from Badajoz are of the 27th. The Central Junta had quitted Seville, and had gone to the Isla de Leon, and had given over to the Junta of Seville the charge of defending the province of Andalusia. This Junta had proposed to that of Badajoz to consider of the appointment of a regency, which subject they had immediately taken into their consideration.

Your Lordship will have observed, from the movements and operations which I have above detailed to you, that it is the enemy's intention to endeavor to obtain possession of the south of Spain; and I have no doubt that in a short time they will be in possession of Seville, and the arsenals, magazines, and manufactures of arms, &c., which had been established in that city. The uncertainty which has attended all the operations of the war in the Peninsula, particularly those which have been carried on latterly, renders it impossible to form any opinion whether the Spanish armies will give the enemy any opposition in the execution of these plans, or to calculate upon the effect which any opposition they have in their power to give might produce.

There is no doubt that if the enemy's reinforcements have not yet entered Spain, and are not considerably advanced within the Spanish frontiers, the operation which they have undertaken is one of some risk; and I have maturely considered of the means of making a diversion in favor of the allies, which might oblige the enemy to reduce his force in Andalusia, and would expose him to risk and loss in this quarter. But the circumstances which are detailed in the enclosed copy of a letter to Mr. Frere have obliged me to refrain from attempting this operation at present. I have not, however, given up all thoughts of it; and I propose to carry it into execution hereafter, if circumstances should permit.

The passes of the Sierra Morena being lost, and the defeat and dispersion of the Spanish armies being the probable consequence of any action in which their imprudence or even necessity or expediency may involve them, I am desirous that His Majesty's government should consider, and should instruct me on the line to be adopted in Portugal on the state of affairs which will then exist in the Peninsula.

It is probable that, although the armies may be lost, and the principal Juntas and authorities of the provinces may be dispersed, the war of partisans may continue. Cadiz may possibly still hold out, and the Central Junta may continue in existence in that town, although without authority, as the French armies will be in possession of the different provinces in which they will be stationed. In this supposed state of affairs, Portugal will have remained untouched; the enemy having evidently preferred the line of operations by the left of the Peninsula to that by the right, which I supposed in my letter of the 14th Nov. he would adopt.

His Majesty's government are informed of the military situation and resources of Portugal. If arms can be supplied for the militia, there is no doubt that there will be in this country not less than a gross force of 90,000 men, regularly organised, besides the whole armed population of the country and the British army.

Since the restoration of the government by H. R. H. the Prince Regent, there is no doubt that much has been done, particularly in the last nine months, towards the enrolment, organisation, and equipment of this large force; but much still remains to be done, with very insufficient means, to render that part of this force which consists of militia (being not less than 50,000 men) equal to a contest with the enemy for the possession of this country; and even if all that is required in this respect were accomplished, there would be wanting throughout this whole army military experience, and that confidence in themselves and in their officers which can result only from experience.

When the affairs of Spain shall be brought to the state which I have above described, and when all regular resistance shall cease, there will exist no probability of a renewal of the contest in that country on such a scale as to afford any chance of a successful result, notwithstanding that the possession of each of the parts of it may be precarious, and may depend upon the strength of the French armed force maintained within it; and that the possession of the whole may be a burden rather than an advantage to the French government.

The question will then arise, whether the continuation of the contest will ' afford any reasonable prospect of advantage against the common enemy, or of benefit to His Majesty's allies.'

From what I have above stated, your Lordship will observe that it is impossible for me to calculate, upon any certain grounds, on the degree of assistance in the defence of this country which we shall receive from the Portuguese troops. We have done every thing for the regulars that discipline could do, which has been extended to the militia as far as the government could afford the expense of keeping these corps embodied; and the regulars have been armed and equipped as far as the means of the country would go, the militia being in the state already known to your Lordship. There is no doubt also of their general detestation of the French government, of their loyalty to their Prince, of their confidence in us, and of their determination, as individuals, to do the utmost in the cause. But still the operations of these troops cannot be calculated upon as they might be if more inured to war, and if they or their officers had any military experience, or if the majority of their officers were of a different description.

Adverting, then, to the probability, in the case supposed likely to exist, that the whole or the greater part of the French army in Spain will be disposable to be thrown upon this country, I should be glad to know whether it is the wish of His Majesty's government that an effort should be made to defend this country to the last; or whether, as soon as I shall find affairs in Spain in the state in which I have above described, I shall turn my mind seriously to the evacuation of the country, and to the embarkation of as large a body of people, military as well as others, as I can carry away. Whatever may be the decision of the government upon this subject, and whatever may be the force with which the enemy shall invade Portugal, I am of opinion that in all events I shall be able to bring away the British army.

There is another point also upon which I wish to have an explanation of the intentions of His Majesty's government.

In the instructions from Lord Castlereagh of the 3d April, I was ordered ' to detach an adequate force,' for the purpose of ' making every effort to assist in the preservation of Cadiz, if Mr. Frere should at any time notify to me the actual consent of the Spanish government to admit a British garrison into that place.' I still consider that paragraph of my original instructions to be in force, and I shall act accordingly, if the supposed case should occur; but I am desirous of having His Majesty's wishes upon that part of the subject at present.

To the Earl of Liverpool.   Viseu, 31st Jan. 1810.

Your Lordship will have observed, from my private communications, that I had already adverted to the subject referred to in your Lordship's dispatch of the 4th inst. I have no doubt that some, possibly a large proportion, of the Portuguese troops, will be desirous of withdrawing from Portugal at the time this country shall be evacuated by the British army ; but it is impossible to devise any mode by which information can be acquired, or any estimate can be formed, of the numbers which would be likely to go. It may be expected, however, that these numbers would depend in some degree upon the objects held out to the troops for the future ; and as they have generally a great objection to embarking in ships, upon the nature of the accommodation afforded to them.

My dispatch of the 14th Nov., and its enclosures, will have pointed out to your Lordship the general nature of the operations which it is probable will be carried on by the enemy in Portugal. I have no doubt that he will have a corps on each side of the Tagus, and that he will occupy the left bank of that river from Almada to its mouth, at the same time that he will attack us on the right bank. Indeed, his recent operations in La Mancha show that he proposes to complete the conquest of the south of Spain, or at all events to insure it before he will commence his attack upon Portugal ; and in that case it is probable that the principal attack will be made by Alentejo, although probably the operations, which must have for their object the possession of Lisbon, will end on the right bank, a large corps being still kept on the left of the river. If I should be right in this conjecture, it will be obvious to your Lordship that it would be impossible for any proportion of the Portuguese troops to make their retreat into Algarve.

The Berlings would afford no provisions, or even water, for any number of men. Sir C. Cotton was obliged to supply the marines stationed by him on those rocks with water from the fleet employed in the blockade of the Tagus ; and I fear that the voyage from the Tagus to the Bayona Islands in craft would be considered too long, even for persons more accustomed than the Portuguese soldiers are to maritime expeditions, and under more pressing obligations to embark than they can be supposed to be.

I am convinced that the mode in which it will be possible to prevail upon the largest number of them to embark will be to have for their reception ships of the same description, supplied in the same manner with provisions, &c., as for the British army; and although from circumstances it may not be possible for His Majesty's government to station in the Tagus a sufficient number of transports for this purpose, it may be possible to station there, or to have there at the moment the embarkation of the army might become expedient, a large fleet of ships of the line.

There are several Portuguese ships in the Tagus, which might be applied to the purpose of receiving troops; but it would be impossible to employ them in this manner without considerable previous preparation, which would of course discover the object; and it would probably be entirely frustrated by early discovery. It is also probable that the members of the government, and the principal families, and even many of the inhabitants of the country, all at least who showed any active hostility against the French upon their departure from Lisbon, would wish to quit the country when the British army should withdraw from it; and all this description of persons would naturally look to the Portuguese ships as the means of their removal. Their application to the accommodation of the Portuguese army for their removal, which would deprive these persons not only of all hopes of getting away themselves, but of the means of making even tolerable terms with the French by capitulation, would of course be resisted by the whole of this class; and the equipment of the ships probably entirely prevented.

I would therefore recommend to His Majesty's government to make their naval arrangements in such a manner as to have a large fleet of ships of the line in the Tagus at the period of the evacuation of Portugal. I would likewise recommend to them to authorise the British Minister at Lisbon to communicate confidentially with the Portuguese government upon the possible necessity of evacuating Portugal, particularly in case resistance should cease in Spain; and upon the measures to be adopted to put the ships in the Tagus in such a state as to carry off all those who should be desirous of quitting the country.

As an additional measure, I propose to strengthen the works of Peniche and of Setuval, and to provision the former. It might be possible for a large number of persons to take shelter at Peniche, and to reach that place even in boats from the Tagus and other parts on the coasts; and they could afterwards be embarked from Peniche without much difficulty, as occasion might offer.

From what I have above stated, your Lordship will observe that I do not imagine that any large number of the troops would be induced to embark in craft, even to go to Peniche; but some might, and many of the people of the country might avail themselves of this resource; and I imagine that, without incurring much expense, the works of Peniche can be put in such a state as that that place could not be taken for a considerable length of time. Setuval could not be secured so easily or so effectually; but it might for a time.

It is very desirable that for these as for other objects the number of officers of engineers with the army should be increased, as we have not now more than a sufficient number to execute the works already ordered in the positions to be eventually taken up by the army, and we have none to spare for others.

The A.G. to Major Lindsay, Elvas.   1st Feb. 1810.

I am instructed to call your attention to the payment of the convalescents, which, as it now stands, is a service of the extraordinaries of the army. The Dep. Paymaster Gen. has made it appear to the Commander of the Forces that this disbursement might be more regularly classed with the ordinaries.

It is his Excellency's pleasure that this expenditure be transferred from the first to the last named class of accounts, which you will do by passing the receipt given to Mr. Pratt for the sum already received for this service, to the possession of the resident Paymaster at Elvas, and consequently requiring the resident Paymaster to give his receipt to the officer of the Commissariat department for the same amount.

The A.G. to Capt. Meacham, Coimbra.   2d Feb. 1810.

Your letters of the 23d and 28th ult. have been submitted to the consideration of the Commander of the Forces. I am in consequence directed to acquaint you, it is not conceived the distance from Coimbra to the cantonments requires your having additional accounts for the accommodation of the officers; they must, therefore, receive their pay as usual from their regiments.

Lord Wellington authorises your obtaining a supply of mats for the comfort of the convalescents, for which you will send in a requisition to the resident Commissary at Coimbra; and pray take every means to have these preserved, as there may be difficulty in replacing any deficiency. The great scarcity of straw has prevented his Lordship giving orders for the supply of that article.

To Vice Adm. the Hon. G. Berkeley.   Leiria, 3d Feb. 1810.

I have received your letter of the 31st Jan., and I can assure you that I have nothing more to say to Mr. Phillips, than to purchase from him his grain. It is not certain that I shall go to Lisbon, and if I do, it will be only for one night; and I am afraid that there will not be much time for business. I shall therefore be much obliged to you if you will communicate to me your wishes, on the points on which you desire to speak to me, as soon as it shall be convenient to you.

To J. Murray, Esq., Commissary General.   Leiria, 3d Feb. 1810.

I am afraid that the gentlemen of the Commissariat, on this road, either do not understand, or have not received your instructions in respect to the use of the covered carriages, English and Spanish; as the carriages here and at Pombal are doing nothing; and Mr. ——, who is here, tells me that he has no instructions respecting the mode in which they are to be used. It is desirable that the plan of which I gave you a memorandum at Coimbra, about 3 weeks ago, for the use of these carriages, should be carried into execution without loss of time.

P.S. I have a letter from Mr. Villiers, in which he suggests, that as many persons, having money which they may be willing to give up for bills upon England, may be gone to Ayamonte, it would be desirable to send an intelligent person there to endeavor to get what may be got there. I wish that you would advert to this circumstance, and send somebody to Ayamonte for the purpose proposed. I also request you to have an account made out of all our receipts for bills and otherwise in December and

January, in order that we may know what the Portuguese fourth will amount to, and that we may pay it.

To Brig. Gen. R. Craufurd.   Obidos, 4th Feb. 1810.

I wrote to you a letter from Viseu on the 31st, which I have just heard has been stolen from the man who carried it, the purport of which was to apprise you of my intentions and wishes, in case the enemy should attack this country.

As my views, in the position which the army now occupy, are to take the offensive in case of the occurrence of certain events, I wish not to lose the possession of the Coa; and I am anxious therefore that you and Gen. Cole should maintain your positions upon that river, unless you should find that the enemy collect a force in Castille which is so formidable as to manifest a serious intention of invading Portugal; in which case it is not my intention to maintain the line of the Coa. In this case I wish that, if you find it necessary, you should retire gradually to Celorico, where you will be joined by the 4th division and the hussars; and both, when necessary, are to withdraw gradually by the valley of the Mondego towards Pinhanços, where they will find the 1st division, under Sir J. Sherbrooke, and then to the Ponte da Murcella. If you should find it necessary to withdraw from the positions you now occupy upon the Coa, I beg of you to bring with you the 12th Portuguese regt., which has been removed from the garrison of Almeida.

I am not sure that this letter adverts to all the points mentioned in my last, which was written with my papers, &c. before me. As I have not the same advantage at present, I beg that in case of any difference between this letter and that which I wrote to you before, you will consider that which I wrote to you on the 31st Jan., if you should receive it, as the guide for your conduct.

P.S. I hope to be with the army again in a few days; but it is really necessary that you should have in writing the instructions which this letter contains, now that I am so far from you.

To Major Gen. the Hon. W. Stewart.   Torres Vedras, 5th Feb. 1810.

The existing government of Spain having called upon me to assist them with troops for the defence of Cadiz, I have to request that, in obedience to His Majesty's instructions, you will embark in command of the 2 companies of artillery lately arrived from England, the 79th, 94th, and 2d batt. 87th regts., and proceed to Cadiz, where you will land and co-operate in the defence of the place, by every means in your power.

I enclose a letter for Mr. Frere, containing certain conditions which I wish should be made with the government, previous to the landing of the troops under your command; but I consider the defence of Cadiz to be so important to His Majesty's interests, that I beg you will not delay the disembarkation of the troops under your command till these conditions shall be complied with, if you should find that the place has actually been attacked.

You will take with you camp equipage for the corps under your command, and a reserve of musket ammunition amounting to 100 rounds for each man, besides the 60 rounds which each man must have with him. You will report to me by every opportunity.

To Vice Adm. the Hon. G. Berkeley.   Torres Vedras, 5th Feb. 1810.

Having received a requisition from Mr. Frere to assist the Spanish government with troops for the defence of Cadiz, I have ordered Major Gen. the Hon. W. Stewart to embark with the 2 companies of the artillery lately arrived at Lisbon, the 79th, 94th, and 2d batt. 87th regts., for that place; and I shall be much obliged to you if you will give directions that transports may be furnished to them.

The A. Q. M. G. at Lisbon will have directions to communicate with the Agent of transports respecting the embarkation of these troops; and I request you to direct that the troops lately arrived may have the transports which brought them out. I also request you to order a suitable convoy to proceed with these troops, and to direct that the transports may be left with them at Cadiz.

To Bart. Frere, Esq.   Torres Vedras, 5th Feb. 1810.

Having come to this part of the country, I have just received from Lord Burghersh your letters of the 30th and 31st Jan.; and I have sent orders that Major Gen. the Hon. W. Stewart, with 2 companies of artillery, the 79th, 94th, and 2d batt. 87th regts., which are the only troops at present at Lisbon, should embark as soon as possible, and proceed to Cadiz.

If the place should actually be attacked, these troops will land immediately, and will co-operate in its defence. If the place should not be actually attacked, I am desirous that the following conditions should be made with the government previous to their being landed; and, at all events, they must be stated to the government as those on which I have detached them from the army.

1st; Although they will be under the orders of the governor of Cadiz, they must be under the immediate and exclusive command of their own commanding officer, who must solely and exclusively determine on all points of their discipline, &c.

2dly; With the exception of the artillery, which it may be necessary to detach to different points, the British troops are to act, as much as possible, in a body, although they are, of course, to take their turn in all garrison duties.

3dly; They, as well as their officers, are to be relieved as often as may be deemed proper, by other troops, or withdrawn entirely.

4thly; These troops are not to be detached from Cadiz or the Isle of Leon.

5thly; They are to be fed from the Spanish stores, according to the ration given to the British troops, of which the commanding officer will furnish the governor of Cadiz with a return.

6thly; The commanding officer of these troops is to be allowed to have a free communication with the transports which have taken the troops to Cadiz, and which will remain at Cadiz.

To Major Gen. the Hon. W. Stewart. Mafra, 7th Feb. 1810.

I have just received your letter of the 6th inst. I had already given directions that an officer of the department of the Adj. Gen. and of the Q. M. Gen. respectively should be sent to Cadiz to place themselves under your orders; and I propose to send there an officer of the Commissariat, and of the Paymaster Gen.'s department. I shall be happy to hear from you on any points on which you wish to have my instructions or my opinion.

It does not appear to me to be necessary to instruct you on any point at present, excepting those referred to in my letter to Mr. Frere of the 5th inst., which I sent open for your perusal, and of which I request you to keep a copy, excepting in the possible case of the approaching reduction of Cadiz. From the local situation of Cadiz, it is impossible that the enemy should have it in his power to cut off the retreat of the British troops to their ships; and you will embark them before the place shall be surrendered. In case of the surrender of Cadiz, you will send the 2d batt. 87th regt., and one company of the artillery, to Gibraltar, and you will return with the remainder of the troops to Lisbon.

I cannot sufficiently recommend to you to endeavor to keep up a good understanding with the Spanish officers. You will find Gen. Castanos, who is at present at the head of the Regency, and Gen. Venegas, who is the governor of Cadiz, highly deserving your confidence; as well as Gen. Whittingham, who is an English officer, and who is, I understand, at present at Cadiz. I have received your letter of the —— ; and I shall send your brother, Capt. J. Stewart, to Cadiz as your Brigade Major.

To the Rt. Hon. J. Villiers. Mafra, 7th Feb. 1810.

I have received your letters of the 29th Jan., and 5th and 6th inst.

I cannot agree to allow the Commissary Gen. of the British army to take upon himself the responsibility of managing the Commissariat of the Portuguese troops, for many reasons, into which it is unnecessary to enter. The plan under which it is proposed that the business should be carried on affords one grand reason for refusing to agree to this proposition, viz., that it would impose upon Great Britain a large expense, which, under existing arrangements, is paid by Portugal.

I don't think the mode proposed in the paper enclosed in your letter is the best by which the pay of the Portuguese officers can be increased. The increase of pay in proportion to the number of men is founded upon an erroneous notion that the officers have the power of keeping their regiments complete; and if it could operate at all, it would operate to prevent the diminution of numbers at the moment, when probably to risk the diminution of numbers would be important to the honor as well as to the interests of the country. Another objection to the proposed plan is its present expense beyond the sum estimated by Marshal Beresford, which His Majesty has engaged to supply, viz., £130,000 per annum. When the expense of the increased pay to the Generals and Staff shall be added to the sum stated in your estimate, it will far exceed £130,000.

Marshal Beresford has spoken to me respecting the proportions of the money received by the Commissary Gen. of the British army to be paid for the expenses of the Portuguese troops. Of course any money the

King's minister chooses to call for he must have; but as far as depends upon my decision, I propose that as heretofore the Commissary Gen. should pay to your order such proportion of the sums received in each month, at the end of each month, as the amount of the expenses for the Portuguese troops to be paid by His Majesty shall bear to the expenses of the British and Portuguese armies united. I have also received your letter of the 3d.

To Major Gen. the Hon. W. Stewart.   Lisbon, 9th Feb. 1810.

Since I wrote to you on the 7th, I have received your letter of the 6th, and I am happy to find that the departments at Lisbon have been able to supply you with the assistance which you required of Staff officers. I propose to add to the number an officer of the Medical staff, as soon as I can communicate with the Inspector General.

The officers of the corps of engineers with this army are fully employed, and we have not a sufficient number for the duty. I am apprehensive also that you will find the Spanish commander at Cadiz by no means disposed to attend to the suggestions of a British engineer. If, however, you should on your arrival there find an officer of that corps to be useful or necessary to you, I beg you to write to Gen. Campbell at Gibraltar, and to request him to send you one of those officers of engineers who have been already employed at Cadiz.

I enclose you a copy of the instructions which I received from His Majesty's government on my taking the command in this country, to regulate my conduct in all communications with the Spanish and Portuguese governments and their ministers; and I earnestly recommend to you a strict attention to these instructions. These instructions, however, are not to prevent your communications with the governor of Cadiz, Gen. Venegas, under whose command you will act.

Lisbon, 9th Feb. 1810.

The instructions alluded to by Lord Wellington are at Viseu, and will be forwarded by the first opportunity.

The purport of them is to direct Lord Wellington to make and to receive all communications to and from the Spanish and Portuguese governments, or their ministers, through the British Ambassadors residing at these Courts, respectively. Mr. Frere is probably in possession of copies of these instructions.

JAMES BATHURST, Lieut. Col. and Mil. Sec.

To Major Gen. the Hon. W. Stewart.   Lisbon, 9th Feb. 1810.

The Regency of Portugal having offered the 20th Portuguese regt. for the service at Cadiz, I have accepted of their offer, and they will be embarked and sent there in the course of 2 days. I enclose the copy of a letter which I have written to Mr. Frere upon this subject.

I beg that you will take this regiment under your command; and I recommend it to your protection. You will find both officers and soldiers obedient and zealous to carry your wishes into execution, and sincerely attached to the cause of Great Britain. The commanding officer of the regiment will furnish the Assist. Commissary attached to you with the statement of the rations which the Portuguese troops are to receive; and they are to receive them in the same manner as the British troops, from the Spanish magazines.

To Bart. Frere, Esq.   Lisbon, 9th Feb. 1810.

In addition to the troops already sent from hence, detailed to you in my letter of the 5th inst., the 20th Portuguese regt., having been offered by the Regency for this service, will be embarked, and will sail from hence immediately. They will likewise be under the command of Major Gen. the Hon. W. Stewart, and are to serve in Cadiz under the same conditions as the British troops.

P.S. The strength of the 20th Portuguese regt. is 1300 R. and F.

To Bart. Frere, Esq.   Lisbon, 9th Feb. 1810.

Since I wrote to you on the 30th Jan. relative to the proposition which had been made to you by the late Spanish government, that the British army should enter Old Castille, I have received a letter from Don F. de Saavedra, written upon the same subject, while he was President of the Junta of Estremadura, and sent by Col. Alava. As Don F. de Saavedra is one of the members of the Regency, I request you to inform that body that I am disposed to do every thing in my power to create a diversion in favor of the Spanish nation; and that I considered circumstances to have altered so far since I wrote to you on the 30th Jan., by the alteration of the government, by the change of the command of the army in Old Castille, by the army remaining in that province, and by other circumstances, that I had ordered the British cavalry to commence its march; and if I should find it practicable and consistent with the instructions which I have received from His Majesty's government, I will endeavor to alarm the enemy in the centre of Spain.

The government, however, must not expect that I shall risk the British army to effect this object. It must be obvious to them that Spain can derive no great advantage from any temporary effect produced by such an operation, without great exertion on the part of the government. They must also see clearly that, in the present situation of affairs, the occurrence of any misfortune to the British army would be fatal to the cause. I trust, therefore, that if I should find that circumstances will not permit me to undertake an operation which shall create a substantial diversion in their favor, the government will be satisfied that I refrain from it only because I am unable to undertake it with any reasonable prospect of advantage.

I beg you likewise to inform them that the assistance which I have sent them to Cadiz, which is a diminution of the effective strength of the British army, takes away from the means which I had of undertaking this operation.

To the Earl of Liverpool.   Lisbon, 9th Feb. 1810.

His Majesty's government will have received from Mr. Frere the accounts of the events which had occurred at Seville and Cadiz between the 24th and 31st Jan., which have ended in the appointment by the Central Junta of Gen. Castaños, Don F. de Saavedra, the Bishop of Orense, Don A. Escano, and Don E. Fernandez to be Regents of Spain; and you will have learned that the seat of this government is at Cadiz.

I enclose copies of the letters which I have received from Mr. Frere upon these subjects. In consequence of these letters, and in conformity with what I understood to be His Majesty's intentions, and from a conviction that I was doing what was best for the cause, I gave orders, immediately upon the receipt of Mr. Frere's letter of the 31st Jan., that the 79th, 94th, and 2d batt. 87th regts., and 2 companies of artillery, being all the disposable troops then at Lisbon, should sail for Cadiz under the command of Major Gen. the Hon. W. Stewart.

I enclose copies of the letters which I wrote to Gen. Stewart upon that occasion and since, and to Mr. Frere upon the subject of this detachment. Since I made this detachment, I have received intelligence which I believe to be true, that the Duque de Alburquerque's corps, which had been at Carmana on the 24th Jan., and was supposed to have retired across the Guadalquivir, had retired upon Cadiz, and had actually arrived at Xerez on the 1st inst.

The French had entered Seville on the 1st, and King Joseph arrived there on the 2d.

The Spanish corps which had been posted for the defence of the Sierra Morena, under Gen. Areyzaga, had separated; a part of them, under the General himself, had retired upon Jaen, which had been fortified; but they abandoned it, and the enemy are now in possession of that town, and this part of Areyzaga's corps are in Granada. Another division retired across the Guadalquivir, and are at Monasterio in Estremadura; and I believe a third division have crossed the Guadalquivir at Seville, and have gone towards the mouth of the Guadiana, with a design of embarking for Cadiz; and a fourth have retired upon the Sierra de Ronda. I understand that it is the intention of the newly formed Spanish government to endeavor to form armies upon each of these corps; and that Gen. Blake is appointed to command the principal corps, which is in Granada.

The Marques de la Romana is appointed to command the army hitherto under the command of the Duque del Parque; and he had proceeded on the 5th inst. as far as Badajoz to take the command of it. It had not at that time commenced its march to cross the Tagus.

The Spanish government had, I understand, immediately upon their formation, removed the French and Spanish ships from the inner harbour to the outer roads of Cadiz, and had destroyed the forts and batteries on the northern shore, of the effect of which I informed your Lordship in a former dispatch. They also gave immediate orders for the complete destruction of the lines of San Roque. These measures were an additional inducement to me to lose no time in sending them the reinforcements which I had at my command, to which I shall add still further reinforcements, if I should find them to be necessary, including a Portuguese regiment of infantry which the Regency have offered, and I have accepted, for this service.

Your Lordship will observe that this situation of affairs in Spain approaches to that which I thought it probable would soon exist in that country, when I addressed you on the 31st Jan. There is, however, so far an improvement, that the Regency have manifested a greater degree of confidence and a more conciliatory spirit towards His Majesty's government, and a greater regard to His Majesty's interests, than the Central Junta. It is composed of persons of integrity, experienced in business, thoroughly acquainted with the existing situation of affairs in Spain, and possessing the confidence of the people. I am apprehensive that these persons have been called to the government at too late a period to effect much good; but I am convinced that they are disposed to do every thing in their power.

In the mean time we have not heard that the reinforcements of the French armies, to any large amount, have arrived in Spain. It would appear, from the accounts which I have received, that the corps of Victor, Mortier, and Sebastiani, and the King's guards and the reserve, amounting in the whole to above 60,000 men, have passed the Sierra Morena; and that Soult's corps is upon the Tagus, between Talavera and Toledo, and Ney's and Kellermann's in Old Castille. These three last are supposed to amount to about 40,000 men.

It is obvious that there is nothing in this situation of the enemy which can affect the British army or this country, even if the Spanish corps, remaining in Granada and in the Sierra de Ronda, should be dispersed. The enemy could not be in a situation for a considerable length of time to attack this country; and although I am of opinion that the time may come when it may be doubtful whether a perseverance in the contest in Portugal will hold out ' any prospect of advantage against the common enemy, or of benefit to His Majesty's allies,' I conceive that it is a question upon which it is difficult for His Majesty's government at this distance to decide. That it must depend upon events in Spain, upon which no calculation can be formed, as well as upon the existing spirit and the prospect of resistance by the people in this country, and in some measure upon the season of the year in which the attack will be made, and upon the preparation which the enemy will have made for it; and that adverting to the certainty that, in all events, the British army will be able to embark, and that its continuance on the Peninsula must be beneficial to His Majesty's and the general interest, as it must draw the attention of the enemy, and must tend to His Majesty's honor, it would probably be best to leave to the decision of the officer commanding the troops in this country the period of the evacuation as a military question, after an explanation by His Majesty's government of their objects in the continuance of the contest. It is desirable that the troops sent to Cadiz should be replaced in this country as soon as may be convenient.

I have come to this part of the country to view the progress of the works which I had ordered to be constructed when here in October; and I propose to return to the army to-morrow.

To Vice Adm. the Hon. G. Berkeley.   Villa Franca, 10th Feb. 1810.

The Regency of Portugal having offered the 20th Portuguese regt. for service at Cadiz, I have to request that you will be so kind as to give directions that transports may be supplied to convey them thither, and a ship of war to convoy them. The regiment consists of 1300 R. and F.; and the officer of the Q. M. Gen.'s department will communicate with the Agent of transports respecting the details of the embarkation.

The A.G. to Capt. Meacham, Coimbra.   11th Feb. 1810.

On the present occasion you will send the perfectly recovered men belonging to the Coimbra station, with the detachment moving towards the army from Elvas, under charge of Capt. Hood of the Guards. As a general system, however, you will put in memorandum, at the bottom of each return, the number esteemed sufficiently re-established to proceed towards the army, for a man in a convalescent state may not be equal to undergo fatigue ; and except in cases of emergency his Excellency does not wish any soldier to be permitted to march till at least a week on the convalescent list. On the back of each state must be written the names of all officers at the hospital station. States to be dispatched on the 4th, 10th, and 18th ; also on the same dates a nominal return of deaths within the period, agreeable to annexed form, addressed to regiments, and under cover to this office.

When you find it requisite to detain any officer, non-commissioned officer, or soldier at the station, immediately report the same, that I may be enabled to communicate with the corps to which such persons may belong.

The A.G. to the Commissary General.   11th Feb. 1810.

I have the honor to enclose letters from Lieut. Gen. Sir J. Sherbrooke and Dr. Franck, on the subject of improving the means of transport of the sick from the cantonments towards the general hospital.

The carpenters from the Staff corps, and also those that can be spared from the Guards, are directed to attend at the Adj. Gen.'s Office to-morrow morning at 8 o'clock, where I have to request you will send proper persons to instruct them how to proceed. It will be necessary that as many of the carts should be finished to-morrow as possible, the whole of the sick from the advanced stations being expected in town to proceed the day following towards the rear.

To Lieut. Gen. Hill.   Santarem, 12th Feb. 1810, 10 A.M.

I received this morning the account of the enemy's probable arrival at Zafra ; and at this moment your letter of this day, acquainting me that a detachment had been at Olivenca on the 10th, and of the probability that they had got possession of that place this day. Their excursion to Zafra appears to me to be the consequence of their incursion into the province of Andalusia : and their existence in safety at Seville depends upon the tenure of the pass of Monasterio, in front of which they will continue to hold a detachment more or less advanced.

If the enemy really intend any serious operation in Estremadura, a corps of their army must have crossed the Tagus, in addition to that which has come in by Monasterio ; and if no troops have crossed the Tagus, you may depend upon it that what has been done is of no consequence, and is not likely to be attended by any results.

I should doubt the taking possession of Olivenca in its present state without ordnance, or stores, or provisions. It is, however, a possible event ; and if it be true, you must urge Gen. Leite to take care of his place of Jurumenha ; and that he and the Junta of Badajoz should prevent the French from collecting provisions at Olivenca. It may be depended upon, that although the Spaniards do not know how to make use of that place, the French will, if they should be able to keep it.

In respect to yourself, I wish you to move forward to Portalegre, attending to your instructions. The difficulty of forage, and the consequences to the cavalry which will result from a want of that necessary article, induce me to wish that, till you shall see more clearly the plans and intentions of the enemy, the 14th dragoons alone should be brought up to Portalegre, and the 1st Royals not farther than the old cantonments of the 16th. You will send them your own orders, as I do not know what your other arrangements will be. I shall only let them know that it is probable you will soon move them.

You may move Col. Campbell's brigade from Thomar, as I have made other arrangements for the defence of the Zezere. In respect to the hospital, I beg that you will tell Col. Lindsay that I think it desirable that, as soon as possible, he should send off to Abrantes all the convalescents able to march from any of the hospitals; and that he should collect in Elvas all the sick of the army.

I shall be at Thomar to-morrow, where I hope to hear from you again.

P.S. I send with this letters for Gen. Leite and the Marques de la Romana, which I beg of you to forward. Gen. Madden's brigade is still at Lisbon, and unable yet to move, but there are 4 squadrons of Portuguese dragoons at Chamusca and in the neighbourhood, which you may take instead of them.

The A.G. to Lieut. Col. Darroch, A.A.G., Lisbon. 13th Feb. 1810.

I enclose extracts from G. O. of the regulations to be observed by detachments on march to the army,* a copy of which you will be so good as to give every officer who leaves Lisbon in such charge. These copies of instructions you will sign, and let it be understood they are intended for the general guidance of officers and soldiers on detachment, and therefore should be promulgated.

To Lieut. Gen. Hill. Thomar, 14th Feb. 1810, 10 P.M.

I have just received your letter of this day; and I do not propose to stop the march of the troops. You will be the best judge of the necessity of so doing, by your knowledge of the state of the roads, &c., forward. I think it would be desirable to make arrangements to move forward your cavalry rather quicker than one squadron each day. I should think that this object might be effected by moving some of the 3d dragoon guards out of Golegao to Santarem during this march, and back again to Golegao when it shall be effected. I beg of you to communicate with Gen. Payne upon this subject.

In respect to money, I took an opportunity when at Lisbon of inquiring how far my orders upon that subject had been obeyed, and I find that £10,000 had been sent to Santarem regularly every week. Of this sum Mr. —— ought to have taken care that a sufficiency was left to pay the troops. I shall now send orders that the money may be sent to Abrantes.

In respect to Mr. ——, I have more than one cause to complain of his conduct lately, and I shall take the whole into consideration when I shall return to head quarters, and I shall give orders respecting it.

Take the artificers of the regiments with you; and tell the magistrates of Abrantes that I hold them responsible not only that you, but that Capt. Patton shall have all the carts that may be required. Your regular supply, however, depends upon the regularity of Mr. ——, and upon his acts, and not upon his talking. You will do well to communicate, at an early period, with the Spanish corps at Alburquerque.

Let me hear from you constantly; and I beg of you particularly to attend to the movements of any corps north of the Tagus, to Castello Branco, and to the bridge of Villa Velha.

* See G.O. 13th June, 1809, p. 293; and G.O. 24th June, 1809, p. 323.

P.S. Don't forget to send the convalescents, artillery, horse and foot, from Elvas, Estremoz, &c., as fast as they shall recover.

To Marshal Beresfcrd.   Thomar, 14th Feb. 1810.

I just write to let you know, that in consequence of events at Badajoz, Hill is about to move forward with his whole corps. I am very anxious about the line of the Zezere, and I wish that you would order out immediately the regiments of militia which we allotted for this service; and the 13th regt. to Thomar, and Gen. Widerhott to his station.

To Brig. Gen. Alex. Campbell.   Thomar, 14th Feb. 1810.

I have received your letters of the 11th and 12th, and I am happy to hear of your arrival in good health. I beg you will join the army at Viseu as soon as may be convenient to you; your aide de camp shall be put in orders as you wish. Let me know by post to Viseu, whether you wish to have the 74th in your brigade instead of the 11th; the 11th is, however, the strongest regiment in the army. Give my tea, &c., to Col. Peacocke, and request him to send them to head quarters occasionally by the messengers.

To Marshal Beresford.   Espinhal, 15th Feb. 1810.

I conclude that you will have heard that the enemy had summoned Ciudad Rodrigo, as well as Badajoz, on the 12th. I cannot believe they are in earnest in intending to attack both these places at the same time. However, we shall see.

I enclose a memorandum of the movements which I have ordered; and I think it would be desirable to order up Gen. Madden's brigade of cavalry. I shall continue the movement of these troops forward, if I should find it necessary; and I wish you would come up as soon as you can. But I beg you to send your staff by different roads, so that the communication may not be cut off by their taking all the mules and horses.

The attempt to relieve Ciudad Rodrigo is a measure deserving of serious consideration; as, in effecting it, we must use the magazine in Almeida, and that place must then fall immediately. I have written to Dom M. Forjaz upon this subject, upon which I wish you would speak to him, as well as upon making a great exertion to feed the troops when they shall be collected.

P.S. I wish that you would make arrangements immediately;

1st; To call out all the militia for whom there are arms.

2dly; To allot a good regiment of militia to garrison Peniche.

3dly; To allot a regiment of militia to be posted at Obidos.

To Brig. Gen. R. Craufurd.   Viseu, 18th Feb. 1810.

I arrived here yesterday, and I have received all your letters respecting Ney's march upon Ciudad Rodrigo, and your letter of the 1st inst., which reached me while I was near Lisbon. I don't understand Ney's movement, coupled as it was with a movement upon Badajoz from the south of Spain. The French are certainly not sufficiently strong for two sieges at the same time, and I much doubt whether they are in a state even to undertake one.

Since my arrival here I have received intelligence of Soult's movement to Plasencia on the 12th; and I conceive that his further movements will explain nearly what is their object, if they have any decided object at present, and will enable me to determine the line which I shall take. It is obvious that the enemy's strength in Castille has been underrated. I was always convinced that the 3 corps of Ney and Kellermann in Castille, and Soult, who had joined them from Talavera, did not amount to less than 40,000 men, which, with the reinforcements expected from France, some of which have certainly arrived, were too much for us. If Soult turns to his left from Plasencia, and crosses the·Tagus, or if he should move upon Castello Branco, we are too forward on this flank. My opinion is that he will cross the Tagus at Alconeta, to give countenance to Mortier's operations against Badajoz.

In answer to your letter of the 1st, I have only to assure you, that in every event I should have taken care to keep your command distinct, as I am convinced that you will be able to render most service in such a situation. You will have heard that Gen. the Hon. W. Stewart is gone to Cadiz; but Gen. Picton is coming to the army, which will render necessary a new arrangement, and will oblige me to deprive you of Col. Mackinnon's brigade. But I shall make up for you the best corps I can, including your own brigade, of which you shall continue to have the separate command.

P.S. Will you inform Gen. Cox that I have returned, and that I am obliged to him for all his letters?

To J. Murray, Esq., Commissary General.   Viseu, 18th Feb. 1810.

As the works carrying on under Lieut. Col. Fletcher may require the employment of persons in the country, and the use of materials, without waiting for the employment of those persons or the purchase of those materials by an officer of the Commissariat, I have to request that all orders for workmanship, labor, or materials, drawn by Lieut. Col. Fletcher upon the Dep. Commissary Gen. at Lisbon, may be paid, Lieut. Col. Fletcher being accountable for the money.

I have also to request that the Dep. Commissary Gen. at Lisbon may be directed to supply Lieut. Col. Fletcher with such numbers of fascines, palisades, and pickets as he may require at such stations as he may point out, without waiting for further orders from me.

To Col. Le Cor.   Viseu, 18th Feb. 1810.

As there is reason to believe that the enemy will attack Portugal by the frontier of Beira, I have formed a corps on the side of Castello Branco, under the orders of Col. Wilson, and another as a second line upon the Zezere, of which I have arranged with Marshal Beresford that you are to take the command. This corps will at present consist of the 13th regt. of infantry, which has already marched from Leiria for those parts; and of 3 regiments of militia of Thomar, Leiria, and Santarem, which are under arms, and which will be placed under your orders.

You will, in the first place, take up your head quarters at Thomar, and you will dispose of the troops under your orders in the most suitable manner for defending the passage of the Zezere. You will communicate with Col. Wilson, who will be in front of your line; with Gen. Hill, who commands a corps of the army which has entered the Alentejo; and also with me.

I believe that the 13th regt. of infantry has been ordered to Villa de Rei, because it was supposed there was no room at Thomar; but as the brigade under Col. Campbell has marched, the 13th regt. may be stationed at Thomar.

To Col. Wilson.   Viseu, 18th Feb. 1810.

I beg that you will, on the receipt of this letter, take measures immediately to have the road called the Estrada Nova broken up at the points described in the enclosed papers, and will station parties at those points to prevent its repair by the enemy. This measure, if carried effectually into execution, will, I understand, close that road, and enable you to concentrate a larger part of your force on the main road from Castello Branco.

I beg that you will pay particular attention to the bridge at Villa Velha, if you should find it necessary to retire from Castello Branco.

To Lieut. Gen. Hill.   Viseu, 18th Feb. 1810.

I have received your letter of the 16th. I had already received from Gen. Cole a copy of the information which Col. Wilson had transmitted. I believe Soult's force is of the strength stated : the question is which way he will turn from Plasencia.

The instructions you have already received are applicable to the possible case of his crossing the Tagus, which it is not improbable he may do at Alconeta. The enemy will then be too strong for you in Estremadura. If Soult should advance upon Castello Branco, which is another not improbable movement, your instructions provide for it, and you must retire upon Abrantes; and if you should find that Col. Wilson is unable to maintain himself in the mountains beyond the Zezere, you must leave the Portuguese militia in garrison at Abrantes, and cross the Zezere at Punhete, and maintain the Zezere as long as you can. If Soult should turn towards the Puerto de Baños, which is not improbable, he will be out of your way entirely. I beg you to endeavor particularly to discover if the enemy, whether Soult or Mortier, or any other, get a bridge up to them; and let me know it immediately.

I enclose a duplicate of a letter which I have written to Col. Wilson, of which, and its enclosures, I beg you to take a copy. Let Col. Le Cor know where you are. Pray have an eye upon the bridge of Villa Velha, and take care that it does not fall into the possession of the enemy in any of the cases supposed.

P.S. You may depend upon it that all the money which I have stated to you has been sent, and it is probable that the Commissary has taken the largest share of it; but there is some money at Elvas, part of which I have desired may be sent to you.

To Marshal Beresford.   Viseu, 18th Feb. 1810.

I have to request that 4 Portuguese engineers, who understand French, may be placed at the disposal of Lieut. Col. Fletcher, chief engineer, with a view to their being employed in the destruction of roads when it may be necessary. If you will direct that these officers may be in readiness to attend Lieut. Col. Fletcher, he will communicate with the chief engineer of the Portuguese army when he shall require their services.

To Lieut. Col. Torrens, Military Secretary.   Viseu, 18th Feb. 1810.

In answer to your letter of the 22d Jan., regarding Campbell's claim for promotion, I have to remind you that H.R.H. the Duke of York promised Campbell, when he arrived in England with the accounts of the battles of Roliça and Vimeiro, that he should be made a Lieut. Colonel, by brevet, as soon as he should have it in his power to appoint him Major of a regiment, and that this promise would have been carried into execution if the regulation of March, 1809, had not been adopted. However, after all, the Commander in Chief must be the best judge of what he can do; and I only submit this circumstance for his consideration.

The A.G. to Dr. Franck, Inspector of Hospitals.   18th Feb. 1810.

You will please to inform your department, when any officer of the Medical staff may have any thing to communicate to the Adj. Gen., such communication is only to be made through you, their superior officer. A letter of intended explanation, written by the members of a Medical board to you, dated 1st Feb., caused by your announcing to them the purport of a letter of the 25th ult. from this office, has been perused by my Lord Wellington, in which his Lordship only finds a confirmation of the truth of the facts in Capt. ——'s case, which before appeared to exist from some former letters, viz. that without inquiring into the state of Capt. ——'s health, or any of the circumstances attending his case, the Board had, on his own desire, allowed that officer to join the army, reporting him fit for duty. From this his Lordship concluded and still believes most fairly, that if Capt. —— had been otherwise disposed, the report would have contained a recommendation that he should remain at Lisbon. By the steps already taken, it was the intention of the Commander of the Forces to caution those officers against this practice. The letter from the Board to their senior officer, of the 1st inst., and that from Dr. —— to the senior of the Adj. Gen.'s department, only induce a repetition of the same caution. In concluding this letter of renewed observation, I am commanded to convey to you his Excellency's desire not to hear any thing further from these officers on the subject in question.

To Marshal Beresford.   Viseu, 19th Feb. 1810.

Since I wrote to you last, you will have heard from Gen. Campbell that I had countermanded the advance of the Portuguese troops, as I found that the enemy had withdrawn from Ciudad Rodrigo; with the exception of Blunt's brigade, and the light battalions, which I thought it best to have up to Coimbra.

I have since received a letter from Gen. Campbell, in which he recommends that Gen. Blunt should be ordered to remain at Monte Mór o

---

G. A. O.   Viseu, 19th Feb. 1810.

2. During the absence from the army of Lieut. Col. Bathurst, all applications and letters hitherto addressed to the Military Secretary are to be sent to Capt. Bouverie or Lord FitzRoy Somerset, and answers will be given by one of those officers.

The warrants signed by the Commander of the Forces are to be countersigned by Capt. Bouverie or Lord FitzRoy Somerset, and either of those officers will sign the duplicate and triplicates to be lodged with the Commissary General.

Velho; and that the light battalions should be moved forward. I have consented to the former; but I have deferred the latter till you shall have arrived.

The accounts which I have of the enemy are, that Junot and Loison, with about 15,000 or 20,000 men, are about to attack the Spaniards at Astorga; Ney's corps, upon drawing off from Ciudad Rodrigo, went towards Salamanca; Soult arrived at Plasencia on the 12th with 16,000 men; and Mortier had, on the 14th, withdrawn his advanced corps from Badajoz, which was all he had there, and had the whole at his head quarters at Talavera Real. I believe he patrolled up to Badajoz again on the 15th. Kellermann's corps is, I believe, still at Valladolid. Soult's next movement will point out nearly what the enemy's intentions are; whether to attack Ciudad Rodrigo or Badajoz; but I should think Ciudad Rodrigo; and yet they are but little prepared for that operation.

The Duque del Parque's army has separated into 3 corps; one, under Gen. O'Donell, has crossed the Tagus at the Barca de Alconeta, and is to be at Alburquerque; another under Mendizabal, is come to Penamacor, and is to cross the Tagus at Villa Velha; a third under Gen. Carrera, of 2000 or 2500 men, remains in the mountains. They are all in want of every thing.

I have written to the government respecting the mode in which the Governor of Estremadura has executed the work on the road from Thomar to Espinhal. It might be made the best, instead of being the worst, military road in Portugal; and it is really a most important line of communication, without which all our combinations for defence, and any offensive measures we may adopt, must be very imperfect. There is not a hill upon the road; it runs along a river; and there are materials close to it which might make it excellent. I enclose the instructions I have sent to Col. Le Cor. Has the 13th regt. been ordered to Thomar? and the 12th to join Col. Wilson?

To Charles Stuart, Esq.*   Viseu, 19th Feb. 1810.

Since I saw you on the 14th, I received on the 15th, at Espinhal, the accounts that the French corps of Ney had appeared before Ciudad Rodrigo on the 12th; but it retired again on the 13th, and has since gone towards Salamanca. Soult on the same day arrived at Plasencia with 16,000 men, and you will recollect that the 12th was the day on which Mortier's corps appeared at Badajoz. The Duc d'Abrantes and Loison have gone with their corps of 15,000 or 20,000 men north of the Duero; and I believe intend to attack the Spanish division under Gen. Garcias at Astorga; and I believe Kellermann is still at Valladolid. I have accounts from that neighbourhood of as late a date as the 15th, which state that Soult had not moved from Plasencia: his next movement will show what are the enemy's intentions.

I wish that you should see a letter which I have written this day to Dom M. Forjaz, which will point out to you a fresh instance of the mode in which directions given to the Portuguese authorities are carried into

* Mr. Stuart (Lord Stuart de Rothesay, K.B.) had succeeded Mr. Villiers (the Earl of Clarendon) as His Majesty's minister at Lisbon.

execution, and the importance of the early and due execution of the work which I had ordered long ago to be performed on the road from Thomar to Espinhal. If it is not done, I must draw in from this frontier, as soon as Soult shall cross the Tagus, if he should cross that river from Plasencia; or I may lose my communication with Hill, or even with Lisbon. If that road were made as it ought to be, I should be at the distance of only 3 marches from the Tagus, of which one only forced; whereas, now, I cannot reach that river by making less than 9 marches.

I have desired the Commissary Gen. to pay Mr. Bell £50,000 on account of aids, of about £100,000 which are due on that account. But we really have not at present more money; and I shall not be able to pay the troops this month; and I must put a stop to all the arrangements which had been made for applying them, founded upon the regular payments for provisions, &c.

I apprised government more than 2 months ago of our probable want of money, and of the necessity that we should be supplied, not only with a large sum, but with a regular sum monthly, equal in amount to the increase of expense occasioned by the increased subsidy to the Portuguese government, and by the increase of our own army. They have not attended to either of those demands; and I must write again. But I wish you would mention the subject in your letters to Lord Wellesley. I propose to dispatch a messenger from hence on Wednesday with letters for England, to be dispatched by the packet of Sunday.

To Lieut. Gen. Hill.   Viseu, 20th Feb. 1810.

I have received your letters of the 17th and 18th.

It is most difficult to form any judgment from the Spanish and Portuguese accounts of the strength of any French corps; and I generally form my estimates of their strength, not only from these accounts, but from intercepted letters, and from my knowledge of their strength at different periods. For this reason, I believed the corps under Soult at Plasencia to be 16,000 men, as reported; but if of this corps 6000 men have come into Estremadura by Arzobispo and Truxillo, it is obvious that there cannot well be 16,000 at Plasencia, unless Soult's corps has been largely reinforced, of which I have no report.

Your position at Portalegre is a very strong one; it cannot be touched by its left or rear at all; or by its right or front, without your having early intelligence of the design. Adverting then to the importance which it is to all the places on the frontier, as well as to the province of Alentejo, that you should continue to hold it as long as may be practicable, I wish you to remain in it as long as you think you can do so with safety, even though the corps at Plasencia should cross the Tagus, which I think is probable, and join that stated to be at Caceres. There is another circumstance which induces me to wish you to stay as long as you can with safety, and that is the necessity of protecting the march of the convalescents from Elvas, whom Gen. Leite has taken upon himself to detain. They must positively come away immediately.

The serious demonstrations, also, which the enemy are now making upon Badajoz will most probably soon become more so, as I understand that they have met with a check in an attack upon the Isla de Leon, and they must therefore confine their operations within more narrow bounds, and choose between Badajoz and the Isla de Leon. If compelled to make this choice, they will probably determine upon an attack upon Badajoz, and they will begin by bringing an army across the Guadiana, and thus cut off our communication with Elvas. The removal of the hospital from Elvas, and from Estremoz to Lisbon or Abrantes, becomes, therefore, an object of great importance, which will be much facilitated by your remaining at Portalegre as long as you can do so with safety to yourself. Major Lindsay was ordered on the 18th to take measures for that purpose, and a letter goes to him, and another to Capt. Beresford this day, upon the same subject.

P.S. You must not send any of your Portuguese troops to Elvas.

To Lieut. Gen. Leite.   Viseu, 20th Feb. 1810.

I have had the honor of receiving your letter of the 15th inst., and I beg that you will allow Major Lindsay to carry into execution the orders which he has received, or may hereafter receive from me, for the disposal of the sick and convalescents, or other movements, &c., of the British army left at Elvas. Much time has elapsed since orders were given for the march of the troops to form the garrison of Elvas, the forts, and the other places which you were directed to occupy: if those who were to have obeyed these orders have disobeyed them, I cannot allow the deficiency of the troops in these places to be made good by leaving these convalescents of the British army. I beg, therefore, that whatever may be the consequences to the forts in question, you will not interfere in the execution of my orders by Major Lindsay.

The A.G. to Lieut. Gen. Hill.   20th Feb. 1810.

Your letter of the 6th inst., so far as referring to Lieut. Col. Drummond's application, has been laid before the Commander of the Forces. His Excellency desires Capt. —— of the — regt. may state the nature of his affairs, and has further commanded me to observe the recent instance of Major —— of the Adj. Gen.'s department has induced a particular caution in granting these applications, and his Lordship trusts it may equally act as a caution to you in forwarding them. My Lord Wellington considers when an officer applies for leave of absence on account of his private affairs, the settlement of those affairs is paramount to every other object, his duty to the service included; but his Lordship cannot understand that an officer is to have leave of absence on account of his private affairs, the settlement of which he can postpone, when a service occurs which it will be agreeable to him to perform, or from which it will not be convenient for him to be absent.

To Marshal Beresford.   Viseu, 21st Feb. 1810.

I have just received your letter of the 18th inst. I take Soult to be stronger than you suppose, as it is now evident that large reinforcements have come into the Peninsula; and it is reported that the corps of troops at Plasencia is 10,000 men. The troops that passed by Truxillo could have been only cavalry and light infantry. I do not know what the French mean to do. They are certainly now too much separated to effect any object; at the same time they are so connected, that it is absolutely impossible that any movement we can make upon them of an offensive description can succeed.

I think that you will do well to retain your cavalry either at or very near Lisbon. I do not care which of the brigades comes, when they shall move. In respect to Almeida, I imagine that salt provisions are not required there, as I never propose to use those which are in store.

I ordered the arms from Elvas to Lisbon months ago; but I have sent for Framingham to know what has been done about them.

P.S. Framingham says that he ordered the arms from Elvas on the 8th Feb.; and that he is almost certain that they are now on their way to Lisbon.

To the Earl of Liverpool. Viseu, 21st Feb. 1810.

In my letter of the 13th Dec., I requested your Lordship to give directions that £100,000 in specie should be sent to Portugal as soon as possible; and another sum of £100,000 in January, and I explained to your Lordship the probable future wants of the army. The *Clyde*, in which the Commissary in Chief had informed the Commissary Gen. of the army that 1,000,000 of dollars were embarked, arrived at Lisbon a few days ago with 500,000 dollars only, the remainder of the sum having been disembarked at Portsmouth.

I beg leave to refer your Lordship to the statement of our probable wants contained in my letter of the 13th Dec. At this moment the troops are one month in arrear, and I am unable to pay them; and money is required to procure supplies from the country, which cannot now be got excepting for ready money.

The sums to be obtained for bills upon England have materially decreased lately; and the expense of raising money in this manner has increased, owing to the fall in the value of the government paper; and this cause will increase in proportion with the probability of the invasion of the country by the enemy. At the same time, the expenses have increased by the additional subsidy to be paid to the government of Portugal. I trust, therefore, that your Lordship, adverting to these circumstances, and to the fact that the difficulty of keeping the troops in order is materially increased by a failure in paying them regularly, and by the necessity of using force to draw supplies from the country, will adopt measures to supply the sums of money, as soon as possible, which I stated would be necessary in my dispatch of the 13th Dec.

I have directed the Commissary Gen. to address the Sec. of the Treasury upon this subject.

To the Earl of Liverpool. Viseu, 21st Feb. 1810.

Immediately after the arrival of the French army at Seville on the 1st and 2d of this month, Marshal Mortier was detached with his corps into Estremadura, through the pass of Monasterio, apparently to disperse the Spanish division of Gen. Areyzaga's corps, which had crossed the Guadalquivir when the enemy passed the Sierra Morena, and had remained at Monasterio. This division went off by its right towards Ayamonte, sending its artillery to Badajoz; and Marshal Mortier continued to advance into Estremadura. On the 12th, his advanced guard appeared before Badajoz, and on the same day a small detachment took possession of Olivença, which town the Spanish government had omitted to occupy or effectually

to destroy its works.   Marshal Mortier's head quarters remained at Talavera Real on the 17th, the date of the last accounts I have received from
that quarter, with his corps between that town and Olivença, and his
advanced posts near Badajoz.

On the 12th inst., Marshal Soult arrived at Plasencia from Talavera de
la Reyna, with a corps stated to be 16,000 men; and a division of his
corps had passed the Tagus at Arzobispo, and entered Lower Estremadura
at Deleytosa, and arrived at Caceres by Truxillo on the 15th.   This corps
is stated to be 6000 men; but I should imagine that if these numbers are
correct, the corps at Plasencia cannot be so strong as is stated.   On the
same day, the 12th inst., Marshal Ney summoned the town of Ciudad
Rodrigo, with a corps stated to consist of 15,000 men.   They opened a
fire upon the town upon that evening, which having produced no effect,
they retired on the morning of the 13th, and have resumed their position
upon the Tormes; and a detachment has been sent to Zamora.   At the
same time a large corps, supposed to be under the command of the Duc
d'Abrantes and Gen. Loison, has marched towards the frontiers of Galicia;
and on the 12th inst. made an attack upon Astorga, in which they were
repulsed.   The French are in possession of the greater part of the
Asturias, and they are certainly in considerable strength in the province
of Leon.   Gen. Kellermann's corps is at Valladolid.

I have not received any accounts from Cadiz or the south of Spain since
the 31st of last month, upon which I can rely.   I understand, however,
that the enemy had separated their army in that quarter, as well as in the
north; Sebastiani being at Granada; and Jaen, Cordova, Carmona, Ecija,
and Seville being occupied by detachments from the corps of Victor and
Sebastiani.   The King is at Seville with his guards, and a detachment
from Victor's corps; and the reserve, under Gen. Dessolles, at Puerto de
Sta Maria.   It is likewise reported that this last corps made an attack on the
12th on the Isla de Leon, in which they were repulsed with considerable loss.

From this statement it is obvious that the French must have received
large reinforcements to their army; and, indeed, all the accounts now
concur in stating, that the conscripts and the corps of the Duc d'Abrantes
have arrived in Spain; and these troops must have been within the scope
of the general operations of the army, when the expedition into the south
of Spain was undertaken in the end of January.

In the divided state of their army, it is probable that the French cannot
accomplish any important military object; and either some additional
reinforcement must arrive, or some of these corps must join, before they
can expect to succeed in any of the objects which it appears they have
undertaken, except possibly in the attack upon Galicia.   From the position of the several corps, however, your Lordship will observe that they
can unite with facility, and particularly those of Marshals Ney, Soult, and
Mortier, and of Gen. Kellermann.

I have not received any positive intelligence respecting the fate of the
only division of Gen. Areyzaga's corps, which remained with him after he
quitted Granada on his retreat to Malaga, leaving at Granada his cannon;
nor of the other divisions of this corps.

The Spanish corps which had been under the Duque del Parque, and had been ordered by the Junta to cross the Tagus in the last month, did not effect that operation. Only one division of infantry and 500 cavalry crossed the river about the 9th or 10th of this month, and is in the neighbourhood of Alburquerque, in Estremadura; another division under Gen. Mendizabal, which was to cross at Villa Velha, in Portugal, was at Penamacor when I last heard of them; and about 2000 men, under Gen. Carrera, are to remain in Castille. The Marques de la Romana, who now com· mands this corps, is still in Badajoz; and the Duque del Parque is gone to Lisbon to embark for Catalonia.

Gen. Hill has advanced with his corps to Portalegre, in conformity with the instructions which I had given him; and the other part of the British army remains in the position which it before occupied.

The facility with which the enemy could unite their corps to co-operate in an attack upon this country, the strength which they have at present, and the probable early arrival of further reinforcements from France, induce me to wish that your Lordship may have carried into execution the intention announced in your dispatch of the 3d Jan., of increasing the transport tonnage in the Tagus to 45,000 tons; and that His Majesty's government may have made arrangements to station in the Tagus a fleet of men of war. The returns which I send by this opportunity will show your Lordship the amount of the force which we should now have to oppose the enemy in the field. I also hope that your Lordship may have sent out the hospital ships, according to my request contained in my letter of the 7th Dec.; and a proportion of horse ships, to remove the best of the horses of the army.

I have the pleasure to inform your Lordship that the 20th Portuguese regt., which is gone to Cadiz, embarked with the utmost cheerfulness, and that none were missing upon the embarkation of the regiment.

To Major Gen. the Hon. G. L. Cole. Viseu, 22d Feb. 1810.

I omitted to desire that my letter to Gen. Hill, by your aide de camp, might be sent open for your perusal. The purport of it was, to desire him to keep his position at Portalegre as long as he thought he could do so with safety, even though the French corps at Plasencia should cross the Tagus, and join that at Caceres. I understand from Gen. Mendizabal, that that corps has withdrawn from Plasencia; which, if it was intended to cross the Tagus, I conclude has been because the boats have all been taken off the river. If you have received Cox's letter of the 19th, you will see that the French have been reinforced sufficiently to make Soult's corps of the strength stated. The intelligence which Cox received from Echavarri's messenger is confirmed by the accounts of the march of the French corps through Bayonne, received from England.

You will see the arrangement which I have made of the divisions upon Gen. Picton's joining the army, which I hope will be satisfactory to you. I have got 2 dozen of excellent port for you, which I do not know how to send you.

To Vice Adm. the Hon. G. Berkeley. Viseu, 22d Feb. 1810.

I have had the pleasure of receiving your letter of the 19th inst.

The baggage of the British army is always an embarrassment, which, like many others, is to be traced to its constitution. The fact is, that regiments come upon service with every thing belonging to every individual in the corps, instead of having a depôt fixed for the reception of the baggage and other incumbrances of the regiment, never wanted on service in the field, and which might be sent to them from the depôt when they should be in any fixed station. The care of this baggage then falls upon persons in my situation, who are obliged to provide for its preservation; and if any of it be lost, there is no end to the complaints upon the subject. Indeed, the loss is not cheap to the public, as they pay for it. For these reasons, and knowing that when we do embark we shall not have much time to spare, I wished to have the baggage out of the way; and as I knew that the embarkation of it, at the moment previous to the embarkation of the army, would create alarm and confusion, I thought it best to have the business done when the reinforcements should come out. Indeed, the desire to have it done at that moment, and the apprehension that the reinforcements might have arrived before my letter upon the subject could reach Lisbon, induced me to desire the Q. M. Gen. to fix upon the transport for each regiment here, in order that there might be no more reference or correspondence. The baggage, which would necessarily be separated among several transports, if embarked in the usual manner with the regiments, is now embarked in one transport for each regiment, of which, of course, it takes up much space. That is an evil which cannot be avoided, unless

G. O.   Viseu, 22d Feb. 1810.

1. The brigade consisting of the 3d batt. 27th, 97th, and 40th regts., is to be Major Gen. Cole's brigade; and that consisting of the 45th, 88th, and 74th regts., Major Gen. Picton's.

2. The 3d division is to consist of the brigades of Major Gen. Picton and Major Gen. Lightburne; the 4th division, of the brigades of Major Gen. Cole and Brig. Gen. Alex. Campbell: Major Gen. Picton is to command the 3d division, and Major Gen. Cole the 4th division, until further orders.

Col. Kemmis is attached as a colonel on the Staff to the brigade of the Hon. Major Gen. Cole, and Col. Mackinnon as a colonel on the Staff to the brigade of Major Gen. Picton, during the time those officers will command the 3d and 4th divisions respectively.

The Portuguese brigade of infantry, consisting of the 9th and 21st regts., now stationed at Coimbra, is attached to the 3d division; and the Portuguese brigade of infantry, consisting of the 3d and 15th regts., now stationed at Lamego, is attached to the 4th division. These brigades will hereafter be ordered to join the divisions to which they belong.

3. The 1st and 2d batts. of Portuguese Chasseurs are attached to the brigade of Brig. Gen. R. Craufurd, which is to be called the Light division. These troops will be ordered to join the division to which they belong.

4. A company 5th batt. 60th regt. is to be attached to each of the brigades of the army according to the plan detailed in the Orders of the 4th May, 1809. The commanding officer of the 5th batt. 60th regt. will detach 3 companies to Lieut. Gen. Hill's division as soon as he shall receive this order, and a route from the Q. M. G. for the purpose; and as the General officers commanding brigades have invariably expressed the highest satisfaction with the uniform good conduct of this valuable body of men, which has always continued effective under many trying circumstances, the Commander of the Forces desires that as far as possible the same companies may be attached as formerly to the same brigades.

Two companies to be attached to Sir J. Sherbrooke's division, one to the brigade of Guards, and one to Brig. Gen. Cameron's brigade; two companies to the 4th division, being one for Major Gen. Cole's, and one for Brig. Gen. A. Campbell's brigades; and three companies, with the head quarters of the regiment, with the 3d division.

5. The A. G. and Q. M. G. will take measures for placing under the orders of Major Gen. Picton an officer belonging to each of their departments; and the Commissary General and Inspector of Hospitals, the same proportion of Commissariat and Medical staff as attached to the other divisions of infantry.

all the transports for each regiment could be immediately fixed upon, which I imagine cannot conveniently be done; or unless I should order a great proportion of the baggage to be destroyed, for which, if I give the order, either I or the public must pay. I must, therefore, in this, as in every other case,. make the best arrangement that circumstances will enable me to make, and be satisfied with something that falls infinitely short of perfection. I shall inquire respecting the quantity of Mr. P——'s baggage.

I am obliged to you for your intelligence respecting the means of communication with Cadiz.

To Charles Stuart, Esq. Viseu, 22d Feb. 1810.

I received your letter of the 19th, and I agree in opinion with you that small duties upon the imports from England, and a more efficient collection of the taxes at present existing in Portugal, and the transmission of the balances in the hands of the collectors of the revenues of the crown to the treasury, or to the military chest, would go far to relieve the difficulties under which the Portuguese government labor : but I understand that the first mentioned was the subject of a treaty between Brazil and the King's ministers, and of course the Portuguese government are unwilling to interfere in it; and in respect to the others, they require only the adoption of a more rigorous system of punishments in order to be carried into execution, as there is really no government in existence of which the regulations are better than those of Portugal.

I doubt whether much can be done in the way of retrenchment. However, upon that point I have not had an opportunity of acquiring much information. I rather think that, adverting to the probability that we shall evacuate the country, and that it will be desirable to carry off as many people as may choose to go, and to have as many ships as may be possible to carry them off, it may be advisable not to put an end to all expense on account of the navy, although even in that view of the subject it would be desirable to draw in the squadron from the Mediterranean.

I have desired the Commissary Gen. to pay £50,000 on account of our debt to the 24th Jan., and I shall, to-morrow, order him to pay the balance of it to the same period. I hope to be able to-morrow to let you know what proportion of our receipts will be applicable in future to Portuguese aids. The increased proportion ought to be calculated from the 1st Jan.; and I shall have that calculation made here, and the amount shall be paid. I am obliged to you for the news, and for Sir Charles's papers, of which I will take care; and they shall be returned to you as you desire.

To the Earl of Liverpool. Viseu, 22d Feb. 1810.

By accident I have omitted to send you the Weekly states according to your desire, which, however, I now enclose, with some remarks upon the last, which will show you nearly how we shall stand in the field.

I likewise enclose an abstract of the last returns of the Portuguese army, which will show you how they will stand in the field. The cavalry in this number, although improved and improving, must not be reckoned for much; and if the whole were reckoned at 20,000 for the field, it would be as much as they would be. Besides these numbers, there are 29,191 militia armed, and 21,985 unarmed. Of the armed, however, there are at least 10,000 whose arms are unfit for service. The Ordenanza are generally unarmed.

To Marshal Beresford.   Viseu, 23d Feb. 1810.

In respect to the employment of the militia of Viseu and Tondella at Obidos and Peniche, do not you think that, adverting to the great strength which the enemy have thrown upon the north of Spain, which will eventually be turned upon the north of Portugal, it would be best to keep those corps for the defence of the northern provinces, and to throw into Peniche and Obidos some of those nearer to these places? I suggest this for your consideration.

I understand from Col. Wilson that he has embodied only one battalion of each of his regiments of militia. My opinion is, that the whole of the militia in the country that have arms ought to be embodied. The corps, when embodied, may be left at their stations, with the exception of those absolutely required elsewhere; but they would acquire some discipline if embodied, as well as be in readiness to move at short notice, which is always worth the expense. I wish you would let me know what orders you gave for the defence of the provinces of Tras os Montes and Minho.

I have no objection to Le Cor's militia remaining in their stations for the present, but they must positively be embodied; and the 13th regt. must be at Thomar. I think Le Cor ought to have a brigade of artillery.

I send you a copy of the orders which I issued yesterday respecting the new organization of the British army, which I beg you to communicate to the parties concerned.

Have you given orders for the artillerymen to be collected for the occupation of our works in the hills? I have written to Fletcher to desire him to see that Rosa and Fisher settle definitively what posts shall be filled with our ordnance, and what by yours; and to have the guns sent to the posts forthwith.

I believe that we ought to take Fort S. Julian for ours, as they are upon travelling carriages, which it might be very inconvenient to lose.

To Charles Stuart, Esq.   Viseu, 23d Feb. 1810.

Since I wrote to you yesterday, I have examined, with the Commissary Gen., the estimate of our expenses, which I find will amount to £190,000 a month. The annual amount of the Portuguese subsidy, and the expenses of the pay of the British officers, being taken at £980,000 *per annum*, comes to about £82,000 a month, making the total monthly expenditure in Portugal £272,000. As all the money received here, on account of His Majesty, passes through the hands of the Commissary Gen., and as it has frequently happened that the monthly supply has not been equal to the demands during the month, I had settled with Mr. Villiers that such a proportion of the monthly supply should be applicable to Portuguese aids, as the total Portuguese subsidy and expenses should bear to the whole of the British expense in Portugal.

We find that the Portuguese expenses of £28,000 are something more than two-sevenths of the whole monthly expense, calculated at £272,000, and we have therefore settled that two-sevenths of the whole monthly supply shall be paid to Mr. Bell for Portuguese aids. As the increased expenses were to commence from the 1st Jan., I have desired the Commissary Gen. to pay the increased proportion of the supplies from the 25th Dec.; and he sends orders accordingly to Mr. Dunmore by this opportunity, and that the account may be cleared, and the balance paid to the 24th Jan. As soon as we shall get an account of our receipts to the 24th Feb., the amount will be made up on the same principles, and the balance shall be paid to that period.

It is obvious that these sums will fall short of those which His Majesty's government have engaged to supply to the Portuguese government, but that is the fault of His Majesty's government in England; and they have been repeatedly informed that it was necessary that they should send out money. The funds for the expenses of the British army are insufficient in the same proportion; and all that I can do is to divide the deficiency in its due proportions between the two bodies which are to be supported by the funds at our disposal.

To Bart. Frere, Esq.   Viseu, 25th Feb. 1810.

I send herewith your brother's 3 maps, which I had still kept; and I beg vou to return them to him.

I have not heard from you since the 31st of last month, not even of the arrival of the British and Portuguese troops. You will have heard of the enemy's attempts upon Ciudad Rodrigo, Badajoz, and Astorga upon the same day, the 12th inst., all of which failed. They still remain at Talavera Real, with their left at Olivença, which the Spaniards had omitted to occupy, or effectually to destroy, and which will answer well for all the ulterior designs of the French, whatever they may be. When Ney retired from Ciudad Rodrigo, he went to Salamanca, and resumed his old position upon the Tormes, holding some troops at Zamora, I suppose to communicate with the corps under Loison and Junot, which had gone towards the frontiers of Galicia. By the last accounts of the 16th, they had not made any impression upon Astorga; but they were in strength in the Asturias, of which they appeared to have the whole, excepting Oviedo. They were also in strength about Benevente. Many of the reinforcements have certainly arrived. Indeed, the corps on the frontier of Galicia is entirely composed of the troops that have lately entered Spain, and I hear of more following them.

Gen. Hill's corps has moved forward to Portalegre, and I shall join it with a reinforcement, if I should have reason to believe that it is desirable to make any movement for the relief of Badajoz.

P.S. I see in a paper of the 9th that my brother * had been driven back to Portsmouth on the 6th.

To the Corregidor of Aveiro.   Viseu, 26th Feb. 1810.

The Commissary Gen. of the British army has informed me that, hav-

---

* The Hon. H. Wellesley (Lord Cowley, K.B.), who had been first named to succeed Mr. Villiers at Lisbon, but was subsequently appointed Ambassador to the Court of Spain.

ing called upon you to supply from the district under your charge certain quantities of straw for the use of the British army, you have refused to do so, stating that there is none in your district. I cannot avoid reminding you that last year the French cavalry found straw in your district for nearly 2 months; and that having had no troops in the district since the last harvest, there must now be in the district as much straw as there was this time last year.

I now order you to draw to Coimbra, within 10 days of the date of this letter, 50,000 rations of straw, to begin the delivery within 5 days after the date; and 50,000 additional rations within 20 days after the date of this letter, for which payment will be made.

If you should fail in obeying this order you will repair to my head quarters, and I shall report you to the government to be punished.

To Major Gen. the Hon. W. Stewart.　　　　　　　Viseu, 27th Feb. 1810.

I have had the honor of receiving your letter of the 15th inst. I approve entirely of your having adopted measures eventually to procure a supply of meat for the British troops; and you will now direct your Commissary to carry those measures into execution. He will pay and charge for this meat in his accounts with the Commissary Gen. of the army. It is desirable, however, that we should not depart from the reasonable principle that the Spanish government should supply with provisions the British and Portuguese troops employed in the defence of Cadiz; and you will accordingly furnish the King's minister with the accounts of the meat which the Commissary will have purchased, and leave him to apply for payment, at such time and in such manner as he may think proper.

I expect to hear from you in case you should apprehend a want of any other article of provisions; and you may depend upon their being sent to Cadiz without loss of time. I approve of your issuing wine to the troops in the same manner as to those composing the army in Portugal.

You must be in every respect the best judge of detaching the troops under your command to any part of the limits in which they are to act; and you will consider the second article of the conditions in my letter of the 5th inst. as intended to strengthen you against the Governor of the garrison, in case he should wish to detach the troops under your command in a manner of which you should not approve. From the character and conduct, however, of the persons in authority in Cadiz, and from your disposition to conciliate them, I expect that you will not be pressed to adopt any measure which you will not think a proper one.

I approve of your detaining Brig. Gen. Bowes :* he is an officer with whom I am well acquainted, and is highly deserving of the confidence which you are disposed to place in him.

I send herewith a warrant, authorising you to convene General Courts Martial, and the warrant for the appointment of a Dep. Judge Advocate, which you will fill up with the name of the officer whom you think proper to appoint to that office.

The warrant under His Majesty's sign manual does not authorise me to depute the power of confirming the sentences of General Courts Martial.

* Afterwards killed in the siege of the Forts at Salamanca, in 1812.

In respect to a Provost, I am authorised by the King's warrant to appoint only one Provost Marshal; but I have appointed several Assist. Provosts, who have the same authority, and you will appoint an Assist. Provost for the troops under your command.

I enclose a copy of the orders which have been issued upon this subject, and I shall further desire the Adj. Gen. to send you a copy of all the general orders which have been issued in this army.

I am much obliged to you for your account of events, and of the situation of affairs at Cadiz, which is very interesting. I had not heard from that quarter since the 31st of last month. I am apprehensive that you will find the Spanish troops in the field not much better than their appearance promises; and you cannot render a more important service to the cause than by precept and example to endeavor to induce the Spanish officers to clothe, discipline, feed, and pay their soldiers; and to establish some system of regimental regulation and economy, by which it may be hoped that the corps may be kept together and in order when on service in the field in the shape of armies. The cavalry in particular is lamentably deficient in discipline, and in every thing which can render that arm useful, or indeed any thing but dangerous to those with whom they may act; and yet it would be difficult, if not impossible, for an army to keep the field in Spain, unless attended by a large body of well disciplined cavalry.

I approve of your having reported your arrival at Cadiz to the Sec. of State.

P.S. Since writing the above, the Commissary Gen. has communicated to me a letter from Mr. O'Meara, from which I observe that he proposes to purchase American salt provisions. From the perusal of your letter, I imagined that you intended that he should purchase cattle from Barbary, to which the paragraph in the commencement of this letter refers. If you should require salt provisions, you will let me know it, and I will send some from Lisbon, where we have large quantities in store, which we cannot make use of. In the mean time, till the salt provisions shall arrive, after I shall receive your requisition for them, you may use the provisions in the transports, which must afterwards be replaced.

To Major Gen. the Hon. W. Stewart.   Viseu, 27th Feb. 1810.

I received yesterday your private letter of the 15th, as well as your dispatch, and I am glad to find that matters are going on at Cadiz to your satisfaction.

I am not acquainted with Venegas, but have always heard a good character of him; and his consent must certainly have been given to the measure of calling for our assistance. You must be a better judge of his conduct than I can be; and adverting to the fact that the seat of the government is within the limit of his command, and that the Duque de Alburquerque, who commands the greater part of the troops, is a senior officer to Venegas, I think it very immaterial whether he does or does not entertain the opinions which O'Farrill's paper attributes to him. If he does entertain them, they are not unnatural opinions for a Spaniard to entertain, by no means uncommon even among the best of the Spaniards, or at all inconsistent with the performance of his duty against the French. I also think that his entertaining these opinions is not inconsistent with his consent to the measure of calling for our assistance to defend Cadiz at the moment the requisition was made; particularly recollecting a letter * which I wrote to Gen. Whittingham in December upon this subject, which I know was shown to Venegas, and which was certainly calculated to inspire confidence rather than mistrust of our designs in regard to Cadiz.

I wrote 'the conditions' in my dispatch of the 5th inst. to Mr. Frere, in the same spirit, as I know that, however important it is to our interests that Cadiz should be defended and maintained, we can effect our object only by convincing the Spaniards that it is essentially their interest (as it really is) to maintain the place; and that we co-operate in its defence with a view to the importance of the preservation of the place for their cause particularly, as well as for the general and the British interests. Upon other points I wish that you and Mr. Frere would consider seriously of the defence of Cadiz, and of the general measures to be adopted in relation to the situation of affairs in Spain at present.

The misfortune throughout the war has been that the Spaniards are of a disposition too sanguine. They have invariably expected only success in objects for the attainment of which they had adopted no measures. They have never looked to, nor prepared for, a lengthened contest; and all those, or nearly all, who have had any thing to do with them, have imbibed the same spirit, and the same sentiments. Without adverting to the enormous armies which are daily pouring into Spain, in addition to those which were before in the country, and were already superior in number to the allies; or to the fact that there is now no army in the field excepting the British army, they are thinking of offensive operations from Cadiz; and they appear to me to hold the Isla de Leon more as the intrenched camp (and hardly even deserving that name) of an army, than as a fortified post, upon the possession of which every thing is to turn in future.

I agree entirely with O'Farrill, that if the Isla de Leon is lost, the town of Cadiz will not, and probably cannot, hold out a week. The Spaniards and we should deceive ourselves if we could suppose that a most serious attack will not sooner or later be made upon this island, or upon the communications between the island and Cadiz, which it would be in vain to expect to resist, without having recourse to all the measures for the defence of these points which art can suggest. It is impossible to say whether the enemy will begin by making this great attack upon Cadiz, or will turn their attention to our situation in Portugal; but sooner or later all that force and art can do to obtain possession of the Isla de Leon will be done, and these efforts can be successfully resisted only by the adoption of similar measures. I would therefore suggest to you to get Capt. Landmann to examine particularly the Isla de Leon, and the communication between the Isla and Cadiz, without loss of time; and to consider of the general principle and plan on which these important possessions ought to be defended. Let him then suggest the construction of the works which appear to him to be most necessary, working always upon the principle and the plan which he would first have laid down for the defence of the Isla, &c.; and supposing always, which he may be sure will be the case,

* See p. 660.

that there will be a sufficient number of men to occupy and defend the works, the construction of which he shall recommend.

When you shall be prepared with these plans, &c., I would suggest to you and Mr. Frere to recommend their adoption, and the immediate execution of the works, to the serious attention of the government, and to press them to provide for the effectual defence of Cadiz, always in the spirit in which I wrote to Gen. Whittingham and of 'the conditions.' Gen. O'Farrill's paper will afford topics in abundance by which this object may be urged; and in fact every man who knows any thing of the state of Spain, and of the sentiments of the people of the country, must be certain that if Cadiz should hold out, and the Mediterranean islands continue in the possession of the patriots, and the colonies continue true to the cause, the Buonapartes may have the military possession of the country, but sooner or later they must lose it. In the same view I would earnestly urge the government to send the fleet to Minorca, and to provide effectually for the defence of that and the other islands. The equipment of the fleet, which ought to be looked to, is a measure for future consideration.

I refer you to my letters to Mr. Frere for information upon the state of affairs in this quarter.

To Bart. Frere, Esq. Viseu, 27th Feb. 1810.

I have received your letter of the 10th inst., and I am glad that the reinforcements sent to Cadiz have given satisfaction. I have written to Gen. Stewart upon the measures to be adopted there and at Minorca, to which letter I beg to refer you.

Since I wrote to you last, I find that a French corps has arrived at Montijo from Arzobispo, Mortier's corps still retaining its position. I have not heard from the Marques de la Romana since I sent his aide de camp, Capt. O'Neil, to him with a communication of my opinion, that unless he had reason to believe that Badajoz required an exertion for its momentary relief, in order to complete the provisions of the place, and was certain that he could effect his object in a short space of time, it was better that I should not collect a larger force south of the Tagus, as he might depend upon it that the consequence of my reinforcing my corps in that quarter would be that the French would reinforce theirs, probably from the southward, and we should be obliged to withdraw, leaving Badajoz in a worse state than we had found it. The same misfortune would occur by the junction of the enemy's reinforcements with their corps in Castille, which would equally oblige me to withdraw the reinforcements which I should now send across the Tagus. That the question would then arise whether any advantage would result to the cause, by inducing the enemy to weaken their corps to the southward, in order to concentrate near Badajoz; upon which I have only to observe that I can expect none, and that I conceive that the enemy cannot be in a situation in which they can do the allies less mischief than in that in which they are at present. All this reasoning depends, however, upon the question whether it is necessary to give Badajoz a little more time, and whether they can improve their situation in a few days. I think I can give them these few days, but no more.

I have heard nothing positive from the northward since I wrote to you on the 25th; but there is a report in this town, stating that the French had entered Lugo. There is nothing new from Castille. Reinforcements have certainly entered Spain in large numbers; and it is said that some have joined Ney's corps. I do not know whether you have been apprised that a post has been established from Faro to Lisbon three times a week, and equally from Lisbon to Faro; and there are boats at Faro to carry the letters to Cadiz, by which means we might hear from you and Gen. Stewart.

To Lieut. Gen. Hill. Viseu, 27th Feb. 1810.

I received only yesterday your letter of the 22d. I have communicated to the Marques de la Romana my opinion, that we should do Badajoz more harm than good, by attempting to remove the enemy to a distance at the present moment, and I shall see what he says in answer to my observations. It is now obvious, however, that your corps must be reinforced, before it can make any offensive movement against the enemy. My opinion is, that the enemy will not make a serious attack upon Badajoz. Indeed, it would be useless to them to make this attack, as they have Olivença, which will answer all their purposes of attack upon Portugal equally with Badajoz, and they lose no time. This view of the subject induces me to instruct you respecting the bridge at Abrantes, in case you should retire from the Alentejo. In this case you will be so kind as to have that bridge taken up, and the boats and all the materials brought over to this side of the river, to a spot where they will be under the fire of our works.

All the boats on the Tagus, from Villa Velha inclusive down to Villa Franca, excepting those of the bridge of Abrantes, above provided for, must be ordered down to Alhandra, 2 miles below Villa Franca, as soon as you shall cross the Tagus. I enclose a paper which will state to you to what persons you are to address yourself to have these boats removed; and you will give them every assistance in your power to effect the object.

P.S. I wish likewise to inform you that arrangements have been made to remove out of the enemy's way the carts, mules, and other means of conveyance, and the provisions, of which the enemy might make use in the invasion of the country. I recommend that you should communicate with Gen. Leite upon this subject, who has the returns of the province of Alentejo in his hands, and settle with him the course which the carts, &c., of the province of Alentejo should take in the event supposed. My opinion is, that those in the southern and eastern parts of the province, that could not collect about Elvas, should go off towards the kingdom of Algarve; and those to the northward to get into the hills about Niza, Portalegre, &c.

You will recollect that part of the province of Portuguese Estremadura is south, or on the left of the Tagus; and if you should cross that river, you should immediately send to the commanding officer of the province of Estremadura, who resides at Lisbon, to desire him to remove from that part of the province which is on the left of the Tagus all carts, mules, &c., and the provisions which they can carry with them; and these should go to Setuval, and under the protection of the castle of Palmella.

The A.G. to Col. Harvey, commg. Portuguese troops, Coimbra.　　　　27th Feb. 1810.

The Commander of the Forces has decided, for the relief of the general hospital, Coimbra, to remove from that station every fortnight a certain proportion of cases towards Lisbon. It is his Excellency's wish that you will be pleased to furnish on these occasions, which will be notified to you by the Military commandant of hospitals, an escort to consist of one subaltern and 20 R. and F. from the Portuguese troops under your command, which guard is proposed to go as far as Leiria, there to be relieved by an equal number of the forces there stationed.

The officer of the Portuguese service is to be put in communication with the senior British officer in charge of the sick, who has received orders to support the detachment in its duty, which it is expected by my Lord Wellington it will execute with propriety and steadiness, and is to consist in preventing the sick from wandering from their carriages on the march, the carriages from halting without necessity, or the native drivers (where such are employed) taking away their animals or carts without regular discharge from the responsible officer.

To Lieut. Gen. Leite.　Confidential memorandum.　　　　28th Feb. 1810.

You are aware of the situation of the frontiers of this Kingdom, and of the necessity which may exist of leaving a part of the country exposed for a time, in order to concentrate our troops on other points of greater and more vital importance.

In contemplation of this necessity, I had proposed to the government some time ago that all the carts, means of transport, &c., in the different provinces should be registered and placed under the direction of the governors in different provinces, in order that they might be removed out of the reach of the enemy, in case it should be necessary at any time to draw the troops from the province.

I have desired Gen. Hill to communicate with you upon this subject in case it should be necessary for him to withdraw from Alentejo, of which, however, there does not appear to be any probability; and I wish you to determine in your own mind to what point the carriages and means of transport, with as much provision as they can carry away, in each Comarca in the province of Alentejo shall go, in case the allied army shall be obliged to withdraw with a view to further operations, and the enemy should be enabled to enter.

It might probably be also desirable that you should give your usual instructions beforehand upon this subject to the heads of the different

G. O.　　　　　　　　　　　　　　　　　　　　Viseu, 28th Feb. 1810.

6. The Commander of the Forces draws the attention of the soldiers of the army to the consequence of the crimes committed by the soldiers thus ordered for execution under the sentence of a General Court Martial. ———, of the — regt., and ———, of the — regt., committed a crime which the Commander of the Forces is concerned to observe is too common in this army; they robbed and ill-treated an inhabitant of this country, whom they met on the road; a crime which the Commander of the Forces is determined in no instance to forgive.

The soldiers of the army have been invariably well treated by the inhabitants of Portugal; and the frequent instances which have occurred of their being robbed and ill-treated, and of murders being committed, by soldiers who straggle from their detachments on a march, are a disgrace to the character of this army, and of the British nation.

The Commander of the Forces is therefore determined in every case of the kind that may occur to have proof adduced of the crime committed; and the sentence of the General Courts Martial, whatever they may be, shall be carried into execution.

The Commander of the Forces is concerned to observe that the crime committed by ———, private in the — regt., is no less common in this army than robbery and murder; and in respect to this crime he is equally determined to carry into execution the sentences of the General Courts Martial whatever they be.

Comarcas, to be carried into execution when they should hear that the enemy are approaching their districts.

While writing upon this subject, I think it proper also to mention to you that I expect that the Capitãos Mór will be prepared with their several companies of Ordenanza to do the enemy all the mischief in their power if he should invade the country; not by assembling in large bodies, but by impeding his communications, by firing upon him from the mountains and strong passes with which the whole country abounds, and by annoying his foraging and other parties that he may send out. His cavalry cannot act in a great part of Alentejo; and by activity, much may be done by the Capitãos Mór in the strong parts of the country.

You must be the best judge upon all these points; and I can only tell you that I shall approve of the measure, if you should decide to admit the Marques de la Romana's troops into Campo Maior, after considering them.

To Lieut. Gen. Hill.   Viseu, 28th Feb. 1810.

Since I wrote to you yesterday, I have received your letter of the 25th. I don't believe that the French corps on the right of the Guadiana is so strong as Lieut. Hay * reports it to be ; but I should think the two corps put together, on both sides the Guadiana, are 24,000 men. However, I do not think they are in a state to meddle with you.

I have written to Gen. Leite on the arrangement on which I wrote to you yesterday, respecting the carts of the country. Respecting the boats on the Tagus, it occurs to me that you might also correspond immediately with the governors of Santarem and Abrantes, and apprise them that circumstances may induce you to desire them to order the boats placed under their charge down the river; and desire them to be prepared to adopt measures to force all the boats to the place to which you will order them ; but desire them not to adopt any measures till they shall receive their ulterior orders from you.

I was afraid that you would be obliged to supply the Portuguese troops, which of course must be done,.if they cannot supply themselves. In the mean time I have written to the government upon this subject.

To Brig. Gen. R. Craufurd.   Viseu, 28th Feb. 1810.

I received last night your letter of the 27th, $1\frac{1}{2}$ A.M.; and, as I have not heard from you since, I conclude that the enemy's advance to Barba de Puerco was only to feel us. Soult's corps, as well as Mortier's, are upon the Guadiana, so that Badajoz would rather appear to be their object. I rather believe, however, that their force is too much separated to effect any military object whatever. Our troops have been well received at Cadiz.

I beg of you to use as much ammunition as you please, and replace it from Almeida; only give notice to your neighbours of what you are about.

To the Earl of Liverpool.   Viseu, 28th Feb. 1810.

Affairs have remained nearly in the same situation since I addressed you

* Sir A. Leith Hay.

on the 21st inst. Marshal Ney's corps remains upon the Tormes, with its advanced posts towards the Agueda. The French had not made any progress in taking Astorga as late as the 20th; and it was supposed that the corps in that quarter would unite with Ney's corps for the attack of Ciudad Rodrigo.

The corps called Marshal Soult's had entered Lower Estremadura by the bridge of Arzobispo : that part of it which was at Plasencia, and was only an advanced guard, crossed the Tagus at the ferry of Serradilla, at which the Spaniards had replaced the boat since the British army were in that neighbourhood in August.

The whole of this corps are now collected on the right of the Guadiana, about Montijo, while Mortier's corps is on the left of that river, between Talavera Real and Olivença. As the rains have not been heavy this winter, the Guadiana is still fordable.

The last accounts I received from Cadiz are of the 15th. The arrival of the British and Portuguese troops had given the greatest satisfaction ; and as the Duque de Alburquerque's corps, consisting of 11,000 men, was in the Isla de Leon, and was likely to be reinforced by a division of Areyzaga's army, which was embarked at Gibraltar, and by another division embarked at Ayamonte, it was expected that there would be 18,000 Spanish troops for the defence of Cadiz, besides the British and Portuguese corps, and the volunteers of the town. The French occupied the country in the neighbourhood, from Rota to Chiclana, with 25,000 men; and Joseph was supposed to be there.

The Spanish corps, called the army of the left, has crossed the Tagus, with the exception of the division under Gen. Carrera, which remains in Castille ; and one division was at Alburquerque ; the other at Castello de Vide, in Portugal, on the 25th inst., when I heard of them last. There appears no doubt that large reinforcements for the enemy's army have arrived in Spain; but I have not received any account upon which I can rely of their amount.

To the Earl of Liverpool. Viseu, 28th Feb. 1810.

I hope that you will have attended to my suggestion to send to the Tagus a fleet of ships of the line; a measure which I really think of the utmost importance. Besides the facility which their assistance will give us in embarking, if it should be necessary, I would wish to draw your Lordship's attention to the possibility that the enemy might combine his attack upon the frontiers of Portugal with a movement of his fleet in the Mediterranean to the Tagus. If he should make this movement, you will probably lose your army, in return for which you would probably blockade his fleet in the Tagus; and, if events should ever turn out favorably again in Spain and Portugal, you might capture it.

However, your loss would be enormous in the mean time, as well as upon the ultimate balance of advantages ; and it may be so easily prevented, that I cannot but hope that you will have adopted the measure I have suggested to you.

P.S. I enclose the last Weekly state.

3 c 2

To the Sec. of the Treasury.   Viseu, 28th Feb. 1810.

I am concerned to have to inform the Lords of the Treasury that a sum of money, amounting to £29,000, has been demanded by Dep. Commissary Gen. ——, and has been paid by Dep. Paymaster Gen. —— out of the military chest at Lisbon, without any warrant or authority from me, or any communication with me, or the Commissary Gen., or Dep. Paymaster Gen. Boys, who is the head of the pay department of this army.

The irregularity of this proceeding is so obvious, that I have declined to enter into any of the circumstances which have induced the parties to commit it, till the money should be replaced in the military chest. I understand, however, that Mr. —— having been at the head of the Commissariat with the army in Portugal, till the end of the month of April, when Mr. Murray took charge of that department, conceives that he has a claim upon the pay department for a sum of money stopped from the pay of the troops who received rations; and he has taken this sum from the military chest in part of discharge of this claim, as I have above stated, without my warrant, or even communication with me.

I must also observe that the stoppage from the pay of the troops, when they receive rations, is the property of the public; and being in the military chest, the amount ought not to have been taken out of the chest without my warrant. Mr. Murray having, since he took charge of the department, paid debts incurred by all his predecessors in office, I do not exactly see what occasion Mr. —— had to call for this sum of money; and at all events supposing the sum was required for a public purpose, application ought to have been made to me for my warrant for its issue.

Although I have thought it proper to bring this subject under the consideration of the Lords of the Treasury, on account of its great irregularity, and because I find from the enclosed correspondence between Mr. Boys and Mr. —— that I cannot get this sum of money replaced in the military chest, I beg that you will inform their Lordships that I have no reason to believe that there is any thing corrupt in the transaction, into which, however, I have refused to examine till the money should be replaced in the military chest.

I have desired Mr. Murray to transmit, for their Lordships' information, copies of the correspondence which he has had with Mr. —— upon this subject.

To Lieut. Gen. Bacellar, Governor of the Province of Beira.   Confidential memorandum.
                                                          1st March, 1810.

At the moment when the enemy may attack this province, the operations of the allied army may have led them to a distance from it, and the enemy may have it in his power to hold a temporary possession of it. It is desirable, therefore, that we should consider at an early moment of the mode of keeping the enemy out of the province as long as possible, supposing the province to be left, in great measure, to its own resources for its defence : 2dly ; of the mode of confining his operations within certain limits, as much as possible, supposing that he should be able to penetrate the frontier : and, 3dly ; of the mode of distressing him as much as possible for provisions and other resources, supposing that he should establish himself within certain districts in the country.

The following suggestions are submitted to Gen. Bacellar with a view to all these objects :

1st; I recommend that the Capitãos Mór of all the districts should be directed to have their companies in the best order and prepared for service. These companies must act independently and separately, each in its own district; unless in cases where 2 or more companies joining can defend a point interesting to the districts to which both belong.

In case it should be necessary, preparations and arrangements must be made for destroying the bridges over the Coa, between Pinhel and Villar Torpim, and at Castello Bom. The bridge at Almeida should also be destroyed eventually; but that measure involves more important consequences, and must not be adopted without orders from me. Whenever a bridge or road is destroyed, a party of the Ordenanza must be stationed to prevent the enemy from repairing it; and a party must, in the event of the British army quitting this part of the country, be stationed on this side of the bridge of Almeida. It will likewise be necessary to have parties of the Ordenanza at the several fords on the Coa, from Castello Bom to the junction with the Douro.

The next point will be the river Mondego. If the enemy should penetrate by passing the Coa, it does not appear that it will be very easy to prevent him from entering the valley of the Mondego. The bridges on the Mondego, in the whole extent of its course from Celorico to Ponte da Murcella, ought to be broken, and arrangements should be made for that purpose, and for posting a party of the Ordenanza at each bridge, in order to prevent the enemy from repairing it, and from spreading to his right across the Mondego into the country north of that river; or if he should take the road north of that river, to prevent him from spreading into the valley south of it.

The bridges upon the Alva, &c., ought likewise to be destroyed, and parties of Ordenanza placed at each of them, if the enemy should penetrate by the left of the Mondego : and those upon the Tavora, upon the Dão, the bridge at Fail, the Ponte da Pedrinha, the bridge at Santa Comba Dão, and the bridges of the Criz, if they should penetrate by the country north of the Mondego. All the bridges upon the Zezere should likewise be destroyed. By these measures, and by the occupation of the ground at the places where the passages shall have been destroyed, if the enemy shall not be stopped, at least he will be confined in his operations, and will not be able to do so much mischief as he otherwise would.

Preparatory measures ought to be adopted to destroy each of these bridges when the necessity of it may exist; and the bridge should be broken only when it appears probable that the enemy may intend to use it.

Besides these measures, the Governor of the province should, at an early period, consider of the place to which the means of transport and the provisions in each Comarca of the province should be sent, in case the enemy should enter the province. Those in the neighbourhood of the Serra d'Estrella should be sent into the Serra; those in the neighbourhood of the Zezere, into the villages along that river; those north of the Mondego, into the Serra de Alcoba. The great object in the preparatory arrangements on this subject should be, that the Commanding officer in the province should make up his mind to what part the means of transport and provisions existing in the different Comarcas in the province should remove, in case the enemy should enter the province by any of the different lines which he might take. He has the register of all the carriages and means of transport; and he would only have to give his orders, all previous arrangements being made, when he should hear of the enemy's movements.

To Charles Stuart, Esq.   Viseu, 1st March, 1810.

I sent off last night my dispatches, and the bag to go to England by the packet of last Sunday; and I now enclose a letter for Lord Liverpool, which I hope may be in time. If it should not be so, I will request you to send it by the first opportunity.

You shall have the accounts made up to 1st March, as soon as we can get an account of our receipts to that period. In respect to the Portuguese deficiency, I made it, in November, from official documents sent to me by the Regency, 6,070,000 dollars, for the year 1809. The revenue received, and expected to be received by the end of the year, was 8,607,337 dollars, and the estimated expenditure was 14,679,250 dollars. From that deficiency was to be subtracted the sum of £500,000, then paid by Great Britain for the troops; and calculating the dollar at 5 shillings, it left a deficiency of about £900,000, which was the sum that I stated to government. Supposing those numbers to be tolerably correct, and to represent the existing state of the Portuguese finance, there would now be to be subtracted from the deficiency the additional £250,000 subsidy; and the deficiency would remain at £650,000 sterling. I believe this to be a tolerably exact account of the deficiency; and I know that I extracted it from the official account with great pains.

It would be most desirable to adopt the measure which you propose respecting the import of British manufactures. In respect to the other measure proposed by Redondo, I am not sufficiently aware of the mode of collecting the revenue, to be certain that they have sufficient checks to make the principle of the measure operate to produce a larger sum into the treasury. Of this, however, we may be certain, that the sum produced will not be smaller than it is, and therefore it might be tried.

Since I wrote to you respecting the use to be made of the Portuguese fleet eventually, I have turned over in my mind the expediency of encouraging a general emigration from this country; and I acknowledge that, upon the whole, I am disposed to doubt it. I think that we ought, and I propose to endeavor, to carry off all the regular army, because we may be very certain, that all that we leave behind will very soon be made French soldiers; but I think that we ought to have in Portugal, and to encourage to remain here, all the gentlemen of the country, as a germ of insurrection, whenever circumstances shall afford them an opportunity to throw off the French yoke, which may be afforded by thousands of events in the Peninsula, in France, and in Europe. If we should encourage the party in general to withdraw, no advantage can be taken of these events hereafter; and we gain no advantage at present by withdrawing them, as they will be only a burden to us, or to the government of Brazil. At the same time I think we are bound to provide for the removal of all who have been concerned in carrying on the government, and who are now or hereafter may be conspicuously active against the French. Pray turn this subject over in your mind, and let me know your opinion upon it.

I believe that the news in Forjaz's letter is nearly correct. I had not heard of the movement of the heavy artillery towards Badajoz from Seville, nor do I believe it. You have omitted to enclose the paper from Dom M. Forjaz respecting the hospital at the Rope walk; and we cannot make out the name of the place which he had proposed for the hospital, as written in your letter. I shall always send my dispatches to you; those of yesterday went to you; and I still hope the enclosed will be in time.

To the Earl of Liverpool.   Viseu, 1st March, 1810.

I have the honor to enclose a letter which I have received from Lieut. Col. Doyle, and upon which I have to request the decision of His Majesty's government.

In the mean time, as I consider it an object of the utmost importance to encourage the desertion of the enemy's troops, I have authorised the payment of 20 dollars to every man who may desert, and will enlist into His Majesty's service; and I have directed Col. Doyle to send such men as he shall agree with on these terms to Gibraltar, Cadiz, or Lisbon.

To the Earl of Liverpool.   Viseu, 1st March, 1810.

I have just received your private letter of the 13th Feb., and I write an answer to it immediately, in order that this may reach Lisbon before the packet sails on Sunday.

Your Lordship will have observed that I sent a detachment to Cadiz, as soon as I heard that the Spaniards were disposed to admit our troops into that garrison, which was as large as I could then make it, and as large as I thought they would be inclined to receive, from what I heard at the time of the disposition of the party in the town. As Gen. Campbell was about to send the 2d batt. 88th regt. from Gibraltar, and as no desire has been expressed from Cadiz that more troops should be sent from hence, and above all, as from the strength of the enemy's corps in the neighbourhood of Cadiz, there does not appear any intention, nor are there means, to make an attack upon the Isla de Leon, which the troops there would not be able to repulse, I have not thought it proper to weaken this army any further, by sending to Cadiz any additional reinforcement.

I agree entirely with Gen. Castaños, that the war has been hitherto carried on on erroneous principles; and I also agree with him that the French will find it most difficult to conquer the country; but I doubt whether any active effort will, or indeed can, be made within Spain itself. It appears to me to be most probable that, in a short time, there will be no resistance to the French troops in any part of Spain, excepting at Cadiz, and in any other of the forts and strongholds which may be able to hold out. But there will be no obedience, and there will remain an universal disposition to revolt, which will break out upon the first, and every opportunity, that will be afforded by the absence or the weakness of the detachments of French troops, which must usually be kept in all parts of the country for the ordinary purposes of government, and, in the end, the French yoke must be shaken off. This disposition of the people will be much encouraged by the continuance of the contest at Cadiz, by the possession by the loyal party of the islands in the Mediterranean and of the fleet, and by the continued loyalty of the colonies.

We are much mistaken, however, if we suppose that the Isla de Leon (without the possession of which I do not think Cadiz would hold out a week) is now in a state to sustain the serious attack which will be made upon it, when the contest shall be brought to that state throughout the Peninsula, that there will be no opposition to the French, excepting at the Isla de Leon. I have written to Gen. W. Stewart upon this subject, and have desired him to order Capt. Landmann of the Engineers, who is there, to look at the island, and fix the principles and the plan on which it must be defended, and the works which ought to be immediately constructed on those principles; and then to alarm the Regency by a representation of the nature of the attack which is likely to be made upon them, and of the inadequacy of their means of resistance at present. From what I hear of them, I think they are likely to attend to this representation, and to order the immediate construction of the works which are necessary for the defence of the island, against an attack in which we may be very certain that all the resources of the art will be resorted to ; and I hope the place will be prepared to resist this attack before it can be made.

This view of the question respecting Cadiz and the Isla has convinced me, as it probably will your Lordship, and indeed every view that I have taken of the British interest in the contest in the Peninsula has convinced me, that the British army ought to remain in the field in Portugal as long as may be practicable, and consistent with its safety.

If we should withdraw from Portugal to go to Cadiz, in the first place, I do not think it quite clear that we should be received there, or that even the best friends of the British alliance would wish to receive us. In the next place, as soon as we shall withdraw from Portugal, the enemy will seize Lisbon on the next day ; the fort of Ciudad Rodrigo cannot hold out a moment; Badajoz will not hold out long ; and the reduction of these two would give the means of taking Elvas and Almeida, which could not be expected to hold out long after we should have withdrawn. Cadiz would then be to be attacked by the whole French army, probably before the Isla could be fortified as it ought to be ; and even if we should be admitted to take a share in its defence, it might be in such a state as to render all our efforts hopeless. In a view, then, to the continuance of the contest at Cadiz, as well as in every other view that I have ever taken of the subject, I consider it highly desirable that we should maintain ourselves in Portugal as long as possible.

Besides the measures for the defence of Cadiz, I have desired Gen. W. Stewart and Mr. Frere to recommend to the Regency to remove the fleet to Mahon, and to provide effectually for the defence of Minorca, and of the other islands in the Mediterranean. Besides this, it is my opinion that we ought to endeavor to retain Peniche, in a view to the continuance of the resistance to the French in the Peninsula. That place is already in such a state that it cannot be taken by a *coup de main;* and if I had engineers to spare, I could soon put it in such a state that it would be very difficult to take it. The possession of this place by the English and the loyal Portuguese would have nearly the same effect in Portugal as the continuance of the contest at Cadiz would have in Spain ; and there are not many days in the year in which the communication with it, by sea, could be prevented. It is worthy of the consideration of the government whether they will continue to occupy this place. If they do, they must leave at least one British battalion in it, and some artillery ; and they may depend upon it that their holding this place will be of use to Cadiz, and to the whole Peninsula.

What I have already written is probably as extensive a consideration of the question respecting Cadiz, as is necessary in the existing situation of the contest in the Peninsula. I shall, however, go one step further, and suppose for a moment that it was possible to renew it with the aid of Spanish armies, &c. &c. ; and knowing what I do of the country and of the disposition of the people, and of the state, and probable future state, of their army, I am decidedly of opinion that the largest British army which Great Britain can afford to supply would do better to carry on its operations through Portugal, and make Lisbon the point of its communication with England, than carry on its operations through the south of Spain, communicating with Cadiz and Gibraltar.

It is useless to trouble you with a consideration of the different topics which bear upon this question. I shall only observe that we can advance with safety nearer to the centre of the scene of operations, and retire with greater ease ; and, I hope, get away with equal safety from the Tagus ; and that, as we now show, we can keep in check, as long as we can remain, a much larger force than we could oppose, if we were in the south of Spain, and it were brought against us.

I can tell you no more than I have already told you about the embarkation of the Portuguese army. If you will let us have a large fleet of ships of war, and 45,000 disposable tons of transports, I shall try, and I think I shall bring them all off ; but I cannot be certain, until the time comes, that I shall be able to bring off a man.

In respect to home politics, I acknowledge that I do not like them much, and I am convinced that the government cannot last. I do not think that any government can stand, after an inquiry into an important measure by a Committee of the House of Commons. However, I am of opinion that the King has a right, and must be supported in the exercise of the right, to choose his own servants, as long as he thinks it proper to persevere in retaining those whom he prefers in his service ; and if no other advantage shall have been gained by the formation of the existing government, it has at least drawn from Lord Grenville opinions which will render the employment of him not inconsistent with the King's ease, if he should think proper to call him to his service.

I assure you that what has passed in Parliament respecting me, has not given me one moment's concern, as far as I am personally concerned ; and indeed I rejoice at it, as it has given my friends an opportunity of setting the public right upon some points on which they had not been informed, and on others on which the misrepresentations had driven the truth from their memories. But I regret that men like Lord —— and others should carry the spirit of party so far as to attack an officer in his absence, should take the ground of their attack from Cobbett and the *Moniteur*, and should at once blame him for circumstances and events over which he could have no control, and for faults which, if they were committed at all, were not committed by him.

To Vice Adm. the Hon. G. Berkeley.   Viseu, 2d March, 1810.

Gen. Payne has informed me that he has given leave to his aide de camp, Fitzgibbon, to go home, on account of an accident which has happened to him, which renders it advisable that he should not ride for some time; and I shall be very much obliged to you if you will be so kind as to ask the Captain of any of the King's ships which may be returning to England to give him a passage. Have you heard any thing of a reinforcement coming for your own squadron? I have frequently urged the measure in official and private letters, as one of essential importance.

P.S. Your son is just arrived from Guarda, in very good health.

Memorandum for the Corregidor of Aveiro.   Viseu, 3d March, 1810.

Inform this gentleman, that as I am responsible for the officers under my command, so must he be, and he is responsible for the magistrates and others placed under his direction; and that if the straw is not produced in the period which I have required it, he must obey the orders which he has received, and repair to my head quarters, or I must be under the necessity of sending for him: that I know that he can afford to give what I have required, and he shall give it, the British Commissary paying for the same; and if he does not do so, I shall make it a particular request that he and the other magistrates of the country may be punished as they deserve for assisting the enemy last year, and for refusing the assistance required, for payment, to the defenders of the country in this year.

To Charles Stuart, Esq.   Viseu, 3d March, 1810.

I enclose answers to the queries in the dispatch from the Marquis Wellesley, referred to in your letter of the 26th Feb., as far as the subject of them comes within my knowledge.

The Commissary Gen. has directions to furnish you with an account of the sums issued by him to the King's ministers at Lisbon; and the dates of the receipts of Mr. Bell, who was authorised by Mr. Villiers to receive those sums.

To Charles Stuart, Esq.   Viseu, 3d March, 1810.

In respect to the Bishop of Tarbes, my opinion is that the Abbé Texeira ought to pay him his pension, subtracting from the account the direct taxes upon it payable to the state, provided the Abbé has paid them; and if he has not paid them, he ought to be made to pay, not only the proportion payable by the Bishop's pension upon the revenue of the Abbaye, but those due by the Abbaye itself.

If, however (as is probable), the Abbaye was plundered by the French during the late invasion, it is reasonable that the Bishop of Tarbes should bear his share of the loss.

I am positively certain that the ministers will be unwilling to go to Parliament to ask for more money for Portugal, and that Parliament will not grant a larger sum, even if the ministers should ask for it. The Portuguese government are perfectly aware of this fact, having been apprised of it by me 3 months ago. It is almost useless, therefore, to discuss the mode in which any further grant to the Portuguese government should be made to them.

If, however, any further grant should be made, I am rather desirous that it should be made to the government, in the same manner as that at present given to them. The truth is, that the British officers and departments are not equal to the management of the detail of a larger service than that which they at present conduct; and I am unwilling to charge them, or, in other words, myself, with the detail of the Portuguese army. Besides, I do not think there is any reason to suspect that the funds, already given to the Portuguese government, have been misapplied in a manner that cannot be corrected by the measures which I have proposed. The fault is in the deficiency of funds, more than in their misapplication.

Another objection which I have to the system proposed for any more grant is, that it does not go far enough. The militia, which are a most important branch of the military of the country, for which the government are now sending out arms, by which the northern provinces are to be exclusively defended, and which are to occupy many important posts in the country, are to continue under the *regie* of the Portuguese government. If it be necessary to take the army under British management, it is equally necessary to take the militia; but I contend for it, that the Portuguese government have paid both army and militia most regularly, more regularly, by far, than they would have been paid by our departments; and in respect to their provisions, all that it required is that the sum of money applicable out of British aids, or out of the general treasury, to pay for provisions, should be disposable under the directions of the person most capable, from his detailed knowledge of the demand for provisions, to dispose of it to advantage.

I am positively certain, as above stated, that government will not give them another shilling; and I think you will do well to discourage the notion that they should get more. At the same time it will be necessary that you should transmit their application to England. The Portuguese government, however, should be informed of the probability that the King will withdraw his assistance, both pecuniary and military, if they do not make an exertion to provide for their own defence: and I must say that they have not made any effort to make up the deficiency of their revenue; and that they might make it good without much difficulty, at least so far as to prevent it from falling upon the military, or upon the defence of the country. If you should think it can do any good, I have no objection to your communicating to the government the substance of this letter as my opinion.

The A.G. to Lieut. Gen. Hill. 3d March, 1810.

I have had the honor to receive and submit to the Commander of the Forces your letter of the 25th inst., and enclosed explanation from Major ——. In reply, I am commanded to observe, in the present system of service the army is employed, many officers have shown an inclination to quit it, which my Lord Wellington has been obliged to resist, although the duty may not be attended with such honor or advantage as the more active service. On this principle leave of absence has invariably been refused, except in such cases where the party applying could declare that to obtain leave was paramount to every other consideration.

Under this impression alone Major —— obtained the leave granted, and it was with much surprise his Lordship found that indulgence became a secondary object, when an opportunity of active service presented a creditable prospect. It appears that as for such occasions Major ——'s business could be postponed, it might equally have been deferred for the performance of the ordinary, which at all times is to be considered as essential as the more active duties of the field. Relative to Major ——'s renewed application, it is his Excellency's pleasure that, should you conceive a compliance with his application to be an object to him, paramount to every other consideration in life, you are authorised to permit that officer's absence from the army for a period equal to the original leave granted.

To the Corregidor of Aveiro. Viseu, 4th March, 1810.

I enclose the duplicate of a letter which I wrote to you 10 days ago, to which you have returned no answer; and you have omitted to obey the orders which I gave you in a former letter, either to supply straw to the Commissary at Coimbra, or to repair to my head quarters. I now send a messenger to bring you to my head quarters forthwith.

To Brig. Gen. R. Craufurd. Viseu, 5th March, 1810.

I received, at Mangualde, on the night before last, your letter of the 2d, mentioning the desertion of the two vedettes. It might be desirable to be stronger in cavalry in front of the Coa; and in case you should think so, Col. Murray has directed Col. Arentschildt to have another troop of hussars at your disposition, which you will call for, if you think them necessary, and station where you may think proper. In case you should find forage scarce, in consequence of the advance of this second troop, take as much as you please from the magazine at Almeida; and desire the Commissary there to let the Commissary Gen. know how much you take, in order that he may adopt measures to keep up that magazine to its full amount.

There is nothing new. The French have withdrawn from Talavera Real, Olivença, &c., near Badajoz, towards Merida, and they occupy Montijo and Puebla. I have no accounts from Cadiz of a later date than the 15th. Our troops and the Portuguese had been well received. The Duque de Alburquerque had there 11,000 men; and about 7000 more were expected by sea, 2000 from Ayamonte, and 5000 from Gibraltar, where they had been embarked; making in all 18,000 Spaniards, 4000 English and Portuguese, and 4500 volunteers of the town; so that I think the Isla de Leon is pretty safe.

G. O. Viseu, 4th March, 1810.

1. The Commander of the Forces has great satisfaction in communicating to the General officers, the officers, non-commissioned officers, and soldiers of the army, who fought the battle of Talavera, the testimonies of the approbation of the Houses of Lords and Commons of their distinguished conduct. [*Here follow the votes of the Houses of Lords and Commons.*]

P.S. I beg you to send here the German deserters whom Gen. Cox has sent to Pinhel.

To Lieut. Gen. Hill.   Viseu, 5th March, 1810.

I have received your letters of the 1st and 2d, and I am much obliged to you for the attention you have paid to the objects which I had recommended to your observation.

If the French are really fitting out boats at Lobon and Puebla (which I should be inclined to doubt, as they would find materials and workmen, with greater facility, and with more convenience, at Merida), it must be with a view to keep up the communication between their corps on the two sides of the Guadiana, in case they should attack Badajoz. They would scarcely find it advantageous to use on the Tagus (where alone we have reason to apprehend the use of a bridge by them) pontoons made at Lobon. However, it is proper to attend to all this work, and to make me acquainted with every thing of the kind that is observed. It is surely impossible that they can have 7000 cavalry in the corps assembled upon the Guadiana!

P.S. Tell Col. Carroll that I am much obliged to him for his letter, and that I shall be glad to hear from him whenever he will favor me with a letter.

To Vice Adm. the Hon. G. Berkeley.   Viseu, 6th March, 1810.

I received only this morning your letters of the 1st and 2d. I had heard of the refusal of the Emperor of Morocco to allow of the export of more than 80 mules, unless upon payment of 70 dollars duty for each. I have refused to pay this sum, as we are really not in want of mules at present.

I hope the government will send us some ships. I think they are mistaken in sending large ships to Cadiz. Not only they can do no good there, but they must quit Cadiz as soon as the French shall re-establish the battery at Sta Catalina, if what we have been told respecting the northern channel being the only one that can be used for large ships be true.

I am very much obliged to you for any suggestion that you will assist me with; and I hope soon to receive a report from Col. Fletcher upon the point to which you refer on the other side of the river. If the ground is what it has been reported to you, it will render our business much more easy than it was before. I passed over the ground, and recollect the swamp, but conceived that the dry ground was more extensive than you have described it to be.

I write to you upon the subject of the guns, &c., in the Russian ships of war. I am much obliged to you for the further measures which you have adopted to expedite our correspondence with Cadiz by Faro. I have no news from Cadiz of a later date than the 15th of last month.

To Vice Adm. the Hon. G. Berkeley.   Viseu, 6th March, 1810.

Having found, upon referring to the returns of the ordnance and ordnance carriages in possession of the Portuguese government, that there are not a sufficient number of guns, with carriages, to arm the different works in front of Lisbon which are now constructing, and which it is intended to construct, to the northward of Lisbon, even with the addition of the heavy ordnance on travelling carriages embarked in the store ships in the Tagus, I shall be much obliged to you if you will place at my disposition the ordnance, the carriages, and the stores belonging to the Russian ships of war still in the Tagus.

If you should consent to adopt this proposition I shall request you further to make them over to Col. Fisher, the commanding officer of the British artillery at Lisbon.

To Charles Stuart, Esq.   Viseu, 6th March, 1810.

I have the honor to enclose a letter from Dom M. Forjaz, which Mr. Villiers transmitted to me shortly previous to his departure from this country, complaining of the conduct of the British soldiers in the neighbourhood of Alemquer, particularly of an occurrence at Villa Nova.

I enclose the report received from Col. Peacocke on the occurrence at Villa Nova, into which he had been directed to inquire. The result of this inquiry is so different from the report forwarded by the Sec. of State to Mr. Villiers, that I am not satisfied with it; and if the Sec. of State will bring forward the persons who gave them the information, to prosecute at a General Court Martial the soldier who committed the act, I will order a General Court Martial to assemble for his trial; but if those persons are unwilling to substantiate upon oath, before a General Court Martial, the information which they have conveyed to the minister of the Police, the inquiry which has been already made must be final; as it is obvious that there are no means in my power of convicting this soldier of a deliberate intention to murder the deceased, or even of proving that he committed the act, because the deceased refused to mend his boots.

It is unfortunately but too true that outrages of all descriptions are committed by the British soldiers in this country, notwithstanding the pains taken by me and the General and other superior officers of the army to prevent them, and to punish those who commit them. It is useless to trouble you with a description of the causes of these evils, upon which I have written fully to the King's ministers. One of them undoubtedly is, the disinclination of the people of this country to substantiate upon oath, before a Court Martial, their complaints of the conduct of the soldiers, without which it is well known that it is impossible for me to punish them : the consequence is, that the criminals are tried, and acquitted for want of evidence ; for it is vain to expect evidence of an outrage from the comrades of the soldier who has committed it.

The records of the embassy at Lisbon must be filled with complaints of the same general nature as that which I now return to you, and with demands from me of evidence on the facts stated; the result of which has invariably been, that no evidence has been adduced to substantiate the complaints made, and those who have committed the outrages complained of have remained unpunished.

I am concerned to add that I know of no means which have not already been adopted to endeavor to keep the British soldiers in order. Detachments are never allowed to march, excepting under the command of an officer ; and the most strict orders have been given for the regulation of the conduct of the soldiers when so employed ; and an officer of the

Provost Marshal establishment is employed whenever the numbers of any detachment will justify such an appointment. But all has hitherto been in vain; the outrages complained of are still perpetrated, and they will continue until the government and people see the necessity of doing their utmost to convict, before a Court Martial, those soldiers of the crimes of which I am sorry to say I am too well convinced they have reason to complain.

To the Rt. Hon. the Speaker of the House of Commons.   Viseu, 6th March, 1810.

I have had the honor of receiving your letter of the 2d Feb., in which you enclosed the resolutions of the House of Commons of the 1st Feb., expressing the approbation of the House of my conduct, and that of the General officers, officers, and troops composing the army under my command in the battle fought at Talavera on the 27th and 28th July last.

In obedience to the orders of the House, I have communicated to the General officers, officers, and troops, this honorable testimony of the approbation of the House; and I beg leave to adopt this mode of expressing to the House the high sense which I entertain of the honor which they have conferred upon me, and upon the army under my command, and to assure them that I shall endeavor to merit their approbation by a zealous discharge of my duty.

I must likewise request you, Sir, to accept my thanks for the kindness towards me in the manner in which you have conveyed to me the pleasure of the House, a kindness of which I had already received repeated proofs during the period that I had the honor of being a member of the House of Commons.

To the Earl of Liverpool.   Viseu, 6th March, 1810.

No material alteration has taken place in the position of the several armies in this part of Spain since I wrote to you on the 28th Feb. The enemy's corps on the Guadiana have concentrated in the neighbourhood of Merida, keeping only advanced posts to the westward of that town, on both sides of the Guadiana, which still continued fordable; it is probable, however, that the rain which has fallen during the last 4 days has filled that river. The enemy's corps in Old Castille also still continues in the same position upon the Tormes and the Agueda; and I have no further intelligence of the progress of the enemy to the northward. A part of the Marques de la Romana's corps has occupied Campo Maior, its left still remaining at Alburquerque.

I have received no intelligence from Cadiz of a later date than the 15th Feb., notwithstanding that measures have been adopted to communicate with that town by Faro, in Algarve.

I have had the honor of receiving your Lordship's dispatch of the 17th Feb., and I am happy to find that the measure which I had adopted in the beginning of February for the defence of Cadiz has been approved of by His Majesty; and your Lordship may depend upon my paying every attention to that object. I have not thought it necessary to send any further reinforcement from this army to Cadiz.

Adverting to the general situation of the enemy's armies, I do not think that they have, at present, in the neighbourhood of Cadiz, such a force as could attack the Isla de Leon with any prospect of success against the troops occupying the Isla de Leon when the last accounts came away. To these, large reinforcements were expected, as well from Ayamonte as from Gibraltar; including another British battalion from the latter.

None of the authorities at Cadiz, whether Spanish or British, had expressed any desire to receive further reinforcements; or any apprehension that the force already in the place was not sufficient to defend it. I understand that there is a party at Cadiz very adverse to receiving the assistance of the British troops in its defence; and, considering the troops already there sufficient for its defence against any attack which may now be reasonably expected, I did not deem it expedient to incur the risk of the refusal of the people of the town, instigated by this party, to admit any reinforcement of British troops which I might send. I have likewise to observe, that the defence of Cadiz and its dependencies is materially aided by the maintenance of our position in Portugal.

Although the Isla de Leon, the possession of which I consider essentially necessary to the possession of Cadiz itself, is naturally a very strong position, and the number of troops now at Cadiz are sufficient to defend it against any body which might attempt to carry it by assault, I do not consider the Isla to be in a state of defence against the serious attack which will certainly be made upon it, sooner or later, directed and assisted by all the resources which art can furnish, and made by all the French troops which can be assembled from all parts of the Peninsula. Time will be required to put the Island in a state of defence to stand against this attack; and I have written to Gen. Stewart upon this subject, and have desired him to consider of and fix the principles and plan of the defence of the Isla; and immediately to represent to the government the probability of their future danger, and to suggest and urge them to construct those works which are most likely to aid them in defeating the enemy in his attack.

In the mean time, the British army in the Peninsula cannot be better employed, even with a view to prevent the enemy from obtaining possession of Cadiz, than in Portugal.

The A.G. to Col. Peacocke, Lisbon.   6th March, 1810.

Your letter of the 2d inst., and accompanying communication from Ensign —— of the —th regt., have been laid before the Commander of the Forces. However my Lord Wellington may feel disposed to commiserate the case of Ensign ——, yet his Excellency, in justice to the service, and the representation of the officer commanding the —th which caused this medical report, cannot require less from that officer than his forthwith repairing to the head quarters of his battalion, now in presence of the enemy; or deciding to retire from a profession, the duties of which he is officially reported hopelessly unequal to perform.

The A.G. to Major Lindsay, Elvas.   6th March, 1810.

I am commanded to express to you my Lord Wellington's approbation of the exertion you have manifested in the rapid removal of the hospital establishment from Elvas. The resignation of Major Murphy as Commandant of detachments, Lisbon, affording his Lordship an opportunity of placing you on the staff, I am authorised by his Excellency to offer you that command, with option at the same time to receive or decline the charge.

To Brig. Gen. R. Craufurd.   Viseu, 8th March, 1810.

I am very much obliged to you for your letter of the 6th, which I received last night. The fact is, that the line of cantonments which we took up, principally with a view to the accommodation of the troops during the winter, and to their subsistence on a point on which it was likely that it might be desirable to assemble the army, will not answer our purpose of assembling upon the Coa, if eventually that should be deemed an object. Neither does our position, as at present occupied, suit the existing organization of the army. For these reasons, I have long intended to alter our disposition, as soon as the season would permit the troops to occupy the smaller villages on the Coa, and as I should be able to bring up the Portuguese light troops of your division to the front. Since we took up the position which we now occupy, our outposts have come in contact with those of the French; and, although there is some distance between the two, still the arrangement of our outposts must be made on a better principle, and the whole of them must be in the hands of one person, who must be yourself. I propose, therefore, as soon as the weather shall allow of an alteration of the disposition of the advanced corps, that your division, with the hussars, which will be put under your orders, should occupy the whole line of the outposts; and, with this view, the Portuguese corps shall be brought up to the front, as soon as the state of the weather will allow them to march.

I am desirous of being able to assemble the army upon the Coa if it should be necessary; at the same time that I am perfectly aware that, if the enemy should collect in any large numbers in Estremadura, we should be too forward for our communication with Gen. Hill even here, much more so upon the Coa. But till they shall collect in Estremadura, and till we shall see more clearly than I can at present what reinforcements they have received, and what military object they have in view, particularly in the existing disposition of their army, I am averse to withdrawing from a position so favorable as the Coa affords to enable us to collect our army to prevent the execution of any design upon Ciudad Rodrigo.

I wish you, then, to consider of the posts to be occupied in front of and upon the Coa, to enable me to effect that object. The left should probably be Castel Rodrigo, and I believe you must have a post of observation as far as Alfaiates on the right. However, you must be a better judge of the detail of this question than I can be; and I wish you to consider of it, in order to be able immediately to carry the plan into execution, when I shall send to you. In the mean time, the state of the weather, which, from all I can learn, is as bad every where as it is here, and the consequence of which must be to fill all the rivers, is no bad security against the effects which might result from the continuance of the existing system of outposts for a few days longer. I intend that the divisions of Gen. Cole and Gen. Picton should support you on the Coa, without waiting for orders from me, if it should be necessary; and they shall be directed accordingly.

I have accounts from Cadiz as late as the 26th. The French had made no attack, and every thing was going on well and quietly. They have retired from the neighbourhood of Badajoz towards Merida, where they had their head quarters. They still threaten to attack Badajoz.

To Vice Adm. the Hon. G. Berkeley.   Viseu, 8th March, 1810.

I am very much obliged to you for your letter of the 5th. I now enclose the report of Col. Fletcher on the ground between Coina and the lake of Albufera, which I am afraid it would be difficult for us to occupy with advantage.

I have very good accounts from Gen. Stewart at Cadiz. My opinion is, that we want the fleet at Lisbon more than they do at Cadiz.

To Charles Stuart, Esq.   Viseu, 8th March, 1810.

I have received your letter of the 3d, but that from Dom M. Forjaz has not yet reached me. He knows that I have always considered it necessary to allow the enemy to have a momentary possession of the left bank of the Tagus, in order to concentrate our force to oppose the serious attack which will certainly be made by the right of that river. In fact, neither Lisbon, nor any thing else of consequence, can be injured by this measure : if we should succeed in maintaining our positions on the right of the river, the enemy on the left must retire; and if we should fail, the latter can do us no mischief, the boats being kept out of their way. They cannot prevent our embarking, and going out of the Tagus; neither can they prevent our using the river for the communications of the army above Lisbon; nor can they injure the town itself, unless they should have, and bring with them, mortars of the largest size, and for sea service. At the same time I am well convinced that, when the enemy shall make a serious attack upon Portugal, he will occupy the left bank of the Tagus from Almada to Traffaria.

In respect to the 15,000 men, in addition to those which government did propose to maintain in this country, I have only to say, that I do not care how many men they send here, provided they will supply us with proportionate means to feed and pay them. But I suspect that they will fall short of, rather than exceed, the 30,000 men. I must observe, however, that it would not become the Portuguese government to call for an additional number of British troops, their own army wanting nearly 10,000 men to complete the establishment, by the last returns I have seen; many of those now in the ranks being untrained recruits, owing to their having omitted to complete their army till the last moment, contrary to my repeated advice and remonstrances. Besides this, they have no money to pay their militia, and no food to give either army or militia, or money to buy it; and I am obliged to feed from the British stores those Portuguese troops acting with the British under Gen. Hill's command, in Alentejo; all from the same unfortunate cause, the disinclination of the government to force those under their authority, and the people of the country, to do their duty. Till they shall make an exertion themselves, I cannot recommend to the King's government to do more than they have done.

I propose, if possible, to keep all the Spanish troops out of Portugal, and to get Romana to do that for which he and his troops are most fit : viz., to hang upon the enemy's rear, his communications and detachments, while we shall be in his front. However, this must depend very much upon the enemy's previous operations ; if he should not take Badajoz before he will attack us, which I think very probable, Romana can remain thereabouts, and operate from thence to great advantage. I have very good accounts from Gen. Stewart to the 26th.

À Dom M. Forjaz. à Viseu, ce 8 Mars, 1810.

Je viens de recevoir vos deux lettres du 4 Mars. Je ferai la revue de la poudre que nous avons en Portugal, et s'il me paraît qu'il n'y en a pas assez, j'en ferai venir encore de l'Angleterre. Je vous suis bien obligé de l'une des deux lettres, et du mémoire que vous m'avez écrit sur la situation actuelle des affaires de la Péninsule, et sur les plans de défense que j'ai faits pour le Portugal.

Je suis d'accord avec vous sur presque toutes les parties de votre mémoire; je crois vraiment que, si nous pouvons faire continuer la guerre sur la Péninsule Portugaise et Espagnole, l'Europe ne sera pas perdue; et je crois aussi que, si nous pouvons nous maintenir en Portugal, la guerre ne finira pas dans la Péninsule. Je suis aussi d'opinion que la position que j'ai choisie pour vider la lutte est bonne; et qu'elle est calculée à défendre l'âme (s'il m'est permis de l'appeler ainsi) du Portugal; mais aussi que, si l'ennemi ne peut pas nous forcer, ou nous faire rétrograder de cette position, il sera obligé de faire une retraite, dans laquelle il courra grand risque d'être perdu, et il sera forcé en tout cas d'abandonner tout le territoire Portugais. S'il nous force à abandonner cette position, nous aurons toujours les moyens de nous embarquer dans le Tage; surtout s'il nous attaque (ce qui est vraisemblable) dans la belle saison.

Mais pour soutenir cette attaque de l'ennemi, qui sera sûrement faite par des forces aussi grandes que l'ennemi peut supporter dans ce pays ci, il est nécessaire de concentrer nos forces, surtout l'infanterie, au point d'attaque principale. Ce point sera sûrement à la droite du Tage; malgré que je m'attende qu'il y aura un corps de l'ennemi, probablement assez considérable, sur la rive gauche de la rivière, qui s'emparera des hauteurs qui s'étendent depuis Almada jusqu'à Traffaria.

Je conviens que cette position de l'ennemi peut avoir des inconvéniens pour nous, le plus grand est celui dont vous faites mention; qu'il sera dans le cas d'exciter des tumultes dans la ville de Lisbonne, ce qui donnerait de l'inquiétude pour les derrières de l'armée dans sa position sur la droite du Tage.

Je ne crois pas qu'il puisse ou passer la rivière dans ces parties là, ou empêcher la navigation, ou faire du mal à la ville de Lisbonne, surtout si l'on ôte tous les canons de gros calibre, qui y sont. Mais il y aura toujours l'inconvénient et le risque dont vous faites mention.

Je compte faire occuper le fort de S. Filippe à Setuval, et le fort de Palmella, surtout pour couvrir la retraite des provisions et des moyens de transport qu'on ôtera de la province d'Estremadure Portugaise; mais je ne crois pas que tout ce que nous pouvons faire puisse apporter un remède aux inconvéniens dont vous faites mention. D'abord il faut que je vous dise, que, si l'armée Anglaise était au complet, et elle ne l'est pas, à cause du détachement dernièrement envoyé à Cadiz, et parceque les autres renforts ne sont pas encore arrivés de l'Angleterre, l'armée Portugaise manque encore de plus de monde.

Quand j'ai estimé qu'il y aurait 30,000 troupes Portugaises pour la position sur la droite du Tage, j'ai compté sur une armée de 50,000 hommes, dont 10,000 seraient dans des garnisons, ou employés autre part; 10,000 malades, et manquant au complet, et 30,000 pour le service. Sur les derniers états que j'ai vus, il y avait 5000 hommes malades et hors de service, et de 9000 ou 10,000 manquant au complet; et je crois que je devrais compter sur 20,000, plutôt que sur 30,000 troupes Portugaises réglées dans les positions.

Malgré ces défalcations, je n'ai pas abandonné mon plan. Après que j'ai eu l'honneur de voir les Gouverneurs du Royaume à Lisbonne, j'ai changé un peu le plan des positions que j'avais arrangées, après avoir fait une reconnaissance plus exacte du terrain; et les positions qu'on prépare à présent pourront être défendues par des troupes moins nombreuses. Mais il vaudrait mieux avoir 60,000 que de 40,000 à 50,000 pour ces positions; et sûrement il n'y aura rien à donner à la rive gauche du Tage.

Mais vous dites que l'Angleterre, qui est si intéressée (et de sa gloire et de sa politique) à supporter la lutte sur la Péninsule, devrait renforcer son armée encore de 10,000 à 15,000 hommes, non seulement pour tenir la rive gauche du Tage, mais aussi pour avoir en réserve un corps qui pourrait être jeté de l'un ou de l'autre côté de la rivière, comme il paraîtrait convenable. En vous écrivant en confidence, je n'ai pas de scrupule à vous dire, que je ne crois pas que l'Angleterre ait les 10,000 ou 15,000 hommes qu'il faudrait avoir pour cet objet. Si elle les avait, vous connaissez aussi bien que moi les difficultés qui existent, de finance et de subsistance, pour le maintien de l'armée que nous avons à présent en Portugal; et pour donner au gouvernement Portugais l'assistance qu'il lui faut. L'Angleterre n'a pas le numéraire qui est nécessaire pour le maintien d'une armée plus grande sur la Péninsule; et vous savez aussi bien que moi, que tout le numéraire qui peut se trouver à Lisbonne et dans la Péninsule est appliqué aux dépenses des armées alliées Portugaises et Anglaises. Dans l'état d'épuisement où sont les ressources de subsistance du pays, nous ne pouvons pas tenter d'augmenter nos armées, sans avoir les moyens de les payer, et de payer pour leur subsistance.

Je vous avouerai aussi qu'il me paraît n'être pas convenable de demander à sa Majesté d'augmenter ses forces en Portugal, quand en même tems je serais obligé de lui dire que l'armée Portugaise n'est pas au complet; qu'une grande partie même de ces soldats qui sont dans les rangs, et sur lesquels il faut compter, ne sont que de nouvelles levées parceque les magistrats du pays n'ont fait que dernièrement les efforts qu'il fallait faire pour avoir des recrues pour l'armée, qui n'est même pas encore au complet.

Cependant votre proposition mérite toute l'attention qui est dûe à vous-même, aussi bien qu'à l'importance de l'objet que vous avez en vue, et auquel nous sommes tous vraiment intéressés. Je vous conseille donc de donner la copie de votre lettre et de votre mémoire, et de cette lettre, à M. Stuart, et de le prier de les envoyer en Angleterre. Je serais bien aise que les ministres de sa Majesté vissent la vraie situation des affaires dans la Péninsule, comme elle est décrite par vous; et la chance qu'il y a qu'elles pourraient encore se rétablir par les efforts et la bravoure des armées alliées auprès de Lisbonne.

To the Earl of Liverpool.   Viseu, 8th March, 1810.

I have the honor to enclose a letter which I have received from Marshal
Beresford, on the subject of your Lordship's dispatch of the 7th Feb.,
relative to the arms for the Portuguese troops, upon which I was desirous
of having Marshal Beresford's report. As I knew that no event had
occurred to the Portuguese troops which could have occasioned the loss of
arms, I could not conceive where the waste had occurred to which your
Lordship refers in your dispatch. Marshal Beresford has accurately stated
the amount of arms received from England in the year 1809, and their
disposal. Of the 30,000 stand of arms which were sent with me from
England in the year 1808, the Portuguese troops received only 8000 stand,
and 3000 stand were delivered to Sir R. Wilson, for the use of the Lusitanian Legion; making a total issued in Portugal of 11,000 stand. The
remainder were given, under the orders of the officers who succeeded to
the command of the army, to the Spanish troops released from confinement;
a considerable number were sent round to Catalonia, and another proportion delivered to the army of Estremadura, under the command of Gen.
Galluzzo.

To Major Gen. the Hon. W. Stewart.   Viseu, 9th March, 1810.

I have had the honor of receiving your letter of the 25th and 26th Feb.,
and I am much obliged to you for the details which it contains.

I shall send a squadron of British cavalry to Cadiz as soon as it is
in my power, by the arrival of the 13th dragoons at Lisbon. I have
directed that a brigade of British light 6 pounder field ordnance, complete
with carriages and ammunition, may be sent round to Cadiz without loss
of time; together with the camp equipage and stores which you have required from the Q. M. G., and any baggage, regimental stores, or recruits
for the regiments at Cadiz, which may be at Lisbon.

To Vice Adm. the Hon. G. Berkeley.   Viseu, 9th March, 1810.

I shall be much obliged to you if you will give directions that transports
may be furnished to receive on board a brigade of light 6 pounder field
ordnance, some camp equipage, &c., for the troops at Cadiz, and to proceed
there as soon as the articles shall be on board.

P.S. Besides the articles above mentioned, I request that any recruits,
or recovered men, that may be at Lisbon, belonging to the regiments under
Gen. Stewart's command, may be sent by this opportunity to Cadiz.

To Charles Stuart, Esq.   Viseu, 10th March, 1810.

I received yesterday, from Baron Tripp, your letter of the 5th inst., with
its enclosures. I have never seen the papers enclosed in your dispatch to
Lord Wellesley of the 4th, and marked A, B, and C.

My letter of the 3d will have pointed out to you the objections which I
have to throw upon the British Commissariat the management of the civil
concerns of the Portuguese army. I know of no English Commissary who
is equal to the task of superintending such a concern. Those we now have
are scarcely equal to the management of the concerns of the British army.

Besides, the immense detail of business which the defective regulations of
the British Commissariat throw upon the Commander in Chief of the
British army, in order to apply a remedy to their defects, renders it quite
impossible for him to undertake the management of a detail equally great
for the Portuguese army; and yet the business can be conducted under
one authority only

Another objection which I have to the alteration is, that it will put out of
employment the whole of the civil branch of the Portuguese army, which,
in my opinion, has conducted one branch of the service infinitely better,
viz., the pay branch, than it could have been conducted by English officers.
As for the other branch, the pecuniary difficulties of the government have
been the cause of failures in it, and the troops have suffered from the want
of provisions; but if the same pecuniary difficulties were to embarrass the
management of an English Commissariat, I know from experience that the
troops would suffer equally, if not in a greater degree, from the want of
provisions.

There is another circumstance to be adverted to, and that is, that the Portuguese army are serving, and are likely to continue to serve, in their own
country; and I cannot but think that the civil branch of the concerns of
that army, connected as they are in some degree with the constitution of
the country, in a greater degree with the property of the Prince, and with
the collection of the revenue, would be better managed by native servants.
I have also to add, that if the management of the civil concerns of the Portuguese army is to be undertaken by the British Commissariat, the detail
of the command of the army must be altered likewise, at least if I am to
continue in the command of the army.

In respect to embarkation, we must consider a little the details of the
subject, and you will then see: 1st; that Peniche and Setuval can be made
use of only as places to receive those who may go to them by sea: 2dly; that
moveable and rich property can be embarked only by the adoption of previous and even early measures for that purpose: 3dly; that the means of
embarkation, which we shall have in our power, will not do more than
carry away the British, and probably a part of the Portuguese army, and
that there will be no room for Spaniards.

The line of operations which we are obliged to adopt for the defence of
Lisbon, and for our own embarkation, necessarily throws us back as far as
below Salvaterra on the Tagus, to which place, and I believe lower, the
Tagus is fordable during the summer; and we should be liable to be
turned and cut off from Lisbon and the Tagus, if we were to take our line
of defence higher up the river. This circumstance obliges us to leave
Peniche out of our line; and although I propose to occupy that place and
improve its defence, as soon as I can get some engineers for the purpose,
the communication can be kept up with it only by sea, after the army shall
take up the position which it is deemed best that it should occupy, to bring
the contest to a decision in this country. The necessity of concentrating
all our force on the right of the Tagus equally obliges us to leave Setuval
out of our line; but I propose to occupy Fort S. Filippe and Outaõ, at
Setuval and Palmella, with which places also the communication must be
kept up by sea, when the army shall take up its position.

I enclose you the copy of a letter which I wrote to Adm. Berkeley * in October last, which will give you a general idea, as well of the probable attack which will be made upon us, as of the proposed system of defence, and its connexion with the different places of embarkation.

When we shall have taken up our position for the defence of Lisbon, the question whether we can hold it will depend upon relative means, and possibly upon the event of a battle. If we should not be able to hold it, I propose to embark the British army, and as many of the Portuguese army as I can bring to consent to embark, under cover of the works which have been, and will be, constructed at S. Julian.

You will observe that one of the events which I consider probable in these operations will be, that the enemy will be in possession of the left bank of the Tagus. Under these circumstances, you will certainly be of opinion that there will be no time, nay, that it will be impossible to embark any quantity of moveable and rich property, unless previous and early measures are adopted for that purpose. The transports which government have proposed to supply to carry away the British army is 45,000 tons, which would not be more than sufficient to carry away the British troops. However, with this tonnage, and with the assistance of the fleet of men of war which I expect we shall have, I can carry away both British and Portuguese armies for a short voyage; but I shall not have a single ton for a Spaniard. Government, in the consideration of this subject, have told me that they could not provide tonnage to carry away the Portuguese army, respecting which, however, they have expressed the greatest anxiety; and they have asked me what could be got at Lisbon, &c. &c. My answer has been, nothing at Lisbon; because I believe that although we may discourage a general emigration, we shall find but too many disposed to emigrate; and that every ship in the Tagus will be occupied by persons who will go, more particularly if it be true that early preparatory measures must be adopted with a view even to this partial emigration.

I have already brought this subject under the consideration of government. My opinion is, that the Portuguese government, &c., ought to be prepared for this embarkation; that it ought to prepare at an early period, if any rich or valuable property is to be carried away, notwithstanding the inconveniences which may attend this system of preparation, in a view to the contest which we are likely to have; and I expect that government will signify their orders upon the subject.

This being the case in regard to the tonnage, I cannot, as an honest man, encourage the Spanish armies to retire upon Portugal, however it may strengthen ourselves at the critical moment. If the Spanish, and even the Portuguese troops were like others, and I could reckon with entire confidence upon their exertions in the hour of trial, I should urge the Marques de la Romana to co-operate with us in the defence of our position, from being certain that we can lose it only from the deficiency of numbers of good troops to defend it. But if he should retire with us towards the Tagus, and if, as is probable, his troops should behave ill, and if consequently we should be obliged to embark, I should have treated him ungenerously and ill to leave him behind. I therefore propose to leave him

* See page 563.

upon the rear of the enemy, as I shall the greatest part of the Portuguese militia, and all those troops of the line which will be in garrisons, in forts, &c. &c.

As for the advantage which the enemy will derive from finding at Lisbon rich and valuable property, I cannot put it in competition with that which they would derive from obtaining the services of a large, and, to a certain degree, disciplined army. To remove this instrument out of their way should be the first object of our attention, and afterwards any thing else of which it may be desirable to deprive them; and those persons and families whom it may be desirable to remove from their reach.

The Spanish troops, you will see from the preceding statement, cannot be removed, from the want of means.

If Capt. Francesi is in the Q. M. Gen.'s department, I have reason to be satisfied with him. He is an Italian. We call him Franciozi, but it may be the same person. He is now at Oporto by my leave.

P.S. I have received Dom M. Forjaz's letter and *mémoire*, to which I have written him an answer, which I have requested him to communicate to you.

The A.G. to Brig. Gen. Baron Low, K.G.L.   10th March, 1810.

In reply to your letter of the 7th inst., I am commanded by my Lord Wellington to inform you, that Major —— has already been granted a leave of absence, on the strength and for the purpose recommended in the annexed proceedings of a Medical board. That indulgence Major —— has not thought proper to take advantage of, according to his Lordship's expectation; but on its expiration submits a new request for 5 months' additional leave. Although Lord Wellington cannot refuse leave, asked under the circumstances of this case as stated, yet it appears that a much shorter period would equally answer the purpose of the proposed experiment; and even under such limit, it must in justice be accompanied by the observation, that there appears but little desire on the part of Major —— to recover so far as to return to duty after his long absence. I am also to explain, that his Excellency conceives it your duty, as senior officer of the King's German Legion, to call the attention of H. R. H. the Duke of Cambridge to this officer's continued absence, and to recommend that another officer may be appointed to fill that situation, the duties of which Brigade Major —— appears either undesiring or unequal to execute.

To J. Murray, Esq., Commissary General.   Viseu, 11th March, 1810.

I have always been of opinion that the bât and forage being a sum of money given to officers of the army to enable them to defray certain extraordinary expenses imposed upon them while on service in the field, it was not the intention of the Legislature that the income tax should be deducted from it; but I gave up my opinion, however confirmed by reflection, upon finding that you had received one of a different tenor, although a verbal one, and therefore liable to be mistaken, from one of the Comptrollers of army accounts.

I now find from the enclosed copy of a letter from tne Under Sec. of State in the War department to the Under Sec. of State in the Foreign department, that the subject has lately been considered by the War office, by the Lords of the Treasury, and by the Sec. of State; and that the result of their consideration of the subject has been an agreement with my opinion, ' that no deduction (of income tax) is made from the allowance of bât and forage, or from other allowances granted specifically to cover certain expenses to which the officers may be supposed to be subjected.'

The stoppage of income tax, which has heretofore been made from the bât and forage of the army, is therefore improper, and ought not to have been made, and must be restored to those from whom it was improperly made; and I beg you not to stop the income tax from the bât and forage now about to be issued to the army.

To Brig. Gen. R. Craufurd. Viseu, 11th March, 1810.

I enclose a memorandum which is circulated to you, Gens. Picton and Cole, to provide for the outposts, and for their support, without further reference to me, on the principles on which I wrote to you the other day.

I have not yet heard from Coimbra respecting the light battalions which are there, but I should think that they would be with you in a few days.

Memorandum for Major Gens. Picton and Cole, and Brig. Gen. R. Craufurd.

Viseu, 11th March, 1810.

The regiment of hussars are to be placed under the orders of Brig. Gen. R. Craufurd, who is to dispose of them, and his division of infantry, in such manner as to observe the enemy's movements upon the Agueda, and between that river and the Coa. He will leave in the rear, in their present quarters, for the sake of forage, such of the hussars as he will not require in front. I beg Gen. Cole to let Gen. Craufurd know what posts of hussars he has in front of, or on, the Coa.

I am desirous of being able to collect the army upon the Coa, in case the enemy should attack Ciudad Rodrigo, only in such force as to afford a prospect that I shall be able to relieve it. Major Gen. Picton and Major Gen. Cole are therefore to support Brig. Gen. Craufurd upon the Coa, in case the enemy should collect in force upon the Agueda, or on this side of that river. In case Brig. Gen. Craufurd should require assistance in infantry to occupy any posts upon the Coa, till the Portuguese brigade of light infantry shall have joined him, I wish Major Gen. Cole to give it to him. I beg Brig. Gen. Craufurd to inform Major Gen. Picton, and Major Gen. Cole, as well as myself, of all that passes in front.

To Vice Adm. the Hon. G. Berkeley. Viseu, 11th March, 1810.

I have given directions to the Commanding officer of the artillery at Lisbon to embark in the ordnance store ships, from which the heavy ordnance and stores will have been disembarked, all the ordnance and military stores belonging to the British army on shore at Lisbon; and I shall be much obliged to you if you will direct that such assistance as may be necessary may be given to him, to enable him to perform this service.

To the Earl of Liverpool. Viseu, 12th March, 1810.

As the Portuguese government have in store but a small quantity of gunpowder, I beg leave to recommend to your Lordship that 2000 barrels of gunpowder may be sent to the Tagus, as soon as may be practicable. I am also desirous of having in the Tagus an additional quantity of 2,000,000 musket ball cartridges. The supply already in Portugal is large; but as I have been obliged to place it in deposits in different parts of the country, on account of the difficulties and uncertainty of conveyance, I am desirous of having in the Tagus this additional quantity.

To the Secretary to the Treasury.   Viseu, 12th March, 1810.

Mr. F. C. Phillips, a merchant, had been employed by the Sec. of State to purchase grain in the Mediterranean for the use of His Majesty's army, and of those of his allies employed in the Peninsula; and having purchased a large quantity of wheat and barley at Malta, Sir Alex. Ball, the late Governor of that island, permitted him to use the transports then stationed there to convey the wheat and barley to Portugal. The grain accordingly arrived in 7 transports in 2 convoys: the first, consisting of 4 vessels, was about 7 weeks; the other, consisting of 3 vessels, about 4 months on their passage.

The Agent of transports at Lisbon, acting under the orders of the Commander in Chief of His Majesty's fleet in the Tagus, has called upon Mr. Phillips to pay for these transports, during the time they have been employed by him, the same sum which they have cost His Majesty, and he has paid the Agent of transports £3422 for the use of 1083 tons, which imported the first cargoes of corn; and the Commissary Gen., who has purchased the grain from Mr. Phillips, has retained in his hands the sum of £3725, to answer the demand of the Transport Board for 677 tons, which imported the second cargo.

I enclose an affidavit sworn by Mr. Phillips on this subject, from which it does not appear that any bargain had been made by Mr. Phillips with Sir Alex. Ball respecting the freight of the transports; and it is probable that Capt. Lambe, the agent of transports at Malta, is the only person who has a knowledge of Sir Alex. Ball's intentions. Whether he intended to give Mr. Phillips the use of the transports without payment of freight, from a view of the advantage which His Majesty's service was likely to derive from the employment of them, or not, I think it almost certain that Sir Alex. Ball never could have proposed that he should pay, and that Mr. Phillips never would have consented to pay, so high a price as the monthly tonnage of the transports paid by His Majesty.

Mr. Phillips was obliged to deliver the grain on the Peninsula at as cheap a rate as grain of the same quality and description could be purchased in the markets there; on no other terms could the Commissary Gen. purchase it; and it is not probable that it could have been in the contemplation of Mr. Phillips to sell grain at Lisbon at the market price of Portugal which was purchased at Malta, and for which freight was to be paid at the high rate paid by His Majesty for the vessels used as transports in his service.

If I am correct in this conjecture, and if there is no evidence that Mr. Phillips did engage to pay this high rate of freight, I beg leave to recommend to their Lordships to order the Commissioners of transports to give directions to their agent at Lisbon to settle with Mr. Phillips for the freight of this grain, according to the ordinary price of freight from Malta to Lisbon; and that the Commissary Gen. should be directed to retain the sum thus settled as the price of the freight, and to pay Mr. Phillips the overplus of that sum out of the money now in his hands.

It will still remain to be ascertained by inquiry from Capt. Lambe and other authorities at Malta, whether the late Sir Alex. Ball made any engagement with Mr. Phillips that he should have the transports without payment of freight.

To the Secretary to the Treasury.   Viseu, 13th March, 1810.

I have had the honor of receiving your letter of the 22d Jan., in answer to mine of the 20th Nov., on the subject of the vouchers required to the accounts of Staff officers.

I do not exactly understand whether it is the pleasure of their Lordships that the accounts of Staff officers, having been examined and certified by the Commissary of Accounts, subject to such observations and queries thereon as their deficiencies in point of vouchers may require, are to be paid by the Commissary Gen., or are to remain unpaid until the Auditors of Public accounts, or ultimately the Board of Treasury, upon the statements of the officers, shall make such allowance for such deficient vouchers as shall appear to be just and equitable under the circumstances of the case.

If the former should be the intention of their Lordships, I presume that they intend to suspend the 19th article of the Instructions to the Commissary Gen., which requires that all bills should be sent to the Commissary of Accounts, who is to certify that they are correct; and that their Lordships intend that the Commissary Gen. should pay the bills of Staff officers, notwithstanding that they are not correct in vouchers, subject to the future decision of the Auditors of Public accounts, or of their Lordships. I request to know whether I am correct in this construction of their Lordships' intention in your letter of the 22d Jan.

I beg leave to submit to their Lordships, that instances daily occur of expenses incurred by Staff officers, for which they cannot produce the voucher required by the Commissary of accounts under his Instructions, viz., the receipt of the party, subscribed by a creditable witness; and it is a hardship upon these officers to oblige them to incur and pay these expenses for the public, and afterwards to prove, at a distance from the scene of action, and in years after the occurrence of the necessity for the payment, before persons entirely unacquainted with the nature of the service, that they could not procure the vouchers which the regulations required.

If, however, it should not be the intention of their Lordships to suspend the 19th article of the Instructions to the Commissary Gen., it becomes still more unjust towards Staff officers to oblige them to incur expenses of this description, the amounts of which cannot be paid till the Auditors of Public accounts, or their Lordships, shall have been convinced that the required voucher could not be obtained or produced.

In my letter of the 20th Nov., I referred to their Lordships' consideration two distinct classes of accountants, suffering under the operation of these Instructions to the Commissary of accounts: Staff officers who had incurred expenses for the public before they knew that these additional vouchers would be required; and Staff officers who had, or who should incur expenses on account of the public, of which, from their nature, the requisite vouchers cannot be procured. Those first mentioned must be involved to the full amount of their demands upon the public under the operation of their Lordships' orders, notwithstanding the apparent injustice of applying to these accounts rules of which the officers could have no knowledge, and which are not observed by the War office in passing accounts of this description for expenses incurred in Great Britain. These last mentioned will be involved only in the amount of expenses for which it is impracticable to produce the required vouchers. I am desirous of knowing the pleasure of their Lordships, upon what is submitted in this letter, by an early opportunity.

To Lieut. Gen. Hill. Viseu, 13th March, 1810.

I have received your letter of the 9th. In order to accelerate the communication between you and me, I have had post mules placed on the direct road from Thomar to Viseu. If, therefore, you should have occasion to send an officer, desire him to come from Thomar by the road of which I enclose the stages. It will save some leagues.

To Charles Stuart, Esq. Viseu, 13th March, 1810.

I have received your letters of the 7th and 10th. I have no means of employing the person whom you mention (—— ——) excepting as a Captain in the Corps of Guides, for which the requisite qualities are intelligence, some honesty, and a knowledge of the Spanish or Portuguese languages, and English or French. I should wish, however, not to employ him, as he would have opportunities of acquiring and conveying to the enemy much useful information. I would recommend to you to send him to England, apprising the government that I had no means of employing him.

The case of Col. —— was as follows. He deserted from the French service to the Marques de la Romana last spring; by whom he was sent to England with a letter of recommendation. Lord Castlereagh sent him to Portugal with directions to Marshal Beresford to employ him in the Portuguese service; Beresford would not employ him excepting in a subaltern situation; and he then came to me, who had no means whatever of employing him. I offered him a commission either in the British or Portuguese service, but he would not accept one of a lower rank than Colonel, which I could not give him; and I then supplied him with money to return to England, as he was apprehensive or unwilling to adopt the alternative proposed for him by Lord Castlereagh, of going into the Spanish service, if Marshal Beresford would not accept of his services in that of Portugal.

We owe you above £120,000 on account of the ' Aids ' to the 24th Feb., but we have no money to pay you. The army is nearly 2 months in arrears. If the ministers do not supply us with money from England, we cannot get on.

The A.G. to Brig. Gen. R. Craufurd. 13th March, 1810.

In compliance with your desire, communicated through the Sec. of the

Board of Claims, I transmit a return of killed, wounded, and missing, in the actions of the 27th and 28th July, at Talavera. Having represented to the Commander of the Forces the difficulties in giving further correct information, to enable you to decide as to the claims of Colonels of regiments on this head of service, I am directed to put you in possession of his Excellency's opinion, that those difficulties cannot be surmounted, as the deficiency of accoutrements of the regiments that were so employed must far exceed the averaged loss of men, as many soldiers were removed, and otherwise escaped from the several temporary hospitals, on the advance of the enemy, who were not able to bring away any part of their arms or accoutrements.

To the Earl of Liverpool.   Viseu, 14th March, 1810.

I enclose the copy of a letter which I wrote many months ago * to the Commander in Chief, on the subject of an important branch of the equipment of the army, which has, I understand, been brought under the consideration of the Treasury, and no answer has yet been returned.

The inconveniences which are the consequence of this delay in giving an answer are increasing daily ; and they will be most seriously and severely felt by the troops, if they should be engaged in operations with the enemy, before arrangements are made to provide for the essential object, the mode of providing for the carriage of their camp kettles, discussed in that letter. I beg only to mention, that the soldiers cannot cook their food unless they have camp kettles.

I also beg again to draw your Lordship's attention to the frequent applications which I have made for money from England, and which have been repeated to the Treasury by the Commissary Gen. It becomes every day more difficult to procure in this country the supplies and means required by the army without paying for them in ready money ; and there is a monthly demand for the Portuguese government amounting to £80,000, without the payment of which their army must disband.

To the Earl of Liverpool.   Viseu, 14th March, 1810.

The enemy's armies have continued nearly in the same positions since I wrote to you last. Marshal Mortier has fixed his head quarters at Zafra, communicating by Almendralejo with the corps called Soult's, which is at Merida.

One of the divisions of the Spanish corps under the Marques de la Romana has gone to Xerez de los Caballeros, with a view to alarm the French for their communication with Andalusia, and another division to Olivença. The left of this corps still continues at Alburquerque.

My last accounts from Cadiz are of the 26th, at which time the 2d batt. 88th regt., and a detachment of artillery and some Spanish troops, had arrived from Gibraltar. The enemy had made no attack. Our troops had retaken possession of Fort Matagorda (which had at first been destroyed) with a view to protect the communication between the outer and inner harbour.

The enemy had repaired Fort Catalina on the northern shore, but it has been discovered that the entrance to the harbour between the Diamond Rock and Los Puercos is equally practicable for large ships with that north of the Diamond.

* 28th Sept. 1809, p. 528.

Nothing of importance has occurred in the north of Spain or in Old Castille. There is a report, to which, however, I do not give credit, that a Spanish corps from Valencia has entered the upper part of La Mancha, and has impeded the communication with Madrid through La Mancha.

The A. G. to Major Gen. the Hon. G. L. Cole.   14th March, 1810.

In reply to your letter of the 12th inst., and enclosures, which have been received and duly submitted, I am directed to communicate to you that it appears to my Lord Wellington that the desired inquiry respecting some reports, supposed to have been made to his Lordship (and heard for the first time at Guarda), is not an inquiry into the conduct of the officer, but an inquiry into the truth of the supposed reports. To this his Lordship never will submit; neither can he submit to be questioned by an officer respecting the reports made to his Lordship by any General or other staff officer, respecting the conduct of any individual placed under the command of such General officer. Having so far decided this point, my Lord Wellington declares that no report of the kind as stated by Major ——, was made to his Lordship by any officer. Lord Wellington, who had the opportunity of seeing all that passed in the battle of Talavera, and having received the reports of the different General officers who commanded divisions, on more than one occasion has expressed satisfaction with the conduct of the whole army; which approval has been repeated by His Majesty upon his Lordship's reports, and has since been expressed in the votes of the two Houses of Parliament. Under these circumstances, it has appeared strange that his Lordship should be called on, at this distance of time, to prove and defend reports supposed to have been made, and to institute an inquiry into the conduct of an officer against whom no charge has been adduced; but that he has heard at Guarda, and thinks, that a report has been made injurious to his character. If Col. —— was aware of any misconduct on the part of Major ——, it was his duty to bring it forward, at the moment the misconduct occurred, and not at this distant period. Should there be any ground for inquiry in Col. ——'s knowledge, which the Commander of the Forces cannot think there is, that officer must make it known, if he chooses that the conduct of the Major and of the — regiment should become subject of inquiry; and not call for and promote an inquiry upon vague grounds, and upon reports supposed to have been made to his Excellency.

To Major Gen. the Hon. G. L. Cole.   Viseu, 15th March, 1810.

I received last night your letter of the 12th, and directions have been sent to Gen. Craufurd that you may be kept informed of what passes directly in your front by the hussars stationed there, as soon as possible. If you should find it necessary, and the weather should not be too bad, I have no objection to your making the disposition of your division which you propose; although I cannot tell you exactly when the Portuguese brigade will join you, as that depends upon their receipt of some articles of clothing and equipments.

To Vice Adm. the Hon. G. Berkeley.   Viseu, 15th March, 1810.

I have sent to Col. Fletcher your observation upon his report, and I shall be very much obliged to you if you will send with him the guide to look at the ground which has been described to you. I have also written to him about the telegraph, upon which I have requested him to speak to you. I have done every thing in my power to prevail upon them to send away the Spanish ships from Cadiz. If I can get them to Mahon, I think I shall do a great deal; and I have begged to secure that island, which is at present a most important object. The Spaniards will never consent to send the ships to Malta, and to propose it will only alarm the jealousy which has but lately been in some degree allayed.

P.S. We have embarked some men in the *Langley* transport, to be taken to the Tagus, when she can get out of the Mondego, and I shall be much obliged to you if you will send this vessel back again.

To Vice Adm. the Hon. G. Berkeley.   Viseu, 15th March, 1810.

I shall be much obliged to you if you will give directions that a passage to England may be furnished to certain officers and non-commissioned officers of the 23d dragoons, as well as to the men belonging to the depôt squadrons of the regiments of cavalry in this country, of which officers and men the Commandant at Lisbon will give the Agent of transports the detail.

To the Earl of Liverpool.   Viseu, 15th March, 1810.

I enclose the last weekly state. I had yesterday a conversation with Gen. Sir J. C. Sherbrooke regarding the state of his health, and he is decidedly of opinion that he cannot last beyond the end of next month; and he is determined to go home at that time, or in the beginning of May. As your Lordship has settled with Gen. Graham that he is to come out to succeed Gen. Sherbrooke, I shall be very much obliged to you if you will arrange with him to be at Lisbon in the first week in May.

To Major Gen. the Hon. G. L. Cole.   Viseu, 16th March, 1810.

I received last night your letter of the 15th, enclosing Cornet Cordemann's of the 14th, from Villar Maior. I think that the enemy's troops near Ciudad Rodrigo, to which Cornet Cordemann refers, are a detachment which went to Alverca on the 10th, whose object apparently was to cut off the Spanish General Carrera, who had pushed himself into the mountains to the eastward of Baños. We should certainly have heard of a collection at, or a movement from Salamanca, from some of the posts on the lower part of the Agueda before we should have heard of it from Villar Maior; and all the intelligence which I have from Chaves, of as late a date as the 8th, would tend to show that the enemy's views were rather directed to that quarter than to this at present. Junot's corps is positively stated to be at Leon; although Loison's has moved towards Salamanca.

To Vice Adm. the Hon. G. Berkeley.   Viseu, 16th March, 1810.

I have reason to believe that Mr. Commissary White will have procured 100,000 dollars at Coruña for bills upon England, which have been sent to him, by the time that a vessel will arrive there to receive that money; and I shall accordingly be much obliged to you if you will dispatch to Coruña a vessel to bring to Lisbon that sum of money.

The A.G. to Officers commanding Divisions.   16th March, 1810.

Adverting to the early approach of the hot season, in which the soldiers will not require blankets as well as great coats, I am directed by the Commander of the Forces to request that, in concert with the General officers in charge of brigades, and officers commanding regiments, you will consider which of those articles it will be expedient to place in store. This may depend much upon the state in which the great coats may be found at the present moment. As the inclement weather may be supposed nearly past, and that the blanket will be more beneficial to the soldier than the great coat during the nights, at the period when it will be necessary to quit cantonments in the villages, it may be deemed expedient to retain the blankets, and to send the great coats into store.

Be pleased, in your report for his Excellency's information, to have annexed the number of blankets or great coats that are to be sent into store by each regiment.

To Vice Adm. the Hon. G. Berkeley.   Viseu, 17th March, 1810.

I am very much obliged to you for your letter of the 14th and its enclosures. It is strange that I should have received no letters from Cadiz since the 26th Feb.

I have desired the Q. M. G. to direct Capt. Mackenzie to arrange with the Agent of transports for the embarkation of the camp equipage in store. I shall be obliged to you if you will desire Lieut. Fleetwood to communicate with Capt. Mackenzie on the subject. This will clear us of Portugal with every thing excepting what we have with the army.

To Charles Stuart, Esq.   Viseu, 17th March, 1810.

I have received your 2 letters of the 13th. The Regency of Portugal having been appointed by orders from Brazil, I do not conceive that any act of their own can legally put out any member, or admit one in the place of another who has absented himself from their meetings. Even if it were desirable that any particular person should belong to the Regency (and I acknowledge that I do not know of any person of a description to be of use to the government in any way), I should doubt the expediency of shaking the foundation of the authority of the Regency, which consists in the soundness of their appointment. My opinion is, therefore, that you ought to confine yourself to making observations on the continued absence of the Marquez das Minas from the Regency, and its supposed cause, and on the bad effects which such conduct must have, as well on the public interests as on the character of the Marquez himself; and to a recommendation that the Regency should suggest to the Prince to appoint a member instead of the Marquez das Minas.

I am entirely ignorant of the general nature, as well as of the detail, of the arrangement made by Mr. Villiers for paying the money from the chest of the ' Aids ' to the Portuguese government; and it is impossible for me to give any opinion how far the system could be relaxed with propriety, so as to give the government the use of the money at an earlier period. My opinion is, that the return signed by Marshal Beresford, on the 1st March, of the number of men in the regiments supposed to be in the service of Great Britain in the month of February, might be a sufficient voucher to you to pay the government for the troops for the month of February, as soon as you should have the money in the chest of the ' Aids ' to enable you to pay them. I do not think you could pay them sooner with propriety ; and it does not occur to me that any other check besides the Marshal's return is necessary. However, I write with diffidence upon this part of the subject, as I am entirely ignorant of the principles, as well as of the detail, of the system established by Mr. Villiers.

My opinion is, that the 30,000 men to be paid should be either 30,000 R. and F., or 30,000 including officers and non-commissioned officers, according to the original estimate of the expense sent from this country to England, which I have not got, and which I never saw, excepting once, when reading Mr. Villiers's dispatches in Mr. Canning's office. It was according to this estimate that Great Britain engaged to pay for the 10,000 men, and then for the 20,000, and lastly for the 30,000 ; and, as we oblige the Portuguese government to abide by it, we are equally bound to abide by it in an instance in which it may not be quite so advantageous to ourselves. I am the person who prevailed upon the British government to grant to Portugal payment for the last 10,000 men, and the £130,000 for the officers ; and I know that the payment for the last was asked for and was granted upon the same principle as the payment for the first was granted. I have no doubt that a great deal might be done to secure further means of embarking the army, and those it may be thought expedient to remove from the country, if timely measures are adopted. I have written to England upon this subject, and I hope that government will have decided upon the line they will adopt, and will instruct us by the first packet. I have not yet returned the interesting papers which you sent me, as I am taking copies of some of them. Have you any plans with them ?

The A.G. to Dr. Franck, Inspector of Hospitals.　　　　　　　18th March, 1810.

I am commanded to inform you, that Mr. ——'s explanations of the complaint made by Col. Drummond and Lord Blantyre, as submitted by you, have proved very unsatisfactory to the Commander of the Forces.

My Lord Blantyre complained that men of the 42d regt. had been sent back to that battalion from general hospital with arms and accoutrements belonging to other corps, notwithstanding repeated orders to the contrary, and that means had been adopted to arrange and register all arms, accoutrements, and necessaries. In answer to these representations, the Commander of the Forces is informed that irregularity had prevailed in the admission of men into general hospital.

This irregularity ought not to have prevailed in any instance, and particularly in respect of the 42d regt., as that regiment did not join the army till the month of September. At all events, the mode of admitting patients into general hospital should not have occasioned their being sent out of hospital in January and February with arms and accoutrements belonging to other regiments. The arrangement and registry of the arms and accoutrements delivered into store, were ordered to prevent the occurrence of irregularity in the re-issue, attributed to a want of necessary system, before those aids.

Unless Mr. —— can give a more satisfactory account than he has hitherto done of the arms, accoutrements, and necessaries of the several soldiers in hospital, he must be responsible for all losses, and must besides expect to be brought to the most rigorous account for disobedience of his Excellency's orders. You will be pleased to require a report from Mr. —— whether all the arms, accoutrements, and necessaries, in his charge at Estremoz, Villa Viçosa, and Elvas (with the exception of those delivered to soldiers on discharge), have been removed to Lisbon. If not, they are to be removed forthwith, and that officer is empowered to make a requisition on the Commissary Gen. for carts for this service.

You will further be pleased to report whether the officers commanding regiments obeyed the order of the 17th Dec.

To Major Gen. the Hon. G. L. Cole.　　　　　　　Viseu, 19th March, 1810.

I received yesterday your 2 letters of the 17th, containing Cornet Cordemann's reports of the 16th and 17th. I desired Capt. Roveria to tell you that I had reason to believe that Cornet Cordemann's report of the 14th was in some degree founded. There is no doubt that the enemy have, since the 12th, collected a large force on the left of the Tormes.

My information from Chaves of the 9th stated that Junot, with another corps, was at Leon; and I conclude that the troops between the Tormes and the Agueda are the corps of Ney, Kellermann, and Loison. I think that the first operation will be to the northward. If they seriously intend to attack Ciudad Rodrigo, it is extraordinary that they should collect a force in the country from which they must draw their subsistence during the continuance of the siege, and keep it there for so many days.

The A.G. to Lieut. Col. Lord Blantyre, 42d regt.   19th March, 1810.

I am directed by my Lord Wellington to enclose a copy of Mr. ——'s reply to your Lordship's representation of the 7th inst. Should you have any thing to observe on the purport of the annexed, you will be pleased, without delay, to communicate the same. You will take occasion, also, to state the date of the entry of the men of the 42d regt. into hospital, who have returned to the corps with arms and accoutrements broken or exchanged. Further, be pleased to mention whether tickets were sent with the soldiers to hospitals, in obedience to the G. O., 17th Dec.

The A.G. to Major ——, — regt., Cadiz.   March, 1810.

I do myself the honor to enclose a correspondence from this office with the Commandant at Lisbon, on the subject of Ensign ——, of the — regt., in consequence of your report to Col. Peacocke, of the 7th Feb., also returned. His Excellency's object in directing these documents to be put in your possession is, that you should, on the arrival of Ensign ——, require that reasonable proportion of duty which justice to the service demands of every officer; but should it still appear that Ensign ——'s constitution is unequal to the fatigues of a soldier's employment, the reports to this effect must be forwarded to the Horse Guards, for the Commander in Chief's decision.

To Brig. Gen. R. Craufurd.   Viseu, 20th March, 1810.

I received last night your letter of the 17th. It is strange that the Governor of Ciudad Rodrigo should have no intelligence of the enemy's movements near his garrison, of which we have received so many accounts. I should believe them not to be true, and that no troops have moved towards the Sierra de Francia excepting those which were at San Felices, and their movement was probably occasioned by that of Carrera.

Mr. Ogilvie and Mr. Drake have been sent to your division as Commissaries. Mr. Ogilvie bears an excellent character. I shall speak to the Commissary Gen. about your wine; and I shall send you some shoes. We have, however, very few in this neighbourhood, as the vagabonds who come from the hospital sell every thing upon the road, and it is generally necessary to supply them with all the requisites for a soldier as they pass through this place. I have, however, ordered forward a large supply, of which you shall have your share.

To Vice Adm. the Hon. G. Berkeley.   Viseu, 20th March, 1810.

I enclose a letter from Col. Peacocke to Lord FitzRoy Somerset, containing one from Mr. J. B. Crispin, of the 8th March, from Faro, from which it appears that that gentleman is not acquainted with the arrangements made by you for the conveyance of the letters for Cadiz from that place, as stated in your letter of the 19th Feb. I shall be very much obliged to you if you will give directions that he may be apprised of them.

To Charles Stuart, Esq.   Viseu, 20th March, 1810.

I have received your letter of the 17th inst. The Commissary Gen. draws for all money required for the service in Portugal, in consequence of orders from England which have been given; because it was supposed that the money which could be procured upon the Peninsula for bills would come into the military chest at a cheaper rate, if only one person, instead of many, should draw the bills upon England. The different departments, however, to which the Commissary Gen. advances money (the heads of which would come into the market with their bills, if it had not been settled that the Commissary Gen.'s bills alone should come into the market) ought to give the Commissary Gen. a bill upon the head of the department in England for every sum of money which they receive here. The Commissary Gen. would send these bills to the Treasury, and they would be settled with the heads of the departments respectively upon which the bills would have been drawn.

This is the mode in which the Dep. Paymaster Gen. of the army and the ordnance are supplied with money, and in which they settle for the advances made to them; and it is the mode in which it would be most regular and satisfactory, and indeed most safe, for the British minister to settle for the sums paid into the chest of the ' Aids.'

After this statement, you will see that I can have no desire to alter the mode of proceeding hitherto adopted. That proposed by the Commissary Gen. to you would be the most regular; but that hitherto in use answers our purposes, and gives us a voucher for the issue of the money, which is all I can require. I confess, however, that if I were in your situation, and feeling, as I do, that the minister must in this, as he is in every other instance of a subsidy, be accountable, I should prefer to give bills for every sum received from the Commissary Gen., to allowing sums to be received from him by Mr. Bell, upon a general order and authority conveyed by a letter.

To the Earl of Liverpool.   Viseu, 20th March, 1810.

I hope your Lordship will excuse me for drawing your attention again to the state of this army for the want of money. I have long been obliged to keep the pay of the troops one month in arrear, contrary to His Majesty's regulations, and the practice and necessities of the service, and we have not money enough to pay them at the end of this month; and, by accounts from Lisbon, up to the 17th, there is no money there which can be sent.

Your Lordship is aware that all the money for the service in Portugal passes through the hands of the Commissary Gen., who pays to the order of His Majesty's minister at Lisbon such portion of the sums in his hands as may be applicable to Portuguese services. The fairest and most proper mode of fixing the sums which should be applicable to Portuguese services in each month was, that that sum should be paid by the Commissary Gen. to the King's minister, which should bear the proportion to the whole sum received by him during the month which the expense of the Portuguese services should bear to the whole expense incurred in the Peninsula, and paid by the Commissary Gen. On this principle the proportion to be paid for Portuguese services, in each month, of the sums passing through the Commissary Gen.'s hands, has been fixed by me lately at two sevenths of the whole, which is about the proportion that the expense of the Portuguese services bears to the whole British expense in the Peninsula. Under this head, there is due to the British minister upon an account closed to the 24th Feb., not less than £160,000, for the payment of which there are not sufficient funds in hand; and the close of another month is approaching. The same proportion of the receipts of this month ought to be allotted for the payment of these services.

It must be obvious to your Lordship that the King's minister cannot perform His Majesty's engagements to the Portuguese government unless money is supplied to him; and the accounts which have been transmitted to England from this country will have convinced His Majesty's government that it will be impossible to keep the Portuguese army together, if the government is not assisted with money to pay it regularly. The want of money to pay the British troops with regularity, and to discharge the demands for their provisions, forage, and means of transport, is also an evil which may be attended by the most serious consequences, in the critical situation in which the army may shortly be placed.

The constitution, and the whole system of the discipline, efficiency, and equipment of the British army, depend upon regular payments. All the soldiers' necessaries, and much of their provisions, and the provisions, equipments, and comforts of the officers, are purchased and paid for out of their pay; and if these articles cannot be paid for, the soldiers will take them without payment, notwithstanding all the exertions of the officers to prevent them.

The quantity of supplies drawn from Portugal for the use of the British and Portuguese armies has been so large, that it is most difficult now to procure any without payment. I have accounts from all quarters of the increasing difficulties in the supply of the troops; and it is reasonable to suppose that the inhabitants of the country are unwilling to part with their provisions, without payment in ready money, to an army which they must expect will, before long, evacuate the country. If not supplied with money in sufficient quantity to pay for the supplies required, the supplies must be taken from the country, without payment, by force. Detachments of the troops must be employed upon this service, instead of in opposing the invasion of the enemy; and fresh opportunities will be afforded for the disorders and outrages to which I have more than once drawn your Lordship's attention, at the moment at which every thing may depend upon the efficiency, discipline, and good order of the troops, and upon the good will of the inhabitants of the country.

I beg to refer your Lordship to my former letters upon this subject, in which I apprised you of the sums which would be necessary by the month of February, and of my opinion that a monthly supply, equal in amount to the increased monthly subsidy to the Portuguese government, ought to be sent to Portugal.

To Brig. Gen. R. Craufurd.　　　　　　　　　　Viseu, 20th March, 1810.

I write to let you know that 800 pairs of shoes are ordered to Celorico for the use of your troops; and the Commissary Gen. tells me that your Commissary has 12,000 dollars. I have spoken to him about your wine.

P.S. 21st March. Since writing the above, I have received your letter of the 18th. I should be glad if I could spare our horses the duty of carrying letters, on which indeed they are employed in no instance, excepting between you and Celorico. We have no Portuguese cavalry near this at present. It is useless to desire you to buy a few horses or mules purposely for the performance of this duty, when you complain of the want of money for other more essential purposes; and unless the 12,000 dollars already sent have reached you, and are sufficient for the present, we have no more which we can send you. I will see, however, if I can't get from the Commissary Gen. 8 or 10 tolerable mules to be employed on this duty. You should make the horses go very short stages. I hope that you will find the caçadores better than you expect they will be. It is impossible to get Elder's corps for you, otherwise you may depend upon it that I should have been happy to make your division so much stronger.

To Vice Adm. the Hon. G. Berkeley.					Viseu, 21st March, 1810.

I find, by a communication from Col. Fisher, that after he shall have landed the heavy ordnance, and the necessary quantity of stores, and occupying the tonnage which these will vacate by placing in those ships the ordnance and military stores now on shore, which they will hold, he will still require 2121 tons. I shall be very much obliged to you if you will desire the Agent of transports to communicate with Col. Fisher, and to arrange for the reception and embarkation of these stores.

I am very anxious to have every thing in such a state that we may either go or stay, according as it may be expedient, in view to the force by which we shall be attacked.

The Agent of transports has mentioned to Col. Murray that he wished to have back the transports from Cadiz. I was desirous that the transports should remain there when first the troops were detached, in order that Gen. Stewart might have it in his power to withdraw when it should be necessary; and I now wish the transports to remain there, in order that we may have the assistance of the troops from Cadiz, if the French should withdraw from their position before Cadiz, when they shall attack Portugal, which I think not an improbable event. However, you will of course give such orders for the transports as you may think best.

The arrangement for the embarkation made by Lieut. Fleetwood is very satisfactory; and the more we conclude upon this subject beforehand, the better shall we execute our business when it comes to the point. I mean, however, to try to prevail upon some, if not all, of the Portu-

G. O.					Viseu, 21st March, 1810.

The Commander of the Forces refers the officers commanding regiments to the orders they received through the Q. M. G., specifying the form in which the returns of the articles of field equipments were to be made, under the Orders of the 31st May, 1809. He requests that the returns may hereafter be made out according to that form. If any articles are returned wanting, a N. B. is to be made at the foot of the return, stating particularly the reason. If any article should become unserviceable, a special report to be made on the subject.

guese infantry at least to evacuate with us, if we should be forced to adopt that measure; and in that case it would be best probably to put them in the transports, and the British troops in the men of war, of which I hope you will soon have a good fleet. We would leave the baggage of the British regiments in the transports, and put nothing but the officers and men in the ships of war, unless you should think it best to take the Portuguese troops into the ships of war.

I hope that Mr. Stuart will soon have directions from government to settle with the Portuguese government for the preparation of their ships for evacuation, in case it should be necessary. I requested the Sec. of State long ago to send out 6 good hospital ships, which I hope will arrive when the weather permits.

The Sec. of State has consented to the measure which I proposed, of not bringing away more than the best of the horses, principally those belonging to the officers of the army. I understood that they would have at Lisbon transports for 600 horses, which would be sufficient for every thing; but there ought to be tonnage for that number which we have in the army of valuable horses. I see that Lieut. Fleetwood talks of dismantling some of the horse ships, which, adverting to their utility, and the expense of fitting them up, it would probably be best to avoid till the last moment.

To Charles Stuart, Esq.   Viseu, 21st March, 1810.

I send some dispatches for England, and some for Cadiz, the last of which I request you to ask the Admiral to forward by a ship of war, as I apprehend that all those which I have sent by the communication which Adm. Berkeley had imagined was arranged between Faro and Cadiz have failed to reach their destination. If the Admiral should be unable to send these dispatches, I shall then request you to ask the Portuguese government to send there one of their vessels.

To the Rt. Hon. H. Wellesley.   Viseu, 21st March, 1810.

I have heard of your arrival at Cadiz, though not from yourself, as I understand that the Captain of the ship which was dispatched from Cadiz, purposely to carry letters from you to Mr. Stuart and me, sailed without your letters. Neither have I heard from Gen. Stewart since the 26th Feb., or from Mr. Frere for a still longer period. I am apprehensive, also, that all my letters to Gen. Stewart and Mr. Frere have miscarried, as I learned yesterday that the communication which Adm. Berkeley had considered certain between Faro and Cadiz had failed entirely. I therefore send to them duplicates by this opportunity.

I have nothing new to tell you from this quarter. The French army is stationed as follows, as far as I can learn. There is a corps under Gen. ——, of 6000 or 7000 men, in the Asturias; they have possession of Oviedo, and have pushed forward as far as the Narcea. Junot's corps, called by the Spaniards 12,000, but which I should imagine is nearer 20,000, is in the kingdom of Leon, threatening Astorga; upon which place, however, they had made no attack as late as the 13th of this month. Ney is upon the Tormes, and between that river and the Agueda, with his own corps, that of Loison, and that of Kellermann. He threatens Ciudad Rodrigo, upon which, however, he had made no attack as late as the 19th. Our advanced posts touch his upon the Agueda. Soult's corps, and a part of Regnier's reserve, are at Merida, and Mortier's corps at Zafra. These threaten Badajoz, upon which they had made no attack as late as the 19th. They have in their front the Marques de la Romana's corps, which has extended its right to Xerez de los Cavalleros, and has its left at Alburquerque. He is well situated for *la petite guerre*. The right wing of the British army is at Portalegre.

The left division of Romana's corps, under Gen. O'Donell, has lately had some success against a French detachment at Caceres. Romana has likewise a small detachment at Coria, on this side of the Tagus, under Gen. Carrera.

The corps of Victor and Sebastiani, the Guard, and the reserve, which usually marches with the King, are in Andalusia; where, I do not know, as we have no intelligence of what is passing to the southward.

I believe that all the reinforcements intended for Spain have arrived, with the exception of the Imperial Guard; and I conclude that operations will commence as soon as the weather holds up. My opinion is, that they will commence on our right and left in Estremadura and Galicia.

It is very desirable that I should be constantly informed of what is passing in other parts of Spain, as far as may be possible; and I wish you would let me have all the intelligence received by the government. Some letters were intercepted lately, which I have reason to believe were interesting: among others one from Berthier to Soult. I should be very glad to have a copy of them.

It is reported that the French are about to withdraw from their position before Cadiz, which I think not unlikely, particularly if there should be any insurrection, or any opposition to them by the people in any part of Spain; or if they should have any reason to apprehend any thing from Blake's corps, or the army said to be in Valencia, while they will be engaged in their operations in the west of the Peninsula. At all events, Cadiz has nothing to apprehend till we shall have been obliged to evacuate Portugal.

If the French should withdraw from their position before Cadiz, I wish you would consider, and let me know your opinion, whether it would be safe to let me have back in Portugal some, at least, of my troops. I am aware that the decision whether any of these troops should be allowed to quit Cadiz does not depend solely upon military considerations; and that much will depend upon the temper and spirit of the people, upon their determination to hold out, and upon the prospect that they will admit us again to their assistance, if we should fail in being able to maintain our ground in Portugal.

To the Earl of Liverpool. Viseu, 21st March, 1810.

I enclose the last weekly state. There is nothing new. I have no intelligence from Cadiz, and I am apprehensive that the measures for keeping up the communication between that place and Faro, which Adm. Berkeley considered effectual, have entirely failed.

I understand, however, that there was a gale of wind at Cadiz in the beginning of the month, in which one Spanish three-decker, two Spanish and one Portuguese 74, were driven on the side of the harbour in possession of the enemy, and were lost. The men were all saved, and were taken out of the ships by the boats of our fleet. Some merchantmen, American as well as English, and one English transport, having on board 130 men of the 4th foot, were likewise lost: I hear that the men of the 4th foot were made prisoners by the enemy. This is the only advantage the enemy acquired from the effects of this gale, excepting a few boats, as I understand that they burnt all the ships that were cast so far on the shore that our seamen could not reach them.

You cannot conceive how much the want of money distresses us; and I cannot imagine why the Treasury cannot purchase bullion in London, and send it to Lisbon, as well as the merchants, who make an enormous profit by the trade. The government would save much if they could send us money. One of the causes of our distress at present is that the late gales have prevented the packets from arriving at Lisbon; and this consequence of the delay in their arrival, which is invariable, is one proof, among many others, that a most profitable trade is carried on in bullion between Falmouth and Lisbon. I understand, also, that my brother had arrived at Cadiz.

To Brig. Gen. R. Craufurd.   Viseu, 23d March, 1810.

I received this morning your letter of the 20th, informing me of the attack on the post at Barba de Puerco, which I imagine ought to have been dated the 21st, and that the attack was made on the night of the 19th. I beg that you will assure Col. Beckwith,* and the officers and soldiers under his command, that their conduct in this affair has augmented the confidence which I have in the troops, when opposed to the enemy in any situation. If the wounded should be unable to march, you had better send them back to the hospital at Coimbra.

I think that the enemy are not likely to disturb you again at present. They have withdrawn Mortier's corps from its position at Zafra to Monasterio, at the entrance of the Sierra Morena, and it is probable that the corps at Merida will not stay long where it is. Something (but I do not know what, as I have not received a letter from any authority at Cadiz since the 26th of last month) has occurred in Andalusia. We hear of an insurrection in the Sierra de Ronda, and of the collection of a large army under Blake in Murcia. However, it is very obvious, from this movement of Mortier's, that the French are not now prepared for an attack upon this country, which, if they are to make it with any effect, must be made on both sides of the Tagus, and with very large force.

I hope that you will find Mr. Downie, whom I propose to send to you,

* Of the 95th or Rifle brigade; afterwards Lieut. Gen. Sir Sidney Beckwith, K.C.B., Commander in Chief at Bombay, where he died.

G. O.   Viseu, 23d March, 1810.

1. The soldiers of the army are desired not to eat roots, particularly the onions which they find growing wild in the fields, and even in the gardens many of them are poisonous, and a serjeant of the 57th regt. has died of the consequences of eating some of them.

as useful as you expected to find Mr. Ogilvie. The latter has charge of a most important department, which cannot well be made over to another; and nothing but the urgency of the case could have induced the Commissary Gen. to allow him to go to you. You will find Mr. Downie, however, very active and intelligent.

I wish that I could send you some money, but we are in the greatest distress, and what is worse, have no hopes of relief. The late gales have prevented the import of specie into Lisbon from Gibraltar and Cadiz, and the delay of the arrival of the packet as usual prevents the negotiation of bills at Lisbon. To this add that government leave me to my own inventions in this, as well as in other respects. If the money were now at Lisbon, a fortnight would elapse before it could possibly reach the army. But I fear there is no chance.

Is it true, as the Governor of Ciudad Rodrigo informs Gen. Cox, that the enemy have withdrawn from that neighbourhood towards Salamanca again?

The 800 pairs of shoes are gone to Celorico for your division. The Caçadores will be at Celorico, I think, to-morrow. Ten mules are gone to Almeida, to enable you to mount hussars for the communication duty.

To Vice Adm. the Hon. G. Berkeley.   Viseu, 23d March, 1810.

I have had the pleasure of receiving your letter of the 18th inst., and I am much obliged to you for the opinions which you have communicated to me. In every case of the kind which you have discussed, I must consider not only what is desirable, but what is practicable; and I must first look a little at the facts of the case, and consider of the means in my power, or likely to be in my power, of their nature, and of the mode in which they will probably operate in the circumstances which will most probably exist.

In case of the occurrence of a great disaster, it will be no justification for me to say that the plan was that of the Portuguese government, and that I would not oppose it, or that you approved and urged it. In the existing temper of the times, and for *me particularly*, such a justification will not be allowed.

It appears to me that we are all agreed that, although it is desirable, it is not essentially necessary, to hold the left bank of the Tagus; and indeed the great inconvenience which will result from the enemy having possession of that point is that stated in Dom M. Forjaz's letter to me, viz., the facility which it will give them to excite, and the probability that they will succeed in exciting, disturbances in Lisbon. I acknowledge that I had not before contemplated this danger, to which I have given a good deal of thought since he drew my attention to it, and I hope that I shall find means of getting the better of it. It is desirable, however, that we should hold the left bank of the Tagus, and certainly, if possible, the communication between Lisbon and Setuval.

You appear to agree in the statement contained in my letter to Dom M. Forjaz, that I have not the means of occupying that part of the country with regular troops; and that it is not expedient to ask, and that it is probable we should not receive, the assistance of more troops from England. But you think that this ground affords advantages, which, if properly improved, might enable the militia, and other irregular force, to hold it against any attack which might probably be made upon it. As far as I know of that ground, there are three positions upon it: one has its left behind the swamp which is in front of Aldea Galega, and its right at Palmella; or the left might be thrown farther back, probably to Coina. The other is that upon which Col. Fletcher lately reported, and you have his report; and the third is with the right at Traffaria, and the left at Almada. Of these, the first only keeps the communication open with Setuval. There is, I understand, a space of between 4 and 5 miles of plain ground to be occupied in each of these positions, which ground affords no natural means of defence, such as rivers, swamps, mountains, &c.; and these deficiencies must be made good by the resources of art. These are the facts as they relate to the ground; and I will now inform you of those which affect the means by which these positions are to be defended.

In the first place, Dom M. Forjaz has misinformed you respecting their description. He has no disposable militia in that quarter; and, in order to hold Palmella and S. Filippe at Setuval, we are obliged to detach a part of the militia from the north side of the river.

In the next place, he has misinformed you of the numbers of the Ordenanza in that part of Portuguese Estremadura. I doubt if there are 1000 instead of 10,000 armed. But if there were 10,000, even with the assistance of 2 or 3 corps of militia, they could not hold the ground, as it has been reported to me to be, even if strengthened by all the resources of art. The consequence of attempting it would be, that they would be driven in confusion to the river, where there must be means prepared to give them a retreat across the river, a part of which means would inevitably fall into the hands of the enemy.

These considerations, and particularly the last, have created a conviction in my mind that, if it were necessary (whereas it is only desirable) to occupy the left bank of the Tagus, the best mode of occupying it would be on the heights from Traffaria to Almada. The loss of one part of this line would not necessarily occasion the immediate loss of the whole. The people employed to defend it would be more immediately under the eye of those capable of directing them, and timely measures might be adopted to withdraw those whose retreat might be necessary, without the risk that any of the boats would fall into the hands of the enemy. But even this measure is impracticable, on account of the want of men to occupy the ground.

That which I proposed for this part of the country was to occupy Forts S. Filippe and Palmella, and Outaõ, and to make the country between these forts the retreat for the Ordenanza, means of transport, &c. &c., of Portuguese Estremadura, which should be ordered thither. They would then be in the rear of the enemy's corps, which should occupy the ground from Almada to Traffaria; and, at all events, this corps would lose its communications, and would find no subsistence in the country, and could not be able to maintain its position for any length of time. I wish I could do more; but, upon a fair calculation of circumstances, probable events and means, I do not think I can, with propriety, undertake, or do otherwise than give my opinion against undertaking, more.

I think it scandalous that the Portuguese regular army should not be 100,000 instead of 50,000 men; more scandalous that they should want near 10,000 men to complete to 50,000; still more scandalous that they have not means to support even the army which they have; and almost as bad as all the rest that Great Britain should not have been able to send arms and clothing for men as soon as the French have been able to send in their reinforcements of made soldiers, which are now upon our frontier. The means however being, as they are, deficient, I must not undertake what is not necessary with insufficient means.

The French endeavored to surprise one of our posts upon the Agueda on the night of the 19th, occupied by 4 companies of the 95th, under Col. Beckwith; they were repulsed in fine style, with some loss. We lost Lieut. Mercer and 3 men killed, and 10 wounded.

To Brig. Gen. R. Craufurd.   Viseu, 24th March, 1810.

I have received your letter of the 22d. I think you were quite right in occupying Barba de Puerco, under the circumstances in which you did occupy that place, and equally so in withdrawing the troops from thence on the night of the 22d, when there was a prospect that they would be attacked by a very superior force. I also agree with you, and intended to write to apprise you of my opinion, that when the Agueda should become fordable, it would be useless and dangerous to occupy Barba de Puerco. These rains will probably keep the river full for some days longer, and in that case I doubt whether the enemy will remain in Barba de Puerco, even if they should have taken possession of the post when you have withdrawn from it.

Adverting to the nature of the bridge at San Felices, they cannot consider it a very safe post for a small corps, and I should doubt their putting there permanently a large one. I am convinced that their object has been to retaliate the check of the night of the 19th.

By accounts of the 21st from Badajoz, it appears Mortier has gone back even to Sta Olalla, and that Soult's corps has retired from Merida to Truxillo, destroying the works they had commenced in the Conventual. Something has occurred in Andalusia. The French have also drawn in the troops which they had down at Ayamonte. We may depend upon it that they will do nothing in this quarter without threatening us at least also upon the left of the Tagus. They are bringing a battering train into Spain from France, which looks like an intention to go regularly to work.

P.S. Do you keep any cavalry in Barba de Puerco? It might be useful to be as near the French posts as possible, in order to encourage and facilitate desertion.

To Charles Stuart, Esq.   Viseu, 24th March, 1810.

I have received your letters of the 21st. Col. —— ought to have gone to England long ago. When I informed him, finally, that I could not give him employment in this country, I gave him money to pay his expenses to England. He is a very silly fellow, and would be entirely useless; and ought not to be suffered to remain at Lisbon.

I do not think the Portuguese government behave very fairly towards Beresford, in burthening him with the task of punishing those magistrates and others who neglect their duty; nor do I know how Beresford will find time to attend to this business, in such a manner as to perform it effectually, or with that justice which will be necessary for his own character and for that of the country. The alteration required is one of system, and ought to be extended, not only to the superior magistrates, but to their inferiors, and even to the people. The latter should be made to understand that their salvation depends upon their obedience to the law and to the orders of their superiors; and that any the slightest disobedience of either would be severely punished, and some examples ought to be made.

I am glad that Dom M. Forjaz is turning his mind to keeping the town in a state of tranquillity in this critical moment, as he may depend upon it that it is impossible, however desirable it may be, to occupy the left bank of the river. We shall be much pressed for numbers even on the right bank; and it would be the height of folly to extend our posts to the left bank, when it does not appear to be necessary. Till I received Dom M. Forjaz's letter, I admit that I did not contemplate the probable insurrections in the town, which, whether on the right or the wrong side, would be equally fatal to us, and would probably oblige me to withdraw, even though pressed by no other military necessity. Thus the people would be the immediate cause of their own subjugation. I conceive, however, that it will be possible to establish in the town a very vigorous system of police, to be well weighed, considered, and arranged beforehand, to be carried into execution at the critical moment. The foundation of this system should be the existing police, which I believe is very good. The town, if not already divided, might be divided into districts; in each district there should be a person employed under the Lieutenant de Police. A certain number of the married inhabitants of each district, not already belonging to any of the military establishments, should be enrolled to be police constables or soldiers, under the direction of this magistrate or officer, to keep the peace of their own district, in case there should be any disturbances in the town. These persons should be armed, but not paid, unless actually called out and employed under a proclamation by the government. They might then, by patrolling the streets of their district constantly, at all hours of the day or night, prevent assemblies of people in the streets or coffee-houses, where all mischief commences. This is an outline upon which Dom M. Forjaz, who has more local knowledge and ability, might work, and bring out a perfect, and, I hope, a simple and practicable system.

The object and pretence for its establishment at present might be stated to be the movements of the French corps upon the frontier; the probability that Portugal would soon be attacked; and the danger and inconvenience which experience had demonstrated to result from popular commotions in all great towns, particularly in the Peninsula, at the moment the armies were engaged upon the frontiers.

If the government should be of opinion that a letter from me, recommending a measure of this description to their consideration, would at all strengthen their hands in carrying it into execution, I will write such a one.

P.S. I have received a letter from the Portuguese government about their money, in which I see they talk of receiving £980,000 sterling a year from the King. I observe they mention the same sum in their letter to you. Now the sum they are to receive in payment for 30,000 men, according to their estimate of the expense of 10,000 given to Mr. Villiers, which, as well as I recollect that estimate, amounts to about, but not quite, £750,000 *per annum;* and £130,000 *per annum* for the expense of increasing the pay of the officers of the army; make a total of £880,000 *per annum.* Besides this, there is a sum of £100,000 *per annum* for the pay and allowances of the British officers lent to Portugal, who are paid from the chest of the 'Aids.' The Portuguese government ought not to touch or to reckon upon this sum as a part of their resources, although Great Britain may fairly, and does reckon it as an aid to Portugal. The sum should remain in the chest of the 'Aids,' to defray the charge of the pay and allowances of the British officers, for which it is given, and who are paid directly from the chest.

I mention this error to you, lest you should not yourself have adverted to it.

To Brig. Gen. R. Craufurd.   Viseu, 26th March, 1810.

I received last night your letter of the 23d. By this time you will have been joined by the 2 battalions of the caçadores, and will be the best judge what to do with them. I believe that Beresford had attached to them Baron Eben, whom you will find a useful officer; but I am not quite certain whether it was to them or to 2 other battalions. You will find the officer who commands the first battalion a very respectable one. The 2d battalion is not so well commanded at present, but Beresford proposes to attach to it Major Nixon, of the 28th regt., who has served in the light infantry, and who has been placed under his orders.

I find, from intercepted letters, that the French are endeavoring to bring up from France, to some station in advance of Burgos (I suppose Valladolid), a battering train. If they should get up a train, they may as well, and, indeed, if I were in their situation, I should prefer to begin by an attack upon Almeida to one upon Ciudad Rodrigo. This deserves attention. In what state is Castel Rodrigo? Can Castello Bom be made a *tête de pont* for a short time?

G. O.   Viseu, 25th March, 1810.

The Commander of the Forces requests that the officers commanding regiments will draw the attention of the soldiers under their command to this example of the consequences of the disgraceful outrages of which too many of the soldiers of this army have been guilty.

The Commander of the Forces repeats his determination to spare no trouble to procure and produce evidence against those who may be guilty of such outrages, and to carry into execution invariably whatever may be the sentence of the Court Martial. His Excellency particularly requests the commanding officers of regiments to revert to the G. O., and to draw the attention of the officers and non-commissioned officers under their command to those orders which have for their object to prevent the commission of those crimes, and to render unnecessary these dreadful punishments, by the preservation of order and regularity among the soldiers, on their marches, in their quarters, and particularly on detachments.

P. S. I should prefer horses to mules for the communication service. But unfortunately we have no money to buy horses at present.

To Brig. Gen. R. Craufurd.   Viseu, 27th March, 1810.

Your letter of the 25th, which I have just received, renders it unnecessary that I should say much in answer to that of the 24th.

Mr. Ogilvie has really business with the head quarters of the army which another could not perform for him; and I am glad to find that you are pleased with the appointment of Mr. Downie. In order that he may be at the head of the department with your division, Mr. Drake is to be relieved by Mr. Purcell, of whom the Commissary Gen. understands that you have a good opinion. Mr. Drake is the senior Assist. Commissary with the army. The Portuguese troops have with them a Commissary, but I imagine that they will require assistance from Mr. Downie, upon which subject he will be instructed.

In respect to the communication, I wish it to be as follows in future: viz., every thing to go from Almeida to Celorico, and from Celorico to Guarda, Trancoso, and head quarters respectively. Orders will go from the Adj. Gen.'s office upon this subject. I shall write by this dispatch to recommend Mr. M'Diarmid for promotion.

I have letters from Cadiz as late as the 17th: all quiet there; but they had at that time no accounts of the insurrection in the Sierra de Ronda. They had made a sortie from one part of the Isla de Leon on the 15th, and had made demonstrations for a general attack upon the enemy's posts on the same morning, which would have been made if the surf had not prevented Gen. Stewart from embarking a part of his corps. I believe that this attack is the real cause of the detachments which have been made into Andalusia from the corps in Estremadura. Nothing has been done yet on the north of the Douro.

To Major Gen. the Hon. W. Stewart.   Viseu, 27th March, 1810.

I have had the honor of receiving your letters of the 11th, and 2 of the 17th.

When an officer is detached from the army in command of a body of troops on a particular service, he must be the best judge of the organization which will suit his purpose. I do not object, therefore, to the organization which you have detailed in your letter of the 11th; although, in general, I disapprove of detaching flank companies from the battalion to which they belong, and I have not allowed of such detachments in this army.

A Brigade Major appears to me to be a necessary appointment in Cadiz, the troops under your command being in 2 bodies.

Lord FitzRoy Somerset has written to the A. A. G. respecting the appointment of an officer to be your secretary; but I shall be obliged to you if you will let me know in what manner, and for what purpose, the appointment is thought necessary by the Assist. Commissary, and by the Assist. Paymaster Gen. detached with you.

I refer you to my letter of the 27th Feb. respecting payment for the fresh meat.

I beg that you will draw a table allowance of 30*s.* a day while you command at Cadiz.

The sum fixed in this army is 9*d. per diem,* to be stopped from the pay of the soldiers in hospital throughout the whole army, as you will observe by the enclosed letter from the War office: it is necessary, therefore, that you should fix the stoppage at 9*d.* in the detachment under your command.

I am concerned to observe that the Spanish troops make no progress in their discipline; and that they are not better in that respect, or improved in efficiency, since you went to Cadiz. I am afraid that much time will elapse before any considerable improvement will be made in the state of these troops, or before several other measures will be adopted by the Spanish government, which are expedient, and even necessary, in the existing situation of their affairs. We must not be discouraged, however, by these untoward circumstances. I have but little doubt that the Spanish troops, bad as their appearance and discipline are, will do their duty in fortified positions; and even if they were worse than they are, and the difficulties of all kinds with which we have to contend were greater than they are, the interests of Great Britain and the world are too deeply involved in this contest for us to recede one step from it, which may not be rendered absolutely necessary by circumstances.

The affairs of the Peninsula have invariably had the same appearance since I have known them; they have always appeared to be lost; means have always appeared inadequate to objects; and the sole dependence of the whole has apparently been upon us. The contest, however, still continues, and is in its third year; and we must continue it as long as we can with the means which the country affords, improving them as much as the people will allow us, as it is obvious that Great Britain cannot give us larger means than we have.

I beg leave to refer you to Mr. Wellesley for an account of the state of affairs in this quarter.

To the Rt. Hon. H. Wellesley.   Viseu, 27th March, 1810.

Since I wrote to you on the 21st, I have received your letters of the 9th and 16th. I was pretty well aware of the state of the Spanish army, but the account you give of the government is not encouraging. However, they can scarcely lose Cadiz at present; and if the measures which I recommended in my letter to Gen. Stewart, of the 27th of last month, are adopted, the French will never be able to get possession of that place.

Since my last, there has been no material alteration in the enemy's position on this side of the Tagus. It is reported by the French that they have taken Astorga by storm, with great loss; but I have not heard of this event from any authority, and I have correspondents in that quarter. The French corps on the Guadiana broke up on the 18th; and that under Mortier marched towards Monasterio, and S^(ta) Olalla in the Sierra Morena; and the other corps which was at Merida retired towards Truxillo. The Marques de la Romana writes me that this movement was occasioned by a serious insurrection in the Sierra de Ronda; that the King, being at Malaga, was surrounded by insurgents, and that he could extricate himself from this situation with difficulty. I should think that affairs could not

be in this state in a part of Andalusia so near to Cadiz, without the knowledge of the Regency. Yet it appears from your letter of the 16th that
nothing was known of this insurrection at Cadiz on that day.

The Marques de la Romana has ordered the *partidas* of Estremadura,
and the right division of his army, under Ballesteros, to follow Mortier
through the Sierra Morena, and to do him as much mischief as may be in
their power. We hear also a great deal of Blake's army in the Alpujarras,
and of a corps from Valencia, operating upon the enemy's communications
with Madrid. But I conclude that there is as little foundation for this
intelligence as for that relating to the insurrection in the Sierra de
Ronda.

When I heard of Mortier's march to the southward, I was in hopes that
something had occurred in Andalusia. If nothing has occurred in that
quarter, they are about to endeavor to press you more closely at Cadiz,
or possibly they are desirous of dispersing Blake's corps in the Alpujarras.
Even with the addition of Mortier's corps, however, to the force near
Cadiz, they cannot hurt that place. I wish that I could be equally certain
of the security of Blake. In the mean time the departure of the French
troops from Estremadura has been a great relief to us in this quarter, and
will give the people in Badajoz, and the Marques de la Romana, time for
further preparations.

I am clearly of opinion that we ought to remove from Cadiz in particular, and from the harbours in the Peninsula in general, every Spanish
ship of war. I was of opinion that they ought to be sent to Mahon; and
I recommended that Minorca in particular, of the Balearic Islands, should
be secured. This opinion was founded upon a notion, 1st, that the Regency had some power, and some means at their disposal ; 2dly, that they
would experience no difficulty in raising the men necessary to secure the
Balearic Islands; and 3dly, that Minorca, in particular, could not be
injured as long as we held the naval superiority in the Mediterranean.
This opinion was in some degree shaken before I received your letters,
by learning accidentally that Lord Collingwood was adverse to sending
the fleet to Minorca, although the reason was not stated; and I now recommend to you to get rid of fleet and prisoners as you can. Let them
go where they please, but do not allow them to remain in Cadiz. I
doubted of Mahon for the prisoners, as I was apprehensive that the garrison would not be sufficiently strong. The same objection would apply
to Ceuta. England is the only safe place for the prisoners.

Whether the fleet is, or is not sent to Minorca, the security of the Balearic Islands is a consideration of the utmost importance, which must not
be lost sight of. You and I (I probably more than you) will be considered responsible for every thing that occurs, although we have no means
in our power, and no power to enforce the execution of what is necessary.
It is desirable that we should advert to every thing, and should recommend
to the consideration of the Spanish government those measures which
appear to us to be necessary. Accordingly, I suggest to you to pass a
note to the Regency, recommending to their serious attention the security
of the Balearic Islands, Minorca particularly : they should send there, in
the first instance, the Viscomte de Gand's corps which is now in Algarve:

they should besides endeavor to raise men in Cadiz, where, by proper measures, they could get thousands.

I shall write to the Marques de la Romana upon this subject, in which he is personally interested, and will suggest to him the expediency of sending 2000 or 3000 men to these Islands; and I will engage to send these men from Lisbon to Cadiz, if means can be found at Cadiz for their further progress. I should think that Blake's army ought not if possible to be weakened. It is a great object to the general cause to preserve it.

In respect to Cadiz itself, the object of the works, the plan and construction of which I recommended in my letter to Gen. Stewart, is to give security to the Isla, employing in its defence a smaller body of men than would be necessary for its security if there were no works. It must be obvious to every body, that if 25,000 men were required for the defence and security of the Isla when not completely fortified, fewer would be necessary if good works should be constructed. But, in truth, when the Spaniards in the Isla shall be attacked in earnest, they will not be able to hold a moment, unless the troops are placed in good works. When I said that Capt. Landmann might be sure of having a sufficient number of men to place in them, I adverted in my own mind to the probable period at which the attack would be made, and to the certainty that as many men as could be required might be raised at Cadiz. It is quite new to my mind that the Spaniards will not make the exertion which is necessary to enable them to defend this important place, with the assistance which I have been able to give them. In respect to further assistance, although ordered to secure Cadiz in a manner which makes me in a measure responsible for the safety of that place, as if nothing was required in Cadiz but British soldiers, I can send no more with propriety.

Those who see the difficulties attending all communications with Spaniards and Portuguese, and are aware how little dependence can be placed upon them, and that they depend entirely upon us for every thing, will be astonished that, with so small a force as I have, I should have been able to maintain myself so long in this country. I certainly should not be able to stay, if I were to weaken it any further; and yet, if I should go from this country, Cadiz would not hold out a month, even if I were to take there a great part of the British army. The French might and could collect there their whole force; and then the serious attack would be made, and the place would really be in danger.

I do not think that Gen. Stewart will be able to hold the Matagorda long; and I have always considered it probable that the enemy would have it in his power to command the communication between the inner and outer harbours, and to prevent us from using it. We ought, therefore, at once to provide for this event by the following measures :

1st; To prepare and establish in the inner harbour all the gun and other vessels which would be necessary for the operations of defence within it.

2dly; To secure the Puntales, and the landing places from the left of the Cortadura to the works of the town.

3dly; To have a good road of communication from the right of the Cortadura along the Isthmus by the right of the existing road.

If there should have been really an insurrection in the Sierra de Ronda, and the French should have been obliged to quit their position before Cadiz, I hope that Gen. Stewart will have seized the peninsula of Trocadero, and endeavored to secure that point by the time the French will return again.

Long before the French passed the Sierra Morena, I desired Gen. Whittingham * to suggest to Venegas to consider of and let us know what naval assistance would be required from Great Britain, particularly of water vessels and of victuallers. This will become most important hereafter when Cadiz shall be seriously attacked. The French will then occupy every point upon the coast, and cut off the supply of provisions, which must be sent for to a great distance; and they will be supplied only by great exertions and arrangements, and by very extensive means. All these matters deserve your attention, and you should suggest them officially. In the existing temper of the times, the loss of this place will be set down to our account, however little is in our power; and we must forget nothing.

P.S. I omitted to tell you that the French attacked one of our posts on the Agueda, occupied by 4 companies of the 95th, on the night of the 19th, and were repulsed with loss. All has been quiet since.

I am astonished at the conduct of the Regency towards ——, who will always be the enemy of the English influence. But I conclude that what has been said, and even done, is only compliment; that they have been urged to it by his friend —— ; and that he will be without employment or influence. It is not worth while to notice this transaction.

To the Earl of Liverpool.   Viseu, 28th March, 1810.

The enemy's corps which I informed you, in my letter of the 14th inst., were in Estremadura, broke up on the 18th inst.; and that commanded by Marshal Mortier went to the southward towards the pass of Monasterio and Sᵗᵃ Olalla in the Sierra Morena; and that of Soult, which was at Merida, retired upon Truxillo. The former was followed by the right divisions of the Marques de la Romana's corps which had been posted at Xerez de los Caballeros, at Olivença, and at Valverde. The left of this corps still continue at Campo Maior and Alburquerque. This movement is supposed to have been occasioned by an insurrection in the Sierra de Ronda; and it has been reported that King Joseph was at Malaga, and all communication with him cut off by the insurgents. I have accounts from Cadiz, however, to as late a date as the 17th of this month, which do not notice these events.

A gale of wind had done much mischief at Cadiz in the early part of this month, of which His Majesty's government will have received the details from His Majesty's minister.

The enemy are not in great strength in the neighbourhood of Cadiz, and appear principally employed in strengthening their own positions, and in establishing themselves upon the peninsula of Trocadero, with an intention to dispossess our troops of the fort of Matagorda, which is situated at the point of that peninsula, and the possession of which gives the command of the communication between the inner and outer harbour.

* See page 660.

Major Gen. Stewart informs me that he had intended to endeavor to dislodge the enemy from their position on the peninsula on the 15th inst., and to destroy the means of attack upon Matagorda which they had prepared, and the buildings which had afforded them cover and facilities in pushing it forward. The surf in the western bay of Puntales had prevented him from embarking there, and a shoal in the eastern bay had delayed the passage over to the Trocadero for such a length of time, that it would have been imprudent to persevere in the attack, which he therefore relinquished. Other attacks were, however, to be made, connected with, and as a diversion of the enemy's attention from this; among others, one upon their posts at S^{ti} Petri, by some Spanish light troops and 4 companies of the 79th regt. under Major Sullivan. The enemy's outposts were driven in, in this quarter. I enclose the report of Major Sullivan to Major Gen. Stewart, with the return of the loss upon this occasion.

If there has been no insurrection in the Sierra de Ronda, it is probable that these preparations and movements on the Isla de Leon and at Cadiz have been the cause of the march of the troops from Estremadura.

The addition of Mortier's corps, however, to the enemy's troops already in the neighbourhood of Cadiz will not enable the enemy to make any serious attack upon the positions on the Isla; and its removal from Estremadura relieves me for the present from all uneasiness respecting the fate of Badajoz, and the other forts in that neighbourhood.

The corps of the Duc d'Abrantes, which is supposed to be composed of about 20,000 men, is in the kingdom of Leon, and threatens Astorga, where there is a Spanish garrison. They had made no attack upon that place as late as the 18th. The French have also a division in the Asturias, which was in possession of Oviedo, Gijon, &c., and had pushed forward towards the frontiers of Galicia. The French corps under the command of Marshal Ney, and that under Loison, and Kellermann's corps, are in Old Castille, and in the same positions on the Tormes, with their advanced posts upon the Agueda.

The advanced posts of the British army, under Brig. Gen. Craufurd, are likewise upon the Agueda, and between that river and the Coa. The French attacked the post at Barba de Puerco, which was occupied by 4 companies of the 95th regt. under Lieut. Col. Beckwith, on the night of the 19th inst. Immediately opposite to Barba de Puerco, on the other side of the river, is San Felices, and between these 2 villages the only bridge on the Agueda below Ciudad Rodrigo; and the recent fall of rain had filled the river, which was no where fordable. The enemy had collected a brigade of infantry at San Felices; and crossed the bridge with 600 men after dark, keeping the remainder on the other side. These followed the piquet of the 95th up from the bridge, and immediately made their attack; but they were repulsed with the loss of 2 officers and 7 men killed, 6 prisoners, and 30 firelocks.

I am sorry to add that Lieut. Mercer of the 95th and 3 men were killed, and 10 were wounded, in this affair, which was highly creditable to Col. Beckwith, and displayed the gallantry and discipline of the officers and troops under his command. The adjutant, Lieut. Stewart, distinguished himself.

To the Rt. Hon. the Commander in Chief.   Viseu, 28th March, 1810.

I have the honor to enclose an extract of my dispatch of this date, to the Sec. of State, giving an account of an attack made by the enemy on the post of Barba de Puerco, occupied by 4 companies of the 95th regt., under Lieut. Col. Beckwith.

I take the liberty of recommending Lieut. and Adj. Stewart to your notice, who distinguished himself on this occasion. I also beg leave to recommend Lieut. M'Diarmid, the senior lieutenant, for promotion.

To the Earl of Liverpool.   Viseu, 28th March, 1810.

I have but little to add to my dispatch of this date.

I have very bad accounts of the Regency at Cadiz, upon which subject, however, I conclude my brother will have sent to government full intelligence.

I enclose to you the copy of a letter which I have received from Col. Roche, which contains a curious account of the flight and dispersion of Areyzaga's army, and their consequences in the different parts of Spain through which he passed, and of the state of affairs at Cadiz. I must do Roche the justice to say that he has invariably transmitted to me the most correct accounts of transactions; that his opinions have always been judicious; and he has been of no party. The packets have not yet arrived, and our distress for money is very great.

The A.G. to Major Gen. the Hon. G. L. Cole.   29th March, 1810.

I have had the honor to receive and submit your letter to the Commander of the Forces. In consequence of the favorable representation therein contained, his Excellency consents to the charges preferred against Assist. Surgeon ——, —— regt., and now returned, being withdrawn, in the expectation that the lenity of his superior and of his commanding officer will have due effect upon him, and induce that officer to attend to his duty more strictly in future.

To Brig. Gen. R. Craufurd.   Viseu, 30th March, 1810.

I have received your letter of the 26th and 27th. I enclose a letter for Gen. Carrera, in which I have requested him to communicate with you. I beg you to observe, however, that very little reliance can be placed on the report made to you by any Spanish General officer at the head of a body of troops. They generally exaggerate on one side or the other, and make no scruple of communicating supposed intelligence, in order to induce those to whom they communicate it to adopt a certain line of conduct. The movement of the French through the Puerto de Baños has been probably occasioned by their desire to oblige Carrera to fall back, and a wish to confine Ciudad Rodrigo on that side. They will find it difficult to cross the Alagon, or to make any impression on that side.

The communication from you to Celorico is very slow. I did not receive your letter of the 27th till last night. It ought to have reached me the night before, at which time only I received that of the 26th. We know that the letters are only 8 hours from Celorico to Viseu, and that on this side of Celorico it is sufficiently regular. Will you be so kind as to have it arranged from Almeida to Celorico? It should go from Almeida at such an hour every morning as to arrive at Celorico by 12 o'clock.

You will see the news from England. The ministers hold out still, but I think they cannot last long.

To Charles Stuart, Esq. Viseu, 30th March, 1810.

I have received your 3 letters of the 26th. I understand that you will send a packet on Sunday, April 1st, for which I have already sent my letters; another on the 5th, for which I will send letters which shall be at Lisbon on Wednesday night; and a third on Monday, 9th April.

The want of provisions at Cadiz is very distressing, more particularly as the Spaniards have made no arrangement to procure a supply. I told Venegas, as long ago as last December, that he ought to advert to the probability that he would be attacked at an early period, and let us know in time what assistance would be required from us in victuallers, water vessels, and other naval means. If they have money and ships to send for grain, Malta can supply their wants with ease.

I don't understand the arrangement which government have made of the command of the troops there. I have hitherto considered them as part of this army, and from the arrangement I made with the Spanish government, they cost us nothing but their pay; and all the money procured at Cadiz for bills was applicable to the service in this country. Their instructions to Gen. Graham alter this entirely; and they have even gone so far as to desire him to take measures to supply the Spaniards with provisions from the Mediterranean, whereas I had insisted that they should feed, and they do actually feed our troops. The first consequence of this arrangement will be, that we shall have no more money from Cadiz. I had considered the troops at Cadiz so much a part of this army, that I had written to my brother to desire to have his opinion whether, if the French withdrew from Cadiz when they should attack Portugal, he thought I might bring into Portugal at least those troops which I had sent there. But I consider this now to be out of the question.

P.S. I have desired that you may have at least half of the 500,000 dollars that came out.

To the Rt. Hon. H. Wellesley. Viseu, 30th March, 1810.

Since I wrote to you on the 27th, I have received accounts from England to the 15th inst., and I have heard that Gen. Graham * is appointed to command at Cadiz. You will find Gen. Graham a most able and active officer, who, I am convinced, will be very desirous to co-operate with you in every thing for the public service. I beg, however, that you will tell Gen. Stewart that the arrangement which has been made for the command at Cadiz was not proposed by me.

There is nothing new since I wrote to you last. I have heard from a person at Alcañices that he had not been able to communicate with Astorga the day before. He does not, however, think that the place is closely invested, but rather that the person he had sent did not adopt the mode to communicate with the place in which he would have succeeded.

The French have passed a division through the Puerto de Baños, by which they have obliged Carrera to retire from Coria across the Alagon.

* The late Lord Lynedoch, G.C.B.

They talk of a part of Mortier's corps, about 1000 men, being caught between 2 of the streams in the Sierra Morena, which had swollen; and being cut off by the guerrillas of Romana's corps, which I do not believe. They also talk of the army of Valencia and Murcia being at Tarancon, in the neighbourhood of Madrid, which I equally discredit.

To the Earl of Liverpool. Viseu, 30th March, 1810.

I have received your letter of the 20th Feb., conveying a copy of your instructions to Gen. Graham, which I acknowledge I think likely to produce confusion at Cadiz, and some difficulties between this army and the corps at Cadiz, and much inconvenience here, unless the General should lay them aside entirely, and in the mean time act upon those which I have given to Gen. W. Stewart.

I enclose a memorandum,* &c., upon the instructions, with the copy of them, with the paragraphs numbered, which will point out the questions that occur to me upon them. I request you to send me your answer to this memorandum; and if I should find that the system which Gen. Graham and I shall have followed is not inconsistent with your Lordship's intentions, I can either alter it or not, as may appear most beneficial to His Majesty's service.

To the Earl of Liverpool. Viseu, 30th March, 1810.

Since I wrote to you on the 28th, I have received your letters to the 13th. I am fully aware of the mutual hatred of the Spanish and Portuguese people towards each other; and you may depend upon it that I adverted to that circumstance when I considered of the propriety of sending to Cadiz a Portuguese regiment. From experience of the manner in which the service of Portuguese troops was received in other Spanish garrisons, I did not consider it probable that this hatred was likely to affect the reception of the Portuguese regiment at Cadiz; and having that regiment at my disposal at the moment a garrison was wanted for Cadiz, I did not think it proper to allow the consideration of the hatred of these nations towards each other to deprive the cause of this timely assistance.

The enclosed letter from Mr. Duff, who generally participates in the feelings of the Spaniards, will show your Lordship that I was not mistaken upon this occasion; and the publications of the day at Cadiz, if they can be supposed to speak the public sentiment, agree in the same opinion. Since that time, all the letters I have received from Cadiz mention the Portuguese troops in terms of praise; but if Gen. Graham should think it better to send them away, I shall be glad to have them again.

To Lieut. Col. Torrens, Military Secretary. Viseu, 31st March, 1810.

I have received your letter of the 7th, and I am very much obliged to the Commander in Chief for the appointment of Pakenham, and for sending us the reinforcements you have stated. I understand that the 9th and Royals have arrived at Lisbon.

I am also much obliged to you for recollecting my wishes in favor of Campbell. I am very anxious for his promotion, which the Duke of York certainly intended he should have.

* This memorandum is not in the Colonial office.

I can give you no news. The French threaten us on all points, and are most desirous to get rid of us. But they threaten upon too many points at a time to give me much uneasiness respecting any one in particular, and they shall not induce me to disconnect my army. I am in a situation in which no mischief can be done to the army, or to any part of it; I am prepared for all events; and if I am in a scrape, as appears to be the general belief in England, although certainly not my own, I'll get out of it.

To Brig. Gen. Cox, Governor of Almeida.   Viseu, 1st April, 1810.

I request you to pay Señor Echevarria all the expenses which he has incurred for the encouragement of desertion from the French army, and for the support of deserters, and to tell him that I request him to encourage desertion by the following measures. Let him send trusty persons to assure soldiers in the French army, induced to desert, that they shall be received here and treated in every respect as British soldiers; that their arms and horses, if they should bring them, shall be bought from them and paid for; that they shall have their option of enlisting into the British service or not; that if they choose to enlist, they shall receive a bounty and shall have the choice of enlisting into any of the foreign corps with this army, or in England; and that, if they do not choose to enlist, measures shall be taken to send them out of the Peninsula, and to facilitate their return to their own country.

I request that all deserters may be sent to the head quarters of the army, and all expenses incurred on their account shall be paid.

To Brig. Gen. Alex. Campbell.   Viseu, 1st April, 1810.

I have received your letter of the 31st March. The War office appoint the agents of the corps called ' foreign corps,' of which I believe yours is one. Ferguson contested this point with the War office, respecting the Sicilian regiment, of which he is Colonel, and he could not succeed. I recommend to you therefore to submit, and ask for your augmentation. No less than 46 deserters have come in since you left this.

Sherbrooke knows something on the subject of the agency of foreign corps, and I will speak to him upon your letter, if I should see him this morning. In the mean time, you might write to your agent to desire him to inquire whether your regiment is called a ' foreign corps.'

P.S. I have spoken to Gen. Sherbrooke, who agrees with me: he says that he has been informed that some Colonels of foreign corps, being British subjects, have appointed their own agents, but he did not find out an instance, and he submitted in the case of the Sicilian regiment: the question is, is yours a foreign corps? We think it is not, as Greenwood was the agent; Disney is the agent for foreign corps.

To Lieut. Gen. Hill.   Viseu, 1st April, 1810.

I have received your letter of the 26th March. We have not more cavalry than is required for the service of the British army, and I cannot allow it to be employed separately from the other troops.

To Vice Adm. the Hon. G. Berkeley.   Viseu, 1st April, 1810.

I am very much obliged to you for your letter of the 25th March.

The alteration of the arrangement for the command at Cadiz, and the orders given by government to send to Lisbon all the transports, which in my opinion they might as well have left to us, render it impossible to draw any part of the corps from thence, whatever may be our necessities. I do not find that the government have sent any hospital ships, notwithstanding my request ; and I shall therefore be much obliged to you if you will allow the fitting up of the number you mention (6) to be continued.

I have not yet heard from Col. Fletcher about the telegraph, since he spoke to you.   I am much obliged to you for the plan for the Portuguese troops.   It will be very useful to them.

To Charles Stuart, Esq.   Viseu, 1st April, 1810.

I have received your letter of the 28th March.   In respect to the Patriarch's prosposal to divide the Kingdom into districts, it is my opinion that the Kingdom is already divided in a very convenient manner ; the magistrates are fully sufficient for the performance of the duty required of them ; the laws and regulations are excellent ; and all that is required is to put the whole in motion, and to carry the laws into execution.   I can have no objection to give Beresford any power ; on the contrary, the greater the power he has, the better it will be for the public service : but, for his own sake, I should think it better to leave the execution of the laws in the hands of the ordinary magistrates.   Settle it, however, in any way you think best.

I agree with you respecting the existing disposition of the inhabitants of Lisbon.   In fact, all they wish for is to be saved from the French : they were riotous last winter, because they imagined, and with some reason, that we intended to abandon them ; and they became quiet as soon as they found that a different system was adopted, and about to be acted upon.   These facts would however lead to a conclusion that they would become riotous if they saw the enemy on the left of the Tagus, and heard of him at no great distance on the right of that river, knowing that we had made all our arrangements to embark.   The riots and insurrections of the town of Lisbon can never do us any good ; and I am therefore anxious that the system which I had proposed to you should be organised.

I have desired that you may have half the money come from England. The arrangement made by government for the command of Cadiz will totally ruin us in the way of money.

Has Lord Wellesley written to you respecting preparations to be made by the government for embarking ?

I shall send off the messenger with the letters for England to-morrow evening, and he will be at Lisbon in the evening or early in the night of Wednesday.   I enclose a letter from Col. ——.

To Lieut. Gen. Hill.   Viseu, 2d April, 1810.

I received last night your letter of the 30th March.   The enemy's detachment which had moved through the Puerto de Baños has retired again into Castille ; and I am convinced that the only object of its movement into Estremadura was to oblige Gen. Carrera to withdraw from Coria, which he did.

I can't understand what advantage the French can derive from the possession of Alcantara, the bridge over the Tagus being irreparably destroyed. It is the worst ferry on the river; I do not believe a gun could get to the boat on either side, which boat is very small, and could not contain 2 horses. The reports which you have on the Portuguese frontier, south of the Tagus, will show you that, the bridge of Alcantara being destroyed, the enemy could not pitch upon a more inconvenient place than that from whence to make their movements; and it is the worst position that they could take for any other purpose: a small corps could not retreat from it.

My opinion is, that they have taken their position at Caceres because they could get no provisions at Truxillo, and because they found they could do so without inconvenience and in safety, as the Marques de la Romana had detached a part of his corps to the Sierra Morena. My opinion therefore is, that the position of the enemy at Caceres has nothing to say to yours or to the Portuguese frontier. It is possible, however, as the Marques de la Romana says, that the position of the enemy at Caceres may annoy the town of Badajoz, in the safety of which we are much interested, and the position of the corps under his command. If you should find this to be really the case, I have no objection to your showing yourself beyond the Sierra, if you should be of opinion that your doing so will be of any advantage to them, and will not be inconvenient to your own troops.

You see what the opinion of people in England is of affairs here. My instructions so far concur with the general sentiment as to forbid any risk, or any unnecessary loss; and you will attend to that in any movement which you may make.

In respect to the relief of Col. Wilson, Marshal Beresford found it necessary to bring the Lusitanian legion, of which Col. Wilson is the commanding officer, out of the mountains, with a view to their discipline; and they are replaced by another regiment; and Col. Le Cor now commands in that part. You will find him equally active and intelligent with Col. Wilson; but you must write to him in French. Communicate with him as soon as you can.

To the Earl of Liverpool.   Viseu, 2d April, 1810.

I have received your letter of the 13th March, and I am much obliged to you for the consideration you have given to our situation in this country, and your discussion of the subject.

The great disadvantage under which I labor is, that Sir J. Moore, who was here before me, gave an opinion that this country could not be defended by the army under his command; and, although it is obvious that the country was in a very different situation at that time from what it is at present; that I am in a very different situation from that in which he found himself; and that, moreover, it can be proved, from the marches and operations of the army under Sir J. Moore, and his dispatches, that little was known of Portugal at that time; yet persons, who ought to be acquainted with these facts, entertain a prejudice against the adoption of any plans for opposing the enemy, of which Portugal is to be the theatre, or its means the instrument, and will not even consider them. I have as much respect as any man can have for the opinion and judgment of Sir J. Moore; and I should mistrust my own, if opposed to his, in a case which he had had an opportunity of knowing and considering. But he positively knew nothing of Portugal, and could know nothing of its existing state. Besides this prejudice, founded on Sir J. Moore's opinion, there is another very general prejudice against any military operation in the Peninsula.

My opinion is, that as long as we shall remain in a state of activity in Portugal, the contest must continue in Spain; that the French are most desirous that we should withdraw from the country, but know that they must employ a very large force indeed in the operations which will render it necessary for us to go away; and I doubt whether they can bring that force to bear upon Portugal without abandoning other objects, and exposing their whole fabric in Spain to great risk. If they should be able to invade it, and should not succeed in obliging us to evacuate the country, they will be in a very dangerous situation; and the longer we can oppose them, and delay their success, the more likely are they to suffer materially in Spain.

All the preparations for embarking and carrying away the army, and every thing belonging to it, are already made, and my intention is to embark it, as soon as I find that a military necessity exists for so doing. I shall delay the embarkation as long as it is in my power, and shall do every thing in my power to avert the necessity of embarking at all. If the enemy should invade this country with a force less than that which I should think so superior to ours as to create the necessity for embarking, I shall fight a battle to save the country, for which I have made the preparations; and if the result should not be successful, of which I have no doubt, I shall still be able to retire and embark the army. In short, the whole of my conduct shall be guided by a fair and cool view of the circumstances of our situation at the moment, and a reference to your Lordship's instructions of the 27th Feb. (A).

I had considered that a doubt might exist of the policy of bringing matters to extremities in this country, and I had brought that subject under the view of the King's government in my dispatches of the 31st Jan. and 9th Feb., to which your Lordship's answer of 27th Feb. is clear and distinct; and I understand from that letter, that if there exists a military necessity for it, I am to evacuate the country; and if there does not exist a military necessity for it, I am not to evacuate the country: in which last understanding is included, of course, the other understanding, that I am not to be frightened away by a force which I shall not consider to be superior to that which I shall have under my command. Your Lordship will observe that, in this plan, there is no intention or desire to attempt a desperate resistance. Am I right in understanding that I am not to quit the country, unless pressed by a force which I shall consider superior to that which I shall have to oppose to the enemy? If I am right, I may be obliged to bring matters to extremities; and I shall now show you, that whatever may be the nature of our operations, or the mode or period at which we shall evacuate Portugal, I have not mistaken the place of embarkation.

Upon reference to the enclosures in my dispatch of 14th Nov., your Lordship will find a discussion on the relative advantage and disadvantage of embarking the army at different places in Portugal, in a letter to Adm. Berkeley; and you will see that it is distinctly stated that the contest for Lisbon and the Tagus cannot be brought to extremities, without giving up all thoughts of embarking at Peniche. I might have said that, connected with an embarkation at Peniche, it cannot be brought to extremities at all with any advantage, as it is obvious that the battle would be fought after Lisbon and the Tagus would be lost, the heart of the country, that alone which is an object to either party, the only point by which we could communicate with England as an army, or the Portuguese with Brazil as a nation.

If I am to bring the question of evacuation to extremities at all, it is therefore obvious that I must preserve the communication with Lisbon, and must give up all thoughts of embarking at Peniche. But I think I am not wrong in my choice of S. Julian, even though I ought not to bring matters to extremities. The government may determine that, not bringing matters to extremities, I shall embark at an early period; or that I shall stay as long as I can, going at last, when the enemy shall move into the country with a force which I shall think so superior to that under my command as to oblige me to evacuate.

In the first case there is no question; all places are alike, S. Julian is as good as Peniche and Oporto, the Mondego and Setuval as good as either. In the second case I must observe, that your Lordship is misinformed of the nature of the position of S. Julian; and I think you have received your information upon the relative strength of these places, and their relative advantage as places of embarkation, from some of those persons who have never considered the subject, and probably have never even looked at either place.

If the weather should prevent the army from embarking at S. Julian, the troops will be in a position from whence nothing could force them. They could withdraw from it the rear guard to the last man, being protected by the works which have been constructed, which are of a strength not to be taken, except by a regular attack. S. Julian, however, is not so strong as Peniche; but the difference in the relative strength of these positions is not sufficient to compensate for other disadvantages in adopting Peniche as a place of embarkation.

In the 1st place; Whether matters are to be brought to extremities or not, we must have our stores and our hospital at Lisbon, and all our communication with Lisbon to the last moment. Peniche has neither the means of giving cover to what we have, nor of providing transports for their removal to the army when wanted; nor are the communications with Peniche sufficiently good to answer the purposes of the constant supply of the army. If we could find cover for all that we have at Peniche, the removal of our stores from Lisbon to that place would soon discover our object, the effect of which discovery would be felt in the conduct of friends as well as of enemies.

2dly; If Peniche is to be used as the place of embarkation for the whole army at the last moment, it must immediately be stored with provisions to provide for the contingency of the weather not suffering the army to quit the place, which is, I assure you, at least as probable at Peniche as it is in the Tagus.

3dly; Adverting to the necessity of keeping a corps upon the Tagus during all our operations, we might experience some inconvenience in forming a junction with that corps, Peniche being the place of embarkation, owing to local circumstances, of which the discussion would be too long at the end of this long letter.

4thly; When we do go, I feel a little anxiety to go, like gentlemen, out of the hall door, particularly after the preparations which I have made to enable us to do so, and not out of the back door, or by the area.

I am willing to be responsible for the evacuation of Portugal, under your Lordship's instructions of the 27th Feb. Depend upon it, whatever people may tell you, I am not so desirous, as they imagine, of fighting desperate battles; if I was, I might fight one any day I please. But I have kept the army for 6 months in two positions, notwithstanding their own desire, and that of the allies, that I should take advantage of many opportunities which the enemy apparently offered of striking a blow against them; in some of which the single operation would certainly have been successful. But I have looked to the great result of our maintaining our position on the Peninsula; and have not allowed myself to be diverted from it by the wishes of the allies, and probably of some of our own army, that I should interfere more actively in some partial affairs; or by the opinion of others, that we ought to quit the country prematurely; and I have not harassed my troops by marches and counter-marches, in conformity to the enemy's movements. I believe that the world in the Peninsula begin to believe that I am right.

I am convinced that, if the Spaniards had followed my advice, Spain would now have been out of danger, and that the conduct which I have pursued has given us at this moment an efficient army, which is the only hope of the Peninsula. I am perfectly aware of the risks which I incur personally, whatever may be the result of the operations in Portugal. All I beg is, that if I am to be responsible, I may be left to the exercise of my own judgment; and I ask for the fair confidence of government upon the measures which I am to adopt.

If government take the opinions of others upon the situation of affairs here, and entertain doubts upon the measures which I propose to adopt, then let them give me their instructions in detail, and I will carry them strictly into execution. I may venture, however, to assure you, that, with the exception of Marshal Beresford, who I believe concurs entirely in all my opinions respecting the state of the contest, and the measures to be adopted here, there is no man in the army who has taken half the pains upon the subject that I have.

To Lieut. Col. Fletcher, R.E. Viseu, 3d April, 1810.

The intention of government in sending out the officers of engineers lately arrived, is to enable us to give some security to Setuval, Palmella, and principally to Peniche. The object in respect to the two first, is to be able to hold them some time as places of refuge for the inhabitants of the country, who might wish, or to whom it might be desirable to evacuate the country. The object in occupying and improving the last mentioned place, is the same; but I think it not impossible that government may be disposed to go a step farther in respect to Peniche, and to make an arrangement for occupying it permanently.

In respect to Peniche, it appears to me that the works which it would be desirable to execute there are:

1st; Something in the way of a counterscarp to cover the existing line wall.

2dly; To build up the breach in the existing wall.

3dly; To make the parapets of a proper height throughout, to fill up the rampart in the bastions, and to make a good rampart communication from each.

4thly; To secure effectually the breach on the left of the line, either by a stockade or the completion of the wall.

5thly; The construction of a redoubt upon the high ground in the rear of the left of the line, which, by crossing its fire with the citadel on the right, would prevent the storm of the line, even though it should be breached.

If government should determine to do any thing permanent at Peniche, these measures will have been a commencement of them; and I request you to employ one or more of the officers under your command upon them, without loss of time.

If it should occur to you that any thing else ought to be done at either of these places, in the view which I have taken of them, of course I expect to receive from you any suggestion that you may think will be useful.

To Vice Adm. the Hon. G. Berkeley. Viseu, 3d April, 1810.

I am much indebted to you for the letter of the 31st. I shall be very much obliged to you if you will send home a transport or transports with the 300 German deserters now at Lisbon; but as I expect many more, I shall be obliged to you if you will send them to England, from time to time, in proportion as they shall arrive at Lisbon. If they should at any time amount to such numbers as that it would be inconvenient to the ships of war to receive them, I will then request you to send home a transport with them.

I shall be very glad to see the *chevaux de frise*. Your nephew is here, and dines with me this day.

I have good accounts from Gen. Murray, of the 10th inst., of our Oporto claims, and it appears to me that all is going on as we could wish. I enclose an extract of his letter to me of the 10th, from which you will see that, although against his opinion and contrary to his wishes, he makes no opposition to the claim of the ships employed in the blockade of the Douro, which of course includes yours. I conclude, that the property being once condemned as prize, or for salvage, there can be no dispute between us about it.

The A.G. to Lieut. Col. ——. 3d April, 1810.

Your letter of the 25th ult. has been laid before the Commander of the Forces. I am in reply instructed to observe, that notwithstanding my Lord Wellington's full assurance that Major ——'s application to return to England is grounded on actual necessity, and that your recommendation to that effect is in consequence perfectly justified, yet his Lordship cannot depart from the regulation established for such cases. Major —— must therefore repair to head quarters, that a Medical board may report on the state of his health, previous to his departure from the army. His Lordship, after perusal of Major ——'s services, which appear to have been extensive and constant, cannot in justice omit to observe, that Major —— will only be allowed to sell the commissions purchased, as such decision has been given at head quarters in reference to officers of equal professional claims.

ADDENDA

TO

THE THIRD VOLUME.

THE PENINSULA.

[The following letters, the drafts of which were found too late for insertion in the order of their dates, are marked with the number of the page to which each in point of date should have been placed.]

To Visc. Castlereagh (p. 185).   London, 7th April, 1809.

Upon referring to Gen. Beresford's private letters to your Lordship and Gen. Stewart, I observe that he is particularly anxious to have the assistance of a larger proportion of British officers than have yet been sent out to him ; and although, at this distance from the scene of action, and with such scanty materials of information as I have in my possession, it is not possible for me to form an opinion respecting the mode in which the number of officers, which this country could afford, could be employed in Portugal, or the degree of utility which would result from the employment of their services in this manner, I think it would be advisable to increase the number now there by 12 or 14 more.

I think it probable that when Gen. Beresford will find that this country cannot afford the number of officers which he would require to discipline the Portuguese troops, he will employ them more in general duties. But even for this purpose the number now in Portugal would not be sufficient. The army in that country would probably not be able to afford any ; and it is therefore desirable, whatever may be the decision ultimately upon the mode of employing them, and whatever may be the numbers required for this employment, that at least 12 or 14 more officers should be sent out without loss of time.

To Visc. Castlereagh (p. 185).   Portsmouth, 13th April, 1809.

The messenger who will deliver you this letter takes up dispatches just arrived from Lisbon in the *Iris,* and I have opened the letter from Cradock to your brother, according to your desire. The progress of events is exactly what was expected it would be, and Cradock appears to have determined to remain in his position in the neighbourhood of Lisbon.

The Captain of the *Iris* informs me that, as he was coming out of the Tagus, he saw a fleet of transports going in, and he spoke a merchantman, by which he was informed that the transports had troops on board.

The wind is still contrary, and it blows so hard that it is impossible to go to sea. It rains, however, and we hope that the rain will change the wind by to-morrow morning.

P.S. If there should be any alteration in the orders to me in consequence of these dispatches, have a telegraph message sent to stop us at daylight in the morning till the messenger will arrive.

To Visc. Castlereagh (p. 189).   Lisbon, 24th April, 1809.

A late regulation respecting the pay of the staff on foreign service having been just transmitted from England, and which differs materially from that which has been acted upon for some years past, particularly with regard to the heads of the staff; viz., the Q. M. G., the A. G., their deputies, and the Military Secretary, who are curtailed of one half of their usual allowance, as will be seen by the enclosed statement, I beg leave to submit to your Lordship the propriety of continuing the customary allowances to these officers, particularly as an assistant in either of these departments has, even in England, the allowance of 15 shillings *per diem*, which is 5 shillings more than the late regulation for the deputies; and as the lowest ranks in them, viz., Dep. Assistants, receive the allowance of 10 shillings *per diem*, which is the same as now allotted to the D. Q. M. G. and the D. A. G.

In some parts of the world where the late regulation formerly prevailed, it was even the custom to issue the additional allowance out of the extraordinaries of the army, which custom has latterly been abolished in order to simplify the accounts, and the whole pay has been drawn for under one head.

I trust your Lordship will consider these circumstances, and that His Majesty's government will be pleased to authorise the issue of the customary pay to these officers; as it is by no means more than adequate to their respective situations as heads of the military departments of the army, through whom the most important duties of the service are carried on, and as the heads of the civil branches of the staff receive a very increased rate of pay and allowances.

To the Rt. Hon. J. Villiers (p. 219).   Coimbra, 7th May, 1809.

I enclose 2 papers omitted in my other dispatches, also a bag of letters from the officers of the army, to be sent to England by the first opportunity.

To the Rt. Hon. J. Villiers (p. 221).   Coimbra, 8th May, 1809.

The bearer is Mr. Viana, who has lately been at Oporto, and has some curious accounts to give you of our *friends* there, and I shall be obliged to you if you will attend to him.

To the Rt. Hon. J. Villiers (p. 256).   Aveiro, 27th May, 1809.

I return your letter to Marshal Soult, which I never had an opportunity of transmitting to him.

To the Rt. Hon. J. Villiers (p. 260).   Coimbra, 30th May, 1809.

I enclose a letter which I have received from Trant, upon which I have referred him to the Regent's ministers; but I send you the letter, that you may give them your opinion upon the subject.

To Visc. Castlereagh (p. 266).   Coimbra, 31st May, 1809.

I beg leave to request that your Lordship would not order any additional supply of spirits or salt meat to be sent out for the use of the army in Portugal, until I shall make a further requisition for them, as there is at present a considerable quantity of each in store.

To Visc. Castlereagh (p. 280). Abrantes, 8th June, 1809.

I forgot to write to you yesterday to tell you that none of the regiments of this army have any spare arms and accoutrements; and if you should send out any recruits, it will be necessary to send arms and accoutrements. The latter of these ought to be supplied by the Colonels of regiments, but probably the best mode of supplying them would be for the Storekeeper to send them out; and pray let them be of buff.

To Visc. Castlereagh (p. 289). Abrantes, 11th June, 1809.

I have the honor to acknowledge the receipt of your Lordship's dispatch of the 25th ult., in which your Lordship conveys to me by His Majesty's command an authority to extend my operations in Spain beyond the provinces immediately adjacent to the Portuguese frontier. It does not appear to be quite certain that Marshal Victor has retired or has made any preparatory arrangements with a view to withdraw from the province of Estremadura, and the accounts which we receive of his movements are so contradictory that I am not enabled to give your Lordship any positive opinion upon the subject, or any satisfactory statement of facts which might enable you to form your own.

Upon my arrival at Coimbra in the end of last month, I dispatched Lieut. Col. Bourke and Lieut. Col. Cadogan to Gen. Cuesta's head quarters to arrange with him a plan of co-operation for the British and Spanish armies with a view to attack Marshal Victor and to oblige him to retire from the menacing position which he had assumed in relation to the seat of government of Portugal and of Spain. I propose now to extend the objects of this co-operation, Gen. Cuesta having expressed himself but little satisfied with the limits which I had assigned to it; but I fear that I must delay to make any movements whatever till the army shall receive a supply of money.

To the Rt. Hon. J. Villiers (P.S. 314). Abrantes, 21st June, 1809.

I am obliged to you for the trouble you have taken respecting the opinions in England regarding our operations. In the present state of the public mind in England, I believe that it will be very difficult to satisfy people with any thing; and the government are so weak that they are afraid to take the lead and to guide the public opinion upon any subject. However, I am very indifferent what the opinion is of our operations. I shall do the best I can with the force given to me; and if the people of England are not satisfied, they must send somebody else who will do better.

I see that Mr. —— accuses me of exaggeration, which is, in other words, lying!!!

To the Rt. Hon. J. Villiers (p. 314). Abrantes, 22d June, 1809.

The enclosed letter from Cadogan contains my dispatches for Lord Castlereagh. If Cadogan should not arrive at Lisbon before the first vessel will sail, pray open the letter and forward the dispatches enclosed in it.

To Visc. Castlereagh (p. 316). Abrantes, 22d June, 1809.

I have the honor to transmit to your Lordship the enclosed memorial from Dr. Fergusson, Dep. Inspector of hospitals, and Chief of the Medical department with the army in the field, which I beg leave to recommend to your Lordship's most favorable consideration, in order that, as head of that department, he may be placed, with regard to allowances, in some degree on a footing with that of the Commissariat, and the other civil departments of the army.

P.S. I hope you will send the remount horses soon. I have given to the 14th and 16th light dragoons 95 horses from the Irish Commissariat, and I believe I shall give some to the other regiments. This arrangement and the draft from the 3d hussars will keep up the regiments for a short time; but it is inconceivable how fast the horses of both cavalry and artillery fall off. When horses, as well as men, are new in war, I believe they are generally the sacrifice of their mutual inexperience. I hope we shall profit by the experience acquired in the expedition to the northward, and that we shall be able to keep up the regiments rather better in future.

To the Rt. Hon. J. Villiers (p. 339).   **Abrantes, 27th June, 1809.**

The result of the inquiry respecting —— ——, the German sent up from Belem, is, that he is a deserter from the Light battalion of the Legion. I enclose a letter from Col. Hawker, of the 14th Light dragoons, respecting the man of the 14th supposed to be a priest, who will be discharged, if those who desire his discharge will pay his debts to his Captain.

To the Rt. Hon. J. Villiers (p. 339).   **Abrantes, 27th June, 1809.**

The money having arrived, the army marches this morning towards Castello Branco and Plasencia. The French retired from the bridge of Almaraz on the 24th, and Gen. Cuesta was about to cross the Tagus. I shall be much obliged to you if you will send me a couple of pounds of black tea by the first courier that comes. I shall also be obliged to you if you will endeavor to give me some general notion of the days of departure of the packets.

Memorandum for Col. Murray, Q.M.G. (p. 401).   **Deleytosa, 8th Aug. 1809.**

1. Orders to be sent to the Commissary Gen., as soon as possible, to send from Lisbon to the army the articles stated in the margin.*

2. These articles must be forwarded by the way of Badajoz, in one or separate convoys, according as may be most convenient, care being taken that the whole should come; and that a list of the articles leaving Lisbon, arriving at Badajoz, and leaving Badajoz, with each convoy, is sent to the army.

3. Mr. Villiers to be applied to, to interfere with the Portuguese go-

---

* 30,000 pairs of shoes.
3,000 stands of arms.
3,000 sets of accoutrements. (Either come or coming in the *Hannah*.)

Linen to make 30,000 shirts. (Must be purchased by the Commissary at Lisbon; ready made shirts would answer better.)
5000 haversacks.

5000 canteens.
500 billhooks.
500 camp kettles.
1,000,000 musket ball cartridges.
Ammunition for 6 pounders in proportion.

vernment to have the articles in question transported to Badajoz, in the manner, by the route, at the time, and by the stages, most convenient to them, and to the people of the country.

4. Applications to the same purport to be made to Señor Lozano de Torres, in respect to the movement of the stores from Badajoz to the army.

5. As soon as the plan of carriage, &c., shall be arranged, and the intelligence shall be received that the convoys have commenced their march from Lisbon, a Commissary to be sent to Badajoz to superintend their receipt, and their further transport from thence in co-operation with the Junta of Badajoz.

6. Orders concerning this memorandum to be sent to all the departments concerned.

N.B. I'll send to Mr. Villiers respecting the business which will be required to be done by the government.

To the Earl of Liverpool (p. 593).   Badajoz, 16th Nov. 1809.

Lest you should not have received the account through any other channel, I enclose 2 accounts which I have received of a naval success in the Mediterranean. I have received several other accounts of the same success, which I believe was achieved by Adm. G. Martin; and I have also reason to believe that the 2 ships, stated by Mr. Frere to have escaped, were chased and destroyed by the fleet off Marseilles. I have not seen Capt. Jenkinson since he was ill, but I understand that he is much better, and I purpose to send him to Lisbon for his recovery.

To the Earl of Liverpool (p. 602).   Badajoz, 20th Nov. 1809.

As the issue of blankets to the troops for the winter season leaves very few in store, I have to request that your Lordship will be pleased to order an additional supply of 35,000 to be sent out to Lisbon for the use of the army under my command.

To the Earl of Liverpool (p. 686).   Viseu, 14th Jan. 1810.

I enclose the name of a French prisoner in whose favor application has been made to me by a Spanish gentleman in order that he may be exchanged, as it is understood here that there is now a cartel agreed upon in England. I should be very much obliged to your Lordship if you will give directions that he may be exchanged.

APPENDIX.

APPENDIX

TO

THE THIRD VOLUME.

No. I. (p. 356.)

Le Maréchal Soult, Duc de Dalmatie, Commandant supérieur des 2me, 5me, et 6me Corps,
au Roi Joseph.   Toro, le 13 Juillet, 1809.

J'éprouve une bien vive satisfaction de voir par la dépêche, en date du 6 de ce mois, dont V. M. a daigné m'honorer, qu'elle partage mon opinion au sujet de la reprise des opérations. Ainsi il ne s'agit plus que de prendre des moyens prompts et efficaces pour que, dans le plus court délai possible, je puisse me remettre en campagne. Avant 15 jours les troupes seront en état d'agir.

S. M. l'Empereur m'a imposé la tâche honorable de chasser les Anglais du continent ; je remplirai son attente et celle de V. M., quelques difficultés que d'ailleurs il y ait à surmonter, si ce que je demande et ce qui est indispensable m'est accordé. Les résultats dédommageront amplement des sacrifices que, pour les obtenir, il faudra faire, et auxquels, sans doute, V. M. est déjà décidée.

Je considère que la position des troupes Impériales en Espagne est infiniment précaire, tant que l'ennemi reste maître des places fortes ; après la prise de Saragosse et celle de Gerona (qui depuis longtemps devraient être au pouvoir de V. M.), il était de la plus grande importance d'entreprendre le siége de Ciudad Rodrigo, afin de couper toute communication aux troupes des provinces méridionales avec celles des provinces du nord, et s'assurer d'une bonne place d'armes pour les opérations en Portugal. Certes si, pendant que j'étais dans ce Royaume, la forteresse de Ciudad Rodrigo eût été prise et celle d'Almeida menacée, ma position eût été beaucoup meilleure, et j'aurais pu, en changeant ma ligne d'opération, me mettre de suite en communication avec l'Espagne. Malheureusement cela n'a pas été fait ; mais il est temps de s'en occuper, et je crois que ce début de campagne sera d'un effet très avantageux sous quelque rapport qu'on le considère.

D'après tous les renseignements, il paraît que l'armée Anglaise qui a agi contre moi était de 26,000 à 30,000 hommes, qui, après m'avoir poursuivi jusqu'à Montalegre et Allariz en Galice, sont retournés en Portugal, et ont paru vouloir diriger leurs opérations sur les frontières d'Espagne entre le Tage et le Douro, en s'appuyant des places de Badajoz, d'Almeida, de Ciudad Rodrigo, même du fort de la Concepcion, qu'on fait rétablir en ce moment, et auquel, dit-on, 2000 hommes soutenus par un corps Anglais travaillent avec beaucoup d'activité. Cette armée n'est pas assez forte pour prendre l'offensive avant que les secours qu'elle a certainement demandés en Angleterre lui soient arrivés (un rapport que j'ai reçu hier annonce qu'un corps de 12,000 à 15,000 Anglais vient de débarquer à Oporto : cela peut être faux) ; avant que les armées Portugaises et Espagnoles soient en état de lui fournir au moins 50,000 auxiliaires, et avant que la récolte soit faite, non seulement pour assurer l'approvisionnement des magasins, mais aussi pour rendre disponibles tous les hommes des Royaumes en état de porter les armes, qui à présent sont retenus par les moissons, et qui bientôt seront en partie employés aux vendanges ou autres travaux de la terre. Ainsi, je ne pense pas qu'avant le mois de Septembre nous ayons de grosses masses à combattre, ni que l'ennemi puisse se livrer à de grandes entreprises. Mais, certainement alors, il agira, s'il n'est prévenu, et si nous lui donnons le temps d'organiser ses moyens et de se réunir.

La Galice et les Asturies sont à présent dans un tel état d'épuisement, qu'il leur faudra plusieurs mois pour se rétablir ; et il n'est pas vraisemblable qu'une forte armée aille s'y réunir, et en fasse ensuite le pivot de ses opérations. Ainsi, pour quelque temps, on n'a, je crois, à craindre de ces deux provinces que des partis, qu'un corps d'observation placé dans le Royaume de Léon pourrait aisément contenir, quand bien même la Romana et la Carrera descendraient avec leurs bandes. Il n'y a non plus à craindre de la rive gauche du Tage que des partis qu'un autre corps d'observation peut aussi maintenir; car l'ennemi n'ira pas faire passer au delà du fleuve sa ligne d'opération, qui serait pour lui la plus dangereuse et la plus longue.

Ainsi, toutes les combinaisons qu'on peut raisonnablement lui prêter, me portent à penser que lorsqu'il reprendra ses opérations (ce qui peut avoir lieu plus tôt que je n'ai dit, et il faut même y compter), il les dirigera par la ligne la plus courte, qui, en même temps, offre les meilleurs débouchés, où il trouvera plusieurs places d'armes pour ses dépôts, et des appuis assurés. Cette ligne ne pourra donc être que celle qui viendra aboutir à Ciudad Rodrigo, dont une direction allant vers Oporto passera par Almeida, place forte soutenue du fort de la Concepcion, et l'autre direction allant sur Lisbonne passera par Guarda, poste avantageux qui est retranché.

Cela admis, je crois qu'il convient, pour remplir la tâche que S. M. l'Empereur m'a imposée (de combattre les Anglais et de les chasser du continent), soit pour le succès des opérations en Espagne, soit pour assurer la conquête des provinces qui sont en état d'insurrection, de débuter' par le siége et la prise de Ciudad Rodrigo, et ensuite par celui d'Almeida, qui pourrait être fort long; car, si, pour trouver les Anglais et les obliger à en venir à une bataille ou à se rembarquer, je dois entrer une deuxième fois en Portugal, ainsi que cela paraît inévitable, je ne puis militairement m'engager dans ce pays où j'aurai des forces considérables contre moi, sans m'être assuré d'une ou de deux places d'armes pour y déposer mes malades et des munitions, et pour protéger mes communications avec l'Espagne.

La prise de Ciudad Rodrigo est encore nécessaire pour désorganiser les projets des armées insurrectionnelles d'Espagne, et les mettre dans l'impossibilité de communiquer entre elles. Elle l'est aussi pour couvrir Madrid; et enfin elle devient indispensable pour ménager par la suite nos forces, et pouvoir ainsi se dispenser d'entretenir sur cette partie de la frontière une armée qui remplisse à la fois ces divers objets.

Ainsi, j'ai l'honneur de proposer à V. M.:

1. De vouloir bien donner des ordres impératifs pour que l'équipage de siége qu'elle a déjà fait préparer, soit en entier réuni à Salamanque avant la fin de ce mois, quelques moyens qu'il faille employer, en serait-il même de vexatoires.

2. De donner des ordres pour qu'un corps d'observation aussi fort que possible, pris dans les troupes qui sont en Aragon et en Catalogne, soit réuni dans le Royaume de Léon, et qu'il y ait un bon chef pour le commander.

3. De faire préparer un autre corps d'observation pour manœuvrer sur les deux rives du Tage, et occuper Plasencia, ou au moins être à portée de cette ville.

4. De laisser à ma' libre disposition les 3 corps d'armée que S. M. l'Empereur a daigné mettre sous mon commandement, afin qu'aussitôt que l'équipage de siége sera près d'arriver à Salamanque, où j'opérerai ma réunion, je puisse le lendemain marcher sur Ciudad Rodrigo, investir la place, ouvrir la tranchée, et offrir la bataille à toute armée ennemie qui voudrait m'arrêter.

5. Que tous les bataillons et détachements quelconques appartenant aux 2me, 5me, et 6me corps d'armée, qui sont répandus dans les provinces de l'intérieur de l'Espagne, soient remplacés et aient ordre de rejoindre leurs régiments, quelque service que d'ailleurs ils remplissent.

6. Que V. M. dispose du surplus des troupes actuellement sur le Tage, qui n'entreront pas dans la composition du corps d'observation, pour former une forte réserve destinée à couvrir Madrid, en même temps qu'elle aurait pour objet de protéger au besoin celui des deux corps d'observation qui demanderait du secours. Cette réserve pourrait être placée vers Salvatierra, entre Salamanque et Avila, occupant ces deux villes, et en outre aurait ordre de maintenir libres mes communications sur les derrières, et de se porter promptement à ma rencontre, si, dans le cas d'une nécessité absolue, je l'appelais. A ce sujet, j'observerai qu'il faut s'attendre que du moment que je porterai mon corps d'observation sur les

frontières du Portugal, pour couvrir le siége de Ciudad Rodrigo, tout ce que les Anglais, les Portugais, et les Espagnols, même l'armée de Cuesta, pourront réunir de forces, se dirigera sur moi, pour secourir la place, et m'obliger à soutenir un combat inégal. Ainsi, il convient que de notre côté nous ayons des forces suffisantes, toutes prêtes à leur opposer, et que nous pressions les opérations.

7. Que V. M. juge à propos de donner des ordres pour qu'il soit promptement travaillé à augmenter la défense du fort de Zamora, et à fortifier quelques autres postes sur le Douro où sont les ponts, devrait-on se borner à construire des ouvrages en terre et à profiter de quelques maisons ou couvents pour préserver des partis les détachements qui défendront ces passages. Une somme de 200,000 francs bien employée suffirait pour toutes ces dépenses.

8. Enfin, que par extraordinaire il soit mis à ma disposition 500,000 francs, même 1,000,000, s'il y a possibilité, pour pourvoir aux dépenses d'urgence de l'artillerie, du génie, de l'administration des vivres, des hôpitaux, et autres dépenses imprévues ou secrètes qu'on sera dans le cas de faire, et dont l'emploi sera justifié après l'opération.

Quant aux subsistances, il serait nécessaire d'avoir à Salamanque 2,000,000 de rations complètes, afin que lorsque Ciudad Rodrigo sera pris, on versât dans la place ce qui ne serait pas consommé, pour en former l'approvisionnement. Il est probable que je trouverai sur les lieux, ou sur les rives du Douro, suffisamment de pain ; mais la viande et le vin, qu'on devrait se procurer par achat, seraient plus difficiles à trouver, et j'éprouverai pour les hôpitaux et les ambulances des embarras non moins grands, si l'administration générale ne vient à mon secours.

Toutes les propositions que j'ai l'honneur de faire à V. M. me paraissent nécessaires pour assurer les succès de la campagne, et même pour que le début en soit éclatant, ainsi que, de jour en jour, les circonstances en font de plus en plus sentir la nécessité. Je pense donc qu'il n'y a pas un instant à perdre pour les mettre en exécution, et, je le répète, quelque violents ou vexatoires que puissent être les moyens qu'on emploiera.

La demande que je fais de 500,000 francs, ou 1,000,000, s'il y a possibilité, n'est pas moins urgente que les autres ; et il faut, à tout prix, obtenir cette somme, V. M. serait elle obligée, pour se la procurer, de faire des sacrifices onéreux, ou de mettre tous les grands qui ont l'honneur d'approcher sa personne, ainsi que les généraux et officiers supérieurs Français qui sont en Espagne, dans le cas de se cotiser pour la former. En mon particulier, j'offre avec bien du plaisir ce que je puis avoir, et, en attendant, j'en ferai usage ; mais malheureusement c'est trop peu. V. M. sait que l'argent est le nerf de la guerre, et que par l'emploi qui en est fait à propos, on se ménage souvent des succès que, sans ce puissant véhicule, on ne serait pas toujours assuré d'obtenir, ou au moins, il en coûterait beaucoup plus d'hommes et une perte de temps qu'on ne saurait remplacer. V. M. est aussi sans doute persuadée que lorsque S. M. l'Empereur sera instruite de l'urgence du besoin, il est infaillible qu'elle enverra les fonds nécessaires pour y pourvoir.

J'ai parlé de l'équipage de siége, mais je dois supposer que son organisation comprendra tout le personnel des armes de l'artillerie et du génie, ainsi que les munitions, outils, et une immense quantité de sacs à terre qu'on sera dans le cas d'employer. Dans cette persuasion, j'ai l'honneur de supplier V. M. de daigner donner ordre aux généraux Senarmont et Léry de mettre la totalité des moyens dont on devra faire usage à la disposition du général Dulauloy pour l'artillerie, et à celle du colonel Garbé pour le génie, en même temps qu'ils prendront les mesures nécessaires pour faire arriver le tout à Salamanque, ainsi que je l'ai proposé.

A présent que j'ai développé toute ma pensée au sujet des opérations à entreprendre, et pour remplir les devoirs qui me sont imposés, il ne me reste qu'à supplier V. M. de pardonner, si j'ai osé, en lui soumettant mes réflexions, y mettre autant de franchise, et lui faire des propositions. La gloire des armes de l'Empereur, dont je suis idolâtre, le zèle ardent dont je suis animé pour son glorieux service, la possibilité que j'entrevois de parvenir par les moyens indiqués à l'entière soumission des provinces d'Espagne et même de Portugal, l'ambition que j'ai de contribuer à ce grand résultat, sans qu'aucune difficulté puisse m'intimider ni m'arrêter, et enfin le désir que j'éprouve d'être agréable à V. M. en me rendant utile, toutes ces considérations m'ont entraîné au delà des bornes où peut-être j'aurais dû m'arrêter, et m'ont suggéré que pour vaincre il fallait d'avance m'en assurer les moyens. Si je me suis trompé, que V. M. daigne me donner ses ordres et j'obéirai.

No. II. (p. 375.)

The battle of Talavera.

Le Maréchal Jourdan à S. A. le Prince de Wagram et Neufchâtel, Major Général.

Bargas, près Tolède, le 30 Juillet, 1809.

Ma depêche, datée de Navalcarnero le 23 courant, aura fait connaître à V. E. les dispositions que le Roi se proposait de prendre pour se préparer à combattre l'armée Anglaise. Le 24 le Roi arriva avec sa réserve à Cabañas sur la route de Tolède à Madrid. Le même jour M. le Maréchal Victor opéra sa retraite sur la rive gauche de la Guadarrama, et vint prendre position à l'embouchure de cette rivière dans le Tage. Pendant ce tems M. le général Sébastiani exécutait son mouvement sur Tolède. Déjà le 24 au soir, la tête de sa colonne était arrivée dans cette ville. Le 25 le Roi donna ordre à l'armée de se porter sur Torrijos. Le 1er corps marchait en tête. Il fut renforcé de la division de cavalerie légère du général Merlin, que le Roi retira du 4me corps. On laissa à Aranjuez et à Tolède ce qui était nécessaire pour défendre ces points.

La cavalerie légère du 1er corps trouva les avant-postes de l'armée Espagnole à Torrijos. On apprit que toute l'armée Espagnole était à Stª Olalla, et qu'elle avait même commencé un mouvement pour se porter sur Tolède. Les avant-postes de l'ennemi furent facilement culbutés. Cuesta, apprenant notre mouvement, crut devoir se retirer sur Talavera, mais son arrière-garde fut atteinte et sabrée en avant de Stª Olalla.

L'armée Française vint camper en entier à Stª Olalla, ayant son avant-garde à El Bravo. Les avant-postes annoncèrent qu'ils étaient en présence des avant-postes de l'armée Anglaise. En effet, cette armée était à Talavera, ayant une avant-garde de quelques bataillons et de 2 régimens de cavalerie à Cazalegas.

Le 27 le Roi dirigea l'armée sur l'Alberche. L'avant-garde de l'armée Anglaise fut chassée de Cazalegas. A 3 heures après midi, l'armée était réunie sur les bords de cette rivière, ayant ses tirailleurs sur la rive droite. On observa les mouvemens de l'ennemi du côté de Talavera. D'ailleurs on crut que l'armée ennemie se retirait sur Oropesa, mais le Duc de Bellune, qui connaît parfaitement les environs de Talavera, crut remarquer que l'ennemi prenait une forte position, sa droite appuyée à Talavera, et sa gauche à un plateau élevé, ayant une avant-garde dans les bois situés sur la rive droite de l'Alberche. Le Roi se décida à marcher de suite á l'ennemi. M. le Duc de Bellune fit attaquer les bois où était l'avant-garde de l'armée Anglaise. Cette avant-garde se défendit vivement, mais elle fut culbutée, et M. le Duc de Bellune s'approcha jusqu'à portée du canon du mamelon où la gauche de l'armée Anglaise était appuyée. Pendant ce tems la division Latour Maubourg, la division Milhaud, et la division Merlin, s'étaient portées sur la rive droite de l'Alberche, et marchaient dans la plaine entre le bois dont on chassait l'avant-garde Anglaise et le Tage; le 4me corps et la réserve suivaient le mouvement.

On crut remarquer que toute l'armée Anglaise se rapprochait du plateau, mais que l'armée Espagnole était en arrière de Talavera. On pensa qu'il était très important de faire tâter, dès le même soir, le plateau où s'appuyait l'aile gauche de l'armée Anglaise, afin de ne pas lui donner le tems de s'y fortifier; mais après quelques tiraillemens, M. le Duc de Bellune, voyant la nuit approcher, et l'ennemi en force, remit la partie au lendemain. L'armée campa à portée du canon de l'armée ennemie.

Le 28 au matin la bataille s'engagea par une nouvelle attaque que M. le Duc de Bellune dirigea sur le plateau. Cette attaque fut des plus vigoureuses. Le 4me corps marchait sur deux lignes contre le centre de l'ennemi, ayant soin de refuser sa gauche, afin d'observer Talavera. La réserve était disposée de manière à pouvoir appuyer les points de la ligne qui en auraient besoin. Cependant les troupes s'ébranlèrent, marchèrent avec une audace peu commune; et après le combat le plus vif, le plus opiniâtre, et le plus meurtrier, l'armée ennemie a été obligée de retrograder et d'abandonner le plateau et Talavera de la Reyna, qui étaient les deux points principaux de la ligne. L'armée Impériale a couché sur le champ de bataille.

Cependant les 2me, 5me, et 6me corps, qui étaient réunis à Salamanque, sous les ordres des Maréchaux Ducs de Dalmatie, de Trévise, et d'Elchingen, sont partis de Salamanque pour Plasencia, et doivent, à l'heure qu'il est, être de bien près sur les derrières de l'armée ennemie. Nous attendons les plus heureux résultats de ces mouvemens, car, avant que les corps fussent réunis, la plus petite partie des forces de S. M. l'Empereur en Espagne a suffi pour battre l'ennemi.

Une partie du 4me corps retourne près Aranjuez pour contenir les mouvemens que le corps Espagnol de Venegas aurait pu faire de ce côté.

Le Maréchal de l'Empire, Jourdan, Major Général de S. M. Catholique, au Maréchal Soult, Duc de Dalmatie.   Bargas, 30 Juillet, 1809.

Eloigné depuis plusieurs jours de Madrid, je vous ai écrit plusieurs fois ; mais comme il est possible que mes lettres aient été interceptées, je vais vous communiquer l'ensemble des opérations de l'armée sous les ordres du Roi, depuis le 23 jusqu'à ce jour.

Le 22 au soir, le Roi apprit que l'armée Anglaise, réunie à celle de Cuesta aux environs de Talavera, se disposait à prendre l'offensive contre M. le Duc de Bellune, qui était campé sur l'Alberche, et qui avait son quartier général à Cazalegas. Le mouvement de l'armée Anglaise et de Cuesta sur M. le Duc de Bellune, devait être soutenu par un corps de 10,000 à 12,000 Portugais, qui des bords du Tiétar s'était porté sur Escalona et sur l'Alberche, afin d'attaquer M. le Duc de Bellune en queue, tandis qu'il le serait de front par l'armée Anglaise et celle de Cuesta. Le Roi, qui avait prévu en partie ces mouvemens, avait donné ordre à M. le général Sébastiani de se replier sur Tolède.

Le 23, le Roi partit de Madrid avec sa réserve, et vint coucher à Navalcarnero. Sa Majesté avait le projet de continuer son mouvement sur Cazalegas, afin de se réunir au Duc de Bellune ; elle avait également le projet d'appeler à Casalegas le 4me corps, lorsqu'il serait arrivé à Tolède. Dans la soirée du 23, M. le Duc de Bellune rendit compte à Sa Majesté, qu'ayant la certitude qu'il serait attaqué le 24, et que ne croyant pas prudent de combattre un ennemi aussi supérieur, il allait se retirer sur Tolède et venir prendre position sur la Guadarrama.

Le Roi ne put donc pas continuer son mouvement sur Cazalegas ; en conséquence Sa Majesté se rendit le 24, à Bargas, près de Tolède. Ce jour-là, la tête du 4me corps arriva à Tolède, et le 25, le 1er corps, le 4me corps, et la réserve furent réunis aux environs de Tolède.

Le 26, le Roi laissa 3,000 hommes pour défendre Tolède, et se mit en marche avec toute l'armée pour prendre l'offensive. Arrivé à Torrijos, on rencontra les avant-postes ennemis ; ils furent culbutés sur le corps de l'armée Espagnole qui était campée à Sta Olalla, où Cuesta avait son quartier général ; l'armée Anglaise était restée à Talavera, ayant une avant-garde à Casalegas. Le même jour, le Roi continua sa marche sur Sta Olalla, où il vint établir son quartier général. L'armée Espagnole se mit en retraite sur Talavera ; son arrière-garde fut atteinte et sabrée.

Le 27, le Roi continua son mouvement en avant ; l'avant-garde de l'armée Anglaise fut rencontrée près de Cazalegas et fut culbutée. L'armée Anglaise et l'armée Espagnole prirent position, la droite à Talavera, et la gauche sur un plateau dont l'accès était extrêmement difficile.

Le Roi fit passer l'Alberche à toute l'armée ; tout ce qui voulut s'opposer à sa marche fut culbuté ; et l'armée Impériale arriva la nuit à portée du canon de l'armée ennemie ; deux heures de jour de plus auraient permis au Roi de faire enlever le plateau auquel s'appuyait l'aile gauche de l'armée ennemie, et, comme ce plateau était la clef de sa position, elle eût été complètement battue.

L'ennemi, qui sentit toute l'importance de cette position formidable, porta pendant la nuit sur ce plateau une nombreuse artillerie, et plaça toute l'armée Anglaise en arrière de cette position, tandis que l'armée Espagnole, forte de 36,000 hommes, occupait les environs de Talavera.

Néanmoins le Roi se décida à attaquer les deux armées ennemies. Le 28, à la pointe du jour, le combat s'engagea par l'attaque du plateau, qui fut faite par les troupes du 1er corps. Nos troupes montèrent à l'assaut avec une valeur peu commune; cependant arrivées à la sommité, elles furent forcées de se replier, ayant été attaquées par des forces supérieures. Elles rentrèrent dans leur première position, et le combat fut suspendu.

Le Roi fut lui-même reconnaître le plateau ; il fut décidé qu'on ferait une nouvelle attaque sur ce point important, qu'il n'y avait pas de possibilité de tourner, mais que cette attaque serait faite par tout le 1er corps, tandis que le 4me attaquerait le centre de l'ennemi. Les troupes se mirent en mouvement à 4 heures après midi ; il s'engagea de suite une action des plus vives ; nos troupes firent des prodiges de valeur. Elles forcèrent l'ennemi à abandonner le plateau, mais elles ne pouvaient jamais s'y maintenir par la facilité que l'ennemi avait d'attaquer nos têtes de colonnes, avec des forces supérieures. L'attaque de centre força également l'ennemi à recéder ; nos troupes couchèrent sur le champ de bataille, après avoir fait éprouver à l'ennemi une perte immense : la nôtre a été considérable. Toute l'infanterie, excepté la réserve, a été engagée ; le terrain n'a pas permis de faire agir la cavalerie.

Le Roi, ayant été prévenu que l'armée de Venegas s'était portée sur Tolède et sur Aranjuez, et qu'elle jetait des partis de cavalerie jusqu'aux portes de Madrid, a cru devoir se rapprocher de sa capitale pour empêcher que Madrid ne fût envahi. Il a aussi été porté à prendre ce parti dans l'espérance que le résultat de la bataille et votre mouvement sur Plasencia engageaient l'armée Anglaise à se séparer de Cuesta et à se reporter sur Plasencia. En conséquence, le 29, le 1er corps prit son ancienne position sur l'Alberche, et Sa Majesté est venue coucher ce même jour avec le 4me corps et la réserve à Sta Olalla ; aujourd'hui elle est venue à Bargas. Là, Sa Majesté est en position de secourir encore une fois, au besoin, le 1er corps, et d'empêcher l'ennemi de rien entreprendre sur Tolède, et faire repentir Venegas de sa témérité, s'il passait le Tage à Aranjuez pour se porter sur Madrid.

Maintenant que je vous ai communiqué, M. le Maréchal, tout ce qui a été fait, et les positions qu'occupe l'armée, Sa Majesté m'ordonne de vous dire, que si, par votre mouvement sur Plasencia, vous ne forcez pas l'armée Anglaise à se séparer de l'armée Espagnole, Sa Majesté aura de la peine à tenir tête à toutes les forces qui sont réunies devant elle ; l'armée de Cuesta est forte de 35,000 hommes, celle de Venegas de 25,000 ; l'armée Anglaise est également au moins de 25,000 ; joignez à cela 12,000 ou 15,000 Portugais aux ordres du général Wilson, vous verrez que tout cela s'élève à 100,000 hommes.

J'oubliais de vous dire que le corps de Wilson s'est avancé jusqu'à Navalcarnero, et qu'au moment où le Roi marchait sur l'armée Anglaise, ce corps a été rappelé.

Sa Majesté espère que vous êtes en pleine marche pour vous porter sur Plasencia, et que, dans le cas où l'armée Anglaise n'y serait pas parvenue, vous la chercherez partout où elle sera, afin de la combattre. Vous sentez que vous n'avez pas un moment à perdre, et que vous devez agir avec la plus grande célérité.

Le Roi désire recevoir fréquemment de vos nouvelles ; il faut tâcher d'établir votre communication avec Avila, afin que Sa Majesté reçoive plus promptement de vos nouvelles.

J'ai l'honneur de vous saluer avec la considération la plus distinguée.

Le Prince de Wagram et Neufchâtel, Major Général, au Maréchal Jourdan, Major Général de S. M. Catholique.   Paris, le 31 Août, 1809.

L'Empereur m'a chargé de faire connaître directement à Votre Excellence ses observations sur la manière dont les affaires ont été conduites en Espagne, relativement aux derniers événements. L'importance de ces remarques m'obligera de les transcrire en partie, et de rendre le reste avec la précision la plus scrupuleuse, pour ne pas courir le risque d'altérer en rien les différentes idées de l'Empereur.

En premier lieu, Sa Majesté a pensé que le Maréchal Duc de Dalmatie n'aurait pas dû être dirigé sur Plasencia, mais qu'il devait venir de Salamanque sur Madrid, par Avila, et que, les 3 corps marchant isolément, la tête serait arrivée dès le 27 ou le 28. Il fallait pendant ce temps là reculer à petites journées, et ne donner la bataille sous Madrid que lorsque toutes nos forces auraient été réunies. La marche du Duc de Dalmatie sur Plasencia était, selon l'Empereur, dangereuse et surtout inutile ; dangereuse, parce que l'autre armée pouvait être battue à Talavera sans qu'on lui portât secours, et qu'on compromettait ainsi la sûreté de tous les corps d'armée en Espagne, tandis que les Anglais n'avaient rien à craindre, puisqu'en 3 heures de temps ils pouvaient se mettre derrière le Tage, et que, en repassant ce fleuve à Talavera, à Almaraz, ou partout ailleurs, ils avaient leur ligne d'opération sur Badajoz à l'abri. Sa Majesté trouve qu'on a compromis les troupes par le mouvement ordonné, sans qu'on pût en obtenir un résultat, même en cas de succès.

L'Empereur pense qu'on avait fait une faute en se divisant en deux armées, de 50,000 hommes chacune, séparées par des montagnes et par une grande étendue de pays, mais que du moins on n'aurait dû ne livrer bataille qu'en même temps ou après.

Le Maréchal Duc de Dalmatie ne pouvait pas être à Plasencia avant le 4 Août, parce qu'il devait y arriver avec tout le 6me corps qui venait d'Astorga, et avait besoin de tout ce temps pour achever cette marche ; au lieu que l'armée du Roi pouvait manœuvrer du côté de Madrid et gagner quelques jours sans livrer bataille ; les Anglais ne se seraient pas compromis, s'ils l'avaient trouvé dans une bonne position.

Enfin arrivé à Talavera, on savait par les prisonniers que l'armée Anglaise était en présence, et l'on ne devait pas l'attaquer sans l'avoir reconnue. Leur droite étant à Talavera, où se trouvaient les Espagnols, on savait que ceux-ci, quoique ne valant rien en plein champ, n'en sont pas moins de bonnes troupes, quand ils peuvent se retrancher dans des maisons. La gauche des Anglais étant sur un plateau, on devait s'assurer si ce plateau ne pouvait pas être tourné, et cette position exigeait donc des reconnaissances préalables, sans lesquelles on compromet les troupes, et on les expose sans nécessité.

Sa Majesté trouve en outre qu'une fois résolu à livrer bataille, il fallait le faire avec plus de vigueur et d'ensemble, et que c'est essuyer un affront que d'être repoussé quand on a eu 12,000 hommes en réserve qui n'ont pas tiré. L'Empereur ajoute qu'on ne doit pas livrer de bataille lorsqu'on n'a pas pu s'assurer d'avance d'avoir les trois quarts des chances en faveur de son succès ; *on ne doit même*, dit encore l'Empereur, *donner une bataille que lorsqu'on n'a plus de nouvelles chances à espérer, puisque de sa nature le sort d'une bataille est toujours douteux ; mais une fois qu'elle est résolue, on doit vaincre ou périr, et les aigles Françaises ne doivent se reployer que lorsque toutes ont fait également leurs efforts.*

Je ne laisserai point ignorer à Votre Excellence que Sa Majesté a été informée d'une circonstance qui a excité son mécontentement : c'est que le Duc de Bellune, à la bataille de Talavera, a pensé que si la réserve avait été mise sous ses ordres, il aurait enlevé la position des Anglais. L'Empereur a donc jugé que c'était par suite des fautes commises que l'armée d'Espagne a été ainsi bravée par 30,000 Anglais. Sa Majesté finit par cette phrase : *Tant qu'on voudra attaquer de bonnes troupes, comme les troupes Anglaises, dans de bonnes positions, sans les reconnaître et s'assurer si on peut les enlever, on conduira des hommes à la mort en pure perte.*

Je remplis le devoir qui m'était imposé par les ordres de l'Empereur ; dans une circonstance aussi délicate qu'importante, il ne m'est pas permis de m'écarter de la ligne qui m'est tracée. Je désire beaucoup que votre réponse me mette à même de donner à Sa Majesté des explications satisfaisantes, et de nature à dissiper l'impression que les circonstances lui ont faite.

No. III. (p. 440.)

Le Maréchal Jourdan, Major Général de S. M. Catholique, au Maréchal Soult, Duc de Dalmatie.   Madrid, le 19 Août, 1809.

Le Roi me charge d'avoir l'honneur de vous prévenir qu'il a reçu une lettre de Son Excellence le Ministre de la Guerre, portant que l'intention de S. M. l'Empereur est qu'on n'entreprenne rien contre le Portugal pendant le mois d'Août, à cause des chaleurs de la saison. L'Empereur pense qu'il faut se préparer à faire cette expédition en Février prochain. S. M. I. et R. demande aussi que le Roi lui fasse connaître, dans un mémoire raisonné, ses pensées et ses vues sur les opérations que l'armée d'Espagne devra entreprendre au mois de Septembre.

Le Roi, qui a reçu votre lettre en date du 14 du courant, m'ordonne de vous observer que, d'après les ordres qu'il vient de recevoir, il ne s'agit plus, comme vous le proposez, d'expulser les Anglais du continent tant qu'ils resteront en Portugal, et qu'il paraît qu'avant d'entreprendre de nouvelles opérations, S. M. l'Empereur veut laisser passer la saison des grandes chaleurs et connaître avant

tout les pensées et les vues du Roi.   S. M. me charge d'ajouter à ces considérations, que dans ce moment les communications avec la France sont très-dange-
reuses et à la veille d'être interceptées. Les courriers sont assassinés, et les divers
détachements sont attaqués et quelquefois enlevés. Enfin, il n'est plus possible de
faire voyager les convois, par l'impossibilité où l'on se trouve de leur donner des
escortes suffisantes. Cependant Madrid se trouve dépourvu de munitions, et l'on
ne peut entreprendre une opération militaire importante avant d'en avoir reçu des
places de dépôt. Les voitures d'artillerie se trouvent, d'après un rapport de M.
le général Senarmont, hors d'état d'entrer en campagne. Elles ont été détruites
par les grandes chaleurs, et le général Senarmont pense qu'il faudra plus d'un
mois pour les réparer. Les fourgons du train sont dans le même état. Les
troupes, surtout la cavalerie, ont le plus grand besoin de repos. Enfin, tous les
approvisionnements en subsistances qui avaient été formés à Madrid, ont été con-
sommés pendant les dernières opérations, et il est indispensable d'en créer de
nouveaux, sans quoi l'armée ne pourrait se soutenir en campagne.

Le Roi pense donc, M. le Maréchal, que dans le moment l'objet principal est de
rendre libres les communications avec la France et avec les places de dépôt. Déjà
des troupes sont parties de Madrid pour disperser les rassemblements qui s'étaient
formés du côté de l'Escurial, de Guadarrama, et de Ségovie, et qui interceptaient
les communications avec Valladolid. Le 4me corps, qui a le plus grand
besoin de repos, a été placé sur la rive droite du Tage, tant pour se reposer que
pour éloigner les rassemblements qui interceptaient l'arrivage des subsistances
destinées à l'approvisionnement de Madrid. S. M. espère que le 6me corps
est arrivé à Salamanque. M. le Duc d'Elchingen arrêtera la marche de la
Romana, il chassera l'ennemi de Salamanque et de Léon, et forcera la Romana à
rentrer dans les montagnes de la Galice. Pendant ce temps, M. le général Kellermann balayera les provinces de Burgos et de Soria, et rétablira les communications avec la France et les places de dépôt; les convois arriveront, on réparera
l'artillerie et le train des équipages, on formera des approvisionnements, les
troupes se reposeront, et quelques chevaux de cavalerie se remettront. D'ici là,
S. M. l'Empereur pourra transmettre ses ordres au Roi, et l'armée sera en état
d'agir lorsque la saison des grandes chaleurs sera passée. Si, avant cette époque,
ce qui est peu probable, l'ennemi prenait l'offensive, alors, par les positions
qu'occupent les divers corps d'armée, on pourrait les réunir en tout ou en partie
en peu de jours sur le point nécessaire, et l'on agirait selon les circonstances.

Le Roi ne peut pas envoyer le 1er corps à Talavera; M. le Duc de Bellune
est dans La Manche à la poursuite de l'armée de Venegas. Le 4me corps
est, ainsi que je vous l'ai dit plus haut, sur la rive droite du Tage; il est, quant à
présent, hors d'état d'entrer en campagne, et d'ailleurs S. M. ne peut pas, dans
les circonstances actuelles, rester à Madrid avec une poignée de troupes autour
d'elle. Son projet est de considérer le 4me corps comme une réserve avec
laquelle S. M. se portera partout où sa présence sera nécessaire. Ainsi le Roi
pense que le 5me corps doit rester dans la position qu'il occupe, et qu'avec
le 2me corps vous devez continuer à observer le Portugal et à chercher à
savoir ce que devient l'armée Anglaise. Les armées ennemies doivent avoir
besoin de plus de temps pour se refaire que l'armée Impériale, puisqu'elles ont
perdu la plus grande partie de leur matériel. Il est donc à présumer qu'avant
qu'elles soient en état de reprendre les opérations, nous serons réparés. Dans ce
cas, si les opérations ont lieu de votre côté, le Roi s'y portera avec le 4me corps,
la Garde, et une brigade de la division Dessolles.

Le Roi ne perd pas de vue le projet du siége de Ciudad Rodrigo, et S. M. pense
qu'il faut se préparer à faire cette opération à la première occasion favorable.
Tous les ordres étaient donnés pour cela; mais les dangers des communications,
la présence de l'ennemi à Salamanque et à Léon, l'invasion par la Romana, dont
les provinces de la Vieille Castille ont été menacées, ont forcé à suspendre
l'exécution de ces ordres.

Le Roi espère que vous parviendrez à enlever le corps de Wilson, puisqu'il se
trouve entre vous et le 5me corps. S. M. ne peut pas faire agir une colonne
de 1,200 à 1,500 hommes d'Avila, puisqu'il n'y a dans cette province qu'environ
1,200 hommes du régiment Royal étranger, qui ont bien de la peine à se soutenir
contre les fréquents détachements de la garnison de Ciudad Rodrigo. Elle a pensé
qu'il serait inutile de faire partir des troupes d'ici pour cette expédition ; car,
lorsqu'elles arriveraient, Wilson sera pris ou échappé.

S. M. est dans l'impossibilité de vous envoyer les 2,000 hommes de cavalerie que vous demandez; à peine y a-t-il 4,000 hommes de cavalerie entre le 1ᵉʳ et le 4ᵐᵉ corps. On ne peut leur en retirer sans les mettre hors d'état d'agir. J'ai écrit à Son Excellence le Ministre de la Guerre, par ordre du Roi, pour demander des secours pour cette arme.

Les ordres sont donnés pour que tous les détachements que vous avez laissés à Valladolid vous soient renvoyés. On a donné l'ordre de vous envoyer des fonds; mais il faut attendre qu'ils soient arrivés de Burgos, où ils ont été arrêtés à cause des dangers des communications.

No. IV. (p. 613.)

The battle of Ocaña.

Le Maréchal Duc de Dalmatie à S. A. le Prince de Wagram et de Neufchâtel, Major Général. Dos Barrios, le 19 Nov. 1809.

Les troupes de S. M. l'Empereur viennent de remporter une victoire signalée. La bataille s'est donnée à Ocaña, où les insurgés Espagnols avaient réuni 55,000 hommes, dont 7000 de cavalerie, et une nombreuse artillerie. Le 4ᵐᵉ corps d'armée réuni au 5ᵐᵉ corps sous les ordres de M. le Maréchal Duc de Trevise, la division de dragons du général Milhaud, la division de cavalerie légère du 5ᵐᵉ corps, commandée par le général Beauregard, et la brigade de cavalerie légère du général Paris, ainsi que la garde du Roi, et 2 bataillons de troupes Espagnoles, sont ce matin partis d'Aranjuez pour se porter à la rencontre de l'armée ennemie, que tous les renseignemens indiquaient en position à Ocaña. A 9 heures l'avant garde a effectivement reconnu cette armée, à 11 heures le combat s'est engagé, et à 2 heures la bataille était gagnée. Les Espagnols ont fait bonne résistance; la supériorité de leur nombre les encourageait; mais ils ont été abordés si franchement par toutes les troupes que leur position leur était enlevée sans la moindre hésitation.

Les charges de cavalerie et d'infanterie qui ont eu lieu les ont mis dans une épouvantable déroute. Toute l'artillerie et les bagages sont restés en notre pouvoir. On compte déjà plus de 50 pièces de canon, 15 drapeaux, et beaucoup de prisonniers, parmi lesquels 3 généraux, 6 colonels, et 700 autres officiers, sont au pouvoir des troupes Impériales. La terre est jonchée de cadavres, et de plus de 40,000 fusils, ainsi que de débris de bagages et effets militaires : à tout instant on amène des prisonniers. Le reste fuit sans armes, sans trop savoir que devenir. Si les Anglais ont encore une armée Espagnole à sacrifier, ils peuvent la présenter; toute l'armée Impériale en Espagne est disponible.

Ce matin le Roi avait donné le commandement de toute la cavalerie à M. le général Sébastiani. Les belles charges qu'il a faites ont justifié ce choix. Il a manœuvré avec précision et audace. M. le général Milhaud s'est aussi très distingué. Tous les chefs de cavalerie méritent d'être cités. Les chevaux légers de la garde Royale ont montré une grande intrépidité.

[*Here follow the recommendations.*]

Notre perte est peu de chose, relativement à l'importance du résultat et de la chaleur du combat. Je ne crois pas qu'elle se lève à 400 hommes, tout compris, &c.

No. V. (p. 719.) (70⅃.)

Le Prince de Wagram et Neufchâtel, Major Général, au Roi Joseph. Paris, le 31 Janvier, 1810.

L'Empereur m'ordonne de ré-expédier pour l'Espagne l'aide de camp de V. M., M. de Clermont Tonnerre, pour porter à la connaissance de V. M. ses intentions au sujet de l'expédition de l'Andalousie.

1. En marchant sur Séville et Cadix, l'Empereur pense qu'il faut avoir soin de mener les équipages de siége nécessaires; car si l'ennemi sait qu'on n'a pas les moyens de le bombarder ni de le miner, cela pourra accroître sa résistance.

2. Il faut prévoir que les Anglais peuvent marcher sur Talavera pour faire diversion; l'Empereur juge donc qu'il est convenable de laisser le 5ᵐᵉ corps d'armée, qui est composé de nos meilleures troupes, pour être opposé aux Anglais,

et de mettre tous les petits corps chargés de garder les communications avec Madrid sous les ordres du commandant du 5me corps, afin qu'il soit à portée de les réunir et·de s'opposer aux entreprises des Anglais. Ce corps pourra se porter sur Alcantara et jusque sur les frontières du Portugal, pour éclairer les mouvements des Anglais et correspondre avec le Maréchal Duc d'Elchingen, commandant le 6me corps d'armée.

3. Si les Anglais ne font pas le mouvement de se porter sur Madrid pour faire diversion, ils peuvent se porter sur Salamanque ; et, dans ce cas, le 6me corps sera renforcé par la division Loison, le 8me corps, et par 12,000 hommes de cavalerie qui rendraient impossible toute opération dans la plaine.

4. Si le corps qui sera opposé aux Anglais n'est pas fortement constitué, si les corps entre la Sierra Morena et Madrid ne sont pas sous le même commandement, si les Anglais conçoivent l'espoir de faire un mouvement offensif, cela encouragera la résistance de Cadix. Le moindre mouvement rétrograde d'un des corps de l'expédition d'Andalousie serait contraire à toute idée militaire, enhardirait l'insurrection et découragerait l'armée Française : il ne faut donc envoyer en Andalousie que les troupes nécessaires ; car, dans cette opération, il faut prévoir la diversion des Anglais.

5. Sa Majesté n'a pas été entièrement satisfaite des projets qui lui ont été soumis ; elle ne trouve pas qu'ils présentent d'assez fortes combinaisons. L'Empereur considère qu'il n'y a de dangereux en Espagne que les Anglais ; que le reste n'est que de la canaille qui ne peut jamais tenir en campagne ; que la communication de Lisbonne avec Séville et Cadix est très-prompte, et que, si on laisse sur le Tage un corps trop faible, on risque de compromettre l'opération.

END OF THE THIRD VOLUME.

London : Printed by WILLIAM CLOWES and SONS, Stamford Street.

Lightning Source UK Ltd.
Milton Keynes UK
UKOW02f0810220317
297238UK00001B/21/P